CIVILIZATION IN THE WEST

SIXTH EDITION

SINCE 1300

ADVANCED PLACEMENT* EDITION

Mark Kishlansky
Harvard University

Patrick Geary
University of California, Los Angeles

Patricia O'Brien
University of California, Los Angeles

PEARSON
Longman

New York   San Francisco   Boston
London   Toronto   Sydney   Tokyo   Singapore   Madrid
Mexico City   Munich   Paris   Cape Town   Hong Kong   Montreal

Senior Acquisitions Editor: Janet Lanphier
Development Editor: Karen Helfrich
Executive Marketing Manager: Sue Westmoreland
Supplements Editor: Kristi Olson
Media Editor: Patrick McCarthy
Production Manager: Donna DeBenedictis
Project Coordination, Text Design, and Electronic Page Makeup: Elm Street Publishing Services, Inc.
Cover Designer/Manager: John Callahan
Cover Image: Master of the St. Barbara Legend (late 15th c.). *A Man and his Wife.* Oil on oak panel, 15 $^1/_2$
    x 11 in. Upton House, Bearsted Collection, Banbury, Oxfordshire, Great Britain. © National Trust/Art
    Resource, NY
Photo Researcher: Photosearch, Inc.
Manufacturing Buyer: Lucy Hebard
Printer and Binder: Quebecor World/Versailles
Cover Printer: Phoenix Color Corporation

For permission to use copyrighted material, grateful acknowledgment is made to the copyright holders on
pp. C-1–C-6, which are hereby made part of this copyright page.

Library of Congress Cataloging-in-Publication Data
Kishlansky, Mark A.
    Civilization in the West/Mark Kishlansky, Patrick Geary, Patricia O'Brien.—6th ed.
        p. cm.
    Includes bibliographical references and index.
    ISBN 0-321-23612-2 (single v. ed.)—ISBN 0-321-23624-6 (v. 1)—ISBN 0-321-23625-4
(v. II)—ISBN 0-321-23621-1 (v. A)—ISBN 0-321-23622-X (v. B)—ISBN 0-321-23623-8 (v. C)
    1. Civilization, Western—History—Textbooks. I. Geary, Patrick J., 1948- II. O'Brien, Patricia,
1945- III. Title.

CB245.K546 2006
909' .09821—dc22

                                                                                2004024450

Please visit us at http://www.ablongman.com/kishlansky

ISBN 0-321-23612-2 (Single volume edition)
ISBN 0-321-23624-6 (Volume I)
ISBN 0-321-23625-4 (Volume II)
ISBN 0-321-23621-1 (Volume A)
ISBN 0-321-23622-X (Volume B)
ISBN 0-321-23623-8 (Volume C)
ISBN 0-321-29235-9 (Advanced Placement* Edition, Since 1300)

*Advanced Placement Program and AP are registered trademarks of The College Board, which was not
involved in the production of, and does not endorse, this book.

2 3 4 5 6 7 8 9 10—QWV—08 07 06

BRIEF CONTENTS

DETAILED CONTENTS

Note: Each chapter ends with Questions for Review, Key Terms, Discovering Western Civilization Online, and Suggestions for Further Reading.

Chapter 11
THE ITALIAN RENAISSANCE   321

Chapter 12
THE EUROPEAN EMPIRES   353

Chapter 13
THE REFORM OF RELIGION   387

Chapter **30**
THE END OF THE COLD WAR AND NEW GLOBAL CHALLENGES, 1970 TO THE PRESENT 929

DOCUMENTS

MAPS

CHRONOLOGIES, GENEALOGIES, AND FIGURES

PREFACE

In planning *Civilization in the West,* our aim was to write a book that students would *want* to read. Throughout our years of planning, writing, revising, rewriting, and meeting together, this was our constant overriding concern. Would students read our book? Would it be effective in conveying information while stimulating the imagination? Would it work for a variety of Western civilization courses with different levels and formats? It was not easy to keep this concern in the forefront throughout the long months of composition, but it was easy to receive the reactions of scores of reviewers to this simple question: "Would students *want* to read these chapters?" Whenever we received a resounding "No!" we began again— not just rewriting but rethinking how to present material that might be complex in argument or detail or that might simply seem too remote to engage the contemporary student. Although all three of us were putting in long hours in front of computers, we quickly learned that we were engaged in a teaching rather than a writing exercise. And though the work was demanding, it was not unrewarding. We hope that you will recognize and come to share with us the excitement and enthusiasm we felt in creating this text. We have enjoyed writing it, and we want students to enjoy reading it.

From the reactions to our first five editions, they have. We have received literally hundreds of cards and letters from adopters and users of *Civilization in the West.* The response has been both overwhelming and gratifying. It has also been constructive. Along with praise, we have received significant suggestions for making each subsequent edition stronger. Topics such as the Crusades, the Enlightenment, and imperialism have been reorganized to present them more clearly. Subjects such as the ancient Hebrews, Napoleon, and German unification have been given more space and emphasis. New features have been added to freshen the book and keep abreast of current scholarship, and more than 100 excerpts from primary sources are presented to give students a feel for the concreteness of the past. We believe that the sixth edition of *Civilization in the West* not only preserves the much-praised quality of its predecessors but also enhances it.

APPROACH

We made a number of decisions early in the project that we believed contributed to our goal. First, we were *not* writing an encyclopedia on Western civilization. Information was not to be included in a chapter unless it related to the themes of that chapter. There was to be no information for information's sake, and each of us was called upon to defend the inclusion of names, dates, and events whenever we met to critique one another's chapters. We found, to our surprise, that by adhering to the principle that information included must contribute to or illustrate a particular point or dominating theme, we provided as much, if not more, material than books that habitually list names, places, and dates without any other context.

Second, we were committed to integrating the history of ordinary men and women into our narrative. We believe that isolated sections, placed at the end of chapters, that deal with the experiences of women or minority groups in a particular era profoundly distort historical experience. We called this technique *caboosing,* and whenever we found ourselves segregating women or families or the masses, we stepped back and asked how we might recast our treatment of historical events to account for a diversity of actors. How did ordinary men, women, and children affect the course of historical events? How did historical events affect the fabric of daily life for men and women and children from all walks of life? We tried to rethink critical historical problems of civilization as gendered phenomena. To assist us in the endeavor, we engaged two reviewers whose sole responsibility was to evaluate our chapters for the integration of those social groups into our discussion.

We took the same approach to the coverage of central and eastern Europe that we did to women and minorities. Even before the epochal events of 1989 that returned this region to the forefront of international attention, we realized that in too many textbooks the Slavic world was treated as marginal to the history of Western civilization. Thus, with the help of a specialist reviewer, we worked to integrate more of the history of eastern Europe into our text than is found in most others, and to do so in a way that presented the regions, their cultures, and their institutions as integral rather than peripheral to Western civilization.

To construct a book that students would *want* to read, we needed to develop fresh ideas about how to involve them with the material, how to transform them from passive recipients to active participants. We borrowed from computer science the concept of being "user-friendly." We wanted to find ways to stimulate the imagination of the student, and the more we experimented with different techniques, the more we realized that the most effective way to do this was visually. It is not true that contemporary students cannot be taught effectively by the written word; it is only true that they cannot be taught as effectively as they can by the combination of words and images. From the beginning, we realized that a text produced in full color was essential to the features we most wanted to use: the pictorial chapter openers; the large number of maps; the geographical tours of Europe at certain times in history; and the two-page special feature essays, each with its own illustration.

The Advanced Placement* Edition

The Advanced Placement* Edition of *Civilization in the West* takes special care to address the needs of the European History AP* course. As the course is primarily focused on European history after 1300, we avoided the inclusion of extraneous material in the textbook. To ensure that students are provided with the appropriate background needed for successful study, we began this volume with an overview chapter titled Western Civilization Before 1300 to introduce early concepts and provide context to later material covered in more detail.

FEATURES

It is hard to have a new idea when writing a textbook. So many authors have come before, each attempting to do something more effective, more innovative than his or her predecessor. However, we feel that the following features enhance students' understanding of Western civilization.

The Visual Record: Pictorial Chapter Openers

It is probably the case that somewhere there has been a text that has used a chapter-opening feature similar to the one we use here. What we can say with certainty is that nothing else we experimented with, no other technique we attempted, has had such an immediate and positive impact on our readers or has so fulfilled our goal of involving the students in learning as *The Visual Record* pictorial chapter openers.

An illustration—a painting, a photograph, a picture, an artifact, an edifice—appears at the beginning of each chapter, accompanied by text through which we explore the picture, guiding students across a canvas or helping them see in an artifact or a piece of architecture details that are not immediately apparent. It is the

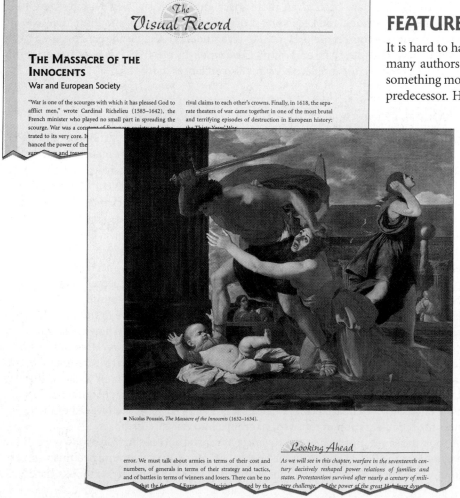

The
Visual Record

THE MASSACRE OF THE INNOCENTS
War and European Society

"War is one of the scourges with which it has pleased God to afflict men," wrote Cardinal Richelieu (1585–1642), the French minister who played no small part in spreading the scourge. War was a constant of European society and penetrated to its very core. It ... hanced the power of the ... sur ... es and trea...

rival claims to each other's crowns. Finally, in 1618, the separate theaters of war came together in one of the most brutal and terrifying episodes of destruction in European history: the Thirty Years' War.

■ Nicolas Poussin, *The Massacre of the Innocents* (1632–1634).

Looking Ahead

error. We must talk about armies in terms of their cost and numbers, of generals in terms of their strategy and tactics, and of battles in terms of winners and losers. There can be no ... that the f... of Eur... decisi... ed by the

As we will see in this chapter, warfare in the seventeenth century decisively reshaped power relations of families and states. Protestantism survived after nearly a century of military challenge, ... the power of the great H... burg dyn...

direct combination of text and image that allows us to achieve this effect, to "unfold" both an illustration and a theme. In some chapters we highlight details, pulling out a section of the original picture to take a closer look. In others we attempt to shock the viewer into the recognition of horror or of beauty. Some chapter-opening images are designed to transport students back in time, to make them ask the question, "What was it like to be there?" All of the opening images have been chosen to illustrate a dominant theme within the chapter, and the dramatic and lingering impression they make helps reinforce that theme. A *Looking Ahead* section provides a brief overview of chapter coverage and further strengthens the connection between the subject of the opener and the major topics and themes of the chapter.

MAP DISCOVERY

Important commercial centers
Major champagne region trade fairs
Major land trade routes
Major sea trade routes
Route of Marco Polo

Medieval Trade Networks
Examine the major trade routes of the High Middle Ages. What commodities and products were plentiful in Europe but scarce in the eastern Mediterranean? What regions were the major wool producers? The major cloth producers? How might silks from the East have arrived in London?

Revised and Improved Map Program

We have taken a similar image-based approach to our *presentation of geography*. When teachers of Western civilization courses are surveyed, no single area of need is cited more often than that of geographical knowledge. Students simply have no mental image of Europe, no familiarity with those geophysical features that are a fundamental part of the geopolitical realities of Western history. We realized that maps, carefully planned and skillfully executed, would be an important component of our text. In this edition, we have revised the entire map program, improving the look of the maps and increasing the sizes of many of them for easier readability.

New! Map Discovery

To complement the standard map program of the text, we have two additional map-based features. A feature, new to this edition, is *Map Discovery*. This feature, which appears two to three times per chapter, offers specially-designed maps with supporting caption information and questions designed to engage students in analyzing the map data and making larger connections to chapter discussions. We have found that focusing students' attention on the details of what a map shows and asking them to consider why that information is important is an effective way to strengthen critical thinking skills, as well as to expand geographical knowledge.

550   **Chapter 18**   The Balance of Power in Eighteenth-Century Europe

GEOGRAPHICAL TOUR
A Grand Tour of Europe in 1714

In the eighteenth century young noblemen from every European nation c... ...tour. Usually in c... ...palaces, castles, an... ...learn a little of the... ...class who were eng... ...prepared for the gr... ...uities—many of th... ...tures to place in the... ...normally religiou...

and music all had an eastern tinge. Nobleman who took the grand tour in the second decade of the century witnessed the redrawing of Europe's political map as well as a new balance of power among the European states.

Within a relatively short span of time at the beginning of the eighteenth century, two treaties brought about a consider...

■ **Map E. France and Spain.** The War of the Spanish Succession permanently separated France and Spain.

■ **Map F. The Holy Roman Empire.** It was still a conglomeration of towns, principalities, and bishoprics, but increasingly the empire was losing political and administrative control over its lands.

the great Habsburg throne and Spain was slowly being sliced to pieces. By 1714 the European territories of the Spanish empire had been reduced to Iberia itself (see **Map E**). But the loss of its European empire was to prove a blessing in disguise for Spain, which now entered a new and unexpected phase of growth and influence. Grand tourists did not always find Spain a congenial destination; a trek across the Pyrenees and on to an arid plain was a deterrent to reaching Madrid and T... ...those...

Catholic countries, German cities were finally recovering from the devastation of the Thirty Years' War.

Increasingly, Habsburg power centered on Austria, Bohemia, and Hungary (see **Map F**). That was especially true during the reign of Leopold I (1655–1705). Withstanding thre... ...des, Leopold was able to... ...and his...

Geographical Tours of Europe

The second map feature is the *Geographical Tours of Europe*. Six times in the book, we pause in the narrative to take a tour of Europe. Sometimes we follow an emperor as he tours his realm; sometimes we examine the impact of a peace treaty; sometimes we follow the travels of a merchant. Whatever the thematic occasion, our intention is to guide the student around the changing contours of the geography of Western history. In order to do this effectively, we worked with our cartographer to develop small, detailed maps to complement the overview map that appears at the beginning of each tour section. We know that only the most motivated students will turn back several pages to locate on a map a place mentioned in the text. Using small maps allows us to integrate maps directly into the relevant text, thus relieving students of the sometimes frustrating experience of attempting to locate not only a specific place on a map but perhaps even the relevant map itself. We have also added labels to all the tour maps and have included in-text references to direct students to relevant maps at specific points in the narrative of the tour. The great number of maps throughout the text, the specially designed geographical tour of Europe feature, and the ancillary programs of map transparencies and workbook exercises combine to provide the strongest possible program for teaching historical geography.

A Closer Look

Another technique we have employed to engage students with historical subjects is the two-page *A Closer Look* special feature that appears in most chapters. The special features focus on an event, phenomenon, or personality chosen to enhance the student's sense that history is something that is real and alive. The features are written more dramatically and sympathetically, with a greater sense of wonder than would be appropriate in the body of the text. The prose style and the accompanying illustration are designed to captivate the reader. To help the student relate personally and directly to a historical event, we have highlighted figures such as Hypatia of Alexandria, Isabella of Castile, and Sigmund Freud.

New! The West and the Wider World

To engage students with historical subjects we have included the new two-page *The West and the Wider World* feature that appears six times in the book. These new essays focus on instances of dynamic cultural encounters and exchanges between the West and the non-West at different points in history. The topics for this new feature were chosen to enhance the student's sense of connections among the events, phenomenon, politics, and products of the West and the wider world. At the end of each feature, we have included questions to spark class discussion and to reinforce such connections.

Documents

Civilization in the West contains selections from primary sources designed to stimulate students' interest in history by allowing them to hear the past speak in its own voice. We have tried to provide a mixture of "canonical" texts along with those illustrating the lives of ordinary people in order to demonstrate the variety of materials that form the building blocks of historical narrative. Each selection is accompanied by an explanatory

A Closer Look
Cathedrals of Light

Once the new posterior has been joined to the anterior
The church flashes with its center made bright
For bright is that which is brightly coupled with bright
And the noble building flooded by the new light shines forth
Which has been accomplished in our time
I Suger, being in charge when it was being done.

With these verses Suger (1081–1151), abbot of the royal monastery of St. Denis, burial place of French kings (on and off) since the Merovingians, celebrated the first Gothic church and

■ The choir of the Basilica of St. Denis.

The West and the Wider World
THE NUTMEG WARS

A seed about the size of an acorn connected Portugal, Holland, and England to a small string of islands in the Pacific Ocean and to the eastern seaboard of North America. It created a series of trading wars among the European powers in the seventeenth century and resulted in a number of trade treaties with the leaders of the Banda Islands, in what is now Indonesia. East and West became linked as great European sailing ships made port at the juncture of the Indian and Pacific Oceans in search of the seeds of the tree *Myristica Fragrans*, which grew only on the Banda Islands and which had the singular virtue of producing two rare spices greatly prized by Europeans: mace and, especially, nutmeg.

Flimsy in appearance, the seeds of the *Myristica Fragrans* could be harvested with no greater effort than the shaking of its branches. The husk of the seed pod yielded the deli-

suggested mystical power. By the end of the century, when the Dutch entered the trade and annual imports grew toward 100 tons, nutmeg was widely believed to be an aphrodisiac, and since aphrodisiacs work on the mind rather than the body, what was believed was all that

that their quest to obtain it led three nations to dispatch their merchants on eighteen-month journeys from which most never returned. If they did not perish during the long sea voyage around the horn of Africa, along the Coromandel Coast of India, and past the great pepper island of Java, they were imperiled by barely submerged razor-sharp volcanic rocks that guarded the Banda Islands on which the trees flourished. Shifting trade winds also made the islands inaccessible six months a year. Only those with good guides or good luck laid anchor there. If the merchants survived the dangers of nature, then they faced those of man. Every European captain claimed his nation held exclusive trading rights to these miraculous seeds, and in the open waters of the Pacific Ocean might made right. More than one great sailing ship had its hull punctured by cannon balls, its mast burned by flaming ar-

■ Engraving of the Banda Islands, based on a sixteenth-century map by Theodore de Bry.

THE RACE OF IRON

Hesiod (fl. ca. 800 B.C.E.), like Homer, is known only from the two poems ascribed to him, Theogony *and* Works and Days *written at the end of the Dark Ages. In his* Works and Days, *he tells of two brothers, himself and Perses, the one just and one unjust, who argue their positions before a group of kings. When the kings find in favor of the unjust brother, Hesiod describes his generation as an Age of Iron, when men lead harsh, brutal lives. And yet he counsels his brother Perses to virtue.*

Focus Questions

What are the primary virtues and vices Hesiod sees in his world? What is the role of the gods in enforcing morality?

Thereafter, would that I were not among the men of the fifth generation, but either had died before or been born afterwards. For now truly is a race of iron, and men never rest from labour and sorrow by day, and from perishing by night; and the gods shall lay sore trouble upon them. But, notwithstanding, even these shall have some good mingled with their evils. The father will not agree with his children,

But you, Perses, listen to right and do not foster violence; for violence is bad for a poor man. Even the prosperous cannot easily bear its burden, but is weighed down under it when he has fallen into delusion. The better path is to go by on the other side towards justice; for Justice beats Outrage when she comes at length to the end of the race. But only when he has suffered does the fool learn this. For Oath keeps pace with wrong judgments. There is a noise when Justice is being dragged in the way where those who devour bribes and give sentence with crooked judgments, take her. And she, wrapped in mist, follows to the city and haunts of the people, weeping, and bringing mischief to men, even to such as have driven her forth in that they did not deal straightly with her. (ll. 212–224)

DISCOVERING WESTERN CIVILIZATION ONLINE

You can obtain more information about Europe and the world between 1870 and 1914 at the Websites listed below. See also the Companion Website that accompanies this text, www.ablongman.com/kishlansky, which contains an online study guide and additional resources.

The European Balance of Power, 1870–1914   **The European Search for Territory and Markets**

Internet Mode...
www.fordham...
This site is part...
secondary sour...
ments among th...

QUESTIONS FOR REVIEW

1. How were rifts in Roman society widened by Rome's expansion into an empire?
2. In what ways were the life and thought of Cicero indicative of an age characterized by civil conflict and the collapse of republican traditions?
3. How was religious reform an important part of Augustus's efforts to restore stability to Roman society?

4. What did the Flavian and Antonine emperors do to keep Rome's vast empire intact and in relative peace?
5. How did Paul of Tarsus transform the teachings of Jesus of Nazareth from an outgrowth of Judaism into a separate spiritual tradition?

---

headnote that identifies the author and work and provides the necessary historical context. Following the headnote are two to three *Focus Questions* to guide students' reading and to spark critical thinking. Most of the extracts relate directly to discussion within the chapter, thus providing the student with a fuller understanding of a significant thinker or event.

Discovering Western Civilization Online

Discovering Western Civilization Online encourages students to further explore Western civilization. These end-of-chapter Website resources link students to documents, images, and cultural sites currently not included in the text.

Questions for Review

Although a standard feature in many texts, the *Questions for Review* in *Civilization in the West* nonetheless are worth noting. They do not provide just a factual review of the chapter. Instead, they prompt students to think critically about the major topics in the chapter and to pull together for themselves some conclusions about the events and peoples of the time.

CHANGES IN THE NEW EDITION

In the sixth edition, we have made significant changes in content and coverage.

Map Discovery

New *Map Discovery* features appear two to three times per chapter, offering specially designed maps with supporting caption information and questions designed to engage students in analyzing map data and making larger connections to chapter discussions.

The West and the Wider World

New two-page *The West and the Wider World* essay features appear six times in the book, exploring instances of dynamic cultural encounters and exchanges between the West and the non-West at different points in history.

Key Terms and Glossary

In each chapter, key terms are highlighted in boldface type to alert students to principal concepts and events discussed in the chapter. A page-referenced list of the key terms is included at the end of the chapter to help students review the main ideas and events covered in the chapter. A new glossary included at the end of the book provides definitions for the key terms.

Content Changes

Chapter 3: Classical and Hellenistic Greece, 500–100 B.C.E. includes additional material on Hellenistic medicine and includes a new feature on representing the Buddha. Chapter 5:

Imperial Rome, 146 B.C.E.–192 C.E. includes a new discussion of the study of science and astronomy in the empire. Chapter 7: The Classical Legacy in the East: Byzantium and Islam includes expanded coverage of Islamic civilization, including additional material on Muslim scientists and philosophers, and a new essay on the secrets of silk production from China introduced into Byzantium. Chapter 9: The High Middle Ages, 900–1300 includes a new section on the expansion of the Mongol Empire and its impact on the West. In Chapter 10: The Later Middle Ages, 1300–1500, there is a new discussion of the impact of events outside Europe on the decline of Italian economic power. Chapter 11: The Italian Renaissance contains a new section on Renaissance science, particularly the biological and life sciences. Chapter 12: The European Empires includes an expanded discussion of the legacy of the Encounters and the origin of the African slave trade. Chapter 17: Science and Commerce in Early Modern Europe includes expanded coverage of the early slave trade and a new feature on European trade competition in the East and the resulting Nutmeg wars. In Chapter 18: The Balance of Power in Eighteenth-Century Europe, a new feature essay explores the formation of the British Raj in India.

Parts of Chapter 20: The French Revolution and the Napoleonic Era, 1789–1815 were re-organized and streamlined to present more succinctly the factors leading to the crisis of the Old Regime and the early stages of the revolution. The chapter now also includes a feature on guillotine justice in the revolution. Chapter 23: State Building and Social Change in Europe, 1850–1914, includes a new section on the new technology and art of photography and an expanded discussion of the Civil War in the United States. In Chapter 24: The Crisis of European Culture, 1871–1914, a new section explores the arts in the shaping of the new consciousness and a new feature essay examines the influence of African art on Western artists and the influence of the industrial West on African art. Parts of Chapter 26: War and Revolution, 1914–1920 were reorganized to better present the Russian Revolution and its impact on the Great War and the discussion of settling the peace was expanded. Chapters 29: The Cold War and Postwar Economic Recovery: 1945–1970 and Chapter 30: The End of the Cold War and New Global Challenges, 1970 to the Present have been reorganized to highlight the significance of postwar economic and social transformations and geopolitical shifts and to better present the developments of the Cold War and its conclusion. Chapter 29 now begins with the origins of the Cold War and includes a new feature on the Post-World War II rise in Japanese manufacturing. Chapter 30 has been updated and also includes expanded coverage of the European Union, analysis of ethnicity and nationalism, terrorism in the early twenty-first century, and a new section on French laws on secularism.

New *The Visual Record* pictorial essays were developed for the sixth edition as well. Chapter 9: The High Middle Ages, 900–1300 opens with a pictorial essay on a Syrian castle and its influence on Edward I and his own castle in Wales; Chapter 12: The European Empires opens with an examination of a portrait of a king; Chapter 30: The End of the Cold War and New Global Challenges, 1970 to the Present begins with an examination of the 1989 fall of the Berlin Wall. We believe that each of these new pictorial essays will help students understand the dominant themes of their respective chapters.

Several new primary source documents were also added to this edition. Chapter 4 includes a new selection from Polybius comparing Rome and Carthage; Chapter 7 includes a new document from the *Alexiad* on a Turkish guest in the court of Alexis I; Chapter 17 has a new selection from Descartes on scientific inquiry into nature; Chapter 18 includes an excerpt from the travel diaries of Captain Cook; Chapter 23 has a new document on managing a household in the nineteenth century; and Chapter 26 includes a war poem from Wilfred Owen.

Other Changes

Icons

Throughout the text, you will see icons that will lead students to additional resources found on MyHistoryLab.com and LongmanWesternCivilization.com. These resources fall into four categories:

The **document** icon directs students to primary source documents that support the material they are reading in the textbook. In addition, the documents offer headnotes and analysis questions that focus students' reading.

The **image** icon leads students to photos, cartoons, and artwork that relate to the topic they are reading. Each image includes a descriptive, contextualized headnote and analysis questions.

The **map** icon refers to interactive maps with headnotes and questions designed to help students visualize the material they are learning. Printable map activities from Longman's outstanding geography workbooks allow students to interact with maps.

The **case study** icon leads to case studies where students can study the material in greater depth by comparing two or more sources.

There are many new features in our text and much that is out of the ordinary. But there are important traditional aspects of the narrative itself that also require mention. *Civilization in the West* is a mainstream text in which most of our energies have been placed in developing a solid, readable narrative of Western civilization that integrates coverage of women and minorities into the discussion. We have highlighted personalities while identifying trends. We have spotlighted social history, both in sections of chapters and in separate chapters, while maintaining a firm grip on political developments. We hope that there are many things in this book that teachers of Western civilization will find valuable. But we also hope that there are things here with which you will disagree, themes that you can develop better, arguments and ideas that will stimulate you. A textbook is only one part of a course, and it is always less important than a teacher. What we hope is that by having done our job successfully, we will have made the teacher's job easier and the student's job more enjoyable.

INSTRUCTOR SUPPLEMENTS

Companion Website (http://www.ablongman.com/kishlansky)

Instructors can take advantage of the Companion Website that supports this text. The instructor section of the Website includes teaching links, downloadable maps and images from the text for use in PowerPoint, PowerPoint lecture outlines, and a link to Supplements Central.

MyHistoryLab (http://www.myhistorylab.com)

MyHistoryLab provides students with an online package complete with the entire electronic textbook, numerous study aids, and a chapter exam. With several hundred primary sources and images, as well as map activities with gradable quizzes and map workbook activities, the site offers students a unique, interactive experience that brings history to life. The comprehensive site also includes a history bookshelf with twenty of the most commonly assigned books in history classes and a history toolkit with tutorials and helpful links. Features include History Toolkit; History Bookshelf; E-Sources; Map Activities; Pre-test and Post-test Self-Study Quizzes with Targeted Feedback; Chapter Review Materials; the textbook online; a Test Bank; and Research Navigator (see p. xxviii).

Delivered in CourseCompass, Blackboard, or WebCT, MyHistoryLab is easy to use and flexible. MyHistoryLab is organized according to the table of contents of your textbook, and because it is part of a course management system, you can customize it by adding your own syllabus, content, and assignments or use the materials as presented.

LongmanWesternCivilization.com (http://www.longmanwesterncivilization.com)

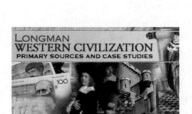

LongmanWesternCivilization.com provides the same Western Civilization resources as MyHistoryLab but without course management or an electronic textbook.

Discovering Western Civilization Through Maps and Views

Created by Gerald Danzer of the University of Illinois at Chicago—the recipient of the American History Association's James Harvey Robinson Prize for his work in the development of map transparencies—and David Buissert, this set of 140 four-color acetates is a unique instructional tool. It contains an introduction to teaching history through maps and a detailed commentary on each transparency. The collection includes cartographic and pictorial maps, views and photos, urban plans, building diagrams, and works of art. Available to qualified college adopters. ISBN 0-673-97499-5

Instructor's Resource Manual

Prepared by David B. Mock of Tallahassee Community College, this edition of the Instructor's Manual contains a chapter summary, key terms, geographic and map items, discussion questions, and an annotated film list for each chapter in the book. ISBN 0-321-31701-7

Test Bank

This edition of the Test Bank, revised by Chris Howell of Walla Walla Community College and University of St. Francis, contains more than 1200 multiple-choice, matching, and completion questions. Multiple-choice items are referenced by topic, text page number, and type (factual or interpretive). ISBN 0-321-31700-9

TestGen-EQ Computerized Testing System

This flexible, easy-to-master computerized testing system includes all of the test items in the printed test bank. The friendly interface allows instructors to easily edit, print, and expand item banks. Tests can be printed in several different formats and can include figures such as graphs and tables. Available on a dual platform CD-ROM. ISBN 0-321-31699-1

History Digital Media Archive CD-ROM

The Digital Media Archive CD-ROM contains electronic images and interactive and static maps, along with media elements such as video. These media assets are fully customizable and ready for classroom presentation or easy downloading into your PowerPoint presentations or any other presentation software. ISBN 0-321-14976-9

Text-Specific Transparency Set

A set of full-color transparency map acetates are taken from the text. ISBN 0-321-31698-3

Penguin-Longman Partnership

The partnership between Penguin Books and Longman Publishers offers a discount on the titles below when they are bundled with any Longman survey textbook. Visit www.ablongman.com/penguin for more information.

Available Titles

Peter Abelard, *The Letters of Abelard and Heloise*
Dante Alighieri, *Divine Comedy: Inferno*
Dante Alighieri, *The Portable Dante*
Anonymous, *The Song of Roland*
Anonymous, *The Epic of Gilgamesh*
Anonymous, *Vinland Sagas*
Aristophanes, *The Knights, Peace, The Birds, Assemblywomen, Wealth*

Louis Auchincloss, *Woodrow Wilson* (Penguin Lives Series)
Jane Austen, *Emma*
Jane Austen, *Pride and Prejudice*
Jane Austen, *Persuasion*
Jane Austen, *Sense and Sensibility*
Edward Bellamy, *Looking Backward*
Richard Bowring, *Diary of Lady Murasaki*
Charlotte Brontë, *Jane Eyre*
Charlotte Brontë, *Villette*

Emily Brontë, *Wuthering Heights*

Benvenuto Cellini, *The Autobiography of Benvenuto Cellini*

Geoffrey Chaucer, *The Canterbury Tales*

Marcus Tullius Cicero, *Cicero: Selected Political Speeches*

Miguel de Cervantes, *The Adventures of Don Quixote*

Bartolome de las Casas, *A Short Account of the Destruction of the West Indies*

René Descartes, *Discourse on Method and The Meditations*

Charles Dickens, *Hard Times*

Charles Dickens, *Great Expectations*

John Dos Passos, *Three Soldiers*

Einhard, *Two Lives of Charlemagne*

Olaudah Equiano, *The Interesting Narrative and Other Writings*

Jeffrey Gantz (tr.), *Early Irish Myths and Sagas*

Peter Gay, *Mozart* (Penguin Lives Series)

William Golding, *Lord of the Flies*

Kenneth Grahame, *The Wind in the Willows*

Grimm & Grimm, *Grimms' Fairy Tales*

Thomas Hardy, *Jude the Obscure*

Herodotus, *The Histories*

Thomas Hobbes, *Leviathan*

Homer, *The Iliad*

Homer, *Odyssey: Revised Prose Translation*

Homer, *Odyssey Deluxe*

The Koran

Lemisch, *B. Franklin*

Primo Levi, *If Not Now, When?*

Machiavelli, *The Prince*

Karl Marx, *The Communist Manifesto*

John Stuart Mill, *On Liberty*

Jean-Baptiste Molière, *Tartuffe and Other Plays*

Charles-Louis Montesquieu, *Persian Letters*

Sir Thomas More, *Utopia and Other Essential Writings*

Sherwin Nuland, *Leonardo DaVinci*

George Orwell, *1984*

George Orwell, *Animal Farm*

Plato, *Great Dialogues of Plato*

Plato, *The Republic*

Plato, *The Last Days of Socrates*

Marco Polo, *The Travels*

Procopius, *The Secret History*

Jean-Jacques Rousseau, *The Social Contract*

Sallust, *The Jugurthine Wars, The Conspiracy of Cataline*

William Shakespeare, *Hamlet*

William Shakespeare, *Macbeth*

William Shakespeare, *The Merchant of Venice* (Pelican Series)

William Shakespeare, *The Merchant of Venice* (Signet Classics)

William Shakespeare, *Othello*

William Shakespeare, *The Taming of the Shrew*

William Shakespeare, *Twelfth Night*

William Shakespeare, *King Lear*

William Shakespeare, *Four Great Comedies: The Taming of the Shrew, A Midsummer's Night Dream, Twelfth Night, The Tempest*

William Shakespeare, *Four Great Tragedies: Hamlet, Macbeth, King Lear, Othello*

William Shakespeare, *Four Histories: Richard II, Henry IV: Part I, Henry IV: Part II, Henry V*

William Shakespeare, *The Tempest*

Mary Shelley, *Frankenstein*

Aleksandr Solzhenitsyn, *One Day in the Life of Ivan Denisovich*

Sophocles, *The Three Theban Plays*

St. Augustine, *The Confessions of St. Augustine*

Robert Louis Stevenson, *The Strange Case of Dr. Jekyll and Mr. Hyde*

Suetonius, *The Twelve Caesars*

Jonathan Swift, *Gulliver's Travels*

Tacitus, *The Histories*

Voltaire, *Candide, Zadig and Selected Stories*

Goethe, *Faust, Part 1*

Goethe, *Faust, Part 2*

Edith Wharton, *Ethan Frome*

M. Willet, *The Signet World Atlas*

Gary Wills, *Saint Augustine* (Penguin Lives Series)

Virginia Woolf, *Jacob's Room*

STUDENT SUPPLEMENTS

Companion Website (http://www.ablongman.com/kishlansky)

The online course companion provides a wealth of resources for students using *Civilization in the West*. Students can access chapter summaries, interactive practice test questions, Web links, and a comprehensive list of recommended readings for every chapter. The Website is a comprehensive online study guide for students.

Research Navigator and Research Navigator Guide

Research Navigator is a comprehensive Website comprising three exclusive databases of credible and reliable source material for research and for student assignments: EBSCO's ContentSelect Academic Journal Database, *The New York Times* Search-by-Subject Archive, and "Best of the Web" Link Library. The site also includes an extensive help section. The Research Navigator Guide provides students with access to the Research Navigator Website and includes reference material and hints about conducting online research. This supplement is free to qualified college adopters when packaged with the text. ISBN 0-205-40838-9

Mapping Western Civilization: Student Activities

Written by Gerald Danzer of the University of Illinois at Chicago, this free map workbook for students is designed as an accompaniment to Discovering Western Civilization Through Maps and Views. It features exercises designed to teach students to interpret and analyze cartographic materials as historical documents. The instructor is entitled to a free copy of the workbook for each copy of the text purchased from Longman. ISBN 0-673-53774-9

Western Civilization Map Workbooks

Prepared by Glee Wilson of Kent State University, these two volumes include map exercises designed to test and reinforce basic geographic literacy and to build critical thinking skills. Available shrink-wrapped at no cost with any Longman survey text. Volume I: 0-321-01878-8, Volume II: 0-321-01877-X

Study Guide

Revised by Paul Brasil of Blue Mountain Community College, this study guide is available in two volumes and offers for each chapter a summary; a glossary list; map and geography questions; and identification, multiple-choice, and critical-thinking questions. Volume I: 0-321-31697-5, Volume II: 0-321-31696-7

Study Card for Western Civilization

Colorful, affordable, and packed with useful information, Allyn & Bacon/Longman's Study Cards make studying easier, more efficient, and more enjoyable. Course information is distilled down to the basics, helping you quickly master the fundamentals, review a subject for understanding, or prepare for an exam. Because they're laminated for durability, you can keep these Study Cards for years to come and pull them out whenever you need a quick review. ISBN 0-321-29233-2

MyHistoryLab (http://www.myhistorylab.com)

MyHistoryLab provides students with an online package complete with the entire Kishlansky textbook, numerous study aids, primary sources, and a chapter exam. With several hundred primary sources and images, as well as map activities with gradable quizzes and map workbook activities, the site offers students a unique, interactive experience that brings history to life. The comprehensive site also includes a history bookshelf with twenty of the most commonly assigned books in history classes and a history toolkit with tutorials and helpful links.

LongmanWesternCivilization.com (http://www.longmanwesterncivilization.com)

This Website provides the same resources as MyHistoryLab but without course management or an electronic textbook included.

Longman Atlas of Western Civilization

This 52-page atlas features carefully selected historical maps that provide comprehensive coverage for the major historical periods. Each map has been designed to be colorful, easy-to-read, and informative, without sacrificing detailed accuracy. This atlas makes history—and geography—more comprehensible. ISBN 0-321-21626-1

A Short Guide to Writing About History, Fourth Edition

Written by Richard Marius, late of Harvard University, and Melvin E. Page, Eastern Tennessee State University, this engaging and practical text helps students get beyond merely compiling dates and facts; it teaches them how to incorporate their own ideas into their papers and to tell a story about history that interests them and their peers. Covering both brief essays and the documented resource paper, the text explores the writing and researching processes, identifies different modes of historical writing, including argument, and concludes with guidelines for improving style. ISBN 0-321-09300-3

SafariX

SafariX Textbooks Online is an exciting new choice for students looking to save money. As an alternative to purchasing the print textbook, you can subscribe to the same content online and save up to 50% off the suggested list price of the print text. With a SafariX WebBook, you can search the text, make notes online, print out reading assignments that incorporate lecture notes, and bookmark important passages for later review. For more information, or to subscribe to the SafariX WebBook, visit www.safarix.com.

ACKNOWLEDGMENTS

We want to thank the many conscientious historians who gave generously of their time and knowledge to review our manuscript. We would like to thank the reviewers of the first five editions as well as those of the current edition. Their valuable critiques and suggestions have contributed greatly to the final product. We are grateful to the following:

Joseph Aieta, III, *Lasell College*; Ken Albala, *University of the Pacific*; Patricia Ali, *Morris College*; Gerald D. Anderson, *North Dakota State University*; Jean K. Berger, *University of Wisconsin, Fox Valley*; Susan Carrafiello, *Wright State University*; Andrew Donson, *University of Massachusetts, Amherst*; Frederick Dotolo, *St. John Fisher College*; Janusz Duzinkiewicz, *Purdue University*; Brian Elsesser, *Saint Louis University*; Bryan Ganaway, *University of Illinois*; David Graf, *University of Miami*; Benjamin Hett, *Hunter College*; Mark M. Hull, *Saint Louis University*; Barbara Klemm, *Broward Community College*; Lawrence Langer, *University of Connecticut*; Elise Moentmann, *University of Portland*; Alisa Plant, *Tulane University*; Salvador Rivera, *State University of New York*; Thomas Robisheaux, *Duke University*; Ilicia Sprey, *Saint Joseph's College*; George S. Vascik, *Miami University, Hamilton*; Vance Youmans, *Spokane Falls Community College*; Achilles Aavraamides, *Iowa State University*; Meredith L. Adams, *Southwest Missouri State*

University; Arthur H. Auten, *University of Hartford;* Suzanne Balch-Lindsay, *Eastern New Mexico University;* Sharon Bannister, *University of Findlay;* John W. Barker, *University of Wisconsin;* Patrick Bass, *Mount Union College;* William H. Beik, *Northern Illinois University;* Patrice Berger, *University of Nebraska;* Lenard R. Berlanstein, *University of Virginia;* Raymond Birn, *University of Oregon;* Donna Bohanan, *Auburn University;* Werner Braatz, *University of Wisconsin, Oshkosh;* Thomas A. Brady, Jr., *University of Oregon;* Anthony M. Brescia, *Nassau Community College;* Elaine G. Breslaw, *Morgan State University;* Ronald S. Brockway, *Regis University;* April Brooks, *South Dakota State University;* Daniel Patrick Brown, *Moorpark College;* Ronald A. Brown, *Charles County Community College;* Blaine T. Browne, *Broward Community College;* Kathleen S. Carter, *High Point University;* Robert Carver, *University of Missouri, Rolla;* Edward J. Champlin, *Princeton University;* Stephanie Evans Christelow, *Western Washington University;* Sister Dorita Clifford, BVM, *University of San Francisco;* Gary B. Cohen, *University of Oklahoma;* Jan M. Copes, *Cleveland State University;* John J. Contreni, *Purdue University;* Tim Crain, *University of Wisconsin, Stout;* Norman Delaney, *Del Mar College;* Samuel E. Dicks, *Emporia State University;* Frederick Dumin, *Washington State University;* Laird Easton, *California State University, Chico;* Dianne E. Farrell, *Moorhead State University;* Margot C. Finn, *Emory University;* Allan W. Fletcher, *Boise State University;* Luci Fortunato De Lisle, *Bridgewater State College;* Elizabeth L. Furdell, *University of North Florida;* Thomas W. Gallant, *University of Florida;* Frank Garosi, *California State University, Sacramento;* Lorne E. Glaim, *Pacific Union College;* Joseph J. Godson, *Hudson Valley Community College;* Sue Helder Goliber, *Mount St. Mary's College;* Manuel G. Gonzales, *Diablo Valley College;* Louis Haas, *Duquesne University;* Eric Haines, *Bellevue Community College;* Paul Halliday, *University of Virginia;* Margaretta S. Handke, *Mankato State University;* David A. Harnett, *University of San Francisco;* Paul B. Harvey, Jr., *Pennsylvania State University;* Neil Heyman, *San Diego State University;* Daniel W. Hollis, *Jacksonville State University;* Kenneth G. Holum, *University of Maryland;* Patricia Howe, *University of St. Thomas;* David Hudson, *California State University, Fresno;* Charles Ingrao, *Purdue University;* George F. Jewsbury, *Oklahoma State University;* Donald G. Jones, *University of Central Arkansas;* William R. Jones, *University of New Hampshire;* Richard W. Kaeuper, *University of Rochester;* David Kaiser, *Carnegie-Mellon University;* Jeff Kaufmann, *Muscatine Community College;* Carolyn Kay, *Trent University;* William R. Keylor, *Boston University;* Joseph Kicklighter, *Auburn University;* Charles L. Killinger, III, *Valencia Community College;* Alan M. Kirshner, *Ohlone College;* Charlene Kiser, *Milligan College;* Alexandra Korros, *Xavier University;* Cynthia Kosso, *Northern Arizona University;* Lara Kriegel, *Florida International University;* Lisa M. Lane, *Mira Costa College;* David C. Large, *Montana State University;* Catherine Lawrence, *Messiah College;* Bryan LeBeau, *Creighton University;* Robert B. Luehrs, *Fort Hays State University;* Donna J. Maier, *University of Northern Iowa;* Margaret Malamud, *New Mexico State University;* Roberta T. Manning, *Boston College;* Lyle McAlister, *University of Florida;* Therese M. McBride, *College of the Holy Cross;* David K. McQuilkin, *Bridgewater College;* Victor V. Minasian, *College of Marin;* David B. Mock, *Tallahassee Community College;* Robert Moeller, *University of California, Irvine;* R. Scott Moore, *University of Dayton;* Ann E. Moyer, *University of Pennsylvania;* Pierce C. Mullen, *Montana State University;* John A. Nichols, *Slippery Rock University;* Thomas F. X. Noble, *University of Virginia;* J. Ronald Oakley, *Davidson County Community College;* Bruce K. O'Brien, *Mary Washington College;* Dennis H. O'Brien, *West Virginia University;* Maura O'Connor, *University of Cincinnati;* Richard A. Oehling, *Assumption College;* James H. Overfield, *University of Vermont;* Catherine Patterson, *University of Houston;* Sue Patrick, *University of Wisconsin, Barron County;* Peter C. Piccillo, *Rhode Island College;* Peter O'M. Pierson, *Santa Clara University;* Theophilus Prousis, *University of North Florida;* Marlette Rebhorn, *Austin Community College;* Jack B. Ridley, *University of Missouri, Rolla;* Constance M. Rousseau, *Providence College;* Thomas J. Runyan, *Cleveland State University;* John P. Ryan, *Kansas City Community College;* Geraldine Ryder, *Ocean County College;* Joanne Schneider, *Rhode Island College;* Steven Schroeder, *Indiana University of Pennsylvania;* Steven C. Seyer, *Lehigh County Community College;* Lixin Shao, *University of Minnesota, Duluth;* George H.

Shriver, *Georgia Southern University;* Ellen J. Skinner, *Pace University;* Bonnie Smith, *University of Rochester;* Patrick Smith, *Broward Community College;* James Smither, *Grand Valley State University;* Sherill Spaar, *East Central University;* Charles R. Sullivan, *University of Dallas;* Peter N. Stearns, *Carnegie-Mellon University;* Saulius Suziedelis, *Millersville University;* Darryl B. Sycher, *Columbus State Community College;* Roger Tate, *Somerset Community College;* Janet A. Thompson, *Tallahassee Community College;* Anne-Marie Thornton, *Bilkent University;* Donna L. Van Raaphorst, *Cuyahoga Community College;* James Vanstone, *John Abbot College;* Steven Vincent, *North Carolina State University;* Richard A. Voeltz, *Cameron University;* Faith Wallis, *McGill University;* Sydney Watts, *University of Richmond;* Eric Weissman, *Golden West College;* Christine White, *Pennsylvania State University;* William Harry Zee, *Gloucester County College.*

Each author also received invaluable assistance and encouragement from many colleagues, friends, and family members over the years of research, reflection, writing, and revising that went into the making of this text.

Mark Kishlansky thanks Ann Adams, Robert Bartlett, Ray Birn, David Buisseret, Ted Cook, Frank Conaway, Constantine Fasolt, James Hankins, Katherine Haskins, Richard Hellie, Matthew Kishlansky, Donna Marder, Mary Beth Rose, Victor Stater, Jeanne Thiel, and the staffs of the Joseph Regenstein Library, the Newberry Library, and the Widener and Lamont Libraries at Harvard.

Patrick Geary thanks Mary, Catherine, and Anne Geary for their patience, support, and encouragement; he also thanks Anne Picard, Dale Schofield, Hans Hummer, Jared Poley, and Richard Mowrer for their able assistance throughout the project.

Patricia O'Brien thanks Elizabeth Sagias for her encouragement and enthusiasm throughout the project and Robert Moeller for his keen eye for organization and his suggestions for writing a gendered history. She is especially grateful to her assistants Susan Beals and Carolyn Drago for keeping her on track throughout the project.

All the authors thank Janet Lanphier, senior acquisitions editor, Karen Helfrich, development editor, and Karin Vonesh, project editor at Elm Street Publishing Services, Inc., for producing a beautiful book. Thanks are also due to Patrick McCarthy, for his work in producing the media supplements that accompany this volume, and Kristi Olson, who worked on the print supplements and Companion Website.

MARK KISHLANSKY
PATRICK GEARY
PATRICIA O'BRIEN

ABOUT THE AUTHORS

MARK KISHLANSKY Mark Kishlansky is Frank B. Baird, Jr., Professor of English and European History at Harvard University, where he has taught Western Civilization and courses in the CORE program for general education. He has also been awarded Harvard's Hoopes Prize for undergraduate teaching. Professor Kishlansky served as Associate Dean of the Faculty from 1999–2001. Before joining the Harvard faculty he taught for sixteen years at the University of Chicago where he was a member of the Committee on Social Thought. Professor Kishlansky is a specialist on seventeenth-century English political history and has written, among other works, *A Monarchy Transformed, The Rise of the New Model Army,* and *Parliamentary Selection: Social and Political Choice in Early Modern England.* From 1984–1991 he was editor of the *Journal of British Studies.* He is currently writing a history of the reign of Charles I entitled *The Death of Kings.* He is the General Editor of Pearson Custom Publishing's primary source databases for Western and World Civilization.

PATRICK GEARY Holding a Ph.D. in Medieval Studies from Yale University, Patrick Geary has broad experience in interdisciplinary approaches to European history and civilization. He has served as the director of the Medieval Institute at the University of Notre Dame as well as director for the Center for Medieval and Renaissance Studies at UCLA where he is currently professor of history. He has also held positions at the University of Florida and Princeton University and has taught at the École des Hautes Études en Sciences Sociales in Paris, at the University of Vienna, and at the Central European University in Budapest. He has coordinated and participated in programs for history teachers in Pennsylvania, Florida, and California, and has co-authored a television series on medieval knights. His many publications include *Readings in Medieval History; Before France and Germany: The Creation and Transformation of the Merovingian World; Furta Sacra: Thefts of Relics in the Central Middle Ages;* and *The Myth of Nations: The Medieval Origins of Europe.*

PATRICIA O'BRIEN Between 1995 and 1999, Patricia O'Brien worked to foster collaborative interdisciplinary research in the humanities as director of the University of California Humanities Research Institute. Between 1999 and 2004, she held the position of Dean of the College of Humanities, Arts, and Social Sciences at the University of California, Riverside. She has also held appointments at the University of California, Irvine, Yale University, and at the École des Hautes Études en Sciences Sociales in Paris. Currently Professor O'Brien is the Executive Dean of the UCLA College of Letters and Sciences. Professor O'Brien is a specialist in modern French cultural and social history and has published widely on the history of crime, punishment, cultural theory, urban history, and gender issues. Representative publications include *The Promise of Punishment: Prisons in Nineteenth-Century France;* "The Kleptomania Diagnosis: Bourgeois Women and Theft in Late Nineteenth-Century France" in *Expanding the Past: A Reader in Social History;* and "Michel Foucault's History of Culture" in *The New Cultural History,* edited by Lynn Hunt. Professor O'Brien's commitment to this textbook grew out of her own teaching experiences in large, introductory Western Civilization courses. She has benefited from the contributions of her students and fellow instructors in her approach to the study of Western Civilization in the modern period.

INTRODUCTION

WESTERN CIVILIZATION BEFORE 1300

Chapter Outline

ÖTZI'S LAST MEAL
Tradition and Innovation in Prehistoric Europe

Most of us never knew our great-grandparents; thus, it seems all the more incredible that we can visit with an ancestor from three hundred generations past—the dawn of civilization. And yet a discovery in the Italian Alps a decade ago has brought us face to face with Ötzi (so-named for the valley where he was found), an ordinary man who faced a cruel death more than five thousand years ago. Ötzi's perfectly preserved body, clothing, tools, and weapons allow us to know how people lived and died in Western Europe before it was Europe—before indeed it was the West.

Ötzi was small by modern European standards: he stood at just 5 feet 4 inches. Around 40 years old, he was probably a senior and respected member of his community. Already he was suffering from arthritis, and tattoos on his left wrist, right knee, calves, ankles, and the lumbar region of his spine

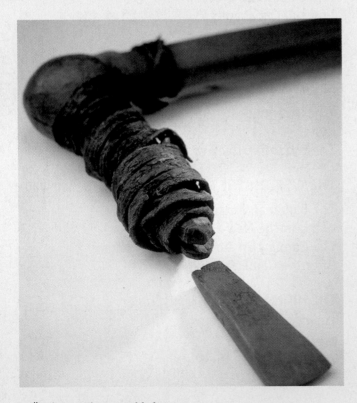

■ Ötzi's ax with copper blade.

suggest that, just as in some nomadic societies today, he and his companions used tattooing as a kind of therapy. He probably lived in a village below the mountain whose inhabitants lived from hunting, simple agriculture, and goat herding.

One spring day around 3000 B.C.E., Ötzi enjoyed what would be his last meal of meat, some vegetables, and flat bread made of einkorn wheat. He dressed warmly but simply: first, a leather breechcloth secured at his waist with a calfskin belt. Over this he put on a knee-length leather upper garment made of long strips of goatskin sewn together with animal sinews. Below, he protected his legs with leather leggings and slipped his feet into sturdy shoes made of bearskin soles, deerhide tops, and lined with soft grasslike socks. On his head was a warm bearskin cap. He was probably in a hurry, and he quickly filled a backpack and took up his usual tools and weapons.

Ötzi traveled light, but he had with him all that he needed to provide for himself. He carried an ax, whose 60-centimeter yew-wood haft ended in a blade of almost pure copper, and a flint knife with an ash-wood handle secured to his belt in a fiber scabbard. In a pouch he carried a tool made of stag antler and limewood with which he could chip new flint tools. He secured his leather backpack on a pack-frame made of a long hazel rod bent into a U shape and reinforced with two narrow wooden slats. Among other things it held birch bark containers, one filled with materials to start a fire, which he could ignite with a flint he carried in his pouch. He also equipped himself with a simple first-aid kit consisting of inner bark from the birch tree, a substance with antibiotic and styptic properties.

For so small a man, Ötzi carried an imposing weapon, but unfortunately for him it was not yet finished. Near his body was found a yew-wood bow almost six feet long and a quiver of arrows. He must have been working on the bow and arrows shortly before he died: the bow's grip was not yet finished, and the bow ends had not yet been prepared to attach the bowstring. In a chamois skin quiver two arrows, equipped with flint heads and fletched with feathers, were ready for use. Twelve other arrow shafts remained unfinished along with his bowstring.

For ten years after the discovery of his body scholars and scientists examined, x-rayed, and studied his remains and speculated on why and how he died. Was he caught by a sudden storm and had he succumbed to hypothermia? Did he fall, injure himself, and die of exposure? And what was he doing so high in the mountains—six hours from the valley where he had his last meal, without adequate food or water—in the first place? For a decade it was thought that the mystery would never be solved. Then, following yet another x ray of his frozen corpse, the truth came out. A sharp-eyed radiologist saw the telltale shadow of a stone point lodged in his back.

Apparently, Ötzi left the lower villages that fateful spring day frightened and in a great hurry. Alone at an altitude of over 10,000 feet, desperately trying to finish his bow and arrows, he was fleeing for his life, but his luck ran out. Ötzi was shot in the back with an arrow. It pierced his shoulder between his shoulder blade and ribs, paralyzing his arm and causing extensive bleeding. He pulled the arrow out but the flint point remained imbedded, and his efforts only increased the pain and the damage. His simple medical kit was of no help. Exhausted, he lay down in a shallow cleft in the snowy rocks. In a matter of hours he was dead, and the snows of centuries quietly buried him.

What does Ötzi's life and death tell us about the story of Western civilization? Although he lived and died at the same time that radically new urban societies and cultures were appearing just east of the Mediterranean, Ötzi still belonged to the Stone Age. His clothing, tools, and weapons all show a perfection of ancient techniques, but nothing innovative. None of his clothing was woven: apparently this basic technology was unknown to his community although it was common in western Asia. The only metal was his precious ax head, and it was of soft copper—Ötzi's society was still ignorant of bronze, a much harder alloy of copper and tin favored in the eastern Mediterranean. And yet, something vital connected Ötzi's world and that distant cradle of civilization: his last meal. Einkorn is not native to western Europe. It originated as a wild grain in the region of the Tigris and Euphrates rivers before being cultivated starting around 10,000 B.C.E. From there, both the grain itself and the technology of its cultivation spread slowly, ultimately reaching Ötzi's world of Alpine villages. If not civilization, then one of the essential components of it had reached this isolated mountain valley. Others

■ Reconstruction of Ötzi with clothing and equipment.

would come in the following centuries: weaving, metal working, urbanization, writing, and ways to kill men and women like Ötzi with greater efficiency.

Looking Ahead

This first introductory chapter begins before Ötzi with the origins of humankind and chronicles the great discoveries that led to the first urban-based civilizations of Mesopotamia and Egypt. From there, the chapter provides an overview of the early and classical periods of Greece and early and Imperial periods of Rome, touches on the transformation of the Classical World and its legacy in the East, and ends with coverage of the Early and High Middle Ages up to 1300. ➤

BEFORE CIVILIZATION

Let's go back even farther, before Ötzi's time. What were the first humans like? The modern species of humans, *Homo sapiens* (thinking human), appeared more than 100,000 years ago. Studies of human DNA from people around the world show that modern humans descend from a common ancestor: a woman who probably lived in Africa. The earliest *Homo sapiens* in Europe, the Neanderthal, were roughly the same size and had the same cranial capacity as we do. They spread throughout much of Africa, Europe, and Asia during the last great ice age.

The Neanderthals were replaced by our subspecies, *Homo sapiens sapiens* (thinking thinking human) 40,000 years ago. Whatever the reason—extinction, evolution, or extermination—this last arrival on the human scene was universally successful. All humans today—whether Scandinavian, African, Japanese, or Native American—belong to this subspecies. Differences in skin color, type of hair, and build are minor variations. Race is not a fact of biology. Racial distinctions are not objective divisions of the human species but arbitrary decisions to group people according to some of these minor variations.

Early *Homo sapiens sapiens* lived in small kin groups of 20 or 30, following game and seeking shelter in tents and caves. These people lived during the **Paleolithic era** (ca. 600,000–10,000 B.C.E.). They worked together for hunting and defense and formed emotional bonds based on more than sex or economic necessity. During the late Paleolithic era (ca. 35,000–10,000 B.C.E.), culture, meaning everything about humans not inherited biologically, was increasingly determinant in human life. Paleolithic people found time to develop speech, religion, and artistic expression. Wall paintings, small clay and stone figurines, and decorated stone and bone tools indicate not just artistic ability but also abstract and symbolic thought.

Around 10,000 B.C.E., hunter-gatherers along the coastal plains of what is today Syria and Israel near the Zagros Mountains between modern Iran and Iraq developed strategies that led to **broad-spectrum gathering.** Rather than constantly traveling in search of food, people stayed put and used the sources of food in their area: fish, wild grains, fruits, and game. People built and rebuilt their mud brick and stone huts over generations rather than moving on. This was known as *sedentarization* (choosing to live in one location). The advantages of settled communities included a decrease in infant mortality and a rise in life expectancy.

The people of the **Neolithic era,** or New Stone Age (ca. 8000–6500 B.C.E.), organized sizable villages. Jericho grew into a fortified town complete with ditch, stone walls, and towers and sheltered 2000 inhabitants. People no longer made long trips to look for favored species of plants and animals where they occurred naturally. Instead, they brought these plants and animals back to the villages to be grown and raised. Agriculture had begun. For the first time, humans could live wherever they could raise their own food rather than where food happened to be. Sedentarization and agriculture led to an increase in population. Population growth demanded more formal organization and led to the development of political

leadership. This leadership and the perception of safety in numbers prevented the traditional breaking away to form communities in the next valley, as had happened when population growth pressured earlier groups. Civilization was just beginning.

Mesopotamia

Around Ötzi's time, civilization was underway in Mesopotamia (which means "between the rivers"). Mesopotamia was a desert plain stretching to the mouth of the Tigris and Euphrates rivers. Until 3500 B.C.E. the people lived in scattered villages. But population in this region, known as Sumer (in what is now Iraq), began to increase. The Sumerian people congregated in urban areas, such as Uruk, to protect themselves from attack and to sustain their increasing population. Nine hundred semicircular towers protected Uruk's 40,000 inhabitants. Within the city walls, social, political, and technological advances of Western civilization were developed.

Technological Advances.   The need to feed, clothe, protect, and govern a growing population led to major discoveries. Canals and dikes harnessed water supplies; plows, sleds, and carts hauled produce to town and to distant markets. The use of bronze tools and weapons enhanced technology. People developed mathematics to understand the movement of the planets and to handle business and government administration. Babylonian mathematics was based on a numerical system from 1 to 60. (Today we still divide hours and minutes into 60 units.) Mathematicians devised multiplication tables, square roots, an algebraic system, and quadratic equations to determine the wages of a variety of workers employed for several days.

Writing.   By 3500 B.C.E., officials were drawing pictographic symbols (**cuneiform**) in clay tablets with sharpened reeds. Eventually writers used cuneiform to depict concepts and sounds. Writing was used in commercial and government activities and in culture and religion. Tablets were used to preserve contracts, maintain administrative records, and record significant events, prayers, myths, and proverbs. Writing allowed centralization and control of government and the ability to communicate over enormous distances, to preserve and transmit information, and to express religious and cultural beliefs. Writing transmitted the achievements of the first civilization to the future.

Temples and Palaces.   Mesopotamians worshiped impersonal gods, each with an area of responsibility and with human characteristics. Humans' role was to serve gods by offering sacrifices to idols, which gave them the gods' protection. Towns first developed around the gods' temples for this purpose. Sumerians did not believe in human immortality. They believed that earthly life and its accomplishments were worthwhile. The temple was one center of the city; the palace was the other. As representative of the city's god, the king was

■ An early Sumerian clay tablet found in Iraq records in cuneiform the barley rations allotted in a five-day week to 40 workers.

the ruler and highest judge. He was responsible for the construction and maintenance of religious buildings and the complex system of canals. He also commanded the army.

King Sargon. The cultural and economic developments of early Mesopotamia occurred within the context of almost constant warfare. From around 3000 B.C.E. until 2300 B.C.E., various rulers fought for control of Sumer (the southern region of Mesopotamia). The population was a mixture of Sumerians and Semites—peoples speaking Semitic languages related to modern Arabic or Hebrew—all jealously protective of their cities and gods.

King Sargon (ca. 2334–2279 B.C.E.) of Akkad was the most important figure in Mesopotamian history: he created the first multiethnic empire in Western civilization. Sargon allowed a variety of territories to be under his control and yet they could keep their own institutions, while using his leaders. His empire extended from the Euphrates to Syria. Sargon used the title "King of the Four Regions" to emphasize the universality of his rule. As with all Mesopotamian states, the Akkadian state did not last long.

Hammurabi's Code of Law. Hammurabi ruled Babylonia from 1792–1750 B.C.E. His code of law dictated rights and obligations of the social classes: the elite, the masses, and the slaves. His code of law provided some legal rights for slaves, who could marry free persons and might eventually obtain freedom. The code also protected women and children. Husbands ruled their households, but they did not have unlimited authority over their wives. Women could initiate their own

■ A seven-foot-high diorite stele, dating from about 1750 B.C.E., is inscribed with the law Code of Hammurabi. The relief at the top shows Hammurabi standing at the left in the presence of the sun god, perhaps explaining his code of laws.

court cases, practice various trades, and hold public positions. Hammurabi's Code included death and mutilation as penalties. If a physician performed a successful eye operation on a member of the elite, the code specified that he receive ten silver coins. However, if the physician caused the loss of the eye, he lost his hand. Hammurabi's extensive use of the law of retaliation was an assertion of royal authority in maintaining justice.

DOCUMENT

Near Eastern Law Codes

Weakened by internal fighting, Babylonia fell to a new and powerful force in Western history, the Hittites. They destroyed the Babylonian state around 1600 B.C.E. and expanded south along the coast. However, the Hittites were stopped at the battle of Kadesh around 1286 B.C.E., when they encountered the army of Egypt of Ramses II.

The Gift of the Nile

The Mesopotamian civilization was characterized by trade, communication, and violent conquest. But Egypt was quite different. Egypt knew self-sufficiency, an inward focus on culture and society, and stability. Egypt's Nile Valley enjoyed fertile soils and security from invasion, which was in great contrast to the conditions in Mesopotamian civilization. Because of this, the Nile Valley was the most stable self-sufficient civilization in the West for more than 2,500 years. These 2,500 years of Egyptian history are divided into four periods:

- Pre- and early dynastic Egypt (ca. 3150–2770 B.C.E.)
- The Old Kingdom (ca. 2770–2200 B.C.E.)
- The Middle Kingdom (ca. 2050–1786 B.C.E.)
- The New Kingdom (ca. 1560–1087 B.C.E.)

The Old Kingdom.   Egyptian life centered on divine kings, or pharaohs. ("Pharaoh," meaning "great house" in Egyptian, is Hebrew for Egyptian king.) The first pharaoh, King Zoser, united upper and lower Egypt around 2686 B.C.E. Pharaohs were responsible for serving as intermediaries to the gods and ensuring the annual flooding of the Nile.

A professional bureaucracy administered land, taxes, and labor to maintain vast public construction projects for the king. This bureaucracy required the ability to read, but women were not allowed formal education and so were excluded. However, women were given some freedoms, such as the right to conduct their own business, including contracts and lawsuits.

Constructing the pyramids, which were tombs for the pharaohs, demanded an extraordinary concentration of resources and created a constant demand for skilled and unskilled labor (70,000 workers). The pyramids transformed Egypt socially, economically, and politically. The expense of constructing pyramids, increasing consumption demands of the wealthy, and the wealth of temples caused extensive economic problems for the country and led to the collapse of royal authority about 2200 B.C.E.

The Middle Kingdom.   Political power shifted to the hands of provincial governors. A less rigidly stratified society emerged when centralized kingship revived about 2000 B.C.E. While pharaohs resumed the construction of pyramids, the projects did not consume as many resources as they had earlier. All literate men gained access to the bureaucracy, and the promise of the afterlife was extended to commoners, reflective of a growing concern for justice. During this time, foreign Semites migrated into Egypt, and some rose to important positions. However, around 1700 B.C.E., the Hyksos, or "rulers of foreign lands," invaded and assumed control of Egypt, introducing new military technology and organization, while retaining Egyptian political traditions.

The New Kingdom.   Ahmose I (1552–1527 B.C.E.) began the New Kingdom, expelled the Hyksos, liberated Egypt, and used his army to expand into Nubia, Canaan, and Syria, reaching to the Euphrates. Egyptian expansion was tentative, as many of the military campaigns in the north were only glorified raids. Still, the campaigns increased trade and contact with peoples outside of Egypt.

The ruler Amenhotep IV (1364–1347 B.C.E.) was controversial because he broke with the customs. He was called the first monotheist because he questioned the religious bases of

■ This bust of Akhenaten, the revolutionary pharaoh who attempted to transform Egyptian religion, breaks with the ancient tradition of Egyptian portraiture, depicting the pharaoh with the symbolic characteristics of both male and female.

his political power by attempting to replace the worship of Amen-Re and other traditional Egyptian gods with the worship of the sun-disk god Aten. Amenhotep changed his own name to Akhenaten ("it pleases Aten"). But his ambition died with him. It was Tutankhamen (1347–1337 B.C.E.) who restored the ancient gods.

Ramses II (1289–1224 B.C.E.) successfully limited Hittite aggression, but the treaty the two states signed marked the failure of a single power to unify the region. The Egyptian and Hittite empires disintegrated because of political, economic, and social conflicts. In the absence of strong Egyptian and Hittite states, the Semitic kingdoms of Syria and Palestine gained their independence.

Between Two Worlds: The Semitic People

Semitic culture, although mostly nomadic during this time, gave rise to the religious and cultural traditions that are central to Western civilization. Groups of Semites entered Syria, Lebanon, Israel, and Palestine after 2000 B.C.E. The nomadic

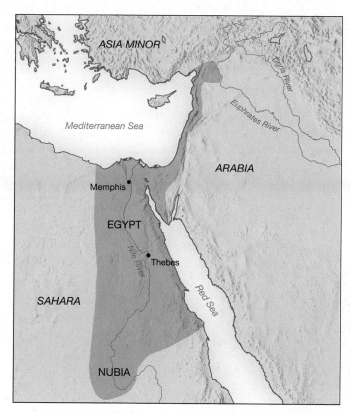

■ The Egyptian Empire. During the New Kingdom, Egyptian power extended from the Nile Valley to include the whole eastern coast of the Mediterranean.

shepherds usually rejected urban culture, pitching tents on the outskirts of towns and moving on when their sheep and goats had exhausted the pasture. But they brought Mesopotamian religious and legal traditions. One such nomad was Abram, who according to later tradition moved with his family from Mesopotamia to the region known as Canaan.

Abraham.   Although Abram rejected Mesopotamian gods, Abram and his successors were not monotheists. They did not deny the existence of other gods. They simply believed that they had a personal pact or covenant with their own god. According to Hebrew tradition, Abram's god promised him that he would be the father of a great nation and as a sign of this promise changed his name to Abraham. Abraham's patriarchal clan (the Greek term "patriarch" means "rule by the father") placed women in subordinate positions.

Exodus.   During the Middle Kingdom and Hyksos period, some of the Semitic wanderers had migrated to Egypt, where many were enslaved. Around the thirteenth century B.C.E., Semitic slaves left Egypt for Sinai and Canaan. They were under the leadership of Moses, a Semite and the founder of the Israelite people. The memory of this departure is known as the Exodus. It became a symbol for the Israelites. Adopting the god Yahweh as their only god in a covenant with Him, they entered Palestine and captured its cities. The Hebrews saw the

Exodus as evidence of the deeds of Yahweh and as imposing ethical demands upon the Hebrew people.

Ark of the Covenant.   During its first centuries, Israel consisted of loosely organized tribes whose only focal point was the religious shrine at Shiloh. The shrine housed no idols, but only a chest known as the Ark of the Covenant, which contained the law of Moses and mementos of the Exodus. By 1050 B.C.E., the Philistines had defeated the Israelites and captured the Ark of the Covenant. Religious leaders responded to the crisis of their loss of the Ark of the Covenant by creating a kingdom, which brought Israel to new military prominence under Saul, David, and later Solomon. Tyrannical kings, higher taxes, and the criticism of prophets undermined support for the monarchy, which eventually split into the kingdoms of Israel in the North and Judah in the South.

A period of decay followed as Assyria conquered the Kingdom of Israel in 722 B.C.E.; the New Babylonians under King Nebuchadnezzar II conquered the Kingdom of Judah in 586 B.C.E., taking a number of Hebrews captive. For fifty years the captives transformed Yahweh into a universal god who had formed a covenant with Abraham and the Hebrew people. When, some fifty years later, the captives were allowed to return to Judaea, their new understanding of their faith and their strengthened identity developed into Judaism. Their religion focused on their monotheism, on the **Torah** or sacred scriptures, on the rebuilt temple in Jerusalem, and their special identity that they sought to keep free from alien influence.

Nineveh and Babylon

In the seventh century B.C.E., the Assyrian state united Mesopotamian and Egyptian civilizations in a single empire that showed an unprecedented degree of integration and governmental centralization. King Assur-dan II took the throne in 934 B.C.E. The Assyrian Empire stretched from the Tigris and Euphrates rivers to the Persian Gulf, along the coast from Syria to beyond the Delta, and up the Nile to Thebes. Assur-dan II rebuilt the army and the agricultural and commercial economy while overseeing the expansion of Assyrian rule.

Tiglath-pileser III (746–727 B.C.E.) was the greatest empire builder of Mesopotamia since Sargon. Tiglath-pileser created an empire that would later be copied by Persia and Macedonia. This was the first true empire. From his palace at Nineveh, Tiglath-pileser created a multiethnic imperial system based on:

- *A modern army.* Tiglath-pileser had the most modern army the world had ever seen. It was the first to use iron weapons on a massive scale. The bronze swords and shields of the enemies were no match. Assyrian armies included infantry, cavalry, chariots, and engineering units for constructing the siege equipment to capture towns. Warfare had become a science.
- *A new military-religious ideology.* Tiglath-pileser created the most developed military-religious ideology of any ancient people. Ashur, the god of the Assyrians, had but

A Closer Look
Discovering the Pharaohs

The English archaeologist Howard Carter had been searching the Valley of the Kings, near Thebes, for the tomb of Tutankhamen for five fruitless years. Years later, he described the events of 26 November 1922, the day that culminated his quest:

> With trembling hands I made a tiny breach in the upper left-hand corner of the door. Darkness and blank space, as far as an iron testing-rod could reach, showed that whatever lay beyond was empty, and not filled like the passage we had just cleared. Candle tests were applied as a precaution against possible foul gases, and then, widening the hole a little, I inserted the candle and peered in, Lord Carnarvon, Lady Evelyn Herbert, and A. R. Callender standing anxiously beside me to hear the verdict. At first I could see nothing, the hot air escaping from the chamber causing the candle flame to flicker, but presently, as my eyes grew accustomed to the light, details of the room within emerged slowly from the mist, strange animals, statues, and gold—everywhere the glint of gold. For the moment—an eternity it must have seemed to the others standing by—I was struck dumb with amazement, and when Lord Carnarvon, unable to stand the suspense any longer, inquired anxiously, "Can you see anything?" it was all I could do to get out the words, "Yes, wonderful things."

■ Rosetta stone.

The "wonderful things" Carter saw were more than 5000 priceless objects, including translucent alabaster jars and cups, painted wooden caskets, life-sized wooden statues of the king, four chariots, three large couches in the forms of animals, a golden throne, a shrine encased in thick sheet gold, and a great number of smaller jars, boxes, baskets, and other burial offerings spread throughout four underground rooms. The burial chamber itself contained the shrine housing the remains of the king, its seals intact. Inside the shrine was another gilt shrine, and within it a third, and a fourth, each more exquisite and precious. Within the last lay the yellow quartzite sarcophagus that held the king's mummified remains in three coffins. The first was of gilded wood; the second, gilded wood with glass paste; the third, 450 pounds of solid gold. The tomb of Tutankhamen, the only royal tomb known to have escaped ancient grave robbers, remains the most spectacular archaeological discovery of all time.

As spectacular as it was, Carter's discovery was not the most important in the history of Egyptology. Actually, Carter's find would have been impossible without a more significant breakthrough that had occurred exactly 100 years earlier and that took place not on the banks of the Nile in Egypt but on those of the Seine in France. Carter was able to discover Tutankhamen's tomb only because an earlier scholar had discovered the secret of Egyptian hieroglyphics. Over the following century, archaeologists, historians, and philologists (scholars who study language) had pieced together the history of ancient Egypt and Tutankhamen's role in it.

The story begins in 1798, when Napoleon Bonaparte invaded Egypt with a view to adding this ancient land to the French Republic. He took with him not just soldiers but also a Commission of Science and Arts composed of more than 100 scientists, engineers, and mathematicians. During their three-year occupation of Egypt, they and their commander were captivated by the splendor of Egypt's ancient monuments. They mapped and sketched hundreds of temples, pyramids, and ruins and brought back to France thousands of objects, many covered with intriguing but unreadable hieroglyphics. Back in France, members of the commission worked for years studying, classifying, and publishing the first comprehensive and systematic survey of Egyptian antiquities. Still the hieroglyphics, and with them the rich history of ancient Egypt, remained a mystery.

The mystery was solved in 1822 by the young scholar Jean François Champollion (1790–1832). Champollion had already mastered Latin, Greek, Hebrew, Syriac, Ethiopic, Arabic, Persian, Sanskrit, and Coptic when, at age 18, he began to devote himself to cracking the mystery of Egyptian writing. His key was a basalt fragment discovered at Rachid (in English, Rosetta) on the west branch of the Nile in 1799 by Napoleon's commission. The stone contains three inscriptions. The uppermost is written in hieroglyphics; the second in what is called *demotic*, the simplified common

script of ancient Egypt; and the third in Greek. Champollion guessed that the three inscriptions might all contain the same text. He spent the next 14 years working from the Greek to the demotic and finally to the hieroglyphics until he had deciphered the whole text and uncovered the basics of ancient Egyptian writing. In 1822 he reported his great discovery to the French Academy of Inscriptions. Champollion's discovery remains the most significant event in Egyptology, and he accomplished it without ever setting foot on Egyptian soil.

In the following century, scholars translated thousands of inscriptions and texts, identifying and dating monuments, tombs, and objects, and gradually compiling a full and accurate picture of Egyptian history, including the reign of the rather obscure Tutankhamen. By the beginning of the twentieth century, archaeologists knew that he had been the successor of Akhenaten, that he had restored the cult of Amen-Ra and the other traditional gods, that he had moved his court back to Thebes, and that he had probably been buried in the nearby Valley of the Kings. In 1906, a British archaeologist working in the valley came across a series of scattered finds that included objects containing hieroglyphic inscriptions pointing to Tutankhamen. An American Egyptologist at the Metropolitan Museum in New York recognized these as the remains of a ritual funeral banquet performed for Tutankhamen. Armed with all of the knowledge accumulated over decades, Carter began a systematic search for the lost tomb. On 26 November 1922, his search ended.

■ Gold coffin of Tutankhamen.

CHRONOLOGY
BETWEEN THE TWO RIVERS

ca. 3500 B.C.E.	Civilization begins; pictograms appear
ca. 3000–2316 B.C.E.	War for control of Sumer
ca. 2700 B.C.E.	Gilgamesh
ca. 2334–2279 B.C.E.	Sargon
1792–1750 B.C.E.	Hammurabi
ca. 1600 B.C.E.	Hittites destroy Old Babylonian state
ca. 1286 B.C.E.	Battle of Kadesh

■ The Assyrian and New Babylonian Empires. The Assyrians united the two great river valley civilizations of Mesopotamia and Egypt into an enormous empire held together by military force.

one command: Enlarge the empire! Warfare was the mission and duty of all.

- *A novel administrative system.* Outside Assyria, the king liquidated traditional leaders whenever possible. He kept close contact with local administrators through a system of royal messengers.
- *A social policy involving large-scale population movements.* To shatter regional identities, which could lead to separatist movements, Tiglath-pileser deported and re-settled conquered peoples.
- *The use of massive terror.* Tiglath-pileser and his successors maintained control of conquered peoples through cruelty and brutality.

The violence of Assyrian rule inspired many of its territories to break from the empire. Babylon, which helped to crush Nineveh in 612 B.C.E., established a new empire based on Hammurabi's Code and the Assyrian imperial system. Under King Nebuchadnezzar II, the city of Babylon reached its height. The city walls were so wide that two chariots could ride abreast on them. In 539 B.C.E., Babylon fell to the Persians. King Cyrus II (ca. 585–ca. 529 B.C.E.) merged the Persians and the Medes while expanding his empire into Syria, Babylon, Egypt, and Nubia. Cyrus allowed peoples such as the Jews, who had been deported by the Babylonians, to re-turn to their homeland. Persians respected local customs and religions and levied relatively light taxes on the people they

conquered. However, the Persians kept political control firmly in the hands of their own appointed governors.

An important part of Perisan civilization was its religion, **Zoroastrianism,** in which its principal god, Ahura Mazda, was the source of all good things. Zoroastrianism focuses on indi-vidual choice of good over evil and a day of final judgment.

The first 3000 years of civilization were more than conquest, exploitation, and cruelty. The progress of these years formed the basic structure of Western civilization. The floodplain civ-ilizations provided the first social and political organizations and complex governments. They built the first cities, city-states, regional states, and multinational empires. They dis-tributed natural resources through irrigation, long-distance trade, and communication. Religious traditions, from poly-theism to monotheism, provided patterns for subsequent Western religious traditions. Mesopotamian astronomy and mathematics and Egyptian engineering and building were fundamental for future civilizations.

THE BIRTH OF GREEK CIVILIZATION, 2500–500 B.C.E.

Western civilization's first epic poem, Homer's *Iliad* (ca. 750 B.C.E.), shows the Greeks' war against the Trojans. In the poem, Homer emphasized the importance of courage, honor, love, loyalty, and coping with the challenges people face in life. These attributes became an enduring heritage of Greek civi-lization; this heritage evolved from the ancient world and still continues in Western civilization.

Greece in the Bronze Age to 800 B.C.E.

The *Iliad* was written at a time of illiterate warriors and im-poverished villages. Still, in the depths of this "Dark Age"— from 1200 to 800 B.C.E.—the memory of a time of rich palaces, teeming cities, and powerful kings lived on. About to emerge from this dark age was an even greater and lasting civilization than before: classical Greece.

Greece is a stark world of mountains and sea that is best suited for small, self-contained agricultural societies. But fluctuations in climate forced isolated communities to build contacts with a wider world in order to survive.

Three Greek Cultures: Cycladic, Minoan, Mycenaean.

Three distinct cultures—the Cycladic, the Minoan, and the Mycenaean—flourished in the Mediterranean prior to the end of the twelfth century B.C.E.

Cycladic. The first culture appeared on the Cyclades, the islands strewn across the bottom of the Aegean from the Greek mainland to the coast of Asia Minor. Many of the largest **Cycladic** settlements were unfortified. This early Bronze Age society faded, but not before influencing its neighbors, especially Crete, the large Mediterranean island to the south.

Minoan. Crete, beginning around 2500 B.C.E., developed a sophisticated centralized civilization termed **Minoan** after the legendary King Minos. The island had great palaces. The walls of the palaces still display frescoes that present vivid images of Cretan life in the late Bronze Age. Some frescoes depict crowds of prosperous Cretans watching as court ladies dance under olive trees.

Palace bureaucrats controlled agricultural production and distribution as well as the work of skilled artisans in their surrounding areas, keeping records in a language known as Linear A. Towns with well-organized street plans, drainage systems, and clear hierarchies of elite and lesser homes dotted the landscape.

Society and religion in Minoan Crete was a stratified system. Peasantry paid a heavy tribute in olive oil and other produce. Taxes went to local and regional palaces and ultimately to the capital, Knossos. The wealth amassed by the elite was consumed by the palace servants and artisans or paid for luxury goods.

Although the system may have been exploitive, it was not militaristic. None of the palaces or towns of Crete was fortified. The frescoes and statues never depict warriors or battles. A key to this unique social tone may be the Cretan religion, and with it the high status of women. However, Cretan religion was not idyllic; hints of human sacrifice were found behind the Knossos palace.

Until the fourteenth century B.C.E., Cretan society was unique. Both men and women shared important roles in religious and public life and built a society without the need for armies or warrior kings. But, around 1450 B.C.E., destruction engulfed all of the Cretan cities except Knossos, which was finally destroyed around 1200 B.C.E.

Mycenaean. The contrast between the islands and the Greek mainland was striking. Around 1600 B.C.E., a powerful warrior civilization arose on the Peloponnesus at Mycenae. The only remains of this **Mycenaean** civilization are 30 graves that tell of a rich and warlike elite. The bronze swords, axes, and armor that fill the graves emphasize the warrior lives of their occupants.

Mycenaean palaces were strongly walled fortresses. From these palaces Mycenaean kings, aided by a military elite, controlled the collection of taxes from subordinate towns. Through their palace administrators, they controlled the production of bronze, the weaving of woolen cloth, and agriculture. Mycenaean administrators transformed Linear A writing into their own language, **Linear B,** which was used for record keeping in palaces—indicating the organization of workers and the quantities of weapons. The Mycenaean culture, however, began to collapse and enter the Dark Ages, a period of disintegration that lasted for 400 years. Between 1100 and 1000 B.C.E., architecture, urban traditions, and writing disappeared along with the elites whose exclusive benefit those achievements had served. The Greece of this Dark Age was poor, rural, and simply organized. The archaeological record is bleak. Pictorial representation of humans and animals almost disappears. Luxury goods and most imports are gone from tombs.

Gradually, beginning in the eleventh century B.C.E., things began to change. New geometric forms of decoration begin to appear on pottery. Cultural changes accompanied the material changes. Around the middle of the eleventh century B.C.E., Greeks in some locations stopped burying their dead and began to practice cremation. Whatever the meaning of these changes, they signaled something new.

By the eighth century B.C.E., the aristocracy had eliminated most kings. Ranking beneath the proud warriors was the populace. Some of this group were slaves. Still, the populace was not entirely excluded from public life. In Homer's *Odyssey,* the hero's son Telemachus summoned an assembly of

■ This sixth-century B.C.E. terra cotta figure from Thebes represents a farmer plowing with a yoke of oxen, an essential agricultural activity in Archaic Greece.

MAP DISCOVERY

Greece in the Bronze Age

What geographical characteristics distinguished Cycladic, Minoan, and Mycenaean civilizations? Given its location, what older civilizations might have exerted a major influence on the civilization of Crete?

the people to listen to his complaints against the noble suitors of his mother. Although the assembly listened to both sides and did nothing, a time was coming when society would give power to the silent farmers and herdsmen of the Dark Age.

Archaic Greece, 800–500 B.C.E.

The Greeks of the Archaic Age (ca. 800–500 B.C.E.) revolutionized political, economic, artistic, and intellectual life. Population growth stressed the cities. In this period, urban life, commerce, and literacy were reborn. New political structures were developed to organize a complex culture that laid many of the foundations of Western civilization. The growing population encouraged greater communication. The availability of leisure time made a lively intellectual climate possible.

In this burst of creativity, the Greeks invented politics and abstract thought and created the concept of the individual. Greeks of the Archaic Age set the agenda for the rest of Western history.

Ethnos and Polis.   Two forms of political organization developed. On the mainland and in the western Peloponnesus, people continued to live in large territorial units called *ethne* (sing. *ethnos*). In each **ethnos,** people lived in villages and small towns scattered across a wide region. The ethnos was governed by an elite, or **oligarchy** (meaning "rule by the few"), made up of major landowners who met from time to time in a town within the region.

A more innovative form of political organization was the **polis** (pl. *poleis*), or city-state. Initially, *polis* meant simply "citadel." Villages clustered around fortifications, which were both protective structures and centers for specific deities. These high, fortified sites—*acropolis* means "high citadel"—were believed to be sacred to specific gods, such as the goddess Athena in Athens and Sparta.

In addition to protection, the polis offered a marketplace, or *agora,* where farmers and artisans could trade and conduct business. The population growth of the eighth century B.C.E. led to the formation of real towns. Each town was independent and was ruled by a monarch or an oligarchy. Each town controlled the surrounding region, the inhabitants of which were on an equal footing with the townspeople. During a political or military crisis, the rulers summoned a group from the community to the agora to witness the decision-making process. In the following centuries, the city-states became centers for that most dramatic Greek experiment in government: democracy.

Writing.   Greeks adopted the Phoenician writing system for the purpose of private, personal use. They made the Semitic characters into arbitrary sounds and added vowels in order to record poetry. Soon the writing system was used to indicate ownership of objects, to record religious vows, and even to entertain.

Warfare.   Within the polis, political power was not the monopoly of the aristocracy. The expansion of the politically active population resulted from the demands of warfare. Battles were often won because of the use of infantrymen. These foot soldiers developed their own warrior pride, equal to but differing from that of the aristocrats.

The democratization of war led gradually to the democratization of political life. The foot soldiers who brought victory were unwilling to accept domination by the aristocracy. Growing demands of the common people, combined with expansion and economic changes, created enormous social and political change.

Colonists and Tyrants.   The turmoil of the seventh century B.C.E. encouraged the Greeks to restructure their political systems and to colonize new territories. Population pressures encouraged voluntary and forced migrations starting about 750 B.C.E. Greek culture spread as far as southern Italy, Sicily, and Thrace. Once established, colonies were politically independent.

Colonization did not solve the problem of political conflict. As opposition to aristocracies grew, individuals supported by those opposed to aristocratic rule seized power. These rulers were known as **tyrants,** a term that originally meant the same as "king." In the later sixth century B.C.E.,

tyrant came to mean those who had achieved power without benefit of official position. The term tyrant did not carry the negative meaning associated with it today. Early tyrants were welcomed by citizens. The weakness of tyrannies was that they depended on the individual qualities of the ruler. Tyrants tended to pass their powers on to their sons and cities came to resent harsh heirs' control of government.

Gods and Mortals.   Greeks made offerings to the gods, pleaded with them for help, and gave them thanks for assistance. The gods, however, were seen as thoroughly human, showing exaggerated human virtues and vices.

Greeks offered sacrifices to the gods on altars. Unlike the temples of other societies, Greek temples were houses of the gods, not centers of ritual. On special occasions, festivals celebrated at sanctuaries honored the gods of the city with athletic contests and feasts. The two greatest pan-Hellenic (meaning "all Greek," from *Hellas,* the Greek word for Greece) sanctuaries were Olympia and Delphi. Because both were remote from centers of political power, they were insulated from interstate rivalry and provided neutral ground for the celebrations.

Olympia was the main sanctuary of Zeus. Beginning in 776 B.C.E., every four years wars and conflicts were suspended while athletes from the Greek world met at Olympia to participate in contests in honor of Zeus. The sports included footraces, wrestling, horse races, and other events. Victors were seen as the ideals of human society, the perfect triumph of body and soul. Delphi, the site of the shrine of Apollo, god

■ A vase painting showing the Pythia, the priestess of Delphi, seated on her tripod. She holds a branch of the laurel plant, which is sacred to her patron, the god Apollo. The petitioner standing at the right will most likely receive an enigmatic reply to his question.

of music, archery, medicine, and prophecy also drew athletes from the Greek world to its athletic contests. Although gods were placated and pampered, they were not privileged or protected. The Greek gods were immortal, superhuman in strength, and able to interfere in human affairs.

Myth and Reason.   The glue holding together the individual and frequently hostile Greek poleis and ethne scattered throughout the Mediterranean was their common myths. The myths provided an explanation for their political, social, and religious practices. Myths were told about every city, shrine, mountain, and island. They explained the origins of cities, festivals, and the world itself. For example, the Greeks believed the seasons occurred because Persephone, a daughter of Zeus, had been carried off by Hades, god of the dead, and for four months each year she had to dwell in his dark kingdom. Myths presented how things had come to be and prescribed how they were to remain. Young Greeks were urged to model themselves on the example of the ancients, as described in the *Iliad* and the *Odyssey*.

Philosophy: The Beginnings of Rational Thought.   By the sixth century B.C.E., Ionian Greeks began to seek explanations for the world around them. The early Ionian Greek philosophers formed ideas by using observation and rational thought, not myth and religion.

Thales of Miletus (ca. 625–ca. 547 B.C.E.) regarded water as the fundamental substance of the universe. Other philosophers considered air or matter to be the primary substance. Heraclitus of Ephesus (ca. 540–ca. 480 B.C.E.) saw the universe not as one unchanging substance but rather as change itself.

Greek society was ready to tolerate nonreligious, rational teaching, which in other times and places would have been thought scandalous.

Art: The Importance of the Individual.   During the Dark Age, the Mycenaean traditions of art entirely disappeared. Then, gradually, changes in art appeared—stylized human and animal figures, such as griffins, and other strange beasts appeared on pottery. But by the eighth century B.C.E., these exotic subjects gave way to the Greek passion for human images taken from their own myths and legends.

Greek sculpture underwent a dramatic change. Sculptors wanted to give their statues originality, to show that the individual sculptor was important. They experimented with natural molding of limbs and body, and they added their signature to their works. Figures such as the Calf-Bearer (ca. 590 B.C.E.) from the Athenian acropolis are daring in their complexity and in the delicacy of execution. These are statues that tell stories. In the Calf-Bearer, a master farmer carries a calf to be sacrificed to Athena. The two gentle heads and the cross formed by the farmer's hands and the calf's legs are individual traits without precedent in ancient art. The statue surpasses the monotony and anonymity of tradition.

■ The Calf-Bearer was commissioned for the temple of Athena, which was destroyed by the Persians in 480 B.C.E. when they captured Athens and burned the Acropolis.

Three Cities: Corinth, Sparta, and Athens

The variety of Greek solutions to the challenges of the Archaic period can best be understood by examining three very different

HECTOR AND ANDROMACHE

The Trojan hero Hector is almost as central to the Iliad of Homer as is Achilles. Unlike the latter, Hector is a dutiful, reliable support to his city and to Andromache, who is not only his wife but his closest and dearest companion. The description of their last meeting is one of the great expressions of the heroic ethos and of the bonds of man and woman in that culture.

Focus Questions

How would you describe the relationship between Hector and Andromache? What is the ideal future that Hector wishes for his son?

At last his own generous wife came running to meet him,
Andromache, the daughter of high-hearted Eëation. . . .
She came to him there, and beside her went an attendant
  carrying
the boy in the fold of her bosom, a little child, only a
  baby,
Hector's son, the admired, beautiful as a star shining . . .
Andromache, stood close beside him, letting her tears fall,
and clung to his hand and called him by name and spoke
  to him:
"Dearest, your own great strength will be your death,
  and you
have no pity on your little son, nor on me, ill-starred,
  who soon must be your widow." . . .
Then tall Hector of the shining helm answered her: "All
  these
things are in my mind also, lady; yet I would feel deep shame
before the Trojans, and the Trojan women with trailing
  garments,

if like a coward I were to shrink aside from fighting. . . .
But it is not so much the pain to come of the Trojans
that troubles me . . . as the thought of you, when some
  bronze-
armored Achaian leads you off, taking away your day of
  liberty in
tears; and in Argos you must work at the loom of
  another." . . .
Then taking up his dear son he tossed him about in his
  arms and
kissed him, and lifted his voice in prayer to Zeus and the
  other immortals:
"Zeus, and you other immortals, grant that this boy, who
  is my
son, may be as I am, pre-eminent among the Trojans,
great in strength, as I am, and rule strongly over Ilion;
And someday let them say of him: 'He is better by far
  than his father,'
as he comes from the fighting; and let him kill his enemy
and bring home the blooded spoils, and delight the heart
  of his mother."

From the *Iliad* of Homer, Book VI.

---

cities. Corinth became an oligarchy, Sparta a military state, and Athens a radical democracy.

Wealthy Corinth. Corinth owed its prosperity to its location near a rich coastal plain and the isthmus (a narrow strip of land) connecting the Peloponnesus to the mainland. In the eighth century B.C.E., Corinthian trade and population growth led to colonization. Colonies reduced the population pressure on the city and provided markets for its grain, pottery, and textiles. More important to Corinthian prosperity was its role in transporting products for other cities. Corinth placed taxes on other cities that carried their products through the isthmus.

The rulers in Corinth were tyrants. Cypselus (ca. 657–627 B.C.E.) and his son Periander (ca. 627–586 B.C.E.) were tyrants, but were popular with most Corinthians. The tyrants laid the foundation for broader political participation. Cypselus divided the population into eight tribes, based not on traditional ethnic divisions but on arbitrary groupings by region.

All of Corinth was divided into three large regions. The population of each region was distributed among each of the eight tribes, which prevented the emergence of political groups based on regional arguments. Ten representatives from each tribe formed a council of 80 men. The council provided a connection between the tyrants and the citizens.

Periander forbade women to wear expensive clothes and jewelry. He introduced laws against idleness and put thousands of Corinthians to work erecting temples. Also, under his leadership the Corinthian fleet developed into a powerful naval force. The benefits tyrants brought their cities could not, however, overcome the negative impression made by the increasingly harsh nature of their rule. Shortly after Periander's death a successful revolt ended the tyranny.

Corinth then was ruled by an oligarchy from the sixth century B.C.E. until 338 B.C.E. The new government continued the tribal and council system. Although an assembly of the *demos*, or the people at large, met occasionally, government was in the hands of eight deliberators, and nine other men from each tribe, who formed the council of 80. The oligarchs had the support of the citizens, and provided an effective government. Corinth flourished, a city more open to commerce and wealth than most, moderate in its political institutions, and eager for stability.

Military Sparta.   In Sparta, the polis consisted of two classes: a small warrior class, the *homoioi,* or equals, who ruled a large population of *helots,* or state serfs.

Plutarch on
Life in Sparta

After Sparta suppressed a revolt by Messinian helots, the Spartans realized the need to structure their society to ensure that warriors could devote themselves to military activities, and not be overtaken by the helots. The legendary lawgiver Lycurgus (seventh century B.C.E.) is attributed with instilling these changes in Sparta where everyone was under the direct supervision and service of the state from birth until death.

In Sparta, public officials examined infants and decided whether they were sufficiently strong to be allowed to live or should be exposed on a hillside to die. From birth until age 7, a boy lived with his mother, but then he entered the state education system, living in barracks with his contemporaries, and enduring 13 years of military training. This was intended to teach men to endure pain and to conquer in battle.

At age 20, each Spartan youth was sent out into the countryside with nothing but a cloak and a knife and forbidden to return until he had killed a helot. This kept helots in constant terror. After this test, the youth also had to prove his financial ability to help support his communal dining group. Those who passed the final qualification became equals, but continued to live with the other warriors. They could marry, but family life was nonexistent because they had to slip out at night to visit their wives.

Spartan girls, like boys, were trained in wrestling, footraces, and spear throwing. This training was based not on a belief in the equality of the sexes but on the desire to improve the physical stamina and childbearing ability of Spartan women. Women owned land and participated in business and agricultural affairs. Since men were entirely involved in the military, women looked after economic and household affairs. The dedication to military life was reinforced by a deliberate rejection of other activities. Equals could not engage in crafts, trade, or any other forms of economic activity. Even though Spartans ruled through terror, throughout antiquity they were praised for their courage, simplicity of life, and service to the state.

Democratic Athens.   Athens enjoyed neither the advantage of a strategic site such as Corinth's nor that of the rich plains of Sparta. However, Athens was one of the few Mycenaean cities to escape destruction at the start of the Dark Age. Until the seventh century B.C.E., Athens escaped the social pressures brought on by population growth. This was due to its arable land and its commercial prosperity.

By the late seventh century B.C.E., Athens suffered from the same class conflict that had shaken other cities. Violence

between groups and families threatened to tear the community apart. In 621 B.C.E., the Athenians granted a judge, Draco, powers to revise traditional laws. His restructuring of procedures for limiting were harsh enough to add the term *draconian* to the Western legal vocabulary. When asked why death was the most common penalty he imposed, Draco explained that minor offenses merited death and he knew of no more severe penalty for major ones.

Still, these measures did not solve the problems of political control. In 594 B.C.E., Solon (ca. 630–ca. 560 B.C.E.) was charged with restructuring the city's government. He restored freedom to Athenians who had been forced into slavery because of their debts. The free peasants were now the basis of Athenian society. Solon divided the society into four classes based on wealth rather than birth. He established a council of 400 members, drawn from all four classes, to which citizens could appeal decisions of the magistrates.

Solon's reforms did not entirely succeed. Peisistratus (b. 527 B.C.E.), an aristocrat supported by the peasants, took control of the city as tyrant. Then, Peisistratus's son, Hippias, ruled. They drew their support from the demos rather than from aristocrats. They claimed divine justification for their rule and made a great show of devotion to the Athenian gods. They promoted annual festivals and began the great tradition of Athenian literature. Hippias was overthrown in 510 B.C.E., which ended the tyrants' rule in Athens.

When the aristocrats tried to recover power, their opponent, Cleisthenes (ca. 570–ca. 507 B.C.E.), "made the demos his

CHRONOLOGY	
ARCHAIC GREECE	
ca. 780–720 B.C.E.	Population increase in Greece
776 B.C.E.	First Olympic Games held
ca. 750–700 B.C.E.	Greeks develop writing system based on Phoenician model; Greeks begin colonizing western Mediterranean
ca. 800–500 B.C.E.	Archaic Age of Greece
ca. 700 B.C.E.	First stone temples appear in Greece
ca. 650 B.C.E.	Cypselus breaks rule of Bacchiads in Corinth; rules city as tyrant
594 B.C.E.	Solon elected chief archon of Athens; institutes social and political reforms
586 B.C.E.	Death of Periander ends tyrants' rule in Corinth
499 B.C.E.	Ionian cities revolt

faction" and pushed through a final constitutional reform that became the basis for Athenian **democracy.** Cleisthenes allowed groups of citizens to elect for their territory the members of the council, military commanders, jurors, and magistrates. As in Corinth, this reorganization integrated people of different social, economic, and regional backgrounds. Aristocrats, merchants, and poor farmers worked together to find common ground for political action. Athens emerged as an integrated democracy with a strong sense of nationalism. Athens was the leading city in the Greek world.

The Coming of Persia

By the end of the sixth century B.C.E. Greek city-states had resolved the crises of class conflict. Greek merchants and artisans had found ways to flourish despite poor soil and uncertain climate. Greek philosophers, poets, and artists had begun to celebrate the human form and the human spirit. Still, these achievements were the product of small, independent, and relatively weak communities on the fringe of the civilized world. The Greeks' insignificance and isolation had kept them out of the sphere of interest of the great empires to the east.

In the second half of the sixth century B.C.E., all this changed. The Persian Empire, under its dynamic king, Cyrus II, began a process of conquest and expansion west into Asia Minor. Cyrus granted the provinces of his empire great autonomy and preserved local forms of government wherever possible, being careful only to impose governors loyal to him. When he absorbed Ionia and the kingdom of Lydia on the coast of Asia Minor, he put tyrants loyal to Persia to rule over the Greek communities. For a few decades these centers of Greek culture and thought accepted foreign control.

In 499 B.C.E., the passion for democracy that had swept much of mainland Greece reached Ionia. Many cities expelled the Persian tyrants and established democracies. The giant Persian Empire responded with force to this Greek revolt. King Darius I (522–486 B.C.E.) gathered a vast force from throughout his empire and by 494 B.C.E. they had recaptured the rebellious cities. Darius disposed of his rebels and then the Persian king turned his vast armies toward the Greek mainland.

CLASSICAL AND HELLENISTIC GREECE, 500–100 B.C.E.

In the fifth century the Greek world met the challenge of external invasion and went on to create the charismatic forms of society, politics, and culture that continue to define Western civilization. However, the Greeks failed to achieve stability or to protect their independence in the long run because of their internal conflicts.

War and Politics in the Fifth Century B.C.E.

A handful of Greek states—Athens, Plataea, and Eretria—resisted the invading Persian armies of Darius I. Divided by municipal rivalries and different political traditions, there

■ The Persian Wars. Greeks fought on both sides in the Persian Wars, while many others remained neutral.

■ This ostrakon was found in the Athenian agora. It was used to cast a vote to choose a person who would be ostracized—banished from Athens for a period of ten years. The name on the first line is Themistocles.

was little cultural or national unity to bring the Greek city-states together to face a common enemy.

The Persian Wars.   After suppressing the revolt of the Ionian Greeks, Darius assembled a large army and invaded the Peloponnesus. The Athenians infantry or **hoplites,** led by Miltiades, decisively defeated the Persians at Marathon. Darius withdrew his troops after they failed to reach Athens before the arrival of Miltiades's soldiers. This victory encouraged Greek unity, convincing all Greeks of the skill of their soldiers, their superior cultural values, and the value of the citizen army. This victory of the Athenians also solidified the democratic reforms of Cleisthenes. (Remember that he started some of the first movements toward democracy by allowing groups of citizens to be involved in electing officials for their own territories.)

Common citizens were determined that the victory at Marathon should not be lost to an aristocratic faction at home. To guard against this danger, the Athenian assembly began to practice **ostracism,** ten-year exile without loss of property, imposed on those who threatened to undermine the constitution of Cleisthenes. Each year every Athenian citizen had the opportunity to write on a potsherd (in Greek, *ostrakon*) the name of the man he most wanted to leave Attica. No charges or accusations had to be made, much less proven. Anyone who had offended the Athenians or who seemed to be a threat to democracy could be ostracized.

The Athenian Empire.   The Spartans had provided crucial military force and leadership, and Sparta had emerged unharmed from the Persian wars. However, the constant threat of a helot revolt left Sparta preoccupied with internal problems.

Athens, on the other hand, was ready to take the lead in bringing the war home to the Persians. In 478 B.C.E., Athens accepted control of the **Delian League,** after the island of Delos, a religious center. Athens's domination of the Delian League assured its prosperity. Athens received cash "contributions" from league members. The new riches made possible the reconstruction of the city that had been burned by the Persians.

As the Persian threat receded after about 449 B.C.E., Athens used the resources of the league to build an empire

enforced by the Athenian fleet. Athens established garrisons throughout Greece and imposed taxes and dominated legal matters and politics. Opposition to Athenian leadership was met with brutality.

Private and Public Life in Athens.   Classical Athens was a vibrant, crowded city. Although Athens is remembered for its contribution to the development of democratic government, most Athenians were excluded from public life in the classical age. More than a fourth of the population were slaves, of both sexes and of all races and backgrounds. Athenians considered slaves to be property, so slaves were at the mercy of their owners. Anyone could be a slave: pirates even captured the great philosopher Plato while he was traveling from Sicily to Athens and sold him into slavery in Egypt. Only a payment by his family saved him from an obscure life in the household of some wealthy Egyptian.

Half of the free population were **metics,** or foreigners, who could neither own land nor participate in politics. Citizen women were excluded from politics and considered citizens only for the purposes of transferring property from man to man and for giving birth to legitimate children. Women were always in the custody of a male guardian. Women were responsible for running households and had limited mobility. Fathers arranged marriages, the purposes of which were procreation of legitimate children and exchange of wealth. The women were not consulted.

Male citizens enjoyed a high degree of self-government. They actively participated in public life. However, political freedom was a constant balancing act between many conflicting obligations—family, tribe, and *deme* (local government unit). Economic and social equality were nonexistent in fifth-century Athens. Although sovereignty formally resided in an assembly of citizens, the actual leadership was in the hands of generals and demagogues. *Demagogues,* or popular leaders, exercised their power through their speaking skills and knowledge of how to get things done. Governing an empire demanded energy and experience, but Athenian democracy was formally run by amateurs.

For more than 30 years, from ca. 495 to 429 B.C.E., one individual dominated Athenian public life: the general Pericles. He was a great orator and military commander who was able to win the confidence of Athens and to lead it during the decades of its greatest glory. The Athenian political system of radical democracy reached its height under the leadership of Pericles.

Pericles.   Pericles was descended from the greatest aristocratic families of Athens but sided with the poor. He learned about government through experience on public works projects that provided income to poorer citizens. He served on the commission that built the Lyceum and the Parthenon, which won him a popular following while giving him knowledge of public finance and Athenian government.

Pericles never ruled Athens. Still, under his influence, Athens abolished the last property requirements for officeholding. He

■ The ruins on the acropolis of Athens are dominated by the Parthenon (center). At the left is the temple of Athena as Victory.

convinced the state to pay those who served on juries, thus making it possible for even the poorest citizens to participate in Athenian government.

Pericles had little fear of Persia but believed that the Athenian Empire had to be preserved at all costs. This policy drew Athens into deadly conflict with Sparta. Treaties delayed major conflicts between the two powers for more than ten years, but the treaties could not prevent the Peloponnesian War. This war would destroy both great powers.

The Peloponnesian War. The Peloponnesian War was actually a series of wars. Athens and Sparta waged two devastating ten-year wars, from 431 B.C.E. to 421 B.C.E. and then again from 414 B.C.E. to 404 B.C.E. At the same time, cities in each alliance took advantage of the wars to revolt against the great powers, eliciting terrible vengeance from both Athens and Sparta. Within many of the Greek city-states, oligarchs and democrats waged bloody civil wars for control of their governments. Before it was over, the Peloponnesian War had become an international war, with Persia entering on the side of Sparta. In the end, there were no real victors.

The first phase of the war was indecisive. In 430 B.C.E., the Spartans received unexpected help in the form of plague, which ravaged Athens for five years. By the time the plague ended in 426 B.C.E., as much as one-third of the Athenian population had died, including Pericles. The defeated Athenian commander, Thucydides, was exiled for his failure. Exhausted by a decade of death and destruction, the two sides contracted peace in 421 B.C.E. Although Athens had maintained its empire, the peace changed nothing.

War broke out again and soon Athens was fighting not just for its empire but for its life. Under the Spartan general Lysander (d. 395 B.C.E.), Sparta and its allies finally closed in on Athens. Lysander captured the Athenian fleet and severed Athens's grain supply. Within months, Athens was entirely cut off from the outside world and starving. In 404 B.C.E., Sparta accepted Athens's surrender. Athens's fortifications came down, its empire vanished. The Peloponnesian War showed the limitations of Athenian democracy. It also demonstrated the catastrophic effects of disunity and rivalry among the Greek cities of the Mediterranean.

Athenian Culture in the Hellenic Age

The Athenians of the classical age started to use critical thinking and reasoning. This was a new way to approach moral ideas and to think about history. As rhetoric became crucial to secure political power, teachers (known as **Sophists**) traveled throughout the Greek city-states offering young citizens an education in rhetoric. They taught them ethics based on reason and logic.

The Examined Life.

The teacher Socrates (ca. 470–399 B.C.E.) was considered by many of his contemporaries as but one more Sophist, but he himself reacted against what he saw as the amoral and superficial nature of sophistic education. "Know thyself" was Socrates's plea. An unexamined life, he argued, was not worth living. He urged his students to understand morality by taking a critical look at their own lives and choices. Socrates refused any pay for his teaching, arguing that he had nothing to teach. He knew nothing, he said, and was superior to the Sophists only because he recognized his ignorance while they professed wisdom.

Socrates's method infuriated his contemporaries. Condemned to death in 399 B.C.E. on trumped-up charges of corrupting the morals of the Athenian youth and introducing strange gods, he accepted the laws of the city and drank the fatal potion of hemlock given him by the executioner.

Scientific Medicine: Hippocrates.

The study of medicine advanced through the work of Hippocates of Cos (460–377 B.C.E.) who firmly believed that illness had physical and rational explanations and who based his medical practice on careful observation rather than on religious or abstract theories. Hippocrates was convinced that the human body needed to be treated as a whole, not just as a series of organs, and he emphasized the importance of rest, diet, and hygiene. Although he traveled throughout Greece, including Athens, in his study and practice, he established a school of medicine on the island of Cos where he taught, establishing a tradition of medicine that continues today.

The First Historians: Herodotus and Thucydides.

Two early historians established the spectrum of how to understand the past. Herodotus (ca. 484–ca. 420 B.C.E.), the first historian, wrote an account of the Persian Wars of the preceding generation. His book of inquiries into the origins and events of the conflict between Greeks and Persians is the first true history. He was more than just a good storyteller or a chronicler of legends. Often, after reporting conflicting accounts, he would conclude, "Both stories are told and the reader may take his choice between them." It was his desire to explain, to go beyond mere storytelling, that earned Herodotus the designation of "the father of history."

DOCUMENT

Herodotus, *Histories*

The story of the Peloponnesian War was recorded by Thucydides, who focused on the Greek world and on political power. For Thucydides, the central subject was human society in action. He showed that the consequences of political self-interest, devoid of other considerations, follow their own natural course to disaster and ruin.

Athenian Drama.

Drama was popular throughout the Greek world. Three types of plays developed. Tragedies dealt with great men who failed because of flaws in their natures. Comedies, more directly topical and political, parodied real Athenians and amused even while making serious points in defense of democracy. Somewhere between tragedies and comedies, satyr plays featured lecherous drunken satyrs (mythical half-man, half-goat creatures) that interacted with gods and men as they roamed the world in search of Dionysus, the god of wine, life blood, and fertility.

Athenian drama became more secular and less mythic as dramatists began to deal with topics of the human condition. Aeschylus (525–456 B.C.E.) wrote tragedies that showed the conflict between duties and loyalties. Sophocles (496–406 B.C.E.) wrote tragedies expressing human character, showing how humans make decisions and carry them out. Sophocles's message was of endurance, acceptance of human responsibility, and acceptance of the ways of the gods who overrule people's plans. Euripides (485–406 B.C.E.) was far more original and daring in his subject matter and treatment of human emotions. His plays abound in plot twists and unexpected, violent outbursts. Passion, not reason, ruled Euripides's world.

Athenian comic playwrights focused their satire on political and social issues. The comic genius Aristophanes (ca. 450–ca. 388 B.C.E.) attacked everything that offended him in his city. He ridiculed statesmen, philosophers, and even the gods. His comedies are full of talking animals and obscene jokes and puns. Yet Aristophanes was a deeply patriotic Athenian, dedicated to the democratic system and to the cause of peace. In *Lysistrata,* written in 411 B.C.E. after Athens had once more renewed the war with Sparta, the women of Greece force their men to make peace by conspiring to refuse them sex as long as war continues. Aristophanes communicated his sympathy for ordinary people, who had to match wits with pompous frauds who attempted to dominate Athens's public life.

From City-States to Macedonian Empire, 404–323 B.C.E.

Conflict cost Greek cities their independence, but a new empire transmitted Greek culture throughout the civilized world and beyond.

Politics After the Peloponnesian War.

Mercenary soldiers, who gradually replaced the citizen hoplites in the course of the Peloponnesian War, weakened the democratic institutions in many city-states as the importance of the hoplites declined. War became more vicious as professional soldiers began to dominate the battlefields. Victorious Sparta sought to rule its new empire with tyrannical oligarchies, a policy that precipitated decades of civil warfare in the Greek world and contributed to the destruction of Spartan armies by Thebes in 371 B.C.E. Although Athens formed several military alliances that were directed against Sparta and later Thebes, by the 330s political instability had fractured political life above the level of the polis.

Philosophy and the Polis.

The failure of Greek political forms, oligarchy and democracy, profoundly affected

Athenian philosophers. Plato (ca. 428–347 B.C.E.), an aristocratic student of Socrates, grew up during the Peloponnesian War and had witnessed the collapse of the empire, the execution of Socrates, and the revival of the democracy and its imperialistic ambitions. From these experiences he developed a hatred for Athenian democracy and a distrust of ordinary people's ability to tell right from wrong. Plato wrote dialogues, a literary genre of imagined discussions between his teacher, Socrates, and a variety of students and opponents, to develop his ideas. Plato's philosophy argues the inadequacy of all existing forms of government and the need to create a new form of government through the proper education of elite philosopher rulers.

According to Plato, the evils of the world, and in particular the vices of government and society, result from ignorance of the truth, which exists in this world only in an inadequate reflection. He believed the philosopher's task was to help people to see the world as it really was and to look beyond it to the ideal world.

Plato's greatest student, Aristotle (384–322 B.C.E.), rejected Plato's view in favor of a philosophy rooted in the natural world. Aristotle's theories are distinguished by clarity of logical thinking, precision in the use of terminology, and respect for the world of experience. For Aristotle, understanding of the world remained basic, and no valid theory could make it unintelligible. Aristotle concluded that the type of government ultimately mattered less than obtaining a balance composed of citizens who were neither extremely wealthy nor extremely poor; moderation was the key to stability and justice.

The Rise of Macedon.   Ruled for centuries by hereditary kings, Maceonia rose to power under Philip II (359–336 B.C.E.) and filled the political vacuum left by the defeat of Sparta, Athens, and Thebes. Philip's army of mercenary soldiers and elite cavalry initiated a relentless campaign against the southern city-states in 346 B.C.E., winning a signal victory at Chaeronea in 338 B.C.E. Philip's League of Corinth established a monarchical empire supported by a wealthy aristocracy, a form of government that persisted until modern times in the Mediterranean region. Philip's assassination left the task of extending the Macedonian Empire to his son, Alexander.

■ This sumptuous gilded cuirass or armor for protecting the front and back was discovered in 1977 in a royal Macedonian tomb originally believed to be that of Philip. Today it is widely believed to have been the tomb of Alexander the Great's half brother Philip III Arrhidaeus, who was killed in 317 B.C.E.

Alexander the Great.   Alexander's military genius, dedication to his troops, reckless disregard for his own safety, and ability to move both men and supplies across vast distances at great speed inspired the war machine developed by Philip and led it on a conquest that stretched from Asia Minor to India. In 334 B.C.E., Alexander captured the Greek cities of Asia Minor. Two months later he defeated the Persian king Darius III at Issus and then headed south toward the Mediterranean coast and Egypt. Alexander captured the Persian capital of Persepolis and became the undisputed ruler of the vast empire.

The conquest of Persia was not enough. Alexander pushed on, intending to conquer the whole world. He subdued the rebellious Asian provinces of Bactria and Sogdiana. He negotiated the Khyber Pass from what is now Afghanistan into the Punjab, crossed the Indus River, and defeated the local Indian king. Everywhere he went, he reorganized or founded cities, entrusting them to loyal Macedonians and other Greeks and settling them with veterans of his campaigns, and then pushed on toward the unknown. Beyond the Hydaspes River, in what is now Pakistan, his Macedonian warriors, worn out by years of bloody conquest and exhausting travel, refused to go farther, even if Alexander himself were to lead them. Furious but impotent, Alexander turned south, following the Indus River to its mouth in the hope that it might turn out to be an extension of the Nile encircling the earth. Upon

THE TWO FACES OF ATHENIAN DEMOCRACY

Early in the Peloponnesian War, Thucydides summarized the virtues of Athenian democracy in the speech he ascribes to Pericles in honor of those who died in the first year of the war. By 416 B.C.E., the sixteenth year of the Peloponnesian War, Athenian imperialism no longer even paid lip service to the ideals of democracy or freedom. Thucydides illustrates this in his reconstructed debate between representatives of the Spartan colony of Melos, which had attempted to remain neutral, and representatives of the Athenians, who demanded their surrender and enslavement.

Focus Questions

What limits did the Athenians place on the ideal of democracy? How did the Athenians justify violence to maintain their empire?

Pericles' Funeral Oration

Our constitution is called a democracy because power is in the hands not of a minority but of the whole people. When it is a question of settling private disputes, everyone is equal before the law; when it is a question of putting one person before another in positions of public responsibility, what counts is not membership of a particular class, but the actual ability which the man possesses. No one, so long as he has it in him to be of service to the state, is kept in political obscurity because of poverty.

The Melian Debate

ATHENIANS: You know as well as we do that, when these matters are discussed by practical people, the standard of justice depends on the equality of power to compel and that in fact the strong do what they have the power to do and the weak accept what they have to accept.

MELIANS: And how could it be just as good for us to be the slaves as for you to be the masters?

ATHENIANS: You, by giving in, would save yourselves from disaster; we by not destroying you, would be able to profit from you.

MELIANS: So you would not agree to our being neutral, friends instead of enemies, but allies of neither side?

ATHENIANS: No, because it is not so much your hostility that injures us; it is rather the case that, if we were on friendly terms with you, our subjects would regard that as a sign of weakness in us, whereas your hatred is evidence of our power.

Ultimately the Melians rejected Athens's demands, and shortly after the Athenians captured the city, they executed all the men and sold the women and children as slaves.

From Thucydides, *History of the Peloponnesian War.*

---

reaching the Indian Ocean he at last turned west, leading his army across the barren Gedrosian desert and finally back to Persepolis in 324 B.C.E. No mortal had ever before accomplished such a feat. Even in his own lifetime, Alexander was venerated as a god.

Alexander recognized that only by merging local and Greek peoples could he forge a lasting empire. At the same time, he sought to bind his vast empire together through a common Greek culture and through the network of more than 35 cities that he created. Modeled on Greek cities of the Mediterranean world, these were well located, spacious cities with paved streets, flowing fountains, and impressive architecture. They became trading as well as administrative centers and, thanks to the Greek veterans settled in them, centers of Hellenistic culture. To these cities flocked not only retired soldiers and merchants but also artists, poets, scholars, physicians, and architects. Traditions of Persian government and religious toleration and openness combined with Greek culture in exciting and novel ways. But whether Alexander's program of Hellenistic civilization could have succeeded is a moot point. In 323 B.C.E., two years after his return from India, he died at Babylon at the age of 32.

The empire did not long outlive the emperor. Vicious fighting soon broke out among his generals and his kin. They all hoped to enhance their positions while preserving a relative balance of power. By 275 B.C.E., three large kingdoms dominated Alexander's former domain. The most stable was Egypt, which Ptolemy I (323–285 B.C.E.), one of Alexander's closest followers, acquired upon Alexander's death and which he and his descendants ruled until Cleopatra VII (51–30 B.C.E.) was defeated by the Roman Octavian in 31 B.C.E. In the east, the Macedonian general Seleucus (246–226 B.C.E.) captured Babylon in 312 B.C.E. and created what would become the Selucid Kingdom. The Antigonid Kingdom included the old Macedonia and parts of Greece.

Alexander's conquests transformed the political map of southern Europe, western Asia, and Egyptian Africa. They swept away or absorbed old traditions of government, brought Greek traditions of urban organization, and replaced indigenous ruling elites with hellenized dynasties. Rulers encouraged commercial and cultural contact, enriching their treasuries and creating a new form of Greek culture even while incorporating elements of the more ancient civilizations they had conquered.

■ The Empire of Alexander the Great. Alexander's conquests united Eurasia from Greece to India into a cultural and, briefly, a political unity.

The Hellenistic World

Despite their many differences, the Hellenistic kingdoms that emerged from Alexander's fractured empire were united by two shared traditions. First, the territories had been governed earlier by Mesopotamian rulers who had established centralized administrative structures and systems of taxation, which were continued in the kingdoms. Second, leaders encouraged the cultivation of Greek urban culture in newly created cities that were based on Greek models, making the new cities the political, economic, and cultural focus of the Hellenistic world.

Urban Life and Culture.

The Hellenistic kingdoms lived in a state of warfare. Kings needed Greek soldiers, merchants, and administrators and competed with their rivals in offering Greeks all the comforts of home. Hellenistic cities were Greek in physical organization, constitution, and language. They boasted temples to the Greek gods and goddesses, theaters, and, most importantly, a *gymnasion,* or combination sports center and school. In the gymnasion, young men competed in Greek sports and absorbed Greek poetry and philosophy.

Hellenistic cities were larger than any earlier Greek cities but were never politically sovereign. The regional kings maintained firm control over the cities; politics was no longer the passion that it had been in the fifth and early fourth centuries B.C.E. In each city, a council elected from among the Greek inhabitants was self-governing in domestic matters. However, while the cities were in theory democracies, kings firmly controlled city government, and participation in the city councils and magistracies became the affair of the wealthy.

The Hellenistic cities were much less closed than were the traditional poleis of the Hellenic world. Greeks from all over were welcomed as soldiers and administrators, regardless of their city of origin. Greeks no longer identified themselves by their city of origin but as "Hellenes," that is, Greeks.

Women in Public Life.

The great social and geographical mobility possible in the new cities extended to women as well as men. Women assumed a greater role in the family, in the economy, and in public life. Marriage contracts emphasized the theoretical equality of husband and wife. In one such contract, the wife was granted "mastery in common with [her husband] over all their possessions." Since women could control their own property, many engaged in business and some became wealthy. Wealth translated into civic influence and power.

The most powerful women in Hellenistic society were queens, especially in Egypt. A tradition of powerful female monarchs ended with Cleopatra VII, the last independent ruler of Egypt, who successfully manipulated the Roman generals Julius Caesar (100–44 B.C.E.) and Mark Antony (81–30 B.C.E.) to maintain Egyptian autonomy.

Alexandria.

The most vibrant center of the rich complex of social change and culture was Alexandria in Egypt. Its location was well suited to be a major international port of Egypt.

Ptolemy I made it not only his political and commercial center but the cultural center for Greek art, science, and scholarship for the whole world. He lavished money on its temples and public buildings. He gathered poets, scientists, and scholars from throughout the Greek-speaking world. The heart of his enterprise was the **Museum** (*Mouseion*) or shrine to the Muses, the goddesses of literature, music, and the arts, and closely attached to it, a library in which he sought to collect all the great works of Greek literature and learning.

Scholars, scientists, and philosophers lived, worked, and taught, free of ordinary cares. They collected all Greek literature and set out to obtain copies of every work, establishing the greatest library of the Ancient World. The Museum scholars invented aspects of writing such as punctuation and accent marks. Their commentaries on sources and their marginal comments became the basis for literary criticism and scholarship. Their efforts preserved much of what is known about classical authors.

Hellenistic Literature.

Hellenistic writers developed new forms of literature, including the romance and the pastoral poem, while continuing earlier Greek drama traditions. Menander's (342–292 B.C.E.) gift was for comedy. His characters were stock figures: slaves and freedmen, soldiers, and wily shepherds. Plots are full of mistaken identities: slaves who turn out to be free-born children kidnapped at birth, for example. Menander's characters are diffused with sympathy and they are credible as human beings. Menander was a master of the happy ending. Menander provided the plots for virtually every subsequent comedy from the Roman theater to television sit-coms.

Art and Architecture.

Temples, porticoes, and public buildings grew in size and ornamentation. Architects experimented with multitiered buildings. Hellenistic rulers provided the funds to undertake major urban renewal projects in older cities. Freestanding statues and magnificent murals and mosaics adorned the public squares, temples, and private homes. Artists displayed more freedom in portraying tension and restlessness as well as individuality in the human form. Mural painters managed multifigure compositions, perspective, and realistic portrayal of landscapes. Sculptors portrayed drapery tightly folded or falling naturally across the human form.

Hellenistic Philosophy: Cynics, Epicureans, and Stoics.

Philosophy, too, flourished in the Hellenistic world. Cynics, Epicureans, and Stoics turned inward, advocating types of morality less directly tied to the state and society. Each philosophy was as much a way of life as a way of thought and offered different answers to the question of how the individual should deal with the whims of fate.

Antisthenes (ca. 450–ca. 350 B.C.E.) established the Cynic tradition, which taught that excessive attachment to the things of this world was the source of evil and unhappiness. The **Cynics'** goal was to reduce their possessions, connections, and pleasures to the absolute minimum.

The **Epicureans** sought freedom from pain rather than from the conventions of ordinary life. Epicurus (341–270 B.C.E.) and his disciples have often been attacked for their emphasis on pleasure. Pleasure was to be pursued rationally, with awareness that today's pleasure could mean tomorrow's suffering. The goal was to reduce desires to those that were simple and attainable. The traditional image of the Epicurean as an indulgent sensualist is a gross caricature. As Epicurus advised one follower, an Epicurean "revels in the pleasure of the body—on a diet of bread and water."

The founder of Stoicism, Zeno (ca. 335–ca. 263 B.C.E.), explained the philosophy: "All men should regard themselves as members of one city and people, having one life and order." According to the **Stoics,** every person had a role in the divinely ordered universe, and all roles were of equal value. True happiness consisted in freely accepting one's role, whatever it was, while unhappiness and evil resulted from attempting to reject one's place in the divine plan.

All three philosophical traditions emphasized the importance of reason and the proper understanding of nature.

CHRONOLOGY CLASSICAL GREECE	
525–456 B.C.E.	Aeschylus
ca. 500–ca. 430 B.C.E.	Phidias
496–406 B.C.E.	Sophocles
490 B.C.E.	Battle of Marathon
485–406 B.C.E.	Euripides
ca. 484–ca. 420 B.C.E.	Herodotus
480 B.C.E.	Battles of Thermopylae and Salamis
478 B.C.E.	Athens assumes control of Delian League
ca. 470–399 B.C.E.	Socrates
ca. 460–430 B.C.E.	Pericles dominates Athens
ca. 450–ca. 388 B.C.E.	Aristophanes
431–421; 414–404 B.C.E.	Peloponnesian War
ca. 428–347 B.C.E.	Plato
384–322 B.C.E.	Aristotle
384–322 B.C.E.	Demosthenes
338 B.C.E.	Philip of Macedon defeats Athens

Mathematics and Science. For mathematics, astronomy, and engineering, the Hellenistic period was a golden age. Euclid and Apollonius of Perga established logical proof of theorems as the basis of geometry. Engineering, astronomy, and medicine flourished. Archimedes applied his understanding of mathematics and engineering to solve practical problems.

Archimedes used mathematics to solve engineering problems and to devise a means of measuring the diameter of the sun. Eratosthenes of Cyrene (ca. 276–194 B.C.E.) calculated the circumference of the earth to within 200 miles. Hipparchus of Nicea (ca. 146–127 B.C.E.) offered an alternative theory, placing the earth at the center of the universe. Backed by more mathematically acceptable arguments, Hipparchus's system remained the dominant theory until the sixteenth century.

For all of the vitality of the Hellenistic civilization, the cities remained parasites on the local societies. No real efforts were made to merge the two and to develop a new civilization. Although some ambitious members of the indigenous elites tried to adopt the customs of the Greeks, in time, the Hellenistic kingdoms' inability to bridge the gap between Greek and indigenous populations proved fatal. In the east, the non-Greek kingdom of Parthia replaced the Seleucids in much of the old Persian Empire. In the west, continuing hostility between kingdoms and within kingdoms prepared the way for their progressive absorption by the new power to the west: Rome.

EARLY ROME AND THE ROMAN REPUBLIC, 800–146 B.C.E.

Italy and the Western Mediterranean developed its civilizations later than the East. In time, however, Rome expanded to incorporate the heritage of Greece into a vast Mediterranean empire.

The Western Mediterranean to 509 B.C.E.

While Greek colonies existed in the western Mediterranean, this region was also the home of two other great civilizations, Punic or Carthaginian and Etruscan, and also saw the rise of a new and awesome power, Rome.

Around 800 B.C.E., Phoenicians arrived in the west and established a series of bases on the coasts along the route to and from Spain and on the islands of Corsica and Sicily. Carthage in North Africa began as a small anchorage for Phoenician ships and as an ideal port whose commercial center was secure from enemies. By the middle of the sixth century B.C.E., it was the center of a real empire and integrated other cities and peoples into its military. This multiethnic empire proved more stable than those created by the Greeks, and it endured for more than three centuries.

Carthage was governed by a mixed constitution that combined elements of monarchical, aristocratic, and popular rule.

■ Greek and Phoenician Colonies and Trade. The western Mediterranean was first colonized by Phoenicians and Greeks who together controlled trade throughout the region.

Ordinary citizens had little involvement in government, but the aristocracy treated the rest of the population generously.

In the seventh century B.C.E., the Greek colonies began to encroach on the Carthaginian Empire, and thus the Greeks and Phoenicians in the western Mediterranean were often at war. Much of this fighting took place over Sicily and centered on rivalry between Syracuse and Carthage.

Early in their struggle with the Sicilian Greeks, the Carthaginians found allies in the third major civilization of the west. These were the **Etruscans,** who in the seventh century B.C.E. dominated the western part of central Italy, known as Etruria (now known as Tuscany).

Italy's First Civilization: Etruscans.

Etruscan civilization was the first great civilization to emerge in Italy. This civilization shared much with the eastern civilizations, including the importance of underworld gods, fertility cults, and the high status of women.

In the mid-sixth century B.C.E., in the face of Greek pressure from the south, 12 Etruscan groups united in a religious and military confederation. Cities, each initially ruled by a king, were the centers of Etruscan civilization. Later, in the place of kings, aristocratic assemblies selected magistrates. The republican institutions provided the foundation for later Roman republican government.

A striking aspect of Etruscan civilization was the elevated status of Etruscan women who played an active public role. They presided over dances and sporting events and were active in political life. When a king died, his successor was consecrated by the Etruscan queen to establish his legitimacy.

The Etruscans developed their naval strength and used it in a military alliance with Carthage against their commercial rivals, the Greeks. Etruria consequently dominated much of the Italian coast from the seventh to the fifth century B.C.E. When their fleet was destroyed at Cumae in 474 B.C.E., a period of rapid decline began. Subsequently Etruscan cities fell to Greek, Celtic, Syracusan, and Roman forces.

From City to Empire, 509–146 B.C.E.

Latin Rome.

Civilization in Italy meant Etruria to the north and Greater Greece to the south. In between lay Latium with a population of aboriginal Ligurians, Latins, and Sabines who lived in scattered villages. In the eighth century B.C.E., 40 Latin villages formed a loose confederation, the Alban League, for military and religious purposes. Later, the Albans established a village on Palatine Hill, whose high ground was strategically important. The Alban village, called Roma Quadrata, was joined by other settlements on nearby hills.

Early Roman society was composed of households, clans, and village councils. The male head of each household, the **paterfamilias,** had the power of life and death over its members and was responsible for the worship of the spirits of the family's ancestors on whom prosperity depended.

Male members of village families formed councils, which were religious organizations but also provided a forum for public discussion. All males participated, including the **plebs,** that is, families not organized into clans. Later the leaders of the clans called themselves **patricians** ("descendants of fathers") and claimed superiority to the plebs.

Assemblies of all members of the village councils approved major decisions, especially declaration of war and the selection of new kings, and so played a real political role. The Senate (assembly of elders) was composed of heads of families who participated in selecting a candidate for king. Kings served as religious leaders, the primary means of communication between gods and men. Royal power remained religious and limited.

Initially, Romans maintained their separate villages. By the seventh century B.C.E., they had begun fortifications and a civic life. That changed in the middle of the seventh century B.C.E., when the Etruscans absorbed Latium into their civilization. Under its Etruscan kings, Rome first entered civilization.

Etruscan Rome.

The Etruscans introduced in Latium and especially in Rome their political, religious, and economic traditions. Etruscan city organization partially replaced Latin tribal structures. Etruscan kings and magistrates ruled Latin towns, increasing the power of traditional Latin kingship. The kings were religious leaders and also led the army, served as judges, and held supreme political power. As Latium became an integral part of the Etruscan world, the Tiber River became an

■ By the middle of the second century B.C.E., the Roman Republic had evolved to the point where private citizens could cast private ballots. This Roman coin of 137 B.C.E. features a Roman voter dropping a stone tablet into a voting urn.

important commercial route, carrying the agricultural produce of Latium throughout Etruria and bringing to Rome the products of Etruscan and Greek workshops. For the first time, Rome began to enter the wider orbit of Mediterranean civilization.

As Rome's importance grew, so did its size. Surrounding villages were added to the original seven. The Etruscans constructed vast fortifications encircling the town. In its architecture, religion, commerce, and culture, Latin Rome was indebted to its Etruscan conquerors.

King Servius Tullius (578–534 B.C.E.) set up a military and political system based only on property holding. Wealthy landowners were organized into five *classis* (from which the word *class* is derived). Each class was divided into military units called centuries. Members of the centuries made decisions about the election of magistrates and the declaration of war.

During the monarchy, the power of the wealthy patricians who owned large estates with slaves grew enormously at the expense of the plebs. The patricians monopolized the Senate, religious rites, and magisterial offices; the plebeians were second-class citizens with no political power.

Around 509 B.C.E., the Roman patricians expelled the last king, Tarquin the Proud, and established a republic (from the Latin *res publica,* "public property"). Monarchy was giving way to oligarchic republics across Etruria.

Rome and Italy.   The patrician oligarchy had engineered the end of the monarchy, and patricians dominated the offices and institutions of the new republic at the expense of the plebs, who, in losing the king, lost their only defender.

Characteristic of republican institutions, power was shared by two or more equals elected for fixed terms. This ensured that no one individual could achieve supreme power at any level. Replacing the king were two consuls. Initially, only the consuls held the supreme power to execute the law. Military commanders directed wars against neighboring cities and peoples. The officeholders consulted with each other and with the Senate in all their actions.

With political and religious power came economic power. The poorer plebs were in debt to wealthy patricians, losing their property and with it the basis for military service and political participation. The plebs organized in response to patrician control. Several times they left the city and refused to return or to serve in the military until conflicts with the patricians were resolved. In time, the plebs created their own assembly, which enacted laws binding on all plebeians. The plebian council elected magistrates called tribunes who protected the plebs from arbitrary patrician power. The conflict between the plebeians and the patricians threatened to tear Roman society apart, just as pressure from hostile neighbors placed Rome on the defensive.

Patricians were unable to meet the military pressure without the assistance of the plebs and so began to make a series of compromises. In 450 B.C.E., a basic Roman law was enacted, the Law of the Twelve Tables, which recognized the basic rights of

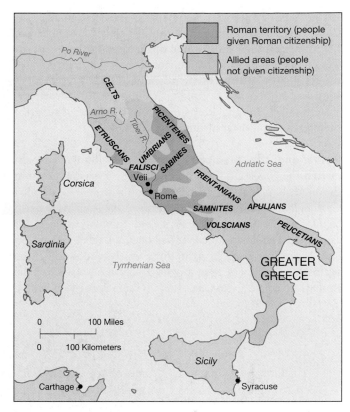

■ Rome in 264 B.C.E. As Rome conquered its neighbors, it either incorporated them directly into its own citizenry or established specific treaties whereby former enemies became Roman allies.

all free citizens. The law was posted publicly and covered private, criminal, sacred, and public matters. Gradually, priesthoods, magistracies, and the Senate opened to plebeians.

In spite of their differences, patricians and plebs presented a united front against their enemies abroad. By the beginning of the fourth century B.C.E., the united patrician-plebeian state was expanding its rule. Roman legions reestablished Roman preeminence in Latium and began a series of wars that brought most of Italy under Roman control. By 265 B.C.E., Rome had absorbed the Hellenistic cities of the south.

The Roman conquest benefited patrician and plebeian alike. While the patricians acquired wealth and power, the plebeians received land. However, into the late third century B.C.E., debt and landlessness remained major problems, creating tensions in Roman society.

The Roman manner of treating conquered populations contributed to Rome's success. In war, no one could match the Roman legions for ruthless, thorough destruction. Yet no conquerors were more generous in victory. Rome extended citizenship to conquered neighbors and offered this possibility to allies. Conquered populations became strong supporters. Rome's colonies drew local populations into the Roman cultural and political orbit; in time, a fortunate few who cooperated with Rome shared the benefits of Roman citizenship. Greeks were scandalized by the Roman tradition of giving citizenship even to freed slaves. By the end of the fourth century B.C.E., some of the sons of the freedmen were finding a place in the Senate. Benevolent treatment of the conquered spurred further conquest. By 264 B.C.E., all of Italy was united under Roman hegemony. Roman expansion finally brought Rome into conflict with the great Mediterranean power of the west, Carthage.

Rome and the Mediterranean.   Once Rome had conquered the Greek cities to the south, it became enmeshed in the affairs of neighboring Sicily, a region with well-established Carthaginian interests. Shortly afterward the Romans invaded Sicily, and Syracuse turned to its old enemy, Carthage, for assistance. The First Punic War had begun. In all, between 265 and 146 B.C.E. Rome fought three costly and brutal wars against Carthage. The first, fought largely as a sea war, led the Romans to create a vast fleet. After 20 years Rome won, taking

over Sicily and Sardinia. In the second, the Carthaginian commander Hannibal (247–183 B.C.E.) brought the war home to the Romans, invading Italy through Spain and across the Alps. Rome suffered disastrous losses and survived due to the support of its allies, the solidarity between patricians and plebs during the war, and the brilliant leadership of its commander, Publius Cornelius Scipio (236–184 B.C.E.). Scipio forced Hannibal from Africa, captured Spain, and defeated the Carthaginian army at Zama, Africa, in 202 B.C.E. The final war was a route: in 146 B.C.E., Scipio's adopted grandson Scipil Aemilianus (184–129 B.C.E.) destroyed Carthage and sold its survivors into slavery. Rome was master of the western shores of the Mediterranean.

In the same year that Carthage was destroyed, Roman armies destroyed Corinth. The victory marked the culmination of Roman imperialist expansion east into the Greek and Hellenistic world. Appealing to Rome's claims as "liberator," cities pressed the Senate to preserve their freedom in the face

THE TWELVE TABLES

The recording of the Twelve Tables in 449 B.C.E. was a great victory for the plebeians, both because it curbed the exercise of arbitrary power by patrician magistrates and because it established the principle of equality before the law.

Focus Questions

What sorts of problems did the law seek to resolve? How did the law regulate and support the importance of the patriarchal family?

Table I. Preliminaries to and Rules for a Trial
If plaintiff summons defendant to court, he shall go. If he does not go, plaintiff shall call witness thereto. Then only shall he take defendant by force.

If defendant shirks or takes to his heels, plaintiff shall lay hands on him. . . .

For a landowner, a landowner shall be surety; but for a proletarian person, let any one who is willing be his protector. . . .

When parties make a settlement of the case, the judge shall announce it. If they do not reach a settlement, they shall state the outline of their case in the meeting place or Forum before noon. . . .

Table III. Execution; Law of Debt
When a debt has been acknowledged, or judgment about the matter has been pronounced in court, thirty days must be the legitimate time of grace. After that, the debtor may be arrested by laying on of hands. Bring him into court. If he does not satisfy the judgment, or no one in court offers himself as surety in his behalf, the creditor

may take the defaulter with him. He may bind him either in stocks or in fetters. . . . The debtor, if he wishes, may live on his own. If he does not live on his own, the person [who shall hold him in bonds] shall give him one pound of grits for each day. . . .

Table IV. Rights of Head of Family
Quickly kill . . . a dreadfully deformed child.

Table VI. Guardianship; Succession
Females shall remain in guardianship even when they have attained their majority . . . except Vestal Virgins. Conveyable possessions of a woman under guardianship of agnates cannot be rightfully acquired by [long-term possession], save such possessions as have been delivered up by her with a guardian's sanction. . . .

Table IX. Public Laws
Laws of personal exception [i.e., bills of attainder] must not be proposed; cases in which the penalty affects the person of a citizen must not be decided except through the greatest assembly and through those whom the censors have placed upon the register of citizens. . . .

Table XI. Supplementary Laws
Intermarriage shall not take place between plebeians and patricians.

of aggressive expansion by their more powerful neighbors. In a series of intermittent engagements, Rome intervened, upsetting the balance of power in the Hellenistic world. Gradually the Roman shadow fell over the eastern Mediterranean.

By 146 B.C.E., the Roman Republic controlled the whole rim of the Mediterranean from Rhodes in the east across Greece, Dalmatia, Italy, southern Gaul, Spain, and North Africa. Even Syria and Egypt, although nominally independent, had to bow to Roman will. Perseverance and determination had brought Rome from obscurity to the greatest power the West had ever known. The republic had endured great adversity. But, it would not survive prosperity.

Republican Civilization

The ideal Roman soldier was the solid foot soldier, and the main fighting force was the infantry. When Rome's wars became international expeditions lasting for years, many soldiers were unable to work their lands during military service and mortgaged their farms in order to support their families. When they returned, they found they had lost their farms to aristocratic moneylenders. Thus, ordinary Romans and Italians lacked even a family farm to support their families. This excluded them from further military service, and they became desperately poor, disfranchised citizens.

The Roman Family. The father was the master of the Roman family, which included his wife, children, and slaves, over whom he exercised the power of life and death. This authority was the foundation of the patriarchal society.

Traditionally, Roman women did not have independent power in their male-dominated world. When a girl married, her father transferred legal guardianship to her husband, thus severing her bonds to her paternal family. A husband could divorce his wife at will, returning her and her dowry to her father. However, wives had informal authority within the family through the moral education of their children and the direction of the household.

Slaves, too, were members of the family. Although slaves were property without personal rights, they lived and worked alongside the free members of the family. Freed slaves remained obligated to their former owner throughout life.

DOCUMENT
Slaves in
Roman Law

In the wake of imperial conquests, the Roman family changed in ways disturbing to many of the oligarchy. Some women took a more active role in public life, and some married women escaped the authority of their husbands. Fewer fathers transferred authority over their daughters to their husbands. Instead, daughters remained under their father's authority as long as he lived. Therefore, at the father's death, the daughters became independent.

Homes grew in size and wealth for those who participated in the wealth of empire. But not every Roman family could afford its own *domus* (family house). In many Roman towns, simple dwellings and luxurious mansions existed side by side.

CHRONOLOGY	
THE ROMAN REPUBLIC	
509 B.C.E.	Expulsion of last Etruscan king; beginning of Roman Republic
ca. 450 B.C.E.	Law of the Twelve Tables
396 B.C.E.	Rome conquers southern Etruria
295 B.C.E.	Rome extends rule north to Po Valley
265–241 B.C.E.	First Punic War
264 B.C.E.	All of Italy under Roman control
218–202 B.C.E.	Second Punic War
149–146 B.C.E.	Third Punic War; Carthage is destroyed

The rich and the poor rubbed shoulders every day, producing a friction that threatened to burst into flame.

Roman Religion. Romans worshipped many gods, the more the better. Every aspect of daily life and work was the responsibility of individual powers. Each family had its household powers, whose proper worship was the responsibility of the paterfamilias. For example, the *Vesta* was the spirit of the hearth fire. The family spirits exercised a binding power, a *religio,* upon the Romans.

Those basic attitudes of religion, piety, and office lay at the heart of Roman reverence for order and authority. Religion was a public, civic activity that served the purpose of binding society together. State-supported cults with priests, Etruscan- and Greek-style temples, and elaborate ceremonies were integral parts of the Roman state and society.

Still, Roman religious tolerance had its limits. Following the Second Punic War, the cult of Dionysus, known in Latin as Bacchus, spread rapidly in Italy. Everything about the cult threatened traditional Roman values: it was Greek; it was dominated by women; and, most significantly, its rituals were secret. Eventually, the cult was banned, its leaders imprisoned and executed. The suppression of the Bacchic cult showed the fear that the oligarchy felt about the changes sweeping Roman civilization.

Republican Writings. As Rome absorbed foreign gods, it also absorbed foreign letters. From the Etruscans the Romans adapted the alphabet, the one in which most Western languages are written to this day. Early Latin inscriptions are largely funeral monuments and some public notices such as the Law of the Twelve Tables. Prior to the third century B.C.E., Romans had no apparent interest in writing or literature. The birth of Latin letters began with Rome's exposure to Greek civilization. The earliest Latin literary works were clearly adaptations, if not simply translations, of Hellenistic genres and texts, particularly the comedies of Menander.

Rome had come a long way since its origins as an outpost of the Alban League. Gradually it had created a political system that could incorporate not only different social and economic groups within the city, but other populations as well. Its power spread due to Roman authoritarianism as well as its genius for creative adaptation, flexibility, and a willingness to give those it conquered a stake in Roman victory. However, when it became a Mediterranean empire, its oligarchy was increasingly unwilling or unable to broaden the base of those participating in the Roman achievement. The result was a century of conflict and civil war that destroyed the republic.

IMPERIAL ROME, 146 B.C.E.–192 C.E.

Rome emerged victorious in the Punic and Macedonian wars against Carthage and Macedon, but the real winners were the members of the oligarchy—the **optimates,** or "the best" as they called themselves—whose wealth and power had grown beyond all imagining. Another group of Romans, the newly enriched Romans, were a second elite, distinguished by their wealth and military service. The losers in the wars included those sold into slavery; the provincials; the Italian allies; and the citizen farmers, or **populares.** These groups suffered from the effects of empire, and they all resorted to violence against the optimates.

Thousands of slaves were the first to revolt against the wealthy optimates. It took the Roman state three years to crush the revolt of the more than 200,000 slaves that began in 135 B.C.E.. The slaves revolted again between 104 and 101 B.C.E., and the worst slave revolt occurred between 74 and 71

B.C.E. Only a full-scale military campaign could defeat them. In addition to slaves, impoverished provincials of Rome's provinces rose up against their masters. Finally, closer to home following the second Punic War, Rome's Italian allies revolted against the way the oligarchy was driving free peasants from the land and replacing them with slaves. These revolts profoundly disturbed the Roman state, because the rebels included not only slaves, provincials, and allies, but even some ordinary Roman citizens. The despair that led ordinary Roman citizens to armed rebellion grew from the social and economic consequences of conquests. While aristocrats acquired land estates worked by slaves, ordinary Romans often lacked even a family farm to support their families.

In the face of the oligarch's unwillingness to deal with the problems facing ordinary citizens, in 133 B.C.E. the tribune Tiberius Gracchus (ca. 163–133 B.C.E.) proposed laws that would distribute public lands claimed by the elites to ordinary citizens and provide funds for them to purchase livestock and equipment. The law passed, but the Senate, which saw Gracchus's moves as a threat to their control of the state, accused him of attempting to make himself ruler of Rome and murdered him and 300 of his supporters.

In 123 B.C.E., Tiberius's brother, Gaius Sempronius Gracchus (153–121 B.C.E.), became tribune and attempted to extend his brother's efforts to shift power away from the Senate. Gaius wanted citizenship for all Latins and wanted to give Italian allies the right to vote. His program amounted to a fundamental change in the Roman constitution and met enormous opposition from the Senatorial elite. Fearing that he would be killed like his brother, he armed his supporters, but was killed along with 3000 of his supporters on the orders of the Senate.

The deaths of Tiberius Gracchus and Gaius Gracchus marked a new beginning in Roman politics. Reformers would

■ Roman slaves sifting grain. Roman victories in the Punic and Macedonian wars brought a huge influx of slaves from the conquered lands. Slaves were pressed into service on the estates and plantations of wealthy landowners.

■ Marcus Tullius Cicero, the famous statesman and orator, fought throughout his career to save the dying Roman Republic.

look not to the Senate or the aristocracy. They would look to the people for their political power.

The End of the Republic

With the Gracchi dead and the core of their reforms dismantled, the Senate appeared victorious against all challengers. However, Rome had not solved the problems of internal conflict between rich and poor, or how to govern its enormous empire.

In 107 B.C.E., the people elected as consul Gaius Marius (157–86 B.C.E.). Marius waged war in Africa and quickly won. He promised land to his impoverished soldiers, but the Senate refused to provide veterans with farms. As a result, Marius's armies shifted their allegiance away from the Roman state and to their popular commander. Soon that pattern of loyalty became the norm. Politicians forged close bonds with the soldiers of their armies.

Marius and the consul Lucius Cornelius Sulla (138–78 B.C.E.) fought the Italians, who were quieted only after Roman citizenship was extended to all Italians. However, in 89 B.C.E. Marius and Sulla became rivals—Marius was the leader of the populares while Sulla represented the optimates. Sulla marched on Rome, initiating a bloody civil war. In the course of this war, Rome was occupied three times—once by Marius and twice by Sulla. After Marius's death, Sulla ruled as dictator from 82 to 79 B.C.E. He reduced the authority of the plebian tribunes and restored oligarchy. Although his changes brought a decade of peace, they did not solve the problems dividing wealthy elites and the poor. If anything, his rule had proven that the only real political option was a dictatorship by a powerful individual with his own army.

Civil Wars.   As the republic slipped toward anarchy, a few voices spoke to return to the earlier principles of government that had led to Rome's greatness. The most important was Marcus Tullius Cicero (106–43 B.C.E.), a great orator and statesman who supported the conservative Senatorial tradition but who hoped to save the republic through harmony and cooperation among the different factions.

Few heeded him. Instead, in the next decades, three strong military commanders, Pompey (106–48 B.C.E.), Crassus (ca. 115–53 B.C.E.), and Julius Caesar (100–44 B.C.E.) continued the tradition of military rule started by Sulla. Pompey, a successful military commander, and the wealthy Crassus, who had defeated the last slave revolt, had been protégés of Sulla, but they sought support instead from the populares. Caesar began his career as a follower of Crassus but gained popularity for his military victories in Gaul. The three formed an uneasy alliance called the **first triumvirate.** After Crassus's death in 53 B.C.E., tensions between Pompey and Caesar erupted into civil war. When Caesar defeated Pompey, Caesar became the political leader of Rome. He started a series of reforms, including adding Italians to the Senate, founding colonies for retired soldiers, and increasing the number of magistracies to broaden political participation. Caesar had declared himself a dictator. Eventually, a group of senators assassinated him because he did not intend to restore the oligarchy. This set off another round of civil wars.

A **second triumvirate** of political leaders stepped in: Antony, Lepidus, and Caesar's grandnephew and adopted son, Ocatvian (63 B.C.E.–14 B.C.E). They succeeded in eliminating the senators responsible for the murder of Caesar, but Lepidus retired and Antony and Ocatvian fought for supreme command. The contest ended in victory for Octavian and the death of Antony and his supporter Cleopatra, queen of Egypt.

Although the last years of the republic were violent, Roman culture flourished. The most prominent figure in the late republic was Cicero. He believed in the Stoic philosophy of divine providence, morality, and duty to one's allotted role in the universe. Cicero found a rational basis for his commitment to public life. For Cicero, humans and gods were bound together in a world governed not simply by

■ The Career of Julius Caesar. Caesar's military career, first against the Gauls and Germans and then against his Roman rivals, took him as far west as the Rhine and east through Greece to Egypt.

might but by justice. The universe, while perhaps not fully intelligible, was nonetheless rational, and reason had to be the basis for society and its laws. Although he was killed by the second triumvirate, even Octavian recognized his integrity and his love of Rome.

The Augustan Age

Octavian's power rested on three factors: his immense wealth, his vast following among the surviving elites, and his total command of the army. Octavian had no intention of rekindling opposition by establishing an overt monarchy. Instead, in 27 B.C.E., he returned the power of the republic to the Senate and the people of Rome. In turn, the Senate granted him the title of *Augustus,* meaning "exalted."

DOCUMENT

Augustus on His Accomplishments

This meant that Augustus, as Octavian was now called, continued to rule no less strongly than before, but he did not rule through any autocratic office or title—he preferred to be called simply the "first citizen." This preserved the form of the traditional Roman magistracies. Augustus, through the power of the plebeian office of tribune, stood as the permanent protector of the Roman people. As either consul or proconsul, he held the command of the army and the basis of the ancient patrician authority. He was the first and greatest emperor.

Augustus's power was absolute. However, by choosing not to exercise it in an absolutist manner, he forged a new constitutional system that worked well for him and for his successors. Augustus's extraordinarily long reign lasted 41 years. Under Augustus and his successors, the empire enjoyed two centuries of stability and peace.

The Empire Renewed.   Key to Augustus's program of renewal was the Senate. He revived this body by admitting wealthy sons of provincials and even of freed slaves while removing those who were unfit or whose families could no longer be of use. Still, the Senate remained a creature of the emperor. Augustus increased the size of the army. He also granted loyal veterans of his armies colonies that helped Romanize the far provinces of the empire and also addressed the land ownership crisis that provoked much of the unrest in the late republic.

Augustus's renewal of Rome rested on religious reform. He restored numerous temples and revived ancient Roman cults. He established a series of public religious festivals, reformed priesthoods, and encouraged citizens to participate in the traditional cults of Rome. Augustus was determined to restore the traditions of Roman piety, morality, sacred order, and faith in the relationship between the gods and Roman destiny. Augustus received special devotion in temples throughout the west dedicated to "Rome and Augustus." In this manner, the emperor became identical to the state, and the state religion was closely akin to emperor worship.

■ This idealized marble portrait statue of the emperor Augustus addressing his army was found in the villa of Livia, wife of Augustus, at Prima Porta in Rome. The carvings on his breastplate recall a diplomatic incident during his reign.

Augustus believed that the declining power of the paterfamilias was at the root of much that was wrong with Rome. So he encouraged marriage, procreation, and the firm control of husbands over wives.

Poetry and the Arts.   Augustus actively patronized those writers who shared his conservative religious and ethical values and he used his power to censor and silence writers he considered immoral. Chief among the favored were the poets Virgil (70–19 B.C.E.) and Horace (65–8 B.C.E.).

In Horace's poems, Augustus is almost a god; his deeds are compared to those of the great heroes of Roman legend and judged superior. Virgil expressed this sentiment in the *Aeneid*, an epic intended to serve for the Roman world the role of the Homeric poems in the Greek. As he reworked the legend of Aeneas—a Trojan hero who escaped the destruction of the city, wandered throughout the Mediterranean, and ultimately came to Latium—Virgil presented a panoramic history of Rome and its destiny.

Augustus strongly opposed the work of Ovid (43 B.C.E.–17 C.E.), the great Latin poet of erotic love. In *Art of Love and Amores,* Ovid cheerfully preached the art of seduction and adultery. He poked irreverent fun at everything from the sanctity of Roman marriage to the serious business of warfare. Although Augustus exiled the poet, Ovid was appreciated by his contemporaries as the greatest poet of the age.

Augustus's Successors.   Augustus's stepson Tiberius (14–37 C.E.) proved to be an unpopular successor but was a competent ruler. The smooth functioning of the empire even under the subsequent members of Augustus's family—Caligula (37–41), Claudius (41–54), and Nero (54–68)—is a tribute to the soundness of Augustus's constitutional changes and the interest that the descendants of Augustus's military and aristocratic supporters had in them.

Nero divided his time between murdering his relatives and associates and squandering his wealth on attempts to gain recognition as a great poet, actor, singer, and athlete. After Nero, four men in quick succession won the office, only to lose their lives just as quickly. Finally, in 70, Vespasian (69–79 C.E.) restored order.

When Vespasian's troops fought their way into Rome in vicious hand-to-hand street fighting, the populace watched with idle fascination. The empire remained stable, which was the greatest achievement of Augustus and his immediate successors.

Administering the Empire.   The imperial government of the vast empire was as oppressive as it was primitive. Taxes, forced labor service, military levies and requisitions, and extortion weighed heavily on its subjects. The daily exercise of government fell to local elites, the army, and members of the imperial household.

Thus, Hellenistic cities continued to manage their own affairs under the supervision of essentially amateur Roman governors. In return for their participation in Roman rule, the elites received Roman citizenship, a prize that carried prestige, legal protection, and the promise of further advancement in the Roman world.

The empire worked because it rewarded those who worked with it and left alone those who paid their taxes and kept quiet. Seldom has a ruling elite made access to its ranks so open to those who cooperated with it. Proper education in Latin and Greek, the ability to hold one's own in philosophical discussion, and the absorption of Roman styles of dress, recreation, and religious cults were essential for ambitious provincials. In the first century B.C.E., the disparate portions of the empire competed not to free themselves from the Romans, but to become Roman themselves.

Science and Medicine in the Empire.   Romans were more interested in practical issues of government than in

MAP DISCOVERY

The Roman Empire, 14 and 117 C.E.

Examine the extent of the Roman Empire in 14 C.E. and in 117 C.E. What civilizations and empires that you have previously studied were incorporated into the Roman Empire by 14 C.E.? By 117 C.E.? Which regions had never before been part of ancient civilizations? What natural geographical features defined the boundaries of the empire in the west, north, south, and east?

speculative science, which they left to the Greek scholars of Alexandria. Three centuries of Greek mathematics, astronomy, and geography came to fruition in the work of Claudius Ptolemaeus (ca.85–ca.165 C.E.), usually known as Ptolemy. He developed a complex model for the universe with which to explain the apparent motion of the Sun, Moon, and planets. Since, like most ancient scientists, he believed the earth to be the center of the universe, he sought a mathematically correct model to explain the apparent motions of the sun and the moon, which appear to move at varying speeds, and of the planets, which appear to move erratically when observed from earth. His solution was to argue that that the

planets move in uniform circular motion in a small circle while at the same time moving uniformly on the circumference of a larger circle. The result was a complex series of cycles and epicycles, but the mathematics work quite well. Ptolemy's theory, which he explained in his treatise know from its influential Arabic translation as the *Almagest* (The Greatest Compilation), remained the accepted model of the solar system for the next 1400 years.

A Greek of more interest to the Romans was Galen, (129–ca. 201 C.E.) who studied medicine in the Eastern Mediterranean before becoming the physician to the Emperor Marcus Aurelius. Galen was an expert in anatomy and trauma and wrote over 500 works. His medical treatises remained the standard for over a thousand years.

Religions from the East: Judaism and Christianity

For many in the empire, the traditional rituals offered to the household gods and the state cults were insufficient ways to express religious devotion. In the first century B.C.E., so-called **mystery cults**—that is, religions promising personal contact with a deity that would bring immortality—spread throughout the empire. Rome tolerated the cults as long as they could be assimilated into the cult of the Roman gods and the genius of the emperor. However, many educated members of the elite were monotheists, believing in a supreme deity.

Jewish Resistance of Polytheistic Cults. For one religious group, belief in Roman gods was impossible. The Jews of Palestine refused the polytheistic cults. Roman conquerors and emperors avoided antagonizing the Jews, who were allowed to worship only one god and were excused from making sacrifices to the Roman gods.

The Jewish community remained deeply divided about its relationship with the wider world and with Rome. Some, called Sadducees, were willing to work with Rome and even adopt some Hellenistic ways as long as the temple service could continue. Others, called the pure ones (Hasidim), rejected all compromise with Rome. Among the Hasidim, the Pharisees taught strict dietary rules and rituals. The most prominent Pharisee, Hillel (ca. 30 B.C.E.–10 C.E.) was a Jewish scholar from Babylon who came to Jerusalem as a teacher of the law. He began a tradition of legal and scriptural interpretation that became the Talmud, and taught a morality of peace and love, not revolt. Other Hasidim, termed Zealots, organized sporadic armed resistance to Roman rule. As ever, armed resistance was met with violent suppression. Throughout the first century B.C.E., clashes between Roman troops and Zealot revolutionaries grew more frequent.

The Origins of Christianity. The complex landscape of the Jewish religious world was complicated by Joshua ben Joseph (ca. 6 B.C.E.–30 C.E.), known to history as Jesus of Nazareth and to his followers as Jesus the Messiah, or the Christ.

PETER ANNOUNCES THE GOOD NEWS

The following passage, attributed to the apostle Peter in the book of Christian Scripture known as the Acts of the Apostles, is probably a close approximation of the earliest Christian preaching. In it, Jesus is presented as the new Moses.

Focus Questions

How does Peter explain Jesus within the Jewish tradition? How does Peter explain the mission of Jesus?

Men of Israel, why do you stare at us, as though by our own power or piety we had made him [a paralytic who has just been cured] walk? The God of Abraham and of Isaac and of Jacob, the God of our fathers, glorified his servant Jesus, whom you delivered up and denied in the presence of Pilate, when he had decided to release him. But you denied the Holy and Righteous One, and asked for a murderer to be granted to you, and killed the Author of life, whom God raised from the dead. To this we are witnesses. And his name, by faith in his name, has made this man strong whom you see and know; and the faith which is through Jesus has given the man this perfect health in the presence of you all.

And now, brethren, I know that you acted in ignorance, as did also your rulers. But what God foretold by the mouth of all the prophets, that his Christ should suffer, he thus fulfilled. Repent therefore, and turn again, that your sins may be blotted out, that times of refreshing may come from the presence of the Lord, and that he may send the Christ appointed for you, Jesus, whom heaven must receive until the time for establishing all that God spoke by the mouth of his holy prophets from of old.

Moses said, "The Lord God will raise up for you a prophet from your brethren as he raised me up. You shall listen to him in whatever he tells you. And it shall be that every soul that does not listen to that prophet shall be destroyed from the people." And all the prophets who have spoke, from Samuel and those who came afterwards, also proclaimed these days.

You are the sons of the prophets and of the covenant which God gave to your fathers, saying to Abraham, "And in your posterity shall all the families of the earth be blessed." God, having raised up his servant, sent him to you first, to bless you in turning every one of you from your wickedness.

From Acts 3: 12–26. The Holy Bible, Revised Standard Version.

CHRONOLOGY
THE END OF THE REPUBLIC

135–81 B.C.E.	Revolts against the republic
133–121 B.C.E.	Gracchi reform programs
107 B.C.E.	Gaius Marius elected consul
91–82 B.C.E.	Social War and civil war (Marius vs. Sulla)
82–79 B.C.E.	Sulla rules as dictator
79–27 B.C.E.	Era of civil wars
63 B.C.E.	Cicero elected consul; first triumvirate (Pompey, Crassus, Caesar)
59 B.C.E.	Caesar elected consul
45 B.C.E.	Caesar defeats Pompey's forces
44 B.C.E.	Caesar is assassinated; second triumvirate (Mark Antony, Lepidus, Octavian)
42 B.C.E.	Octavian and Mark Antony defeat Cassius and Brutus at Philippi
31 B.C.E.	Octavian defeats Mark Antony and Cleopatra at Actium
27 B.C.E.	Octavian is declared Augustus

Jesus left no body of sacred texts, and what is known about the man and the first generation of his followers comes from Greek texts written between the middle of the first century and the middle of the second. The texts include gospels, accounts of Jesus' life; letters, or epistles; and historical narratives and visionary writings by his early disciples. From such sources, it is difficult to separate the actual historical figure of Jesus from the images of him that developed within the communities in the following century.

Jesus came from Galilee. While Jesus preached the imminent coming of the kingdom, he did so in a nonpolitical manner. He preached a message of peace and love of God and neighbor. His teachings were entirely within the Jewish tradition and resembled those of Hillel—with one major exception. While many contemporary religious leaders announced the imminent coming of the messiah, Jesus' closest followers saw him as the messiah and expected him to liberate the Jewish people.

Jesus became a figure of controversy, a catalyst for violence. Ultimately the Roman procurator, Pontius Pilate, decided that he posed a threat to law and order. Pilate ordered Jesus put to death by crucifixion, a common Roman form of execution for slaves, pirates, and troublemakers. Jesus' death did not deter his followers who announced that three days after his death he had risen. They took his resurrection as proof that he was the messiah. A group of followers formed another Jewish sect known as Christianity.

Christianity spread beyond its origin as a Jewish sect because of the work of Paul of Tarsus (ca. 5–ca. 67 C.E.). He saw Christianity as a separate tradition, completing and perfecting Judaism but intended for the whole world. The Christian message of salvation was to be preached to all nations and people, for "there is neither Jew nor Greek, slave nor free, male or female, for all are one in Christ Jesus."

Paul spread his message throughout the eastern Mediterranean world and Rome. He won converts, established churches, and expressed the first coherent system of beliefs of the Christian sect. His teachings were radically new: God had created the human race in the image of God and destined it for eternal life. However, by the deliberate sin of Adam and Eve, humans had lost eternal life and introduced evil and death into the world. Salvation from sin was accomplished by Jesus, the son of God, through his faith.

The Christians' refusal to acknowledge the existence of the other gods or participate in the cult of the emperor was intolerable. Judaism was tolerated because it was not seeking to convert others. Christianity was an aggressive and successful cult, viewed not as religion, but as subversion. Romans destroyed Christian sacred Scriptures and executed those who refused to sacrifice to the imperial genius. But instead of decreasing the cult's appeal, persecution only aided it. The strength of their convictions convinced others of the truth of their religion.

As time went on, a hierarchy developed. The leader of each community was the bishop, assisted by priests, deacons, and deaconesses. Gradually, the exalted position of the bishop and his assistants led to a distinction between the clergy—that is, those who served at the altar—and the laity, the rank and file of Christians. Women, who had played central roles in Jesus' ministry, were excluded from positions of authority within the clergy.

Although Christianity spread rapidly throughout the eastern Mediterranean in the first and second centuries, the empire's rulers viewed it as only a minor irritation. Its fundamental role in the transformation of the Roman world would not become clear until the third and fourth centuries.

THE TRANSFORMATION OF THE CLASSICAL WORLD

The empire created by Augustus encountered grave problems both from within and without by the end of the second century. It survived, but transformed into an autocratic, Christian empire far different from its origins.

The Crisis of the Third Century

From the reign of Septimus Severus (193–211) to the time of Diocletian (284–305), both internal and external challenges shook the Roman Empire. It survived, but its social, political, and economic structures were radically transformed. Its fundamental problems were many: it was too vast, its economic system underdeveloped, and it had never developed a regular system of imperial succession or an adequate power base. Only an emperor able to lead armies to victory could hold it together.

Throughout much of the late second and third centuries, emperors failed dismally to lead their armies to victory, and frustrated provincial armies elected emperors on their own. Exercising their newly discovered power, armies supported whichever imperial candidate promised them the greatest riches. Emperors who could not meet the demands were killed by their troops. In fact, the army was much more effective at

killing emperors than enemies. Between 235 and 284, 17 of the 20 more or less legitimate emperors were assassinated or killed in civil war.

The crisis of the third century did not result only from economic and political instability within the empire. Rome's internal imperial crises coincided with an increase in attacks from the Persian Empire to the east, from Berber tribes in North Africa, and from Germanic peoples along the Rhine and Danubian frontiers in Europe.

The central administration of the empire simply could not deal effectively with the numerous barbarian attacks. Taxes to support the army rose constantly, but these armies were as much a threat as the barbarians themselves. Many ordinary farmers were driven to banditry, terrorizing the countryside, but also sometimes protecting peasants from greedy tax collectors and military commanders. Although these resistance movements were always ruthlessly crushed, they continued to reappear—a sign of the desperation of ordinary people.

The Barbarian Menace. The most serious attacks on the Roman Empire in the west came from various German peoples. Traditionally organized in small tribal groups, these societies were profoundly affected by their contact with Rome. Barbarian commanders were recruited into the Roman army, allowing them to increase their wealth and power and put together large, dangerous armies and tribal confederations that threatened their barbarian neighbors and the Roman provinces. New peoples emerged in the course of the second and third centuries, including the Goths along the lower Danube, the Alemanni on the upper Rhine, and the Franks on the lower Rhine near the North Sea. These confederations alternatively served and fought the Romans.

The Empire Restored

The emperors Aurelian (270–275) and especially his successor Diocletian (284–305) stopped the disintegration of the Roman Empire through a fundamental restructuring of its political and ideological foundations. First, Diocletian reorganized the military and civil bureaucracies. He separated military and civilian offices, making them more efficient and modeling the civil bureaucracy on the military. Second, he recognized that the empire was too large for one man to administer. Therefore he divided the empire into two parts each ruled by an emperor and an assistant called caesar. In theory, this new system (the **tetrarchy** or rule by four) made revolts and assassinations less likely to be successful, since a person would have to kill all four rulers in order to seize power. Since each caesar was to succeed the senior emperor, the system also was intended to create orderly succession for the first time. Third, he attempted to stop runaway inflation by instituting wage and price controls throughout the empire. Finally, he elevated the rituals surrounding the emperor to those of a god, thus tying the identity of the living emperors to religious worship and demanding veneration from all citizens as part of the ideology of the state.

■ The tetrarchy was an attempt to regulate the succession. Here, the emperors Diocletian and Maximian are depicted with their caesars—Constantius of the west and Galerius of the east—who were their respective sons-in-law.

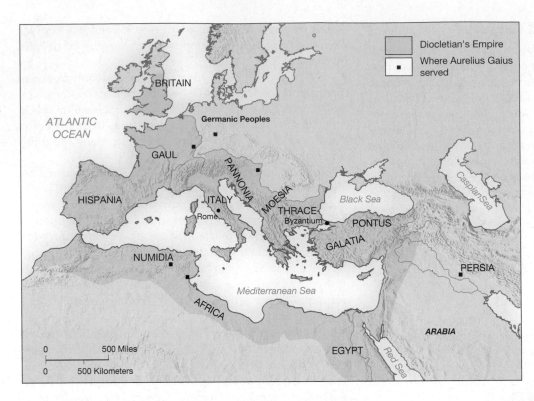

■ The Empire Under Diocletian. Under pressure from external enemies, Rome pulled back from parts of western Europe, the Balkans, and Mesopotamia. This map shows the extent of the empire in 305, at the end of Diocletian's reign.

His military and administrative reforms were successful; his price controls largely failed; his religious program was a disaster. The one group that stubbornly opposed his religious reform were the Christians. Failure of the Christians to support the cult of the deified emperor led to their persecution, the most thorough in Roman history.

Constantine, the Emperor of God.   In 305, in the midst of the Great Persecution, Diocletian resigned. Instead of the anticipated orderly succession, a civil war ensued. Constantine (306–337), the winner, was the son of one of Diocletian's caesars.

Constantine rescinded the persecution of Christians and granted Christian clergy the same privileges enjoyed by pagan priests. Constantine then converted to Christianity. During his reign, Christianity grew from a persecuted minority to the most favored cult in the empire.

Almost as important as Constantine's conversion to Christianity was his decision to establish his capital not in Rome, but in Byzantium. He called it the New Rome. Later it was known as Constantinople, the city of Constantine. For the next 11 centuries, Constantinople served as the heart of the Roman and then the Byzantine world. From his new city, Constantine transformed the empire into a Christian state and Christianity into a Roman state religion. In 341, pagan sacrifice was banned and by 355 the temples had been closed.

The Triumph of Christianity.   Under Constantine and his successors, Christianity rapidly became the established religion. Constantine made enormous financial contributions to Christian communities to repay them for their losses during the

■ This head of Constantine, seven times life size, was part of an immense seated statue intended to portray not the emperor as he was but rather the divinity that resided in him.

■ The Spread of Christianity. Christian churches appeared first in the major cities of the empire and spread only gradually into the countryside, in part due to the establishment of monasteries.

persecutions. At the same time, he attempted to make himself the de facto head of the Christian Church. Constantine and his successors sought to use the cult of the one God to strengthen their control over the empire.

Over the course of the fourth century, the number of Christians rose from 5 to 30 million. Conversions resulted both from positive incentives of participating in the new state religion and negative pressures including persecution and even execution of polytheists.

Imperial Christianity

The Christian Church of the later Roman Empire was well organized under the leadership of the bishops, but the Church remained divided by significant differences. Two of the most important issues were the nature of Christ and the means by which people were saved. Generally, Christians saw God as a Trinity, at once one and three. Was Christ just a man, chosen by God as a divine instrument, or was he God, and if so, had he simply appeared to be human? Followers of Arius (250–336), called **Arians,** believed that Jesus was merely human, and disagreements deeply divided the Christian world. The council of Nicaea called by Constantine in 325 declared that Jesus was divine and condemned Arius and his followers, but the Arian position continued to attract followers in the Roman Empire and in the barbarian world on its borders.

Western Christians were not as deeply concerned with the **Christological controversies** as were the easterners. For westerners, the great question was less the nature of God than the mechanism of salvation and the role of humans in the salvation process.

Augustine of Hippo (354–430), a North African rhetorician and convert to Christianity, set the course of Western Christianity and political philosophy for the next thousand years. Augustine elaborated a new Christian understanding of human society and the individual's relationship to God, which dominated Western thought for the next 15 centuries. He rejected the elitist attempts to identify the true church with any earthly community. Salvation was free, a gift not earned by virtuous lives but freely granted by God to the elect. He also insisted that the community of the elect could not be equated with any human organization, even the Christianized Roman Empire.

Just as it became easier to be Christian in the empire, some men and women sought a more difficult life by radically rejecting society's values in favor of absolute dedication to God. Thousands rejected the worldliness of civilization and the easy life of the average Christian to lead a monastic life in the wildernesses of the empire. Monastic living involved communities of Christians dedicated to rigorous prayer under the command of abbots who ruled the communities. In the east, monasteries were often in or near cities and monks took active parts in the political life of their societies, following the

LOVE IN THE TWO CITIES

Augustine took more than 14 years to write his masterpiece, The City of God. *Initially, he intended to write simply a defense of Christianity from the charge that the disasters of his age, culminating in the sack of Rome in 410, resulted from Rome's abandoning its traditional gods. In time the work grew into a wide-ranging inquiry into the nature of human society. In the following passage, he summarizes his conclusion that human society and divine society are based on fundamentally different foundations.*

Focus Questions

Why, in Augustine's estimation, are all human societies fundamentally flawed? On what does Augustine believe the perfect society should be based?

What we see, then, is that two societies have issued from two kinds of love. Worldly society has flowered from a selfish love which dared to despise God, whereas the communion of saints is rooted in a love of God that is ready to trample on self. In a word, this latter relies on the Lord, whereas the other boasts that it can get along by itself. The city of man seeks the praise of men, whereas the heights of glory for the other is to hear God in the witness of conscience. The one lifts up its head in its own boasting; the other says to God: "Thou art my glory, thou liftest up my head" (Psalm 3:4).

In the city of the world, both the rulers themselves and the people they dominate are dominated by the lust for domination; whereas in the City of God all citizens serve one another in charity, whether they serve by the responsibilities of office or by the duties of obedience. The one city loves its leaders as symbols of its own strength; the other says to its God: "I love thee, O Lord, my strength" (Psalm 17:2). Hence, even the wise men in the city of man live according to man, and their only god has been the gods of their bodies or of the mind or of both, though some of them have reached a knowledge of God, "they did not glorify him as God or give thanks but became vain in their reasonings, and their senseless minds have been darkened. For while professing to be wise" (that is to say, while glorying in their own wisdom, under the domination of pride), "they have become fools, and they have changed the glory of the incorruptible God for an image made like to corruptible man and to birds and four-footed beasts and creeping things" (meaning that they either led their people, or imitated them, in adoring idols shaped like these things), "and they worshipped and served the creature rather than the Creator who is blessed forever" (Romans 1:21–25). In the City of God, on the contrary, there is no merely human wisdom, but there is a piety which worships the true God as He should be worshipped and has as its goal that reward of all holiness whether in the society of saints on earth or in that of angels of heaven, which is "that God may be all in all" (1 Corinthians 15:28).

From Saint Augustine, *The City of God.*

---

lead of Basil the Great. Benedict of Nursia (ca. 480–547) created the most popular type of monasticism in the west: Monks lived a life of poverty, chastity, and obedience, and the day was divided between prayer and meditation. Unlike in the east, western monks and abbots remained largely aloof from secular politics.

A Parting of the Ways

The vulnerability of the Constantinian system became clear shortly after 376 when the Huns, a nomadic horse-riding people from central Asia, swept into the Black Sea region and threw the entire barbarian world once more into chaos. The Huns destroyed the Gothic confederation. Some of the refugees, the Visigoths, as they came to be known, turned to the empire for assistance. But the Roman authorities treated them brutally. In despair, the Visigoths rose up against the Romans, and against all odds, they succeeded. They annihilated an imperial army at Adrianople in 378, and the emperor Valens was killed. His successor, Theodosius, was forced to allow the Visigoths to settle along the Danube and to be governed by their own leaders despite the fact that they lived within the boundaries of the empire. Never before had a barbarian people been allowed to settle as a political unit within the empire.

The Barbarization of the West.   Rome did not fall. It was transformed. Romans participated in and even encouraged the transformation. Roman accommodation of the Visigoths set the pattern for additional settlement of barbarians in the western half of the empire. By this time, barbarians made up the bulk of the imperial army. In the late fourth and fifth centuries, emperors accepted whole barbarian peoples as integral parts of the Roman army and settled them within the empire.

The Visigoths wandered through Italy, sacking Rome in 410 before settling into southern Gaul and Northern Spain. The Vandals crossed over to Africa and conquered a kingdom along the Mediterranean coast. Alemanni and Franks crossed the Rhine as federated Roman armies to settle areas of Northern Gaul. Another threat appeared in the 430s, when the Huns invaded the empire under their charismatic leader Attila (ca. 406–453). Eventually, Attila withdrew from Italy. During this time, as the military became increasingly composed of barbarian peoples and the civilian authorities were powerless to protect their communities, bishops began to play wider political roles in their communities. This was especially true of the bishop of Rome, the pope.

The Huns collapsed after the death of Attila in 453, but imperial power did not revive in Italy and the last incompetent western emperors were pushed aside by barbarian generals. In 489, the Ostrogothic king Theodoric invaded Italy with eastern imperial blessing and established himself as ruler of Italy.

The New Barbarian Kingdoms.

The establishment of barbarian kingdoms within the Roman world meant the end of the western empire as a political entity. However, the emperors, from their capital in Constantinople, continued to give western barbarian kings or war leaders official status within the empire as Roman generals or patricians. Local Roman elites considered the leaders rude and uncultured barbarians. Moreover, most were Arians while the local Romans were orthodox Christians. Nevertheless, the aristocrats found that the barbarian rulers could be made to serve their own interests more easily than better-educated imperial bureaucrats.

In spite of the creation of the barbarian kingdoms, cultural and political leadership at the local level remained firmly in the hands of the aristocracy. Aristocratic bishops monopolized the role of mediators of divine power, just as their lay brothers, in cooperation with barbarian military leaders, monopolized the role of mediators of secular power. Barbarian military leaders needed local ties by which to govern the large indigenous populations over whom they ruled. During the fifth century, the imperial presence simply faded away as barbarian kings came to rule in the name of the emperor.

The eastern half of the empire, in contrast to the west, managed to survive and even to prosper in the fifth and sixth centuries. In the east, the trends toward militarization and barbarization of the administration were reversed, the strength of the imperial government was reaffirmed, and the vitality and integrity of the empire were restored.

The divergence in religious power between east and west was characteristic of the growing differences between the two halves of the Roman Empire at the close of late antiquity. In the east, emperors continued to rule from Constantinople for another thousand years, but the extent of their authority gradually waned. Furthermore, their empire was so profoundly Hellenized in nature that it is properly called Byzantine (from the original name of Constantinople) rather than Roman. The west experienced a transformation even more profound than that of the east. The triple heritage of late Roman political and military forms, barbarian society, and Christian culture coalesced into a new civilization. In culture, politics, and patterns of urban and rural life, the west and the east had gone their separate ways, and their paths diverged ever more in the centuries ahead.

THE CLASSICAL LEGACY IN THE EAST: BYZANTIUM AND ISLAM

From the sixth century onward, the heritage of classical civilization developed in different directions in the eastern and western parts of the former Roman Empire. In the end, the Byzantine Empire and the Islamic world adapted this heritage in new and vital ways.

The Byzantines

The emperor Justinian (527–565) temporarily restored the fortunes of the Byzantine state by conquering parts of the empire lost to the Germanic tribes. He took back northern Africa, Italy, and a part of Spain. The enormous expense of Justinian's ambitious military policy was passed on in taxes to the residents of the empire. Justinian is also credited with codifying the Roman legal system, and his code provided the model of many European legal systems. Anthemius and Isidorus combined their knowledge of mathematics, geometry, kinetics, and physics to build the Church of the Holy Wisdom in Constantinople, one of the largest and most innovative churches ever constructed.

Justinian's achievements strained the treasury. Bankrupt successors were unable to deal with assaults on the borders of the empire. The Sassanid Empire captured Egypt, Palestine, and Syria. The emperor Heraclius recaptured the eastern territories from the Sassanids, but the weakened Byzantine state could not defend its easternmost regions from the Muslims indefinitely. A new power had emerged that would challenge and ultimately absorb much of the eastern Roman Empire. As a result, the east became increasingly less Roman and more Greek or, specifically, more Byzantine.

For more than 700 years the Byzantine Empire played a major role in Western history. From the seventh through the tenth centuries, when most of Europe was too weak and disorganized to defend itself against the expansion of Islam, the Byzantines were the bulwark of Christianity. When organized government had virtually disappeared in the west, the Byzantine Empire provided a model of a centralized bureaucratic state ruled according to principles of Roman law.

When, beginning in the fourteenth century, western Europeans began once more to appreciate the heritage of Greek and Roman art and literature, they turned to Constantinople. There the manuscripts of Greek writers such as Plato and Homer had been preserved and contributed to a rebirth of classical culture in the west. When the Slavic north sought its cultural and religious orientation, it looked to the culture of Byzantine orthodoxy. Most importantly, when urban civilization had almost disappeared from the rest of Europe, Greeks and Latins could still look

The Byzantine Empire Under Justinian. Justinian's reconquests of North Africa, Italy, and the coast of Spain severely strained the empire's resources.

"to the City," *eis ten polin,* or as the Turks pronounced it, *Istanbul.*

The Byzantine world was intensely individualistic. Byzantine individualism meant that individuals and small family groups stood as isolated units in a society characterized, until the mid-eleventh century, by the direct relationship between an all-powerful emperor and citizens of all ranks. In part, this individualism resulted from the Byzantine form of government—autocracy. As long as the empire remained a civilian autocracy, it was even possible for a woman to rule.

Male or female, emperors were above and beyond their subjects. Like God the Father, the emperor was separated from the people by an unbridgeable gulf. For great lords and peasants alike, the only proper attitude toward such a ruler was adoration and humility. While the emperor was the source of all authority, the administration of the empire was carried out by a bureaucracy composed of military and civilian officers.

Byzantine society was organized at the lowest level by that of the nuclear family. Single-family dwellings replaced the public spaces and buildings of antiquity. Communal celebrations either disappeared or were absorbed into the ritual of imperial dignity. Daily life focused on the private home, which served as both shelter and workplace.

Villages were the basic elements in the imperial system. The village court handled local affairs and tax assessments, and dealt directly with the imperial bureaucracy. Like the villages, Byzantine towns were isolated by the mountainous terrain. The empire's cities were centers for the manufacture of highly desirable luxury goods. The secret of silk manufacture had been smuggled out of China by a Christian monk who

had hidden silkworms in his staff during his journey home. (See "The West and the Wider World: Industrial Espionage in the Sixth Century, pp. lxxvi–lxxvii.) Imperial workshops in Constantinople and workshops in Corinth and Thebes produced fine silks and other luxury products marketed throughout the Mediterranean. Constantinople was ideally situated to develop into the greatest commercial center of the west because of its location on the water. All the products for the Slavic, Latin, and Islamic worlds passed through the city and were subjected to a tax that benefited the empire.

Byzantine culture was held together by **Orthodox Christianity.** The patriarch of Constantinople became the center of Orthodox Christianity, although the emperors in Constantinople appointed and dismissed patriarchs at will and were the true heads of the Church.

The essence of Orthodox religion was the liturgy, or ceremonies, of the Church, which provided, it was said, a foretaste of heaven. Adoration of God and veneration of the emperor were the cornerstone of imperial propaganda. Everything and everyone was in the proper place, and order and stability reigned in this world as a reflection of the eternal order of the next. Stability and permanence in the face of possible crisis and disruption calmed and reassured the liturgically oriented society.

The one aspect of religious life not entirely under control of the emperor was **monasticism.** By the eleventh century there were at least 300 monasteries within Constantinople. Monasteries were often wealthy and powerful and their religious appeal was a different kind of authority that clashed with the control that the emperor had over all aspects of Byzantine life. Icons, religious images thought to have mystic powers as intermediaries of the saints, strengthened the religious appeal of the monks. The emperors and their supporters, termed **iconoclasts** (literally, "breakers of images"), objected to the role of sacred images in worship. The attack on the images, iconoclasm, was an assault on monastic independence. Those who kept icons were persecuted.

Islam

Abu al-Qasim Muhammad ibn 'Abd Allah ibn 'Abd al-Muttalib ibn Hashim (ca. 570–632)—or more simply, Muhammad—united the tribes of the Arabian Peninsula and propelled them on an unprecedented mission of conquest. Within a century of Muhammad's death, the world of *Islam*, a word that means "submission to the will of God," included the ancient Near East and extended from Asia south into India, west across Africa to the Atlantic, north through Spain, and along the Mediterranean coast. The Arabian conquerors and their subject populations created a vital civilization from a mix of Arabian, Roman, Hellenistic, and Sassanid traditions.

By the sixth century C.E., Arabic-speaking peoples from the Arabian Peninsula had spread through the Syrian Desert as far north as the Euphrates. Those who lived on the fringes of the Byzantine and Sassanid empires were absorbed into the cultural and political spheres of those two great powers. Within both empires the distinction between Arab and non-Arab populations was blurred. Except for a different language and a hazy idea of common kinship, nothing differentiated Arabs from their neighbors.

The interior of the Arabian Peninsula was much less directly affected by the great empires to the north or the Arabian kingdoms to the south. The nomadic Bedouin roamed the peninsula in search of pasture for their flocks. Theirs was a life of independence, simplicity, and danger. Kin relationships, not the government, protected individuals. The patriarch of each family held final say over his kin. The individual was unimportant in Bedouin society. Private land ownership was unknown. Goods and women were taken in raids against other tribes.

Some of the Arabs of the more settled south, as well as inhabitants of towns along caravan routes, were Christian or Jewish. Those groups were looked down upon by the nomadic Bedouin, who remained pagan. Rivalry and feuding among tribes could be set aside at a mutually accepted site such as a religious sanctuary, or *haram,* that was declared neutral by a holy man. There enemies could meet to settle differences under the direction of the holy man. One of these sanctuaries was located in the city of Mecca where the Quraysh tribe guarded a sacred black rock. With its neutrality guaranteed, Mecca grew into a major center for all Arabs, although the Quraysh regulated the commerce.

Muhammad, Prophet of God. More is known about Muhammad's life than about that of Moses, Jesus, Buddha, or any of the other great religious reformers of history. Still, it is difficult to discern truth from legend in Muhammad's early years since such stories were written down only long after his death.

He was born a member of the Quraysh. He married Khadijah, a wealthy widow, and entered the ranks of the Quraysh merchants of Mecca. The traditions of Judaism and Christianity were well known to him through contact with

■ Arabic manuscripts were decorated with intricate geometric designs. This page from an eighth- or ninth-century copy of the Qur'an illustrates the elegance and formality of the Kufic form of Arabic calligraphy. Vowel marks appear as dots of various colors.

The West and the Wider World

INDUSTRIAL ESPIONAGE IN THE SIXTH CENTURY

The Emperor Justinian not only laid the political, institutional, and cultural foundations of Byzantium, but in a daring act of industrial espionage and smuggling, he also established what remained for centuries one of its most important export industries: silk manufacture. In the year 950 Bishop Liutprand of Cremona, emissary of the Emperor Otto I to the Byzantine court, was returning home from Constantinople after a humiliating encounter with Emperor Nicephorus when, as a final insult, his baggage was inspected and five valuable pieces of purple silk confiscated: the German emperor was deemed unworthy of the precious purple cloth. Liutprand fumed and complained but could do nothing: silk, the most prized cloth in the world, was available only from Byzantium or the Far East. Its manufacture was a closely guarded secret and a state monopoly. But Justinian had stolen the secret in the sixth century, and his Byzantine successors had maintained their monopoly for four hundred years.

Silk is a miracle fabric: a single filament of silk is as strong as steel of the same thickness. It is also much less dense than cotton or wool and much more moisture absorbent, able to take in three times its own weight without appearing damp. It is durable, dyes beautifully, and resists mold and mildew. No wonder it has been a prized commodity for the past five thousand years. However, its production is extraordinary. Silk is produced from the cocoons of silkworm moths. The worms feed on mulberry leaves before spinning their cocoons in one continuous thread that can be as long as 1000 feet long. Before the worms can hatch into moths and destroy the cocoon, they are killed with hot air or steam and then the cocoon is softened and unraveled.

This laborious process was first discovered in China, the native habitat of the silkworm, and the Chinese monopolized its production for the first three thousand years. Exports were strictly controlled. Only finished cloth could be exported, and no one was allowed to export eggs, cocoons, or silkworms under penalty of death. Only very gradually did this monopoly break down in Asia: Around 200 B.C.E. Chinese emigrants to Korea brought with them silkworms and mulberry plants and began Korean silk production. Japan and India acquired the secret technology around 300 C.E., but they were as careful as the Chinese to avoid further proliferation of the technique, especially further west.

And the West was mad for silk. Already in antiquity caravan routes along what today is called the Silk Road reached from the western Chinese city of Xian across modern Afghanistan and into modern Iraq and Syria, ending in Damascus. Sea routes also connected Egypt and India through the Red Sea, providing an alternative route for silk to reach the Mediterranean world. Ancient Persians particularly admired the material and even unwove Chinese cloths so that they could reuse the precious filaments to reweave them into clothing and textiles of their own. Alexander the Great was so impressed

■ Eastern Han (25–220) tomb decoration showing silk weavers.

with the splendid silk robes worn by the vanquished Persian Emperor Darius III that he demanded vast amounts of the material from the conquered Persians as spoils of war. The Romans first became aware of silk around 50 B.C.E., and the cloth became enormously popular (and enormously expensive). It was literally worth its weight in gold. Aristocratic women and particularly empresses amassed vast quantities of silk shawls and scarves. The conspicuous use of silk was a barometer of Roman morals: severe emperors such as Aurelian forbade his wife to own so much as a single silk shawl, while others like Caligula enjoyed wearing silk himself.

But where did silk come from? Although Aristotle was aware that the threads came from the cocoons of the silkworm, Romans had only a vague idea of its origins. Their best guess was that it grew on trees. And they certainly had no means of manufacturing it, being content with importing raw silk and then weaving and dying it according to their own taste. Thus Roman desire for silk was at the mercy of those who controlled the silk route from China and India, their enemies the Persians.

All this changed around 530 when a group of monks from India appeared before the Emperor Justinian. These men, Nestorian Christians from a region of India that specialized in silk production, explained to the emperor that they could make it possible for the empire to free itself from its dependency on Persia to supply its appetite

■ This Byzantine silk cloth, showing a hero or charioteer driving a quadringa (four horse chariot) was found in Charlemagne's tomb—probably a gift from the Byzantine court to the Frankish emperor.

for silk. They revealed to him the origin of silk and the process of recovering it from cocoons. With his encouragement, they returned home and smuggled back to the empire silkworm eggs and mulberry seeds, according to legend, hidden in their hollow walking staffs. Soon, Byzantine silk production was underway, but the Byzantines, in the tradition of the Chinese and Indians before them, maintained silk manufacture as a strictly controlled state monopoly. Silk's beauty, its rarity, and its prestige were too great an economic and political asset to allow uncontrolled production. For centuries,

until its monopoly was broken by Muslim silk production in Spain and eventually Italy, silks could be used not simply as commodities but as tools of politics to honor, or to shame, Byzantium's neighbors.

⬛ Questions for Discussion

Why do you suppose that Western elites so desired Chinese and Indian silk? Was there a relationship between the expansion of Western religions such as Christianity and Islam into Asia and the end of the Asian silk monopoly?

merchants and traders. In his thirties, he devoted time to meditation. In the month of Ramadan in the year 610, he reported a vision of a man, his feet astride the horizon. The figure commanded: "O Muhammad! Thou art the Messenger of God. Recite!" This was Muhammad's first revelation that he was Allah's messenger. His early teachings stressed the absolute unity of God, the evils of idolatry, and the threat of divine judgment. Further revelations to Muhammad were memorized and later written down in what came to be the Qur'an.

To Muhammad and his followers, the Qur'an was the final and perfect revelation of Allah, the God of Abraham and Jesus, and Muhammad was the last and greatest prophet. Allah's revelation emphasized his power and transcendence and that the duty of humans is worship. Muslims regard the whole Qur'an as the exact and complete revelation of God, literally true, and forming a unified whole. It is the fundamental law of conduct for Islamic society. Muhammad, known as the Prophet, emphasized constantly that he was simply God's messenger and that he merited no special veneration or worship.

DOCUMENT

The Holy Qur'an

Muhammad began to carry his message to the Arabs of Mecca. Initially, such revelations of divine power and judgment convinced very few of Mecca's merchant elite. Muhammad's earliest followers came primarily from his own family and from among the moderately successful members of the Meccan community. Muhammad began to insist that those who did not accept Allah as the only God were damned. With this proclamation, toleration gave way to hostility. Muhammad and his followers were ostracized and even persecuted.

In 622, Muhammad was invited to settle factional disputes in the small trading city of Medina. His secret journey to Medina is called the **Hijra** and marks the beginning of the Islamic calendar. There he organized his followers from Mecca and Medina into the **Umma,** a community that transcended the old bonds of tribe and clan. He turned Medina into a haram like Mecca with himself as the holy man. Muhammad was seen as God's messenger, and his authority was absolute. His goal was to extend that authority beyond his adopted town of Medina to Mecca, and ultimately to the whole Arab world.

First, he gained firm control of Medina at the expense of its Jewish clans. The monotheists rejected his attempt to transform Judaic and Christian traditions into an Arab faith. Muhammad expelled most and executed others in the name of political and religious unity. Muhammad then used the unified community to attack the Quraysh in Mecca. He destroyed the Meccan trade network then took the city in 629.

■ A manuscript illustration showing a party of Muslim pilgrims on their way to Mecca. Every able Muslim man is required to make the pilgrimage once in his lifetime.

The message of Islam spread rapidly through the Arabic tribes. Believers were attracted to the new religion not simply through descriptions of the delights of heaven and the pains of hell but because it offered a specifically Arabic religious and cultural vision.

There were also economic reasons. Since Mecca was now the sacred city of Islam and was cleansed of idols, it was the center of Islamic pilgrimage. It regained its central position in Arabian trade, and the Quraysh rushed to accept Allah as the sole god. Converts to Islam were permitted to participate in the holy wars that forcibly brought other tribes into the Umma.

Islam brought a transformation of the rights of women in Arabian society. Men continued to dominate Islamic society, and women remained subordinate to men. In some areas, Muslim women adopted the Syriac Christian practice of wearing a veil. However, Islam guaranteed women more rights than they had previously enjoyed. Brides, and not their fathers, received the dowry from their husbands, thus making marriage more a partnership than a sale. Islamic women acquired inheritance and property rights and gained protection against mistreatment in marriage.

The Spread of Islam.   Muhammad died in 632, leaving no successor. Immediately his closest followers selected Abu Bakr (632–634) to be **caliph,** or successor of the Prophet. Abu Bakr and his successors faced major obstacles.

Many tribes felt a personal loyalty to only Muhammad, not his successors. To maintain the Umma, Muhammad's immediate successors called for a holy war against tribes that had given up their faith in Islam. Muslim forces defeated tribe after tribe and brought them back into the Umma. But long-term survival demanded expansion. Muslim armies gained control of all of Arabia, then extended their campaign to conquests of the neighboring Sassanid and Byzantine empires. Internal disruption within the Byzantine Empire, particularly over religious disputes, paved the way for the Islamic invasion.

Many Christians and Jews in Syria, Palestine, Egypt, and North Africa shared the view of the Muslim conquest as liberation rather than enslavement. Jews and Christians were second-class citizens in the Islamic world, but at least they were allowed to practice their religion in peace.

By 650, Islam stretched from Egypt to Asia Minor, from the Mediterranean to the Indus River. Although Constantinople survived, the Muslim conquests left the once-vast empire a small state reduced to little more than Greece, western Asia Minor, southern Italy, and the Balkans. Discord within the Islamic community, however, led to the murder of the third caliph, 'Uthman (d. 656), and his successor and Muhammad's beloved son-in-law, 'Ali (656–661), at the hands of the old Meccan elite, especially the Umayyad clan, which monopolized the caliphate and established their capital at Damascus in Syria.

■ The Spread of Islam. The rapid spread of Islam created within a century a unified cultural and economic zone from India to the Atlantic Ocean.

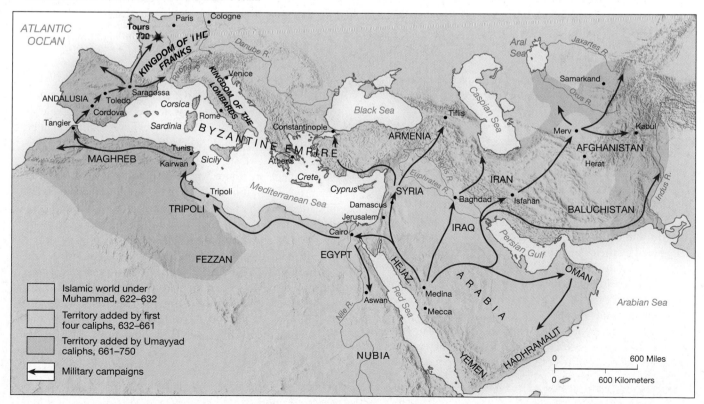

Successors to Muhammad: The Umayyads and 'Abbasids. The Umayyads extended the Islamic Empire to its farthest reaches—to the borders of China, and along the coast of the Mediterranean to Spain. The Umayyads tried to keep a strictly Arab elite within their state. As the number of non-Arab converts to Islam grew, dissatisfaction with the concept of Arab—especially Quraysh—dominance festered. Demands for greater equality among all Muslims came together in a broad movement that unseated the Umayyads.

Muslims unhappy with the Umayyads, especially non-Arab converts from Iraq, rallied around distant relatives of Muhammad known as the 'Abbasids. In 750, the 'Abbasids replaced the Umayyads as rulers everywhere but in Spain. At the outset, the 'Abbasids represented the reform movement and set out to govern according to strict religious principles, unlike the Umayyad rulers. The 'Abbasids created a new capital in Baghdad, a recognition of the new importance of Iraq and Persia in the new government. The 'Abbasids claimed absolute rights of government based on the righteousness of their claims to power. They created a centralized bureaucracy.

But by the tenth century, the 'Abbasid caliphs lost absolute control over Islam. Local military commanders took over provincial governments. Various Shi'ite movements loyal to the memory of 'Ali successfully established separatist governments. External invasions led to the final collapse of the 'Abbasids.

Turks conquered Baghdad in 1055, while much of northern Africa fell to Moroccan Berbers. The invasions disrupted the commercial and economic systems of the Islamic Empire.

The Islamic conquest of the seventh century brought peace to the vast regions from the Mediterranean to India for the first time in centuries and set the stage for agricultural and cultural recovery. The conquest in the name of Allah created a vast religious and commercial zone in which ideas and cultures flowed. The Arabians soon lost political control of the Islamic movement, but their religious tradition and its emphasis on worship of the one God remains an enduring legacy in world civilization.

The Byzantine Decline, 1000–1453

In the tenth and eleventh centuries, the Byzantine Empire temporarily regained some power in the eastern Mediterranean. Armies of the Macedonian dynasty had invaded Italy, Syria, and Asia Minor, reconquering areas lost to western barbarians and eastern Muslim armies.

The Disintegration of the Empire. The successes of the Macedonian emperors set the stage for serious problems. Military expansion and economic growth allowed new elites to become autonomous powers and to position themselves

THE QUR'AN

The following passages from the Qur'an express the central importance of the revelation of Allah, compassion for Jews and Christians as sharers in the belief in the one God, and the condemnation of polytheistic idolaters.

Focus Questions

What are the characteristics of the righteous according to the Qur'an? How does the attitude of Islam differ toward Christians, Jews, and polytheists?

In the name of Allah, the compassionate, the Merciful This Book is not to be doubted. It is a guide to the righteous, who have faith in the unseen and are steadfast in prayer; who bestow in charity a part of what We give them; who trust what has been revealed to you [Muhammad] and to others before you, and firmly believe in the life to come. These are rightly guided by their Lord; these shall surely triumph.

As for the unbelievers, whether you forewarn them or not, they will not have faith. Allah has set a seal upon their hearts and ears; their sight is dimmed and a grievous punishment awaits them. . . .

Men, serve your Lord, who has created you and those who have gone before you, so that you may guard yourselves against evil; who has made the earth a bed for you

and the sky a dome, and has sent down water from heaven to bring forth fruits for your sustenance. Do not knowingly set up other gods besides Him. . . .

Believers, Jews, Christians, and Sabaeans [ancient rulers of Yemen believed to be monotheists]—whoever believes in Allah and the Last Day and does what is right—shall be rewarded by their Lord; they have nothing to fear or to regret. . . .

Yet there are some who worship idols, bestowing on them the adoration due to Allah (though the love of Allah is stronger in the faithful). But when they face their punishment the wrongdoers will know that might is His alone and that Allah is stern in retribution. When they face their punishment the leaders will disown their followers, and the bonds which now unite them will break asunder. Those who followed them will say: "Could we but live again, we would disown them as they have disowned us now."

Thus Allah will show them their own works. They shall sigh with remorse, but shall never come out of Hell.

From Qur'an, sura 2.

■ Muslim astronomers made many advances. They perfected the astrolabe, an instrument used to observe and calculate the positions of heavenly bodies.

between the imperial administration and the people. In the eleventh century, emperors granted imperial estates to great magnates in return for military service. This created a military aristocracy that stood between the peasantry and the imperial government.

As generals became dissatisfied with the civilian central administration, they turned their armies against the emperors. To defend itself against both the Muslims without and the generals within, the central government spent vast sums on mercenary armies. The armies plundered the empire they were hired to protect. Further danger came from other, independent Normans who, under their commander, Robert Guiscard (ca. 1015–1085), conquered Byzantine Bari, southern Italy, and then Muslim Sicily. The hostility between military aristocracy and imperial administration destroyed the tradition of civilian government. Under increasing pressure from local magnates and desperate imperial tax collectors, villages made deals with powerful patrons to represent them

in return for the surrender of their independence. Through the same process, landlords and patrons exercised a political role, which ended the state's monopoly on public power.

At the same time that civil war and external pressure were destroying the provincial administration, Byzantine disdain for commerce was weakening the empire's ability to control its income from customs duties. Merchants from Amalfi, Bari, and then Venice came to dominate Byzantine commerce.

In 1071, at Manzikert in Anatolia, the emperor Romanus IV (1067–1071) and his unreliable mercenary army fell to the Seljuk Turks. Anatolia was lost and the gradual erosion of the empire in both the west and the east had begun.

The Conquests of Constantinople and Baghdad. At the end of the eleventh century, the Comnenian dynasty (1081–1185) briefly halted the political and economic chaos of the empire. Rather than fighting the tendency of the centralized state to devolve into a decentralized aristocratic one, Alexius I Comnenus (1081–1118) tied the aristocracy to his family, thus making it an imperial government. In the short run, the process was successful. Still, by the late twelfth century, the empire was a vulnerable second-rate power.

Byzantine authority faced not only military but cultural threats from the west. In the eleventh century, the papacy in Rome claimed supreme authority throughout Christendom. Disagreements between the patriarchs of Constantinople and the popes of Rome prevented cooperation between the two Christian worlds and led to deterioration of relationships between Greeks and Latins. The disagreements came to a head in 1054, when the papal representative met with the patriarch of Constantinople. The papal representative excommunicated the patriarch and all his followers. The patriarch responded by excommunicating the papal representative and all connected with him. The split between the churches of Rome and Constantinople continues today.

The full fury of the western society reached the empire when the emperor Alexius called on western Christians for support against the Muslims. To his horror, adventurers of every sort eager to conquer land and wealth in the name of the cross flooded the empire. The crusaders were uncouth and barbarous, yet effective. The First Crusade took advantage of division in the Muslim world to conquer Palestine and establish a Latin kingdom in Jerusalem in 1099.

While crusaders threatened Byzantine territories, Venetian merchants imposed a stranglehold on Byzantine trade. Anti-Latin sentiment reached the boiling point in 1183 in the riots that broke out in that year. In 1204, another crusade turned aside from its goal of capturing Jerusalem and instead captured Constantinople. After pillaging the city for three days, the westerners established one of their own as emperor and installed a Venetian as patriarch. This was the worst and most enduring western affront to the Byzantine world.

The Byzantines held on to a portion of their empire and before long the Latins were bickering among themselves. In 1261, the ruler of Nicaea recaptured Constantinople and

CHRONOLOGY
THE BYZANTINE EMPIRE AND THE RISE OF ISLAM

527–565	Reign of Justinian
610	Muhammad's vision
662	The Hijra, Muhammad's journey from Mecca to Medina
726–787	First phase of iconoclast dispute
732	Muslim advance halted by Franks
750	'Abbasids overthrow Umayyads; take control of Muslim world
802–843	Second phase of iconoclast dispute
843	Empress Theodora ends iconoclast persecution; restores image veneration
867–1059	Macedonian dynasty rules Byzantine Empire; begins recovering lands from Muslims
1054	Schism splits churches of Rome and Constantinople
1071	Robert Guiscard captures Sicily and southern Italy
	Battle of Manzikert
	Seljuk Turks defeat Byzantines
1099	First Crusade establishes Latin kingdom in Jerusalem
1221	Genghis Khan leads Mongol army into Persia
1453	Constantinople falls to Ottomans

crowned himself the emperor. Still, the restored empire consisted of little more than the district around Constantinople, Thessalonica, and the Peloponnesus. The restored empire's survival for almost 200 years was not due to its own strength, but to the internal problems of the Islamic world.

The weaknesses of the Byzantine Empire were paralleled by those of the 'Abbassid caliphate. Both fell prey to new invading and migrating armies from Central Asia. The caliphs of Baghdad succumbed to invaders from the barbarous fringes of their empire. In 1221, the Mongol prince known as Genghis Khan led his conquering army into Persia from central Asia. In 1258, a Mongol army captured Baghdad and executed the last 'Abbasid caliph. The Mongol armies moved west, shattering the Seljuk principalities in Iraq, Anatolia, and Syria.

From the ruins of the Seljuk kingdom arose a variety of small Turkish principalities. After the collapse of the Mongol Empire, one of the principalities, the Ottoman, expanded

considerably. By 1450, the Ottoman stranglehold on Constantinople was complete. Mehmed the Conqueror (1452–1481) could as easily be seen as its restorer. He rededicated the Hagia Sophia church to the worship of one god. Once more Constantinople was the center of a great Mediterranean empire. In the following centuries, Ottoman rule stretched from Vienna to the Caspian Sea and from the Persian Gulf to the Strait of Gibraltar.

THE WEST IN THE EARLY MIDDLE AGES, 500–900

While the Byzantine and Islamic civilizations continued the urban culture of Antiquity, western Europe became a largely rural society dominated by military states in numerous competing kingdoms.

The Barbarian Kingdoms, 500–750

By the sixth century, what had once been the Roman Empire in the west was an assortment of individual kingdoms ruled by descendants of Germanic military commanders who, while proud of titles granted by the Byzantine emperors, no longer followed their commands. The inhabitants of their kingdoms were overwhelmingly the indigenous Roman provincial population plus small minorities of barbarian warriors. The barbarian kingdoms attempted to create from these disparate elements new political and social forms, only a few of which proved to be enduring.

The Gothic Kingdoms.   There were two Gothic kingdoms in the sixth century, the Ostrogothic kingdom of Italy and the Visigothic kingdom of Toulouse. Theodoric, king of the

■ A gold solidus coin bears a portrait of Theodoric. His left hand holds a globe on which stands a personification of victory. The inscription reads "King Theodoric," but the absence of a robe and diadem shows that he was not considered the equal of the emperor.

Ostrogoths, was the most successful Gothic monarch. He established a bipartite government in Italy that in which he ruled the indigenous population according to Roman civil tradition and his Arian, Gothic following as king of the Goths. On Theodoric's death, disputes broke out between the Goths who favored progressive Romanization and those who feared loss of Gothic identity. Taking advantage of the situation, the Byzantine emperor Justinian ordered an invasion of Italy. Twenty years of warfare followed, made worse by a terrible plague that killed over a third of the population. Finally the Goths were defeated and ceased to exist as an independent people, but the Byzantine victors were soon ousted by another Barbarian people, the Lombards.

Visigothic Spain. The Visigoths of Gaul and Spain tried to unify the population of their kingdom through law and religion. Religious unity was a difficult goal. The Visigoths were Arian Christians and for more than a century resisted and distrusted the orthodox faith of the majority of the population. That mistrust proved fatal. In 507, Gallo-Roman aristocrats supported the Frankish king Clovis in his successful conquest of the Visigothic kingdom of Toulouse. Defeat drove the Visigoths deeper into Spain, where they gradually forged a unified kingdom based on Roman administrative tradition and Visigothic kingship.

The religious unity was finally achieved when the king and the Gothic aristocracy embraced Orthodox Christianity. The conversion further blurred the differences between Visigoths and Roman provincials in the kingdom. It also initiated an unprecedented use of the Church and its ideology to strengthen the monarchy. Visigothic distrust focused on the Jewish population. All Jews were commanded to accept baptism or leave the kingdom.

Rivalry within the aristocracy weakened the kingdom and left it vulnerable to attack from without. In 711, Muslims from North Africa conquered the Visigothic kingdom. Jews rejoiced in the religious toleration brought by Islam, and many members of the Christian elite converted to Islam and retained their positions of authority under the new regime.

The Anglo-Saxons. In Britain, Germanic warriors invited in to protect the Roman population soon took over and carved out small kingdoms for themselves. Although independent, the little kingdoms—from 5 to as many as 11—maintained identity as a group. Unlike the Goths, none of these peoples had previously been integrated into the Roman world. Thus, rather than fusing Roman and Germanic traditions, they eradicated Roman traditions. Urban life disappeared, and with it the Roman traditions of administration, taxation, and culture.

In their place developed a world whose central values were honor and glory, whose primary occupation was fighting, and whose economic system was based on plunder and the distribution of riches. It was a society dominated by petty kings and their aristocratic war leaders.

The Anglo-Saxons were pagans, but eventually converted to Christianity. King Oswy of Northumbria (d. 670) accepted

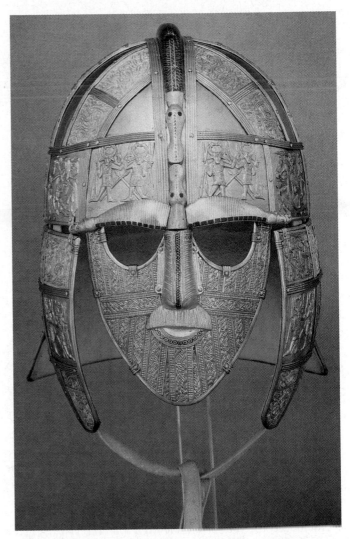

■ The elaborate helmet of a seventh-century Anglo-Saxon king, recovered from his ship burial at Sutton Hoo on the southeast coast of England, shows the wealth and culture of these rulers.

the customs of the Roman Church—allying himself and all of Anglo-Saxon England with the centralized, hierarchical form of Christianity. Contact with the Continent, and especially with Rome, increased. The monasteries became centers of learning, culminating in the writings of Bede (673–735), the greatest scholar of his time. Through his writings, he was responsible for the popularization of dating history from before or after the birth of Jesus.

The Franks. In the fourth century, small Germanic tribes came together in a confederation known as the Franks. Their primary purpose was to supply soldiers for the Roman frontier defenses, and their leaders rose to important positions in the Roman army. In 486, Clovis, leader of the Salian Franks and commander of the barbarized Roman army, successfully overthrew the last Roman commander in the west. Clovis's early conversion to Orthodox Christianity helped ensure the effectiveness of the Gallo-Roman cooperation. The king's baptism convinced many of his subjects to convert as well, paving the way for the assimilation of Franks and Romans into a new society. Clovis's descendants, the Merovingians, became the royal dynasty of the Franks for more than two centuries and ruled with the assistance of aristocratic supporters. Frankish society became the model for European social and political organization for more than a thousand years.

Living in the New Europe

Early medieval society encompassed a peasantry controlled by a small aristocracy of landowners.

The Peasants. Three changes transformed rural society during the early Middle Ages. First, Roman slavery virtually disappeared. Second, the household emerged as the primary unit of social and economic organization. Third, Christianity spread throughout the rural world.

As the empire ceased to expand, the supply of slaves dwindled. Owners abandoned the practice of keeping gang slaves in favor of the less complicated practice of establishing slave families on individual plots of land. Gradually, slaves intermarried and, although nominally free, found themselves in an economic situation much like that of slaves. By the ninth century, the distinction between slaves and free peasants was blurred.

The second change of European peasant society was the formation of the household. When individual slaves and their spouses were placed on estates, which they and their children were expected to cultivate, the household became the basic unit of Western economy. However, the household was also the first level of government. The head of the household exercised authority over its other members. Peasant life centered on the house, the village, and the field. The hovel was heated by the body warmth of the cattle and sheep and by a hearth fire. Smoke escaped not through a chimney, but through a hole in the roof. Occasionally, peasants used new tools or technical innovations in their labor. Some lords established water mills for grinding.

During this period the peasantry became Christian. In antiquity Christianity had been an urban phenomenon. Christianity penetrated more deeply into rural society with the establishment of parishes, or rural churches. The presence of priests in each village had a profound effect on the daily lives of Europe's peasants. Christian ritual came to be a regular part of peasant life.

The European Aristocracy. At the same time that a homogeneous peasantry was emerging from the blend of slaves and free farmers, a homogeneous aristocracy was evolving out of the mix of Germanic and Roman traditions. The aristocrats were largely independent of their kings. The freedom of the aristocracy meant freedom from royal governance.

Roman aristocrats monopolized the office of bishop and became identified with the sacred and political traditions associated with the Church. In Spain and Italy, the religious differences separating Arians and Orthodox Christians impeded the fusion of the Germanic and Roman aristocracies. The Roman aristocratic tradition of great landholders became an integral part of the identity of the Frankish elite.

Aristocratic family structures were loosely knit clans. The aristocratic lifestyle focused on feasting, on hospitality, and on the male activities of hunting and warfare. In southern Europe, great nobles lived in spacious villas. In the north, Frankish and Anglo-Saxon nobles lived in great wooden halls, richly decorated but lacking fortifications.

The religious life opened to aristocratic women possibilities of autonomy and authority previously unknown in the West. Women exercised such authority over mixed monasteries, in which men and women lived in separate quarters but recognized the rule of the abbess.

Governing Europe. The aristocracy and the kings shared an uneasy partnership. During times of war, the king's powers were absolute. At other times, his authority was strictly limited. Better hope for authority stemmed from the king's role as protector of the Church, and many royal advisers were drawn from the ranks of the clergy.

Kings had no fixed location but wandered from one part of their kingdoms to another. Local authority in the king's absence was held by the aristocracy. Among the Franks, local representatives of the king were called *counts*. In Anglo-Saxon England, the royal appointees were called *ealdormen*.

Kings could rule only in cooperation with aristocrats. Aristocrats were primarily concerned with maintaining and expanding their own spheres of control and independence. They perceived royal authority over them or their dependents as a threat. Still, they needed kings. Strong kings brought victory against external foes and thus maintained the flow of booty to the aristocracy.

The Carolingian Achievement

The most successful of the Frankish aristocratic factions was that led by Charles Martel (ca. 688–741) and his heirs, known as the Carolingians. Charles Martel crushed rivals in his own family, subdued competing aristocrats, and united the Frankish realm. He was successful because he molded the Frankish military into the most effective military force of the time. However, he looked beyond military power to the control of religious and cultural institutions. He supported Anglo-Saxon missionaries who were trying to introduce on the Continent the Roman form of Christianity they knew in England.

The alliance with the papacy solidified during the lifetime of Charles's son Pippin III (ca. 714–768). Pippin inherited his father's power. However, since he was not of the royal family, he had no more right to supreme authority than any other powerful aristocrat. Building on his increasingly close relationship with the papacy and the Frankish church dominated by his supporters, Pippin sought legitimacy in religious authority. The pope declared that the individual who exercised the power of king ought to have the title, and Pippin was duly anointed king of the Franks by representatives of the pope.

The alliance between the new dynasty and the papacy marked the first union of royal legitimacy and ecclesiastical sanction in European history. Now the office of king required the active participation of the Church.

Charlemagne. Pippin's son Charlemagne was the heir of the political, religious, and social revolutions begun by his grandfather and father. Charlemagne changed the West more profoundly than anyone since Augustus.

DOCUMENT

Einhard, *Life of Charlemagne*

Charlemagne engaged in a number of successful military ventures: conquest of the kingdom of the Lombards in Italy, incorporation of the Saxons, annexation of the buffer zone between the kingdom of the Franks and the Islamic caliphate in Spain, and the destruction of the Avars. In wars of aggression, his armies were invincible.

War booty fueled Charlemagne's renewal of European culture. As a Christian king, he considered it his duty to reform the spiritual life of his kingdom and to bring it into line with his concept of the divinely willed order. To achieve this goal he needed a dedicated and educated clergy.

Charlemagne recruited leading intellectuals from England, Spain, Ireland, and Italy to the royal court to lead a thorough educational program. He supported schools in great monasteries for the training of young clerics and laymen. The schools needed books. Charlemagne's educational reformers scoured Italy for fading copies of works by Virgil, Horace, and Tacitus.

The reformers of this era laid the necessary foundation for what has been called the **Carolingian Renaissance.** Their successors in the ninth century built on that foundation to make creative contributions in theology, philosophy, historiography, and literature. In the later ninth century, great aristocrats were highly literate and collected their own libraries. Elite women participated fully in the Carolingian Renaissance.

Charlemagne invited Italian and Byzantine artists and artisans to his kingdom to teach a form of representational art that would educate as well as decorate. The synthesis of Mediterranean and northern artistic traditions produced a dynamic, plastic style of representation that could serve also for religious education.

Charlemagne and his son Louis the Pious (814–840) also worked to establish the Benedictine rule as the norm for monastic life. They tried to ensure that parish clergy were competent and committed to serving the needs of the people. Charlemagne also appointed counts throughout Europe. He thus created what might be termed an *imperial aristocracy*—truly international in scope.

Charlemagne recognized that the only universal system that might unify the kingdom was Roman Christianity. The system of counts and **missi dominici** (emissary teams composed of bishops and counts that examined the state of each county) provided the most effective system of government prior to the thirteenth century and served as the model for subsequent medieval rulers.

■ Charlemagne's Empire, 814. Either directly or indirectly, Charlemagne ruled a vast empire that included almost all of the western Roman Empire except for Spain and Britain.

On Christmas Day 800, the pope proclaimed Charlemagne emperor, thus reviving the Roman Empire in the West after more than three centuries. Charlemagne saw his title of emperor as a reflection of his accomplishments, not as a political title indicating the foundation of his authority. The imperial coronation of 800 took on great significance. His son Louis attempted to make his imperial title the sole basis for his rule, and for the next six hundred years Germanic kings traveled to Rome to receive the imperial title from the pope. This strengthened papal claims to give or take away the throne from emperors.

After the Carolingians

Charlemagne remained dependent on the Frankish aristocracy. Wars of conquest under Charlemagne dried up the supply of wealth. Aristocratic supporters had to be rewarded with estates within the empire, and aristocrats became enormously wealthy and powerful.

Competition among Charlemagne's descendants as well as grants to the aristocracy weakened central authority. Only one of Charlemagne's sons, Louis, survived him and so inherited the empire. Louis's three sons divided the empire among them. In time, the western kingdom became France and the eastern kingdom became Germany. The middle kingdom in-

■ The Division of Charlemagne's Empire. Internal tensions, dynastic competition, and external pressures led to the disintegration of Charlemagne's Empire and the emergence of what would become France and Germany.

cluded what are now Holland, Belgium, Luxembourg, Lorraine, Switzerland, and northern Italy.

Charlemagne's heirs could not provide the peace and public control that Charlemagne had established. The Frankish armies were too clumsy and slow to deal with attacks. Increasingly, the magnates transformed the offices of count and bishop into inherited familial positions. They also determined who would reign in their kingdoms and sought kings who posed no threat. Thus, during the late ninth and tenth centuries, much of Europe found its equilibrium at the local level as public powers, judicial courts, and military authority became the private possession of wealthy families.

After the demise of the Carolingian Empire, the West found stability at a local but more permanent level. Carolingian religious reform, classical learning, and political ideology were preserved in the following centuries. During the late ninth and tenth centuries, Western Christian civilization spread north and east. By the year 1000, Scandinavia, Poland, Bohemia, and even Hungary had become Christian kingdoms with national churches whose bishops were approved by the pope.

The Carolingian synthesis left a powerful and enduring legacy. Only the Franks found a lasting means of synthesizing Roman and Germanic societies. The key elements of the synthesis were Orthodox Christianity, Roman administration, and Frankish military kingship.

THE HIGH MIDDLE AGES

Dynamic change in society, intellectual life, and government transformed Europe in the centuries following the start of the second millennium.

The Countryside

Between the tenth and fourteenth centuries, enormous transformations recreated the rural landscape. Population more than doubled, the amount of land under cultivation increased, and agricultural technology improved crop yields and increased the wealth of landowners. The status of those working the land changed as well: in western Europe peasants who had been reduced to semi-free serfdom acquired freedom, while in much of eastern Europe traditionally free peasants lost that freedom.

The Peasantry: Serfs and Freemen.   In the course of the tenth century the gradations in social status between slaves and poor free peasants disappeared and the peasantry formed a homogeneous social category loosely described as serfdom. While **serfs** were not slaves in a legal sense, their degraded status, their limited or nonexistent access to public courts of law, and their dependency on their lords left them in a situation similar to that of slaves. Each year, serfs had to hand over to their lords certain fixed portions of their meager harvests. In addition, they were required to make ritual payments symbolizing their subordination.

Agricultural technology gradually changed the ways that peasants worked their land and the amount of food that they could produce. Traditionally, Europeans worked their fields with simple plows that broke up light soils but were unable to turn the heavy clay soils of northern Europe, which required backbreaking labor with hoes and shovels to cultivate. Between the ninth and the twelfth centuries, a heavier plow became common in Europe. Later, peasants began rotating crops, which resulted in increased yield. Women took charge of the domestic tasks that included wool carding, spinning, weaving, and bearing and raising children. During harvest time, women worked in the fields alongside the men. Still, even with improvements, inadequate agricultural methods and inefficient storage systems left the peasantry in constant threat of famine. A bad year could send mobs of desperate peasants roaming the land in search of food.

Labor was increasingly in demand, and lords often made arrangements with groups of peasants to bring new land under cultivation. So, peasant villages acquired from their lord the privilege of dealing with him and his representatives collectively rather than individually. In the twelfth and thirteenth centuries, many serfs in western Europe purchased their freedom from their lords, transforming their servile payments into payments of rent, and purchased their own land. By the fourteenth century, serfs were a rarity in many parts of western Europe.

Yet, freedom often meant freedom from the protection that lords had provided. It meant the freedom to fail and even to starve. Successful peasants acquired land, employed their own workers, and established some wealth; unsuccessful landless and starving peasants roamed the countryside.

Even as western serfs acquired a precious though fragile freedom, the free peasantry in much of eastern Europe and Spain were losing it. Princes, churches, and aristocrats began to build great landed estates. By the thirteenth century, lords acquired political and economic control over the peasantry. In all the regions, the decline of the free peasantry accompanied the decline of public authority.

The Aristocracy: Warriors and Heiresses.   A tiny minority of elite warrior landowners composed the upper classes of European society, descendants of the old Carolingian and local aristocracies and a few fortunate individuals who had been able to marry into the old families or acquire royal favor. By the tenth century, such men were increasingly termed *knights.* Initially, a knight was simply any mounted warrior; however, in France, northern Italy, England, and much of Spain, the term knight worked its way up the social ladder. From northern France, the ideals of knighthood, or **chivalry,** spread across Europe, influencing aristocrats as far east as Byzantium.

The essence of the knightly lifestyle was fighting. Inheritance was usually limited to the eldest sons; daughters were given a dowry but did not share in inheritance. Such noble families could dominate the surrounding countryside. By the twelfth century, nobles lived safely behind castle walls, often even independent of the local counts, dukes, and kings.

■ A knight receives a token from a lady in this image from a manuscript from ca. 1300 that contains the works of more than 100 German courtly love poets. The ideals of chivalry and courtly love glorified women in literature and song, but in real life the subordinate status of women reflected the values of a martial society.

For the sons of nobles, preparation for a life of warfare began early. They learned about honor, loyalty, and family tradition. The culmination of this education for English and French nobles came in a ceremony of knighting. An adolescent from age 16 to 18 received a sword from an older, experienced warrior. No longer a boy, he now became a youth, ready to enter the world of fighting for which he had trained.

The length of time one remained a youth could extend into one's thirties. During this time, the knight led the life of a warrior. It was an extraordinarily dangerous lifestyle. Many youths did not survive to the next stage in a knight's life—that of acquiring land, wife, and honor. The period between childhood and maturity was no less dangerous for noblewomen than for men. Many noblewomen died in childbirth, often literally exhausted by frequent successive births.

The nobility was essentially a society of heirs whose power was based on inherited land and serfs and kin alliances with other noble families. In addition, individual knights, termed **vassals,** often formed bonds with greater aristocrats to whom they swore personal loyalty as their lord and promised military assistance. In return, the lord swore to protect his vassal. In addition, he might grant him a **fief,** a parcel of productive land and the serfs and privileges attached to it. Individual lords often had considerable numbers of vassals. The networks formed another type of social and political bond which in the thirteenth and fourteenth centuries would be transformed by lawyers and rulers into a kind of political system.

The aristocratic domination began to decline from the middle of the twelfth century. Counts, dukes, and kings undermined noble autonomy by reasserting traditional public control over justice and warfare. By the thirteenth century, the old ideal of the independent nobleman living from his own estates and serving his feudal lord for honor and glory was largely a myth.

The Church: Saints and Monks.

The religious appeals of the peasantry concerned fertility of land, animals, and women; protection from the ravages of climate and the warrior elite; and supernatural cures for the ailments and disabilities of their harsh life. The nobility sought religious sanction for their positions and prayers for their souls in this life and the next. The rural church of the High Middle Ages met the needs of both.

Most medieval people, whether peasants or lords, lived in a world in which religion meant action, that is, the liturgical celebrations performed by the clergy. Extensive religious education and learning was less important for the priests who performed baptisms, solemnized marriages, and conducted funerals than their ability to perform the rites of the Church. However, ordinary lay people wanted priests who would not extort them by selling the sacraments and would not seduce their wives and daughters.

Monasteries were elite religious institutions responsible for praying for the souls of mortals. In particular, monastic communities commemorated and prayed for those members of noble families who, through donations of land, had become especially associated with the monastic community. Monasteries continued the ritual remembrance of the family, providing it with a history and forming an important part of its material as well as spiritual prestige.

In addition, monasteries directed the cult of the saints, that is, men and women who during their lives had shown that they enjoyed special favor with God. After their deaths, through their bodies preserved as relics in the monasteries, they continued to live among mortals even while participating in the heavenly court. Thus they could be approached just like local earthly lords and be won over through offerings and bribes. As the recipients of gifts to the saints, monastic communities became wealthy and powerful institutions.

Benedictine monasteries developed a religious culture that was one of the greatest achievements of the Middle Ages. The essence of the monastic life was the passionate pursuit of God. The goal was not simply salvation but perfection, and this required discipline of the body through a life of chastity and poverty and discipline of the spirit through obedience and learning.

Monks spent much of their day in communal prayer, praising God and asking for his aid and that of his saints on behalf of themselves, their secular patrons, their families, and all of society. They valued serious study as a means of improving their ability to pray.

The monastery of Cluny became the first international organization of monastic centers. The abbots of Cluny were among the most powerful and influential people in Europe during the eleventh and twelfth centuries—considered as equals to kings, popes, and emperors.

Some monastic reformers called for a return to simplicity, separation from the rest of society, and a deeper spirituality. In 1098, Robert of Molesme and a small group of monks from a Benedictine monastery in France established a new monastery at Cîteaux where they sought to lead a life of strict observance of the rule of Benedict. This rigorous form of monasticism reached from England to Vienna by the end of the Middle Ages. By establishing themselves in remote areas, organizing their estates in an efficient manner, and gaining a great reputation for asceticism, the Cistercians became enormously wealthy and successful leaders in the economic changes taking place in the twelfth and thirteenth centuries.

Since Church property was often the focus of aristocratic greed, the decline of public power and the rise of aristocratic autonomy and violence were particularly marked in southern France. There, beginning in the tenth century, churchmen organized movements to protect peasants, merchants, and clerics from aristocratic violence and to limit warfare. During the eleventh century, the goals of warfare were shifted from attacks against other Christians to the defense of Christian society. That redirection produced the **Crusades,** religious wars of conquest directed against Europe's non-Christian neighbors.

Crusaders: Soldiers of God.

The Crusades left a troubling legacy in world civilization. In order to direct noble violence away from Christendom, in 1095 Pope Urban II (1088–1099) urged western knights to use their arms to free the Holy Land from Muslim occupation. In return, he promised to absolve them from all of the punishment due for their sins in this life or the next. Nobles and commoners responded with enthusiasm. The commoners left a swath of destruction in their wake, beginning by murdering Jews in Europe and then pillaging their way east. Few mourned when these crusaders were destroyed by the Muslims. The nobles by contrast were remarkably successful. After terrible hardships, the crusaders took Jerusalem in 1099 and established a Latin kingdom in Palestine. For more than two centuries, bands of Western warriors went on armed pilgrimages to defend that precarious kingdom.

The new Latin Kingdom of Jerusalem was the first experiment in European overseas colonization. Its rulers, a tiny minority of western Knights, ruled a vastly larger population of Muslims and eastern Christians. Although the Christian rulers were not harsh, they made little effort to absorb or even to understand the native population. Crusaders were

MAP DISCOVERY

The Crusades

Examine the religious divisions of Europe and the major crusade routes. What different geographical and political obstacles did crusaders face depending on whether they travelled by land or by water? How did the divisions of Christianity and Islam affect the course of the Crusades?

uninterested in converting Muslims, and their efforts to impose Roman forms of Christian worship and organization alienated the indigenous Christian population of the kingdom. The Latin kingdom played a negligible role as a bridge between the eastern and western worlds. More pacific contacts in Sicily and Spain were the primary paths of real cultural exchange. The crusaders remained isolated, supported by the regular supplies brought by Italian merchants (and by periodic infusions of fighters in the form of individuals or as part of subsequent organized Crusades).

The Latin Kingdom survived less than a century before the crusaders were pushed to coastal towns supplied by Italian merchants. Subsequent crusades attempted to recapture Jerusalem and reestablish the kingdom, but the violent and bloody clashes accomplished only short-term victories at best and many ended in disaster.

Crusades often appealed to younger sons of the nobility who saw in them opportunities to obtain land and enhance their social status. Although often glorified, Crusades were more noble military exercises in greed than in piety. The crusading ethic often included anti-Semitism and indiscriminant

slaughter of innocents. When kings of more centralized states came to see the Crusades as wasteful, the era of the Crusade came to an end.

Medieval Towns

Towns represented the social opposite of the rural countryside. Serfdom did not exist there, nor did most towns recognize the authority of the military aristocracy. Towns were, however, the purveyors of manufactured goods and services sought by all members of rural society.

Italian Cities. The coastal cities of Amalfi, Bari, Genoa, and especially Venice had continued to play important roles in commerce both with the Byzantines and with the new Muslim societies since late antiquity. For Venice, the role was facilitated by its official status as a part of the Byzantine Empire, which gave it access to Byzantine markets. The geographical isolation of most of those cities from prosperous hinterlands gave them an additional advantage as commercial centers. With nothing of their own to trade but perhaps salt and, in

In this illustration from a four-teenth-century manuscript, the Venetian merchant Marco Polo (1254–1324), with his father and uncle, is seen departing from Venice for points east in 1271. Marco traveled as far as China and did not return home to Venice until 24 years later.

Venice, glass, they served as go-betweens for the transport of eastern spices, silks, and ivories. In order to protect their merchant ships, Italian coastal cities developed their own fleets and, by the eleventh century, they were major military forces in the Mediterranean. Venice's fleet became the primary protector of the Byzantine Empire.

Italian towns established permanent merchant colonies in the east. When necessary, they did not hesitate to use military force to win concessions. In 1088, the Venetians sacked the capital of Tunis in North Africa in order to force concessions to their merchants.

The Crusades were economic opportunities for the Italians, who had no scruples about trading with Muslims. Furthermore, only the Italians had the ships and the expertise to transport the crusaders by sea. That mode of transportation offered the crusaders hope of success, since every crusade but the first that had followed an overland route had ended in failure. The crusaders paid the Italian merchants handsomely for their assistance. They also granted them economic and political rights in Palestinian port cities. The culmination of the relationship between the northern crusaders and the Italians was the Fourth Crusade, which was sidetracked by the Venetians into capturing and sacking Constantinople. The Byzantine Empire never recovered from that disaster, and Venice emerged as the undisputed Mediterranean power.

By the thirteenth century, Italian merchants had spread far beyond the Mediterranean—to Morocco, Persia, London, and Scandinavia. Italian merchants developed the practices of double entry bookkeeping, limited liability partnership, commercial insurance, international letters of exchange, credit, and interest-bearing loans.

The strength of the Italian towns was that they moved from a rural value system to wealth in commercial ventures. By the twelfth century, wealthy citizens were indiscriminately termed *magnates*. The rest of the town's population was called *populars*. The difference between the two was economic. In the eleventh and early twelfth centuries, many Italian towns bought off or expelled their traditional lords such as counts and bishops, thus allowing the magnates and populars of the cities to create their own governing institutions or communes.

During the twelfth and thirteenth centuries, Italy experimented with self-government as urban populations banded together in communes of citizens. The small communities of citizens developed a sense of patriotism, local pride, and independence. Their citizens sought to surpass each other in the construction of beautiful plazas, town halls, and sumptuous urban palaces. The communes also sought to control civic life: prices, markets, sanitation, and medical care. Who might wear what forms of dress and jewelry? How many inches of lace might the wife of a merchant wear on her dress? Such questions were considered appropriate topics of public legislation.

The unity and patriotism of the Italian cities shown to the rest of the world were matched in intensity by the violence of their internal disputes. Magnates argued among themselves and with the populace for control of the town. The conflicts frequently turned violent as citizens took sides on wider issues of Italian and European politics.

■ Medieval Trade Networks. Italian, Flemish, and German merchants tied northern and southern Europe to the eastern Mediterranean and beyond through networks of trade routes and markets that crossed religious, cultural, and political boundaries.

Feuds fought between noble families and their vassals in city streets were frequent events in Italian towns. In order to maintain civic life in spite of the conflicts, cities established complex systems of government in which officers were selected by a series of elections and lotteries designed to prevent any one faction from seizing control.

Generally, executive authority was vested in consuls. When the consuls proved unable to overcome the partisan politics of the factions, many towns turned to hiring nonpolitical professional city managers from outside the community. Their salaries were paid every two months, the last third not being handed over until after a final audit of their term.

Northern Towns.   Commercial activity in northern Europe centered around the northern seas, the Baltic and the North. The greatest concentration of urbanism in northern Europe was located in the Low Countries at the mouth of the Rhine River. Town growth was based on the development of the woolen cloth industry. The social organization of northern European towns differed from that of Italian towns because they lacked an aristocratic group of magnates. At the top of the society of northern towns were the wholesale merchants or patricians who purchased raw materials and sold the finished products. The wholesale merchants monopolized urban government. Next were the masters of the craft **guilds** who controlled the production of woolen cloth through the processes of

weaving and dyeing. At the bottom were the unskilled and semiskilled laborers in the employ of the guild masters.

Providing a conduit for the exchange of goods between the northern towns and the Italian towns were the fairs of Champagne, annual markets located in the center of Europe in eastern France. Products from north and south, both luxuries and more mundane items, were bought and sold at the fairs.

Medieval Trade Routes and Fairs

Urban Intellectuals.   The urban world of the twelfth and thirteenth centuries created forms of religious and cultural expression particularly suited to it. During the eleventh century, cathedrals became centers of learning as young clerics sought training in schools established by bishops. At Bologna in Italy, students of Roman law began the first university, essentially a guild of students who hired professors and regulated the system of legal studies. In northern Europe, Paris emerged as the greatest educational center. Unlike Bologna, the guilds of the university at Paris were composed of masters.

From the later twelfth century, the works of Aristotle began to be translated into Latin, and the professors at Paris began to try to apply Aristotelian philosophy to their understanding of the world and, especially, their Christian faith. The synthesis of this pagan philosopher into Christianity was complex and controversial. Ultimately, theologians such as Thomas Aquinas bridged the chasm between Aristotle and

SAINT FRANCIS OF ASSISI ON HUMILITY AND POVERTY

By 1223, Francis of Assisi's desire to lead a life of radical poverty and simplicity in conformity with the life of Jesus in the Gospels had inspired thousands to follow his example, and he was obligated to prepare a rule by which his order of Friars Minor would be governed. That simple rule emphasizes his fundamental concerns of humility and poverty.

Focus Questions

How are the friars to provide for the necessities of life according to Francis's rule? How is Francis's form of poverty different from the poverty of the Benedictine tradition?

1. This is the rule and way of living of the Minorite brothers: namely to observe the holy Gospel of our Lord Jesus Christ, living in obedience, without personal possessions, and in chastity. Brother Francis promises obedience and reverence to our lord pope Honorius, and to his successors who canonically enter upon their office and to the Roman Church. And the other brothers shall be bound to obey brother Francis and his successors.

2. If any persons shall wish to adopt this form of living and shall come to our brothers, they shall send them to their provincial ministers. . . . The ministers shall say unto them the word of the holy Gospel, to the effect that they shall go and sell all that they have and strive to give it to the poor. But if they shall not be able to do this, their good will is enough. . . . And those who have now promised obedience shall have one gown with a cowl, and another, if they wish it, without a cowl. And those who are compelled by necessity, may wear shoes. . . .

3. I firmly command all the brothers by no means to receive coin or money, of themselves or through an intervening person. But for the needs of the sick and for clothing the other brothers, the ministers alone and the guardians shall provide through spiritual friends, as it may seem to them that necessity demands.

4. Those brothers to whom God has given the ability to labor, shall labor faithfully and devoutly. . . . As a reward, they may receive for themselves and their brothers the necessaries of life, but not coin or money, and this humbly, as becomes the servants of God and the followers of most holy poverty.

5. The brothers shall appropriate nothing to themselves, neither a house, nor a place, nor anything; but as pilgrims and strangers in this world, in poverty and humility, serving God, they shall confidently go seeking for alms. Nor need they be ashamed, for the Lord made Himself poor for us in this world. . . .

6. I firmly command all the brothers not to have suspicious relations or to take counsel with women. And, with the exception of those whom special permission has been given by the Apostolic Chair, let them not enter nunneries. Neither may they become fellow god-parents with men or women, lest from this cause a scandal may arise among the brothers or concerning brothers.

From *The Rule of St. Francis of Assisi.*

---

ecclesiastical orthodoxy, insisting that human reason, even when unaided by divine revelation or scripture, was a valuable tool for finding and understanding truth.

Urban life, with its increasing focus on business and wealth, created strains in traditional Christianity that monasticism, with its demands for isolation, could not meet. New religious groups focusing on the importance of poverty sprang up across Europe. Some were regarded by the Church as dangerous and labeled as heretical. Others, such as the Order of Friars Minor founded by Francis of Assisi (1182–1226) and the Order of Preachers established by Dominic (1170–1221), became powerful means of religious renewal within the Church. The Franciscans devoted themselves to public preaching and to education. Similarly, the Dominicans were dedicated to combating heresy through educated debating and preaching. Both orders became mainstays of European universities.

The Invention of the State

Two types of political entities existed in the Middle Ages. The papacy and the Germanic Empire laid claim to universal authority. Kingdoms such as France and England were more limited in their concept of government but proved more successful in the long run.

The Universal States: Empire and Papacy. The Frankish world east of the Rhine River had been less affected than the kingdom of the West Franks by the onslaught of Vikings, Magyars, and Saracens. The eastern Frankish kingdom had preserved many of the Carolingian religious, cultural, and institutional traditions. In 919, Duke Henry I of Saxony (919–936) was elected king, and his son Otto I (936–973) laid the foundation for the revival of the empire. Otto inflicted a devastating defeat on the Magyars in 955, subdued the other dukes, and tightened his control over the kingdom. He accomplished that largely through the extensive use of bishops and abbots, whom he appointed as his agents and sources of loyal support. In 951, Otto invaded and conquered Lombardy. Eleven years later he entered Rome, where he was crowned emperor by the pope.

The Empire.   Otto, known to history as "the Great," established the main outlines of German imperial policy for the next 300 years, which included conflict with the German aristocracy, reliance on bishops and abbots as imperial agents, and preoccupation with Italy. Magnates elected the German kings, who were then consecrated as emperors by the pope. Royal fathers brought about the election of their sons, attempting to turn the kingship into a hereditary office. However, the royal families could not manage to produce male heirs in each generation, and thus the magnates continued to exercise real power in royal elections. Because of the elective tradition, German emperors were never able to establish effective control over the German magnates outside their own duchies.

Otto the Great had entered Italy to secure his southern flank. His successors eventually abandoned Germany altogether. As emperors, they had to be crowned by the pope, which was possible only if they controlled Rome. The preoccupation with Italy was a natural outcome of the nature of the empire. An imperial office without Italy was unthinkable. Thus the emperors found themselves drawn into papal and Italian politics, frequently with disastrous results. Germany became merely a source of men and material with which to fight the Lombard towns and the pope. From the eleventh through the thirteenth centuries, emperors granted German princes autonomy in return for that support.

The Papacy.   In the later tenth and early eleventh centuries, emperors had intervened in papal elections, deposed and replaced corrupt popes, and worked to ensure that bishops and abbots within the empire would be educated churchmen. The most effective reformer was Emperor Henry III (1039–1056), an emperor who took seriously his role as the anointed of the Lord to reform the Church in Germany and in Rome. When three rivals claimed the papacy, Henry deposed all three and installed the first of a series of German popes. The most effective was Henry's own cousin, Leo IX (1049–1054). Leo condemned the practice of buying Church offices and fostered monastic reforms such as that of Cluny. He also encouraged the efforts of a group of young reformers drawn from across Europe.

In the next decades, the more radical reformers advocated a widespread renewal of the Christian world, led by popes. The reformers sought to reform the morals of the clergy and to eliminate married priests. They tried to free churches and monasteries from lay control by forbidding lay men and women from owning churches and monasteries. Most importantly, they insisted that the pope, not the emperor, was the supreme representative of God on earth and as such had the right to exercise universal sovereignty.

Every aspect of the reform movement met with strong opposition throughout Europe. However, its effects were most dramatic in the empire because of the central importance of the Church in the emperor's control of his empire. Henry III's son Henry IV (1056–1106) clashed head-on with the leading radical reformer and former protégé of Leo IX, Pope Gregory VII (1073–1085), over the emperor's right to appoint and to install or invest bishops in their offices.

The Investiture Controversy.   The conflict between emperors and popes over investiture changed the face of European political history. Legal scholars for both sides searched Roman and Church law for arguments to bolster their claims, thus encouraging the revival of legal studies at Bologna. Both sides composed carefully worded propaganda aimed at secular and religious audiences. Gradually, the idea of the separate spheres of church and state emerged for the first time in European political theory.

The decline of royal rule in the empire that began with the investiture controversy continued as emperors abandoned political power north of the Alps in order to pursue their ambitions in Italy. Frederick I Barbarossa (1152–1190) spent much of his reign attempting to reimpose imperial authority on and to collect imperial incomes from the rich towns of northern Italy. For this he needed the support of the German princes, and he granted them extraordinary privileges in return for their cooperation south of the Alps. In 1156, he gave Henry Jasomirgott (ca. 1114–1177) virtual autonomy in the newly created duchy of Austria. Still, the combined efforts of the Lombard towns and the papacy were too much for Frederick and his armies to win a decisive victory. By the time of Frederick's death in Germany in 1190, the emperor was more a feudal lord than a sovereign, and in Italy his authority was disputed by the papacy and the towns. In 1230, Frederick II (1215–1250) conceded to each German prince sovereign rights in his own territory. From the thirteenth to the nineteenth centuries, the princes ruled their territories as independent states, leaving the office of emperor a hollow title.

The investiture controversy ultimately compromised the authority of the pope as well as that of the emperor. First, the series of compromises established a powerful tradition in Western political thought: the definition of separate spheres of authority for secular and religious government. While in the short run popes exercised enormous political influence, they were increasingly unable to make good their claims to absolute authority.

Over the centuries, the popes had acquired large amounts of land in central Italy and in the Rhone Valley that formed the nucleus of the Papal States. In every corner of Europe, bishops and clergy were agents of papal programs. The elaboration of systematic canon law created a system of courts and legal institutions more sophisticated than that of any secular monarch. Church courts claimed jurisdiction over all clerics and over all baptized Christians in such fundamental issues as legitimacy of marriages, inheritances, and oaths.

With Innocent III (1198–1216), the papacy reached the height of its powers. Innocent made and deposed emperors,

CHRONOLOGY
PROMINENT POPES AND RELIGIOUS FIGURES OF THE HIGH MIDDLE AGES

1049–1054*	Pope Leo IX
1073–1085	Pope Gregory VII
1088–1099	Pope Urban II
1098–1179	Hildegard of Bingen
1119–1124	Pope Calixtus II
1170–1221	Saint Dominic
1182–1226	Saint Francis of Assisi
1198–1216	Pope Innocent III
1225–1274	Saint Thomas Aquinas
1294–1303	Pope Boniface VIII

*Dates for popes are dates of reign.

excommunicated kings, and placed whole countries under the suspension of all religious services when rulers dared to contradict him. Still, he found time to support Francis of Assisi and Dominic and, in 1215, to call the Fourth Lateran Council, which culminated the reforms of the past century and had a lasting effect on the spiritual life of clergy and laity.

During the thirteenth century, the popes were unable to assert their claims to universal supremacy. This was true in Italy, and in the emerging kingdoms north of the Alps. The old claims of papal authority rang increasingly hollow. There was a new political tradition that was much more limited but ultimately more successful than either the empire or the papacy: the medieval nation-state.

The Nation-States: France and England.
Kings, unlike emperors, claimed only regional rather than universal authority. The kings of France began as regional aristocrats surrounded by peers who were in many cases more powerful than the kings. France was favored by a dynasty, the Capetians, who continuously provided male heirs. From their capital at Paris, the Capetians slowly built a more centralized kingdom. The founder of a united France was King Philip II Augustus (1180–1223) who acquired enormous territories by marriage alliances, warfare, and crusade. He established a new administrative system based on salaried agents who administered justice and collected royal taxes. Gradually, the power and independence of the regional aristocrats in France declined and the French monarchy became the most powerful state in Europe, able to have its own way with other kings, with the German emperor, and even with the pope.

The centralized kingdom of England was the creation of the Norman Conquest of 1066. William the Conqueror retained portions of the administrative system of Anglo-Saxon England while imposing the French system of feudal vassalage. All land in England was held directly by the king. William's successors created a central treasury system and a central court. The most important legal reformer was Henry II (1154–1189). Henry successfully imposed the jurisdiction of royal courts over both aristocratic and ecclesiastical tribunals. Under King John (1199–1216) and Henry III (1216–1272), the barons of England were able to gain some voice in government. John was forced to accept the **Magna Carta,** or great charter of liberties, that placed the English king under the rule of law. King Edward I (1272–1307) formalized the participation of barons in government by the creation of a parliament. As the wealth of the towns made them attractive sources of revenue, urban representatives also became customary participants in the royal court assembly or parliament.

By 1300, England and France had become the most centralized governments of western Europe. Because their governments could make more efficient use of their national resources, they were also the most powerful. Elsewhere, as in the Iberian peninsula, as Christian rulers of Castile, Aragon, and Leon expanded their territories at the expense of the Islamic rulers in the south, they looked to the French royal model. So too did monarchies such as Hungary, Bohemia, and Poland in central Europe, for whom French manners and style set the tone for court life.

The Mongol Empire.
Early in the fourteenth century a new and enormously powerful empire arose in Central Asia that connected for the first time much of Eurasia from China to Europe. The Mongols were nomadic herdsmen whose loose confederations of clans roamed the steppe lands of northern Asia. The brilliant war leader Temujin (ca. 1167–1227) united the Mongol clans (his title, Genghis Khan means "universal ruler") and led the Mongols to victory over the ancient Chinese Empire, while others under his command conquered westward. By the reign of Kublai Khan (1216–1294) the Mongol Empire extended from the East China Sea in the East to the Black Sea in the West, creating a vast commercial zone from Hungry to Korea, spanning both ends of the ancient silk route, and tying Mediterranean commerce through the Black Sea to the riches of China and India. The Mongol Empire was the first and only world empire to unite Eastern and Central Asia as well as parts of Europe.

By 1300, Europe had achieved a level of population density, economic prosperity, cultural sophistication, and political organization greater than at any time since the Roman Empire. Across Europe, a largely free peasantry cultivated a spectrum of crops for local consumption and for commercial markets. Cities bustled with manufacturing and commercial activities that connected Europeans from Scandinavia to the Mediterranean, while adventurous Italian merchants carried Europe's products into Africa and as far east as China. In royal and papal chanceries, university-trained lawyers worked to expand the rule of law over recalcitrant nobles, to keep the peace, and to preserve justice. Once more, western Europe had become a dominant force in world civilization.

QUESTIONS FOR REVIEW

1. What were some of the advances in early Mesopotamian and Babylonian cultures that contributed to the basic structure of Western civilization?
2. How did the Corinthian, Spartan, and Athenian cultures differ, and why did these city-states evolve in such different directions?
3. What factors explain Alexander the Great's success in expanding his empire?
4. What was the significance of the Punic Wars? How did their outcomes affect Rome's position as an imperial power?

5. How did Paul of Tarsus transform the teachings of Jesus of Nazareth from an outgrowth of Judaism into a separate spiritual tradition?
6. In what ways did Diocletian restore the empire? Were these reforms effective?
7. What were Muhammad's accomplishments?
8. What were Charlemagne's achievements?
9. What were the roles of peasants, knights, and clergymen, and how did they differ?

KEY TERMS

Arians, *p. lxxi*

broad-spectrum gathering, *p. xxxvi*

caliph, *p. lxxix*

Carolingian Renaissance, *p. lxxxv*

chivalry, *p. lxxxvii*

Christological controversies, *p. lxxi*

Crusades, *p. lxxxviii*

cuneiform, *p. xxxvi*

Cycladic, *p. xliii*

Cynics, *p. lvi*

Delian League, *p. l*

democracy, *p. xlix*

Epicureans, *p. lvi*

ethnos, *p. xlv*

Etruscans, *p. lviii*

fief, *p. lxxxviii*

first triumvirate, *p. lxiii*

guilds, *p. xci*

Hijra, *p. lxxviii*

hoplites, *p. l*

iconoclasts, *p. lxxv*

Linear B, *p. xliii*

Magna Carta, *p. xciv*

metics, *p. l*

Minoan, *p. xliii*

missi dominici, *p. lxxxv*

monasticism, *p. lxxiv*

Museum, *p. lvi*

Mycenaean, *p. xliii*

mystery cults, *p. lxvii*

Neolithic era, *p. xxxvi*

oligarchy, *p. xlv*

optimates, *p. lxii*

Orthodox Christianity, *p. lxxiv*

ostracism, *p. l*

Paleolithic era, *p. xxxvi*

paterfamilias, *p. lviii*

patricians, *p. lviii*

plebs, *p. lviii*

polis, *p. xlv*

populares, *p. lxii*

second triumvirate, *p. lxiii*

serfs, *p. lxxxvi*

Sophists, *p. lii*

Stoics, *p. lvi*

tetrarchy, *p. lxix*

Torah, *p. xxxix*

tyrants, *p. xlv*

Umma, *p. lxxviii*

vassals, *p. lxxxvii*

Zoroastrianism, *p. xlii*

DISCOVERING WESTERN CIVILIZATION ONLINE

To further explore Western civilization before 1300 consult the following Websites. Since Web resources are constantly being updated, also go to www.ablongman.com/kishlansky for further suggestions.

Before Civilization

history.evansville.net/referenc.html#West
A site that provides a directory of Western civilization Websites and pages for further exploration.

www.geocities.com/Tokyo/2384/links.html
Links to prehistoric rock art throughout the world.

www.taisei.co.jp/cg_e/ancient_world/ur/aur.html
The city of Mesopotamia (Ur) reproduced with computer graphics.

history.evansville.net/egypt.html
Award-winning site for Egyptian history.

The Birth of Greek Civilization, 2500–500 B.C.E.

www.pantheon.org/mythica.html
A site devoted to mythology with excellent resources on Greek myth.

www.pbs.org/empires/thegreeks/
A Public Broadcasting System site devoted to ancient Greece.

www.indiana.edu/~kglowack/athens/
An excellent site devoted to Athens.

Classical and Hellenistic Greece, 500–100 B.C.E.

www.history.boisestate.edu/westciv/alexander/
Dr. Ellis L. Knox's page devoted to Alexander the Great.

www.perseus.tufts.edu/GreekScience/Students/Jesse/CLOCK1A.html
A history of clocks in the Hellenistic world.

Early Rome and the Roman Republic, 800–146 B.C.E.

www.providence.edu/dwc/rome.htm
A course Web page with links to every aspect of Roman history and civilization.

www.uky.edu/ArtsSciences/Classics/wlgr/wlgr-romanlegal.html
A site devoted to women in Rome and Greece.

Imperial Rome, 146 B.C.E.–192 C.E.

www.carthage.edu/outis/augustus.html
A Web page devoted to the Emperor Augustus with links to archaeology and art of the Augustan age.

corinth.sas.upenn.edu/corinth.html
A computer reconstruction of Roman Corinth.

The Transformation of the Classical World

shsu.edu/~eng_wpf/con-hist.html
Links connecting to sites concerning Constantine.

www.nipissingu.ca/department/history/muhlberger/4505/show.htm
Images of people and places of late antiquity.

The Classical Legacy in the East: Byzantium and Islam

www.fordham.edu/halsall/Byzantium/
A major site with links to every aspect of Byzantine civilization maintained by Paul Halsall.

metmuseum.org/explore/Byzantium/byzhome.html
A site dedicated to Byzantine art and history at the Metropolitan Museum.

The West in the Early Middle Ages, 500–900

www.georgetown.edu:80/labyrinth/labyrinth-home.html
Labyrinth is the central Website for all medieval studies.

metmuseum.org/collections/view50.asp?dep=17
A look at some of the Metropolitan Museum's collection of medieval art, including migration period jewelry.

The High Middle Ages

georgetown.edu/labyrinth/subjects/women/women.html
Links to resources on medieval women.

castlesontheweb.com/
A whole Website dedicated to castles, abbeys, and medieval churches.

georgetown.edu/labyrinth/subjects/british_isles/england/england.html
The Labyrinth site with links to every aspect of medieval England.

SUGGESTIONS FOR FURTHER READING

Before Civilization

A. Bernard Knapp, *The History and Culture of Ancient Western Asia and Egypt* (Belmont, CA: Wadsworth Publishing Company, 1990). A good general survey of the entire period.

Barbara S. Lesko, ed. *Women's Earliest Records from Ancient Egypt and Western Asia: Proceedings of the Conference on Women in the Ancient Near East* (Atlanta: Scholars Press, 1989). Important collection of essays on all aspects of women in ancient societies.

The Birth of Greek Civilization, 2500–500 B.C.E.

M. I. Finley, *Early Greece: The Bronze and Archaic Ages,* 2nd ed. (New York: W. W. Norton, 1982). A very readable overview by a leading Greek historian.

William Taylour, *The Mycenaeans* (London: Thames & Hudson, 1990). General overview of Mycenaean civilization and daily life based on archaeology.

Classical and Hellenistic Greece, 500–100 B.C.E.

Yvon Garlan, *Slavery in Ancient Greece* (Ithaca, NY: Cornell University Press, 1988). A basic study of Greek slavery.

James L. O'Neil, *The Origins and Development of Ancient Greek Democracy* (Lanham, MD: Rowman & Littlefield, 1995). Greek democracy with a focus on Athens.

S. B. Pomeroy, *Families in Classical and Hellenistic Greece: Representation and Realities* (Oxford: Oxford University Press, 1999). A history of the family in Greece by a leading feminist historian.

Early Rome and the Roman Republic, 800–146 B.C.E.

Many of the works of Polybius, Livy, Cato, Caesar, Cicero, and other Roman authors are available in English translation from Penguin Books.—*Roman Civilization, Selected Readings, Vol. I: The Republic* (1951) by Naphtali Lewis and Meyer Reinhold contains a wide selection of documents with useful introductions.

Nigel Bagnall, *The Punic Wars* (London: Hutchinson, 1990). Survey of the wars between Rome and Carthage.

Graeme Barker and Tom Rasmussen, *The Etruscans* (Oxford: Blackwells Publishers, 2000). An introduction to Etruscan studies and history.

Imperial Rome, 146 B.C.E.–192 C.E.

Major selections of the works of Caesar, Cicero, Tacitus, Plutarch, Suetonius, and Marcus Aurelius are available in English translation from Penguin Books. *Roman Civilization Selected Readings, Vol. II: The Empire* (1951) by Naphtali Lewis and Meyer Reinhold contains a wide selection of documents with useful introductions.

Philippe Ariès and Georges Duby, eds., *History of Private Life. Vol. 1: From Pagan Rome to Byzantium* (Cambridge, MA: Harvard University Press, 1986). Essays on the interior, private life of Romans and Greeks by leading French and British historians.

Schuyler Brown, *The Origins of Christianity: A Historical Introduction of the New Testament*. Revised edition (Oxford: Oxford University Press, 1993). A balanced and comprehensive introduction to early Christianity.

Ramsay MacMullen, *Paganism in the Roman Empire* (New Haven, CT: Yale University Press, 1981). A description of the varieties and levels of pagan religion in the Roman world.

The Transformation of the Classical World

A. H. M. Jones, *The Later Roman Empire, 284–602: A Social, Economic, and Administrative Survey,* 2 vols. (Baltimore: Johns Hopkins University Press, 1986). The standard detailed survey of late antiquity by an administrative historian.

Herwig Wolfram, *The Roman Empire and Its Germanic Peoples* (Berkeley: University of California Press, 1997). Important general survey of the place of the barbarians in the Roman world.

The Classical Legacy in the East: Byzantium and Islam

Bernard Lewis, *The Muslim Discovery of Europe* (New York: W. W. Norton, 1985). Views of the West by Muslim travelers.

Fatima Mernissi, *Women and Islam: An Historical and Theological Enquiry* (Oxford: Basil Blackwell, 1991). Sympathetic study of women in Islam.

Warren T. Treadgold, *A Concise History of Byzantium* (New York: St. Martin's Press, 2001). An up-to-date survey of Byzantine history.

The West in the Early Middle Ages, 500–900

Roger Collins, *Early Medieval Europe: 300–1000* (Basingstoke, England: Macmillan Education, 1991). A brief survey of the barbarian kingdoms in late antiquity and the early Middle Ages, with an emphasis on political history.

Julia Bolton Holloway, Constance S. Wright, and Joan Bechtold, *Equally in God's Image: Women in the Middle Ages* (New York: P. Lang, 1990). Studies of medieval women from the end of antiquity to the Renaissance.

The High Middle Ages

Richard W. Kauper, *Chivalry and Violence in Medieval Europe (Oxford: Oxford University Press, 2001)*. A comprehensive look at the relationship between chivalry and medieval violence.

Jonathan Riley-Smith, ed. *The Oxford Illustrated History of the Crusades* (Oxford: Oxford University Press, 2001). A comprehensive, collectively authored introduction to crusade history.

For a list of additional titles related to this chapter's topics, please see http://www.ablongman.com/kishlansky.

Chapter 10

THE LATER MIDDLE AGES, 1300–1500

Chapter Outline

Saint Vitus Cathedral in Prague was the masterpiece of the architect Peter Parler, whose work was supported by Emperor Charles IV. What did the stonemason and the prince have in common? The Visual Record shows how both were spinning webs across Europe. ➤

The Visual Record

WEBS OF STONE AND BLOOD
European Civilization at the End of the Middle Ages

Like a delicate basket of woven stone, the Gothic vaulting in the choir of Saint Vitus Cathedral in Prague encloses and unifies the sacred space over which it floats. In a similar manner, the great aristocratic families of the fourteenth and fifteenth centuries spun webs of estates, hereditary principalities, and fiefs across Europe. In art as in life, dynamic individuals reshaped the legacy of the past into new and unexpected forms.

In France, where Gothic architecture originated in the twelfth century, architects had long used stone springers and vaults, but only to emphasize verticality and lift the eyes of the faithful to the heavens. Throughout the thirteenth and fourteenth centuries, French architects vied with one another to raise their vaults ever higher but never rethought the basic premise of their design. Peter Parler (1330–1399), the architect of Saint Vitus, approached the design of his cathedral in a novel way. He used intersecting vaults not simply for height but also to bind together the interior space of the edifice in a net of intersecting stone arches. The ability to rethink the architectural heritage of the past marked Peter Parler as the greatest architectural genius of the fourteenth century.

Emperor Charles IV (1355–1378), the head of the most successful web-spinning aristocratic family of the Later Middle Ages, recognized Parler's talent and enlisted him in making his Bohemian capital one of the most splendid cities of Europe.

Along with his innovations in architecture, Peter Parler also opened new directions in sculpture. Again breaking with French tradition, in which sculptors sought to present their subjects as ideal types, Parler concentrated on realism and individual portraiture in his work. The carved heads of Bohemia's kings, queens, prelates, and princes that peer down from the ambulatory of Saint Vitus are real people, with their blemishes, their virtues, and their vices marked in their faces. The interest in the individual was entirely appropriate in the late fourteenth century—a time when kings and peasants, saints and heretics, lords and merchants sought to make their mark by stepping out of their traditional roles. The characters of the age had personalities as marked as those of Parler's individualistic sculptures. Their epithets tell much: John "the Valiant" of Brittany; Philip "the Bold" of Burgundy; his son John "the Fearless"; the Habsburg John "the Parricide"; Charles II "the Bad" of Navarre; Pedro IV "the Cruel" of Aragon; Charles VI "the Mad" of France. Powerful and ambitious men and women fought for political dominance, religious visionaries and

■ The head of Charles IV from St. Vitus Cathedral.

preachers announced new and daring revelations, and thinkers and artists broke with hallowed philosophical and literary traditions. Parler had no doubt about his own importance in that age of individuals. His own portrait bust looks down from the cathedral beside those of kings and queens.

Parler was born into a well-known family of stonemasons near the German town of Württemberg. He learned his craft from his father but at a young age surpassed the elder Parler, not simply in the execution of stone constructions but also in their design. A century earlier, a young man of such recognized talent would almost certainly have gravitated from his native Swabia to France, then the cultural center of Europe. However, although French language, styles, and tradition continued to inspire Europeans everywhere throughout the fourteenth century, by mid-century France was increasingly troubled by dynastic problems, war, economic decline, and the ravages of disease. It was no longer the magnet that drew the greatest artists, architects, and thinkers. Thus, at the age of 23, the brilliant and ambitious young architect looked to the east rather than to the west and cast his lot with the splendid court of Charles IV, king of Bohemia and soon to be Holy Roman Emperor.

Charles invited Parler to complete his great Prague cathedral, which had been begun by a French architect and modeled on the great cathedrals of France. With Charles's patronage, Parler modified the building program to incorporate his original vision of architecture and portraiture. He went on to direct the construction of churches, bridges, and towers in Prague and throughout Bohemia. Within a generation, Parler's students had spread his refinement of Gothic architecture and sculpture throughout the

■ St. Vitus Cathedral.

Holy Roman Empire—to Austria, Bavaria, Swabia, Alsace, Poland, and Italy. Parler, the weaver of stone, and Charles, the weaver of politics, were emblematic of their age.

Looking Ahead

This chapter explores the tensions, crises, and creativity of Parler's age. It examines the rise of central Europe as a main stage of cultural and political action, follows the disasters of the Hundred Years' War, the Black Death, and the Great Schism, and reviews the religious, artistic, and literary creativity of the Later Middle Ages. ➤

POLITICS AS A FAMILY AFFAIR

Like those of his architect, Charles's roots were in the Rhineland and his cultural inspiration in France. The ancestral estates of his family, the house of Luxembourg, lay on the banks of the Moselle River. Between 1250 and 1350, the Luxembourg family greatly expanded its political and geographical powers by involving itself in the dynastic politics of the decaying Holy Roman Empire. At the height of his power, Charles controlled a patchwork of lands that included Luxembourg, Brabant, Lusatia, Silesia, Moravia, Meissen, and Brandenburg. His daughter married Richard II of England. A son succeeded him in Bohemia and another obtained the Hungarian crown.

Such fragmented and shifting territorial bases were typical of the great families of the fourteenth and fifteenth centuries. Everywhere, family politics threatened the fragile institutional developments of the thirteenth century. Aristocrats competed for personal power and used public office, military command, and taxing power for private ends. What mattered was neither territorial boundaries nor political divisions but marriage alliances, kinship, and dynastic ambitions.

The Struggle for Central Europe

In addition to the Luxembourgs, four other similarly ambitious families competed for dominance in the empire. First were the Wittelsbachs, the chief competitors of the Luxembourgs. The Wittelsbachs had originated in Bavaria but had since spread across Europe. In the west the Wittelsbachs had acquired Holland, Hainaut, and Frisia, while in the east they temporarily held Tyrol and Brandenburg. Next were the Habsburgs, allies of the Luxembourgs, who had begun as a minor comital family in the region of the Black Forest. They expanded east, acquiring Austria, Tyrol, Carinthia, and Carniola. When Rudolf I of Habsburg (1273–1291) was elected emperor in 1273, Otakar II, king of Bohemia (1253–1278) and head of the powerful Premysl family, dismissed Rudolf as "poor." Compared to the Premysls, perhaps he was. At its height, the Premysl family controlled not only Bohemia but also Moravia, Austria, and a miscellany of lands stretching from Silesia in the north to the Adriatic Sea. Finally, the house of Anjou—descendants of Charles of Anjou, the younger brother of the French king Louis IX, who had become king of Naples—created a similar eastern network. Charles's son Charles Robert secured election as king of Hungary in 1310. His son Louis (1342–1382) added the crown of Poland (1370–1382) to the Hungarian crown of Saint Stephen. The protracted wars and maneuvers that the families conducted for dominance in the empire resembled nothing so much as the competition that had taken place three centuries earlier for dominance in feudal France.

Eastern Expansion.   For more than a century, not only great princes but also monks, adventurers, and simple peasants streamed into the kingdoms and principalities of eastern Europe. Since the early thirteenth century, the Teutonic orders had used the sword to spread Christianity along the Baltic coast. By the early fourteenth century, the knight-monks had conquered Prussia and the coast as far east as the Narva River (now well within Russia), where they reached the borders of the Christian principality of Novgorod. The pagan inhabitants of the regions had to choose between conversion and expulsion. When they fled, their fields were turned over to land-hungry German peasants. Peasants from the Rhineland, Westphalia, and Saxony were able to negotiate advantageous contracts with their new lords, guaranteeing them greater freedom than they had known at home.

By the fifteenth century, religious and secular German lords had established a new agrarian economy, modeled on western European estates, in regions previously unoccupied or sparsely settled by the indigenous Slavic peoples. That economy specialized in the cultivation of grain for export to the west. Each fall, fleets of hundreds of ships sailed from the ports of Gdansk and Riga to ports in the Netherlands, England, and France. Returning flotillas carried Flemish cloth and tons of salt for preserving food to places as far as Novgorod. The influx of Baltic grain into western Europe caused a decline in domestic grain prices and a corresponding economic slump for landlords throughout the fourteenth and fifteenth centuries.

Central European Kingdoms.   Farther south, the Christian kingdoms of Poland, Bohemia, and Hungary beckoned different sorts of westerners. Newly opened silver and copper mines in Bohemia, Silesia, southern Poland, and Hungarian Transylvania needed skilled miners, smelters, and artisans. Many were recruited from the overpopulated regions of western Germany. East–west trade routes developed to export those metals, giving new life to the Bohemian towns of Prague and Brno, the Polish cities of Krakow and Lvov, and Hungarian Buda and Bratislava. Trade networks reached south to the Mediterranean via Vienna, the Brenner Pass, and Venice. To the north, trade routes extended to the Elbe River and the trading towns of Lübeck and Bremen. The Bavarian towns of Augsburg, Rothenburg, and Nuremberg flourished at the western end of the network. To the east, Lvov became a great trading center connecting southern Russia with the west.

The wealth of eastern Europe, its abundant land, and its relative freedom attracted both peasants and merchants. The promise of profitable marriages with eastern royalty drew ambitious aristocrats. Through such a marriage, for example, Charles Robert of Anjou became king of Hungary after the extinction of that realm's ancient royal dynasty. Similarly, Charles Robert's son Louis inherited the Polish crown in 1370 after the death of Casimir III, the last king of the Polish Piast dynasty. Nobles of the eastern European kingdoms were pleased to confirm the election of such outsiders. The elections prevented powerful German nobles from claiming succession to the Bohemian, Hungarian, and Polish thrones. At the same time, the families of the western European aristocracy did not have sufficiently strong local power bases to challenge the autonomy

MAP DISCOVERY

Central and Eastern Europe, ca. 1378

Examine this complex map of rival dynasties in fourteenth-century Europe. How do you explain the discontinuous territorial holdings of these great competing families? To what extent could the regions of the Holy Roman Empire be considered a state in 1378? Based on the text discussion, where might the Habsburgs be expected to extend and consolidate their power in the east?

of the eastern nobility. For the outsiders, eastern alliances meant the expansion of family power and the promise of glory.

Charles IV (1347–1378) was typical of the restless dynasts. His grandfather, Emperor Henry VII (1308–1313), had arranged for his son, John of Luxembourg, to marry Elizabeth (d. 1330), the Premysl heiress of Bohemia, and thus acquire the Bohemian crown in 1310. John was king in name only. He spent most of his career fighting in the dynastic wars of the empire and of France. However, by mastering the intricate politics of the decaying Holy Roman Empire, he arranged the

deposition of the Wittelsbach emperor Louis IV (1314–1347) and in 1346 secured the election of Charles as king of the Romans, or heir of the empire. The following year the Bohemian crown passed to Charles.

Although born in Prague and deeply committed to what he called "the sweet soil of my native land," Charles had spent most of his youth in France, where he was deeply influenced by French culture. However, upon his return to Prague in 1333 he rediscovered his Czech cultural roots. As king of Bohemia, he worked to make Prague a cultural center by combining French

■ Emperor Charles IV presenting sacred relics to the Church of Karlstein in Prague, built by Charles to house the crown jewels of the Holy Roman Empire.

and Czech traditions. He imported artisans, architects, and artists such as Peter Parler to transform and beautify his capital. In 1348 he founded a university in Prague, the first in the empire, modeled on the University of Paris. Keenly interested in history, Charles provided court historians with the sources necessary to write their histories of the Bohemian kingdom. "It is to the great profit of the state that young princes be taught history," he wrote, "lest through ignorance they should become degenerate inheritors of an ancient greatness."

Charles took a more active role in the cultural renewal than perhaps any European king since Alfred of England, fostering a literary renaissance in both Latin and Czech. Although he had forgotten his native Czech during his long stay in France, he soon learned to read and write it, along with French, German, Italian, and Latin. He authored a number of religious texts, fostered the use of the Czech language in religious services, and initiated a Czech translation of the Bible. He even composed his own autobiography, perhaps the first lay person to do so in medieval Europe.

The effects of Charles's cultural policies were far-reaching, but in directions he never anticipated. His interests in Czech culture and religious reform bore unexpected fruit during the reign of his son Sigismund, Holy Roman Emperor (1433–1437) and king of Hungary (1387–1437), Germany (1410–1437), and Bohemia (1419–1437). During Sigismund's reign, Czech religious and political reformers came into open conflict with the powerful German-speaking minority in the University of Prague. Led by the theologian Jan Hus (ca. 1372–1415), the reform movement ultimately challenged the authority of the Roman Catholic Church and became the direct predecessor of the great reformation of the sixteenth century.

Even while building up his beloved city of Prague, Charles was dismantling the Holy Roman Empire. By the fourteenth century, the title of emperor held little political importance, although as an honorific title it was still bitterly contested by the great families of the empire. Charles sought to end such disputes and at the same time to solidify the autonomy of the kingdoms, such as Bohemia, against the threats of future imperial candidates. In 1356 he issued the **Golden Bull**, an edict that officially recognized what long had been the reality, namely, that the various German princes and kings were autonomous rulers. The bull also established the procedure by which future emperors would be elected. Thereafter, the emperor was chosen by seven great princes of the empire without the consultation or interference of the pope—a tradition of interference that dated to the coronation of Charlemagne. The procedure made disputed elections less likely, but it acknowledged that the office itself was less significant.

The same process that sapped the power of the emperor also reduced the significance of the princes. The empire fragmented into a number of large kingdoms and duchies such as Bohemia, Hungary, Poland, Austria, and Bavaria in the east and more than 1600 autonomous principalities, free towns, and sovereign bishoprics in the west. The inhabitants of the territories, often ruled by foreigners who had inherited sovereign powers through marriage, organized themselves into estates—political units of knights, burghers, and clergy—to present a united front in dealing with their prince. The princes in turn did not enjoy any universally recognized right to rule and were forced to negotiate with their estates for any powers they actually enjoyed.

The disintegration of the empire left political power east of the Rhine widely dispersed for more than 500 years. While this meant that Germany did not become a nation-state until the nineteenth century, decentralization left late medieval Germany as a fertile region of cultural and constitutional creativity. In that creative process the office of emperor played no role. After the Habsburg family definitively acquired the imperial office in 1440, the office of emperor ceased to have any role in Germany. Rather, the office became one of the building blocks of the great multinational Habsburg Empire of central Europe, an empire that survived until 1918.

A Hundred Years of War

The political map of western Europe was no less a patchwork quilt of family holdings than was the empire. On the Iberian Peninsula, the gradual Christian reconquest bogged down as the three Christian monarchies of Castile, Aragon, and Portugal largely ignored the remaining Muslim kingdom of Granada. Instead, dynastic rivalries, expansionist adventures in Sicily and Italy, internal revolts of nobility and peasants, and futile wars against one another commanded the energy and attention of the Christian kingdoms. Only when Ferdinand of Aragon married Isabella of Castile in 1469 did something like a unified Spain begin to emerge from that world of familial rivalries.

North of the Pyrenees, the situation was even more critical. The same kinds of familial rivalries that destroyed the empire as a political entity threatened to overwhelm the feudal monarchies of France and England in the fourteenth and fifteenth centuries. In both kingdoms, weakening economic climates and demographic catastrophe exacerbated dynastic crises and fierce competition. The survival of the English and French monarchies was due to luck, to a longer tradition of bureaucratic government, and—in the minds of contemporaries—to the hand of God. Three long-simmering disputes triggered the series of campaigns collectively termed the **Hundred Years' War.** The first issue was conflicting rights to Gascony in southern France. Since the mid-thirteenth century, the kings of England had held Gascony as a fief of the French king. Neither monarchy was content with this arrangement, and for the next 75 years kings quarreled constantly over sovereignty in the region.

The second point of contention was the close relationship between England and the Flemish cloth towns. The manufacturing centers were the primary customers for English wool. Early in the fourteenth century, Flemish artisans rose up in a series of bloody revolts against the aristocratic cloth dealers who had long monopolized power. The count of Flanders and the French king supported the wealthy merchants, while the English sided with the artisans.

The third dispute concerned the royal succession in France. Charles IV (1322–1328), the son of Philip IV the Fair, died without an heir. The closest descendant of a French king was the grandson of Philip the Fair, King Edward III of England (1327–1377). Edward, however, was the son of Philip's daughter Isabella. The French aristocracy, which did not want an English king to inherit the throne and unite the two kingdoms, pretended that according to ancient Frankish law, the crown could not pass through a woman. Instead, they preferred to give the crown to a cousin of the late king, Philip VI (1328–1350),

■ The Hundred Years' War. The English and their Burgundian allies almost succeeded in surrounding and conquering France in the fifteenth century.

who became the first of the Valois kings of France. At first the English voiced no objection to Philip's accession, but in 1337, when the dispute over Gascony again flared up and Philip attempted to confiscate the region from his English "vassal" Edward III, the English king declared war on Philip. Edward's stated goal was not only to recover Gascony but also to claim the crown of his maternal grandfather.

Chivalry and Warfare. Although territorial and dynastic rivalry were the triggers that set off the war, its deeper cause was chivalry. The elites of Europe were both inspired by and trapped in a code of conduct that required them not only to maintain their honor by violence but also to cultivate violence to increase that honor. The code had been appropriate in a period of weak kingship, but by the late thirteenth century, the growth of courts and royal power in France and in England left little room for private vengeance and vendettas. Nobles were now more often royal retainers than knights errant traveling about the countryside righting wrongs. Government was increasingly an affair of lawyers and bureaucrats, and war an affair of professionals. Yet kings and nobles alike still agreed with the sentiment expressed by a contemporary poet: "The glory of princes is in their pride and in undertaking great peril." By the fourteenth century, only war provided sufficient peril.

Edward III of England and his rival Philip VI of France both epitomized the chivalrous knight. Both gloried in luxurious

GENEALOGY
THE FRENCH AND ENGLISH SUCCESSIONS

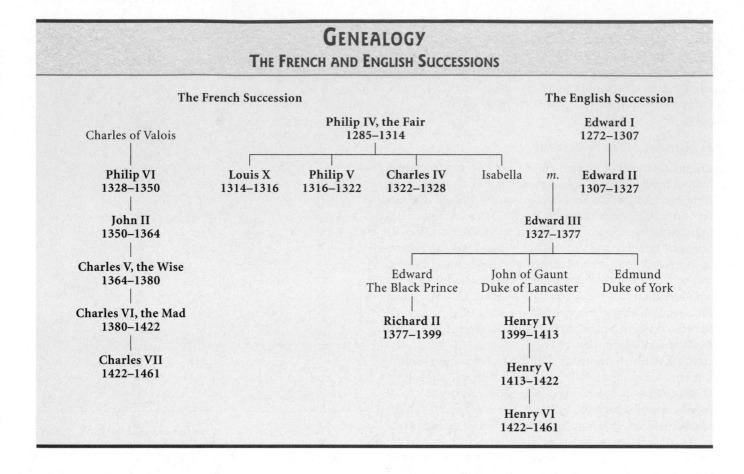

The French Succession

The English Succession

Philip IV, the Fair
1285–1314

Edward I
1272–1307

Charles of Valois

Philip VI
1328–1350

Louis X
1314–1316

Philip V
1316–1322

Charles IV
1322–1328

Isabella   *m.*   Edward II
1307–1327

John II
1350–1364

Edward III
1327–1377

Charles V, the Wise
1364–1380

Edward
The Black Prince

John of Gaunt
Duke of Lancaster

Edmund
Duke of York

Charles VI, the Mad
1380–1422

Richard II
1377–1399

Henry IV
1399–1413

Charles VII
1422–1461

Henry V
1413–1422

Henry VI
1422–1461

living and conspicuous consumption. Captivated by the romantic tales of King Arthur and the Round Table, Edward created the Order of the Garter, a select group of nobles who were to embody the highest qualities of chivalry. For a ruler such as Edward, obsessed with knightly glory, war with France was the ideal way to win honor and fame.

In spite of his chivalric ideals, Edward was practical when it came to organizing and financing his campaigns. Philip shared Edward's ideals but lacked his rival's practicality and self-assurance. Before his elevation to the throne, Philip had been a valiant and successful warrior, fond of jousting, tournaments, and lavish celebrations. After his coronation he continued to act like a figure from a knightly romance, surrounding himself with aristocratic advisers who formed the most brilliant court of Europe, dispensing the royal treasure to his favorites, and dreaming of leading a great crusade to free the Holy Land. However, as the first French king in centuries elected rather than born into the right of succession, Philip treated the magnates from whose ranks he had come with excessive deference. He hesitated to press them for funds and deferred to them on matters of policy even while missing opportunities to raise other revenue from towns and merchants. Finally, although a competent warrior, Philip was no match in strategy or tactics for his English cousin.

Still, the sheer size and wealth of France should have made it the favorite in any war with England. Its population of roughly 16 million made it by far the largest and most densely populated kingdom in Europe. At the start of the war, Philip could rely on an income roughly three to five times greater than that of Edward. However, the inequalities mattered little because the French king had no means of harnessing the resources of his kingdom. His greater income was matched by greater expenses, and he had no easy way to raise extraordinary funds for war. In contrast, the English king could use Parliament as an efficient source of war subsidies. Edward could also extract great sums from taxes on wool exports. Even after the invasion of France, Philip had to rely on manipulation of the coinage, confiscation of Italian bankers' property, and a whole range of nuisance taxes to finance his campaigns.

War was expensive. In spite of chivalrous ideals, nobles no longer fought as vassals of the king but rather as highly paid mercenaries. The nature of that service differed greatly on the two sides of the Channel. In France, tactics and personnel had changed little since the twelfth century. The core of any army was the body of heavily armored nobles who rode into battle with their lords, supported by lightly armored knights. Behind them marched infantrymen recruited from towns and armed with pikes. Although the French also hired mercenary Italian crossbowmen, the nobles despised them and never used them effectively.

In contrast, centuries of fighting against Welsh and Scottish enemies had transformed and modernized the English armies and their tactics. The great nobles continued to serve as heavily armored horsemen, but professional companies of foot soldiers raised by individual knights made up the bulk of the army. The professional companies consisted largely of pikemen and, most importantly, of longbowmen. Although not as accurate as the crossbow, the English longbow had a greater range. Moreover, when massed archers fired volleys of arrows into enemy ranks, they proved extremely effective against enemy pikemen and even lightly armored cavalry.

English Successes. The first real test of the two armies came at the Battle of Crécy in 1346. There an overwhelmingly superior French force surrounded the English army. Massing their archers on a hill, the English rained arrows down on the French cavalry, which attacked in a glorious but suicidal manner. Typical of the French chivalric behavior was that of King John of Bohemia, father of Charles IV, both of whom were fighting as mercenaries of the French king. Although he was totally blind, John requested and received the privilege of commanding the vanguard of the first French division. He had his men tie their horses together and lead him into battle so that he might strike a blow. The next day his body and those of all his men were found on the field, their mounts still bound together.

The English victory was total. By midnight they had repelled 16 assaults, losing only 100 men while killing more than 3000 French. The survivors, including Philip VI, fled in disorder. Strangely enough, the French learned nothing from the debacle. In 1356 Philip's successor, John II (1350–1364), rashly attacked an English army at Poitiers and was captured. In 1415 the French blundered in a different way at Agincourt. Then, most of the heavily armored French knights dismounted and attempted to charge the elevated English position across a soggy, muddy field. Barely able to walk and entirely unable to rise again if they fell, all were captured. Out of fear that his numerically inferior English army would be overwhelmed if the French recovered their breath, the English king ordered more than 1500 French nobles and 3000 ordinary soldiers killed. He held more than 1000 of the greatest nobles for ransom. English losses were less than 100.

Pitched battles were not the worst defeats for the French. More devastating were the constant raiding and systematic destruction of the French countryside by the English companies. The relief effort launched in 1339 by Pope Benedict XII (1334–1342) gives some idea of the scale of destruction. Papal agents, sent to aid victims of the English invasion, paid out more than 12,000 pounds—the equivalent of one-third of the English annual royal income—to peasants in just one region of northern France. The funds distributed were simple charity and far from adequate compensation. Villagers estimated that their actual losses were perhaps seven times greater than what they received.

Raiding and pillaging continued for decades, even during long truces between the French and English kings. During periods of truce, unemployed free companies of French and English mercenaries roamed the countryside, supporting themselves by banditry while awaiting the renewal of more formal hostilities. Large swaths of France were left uncultivated for years because peasants were killed or terrorized into flight. Never had the ideals of chivalric conduct been so distant from the brutal realities of warfare.

The French kings were powerless to prevent the destruction, just as they were unable to defeat the enemy in open battle. Since the kings were incapable of protecting their subjects or of leading their armies to victory, the "silken thread binding together

■ The battle of Agincourt (1415) was one of the great battles of the Hundred Years' War. The heavily armored French cavalry met defeat at the hands of a much smaller force of disciplined English pikemen and longbowmen.

the kingdom of France," as one observer put it, began to unravel, and the kingdom so painstakingly constructed by the Capetian monarchs began to fall apart. Not only did the English make significant territorial conquests, but the French nobles began behaving much like those in the Holy Roman Empire, carving out autonomous lordships. Private warfare and castle building, never entirely eradicated even by Louis IX and Philip IV, increased as the royal government lost its ability to control the nobility. Whole regions of the kingdom slipped entirely from royal authority. Duke Philip the Good of Burgundy (1396–1467) allied himself with England against France and profited from the war to form a far-flung lordship that included Flanders, Brabant, Luxembourg, and Hainaut. By the time of his death, he was the most powerful ruler in Europe. Much of the so-called Hundred Years' War was actually a French civil war.

During this century of war, the French economy suffered even more than the French state. Trade routes were broken and commerce declined as credit disappeared. French kings repeatedly seized the assets of Italian merchant bankers in order to finance the war. Such actions made the Italians, who had been the backbone of French commercial credit, extremely wary about extending loans in the kingdom. The kings then turned to French and Flemish merchants, extorting from them forced loans that dried up capital that might otherwise have been returned to commerce and industry. Politically and economically, France seemed doomed.

Joan of Arc and the Salvation of France.   The flower of French chivalry did not save France. Instead, at the darkest moment of the long and bloody struggle, salvation came at the hands of a simple peasant girl from the county of Champagne. By 1429, the English and their Burgundian allies held virtually all of northern France, including Paris. Now they were besieging Orléans, the key to the south. The heir to the French throne, the dauphin, was the weak-willed and uncrowned Charles VII (1422–1461). To him came Joan of Arc (1412–1431), an illiterate but deeply religious girl who bore an incredible message of hope. She claimed to have heard the voices of saints ordering her to save Orléans and have the dauphin crowned according to tradition at Reims.

Charles and his advisers were more than skeptical about the brash peasant girl who announced her divinely ordained mission to save France. Finally convinced of her sincerity, if not of her ability, Charles allowed her to accompany a relief force to Orléans. The French army, its spirit buoyed by the belief that Joan's simple faith was the work of God, defeated the English and ended the siege. That victory led to others, and on 16 July 1429 Charles was crowned king at Reims.

After the coronation, Joan's luck began to fade. She failed to take Paris, and in 1431 she was captured by the Burgundians, who sold her to the English. Eager to get rid of the troublesome girl, the English had her tried as a heretic. Charles did nothing to save his savior. After all, the code of chivalry did not demand that a king intervene on behalf of a mere peasant girl, even if she had saved his kingdom. She was burned at the stake in Rouen on 30 May 1431.

■ A fifteenth-century portrait of Joan of Arc. The Maid of Orléans was tried for heresy and executed in 1431. Later, in 1456, Pope Calixtus III pronounced her innocent. Pope Benedict XV formally declared her a saint in 1920.

Despite Joan's inglorious end, the tide had turned. The French pushed the English back toward the coast. In the final major battle of the war, fought at Formigny in 1450, the French used a new and telling weapon to defeat the English— gunpowder. Rather than charging the English directly, as they had done so often before, they mounted a cannon and pounded the English to bits. Gunpowder completed the destruction of the chivalric traditions of warfare begun by archers and pikemen. By 1452 English continental holdings had been reduced to the town of Calais. Although the English kings continued to call themselves kings of France until the eighteenth century, it was a hollow title. The continental warfare of more than a century was over.

The English Wars of the Roses.   Although war on the Continent had ended, warfare in England was just beginning. In some ways, the English monarchy had suffered even more from the Hundred Years' War than had the French. At the outset, English royal administration had been more advanced than the French. The system of royal agents, courts, and parliaments had

■ A fourteenth-century manuscript illustration shows bankers counting gold coins. Italian banks helped finance armies on both sides of the Hundred Years' War, and the two largest banking firms were bankrupted when Edward III of England failed to repay the loans.

created the expectation that the king could preserve peace and provide justice at home while waging successful and profitable wars abroad. As the decades dragged on without a decisive victory, the king came to rely on the aristocracy, enlisting its financial assistance by granting the magnates greater power at home.

War created powerful and autonomous aristocratic families with their own armies. Under a series of weak kings those families fought among themselves. Ultimately, they took sides in a civil war to determine the royal succession. For 30 years, from 1455 to 1485, supporters of the house of York, whose badge was the white rose, fought the rival house of Lancaster, whose symbol was the red rose, in the sort of dynastic struggle that would not have seemed out of place in the disintegrating German Empire. The English Wars of the Roses, as the conflict came to be called, finally ended in 1485 when Henry Tudor of the Lancastrian faction defeated his opponents. He inaugurated a new era as Henry VII (1485–1509), the first king of the Tudor dynasty.

By the end of the fifteenth century, England and France had survived with their central monarchical institutions largely intact, although their aristocracies still shared an important role in the exercise of power.

LIFE AND DEATH IN THE LATER MIDDLE AGES

The violence and pageantry of late medieval warfare played out against a backdrop of extraordinary social upheaval. By the end of the thirteenth century, population growth in the West had strained available resources to the breaking point. All arable land was under cultivation, and even marginal moorland, rocky mountainsides, and arid plains were being pressed into service to feed a growing population. At the same time, kings and nobles demanded ever higher taxes and rents to finance their wars and extravagant lifestyles. The result was a precarious balance in which a late frost, a bad harvest, or hungry mercenaries could mean disaster. Part of the problem could be alleviated by importing grain from the Baltic or from Sicily, but that solution carried risks of its own. Transportation systems were too fragile to ensure regular supplies, and their rupture could initiate a cycle of famine, disease, and demographic collapse. Population began to decline slowly around 1300, and the downturn became catastrophic within the following 50 years. In the period between 1300 and 1450, Europe's population fell by more than 30 percent. It did not recover until the seventeenth century.

Dancing with Death

Between 1315 and 1317, the first great famine of the fourteenth century, triggered by crop failures and war, struck Europe. People died by the thousands. Urban workers, because they were chronically undernourished, were particularly hard hit. In the Flemish cloth town of Ypres, whose total population was less than 20,000, the town ordered the burial of 2794 paupers' corpses within a five-month period. Although it was the greatest famine in medieval memory, it was not the last. The relatively prosperous Italian city of Pistoia, for example, recorded 16 different famines and food shortages in the fourteenth and fifteenth centuries.

Disease accompanied famine. Crowded and filthy towns, opposing armies with their massed troops, and overpopulated countrysides provided fertile ground for the spread of infectious disease. Moreover, the greatly expanded trade routes of the thirteenth and fourteenth centuries that carried goods and grain between the East and the West also provided highways for deadly microbes. At Pistoia again, local chroniclers of the fourteen and fifteenth centuries reported 14 years of sickness, fevers, epidemic, and plague.

Between 1347 and 1352, from one-half to one-third of Europe's population died from a virulent combination of bubonic, septicemic, and pneumonic plagues known to history as the **Black Death**. The disease, carried by the fleas of infected rats, traveled the caravan routes from central Asia. It arrived in Messina, Sicily, aboard a merchant vessel in October 1347. From there the Black Death spread up the boot of Italy and then into southern France, England, and Spain. By 1349 it had reached northern Germany, Portugal, and Ireland. The following year the Low Countries, Scotland, Scandinavia, and Russia fell victim.

Plague victims died horribly. Soon after being bitten by an infected flea, they developed a high fever, began coughing, and suffered excruciatingly painful swellings in the lymph nodes of the groin or armpits. The swellings were known as *buboes,* from which the disease took its name. In the final stages, the victims began to vomit blood. The bubonic form of the disease usually killed within five days. The septicemic form, which attacked the blood, was more swift and deadly. Those infected by the airborne, pneumonic form usually died in less than three days; in some cases, within a matter of hours.

The plague was all the more terrifying because its cause, its manner of transmission, and its cure were totally unknown until the end of the nineteenth century. Preachers saw the plague as divine punishment for sin. Ordinary people frequently accused Jews of causing it by poisoning drinking water. The medical faculty of Paris announced that it was the result of the conjunction of the planets Saturn, Jupiter, and Mars, which caused a corruption of the surrounding air.

Responses to the plague were equally varied. Across Europe, terrified people thought that by joining penitential groups that prayed, fasted, and even whipped themselves, they could turn away divine wrath through self-mortification. Others thought it best to abandon themselves to pleasure, either out of despair or in the hope that a pleasant life of eating and drinking would in some way ward off the terror of the plague. In many German towns, terrified Christian citizens looked for outside scapegoats and slaughtered the Jewish community. Cities, aware of the risk of infection although ignorant of its process, closed their gates and turned away outsiders. Individuals with means fled to country houses or locked themselves in their homes to avoid contact with others. Nothing worked. The Italian author Giovanni Boccaccio (1313–1375) remarked on the wide range

■ A page from the fourteenth-century psalter and prayer book of Bonne of Luxembourg, Duchess of Normandy. The three figures of the dead shown here contrast with three living figures on the facing page of the psalter to illustrate a moral fable.

of opinions on how to deal with the plague, "Of the people who held these various opinions, not all of them died. Nor, however, did they all survive."

As devastating as the first outbreak of the plague was, its aftershocks were even more catastrophic. Once established in Europe, the disease continued to return roughly once each generation. Pistoia, for example, which probably lost roughly two-thirds of its population in 1348, suffered recurrences in 1389; in 1393; in 1399 when one-half of the population died; and again in 1410, 1416, 1418, 1423, 1436, and 1457. The rueful call, "Bring out your dead," resounded for centuries in European cities. The last outbreak of the plague in Europe was the 1771 epidemic in Moscow that killed 60,000.

The Black Death, along with other epidemics, famines, and war-induced shortages, affected western much more than eastern Europe. The culminating effect of the disasters was a darker, more somber vision of life than that of the previous centuries. The vision ultimately found its expression in the Dance of Death, an increasingly popular image in art and literature first depicted in the murals of the Church of the Holy Innocents in Paris around 1485. Naked, rotting corpses dance

THE BLACK DEATH IN FLORENCE

Giovanni Boccaccio set his Decameron *in Florence at the height of the Black Death. His eyewitness description of the plague is the most graphic account of the disease and its effects on society.*

Focus Questions

In what different ways did people try to live so as to escape the plague? What were the effects of the plague on the social fabric?

I say, then, that the sum of thirteen hundred and fifty-eight years had elapsed since the fruitful Incarnation of the Son of God, when the noble city of Florence, which for its great beauty excels all others in Italy, was visited by the deadly pestilence. Some say that it descended upon the human race through the influence of the heavenly bodies, others that it was a punishment signifying God's righteous anger at our iniquitous way of life. But whatever its cause, it had originated some years earlier in the East, where it had claimed countless lives before it unhappily spread westward, growing in strength as it swept relentlessly on from one place to the next. . . . Against these maladies, it seemed that all the advice of physicians and all the power of medicine were profitless and unavailing. . . . Some people were of the opinion that a sober and abstemious mode of living considerably reduced the risk of infection. They therefore formed themselves into groups and lived in isolation from everyone else. . . . Others took the opposite view, and maintained that an infallible way of warding off this appalling evil was to drink heavily, enjoy life to the full, go round singing and merrymaking, gratifying all of one's cravings whenever the opportunity offered, and shrug the whole thing off as one enormous joke. . . . There were many other people who steered a middle course between the two already mentioned, neither restricting their diet to the same degree as the first group, nor indulging so freely as the second in drinking and other forms of wantonness, but simply doing no more than satisfy their appetite. Instead of incarcerating themselves, these people moved about freely, holding in their hands a posy of flowers, or fragrant herbs, or one of a wide range of spices, which they applied at frequent intervals to their nostrils, thinking it an excellent idea to fortify the brain with smells of that particular sort, for the stench of dead bodies, sickness, and medicines seemed to fill and pollute the whole of the atmosphere.

Some people pursuing what was possibly the safer alternative callously maintained that there was no better or more efficacious remedy against the plague than to run away from it. . . .

Of the people who held these various opinions, not all of them died. Nor, however, did they all survive. On the contrary, many of each different persuasion fell ill here, there, and everywhere, and having themselves, when they were fit and well, set an example to those who were as yet unaffected, they languished away with virtually no one to nurse them. This scourge had implanted so great a terror in the hearts of men and women that brothers abandoned brothers, uncles their nephews, sisters their brothers, and in many cases wives deserted their husbands. But even worse, and almost incredible, was the fact that fathers and mothers refused to nurse and assist their own children, as though they did not belong to them.

From Giovanni Boccaccio, *The Decameron*.

with great animation before the living. The latter, depicted in the dress of all social orders, are immobile, surprised by death, reluctant but resigned.

Although no solid statistics exist from the fourteenth century, the plague certainly killed more people than all of the wars and famines of the century. It was the greatest disaster ever to befall Europe. The Black Death touched every aspect of life, hastening a process of social, economic, and cultural transformation already underway. The initial outbreak shattered social and economic structures. Fields were abandoned, workplaces stood idle, international trade was suspended. Traditional bonds of kinship, village, and even religion were broken by the horrors of death, flight, and failed expectations. "People cared no more for dead men than we care for dead goats," wrote one survivor. Brothers abandoned brothers, wives deserted husbands, and terror-stricken parents refused to nurse their own children. Nothing had prepared Europe for the catastrophe. In spite of learned Parisian professors who proclaimed it the result of the movement of the planets and the popular preachers who argued that it was punishment for human sins, no teaching of the Church or its leaders could adequately explain it. Likewise, in spite of desperate attempts by others to fix the blame on Jews or strangers, no one but God could be held responsible. Survivors stood alone and uncertain before a new world. Across Europe, moralists reported a general lapse in traditional ethics, a breakdown in the moral codes. The most troubling aspect of the breakdown was what one defender of the old order termed "the plague of insurrection" that spread across

Europe. That plague was brought on by the dimming of the hopes held by the survivors of the Black Death.

The Plague of Insurrection

Initially, even that darkest cloud had a silver lining. Lucky survivors of the plague soon found other reasons to rejoice. Property owners, when they finished burying their dead, discovered that they were far richer in land and goods. At the other end of the social spectrum, the plague had eliminated the labor surplus. Peasants were suddenly in great demand. For a time at least, they were able to negotiate substantially higher wages and an improved relationship with landlords. An English thresher who before 1349 had been paid around three pence a day could hope to earn 25 percent more after the plague.

The peasants' hopes were short-lived. The rise in expectations produced by the redistribution of wealth and the labor shortage created new tensions. Landlords sought laws forcing peasants to accept preplague wages and tightened their control over serfs in order to prevent them from fleeing to cities or other lords. At the same time, governments attempted to benefit from laborers' greater prosperity by imposing new taxes. In cities, where the plague had been particularly devastating, the demographic decline sharply lowered the demand for goods and thus reduced the need for manufacturing and production of all kinds. Like rural landowners, master craftsmen sought legislation to protect their incomes. New laws reduced production by restricting access to trades and increased masters' control over the surviving urban laborers. Social mobility, once a characteristic of urban life, slowed to a halt. Membership in guilds became hereditary, and young

MAP DISCOVERY

Spread of the Black Death and Peasant Revolts

How closely did the spread of the Black Death follow the medieval trade networks shown in the map on p. 272? What was the general direction and average annual speed of the disease's spread? Was the Black Death only a disaster to western Europe? Note the locations of peasant revolts. Based on the chapter discussion, what similarities and differences existed among the groups that revolted in the Later Middle Ages? Was there a relationship between the devastation of the plague and the outbreak of revolts?

■ Amid the disasters of the Hundred Years' War and the Black Death, the fourteenth century witnessed numerous peasant revolts. This manuscript illustration shows armed rioters ransacking the house of a wealthy Paris merchant.

apprentices or journeymen had little hope of ever rising to the level of independent master craftsmen.

The new tensions led to violence when kings added their demands for new war taxes to the landlords' and masters' attempts to erase the peasants' and workers' recent gains. The first revolts took place in France, where peasants and townspeople, disgusted with the incompetence of the nobility in their conduct of the war against England, feared that their new wealth would be stolen from them by corrupt and incompetent aristocrats.

The Jacquerie.   In 1358, in order to ransom King John II from the English, the French government attempted to increase taxes on the peasantry. At the same time, local nobles increased their rents and demands. Peasants in the area of Beauvais, north of Paris, fearing they would lose the modest level of prosperity they had gained over the previous ten years, rebelled against their landlords. The revolt—known as the **Jacquerie** for the archetypal French peasant, Jacques Bonnehomme—was a spontaneous outburst directed against the nobility, whom the peasants saw as responsible for all their ills. Without real leadership or a program, peasants attacked as many nobles as they could find, killing them along with their wives and children and burning their homes and castles.

The peasants' brutality deeply shocked the upper classes, whose own violence was constrained by the chivalric code. One chronicler reported in horror, "Among other evil deeds, they killed a knight and quickly began to roast him before the eyes of his wife and children. After 10 or 12 had raped the noble lady, they wanted to force her to eat her husband's flesh. They then put her to death horribly." Because the Church largely supported the power structure, the uprising was also strongly anticlerical. Churches were burned and priests killed. Success bred further attacks, and the disorganized army of peasants began to march south toward Paris, killing, looting, and burning everything associated with the despised nobility.

In the midst of this peasant revolt, Etienne Marcel (ca. 1316–1358), a wealthy Parisian cloth merchant, led an uprising of Parisian merchants who sought to take control of royal finances and force fiscal reforms on the dauphin, the future Charles V. Although initially the rebels were primarily members of the merchant and guild elite, Marcel soon enlisted the support of the radical townspeople against the aristocracy. He even made overtures to the leaders of the Jacquerie to join forces. For a brief time, it appeared that the aristocratic order in France might succumb. However, in the end, peasant and merchant rebels were no match for professional armies. The Jacquerie met its end at Meaux, outside Paris, where an aristocratic force cut the peasants to pieces. Survivors were systematically hunted down and hung or burned alive. The Parisian revolt met a similar fate. Aristocratic armies surrounded the city and cut off its food supply. Marcel was assassinated and the dauphin Charles regained the city.

The English Peasants' Revolt.   The French revolts set the pattern for similar uprisings across Europe. Rebels were usually relatively prosperous peasants or townspeople whose economic situations were threatened by aristocratic attempts to turn back the clock to the period before the Black Death. In 1381, English peasants, reacting to new and hated taxes, rose in a less violent but more coordinated revolt known as the Great Rebellion. Peasant revolts took place in the northern Spanish region of Catalonia in 1395 and in Germany throughout the fourteenth and fifteenth centuries. The largest was the great Peasant's Revolt of 1524. Although always ruthlessly suppressed, European peasant uprisings continued until the peasant rebellion of 1626 in upper Austria. The outbursts did not necessarily indicate the desperation of Europe's peasantry, but they did reflect the peasants' new belief that they could change their lives for the better through united action.

Urban Uprisings. Urban artisans imitated the example of their rural cousins. Although there had been some uprisings in the Flemish towns before the Black Death, revolts of townspeople picked up momentum in the second half of the fourteenth century. In general, the town rebels were not the destitute urban poor any more than the peasant rebels had been the landless rural poor. Instead, they were generally independent artisans and small tradesmen who wanted to break the control of the powerful guilds.

The one exception to the pattern was the Ciompi revolt of 1378 in Florence. There the wool workers rioted and forced recognition of two guilds of laborers alongside the powerful guilds of masters. The workers and artisans controlled city government until 1382, when mercenaries hired by the elite surrounded the workers' slums and crushed them in bloody house-to-house fighting. In spite of the brutal suppression and ultimate failure of popular revolts, they became permanent, if intermittent, features of the European social landscape. The line from the Jacquerie runs to the storming of the Bastille 431 years later, and beyond.

Living and Dying in Medieval Towns

Population decline, war, and class conflict in France and the Low Countries fatally weakened the vitality of the commercial and manufacturing system of northwestern Europe. The same events reduced the market for Italian goods and undermined the economic strength of the great Italian cities. The Hundred Years' War bankrupted many of Florence's greatest banking houses, such as the Bardi and Peruzzi, who lent to both French and English kings. Commercial activity declined as well. While in the 1330s Venice had sent between four and nine trading galleys to Flanders each year, by the 1390s the city was sending only three to five. Genoa, which earlier had led in the trade with the cloth towns of the north, saw the economic activity of its port decline by roughly one-third to one-half during the same period. While Italians did not disappear from northern cities, they no longer held a near monopoly on northern trade.

Events outside of Europe also led to the decline of Italian economic power. In the course of the fourteenth and fifteenth

centuries, the Mongol Khanates gradually lost power or were absorbed into local traditions. In China, adherents of the White Lotus sect, a millenarian, messianic offshoot of Buddhism, led the revolt that established the Ming dynasty. In western Asia Tamerlane (1370–1405), a Muslim of Mongolian descent, briefly and brutally restored the Khanate but after his death Turkish peoples divided his vast lands among tribal rulers. In Russia, the Duke Ivan I of Moscow (1328–1341) rose to power by persuading the Mongols to appoint him as the sole collector of tribute from the various Slavic states. A century later his successor Prince Ivan III the Great (1462–1505) led a successful revolt against the remnants of Mongol rule, subjugated the other Russian princes to himself and assumed the title of tsar (or caesar). The disintegration of the Mongol Empire and the rise of new, aggressive kingdoms also caused disruptions of the Silk Route and Italian trade with China and India. Soon, Europeans would begin to look for alternative routes to the East.

Economic Shifts. The setbacks of the Italians worked to the advantage of German towns in the disintegrating empire. Along the Baltic Sea, in Scandinavia, and in northern Germany, towns such as Lübeck, Lüneburg, Visby, Bremen, and Cologne formed a commercial and political alliance to control northern trade. During the second half of the fourteenth century, the **Hanseatic League**—the word *Hansa* means "company"—monopolized

■ The Hanseatic League. Merchant cities formed a powerful confederation that dominated northern trade from Sweden to central Europe.

the northern grain trade and forced Denmark to grant its members exclusive rights to export Scandinavian fish throughout Europe. Hanseatic merchants established colonies from Novgorod to London and Bruges, and even to Venice. They carried dried and salted fish to Prague and supplied grain from Riga to England and France.

English towns also profited from the decline of Flanders and France. The population decline of the fourteenth century led many English landowners to switch from traditional farming to sheep raising, since pasturing sheep required few workers and promised cash profits. While surviving peasants were driven off the land and forced to beg for a living, lords produced more wool than ever before. However, instead of exporting the wool to Flanders to be made into cloth, the English began to make cloth themselves. Protected by high tariffs on imports and low duties on exports, England had become a major exporter of finished cloth by the middle of the fifteenth century.

Addressing Poverty and Crime.   The new social and economic circumstances of European towns accentuated the gulf between rich and poor. The streets and markets of fifteenth-century towns bustled with the sights and sounds of rich Hanseatic merchants, Italian bankers, and prosperous local tradesmen. The back alleys and squatter settlements on the edges of the towns teemed with a growing mass of desperate and despairing workers and their families. The combination of economic depression, plague, and rural crisis deepened the misery of the growing population of urban poor. Driven both by mounting compassion for the urban poor and by a growing fear of the violent potential of that ever-increasing population, medieval towns developed novel systems to deal with poverty. The first was public assistance, the second was social control and repression.

Traditionally, charity had been a religious act that focused more on the soul of the giver than on the effect on the life of the recipient. The same had been true of charitable organizations such as confraternities and hospitals. Confraternities were pious religious organizations of lay people and clergy who ministered to the poor and sick. Hospitals were all-purpose religious institutions providing lodging for pilgrims, the elderly, and the ill. By the fourteenth century, such pious institutions had become inadequate to deal with the growing numbers of poor and ill. Towns began to assume control over a centralized system of public assistance. New, specialized institutions appeared for the care of different categories of the poor, including the ill, women in childbirth, the aged, orphans, and travelers. Pesthouses were founded in which plague victims could be isolated. Hospitals also distributed food to the poor. In 1403, the hospital of the Holy Spirit in Cologne supported more than 1400 paupers per week. Seventy years later, that number had grown to almost 5000.

Although men and women who had taken religious vows staffed the institutions, city governments contributed to their budgets and oversaw their finances. Cities also attempted to rationalize the distribution of charity according to need and merit. Antwerp, for example, established a centralized relief service, which distributed badges to those deemed worthy of public assistance. Only those who presented their badges could receive food. The system spread throughout Europe in the fourteenth century.

At the same time that towns began to organize public assistance, they attempted to control more strictly the activities of the urban poor. In the fourteenth century, Nuremberg forbade begging to everyone except those who had received a special license. In Strasbourg, blind beggars organized an official "Confraternity of Strasbourg Beggars" on the model of other professional guilds, with its own officers, regulations, and membership requirements. Many towns, fearing wandering professional beggars and landless peasants, allowed them to remain only three days before being expelled.

One consequence of poverty was increased crime. Fear of the poor led to repressive measures and harsh punishments. Traditionally, in much of Europe, crimes such as robbery, larceny, and even manslaughter had been punishable by fines

■ Breaking on the wheel was a particularly gruesome punishment inflicted on condemned criminals during the Later Middle Ages. The criminal's broken limbs are threaded through the spokes of the wheel and tied with ropes. The mocking executioner holding leftover rope stands at the right. To the left are three seemingly sympathetic spectators.

and payments to the victim or the victim's heirs. Elsewhere, as in France and England, where corporal punishment had been the normal penalty for major crimes, hanging, blinding, and the loss of a hand or foot had been the most common punishments. During the Later Middle Ages, gruesome forms of mutilation and execution became common for a long list of offenses. Petty larceny was punished with whipping, cutting off ears or thumbs, branding, or expulsion. In some towns, robbery of an amount greater than three pence was punished with death. Death by hanging might be replaced by more savage punishments such as breaking on the wheel. In that particularly brutal torture, the prisoner's limbs and back were first broken with a wagon wheel. Then the criminal was tied to the wheel and left on a pole to die. Drowning, boiling, burning, and burial alive—a particularly common punishment for women— were other frequently used methods of execution.

The frequency of such punishments increased with their severity. In Augsburg, until the middle of the thirteenth century, executions were so rare that the city did not even have a public executioner before 1276. However, in the following two centuries, the city fathers increased executions in an attempt to control what they perceived as an ever rising crime rate, largely attributed to the growing masses of the poor. In 1452, the skulls of 250 hanged persons were found in pits on the gallows hill. At the same time, the bodies of 32 thieves twisted in the wind above.

THE SPIRIT OF THE LATER MIDDLE AGES

The Dance of Death and the gallows were not the only images of later medieval life. The constant presence of death made life more precious. Europeans celebrated life with a vigor and creativity characterized by a growing sense of individuality, independence, and variety. During the fourteenth century, the Church failed to provide unified spiritual and cultural leadership to Europe. The institutional division of the Church was paralleled by divisions over how to lead the proper Christian life. Many devout Christians developed independent lifestyles intended to bring them closer to God without reliance on the Church hierarchy. They elaborated beliefs that the Church branded as heresy. Others called into question the philosophical bases of theological speculation developed since the time of Abelard and Aquinas. Finally, the increasing pluralism of European culture gave rise to new literary traditions that both celebrated and criticized the medieval legacy of Christianity, chivalry, and social order.

The Crisis of the Papacy

DOCUMENT

Pope Boniface
VIII, *Unam
Sanctam*

The universal empire as well as its traditional competitor, the universal Church, declined in the Later Middle Ages. The papacy never recovered from the humiliating defeat Pope Boniface VIII suffered at the hands of King Philip the Fair in 1303. The ecclesiastical edifice created by the thirteenth-century popes

was shaken to its foundations, first by becoming a virtual appendage of the French monarchy and then by a dispute that for more than 40 years gave European Christians a choice between two, and finally three, claimants to the chair of Saint Peter.

In 1305 the College of Cardinals elected as pope the bishop of Bordeaux. The new pope, who took the name Clement V (1305–1314), was close to Philip IV of France and had no desire to meet the fate of his predecessor, Pope Boniface VIII. Thus Clement took up residence, not in Rome, but in the papal city of Avignon on the east bank of the Rhone River. Technically, Avignon was a papal estate within the Holy Roman Empire. Actually, with France just across the river, the pope at Avignon was under French control.

The Avignon Papacy. For the next 70 years, French popes and French cardinals ruled the Church. The traditional enemies of France, as well as religious reformers who expected leadership from the papacy, looked on the situation with disgust. The Italian poet Petrarch (1304–1374) denounced what he termed the "Babylonian captivity" of the papacy in especially bitter tones:

> Now I am living in France, in the Babylon of the West. The sun in its travels sees nothing more hideous than this place on the shores of the wild Rhone. Here reign the successors of the poor fishermen of Galilee; they have strangely forgotten their origin.

Although Petrarch went on to accuse the popes and their courtiers of every possible crime and sin, the Avignon popes were no worse than any other great lords of the fourteenth century. In pursuit of political and financial rewards, they had simply lost sight of their roles as religious leaders.

The popes of Avignon were more successful in achieving their financial goals than in winning political power. Although they attempted to follow an independent course in international affairs, their French orientation eroded their influence in European politics, especially in the Holy Roman Empire. Pope John XXII (1316–1334), one of the most unpleasant and argumentative persons ever to hold the chair of Peter, tried to block the election of the Wittelsbach Louis of Bavaria as emperor. Louis ignored the pope, invaded Italy, and was proclaimed emperor by the people of Rome. In 1338, the German electors solemnly declared that the imperial office was held directly from God and did not require papal confirmation—a declaration later upheld in the Golden Bull. No longer could the popes exert any direct influence in the internal affairs of Europe's states.

Frustrated politically, the Avignon popes concentrated on perfecting the legal and fiscal systems of the Church and were enormously successful in concentrating the vast financial and legal power of the Church in the papal office. From the papal court, or curia, they created a vast and efficient central bureaucracy whose primary role was to increase papal revenues.

Revenues came from two main sources. The less lucrative but ultimately more important source was the sale of indulgences. The Church had long taught that sinners who repented might be absolved of their sins and escape the fires of hell. However, they still had to suffer temporary punishment. That punishment, called *penance,* could take the form of fasting, prayer, or performance of some good deed. Failing to do penance on earth, absolved sinners would have to endure a period in purgatory before they could be admitted to heaven. However, since the saints had done more penance than was required to make up for the temporal punishments due them, they had established a treasury of merit—a sort of spiritual bank account. The pope was the "banker" and could transfer some of the positive balance to repentant sinners in return for some pious act, such as contributing money to build a new church. The so-called **indulgences** could be purchased for one's own use or to assist the souls of family members already in purgatory. Papal "pardoners," working on commission, used high-pressure sales pitches to sell indulgences across Europe.

The second and major source of papal income was the sale of Church offices, or benefices. Popes claimed the right to appoint bishops and abbots to all benefices and to collect a hefty tax for the appointment. The system encouraged pluralism, that is, individuals could acquire numerous ecclesiastical benefices scattered across Europe in the same way that lay lords held multiple fiefs and territories from France to Poland. Like the pope, papal appointees often viewed their offices merely as sources of income, leaving pastoral duties, when they were performed at all, to hired local clergy.

The Great Schism. In 1377, Pope Gregory XI (1370–1378) returned from Avignon to Rome but died almost immediately upon arrival. Thousands of Italians, afraid that the cardinals would elect another Frenchman, surrounded the church where they were meeting and demanded an Italian pope. The terrified cardinals elected an Italian, who took the name of Urban VI (1378–1389). Once elected, Urban attempted to reform the curia, but he did so in a most undiplomatic way, insulting the cardinals and threatening to appoint sufficient non-French bishops to their number to end French control of the curia. The cardinals soon left Rome and announced that because the election had been made under duress, it was invalid and Urban should resign. When he refused, they held a second election and chose a Frenchman, Clement VII (1378–1394), who took up residence in Avignon. The Church now had two heads, both with reasonable claims to the office.

The chaos created by the so-called **Great Schism** divided Western Christendom. In every diocese, when a bishop died his successor had to be appointed by the pope. But by which pope? To whom did taxes go? Who received the income from the sale of indulgences or benefices? Did appeals in the Church courts go to Rome or to Avignon? More significantly, since each pope excommunicated the supporters of his opponent, everyone in the West was under a sentence of excommunication. Could anyone be saved?

Communities were divided. When the city of Bruges officially accepted the Avignon pope, many citizens left their homes and professions to live in cities loyal to Rome. Not surprisingly, countries tended to side with one or the other

MAP DISCOVERY

The Great Schism

Consider the divisions of Europe during the Great Schism. What political considerations might have explained the varying loyalties to Rome and to Avignon? Compare this map with the map on p. 293 and speculate on the influence of princely families on the divisions. What effect might such divisions have had on the emperor's power in the Holy Roman Empire?

contender for political reasons. France recognized Clement. France's traditional enemies, England and the empire, recognized Urban. England's traditional enemy, Scotland, accepted Clement. Most of Italy sided with Urban, but the Angevin kingdom of Naples and Sicily recognized Clement, as did most of Spain.

Nothing in Church law or tradition offered a solution to this crisis. Nor did unilateral efforts to settle the crisis succeed. Twice France invaded Italy in an attempt to eliminate Urban but failed both times. Professors at the University of Paris argued that both popes should abdicate, but neither was willing to do so. Moreover, the situation perpetuated itself. When Urban and Clement died, cardinals on both sides elected successors. By the end of the fourteenth century, France and the empire were exasperated with their popes and even the cardinals were determined to end the stalemate.

Conciliarism. Church lawyers argued that a general council alone could end the schism. Both popes opposed the "**conciliarism**" because it suggested that an assembly of the Church rather than the pope held supreme authority. However, in 1408 cardinals from both sides summoned a council in the Italian city of Pisa. The council deposed both rivals and elected a new pope. But the solution only made matters worse, since neither rival accepted the decision of the council. Europe now had to contend with not two popes but three, each claiming to be the true successor of Saint Peter.

Six years later the Council of Constance managed a final solution. There, under the patronage of the emperor-elect Sigismund (1410–1437), cardinals, bishops, abbots, and theologians from across Europe met to resolve the crisis. Their goal was not only to settle the schism but also to reform the Church to prevent a recurrence of such a scandal. The participants at Constance hoped to restructure the Church as a limited monarchy in which the powers of the pope would be controlled through frequent councils. The Pisan and Avignon popes were deposed. The Roman pope, abandoned by all of his supporters, abdicated. Before doing so, however, he formally convoked the council in order to preserve the tradition that a general council had to be called by the pope. Finally, the council elected as pope an Italian cardinal not aligned with any of the claimants. The election of the cardinal, who took the name Martin V (1417–1431), ended the schism.

The relief at the end of the Great Schism could not hide the very real problems left by over a century of papal weakness. The prestige of the papacy had been permanently compromised. Everywhere the Church had become more national in character. The conciliarist demand for control of the Church, which had ended the schism, lessened the power of the pope. Moreover, during the century between Boniface VIII and Martin V, new religious movements had taken root across Europe, movements that the political creatures who had occupied the papal office could neither understand nor control. The Council of Constance, which brought an end to the schism, also condemned Jan Hus, the leader of the Czech reform movement and the spiritual founder of the Protestant reformation of the sixteenth century. The disintegration of the Church loomed ever closer as pious individuals turned away from the organized Church and sought divine help in personal piety, mysticism, or even magic.

Discerning the Spirit of God

When Joan of Arc first appeared before the dauphin in 1429, he feared that she was a witch. Only a physical examination by matrons, which determined that she was a virgin, persuaded him otherwise—witches were believed to have had intercourse with the devil. In 1431, the English burned Joan as a heretic. For the two years between 1429 and 1431 and long afterward, many venerated her as a saint. Everyone in the Later Middle Ages was familiar with witches, saints, and heretics. Distinguishing among them was often a matter of perspective.

Witchcraft. Accusations of witchcraft were relatively rare in the Middle Ages. The age of witch hunts occurred in the sixteenth and seventeenth centuries. During the Middle Ages, people believed magic existed in a wide variety of forms, but its definition was fluid and its practitioners were not always considered witches. Alchemists and astrologers held honored places in society, while simple practitioners of folk religion, medicine, and superstition were condemned—particularly when they were poor women.

Witches, believed to have made a contract with the devil, were condemned as a type of heretic and were persecuted like other heretics. Only at the end of the fifteenth century, with the publication of *The Witch Hammer*, a great handbook for inquisitors, did the European witch craze begin in earnest. Earlier, authorities had been more fearful of those people who sought their own pacts, not with the devil, but with God.

Lay Piety. Even as Europeans were losing respect for the institutional Church, people everywhere were seeking closer and more intimate relationships with God. Distrusting the formal institutions of the Church, lay persons and clerics turned to private devotions and mysticism to achieve union with the divine. They developed their own forms of devotion based on translations of the Bible into their native languages. They looked for a direct relationship with God, thus minimizing the importance of the Church hierarchy. Most, like the Beguines and Beghards of northern Europe, stayed within the Church. Others, among them many female mystics, maintained an ambiguous relationship with the traditional institutions of Christianity. A few, such as the Brethren of the Free Spirit, broke sharply with it.

In the fourteenth and fifteenth centuries, a great many pious lay men and women chose to live together in order to strive for spiritual perfection without entering established religious orders. The female Beguines and male Beghards of northern cities often formed miniature towns-within-towns. The Brethren of the Common Life in the Rhineland and Low Countries dedicated themselves to preaching, charity, and a pious life. In the early fifteenth century, an unknown member of the Brethren wrote the *Imitation of Christ,* a book of spiritual direction that continues to be the most widely read religious text after the Bible.

Christians of the Later Middle Ages sought to imitate Christ and venerated the Eucharist, or communion wafer, which the Church taught was the actual body of Christ. Male mystics focused on imitating Christ in his poverty, his suffering, and his humility. The Spiritual Franciscans made radical poverty the cornerstone of their belief and the yardstick by which to judge Christian action. The furor between the Spiritual Franciscans and the more moderate Conventuals led Pope John XXII to condemn radical poverty in 1323 and to begin persecuting the Spirituals as heretics. As the wealth and luxury of the Church hierarchy increased, so did the spiritual reaction against it.

A Woman Before the Inquisition

In 1320, Jacques Fournier (ca. 1280–1342), bishop of Pamiers in France and the future Pope Benedict XII, interrogated the villagers of Montaillou in southern France about their involvement in the Cathar heresy, a dualist religion present in the region since the eleventh century. The following excerpt is from the testimony of Béatrice de Planissoles, a member of the lower nobility and a prominent inhabitant of the village.

Focus Questions

What does Béatrice mean by "good Christians"? What makes the Cathars willing to accept death?

Twenty-six years ago during the month of August, I was the wife of the late knight Bérenger de Roquefort, castellan of Montaillou. The late Raimond Roussel was the intendant and the stewart of our household which we held at the castle of Montaillou. He often asked me to leave with him and to go to Lombardy with the good Christians who are there, telling me that the Lord had said that man must quit his father, mother, wife, husband, son and daughter and follow him, and that he would give him the kingdom of heaven. When I asked him, "How could I quit my husband and my sons?" he replied that the Lord had ordered it and that it was better to leave a husband and sons whose eyes rot than to abandon him who lives for eternity and who gives the kingdom of heaven.

When I asked him, "How is it possible that God created so many men and women if many of them are not saved?" he answered that only the good Christians will be saved and no others, neither religious nor priests, nor anyone except these good Christians. Because, he said, just as it is impossible for a camel to pass through the eye of a needle, it is impossible for those who are rich to be saved. This is why the kings and princes, prelates and religious, and all those who have wealth, cannot be saved, but only the good Christians. . . . He also told me that all spirits sinned at the beginning with the sin of pride, believing that they could know more and be worth more than God, and for that they fell to earth. These spirits later take on bodies, and the world will not end before all of them have been incarnated into the bodies of men and women. Thus it is that the soul of a newborn child is as old as that of an old man.

He also said that the souls of men and women who were not good Christians, after leaving their bodies, enter the bodies of other men and women a total of nine times. If in these nine bodies they do not find the body of a good Christian, the soul is damned. If, on the contrary, they find the body of a good Christian, the soul is saved.

I asked him how the spirit of a dead man or woman could enter the mouth of a pregnant woman and from there into the mouth of the fruit that she carries in her womb. He answered that the spirit could enter the fruit of the woman's womb by any part of her body.

Thus he urged me to leave with him so that we could go together to the good Christians, mentioning various noble women who had gone there. Alesta and Serena, women of Châteauverdun, painted themselves with colors which made them appear foreign, so that they could not be recognized and went to Toulouse. When they arrived at an inn, the hostess wanted to know if they were heretics and gave them live chickens, telling them to prepare them because she had things to do in town, and left the house. [Cathars avoided killing and eating animals.] When she had returned she found the chickens still alive and asked them why they had not prepared them. They responded that if the hostess would kill them, they would prepare them but that they would not kill them. The hostess heard that and went to tell the inquisitors that two heretics were in her establishment. They were arrested and burned. When it was time to go to the stake, they asked for water to wash their faces, saying that they would not go to God painted thusly.

I told Raimond that they would have done better to abandon their heresy than to allow themselves to be burned, and he told me that the good Christians did not feel fire because fire with which they are burned cannot hurt them.

Women developed their own form of piety, which focused not on wealth and power but on spiritual nourishment, particularly as provided by the Eucharist. For women mystics, radical fasting became preparation for the reception of the Eucharist, often described in highly emotional and erotic terms. After a long period of fasting, Lukardis of Oberweimar (d. 1309) had a vision in which Christ appeared to her as a handsome youth and blew into her mouth. In the words of her biographer, "She was infused with such sweetness and such inner fruition that she felt as if drunk." From the age of 23, Catherine of Siena (d. 1380) subsisted entirely on the Eucharist, cold water, and bitter herbs that she sucked and then spat out. She wrote of the importance of the Eucharist, "We must attach ourselves to the breast of Christ crucified, which is the source of charity, and by means of that flesh we draw milk." For pious women, fasting and devotion to the

Eucharist did not mean rejection of the body but rather were attempts to use their senses to approach perfect union with God, who was for them both food and drink.

Heresy and Revolt

Only a thin line separated the saint's heroic search for union with God from the heretic's identification with God. The radical Brethren of the Free Spirit believed that God was all things and that all things would return to God. Such pantheism denied the possibility of sin, punishment, and the need for salvation. Members of the sect were hunted down, and many were burned as heretics. Local bishops and clergy often confused Beguines, Beghards, and Brethren of the Common Life with adherents of the Free Spirit movement. The specter of the Inquisition, the ecclesiastical court system charged with ferreting out heretics, hung over all such communities.

John Wycliffe.   When unorthodox Christians were protected by secular lords, the ecclesiastical courts were powerless. Such was the case with John Wycliffe (ca. 1330–1384), an Oxford theologian who attacked the doctrinal and political bases of the Church. He taught that the value of the sacraments depended on the worthiness of the priest administering them. He also insisted that God conferred ecclesiastical authority on individuals, but that an individual, be he priest, bishop, or pope, who was sinful forfeited the right to exercise that authority. He also taught that Christ was present in the

■ In this illustration from a fifteenth-century chronicle, Jan Hus, wearing a heretic's hat, is shown being burned at the stake.

Eucharist only in spirit, that indulgences were useless, and that salvation depended on divine predestination rather than individual merit. Normally, those teachings would have led him to the stake. But he had also attacked the Church's right to wealth and luxury, an idea whose political implications pleased the English monarchy and nobility. Wycliffe's own exemplary manner of life and his teaching that the Church's role in temporal affairs should be severely limited made him an extremely popular figure in England. Thus he was allowed to live and teach in peace. Only under Henry V (1413–1422) were Wycliffe's followers, known as Lollards, vigorously suppressed by the state.

Before that condemnation took place, however, Wycliffe's teachings reached the kingdom of Bohemia through the marriage of Charles IV's daughter Anne of Bohemia to the English king Richard II. Anne took with her to England a number of Bohemian clerics, some of whom studied at Oxford and absorbed the political and religious teachings of Wycliffe, which they then took back to Bohemia. In Prague, some of Wycliffe's less radical teachings took root among the theology faculty of the new university. Wycliffe's ideas were particularly popular with Czech professors of theology, who were demanding not only a reform of religious teaching and practice but also a reduction of the influence of German professors in the University of Prague.

Jan Hus.   The leading proponent of Wycliffe's teachings in Prague was Jan Hus (1373–1415), an immensely popular young master and preacher. Although Hus rejected Wycliffe's ideas about the priesthood and the sacraments, he and other Czech preachers attacked indulgences and demanded a reform of Church liturgy and morals. They grafted those religious demands onto an attack on German dominance of the Bohemian kingdom. The attacks outraged both the Pisan pope John XXIII (1410–1415) and the Bohemian king Wenceslas IV (1378–1419), who favored the German faction. The pope excommunicated Hus, and the king expelled the Czech faculty from the university. Hus believed that he was not a heretic and that a fair hearing would clear him. He therefore agreed to travel to the Council of Constance under promise of safe conduct from the emperor-elect Sigismund to defend his position. There he was tried on a charge of heresy, convicted, and burned at the stake.

News of Hus's execution touched off a revolt in Bohemia. Unlike the peasant revolts of the past, however, the revolt had broad popular support throughout all levels of Czech society. Peasants, nobles, and townspeople saw the attack on Hus and his followers as an attack on Czech independence and national interest by a Church and an empire controlled by Germans. The rebels slaughtered the largely German city council and defeated an army sent by emperor-elect Sigismund to crush the revolt. Soon a radical faction known as the Taborites was demanding the abolition of private property and the institution of a communal state. Although moderate **Hussites** and Bohemian Catholics combined to defeat the radicals in 1434, most of Bohemia remained

Hussite throughout the fifteenth century. The sixteenth-century reformer Martin Luther declared himself a follower of Jan Hus.

Religious Persecution in Spain

A different anxiety about religious unity existed in the Iberian peninsula, where since the eleventh century Christian conquest had brought thousands of Jews and Muslims under Christian rule. These populations were the key to the economic and cultural vitality of the peninsula, and the kings of Castile, Aragon, and other Iberian monarchies initially took pains to protect their non-Christian subjects. However, in the fourteenth and fifteenth centuries, these protections disappeared in the face of rising xenophobia.

Jews had been a part of the Iberian population since Roman times and, while persecuted by the Visigoths, they had flourished under more benign Islamic rule. As the Conquest

---

CONVIVENCIA

By the High Middle Ages the position of Jews in western Europe was difficult. They had been expelled from England and from France. In Spain, under a system known as Convivencia, *or living together, they still enjoyed royal protection. However, as this text, known as* Las Siete Partidas, *issued in 1263 by King Alfonso X of Castile and in force through the fourteenth and fifteenth centuries shows, hostility, fueled by unfounded rumors of ritual murder, was making Jewish life increasingly precarious.*

Focus Questions

What beliefs and prejudices led to Christians' intolerance toward Jews? What protections did Jews receive from the king?

Jews should pass their lives among Christians quietly and without disorder, practicing their own religious rites, and not speaking ill of the faith of Our Lord Jesus Christ, which Christians acknowledge. Moreover, a Jew should be very careful to avoid preaching to, or converting any Christian, to the end that he may become a Jew, by exalting his own belief and disparaging ours. Whoever violates this law shall be put to death and lose all his property. And because we have heard it said that in some places Jews celebrated, and still celebrate Good Friday, which commemorates the Passion of Our Lord Jesus Christ, by way of contempt; stealing children and fastening them to crosses, and making images of wax and crucifying them, when they cannot obtain children; we order that, hereafter, if in any part of our dominions anything like this is done, and can be proved, all persons who were present when the act was committed shall be seized, arrested and brought before the king; and after the king ascertains that they are guilty, he shall cause them to be put to death in a disgraceful manner, no matter how many there may be.

We also forbid any Jew to dare to leave his house or his quarter on Good Friday, but they must all remain shut up until Saturday morning; and if they violate this regulation, we decree that they shall not be entitled to reparation for any injury or dishonor inflicted upon them by Christians.

Saturday is the day on which Jews perform their devotions, and remain quiet in their lodgings, and do not make contracts or transact any business; and for the reason that they are obliged by their religion, to keep it, no one should on that day summon them or bring them into court. Wherefore we order that no judge shall employ force or any constraint upon Jews on Saturday, in order to bring them into court on account of their debts; or arrest them; or cause them any other annoyance; for the remaining days of the week are sufficient for the purpose of employing compulsion against them, and for making demands for things which can be demanded of them, according to law. Jews are not bound to obey a summons served upon them on that day; and, moreover, we decree that any decision rendered against them on Saturday shall not be valid; but if a Jew should wound, kill, rob, steal, or commit any other offense like these for which he can be punished in person and property, then the judge can arrest him on Saturday.

We also decree that all claims that Christians have against Jews, and Jews against Christians shall be decided and determined by our judges in the district where they reside, and not by their old men. And as we forbid Christians to bring Jews into court or annoy them on Saturday; so we also decree that Jews, neither in person, nor by their attorneys, shall have the right to bring Christians into court, or annoy them on this day. And in addition we forbid any Christian, on his own responsibility, to arrest wrong any Jew either in his person or property, but where he has any complaint against him he must bring it before our judges; and if anyone be so bold as to use violence against the Jews, or rob them of anything he shall return them double the value of the same.

Las Siete Partidas, tr. Samuel Parsons Scott (Chicago: Published for the Comparative Law Bureau of the American Bar Association by Commerce Clearing House, Inc., 1931).

of Spain progressed, Jewish artisans, merchants, farmers, physicians, royal advisers, and moneylenders formed an important community in these new kingdoms. Because they were under direct control (and taxation) of the king rather than of local authorities, they enjoyed special royal protection and considerable rights of self-government, although they continued to be mistrusted by their Christian neighbors and were denigrated as "Christ killers" and suspected of all sorts of crimes.

Life for Muslims in Christian Spain was more difficult. Early, benign treatment by conquerors was condemned by northern clergy in their entourages, particularly by Cluniac monks. Too, Muslims under Christan rule were co-religionists of independent Muslim states in the peninsula, and Christian rulers feared subversion and revolt, such as actually did occur in Castile in 1264.

Nevertheless, through the thirteenth century, while kings of England and France expelled Jews from their kingdoms and in Germany they were subject to sporadic pogroms and massacres, Spanish Jewish and Muslim communities managed to survive. This fragile existence was shattered in the fourteenth and fifteenth centuries. The causes were complex: a declining economy, political unrest, Christian triumphalism as the reconquest moved into its last stages, and nascent nationalism all increased intercultural tensions. In 1391, mendicant friars inflamed Aragon with preaching against Jews and caused widespread violent attacks. Thereafter, in towns across Spain Christians rose up in arms against their Jewish neighbors in riots animated both by a hatred of Jews and a protest against the king. Thousands died and thousands more were forced to convert.

The Muslim population fared no better. In the fifteenth century Muslims faced conversion or expulsion, first to Granada and, after that last Muslim principality fell in 1492, to North Africa. Those who resisted were hunted down, their villages destroyed, and their populations dispersed.

In time, even Muslim and Jewish converts (termed respectively *moriscos* and *conversos*) found that Christian baptism was not necessarily a protection. Most moriscos remained secretly faithful to Islam and were ruthlessly persecuted and expelled. Many conversos also continued to practice their faith in secret for generations. However, many descendants of Jewish converts became sincere Christians: their ranks included bishops, inquisitors, and even saints (such as Teresa of Ávila). Nevertheless, Spaniards became obsessed with fears of anyone descended from Jews or Muslims and instituted legal sanctions against anyone who could not prove "purity of blood," that is, who might have Jewish or Muslim ancestors.

William of Ockham and the Spirit of Truth

The critical and individualistic approach that characterized religion during the Later Middle Ages was also typical of the philosophical thought of the period. The delicate balance between faith and reason taught by Aquinas and other intellectuals in the thirteenth century disintegrated in the fourteenth. As in other areas of life, intellectuals questioned the basic suppositions of their predecessors, directing intellectual activity away from general speculations and toward particular, observable reality.

The person primarily responsible for the new intellectual climate was the English Franciscan William of Ockham (ca. 1300–1349). Ockham was no ivory-tower intellectual. He was a dedicated Spiritual Franciscan whose defense of radical poverty led to his excommunication by the cantankerous Pope John XXII. Excommunication drove Ockham to the court of John's enemy, the emperor Louis IV, where he became a dedicated propagandist for the imperial cause. There he developed a truly radical political philosophy. Imperial power, Ockham argued, derived not from the pope but from the people. He believed that people should be free to determine their own form of government and to elect rulers. They should be able to make their choice directly, as in the election of the emperor by electors who represent the people, or implicitly, through continuing forms of government. In either case, Ockham believed, government should be entirely secular and neither popes nor bishops nor priests should have any role. Ockham went still further. He denied the absolute authority of the pope, even in spiritual matters. Rather, Ockham argued, parishes, religious orders, and monasteries should send representatives to regional synods that in turn would elect representatives to general councils. Both laypersons and clergy would serve on the councils, which were to act rather like parliaments, tempering papal absolutism.

As radical as Ockham's political ideas were, his philosophical outlook was even more extreme and exerted a more direct and lasting influence. The Christian Aristotelianism that developed in the thirteenth century had depended on the validity of general concepts, called *universals,* that could be analyzed through the use of logic. Aquinas and others who studied the eternity of the world, the existence of God, the nature of the soul, and other philosophical questions believed that people could reach general truths by abstracting universals from particular, individual cases. Ockham argued that universals were merely names, no more than convenient tags for discussing individual things. He stated that universals had no connection with reality and could not be used to reason from particular observations to general truths. Ockham's radical **nominalism** (from the Latin *nomen,* "name") thus denied that human reason could aspire to certain truth. For Ockham and his followers, philosophical speculation was essentially a logical, linguistic exercise, not a way to certain knowledge.

Ockham died in 1349, a victim of the plague, but his political and philosophical teachings lived on. His ideas on Church governance by a general council representing the whole Christian community offered the one hope for a solution to the Great Schism that erupted shortly after his death. Conciliarists such as Pierre d'Ailly (1350–1420) and Jean de Gerson (1363–1429) drew on Ockham's attack on papal absolutism to propose an alternative church. The Council of Constance, which ended the schism, was the fruit of Ockham's political theory, as were the various organizational structures of the Protestant churches of the sixteenth century.

Just as Ockham's political theory dominated the later four-teenth century, his nominalist philosophy won over the philosophical faculties of Europe. Since he had discredited the power of Aristotelian logic to increase knowledge, the result was, on the one hand, a decline in abstract speculation, and on the other hand, a greater interest in scientific observation of individual phenomena. The next generation Parisian professors, trained in the tradition of Ockham, laid the foundation for scientific studies of motion and the universe that led to the scientific discoveries of the sixteenth and seventeenth centuries.

Vernacular Literature and the Individual

Just as the religious and philosophical concerns of the later Middle Ages developed within national frameworks and criticized accepted authority from the perspective of individual experience, the vernacular (as opposed to Latin) literatures of the age began to explore the place of the individual within an increasingly complex society. Across Europe, authors reviewed the traditional values of society with a critical eye, reworking and transforming traditional literary genres into statements both personal and profound.

Italy. In Italy, a trio of Tuscan poets, Dante Alighieri (1265–1321), Francesco Petrarch (1304–1374), and Giovanni Boccaccio (1313–1375), not only made Italian a literary language but composed in it some of the greatest literature of all time. Dante, the first and greatest of the three, was born into a modest but respectable Florentine family, and after receiving an excellent education entered the public life of his city. At the same time, he began writing poetry and quickly acquired a reputation for his ability to express in love lyrics a new sensitivity and individual expression. In 1301, he fell victim to the viciousness of Florentine politics and was exiled from his beloved city for the remainder of his life. For two decades he traveled throughout Italy, residing in the courts of friendly princes and writing philosophical treatises and literary works, which culminated in his *Divine Comedy,* written during the last years of his life.

The Divine Comedy is a view of the whole Christian universe, populated with people from antiquity and from Dante's own day. The poem is both a sophisticated summary of philosophical and theological thought at the beginning of the four-

DOCUMENT

Dante, *Divine Comedy*

teenth century and an astute political commentary on his times. The poet sets this vision within a three-part poetic journey through hell (*Inferno*), purgatory (*Purgatorio*), and heaven (*Paradiso*). In each part, Dante adopts a poetic style appropriate to the subject matter. His journey through hell to witness the sufferings of the damned is described in brutal, immediate language that lets readers almost feel the agony of the condemned, each of whom receives an eternal punishment appropriate to his or her sins. The violent conquerors Alexander the Great and Attila the Hun, for example, wallow for all eternity in boiling blood as punishment for spilling the blood of so many others.

■ A miniature painted by Guglielmo Giraldi to illustrate Canto VIII of Dante's *Inferno* shows Dante and Virgil being ferried across the River Styx by the boatman Phlegyas.

In purgatory, Dante meets sinners whose punishments will someday end. Those he described in a language of dreams and imagination, of nostalgic recollections cast in a misty landscape of the memory. On a ledge populated by hoarders and wasters, for example, the poet hears but does not see Hugh Capet, founder of the French Capetian dynasty, who describes a vision of his greedy descendants who devastate Italy to gain riches. Dante described paradise in a symbolic language that is nonphysical and nonrepresentational. In the face of transcendent perfection, human imagery and poetry fail. In his final vision of heaven, he sees the reflected light of a mystical rose in which the saints are ranked. Those include both religious leaders such as Bernard of Clairvaux and political leaders such as Emperor Henry VII, grandfather of Charles IV. *The Divine Comedy* is Dante's personal summary of all that was good and bad in medieval culture and politics.

England.   English literature emerged from more than two centuries of French cultural domination with the writings of William Langland (ca. 1330–1395) and Geoffrey Chaucer (ca. 1343–1400). Both presented images of contemporary society with a critical and often ironic view. In *Piers Plowman*, Langland presents society from the perspective of the peasantry. Chaucer's work is much more sophisticated and wide-ranging, weaving together the whole spectrum of late medieval literature and life.

Chaucer was born into a London merchant family and spent a long and successful career as a courtier, serving English aristocrats and finally the king both in England and on the Continent. His travels brought him into contact with the literary and philosophical traditions of all of Europe, and he mastered every genre, always molding them with wit and imagination into something new.

Dante had set his great poem within a vision of the other world. Chaucer placed his tales in the mouths of a group of 30 pilgrims traveling to the tomb of Thomas à Becket at Canterbury. The pilgrims represent every walk of life and spectrum of medieval society: a simple knight, a vulgar miller, a lawyer, a lusty widow, a merchant, a squire, a physician, a nun, her chaplain, and a monk, among others. Each pilgrim is at once strikingly individual and representative of his or her profession or station in life. The tales that they tell are drawn from folklore, Italian literature, the lives of the saints, courtly romance, and religious sermons. However, Chaucer played with the tales and their genres in the retelling. He used them to contrast or illuminate the persons and characters of their tellers, as well as to comment in subtle and complex ways on the literary, religious, and cultural traditions of which they were part. His knight, for example, tells a tale of chivalric love taken from Boccaccio. However, in Chaucer's version, the tale becomes both more real and vivid and more humorous as he plays with the traditional genre of courtly love poetry. The Wife of Bath, a forceful woman who has survived five husbands, argues for the superiority of married life over celibacy, particularly when the wife controls the marriage. Her tale, which takes a form common in religious sermons, continues her argument. It is a retelling of a fairy tale in which a woman is released from a spell by a knight. She offers him the choice of having her ugly and faithful or beautiful and free to bestow her favors where she will. The knight courteously leaves the decision to her and is rewarded by her promise to be both fair and faithful. In his mastery of the whole heritage of medieval culture and his independent use of that heritage, Chaucer proved himself the greatest English writer before Shakespeare.

France.   Much of Italian and English literature drew material and inspiration from French, which continued into the fifteenth century to be the language of courtly romance. In France, literature continued to project an unreal world of allegory and nostalgia for a glorious if imaginary past. Popular literature, developed largely in the towns, often dealt with courtly themes, but with a critical and more realistic eye.

In that literary world appeared a new and extraordinary type of poet, a woman who earned her living with her pen, Christine de Pisan (1364–ca. 1430). Married at 16 and widowed at 25, de Pisan was left virtually impoverished, with the responsibility for supporting herself, her three children, her mother, and a niece. Rather than remarrying, she decided to earn her way as an author—an unheard-of decision for a woman of the fourteenth century. Beginning her education from scratch, she absorbed history and literature and began writing the sorts of conventional love poems popular with the French aristocracy. From there she moved to autobiographical poetry in which she described how fortune had changed her life. Her success was immediate and tremendous. Kings, princes, and aristocrats from England to Italy bought copies of her works and tried to attract her to their courts.

As a professional woman of letters, de Pisan fought the stereotypical medieval image of women as weak, sexually aggressive temptresses. With wit and reason she argued that women could be virtuous and showed the fallacies of traditional antifeminist preaching, poetry, and belief. She appealed to women to develop their own sense of self-worth directly from experience and not to rely on the advice of men, who, no matter how well read, could not have any direct, accurate knowledge of the meaning of being a woman. In her *Hymn to Joan of Arc,* she saluted her famous contemporary for her accomplishments: bringing dignity to women, striving for justice, and working for peace in France.

CHRONOLOGY
THE LATER MIDDLE AGES, 1300–1500

1305–1377	Babylonian Captivity (Avignon papacy)
1337–1452	Hundred Years' War
1347–1352	Black Death spreads throughout Europe
1358	Jacquerie revolt of French peasants; Etienne Marcel leads revolt of Parisian merchants
1378	Ciompi revolt in Florence
1380	Death of Catherine of Siena
1378–1417	Great Schism divides Christianity
1381	Great Rebellion of English peasants
1409–1410	Council of Pisa
1414–1417	Council of Constance ends Great Schism
1415	Jan Hus executed
1431	Death of Joan of Arc
1455–1485	English Wars of the Roses

Although Christine de Pisan was the exception rather than the rule, her life and writing epitomized the new possibilities and new interests of the fifteenth century. They included an acute sense of individuality, a willingness to look for truth not in the clichés of the past but in actual experience, and a readiness to defend one's views with tenacity. Although an heir of the medieval world, de Pisan, like her contemporaries, already embodied the attitudes of a new age. That new age was reflected in a second tradition in fifteenth-century France, that of realist poetry. Around 1453, just as the English troops were enduring a final battering from the French artillery, Duke Charles of Orléans (1394–1465) organized a poetry contest. Each contestant was to write a ballad that began with the contradictory line, "I die of thirst beside the fountain." The duke, himself an outstanding poet, wrote an entry that embodied the traditional courtly themes of love and fortune:

> *I die of thirst beside the fountain,*
> *Shaking from cold and the fire of love;*
> *I am blind and yet guide the others;*
> *I am weak of mind, a man of wisdom;*
> *Too negligent, often cautious in vain,*
> *I have been made a spirit,*
> *Led by fortune for better or for worse.*

An unexpected and very different entry came from the duke's prison. The prisoner-poet François Villon (1432–ca. 1464) was a child of the Paris streets, an impoverished student, a barroom brawler, a killer, and a thief who spent much of his life trying to escape the gallows. He was also the greatest realist poet of the Middle Ages. His entry read:

> *I die of thirst beside the fountain,*
> *Hot as fire, my teeth clattering,*
> *At home I am in an alien land;*

> *I shudder beside a glowing brazier,*
> *Naked as a worm, gloriously dressed,*
> *I laugh and cry and wait without hope,*
> *I take comfort and sad despair,*
> *I rejoice and have no joy,*
> *Powerful, I have no force and no strength,*
> *Well received, I am expelled by all.*

The duke focused on the sufferings of love, the thief on the physical sufferings of the downtrodden. The two poets represent the contradictory tendencies of literature in the Later Middle Ages. From Prague to Paris, vernacular languages everywhere had come into their own. Poets used their native tongues to express a spectrum of sentiments and to describe a spectrum of emotions and values. The themes and ideas expressed ranged from the polished, traditional values of the aristocracy, trying to maintain the ideals of chivalry in a new and changed world, to the views of ordinary people, by turns reverent or sarcastic, joyful or despondent.

CONCLUSION

Late in life, Christine de Pisan relinquished her independence to enter a convent. Charles of Orléans was so moved by Villon's poetry that he released him from prison. The pope and the Hussites came to terms. King Charles VII ordered a new investigation into Joan of Arc, which absolved her—posthumously—of the charge of heresy. The religious, political, and cultural systems of the later Middle Ages remained sufficiently flexible to absorb the contradictory tendencies that they had created. The flexibility would not last. In the next century, the political, religious, and cultural landscapes of Europe would be transformed by the new impulses born in the Later Middle Ages.

■ Christine de Pisan presenting a manuscript of her poems to Isabeau of Bavaria, the wife of King Charles VI of France.

The fourteenth and fifteenth centuries saw demographic collapse brought on by plague and accentuated by overpopulation and the ravages of warfare. They saw the transformation of the masses of the poor from the objects of Christian charity to the objects of fear and mistrust. During those centuries, warfare in France, England, Italy, and elsewhere evolved from elite battles to devastating professional campaigns of mass destruction capable of leaving whole countries in ruins for decades. Peasants fought for survival; aristocrats and wealthy merchants fought for greater power, prestige, and wealth on an international scale. Family alliances and merchant companies bound Europe together in a web of blood and money.

As the inherited forms of social and political organization strained to absorb those new conditions, individuals sought their own answers to the problems of life and death, using the legacy of the past, but using it in novel and creative ways. Dynasts created new principalities without regard for ancient allegiances. Mystics and heretics sought God without benefit of traditional religious hierarchies, and poets and philosophers sought personal expression outside the confines of inherited tradition.

The legacy of the Later Middle Ages was a complex and ambiguous one. The thousand years of synthesis of classical, barbarian, and Christian traditions did not disappear. The bonds holding the world together were not yet broken. But the last centuries of the Middle Ages bequeathed a critical detachment from that heritage expressed in the revolts of peasants and workers, the preaching of radical religious reformers, and the poems of mystics and visionaries.

QUESTIONS FOR REVIEW

1. What social and political forces prevented both the Holy Roman Emperors and the French kings from uniting the lands they ruled?
2. How did disease transform social relations in fourteenth-century Europe?
3. Why did a division in the papacy mean both political chaos and spiritual fear for Europeans?
4. How did the vernacular literature of Dante, Chaucer, and Christine de Pisan represent a departure from previous literary traditions?

KEY TERMS

Black Death, *p. 302*

conciliarism, *p. 310*

Golden Bull, *p. 296*

Great Schism, *p. 309*

Hanseatic League, *p. 306*

Hundred Years' War, *p. 297*

Hussites, *p. 312*

indulgences, *p. 309*

Jacquerie, *p. 305*

nominalism, *p. 314*

DISCOVERING WESTERN CIVILIZATION ONLINE

You can obtain more information about the Later Middle Ages at the Websites listed below. See also the Companion Website that accompanies this text, www.ablongman.com/kishlansky, which contains an online study guide and additional resources.

Politics as a Family Affair

Web Gallery of Art: Bohemian School
www.kfki.hu/~arthp/tours/mini/Bohemian.html
Overview of art and architecture in Bohemia under the patronage of Charles IV.

The Hundred Years' War History Page
geocities.com/Wellesley/Veranda/1912/hundred/history.htm#top
A Web page devoted to the Hundred Years' War.

Life and Death in the Later Middle Ages

Internet Resources on the Black Death
www.historyguide.org/ancient/death.html
An annotated list of Web links to sites about the Great Plague of the fourteenth century.

The Spirit of the Later Middle Ages

Avignon: The Medieval and Papal Period
www.avignon.com/anglais/avi003.html
A brief introduction to Avignon and the papal palaces.

SUGGESTIONS FOR FURTHER READING

General Reading

Robert Bartlett, *The Making of Europe: Conquest, Colonization, and Cultural Change, 950–1350* (Princeton, NJ: Princeton University Press, 1993). A comparative study of Europe's expansion into the Celtic, Islamic, and Slavic worlds in the Later Middle Ages.

Johan Huizinga, *The Autumn of the Middle Ages*, trans. Rodney J. Payton and Ulrich Mammitzsch (Chicago: University of Chicago Press, 1996). An important new translation of the classic interpretation of culture and society in the Burgundian court in the Later Middle Ages.

Daniel Waley, *Later Medieval Europe: From Saint Louis to Luther* (London: Longman, 1985). A brief introduction with a focus on Italy.

Politics as a Family Affair

Richard W. Kaeuper, *Chivalry and Violence in Medieval Europe* (Oxford: Oxford University Press, 1999). A fine analysis of the complex relationship between chivalric ethos and the violence of aristocratic society in the Middle Ages.

Joachim Leuschner, *Germany in the Late Middle Ages* (Amsterdam: Elsevier, 1980). An introduction to late medieval German history.

Jean W. Sedlar, *East Central Europe in the Middle Ages, 1000–1500* (Seattle: University of Washington Press, 1994). A thematic introduction to the medieval history of the region that today comprises Poland, the Czech Republic, Slovakia, Hungary, Romania, Bulgaria, Albania, and the former Yugoslavia.

Life and Death in the Later Middle Ages

P. Dollinger, *The German Hansa* (Stanford, CA: Stanford University Press, 1970). A brief history of the Hansa intended for the nonspecialist.

Bronislaw Geremek, *The Margins of Society in Late Medieval Paris*, trans. Jean Birrell (Cambridge: Cambridge University Press, 1987). A landmark study of the urban poor in the Later Middle Ages.

Edward S. Hunt and James M. Murray, *A History of Business in Medieval Europe, 1200–1550* (Cambridge: Cambridge University Press, 1995). A brief and readable history of medieval business practice.

David Nicholas, *The Growth of the Medieval City: From Late Antiquity to the Early Fourteenth Century* (London, New York: Longman, 1997). A comprehensive survey of medieval towns.

Teofilo F. Ruiz, *Spanish Society 1400–1600* (Harlow: Longman, 2001). A sensitive and original survey of Spanish society at the end of the Middle Ages.

Philip Zieger, *The Black Death* (New York: Sutton Publishing, 1999). A reliable introduction to the plague in the fourteenth century.

The Spirit of the Later Middle Ages

Renate Blumenfeld-Kosinski, ed., trans. Kevin Brownlee, *The Selected Writings of Christine De Pizan: New Translations, Criticism* (New York: Norton, 1997). A selection of de Pizan's works and of scholarship on her. The place to start for learning about her.

Eamon Duffy, *The Stripping of the Altars: Traditional Religion in England, 1400–1580* (New Haven: Yale University Press, 1992). A revisionist study of local religion at the end of the Middle Ages.

David A. Fein, *François Villon Reconsidered* (New York: Macmillan, 1997). Villon's poetry and his life examined by an authority.

Malcolm Lambert, *Medieval Heresy: Popular Movements from the Gregorian Reform to the Reformation*, 2nd ed. (Oxford: Blackwell, 1992). A comprehensive survey of heretical movements from the eleventh to the sixteenth centuries.

Caroline Walker Bynum, *Holy Feast and Holy Fast: The Religious Significance of Food to Medieval Women* (Berkeley: University of California Press, 1987). An imaginative and scholarly examination of the role of food in the spirituality of medieval women.

Scott L. Waugh and Peter D. Diehl, eds., *Christendom and Its Discontents: Exclusion, Persecution, and Rebellion, 1000–1500* (New York: Cambridge University Press, 1995). Important collection of essays on heresy and dissent in western Europe.

For a list of additional titles related to this chapter's topics, please see http://www.ablongman.com/kishlansky.

Chapter 11
THE ITALIAN RENAISSANCE

Chapter Outline

A Renaissance city was a community that shared not only space but also ritual events. These could be both celebrated and memorialized. Examine The Visual Record to see how the artist Gentile Bellini immortalized an important event in the life of Venice. ➤

A Civic Procession
Community Building in Renaissance Venice

It is 25 April 1444, the day Venice celebrates its patron, Saint Mark, with a procession through the square that bears his name. Processions are a common form of civic ritual by which a community defines itself. The special features that identify Venice for its citizens are all on display. City flags and emblems are mounted on poles, and clothes bear the insignia of various orders and groups. The procession recreates all forms of communal life. Here are the religious orders (the white-clad brothers of the Confraternity of Saint John are passing before us now), and the civic leaders can be seen just behind them. Musicians entertain both marchers and onlookers. A band files by on the right. The procession is orderly, but it is by no means contrived. It is not staged, as would be a modern ceremony, and this is evident in the relaxed attitude of ordinary citizens who gather in the middle of the square. There is no apparent drama to observe, and they walk and talk quite naturally. So, too, do the participants. In the lower left-hand corner of the painting shown here, some friars are reading music; at the lower right, members of the confraternity carry their candles negligently.

Yet this painting, *The Procession of the Relic of the Holy Cross* (1496) by Gentile Bellini (ca. 1429–1507), was commissioned to commemorate a miracle rather than a civic procession. On the evening before Saint Mark's Day, a visiting merchant and his son were touring the square when the boy fell and cracked his skull. The doctors who treated him regarded the case as hopeless and prepared the father for his son's death. The next morning, the Brothers of the Confraternity of Saint John paraded their relic of a piece of the cross on which Jesus was crucified. The merchant approached the golden altarpiece containing the relic, dropped to his knees, and prayed that Saint Mark would miraculously cure his son. He is the red-clad figure kneeling just to the right of center, where the line of brothers breaks. The next day the boy revived.

The Brothers of Saint John commissioned Bellini to commemorate the event. He came from the most distinguished family of painters in Venice. His father, Jacopo, had studied in Florence and had brought his sons into his workshop as young boys. Until the age of thirty, Gentile worked on his father's commissions, learning the difficult craft of painting. Art was a family business in fifteenth-century Italy. The large workshops, with their master and apprentices, turned out vast canvasses with assembly-line precision. The master created the composition and sketched it; his skilled assistants, like the Bellini brothers, worked on the more complex parts; and young apprentices painted backgrounds. The master was first and foremost a businessman, gaining commissions to sustain his family and his workers. The Bellinis were connected to the Confraternity of Saint John, and it was only natural that Gentile would receive the lucrative contract.

Although *The Procession of the Relic of the Holy Cross* was designed to recreate a central moment in the history of the confraternity, it is not the confraternity that dominates the picture. Miracles were part of civic life, and each town took pride in the special manifestations of heavenly care that had taken place within it. Thus it is Venice that is the centerpiece

■ *The Procession of the Relic of the Holy Cross* (1496) by Gentile Bellini.

of Bellini's canvas. Dominating the painting is the Basilica of San Marco, with its four great horses over the center portico and the winged lion—the city's symbol—on the canopy above. The procession emanates from the duke's palace to the right of the church, and the great flags of the city are seen everywhere. By the end of the fifteenth century, Venice was one of the greatest powers on earth, the center for international trade and finance. Home to the largest concentration of wealthy families anywhere in Europe, it could well afford the pomp and splendor of its processions.

Looking Ahead

The achievements of God and the achievements of humans blend together in Bellini's painting as they blended together in that era of remarkable accomplishments that historians call the Renaissance. In this chapter we shall see how philosophy, art, architecture, and literature enjoyed a remarkable development in the Italian city-states and how Renaissance ideals were exported throughout the Continent and came to define the age. ➤

RENAISSANCE SOCIETY

Perhaps the most surprising result of the Black Death was the way in which European society revived itself in the succeeding centuries. Even at the height of the plague, a spirit of revitalization was evident in the works of artists and writers. Petrarch (1304–1374), the great humanist poet and scholar, was among the first to differentiate the new age in which he was living from two earlier ones: the classical world of Greece and Rome, which he admired, and the subsequent Dark Ages, which he detested. That spirit of self-awareness is one of the defining characteristics of the **Renaissance.** "It is but in our own day that men dare boast that they see the dawn of better things," wrote Matteo Palmieri (1406–1475). Like many others, Marsilio Ficino (1433–1499), a Florentine physician and philosopher who translated Plato and dabbled in astrology, dubbed his times a golden age: "This century, like a golden age, has restored to light the liberal arts, which were almost extinct: grammar, poetry, rhetoric, painting, sculpture, architecture, and music." The Renaissance was a new age by self-assertion. In that self-assertion, wave after wave of artistic celebration of the human spirit found its wellspring and created a legacy that is still vibrant 500 years later.

What was the Renaissance? A French word for an Italian phenomenon, *renaissance* literally means "rebirth." The word captures both the emphasis on humanity that characterized Renaissance thinking and the renewed fascination with the classical world. But the Renaissance was an age rather than an event. There is no moment at which the Middle Ages ended, and late medieval society was artistically creative, socially well developed, and economically diverse. Yet eventually the pace of change accelerated, and it is best to think of the Renaissance as an era of rapid transitions. Encompassing the two centuries between 1350 and 1550, it passed through three distinct phases. The first, from 1350 to 1400, was characterized by a declining population, the uncovering of classical texts, and experimentation in a variety of art forms. The second phase, from 1400 to 1500, was distinguished by the creation of a set of cultural values and artistic and literary achievements that defined Renaissance style. The large Italian city-states developed stable and coherent forms of government, and the warfare between them gradually ended. In the final period, from 1500 to 1550, invasions from France and Spain transformed Italian political life, and the ideas and techniques of Italian writers and artists radiated to all points of the Continent. Renaissance ideas and achievements spread throughout western Europe and were particularly important in Holland, but they are best studied where they first developed, on the Italian peninsula.

The Urban Environment

The Italian peninsula differed sharply from other areas of Europe in the extent to which it was urban. By the late Middle Ages nearly one in four Italians lived in a town, in contrast to one in ten elsewhere. Not even the plague did much to change that ratio. There were more Italian cities and more people in them. By 1500, seven of the ten largest cities in the West were in Italy. Naples, Venice, and Milan, each with a population of more than 100,000, led the rest. But not every city was a great metropolis, and it was the numerous smaller towns, with populations nearer to 1000, that gave the Italian peninsula its urban character. Cities also served as convenient centers of judicial and ecclesiastical power.

Cities acted as central places around which a cluster of large and small villages was organized. Urban areas, especially the small towns, provided markets for the agricultural produce of the countryside and for the manufactured goods of the urban artisans. This allowed for the specialization in agricultural and industrial life that increased both productivity and wages. Cities also caught the runoff of rural population, especially the surplus of younger sons and daughters who could not be accommodated on the farms. Cities grew by migration rather than by natural increase. Thus the areas surrounding a city were critical to its prosperity and survival. The urban system was a network of cities encompassed by towns and encircled by rural villages. Florence, the dominant city in the region of Tuscany, exemplifies that relationship. Although it possessed two-thirds of its region's wealth, Florence contained only 14 percent of the regional population. The surrounding countryside was agriculturally rich because marketing costs were low and demand for foodstuffs was high. Smaller cities channeled their local produce and trade to Florence.

Although cities may have dominated Renaissance Italy, by present standards they were small in both area and population. Despite the city's wealth, great banks, magnificent palaces, and piazzas, a person could walk across fifteenth-century Florence in less than half an hour. In 1427 its population was 37,000, only half its pre-plague size. Most Italian cities contained large fields for agricultural production, and within the outer walls of Florence were gardens and fields of grain. Inside the inner city walls the people crowded together into tightly packed quarters. The intensity of the stench from raw sewage, rotting foodstuffs, and animals being brought to slaughter was equaled only by the din made by hoofs and wooden cartwheels on paving stones.

Urban populations were organized far differently from rural ones. On the farms, the central distinctions involved ownership of land. Some farmers owned their estates outright and left them intact to their heirs. Others were involved in a sharecropping system by which absentee owners of land supplied working capital in return for half of the farm's produce. A great gulf in wealth separated owners from sharecroppers, but within the groups the gaps were not as great. There were gradations, but those ordinarily were temporary conditions that bad harvests, generous dowries, or divided inheritances balanced out over time.

In the city, however, distinctions were based first on occupation, which largely corresponded to social position and wealth. Cities began as markets, and the privilege to participate in the market defined citizens. City governments provided protection

MAP DISCOVERY

Largest Cities in Western Europe, ca. 1500

Examine the locations of western Europe's largest cities at the beginning of the sixteenth century. Where were these cities concentrated? What was the least urbanized part of Europe? Based on this information, why do you suppose the Mediterranean Sea was considered the center of Europe? What was distinctive about the Holy Roman Empire?

for consumers and producers by creating monopolies through which standards for craftsmanship were maintained and profits for craftsmen were guaranteed. The monopolies were called guilds or companies. Each large city had its own hierarchy of guilds. At the top were the important manufacturing groups— clothiers, metalworkers, and the like. Just below them were bankers, merchants, and the administrators of civic and Church holdings. At the bottom were grocers, masons, and other skilled workers. Roughly speaking, all of those within the guild structure, from bottom to top, lived comfortably. Yet the majority of urban inhabitants were not members of guilds. Many managed to eke out a living as wage laborers; many more were simply destitute. As a group, the poor constituted as much as half of the entire population. Most were dependent upon civic and private charity for their survival.

The disparities between rich and poor were overwhelming. The concentration of wealth in the hands of an ever-narrowing group of families and favored guilds characterized every large city. One reason for that was the extreme instability of economic life. Prices and wages fluctuated wildly in response to local circumstance. After an epidemic of plague, wages climbed and the prices of consumer goods tumbled. A bad harvest sent food prices skyrocketing. Only those able to even out the extreme swings by stockpiling goods in times of plenty and consuming them in times of want were safe. Capital, however initially accumulated, was the key to continued wealth. Monopolies ensured the profitability of trade and manufacturing, but only those with sufficient capital could engage in either. In Florence, for example, 10 percent of the families controlled 90 percent of the wealth, with an even more extreme concentration at the top. The combined wealth of the richest 100 Florentine families was greater than the combined wealth of 87 percent of the city's population.

Production and Consumption

The concentration of wealth and the way in which it was used defined the Renaissance economy. Economic life is bound up in the relationship between resources and desires, or, as economists would have it, supply and demand. The late medieval economy, despite the development of international banking and long-distance trade, was still an economy of primary producers: between 70 and 90 percent of Europe's population was involved in subsistence agriculture. Even in Italy, which contained the greatest concentration of urban areas in the world, agriculture predominated. The manufacture of clothing was the only other significant economic activity. Moreover, most of what was produced was for local consumption rather than for the marketplace. The relationship between supply and demand was precisely measured by the full or empty stomach. Even in good times, more than 80 percent of the population lived at subsistence level with food, clothing, and shelter their only expenses. Thus, when the market economy of the Renaissance is discussed, it actually is the circumstances of the few rather than the many that is under discussion.

The defining characteristic of the early Renaissance economy was population change. Recurring waves of plague kept population levels low for more than a century. Between 1350 and 1450, one in every six years was characterized by an unusually high mortality rate. At the end of that period, for example, Florence's population was only a quarter of what it had been at the beginning. The dramatic reduction in population depressed economic growth. Until 1460 the major sectors of the economy were stagnant. The general economy did not revive until the sustained population increase toward the end of the fifteenth century. Until then, in both agriculture and manufacturing, supply outstripped demand.

On the farms, overabundance resulted from two related developments, the concentration of surviving farmers on the best land and the enlargement of their holdings. In the shops, finished products outnumbered the consumers who survived the epidemics. Overproduction meant lower prices for basic commodities, and the decline in population meant higher wages for labor. The result was that, at the lowest levels of society, survivors found it easier to earn their living and even to

■ Cloth making was a major contributor to European economic growth during the Middle Ages. In this 1470 portrait of Cloth Merchants' Street in Bologna, a tailor (center) measures a prospective client.

create a surplus than had their parents. For a time, the lot of the masses improved.

But for investors, such economic conditions meant that neither agriculture nor cloth making were particularly attractive. Expensive investments in land or equipment for sharecropping were paid back in inexpensive grain. High wages for the few surviving skilled workers brought a return only in cheap cloth. In such circumstances, consumption was more attractive than investment. It was not merely the perceived shortage in profitable investments that brought on the increase in conspicuous consumption during the fifteenth century. In the psychological atmosphere created by unpredictable, swift, and deadly epidemics, luxurious living seemed an appropriate response. Moreover, although tax rates increased, houses and personal property remained exempt, making luxury goods attractive investments. Even those at the lowest levels of society eagerly purchased whatever their meager means permitted.

For those reasons, the production and consumption of luxuries soared. By the middle of the fourteenth century,

Florence was known for its silks and jewelry as much as for its cloth. Venice became a European center for the glass industry, especially for the finely ground glass that was used in eyeglasses. Production of specialty crops such as sugar, saffron, fruits, and high-quality wine expanded. International trade increasingly centered on acquiring Eastern specialities, resulting in the serious outflow of gold and silver that enriched first the Byzantine and then the Ottoman emperors.

The Experience of Life

Luxury helped improve a life that for rich and poor alike was short and uncertain. Nature was still people's most potent enemy. Renaissance children who survived infancy found their lives governed by parentage and by gender. In parentage, the great divide was between those who lived with surplus and those who lived at subsistence. The first category encompassed the wealthiest bankers and merchants down to those who owned their own farms or engaged in small urban crafts. The vast majority of urban and rural dwellers comprised the second category. About the children of the poor we know very little other than that their survival was unlikely. If they did not die at birth or shortly afterward, they might be abandoned—especially if female—to the growing number of orphanages in the cities, waste away from lack of nutrition, or fall prey to ordinary childhood diseases for which there were no treatments. Eldest sons were favored; younger daughters were disadvantaged. In poor families, however, this favoritism meant little more than early apprenticeship to day labor in the city or farm labor in the countryside. Girls were frequently sent out as domestic servants far from the family home.

Childhood.   Children of the wealthy had better chances for survival than did children of the poor. For children of the wealthy, childhood might begin with "milk parents," life in the home of the family of a wet nurse who would breast-feed the baby through infancy. Only the very wealthy could afford a live-in wet nurse, which would increase the child's chances of survival. Again, daughters were more likely to be sent far from home and least likely to have their nursing supervised. The use of wet nurses not only emancipated parents from the daily care of infants, it also allowed them to resume sexual relations. Nursing women refrained from sex in the belief that it affected their milk.

During the period between weaning and apprenticeship, Renaissance children lived with their families. There was no typical Renaissance family. Nuclear families—parents and their children under one roof—were probably more common than extended families, which might include grandparents and other relatives. But the composition of the family changed over the course of the life cycle and included times in which married children or grandparents were present and other times when a single parent and small children were the only members. Moreover, even nuclear families commonly contained stepparents and stepchildren as well as domestic

servants or apprentices. Thus a child returning to the parental household was as likely to form emotional bonds with older siblings as with parents.

The family was an economic unit as well as a grouping of relatives. Decisions to abandon children, to send them away from the household when very young, or to take in domestic servants were based on economic calculations. In the competition for scarce resources, the way in which children were managed might determine the survival of the family unit. Sons could expect to be apprenticed to a trade, probably between the ages of 10 and 13. Most, of course, learned the crafts of their fathers, but not necessarily in their father's shop. By adolescence those fortunate boys, who might have had some rudimentary schooling, were earning token wages that contributed to family income. Sons inherited the family business and its most important possessions—tools of the trade or beasts of labor for the farm. Inheritance customs varied. In some places only the eldest son received the equipment of the family occupation; in others, such as Tuscany, all the sons shared it. Still, in the first 15 years of life, the most-favored children would have spent between one-third and one-half of their time outside the household in which they had been born.

Marriage and the Family.   Expectations for daughters centered on their chances of marriage. For a girl, dowry was everything. If a girl's father could provide a handsome one, her future was secure; if not, the alternatives were a convent, which would take a small bequest, or a match lower down the social scale, where the quality of life deteriorated rapidly. Daughters of poor families entered domestic service in order to have a dowry provided by their masters. The dowry was taken to the household of the husband. There the couple resided until they established their own separate family. If the husband died, it was to his parental household that the widow returned.

DOCUMENT

The Office and Dutie of an Husband

Women married in late adolescence, usually around the age of 20. Among the wealthy, marriages were perceived as familial alliances and business transactions rather than love matches. The dowry was an investment on which fathers expected a return, and while the bride might have some choice, it was severely limited. Compatibility was not a central feature in matchmaking. Husbands were, on average, ten years older than their wives and likely to leave them widows. In the early fifteenth century, about one-fourth of all adult women in Florence were widows, many without prospects of remarriage.

Married women lived in a state of nearly constant pregnancy. Alessandra Strozzi, whose father was one of the wealthiest citizens of Florence, married at the age of 16, gave birth to eight children in ten years, and was widowed at the age of 25. Not all pregnancies produced children. The rates of miscarriages and stillbirths were very high, and abortions and infanticide were not unknown. Only among the families who hovered between surplus and subsistence is there any evidence of attempts to control pregnancies. The efforts, which relied upon techniques such as the rhythm method and withdrawal,

ON THE FAMILY

Leon Battista Alberti wrote a number of important tracts that set out the general principles of a subject, including On Architecture, *which was considered the basic text for 300 years. His writings on the family bring insight into the nature of a patriarchal, male-dominated institution.*

Focus Questions

According to Alberti, why is it important for men to look for an "honorable manner" when choosing a wife? What role would Alberti see the wife playing in a marriage?

They say that in choosing a wife one looks for beauty, parentage, and riches. . . . Among the most essential criteria of beauty in a woman is an honorable manner. Even a wild, prodigal, greasy, drunken woman may be beautiful of feature, but no one would call her a beautiful wife. A woman worthy of praise must show first of all in her conduct, modesty, and purity. Marius, the illustrious Roman, said in that first speech of his to the Roman people: "Of women we require purity, of men labor." And I certainly agree. There is nothing more disgusting than a coarse and dirty woman. Who is stupid enough not to see clearly that a woman who does not care for neatness and cleanliness in her appearance, not only in her dress and body but in all her behavior and language, is by no means well mannered? How can it be anything but obvious that a bad-mannered woman is also rarely virtuous? We shall consider elsewhere the harm that comes to a family from women who lack virtue, for I myself do not know which is the worse fate for a family, total celibacy or a single dishonored woman. In a bride, therefore, a man must first seek beauty of mind, that is, good conduct and virtue.

In her body he must seek not only loveliness, grace, and charm but must also choose a woman who is well made for bearing children, with the kind of constitution that promises to make them strong and big. There's an old proverb, "When you pick your wife, you choose your children." All her virtues will in fact shine brighter still in beautiful children. It is a well-known saying among poets: "Beautiful character dwells in a beautiful body." The natural philosophers require that a woman be neither thin nor very fat. Those laden with fat are subject to coldness and constipation and slow to conceive. They say that a woman should have a joyful nature, fresh and lively in her blood and her whole being. They have no objections to a dark girl. They do reject girls with a frowning black visage, however. They have no liking for either the undersized or the overlarge and lean. They find that a woman is most suited to bear children if she is fairly big and has limbs of ample length. They always have a preference for youth, based on a number of arguments which I need not expound here, but particularly on the point that a young girl has a more adaptable mind. Young girls are pure by virtue of their age and have not developed any spitefulness. They are by nature modest and free of vice. They quickly learn to accept affectionately and unresistingly the habits and wishes of their husbands.

From Leon Battista Alberti, *On the Family.*

---

were not particularly effective. The rhythm method was especially futile because of the misunderstanding of the role of women in conception. It was not yet known that the woman contained an egg that was fertilized during conception. Without this knowledge it was impossible to understand the cycle of ovulation. Practically speaking, family size was limited on the one end by late marriages and on the other by early deaths.

Life experiences differed for males. Men married later—near the age of 25 on the farms, nearer the age of 30 in the cities—because of the cost of setting up in trade or on the land. Late marriage meant long supervision under the watchful eye of father or master, an extended period between adolescence and adulthood. The reputation that Renaissance cities gained for homosexuality and licentiousness must be

viewed in light of the advanced age at which males married. The level of sexual frustration was high, and its outlet in ritual violence and rape was also high.

The establishment of one's own household through marriage was a late rite of passage, considering the expectations of early death. Men came of age at 30 but were thought to be old by 50. Thus for men marriage and parenthood took place in middle age rather than in youth. Valued all their lives more highly than their sisters, male heads of households were the source of all power in their domiciles, in their shops, and in the state. They were responsible for overseeing every aspect of the upbringing of their children, even choosing wet nurses for their infants and spouses for their daughters. But their wives were essential partners who governed domestic life. Women labored not only at the hearth, but in the fields and shops as

■ Double portraits of husbands and wives showed the union of individuals and of families. In this ca. 1465 diptych of Frederico da Montefeltro, the Duke of Urbino, and his wife Battista Sforza, artist Piero della Francesca shows the couple facing each other against the distant backdrop of the territory they ruled. Their union joined the Montefeltro family ruling the small duchy of Urbino in central Italy with the powerful Sforza family that ruled Milan. The wealthy couple was also a generous patron of the artist.

well. Their economic contribution to the well-being of the family was critical, both in the dowry they brought at marriage and in the labor they contributed to the household. If their wives died, men with young children remarried quickly. While there were many bachelors, there were few widowers.

In most cases death came suddenly. Epidemic diseases, of which plague was the most virulent, struck with fearful regularity. Even in the absence of a serious outbreak, there were always deaths in town and country attributable to the plague. Epidemics struck harder at the young—children and adolescents, who were the majority of the population—and hardest in the summer months, when other viruses and bacteria weakened the population. Influenza must have been the second largest cause of death, although that can only be speculated in the absence of proper records. Medical treatment was more likely to hasten death than to prolong life. Lorenzo de' Medici's physician prescribed powdered pearls for the Florentine ruler's gout. After that Lorenzo complained more of stomach pains than of gout. Such remedies revealed a belief in the harmony of nature and the healing power of rare substances. The remedies were not silly or superstitious, but they were not effective either. Starvation was rare, less because of food shortage than because the seriously undernourished were more likely to succumb to disease than to famine. In urban areas, the government would intervene to provide grain from public storehouses at times of extreme shortage; in the countryside, large landholders commonly exercised the same function.

The Quality of Life

Although life may have been difficult during the Renaissance, it was not unfulfilling. Despite constant toil and frequent hardship, people of the Renaissance had reason to believe that their lives were better than those of their ancestors and that their children's lives would be better still. On the most basic level, health improved and, for those who survived plague, life expectancy increased. Better health was related to better diet. Improvement came from two sources: the relative surplus of grain throughout the fifteenth century and the wider variety of foods consumed. Bread remained the most widely consumed foodstuff, but even subsistence consumers were beginning to supplement their diet with meat and dairy products. There was more pork and lamb in the diet of ordinary people in the fifteenth century than there would be for the next 400 years. At the upper levels of society, sweet wine and citrus fruits helped offset the lack of vegetables. The diversification of diet resulted from improvements in transportation and communication, which brought more goods and services to a growing number of towns in the chain that linked the regional centers to the rural countryside.

The towns and cities also introduced a new sense of social and political cohesiveness. The city was something to which people belonged. In urban areas they could join social groups of their own choosing and develop networks of support not possible in rural environments. Blood relations remained the primary social group. Kin were the most likely source of aid in times of need, and charity began at home. Kin groups extended well beyond the immediate family, with both cousins and in-laws laying claim to the privileges of blood. The urban family could also depend upon the connections of neighborhood. In some Italian cities, wealth or occupation determined housing patterns. In others, such as Florence, rich and poor lived side by side and identified themselves with their small administrative unit and with their local church. Thus they could participate in relationships with others both above and below them on the social scale. From their superiors they gained connections that helped their families; from their inferiors they gained devoted clients. The use of both in such important functions as godparenting demonstrates how the urban family built a complex set of social relations.

As in the Middle Ages, the Church remained the spatial, spiritual, and social center of people's lives. Though Renaissance society became more worldly in outlook, this worldliness took place within the context of an absorbing devotional life. There was not yet any separation between faith and reason. The Church provided explanations for both the mysterious and the mundane. The clergy performed the rituals of baptism, marriage, and burial that measured the passage of life. Religious symbols also adorned the flags of militia troops, the emblems of guilds, and the regalia of the city itself. The Church preserved holy relics that were venerated for their power to protect the city or to endow it with particular skills and resources. Through its holy days as much as through its rituals, the Church helped to channel leisure activities into community celebrations.

A growing sense of civic pride and individual accomplishment were underlying characteristics of the Italian Renaissance, enhanced by the development of social cohesion and community solidarity that both Church and city-state fostered. It is commonly held that the Renaissance was both elitist and male dominated, that it was an experience separate from that of the society at large. There can be no question that it was the rich who commissioned works of art and that it was the highly skilled male craftsmen who executed them. But neither lived in a social vacuum. The Renaissance was not the result of the efforts of a privileged few. Family values that permitted early apprenticeships in surrogate households and that emphasized the continuity of crafts from one generation to the next made possible the skilled artists of the Renaissance cities. The stress on the production of luxury goods placed higher value upon individual skills and therefore upon excellence in workmanship. Church and state sought to express social values through representational art. One of the chief purposes of wall murals was to instruct the unlettered in religion, to help them visualize the central episodes in Christian history and thus increase the pleasure they derived from their faith. The grandiose architecture and statuary that adorned central places were designed to enhance civic pride, nurture loyalty, and communicate the protective power of public institutions.

For ordinary people, the world of the Renaissance was not much different from the world of the Middle Ages. Although urban areas grew, providing a wider variety of occupations and a varied material life, most people continued to scratch a meager living from the soil. The crucial difference from generation to generation was the degree of infectious diseases and the rate of rising or falling population. For the lucky ones there was surplus, for the unfortunate there was dearth. Within those confines, men were privileged over women, having greater security, status, and monopolizing power. But the tightly knit organization of family life protected the weak and the poor, while the Church provided faith, hope, and charity.

RENAISSANCE ART

In every age, artistic achievement represents a combination of individual talent and predominant social ideals. Artists may be at the leading edge of the society in which they live, but it is the spirit of that society that they capture in word, song, or image. Artistic disciplines also have their own technical development. Individually, Renaissance artists were attempting to solve problems of perspective and three-dimensionality that had defeated their predecessors. But the particular techniques or experiments that interested them owed as much to the social context as they did to the artistic one. For example, the urban character of Italian government led to the need for civic architecture—public buildings on a grand scale. The celebration of individual achievement led to the explosive growth of portraiture. Not surprisingly, major technological breakthroughs were achieved in both areas. Nor should the brilliance of the artists themselves be underestimated. To deny genius is to deprecate humanity. What needs to be explained is not the existence of a Leonardo or a Michelangelo but their coexistence.

The relationship between artist and social context was all the more important in the Renaissance, when artists were closely tied to the crafts and trades of urban society and to the demands of clients who commissioned their work. Although it was the elite who patronized art, it was skilled tradesmen who produced it. Artists normally followed the pattern of any craftsman—an apprenticeship begun as a teenager and a long period of training and work in a master's shop. That form of education gave the aspiring artist a practical rather than a theoretical bent and a keen appreciation for the business side of art. Studios were identified with particular styles and competed for commissions from clients, especially the Church. Wealthy individuals commissioned art as investments, as marks of personal distinction, and as displays of public piety. They got what they paid for, usually entering into detailed contracts that stipulated the quality of materials and the amount of work done by the master. Isabella d'Este (1474–1539), one of the great patrons of Renaissance artists, wrote hundreds of letters specifying the details of the works she commissioned. She once sent an artist threads of the exact dimensions of the pictures she had ordered. Demand for art was high. The vast public works projects needed buildings, the new piazzas (public squares) and palazzos (private houses) needed statuary, and the long walls of churches needed murals.

The survival of so many Renaissance masterpieces allows us to reconstruct the stages by which the remarkable artistic achievements of the era took place. Although advances were made in a variety of fields during the Renaissance, the three outstanding areas were architecture, sculpture, and painting. While modern artists would consider each a separate discipline, Renaissance artists crossed their boundaries without hesitation. Not only could the artists work with a variety of materials, their intensive and varied apprenticeships taught them to apply the technical solutions of one field to the problems of another. Few Renaissance artists confined themselves to one area of artistic expression, and many created works of enduring beauty in more than one medium. Was the greatest achievement of Michelangelo his sculpture of David, his paintings on the ceiling of the Sistine Chapel, or his design for the dome of Saint Peter's? Only a century of interdisciplinary cross-fertilization could have prepared the artistic world for such a feat.

An Architect, a Sculptor, and a Painter

The century that culminated in Michelangelo's extraordinary achievements began with the work of three Florentine masters who deeply influenced one another's development: Brunelleschi (1377–1446), Donatello (1386–1466), and Masaccio (1401–1428). In the Renaissance, the dominant artistic discipline was architecture. Buildings were the most expensive investment patrons could make, and the technical knowledge necessary for their successful construction was immense. Not only did the architect design a building, he also served as its general contractor, its construction supervisor, and its inspector. Moreover, the architect's design determined the amount and the scale of the statuary and decorative paintings to be incorporated. By 1400 the Gothic style of building had dominated western Europe for more than two centuries. Its pointed arches, vaulted ceilings, and slender spires had simplified building by removing the heavy walls formerly thought necessary to support great structures. Gothic construction permitted greater height, a characteristic especially desirable in cathedrals, which stretched toward the heavens. But although the buildings themselves were simplified, the techniques for erecting them became more complex. By the fifteenth century, architects had turned their techniques into

■ Raphael's fresco *The School of Athens* (1510–1511) exemplifies the Renaissance admiration for the classical heritage, depicting a gathering of philosophers and scientists of antiquity assembled around Plato and Aristotle and including likenesses of contemporaries such as Leonardo, Michelangelo, and Raphael himself among the crowd.

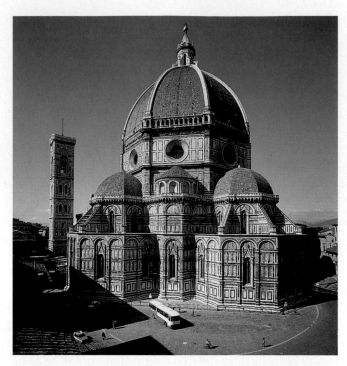

■ Florence Cathedral was begun by Arnolfo di Cambio in 1296. The nave was finished about 1350 and the dome, designed by Brunelleschi, was added in the 1420s. This view shows the dome and the apse end of the cathedral.

an intricate style. They became obsessed by angular arches, elaborate vaultings and buttresses, and long, pointed spires.

It was Brunelleschi who decisively challenged the principles of Gothic architecture by recombining its basic elements with those of classical structures. His achievement was less an innovation than a radical synthesis of old and new. Basing his designs on geometric principles, Brunelleschi reintroduced planes and spheres as dominant motifs. His greatest work was the dome on the cathedral in Florence, begun in 1420. His design was simple but bold. The windows at the base of the dome of the cathedral illustrate Brunelleschi's geometric technique. Circular windows are set inside a square of panels, which in turn are set inside a rectangle. The facades are dominated by columns and rounded arches, proportionally spaced from a central perspective. Brunelleschi is generally credited with having been the first Renaissance artist to have understood and made use of perspective, though it was immediately put to more dramatic effect in sculpture and painting.

The sculptor's study was the human form in all of its three-dimensional complexity. The survival of Roman and Hellenistic pieces, mostly bold and muscular torsos, meant that the influence of classical art was most direct in sculpture. Donatello translated the classical styles into more naturalistic forms. His technique is evident in the long flowing robes that distinguish most of his works. Donatello sculpted the cloth, not in the stylized angularity of the past in which the creases were as sharp as sword blades, but in the natural fashion in which cloth hung. Donatello also revived the freestanding statue, which demanded greater attention to human anatomy

because it was viewed from many angles. *Judith Slaying Holofernes* (1455) is an outstanding example of Donatello's use of geometric proportion and perspective. Each side of the piece captures a different vision of Judith in action. In addition, Donatello led the revival of the equestrian statue, sculpting the Venetian captain-general Gattamelata for a public square in Padua. The enormous bronze horse and rider (1445–1450) borrowed from surviving first- and second-century Roman models but relied upon the standpoint of the viewer to achieve its overpowering effect. The use of **linear perspective,** a technique applying principles of geometry to create the illusion of depth and dimension on a flat surface, was also a characteristic of Donatello's dramatic works. His breathtaking bas-relief altar scenes of the miracles of Saint

■ Donatello's bronze statue *Judith Slaying Holofernes* symbolized the Florentines' love of liberty and hatred of tyranny.

Anthony in Padua, which resemble nothing so much as a canvas cast in bronze, utilize linear perspective and architectural elements to make the flattened relief panels spring to life.

The altar scenes clearly evince the unmistakable influence of the paintings of Masaccio. Although he lived fewer than 30 years, Masaccio created an enduring legacy. His frescoes in the Brancacci Chapel in Florence were studied and sketched by all the great artists of the next generation, who unreservedly praised his naturalism. What most claims the attention of the modern viewer is Masaccio's shading of light and shadow and his brilliant use of linear perspective to create the illusion that a flat surface has three dimensions. Masaccio worked with standard Christian themes, but he brought an entirely novel approach to them all. In an adoration scene he portrayed a middle-aged Madonna and a dwarfish baby Jesus; in a painting of Saint Peter paying tribute money he used his own likeness as the face of one of the Apostles. His two best-known works are *The Expulsion of Adam and Eve* (ca. 1425) and *The Holy Trinity* (1425). In *The Expulsion of Adam and Eve*, Masaccio has left an unforgettable image of the fall from grace in Eve's primeval anguish. Her deep eyes and hollow mouth are accentuated by casting the source of light downward and shading what otherwise would be lighted. In *The Holy Trinity*, Masaccio provides the classic example of the use of linear perspective. In the painting, the ceiling of a Brunelleschi-designed temple recedes to a vanishing point beyond the head of God, creating the simultaneous illusion of height and depth.

Renaissance Style

By the middle of the fifteenth century, a recognizable Renaissance style had triumphed. Florence continued to lead the way, although ideas, techniques, and influences had spread throughout the Italian peninsula and even to the north and west. The outstanding architect of the period was Leon Battista Alberti (1404–1472), whose treatise *On Architecture* (1452) remained the most influential work on the subject until the eighteenth century. Alberti consecrated the geometric principles laid down by Brunelleschi and infused them with a humanist spirit. He revived the classical dictum that a building, like a body, should have an even number of supports and, like a head, an odd number of openings, which furthered precise geometric calculations in scale and design. But it was in civic architecture that Alberti made his most significant contributions. There he demonstrated how classical forms could be applied to traditional living space by being made purely decorative. His facade of the Palazzo Rucellai uses columns and arches not as building supports, but as embellishments that give geometric harmony to the building's appearance.

No sculptor challenged the preeminence of Donatello for another 50 years, but in painting there were many contenders for the garlands worn by Masaccio. The first was Piero della Francesca (ca. 1420–1492) who, though trained in the tradition of Masaccio, broke new ground in his concern for the visual unity of his paintings. From portraits to processions to his stunning fresco *The Resurrection* (ca.

■ In this fresco, *The Expulsion of Adam and Eve* (ca. 1425), Masaccio's mastery of perspective helps create the illusion of movement, as an angel drives the grieving Adam and Eve out of paradise into the world.

■ Botticelli's *Primavera* (Spring), also called *Garden of Venus*. Venus, in the center, is attended by the three Graces and by Cupid, Flora, Chloris, and Zephyr. Botticelli's figures have a dreamlike quality, an unreality highlighted by their beautiful faces and lithe figures.

1463), Piero concentrated upon the most technical aspects of composition. He was influenced by Alberti's ideas about the geometry of form, and it is said that his measurements and calculations for various parts of *The Resurrection* took more time than the painting itself. Another challenger was Sandro Botticelli (1445–1510), whose classical themes, sensitive portraits, and bright colors set him apart from the line of Florentine painters with whom he studied. His mythologies, *The Birth of Venus* and *Spring* (both ca. 1478), depart markedly from the naturalism inspired by Masaccio. Botticelli's paintings have a dreamlike quality, an unreality highlighted by the beautiful faces and lithe figures of his characters.

Botticelli's concern with beauty and personality is also seen in the paintings of Leonardo da Vinci (1452–1519), whose creative genius embodied the Renaissance ideal of the "universal man." Leonardo's achievements in scientific, technical, and artistic endeavors read like a list of all of the subjects known during the Renaissance. His detailed anatomical drawings and the method he devised for rendering them, his botanical observations, and his engineering inventions (including models for the tank and the airplane) testify to his unrestrained curiosity. His paintings reveal the scientific application of mathematics to matters of proportion and perspective. The dramatic fresco *The Last Supper* (ca. 1495–1498), for example, takes the traditional scene of Jesus and his disciples at a long table and divides it into four groups of three, each with its own separate action, leaving Jesus to dominate the center of the picture by balancing its two sides. Leonardo's psychological portrait *La Gioconda* (1503–1506), popularly

DOCUMENT

Vasari on Leonardo da Vinci

called the *Mona Lisa*, is quite possibly the best-known picture in the Western world.

From Brunelleschi to Alberti, from Masaccio to Leonardo da Vinci, Renaissance artists placed a unique stamp upon visual culture. By reviving classical themes, geometric principles, and a spirit of human vitality, they broke decisively from the dominant medieval traditions. Art became a source of individual and collective pride, produced by masters but consumed by all. Cities and wealthy patrons commissioned great works of art for public display. New buildings rose everywhere, adorned with the statues and murals that still stand as a testimony to generations of artists.

Michelangelo

The artistic achievements of the Renaissance culminated in the creative outpourings of Michelangelo Buonarroti (1475–1564). It is almost as if the age itself had produced a summation of how it wished to be remembered. Uncharacteristically, Michelangelo came from a family of standing in Florentine society and gained his apprenticeship over the opposition of his father. He claimed to have imbibed his love of sculpture from the milk of his wet nurse, who was the wife of a stonecutter. In 1490, Michelangelo gained a place in the household of Lorenzo de' Medici, thus avoiding the long years of apprenticeship during which someone else's style was implanted upon a young artist.

In 1496, Michelangelo moved to Rome. There his abilities as a sculptor brought him a commission from a French cardinal for a religious work in the classical style, which

■ Leonardo da Vinci's *La Gioconda,* or *Mona Lisa.*

Although Michelangelo always believed himself to be primarily a sculptor, his next outstanding work was in the field of painting. In 1508, Pope Julius II commissioned Michelangelo to decorate the small ceremonial chapel that had been built next to the new papal residence. The initial plan called for figures of the 12 apostles to adorn the ceiling, but Michelangelo soon launched a more ambitious scheme: to portray, in an extended narrative, human creation and those Old Testament events that foreshadowed the birth of Jesus. Everything about the execution of the Sistine Chapel paintings was extraordinary. First, Michelangelo framed his scenes within the architecture of a massive classical temple. In this way he was able to give the impression of having flattened the rounded surface on which he worked. Then, on the two sides of the central panels, he represented figures of Hebrew prophets and pagan Sybils as sculptured marble statues. Finally, within the center panels came his fresco scenes of the events of the creation and of human history from the Fall to the Flood. His representations were simple and compelling: the fingers of God and Adam nearly touching; Eve with one leg still emerging from Adam's side; the half-human snake in the temptation. All are majestically evocative.

The *Pietà,* the *David,* and the paintings of the Sistine Chapel were the work of youth. Michelangelo's crowning

■ Michelangelo, *Pietà* (1498–1499). The sculptor's contract for the piece called for it to be "the most beautiful work in marble which exists today in Rome." Michelangelo made several trips to Carrara to find the highest quality marble for the *Pietà.*

Michelangelo named the **Pietà.** Although it was his first attempt at sculpting a work of religious art, Michelangelo would never surpass it in beauty or composition. The *Pietà* created a sensation in Rome, and by the time that Michelangelo returned to Florence in 1501, at the age of 26, he was already acknowledged as one of the great sculptors of his day. He was immediately commissioned to work on an enormous block of marble that had been quarried nearly a half-century before and had defeated the talents of a series of carvers. He worked continuously for three years on his *David* (1501–1504), a piece that completed the union between classical and Renaissance styles. Michelangelo's giant nude gives eloquent expression to his belief that the human body was the "mortal veil" of the soul.

■ The creation of Adam and Eve, a detail from Michelangelo's frescoes on the ceiling of the Sistine Chapel. The Sistine frescoes had become obscured by dirt and layers of varnish and glue applied at various times over the years. In the 1980s they were cleaned to reveal their original colors.

achievement—the building of Saint Peter's—was undertaken at the age of 71. The purpose of the church was to provide a suitable monument for the grave of Saint Peter. The basework had already been laid, and drawings for the building's completion had been made 30 years earlier by Donato Bramante. Michelangelo altered the plans in an effort to bring more light inside the church and provide a more majestic facade outside. His main contribution, however, was the design of the great dome, which centered the interior of the church on Saint Peter's grave. More than the height, it is the harmony of Michelangelo's design that creates the sense of the building thrusting upward like a Gothic cathedral of old. The dome on Saint Peter's was the largest then known and provided the model, in succeeding generations, for Saint Paul's Cathedral in London and the U.S. Capitol building in Washington, DC.

Renaissance art served Renaissance society. It reflected both its concrete achievements and its visionary ideals. It was a synthesis of old and new, building upon classical models, particularly in sculpture and architecture, but adding newly discovered techniques and skills. Demanding patrons such as Pope Julius II, who commonly interrupted Michelangelo's work on the Sistine Chapel with criticisms and suggestions, fueled the remarkable growth in both the quantity and quality of Renaissance art. When Giorgio Vasari (1511–1574) came to write his *Lives of the Most Eminent Painters, Sculptors, and Architects* (1550), he found more than 200 artists worthy of distinction. But Renaissance artists did more than construct and adorn buildings and celebrate and beautify spiritual life. Inevitably their work expressed the ideals and aspirations of the society in which they lived, the new emphasis upon learning and knowledge; upon the here and now rather than the hereafter; and, most importantly, upon humanity and its capacity for growth and perfection.

RENAISSANCE IDEALS

Renaissance thought went hand in glove with Renaissance art. Scholars and philosophers searched the works of the ancients to find the principles on which to build a better life. They scoured monastic libraries for forgotten manuscripts, discovering among other things Greek poetry and history, the works of Homer and Plato, and Aristotle's *Poetics*. Their rigorous application of scholarly procedures for the collection and collation

The Renaissance Man

Giorgio Vasari celebrated the creativity of the artists who made Italy the center of cultural activity in the Later Middle Ages. His commemoration of their achievements through the medium of biographies helped to create the aura that still surrounds Renaissance art.

Focus Questions

What makes Leonardo such an exemplary "Renaissance man"? Does Vasari see Leonardo as someone who excels in many separate fields, or does he see the different arts and sciences as unified?

The most heavenly gifts seem to be showered on certain human beings. Sometimes supernaturally, marvelously, they all congregate in one individual. Beauty, grace, and talent are combined in such bounty that in whatever that man undertakes, he outdistances all other men and proves himself to be specially endowed by the hand of God. He owes his pre-eminence not to human teaching or human power. This was seen and acknowledged by all men in the case of Leonardo da Vinci, who had, besides the beauty of his person (which was such that it has never been sufficiently extolled), an indescribable grace in every effortless act and deed. His talent was so rare that he mastered any subject to which he turned his attention. Extraordinary strength and remarkable facility were here combined. He had a mind of regal boldness and magnanimous daring. His gifts were such that his celebrity was worldwide, not only in his own day, but even more after his death, and so will continue until the end of time.

Leonardo was frequently occupied in the preparation of plans to remove mountains or to pierce them with tunnels from plain to plain. By means of levers, cranes, and screws, he showed how to lift or move great weights. Designing dredging machines and inventing the means of drawing water from the greatest depths were among the speculations from which he never rested. Many drawings of these projects exist which are cherished by those who practice our arts. . . .

Leonardo, with his profound comprehension of art, began many things that he never completed, because it seemed to him that perfection must elude him. He frequently formed in his imagination enterprises so difficult and so subtle that they could not be entirely realized and worthily executed by human hands. His conceptions were varied to infinity. In natural philosophy, among other things, he examined plants and observed the stars—the movements of the planets, the variations of the moon, and the course of the sun. . . .

From Giorgio Vasari, *Lives of the Most Eminent Painters, Sculptors, and Architects.*

---

of those texts was one of the most important contributions of the Renaissance intellectuals who came to be known as **humanists.** Humanism developed in reaction to an intellectual world that was centered on the Church and dominated by otherworldly concerns. Humanism was secular in outlook, though by no means was it antireligious.

Humanists celebrated worldly achievements. Pico della Mirandola's *Oration on the Dignity of Man* (1486) is the best known of a multitude of Renaissance writings influenced by the discovery of the works of Plato. Pico believed that people could perfect their existence on earth because humans were divinely endowed with the capacity to determine their own fate: "O highest and most marvelous felicity of man! To him it is granted to have whatever he chooses, to be whatever he wills."

Thus humanists studied and taught the humanities—the skills of disciplines such as **philology,** the art of language, and **rhetoric,** the art of expression. Although they were mostly laypeople, humanists applied their learning to both religious and secular studies. Humanists were not antireligious. Although they reacted strongly against Scholasticism (see Chapter 14), they were heavily indebted to the work of medieval churchmen, and most were devoutly religious. Nor were they hostile to the Church. Petrarch, Leonardo Bruni, and Leon Battista Alberti were all employed by the papal court at some time in their careers, as was Lorenzo Valla, the most influential of the humanists. Their interest in human achievement and human potential must be set beside their religious beliefs. As Petrarch stated quite succinctly: "Christ is my God; Cicero is the prince of the language I use."

Humanists and the Liberal Arts

The most important achievements of humanist scholars centered on ancient texts. It was the humanists' goal to discover as much as had survived from the ancient world and to provide texts of classical authors that were as full and accurate as possible.

Studying the Classical World.   Although much was already known of the Latin classics, few of the central works of ancient Greece had been uncovered. Humanists preserved that heritage by reviving the study of the Greek language and by translating

Greek authors into Latin. After the fall of Constantinople in 1453, Italy became the center for Greek studies as Byzantine scholars fled the Ottoman conquerors. Humanists also introduced historical methods in studying and evaluating texts, establishing principles for determining which of many manuscript copies of an ancient text was the oldest, the most accurate, and the least corrupted by copyists. That was of immense importance in studying the writings of the ancient Fathers of the Church, many of whose manuscripts had not been examined for centuries. They believed that the study of the "liberal arts" should be undertaken for its own sake. That belief gave a powerful boost to the ideal of the perfectability of the individual that appeared in so many other aspects of Renaissance culture.

Humanists furthered the secularization of Renaissance society through their emphasis on the study of the classical world. The rediscovery of Latin texts during the Later Middle Ages spurred interest in all things ancient. Petrarch, who is rightly called the father of humanism, revered the great Roman rhetorician Cicero above all others. For Petrarch, Cicero's legacy was eloquence. He stressed that in his correspondence with the leading scholars of his day and taught it to those who would succeed him. From 1350 to 1450, Cicero was the dominant model for Renaissance poets and orators. The leading humanist in the generation after Petrarch was Leonardo Bruni (1370–1444), who was reputed to be the greatest Greek scholar of his day. He translated both Plato and Aristotle and did much to advance mastery of classical Greek and foster the ideas of Plato in the late fifteenth century.

Philology and Lorenzo Valla. The study of the origins of words, their meaning, and their proper grammatical usage may seem an unusual foundation for one of the most vital of all European intellectual movements. But philology was the humanists' chief concern and can be best illustrated by the work of Lorenzo Valla (1407–1457). Valla was brought up in Rome, where he was largely self-educated, although according to the prescriptions of the Florentine humanists. Valla entered the service of Alfonso I, king of Naples, and applied his humanistic training to affairs of state. The kingdom of Naples bordered on the Papal States, and its kings were in continual conflict with the papacy. The pope asserted the right to withhold recognition of the king, a right that was based upon the jurisdictional authority supposedly ceded to the papacy by the Emperor Constantine in the fourth century. The so-called Donation of Constantine had long been a matter of dispute, and its authenticity had been challenged frequently in the Middle Ages. But those challenges were made on political grounds, and the arguments of papal supporters were as strenuous as those of papal opponents. Valla settled the matter definitively. Applying historical and philological critiques to the text of the Donation, Valla proved that it could not have been written earlier than the eighth century, 400 years after Constantine's death. He exposed words and terms that had not existed in Roman times, such as *fief* and *satrap,* and thus proved beyond doubt that the Donation was a forgery and papal claims based upon it were without merit.

■ Melozzo da Forlì, *Sixtus IV Appoints Platina as Prefect of the Vatican Library* (1475). The importance of the humanists was represented in this fresco of the Pope appointing a librarian for the newly established Vatican Library.

Civic Humanism. Valla's career demonstrates the impact of humanist values on practical affairs. Although humanists were scholars, they made no distinction between an active and a contemplative life. A life of scholarship was a life of public service. They saw their studies as means of improving themselves and their society: "Man is born in order to be useful to man." That **civic humanism** is best expressed in the writings of Leon Battista Alberti (1404–1472), whose treatise *On the Family* (1443) is a classic study of the new urban values, especially prudence and thrift. Alberti extolled the virtues of "the fatherland, the public good, and the benefit of all citizens." An architect, a mathematician, a poet, a playwright, a musician, and an inventor, Alberti was one of the great virtuosi of the Renaissance.

Alberti's own life might have served as a model for the most influential of all Renaissance tracts, Baldesar Castiglione's *The Courtier* (1528). While Alberti directed his lessons to the private lives of successful urban families, Castiglione (1478–1529) directed his to the public life of the aspiring elite. In Castiglione's view, the perfect courtier was as much born as made: "Besides his noble birth I would have the Courtier endowed by nature not only with talent and beauty of person and feature, but with a certain grace and air that shall make him at first sight pleasing." Everything that the courtier did was to maintain his pleasing grace and his public reputation. *The Courtier* was an etiquette book, and in it Castiglione prescribed every detail of the education necessary for the ideal state servant, from table manners to artistic attainments. Although each talent was to be acquired through careful study and application, it was to be manifested with *sprezzatura,* a natural ease and superiority that was the essence of the gentleman.

Renaissance Science

As the spirit of the Renaissance looked back to the classical world and ahead to the achievements that would come from the adaptation of ancient wisdom, so Renaissance scientific inquiry was focused in two directions. The first was text-based knowledge derived from recovered works mainly from classical Greece; the second was experiment-based knowledge achieved through observation. Texts dominated the life sciences, especially medicine and biology; experimentation enriched the physical sciences such as engineering and cartography. But it is important to realize that both ways of knowing blended together. Doctors were instructed by the classics but increasingly learned their anatomy by dissection. Navigators carried the works of Ptolemy on voyages of discovery but amended his maps and charts with what they found in practice.

The biological sciences were given new life by the recovery of the writings of Hippocrates and Galen. Medicine became a subject for learned inquiry and the medical school at Padua was considered the greatest in Europe. The work of Hippocrates concerned diagnosing common diseases and attempting to find treatments. Galen's studies of the human body, rediscovered, formed the basis for a new interest in anatomy and led to experiments in human dissection in the most advanced universities. Such experimentation improved knowledge of the skeleton and the placement of the organs, which led to medical advances in setting broken bones and treating injuries. Galen taught that the body was composed of humors that corresponded to the four elements of life—earth, air, water, and fire. In the healthy body the humors were well mixed together, but in the diseased body there was an imbalance. This understanding explains why doctors attempted to cure disease by the use of leeches or the practice of "bleeding," cutting open a vein and allowing blood to run out. The extraction of blood was believed to aid in restoring the balance of the humors and thus the health of the body.

While the life sciences were advanced through attention to ancient texts, engineering developed through the experiences of Renaissance craftsmen and artists who were attempting to solve practical problems of proportion, stability, and height in the buildings, bridges, and ultimately domes that they built. Most of the important advances in engineering were actually made in the service of military ventures. The science of ballistics advanced through greater mathematical precision in studying the relationship between speed and trajectory in the shooting of artillery. It was Leonardo da Vinci who attempted to apply a theory of mechanics to Renaissance warfare, and he made drawings for the creation of war machines such as tanks and flying machines such as airplanes, though, of course, neither were produced during his lifetime. But he was expert in building working models of machines, in advising princes on their fortifications, and suggesting improvements in the art of gunnery. All of his contributions were made by experimentation rather than through text-based learning. Wherever he went, Leonardo built workshops to construct models and kept careful notebooks of the results of his trials. This spirit of experimentation would ultimately lead to the birth of a recognizably scientific method in the next century.

Machiavelli and Politics

At the same time that Castiglione was drafting a blueprint for the idealized courtier, Niccolò Machiavelli (1469–1527) was laying the foundation for the realistic sixteenth-century ruler. No Renaissance work has been more important or more controversial than Machiavelli's *The Prince* (1513). Its vivid prose, its epigrammatic advice—"Men must either be pampered or crushed"—and its clinical dissection of power politics have attracted generation after generation of readers. With Machiavelli began the science of politics.

DOCUMENT

Machiavelli, *The Prince*

■ Portrait of Niccolò Machiavelli, who expounded his theory of statecraft in *The Prince.*

THE LION AND THE FOX

Niccolò Machiavelli wrote The Prince *in 1513 while he was under house arrest. It is one of the classics of Western political theory in which the author separates the political from the moral.*

Focus Questions

According to Machiavelli, why is honesty not always the best policy? For a ruler, how valuable a tactic is a show of strength?

Everyone understands how praiseworthy it is in a prince to keep faith, and to live uprightly and not craftily. Nevertheless we see, from what has taken place in our own days, that princes who have set little store by their word, but have known how to overreach men by their cunning, have accomplished great things, and in the end got the better of those who trusted to honest dealing.

Be it known, then, that there are two ways of contending—one in accordance with the laws, the other by force; the first of which is proper to men, the second to beasts.

But since the first method is often ineffectual, it becomes necessary to resort to the second. A prince should, therefore, understand how to use well both the man and the beast. . . . But inasmuch as a prince should know how to use the beast's nature wisely, he ought of beasts to choose both the lion and the fox; for the lion cannot guard himself from the toils, nor the fox from wolves. He must therefore be a fox to discern toils, and a lion to drive off wolves.

To rely wholly on the lion is unwise; and for this reason a prudent prince neither can nor ought to keep his word when to keep it is hurtful to him and the causes which led him to pledge it are removed. If all men were good, this would not be good advice, but since they are dishonest and do not keep faith with you, you in return need not keep faith with them.

From Niccolò Machiavelli, *The Prince.*

Machiavelli came from an established Florentine family and entered state service as an assistant to one of his teachers, who then recommended him for the important office of secretary to the Council of Ten, the organ of Florentine government that had responsibility for war and diplomacy. Machiavelli devoted all his energies and his entire intellect to his career. He was a tireless correspondent, and he began to collect materials for various tracts on military matters. He also planned out a prospective history in which to celebrate the greatness of the Florentine Republic that he served.

But as suddenly as Machiavelli rose to his position of power and influence, he fell from it. The militia that he had advocated and in part organized was soundly defeated by the Spaniards, and the Florentine Republic fell. Machiavelli was summarily dismissed from office in 1512 and was imprisoned and tortured the following year. Released and banished from the city, he retired to a small country estate and turned his restless energies to writing. Immediately he began work on what became his two greatest works, *The Prince* and the *Discourses on Livy* (1519).

Machiavelli has left a haunting portrait of his life in exile, and it is important to understand how intertwined his studies of ancient and modern politics were.

On the coming of evening, I return to my house and enter my study; and at the door I take off the day's clothing, covered with mud and dust, and put on garments regal and courtly; and reclothed appropriately, I enter the ancient courts of ancient men, where, received by them with affection, I feed on that food which only is mine and which I was born for. For four hours of

time I do not feel boredom, I forget every trouble, I do not dread poverty, I am not frightened by death; entirely I give myself over to them.

In this state of mind *The Prince* was composed.

The Prince is a handbook for a ruler who would establish a lasting government. It attempts to set down principles culled from historical examples and contemporary events to aid the prince in attaining and maintaining power. By study of those precepts and by their swift and forceful application, Machiavelli believed that the prince might even control fortune itself. *The Prince* is purely secular in content and philosophy. Where the medieval writer of a manual for princes would have stressed the divine foundations of the state, Machiavelli asserted the human bases: "The chief foundations on which all states rest are good laws and good arms." What made *The Prince* so remarkable in its day, and what continues to enliven debate over it, is that Machiavelli was able to separate all ethical considerations from his analysis. Whether that resulted from cynicism or from his own expressed desire for realism, Machiavelli uncompromisingly instructed the would-be ruler to be half man and half beast—to conquer neighbors, to murder enemies, and to deceive friends. Steeped in the humanist ideals of fame and *virtù*—a combination of virtue and virtuosity, of valor, character, and ability—he sought to reestablish Italian rule and place government upon a stable, scientific basis that would end the perpetual conflict among the Italian city-states.

The careers of Lorenzo Valla and Niccolò Machiavelli both illustrate how humanists were able to bring the study of the liberal arts into the service of the state. Valla's philological studies had a vital impact on diplomacy; Machiavelli's historical studies were directly applicable to warfare. Humanists created a demand for learning that helps account for the growth of universities, the spread of literacy, and the rise of printing. They also created a hunger for knowledge that characterized intellectual life for nearly two centuries.

THE POLITICS OF THE ITALIAN CITY-STATES

Like studs on a leather boot, **city-states** dotted the Italian peninsula. They differed in size, shape, and form. Some were large seaports, others small inland villages; some cut wide swaths across the plains, others were tiny islands. The absence of a unifying central authority in Italy, resulting from the collapse of the Holy Roman Empire and the papal schism, allowed ancient guilds and confraternities to transform themselves into self-governing societies. By the beginning of the fifteenth century the Italian city-states were the center of power, wealth, and culture in the Christian world.

That dominion rested on several conditions. First, Italy's geographical position favored the exchange of resources and goods between the East and the West. Until the fifteenth century, and despite the crusading efforts of medieval popes, the East and the West fortified each other. A great circular trade had developed, encompassing the Byzantine Empire, the North African coastal states, and the Mediterranean nations of western Europe. The Italian peninsula dominated the circumference of that circle. Its port cities, Genoa and Venice especially, became great maritime powers through their trade in spices and minerals. Second, just beyond the peninsula to the north lay the vast and populous territories of the Holy Roman Empire. There the continuous need for manufactured goods, especially cloths and metals, was filled by long caravans that traveled from Italy through the Alps. Milan specialized in metal crafts. Florence was a financial capital as well as a center for the manufacture of fine luxury goods. Finally, the city-states and their surrounding areas were agriculturally self-sufficient.

Because of their accomplishments, there has been a tendency

MAP DISCOVERY

Italy, 1494

Notice how Italy was organized into city-states at the end of the fifteenth century. Which were the largest city-states? Which city-states seem most susceptible to foreign invasion? Which states had the best positioning for trade? When the wars of Italy began in 1494 (discussed later in this chapter), France sided with Milan against Naples, Florence, and the Papal States. Based on the positions of the combatants, what do you think would have been the likeliest route for the French invasion? Which city-states could the French avoid fighting?

to think of the Italian city-states as small nations. Even the term *city-state* implies national identity. Each city-state governed itself according to its own rules and customs, and each defined itself in isolation from the larger regional or tribal associations that once prevailed. Indeed, the struggles of the city-states against one another speak eloquently of their local self-identification. Italy was neither a nation nor a people.

The Five Powers

Although there were dozens of Italian city-states, by the early fifteenth century five had emerged to dominate the politics of the peninsula. In the south was the kingdom of Naples, the only city-state governed by a hereditary monarchy. Its politics were mired by conflicts over its succession, and it was not until the Spaniard Alfonso I of Aragon (1442–1458) secured the throne in 1443 that peace was restored. Bordering Naples were the Papal States, whose capital was Rome but whose territories stretched far to the north and lay on both sides of the spiny Apennine mountain chain that extends down the center of the peninsula. Throughout the fourteenth and early fifteenth centuries, the territories under the nominal control of the Church were largely independent and included such thriving city-states as Bologna, Ferrara, and Urbino. Even in Rome the weakened papacy had to contend with noble families for control of the city.

The three remaining dominant city-states were clustered together in the north. Florence, center of Renaissance culture, was one of the wealthiest cities of Europe before the devastations of the plague and the sustained economic downturn of the late fourteenth century. The city itself was inland and its main waterway, the Arno, ran to the sea through Pisa, whose subjugation in 1406 was a turning point in Florentine history. Nominally Florence was a republic, but during the fifteenth century it was ruled in effect by its principal banking family, the Medici.

To the north of Florence was the duchy of Milan, the major city in Lombardy. It too was landlocked, cut off from the sea by Genoa. But Milan's economic life was oriented northward to the Swiss and German towns beyond the Alps, and its major concern was preventing foreign invasions. The most warlike of the Italian cities, Milan was a despotism, ruled for nearly two centuries by the Visconti family.

The last of the five powers was the republic of Venice. Ideally situated at the head of the Adriatic Sea, Venice became the leading maritime power of the age. Until the fifteenth century, Venice had been less interested in securing a landed empire than in dominating a seaborne one. Its outposts along the Greek and Dalmatian coasts, and its favored position in Constantinople, were the source of vast mercantile wealth. The republic was ruled by a hereditary elite—headed by an elected **doge,** who was the chief magistrate of Venice—and a variety of small elected councils.

The political history of the Italian peninsula during the late fourteenth and early fifteenth centuries is one of unrelieved turmoil. Everywhere, the governments of the city-states were threatened by foreign invaders, internal conspiracies, or popular revolts. By the middle of the fifteenth century, however, two trends were apparent amid the political chaos. The first was the consolidation of strong centralized governments within the large city-states. The governments took different forms but yielded a similar result—internal political stability. The return of the popes to Rome after the Great Schism restored the pope to the head of his temporal estates and began a long period of papal dominance over Rome and its satellite territories. In Milan, one of the great military leaders of the day, Francesco Sforza (1401–1466), seized the reins of power. The succession of King Alfonso I in Naples ended a half century of civil war. In both Florence and Venice, the grip that the political elite held over high offices was tightened by placing greater power in small advisory councils and, in Florence, by the ascent to power of the Medici family. That process, known as the rise of signorial rule, made possible the establishment of a balance of power within the Italian peninsula.

It was the leaders of the Italian city-states who first perfected the art of diplomacy. Constant warfare necessitated continual alliances, and by the end of the fourteenth century the large city-states had begun the practice of keeping resident ambassadors at the major seats of power. That enhanced communication, a principal challenge in Renaissance diplomacy, and also provided leaders with accurate information about the conditions of potential allies and enemies. Diplomacy was both an offensive and a defensive weapon, especially because the city-states hired their soldiers as contract labor. The mercenary armies, whose leaders were known as **condottieri** from the name of their contract, were both expensive and dangerous to maintain. If they did not bankrupt their employers, they might desert them or, even worse, turn on them.

Venice: A Seaborne Empire

Water was the source of the prosperity of Venice. Located at the head of the Adriatic Sea, the city was formed by a web of lagoons. Through its center snaked the Grand Canal, whose banks were lined with large and small buildings that celebrated its civic and mercantile power. At the Piazza San Marco stood the vast palace of the doge, elected leader of the republic, and the Basilica of Saint Mark, a domed church built in the Byzantine style. At the Rialto were the stalls of the bankers and moneylenders, less grand perhaps but no less important. There, too, were the auction blocks for the profitable trade in European slaves, eastern European serfs, and battlefield captives who were sold into service in Egypt or Byzantium. On the eastern edge of the island city was the Arsenal, erected in the twelfth century to house the shipbuilding and arms manufacturing industries. Three centuries later it was the industrial marvel of the world, where the Venetian great galleys were constructed with assembly-line precision.

Its prosperity based on trade rather than conquest, Venice enjoyed many natural advantages. Its position at the head of the Adriatic permitted access to the raw materials of both the East and the West. The rich Alpine timberland beyond the city provided the hardwoods necessary for shipbuilding. The hinterland population were steady consumers of grain, cloth, and the new manufactured goods—glass, silk, jewelry, and cottons—that came pouring onto the market in the Later Middle Ages.

But the success of Venice owed more to its own achievements than to its rich inheritances. "It is the most triumphant city I have ever seen," wrote the Frenchman Philippe de Commynes at the end of the fifteenth century. The triumph of the Venetian state was the triumph of dedicated efficiency. The heart of its success lay in the way in which it organized its trade and its government. The key to Venetian trade was its privileged position with the Byzantine Empire. Through a treaty with the Byzantines, Venetian traders gained a competitive edge in the spice trade with the East. Venetians were the largest group of resident Europeans in Constantinople, and their personal contacts with Eastern traders were an important part of their success. The spice trade was so lucrative that special ships were built to accommodate it. The galleys were constructed at public expense and doubled as the Venetian navy in times of war. By controlling the ships, the government strictly regulated the spice trade.

Like its trade, Venetian government was also designed to disperse power. Although it was known as the Most Serene Republic, Venice was not a republic in the sense that the term is used today; rather, it was an oligarchy—a government administered by a restricted group. Political power was vested in a Great Council whose membership had been fixed at the end of the thirteenth century. All males whose fathers enjoyed the privilege of membership in the Great Council were registered at birth in the "Book of Gold" and became members of the Great Council when adults. There were no further distinctions of rank within the nobility, whose members varied widely in wealth and intermarried freely with other groups in the society. From the body of the Great Council, which numbered about 2500 at the end of the fifteenth century, was chosen the Senate—a council about one-tenth the size, whose members served a one-year term. It was from the Senate that the true officers of government were selected: the doge, who was chosen for life; and members of a number of small councils, who administered affairs and advised the doge. Members of the councils were chosen by secret ballot in an elaborate process by which nominators were selected at random. Terms of office on the councils were extremely short in order to limit factionalism and to prevent any individual from gaining too much power. Venetian-style republicanism was admired throughout Europe.

With its mercantile families firmly in control of government and trade, Venice created an overseas empire in the East during the thirteenth and fourteenth centuries. Naval supremacy, based largely on technological advances that made long-distance and winter voyages possible, allowed the Venetians to offer protection to strategic outposts in return for either privileges or tribute. But in the fifteenth century, Venice turned to the West. In a dramatic reversal of its centuries-old policy, it began a process of conquest in Italy, an empire on terra firma, as Venetian islanders called it. There were several reasons for this

new policy. First, the Venetian navy was no longer the unsurpassed power that it once had been. More importantly, mainland expansion offered new opportunities for Venice. Not all Venetians were traders, and the new industries that were being developed in the city could readily benefit from control of mainland markets. So could those Venetian nobles employed to administer the conquered lands. They argued persuasively that the supply of raw materials and foodstuffs on which Venetian trade ultimately depended should be secured by the republic itself. Most decisively of all, opportunity was knocking. In Milan, Visconti rule was weakening and the Milanese territories were ripe for picking.

Venice reaped a rich harvest. For the first half of the fifteenth century, the Most Serene Republic engaged in unremitting warfare. Its successes were remarkable. It pushed out to the north to occupy all the lands between the city and the Habsburg territories; it pushed to the east until it straddled the entire head of the Adriatic; and it pushed to the west almost as far as Milan itself. Venetian victories resulted from both the traditional use of hired mercenaries and from the Venetians' own ingenuity at naval warfare. Although Venice was creating a landed empire, the course of expansion, especially in Lombardy, was along river routes. At the Arsenal were built new oared vessels armed with artillery for river sieges. Soon the captured territories were paying for continued expansion. The Western conquests in particular brought large populations under Venetian control, which, along with their potential as a market, provided a ready source of taxation. By the end of the fifteenth century, the mainland dominions of Venice were contributing nearly 40 percent of the city's revenue at a cost far smaller than that of the naval empire a century earlier. Venice had become the most powerful city-state in Italy.

Florence: Spinning Cloth into Gold

"What city, not merely in Italy, but in all the world . . . is more proud in its palazzi, more bedecked with churches, more beautiful in its architecture, more imposing in its gates, richer in its piazzas, happier in its wide streets, greater in its people, more glorious in its citizenry, more inexhaustible in wealth, more fertile in its fields?" So boasted the humanist Coluccio Salutati (1331–1406) in 1403 during one of the most calamitous periods in Florentine history. Salutati's boastings were not unusual; the Florentines' mythical view of their homeland as savior of Christianity and as heir to the republican greatness of Rome was everywhere apparent. And it seemed to be most vigorously expressed in the city's darkest moments.

Florentine prosperity was built on two foundations: money and wool. Beginning in the thirteenth century, Florentine bankers were among the wealthiest and most powerful in the world. Initially their position was established through support of the papacy in its long struggle with the Holy Roman Empire. Florentine financiers established banks in all the capitals of Europe and the East, though their seats in Rome and Naples were probably most important. In the

Middle Ages, bankers had served more functions than simply handling and exchanging money. Most were also tied to mercantile adventures and underwrote industrial activity. So it was in Florence, where international bankers purchased high-quality wool to be manufactured into the world's finest woven cloth. At its height before the plague, the cloth industry employed nearly 30,000 workers, providing jobs at all levels of society, from the rural women who spun the wool into yarn at piecework wages to the highly paid weavers and dyers whose skills made Florentine cloth so highly prized.

The activities of both commerce and cloth manufacture depended on external conditions, and thus the wealth of Florence was potentially unstable. In the mid-fourteenth century instability came with the plague that devastated the city. Nearly 40 percent of the entire population was lost in the single year 1348, and recurring outbreaks continued to ravage the already weakened survivors. Loss of workers and loss of markets seriously disrupted manufacturing. By 1380, cloth production had fallen to less than a quarter of pre-plague levels. On the heels of plague came wars. The property of Florentine bankers and merchants abroad was an easy target. Thirty years of warfare with Milan, interrupted by only a single decade of peace (1413–1423), resulted in total bankruptcy for many of the city's leading commercial families. More significantly, the costs of warfare, offensive and defensive, created a massive public debt. Every Florentine of means owned shares of the debt, and the republic was continually devising new methods for borrowing and staving off crises of repayment. Small wonder that the republic turned for aid to the wealthiest banking family in Europe, the Medici.

The ability of the Medici to secure a century-long dynasty in a government that did not have a head of state is just one of the mysteries surrounding the history of the remarkable family. Cosimo de' Medici (1389–1464) was one of the richest men in Christendom when he returned to the city in 1434 after a brief exile. His leading position in government rested upon supporters who were able to gain a controlling influence on the Signoria, the ruling Council in Florence's republican form of government. Cosimo built his party carefully, recruiting followers among the artisans whom he employed and even paying delinquent taxes to maintain the eligibility of his voters. Most importantly, emergency powers were invoked to reduce the number of citizens qualified to vote for the Signoria until the majority were Medici backers.

Cosimo was a practical man. He raised his children along humanist principles and was a great patron of artists and intellectuals. He collected books and paintings, endowed libraries, and spent lavishly on his own palace, the Palazzo Medici, which after his death was transformed into the very center of Florentine cultural life. Cosimo's position as an international banker brought him into contact with the heads of other Italian city-states and enabled him to negotiate peace treaties.

It was Cosimo's grandson Lorenzo (1449–1492) who linked the family's name to that of the age. Lorenzo was trained to office as if he had been a prince rather than a citizen of a republic. His own father ruled for five years and used his son as a diplomat in order to acquaint him with the leaders of Europe. Diplomacy was Lorenzo's greatest achievement. He held strong humanist values instilled in him by his mother, Lucrezia Tornabuoni, who organized his education. He wrote poetry and drama and even entered competitions for architectural designs. But Lorenzo's chief contribution to artistic life as it reached its height in Florence was to facilitate its production. He brought Michelangelo and other leading artists to his garden; he brought Pico della Mirandola and other leading humanists to his table. He secured commissions for Florentine artists throughout the Italian peninsula, ensuring the spread of their influence and the continued regeneration of artistic creativity in Florence itself.

Lorenzo was generally regarded as the leading citizen of Florence, and that was true in terms of both his wealth and his influence. He did not rule from high office, though he maintained the party that his grandfather had built and even extended it through wartime emergency measures. His power was based on his personality and reputation, a charisma enhanced when he survived an assassination attempt in which his brother was killed. His diplomatic abilities were the key to his survival. Almost immediately after Lorenzo came to power, Naples and the papacy began a war with Florence, a

■ The patriarch of a great Florentine banking family, Cosimo de' Medici, portrayed here by Pontormo, was the dominant force in the city's politics from 1434 until his death in 1464.

■ A view of Florence in 1490. The Duomo of the Florence Cathedral dominates the small city, which is already built up on both sides of the Arno River.

war that was costly to the Florentines in both taxation and lost territory. In 1479, Lorenzo traveled to Naples and personally convinced the Neapolitan king to sign a separate treaty, which restored the Italian balance of power and ensured continued Medici rule in Florence. Soon Lorenzo even had a treaty with the pope that allowed for the recovery of lost territories and the expansion of Florentine influence. But two years after his death, the Italian peninsula was plunged into wars that turned it from the center of European civilization into one of its lesser satellites.

The End of Italian Hegemony, 1450–1527

In the course of the Renaissance, western Europe was Italianized. For a century, the city-states dominated the trade routes that connected the East and the West. Venetian and Genoese merchants exchanged spices and minerals from the Black Sea to the North Sea, enriching the material life of three continents. They brought wool from England and Spain to the skilled artisans in the Low Countries and Florence. Italian manufactures such as Milanese artillery, Florentine silk, and Venetian glass were prized above all others. The ducat and the florin, two Italian coins, were universally accepted in an age when every petty prince minted his own money. The Italian peninsula exported culture in the same way that it exported goods. Humanism quickly spread across the Alps, aided by the recent invention of printing (which the Venetians soon dominated), while Renaissance standards of artistic achievement were known worldwide and everywhere imitated. The city-states shared their technology as well. The compass and the navigational chart, projection maps, double entry bookkeeping, eyeglasses, the telescope—all profoundly influenced what could be achieved and what could be hoped for. In this spirit, Christopher Columbus—a Genoese seaman—successfully crossed the Atlantic under the Spanish flag, and Amerigo Vespucci—a Florentine merchant—gave his name to the newly discovered continents.

Political and Military Unrest.   But it was not in Italy that the rewards of innovation or the satisfactions of achievement were enjoyed. There the seeds of political turmoil and military imperialism, combined with the rise of the Ottoman Turks, were to reap a not-unexpected harvest. In 1454, the five powers agreed to the Peace of Lodi, which established two balanced alliances, one between Florence and Milan, the other between Venice and Naples. The states, along with the papacy, pledged mutual nonaggression, a policy that lasted for nearly 40 years. But the Peace of Lodi did not bring peace. It only halted the long period in which the major city-states struggled against one another. Under cover of the peace, the large states continued the process of swallowing up their smaller neighbors and creating quasi-empires. It was a policy of imperialism as aggressive as that of any in the modern era. Civilian populations were overrun, local leaders exiled or exterminated, tribute monies taken, and taxes levied. Each of the five states either increased its mainland territories or strengthened its hold upon them.

By the end of the fifteenth century the city-states eyed one another greedily and warily. Each expected the others to begin a peninsulawide war for hegemony and took the steps

■ Paolo Uccello, *Niccolò da Tolentino at the Battle of San Romano* (ca. 1435–1450). The painting represents the early stages of a 1432 battle between the Florentines and the Sienese at San Romano. The Florentine condottiere, Niccolò da Tolentino, on a white horse, dominates the center of the scene.

that ultimately ensured the contest. Perhaps the most unusual aspect of the imperialism of the city-states was that it had been restricted to the Italian peninsula. Each of the major powers shared the dream of recapturing the glory that was Rome. Although the Venetians had expanded abroad, their acquisitions had not come through conquest or occupation. In their Greek and Dalmatian territories, local law and custom continued to govern under the benevolent eye of Venetian administrators. But in their mainland territories, the Venetians were as ruthless as the Florentines were in Pisa or as Cesare Borgia was in Romagna when he consolidated the Papal States by fire and sword. Long years of siege and occupation had militarized the Italian city-states. Venice and Florence balanced their budgets on the backs of their captured territories, Milan had been engaged in constant war for decades, and even the papacy was militarily aggressive.

The Italian Decline. The Italians were no longer alone. The most remarkable military leader of the age was not a Renaissance *condottieri* but an Ottoman prince, Mehmed II (1451–1481), who conquered Constantinople and Athens and threatened Rome itself. The rise of the Ottomans (whose name is derived from that of Osman, their original tribal leader) is one of the most compelling stories in world history. Little more than a warrior tribe at the beginning of the fourteenth

century, 150 years later the Ottomans had replaced stagnant Byzantine rule with a virile and potent empire. First they gobbled up towns and cities in a wide arc around Constantinople. Then they fed upon the Balkans and the eastern kingdoms of Hungary and Poland. By 1400, they were a presence in all the territory that stretched from the Black Sea to the Aegean; by 1450, they were its master.

Venice was most directly affected by the Ottoman advance. Not only was its favored position in Eastern trade threatened, but during a prolonged war at the end of the fifteenth century, the Venetians lost many of their most important commercial outposts. Ottoman might closed off the markets of eastern Europe. Islands in the Aegean Sea and seaports along the Dalmatian coast fell to the Turks in alarming succession. By 1480, Venetian naval supremacy was a thing of the past. (See "A Closer Look: The Fall of Constantinople," pp. 348–349.)

The Italian city-states might have met this challenge from the East had they been able to unite in opposing it. Successive popes pleaded for holy wars to halt the advance of the Turks, which was compared in officially inspired propaganda to an outbreak of plague. The fall of Constantinople in 1453 was an event of epochal proportions for Europeans, many believing that it foreshadowed the end of the world. "A

CASE STUDY

Two Views on the Fall of Constantinople

THE SIEGE OF CONSTANTINOPLE

Mehmed II (1432–1481) was one of the great military geniuses of world history. He consolidated the expansion of the Ottoman Empire in Asia Minor and in 1453 organized the siege of Constantinople. He personally directed the combined land and naval assault and brilliantly improvised the tactics that led to the fall of the city. The fall of Constantinople to the Ottomans was a watershed. Kritovoulos was a Greek who entered the service of Mehmed II, probably after the siege. Though he was not an eyewitness of the fall of Constantinople, he gathered numerous accounts together in composing his history. In this selection he refers to the defenders of the city as Romans because Constantinople was what remained of the Roman Empire.

Focus Questions

How did Mehmed get his ships into the harbor at Constantinople? Why was Mehmed's scheme for moving the ships so important in the siege of Constantinople?

Sultan Mehmed considered it necessary in preparation for his next move to get possession of the harbor and open the Horn for his own ships to sail in. So, since every effort and device of his had failed to force the entrance, he made a wise decision, and one worthy of his intellect and power. It succeeded in accomplishing his purpose and in putting an end to all uncertainties.

He ordered the commanders of the vessels to construct as quickly as possible glideways leading from the outer sea to the inner sea. . . . He brought up the ships and placed large cradles under them, with stays against each of their sides to hold them up. And having under-girded them well with ropes, he fastened long cables to the corners and gave them to the soldiers to drag, some of them by hand, and others by certain machines and capstans.

So the ships were dragged along very swiftly. And their crews, as they followed them, rejoiced at the event and boasted of it. Then they manned the ships on the land as if they were on the sea. Some of them hoisted the sails with a shout, as if they were setting sail, and the breeze caught the sails and bellied them out. Others seated themselves on the benches, holding the oars in their hands and moving them as if rowing. And the commanders, running along by the sockets of the masts with whistlings and shouting, and with their whips beating the oarsmen on the benches, ordered them to row. The ships, borne along over the land as if on the sea, were some of them being pulled up the ascent to the top of the hill while others were being hauled down the slope into the harbor, lowering the sails with shouting and great noise.

It was a strange spectacle, and unbelievable in the telling except to those who actually did see it—the sight of ships borne along on the mainland as if sailing on the sea, with their crews and their sails and all their equipment. I believe this was a much greater feat than the cutting of a canal across at Athos by Xerxes, and much stranger to see and to hear about.

The Romans, when they saw such an unheard-of thing actually happen, and warships lying at anchor in the Horn—which they never would have suspected—were astounded at the impossibility of the spectacle, and were overcome by the greatest consternation and perplexity. They did not know what to do now, but were in despair. In fact they had left unguarded the walls along the Horn for a distance of about thirty stadia, and even so they did not have enough men for the rest of the walls, either for defense or for attack, whether citizens or men from elsewhere. Instead, two or even three battlements had but a single defender.

And now, when this sea-wall also became open to attack and had to be guarded, they were compelled to strip the other battlements and bring men there. This constituted a manifest danger, since the defenders were taken away from the rest of the wall while those remaining were not enough to guard it, being so few.

From Kritovoulos, *The History of Mehmed the Conqueror.*

thing terrible to relate and to be deplored by all who have in them any spark of humanity. The splendor and glory of the East has been captured, despoiled, ravaged and completely sacked by the most inhuman barbarians," the Venetian doge was informed. Yet it was Italians rather than Ottomans who plunged the Italian peninsula into the wars from which it never recovered.

The Wars of Italy (1494–1529) began when Naples, Florence, and the Papal States united against Milan. At first the alliance seemed little more than another shift in the balance of power. But rather than call upon Venice to redress the situation, the Milanese leader, Ludovico il Moro, sought help from the French. An army of French cavalry and Swiss mercenaries, led by Charles VIII of France (1483–1498), invaded the

A Closer Look
The Fall of Constantinople

The prayers of the devout were fervent on Easter Sunday in 1453. The Christians of Constantinople knew that it was only a matter of time before the last remaining stronghold of the Byzantine Empire came under siege. For decades the ring of Ottoman conquests had narrowed around the holy city until it alone stood out against the Turkish sultan. Constantinople, the bridge between Europe and Asia, was tottering. The once teeming center of Eastern Christianity had never recovered from the epidemics of the fourteenth century, and now dwindling revenues matched the dwindling population.

Perhaps it was that impoverishment that had kept the Turks at bay. Constantinople was still the best fortified city in the world. Shaped like the head of a horse, it was surrounded by water on all but one side, and that side was protected by two stout rings of walls separated by a trench lined with stones. No cannon forged in the West could dent the battlements, and no navy could hope to force its way through the narrow mouth of the Golden Horn. Thus an uneasy peace existed between sultan and emperor. It was shattered in 1451 with the accession of a new sultan, the 19-year-old Mehmed II. Mehmed's imagination was fired by the ancient prophecies that a Muslim would rule the East. Only Constantinople was a fitting capital for such an empire, and Mehmed immediately began preparations for its conquest.

In 1452 Mehmed had constructed a fortress at the narrow mouth of the Bosporus and demanded tribute from all ships that entered the Golden Horn. The Byzantine emperor sent ambassadors to Mehmed to protest that aggression; Mehmed returned their severed heads. When the first Venetian convoy refused to lower its sails, Mehmed's artillery efficiently sank one of the galleys with a single shot. The Turks now controlled access to the city for trade and supplies. An attack the following spring seemed certain.

The emperor appealed far and wide for aid: to the Venetians and Genoese to protect their trade and to the pope to defend Christianity. The Europeans were willing, but as yet they were unable. They did not think that the Ottomans could assemble an army before summer. By then an Italian armada could dislodge the Ottoman fortress and reinforce the city with trained fighting men.

But they hadn't reckoned with Mehmed. While the Italians bickered over the cost of the expedition and Christians everywhere made ready to celebrate Holy Week, the Ottomans assembled a vast army of fighters and laborers and a huge train of weapons and supplies. Among them was the largest cannon ever cast, with a 26-foot barrel that shot a 1200-pound ball. Fifty teams of oxen and 200 men took two months to pull it in place.

Mehmed's forces—which eventually numbered more than 150,000, of which 60,000 were soldiers—assembled around the walls of Constantinople on 5 April. During the next week a great flotilla sailed up the Bosporus and anchored just out of reach of the Byzantine warships in the Golden Horn. A census taken inside the city revealed that there were only 7000 able-bodied defenders—about 5000 Greek residents and 2000 foreigners, mostly Genoese and Venetians. The Italians were the only true soldiers among them.

Although the defenders were vastly outnumbered, they still held the military advantage. As long as their ships controlled the entrance to the Golden Horn, they could limit the Ottoman attack to only one side of the city, where all of the best defenders could be massed. The Byzantines cast a boom—an iron chain supported by wooden floats—across the mouth of the Horn to forestall a naval attack. By the middle of April, the Turks had begun their land assault. Each day great guns pounded the walls of the city, and each night residents worked frantically to repair the damage. Everyone contributed. Old women wove baskets in which children carried stones. Monks and nuns packed mud and cut branches to shore up the breaches in the wall. The Turks suffered heavily each time they attempted to follow a cannon shot with a massed charge, but the attack took its toll among the defenders as well. No one was safe from the flaming arrows and catapulted stones flung over the city's walls. Choking black smoke filled the air as the huge cannon shook the foundations of the city and treated its stout stone walls as if they were plaster. Nevertheless, for the first month of siege the defenders held their own.

The stubborn defense of the city infuriated Mehmed. As long as there was only one point of attack, the defenders could resist indefinitely. The line of assault had to be extended, and this could only be done by sea. With the boom effectively impregnable and with Italian seamen superior to the Turks, the prospects seemed dim. But what could not be achieved by force might be achieved by intelligence. Mehmed devised a plan to carry a number of smaller ships across land and then to float them behind the Christian fleet. Protected by land forces, the ships could be used as a staging point for another line of attack. Thousands of workers built huge wooden rollers, which were greased with animal fat. Under cover of darkness and the smoke of cannon fire, 72 ships were pulled up the steep hills and pushed down into the sea. Once they were safely anchored, a pontoon bridge was built and cannons were trained on the seaward walls of the city.

By then the city had withstood siege for nearly six weeks without any significant reinforcement. At the end of May there was a sudden lull. A messenger from the sultan arrived to demand surrender. The choice was clear. If the city was taken by force, the customary three days of unrestricted pillage would be allowed; if it yielded, the sultan pledged to protect the property of all who desired to remain under his rule. The emperor replied feebly that no one who had ever laid siege to Constantinople had enjoyed a long life. He was ready to die in defense of his capital.

On 30 May the final assault began. Mehmed knew that his advantage lay in numbers. First, he sent in waves of irregular troops, mostly captured slaves and Christians, who suffered

■ This fifteenth-century illustration shows the siege of Constantinople by the Turks.

great losses and were finally driven back by the weakened defenders. Next, better-trained warriors attacked and widened the breaches made by the irregulars. Finally came the crack Janissaries, the sultan's elite warriors, disciplined from birth to fight. It was the Janissaries who found a small door left open at the base of the wall. In they rushed, quickly overwhelming the first line of defenders and battering their way through the weaker second walls. By dawn the Ottoman flag

was raised over the battlements and the sack of Constantinople had begun.

There was no need for the customary three days of pillage. By the end of the first day there was nothing left worth taking. The churches and monasteries had been looted and defaced, the priests and nuns murdered or defiled, and thousands of civilians had been captured to be sold into slavery. Large areas of the city smoldered from countless fires. The bastion of Eastern Christendom was no more.

Italian peninsula in 1494. With Milanese support, the French swept all before them. Florence was forced to surrender Pisa, a humiliation that led to the overthrow of the Medici and the establishment of French sovereignty. The Papal States were next to be occupied, and within a year Charles had conquered Naples without engaging the Italians in a single significant battle. Unfortunately, the Milanese were not the only ones who could play at the game of foreign alliances. Next, it was the turn of the Venetians and the pope to unite and call upon the services of King Ferdinand of Aragon and the Holy Roman Emperor. Italy was now a battleground in what became a total European war for dynastic supremacy. The city-states used their foreign allies to settle old scores and to extend their own mainland empires. At the turn of the century Naples was dismembered. In 1509, the pope conspired to organize the most powerful combination of forces yet known against Venice. All the "terra firma" possessions of the Most Serene Republic were lost, but by a combination of good fortune and skilled diplomacy Venice itself survived. Florence was less fortunate, becoming a pawn first of the French and then of the Spanish. The final blow to Italian hegemony was the sack of Rome in 1527, when German mercenaries fulfilled the fears of what the "infidels" would do to the Holy City.

Surveying the wreckage of the Italian wars, Machiavelli ended *The Prince* with a plea for a leader to emerge to restore Italian freedom and recreate the unity of the ancient Roman Republic. He concluded with these lines from Petrarch:

> *Then virtue boldly shall engage*
> *And swiftly vanquish barbarous rage,*
> *Proving that ancient and heroic pride*
> *In true Italian hearts had never died.*

CONCLUSION

The revival of "ancient and heroic pride" fueled the Italian Renaissance. The sense of living in a new age, the spirit of human achievement, and the curiosity and wonderment of writers and artists all characterized the Renaissance. The desire to recreate the glories of Rome was not Machiavelli's alone. It could be seen in the palaces of the Italian aristocracy; in the papal rebuilding of the Holy City; and in the military ambitions of princes. But the legacy of empire, of "ancient and heroic pride," had passed out of Italian hands.

QUESTIONS FOR REVIEW

1. What social and cultural conditions were peculiar to the Italian peninsula, and how might those conditions have contributed to the Renaissance?
2. What were the principal characteristics of the Renaissance style in the visual arts?
3. What is humanism, and why was the study of languages so important to the humanists?
4. In what ways did the ideas of Niccolò Machiavelli reflect the reality of politics in the city-states of Renaissance Italy?

KEY TERMS

city-states, *p. 341*

civic humanism, *p. 338*

condottieri, p. 342

doge, *p. 342*

humanists, *p. 337*

linear perspective, *p. 332*

philology, *p. 337*

Pietà, p. 335

Renaissance, *p. 324*

rhetoric, *p. 337*

DISCOVERING WESTERN CIVILIZATION ONLINE

You can obtain more information about the Italian Renaissance at the Websites listed below. See also the Companion Website that accompanies this text, www.ablongman.com/kishlansky, which contains an online study guide and additional resources.

Renaissance Society

NM's Creative Impulse: Renaissance

www.history.evansville.net/renaissa.html#Resources
A site of links to a wide array of subjects relating to the era of the Renaissance. A good starting point.

The Florentine Republic

www.mega.it/eng/egui/epo/secrepu.htm
The history of the Florentine Republic with links to major tourist attractions and buildings. Brief biographies of important Florentine citizens can also be found.

The History of Costume—Index

www.siue.edu/COSTUMES/COSTUME5_INDEX.HTML
Part of a site devoted to the history of dress. This page shows examples of the clothing worn by different classes as well as in different countries during the fifteenth and sixteenth centuries.

Renaissance Art

Renaissance Art

www.anu.edu.au/ArtHistory/renart/pics.art/index_1.html
A pictorial guide to the major artists of the Italian Renaissance and their works. Thumbnail representations lead to links on specific pieces.

Leon Battista Alberti—Great Buildings Online

www.greatbuildings.com/architects/Leon_Battista_Alberti.html
A page devoted to Alberti's architecture with a brief biography and links to pictures.

Michelangelo Buonarroti

www.mega.it/eng/egui/pers/micbuon.htm
A Website devoted to Michelangelo with a variety of links to text and images of Renaissance Florence.

WebMuseum: The Italian Renaissance (1420–1600)

www.ibiblio.org/wm/paint/tl/it-ren/
Reproductions of Renaissance art, with accompanying text.

SUGGESTIONS FOR FURTHER READING

General Reading

P. Burke, *Culture and Society in Renaissance Italy* (Princeton, NJ: Princeton University Press, 1999). A good introduction to social and intellectual developments.

Paul Grendler, ed., *Encyclopedia of the Renaissance* (New York: Scribners, 1999). A valuable reference work for all aspects of the Renaissance.

Denys Hay, *The Italian Renaissance* (Cambridge, England: Cambridge University Press, 1977). The best first book to read, an elegant interpretive essay.

Renaissance Society

Carlo Cipolla, *Before the Industrial Revolution: European Society and Economy, 1000–1700*, 3rd ed. (New York: W. W. Norton, 1994). A sweeping survey of social and economic developments across the centuries.

J. R. Hale, *Renaissance Europe: The Individual and Society* (Berkeley: University of California Press, 1978). A lively study that places the great figures of the Renaissance in their social context.

D. Herlihy and C. Klapisch-Zuber, *Tuscans and Their Families* (New Haven, CT: Yale University Press, 1985). A difficult but rewarding study of the social and demographic history of Florence and its environs.

Margaret L. King, *Women of the Renaissance* (Chicago: University of Chicago Press, 1991). A study by a leading women's historian.

Renaissance Art

Michael Baxandall, *Painting and Experience in Fifteenth-Century Italy* (Oxford, England: Oxford University Press, 1972). A study of the relationship between painters and their patrons and of how and why art was produced.

Anthony Grafton, *Leon Battista Alberti: Master Builder of the Italian Renaissance* (New York: Hill and Wang, 2000). A lucid biographical study of a truly renaissance man.

Frederick Hartt, *History of Italian Renaissance Art* (Englewood Cliffs, NJ: Prentice-Hall, 1974). The most comprehensive survey, with hundreds of plates.

Howard Hibbard, *Michelangelo* (New York: Harper & Row, 1974). A compelling biography of an obsessed genius.

Lisa Jardine and Jerry Brotton, *Global Interests: Renaissance Art Between East and West* (Ithaca, NY: Cornell University Press, 2000). A bold argument about Renaissance art and its relation to Ottoman culture.

Michael Levey, *Early Renaissance* (London: Penguin, 1967). A concise survey of art, clearly written and authoritative.

Linda Murray, *High Renaissance and Mannerism* (London: Thames & Hudson, 1985). The best introduction to late Renaissance art.

Renaissance Ideals

Hans Baron, *The Crisis of the Early Italian Renaissance* (Princeton, NJ: Princeton University Press, 1966). One of the most influential intellectual histories of the period.

George Holmes, *The Florentine Enlightenment*, 2nd ed. (Oxford: Clarendon Press, 1992). A new edition of the best study of intellectual developments in Florence.

Quentin Skinner, *Machiavelli* (Oxford: Oxford University Press, 1981). A brief but brilliant biography.

The Politics of the Italian City-States

Gene Brucker, *Florence, The Golden Age 1138–1737* (Berkeley: University of California Press, 1998). The best single-volume introduction to Florentine history with excellent illustrations.

J. R. Hale, *Florence and the Medici* (London: Thames & Hudson, 1977). A compelling account of the relationship between a city and its most powerful citizens.

Frederic C. Lane, *Venice: A Maritime Republic* (Baltimore, MD: Johns Hopkins University Press, 1973). A complete history of Venice that stresses its naval and mercantile developments.

Lauro Martines, *Power and Imagination: City-States in Renaissance Italy* (New York: Alfred A. Knopf, 1979). An important interpretation of the politics of the Italian powers.

Eugene F. Rice, Jr., *The Foundations of Early Modern Europe, 1460–1559*, 2nd ed. (New York: W. W. Norton, 1994). The best short synthetic work.

Charles Stinger, *The Renaissance in Rome* (Bloomington, IN: University of Indiana Press, 1998). A thorough account of one of the great ages in the history of Rome.

For a list of additional titles related to this chapter's topics, please see http://www.ablongman.com/kishlansky.

Chapter 12
THE EUROPEAN EMPIRES

Chapter Outline

Kings were mythical figures even in life. Only the bravest and the ablest artists attempted to represent them on canvas. In The Visual Record, you will see one of the most famous images of a king in all of European history. ➤

ASTRIDE THE WORLD

The Age of Monarchies

Henry VIII lived large. He was a bear of a man, famed for his ability to hunt all day while wearing out a pack of trained horses, for his prowess in wrestling bouts, including one with King Francis I of France, and, of course, for having six wives. His accomplishments as leader were equally impressive. Bequeathed a surplus by his father, Henry spent lavishly in an attempt to restore England to European prominence. He allied with Spain to fight France and with France to fight Spain and ran an expensive but futile campaign to be elected Holy Roman Emperor. He sponsored humanist thinkers and brought them to his court from all over Europe. He also encouraged the new learning at the Universities of Oxford and Cambridge and during his reign one of the classic works of English literature, Sir Thomas More's *Utopia*, was written. Henry's generals decisively defeated the Scots, England's troublesome northern neighbor, and his ministers successfully completed the integration of Wales into the English crown.

In 1532, when his attempt to secure an annulment of his first marriage failed, Henry dissolved England's ties to the Church of Rome declaring that "this realm of England is an Empire"—the first statement of British imperial ambition. He had Parliament declare him Supreme Head of the Church in England and then helped himself to the vast holdings of the Catholic religious orders. Perhaps as much as a third of all of the land in England was forfeited to the crown when the monasteries and chantries were dissolved. Though Henry VIII shared his plunder with his loyal nobility and gentry, the lion's share was his. Henry's own religious beliefs remained shrouded in mystery, but he guided his nation toward the Protestantism that would bloom under his son Edward VI and his daughter Elizabeth I.

Henry VIII has passed through the ages as the very symbol of a monarch, an image captured by the German portrait painter Hans Holbein. Holbein was born into a family of painters and settled among the Swiss in Basel to practice his craft before being invited to the English court in the mid-1530s. His great skill was in rendering subjects true to life and his paintings of the Henrician court and its leading members such as Thomas More and Thomas Cromwell rival the works of Italian Renaissance

portraiturists. But none were more memorable than the artist's numerous studies of Henry himself. Holbein was able to capture both the ferocity and the grandeur of the king.

Ironically, one of Holbein's most powerful, and most famous, portraits of Henry did not survive the seventeenth century. Part of a mural that Holbein painted in Henry's Whitehall Palace in 1537, the original work was lost when the palace burned in 1698. However, Holbein's followers had copied the grand painting, and earlier sketches of it by Holbein himself also survived, and so we still have a strong visual record of Holbein's vision of the king. The image shown here is a vibrant copy of the Whitehall Palace original, painted on oak panels, likely in the mid-sixteenth century. In this portrait, Henry stands with straight legs astride suggesting the solidity of tree trunks, one arm bent at the elbow as if in defiance of all comers. There is not even a suggestion of doubt as the king thrusts out his chest and fixes the viewer with a penetrating stare. The artist represents the sumptuousness of Henry's court in the monarch's clothing. Fabric literally encases him, flowing in folds and gathers of intricate design and the costliest material. Furs drape over his doublet and elaborately embroidered red cloak. Enormous rubies bedeck not only his great gold chain, but his hat and vest, running down both sleeves, all to create an overwhelming sense of opulence. Even the protruding codpiece is meant to convey the potency of a king who had finally sired a male heir. Every detail conveys the impression of a monarch at the height of his power.

Looking Ahead

This image of Henry VIII is among the most recognizable from an age of monarchy that began in the sixteenth century and coincided with the consolidations of nations in western Europe and their expansion into all corners of the globe. Everywhere small principalities and kingdoms were absorbed by their larger and more powerful neighbors, and Europe's military might was on display as far east as India and as far west as Peru. Though England played but a small part in a century dominated by Spain and France, even its monarch could believe that he bestrode the world like a colossus. ➤

■ Henry VIII portrait, after Hans Holbein.

EUROPEAN ENCOUNTERS

The sixteenth century was an age of exploration. Knowledge bequeathed from the past created curiosity about the present. Technological change made long sea voyages possible, and the demands of commerce provided incentives. Ottoman expansion on the southern and eastern frontiers of the Continent, however, threatened access to the goods of the East on which Europeans had come to rely. Spices were rare and expensive, but they were not merely luxuries. While nobles and rich merchants consumed them lavishly to enhance their reputations of wealth and generosity, spices had many practical uses. Some acted as preservatives, some as flavorings, and others were used as perfumes to battle the noxious gases that rose from urban streets and invaded homes and workplaces. The drugs of the East, the nature of which we can only guess at, helped soothe chronic ill health. The demand for all of the "spices" continued to rise at a greater rate than their supply. There was more than a fortune to be made by anyone who could participate in the trade.

Eastern spices were expensive. Most European manufactured goods had little utility in the East. Woven wool, which was the staple of Western industry, was too heavy to be worn in Eastern climes. Both silk and cotton came from the East and were more expertly spun there. Even Western jewelry relied upon imported stones. Metalwork was an attractive commodity for export, but providing Ottomans or other Muslims with weapons to wage holy wars against Christian Europe posed problems of policy and morality. And once the Ottomans began to cast great bronze cannons of their own, European arms were less eagerly sought. Western gold and silver flowed steadily east. As supplies of precious metals dwindled, economic growth in Europe slowed. Throughout the fifteenth century, ever-larger amounts of Western specie were necessary to purchase ever-smaller amounts of Eastern commodities. Europe faced a severe shortage of gold and silver, a shortage that threatened its standard of living and its prospects for economic growth. The search was on to discover new sources of gold.

Africa and a Passage to India

It was the Portuguese who made the first dramatic breakthroughs in exploration and colonization. Perched on the southwestern tip of Europe, Portugal was an agriculturally poor and sparsely populated nation. Among its few marketable commodities were fish and wine. The Portuguese had long been sea explorers, especially in the Atlantic Ocean, where they had established bases in the Azores and Madeira islands. Their small ships, known as **caravels**, were ideal for ocean travel, and their navigators were among the most skillful in the world. Yet they were unable to participate in the lucrative Mediterranean trade in bullion and spices until the expanding power of the Ottomans threatened the traditional eastern sea routes.

Prince Henry the Navigator. In the early fifteenth century, the Portuguese gained a foothold in northern Africa and used it to stage voyages along the continent's unexplored western coast. Like most explorers, the Portuguese were motivated by an unselfconscious mixture of faith and greed. Establishing southern bases would enable them to surround their Muslim enemies and give them access to the African bullion trade. The Portuguese navigator Bartolomeu Dias (ca. 1450–1500) summarized those goals succinctly: "To give light to those who are in darkness and to grow rich." Under the energetic leadership of Prince Henry the Navigator (1394–1460), the Portuguese pushed steadily southward. Prince Henry studied navigational techniques, accumulated detailed accounts of voyages, and encouraged the creation of accurate maps of the African coastline.

Prince Henry's systematic program paid off in the next generation. By the 1480s, Portuguese outposts had reached almost to the equator, and in 1487 Bartolomeu Dias rounded the tip of Africa and opened the eastern African shores to Portuguese traders. The aim of the enterprises was access to Asia rather than Africa. Dias might have reached India if his crew had not mutinied and forced him to return home. A decade later, Vasco da Gama (ca. 1460–1524) rounded the Cape of Good Hope and crossed into the Indian Ocean. His journey took two years, but when he returned to Lisbon in 1499 laden with the most valuable spices of the East, Portuguese ambitions were achieved. Larger expeditions followed, one of which, blown off course, touched the South American coast of Brazil. Brazil was soon subsumed within the Portuguese dominions.

Spanish and Portuguese Explorations, 1400–1600

The Beginnings of the Slave Trade. The exploration of the African coast also brought the Portuguese into contact with Muslim traders who had developed connections between North Africa and the middle of the continent. They bartered for gold, ivory, and exotic spices, exchanging colorful cloth, metalwork, and other manufactured goods. They also bartered for slaves. Slavery was a common feature of the cultures that interacted in Africa. Europeans had used slaves in ancient times and had developed a theory that justified slavery by capture. Muslims were dependent upon them for their armies and bought many slaves from European sources. Africans enslaved those who were captured in tribal wars and sold them out of Africa, first to Muslim traders and then to the Portuguese. There was nothing new about slavery in the West, especially if the slaves were not Christians. The popes who granted Portugal a monopoly on European trade in Africa also sanctioned the trade in African slaves upon the condition that those enslaved had not converted to Christianity.

The slave trade began almost immediately. At first African slaves were imported to Europe as a curiosity and were purchased by wealthy families. But the discovery of the Azores and the Canary Islands provided a much more valuable use for the enslaved Africans. Their ability to labor in intense heat

MAP DISCOVERY

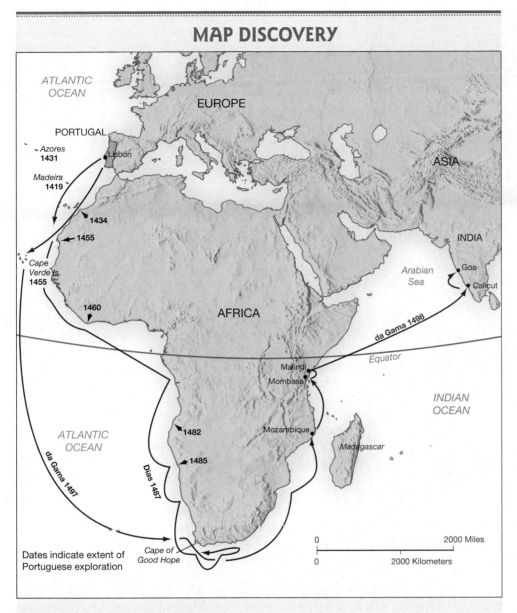

Portuguese Explorations

Examine the routes of the Portuguese explorers. What was their strategy of exploration? How long did it take for explorers to round the tip of Africa? What was the ultimate goal of Portuguese seafarers?

the right to trade in slaves was sold to private entrepreneurs, and they were less scrupulous in their methods. Soon the Portuguese were simply conducting raids on coastal villages to capture as many Africans as they could cram on to their boats.

In these early decades, slaves were viewed as just another trading commodity and valued only in regard to their profit. Ships were still small, voyages still risky, and capital still scarce. Traders carried whatever items were most in demand, and the agricultural use of African slaves was limited by the small amount of commercial agriculture undertaken by Europeans. The Portuguese held a monopoly on transporting slaves from Africa, but the trade soon centered in Seville where Italians dominated it. This was a significant, if unplanned development. Seville would soon become the center of the Spanish overseas empire, and the Spanish colonies in America would soon become the destination for most of the African slaves bought by Europeans.

The Asian Trade. The Portuguese came to the East as traders rather than as conquerors. Building on their experience in West Africa, they developed a policy of establishing military outposts to protect their investments and subduing native populations only when necessary. Throughout the East the Portuguese took advantage of local feuds to gain allies, and they established trading compounds that were easily defensible. The Portuguese general Alfonso de Albuquerque (1453–1515) understood the need for strategically placed garrisons and conquered the vital ports of the Middle East and India. By the first decade of the sixteenth century, the Portuguese were masters of a vast empire, which spanned both the eastern and western coasts of Africa and the western shores of India. Most importantly, the Portuguese controlled Ceylon and Indonesia, the precious Spice Islands from which came cloves, cinnamon, and pepper.

fitted them for agricultural work in the new sugar fields that were being developed in these Atlantic islands. By the 1470s it was estimated that over a thousand African slaves a year were being imported into Portugal and that a significant percentage of those were sold to Spanish masters who also saw their value in farming. Originally, the slaves were purchased either from Muslim traders or directly from African tribal leaders. As the trade became more sophisticated and more competitive, slaves could no longer by bartered for trinkets. Horses became the preferred medium of exchange, and Prince Henry the Navigator financed the trade until his death. Thereafter,

■ This sixteenth-century map of Java and the Moluccas shows European traders bartering for spices. At the upper left, a ship laden with the rich cargo sails for markets in Europe.

Almost overnight, Lisbon became one of the trading capitals of the world, tripling in population between 1500 and 1550.

It was northern Europe that was to harvest what Portugal had sown. The long voyages around Africa were costly and dangerous. Moreover, the expense of maintaining a far-flung empire ate into the profits of trade at the same time that the increased volume necessary to make the voyages worthwhile drove down spice prices. Between 1501 and 1505, more than 80 ships and 7000 men sailed from Portugal to the East. The vast commitment was underwritten by Flemish, German, and Italian bankers. Soon Antwerp replaced Lisbon as the marketplace for Asian spices. Ironically, it was in the accidental discovery of Brazil rather than in Asia that the Portuguese were rewarded for the enterprise of their explorers.

Mundus Novus

While most of Portugal's resources were devoted to the Asian trade, those of the Spanish kingdom came to be concentrated in the New World. Although larger and richer than its eastern neighbor, Spain had been segmented into a number of small kingdoms and principalities and divided between Christians and Muslims. Not until the end of the fifteenth century, when the crowns of Aragon and Castile were united and the Muslims expelled from Granada, could the Spanish concentrate their resources. By then they were far behind in establishing commercial enterprises. With Portugal dominating the African route to India, Queen Isabella of Castile was persuaded to take an interest in a western route by a Genoese adventurer, Christopher Columbus (ca. 1446–1506). That interest resulted in one of the greatest accidents of history. (See "A Closer Look: Isabella of Castile," pp. 360–361.)

Christopher Columbus.   Like all well-informed people of his day, Columbus believed that the world was round. By carefully calculating routes and distances, he concluded that a western track would be shorter and less expensive than the path that the Portuguese were breaking around Africa. Columbus's conclusions were based partly on conventional knowledge and partly on his own self-assurance. All were wholly erroneous. He misjudged the size of the globe by 25 percent and the distance of the journey by 400 percent. But he persevered against all odds. Columbus sailed westward into the unknown in 1492, and on 12 October he landed in the Bahamas, on an island that he named San Salvador. He had encountered a *Mundus Novus,* a New World.

DOCUMENT

Christopher Columbus, Letter from the New World

Initially, Columbus's discovery was a disappointment. He had gone in search of a western passage to the Indies and he had failed to return to Spain laden with Eastern spices. Despite his own belief that the islands he had discovered lay just off the coast of Japan, it was soon apparent that he had found an altogether unknown landmass. Columbus's own explorations and those of his successors continued to focus on discovering a route to the Indies. That was all the more imperative once the Portuguese succeeded in finding the passage around Africa. In 1494, the **Treaty of Tordesillas** had confirmed Portugal's right to the eastern route to the Indies as well as to any undiscovered lands east of an imaginary line fixed west of the Cape Verde Islands. That entitled Portugal to Brazil; the Spanish received whatever lay west of the line. At the time few doubted that Portugal had the better end of the bargain.

But Spanish-backed explorations soon proved the value of the new lands. Using the Caribbean Islands as a staging ground, successive explorers uncovered the vast coastline of Central and South America. In 1513, Vasco Núñez de Balboa (1475–1517) crossed the land passage in Panama and became the first European to view the Pacific Ocean. The discovery of this ocean refueled Spanish ambitions to find a western passage to the Indies.

Ferdinand Magellan.   In 1519, Ferdinand Magellan (ca. 1480–1521), a Portuguese mariner in the service of Spain, set sail in pursuit of Columbus's goal of reaching the Spice Islands by sailing westward. His voyage, which he did not live

A MOMENTOUS DISCOVERY

Christopher Columbus seemingly needs no introduction. His name has forever been associated with the European discovery of the New World, although the meaning of that discovery has continually been contested. In the summer of 1492, Columbus sailed west from the Canary Islands believing that he would reach the coast of China. Instead he landed on an island in the Caribbean. This passage, from a letter addressed to the royal treasurer of Spain, contains his first impressions of the people he encountered.

Focus Questions

How do the indigenous people respond to Columbus and his men? Why is Columbus so interested in the tools and clothing of the natives?

A letter addressed to the noble Lord Raphael Sanchez, *Treasurer to their most invincible Majesties, Ferdinand and Isabella, King and Queen of Spain, by Christopher Columbus, to whom our age is greatly indebted, treating of the islands of India recently discovered beyond the Ganges, to explore which he had been sent eight months before under the auspices and at the expense of their said Majesties.*

The inhabitants of both sexes in this island, and in all the others which I have seen, or of which I have received information, go always naked as they were born, with the exception of some of the women, who use the covering of a leaf, or small bough, or an apron of cotton which they prepare for that purpose. None of them are possessed of any iron, neither have they weapons, being unacquainted with, and indeed incompetent to use them, not from any deformity of body (for they are well-formed), but because they are timid and full of fear.

They carry however in lieu of arms, canes dried in the sun, on the ends of which they fix heads of dried wood sharpened to a point, and even these they dare not use habitually; for it has often occurred when I have sent two or three of my men to any of the villages to speak with the natives, that they have come out in a disorderly troop, and have fled in such haste at the approach of our men, that the fathers forsook their children and the children their fathers. This timidity did not arise from any loss or injury that they had received from us; for, on the contrary, I gave to all I approached whatever articles I had about me, such as cloth and many other things, taking nothing of theirs in return: but they are naturally timid and fearful. As soon however as they see that they are safe, and have laid aside all fear, they are very simple and honest, and exceedingly liberal with all they have; none of them refusing any thing he may possess when he is asked for it, but on the contrary inviting us to ask them. They exhibit great love towards all others in preference to themselves: they also give objects of great value for trifles, and content themselves with very little or nothing in return.

Such are the events which I have briefly described. Farewell.

Lisbon, the 14th of March.

CHRISTOPHER COLUMBUS,
Admiral of the Fleet of the Ocean.

Christopher Columbus, *Letter from the First Voyage* (1493).

to complete, remains the most astounding of the age. After making the Atlantic crossing, Magellan resupplied his fleet in Brazil. Then his ships began the long southerly run toward the tip of South America, though he had no idea of the length of the continent. Suppressing mutinies and overcoming shipwrecks and desertions, Magellan finally found the straits that still bear his name. That crossing was the most difficult of all; the 300 miles took 38 terrifying days to navigate.

The Pacific voyage was equally remarkable. The sailors went nearly four months without taking on fresh food or water. Survival was miraculous. "We drank yellow water and often ate sawdust. Rats were sold for half a ducat a piece."

When Magellan finally reached land, in the Philippines, his foolhardy decision to become involved in a local war cost him his life. It was left to his navigator, Sebastian Elcano (ca. 1476–1526), to complete the journey. In 1522, three years and one month after setting out, Elcano returned to Spain with a single ship and 18 survivors of the crew of 280. But in his hold were spices of greater value than the cost of the expedition, and in his return was practical proof that the world was round.

The circumnavigation of Magellan and Elcano brought to an end the first stage of the Spanish exploration of the New World. Columbus's dreams were realized, but the vastness of the Pacific Ocean made a western passage to the Indies uneconomical. In 1529, the Spanish crown relinquished to the Portuguese its claims to the Spice Islands for a cash settlement. By then, trading spices was less alluring than mining gold and silver.

The Spanish Conquests

At the same moment that Magellan's voyage closed one stage of Spanish exploration, the exploits of Hernando Cortés (1485–1547) opened another. The Spanish colonized the New

A Closer Look
Isabella of Castile

"It is bittersweet to reign" was the motto of her predecessor, Henry IV. It was also the legacy of Isabella of Castile. She was beloved in life and revered after death; indeed, until recently there was a movement to have her canonized as a saint in the Catholic Church. Her achievements were staggering. Her reign ended nearly a half century of internecine and dynastic warfare in Castile. Through her marriage to Ferdinand of Aragon she united the two largest kingdoms on the Spanish peninsula. With their combined resources, Isabella and Ferdinand were able to accomplish what their predecessors had only dreamed of for 500 years: the final reconquest of Spanish lands held by the Moors. By her financial support to a Genoese explorer named Christopher Columbus, Isabella gained for Castile title to the richest discovery in history.

But those accomplishments were not without cost. For Isabella, a united Spain was a Catholic Spain. The reconquista was conducted as a holy war of Christian against Muslim. It was as brutal as it was successful. Isabella was directly involved in planning the military campaign and attending to the details of logistics and strategy. She ended centuries of religious diversity by expelling both the Muslims and the Jews. She also accepted the need to purify Catholicism and encouraged the work of the Inquisition in examining the beliefs of converts known as *conversos*. That resulted in the exile or execution of thousands of former Muslims and Jews and blackened forever the reputation of the Spanish church.

Isabella of Castille was not raised to rule. She had two older brothers and was given a "woman's" education as a child. While her brother Alfonso struggled with Latin and French, she was taught only Castilian. While he learned to wield a sword, she learned to manipulate a needle. Isabella mastered sewing and the decorative arts of needlepoint and embroidery. Even as queen she sewed Ferdinand's shirts as a mark of respect and wifely devotion. But if she accepted the education that was offered to her, she had a streak of independence as well. She loved to hunt and refused to give up horses for donkeys as befitted a noblewoman. She also refused to accept the husband that her half-brother Henry IV had chosen for her. Isabella was a valuable pawn in the international game of diplomacy. She had a reputation for great beauty—her strawberry-blond hair and turquoise eyes were uncommon and much admired in Spain—and that, plus the fact that she had been named heir to the Castilian throne in 1468, brought a number of suitors. Henry betrothed her to Alfonso of Portugal, but Isabella had set her heart on Ferdinand of Aragon. In 1469, the two teenagers eloped, setting off a succession crisis in Castile and ultimately a civil war for the crown in which Isabella triumphed.

Ferdinand and Isabella enjoyed three decades of a happy marriage. Despite their travels, they were nearly inseparable. They ruled their kingdoms as partners and shared the joys and sorrows of their days. They endured the death of their only son,

Juan, in 1497, and of his sister Isobel the following year. Three girls outlived their mother, but the eldest, Isabella's heir, Juana, had exhibited such erratic behavior that she was widely believed mentally incompetent. Her claims to the throne were ultimately set aside. Their youngest daughter, Catherine, the queen's favorite, was married to an English prince in 1501. Her mother would not live to see her divorced by Henry VIII.

At the time of their marriage, neither Ferdinand nor Isabella could have known that the union of their crowns was the first step in making Spain the most powerful nation in Europe. The two economies were complementary: Aragon with its long Mediterranean coastline was mercantile and Castile with its vast plain and fertile valleys was agricultural. Both were to benefit by the reconquest of Granada, which joined Spain's Atlantic and Mediterranean seaboards in the southeast. Isabella herself directed the military campaign. During eight years of battle, she guided Christian forces from the front, organizing supplies, reinforcements, and arms. She took special care of the wounded, setting up hospital tents that she visited. "The dead weigh on me heavily," she confessed to Ferdinand, "but they could not have gone better employed." Isabella was present at the siege of Granada, viewing the battlements personally and receiving the surrendered keys to the city on 2 January 1492.

The conquest of Granada drove the Muslims south into North Africa. It completed one part of the queen's program for religious unity. The second part was accomplished by decree. In April 1492, all Jews were given three months to depart the Spanish kingdoms. They were prohibited from removing arms, horses, or precious metal, making them not only homeless, but destitute. From the beginning of her reign, Isabella had persecuted the Jewish minority in her realm. They were made to wear distinguishing badges and denied civil rights that they had long enjoyed. At the same time, the work of the Spanish Inquisition under the direction of the zealous Cardinal Tomás de Torquemada had increased anti-Semitic tensions within Castile. Using threats and torture, Torquemada exposed loyal conversos as secret Jewish agents. He encouraged confiscation of converso property and attacks against Jewish communities. Although the queen at first intervened to maintain civic order, she, too, believed that the Jews constituted a disloyal fifth column within her state. But as long as she was at war with the Muslims, she needed Jewish financiers and administrators.

■ Flemish tapestry showing Isabella and Ferdinand attended by courtiers and ladies-in-waiting.

Once the war had ended, expulsion followed. Paradoxically, the first of the representatives of the old wealth of Castile boarded ship on the same day as a Genoese explorer, Christopher Columbus, set sail under the Castilian flag to uncover the new wealth of Castile. Columbus had approached Isabella twice before, but on both occasions his proposals had been rejected. Isabella's councillors were opposed both to Columbus's plan of sailing west to reach the Indies and to the concessions he demanded should he be successful. Although crown finances were depleted by the war and Isabella did not want to bargain with an Italian adventurer, she realized that she would risk little to gain much. The decision was the most important of her reign. Through the discoveries made by Columbus and his successors, Castile reaped the greatest windfall in European history.

■ Looking downward from North America, this "inverted" map of Brazil from ca. 1547 depicts everyday activities and incidents of European cruelty against the indigenous people.

World along the model of their reconquest of Spain. Individuals were given control over land and the people on it in return for military service. The interests of the crown were threefold: to convert the natives to Christianity; to extend sovereignty over new dominions; and to gain some measure of profit from the venture. The colonial entrepreneurs had a singular interest—to grow rich. By and large, the colonizers came from the lower orders of Spanish society. Even the original captains and governors were drawn from groups, like younger sons of the nobility, that would have had little opportunity for rule in Castile. They undertook great risks in expectation of great rewards.

Thus many of the protective measures taken by the crown to ensure orderly colonization and fair treatment of the natives were ineffective in practice. During the first decades of the sixteenth century, Spanish captains and their followers subdued the Indian populations of the Caribbean Islands and put them to work on the agricultural haciendas that they had carved out for themselves. As early as 1498, Castilian women began arriving in the New World. Their presence helped change the character of the settlement towns from wild frontier garrisons to civilized settlements. Younger daughters of the lesser nobility, guided and guarded by chaperones, came to find husbands among the successful **conquistadores**. Some of the women ultimately inherited huge estates and participated fully in the forging of Spanish America.

Life on the hacienda, even in relative ease with a Castilian wife and family, did not always satisfy the ambitions of the Spanish colonizers. Hernando Cortés was one such conquistador. Having participated in the conquest of Cuba, Cortés sought an independent command to lead an expedition into the hinterland of Central America, where a fabulous empire

■ A sixteenth-century Indian drawing of Cortés marching on the Aztec capital at Tenochtitlán. Cortés, the bearded figure third from right, is accompanied by the Indian princess Malinche, who served as his interpreter, and the Moorish servant Estevanico. Barefoot soldiers and Indian porters bring up the rear.

Cortés's Letter to Charles V

was rumored to exist. Gathering a force of 600 men, Cortés sailed across the Gulf of Mexico in 1519; established a fort at Vera Cruz, where he garrisoned 200 men; and then sank his boats so that none of his company could turn back. With 400 soldiers, he began his quest. The company marched 250 miles through steamy jungles and over rugged mountains before glimpsing the first signs of the great Aztec civilization.

The Aztec Empire was a loose confederation of native tribes that the Aztecs had conquered during the previous century. They were ruled by the emperor Montezuma II (1502–1520) from his capital at Tenochtitlán, a marvelous city built of stone and baked clay in the middle of a lake. Invited to an audience with the Aztec emperor, Cortés and his men saw vast stores of gold and silver.

The conquest of the Aztecs took almost a year. Nearly 100,000 natives from the tribes that the Aztecs had conquered supported the Spanish assault. Cortés's cavalry terrified the Aztecs. They had never seen horses or iron armaments. Cortés also benefited from the Aztec practice of taking battlefield captives to be used in religious sacrifices. That allowed many Spanish soldiers, who would otherwise have been killed, to be rescued and to fight again.

By 1522, Cortés was master of an area larger than all of Spain. But the cost in native lives was staggering. In 30 years a population of approximately 25 million had been reduced to

THE HALLS OF MONTEZUMA

Bernal Díaz del Castillo (ca. 1492–1581) was one of the soldiers who accompanied Hernando Cortés on the conquest of the Aztecs. Díaz wrote The True History of the Conquest of New Mexico *to refute what he regarded as inaccurate accounts of the conquest. In this passage he describes the Aztec gods from a Christian point of view and shows how difficult it was for the Europeans to understand the different cultures they were encountering.*

Focus Questions

Díaz describes the Aztec gods as devils and idols. What does this reveal about the Europeans' way of thinking? Why would Cortés want to see Montezuma's gods, and why does Montezuma show them to him?

Then Cortés said to Montezuma . . . "Your Highness is indeed a great prince, and it has delighted us to see your cities. Now that we are here in your temple, will you show us your gods?"

Montezuma replied that he would first have to consult with his priests. After he had spoken with them, he bade us enter a small tower room, a kind of hall where there were two altars with very richly painted planks on the ceiling. On each altar there were two giant figures, their bodies very tall and stout. The first one, to the right, they said was Uichilobos, their god of war. It had a very broad face with monstrous, horrible eyes, and the whole body was covered with precious stones, gold, and pearls that were stuck on with a paste they make in this country out of roots. The body was circled with great snakes made of gold and precious stones, and in one hand he held a bow and in the other some arrows. A small idol standing by him they said was his page; he held a short lance and a shield rich with gold and precious stones. Around the neck of Uichilobos were silver Indian faces and things that we took to be the hearts of these Indians, made of gold and decorated with many precious blue stones. There were braziers with copal incense, and they were burning in them the hearts of three Indians they had sacrificed that day. All the walls and floor were black with crusted blood, and the whole place stank.

To the left stood another great figure, the height of Uichilobos, with the face of a bear and glittering eyes made of their mirrors, which they call *tezcal*. It was decorated with precious stones the same as Uichilobos, for they said that the two were brothers. This Tezcatepuca was the god of hell and had charge of the souls of the Mexicans. His body was girded with figures like little devils, with snake-like tails. The walls were so crusted with blood and the floor was so bathed in it that in the slaughterhouses of Castile there was no such stink. They had offered to this idol five hearts from the day's sacrifices. . . .

Our captain said to Montezuma, half laughingly, "Lord Montezuma, I do not understand how such a great prince and wise man as yourself can have failed to come to the conclusion that these idols of yours are not gods, but evil things—devils is the term for them. . . . "

The two priests with Montezuma looked hostile, and Montezuma replied with annoyance, "Señor Malinche, if I had thought that you would so insult my gods, I would not have shown them to you. We think they are very good, for they give us health, water, good seedtimes and weather, and all the victories we desire. We must worship and make sacrifices to them. Please do not say another word to their dishonor."

From Bernal Díaz, *The True History of the Conquest of New Mexico* (1552–1568).

less than 2 million. Most of the loss was due to exposure to European diseases such as smallpox, typhoid, and measles, against which the natives were helpless. Their labor-intensive system of agriculture could not survive the rapid decrease in population, and famine followed pestilence.

This tragic sequence was repeated everywhere the Europeans appeared. In 1531, Francisco Pizarro (ca. 1475–1541) matched Cortés's feat when he conquered the Peruvian empire of the Incas. That conquest vastly extended the territory under Spanish control and became the true source of profit for the crown when a huge silver mine was discovered in 1545 at Potosí in what is now southern Bolivia. The gold and silver that poured into Spain in the next quarter century helped support Spanish dynastic ambitions in Europe. During the course of the sixteenth century, more than 200,000 Spaniards migrated across the ocean. Perhaps one in ten were women who married and set up families. In succeeding generations, the settlers created huge haciendas built on the forced labor of black African slaves, who proved better able to endure the rigors of mining and farming than did the natives.

The Legacy of the Encounters

By the seventeenth century, long-distance trade had begun to integrate the regions of the world into a single marketplace. Slaves bought in Africa mined silver in South America. The bullion was shipped to Spain, where it was distributed across Europe. Most went to Amsterdam to settle Spanish debts, Dutch bankers having replaced the Italians as the paymasters of Europe. From Holland the silver traveled east to the Baltic Sea—the Dutch lifeline where vital stores of grain and timber were purchased for home consumption. Even more of this African-mined Spanish silver, traded by the Dutch, was carried to Asia to buy spices in the Spice Islands, cottons in India, and silk in China. Millions of ounces of silver flowed from South America to Asia via the European trading routes. On the return voyage, Indian cottons were traded in Africa to purchase slaves for the South American silver mines.

Gold, God, and Glory.   Gold, God, and glory neatly summarized the motives of the European explorers. Perhaps it is

MAP DISCOVERY

Claims of Spain and Portugal to Overseas Empires

Examine the voyages of discovery and the claims to overseas empires. How did Portuguese and Spanish exploration differ? What was the effect of the Treaty of Tordesillas on their travel and claims? Why was it believed at the time that Portugal was the more powerful empire?

not necessary to delve any further. The gold of Africa and the silver of South America enriched the Western nations. Christian missions arose wherever the European empires touched down: among Africans, Asians, and Native Americans. And glory there was in plenty. The feats of the European explorers were recounted in story and song. The *Lusiads* (1572) by Luiz de Camões (ca. 1524–1580), one of the greatest works of Portuguese literature, celebrated the new age. "They were men of no ordinary stature, equally at home in war and in dangers of every kind: they founded a new kingdom among distant peoples, and made it great." In the achievement of exploration and conquest, the modern world had finally surpassed the ancients. "Let us hear no more then of Ulysses and Aeneas and their long journeyings, no more of Alexander and Trajan and their famous victories. My theme is the daring and renown of the Portuguese, to whom Neptune and Mars alike give homage."

The feats of exploration were worthy of celebration. In less than 50 years, tenacious European seafarers found passages to the east and continents to the west. In doing so they overcame terrors both real and imagined. Hazardous journeys in uncharted waters took their toll in men and ships. The odds of surviving a voyage of exploration were no better than those of surviving an epidemic of plague. Nearly two-thirds of da Gama's crew perished on the passage to India. The 40 men that Columbus left on Hispaniola, almost half his company, disappeared without a trace. Only one of the five ships that set out with Magellan in 1519 returned to Spain. "If you want to learn how to pray, go to sea" was a Portuguese proverb that needed no explanation.

Yet all of these dangers were overcome. The expansion of Europe was a feat of technology. Advances in navigational skills, especially in dead reckoning and later in calculating latitude from the position of the sun, were essential preconditions for covering the distances that were to be traveled. So were the more sophisticated ship designs. The magnetic compass and the astrolabe were indispensable tools. New methods for the making of maps and charts, and the popular interest in them, fueled both ambitions and abilities. It was a mapmaker who named the newly found continents after Amerigo Vespucci (1451–1512), the Italian explorer who voyaged to Brazil for the Portuguese. It may have been an accident that Columbus found the New World, but it was no coincidence that he was able to land in the same place three more times.

The Columbian Exchange. The encounters between Europeans and native Americans were a cultural and intellectual event of the first magnitude, likely stirring the imaginations of native tribesmen as much as those of European writers. But it was also an ecological and biological event with enormous consequences—a transfer of microbes, animals, and plants known as the **Columbian Exchange**.

The mixing of populations that had historically remained separate had effects that no one could have foreseen. First and foremost were issues of public health. Although it is believed that the Americas were originally settled by migration across a land bridge that connected Russia to Alaska, those who made the trek were few and over many generations lost their immunity to diseases that they may have encountered in Europe. When the Spanish explorers arrived in the Caribbean islands, they carried agents of common diseases such as measles, smallpox, and influenza that raged in European population centers and killed many thousands each year but to which survivors carried a lifetime immunity. The native populations of the Americas endured their first exposure to these diseases all at once and millions succumbed in the first half-century of contact. Similarly, it was believed that Europeans first contracted the venereal disease syphilis through sexual encounters with American women. Though experts still debate whether syphilis originated in the New World, there was an epidemic of the disease in western Europe after the explorers returned home.

Disease was not the only unanticipated exchange that resulted from the encounters. On their ships the Spanish explorers brought horses, pigs, cows, and other domesticated animals unknown in the Americas. Not only did these new animals change patterns of work among the native populations, but they also changed dietary customs. Pork and beef gradually entered the diet of those who traded with the colonists and ultimately into that of the general population.

Nor was the exchange one-sided. Beginning in the 1550s, men who in later centuries would be called botanists and zoologists began to make the voyage to the Americas, hoping to discover new plants and animals that could be exported to Europe. Some catalogued thousands of unknown species, a small number of which were suited to the different climates and soils of Europe. Among the most important of these species were a number of foodstuffs that ultimately had a transforming effect on the European diet. A small yellow fruit from the Americas took root in southern Italy, where the hot sun and rich clay provided a perfect growth environment. The Italians called it *pomodoro*—the yellow apple—but the native Americans called it *tomato*. Central Europe proved a welcoming place to grow another South American plant, the potato—a food so nutritious that laborers could nearly survive on it alone. It was to become a staple of the German diet and later was to be both a boon and a bane in Ireland. South American chili peppers found their market in Hungary, where they were dried and powdered to be used as a condiment called paprika. Even the French found their diet enhanced by products of the New World; the popular cocoa bean, after generations of refinement, was used to make chocolate.

European Reflections. Riches and converts, power and glory, all came in the wake of exploration. But in the process of exploring new lands and new cultures, Europe also discovered itself. It learned something of its own aspirations. Early Portuguese voyagers went in quest of the mythical Prester John, a saintly figure who was said to rule a heaven on earth in the middle of Africa. The first children born on Madeira were

■ Contact with cultures of the New World forced Europeans into a different way of thinking about
the old world. In this detail from *The Cognoscenti,* a seventeenth-century Flemish painting,
English scholars and navigators examine European encounters with new lands and new cultures.

named Adam and Eve, though that slave plantation of sugar
and wine was an unlikely Garden of Eden. The optimism of
those who searched for the fountain of youth in the Florida
swamps was not only that they would find it there, but that a
long life was worth living. Contact with the cultures of the
New World also forced a different kind of thinking about life
in the old one. The supposed customs of strange lands also
provided the setting for one of the great works of English
social criticism, Sir Thomas More's *Utopia* (1516).

Europe also discovered and revealed a darker side of itself
in the age of exploration. Accompanying the boundless optimism and assertive self-confidence that made so much possible was a tragic arrogance toward and callous disregard of native races. Portuguese travelers described Africans as
"dog-faced, dog-toothed people, satyrs, wild men, and cannibals." Such attitudes helped justify enslavement. The
European conquests were both brutal and wasteful. The
Dominican priest Bartolomé de Las Casas (1474–1566)

championed the cause of the native inhabitants at
the court of the Spanish kings. His *Apologetic History
of the Indies* (1550) highlighted the complexity of native society even as he witnessed its destruction. The
German artist Albrecht Dürer (1471–1528) mar-
veled at the "subtle ingenuity of the men in those
distant lands" after viewing a display of Aztec art.

DOCUMENT

Laws on Good
Treatment of
the Indians

But few Europeans were so enlightened about native society.
Although Europeans encountered heritages that were in some
ways richer than their own, only the most farsighted Westerners
could see that there was more value in the preservation of the
heritages than in their demolition. The Portuguese spice trade
did not depend upon the indiscriminate destruction of eastern
ports. The obliteration of millions of Aztecs and Incas was not a
necessary result of the fever for gold and silver. The destruction
was wanton. It revealed the rapaciousness, greed, and cruelty of
the Portuguese and Spanish conquerors. Those were the impulses of the Crusades rather than of the Renaissance.

GEOGRAPHICAL TOUR
Europe in 1500: The Age of the New Monarchies

Just as the map of the world was changing as a result of the voyages of exploration, so the map of Europe was changing as a result of the activities of princes. The early sixteenth century was the age of the prince, the first great stage of nation building that would last for the next 300 years. The **New Monarchies**, as they are sometimes called, consolidated territories that were divided culturally, linguistically, and historically. The states of Europe were political units, and they were forged by political means: by diplomacy, by marriage, and, most commonly, by war. The national system that we take for granted when thinking about Europe is a relatively recent development. Before we can observe its beginnings, we must first have a picture of Europe as it

existed in 1500 (see **Map A**). At that time it was composed of nearly 500 distinct political units.

Europe is a concept. Like all concepts, it is difficult to define. The vast plain that stretches from the Netherlands to the steppes of Russia presents few natural barriers to migration. Only in the south did geographical forces stem the flow of humanity. The Carpathian Mountains created a basin for the settlement of Slavic peoples that extended down to the Black Sea. The Alps provided a boundary for French, Germanic, and Italian settlements. The Pyrenees defined the Iberian Peninsula, with a mixture of African and European peoples.

Boundaries of Eastern Europe

In the East, three great empires had created the political geography that could be said to define a European boundary: the Mongol, the Ottoman, and the Russian. During the early Middle

■ **Map A. Europe in 1500.** While the western part of Europe had taken on its modern features, central and eastern Europe continued to change their boundaries.

■ **Map B. Eastern Europe.** This map shows eastern Europe before the consolidation of Russia. The Duchy of Lithuania had reached the height of its power and stretched from the Baltic to the Black Sea.

Ages, Mongol warriors had swept across the Asian steppes and conquered most of central and southern Russia. By the sixteenth century, the Mongol Empire was disintegrating, its lands divided into a number of separate states called *khanates*. The khanate of the Crimea, with lands around the northern shores of the Black Sea, created the southeastern border of Europe (see **Map B**).

The Ottoman territories defined the southern boundary. By 1450, the Ottomans controlled all of Byzantium and Greece, dominating an area from the Black Sea to the Aegean. Fifty years later, they had conquered nearly all the lands between the Aegean and the Adriatic seas. A perilous frontier was established on the Balkan Peninsula. There the principalities of Moldavia, Wallachia, Transylvania, and Hungary (see **Map B**) held out against the Ottomans for another quarter century before being overrun.

The Russian state defined the eastern boundary of Europe. Russia too had been a great territorial unit in the Middle Ages, centered at Kiev in the west and stretching eastward into Asia. The advance of the Mongols in the thirteenth century had contracted the eastern part of Russia, and its western domains had disintegrated under the practice of dividing the ruling prince's inheritance among his sons. In 1500, Europe reached as far east as the principality of Muscovy. There the heritage of East and West mingled. In some periods of history, Russia's ties with the West were most important; at other times, Russia retreated into isolation from Europe.

The northern borders of eastern Europe centered on the Baltic Sea, one of the most important trading routes of the early modern era (see **Map B**). On the northern coasts lay the

Scandinavian nations of Sweden, Norway, and Denmark. These loosely confederated nations had a single king throughout the fifteenth century. Denmark, the southernmost of the three, was also the richest and most powerful. It enjoyed a favorable trading position on both the North and Baltic seas and social and economic integration with the Germanic states on its border. On the southern side of the Baltic Sea lay the dominions of the Teutonic Knights, physically divided by the large state of Poland-Lithuania. The Teutonic territories, in the valuable Baltic region of Prussia, had been colonized by German crusaders in the thirteenth century.

Poland-Lithuania comprised an enormous territory that covered the length of Europe from the Baltic to the Black Sea (see **Map B**). The crowns of the two nations had been joined at the end of the fourteenth century, and their dynastic history was tied up with the nations of Bohemia and Hungary to their west and south. While Bohemia was increasingly drawn into the affairs of central Europe, Hungary remained more eastern in orientation, partly because the Bohemians gave nominal allegiance to the Holy Roman Emperor and partly because the Ottoman conquests had engulfed a large part of the Hungarian territories. At the end of the fifteenth century, Poland, Lithuania, Bohemia, and Hungary were all ruled by the same family, the Jagiellons.

Mongols and Ottomans to the south, Russians in the east, Scandinavia in the north, Poland-Lithuania in the center, and Hungary in the west: such were the contours of the eastern portion of Europe. Its lands were, on the whole, less fertile than those farther west, and its climate was more severe. It was a sparsely populated region. Its wealth lay in the Baltic fisheries, in the Hungarian and Bohemian silver mines, and in the enormous Russian forests, where wood and its by-products were plentiful. Except in the southern portions of Poland and central Bohemia, the region was agriculturally poor.

Central Europe

The middle of the continent was defined by the Holy Roman Empire and occupied almost entirely by Germanic peoples (see **Map C**). In length, the empire covered the territory from the North and Baltic seas to the Adriatic and the Mediterranean, where the Italian city-states were located. In width, it stretched from Bohemia to Burgundy. Politically, central Europe comprised a bewildering array of principalities, Church lands, and free towns. By the end of the fifteenth century, the Holy Roman Empire was an empire in name only. The large states of Brandenburg, Bohemia, and Bavaria resembled the political units of the East. In the south, the Alps provided an effective physical boundary, which allowed the Archduchy of Austria and the Swiss Confederation to follow their own separate paths. Stretching across the center of the empire, from the Elbe River to the North Sea, were a jumble of petty states. Great cities such as Nuremberg and Ulm in the south, Bremen and Hamburg in the north, and Frankfurt and Cologne in the west were free municipalities. Large sections of the northwestern part of the empire were governed by the Church through resident bishops.

■ **Map C. Central Europe.** This map of Central Europe shows the boundaries of the Holy Roman Empire.

Farther to the west were the prosperous Low Countries: Holland and its port of Amsterdam, Brabant and its port of Antwerp. In the southwest, the empire extended in some places as far as the Rhone River and included the rich estates of Luxembourg, Lorraine, and Burgundy (see **Map C**).

The riches of the empire made it the focal point of Europe. Nearly 15 million people lived within its borders. Its agriculture varied from the olive- and wine-producing areas in the southwest to the great granaries in its center. Rich mineral deposits and large reserves of timber made the German lands industrially advanced. The European iron industry was centered there, and the empire was the arms manufacturer for the Western world. The empire was also a great commercial center, heir to the Hanseatic League of the Middle Ages. Its northern and western ports teemed with trade, and its merchants were replacing the Italians as the leading international bankers.

Like the empire, the Italian peninsula was divided into a diverse collection of small city-states (see **Map C**). During the course of the fifteenth century, five city-states had emerged as most powerful (see Chapter 11). In the north were Florence, Venice, and the Duchy of Milan. In the south was Rome, spiritual center of Catholicism and residence of the pope. Although Roman and papal governments were separate jurisdictions, in fact their fates were bound together. Papal lands stretched far to

the north of Rome, and wars to defend or expand them were Roman as well as papal ventures. The kingdom of Naples—the breadbasket of the Mediterranean—occupied the southernmost part of Italy and included the agriculturally rich island of Sicily.

Western Europe

The Iberian Peninsula, the French territories, and the British Isles formed the westernmost borders of Europe (see **Map D**). Separated from France in the north by the Pyrenees, the Iberian Peninsula is surrounded by the Atlantic Ocean and the Mediterranean Sea on the west and east. But neither its protective mountain barrier nor its ample coastline was its most significant geographical feature during its formative period. Rather, it was the fact that Iberia is separated from North Africa only by the easily navigable Strait of Gibraltar. During the Middle Ages, the peninsula was overrun by North African Muslims, whom the Spanish called Moors. From the eighth to the fifteenth centuries, Iberian history was dominated by the **reconquista**—the recapture and re-Christianization of the conquered territories. The reconquest was finally completed in 1492, when the Moors were pushed out of Granada and the Jews were expelled from Spain. At the end of the fifteenth century, the Iberian Peninsula contained several separate kingdoms. The most important were Portugal—the only Continental nation to have the same borders in 1500 as it does today—on the western coast; Aragon,

■ **Map D. Western Europe.** Western Europe was already consolidated into nation-states.

with its Mediterranean ports of Barcelona and Valencia; and Castile, the largest of the Iberian states (see **Map D**). The marriage of King Ferdinand of Aragon and Queen Isabella of Castile in 1469 had joined the crowns of Aragon and Castile, but the two kingdoms remained separate.

The remnants of ancient Gaul were also favored by a maritime location. Like those of Iberia, French coasts are located along the Mediterranean Sea and the Atlantic Ocean. France's eastern boundaries touched the empire; its southern mountain border touched Spain. To the northwest, Britain was less than 30 miles from France across the English Channel. Toward the end of the fifteenth century, France was still divided into many smaller fiefs. The royal domain centered on Paris and extended to Champagne in the east and Normandy in the west (see **Map D**). South of this area, however, from Orléans to Brittany, were principalities that had long been contested between England and France. Nor was the rich central plain yet integrated into the royal domain. Agriculturally, French lands were the richest in Europe. France enjoyed both Mediterranean and Atlantic climates, which suited the growing of the widest variety of foodstuffs. Its population of approximately 13 million was second only to that of the empire.

Across the Channel lay Britain (composed of England, Scotland, and Wales) and Ireland (see **Map D**). Britain had been settled by an array of European colonizers—Romans, Danes, Angles, and Saxons—before being conquered in the eleventh century by the French Normans. From that time, it was protected by the rough waters of the English Channel and the North Sea and allowed to develop a distinct cultural and political heritage. Wales to the west and Scotland to the north were still separate nations at the beginning of the sixteenth century. Both were mountainous lands with harsh climates and few natural advantages. They were sparsely populated. Although Ireland, too, was sparsely populated, it contained several rich agricultural areas especially suited for dairying and grazing.

In 1500, Europe exhibited a remarkable diversity of political and geographical forms. Huge states in the east, tiny principalities in the center, emerging nations in the west, all seemingly had little in common. There was as yet no state system and no clear group of dominant powers. The western migration of the Germanic peoples appeared to be over, but their consolidation was as yet unimagined. The Iberians struggled to expel the Moors, the Hungarians to hold back the Ottomans. Everywhere one looked there was fragmentation and disarray. Yet in less than a half century the largest empire yet known in the West would be formed. States would come to be consolidated and dynasties established all over the Continent. And with the rise of the state would come the dream of dominion, an empire over all of Europe. ∎

THE FORMATION OF STATES

It was Machiavelli who identified the prince as the agent of change in the process of state formation. He believed that the successful prince could bring unity to his lands, security to his borders, and prosperity to his subjects. The unsuccessful prince brought nothing but ruin.

A process as long and as complex as the formation of nations, however, depends on more than the will of individuals. Factors such as geography, population, and natural resources are all important. So too are the structures through which human activity is channeled. The ways in which families are organized and wealth is transmitted from generation to generation can result in large estates with similar customs or small estates with varying ones. The manner in which social groups are formed and controlled can mean that power is centralized or dispersed. The beliefs of ordinary people and the way they practice them can define who is a part of a community and who is not. All these elements and many others affected the way in which European states began to take shape at the end of the fifteenth century. Despite these complexities, we should not lose sight of the simple truth of Machiavelli's observations. In the first stages of the consolidation of European nations, the role of the prince was crucial.

Indeed, in the middle of the fifteenth century there were many factors working against the formation of large states in Europe. The most obvious involved simple things such as transportation and communication. The distance that could be covered quickly was very small. In wet and cold seasons, travel was nearly impossible. The emperor Charles V sat in Burgundy for two months awaiting a favorable wind to take him to his newly inherited kingdom of Spain. Similarly, directives from the center of the states to the localities were slow to arrive and slower still to be adopted. Large areas were difficult to control and to defend. Distinct languages or dialects also made for difficulties in communication. Only the most educated could use Latin as a common written language. Separate languages contributed to separate cultures. Customary practices, common ancestry, and shared experiences helped define a sense of community through which small states defined themselves.

To the natural forces that acted to maintain the existence of small units of government were added invented ones. To succeed, a prince had to establish supremacy over a number of rivals. For the most part, states were inherited. In some places it was customary to follow the rule of primogeniture—inheritance by the eldest son. In others, estates were split among sons, or among children of both sexes. Some traditions, like those of the French, excluded inheritance through women; others, like the Castilian, treated women's claims as equal to men's. Short lives meant prolonged disputes about inheritance. Rulers had to defend their thrones from any number of rivals with strong claims to legitimacy.

Rulers also had to defend themselves from the ambitions of their mightiest subjects. Dukes could dream only one dream. The constant warfare of the European nobility was one of the central features of the Later Middle Ages. To avoid resort to arms, princes and peers entered into all manner of alliances, using their children as pawns and the marriage bed as the chessboard. Rulers also faced independent institutions within their states, powerful organizations that had to be won over or crushed. The long process of taming the Church was well advanced by the end of the fifteenth century and about to enter a new stage. Fortified towns presented a different problem. They possessed both the manpower and wealth necessary to raise and maintain armies. They also jealously guarded their privileges. Rulers who could not tax their towns could not rule their state. Finally, most kingdoms had assemblies that represented the propertied classes, especially in matters of taxation. Some, such as the English Parliament and the Spanish Cortes, were strong; others, such as the Imperial Diet and the French Estates-General, were weak. But everywhere they posed an obstacle to the extension of the power of princes.

In combination, these factors slowed and shaped the process of state formation. But neither separately nor together were they powerful enough to overcome it. The fragmentation of Europe into so many small units of government made some consolidation inevitable; and as the first large states took shape, the position of smaller neighbors grew ever more precarious.

This was especially true by the end of the fifteenth century because of the increase in the destructive power of warfare. Technological advances in cannonry and in the skills of gunners and engineers made medieval fortifications untenable. The fall of Constantinople was as much a military watershed as it was a political one. Gunpowder decisively changed battlefield tactics. It made heavy armor obsolete and allowed for the development of a different type of warfare. Lightly armored horses and riders could not only inflict more damage upon one another, but they were now mobile enough to be used against infantry. Infantry armed with long pikes or small muskets became the crucial components of armies that were growing ever larger. Systems of supply were better, sources of small arms were more available, and the rewards of conquest were more tangible. What could be inherited or married could be conquered.

Eastern Configurations

The interplay of factors that encouraged and inhibited the formation of states is most easily observed in the eastern parts of Europe. There the different paths taken by Muscovy and Poland-Lithuania stand in contrast. At the beginning of the sixteenth century, the principality of Muscovy was the largest European political unit. Muscovy had established itself as the heir to the ancient state of Russia through conquest, shrewd political alliances, and the good fortune of its princes to be blessed with long reigns. Muscovy's growth was phenomenal. Under Ivan III, "the Great" (1462–1505), Muscovy expanded to the north and west. During a long series of wars it annexed Novgorod and large parts of Livonia and Lithuania. Its military successes were almost unbroken, but so too were its diplomatic triumphs. Ivan the Great preferred pacification to conquest, though when necessary he could conquer with great brutality. Between 1460 and 1530, Muscovy increased its landed territory by 1.5 million square miles.

A number of factors led to the rise of Muscovy. External threats had diminished. First, the deterioration of the Mongol

Empire that had dominated south-central Russia allowed Ivan to escape the yoke of Mongol rule that the Russian princes had worn for centuries. Second, the fall of Constantinople made Muscovy the heir to Eastern Christendom, successor to the Roman and Byzantine empires. Ivan's marriage to Sophia, niece of the last emperor of Byzantium, cemented the connection. Sophia brought both Italian artisans and Byzantine customs to the Russian court, helping Ivan open his contacts with the wider world.

Territorial conquests and the decline of Byzantium were not the only important features of the consolidation of the Muscovite state. Ivan the Great was fortunate in having no competitors for his throne. He was able to use other social groups to help administer the new Muscovite territories without fear of setting up a rival to power. Ivan extended the privileges of his nobility and organized a military class that received land as a reward for fidelity. He also developed a new theory of sovereignty that rested on divine rather than temporal power. Traditionally, Russian princes ruled their lands by patrimony. They owned both estates and occupants. Ivan the Great extended that principle to cover all lands to which there was an ancient Russian claim and combined it with the religious authority of the Orthodox Church. Both he and his successors ruled with the aid of able Church leaders who were usually part of the prince's council.

Ivan the Terrible.   What made the expansion of Muscovy so impressive was that land once gained was never lost. The military and political achievements of Ivan the Great were furthered by his son Vasili and his more famous grandson Ivan IV, "the Terrible" (1533–1584). Ivan IV defeated the Mongols on his southeastern border and incorporated the entire Volga river basin into Muscovy. But his greatest ambition was to gain a port on the Baltic Sea and establish a northern outlet for commerce. His objective was to conquer Livonia. Nearly three decades of warfare between Muscovy and Poland-Lithuania—with which Livonia had allied itself—resulted in large territorial gains, but Muscovy always fell short of the real prize. And Ivan's northern campaigns seriously weakened the defense of the south. In 1571, the Crimean Tatars advanced from their territories on Muscovy's southwestern border and inflicted a powerful psychological blow when they burned the city of Moscow. Although the Tatars were eventually driven off Muscovite soil, expansion in both north and south was at an end for the next 75 years.

By the reign of Ivan IV, Muscovite society was divided roughly into three groups: the hereditary nobility known as the *boyars,* the military service class, and the peasantry who were bound to the land. There was no large mercantile presence in Muscovy and its urban component remained small. The boyars, who were powerful landlords of great estates, owed little to the tsar. They inherited their lands and did not necessarily benefit from expansion and conquest. Members of the military service class, on the other hand, were bound to the success of the crown. Their military service was a requirement for the possession of their estates, which were granted out of lands gained through territorial expansion. Ivan IV used members of the military service class as legislative advisers and elevated them in his parliamentary council (the Zemsky Sobor), which also included representatives of the nobility, clergy, and towns.

Unlike his grandfather, Ivan IV had an abiding mistrust of the boyars. They had held power when he was a child, and it was rumored that his mother had been poisoned by them. It was in his treatment of the boyars that he earned the nickname "the Terrible." During his brutal suppression of supposed conspiracies, several thousand families were massacred by Ivan's own orders and thousands more by the violent excesses of his agents. Ivan constantly imagined plots against himself, and many of the men who served him met horrible deaths. He also forcibly relocated boyar families, stripping them of their lands in one place but granting them new lands elsewhere.

All those measures contributed to the breakdown of local networks of influence and power and to a disruption of local governance. But they also made possible a system of central administration, one of Ivan IV's most important achievements. He created departments of state to deal with the various tasks of administration, which resulted in more efficient management of revenues and of the military. Ivan IV promoted the interests of the military service class over those of the boyars, but he did not destroy the nobility. New boyars were created, especially in conquered territories, and those new families owed their positions and loyalty to the prince. Both the boyars and the military benefited from Ivan's policy of binding the great mass of people to the land. Russian peasants had few political or economic rights in comparison to those of Western peasants, but during the early sixteenth century even the meager rights Russian peasants had were curtailed. The right of peasants to move from the estate of one lord to that of another was suspended, all but binding the peasantry to the land. The serfdom made possible the prolonged absence of military leaders from their estates and contributed to the creation of the military service class. But it also made imperative the costly system of coercing agricultural and industrial labor. In the long term, serfdom retarded the development of the Muscovite economy by removing incentive from large landholders to make investments in commerce or to improve agricultural production.

Poland-Lithuania. The growth of an enlarged and centralized Muscovy stands in contrast to the experiences of Poland-Lithuania during the same period. At the end of the fifteenth century, Casimir IV (1447–1492) ruled the kingdom of Poland and the grand duchy of Lithuania. His son Vladislav II ruled Bohemia (1471–1516) and Hungary (1490–1516). Had the four states been permanently consolidated they could have become an effective barrier to Ottoman expansion in the south and Russian expansion in the east. But the union of crowns had never been the union of states. The union of crowns had taken place during the previous century by political alliances, diplomatic marriages, and the consent of the

■ A miniature painted by a Krakow artist about 1510 depicts the final act of the coronation rite. The king in majesty is surrounded by his court while a *Te Deum* is sung. The knights in the foreground bear the standards of Poland and Lithuania.

nobility. Such arrangements kept peace among the four neighbors, but they kept any one of them from becoming a dominant partner.

While the Polish-Lithuanian monarchs enjoyed longevity similar to that of the Muscovites, those who ruled Hungary and Bohemia were not so fortunate: by the sixteenth century a number of claimants to both crowns existed. The competition was handled by diplomacy rather than war. The accession of Vladislav II, for example, was accompanied by large concessions, first to the Bohemian towns and later to the Hungarian nobility. The formal union of the Polish and Lithuanian crowns in 1569 also involved the decentralization of power and the strengthening of the rights of the nobility in both countries. In the end, the states split apart. The Russians took much of Lithuania, the Ottomans much of Hungary. Bohemia, which in the fifteenth century had been ruled more by its nobles than its king, was absorbed into the Habsburg territories after 1526.

There were many reasons why a unified state did not appear in east-central Europe. In the first place, external forces disrupted territorial and political arrangements, and wars with the Ottomans and the Russians absorbed resources. Second, the princes faced rivals to their crowns. Although Casimir IV was able to place his son on the thrones of both Bohemia and Hungary, he managed to do so against the powerful claims of the Habsburg princes, who continued to intrigue against the Jagiellons. The contests for power necessitated concessions to leading citizens, which decreased the ability of the princes to centralize their kingdoms or to effect real unification among them. The nobility of Hungary, Bohemia, and Poland-Lithuania all developed strong local interests that increased over time. In Bohemia, Vladislav II was king in name only, and even in Poland the nobility won confirmation of its rights and privileges from the monarchy. War, rivalries for power, and a strong nobility prevented any one prince from dominating the area as the princes of Muscovy dominated theirs.

The Western Powers

Just as in the east, there was no single pattern to the consolidation of the large western European states. They, too, were internally fragmented and externally imperiled. While England had to overcome the ruin of decades of civil war, France and Spain faced the challenges of invasion and occupation. Western European princes struggled against powerful institutions and individuals within their states. Some they conquered, others they absorbed. Each nation formed its state differently: England by administrative centralization, France by good fortune, and Spain by dynastic marriage. Yet in 1450 few imagined that any one of these states would succeed.

The Taming of England. Alone among European states, England suffered no threat of foreign invasion during the fifteenth century. The island fortress might easily have become the first consolidated European state were it not for the ambitions of the nobility and the weakness of the crown. For thirty years, the English aristocracy fought over the spoils of a helpless monarch. The Wars of the Roses (1455–1485), as they came to be called, were as much a free-for-all among the English peerage as they were a contest for the throne between the houses of Lancaster and York. At their center was an attempt by the dukes of York to wrest the crown from the mad and ineffective Lancastrian king Henry VI (1422–1461). All around the edges was the continuation of local and family feuds that had little connection to the dynastic struggle.

Three decades of intermittent warfare had predictable results. The houses of Lancaster and York were both destroyed. Edward IV (1461–1483) succeeded in gaining the crown for the House of York, but he was never able to wear it securely. When he died, his children, including his heir, Edward V (1483), were placed in the protection of their uncle Richard III (1483–1485). It was protection that they did not survive. The two boys disappeared, reputedly murdered in the Tower of London, and Richard declared himself king. Richard's usurpation led to civil war, and he was killed by the forces of Henry Tudor at the battle of Bosworth Field in 1485. By the end of the Wars of the Roses, the monarchy had lost both revenue and prestige, and the aristocracy had stored up bitter memories for the future.

It was left to Henry Tudor to pick up the pieces of the kingdom. As legend has it, he picked up the crown off a bramble bush. The two chief obstacles to his determination to consolidate the English state were the power of the nobility and the poverty of the monarchy. No English monarch had held secure title to the throne for more than a century. Henry Tudor, as Henry VII (1485–1509), put an end to the dynastic instability at once. He married Elizabeth of York, in whose heirs would rest the legitimate claim to the throne. Their children were indisputable successors to the crown. He also began the long process of taming his over-mighty subjects. Traitors were hung and turncoats rewarded. He and his son Henry VIII (1509–1547) adroitly created a new peerage, which soon was as numerous as the old feudal aristocracy. The new nobles owed their titles and loyalty to the Tudors. They were favored

■ Portrait of Anne Boleyn, the second wife of Henry VIII, by an unknown artist. Anne lost favor with Henry when she delivered a daughter instead of the son he expected. Anne made other enemies at court and in 1536 was convicted of adultery and beheaded.

LAST WORDS

Anne Boleyn was the second wife of Henry VIII and the mother of Elizabeth I. Henry's desire to have a son and his passion for Anne resulted in his divorce from Catherine of Aragon and England's formal break with the Roman Catholic Church. When Anne bore only a daughter, she too became dispensable. She was convicted of adultery and incest and executed in 1536. Here are her last words.

Focus Questions

How does Anne respond in her scaffold speech to the charges against her? What does Anne mean when she condemns "the cruel law of the land" at the same time as she praises "the King my sovereign lord"?

Good friends, I am not come here to excuse or to justify myself, for as much as I know full well that aught that I could say in my defense doth not appertain unto you, and that I could draw no hope of life from the same. But I come here only to die, and thus to yield myself humbly to the will of the King my lord. And if in my life I did ever offend the King's grace, surely with my death I do now atone for the same. And I blame not my judges, nor any other manner of person, nor anything save the cruel law of the land by which I die. But be this, and be my faults as they may, I beseech you all, good friends, to pray for the life of the King my sovereign lord and yours, who is one of the best princes on the face of the earth, and who hath always treated me so well that better could not be; wherefore I submit to death with a good will, humbly asking pardon of the world.

Anne Boleyn, scaffold speech.

---

with offices and spoils and were relied upon to suppress both popular and aristocratic rebellions.

The financial problems of the English monarchy were not so easily overcome. In theory and practice an English king was supposed to live "of his own," that is, off the revenues from his own estates. In normal circumstances, royal revenue did not come from the king's subjects. The English landed classes had established the principle that only on extraordinary occasions were they to be required to contribute to the maintenance of government. The principle was defended through their representative institution—the Parliament. When the kings of England wanted to tax their subjects, they had first to gain the assent of Parliament. Although Parliaments did grant requests for extraordinary revenue, especially for national defense, they did so grudgingly. The English landed elites were not exempt from taxation, but they were able to control the amount of taxes they paid.

The inability of the crown to extract its living from its subjects made it more dependent on the efficient management of its own estates. Thus English state building depended upon the growth of centralized institutions that could oversee royal lands and collect royal customs. Gradually, medieval institutions such as the Exchequer were supplanted by newer organs that were better able to adjust to modern methods of accounting, record keeping, and enforcement. Henry VII sent ministers to view and value royal lands. He ordered the cataloging and collection of feudal obligations. Ship cargoes were inspected thoroughly and every last penny of customs charged. Whether Henry's reputation for greed and rapacity was warranted, it was undeniable that he squeezed as much as could be taken from a not very juicy inheritance. His financial problems limited both domestic and foreign policy.

It was not until the middle of the next reign that the English monarchy was again solvent. As a result of his dispute with the papacy over his divorce from Catherine of Aragon and marriage to Anne Boleyn, Henry VIII confiscated the enormous wealth of the Catholic church, and with one stroke solved the crown's monetary problems (see Chapter 13). But the real contribution that Henry and his chief minister, Thomas Cromwell (ca. 1485–1540), made to forming an English state was the way in which the windfall was administered. Cromwell accelerated the process of centralizing government that had begun under Edward IV. He divided administration according to its functions by creating separate departments of state, modeled upon courts. The new departments were responsible for record keeping, revenue collection, and law enforcement. Each had a distinct jurisdiction and a permanent, trained staff. Cromwell coordinated the work of the distinct departments by expanding the power of the Privy Council, which included the heads of the administrative bodies. Through a long evolution, the Privy Council came to serve as the king's executive body. Cromwell also saw the importance of Parliament as a legislative body. Through Parliament, royal policy could be turned into statutes that had the assent of the political nation. If Parliament was well managed, issues that were potentially controversial could be defused. Laws passed by Parliament were more easily enforced locally than were proclamations issued by the king. By the end of Henry VIII's reign, the English monarchy was strong enough to withstand the succession of a child king, precisely the circumstance that had plunged the nation into civil war a century earlier.

The Unification of France.   Perhaps the most remarkable thing about the unification of France is that it took place at all. The forces working against the consolidation of a French state were formidable. France was surrounded by aggressive and powerful neighbors with whom it was frequently at war. Its greatest nobles were semi-independent princes who were constant rivals for the throne and consistent opponents of the extension of royal power. The French people were deeply suspicious of the pretensions of the monarchy. Provincialism was not simply negative; it was a fierce pride of and loyalty toward local customs and institutions that had deep roots within communities. Furthermore, France was splintered by profound regional differences. The north and south were divided by culture and by language (the *langue d'oc* in the south and the *langue d'oïl* in the north). As late as the fifteenth century, a French king needed a translator to communicate with officials from his southern lands.

The first obstacles that were overcome were the external threats to French security. For more than a century, the throne of France had been contested by the kings of England. The so-called Hundred Years' War, which was fought intermittently between 1337 and 1453, originated in a dispute over the inheritance of the French crown and English possessions in Gascony in southern France (see Chapter 10). The war was fought on French soil, and by the early fifteenth century English conquests in north-central France extended from Normandy to the borders of the Holy Roman Empire. Two of the largest French cities, Paris and Bordeaux, were in English hands.

Nor was England the only threat to the security of the French monarchy. On France's eastern border, in a long arching semicircle, were the estates of the dukes of Burgundy. The dukes of Burgundy and the kings of France shared a common ancestry—both were of the House of Valois. Still, the sons of brothers in one generation were only cousins in the next, and the two branches of the family grew apart. The original Burgundian inheritance was in the southeast, centered at Dijon. A good marriage and good fortune brought to the first duke the rich northern province of Flanders. For the next hundred years, the aim of the dukes of Burgundy was to unite their divided estates. While England and France were locked in deadly embrace, Burgundy systematically grew. It absorbed territory from both the Holy Roman Empire and France. To little pieces gained through marriages were added little pieces taken through force. As the second half of the fifteenth century began, the court of the duke of Burgundy was the glittering jewel of Europe, the heir of the Italian Renaissance. Wealthy and powerful, it stood poised to achieve what had once only been dreamed: the unification of the Burgundian lands. The conquest of Lorraine finally connected the ducal estates in one long, unbroken string.

But it was a string stretched taut. The power of Burgundy threatened its neighbors in all directions. Both France and the empire were too weak to resist its expansion, but the confederation of Swiss towns to the southwest of Burgundy was not. Fearing a Burgundian advance against them, a number of independent Swiss towns pooled their resources to raise a large army. In a series of stunning military victories, Swiss forces repelled the Burgundians from their lands and demolished their armies. Charles the Bold, the last Valois duke of Burgundy, fell at the Battle of Nancy in 1477. His estates were quickly dismembered. France recovered its ancestral territories, including Burgundy, and through no effort of its own was now secure on its eastern border.

The king most associated with the consolidation of France was Louis XI (1461–1483). He inherited an estate exhausted by warfare and civil strife. More by chance than by plan, he vastly extended the territories under the dominion of the French crown and, more importantly, subdued the nobility. Louis XI was as cunning as he was peculiar. In an age in which royalty was expressed through magnificence, Louis sported an old felt hat and a well-worn coat. His enemies constantly underestimated his abilities, which earned him the nickname "the Spider." But during the course of his reign, Louis XI gradually won back what he had been forced to give away. Years of fighting both the English and each other left the ranks of the French aristocracy depleted. As blood spilled on the battlefields, the stocks of fathers and sons ran low. Estates, to which

■ This painting by an anonymous Flemish artist of the wedding of Philip the Good, duke of Burgundy, and Isabella of Portugal evokes the courtly style and aspirations of fifteenth-century Burgundy.

THE KINGDOM OF FRANCE

Claude de Seyssel (ca. 1450–1519) was a legal scholar and professor at the University of Turin. He came from the duchy of Savoy, a small state that mixed French and Italian peoples and culture. Seyssel thus learned about the French monarchy as an outsider and wrote The Monarchy of France *as a book of counsel for French kings. In this passage he explains and defends the Salic law, which prohibited legitimate title to the French throne from passing through a woman. The legal documents that supposedly established Salic law were fakes.*

Focus Questions

Why is it "excellent" that the French throne cannot pass to a woman? What conditions are desirable in order for a state to be stable and prosper?

Without going too deeply into the disputes of the philosophers, we may presuppose three kinds of political rule: monarchy under a single person, aristocracy under a certain number of the better sort, and democracy the popular state. Of these, according to the true and most widespread opinion, monarchy is the best if the prince is good and has the sense, the experience, and the good will to govern justly. That rarely comes to pass, however, because with such authority and license it is hard to follow the right course and hold fairly the balance of justice. The second state seems the more reasonable and praiseworthy since it is more lasting, better founded, and easier to bear, being comprised of the persons selected by the assembly or a part of them. Such persons are, moreover, subject to corruption and change, at least to the extent that, when there are several bad and inadequate men among them, the better sort, being their superiors, can repress their boldness and thwart their unreasonable enterprises. As to the popular state, it has always been turbulent, dangerous, and hostile to the better sort. Nevertheless, the aristocratic state is often transformed into oligarchy, a monopoly by covetous and ambitious folk, who, though chosen as the wisest and most prudent of the people to rule and to govern the people well, care only for their particular profit. So when all is said, none of these states can possibly be perpetual, for ordinary in the course of time they get worse, especially when they go on growing, so that often one [by disorder] rises from the other.

The first special trait that I find good is that this realm passes by masculine succession and, by virtue of the law which the French call Salic, cannot fall into the hands of a woman. This is excellent, for by falling into the feminine line it can come into the power of a foreigner, a pernicious and dangerous thing, since a ruler from a foreign nation is of a different rearing and condition, of different customs, different language, and a different way of life from the men of the lands he comes to rule. He ordinarily, therefore, wishes to advance those of his nation, to grant them the most important authority in the handling of affairs, and to prefer them to honors and profits. Moreover, he always has more love for and faith in them and so conforms more to their customs and ways than to the customs of the land to which he has newly come, whence there always follows envy and dissension between the natives and the foreigners and indignation against the princes, as has often been seen by experience, and is seen all the time. When the succession goes from male to male, the heir is always certain and is of the same blood as those who formerly ruled, so the subjects have the very same love and reverence for him as for his predecessors. Even though he be related only distantly and the dead king have daughters, yet without deviation or scruple the people turn to him as soon as the other has ceased to be, and there is no disturbance or difficulty. So it went at the death of King Charles VIII and of King Louis XII recently deceased. Although in former times there were great quarrels and differences on such occasions, which brought great wars, persecutions, and desolations to the realm, nevertheless, these differences were not the reason for the troubles but the pretext, although well known to be frivolous and ill founded. In the end matters must have been redressed and so established that there can never again be dissensions and difficulties on this score. [In order to demonstrate what I said about the perfection of the monarchy of France I have included in this account] the state of France as it is now, joining the old laws, customs, and observances with the new and more recent.

From Claude de Seyssel, *The Monarchy of France* (1515).

no male heirs existed, fell forfeit to the king. In that manner, the crown absorbed Anjou and Maine in the northwest and Provence in the south. More importantly, Louis XI ultimately obtained control of the two greatest independent fiefs, Brittany and Orléans. He managed the feat by arranging the marriage of his son Charles to the heiress of Brittany and of his daughter Jeanne to the heir of Orléans. When in 1527 the lands of the duke of Bourbon fell to the crown, the French monarch ruled a unified state.

The consolidation of France was not simply the result of the incorporation of diverse pieces of territory into the domain of the king. More than in any other state, the experience in France

MAP DISCOVERY

The Unification of France

Notice how France grew piecemeal rather than by acquiring large additions of adjacent estates. Which monarch added the most land to the state? Contrast the acquisitions made by Louis XI and those made by the Bourbons. Notice how France was not a unified geographical unit even after its so-called unification.

for consolidation. Because of the strength of the nobles, most taxation fell only on the commoners, the so-called third estate. The *taille* was a direct tax on property from which the nobility and clergy were exempt. The *gabelle* was a consumption tax on the purchase of salt in most parts of the kingdom, and the *aide* was a tax on a variety of commodities, including meat and wine. The consumption taxes were paid by all members of the third estate no matter how poor they might be. Although there was much complaint about taxes, the French monarchy established a broad base for taxation and a high degree of compliance long before any other European nation.

Along with money went soldiers, fighting men necessary to repel the English and to defend the crown against rebels and traitors. Again the French monarchy was the first to establish the principle of a national army, raised and directed from the center but quartered and equipped regionally. From the nobility were recruited the cavalry, from the towns and countryside the massive infantry. Fortified towns received privileges in return for military service to the king. Originally, towns were required to provide artillery, but constant troubles with the nobility had led the kings of France to establish their own store of heavy guns. The towns supplied small arms, pikes, and swords, and later pistols and muskets. By the beginning of the sixteenth century, the French monarch could raise and equip an army of his own.

demonstrated how a state could be formed without the designs of a great leader. Neither Louis XI nor his son Charles VIII (1483–1498) was a nation builder. Louis's main objective was always to preserve his estate. His good fortune saved him from the consequences of many ill-conceived policies. But no amount of luck could make up for Louis's failure to obtain the Burgundian Low Countries for France after the death of Charles the Bold in 1477. The marriage of Mary of Burgundy to Maximilian of Habsburg was one of the great turning points in European history. It initiated the struggle for control of the Low Countries that endured for more than two centuries.

The long years of war established the principle of royal taxation that was so essential to the process of state building in France. It enabled the monarchy to raise money for defense and

The Marriages of Spain.   Before the sixteenth century there was little prospect of a single nation emerging on the Iberian Peninsula. North African Muslims, called Moors, occupied the province of Granada in the south, while the stable kingdom of Portugal dominated the western coast. The Spanish peoples were divided among a number of separate states. The two most important were Castile, the largest and wealthiest kingdom, and Aragon, which was composed of a number of quasi-independent regions, each of which maintained its own laws and institutions. Three religions and four languages (not including dialects) widened the political divisions. Furthermore, the different states had different outlooks. Castile was, above all, determined to subjugate the last of Islamic Spain and to convert its large Jewish population to Christianity. Aragon played in the high-stakes game for power in the Mediterranean, claiming sovereignty over Sicily and Naples and exercising that sovereignty whenever it could.

A happy teenage marriage brought together the unhappy kingdoms of Castile and Aragon. When Ferdinand of Aragon and Isabella of Castile secretly exchanged wedding vows in 1469, both their homelands were rent by civil war. In Castile, Isabella's brother, Henry IV (1454–1474), struggled unsuccessfully against the powerful Castilian nobility. In Aragon, Ferdinand's father, John II (1458–1479), faced a revolt by the rich province of Catalonia on one side and the territorial ambitions of Louis XI of France on the other. Joining the heirs increased the resources of both kingdoms. Ferdinand took an active role in the pacification of Castile, while Castilian riches allowed him to defend Aragon from invasion. In 1479, the two crowns were united and the Catholic monarchs, as they were called, ruled the two kingdoms jointly. But the unification of the crowns of Castile and Aragon was not the same as the formation of a single state between them. Local privileges were zealously guarded, especially in Aragon, where the representative institutions of the towns—the Cortes—were aggressively independent. Their attitude is best expressed in the oath of the townspeople of Saragossa: "We accept you as our king provided you observe all our liberties and laws; and if not, not." The powerful Castilian nobility never accepted Ferdinand as their king and refused him the crown after Isabella's death.

But Ferdinand and Isabella (1479–1516) took the first steps toward forging a Spanish state. Their most notable achievement was the final recovery of the lands that had been conquered by the Moors. For centuries, the Spanish kingdoms had fought against the North African Muslims, who had conquered large areas of the southern peninsula. The reconquista was characterized by short bursts of warfare followed by long periods of wary coexistence. By the middle of the fifteenth century, the Moorish territory had been reduced to the province of Granada, but civil strife in Castile heightened the possibility of a new Moorish offensive. "We no longer mint gold, only steel," was how a Moorish ruler replied to Isabella's demand for the traditional payment of tribute money. The final stages of the reconquista began in 1482 and lasted for a decade. The struggle was waged as a holy war and was financed in part by grants from the pope and the Christian princes of Europe. It was a bloody undertaking. The Moorish population of nearly 500,000 was reduced to 100,000 before the town of Granada finally fell and the province was absorbed into Castile.

The reconquista played an important part in creating a national identity for the Christian peoples of Spain. In order to raise men and money for the war effort, Ferdinand and Isabella mobilized their nobility and town governments and created a central organization to oversee the invasion.

Ferdinand was actively involved in the warfare, gaining the respect of the hostile Castilian nobles in the process. The conquered territories were used to reward those who had aided the effort, though the crown maintained control and jurisdiction over most of the province. But the idea of the holy war also had a darker side and an unanticipated consequence. The Jewish population that had lived peacefully in both Castile and Aragon became another object of hostility. Many Jews had risen to prominence in government and in skilled professions. Others, who had accepted conversion to Christianity and were known as *conversos,* had become among the most powerful figures in Church and state.

Both groups were now attacked. The conversos fell prey to a special Church tribunal created to examine their sincere devotion to Catholicism. This was the **Spanish Inquisition**, which, though it used traditional judicial practices—torture to gain confessions, public humiliation to show contrition, and burnings at the stake to maintain purity—used them on a scale never before seen. Thousands of conversos were killed, and many more families had their wealth confiscated to be used for the reconquista. In 1492, the Jews themselves were expelled from Spain. Although the reconquista and the expulsion of the Jews inflicted great suffering upon victims and incalculable loss to the Castilian economy, both events enhanced the prestige of the Catholic monarchs.

In many ways, Ferdinand and Isabella had trodden the paths of the medieval monarchy. They relied upon personal contact with their people more than upon the use of a centralized administration. They frequently dispensed justice personally, sitting in court and accepting petitions from their subjects. Quite remarkably, they had no permanent residence and traveled the length and breadth of their kingdoms. Isabella is said to have visited every town in Castile, and it is entirely possible that a majority of the population of both kingdoms actually saw their monarchs at one time or another. Queen Isabella was venerated in Castile, where women's right to inheritance remained strong. Ferdinand's absences from Aragon were always a source of contention between him and the Cortes of the towns, yet he was careful to provide regents to preside in his absence and regularly returned to visit his native kingdom. He was not an absentee monarch.

The joint presence of Ferdinand and Isabella in the provinces of Spain was symbolic of the unity that they wanted to achieve. Despite the great obstacles, they were intent on bringing about a more permanent blending. Ferdinand made Castilian the official language of government in Aragon and even appointed Castilians to Aragonese posts. He and Isabella actively encouraged the intermarriage of the two aristocracies and the expansion of the number of wealthy nobles who held land in both kingdoms. A single coinage, stamped with the heads of both monarchs, was established for both kingdoms. Nevertheless, the measures did not unify Spain or erase the centuries' long tradition of hostility among the diverse Iberian peoples.

It was left to the heirs of Ferdinand and Isabella to forge together the Spanish kingdoms, and the process was a painful

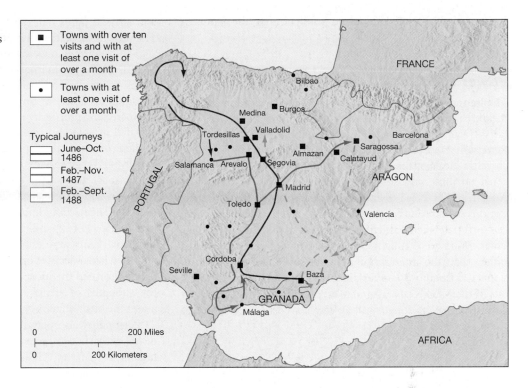

■ The Travels of Ferdinand and Isabella. Early modern monarchs did not reside solely in a capital city but moved around their territories to consolidate their power and assure the loyalty of their subjects.

one. The hostility to a foreign monarch that both the Castilian nobility and the Aragonese towns had shown to Ferdinand and Isabella increased dramatically at the accession of their grandson, who became the Emperor Charles V (1516–1556). Charles had been born and raised in the Low Countries, where he ruled over Burgundy and the Netherlands. Through a series of dynastic accidents, he became heir to the Spanish crown with its possessions in the New World and to the vast Habsburg estates that included Austria. Charles established his rule in Spain gradually. For a time he was forced to share power in Castile and to suppress a disorganized aristocratic rebellion.

Because of his foreign obligations, Charles was frequently absent from Spain. During those periods he governed through regents and royal councils that did much to centralize administration. Although Castile and Aragon had separate councils, they were organized similarly and had greater contact than before. Charles V realized the importance of Spain, especially of Castile, in his empire. He learned Castilian and spent more time there than in any other part of his empire, calling it "the head of all the rest." Like Ferdinand and Isabella, he traveled throughout Castile and Aragon; unlike them, he established a more permanent bureaucratic court, modeled on that of Burgundy, and placed able Spaniards at the head of its departments. That smoothed over the long periods when Charles was abroad, especially the thirteen years between 1543 and 1556.

Yet neither his personal efforts to rule as a Spanish monarch nor those of his able administrators were the most important factor in uniting the Spanish kingdoms of Iberia. Rather it was the fact that Charles V brought Spain to the forefront of European affairs in the sixteenth century. Spanish prowess, whether in arms or in culture, became a source of

national pride that helped erode regional identity. Gold and silver from the New World helped finance Charles's great empire. Whether or not he dreamed of uniting all of Europe under his rule, Charles V fulfilled nearly all of the ancient territorial ambitions of the Spanish kingdoms. In Italy, he prosecuted Aragonese claims to Sicily and Naples; in the north he held on firmly to the kingdom of Navarre, which had been annexed by Ferdinand and which secured Spain's border with France. In the south, he blocked off Ottoman and Muslim expansion. The reign of Charles V ushered in the dawn of Spain's golden age.

THE DYNASTIC STRUGGLES

The formation of large states throughout Europe led inevitably to conflicts among them. Long chains of marriages among the families of the European princes meant that sooner or later the larger powers would lay claim to the same inheritances and test the matter by force. Thus the sixteenth century was a period of almost unrelieved general warfare that took the whole of the Continent as its theater. Advances in technology made war more efficient and more expensive. They also made it more horrible. The use of artillery against infantry increased the number of deaths and maiming injuries, as did the replacement of the arrow with the bullet. As the size of armies increased, so did casualties. Nearly 60,000 men met at Marignano in 1515, where it took 30 French cavalry charges and 28 consecutive hours of battle before the Swiss infantry was driven from the field. The slaughter of French nobility at Pavia in 1525 was the largest in a century, while the Turkish sultan Suleiman the Magnificent recorded the burial of 24,000 Hungarian soldiers after the battle of Mohacs in 1526.

Power and Glory

The frequency with which offensive war was waged in the sixteenth century raises a number of questions about the militaristic values of the age. Valor remained greatly prized—a Renaissance virtue inherited from the crusading zeal and chivalric ideals of the Middle Ages. Princes saw valor as a personal attribute and sought to do great deeds. Ferdinand of Aragon and Francis I of France (1515–1547) won fame for their exploits in war. Charles the Bold and Louis II of Hungary were less fortunate: their battlefield deaths led to the breakup of their states. Wars were fought to further the interests of princes rather than the interests of national sovereignty or international Christianity. Wars certainly were not fought in the interests of their subjects. States were an extension of a prince's heritage: what rulers sought in battle was a part of the historical

■ Titian, *Charles V on Horseback* (1548). The portrait commemorates the Emperor's victory in the Battle of Mülberg in 1547. The portrait is less that of a victorious hero, but rather that of a forceful individual girded to contend against his enemies.

and familial rights that defined themselves and their subjects. The wars of the sixteenth century were dynastic wars.

The New Monarchs waged war and defended their territories in new ways. Internal security depended on locally raised forces or hired mercenaries. Both required money, which was becoming available in unprecedented quantities as a result of the increasing prosperity of the early sixteenth century and the windfall of gold and silver from the New World. Professional soldiers, of whom the Swiss and Germans were the most noteworthy, sold their services to the highest bidders. Developments in transport and supply enabled campaigns to take place far from the center of a state. Finally, communications were improving. The need for knowledge about potential rivals or allies had the effect of expanding the European system of diplomacy. Resident agents were established in all the European capitals, and they had a decisive impact upon war and peace. Their dispatches formed the most reliable source of information about the strengths of armies or the weaknesses of governments, about the birth of heirs or the death of princes.

Personality also played a part in the international warfare of the early sixteenth century. The three most consistent protagonists—Charles V, Francis I, and Henry VIII—were of similar age and outlook. Each came unexpectedly to his throne in the full flush of youth, eager for combat and glory. The three were self-consciously rivals, each jealous of the other's successes, each triumphant in the other's failures. Henry VIII and Francis I held wrestling bouts when they met in 1520. Francis I challenged Charles V to single combat after the French king's humiliating imprisonment in Madrid in 1526. As the three monarchs aged together, their youthful wars of conquest matured into strategic warfare designed to maintain a continental balance of power.

The Italian Wars

The struggle for supremacy in Europe in the sixteenth century pitted the French House of Valois against the far-flung estates of the Habsburg Empire. Yet the wars took place in Italy. The rivalries among the larger Italian city-states proved fertile ground for the newly consolidated European monarchies. Both French and Spanish monarchs had remote but legitimate claims to the kingdom of Naples in southern Italy. In 1494, the French king, Charles VIII, took up an invitation from the ruler of Milan to intervene in Italian affairs. His campaign was an unqualified, if fleeting, success. He marched the length of the Italian peninsula, overthrew the Medici in Florence, forced the pope to open the gates of Rome, and finally seized the crown of Naples. The occupation was accomplished without a single great battle and lasted until the warring Italian city-states realized that they had more to fear from the French than from one another. Once that happened, Charles VIII beat a hasty retreat. But the French appetite for Italian territory was not sated. Soon a deal was struck with Ferdinand of Aragon to divide the kingdom of Naples in two. In the end, Spain wound up with all of Naples and France was left with nothing but debts and grievances.

Thus, when Francis I came to the French throne and Charles V to the Spanish, Naples was just one of several potential sources of friction. Not only had Ferdinand betrayed the French in Naples, he had also broken a long-standing peace on the Franco-Spanish border by conquering the independent but French-speaking kingdom of Navarre. Francis could be expected to avenge both slights. Charles, on the other hand, was the direct heir of the dukes of Burgundy. From his childhood he had longed for the restoration of his ancestral lands, including Burgundy itself, which had been gobbled up by Louis XI after the death of Charles the Bold. Competition between Francis and Charles became all the more ferocious when Charles's grandfather, the Holy Roman Emperor Maximilian I (1486–1519), died in 1519. Both monarchs launched a vigorous campaign for the honor of succeeding him.

For nearly a century the Holy Roman Emperor had come from the Austrian ruling family, and there was little reason to

■ Jean Clouet, *Portrait of Francis I* (sixteenth century). Rivalry between Francis and Charles V plunged Europe into decades of war.

■ The Italian Wars with Key Battle Sites. Italy was overrun in the sixteenth century and became a battleground for the dynastic struggles of the French, the Spanish, and the Imperial forces.

believe that Charles V, who now inherited the Habsburg lands in Austria and Germany, would not also succeed to the eminent but empty dignity. Nevertheless, the electors were willing to be bribed by French agents who supported Francis's candidacy, and even by English agents who supported Henry VIII. Charles spent the most of all, and his eventual election not only aggravated the personal animosity among the monarchs, but added another source of conflict in Italy. When Louis XII (1498–1515) succeeded Charles VIII as king of France, he had laid claim to the duchy of Milan through an interest of his wife's, though he was unable to enforce it. Francis I proved more capable. In 1515, he stunned all of Europe by crushing the vaunted Swiss mercenaries at the battle of Marignano. But the duchy of Milan was a territory under the protection of the Holy Roman Emperor, and it soon appealed for Imperial troops to help repel the French invaders. Milan was strategically important to Charles V, as it was the vital link between his Austrian and Burgundian possessions. Almost as soon as he took up the imperial mantle, Charles V was determined to challenge Francis I in Italy.

The key to such a challenge was the construction of alliances among the various Italian city-states and most especially with England, whose aid both Charles and Francis sought to enlist in the early 1520s. Henry VII had found foreign alliances a ready source of cash, and he was always eager to enter into them as long as they did not involve raising armies and fighting wars.

■ The Battle of Pavia in 1525, shown in this tapestry, gave Spain a decisive victory over its French rivals. Francis I was captured and imprisoned in Madrid where he was forced to accept a humiliating peace treaty.

Henry VIII was made of sterner stuff. He longed to reconquer France and to cut a figure on the European scene. Despite the fact that his initial Continental adventures had emptied his treasury without fulfilling his dreams, Henry remained eager for war. He was also flattered to find himself the object of attention by both Valois and Habsburg emissaries. Charles V made two separate trips to London, while Henry crossed the Channel in 1520 to meet Francis I in one of the gaudiest displays of conspicuous consumption that the century would witness, appropriately known as the Field of the Cloth of Gold.

The result of the diplomatic intrigues was an alliance between England and the Holy Roman Empire. English and Burgundian forces would stage an invasion of northern France while Spanish and German troops would again attempt to dislodge the French forces from Italy. The strategy worked better than anyone could have imagined. In 1523, Charles's forces gained a foothold in Milan by taking the heavily fortified town of Pavia. Two years later Francis was ready to strike back. At the head of his own royal guards, he massed Swiss mercenaries and French infantry outside Pavia and made ready for a swift assault. Instead, a large imperial army arrived to relieve the town, and in the subsequent battle the French suffered a shattering defeat. Francis I was captured.

The victory at Pavia, which occurred on Charles V's twenty-fifth birthday, seemingly made him master of all of Europe. His ally Henry VIII urged an immediate invasion and dismemberment of France and began raising an army to spearhead the attack. But Charles's position was much less secure than it appeared. The Ottomans threatened his Hungarian territories, and the Protestants threatened his German lands. He could not afford a war of conquest in France. His hope now was to reach an agreement with Francis I for a lasting European peace, and for that purpose the French king was brought in captivity to Madrid.

It is doubtful that there was ever any real chance for peace between Habsburg and Valois after the battle of Pavia. Francis's personal humiliation and Charles's military position were both too strong to allow for a permanent settlement in which Habsburgs ruled in Milan and Naples. But it was neither political nor personal considerations that were the source of another 30 years of continuous European warfare. Rather it was Charles's demand that Burgundy be returned to him. Although Francis was hardly in a position to bargain, he held out on this issue for as long as possible and secretly prepared a disavowal of the final agreement before it was made. By the Treaty of Madrid in 1526, Francis I yielded Burgundy and recognized the Spanish conquest of Navarre and Spanish rule in Naples. The agreement was sealed by the marriage of Francis to Charles's sister, Eleanor of Portugal. But marriage was not sufficient security for such a complete capitulation. To secure his release from Spain, Francis was required to leave behind as hostages his seven- and eight-year-old sons until the treaty was fulfilled. For three years, the children languished in Spanish captivity.

No sooner had he set foot upon French soil than Francis I renounced the Treaty of Madrid. Despite the threat that it posed to his children, Francis argued that the terms had been extracted against his will, and he even gained the approval of the pope for violating his oath. Setting France on a war footing, he began seeking new allies. Henry VIII, disappointed with the

Germany, the French and English were preparing to strike in the Low Countries, and the Italian wars continued. In 1527, Charles's unpaid German mercenaries stormed through Rome, sacked the papal capital, and captured the pope. Christian Europe was mortified.

The struggle for European mastery ground on for decades. The Treaty of Cateau-Cambrésis in 1559 brought to a close 60 years of conflict. In the end the French were no more capable of dislodging the Habsburgs from Italy than were the Habsburgs of forcing the Ottomans out of Hungary. The great stores of silver that poured into Castile from the New World were consumed in the fires of Continental warfare. In 1557, both France and Spain declared bankruptcy to avoid foreclosures by their creditors. For the French, the Italian wars were disastrous. They seriously undermined the state's financial base, eroded confidence in the monarchy, and thinned the ranks of the ruling nobility. The adventure begun by Charles VIII in search of glory brought France nearly to ruin. It ended with fitting irony. After the death of Francis I, his son Henry II (1547–1559) continued the struggle. Henry never forgave his father for abandoning him in Spain, and he sought revenge on Charles V, who had been his jailer. He regarded the Treaty of Cateau-Cambrésis as a victory and celebrated it with great pomp and pageantry. Among the feasts and festivities were athletic competitions for the king's courtiers and attendants. Henry II entered the jousting tournament and was killed there.

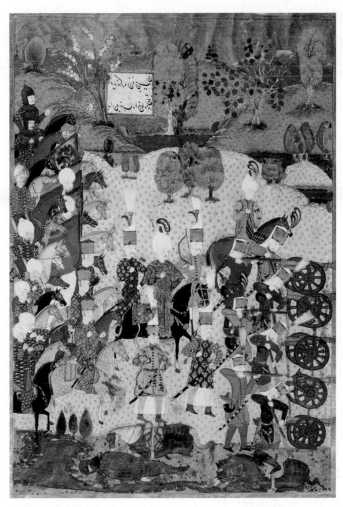

■ This Ottoman painting depicts the defeat of the Hungarians at the hands of the sultan's army at Mohacs in 1526. The prominence of artillery and muskets in the painting reflects the impact of technological advances on warfare.

meager spoils of his last venture, switched sides. So too did a number of Italian city-states, including Rome. Most importantly, Francis I entered into an alliance with the Ottoman sultan, Suleiman the Magnificent (1520–1566), whose armies were pressing against the southeastern borders of the Holy Roman Empire. In the year following Pavia, the Ottomans secured an equally decisive triumph at Mohacs, captured Budapest, and threatened Vienna, the eastern capital of the Habsburg lands. Almost overnight Charles V had been turned from hunter into hunted. The Ottoman threat demanded immediate attention in

CONCLUSION

Charles V died in his bed. The long years of war made clear that the dream to dominate Europe could only be a dream. He split apart his empire and granted to his brother, Ferdinand I (1558–1564), the Austrian and German lands and the mantle of the Holy Roman Empire. To his son Philip II (1556–1598) he ceded the Low Countries, Spain and the New World, Naples, and his Italian conquests. In 1555, Charles abdicated all of his titles and retired to a monastery to live out his final days. The cares of an empire that once stretched from Peru to Vienna were lifted from his shoulders. Beginning with his voyage to Castile in 1517, he had made ten trips to the Netherlands, nine to Germany, seven to Italy, six to Spain, four to France, two to England, and two to Africa. "My life has been one long journey," he told those who witnessed him relinquish his crowns. On 21 September 1558, he finally rested forever.

QUESTIONS FOR REVIEW

1. What impulses in European society were revealed by the global exploration and conquests of the Portuguese and the Spanish?
2. What qualities characterized the "New Monarchies" and what are some of the best examples of such princely states?
3. How and why did the experience of political and territorial unification differ in England, France, and Spain?
4. How did war between the great European monarchies contribute to unity within each?

KEY TERMS

caravels, *p. 356*	New Monarchies, *p. 367*	Treaty of Tordesillas, *p. 358*
Columbian Exchange, *p. 365*	reconquista, *p. 369*	
conquistadores, *p. 362*	Spanish Inquisition, *p. 378*	

DISCOVERING WESTERN CIVILIZATION ONLINE

You can obtain more information about the European empires at the Websites listed below. See also the Companion Website that accompanies this text, www.ablongman.com/kishlansky, which contains an online study guide and additional resources.

European Encounters

Discoverers Web

www.win.tue.nl/cs/fm/engels/discovery/

A site devoted to all ages of discovery with maps, short biographies, and time lines. There are links to the writings of Columbus, Cortés, and others of the early voyagers.

The Columbus Navigation Homepage

www1.minn.net/~keithp/

Everything you ever wanted to know about Christopher Columbus.

1492: An Ongoing Voyage

www.loc.gov/exhibits/1492

A Library of Congress online exhibit on the causes and consequences of European exploration and expansion.

Christopher Columbus—A Culinary History

www.castellobanfi.com/features/story_3.html

A site devoted to the food and drink associated with a long ocean voyage in the fifteenth century.

Medieval Sourcebook: Exploration and Expansion

www.fordham.edu/halsall/sbook1z.html

Dozens of primary sources relating to the voyages of discovery.

The Formation of States

Henry VIII: Intrigue in the Tudor Court

www.archsoc.com/games/Henry.html

A board game that teaches both history and strategy.

SUGGESTIONS FOR FURTHER READING

General Reading

David Nicholas, *The Transformation of Europe 1300–1600* (New York: Oxford University Press, 1999). A comprehensive survey that emphasizes continuities between the sixteenth century and the preceding period.

Eugene Rice, *The Foundations of Early Modern Europe, 1460–1559,* 2nd ed. (New York: Norton, 1994). An outstanding synthesis.

European Encounters

C. R. Boxer, *The Portuguese Seaborne Empire, 1415–1825* (London: Hutchinson, 1968). The best history of the first of the explorer nations.

J. H. Elliott, *The Old World and the New, 1492–1650* (Cambridge: Cambridge University Press, 1970). A brilliant look at the reception of knowledge about the New World by Europeans.

Felipe Fernandez-Armesto, *Columbus* (Oxford: Oxford University Press, 1991). The best of the recent studies. Reliable, stimulating, and up-to-date.

Anthony Pagden, *Lords of All the World: Ideologies of Empire in Spain, Britain and France, c. 1500–c. 1800* (New Haven, CT: Yale University Press, 1995). A fresh look at the ideas behind the European encounter with the New World.

Hugh Thomas, *Rivers of Gold: The Rise of the Spanish Empire* (London: Widenfeld & Nicholson, 2004). A breathtaking retelling of Spain's New World Empire.

Geographical Tour—Europe in 1500: The Age of the New Monarchies

N. J. G. Pounds, *An Historical Geography of Europe, 1500–1800* (Cambridge: Cambridge University Press, 1990). A remarkable survey of the relationship between geography and history.

Daniel Waley, *Later Medieval Europe* (London: Longman, 1985). A good brief account.

The Formation of States

S. B. Chrimes, *Henry VII* (Berkeley: University of California Press, 1972). A traditional biography of the first Tudor.

Robert O. Crummey, *The Formation of Muscovy, 1304–1613* (London: Longman, 1987). The best one-volume history.

Norman Davies, *God's Playground: A History of Poland, Vol. 1, The Origins to 1795* (New York: Columbia University Press, 1982). The best treatment in English of a complex history.

Bernard Guenée, *States and Rulers in Later Medieval Europe* (London: Basil Blackwell, 1985). An engaging argument about the forces that helped shape the state system in Europe.

Henry Kamen, *The Spanish Inquisition: A Historical Revision* (New Haven, CT: Yale University Press, 1998). The most recent assessment of the power and activities of the Inquisition.

Paul M. Kendall, *Louis XI: The Universal Spider* (New York: Norton, 1971). A highly entertaining account of an unusual monarch.

John Lynch, *Spain, 1516–1598: From Nation State to World Empire* (Cambridge, MA: Blackwell, 1994). The most up-to-date survey.

J. H. Shennan, *The Origins of the Modern European State, 1450–1725* (London: Hutchinson, 1974). An analytic account of the rise of the state.

The Dynastic Struggles

J. R. Hale, *War and Society in Renaissance Europe* (Stroud, England: Sutton, 1998). Assesses the impact of war on the political and social history of early modern Europe.

William Maltby, *The Reign of Charles V* (New York: Palgrave, 2002). The most recent study of one of Europe's great emperors.

David Potter, *A History of France, 1460–1560* (London: Macmillan, 1995). A reliable survey that connects medieval and early modern developments.

J. J. Scarisbrick, *Henry VIII* (New Haven: Yale University Press, 1997). The definitive biography.

For a list of additional titles related to this chapter's topics, please see http://www.ablongman.com/kishlansky.

Chapter 13

THE REFORM OF RELIGION

Chapter Outline

In the Middle Ages, Holy Scripture was just that—written manuscripts of parts of the Bible. But with the invention of moveable type, Bibles became more uniform and more available. Turn the page to examine the greatest printed Bible of them all in The Visual Record. ➤

SOLA SCRIPTURA
The Bible and the Reformation

"In the beginning was the word, and the word was with God, and the word was God." In no other period of European history was this text of the apostle John so appropriate. Men and women shared a consuming desire to hear and to read the Word of God as set down in the Bible. In the early sixteenth century, Europeans developed an insatiable appetite for the Bible. Scriptures rolled off printing presses in every shape and form, from the great vellum tomes of Gutenberg pictured here to pocket Bibles that soldiers carried into battle. They came in every imaginable language. Before 1500 there were 14 complete Bibles printed in German, 4 each in Italian, French, and Spanish, 1 in Czech, and even 1 in Flemish. There were hundreds more editions in Latin, the official Vulgate Bible first translated by Saint Jerome in the fourth century. Whole translations and editions of the Bible were only part of the story. Separate sections, especially the Psalms and the first books of the Old Testament, were printed by the thousands. There were 24 French editions of the Old Testament before an entirely new translation appeared in 1530. When Martin Luther began his own German translation of the Bible in 1522, it immediately became an international best seller. In 25 years it went into 430 editions. It is estimated that 1 million German Bibles were printed in the first half of the sixteenth century—a time when Europe had a German-speaking population of about 15 million people, 90 percent of whom were illiterate.

Bible owning was no fad. It was but one element in a new devotional outlook that was sweeping the Continent and that would have far-reaching consequences for European society during the next 150 years. A renewed spirituality was everywhere to be seen. It was expressed in a desire to change the traditional practices and structures of the Roman Church. It was expressed in a desire to have learned and responsible ministers to tend to the needs of their parishioners. It was expressed in a desire to establish godly families, godly cities, and godly kingdoms. Sometimes it took the form of sarcasm and bitter denunciations; sometimes it took the form of quiet devotion and pious living. The need for reform was everywhere felt; the demand for reform was everywhere heard. It came from within the Roman Church as much as from without.

The inspiration for reform was based on the Word of God. Scholars, following humanist principles, worked on biblical translations in an attempt to bring a purer text to light. Biblical commentary dominated the writings of churchmen as never before. Woodcut

■ Pages from a Gutenberg Bible printed in the 1450s.

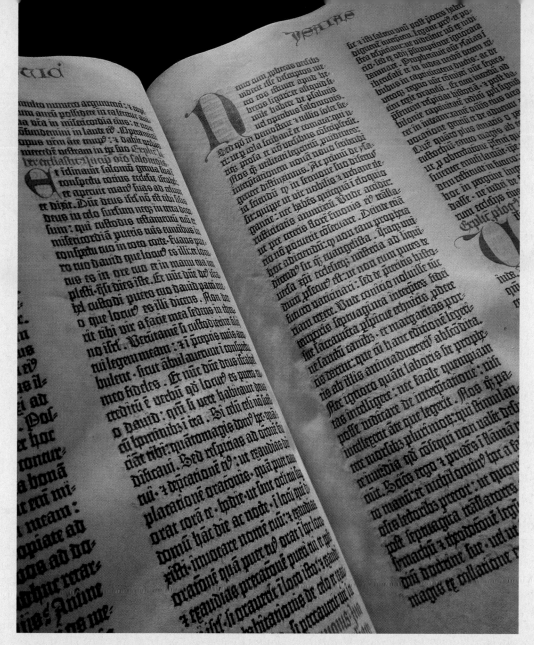

■ Detail of pages from a Gutenberg Bible.

pictures depicting scenes from the life of Jesus or from the Old Testament were printed in untold quantities for the edification of the unlettered. For the first time, common people could, in their own dwellings, contemplate representations of the lives of the saints. Many of the Bibles that were printed in vernacular—that is, in the languages spoken in the various European states rather than in Latin—were interleaved with illustrations of the central events of Christian history. Preachers spoke to newly aware audiences and relied on biblical texts to draw out their message. Study groups, especially in urban areas, proliferated so that the literate could read and learn together. Bible reading became a part of family life, one that mothers and fathers could share with their children and their servants.

Looking Ahead

Sola Scriptura—*by the word alone*—*became the battle cry of religious reform. As we will see in this chapter, in the early decades of the sixteenth century Europeans experienced one of the greatest of all religious rebirths: the Protestant Reformation. The* **Reformation** *was a movement to purify the Catholic Church that resulted in the creation of new religions denominations in Europe collectively known as Protestants from their protest against Roman Catholic practices. But the Catholic Church experienced its own renewal as well. Figures such as Luther, Calvin, and Ignatius of Loyola were part of the most remarkable generation of religious leaders since the foundation of Christianity.* ➤

THE INTELLECTUAL REFORMATION

There is nothing as powerful as an idea whose time has come. But the coming of ideas has a history as complex as the ideas themselves. In the early sixteenth century, reformers throughout western Europe preached new ideas about religious doctrine and religious practice. At first the ideas took the form of a sustained critique of the Roman Catholic Church, but soon they developed a momentum of their own. Some reformers remained within traditional Catholicism; others moved outside and founded new Protestant churches. Whether Catholic or Protestant, wherever the movement for religious reform appeared it was fed by new ideas. But if new ideas were to supplant old ones, they had to be communicated—not only heard and repeated but accurately recorded and understood. That was made possible by the development of the technology of printing, which appeared in Germany in the late fifteenth century and rapidly spread across Europe in the succeeding decades. Yet printing was as much a result as it was a cause of the spread of ideas. The humanist call for a return to the study of the classics and for the creation of accurate texts, first heard in Italy, aroused scholars and leaders in all of the European states. Their appetite for manuscripts exhausted the abilities of the scribes and booksellers who reproduced texts. Printing responded to that demand.

The Print Revolution

The development of printing did not cause religious reform, but it is difficult to see how reform would have progressed in its absence. The campaign to change the doctrine and practice of Catholicism was waged through the press, with millions of flyers and pamphlets distributed across Europe to spread the new ideas. One-third of all books sold in Germany between 1518 and 1525 were written by Luther. But the ways in which printing came to be used by religious reformers could hardly have been foreseen by the artisans, bankers, and booksellers who together created one of the true technological revolutions in Western history.

Printing was not invented. It developed as a result of progress made in a number of allied industries, of which papermaking and goldsmithing were the most important. Scholars and university students needed copies of manuscripts. Their need led to the development of a trade in bookselling that flourished in almost every university town. The process of reproduction was slowed by difficulties in obtaining the sheepskins and calfskins on which the manuscripts were written. It took the skins of 300 sheep to produce a single Bible. In the early fifteenth century, copyists began to substitute paper made from linen rags for the expensive vellum skins. A number of German artisans experimented with using movable metal type to make exact reproductions of manuscripts on paper. Paper took a better impression and provided an absolutely smooth surface, which was essential for pressing the image. In the 1450s, in Mainz, Johannes Gutenberg (ca.

■ An early German print shop. The man at the left operates the screw press while an apprentice (right) stacks the printed sheets. The man in the back is setting type for the next impression.

1400–1468) and his partners succeeded and published their famous Bibles.

The association of early printing with goldsmithing resulted from the high level of technical skill that was necessary to create the hard metal stamps from which the softer metal type was produced. Printing was an expensive business. The investment in type and in paper was considerable. Only the press itself was cheap. Any corn or wine press could be used to bring the long flat sheets of paper down upon a wooden frame filled with ink-coated metal type. Booksellers initially put up the capital needed to cast the stamps, mold the type, and buy the paper. They bound the printed pages and found the markets to distribute them. At first sales were slow. Printed books were considered inferior to handwritten manuscripts. Nor at first were printed books less expensive. Bibles like those printed by Gutenberg were major investments, equivalent to purchasing a house today. Many printing shops quickly went bankrupt as they misjudged their markets and were unable to pay back their loans.

Still, once it was begun, printing spread like wildfire. By 1480, more than 110 towns had established presses, most in Italy and Germany. After that the pace quickened. By the beginning of the

MAP DISCOVERY

Dates indicate the first occurrence of printing.

The Spread of Printing

Examine the locations and dates of early printing. Where were the earliest printing presses concentrated? How did printing spread? Why do you think Rome had a press established before Florence?

sixteenth century, Venice and Paris were the centers of the industry, with the Paris presses producing more than three hundred new titles annually. Most of the early printed works were either religious or classical. Bibles, church service books, and the commentaries of the Church fathers were most common. Cicero topped the list of classical authors.

What is most amazing about the printing revolution is how rapidly printing came to be a basic part of life. In the first 40 years after the presses began, perhaps as many as 20 million books were produced and distributed. Printing changed the habits of teachers and students, and therefore the possibilities

of education. It altered the methods by which the state conducted its business. It affected both legal training and legal proceedings. Compilations of laws could now be widely distributed and more uniformly enforced. Printing had a similar effect on the development of scientific study. The printing press popularized the discoveries of the New World and contributed to the reproduction of more accurate charts and maps, which in turn facilitated further discovery. Printing also helped standardize language—both Latin and vernacular—by frequent repetition of preferred usage and spelling. Perhaps most importantly, printing created an international intellectual community whose ideas could be dispersed the length and breadth of the Continent. The printing press enhanced the value of ideas and of thinking. Nothing could be more central to the reform of religion.

Christian Humanism

Many of the ideas that spread across Europe as the result of the printing revolution originated in Italian humanism (see Chapter 11). The revival of classical literature, with its concern for purity in language and eloquence in style, was one of the most admired achievements of the Renaissance. Students from all over Europe who descended upon Italian universities to study medicine and law came away with a strong dose of philology, rhetoric, moral philosophy, and the other liberal arts. Their heads were filled with the new learning. By the beginning of the sixteenth century, the force of humanism was felt strongly in northern and western Europe, where it was grafted to the dominant strains of traditional theological teaching. The combination was a new and powerful intellectual movement known as **Christian humanism.**

Although the humanism of the north differed from that of the Italian city-states, this is not to say that northern humanists were Christians and Italian humanists were not. But Italian intellectual interests were in secular subjects, especially in mastering classical languages and in translating classical texts. Italian humanists had established techniques for the recovery of accurate texts and had developed principles for compiling the scholarly editions that now poured forth from the printing presses. Christian humanists applied the techniques to the study of the authorities and texts of the Church. Most of the new humanists had been trained in Italy, where they devoted themselves to the mastery of Greek and Latin. They had imbibed the idea that scholars, using their own critical faculties, could establish the authority of texts and the meaning of words. Building upon the patient work of their predecessors and the advantages offered by printing, the new generation of humanists brought learning to educated men and women throughout Europe.

Christian humanism was a program of reform rather than a philosophy. It aimed to make better Christians through better education. Humanists were especially interested in the education of women. "For what is more fruitful than the good education and order of women, the one half of all mankind," wrote Thomas More (1478–1535). Humanists helped found schools for girls and advocated that they be trained in the same subjects as boys. Thomas More raised his daughters to be among the educated elite of England, and they enjoyed international renown. The Spanish humanist Juan Luis Vives (1492–1540) wrote *The Instruction of a Christian Woman* (1523), a handbook for women of the elite orders commissioned by Catherine of Aragon. Renowned women scholars even held places at Italian universities. Humanist educational principles posed an implicit challenge to Roman Catholicism. Schools had once been the monopoly of the Church, which used them to train clergymen. The Church had founded them and kept them afloat in good times and in bad. Literacy itself had been preserved over the centuries so that the gospel could be propagated.

By the sixteenth century those purposes had been transformed. Schools now trained many who were not destined for careers in the Church, and literacy served the needs of the state, the aristocracy, and the merchant classes. More importantly, as the humanists perfected their techniques of scholarship, the Church continued to rely upon traditional methods of training and traditional texts. The dominant manner of teaching at the schools and universities was known as Scholasticism. Passages of biblical texts were studied through the commentaries of generations of Church fathers. Rote memorization of the opinions of others was more highly valued than critical thinking. Argument took place by formal disputation of questions on which the Church fathers disagreed. Disputed questions became more and more obscure. Even if Scholastics did not debate the question, "How many angels can dance on the head of a pin?" it seemed to many humanists that they might as well have. The Vulgate Bible was used throughout Western Christendom. It was now a thousand years old.

The Humanist Movement

Many humanist criticisms of Church teaching focused on its failure to inspire individuals to live a Christian life. Humanist writers were especially scathing about popular practices that bordered on superstition, such as pilgrimages to holy places or the worship of relics from the early history of the Church. Such beliefs became the butt of popular humor: "If the fragments [of the Lord's Cross] were joined together they would seem a full load for a freighter. And yet the Lord carried his whole cross." Christian humanists wanted to inspire Christians. As the great Dutch humanist Desiderius Erasmus observed, "To be learned is the lot of only a few; but no one is unable to be a Christian, no one is unable to be pious." The ironic strain in humanist writing is most closely associated with Erasmus, but it is also visible in the humanist social criticism of Sir Thomas More's *Utopia*. (See "A Closer Look: Utopia," pp. 394–395.)

DOCUMENT

Sir Thomas More, *Utopia*

Christian humanism was an international movement. The humanists formed the elite of the intellectual world of the sixteenth century, and their services were sought by princes and peers as well as by the most distinguished universities. In fact, the New Monarchs supported the humanists and protected them from their critics. Marguerite of Navarre, sister of Francis I, was an accomplished writer who frequently interceded on behalf of the leading French humanists. Ferdinand of Aragon, Henry VIII, and the Holy Roman Emperors Maximilian I and Charles V all brought humanists to their courts and aided their projects. Maria of Hungary and Mary and Elizabeth Tudor were trained in humanist principles and participated in humanist literary achievements.

The centerpiece of humanist reforms was the translation of Christian texts. Armed with skills in Greek and Latin, informed by scholars of Hebrew and Aramaic, humanist writers prepared new editions of the books of the Bible and of the writings of the early Church fathers. Their favorite method was side-by-side translation. The Polyglot—literally "many languages"—Bible that was produced in 1522 at the University of Alcala took a team of scholars 15 years to complete. They gathered together copies of all known biblical manuscripts and rigorously compared their texts. They established the principle that inconsistencies among Latin manuscripts were to be resolved by reference to Greek texts, and difficulties in Greek texts by reference to Hebrew texts. The result was six elegantly printed volumes that allowed scholars to compare the texts. The Old Testament was printed in three parallel columns of Hebrew, Latin Vulgate, and Greek. The New Testament was printed in double columns, with the Greek text on one side and the Vulgate on the other. The Greek edition of the Bible and its establishment as a text superior to the Vulgate caused an immediate sensation throughout humanist and Church circles.

The Wit of Erasmus

Although the Polyglot Bible contained the first completed Greek edition of the New Testament, it was not the first published one. That distinction belongs to the man whose name is most closely associated with the idea of Christian humanism: Desiderius Erasmus of Rotterdam (ca. 1466–1536). Orphaned at an early age, Erasmus was educated by the Brothers of the Common Life, a lay brotherhood that specialized in schooling children and preparing them for a monastic life. Marked out early by his quick wit, pleasant though strong personality, and extraordinary intellectual gifts, Erasmus entered a monastery and was then allowed to travel to pursue his studies, first in France and then in England.

In England, Erasmus learned of new techniques for instructing children both in classical knowledge and in Christian morals, and he became particularly interested in the education of women. He dedicated a number of his later writings to women patrons who were accomplished humanist scholars. While in England, Erasmus decided to compose a short satire on the lines of his conversations with Thomas More, extolling what was silly and condemning what was wise. The result was *In Praise of Folly* (1509), a work that became one of the first best sellers in publishing history.

Before his visit to England, Erasmus had worked solely on Latin translations, but he came to realize the importance of recovering the Greek texts of the early Church fathers. At the age of 30, he began the arduous task of learning ancient Greek and devoted his energies to a study of the writings of Saint Jerome, the principal compiler of the Vulgate, and to preparing an edition of the Greek text of the Bible. Erasmus's New Testament and his edition of the writings of Saint Jerome both appeared in 1516. Coming from the pen of the most renowned intellectual in Europe, they were an immediate success.

Erasmus devoted his life to restoring the direct connection between the individual Christian and the textual basis of

A DUTCH WIT

In Praise of Folly *(1500) was a witty satire on the abuses to be found in the Catholic Church. Desiderius Erasmus wrote it on a lark to be presented to his friend, Sir Thomas More, on whose name its Greek title puns. It was probably the first best seller of the age of printing.*

Focus Questions
How do the follies of priests and theologians differ, and how are they similar? Is this piece a satire of religion?

These various forms of foolishness so pervade the whole life of Christians that even the priests themselves find no objection to admitting, not to say fostering, them, since they do not fail to perceive how many tidy little sums accrue to them from such sources. But what if some odious philosopher should chime in and say, as is quite true: "You will not die badly if you live well. You are redeeming your sins when you add to the sum that you contribute a hearty detestation of evil doers: then you may spare yourself tears, vigils, invocations, fasts, and all that kind of life. You may rely upon any saint to aid you when once you begin to imitate his life."

As for the theologians, perhaps the less said the better on this gloomy and dangerous theme, since they are a style of man who show themselves exceeding supercilious and irritable unless they can heap up six hundred conclusions about you and force you to recant; and if you refuse, they promptly brand you as a heretic—for it is their custom to terrify by their thunderings those whom they dislike. It must be confessed that no other group of fools are so reluctant to acknowledge Folly's benefits toward them, although I have many titles to their gratitude, for I make them so in love with themselves that they seem to be happily exalted to the third heaven, whence they look down with something like pity upon all other mortals, wandering about on the earth like mere cattle.

From Erasmus, *In Praise of Folly.*

A Closer Look
Utopia

"It is a general rule that the more different anything is from what people are used to, the harder it is to accept." So warned the imaginary traveler, Raphael Hythloday as he described Utopia, a fabulous society he had visited in the New World. Utopian society was different indeed. In Utopia, all property was held in common; there were no social classes; families were extended to include grandparents, in-laws, and flocks of children; and all work and most social activities were regulated by the state. Utopians were rarely tempted to sin. Everyone wore the same practical clothes to abolish vanity. "No matter how delicate the thread, they say a sheep wore it once and still was nothing but a sheep." Everyone ate the same food in large common halls to abolish jealousy. "A man would be stupid to take the trouble to prepare a worse meal at home when he had a sumptuous one near at hand in the hall." To abolish greed, Utopians scorned gold and silver. "Criminals who are to bear through life the mark of some disgraceful act are forced to wear golden rings on their ears, golden bands on their fingers, golden chains around their necks, and even golden crowns on their heads." Utopians lived harmoniously in planned cities, honored their elders, cared for their sick, and brought up their children to love learning and respect hard work. They "lead a life as free of anxiety and as full of joy as possible."

There were many ways in which Christian humanists attempted to instruct their contemporaries to lead a joyful life. None has proved more enduring than the imaginary community Sir Thomas More created in *Utopia*, a social satire so convincing that a Catholic priest sought to become its bishop and sea travelers tried to learn its location. More's creation has proven so compelling that it has given its name to the entire genre of dreamworlds that followed in its wake. His vision of a carefully planned and permanently contented society has passed into our language, but in a way that would not have pleased the author. Now, utopian has a wistful ring. It is a label for impractical ideals that will never come to pass, a name for well-meaning but misguided daydreams. For More, as for his generation of humanists, the goal of teaching Christians to lead a Christian life was neither wistful nor impractical.

Sir Thomas More was a London lawyer by vocation but a humanist scholar by avocation. His father practiced law and planned a similar career for his son. But More's stay at Oxford University coincided with the first flush of humanist enthusiasm there, especially in the study of Greek. More proved so able that his father removed him to London in fear that reading Greek would turn him away from Catholicism. More was as good at law school as he had been at the university, and he was soon singled out as one of the best lawyers of his day. But in his spare time he continued to study the classics and became part of the growing humanist circle in London. There he met Erasmus, who was to become his lifelong friend.

Erasmus left a vivid portrait of More. "His complexion is fair, his face being rather blond than pale; his hair is auburn inclining to black, his eyes a bluish gray. It is a face more expressive of pleasantry than of gravity or dignity. He seems to be born and made for friendship, his extraordinary kindness and sweetness of temper are such as to cheer the dullest spirit."

More wrote *Utopia* in 1516, before he embarked upon the public career that would result in his becoming Chancellor of England, Speaker of the House of Commons, Privy Councilor and companion to Henry VIII, and finally a victim of the king's divorce and assumption of the title Supreme Head of the Church of England. More's life was ended on the chopping block, and his death was mourned by humanists throughout Europe.

The community that More described in *Utopia* combined Plato's republic with a Christian monastery and was wrapped about by travelers' tales of the New World. But More's Utopia resembled nothing so much as England. The real and the imaginary, the serious and the absurd intermingle to disguise the author's point of view. *Utopia* is written in the form of a dialogue in which the author pretends to be one of the characters. On a visit to Antwerp, the character More is introduced to an imaginary traveler named Raphael Hythloday. During a long evening, Hythloday related a tale of a remarkable society that he encountered on his voyages. Utopia was a self-sufficient island, protected from invasion by the sea and thus able to develop its social customs without interference.

Hythloday contrasted the practices of the Utopians with those of contemporary Europeans. For example, where European peasants or craftsmen worked for fourteen hours a day, Utopians worked for only six. But all Utopians worked. There were no idle aristocrats with their marauding retainers, no priests and monks and nuns, no beggars unable to find jobs. Moreover, there was no surplus of workers in one field and shortage in another. For two years, each Utopian worked on a farm. After that, Utopians practiced a craft according to the needs of the city. Both males and females were educated to serve the community. Women were trained in less strenuous but no less essential trades such as weaving or spinning. The population of cities was strictly controlled so that there was neither poverty nor homelessness. In their spare time Utopians engaged in uplifting activities such as music, gardening, or artistic pursuits. Severe punishment awaited transgressors, but in contrast to the European practice of executing thieves, Utopian criminals were enslaved so that they could work for the restitution of the wrongs that they committed. Even as slaves they lived well, with good food and much leisure. Though they had not the benefit of Christian religion, the Utopians believed in a single divinity as well as an afterlife and their worship was simple and natural.

More's *Utopia* was written in Latin, but the name of the island and its central places were all Greek words. For More's humanist friends the joke was plain. Utopia meant "nowhere" in Greek and Hythloday meant "peddler of nonsense." Humanist interest in the New

■ A woodcut of the island of Utopia by Ambrosius Holbein, from the 1518 edition of Sir Thomas More's *Utopia*.

World and in the strange native customs of the Amerindians made it a logical setting for an idealized community. But *Utopia* was a model for a Christian community, one in which the seven deadly sins had all been abolished and replaced by a life led according to the Golden Rule, where people did attempt to do to others what they wished done to themselves. By ironic contrast with the unfulfilling life led by Europeans,

grasping for riches, the simple life of the Utopians held great attraction. By comparing the success of heathen Utopians with the failure of Christian Europeans, More called upon his contemporaries to reform their own lives. The purpose of *Utopia* was not to advocate the abolition of wealth and property but to demonstrate that a society founded upon Christian principles would become truly Christian.

■ Hans Holbein's 1523 portrait depicts Erasmus in profile, absorbed in his work rather than looking in the direction of the viewer.

Christian doctrine. Although he is called the father of biblical criticism, Erasmus was not a theologian. He was more interested in the practical impact of ideas than in the ideas themselves. His scathing attacks upon the Scholastics, popular superstition, and the pretensions of the traditionalists in the Church and the universities all aimed at the same goal: to restore the experiences of Christ to the center of Christianity. Many of Erasmus's popular writings were how-to books—how to improve one's manners, how to speak Latin properly, how to write letters—he even propounded 22 rules on how to lead a Christian life. Although his patrons were the rich and his language was Latin, Erasmus also hoped to reach men and women lower down the social order, those whom he believed the Church had failed to educate. "The doctrine of Christ casts aside no age, no sex, no fortune or position in life. It keeps no one at a distance."

THE LUTHERAN REFORMATION

On the surface, the Roman Catholic Church appeared as strong as ever at the end of the fifteenth century. The growth of universities and the spread of the new learning had helped create a better-educated clergy. The printing press proved an even greater boon to the Church than it had to the humanists by making widely available both instructional manuals for priests and up-to-date service books for congregations. The prosperity of European societies enhanced the prosperity of the Church. In Rome, successive late medieval popes had managed to protect Church interests in the wake of the disintegration of the autonomous power of the Italian city-states. That was a remarkable feat. Popes had become first diplomats and then warriors in order to repel French and Spanish invaders. Although Rome had been invaded, it had never been conquered. And it was more beautiful than ever, as the greatest artists and artisans of the Renaissance had built and adorned its churches. Pilgrims came in the hundreds of thousands to bask in its glory. On the surface all was calm.

Yet everywhere in Europe the cry was for reform. Reform the venal papacy and its money-sucking bishops. Reform the ignorant clergy and the sacrilegious priests. Raise up the fallen nuns and the wayward friars. Wherever people turned, they saw abuses. Parish livings were sold to the highest bidder to raise money. That was simony. Rich appointments were given to the kinsmen of powerful Church leaders rather than to those most qualified. That was nepotism. Individual clergymen accumulated numerous positions whose responsibilities they could not fulfill. That was pluralism. Some priests who took the vow of chastity lived openly with their concubines. Some mendicants who took the vow of poverty dressed in silk and ate from golden plates.

Yet the cry for reform that pierced the states of Europe at the beginning of the sixteenth century was a cry not so much of anguish as of hope. It came at a moment when people from all walks of life demanded greater spiritual fulfillment and held those whose vocation it was to provide such fulfillment to higher standards of achievement. It was expectation rather than experience that powered the demands for reform.

The Spark of Reform

Europe was becoming more religious. The signs of religious fervor were everywhere. Cities hired preachers to expound the gospel. Pilgrims to the shrines of saints clogged the roadways every spring and summer. It is estimated that 140,000 people visited the relics at Aachen on one day in 1496. Rome remained the greatest attraction, but pilgrims covered the Continent. The shrine of the apostle Saint James at Compostela in Spain was believed to cure the ill. Endowments of masses for the dead increased. Henry VII of England provided money for 10,000 masses to be said for his soul. Even moderately well-to-do city merchants might bequeath funds for several hundred. The chantries, where such services were performed, became overburdened by the "arithmetical piety," as there were neither enough priests nor enough altars to supply the demand.

People wanted more from the Church than the Church could possibly give them. Humanists condemned visits to the shrines as superstitious; pilgrims demanded that the relics be made more accessible. Reformers complained of pluralism;

the clergy complained that they could not live on the salary of a single office. In one English diocese, 60 percent of all parish incomes were inadequate to live on. Civic authorities demanded that the established Church take greater responsibility for good works; the pope demanded that civic authorities help pay for them.

Contradiction and paradox dominated the movements for reform. Although the most vocal critics of the Church complained that its discipline was too lax, for many ordinary people its demands were too rigorous. The obligations of penance and confession weighed heavily upon them. Church doctrine held that sins had to be washed away before the souls of the dead could enter heaven. Until then they suffered in purgatory. Sins were cleansed through penance—the performance of acts of contrition assigned after confession. Despite the rule that confession must be made at least annually, it is doubtful if many Catholics entered the confessional for years on end. This is not to say that they were unconcerned about their sins or did not desire to do penance for them. Rather, it was the ordeal of the confession itself that kept many people away. "Have you skipped mass? Have you dressed proudly? Have you thought of committing adultery? Have you insulted or cursed your parents? Have you failed to offer prayers, give alms, and endow masses for departed parents?" These were just a few of the uncomfortable questions that priests were instructed to pose in confession. In towns, merchants were asked about their trading practices, shopkeepers about the quality of their goods. Magistrates were questioned about their attitudes to the clergy, intellectuals about their attitudes to the pope.

Thus it is hardly surprising that the sale of **indulgences** became a popular substitute for penance and confession. An indulgence was a portion of the treasury of good works performed by righteous Christians throughout the ages. They could be granted to those who desired to atone for their sins. Strictly speaking, an indulgence supplemented penance rather than substituted for it. It was effective only for the contrite— for sinners who repented of their sins. But as the practice of granting indulgences spread, the subtle distinction largely disappeared. Indulgences came to be viewed as pardons and the gift given to the Church in return as payment. "So soon as coin in coffer rings, the soul from purgatory springs." Indulgences were bought by the living to cleanse the sins of the dead, and some people even bought indulgences in anticipation of sins they had not yet committed.

By the sixteenth century, to limit abuses by local Church authorities, only the pope, through his agents, could grant indulgences. And their sale had become big business. Indulgences were one of the first items printed on Gutenberg's press. Popes used special occasions to offer an indulgence for pilgrimages to Rome or for contributions to special papal projects. Other indulgences were licensed locally, usually at the shrines of saints or at churches that contained relics, which was one reason why pilgrimages became increasingly popular. Frederick III, "the Wise" (1463–1525), ruler of Saxony, was one of the largest collectors of relics in Europe. At

■ An anonymous caricature of Johann Tetzel, whose sale of an indulgence inspired Martin Luther's Ninety-five Theses. Tetzel answered with 122 theses of his own but was rebuked and disowned by the Catholics.

its height, his collection contained 17,000 different items, including a branch of Moses' burning bush, straw from Christ's manger, and 35 fragments of the true cross. Together, his relics carried remission for sins that would otherwise have taken more than a quarter of a million years in purgatory to be cleansed.

The indulgence controversy was a symptom rather than a cause of the explosion of feelings that erupted in the small German town of Wittenberg in the year 1517. In that year, the pope was offering an indulgence to help finance the rebuilding of Saint Peter's Basilica in Rome. The pope chose Prince Albert of Brandenburg (1490–1545) to distribute the indulgence in Germany, and Albert hired the Dominican friar Johann Tetzel (ca. 1465–1519) to preach its benefits. Tetzel offered little warning about the theological niceties of indulgences to those who paid to mitigate their own sins or alleviate the suffering of their ancestors whose souls resided in purgatory.

Enthusiasm for the indulgence spread to the neighboring state of Saxony, where Frederick banned its sale. His great collection of relics carried their own indulgences, and Tetzel offered unwelcome competition. But Saxons flocked into Brandenburg to make their purchases. By the end of October, Tetzel was not very far from Wittenberg Castle, where Frederick's relics were housed. On All Saints' Day the relics would be opened to view and, with the harvest done, one of the largest crowds of the year would gather to see them. On the night before, Martin Luther (1483–1546), a professor of theology at Wittenberg University, posted on the door of the castle church Ninety-five Theses attacking indulgences and their sale.

Aside from the timing of Luther's action, there was nothing unusual about the posting of theses. In the Scholastic tradition of disputation, scholars presented propositions, or theses, for debate and challenged all comers to argue with them in a public forum. Luther's theses were controversial, but—as that was the whole point of offering them for discussion—they were meant to be. Only circumstance moved Luther's theses from the academic to the public sphere. Already there was growing concern among clergy and theologians about Tetzel's blatant sale of indulgences. Hordes of purchasers believed that they were buying unconditional remission of sin. In the late summer and early fall of 1517, the frenzy to buy indulgences had reached gold-rush proportions, and individual priests and monks began to sound the alarm: an indulgence without contrition was worthless.

Luther's theses focused that concern and finally communicated it beyond the walls of the Church and university. The theses were immediately translated into German and spread throughout the Holy Roman Empire by humanists who had long criticized practices such as the sale of indulgences as superstitious. Prospective buyers became wary; past purchasers became angry. They had been duped again by the Church, by the priests who took their money, and by the Italian pope who cared nothing for honest, hardworking Germans. But Prince Albert and the pope needed the income. They could not stand by while sales collapsed and anticlerical and antipapal sentiment grew. Luther and his theses would have to be challenged.

Martin Luther's Faith

Martin Luther was not a man to challenge lightly. Although he was only an obscure German professor, he had already marked himself out to all who knew him. In his youth, Luther was an exceptionally able student whose father sent him to the best schools in preparation for a career in law. But Martin had his own ideas about his future, which were made more vivid when he was nearly struck by lightning. Against the wishes of his father, he entered an Augustinian monastery, wholeheartedly followed the strict program of his order, and was ordained a priest in 1507. Intellectually gifted, he went on to study at the university, first at Erfurt and then at Wittenberg, where he received his doctorate and was appointed to the theology faculty in 1512.

A professor at the age of 29, he also served as priest at the castle church, where he preached each week. He attracted powerful patrons in the university and gained a reputation as an outstanding teacher. He began to be picked for administrative posts and became overseer of 11 Augustinian monasteries. His skills in disputation were so widely recognized that he was sent to Rome to argue a case on behalf of his order. Each task he was given he fulfilled beyond expectation; at every step he proved himself ready to go higher.

In all outward appearances, Luther was successful and contented. But beneath this tranquil exterior lay a soul in torment. As he rose in others' estimation, he sank in his own. Through beating and fasting he mortified his flesh. Through vigil and prayer he nourished his soul. Through study and contemplation he honed his intellect. Still he could find no peace. Despite his devotion, he could not erase his sense of

■ A portrait of Martin Luther (1483–1546) as he appeared later in his life.

sin; he could not convince himself that the righteousness God demanded of him was a righteousness he could achieve. "I was one who terribly feared the last judgment and who nevertheless with all my heart wished to be saved."

Knowledge of his salvation came to Luther through study. His internal agonies led him to ponder over and over again the biblical passages that described the righteousness of God. In the intellectual tradition in which he had been trained, that righteousness was equated with law. The righteous person either followed God's law or was punished by God's wrath. It was that understanding that tormented him. "I thought that I had to perform good works till at last through them Jesus would become a friend and gracious to me." But no amount of good works could overcome Luther's feelings of guilt for his sins. Like a man caught in a net, the more he struggled the more entangled he became. For years he wrestled with his problem. Almost from the moment he began lecturing in 1512 he searched for the key to the freedom of his own soul.

Even before he wrote his Ninety-five Theses, Luther had made the first breakthrough by a unique reading of the writings of Saint Paul. "I pondered night and day until I understood the connection between the righteousness of God and the sentence 'The just shall live by faith.' Then I grasped that the justice of God is the righteousness by which through grace and pure mercy, God justifies us through faith. Immediately I felt that I had been reborn and that I had passed through wide open doors into paradise!" Finally he realized that the righteousness of God was not a burden that humans carried, but a gift that God bestowed. It could not be earned by good works but was freely given. It was this belief that fortified Luther during his years of struggle with both civil and Church powers.

Over the next several years, Luther refined his spiritual philosophy and drew out the implications of his newfound beliefs. His religion was shaped by three interconnected tenets. First came justification by faith alone—*sola fide.* An individual's everlasting salvation came from faith in God's goodness rather than from the performance of good works. Sin was ever present and inescapable. It could not be washed away by penance, and it could not be forgiven by indulgence. Second, faith in God's mercy came only through the knowledge and contemplation of the Word of God—*sola scriptura.* All that was needed to understand the justice and mercy of God was contained in the Bible, the sole authority in all things spiritual. Reading the Word, hearing the Word, expounding upon and studying the Word—that was the path to faith, and through faith to salvation. Third, all who believed in God's righteousness and had achieved their faith through the study of the Bible were equal in God's eyes. No longer was it necessary for men and women to renounce their worldly existence and take up a life consumed by spiritual works. Neither pope nor priest, neither monk nor nun, could achieve a higher level of spirituality than the most ordinary citizen. The priesthood was of all believers. Each followed his or her own calling in life and found his or her own faith through Scripture. Ministers and preachers were valuable because they could help others learn God's Word. But they could not confer faith.

Luther's spiritual rebirth and the theology that developed from it posed a fundamental challenge to the Roman Catholic Church. The doctrine of justification by faith alone called into question the Church's emphasis upon the primacy of works—that is, receiving the sacraments administered by the priests and performing acts of charity and devotion. The doctrine that faith was achieved through Scripture weakened the mediating power of the Church by making salvation an individual rather than a collective event. The doctrine of the equality of all believers struck at the vast establishment of religious houses as well as the spiritual hierarchy of the Church from the lowest priest to the pope. Although for centuries the Roman Catholic Church had met doctrinal challenges and had absorbed many seemingly unorthodox ideas, Luther's theology could not be among them. It struck too deeply at the roots of belief, practice, and structure. If Luther was right, then the Roman Catholic Church must be wrong.

Yet for all of the transforming power of the apparently simple ideas, it was not Luther alone who initiated the reform of religion. Before Luther, countless thousands strove for salvation. Justification by faith alone provided an alternative to the combination of works and faith that many Roman Catholics found too difficult to fulfill. Luther's insistence that faith comes only through the study of the Word of God was facilitated by the new learning and the invention of printing.

The printing press prepared the ground for the dissemination of his thought as much as it disseminated it. That was a result of the Renaissance. Luther's hope for the creation of a spiritual elite, confirmed in their faith and confident of their salvation, readily appealed to the citizens of hundreds of German towns who had already made of themselves a social and economic elite. That was a result of the growth of towns. The idea of the equality of all believers meant that all were equally responsible for fulfilling God's commandments. That set secular rulers on an equal footing with the pope at a moment in Western history when they were already challenging papal power in matters of both Church and state. That was a result of the formation of states. For all of the painful soul-searching by which he came to his shattering insight, there was embodied in Luther the culmination of changes of which he was only dimly aware.

Lutheranism

The first to feel the seriousness of Luther's challenge to the established order was the reformer himself. The head of his order, a papal legate, and finally the Emperor Charles V all called for Luther to recant his views on indulgences. Excommunicated by Pope Leo X in 1521, Luther was ordered by Charles V to appear before the diet, or assembly, in Worms. The emperor demanded that Luther retract his teachings. Infuriatingly, Luther replied that, if he could be shown the places in the Bible that contradicted his views, he would gladly change them. "I cannot and I will not retract anything, since it is neither safe nor right to go against conscience. I cannot do otherwise." In fact, during the three years between the posting of his theses and his appearance before the emperor, Luther came to conclusions much more radical than his initial attack on indulgences. Preparing to contend with papal representatives about the pope's right to issue indulgences, Luther came to believe that the papacy was a human rather than a divine invention. Therefore he denounced both the papacy and the general councils of the Church. In his *Address to the Christian Nobility of the German Nation* (1520), he called upon the princes to take the reform of religion into their own hands. No longer was there hope of compromise. Charles V declared Luther an enemy of the empire. In both Church and state he was now an outlaw.

But Luther had attracted powerful supporters as well as powerful enemies. Prince Frederick III of Saxony consistently intervened on his behalf, and the delicate international situation forced Luther's chief antagonists to move more slowly than they might have wanted. The pope hoped first to keep Charles V off the imperial throne and then to maintain a united front with the German princes against him. Charles V, already locked in his lifelong struggle with the French, needed German military support and peace in his German territories. Those factors consistently played into Luther's hands.

While pope and emperor were otherwise occupied, Luther refined his ideas and thus was able to hold his own in the theological debates in which he won important converts. More

DOCUMENT

Martin Luther,
The German
Mass

importantly, as time passed Luther's reputation grew, not only in Germany, but all over Europe. Between 1517 and 1520 he published 30 works, all of which achieved massive sales. Yet Luther alone could not sustain what came to be called Lutheranism. The Roman Catholic Church had met heresy before and knew how to deal with it. What turned Luther's theology into a movement—which after 1529 came to be known as Protestantism—was the support he received among German princes and within German cities.

Princes and Cities.   There were many reasons that individual princes turned to Luther's theology. First and foremost was sincere religious conviction. Matters of the hereafter were a pressing concern in a world in which the average life span was 30 years and nearly all natural phenomena were inexplicable. And they were more pressing still among the educated elites inspired by the new learning and confident of their power to reason critically. Yet there were secular reasons as well. The formation of large states had provided a model for civil government. On a smaller scale, German princes worked to centralize their administration, protect themselves from predatory neighbors, and increase their revenues. They had long suffered under the burden of papal exactions. Taxes and gifts flowed south to a papacy dominated by Italians. Luther's call for civil rulers to lead their own churches meant that civil rulers could keep their own revenues.

The Reformation spread particularly well in the German cities, especially those the emperor had granted the status of freedom from the rule of any prince. Once Protestant ideas were established, entire towns adopted them. The cities had long struggled with the tension of the separate jurisdictions of state and Church. Much urban property was owned by the Church and thus exempt from taxation and law enforcement, and the clergy constituted a significant proportion of urban populations. Reformed religion stressed the equality of clergy and laity, and thus the indisputable power of civil authorities. Paradoxically, it was because the cities contained large numbers of priests that Luther's ideas reached them quickly. Many of his earliest students served urban congregations and began to develop doctrines and practices that, though based on Luther's ideas, were adapted to the circumstances of city life. The reform clergy became integrated into the life of the city in a way that the Catholic clergy had not. They married the daughters of citizens, became citizens themselves, and trained their children in the guilds. Moreover, the imperial free cities were also the center of the printing trade and home to many of the most noted humanists who were initially important in spreading Luther's ideas.

LUTHER ON MARRIAGE

Martin Luther wrote thousands of pages of theological and devotional literature in establishing a new religious movement. His simple style and everyday examples made his message accessible to hundreds of thousands of ordinary people. In this selection from his tract On Good Works *(1520), he compares the relationship of the husband and wife to that of the Christian and Christ.*

Focus Questions

Why are "good works" not of primary importance in a Christian's relationship with God? Does Luther leave a role for the Church in his ideal of the relationship between a Christian and God?

We can understand this whole matter [of good works] by an obvious human example. When husband and wife are fond of one another and live together in love and in confidence in one another, and each believes truly in the other, who shall teach them how they should act, what they should do or leave undone, say or not say, think or not think? Their own insight tells them all that need be, and more too. There is no distinction in their "works" for one another. They do the long, hard, and heavy tasks as willingly as the slight and easy things, and moreover they act with glad, peaceful, and secure hearts and are altogether free and unconstrained. But when doubt comes they begin to ask what is best, and begin to distinguish between their acts in order to gain the other's favor, and go about with troubled and heavy hearts, perhaps well-nigh in despair or driven to downright desperation.

So the Christian who lives in confidence toward God knows what things he should do, and does all gladly and freely, not with a view to accumulating merit and good works, but because it is his great joy to please God and to serve him without thought of reward, contented if he but do God's will. On the contrary, he who is not at one with God, or is in doubt, will begin to be anxious how he may satisfy God and justify himself by his works. He runs off on a pilgrimage to St. James of Compostella, to Rome, to Jerusalem—here, there, anywhere; prays to St. Bridget, or some other saint, fasts this day and that, confesses here and confesses there, asks this man and that, but finds no peace.

From Martin Luther, *On Good Works.*

Luther's message held great appeal for the middle orders in the towns. While it was necessary for the leader of a state to support reform if it was to survive, in the cities it was the petty burghers, lesser merchants, tradesmen, and artisans who led the movements that ultimately gained the approval of city governments. The groups resented the privileges given to priests and members of religious orders who paid no taxes and were exempt from the obligations of citizenship. The level of anti-clericalism, always high in Germany, was especially acute in cities that were suffering economic difficulties. Pressure from ordinary people and petty traders forced town leaders into action. The evangelism of reforming ministers created converts and an atmosphere of reform. Support from members of the ruling oligarchy both mobilized the pressures and capitalized upon them. Town governments secured their own autonomy over the Church, tightening their grip upon the institutions of social control and enhancing the social and economic authority of their members. Once Protestant, city governments took over many of the religious houses, often converting them into schools or hostels for the poor. Former monks were allowed to enter trades and to become citizens. Former nuns were encouraged to marry. Luther himself married an ex-nun after the dissolution of her convent.

The Appeal for Women. Religious reform appealed to women as well as men, but it affected them differently. Noblewomen were among the most important defenders of Protestant reformers, especially in states in which the prince opposed it. Marguerite of Navarre (1492–1549), sister of Francis I, frequently intervened with her brother on behalf of individual Lutherans who fell afoul of Church authorities. She created her own court in the south of France and stocked it with both humanists and Protestants. Her devotional poem *Mirror of the Sinful Soul* (1533) inspired women reformers and was translated into English by Elizabeth I. Mary of Hungary (1505–1558) served a similar role in the Holy Roman Empire. Sister of both Charles V and Ferdinand I, queen of Hungary, and later regent of the Netherlands, she acted as patron to Hungarian reformers. Although Mary was more humanist than Protestant, Luther dedicated an edition of the Psalms to her, and she read a number of his works. Her independent religious views infuriated both of her brothers. Bona (1493–1558), wife of Sigismund I of Poland, was especially important in eastern reform. An Italian by birth, Bona was a central figure in spreading both Renaissance art and humanist learning in Poland. She became one of the largest independent landowners in the state and initiated widespread agricultural and economic reforms. Her private confessor was one of Poland's leading Protestants.

Luther's reforms also offered much to women who were not so highly placed in society. The doctrine of the equality of all believers put men and women on an equal spiritual footing, even if it did nothing to break the male monopoly of the ministry. But the most important difference that Protestantism made to ordinary women was in the private rather than the public sphere. Family life became the center of faith when salvation was removed from the control of the

■ A portrait of Marguerite de Valois, queen of Navarre, the cultured and talented sister of King Francis I.

Church. Luther's marriage led him to a deeper appreciation of the importance of the wife and mother in the family's spirituality. "Next to God's word there is no more precious treasure than holy matrimony."

By following humanist teaching on the importance of educating women of the upper orders and by encouraging literacy, the reformers did much that was uplifting. Girls' schools were founded in a number of German cities, and townswomen could use their newly acquired skills in their roles as shopkeepers, family accountants, and teachers of their children. But there were losses as well as gains. The attack on the worship of saints, and especially of the Virgin Mary, removed female images from religion. Protestantism was male dominated in a way that Catholicism was not. Moreover, the emphasis upon reading the Bible tended to reinforce the image of women as weak and inherently sinful. The dissolution of the convents took away from women the one institution that valued their gender and allowed them to pursue a spiritual life outside marriage.

The Spread of Lutheranism

By the end of the 1520s, the Holy Roman Empire was divided between cities and states that accepted reformed religion and

MAP DISCOVERY

Intensity of green represents the approximate strength of Lutheranism

The Spread of Lutheranism

Observe the extent of Lutheranism across Europe in the sixteenth century. Where was Lutheranism concentrated? Notice how Lutheranism swept through entire states. How was Europe divided between Protestants and Catholics?

those that adhered to Roman Catholicism. Printing presses, traveling merchants, and hordes of students who claimed—not always accurately—to have attended Luther's lectures or sermons spread the message. Large German communities across northern Europe, mostly founded as trading outposts, became focal points for the penetration of reformist ideas. In Livonia, the Teutonic Knights established a Lutheran form of worship that soon took hold all along the shores of the Baltic. Lutheran-inspired reformers seized control of the Polish port city of Gdansk, which they held for a short time, while neighboring Prussia officially established a Lutheran church. Polish translations of Luther's writings were disseminated into

Poland-Lithuania, and Protestant communities were established as far south as Krakow.

Merchants and students carried Luther's ideas into Scandinavia, but there the importance of political leaders was crucial. Christian III (1534–1559) of Denmark had been present at the Diet of Worms when Luther made his famous reply to Charles V. Christian was deeply impressed by the reformer, and after a ruinous civil war, he confiscated the property of the Catholic Church in Denmark and created a reformed religion under Luther's direct supervision.

Paradoxically, Lutheranism came to Sweden as part of an effort to throw off the yoke of Danish dominance. There, too, direct connection with Luther provided the first impulses. Olaus Petri (1493–1552) had studied at Wittenberg and returned to preach Lutheran doctrine among the large German merchant community in Stockholm. He was a trained humanist who used both Erasmus's Greek New Testament and Luther's German one to prepare his Swedish translation (1526). When Gustav I Vasa (1523–1560) led a successful uprising against the Danes and became king of Sweden, he encouraged the spread of Protestant ideas and allowed Petri to continue his Swedish translations of the mass and the Lutheran service. Under the protection of the monarchy, Lutheranism flourished in Scandinavia, where it remains the dominant religion to this day.

As important as Protestant ideas were in northern and central Europe, it was in the Swiss towns of the Holy Roman Empire that they proved most fertile. Here was planted the second generation of reformers, theologians who drew radical new conclusions from Luther's insights. In the east, Huldrych Zwingli (1484–1531) brought reformed religion to the town of Zurich. Educated at the University of Basel and deeply influenced by humanist thought early in his career, Zwingli was a preacher among the Swiss mercenary troops that fought for

■ Huldrych Zwingli was a scholarly humanist deeply influenced by Erasmus. He led the Reformation in Zurich, the most important Swiss town.

the empire. In 1516, he met Erasmus in Basel and under his influence began a study of the Greek writings of the Church fathers and of the New Testament. Zwingli was also influenced by reports of Luther's defiance of the pope, for his own antipapal views were already developing. Perhaps most decisively for his early development, in 1519 Zwingli was stricken by plague. In his life-and-death struggle he came to a profoundly personal realization of the power of God's mercy.

Those experiences became the basis for the reform theology Zwingli preached in Zurich. He believed that the Church had to recover its earlier purity and to reject the innovations in practices brought in by successive popes and general councils. He stressed the equality of believers, justification by faith alone, and the sufficiency of the gospel as authority for church practice. He attacked indulgences, penance, clerical celibacy, prayers to the Virgin, statues and images in churches, and a long list of other abuses. He also stressed that the mass was to be viewed as a commemorative event rather than one that involved the real presence of Christ. He preferred to call the service the Lord's Supper. His arguments were so effective that the town council adopted them as the basis for a reform of religion.

The principles Zwingli preached quickly spread to neighboring Swiss states. He participated in formal religious disputations in both Bern and Basel. In both places, his plea for a simple, unadorned religious practice met widespread approval.

Practical as well as theological, Zwingli's reforms were carried out by the civil government with which he allied himself. That was not the same as the protection that princes had given to Lutherans. Rather, in the places that came under Zwingli's influence there was an important integration of church and state. Zwingli organized a formal military alliance of the Protestant Swiss towns. For him, the Bible carried a social message, and it is fitting that he died on the battlefield defending the state. He stressed the divine origins of civil government and the importance of the magistrate as an agent of Christian reform: "A church without the magistrate is mutilated and incomplete." That theocratic idea—that the leaders of the state and the leaders of the church were linked together—became the basis for further social and political reform.

THE PROTESTANT REFORMATION

By the middle of the 1530s, Protestant reform had entered a new stage. Luther did not intend to form a new religion; his struggle had been with Rome. Before he could build, he had to tear down—his religion was one of protest. Most of his energy was expended in attack and counterattack. The second generation of reformers faced a different task. The new reformers were the church builders who had to systematize doctrine for a generation that had already accepted religious reform. Their challenge was to draw out the logic of reformed ideas and to create enduring structures for reformed churches. The problems they faced were as much institutional as doctrinal. How was the new church to be governed in the absence of the traditional hierarchy? How could discipline be enforced when members of the reformed community went astray? What was the proper relationship between the community of believers and civil authority? Whatever the failings of the Roman Catholic Church, it had ready answers to those critical questions. The first generation of reformers had thrown out the stagnant bathwater of ecclesiastical abuses; it was left to the second generation to discover if they had thrown out the baby and the bathtub as well.

Geneva and Calvin

The Reformation came late to Geneva. In the sixteenth century, Geneva was under the dual government of the Duchy of Savoy, which owned most of the surrounding rural areas, and the Catholic bishop of the town, who was frequently a Savoy client. The Genevans also had their own town council, which traditionally struggled for power against the bishop. By the 1530s the council had gained the upper hand. The council confiscated Church lands and institutions, secularized the Church's legal powers, and forced the bishop and most of his administrators to flee the city. War with Savoy inevitably followed, and Geneva would certainly have been crushed into submission had it not been for its alliance with neighboring Bern, a potent military power among the Swiss towns.

Geneva was saved and was free to follow its own course in religious matters. Under Zwingli's influence, Bern had become

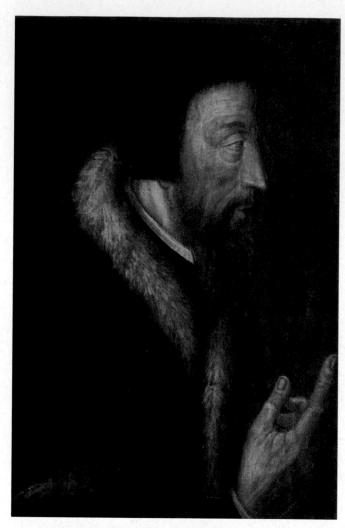

■ John Calvin preached a disciplined form of religion that appealed to a generation that was already influenced by Luther.

for heresy. The events left an indelible impression upon him. In 1535, he left France for Basel, where he wrote and published the first edition of his *Institutes of the Christian Religion* (1536), a defense of French Protestants against persecution. Directed to Francis I, it set out "the whole sum of godliness and whatever it is necessary to know of the doctrine of salvation." Calvin returned briefly to France to wind up his personal affairs and then decided to settle in Strasbourg, where he could retire from public affairs and live out his days as a scholar.

To Calvin, providence guided all human action. He could have no better evidence for that belief than what happened next. War between France and the Holy Roman Empire clogged the major highways to Strasbourg. Soldiers constantly menaced travelers, and Protestants could expect the worst from both sides. Thus Calvin and his companions detoured around the armies and passed through Geneva. How Calvin's presence there came to be known remains a mystery, but when Guillaume Farel (1489–1565), one of Geneva's leading Protestant reformers, heard of it, he quickly made his way to the inn where Calvin was staying. Farel implored Calvin to remain in Geneva and lead its reformation. Calvin was not interested. Farel tried every means of persuasion he knew until, in exasperation, Farel declared that God would curse Calvin's retirement if, Calvin wrote, "I should withdraw and refuse to help when the necessity was so urgent. By this imprecation I was so terror-struck that I gave up the journey that I had undertaken." For a quarter of a century, Calvin labored to bring order to the Genevan church.

Calvin's greatest contributions to religious reform came in church structure and discipline. He had studied the writings of the first generation of reformers and accepted without question justification by faith alone and the biblical foundation of religious authority. Like Luther and Zwingli, he believed that salvation came from God's grace. But more strongly than his predecessors he believed that the gift of faith was granted only to some and that each individual's salvation or damnation was predestined before birth. "We call predestination God's eternal decree. For all are not created in equal condition; rather, eternal life is foreordained for some, eternal damnation for others." The doctrine of **predestination** was a traditional one, but Calvin emphasized it differently and brought it to the center of the problem of faith. "Many are called but few are chosen," Calvin quoted from the Bible. Those who were predestined to salvation, "the elect," were obliged to govern; those who were predestined to damnation were obliged to be governed. Thus, for the church that Calvin erected, discipline was the central concern.

Calvin on Predestination

Calvin structured the institution of the Genevan church in four parts. First were the pastors who preached the Word to their congregations. There were fewer than 10 pastors in Geneva in the early 1540s and fewer than 20 by the time of Calvin's death—a far cry from the 500 priests who had administered the sacraments there under Catholicism. While the pastors preached, the doctors, the second element in Calvin's church, studied and wrote. The doctors were scholars who

Protestant, and it might have been expected that Geneva would adopt that model even though French rather than German was the predominant language of the city. Some Protestant preachers arrived in Geneva to propagate reformed religion, and after a public disputation the town council abolished the mass. In 1536, the adult male citizens of the city voted to become Protestant. But as yet there was no reformer in Geneva to establish a Protestant program and no clear definition of what that program might be.

Martin Luther had started out to become a lawyer and ended up a priest. John Calvin started out to become a priest and ended up a lawyer. The difference tells much about each man. Calvin (1509–1564) was born in France, the son of a bishop's secretary. His education was based on humanist principles, and he learned Greek and Hebrew, studied theology, and received a legal degree from the University of Orléans. Around the age of 20 he converted to Lutheranism. He described the experience as "unexpected," but it had predictable results. Francis I had determined to root Protestants out of France, and Calvin fled Paris. Persecution of Protestants continued in France, and one of Calvin's close friends was burned

THE ETERNAL DECREE

John Calvin was born in France but led the Reformation in the Swiss town of Geneva. He was one of the leaders of the second generation of reformers, whose task was to refine the structure of church doctrine. Calvinism was propounded in the Institutes of the Christian Religion *(1534), from which this section on the doctrine of predestination is taken.*

Focus Questions

According to Calvin, why is everyone contaminated by sin? What power do humans have over their spiritual destiny?

We must be content with this—that such gifts as it pleased the Lord to have bestowed upon the nature of man he vested in Adam; and therefore when Adam lost them after he had received them, he lost them not only from himself but also from us all. . . . Therefore from a rotten root rose up rotten branches, which sent their rottenness into the twigs that sprang out of them; for so were the children corrupted in their father that they in turn infected their children. . . .

And the apostle Paul himself expressly witnesseth that therefore death came upon all men, because all men have sinned and are wrapped in original sin and defiled with the spots thereof. And therefore the very infants themselves, since they bring with them their own damnation from their mothers' womb, are bound not by another's but by their own fault. For although they have not as yet brought forth the fruits of their own iniquity, yet they have the seeds thereof enclosed within them; yea, their whole nature is a certain seed of sin, therefore it cannot but be hateful and abominable to God. . . .

Predestination we call the eternal decree of God, whereby he has determined with himself what he wills to become of every man. For all are not created to like estate; but to some eternal life and to some eternal damnation is foreordained. Therefore as every man is created to the one or the other end, so we say that he is predestinate either to life or to death.

From John Calvin, *Institutes of the Christian Religion.*

---

mastered the difficult portions of the Bible and who increased the stock of learned pastors by their teaching. In the beginning, Calvin was the only Genevan doctor, but after he helped to establish the University of Geneva in 1559, there was a ready supply of learned theologians.

Pastors and doctors made up the top tier of the official church; deacons and elders the lower. Deacons, the third element in Calvin's four-part structure, were laymen chosen by the congregation to oversee the institutions of social welfare run by the church. Those institutions included the hospitals and schools that cared for the sick and the poor and instructed the young. The last element was the elders of the church, who were its governors in all moral matters. They were the most controversial part of Calvin's establishment and the most fundamental. They had the power to discipline. Chosen from among the elite of the city, the 12 elders enforced the strict Calvinist moral code that extended into all aspects of private life. The elders and the pastors met each week in a body known as the consistory to examine violations of God's laws; for them was reserved the ultimate sanction of excommunication. Offenses ranged from trivial superstitions—a woman wrapping a walnut containing a spider around the neck of her sick husband—to cases of blasphemy. Sexual offenses were the most common. Adultery and fornication were vigorously suppressed, and prostitutes, who had nearly become a recognized guild in the early sixteenth century, were expelled from Geneva.

The structure that Calvin gave to the Genevan church soon became the basis for reforms throughout the Continent. The Calvinist church was self-governing, independent of the state, and therefore capable of surviving and even flourishing in a hostile environment. Expanded in several subsequent editions, *The Institutes of the Christian Religion* became the most influential work of Protestant theology. It had begun as an effort to extend Protestantism to France, and Calvin never abandoned hope that his homeland would be converted. Waves of Calvinist-educated pastors returned to France in the mid-sixteenth century and established churches along Calvinist lines. Calvinism spread north to Scotland and the Low Countries, where it became the basis for Dutch Protestantism, and east to Poland, where it flourished in Lithuania and Hungary. It reached places untouched by Luther and revitalized reform where Lutheranism had been suppressed. Perhaps its greatest impact was in Britain, where the Reformation took place not once but twice.

The English Reformation

The king of England wanted a divorce. Henry VIII had been married to Catherine of Aragon (1485–1536) as long as he had been king, and she had borne him no male heir to carry on his line. Catherine of Aragon had done her duty: in ten years she had given birth to six children and endured several miscarriages. Yet only one daughter, Mary, survived. Nothing

■ This painting depicts a Calvinist service in Lyon, France, in 1564. The men and women are segregated, and the worshipers are seated according to rank. An hourglass times the preacher's sermon.

so important as the lack of a male heir could happen by accident, and Henry came to believe that it was God's punishment for his marriage. Catherine had been married first to Henry's older brother, who had died as a teenager, and there was at least one scriptural prohibition against marrying a brother's wife. A papal dispensation had been provided for the marriage, and now Henry wanted a papal dispensation for an annulment. For three years his case ground its way through the papal courts. Catherine of Aragon was the aunt of the Emperor Charles V, and the emperor had taken her side in the controversy. With imperial power in Italy at its height, the pope was content to hear all of the complex legal and biblical precedents argued at leisure.

By 1533, Henry could wait no longer. He had already impregnated Anne Boleyn (ca. 1507–1536), one of the ladies-in-waiting at his court. If the child—which Henry was certain would be a boy—was to be legitimate, a marriage would have to take place at once. Legislation was prepared in Parliament to prevent papal interference in the decisions of England's courts, and Thomas Cranmer (1489–1556), archbishop of Canterbury, England's highest ecclesiastical officer, agreed to annul Henry's first marriage and celebrate his second. That was the first step in a complete break with Rome. Under the guidance of Thomas Cromwell (ca. 1485–1540), the English Parliament passed statute after statute that made Henry supreme head of the church in England and owner of its vast

wealth. Monasteries were dissolved and a Lutheran service was introduced. England's first reformation came as a result of the "King's Great Matter." On 7 September 1533, Anne Boleyn gave birth not to the expected son, but to a daughter, the future Queen Elizabeth I.

The Church of England.   Henry's reformation was an act of state, but the English Reformation was not. There was an English tradition of dissent from the Roman Church that stretched back to the fourteenth century and that had survived even the most determined efforts to suppress it. Anticlericalism was especially virulent in the towns, where citizens refused to pay fees to priests for performing services such as burial. And humanist ideas flourished in England, where Thomas More, John Colet, and a host of others supported both the new learning and its efforts to reform spiritual life. The English were as susceptible as other Europeans to Luther's ideas, which crossed the Channel with German merchants and English travelers. Luther's attack on ritual and the mass and his emphasis on Scripture and faith found many recruits in London and the northern port towns.

Protestantism had grown slowly in England because it had been vigorously repressed. Like Francis I and Charles V, Henry VIII had viewed actual attacks on the established church as potential attacks on the established state. The consolidation of the Tudor monarchy was too recent for him not to be concerned with its stability. Henry had earned the title "Defender of the Faith" from the pope in 1521 for authoring an attack on Luther. Bonfires of Lutheran books had lighted the English skies. Small groups of Protestants at Cambridge and Oxford universities had been sniffed out and hunted down by Henry's agents. Some had made public recantations; some had fled to the Continent; one—Thomas Bilney—went to the stake. The first published English translation of the New Testament, made by William Tyndale in 1525, had to be smuggled into England. As sensitivity to the abuses of the Church grew and Lutheran ideas spread, official censorship and persecution sharpened.

Henry's divorce unleashed a groundswell of support for religious change. The king's own religious beliefs remained a secret, but Anne Boleyn and Thomas Cromwell sponsored Lutheran reforms and Thomas Cranmer put them into practice. Religion was legislated through Parliament, and the valuable estates of the Church were sold to the gentry. The practices found favor with both the legal profession and the landed elites and made Protestantism more palatable among those conservative groups. It was in the reign of Edward VI (1547–1553), Henry's son by his third wife, that the central doctrinal and devotional changes were made. Although they were Protestant in tenor, there remained compromises and deliberate ambiguities. The chantries were abolished, and with them masses for the dead. Church service was now conducted in English, and the first two English prayer books were created. The mass was reinterpreted along Zwinglian lines and became the Lord's Supper, the altar became the communion table, and the priest became the minister. Preaching became the center of the church service, and concern over the education of learned ministers resulted in commissions to examine and reform the clergy.

Beginning in the 1530s, state repression turned against Catholics. Those who would not swear the new oaths of allegiance or recognize the legality of Henry VIII's marriage suffered for their beliefs as the early Protestants had suffered for theirs. Thomas More and more than 40 others paid with their lives for their opposition. Others took up arms against the government, marrying economic and political grievances to religious ones. An uprising in the north in 1536, known as the Pilgrimage of Grace, posed the most serious threat to the English Crown since the Wars of the Roses. Gentry and common people opposed the dissolution of the monasteries and feared for provision for their spiritual needs. Henry's ability to suppress the Pilgrimage of Grace owed more to his political power than to the conversion of his governing classes to Protestantism. Edward VI's government faced a similar uprising in 1549 when it attempted to introduce a new and more Protestant prayer book. Catholicism continued to flourish in England, surviving underground during the reigns of Henry and Edward and reemerging under Mary I (1553–1558).

The Successors of Henry VIII. Mary Tudor was her mother's child. The first woman to rule England, she held to the Catholic beliefs in which Catherine of Aragon had raised her, and she vowed to bring the nation back to her mother's church. When Edward VI died, the English ruling elite opted for political legitimacy rather than religious ideology in supporting Mary against a Protestant pretender to the throne. The new queen was as good as her word. She reestablished papal sovereignty, abolished Protestant worship, and introduced a crash program of education in the universities to train a new generation of priests. The one thing that Mary could not achieve was restoration of monastic properties and Church lands: they had been scattered irretrievably and any attempt at confiscation from the landed elite would surely have been met with insurrection. Mary had to be content with reestablishing orthodoxy. She fought fire with fire. Catholic retribution for the blood of their martyrs was not long in coming. Cranmer and three other bishops were burned for heresy, and more than 270 others, mostly commoners, were consigned to the flames.

Nearly 800 Protestants fled the country rather than suffer a similar fate. The Marian exiles, as they came to be called, settled in a number of reformed communities, Zurich, Frankfurt, and Geneva among them. There they imbibed the second generation of Protestant ideas, especially Calvinism, and from there they began a propaganda campaign to keep reformed religion alive in England. It was the Marian exiles who were chiefly responsible for the second English reformation, which began in 1558 when Mary died and her half-sister, Elizabeth I (1558–1603), came to the throne.

Under Elizabeth, England returned to Protestantism. The rapid reversals of established religion were more than disconcerting to laity and clergy alike. Imagine the experience of ordinary churchgoers. For all their lives they had prayed to the Virgin Mary for aid and comfort. One day all images of the Virgin disappeared from the church. The Latin mass was replaced by a whole new English service. Then the Latin mass returned and back came the images of the Virgin. Five years later the Virgin was gone again and the English service was restored. Imagine the plight of a clergyman who questioned the vow of chastity in the 1540s. Prohibited from marrying under Henry VIII, he was encouraged to marry under Edward VI. When Mary came to the throne, he had to put his wife aside and deny the legitimacy of his children. At Elizabeth's accession he was married again—if he could find his wife and if she had not taken another husband. The Elizabethan reforms put an end to those uncertainties.

But what was reestablished was not what had come before. Even the most advanced reforms during Edward's reign now seemed too moderate for the returning exiles. Against Elizabeth's wishes, the English church adopted the Calvinist doctrine of predestination and the simplification (but not wholesale reorganization) of the structure of the church. But it did not become a model of thoroughgoing reformation. The Thirty-nine Articles (1563) continued the English tradition of compromising points of disputed doctrine and of maintaining traditional practices wherever possible. The Calvinism that the exiles learned abroad was more demanding than the Calvinism that the queen practiced at home.

The Reformation of the Radicals

Schism breeds schism. That was the stick with which Catholic Church and civil authorities beat Luther from the beginning. By attacking the authority of the established church and flouting the authority of the established state, he was fomenting social upheaval. It was a charge to which he was particularly sensitive. He insisted that his own ideas buttressed rather than subverted authority, especially civil authority, under whose protection he had placed the Church. As early as 1525, peasants in Swabia appealed to Luther for support in their social rebellion. They based some of their most controversial demands, such as the abolition of tithes and labor service, on biblical authority. Luther offered them no comfort. "Let every person be subject to the governing authorities with fear and reverence," he quoted from the Bible while instructing rebels to lay down their arms and await their just rewards in heaven.

But Luther's ideas had a life of their own. He clashed with Erasmus over free will and with Zwingli over the mass. Toward the end of his life he felt he was holding back the floodgates against the second generation of Protestant thinkers. Time and again serious reformers wanted to take one or another of his doctrines further than he was willing to go himself. The water was seeping in everywhere.

The most dangerous threat to the establishment of an orthodox Protestantism came from groups who were described, not very precisely, as **Anabaptists.** *Anabaptist* was a term of abuse. Although it identified people who practiced adult baptism—literally, "baptism again"—the label was mainly used to tar religious opponents with the brush of extremism. For more than a hundred years it defined the outcast from the Protestant fold. New ideas were branded Anabaptist to discredit them; religious enthusiasts were labeled Anabaptists to expel them. Catholics and Protestants both used the term to describe what they were not, and thereby defined what they were.

Anabaptists appeared in a number of German and Swiss towns in the 1520s. Taking seriously the doctrine of justification by faith, Anabaptists argued that only believers could be members of the true church of God. Those who were not of God could not be members of his church. While Catholics, Lutherans, and Calvinists incorporated all members of society into the church, Anabaptists excluded all but true believers. As baptism was the sacrament through which entry into the church took place, Anabaptists reasoned that it was a sacrament for adults rather than infants. Although the practice was as much symbolic as substantive, it was a practice that horrified others. Infant baptism was a core doctrine for both Catholics and Protestants. It was one of only two sacraments that remained in reformed religion. It symbolized the acceptance of Christ, and without it eternal salvation was impossible. Luther, Zwingli, and Calvin agreed that infant baptism was biblical in origin and all wrote vigorously in its defense. It was a doctrine with practical import. Unbaptized infants who died could not be accepted in heaven, and infant mortality was appallingly common.

Thus the doctrine of Anabaptism posed a psychological as well as a doctrinal threat to the reformers. But the practice of adult baptism paled in significance to many of the other conclusions that religious radicals derived from the principle of *sola scriptura*—by the Word alone. Some groups argued the case that since true Christians were only those who had faith, all others must be cast out of the church. Those true Christians formed small separate sects. Many believed that their lives were guided by the Holy Spirit, who directed them from within. Both men and women could give testimony of revelations that appeared to them or of mystical experiences. Some went further and denied the power of civil authority over true believers. They would have nothing to do with the state, refusing to pay taxes, perform military obligations, or

■ This engraving from the *Chronicle of the Peasants' War* by Abbot Murer presents a Catholic interpretation of the peasants' actions as they pillaged the Monastery of Weissenau.

■ Anabaptist leaders persecuted at Münster endured the torture of being confined in cages hung from the church belfry.

give oaths: "The Sword must not be used by Christians even in self-defense. Neither should Christians go to law or undertake magisterial duties." Some argued for the community of goods among believers and rejected private property. Others literally followed passages in the Old Testament that suggested polygamy and promiscuity.

Wherever they settled, the small bands of believers were persecuted to the brutal extent of the laws of heresy. Catholics burned them, Protestants drowned them, and they were stoned and clubbed out of their communities. Although Anabaptists were never a large group within the context of the Protestant churches, they represented an alternative to mainstream views—whether Lutheran or Calvinist—that was both attractive and persistent. There was enough substance in their ideas and enough sincerity in their patient sufferings that they continued to recruit followers as they were driven from town to town, from Germany into the Swiss cities, from Switzerland into Bohemia and Hungary.

There, on the eastern edges of the Holy Roman Empire, the largest groups of Anabaptists finally settled. Although all practiced adult baptism, only some held goods in common or remained pacifist. Charismatic leaders such as Balthasar Hubmaier (1485–1528) and Jacob Hutter (d. 1536) spread Anabaptism to Moravia in southern Bohemia, where they converted a number of the nobility to their views. They procured land for their communities, which came to be known as the Moravian Brethren. The Moravian Anabaptists ultimately split on the question of pacifism when the advancing Turkish armies posed the problem starkly. Anabaptists remained a target of official persecution, and Hubmaier, Hutter, and a number of

other leaders met violent deaths. But the Moravian communities were able to survive and to spread their movement throughout Hungary and Poland. Independent groups existed in England and throughout northwest Europe, where Menno Simons (1496–1561), a Dutch Anabaptist, spent his life organizing bands of followers who came to be known as Mennonites.

THE CATHOLIC REFORMATION

Like a rolling wave, Protestant reform slapped up across the face of Europe, but the rock of the Roman Catholic Church endured. Although pieces of the universal church crumbled away in northern Germany, Switzerland, Bohemia, Scandinavia, England, and Scotland, the dense mass remained in southern Germany, Italy, Poland-Lithuania, Spain, France, and Ireland. Catholics felt the same impulses toward a more fulfilling religious life as did Protestants and complained of the same abuses of clerical, state, and papal powers. But the Catholic response was to reform the Church from within. A new personal piety was stressed, which led to the founding of additional spiritual orders. The ecclesiastical hierarchy became more concerned with pastoral care and initiated reforms of the clergy at the parish level. The challenge of converting other races, Asians and Native Americans especially, led to the formation of missionary orders and to a new emphasis on preaching and education. Protestantism itself revitalized Catholicism. Pope and emperor met the challenge of religious reform with all of the resources at their disposal. If anything, Roman Catholicism was stronger at the end of the era of religious reformation than it had been at the beginning.

The Spiritual Revival

The quest for individual spiritual fulfillment dominated later medieval Roman Catholicism. Erasmus, Luther, and Zwingli were all influenced by a Catholic spiritual movement known as the **New Piety.** It was propagated in Germany by the Brethren of the Common Life, a lay organization that stressed the importance of personal meditation upon the life of Jesus. *The Imitation of Christ* (1427), the central text of the New Piety, commonly attributed to Thomas à Kempis (1379–1471), was among the most influential works of the later Middle Ages, with 70 editions printed before 1500. The Brethren taught that a Christian life should be lived according to Jesus' dictates as expressed in the Sermon on the Mount. They instructed their pupils to lead a simple ascetic life with personal devotion at its core. Those were the lessons that the young Erasmus found so liberating and the young Luther so stifling.

The New Piety, with its emphasis on a simple personal form of religious practice, was a central influence upon Christian humanism. It is important to realize that humanism developed within the context of Catholic education and that many churchmen embraced the new learning and supported educational reform or patronized works of humanist scholarship. The Polyglot Bible, the first new translation project of the sixteenth century, was organized by Cardinal Jiménez de Cisneros (1436–1517), Archbishop of Toledo and Primate of Spain. The greatest educational reformer in England, John Colet (1467–1519), was dean of Saint Paul's, London's cathedral church. Without any of his famed irony, Erasmus dedicated his Greek Bible to the pope. Although they set out to reform education and to provide better texts through which Christian learning could be accomplished, the leading Christian humanists remained within the Catholic Church even after many of their criticisms formed the basis of Protestant reforms.

The combination of piety and humanism imbued the ecclesiastical reforms initiated by Church leaders. Archbishop Jiménez de Cisneros, who also served as Inquisitor-General of the Spanish Inquisition, undertook a wide-ranging reorganization of Spanish religious life in the late fifteenth century. Although not every project was successful, Jiménez de Cisneros's program took much of the sting out of Protestant attacks on clerical abuse, and there was never a serious Protestant movement in Spain.

The most influential reforming bishop was Gian Matteo Giberti (1495–1543) of Verona. Like Jiménez de Cisneros, Giberti believed that a bishop must be a pastor rather than an administrator. After a period of service in Rome, Giberti returned to live in his diocese and made regular visits to all of its parishes. Using his own frugal life as an example, Giberti rigorously enforced vows, residency, and the pastoral duties of the clergy. "The priests in this diocese are marked men; the unworthy are removed from their offices; the jails are full of their concubines; sermons for the people are preached incessantly and study is encouraged," came the report after one of

■ Tintoretto, *Crucifixion* (1565). Tintoretto's composition, dominated by the figure of the crucified Christ at the center, looking down as if from heaven, suggests the spiritual renewal and peak of religious feeling that marked the Catholic Reformation in Europe.

HEAVENLY VISION

Teresa of Ávila was a Carmelite nun whose life became a model of spirituality for Spanish Catholics in the seventeenth century. She founded a number of monasteries and convents and wrote popular devotional literature. Her autobiography was published after her death.

Focus Questions

How does Teresa explain God's sympathy for humans? How does she see God's manner as different from that of earthly rulers?

My love of, and trust in, our Lord, after I had seen Him in a vision, began to grow, for my converse with Him was so continual. I saw that, though He was God, He was man also; that He is not surprised at the frailties of men; that He understands our miserable nature, liable to fall continually, because of the first sin, for the reparation of which He had come. I could speak to Him as a friend, though He is my Lord, because I do not consider Him as one of our earthly lords, who affect a power they do not possess, who give audience at fixed hours, and to whom only certain persons may speak. If a poor man have any business with these, it will cost him many goings and comings, and currying favour with others, together with much pain and labour before he can speak to them. Ah, if such a one has business

with a king! Poor people, not of gentle blood, cannot approach him, for they must apply to those who are his friends; and certainly these are not persons who tread the world under their feet; for they who do this speak the truth, fear nothing, and ought to fear nothing; they are not courtiers, because it is not the custom of a court, where they must be silent about those things they dislike, must not even dare to think about them, lest they should fall into disgrace.

O my Lord! O my King! who can describe Thy Majesty? It is impossible not to see that Thou art Thyself the great Ruler of all, that the beholding of Thy Majesty fills men with awe. But I am filled with greater awe, O my Lord, when I consider Thy humility and the love Thou hast for such as I am. We can converse and speak with Thee about everything whenever we will; and when we lose our first fear and awe at the vision of Thy Majesty, we have a greater dread of offending Thee—not arising out of the fear of punishment, O my Lord, for that is as nothing in comparison with the loss of Thee!

From The Life of St. Teresa of Ávila (1611).

his tours. He founded almshouses to aid the poor and orphanages to house the homeless. In Verona, Giberti established a printing press, which turned out editions of the central works of Roman Catholicism, especially the writings of Augustine.

The most important indication of the reforming spirit within the Roman Church was the foundation of new religious orders in the early sixteenth century. Devotion to a spiritual life of sacrifice was the chief characteristic of the lay and clerical orders that had flourished throughout the Middle Ages. In one French diocese, the number of clergy quadrupled in the last half of the fifteenth century, and while entrants to the traditional orders of Franciscans and Dominicans did not rise as quickly, the growth of lay communities such as the Brethren of the Common Life attested to the continuing appeal of Catholic devotionalism.

Devotionalism was particularly strong in Italy, where new orders received papal charters. The Capuchins were founded by the Italian peasant Matteo de Bascio (ca. 1495–1552). He sought to follow the strictest rule of the life of Saint Francis of Assisi, a path that even the so-called Observant Franciscans had found too arduous. Bascio won admiration for his charitable works among the poor and the victims of the plague in

the late 1520s and ultimately secured approval for the establishment of a small community devoted to penance and good works.

The spiritual revival spread all over Catholic Europe and was not limited to male orders. In Spain, Saint Teresa of Ávila (1515–1582) led the reform of the Carmelites. From an early age she had had mystical visions and had entered a convent near her home. But her real spiritual awakening came when she was 40. She believed that women had to withdraw totally from the world around them in order to achieve true devotion. Against the wishes of the male superiors of her order, she founded a convent to put her beliefs into practice and began writing devotional tracts such as *The Way of Perfection* (1583). Teresa was ultimately granted the right to establish convents throughout Castile, and she supervised the organization of 16 religious houses for women. In 1535, Angela Merici (ca. 1474–1540) established another female order. The Ursulines were one of the most original of the new foundations, composed of young unmarried girls who remained with their families but lived chaste lives devoted to the instruction of other women. The group met monthly and submitted to the discipline of a superior, but otherwise they rejected both the cloistered monastic life and vows. The Ursuline movement,

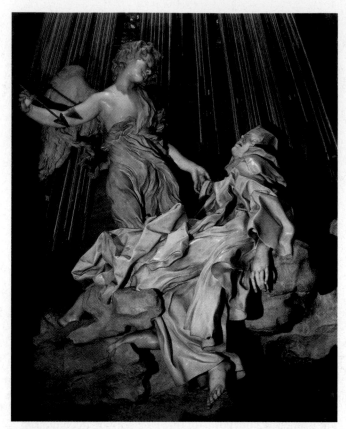

■ Gian Lorenzo Bernini, *The Ecstasy of St. Teresa.* In this work, depicting the ecstatic vision of St. Teresa of Ávila, the sixteenth-century Spanish Carmelite reformer, the saint floats toward heaven on seemingly weightless marble as an angel is about to pierce her breast with a burning arrow. The artist's creation depicts a mystic vision St. Teresa experienced and described in her writings.

begun in northern Italy, spread into France and helped provide women with education and with moral role models.

Loyola's Pilgrimage

At first sight, Saint Ignatius Loyola (1491–1556) appears an unlikely candidate to lead one of the most vital movements for religious reform in the sixteenth century. The thirteenth child of a Spanish noble family, Loyola trained for a military life in the service of Castile. He began his career as an administrative official and then became a soldier. In 1521, he was one of the garrison defenders when the French besieged Pamplona. A cannonball shattered his leg, and he was carried home for a long enforced convalescence. There he slowly and carefully read the only books in the castle, a life of Jesus and a history of the saints. His reading inspired him. Before he had sought glory and renown in battle. But when he compared the truly heroic deeds of the saints to his own vainglorious exploits, he decided to give his life over to spirituality.

Loyola was not a man to do things by halves. He resolved to model his life on the sufferings of the saints about whom he had read. He renounced his worldly goods and endured a

year-long regimen of physical abstinence and spiritual nourishment in the town of Manresa. He deprived himself of food and sleep for long periods and underwent a regimen of seven hours of daily prayer, supplemented by nearly continuous religious contemplation. "But when he went to bed, great enlightenment, great spiritual consolations often came to him, so that he lost much of the time he had intended for sleeping." During that period of intense concentration he first began to have visions, which later culminated in a mystical experience in which Jesus called him directly to his service.

Like Luther, Loyola was tormented by his inability to achieve grace through penance, but unlike Luther he redoubled his efforts. At Manresa, Loyola encountered *The Imitation of Christ,* which profoundly influenced his conversion. He recorded the techniques he used during this vigil in *The Spiritual Exercises,* which became a handbook for Catholic devotion. In 1523, crippled and barefoot, he made a pilgrimage to Jerusalem, where he intended to stay and battle the infidel. But he was dissuaded from that course and returned to Spain intent upon becoming a priest.

By this time, Loyola had adopted a distinctive garb that attracted both followers and suspicion. Twice the Spanish ecclesiastical authorities summoned him to be examined for heresy. In 1528, he decided to complete his studies in France. Education in France brought with it a broadening of horizons that was so important in the movement that Loyola was to found. He entered the same college that Calvin had just left, and it is more than likely that he came into contact with the Protestant and humanist ideas that were then in vogue. Given his own devotional experiences, Protestantism held little attraction. While in France, Loyola and a small group of his friends decided to form a brotherhood after they became priests. They devoted themselves to the cure of souls and took personal vows of poverty, chastity, and obedience to the pope. On a pilgrimage to Rome, Loyola and his followers again attracted the attention of ecclesiastical authorities. Loyola explained his mission to them and in 1540 won the approval of Pope Paul III to establish a new holy order, the Society of Jesus.

DOCUMENT

Ignatius Loyola, Rules for Thinking with the Church

Loyola's Society was founded at a time when the spiritual needs of the Church were being extended beyond the confines of Europe. Loyola volunteered his followers, who came to be known as Jesuits, to serve in the remotest parts of the world, and that offer was soon accepted. One disciple, Francis Xavier (1506–1552), was sent to Portugal, where he embarked on an expedition to the East. For ten years, Xavier made converts to Catholicism in the Portuguese port cities in the East, and then in India and Japan. Other Jesuits became missionaries to the New World, where they offered Christian consolation to the Native American communities. By 1556, the Society of Jesus had grown from 10 to 1000, and Loyola had become a full-time administrator in Rome.

Loyola never abandoned the military images that had dominated his youth. He thought of the world as an all-consuming struggle between the forces of God and Satan: "It is became one of the Jesuits' most important functions. Loyola lived to see the establishment of nearly a hundred colleges and seminaries and the spread of his order throughout the world. He died while at prayer.

The Counter-Reformation

The Jesuits were both the culmination of one wave of Catholic reform and the advance guard of another. They combined the piety and devotion that stretched from medieval mysticism through humanism, diocesan reforms, and the foundations of new spiritual orders. But they also represented an aggressive Catholic response that was determined to meet Protestantism head on and repel it—the **Counter-Reformation.** This was the Church Militant. Old instruments like the Inquisition were revived, and new weapons such as the Index of prohibited books were forged. But the problems of fighting Protestantism were not only those of combating Protestant ideas. Like oil and water, politics and religion failed to combine. The emperor and the hierarchy of the German church, where Protestantism was strong, demanded thoroughgoing reform of the Catholic Church; the pope and the hierarchy of the Italian church, where Protestantism was weak, resisted the call. As head of the Catholic Church, the pope was distressed by the spread of heresy in the lands of the empire. As head of a large Italian city-state, the pope was consoled by the weakening of the power of his Spanish rival. Brothers in Christ, pope and emperor were mortal enemies in everything else. Throughout the Catholic states of Germany came the urgent cry for a reforming council of the Church. But the voices were muffled as they crossed the Alps and made their way down the Italian peninsula.

■ Rubens's (1577–1640) *The Miracles of Saint Ignatius Loyola.* Founder of the Society of Jesus, Loyola prepared his Jesuit recruits for an active, rather than a contemplative, life.

my will to conquer the whole world and all of my enemies." He enlisted his followers in military terms. The Jesuits were "soldiers of God" who served "beneath the banner of the Cross." Loyola's most fundamental innovation in those years was the founding of schools to train recruits for his order. Jesuit training was rigorous. The period of the novitiate was extended and a second period of secular education was added. Since they were being prepared for an active rather than a contemplative life, Jesuits were not cloistered during their training. At first Loyola wanted to train only those who wanted to be missionaries. When that proved impractical, Jesuit schools were opened to the laity and lay education

At the instigation of the emperor, the first serious preparations for a general council of the Church were made in the 1530s. The papacy warded it off. The complexities of international diplomacy were one factor—the French king was even less anxious to bring peace to the empire than was the pope—and the complexities of papal politics were another. The powers of a general council in relation to the powers of the papacy had never been clarified. Councils were usually the product of crises, and crises were never the best times to settle constitutional matters. Hard cases make bad law. After the advent and

CHRONOLOGY
THE REFORMATION AND THE COUNTER-REFORMATION

1517	Luther writes his Ninety-five Theses
1521	Luther is excommunicated and declared an enemy of the empire; Henry VIII receives title Defender of the Faith
1523	Zwingli expounds his faith in formal disputation
1533	Henry VIII divorces Catherine of Aragon, marries Anne Boleyn, and breaks with the church of Rome
1536	Calvin publishes *Institutes of the Christian Religion*
1540	Loyola receives papal approval for Society of Jesus
1545–1563	Council of Trent
1553	Mary I restores Catholicism in England
1563	Elizabeth I enacts the Thirty-nine Articles, which restores Protestantism to England

Those factors ensured that when a general council of the Church did finally meet, its task would not be an easy one. The emperor wanted the council in Germany; the pope wanted it in Italy. The northern churches, French and German alike, wanted reforms of the papacy; the papacy wanted a restatement of orthodox doctrine. The Spanish church wanted reform along the principles set down by Jiménez de Cisneros—for example, that bishops must be made resident in their dioceses. The papacy needed bishops to serve as administrators in Rome. Many princes whose states were divided among Catholics and Protestants wanted compromises that might accommodate both. Ferdinand I, King of Bohemia, saw the council as an opportunity to bring the Hussites back into the fold. He wanted to allow the laity to take communion in both kinds and the clergy to marry. Charles V and the German bishops wanted the leading Protestant church authorities to offer their own compromises on doctrine that might form a basis for reuniting the empire. The papacy wanted traditional Church doctrine reasserted.

The general council of the Church that finally met in Trent from 1545 to 1563 thus had nearly unlimited potential for disaster. It began in compromise—Trent was an Italian town under the government of the emperor—but ended in total victory for the views of the papacy. For all of the papacy's seeming weaknesses—the defections of England and the rich north German territories cut into papal revenues and Italy was under Spanish occupation—an Italian pope always held the upper hand at the council. Fewer than a third of the delegates came from outside Italy. The French looked upon the council suspiciously and played only a minor role, and the emperor forbade his bishops to attend after the council moved to Bologna. While 270 bishops attended one or another of the council's sessions, 187 of them were Italians.

DOCUMENT

Council of Trent

spread of Protestantism, successive popes had little reason to believe that in that gravest crisis of all a council would be mindful of papal prerogatives. In fact, Catholic reformers were as bitter in their denunciations of papal abuses as were Protestants. The second attempt to arrange a general council of the Church occurred in the early 1540s. Again the papacy warded it off.

■ The Council of Trent met from 1545–1563 and corrected a number of abuses of the Church, including the sale of indulgences, and stressed the obligations of priests and bishops to preach to their congregations. No concessions, however, were made to Protestants. This painting is attributed to Titian.

Yet for all of the difficulties, the councillors at Trent made some real progress. They corrected a number of abuses, of which the sale of indulgences was the most substantive. They formulated rules for the better regulation of parish priests and stressed the obligation of priests and bishops to preach to their congregations. Following the work of Jiménez de Cisneros and Giberti, they emphasized the pastoral function of the clergy. On the heels of the success of the Jesuits, they ordered seminaries to be founded in all dioceses where there was not already a university so that priests could receive sufficient education to perform their duties. They prepared a new modern and uniform Catholic service and centralized and updated the Index of prohibited books to include Protestant writings from all over the Continent.

The Council of Trent made no concessions whatever to Protestants, moderate or radical. The councillors attempted to turn back every doctrinal innovation of the previous 40 years. Although Protestant theologians attended one of the council's sessions, their views were totally repudiated and efforts at compromise, which were supported by a number of Catholics on the council, were rejected. The councillors upheld justification by faith and works over justification by faith alone. They confirmed the truth of Scripture and the traditions of the Church against Scripture alone. They declared the Vulgate the only acceptable text of the Bible and encouraged vast bonfires of Greek and Hebrew Scriptures in an effort to undo the great scholarly achievements of the humanists. They reaffirmed the seven sacraments and the doctrine of the miracle

MAP DISCOVERY

Religious Divisions of Europe

- Catholic
- Lutheran
- Calvinist
- Anglican
- Islamic
- Anabaptist
- Eastern Orthodox
- Bohemian and Moravian Brethren (Hussite)

The Religious Divisions of Europe, ca. 1555

Which was the largest religious denomination by the middle of the sixteenth century? Which states were most at risk of internal religious warfare? Notice the difference in the ways in which Lutheranism and Calvinism spread. Where did Catholicism remain untouched by the new religions?

of the Eucharist. They upheld clerical celibacy. The redefinition of traditional Roman Catholicism drew the doctrinal lines clearly and ended decades of confusion. But it also meant that the differences between Catholics and Protestants could now be settled only by the sword.

The Empire Strikes Back

Warfare dominated the reform of religion almost from its beginning. The burnings, drownings, and executions by which both Catholics and Protestants attempted to maintain religious purity were but raindrops compared to the sea of blood that was shed in sieges and on battlefields beginning in the 1530s. Neither side was capable of waging an all-out war against the other, but they fought intermittently for 25 years. The Catholic divisions were clear. The Holy Roman Empire continued to be engaged in the west with its archenemy France, and in the south with the ever-expanding Ottoman Empire. Charles V needed not only peace within his own German realms, but also positive support for his offensive and defensive campaigns. He could never devote his full resources to suppressing Protestant dissent.

Yet there was never a united Protestant front to suppress. The north German towns and principalities that accepted Lutheranism in the 1520s had had a long history of warfare among themselves. Princes stored up grievances from past wars and contested inheritances; cities stored up jealousies from commercial rivalries and special privileges. Added to that was the division between Luther and Zwingli over doctrinal issues that effectively separated the German and Swiss components of the Reformation from each other. Each faction formed its own political league, and the division almost certainly cost Zwingli his life in 1531, when Zurich was left to stand by itself against imperial allies.

Although both the Protestant and the Catholic sides were internally weak, it was the greater responsibilities of Charles V that allowed for the uneasy periods of peace. Each pause gave the Protestant reformers new life. Lutheranism continued to spread in the northern part of the Holy Roman Empire, and Zwinglian reform in the south. Charles V asked the papacy to convoke a general council and the Protestants to stop evangelizing in new territories. But Protestant leaders were no more capable of halting the spread of the Reformation than were Catholics. Thus each violation of each

Religious Diversity in Western Europe

uneasy truce seemed to prove treachery. In 1546, just after Luther's death, both sides raised armies in preparation for renewed fighting. In the first stage of war, Charles V scored a decisive victory, capturing the two leading Protestant princes and conquering Saxony and Thuringia, the homeland of Lutheran reform.

Charles V's greatest victories were always preludes to his gravest defeats. The remaining Protestant princes were driven into the arms of the French, who placed dynastic interests above religious concerns. Again Europe was plunged into general conflict, with the French invading the German states from the west, the Turks from the south, and the Protestant princes from the north. Charles V, now an old and broken man, was forced to flee through the Alps in the dead of winter and was brought to the bargaining table soon after. Through the Peace of Augsburg in 1555, the emperor agreed to allow the princes of Germany to establish the religion of their people. Protestant princes would govern Protestant states, Catholic princes Catholic states. The Peace of Augsburg ended 40 years of religious struggle in Germany.

CONCLUSION

In 1547, the then-victorious Charles V stood at the grave of Martin Luther. Luther had been buried in the shadow of the church in which he had been baptized, and now other shadows darkened his plot. Imperial troops were masters of all Saxony and were preparing to turn back the religious clock in Luther's homeland. The emperor was advised to have Luther's body exhumed and burned to carry out 25 years too late the Edict of Worms that had made Luther an outlaw from church and state. But Charles V was no longer the self-confident young emperor who had been faced down by the Saxon monk on that long-ago day. Popes had come and gone, and his warrior rivals Francis I and Henry VIII were both dead. He alone survived. He had little stomach for the petty revenge that he might now exact upon the man who more than any other had ruined whatever hope there might have been for a united empire dominant over all of Europe. "I do not make war on dead men," Charles declared as he turned away from the reformer's grave. But the ghosts of Luther and Zwingli, of Calvin and Ignatius of Loyola were not so easily laid to rest. For another century, they would haunt a Europe that could do nothing else but make war on dead men.

QUESTIONS FOR REVIEW

1. How did humanism prepare the way for the Protestant Reformation?
2. What motivated Martin Luther?

3. What were the differences among the reforming ideas of Luther, Zwingli, and Calvin?
4. How did the Catholic Church respond to the challenges posed by the Protestant Reformation?

KEY TERMS

Anabaptists, *p. 408*

Christian humanism, *p. 392*

Counter-Reformation, *p. 413*

indulgences, *p. 397*

New Piety, *p. 410*

predestination, *p. 404*

Reformation, *p. 389*

sola fide, p. 399

sola scriptura, p. 389

DISCOVERING WESTERN CIVILIZATION ONLINE

You can obtain more information about the reform of religion at the Websites listed below. See also the Companion Website that accompanies this text, www.ablongman.com/kishlansky, which contains an online study guide and additional resources.

The Lutheran Reformation

Lutherstadt Wittenberg, Martin Luther

www.wittenberg.de/e/seiten/personen/luther.html

A site devoted to Martin Luther and the city of Wittenberg. Texts of the famous Ninety-five Theses and other of Luther's writings as well as pictures of locations associated with the Lutheran reformation.

The Protestant Reformation

The Reformation Guide

www.educ.msu.edu/homepages/laurence/reformation/index.htm

The Reformation guide is the best starting place for information about all aspects of the Protestant Reformation. Dozens of links to follow.

Discovery and Reformation

www.wsu.edu/~dee/REFORM/REFORM.HTM

A primarily text-based site created by Washington State University, with profiles of key individuals and explanations of the issues at stake.

Project Wittenberg

www.iclnet.org/pub/resources/text/wittenberg/wittenberg-home.html

The home page of Project Wittenberg, containing a large number of texts (including hymns) by Luther and other Reformers.

Tudor History

tudorhistory.org/

A site with links to a variety of subjects relating to England under the Tudors. Biographies of the kings and queens, bibliographies, maps, and documents.

Reformation Picture Gallery

www.mun.ca/rels/hrollmann/reform/pics/pics.html

Contemporary pictures of leading reformers and the places associated with the Protestant Reformation. Excellent reproductions, especially from woodcuts.

Internet Modern History Sourcebook: Reformation Europe

www.fordham.edu/halsall/mod/modsbook02.html

Sources for both the Reformation and Counter-Reformation with links to other valuable sites.

SUGGESTIONS FOR FURTHER READING

General Reading

Owen Chadwick, *The Reformation* (London: Penguin Books, 1972). An elegant and disarmingly simple history of religious change.

Diarmaid MacCulloch, *The Reformation* (London: Viking, 2003). A vastly impressive survey of the Reformation from a leading scholar.

Steven Ozment, *The Age of Reform, 1250–1550* (New Haven, CT: Yale University Press, 1980). An important interpretation of an epoch of religious change.

The Intellectual Reformation

E. Eisenstein, *The Printing Revolution in Early Modern Europe* (Cambridge: Cambridge University Press, 1983). An abridged edition of a larger work that examines the impact of printing upon European society.

Adrian Johns, *The Nature of the Book: Print and Knowledge in the Making* (Chicago: University of Chicago Press, 1998). A major new synthesis with an unusual interpretation.

R. W. Scribner, *For the Sake of Simple Folk* (Cambridge: Cambridge University Press, 1994). A study of the impact of the Reformation on common people. Especially good on the iconography of reform.

James Tracy, *Erasmus of the Low Countries* (Berkeley, CA:, 1996). A brief biography of the great Dutch humanist.

The Lutheran Reformation

Roland Bainton, *Here I Stand* (New York: New American Library, 1968). The single most compelling biography of Luther.

Bernd Moeller, *Imperial Cities and the Reformation* (Durham, NC: Labyrinth Press, 1982). A central work that defines the connection between Protestantism and urban reform.

Heiko Oberman, *Luther: Man Between God and the Devil* (New York: Doubleday, 1992). English translation of one of the best German biographies of Luther. Sets Luther within the context of late medieval spirituality.

G. R. Potter, *Huldrych Zwingli* (New York: St. Martin's Press, 1984). A difficult but important study of the great Swiss reformer.

Lyndal Roper, *The Holy Household: Women and Morals in Reformation Augsburg* (Oxford: Oxford University Press, 1991). The best work to show the impact of the Reformation on family life and women.

R. W. Scribner, *The German Reformation* (Atlantic Highlands, NJ: Humanities Press, 1986). An excellent introduction, especially to the social history of the Reformation.

The Protestant Reformation

William Bousma, *John Calvin* (Oxford: Oxford University Press, 1988). A study that places Calvin within the context of the social and intellectual movements of the sixteenth century.

Claus-Peter Clasen, *Anabaptism, A Social History, 1525–1618* (Ithaca, NY: Cornell University Press, 1972). An important study of the Anabaptist movement.

A. G. Dickens, *The English Reformation*, 2d ed. (London: Batsford, 1989). The classic study of reform in England.

J. J. Scarisbrick, *Henry VIII* (Berkeley: University of California Press, 1968). The classic biography of the larger-than-life monarch.

The Catholic Reformation

Jean Delumeau, *Catholicism Between Luther and Voltaire* (Philadelphia: Westminster Press, 1977). An important reinterpretation of the Counter-Reformation.

Carlos Eire, *From Madrid to Purgatory* (Cambridge: Cambridge University Press, 1995). A brilliant study of the Spanish culture of death during the Counter-Reformation.

W. W. Meissner, *Ignatius of Loyola: The Psychology of a Saint* (New Haven, CT: Yale University Press, 1994). A searching study of the founding spirit of the Counter-Reformation.

John W. O'Malley, *Trent and All That: Renaming Catholicism in the Early Modern Era* (Cambridge, MA: Harvard University Press, 2000). A re-examination of Catholicism in the century surrounding the Council of Trent.

A. D. Wright, *The Counter-Reformation* (New York: St. Martin's Press, 1984). A comprehensive survey.

For a list of additional titles related to this chapter's topics, please see http://www.ablongman.com/kishlansky.

Chapter 14

EUROPE AT WAR, 1555–1648

Chapter Outline

War dominated European society in the early modern era. Artists such as Nicolas Poussin used classical themes to illustrate the devastating impact of war. In The Visual Record, you will see a powerful example of the horror it invoked. ➤

THE MASSACRE OF THE INNOCENTS
War and European Society

"War is one of the scourges with which it has pleased God to afflict men," wrote Cardinal Richelieu (1585–1642), the French minister who played no small part in spreading the scourge. War was a constant of European society and penetrated to its very core. It dominated all aspects of life. It enhanced the power of the state; it defined gender roles; it consumed lives and treasure and commodities ravenously. War affected every member of society from combatants to civilians. There were no innocent bystanders. Grain in the fields was destroyed because it was food for soldiers; houses were burned because they provided shelter for soldiers. Civilians were killed for aiding the enemy or holding out against demands for their treasure and supplies. Able-bodied men were taken forcibly to serve as conscripts, leaving women to plant and harvest best as they could.

There was nothing new about war in the middle of the sixteenth century. The early part of the century had witnessed the dynastic struggle between the Habsburgs and the House of Valois as well as the beginnings of the religious struggle between Catholics and Protestants. But the wars that dominated Europe from 1555 to 1648 brought together the worst of both of the conflicts. War was fought on a larger scale, it was more brutal and more expensive, and it claimed more victims, civilians and combatants alike. During this century, war extended throughout the Continent. Dynastic strife, rebellion, and international rivalries joined together with the ongoing struggle over religion. Ambition and faith were an explosive mixture. The French endured 40 years of civil war; the Spanish, 80 years of fighting with the Dutch. The battle for hegemony in the east led to dynastic strife for decades on end as Poles, Russians, and Swedes pressed their rival claims to each other's crowns. Finally, in 1618, the separate theaters of war came together in one of the most brutal and terrifying episodes of destruction in European history: the Thirty Years' War.

Neither the ancient temple nor the Roman costume can conceal the immediacy of the picture shown here. It is as painful to look at now as it was when it was created more than 350 years ago. Painted by Nicolas Poussin (1594–1665) at the height of the Thirty Years' War, *The Massacre of the Innocents* remains a horrifying composition of power, terror, and despair. The cruel and senseless slaughter of the innocent baby that is about to take place is echoed throughout the canvas. In the background between the executioner's legs can be seen a mother clasping her own child tightly and anticipating the fall of the sword. In the background on the right, another mother turns away from the scene and carries her infant to safety. In the foreground strides a mother holding her dead child. She tears at her hair and cries in anguish. To a culture in which the image of mother and child—of Mary and Jesus—was one of sublime peacefulness and inexpressible joy, the contrast could hardly be more shocking.

The picture graphically displays the cruelty of the soldier, the helplessness of the child, and the horror of the mother. By his grip on the mother's hair and his foot on the baby's throat, the warrior shows his brute power. The mother's futile effort to stop the sword illustrates her powerlessness. She scratches uselessly at the soldier's back. Naked, the baby boy raises his hands as if to surrender to the inevitable, as if to reinforce his innocence.

To study Europe at war, we must enter into a world of politics and diplomacy, of issues and principles, of judgment and

■ Nicolas Poussin, *The Massacre of the Innocents* (1632–1634).

error. We must talk about armies in terms of their cost and numbers, of generals in terms of their strategy and tactics, and of battles in terms of winners and losers. There can be no doubt that the future of Europe was decisively shaped by the century of wholesale slaughter during which dynastic and religious fervor finally ran its course.

Looking Ahead

As we will see in this chapter, warfare in the seventeenth century decisively reshaped power relations of families and states. Protestantism survived after nearly a century of military challenge, and the power of the great Habsburg dynasty was finally crushed. In its place rose France, England, and Holland, and a new chapter of European conflict began. ➤

THE CRISES OF THE WESTERN STATES

"Un roi, une foi, une loi"—one king, one faith, one law. That was a prescription that members of all European states accepted without question in the sixteenth century. Society was an integrated whole, equally dependent upon monarchical, ecclesiastical, and civil authority for its effective survival. A European state could no more tolerate the presence of two churches than it could the presence of two kings. But the Reformation had created two churches.

In Germany, where the problem first arose, the Peace of Augsburg (1555) enacted the most logical solution. The religion of the ruler was to be the religion of the subjects. Princes, town governments, and bishops would determine faith. Not surprisingly, the policy was more convenient for rulers than for the ruled. Sudden conversions of princes, a hallmark of Protestantism, threw the state into disarray. Those closely identified with Catholicism and those who firmly believed in its doctrines had no choice but to move to a neighboring Catholic community and begin again. Given the dependence of ordinary people upon networks of kin and neighbors, enforced migration was devastating. Protestant minorities in Catholic states suffered the same fate. The enmity between the two groups came as much from bitter experience as from differences of belief.

Thus compromises that might have brought Protestants back into a reformed Catholic Church were doomed from the start. Doomed too was the practical solution of toleration. To the modern mind, toleration seems so logical that it is difficult to understand why it took over a century of bloodshed before it came to be grudgingly accepted by those countries most bitterly divided. But toleration was not a practical solution in a society that admitted no principle of organization other than one king, one faith. In such a world, toleration was even more threatening than warfare. Pope Clement VIII (1592–1605) described liberty of conscience as "the worst thing in the world." Those who advocated limited forms of toleration were universally despised. Those occasions during which toleration was a reluctant basis for a cease-fire were moments for catching breath before resuming the struggle for total victory. Only Poland-Lithuania, Hungary, and a few German states experimented with religious toleration during the sixteenth century.

The crises of the western European states that stretched from the middle of the sixteenth century to the middle of the seventeenth were as much internal and domestic as they were external and international. In France, a half century of religious warfare sapped the strength of both the monarchy and the nation. In Spain, the protracted revolt of the Netherlands drained men, money, and spirit from the most powerful nation in Europe. Decades of intermittent warfare turned the golden age of Spain to lead and hastened the decline of the Spanish Empire. Each crisis had its own causes and its own history. Yet it was no coincidence that they occurred together or that they starkly posed the conflict between the authority of the state and the conscience of the individual. The century between the Peace of Augsburg (1555) and the Peace of Westphalia (1648) was the century of total war.

The French Wars of Religion

No wars are more terrible than civil wars. They tear at the very fabric of society, rending its institutions and destroying the delicate web of relationships that underlie all communal life. The nation is divided; communities break into factions; families are destroyed. Civil wars are wars of passion. Issues become elevated into causes and principles that form the rallying cry of heroic self-sacrifice or wanton destruction. Civil wars feed on themselves. Each act of war becomes an outrage to be revenged, each act of revenge a new outrage. Passions run deep and, however primitive, the rules for the civilized conduct of war are quickly broken. The loss of lives and property is staggering, but the loss of communal identity is greater still. Generations pass before societies recover from their civil wars. Such was the case with the **French wars of religion.**

The Spread of Calvinism and Religious Division.
Protestantism came late to France. It was not until after Calvin reformed the church in Geneva and began to export his brand of Protestantism that French society began to divide along religious lines. By 1560 there were more than 2000 Protestant

CHRONOLOGY
THE FRENCH WARS OF RELIGION

1559	Death of Henry II
1560	Protestant duc de Condé sentenced to death
1562	First battle of French wars of religion
1563	Catholic duc de Guise assassinated
1572	Saint Bartholomew's Day Massacre
1574	Accession of Henry III
1576	Formation of Catholic League
1584	Death of duc d'Anjou makes Henry of Navarre heir to throne
1585	War of the three Henrys
1588	Duc de Guise murdered by order of Henry III
1589	Catherine de Médicis dies; Henry III assassinated
1594	Henry IV crowned
1598	Edict of Nantes

congregations in France, whose membership totaled nearly 10 percent of the French population. Calvin and his successors concentrated their efforts on large provincial towns and had their greatest success among the middle ranks of urban society—merchants, traders, and artisans. They also found a receptive audience among aristocratic women, who eventually converted their husbands and their sons.

The wars of religion, however, were brought on by more than the rapid spread of Calvinism. Equally important was the vacuum of power that had been created when Henry II (1547–1559) died in a jousting tournament. Surviving Henry were his extraordinary widow, Catherine de Médicis, three daughters, and four sons, the oldest of whom, Francis II (1559–1560), was only 15. Under the influence of his beautiful young wife, Mary, Queen of Scots, Francis II allowed the Guise family to dominate the great offices of state and to exclude their rivals from power. The Guises

■ Catherine de Médicis (1519–1598), the wife of Henry II of France, was the real power behind the throne during the reigns of her sons Charles IX (1560–1574) and Henry III (1574–1589). Her overriding concern was to ensure her sons' succession and to preserve the power of the monarchy.

MAP DISCOVERY

Religious Divisions in France During the Wars of Religion

What was the dominant religion of France? Notice the relationship between the location of Paris and the Huguenot strongholds. Based on region of influence, which religion controlled trade with England and in the Mediterranean?

Map labels: ENGLAND, Calais, English Channel, HOLY ROMAN EMPIRE, Seine R., CHAMPAGNE, NORMANDY, Paris, Rhine R., BRITTANY, Nantes, Loire R., POITOU, Bay of Biscay, Lyon, PERIGORD, Bordeaux, Rhône R., DAUPHINÉ, Garonne R., Avignon, GASCOGNE, LANGUEDOC, PROVENCE, NAVARRE, Mediterranean Sea

Lands of the Catholic League
Protestant Huguenot lands
Disputed lands

0   100 Miles
0   100 Kilometers

controlled the two most powerful institutions of the state, the army and the Church.

The Guises were staunchly Catholic, and among their enemies were the Bourbons, princes of the blood with a direct claim to the French throne but also a family with powerful Protestant members. The revelation of a Protestant plot to remove the king from Paris provided the Guises with an opportunity to eliminate their most potent rivals. The Bourbon duc de Condé, the leading Protestant peer of the realm, was sentenced to death. But five days before Condé's execution, Francis II died and Guise power evaporated. The new king, Charles IX (1560–1574), was only ten years old and firmly under the grip of his mother, Catherine de Médicis, who now declared herself regent of France. (See "A Closer Look: The Monstrous Regiment of Women," pp. 424–425.)

Civil War. Condé's death sentence convinced him that the Guises would stop at nothing to gain their ambitions. Force would have to be met with force. Protestants and Catholics alike raised armies, and in 1562 civil war erupted. Once the wars began, the leading Protestant peers fled the court, but the position of the Guises was not altogether secure. Henry Bourbon,

A Closer Look
The Monstrous Regiment of Women

"To promote a woman to bear rule, superiority, dominion or empire above any realm, nation, or city is repugnant to nature, contumely to God, and the subversion of good order, of all equity and justice." So wrote the Scottish theologian John Knox (1513–1572) in *The First Blast of the Trumpet Against the Monstrous Regiment of Women* (1558). Although he made his points more emphatically than many others, Knox was only repeating the commonplace notions of his day. He could quote Aristotle and Aquinas as well as a host of secular authorities to demonstrate female inadequacies: "Nature, I say, doth paint them forth to be weak, frail, impatient, feeble, and foolish." He could quote Saint Paul along with the ancient Fathers of the Church to demonstrate the "proper" place of women—"Man is not of the woman, but the woman of the man."

But no stacking up of authorities, no matter how numerous or revered, could erase the fact that all over Europe in the sixteenth century women could and did rule. In the Netherlands, Mary, Queen of Hungary (1531–1552), and Margaret of Parma (1559–1567) were successful regents. Jeanne d'Albret (1562–1572) was queen of the tiny state of Navarre, territory claimed by both France and Spain but kept independent by that remarkable woman. Catherine de Médicis (1560–1589), wife of one king of France and mother of three others, was the effective ruler of that nation for nearly 30 years. Mary, Queen of Scots (1542–1587), was the nominal ruler of Scotland almost from her birth. England was ruled by two very different women, the Catholic Mary I (1553–1558) and her Protestant half-sister Elizabeth I (1558–1603).

The problems faced by this long list of queens and regents were more than just the ordinary cares of government. The belief that women were inherently inferior in intelligence, strength, and character was so pervasive that, for men like Knox, a woman ruler was almost a contradiction in terms. Yet this was not the view taken by everyone, and female rule had its defenders as well as its detractors. One set of objections was overcome by the traditional medieval theory of the two bodies of the monarch. That argument was developed to reconcile the divine origins and functions of monarchs with their very real human frailties. In the theory of the two bodies, there was the body natural and the body politic. Both were joined together in the person of the ruler, but the attributes of each could be separated. Rule of a woman did nothing to disrupt this notion. In fact, it made it easier to argue that the frailties of the body natural of a woman were in no way related to the strengths of the body politic of a monarch.

While such ideas might help a female ruler win the acceptance of her subjects, they did little to invigorate her own sense of her role. Female rulers often strained against the straitjacket that definitions of gender placed them in. When angered, Elizabeth I would proclaim that she had more courage than her father, Henry VIII, "though I am only a woman." Mary, Queen of Scots, once revealed that her only regret was that she "was not a man to know what life it was to lie all night in the fields or to walk with a buckler and a broadsword." Some queens assumed masculine traits, riding in armor or leading forces to battle. Elizabeth's presence in armor at the threat of the landing of the Spanish Armada was viewed as one of the heroic moments of her reign. Other women rulers combined characteristics that were usually separated by gender definitions. Margaret of Parma was considered one of the most accomplished horse riders of her day. After leading her courtiers through woods and fields at breakneck speed, she would then attend council meetings and work on her needlepoint. Mary, Queen of Scots, loved hawking, a traditional kingly sport, in the Scottish wilds. After relishing the hawk's destruction of its prey, she liked to negotiate matters of state by beginning with tears and entreaties and ending with accusations and threats. The effect was more than disconcerting.

Women were no more or less successful as rulers than were men. Women's achievements, like men's, depended upon strength of character and the circumstances of the times. All the women rulers of the sixteenth century had received outstanding educations. Whether raised Catholic or Protestant, each was trained in Latin as well as modern languages, in the liberal arts, and in fine arts. Mary and Elizabeth Tudor of England wrote poetry and played musical instruments with considerable accomplishment. Mary, Queen of Scots, who was raised at the court of France, was considered particularly apt at learning, praise not often accorded a foreigner by the French. Catherine de Médicis, orphaned as an infant, was raised in convents and instructed in the new learning by Italian nuns. It was said that her political instincts were in her blood: Machiavelli had dedicated *The Prince* to her father. Marguerite of Navarre chose one of the leading French humanists to supervise the training of her daughter, Jeanne d'Albret.

Mary, Queen of Scots, was the only one of the female rulers born to rule. She was the sole survivor of her father, who died shortly after her birth. Mary and Elizabeth Tudor came to their thrones after the death of their younger brother Edward VI; Mary of Hungary and Margaret of Parma came to theirs as princesses of the House of Habsburg. The rule of Catherine de Médicis was the most unexpected of all. Her vigorous husband, Henry II, died during a jousting tournament, and her eldest son, Francis II, husband of Mary, Queen of Scots, died the following year. Instead of retirement as a respected queen dowager (the widow of a previous king), Catherine de Médicis was forced into the vortex of French politics to protect the rights of her ten-year-old son, Charles IX.

For most of the queens and regents, marriage was of central importance to their position. Both Mary, Queen of Hungary, and Mary, Queen of Scots, married kings whose reigns were exceedingly brief. Lewis of Hungary died at the battle of Mohács in 1526, just four years after Mary had become his queen. Mary, Queen of Scots, was widowed even sooner, and throughout the rest of her remarkable career schemed to remarry. To strengthen her claim to the throne of England, she married the Scottish Lord Darnley. When he proved unsatisfactory to her plans, she plotted his murder and then married one of his assassins. When that husband died, she sought a match with a powerful English

■ The Latin inscription in this portrait of Mary, Queen of Scots, indicates that it was painted when she had been a prisoner in England for ten years.

lord who might help her capture Elizabeth's throne. The intrigues finally led to her execution in England in 1587. Mary Tudor married Philip II of Spain in hope of reestablishing Catholicism in England through a permanent alliance with the most powerful Catholic state in Europe. Her dreams went unfulfilled when she failed to produce an heir, and the throne passed to her sister, Elizabeth, who, alone among the women rulers of the period, did not marry.

Unfortunately, the accomplishments of women rulers did little to dispel prejudices against women as a whole or to alter the definition of gender roles. Except for Mary, Queen of Scots, whose principal achievement was to provide an heir to the English throne, all the queens and regents of the sixteenth century were successful rulers. Margaret of Parma steered the careful middle course in the conflict between Spain and the Netherlands. She opposed the intervention of the Duke of Alba, and, had her advice been followed, the 80 years of war between Spain and the Netherlands might have been avoided. Catherine de Médicis held the crown of France on the heads of her sons, navigated the treacherous waters of civil war, and provided the model for religious toleration that finally was adopted in the Edict of Nantes. Elizabeth I of England became one of the most beloved rulers in that nation's history. A crafty politician who learned to balance the factions at her court and who turned the aristocracy into a service class for the crown, she brought nearly a half century of stability to England at a time when the rest of Europe was in flames.

■ Painting of the Saint Bartholomew's Day Massacre. The massacre began in Paris on 24 August 1572, and the violence soon spread throughout France.

king of Navarre, was the next in line to succeed to the throne should Charles IX and his two brothers die without male heirs. Henry had been raised in the Protestant faith by his mother, Jeanne d'Albret, whose own mother, Marguerite of Navarre, was among the earliest protectors of the French Protestants. The objectives of the **Huguenots,** as the French Calvinists came to be called, were less clear-cut. The townspeople wanted the right to practice their faith, the clergy wanted the right to preach and make converts, and the nobility wanted their rightful place in local government. Almost from the beginning, the Huguenots were on the defensive, fighting to preserve what they already had and to avoid annihilation.

The inconclusive nature of the early battles might have allowed for the pragmatic solution sought by Catherine de Médicis had it not been for the assassination of the duc de Guise in 1563 by a Protestant fanatic. That act added a personal vendetta to the religious passions of the Catholic leaders. They encouraged the slaughter of Huguenot congregations and openly planned the murder of Huguenot leaders. Protestants gave as good as they got. In open defiance of Valois dynastic interests, the Guises courted support from Spain, while the Huguenots imported Swiss and German mercenaries to fight in France. Noble factions and irreconcilable religious differences were pulling the government apart.

The Saint Bartholomew's Day Massacre. By 1570 Catherine was ready to attempt another reconciliation. She announced her plans for a marriage between her daughter Margaret and Henry of Navarre, a marriage that would symbolize the spirit of conciliation between the crown and the Huguenots. The marriage was to take place in Paris during August 1572. The arrival of Huguenot leaders from all over

France to attend the marriage ceremony presented an opportunity of a different kind to the Guises and their supporters. If leading Huguenots could be assassinated in Paris, the Protestant cause might collapse and the truce that the wedding signified might be turned instead into a Catholic triumph.

DOCUMENT

Massacre of St. Bartholomew

Saint Bartholomew was the apostle that Jesus described as a man without guile. Ironically, it was on his feast day that the Huguenots who had innocently come to celebrate Henry's marriage were led like lambs to the slaughter. On 24 August 1572, the streets of Paris ran red with Huguenot blood. Although frenzied, the slaughter was inefficient. Henry of Navarre and a number of other important Huguenots escaped the carnage and returned to their urban strongholds. In the following weeks, the violence spread from Paris to the countryside and thousands of Protestants paid for their beliefs with their lives. Until the French Revolution, no event in French history would evoke as much passion as the memory of the Saint Bartholomew's Day Massacre.

One King, Two Faiths

The Saint Bartholomew's Day Massacre was a transforming event in many ways. In the first place, it prolonged the wars. A whole new generation of Huguenots now had an emotional attachment to the continuation of warfare: their fathers and brothers had been mercilessly slaughtered. By itself, the event was shocking enough; in the atmosphere of anticipated reconciliation created by the wedding, it screamed out for revenge. And the target for retaliation was no longer limited to the Guises and their followers. By accepting the results of the massacre, the monarchy sanctioned it and spilled Huguenot blood on itself. For more than a decade, Catherine de Médicis had maintained a distance between the crown and the leaders of the Catholic movement. That distance no longer existed.

The Theory of Resistance. The Huguenots could not continue to maintain the fiction that they were fighting against the king's evil advisers rather than against the king. After Saint Bartholomew's Day, Huguenot theorists began to develop the idea that resistance to a monarch whose actions violated divine commandments or civil rights was lawful. For the first time, Huguenot writers provided a justification for rebellion. Perhaps most importantly, a genuine revulsion against the massacres swept the nation. A number of Catholic peers now joined with the Huguenots to protest the excesses of the crown and the Guises. Those Catholics came to be called **politiques** from their desire for a practical settlement of the wars. They were led by the duc d'Anjou, next in line to the throne after Henry III (1574–1589) became king.

Against them, in Paris and a number of other towns, the Catholic League was formed, a society that pledged its first allegiance to religion. The League took up where the Saint Bartholomew's Day Massacre left off, and the slaughter of ordinary people who unluckily professed the wrong religion continued. Matters grew worse in 1584, when Anjou died. With each passing year it was becoming apparent that Henry III would produce no male heir. After Anjou's death, the Huguenot

Henry of Navarre was the next in line for the throne. Catholic Leaguers talked openly of altering the royal succession and began to develop theories of lawful resistance to monarchical power. By 1585, when the final civil war began—the war of the three Henrys, named for Henry III, Henry Guise, and Henry of Navarre—the crown was in the weakest possible position. Paris and the Catholic towns were controlled by the League, the Protestant strongholds by Henry of Navarre. King Henry III could not abandon his capital or his religion, but neither could he gain control of the Catholic party. The extremism of the Leaguers kept the politiques away from court, and without the politiques, there could be no settlement.

In December 1588, Henry III summoned Henry Guise and Guise's brother to a meeting in the royal bedchamber. There they were murdered by the king's order. The politiques were blamed for the murders—revenge was taken on a number of them—and Henry III was forced to flee his capital. Paris was still firmly in the hands of the League, and Henry was in danger of becoming a king without a country. He made a pact with Henry of Navarre, and together royalist and Huguenot forces besieged Paris. All supplies were cut off from the city and only the arrival of a Spanish army prevented its fall. In 1589, Catherine de Médicis died, her ambition to reestablish the authority of the monarchy in shambles, and in the same year a fanatic priest gained revenge for the murder of the Guises by assassinating Henry III.

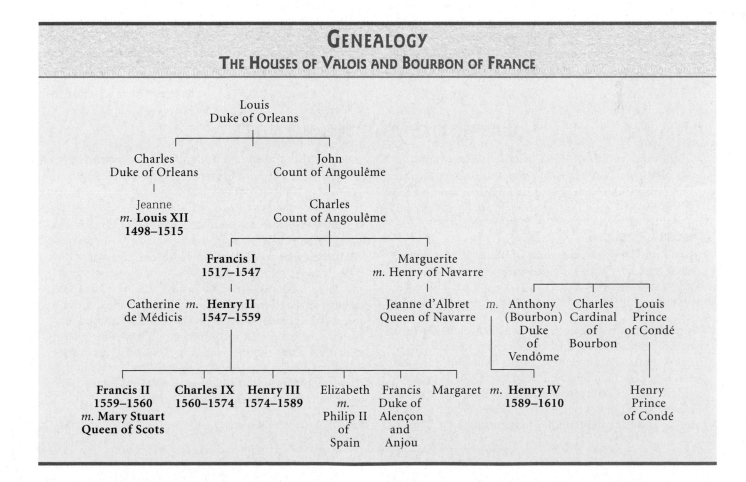

GENEALOGY
THE HOUSES OF VALOIS AND BOURBON OF FRANCE

■ Although he probably never said, "Paris is worth a mass" it was Henry IV's conversion to Catholicism that ended the French wars of religion.

Henry IV. Now Henry of Navarre came into his inheritance. After nearly 30 years of continuous civil war, it was certain that a Huguenot could never rule France. The League had already proclaimed a Catholic rival as king, and the pope excommunicated Henry of Navarre and absolved France from loyalty to him. If Henry was to become king of all France, he would have to become a Catholic king. It is not clear when Henry made the decision to accept the Catholic faith—"Paris is worth a mass," he reportedly declared—but he did not announce his decision at once. Rather he strengthened his forces, tightened his bonds with the politiques, and urged his countrymen to expel the Spanish invaders. He finally made his conversion public and in 1594 was crowned Henry IV (1589–1610). A war-weary nation was willing to accept the sincerity of its new king rather than endure a seemingly endless struggle. Most of the leading peers on both sides were nearly bankrupt, and Henry IV was willing to pay large cash settlements to all those who would return to their estates and pledge allegiance to him.

Resistance to the reestablishment of the monarchy continued for several years, but Henry IV was a strong and capable ruler. He declared war on Spain to unite his nation against foreign aggression, and he carefully reestablished the balance of

CATHOLICS AND HUGUENOTS

The Edict of Nantes (1598) was a milestone in the development of religious toleration in Europe. It was granted by King Henry IV to the Huguenots at the end of the French wars of religion. The Edict of Nantes established the rights of Protestants and was in effect for nearly a century.

Focus Questions

How much religious toleration is Henry IV granting? What authority does the Edict give to Catholics, and what to Protestants?

We ordain that the Catholic, Apostolic and Roman religion shall be restored and re-established in all places and districts of this our kingdom and the countries under our rule, where its practice has been interrupted, so that it can be peacefully and freely practiced there, without any disturbance or hindrance. We forbid very expressly all persons of whatever rank, quality or condition they may be, under the aforesaid penalties, to disturb, molest or cause annoyance to clerics in the celebration of the Divine worship. . . .

And in order not to leave any cause for discords and disputes between our subjects, we have permitted and we permit those of the so-called Reformed religion to live and dwell in all the towns and districts of this our kingdom and the countries under our rule, without being annoyed, disturbed, molested or constrained to do anything against their conscience, or for this cause to be sought out in their houses and districts where they wish to live, provided that they conduct themselves in other respects according to the provisions of our present Edict. . . .

From the Edict of Nantes.

aristocratic factions at his court. The League collapsed, and moderate Catholics rallied around the king. Although Huguenots and Calvinists everywhere were shocked by Henry's conversion, they were hardly in a position to wage a successful war against their former leader. Henry's accession gave them their first real hope for an enduring settlement with the crown.

In 1598, Henry proclaimed the **Edict of Nantes,** which granted limited toleration to the Huguenots. It was the culmination of decades of attempts to find a solution to the existence of two religions in one state. It was a compromise that satisfied no one, but it was a compromise that everyone could accept. One king, two faiths was as apt a description of Henry IV as it was of the settlement. Yet neither Henry's conversion nor the Edict of Nantes stilled the passions that had spawned and sustained the French wars of religion. Sporadic fighting between Catholics and Huguenots continued, and fanatics on both sides fanned the flames of religious hatred. Henry IV survived 18 attempts on his life before he was finally felled by an assassin's knife in 1610, but by then he had reestablished the monarchy and brought a semblance of peace to France.

The World of Philip II

By the middle of the sixteenth century, Spain was the greatest power in Europe. The dominions of Philip II (1556–1598) of Spain stretched from the Atlantic to the Pacific; his continental territories included the Netherlands in the north and Milan and Naples in Italy. In 1580, Philip became king of Portugal, uniting all the states of the Iberian peninsula. With the addition of Portugal's Atlantic ports and its sizable fleet, Spanish maritime power was now unsurpassed. Spain was also a great cultural and intellectual center. The fashions and tastes of its golden age dominated all the courts of Europe.

Great power meant great responsibilities, and few monarchs took their tasks more seriously than did Philip II. Trained from childhood for the cares of office, he exceeded all expectations. Philip II earned his reputation as "King of Paper" by maintaining a grueling work schedule. Up at eight and at mass soon afterward, he met with his advisers and visitors on official business until noon. After a brief lunch, he began the real business of the day, the study of the mountains of papers that his empire generated. Although summaries were prepared of the hundreds of documents he handled each day, Philip II frequently read and annotated the longer originals. No detail was too small to escape his attention. His workday often lasted ten hours or longer. Even when he was traveling, his secretaries carried huge chests of state papers that Philip studied in his carriage and annotated on a portable desk that always accompanied him.

There was good reason why the slightly stooped king appeared as if he had the weight of the world on his shoulders. In the Mediterranean, Spain alone stood out against the expansion of Ottoman power. The sultan's navy continually threatened to turn the Mediterranean into a Turkish lake, while his armies attempted to capture and hold Italian soil. All Europe shuddered at the news of each Ottoman advance. Popes called for holy wars against the Turks, but only Philip heeded the cry. From nearly the moment that he inherited the Spanish crown, he took up the challenge of defending European Christianity. For more than a

■ The defeat of the immense armada that Philip II sent to invade England in 1588 dealt a serious blow to Spain's standing in Europe.

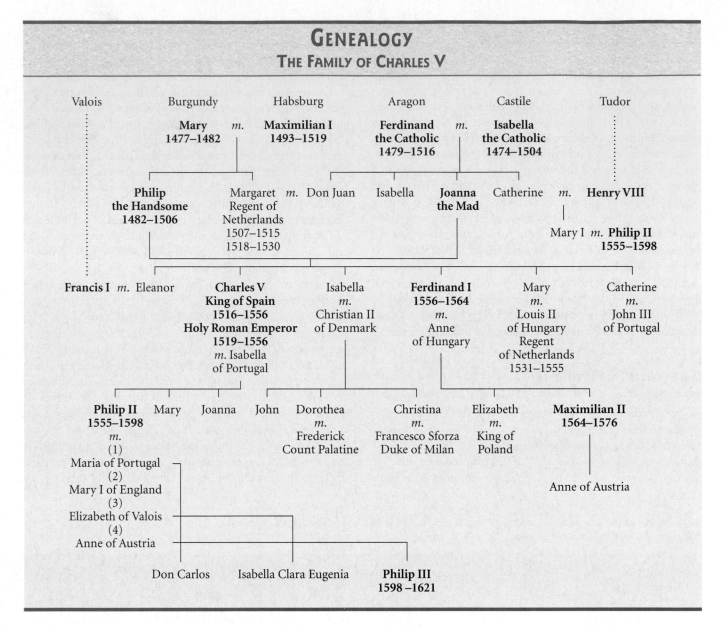

GENEALOGY
THE FAMILY OF CHARLES V

Valois — Burgundy — Habsburg — Aragon — Castile — Tudor

Mary 1477–1482 *m.* **Maximilian I** 1493–1519

Ferdinand the Catholic 1479–1516 *m.* **Isabella the Catholic** 1474–1504

Philip the Handsome 1482–1506 — Margaret *m.* Don Juan — Isabella — **Joanna the Mad** — Catherine *m.* **Henry VIII**

Margaret, Regent of Netherlands 1507–1515 1518–1530

Mary I *m.* **Philip II** 1555–1598

Francis I *m.* Eleanor — **Charles V King of Spain** 1516–1556 **Holy Roman Emperor** 1519–1556 *m.* Isabella of Portugal — Isabella *m.* Christian II of Denmark — **Ferdinand I** 1556–1564 *m.* Anne of Hungary — Mary *m.* Louis II of Hungary Regent of Netherlands 1531–1555 — Catherine *m.* John III of Portugal

Philip II 1555–1598 *m.*
(1) Maria of Portugal
(2) Mary I of England
(3) Elizabeth of Valois
(4) Anne of Austria

Mary — Joanna — John — Dorothea *m.* Frederick Count Palatine — Christina *m.* Francesco Sforza Duke of Milan — Elizabeth *m.* King of Poland — **Maximilian II** 1564–1576

Anne of Austria

Don Carlos — Isabella Clara Eugenia — **Philip III** 1598–1621

---

decade, Philip maintained costly coastal garrisons in North Africa and Italy and assembled large fleets and larger armies to discourage or repel Turkish invasions. The sparring could not go on indefinitely, and in 1571 both sides prepared for a decisive battle. A combined Spanish and Italian force of more than 300 ships and 80,000 men met an even larger Ottoman flotilla off the coast of Greece. The Spanish naval victory at Lepanto was considered one of the great events of the sixteenth century, celebrated in story and song for the next 300 years. Although the Turks continued to menace the Mediterranean islands, Lepanto marked the end of Ottoman advances.

Philip was equally aggressive against the English Protestants. For a brief time he had been king in England through his marriage to Mary I (1553–1558). He encouraged Mary's efforts to restore the Catholic Church in England and supported her policies of repression. When Mary died and Elizabeth I (1558–1603) rejected his marriage proposal, his limited rule in England came to an end. From then on,

England and Spain entered a long period of hostility. English pirates raided Spanish treasure ships returning to Europe, and Elizabeth covertly aided both French and Dutch Protestants. Finally, in 1588, Philip decided upon invasion. A great fleet set sail from the Portuguese coast to the Netherlands, where a large Spanish army stood waiting to be conveyed to England.

The **Spanish Armada** was composed of more than 130 ships, many of them the pride of the Spanish and Portuguese navies. They were bigger and stronger than anything possessed by the English, whose forces were largely merchant vessels hastily converted for battle. But the English ships were faster and more easily maneuverable in the unpredictable winds of the English Channel. They also contained guns that could easily be reloaded for multiple firings, while the Spanish guns were designed to discharge only one broadside before hand-to-hand combat ensued. With those advantages the English were able to prevent the Armada from reaching port in the Netherlands and

DOCUMENT

Reports on the Spanish Armada

to destroy many individual ships as they were blown off course. The defeat of the Spanish Armada was less a military than a psychological blow to Philip II: he could more easily replace ships than restore confidence in Spanish power.

The Burgundian Inheritance

Confidence was all the more necessary when Philip II faced the gravest crisis of his reign: the revolt of the Netherlands. Although Philip's father, Charles V, had amassed a great empire, he had begun only as the duke of Burgundy. Charles's Burgundian inheritance encompassed a diverse territory in the northwestern corner of Europe. The 17 separate provinces of the territory were called the Netherlands, or the Low Countries, because of the flooding that kept large portions of them under water. The Netherlands was one of the richest and most populous regions of Europe, an international leader in manufacturing, banking, and commerce. Antwerp and Amsterdam were bustling port cities with access to the North Sea; inland were the prosperous industrial towns of Ghent and Brussels. The preeminence of the Netherlands was all the more remarkable because the provinces themselves were divided geographically, culturally, and linguistically. Rivers, lakes, and flooded plains separated the southern provinces,

where French was the background and language of the inhabitants, from the northern ones, where Germans had settled and Dutch was spoken. Charles V attempted to unify the provinces by removing them from the jurisdiction of the Holy Roman Empire and establishing a separate regency under his eldest son, Philip II. Thus the future of the Netherlands was tied to Spain and the New World when Philip II set sail for Castile in 1559 to claim the crown of Spain.

Although Philip II had every intention of returning to the Low Countries, in fact the Netherlands had seen the last of their king. Philip left his half-sister, Margaret of Parma, as regent, providing her with a talented group of Spanish administrators to carry out policies that were to be formulated in Madrid. As Philip's own grasp on the affairs of the Netherlands loosened, so did the loyalty of the native nobility to the absent monarch. The resentments that built up were traditional ones—hostility to foreigners, distrust of royal advisers, and contempt for policies that lacked understanding of local conditions. All of the discontents came together over Philip's religious policies.

The Low Countries had accepted the Peace of Augsburg in a spirit of conciliation in which it was never intended. There Catholics, Lutherans, Anabaptists, and Calvinists peaceably coexisted. As in France, the situation changed dramatically with the spread of Calvinism. The heavy concentration of urban populations in the Low Countries provided the natural habitat for Calvinist preachers, who made converts across the entire social spectrum. As Charles V, Holy Roman Emperor, he may have made his peace with Protestants, but as Charles I, king of Spain, he had not. Charles V had maintained the purity of the Spanish Catholic Church through a sensible combination of reform and repression.

Philip II intended to pursue a similar policy in the Low Countries. With papal approval he initiated a scheme to reform the hierarchy of the Church by expanding the number of bishops, and he invited the Jesuits to establish schools for orthodox learning. Simultaneously, he strengthened the power of the Inquisition and ordered the enforcement of the decrees of the Council of Trent. The Protestants sought the protection of their local nobility who—Catholic or Protestant—

MAP DISCOVERY

Habsburg Lands at the Abdication of Charles V

Notice how dispersed were the states controlled by Charles V when he abdicated the throne in 1556. Why do you think he divided his empire between his son Philip II and his brother Ferdinand I? What made it possible for the Netherlands to revolt from Spanish control?

had their own reasons for opposing provincial nobility, and magistrates resented both the policies that were being pursued and the fact that they disregarded local autonomy. Town governors and noblemen refused to cooperate in implementing the new laws. Leading Protestants such as Prince William of Orange, one of the largest landholders in the Netherlands, and Count Egmont, an outstanding military leader, urged Margaret to adopt a policy of toleration along the lines of the Peace of Augsburg and made clear that they would resign from office rather than support anything else.

The Revolt of the Netherlands

The passive resistance of nobles and magistrates was soon matched by the active resistance of the Calvinists. Unable to enforce Philip's policy, Margaret and her advisers agreed to a limited toleration. But in the summer of 1566, before it could be put into effect, bands of Calvinists unleashed a storm of iconoclasm in the provinces, breaking stained glass windows and statues of the Virgin and the saints, which they claimed were idolatrous. Catholic churches were stormed and turned into Calvinist meeting houses. Local authorities were helpless in the face of determined Calvinists and apathetic Catholics; they could not protect Church property. Iconoclasm gave way to open revolt. Fearing social rebellion, even the leading Protestant noblemen took part in suppressing the riots.

Rebellion and War. In Spain, the events in the Netherlands were treated for what they were: open rebellion. Despite the fact that Margaret had already restored order, Philip II was determined to punish the rebels and enforce the heresy laws. A large military force under the command of the Duke of Alba (1507–1582)—whose record of success was matched only by his record of brutality—was sent from Spain as an army of occupation. As befit a warrior who had made his reputation leading imperial troops against the Lutherans, Alba gave no quarter to the Protestants of the Netherlands. "Everyone must be made to live in constant fear of the roof breaking down over his head," he wrote.

Alba lured Count Egmont and other Protestant noblemen to Brussels, where he publicly executed them in 1568. He also established a military court to punish participants in the rebellion, a court that came to be called the Council of Blood. The Council handed down more than 9000 convictions, a thousand of which carried the death penalty. As many as 60,000 Protestants fled beyond Alba's jurisdiction. Alba next made an example of several small towns that had been implicated in the iconoclasm. He allowed his soldiers to pillage the towns at will before slaughtering their entire populations and razing them to the ground. By the end of 1568, royal policy had gained a sullen acceptance in the Netherlands, but the hostilities did not end. For the next 80 years, with only occasional truces, Spain and the Netherlands were at war.

■ Portrait of Philip II by Titian (ca. 1554). Philip tried for 12 years to suppress rebellion in the Protestant Netherlands, and he sent troops to aid Catholic forces in battle with the Huguenots in France. He fared badly in his attempts to deal with England, his Spanish Armada suffering a humiliating defeat in 1588 that marked the beginning of the decline of Spanish power.

The Protestants Rebel. Alba's policies drove the Protestants into rebellion. That forced the Spanish government to maintain its army by raising taxes from those provinces that had remained loyal. Soon the loyal provinces too were in revolt, not over religion, but over taxation and local autonomy. Tax resistance and fear of an invasion from France left Alba unprepared for the series of successful assaults Protestants launched in the northern provinces during 1572. Protestant generals established a permanent base in

DOCUMENT

Michel de Montaigne, *Essays*

CANNIBALS

Michel de Montaigne (1533–1592) came from a wealthy family in the Bordeaux region of France and ultimately in-
herited the chateau from which his name derives. Before his early retirement he worked in the legal profession. His
Essays (1572–1588) combined humanist learning with the new philosophy of skepticism. The following excerpt, from
"Of Cannibals," shows both his penetrating intelligence and his detached observation of the world around him.

Focus Questions

In what ways does Montaigne profess sympathy with
the inhabitants of the New World? What constitutes
barbarism for him?

These nations, then, seem to me barbarous in this sense, that they have been fashioned very little by the human mind, and are still very close to their original naturalness. The laws of nature still rule them, very little corrupted by ours; and they are in such a state of purity that I am some-times vexed that they were unknown earlier, in the days when there were men able to judge them better than we. I am sorry that Lycurgus and Plato did not know of them; for it seems to me that what we actually see in these na-tions surpasses not only all the pictures in which poets have idealized the golden age and all their inventions in imagining a happy state of man, but also the conceptions and the very desire of philosophy. . . .

For the rest, they live in a country with a very pleasant and temperate climate, so that according to my witnesses it is rare to see a sick man there; and they have assured me that they never saw one palsied, bleary-eyed, toothless, or bent with age. They are settled along the sea and shut in on the land side by great high mountains, with a stretch about a hundred leagues wide in between. They have a great abun-dance of fish and flesh which bear no resemblance to ours, and they eat them with no other artifice than cooking.

They have their wars with the nations beyond the mountains, further inland, to which they go quite naked, with no other arms than bows or wooden swords ending in a sharp point, in the manner of the tongues of our boar spears. It is astonishing what firmness they show in their combats, which never end but in slaughter and bloodshed; for as to routs and terror, they know nothing of either.

Each man brings back as his trophy the head of the en-emy he has killed, and sets it up at the entrance to his dwelling. After they have treated their prisoners well for a long time with all the hospitality they can think of, each man who has a prisoner calls a great assembly of his ac-quaintances. He ties a rope to one of the prisoner's arms by the end of which he holds him, a few steps away, for fear of being hurt, and gives his dearest friend the other arm to hold in the same way; and these two, in the presence of the whole assembly, kill him with their swords. This done, they roast him and eat him in common and send some pieces to their absent friends. This is not, as people think, for nour-ishment, as of old the Scythians used to do; it is to betoken an extreme revenge. And the proof of this came when they saw the Portuguese, who had joined forces with their ad-versaries, inflict a different kind of death on them when they took them prisoner, which was to bury them up to the waist, shoot the rest of their body full of arrows, and after-ward hang them. They thought that these people from the other world, being men who had sown the knowledge of many vices among their neighbors and were much greater masters than themselves in every sort of wickedness, did not adopt this sort of vengeance without some reason, and that it must be more painful than their own; so they began to give up their old method and to follow this one.

I am not sorry that we notice the barbarous horror of such acts, but I am heartily sorry that, judging their faults rightly, we should be so blind to our own. I think there is more barbarity in eating a man alive than in eating him dead; and in tearing by tortures and the rack a body still full of feeling, in roasting a man bit by bit, in having him bitten and mangled by dogs and swine (as we have not only read but seen within fresh memory, not among an-cient enemies, but among neighbors and fellow citizens, and what is worse, on the pretext of piety and religion), than in roasting and eating him after he is dead. . . .

So we may well call these people barbarians, in respect to the rules of reason, but not in respect to ourselves, who surpass them in every kind of barbarity.

Their warfare is wholly noble and generous, and as ex-cusable and beautiful as this human disease can be; its only basis among them is their rivalry in valor. They are not fighting for the conquest of new lands, for they still enjoy that natural abundance that provides them without toil and trouble with all necessary things in such profusion that they have no wish to enlarge their boundaries. They are still in that happy state of desiring only as much as their natural needs demand; anything beyond that is superflu-ous to them. . . . Truly here are real savages by our stan-dards, for either they must be thoroughly so, or we must be; there is an amazing distance between their character and ours.

From Montaigne, "Of Cannibals."

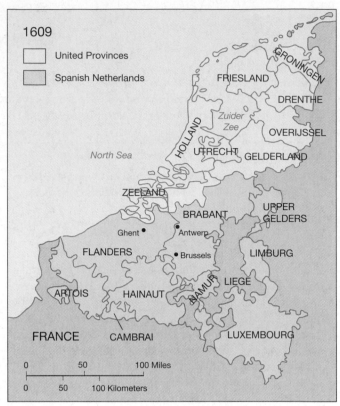

■ The Revolt of the Netherlands, 1555. The consolidation of the Low Countries under Charles V brought together lands with different languages, cultures, and forms of government.

■ The Revolt of the Netherlands, 1609. By the beginning of the seventeenth century, the union had broken apart and the northern provinces had won independence from Spain.

the northwestern provinces of Holland and Zeeland. By 1575 the Protestants had gained a stronghold that they would never relinquish. Prince William of Orange assumed the leadership of the two provinces that were now united against the tyranny of Philip's rule.

Spanish government was collapsing all over the Netherlands. William ruled in the north and the States-General, a parliamentary body composed of representatives from the separate provinces, ruled in the south. Margaret of Parma had resigned in disgust at Alba's tactics, and Alba had been relieved of his command when his tactics had failed. No one was in control of the Spanish army. The soldiers, who had gone years with only partial pay, now roamed the southern provinces looking for plunder. Brussels and Ghent both had been targets, and in 1576 the worst atrocities of all occurred when mutinous Spanish troops sacked Antwerp. One of the wealthiest cities in Europe, home to the most important mercantile and banking establishments in the world, Antwerp was torn apart like a roasted pig. The rampage lasted for days. When it ended, more than 7000 people had been slaughtered and nearly a third of the city burned to the ground.

The "Spanish fury" in Antwerp effectively ended Philip's rule over his Burgundian inheritance. The Protestants had established a permanent home in the north. The States-

General had established its ability to rule in the south, and Spanish policy had been totally discredited. To achieve a settlement, the Pacification of Ghent of 1576, the Spanish government conceded local autonomy in taxation, the central role of the States-General in legislation, and the immediate withdrawal of all Spanish troops from the Low Countries. Five southern provinces pledged to remain Catholic and to accept the authority of the king's regent. The rift between the provinces was soon followed by a permanent split. In 1581, one group of provinces voted to depose Philip II, while a second group decided to remain loyal to him.

Philip II refused to accept the dismemberment of his inheritance and refused to recognize the independent Dutch state that now existed in Holland. Throughout the 1580s and 1590s, military expeditions attempted to reunite the southern provinces and to conquer the northern ones. But Spanish military successes in the south were outweighed by the long-term failure of their objectives in the north. In 1609, Spain and the Netherlands concluded the Twelve Years' Truce, which tacitly recognized the existence of the state of Holland. By the beginning of the seventeenth century, Holland was not only an independent state, it was one of the greatest rivals of Spain and Portugal for the fruits of empire.

CHRONOLOGY
REVOLT OF THE NETHERLANDS

1559	Margaret of Parma named regent of the Netherlands
1566	Calvinist iconoclasm begins revolt
1567	Duke of Alba arrives in Netherlands and establishes Council of Blood
1568	Protestant Count Egmont executed
1572	Protestants capture Holland and Zeeland
1573	Alba relieved of his command
1576	Sack of Antwerp; pacification of Ghent
1581	Catholic and Protestant provinces split
1585	Spanish forces take Brussels and Antwerp
1609	Twelve Years' Truce

THE STRUGGLES IN EASTERN EUROPE

In eastern Europe, dynastic struggles outweighed the problems created by religious reform. Muscovy remained the bulwark of Eastern Orthodox Christianity, immune from the struggles over the Roman faith. Protestantism did spread into Poland-Lithuania, but unlike its reception in the west, its presence was tolerated by the Polish state. The spread of dissent was checked not by repression, but by a vigorous Catholic reformation led by the Jesuits. The domestic crises in the east were crises of state rather than of church. In Muscovy, the disputed succession that followed the death of Ivan the Terrible plunged the state into anarchy and civil war. Centuries of conflict between Poland-Lithuania and Muscovy came to a head with the Poles' desperate gamble to seize control of their massive eastern neighbor. War between Poland-Lithuania and Muscovy inevitably dominated the politics of the entire region. The Baltic states, of which Sweden was to become the most important, had their own ambitions for territory and economic gain. They soon joined the fray, making alliances in return for concessions and conquering small pieces of the mainland.

Kings and Diets in Poland

Until the end of the sixteenth century, Poland-Lithuania was the dominant power in the eastern part of Europe. It was economically healthy and militarily strong. Through its Baltic ports, especially Gdansk, Poland played a central role in international commerce and a dominant role in the northern grain trade. The vast size of the Polish state made defense difficult, and during the course of the sixteenth century it had lost lands to Muscovy in the east and to the Crimean Tatars in the south. But the permanent union with Lithuania in 1569 and the gradual absorption of the Baltic region of Livonia more

■ This sixteenth-century painting, *The Milch Cow,* satirically depicts the Netherlands [Flanders] as a cow in which the major European powers have a stake. Philip II of Spain is trying to ride the cow; Elizabeth I of England is attempting to feed it; William of Orange is trying to milk it; and the King of France is holding on to its tail while collecting its droppings.

■ Eastern Europe (ca. 1550) after the Consolidation of Russia and the Growth of Poland. The eastern part of Europe was still sparsely populated and economically underdeveloped.

than compensated for the losses. Matters of war and peace, of taxation and reform, were placed under the strict supervision of the Polish Diet, a parliamentary body that represented the Polish landed elite. The Diet also carefully controlled religious policy. Roman Catholicism was the principal religion in Poland, but the state tolerated numerous Protestant and Eastern creeds. In the Warsaw Confederation of 1573, the Polish gentry vowed, "We who differ in matters of religion will keep the peace among ourselves."

The biological failure of the Jagiellon monarchy in Poland ended that nation's most successful line of kings. Without a natural heir, the Polish nobility and gentry, who officially elected the monarch, had to peddle their throne among the princes of Europe. When Sigismund III (1587–1632) was elected to the Polish throne in 1587, he was also heir to the crown of Sweden. Sigismund accepted the prohibitions against religious repression that were outlined in the Warsaw Confederation, but he actively encouraged the establishment of Jesuit schools, the expansion of monastic orders, and the strengthening of the Roman Catholic Church.

All those policies enjoyed the approval of the Polish ruling classes. But the Diet would not support Sigismund's efforts to gain control of the Swedish crown, which he inherited in 1592 but from which he was deposed three years later. If Sigismund triumphed in Sweden, all Poland would get was a part-time monarch. The Polish Diet consistently refused to give the king

the funds he would need to invade Sweden successfully. Nevertheless, Sigismund mounted several unsuccessful campaigns against the Swedes that sapped Polish money and manpower.

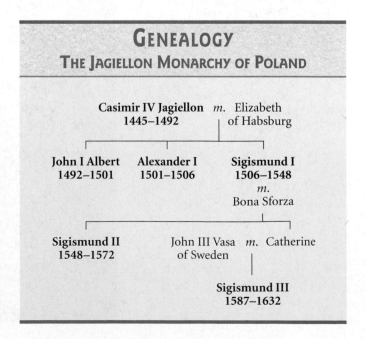

GENEALOGY
THE JAGIELLON MONARCHY OF POLAND

Casimir IV Jagiellon   *m.*   Elizabeth
1445–1492   of Habsburg

John I Albert   **Alexander I**   **Sigismund I**
1492–1501   1501–1506   1506–1548
                                        m.
                                     Bona Sforza

Sigismund II   John III Vasa   *m.* Catherine
1548–1572   of Sweden

Sigismund III
1587–1632

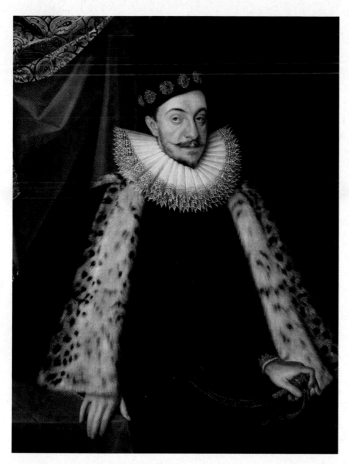

■ Portrait of Sigismund III, who was elected to the Polish throne in 1587. Also the hereditary heir to the Crown of Sweden, Sigismund brought Poland into war with Sweden in an effort to reclaim his crown.

Muscovy's Time of Troubles

The wars of Ivan the Great and Ivan the Terrible in the fifteenth and sixteenth centuries were waged to secure agricultural territory in the west and a Baltic port in the north; both objectives came at the expense of Poland-Lithuania. But following the death of Ivan the Terrible in 1584, the Muscovite state began to disintegrate. For years it had been held together only by conquest and fear. Ivan's conflicts with the boyars, the hereditary nobility, had created an aristocracy unwilling and unable to come to the aid of his successors. By 1601, the crown was plunged into a crisis of legitimacy known as the **Time of Troubles.** Ivan had murdered his heir in a fit of anger and left his half-witted son to inherit the throne, which led to a vacuum of power at the center as well as a struggle for the spoils of government. Private armies ruled great swaths of the state and pretenders to the crown—all claiming to be Dimitri, the lost brother of the last legitimate tsar—appeared everywhere. Ambitious groups of boyars backed their own claimants to the throne. So, too, did ambitious foreigners who eagerly sought to carve up Muscovite possessions.

Muscovy's Time of Troubles was Poland's moment of opportunity. While anarchy and civil war raged, Poland looked to regain the territory that it had lost to Muscovy during the previous century. Sigismund abandoned war with Sweden in order to intervene in the struggle for the Russian crown. Polish forces crossed into Muscovy and Sigismund's generals backed one of the strongest of the false Dimitris, but their plan to put him on the throne failed when he was assassinated. Sigismund used the death of the last false Dimitri as a pretext to assert his own claim to the Muscovite crown. More Polish forces poured across the frontier. In 1610, they took Moscow and Sigismund proclaimed himself tsar, intending to unite the two massive states.

The Russian boyars, so long divided, now rose against the Polish enemy. The Polish garrison in Moscow was starved into submission, and a native Russian, Michael Romanov (1613–1645), was chosen tsar by an assembly of landholders, the Zemsky Sobor. He made a humiliating peace with the Swedes—who had also taken advantage of the Time of Troubles to invade Muscovy's Baltic provinces—in return for Swedish assistance against the Poles. Intermittent fighting continued for another 20 years. In the end, Poland agreed to peace and a separate Muscovite state, but only in exchange for large territorial concessions.

The Rise of Sweden

Sweden's rise to power during the seventeenth century was as startling as it was swift. Until the Reformation, Sweden had been

■ The Rise of Russia. Russia grew through the addition of large units of territory comprising millions of square acres.

■ Michael Romanov was chosen to be tsar in 1613. His father, the Patriarch Philaret of Moscow, acted as joint ruler with Michael until the patriarch's death in 1633.

consolidated their hold on the Livonian coast. By occupying the most important ports on the Gulf of Finland, Sweden could control a sizable portion of the Muscovite trade. As the Swedes secured the northern Livonian ports, more of the Muscovy trade moved to the south and passed through Riga, which would have to be captured or blockaded if the Swedes were to control commerce in the eastern Baltic.

Sigismund's aggressive alliance with the Polish Jesuits persuaded the Swedish nobility that he would undermine their Lutheran church. Sigismund was deposed in favor of his uncle Charles IX (1604–1611). War with Poland resulted from Sigismund's efforts to regain the Swedish crown. The Swedes used the opportunity to blockade Riga and to occupy more Livonian territory. The Swedish navy was far superior to any force that the Poles could assemble, but on land Polish forces were masters. The Swedish invasion force suffered a crushing defeat and had to retreat to its coastal enclaves. The Poles now had an opportunity to retake all of Livonia but, as always, the Polish Diet was reluctant to finance Sigismund's wars. Furthermore, Sigismund had his eyes on a bigger prize. Rather than follow up its Swedish victory, Poland invaded Muscovy.

Meanwhile, the blockade of Riga and the assembly of a large Swedish fleet in the Baltic threatened Denmark. The Danes continued to claim sovereignty over Sweden and took the opportunity of the Polish-Swedish conflict to reassert it. In 1611, under the energetic leadership of the Danish king Christian IV (1588–1648), Denmark invaded Sweden from

■ The Rise of Sweden. For the only time in its history, Sweden acquired territories on the European mainland.

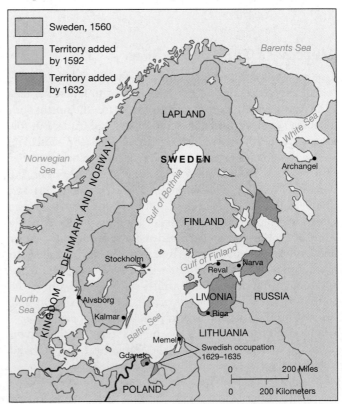

part of the Scandinavian confederation ruled by the Danes. Although the Swedes had a measure of autonomy, they were very much a junior partner in Baltic affairs. Denmark controlled the narrow sound that linked the Baltic with the North Sea, and its prosperity derived from the tolls it collected on imports and exports. When, in 1523, Gustav I Vasa led the uprising of the Swedish aristocracy that ended Danish domination, he won the right to rule over a poor, sparsely populated state with few towns or developed seaports. The Vasas ruled Sweden in conjunction with the aristocracy. Although the throne was hereditary, the part played by the nobility in elevating Gustav I Vasa (1523–1560) gave the nobles a powerful voice in Swedish affairs. Through the council of state, known as the Rad, the Swedish nobility exerted a strong check on the monarch. Sweden's aggressive foreign policy began accidentally. When in the 1550s the Teutonic Knights found themselves no longer capable of ruling in Livonia, the Baltic seaports that had been under their dominion scrambled for new alliances. Muscovy and Poland-Lithuania were the logical choices, but the town of Reval, an important outlet for Russian trade near the mouth of the Gulf of Finland, asked Sweden for protection. After some hesitation, since the occupation of territory on the southern shores of the Baltic would involve great expense, Sweden fortified Reval in 1560. A decade later, Swedish forces captured Narva, farther to the east, and

GENEALOGY
THE HOUSE OF VASA OF SWEDEN

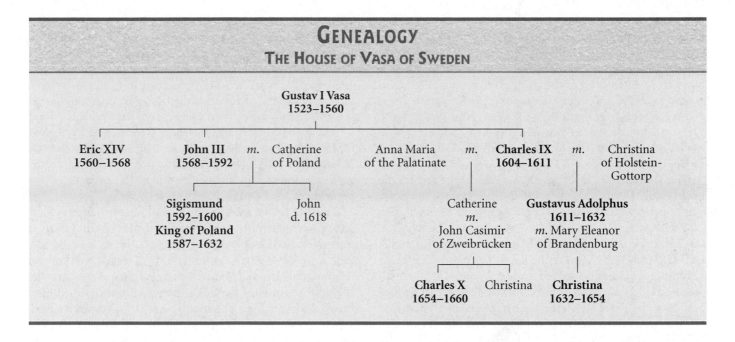

Gustav I Vasa
1523–1560

Eric XIV   **John III**   *m.*   Catherine   Anna Maria   *m.*   **Charles IX**   *m.*   Christina
1560–1568   **1568–1592**   of Poland   of the Palatinate   **1604–1611**   of Holstein-
                                                                                                        Gottorp

Sigismund   John   Catherine   **Gustavus Adolphus**
1592–1600   d. 1618   *m.*   **1611–1632**
King of Poland   John Casimir   *m.* Mary Eleanor
1587–1632   of Zweibrücken   of Brandenburg

Charles X   Christina   **Christina**
1654–1660   **1632–1654**

---

both the east and the west. The Danes captured the towns of Kalmar and Alvsborg and threatened to take Stockholm. To end the Danish war, Sweden accepted humiliating terms in 1613, renouncing all claims to the northern coasts and recognizing Danish control of the Arctic trading route.

Paradoxically, the setbacks became the springboard for Swedish success. Fear of the Danes led both the English and the Dutch into alliances with Sweden. The countries all shared Protestant interests, and the English were heavily committed to the Muscovy trade, which was still an important part of Swedish commerce. Fear of the Poles had a similar effect upon Muscovy. In 1609, the Swedes agreed to send 5000 troops to Muscovy to help repel the Polish invasion. In return, Muscovy agreed to cede to Sweden its Baltic possessions. This was accomplished in 1617, giving Sweden complete control of the Gulf of Finland.

In 1611, during the middle of the Danish war, Charles IX died and was succeeded by his son Gustavus Adolphus (1611–1632). Unlike his father and cousin before him, who had come by chance to the Swedish throne, Gustavus Adolphus was raised to be king. Gruff and affable by turns, he was one of the leading Protestant princes of his day, in every way a match for Christian IV of Denmark. Gustavus's greatest skills were military, and he inherited an ample navy and an effective army. Unlike nearly every other European state, Sweden raised its forces from its own citizens. Gustavus introduced new weapons such as the light mobile gun and reshaped his army into standard-size squadrons and regiments, which were easier to administer and deploy.

The calamitous wars inherited from his father occupied Gustavus during the early years of his reign. He was forced to conclude the humiliating peace with the Danes in 1613 and to go to war with the Russians in 1614 in order to secure the Baltic coastal estates that had been promised in 1609. Gustavus's first military initiative was to resume war with Poland in order to force Sigismund to renounce his claim to the Swedish throne. In 1621, Gustavus landed in Livonia and within two weeks had captured Riga, the capstone of Sweden's Baltic ambitions. Occupation of Riga increased Swedish control of the Muscovy trade and deprived Denmark of a significant portion of its customs duties. Gustavus now claimed Riga as a Swedish port and successfully demanded that ships sailing from there pay tolls to Sweden rather than Denmark. The capture of Riga firmly established Sweden as a coequal Baltic power.

By the mid-seventeenth century, the Sweden of Gustavus Adolphus was well on its way to international prominence. The capture of Riga gave Sweden complete control of the eastern Baltic and ended Polish pretensions to the Swedish throne. A negotiated settlement with the Danes over the collection of tolls enhanced Swedish prestige and increased Sweden's commercial prosperity. Moreover, Gustavus's marriage into the family of the Protestant rulers of Prussia gave Sweden a presence in Germany as well. For the time being, Sweden faced east. But the storm clouds of religious warfare were already bursting over the Holy Roman Empire. Gustavus Adolphus now took his place among the Protestant princes of Europe, and Sweden ranked among the leading Protestant powers.

THE THIRTY YEARS' WAR, 1618–1648

Perhaps it was just a matter of time before the isolated conflicts that dotted the corners of Europe were joined together. In 1609, Spain and the Dutch Republic had signed a truce that was to last until 1621. In more than 40 years of nearly continuous fighting, the Dutch had carved out a state in the northern Netherlands. They used the truce to consolidate their position and increase their prosperity, largely at the expense of

Spain and Portugal. Thus, to the insult of rebellion was added the injury of commercial competition. Spain had reluctantly accepted Dutch independence, but Philip III (1598–1621) never abandoned the objective of recovering his Burgundian inheritance. By the start of the seventeenth century, Philip had good reasons for hope. Beginning in the 1580s, Spanish forces had reconquered the southern provinces of the Netherlands. The prosperous towns of Brussels, Antwerp, and Ghent were again under Spanish control, and they provided a springboard for another invasion.

The Twelve Years' Truce gave Spain time to prepare for the final assault. During this time, Philip III attempted to resolve all of Spain's other European conflicts so that he could then give full attention to a resumption of the Dutch war. Circumstance smiled upon his efforts. In 1603, the pacific James I (1603–1625) came to the English throne. Secure in his island state, James I desired peace among all Christian princes. He quickly concluded the war with Spain that had begun with the invasion of the Spanish Armada and entered into negotiations to marry his heir to a Spanish princess. In 1610, the bellicose Henry IV of France was felled by an assassin's knife. French plans to renew war with Spain were abandoned with the accession of the eight-year-old Louis XIII (1610–1643). As the sands of the Twelve Years' Truce ran out, Spain and the Netherlands readied for war. But not even the greatest empire in Europe could control its own destiny. War was in the air all over the Continent, and not everyone could wait until 1621. The **Thirty Years' War** was about to begin.

Bohemia Revolts

The Peace of Augsburg had served the German states well. The principle that the religion of the ruler was the religion of the state complicated the political life of the Holy Roman Empire, but it also pacified it. Although rulers had the right to enforce uniformity on their subjects, in practice many of the larger states tolerated more than one religion. By the beginning of the seventeenth century, Catholicism and Protestantism had achieved a rough equality within the German states, symbolized by the fact that of the seven electors who chose the Holy Roman Emperor, three were Catholic, three Protestant, and the seventh was the emperor himself, acting as king of Bohemia. The situation was not unwelcome to the leaders of the Austrian Habsburg family who succeeded Emperor Charles V. By necessity, the eastern Habsburgs were more tolerant than their Spanish kinfolk. Protestants fought the Ottomans with as much zeal as did Catholics, and the Ottomans were the empire's more potent enemy. The unofficial policy of toleration not only helped the Austrian Habsburgs defend their state, it allowed them to expand it. The head of their house was elected king of Bohemia and king of Hungary, both states with large Protestant populations.

A Fatal Election. In 1617, Mathias, the childless Holy Roman Emperor, began making plans for his cousin, Ferdinand Habsburg, to succeed him. In order to ensure a Catholic majority among the electors, the emperor relinquished his Bohemian title and pressed for Ferdinand's election as the new king of Bohemia. Ferdinand was Catholic, very devout, and very committed. He had been educated by Jesuits and practiced what had been preached to him. On his own estates, Ferdinand abandoned the policy of toleration. Jesuit schools were founded and the precepts of the Council of Trent were enforced. Protestant preachers were barred from their offices, Protestant books were publicly burned, and thousands of common people were forced to flee, many into nearby Bohemia, where Protestants constituted the majority of the population.

Thus Ferdinand's election as king of Bohemia was no foregone conclusion. Although in the end the Protestant nobles of Bohemia could not prevent his election, they forced the new king to accept the strictest limitations upon his political and religious powers. But once elected, Ferdinand had not the slightest intention of honoring the provisions that had been thrust upon him. His opponents were equally strong willed. When Ferdinand violated Protestant religious liberties, a group of noblemen marched to the royal palace in Prague in

CHRONOLOGY The Thirty Years' War	
1618	Defenestration of Prague
1619	Ferdinand Habsburg elected Holy Roman Emperor; Frederick of the Palatinate accepts the crown of Bohemia
1620	Catholic victory at battle of White Mountain
1621	End of Twelve Years' Truce; war between Spain and Netherlands
1626	Danes form Protestant alliance under Christian IV
1627	Spain declares bankruptcy
1630	Gustavus Adolphus leads Swedish forces into Germany
1631	Sack of Magdeburg; Protestant victory at Breitenfeld
1632	Protestant victory at Lützen; death of Gustavus Adolphus
1635	France declares war on Spain
1640	Portugal secedes from Spain
1643	Battle of Rocroi; French forces repel Spaniards
1648	Peace of Westphalia

WAR IS HELL

No source has better captured the brutality of the Thirty Years' War than the novel Simplicissimus *(1669). In a series of loosely connected episodes, the hero (whose name means "the simplest of the simple") is snatched from his village to serve in marauding armies whose confrontations with local villagers are usually more horrifying than the episode narrated here.*

Focus Questions

How do the peasants respond to the troopers' actions? What does this passage suggest about the breadth of the average villager's experience?

These troopers were even now ready to march, and had the pastor fastened by a rope to lead him away. Some cried, "Shoot him down, the rogue!" Others would have money from him. But he, lifting up his hands to heaven, begged, for the sake of the Last Judgment, for forbearance and Christian compassion, but in vain; for one of them rode down and dealt him such a blow on the head that he fell flat, and commended his soul to God. Nor did the remainder of the captured peasants fare any better. But even when it seemed these troopers, in their cruel tyranny, had clean lost their wits, came such a swarm of armed peasants out of the wood, that it seemed a wasps'-nest had been stirred. And these began to yell so frightfully and so furiously to attack with sword and musket that all my hair stood on end; and never had I been at such a merrymaking before: for the peasants of the Spessart and the Vogelsberg are as little wont as are the Hessians and men of the Sauerland and the Black Forest to let themselves be crowed over on their own dunghill. So away went the troopers, and not only left behind the cattle they had captured, but threw away bag and baggage also, and so cast all their booty to the winds lest themselves should become booty for the peasants: yet some of them fell into their hands. This sport took from me well-nigh all desire to see the world, for I thought, if 'tis all like this, then is the wilderness far more pleasant.

From Hans Von Grimmelshausen, The Adventurous Simplicissimus.

May 1618, found two of the king's chief advisers, and hurled them out of an upper-story window. The officials' lives—if not their dignity—were preserved by the pile of manure in which they landed.

The Defenestration of Prague, as the incident came to be known, initiated a Protestant counteroffensive throughout the Habsburg lands. Fear of Ferdinand's policies led to Protestant uprisings in Hungary as well as Bohemia. Those who seized control of the government declared Ferdinand deposed and the throne vacant, but they had no candidate to accept their crown. When Emperor Mathias died in 1619, the stalemate was broken. Ferdinand succeeded to the imperial title as Ferdinand II (1619–1637) and Frederick V, one of the Protestant electors, accepted the Bohemian crown.

Frederick V, the "Winter King."

Frederick was a sincere but weak Calvinist whose credentials were much stronger than his abilities. His mother was a daughter of Prince William of Orange and his wife, Elizabeth, a daughter of James I of England. It was widely believed that it was Elizabeth's resolution that she would "rather eat sauerkraut with a King than roast meat with an Elector" that decided the issue. No decision could have been more disastrous for the fate of Europe. Frederick ruled a geographically divided German state known as the Palatinate. One hundred miles separated the two segments of his lands, but both were strategically important. The Lower Palatinate bordered on the Catholic Spanish Netherlands and the Upper Palatinate on Catholic Bavaria.

Once Frederick accepted the Bohemian crown, he was faced with a war on three fronts. It was over almost before it began. Ferdinand II had no difficulty enlisting allies to recover the Bohemian crown, since he could pay them with the spoils of Frederick's lands. Spanish troops from the Netherlands occupied the Lower Palatinate, and Bavarian troops occupied the Upper Palatinate. Frederick, on the other hand, met rejection wherever he turned. Neither the Dutch nor the English would send more than token aid—both had advised him against breaking the imperial peace. The Lutheran princes of Germany would not enter into a war between Calvinists and Catholics, especially after Ferdinand II promised to protect the Bohemian Lutherans.

At the Battle of the White Mountain in 1620, Ferdinand's Catholic forces annihilated Frederick's army. Frederick and Elizabeth fled north, first to Denmark and then to Holland. Bohemia was left to face the wrath of Ferdinand, the victorious king and emperor. The retribution was horrible. Mercenaries who had fought for Ferdinand II were allowed to sack Prague for a week. Elective monarchy was abolished, and Bohemia became part of the hereditary Habsburg lands. Free peasants were enserfed and subjected to imperial law. Those nobles who had supported Frederick lost their lands and their privileges. Calvinism was repressed and thoroughly rooted out, consolidating forever the Catholic character of Bohemia. Frederick's estates were carved up and his rights as elector transferred to the Catholic duke of Bavaria. The Battle of the White Mountain was a turning point in the history of central Europe.

The War Widens

For the Habsburgs, religious and dynastic interests were inseparable. Ferdinand II and Philip III of Spain fought for their beliefs and for their patrimony. Their victory gave them more than they could have expected: Ferdinand swallowed up Bohemia and strengthened his position in the empire, and Philip gained possession of a vital link in his supply route between Italy and the Netherlands. The Habsburgs were now more dangerous than ever. Ferdinand's aggressive Catholicism threatened the Protestant princes of Germany, who prudently began to seek allies outside the empire. Spanish expansion threatened France. The occupation of the Lower Palatinate placed a ring of Spanish armies around the French borders from the Pyrenees to the Low Countries. The French too searched for allies. But French opinion remained divided over which was the greater evil: Spain or Protestantism.

The Danes Respond.   Frederick, now in Holland, refused to accept the judgment of battle. He lobbied for a grand alliance to repel the Spaniards from the Lower Palatinate and to restore the religious balance in the empire. Although his personal cause met with little sympathy, his political logic was impeccable, especially after Spain again declared war upon the Dutch in 1621. A grand Protestant alliance—secretly supported by the French—brought together England, Holland, a number of German states, and Denmark. It was the Danes who led this potentially powerful coalition. In 1626, a large Danish army under the command of King Christian IV engaged imperial forces on German soil. But Danish forces could not match the superior numbers and the superior leadership of the Catholic mercenary forces under the command of the ruthless and brilliant Count Albrecht von Wallenstein (1583–1634). In 1629, the Danes withdrew from the empire and sued for peace.

If the Catholic victory at the White Mountain in 1620 threatened the well-being of German Protestantism, the Catholic triumph over the Danes threatened its survival. More powerful than ever, Ferdinand II determined to turn the religious clock back to the state of affairs that had existed when the Peace of Augsburg was concluded in 1555. He demanded that all lands that had then been Catholic but had since become Protestant be returned to the fold. He also proclaimed that as the Peace of Augsburg made no provision for the toleration of Calvinists, they would no longer be tolerated in the empire. Those policies together constituted a virtual revolution in the religious affairs of the German states, and they proved impossible to impose. Ferdinand succeeded in only one thing—he united Lutherans and Calvinists against him.

Protestant Gains.   In 1630, King Gustavus Adolphus of Sweden decided to enter the German conflict. To protect Swedish interests, he reasoned, he must defend the Protestant states of northern Germany. Moreover, France was willing to pay much of the cost of a war against Ferdinand. The French too felt the pressure of increasing imperial and Spanish power. Gustavus Adolphus had more success gaining the support of Catholic France than he did gaining the support of the Protestant German princes. Saxony and Brandenburg, the two largest states, feared the consequences of renewed war. Gustavus believed that he could defend the north German states from Ferdinand's

■ Gustavus Adolphus of Sweden, shown at the battle of Breitenfeld in 1631. The battle was the first important Protestant victory of the Thirty Years' War. Gustavus died on the battlefield at Lützen in the following year.

FIRE AND SWORD

No event of the Thirty Years' War had a greater effect on public opinion than the annihilation of the Protestant city of Magdeburg in 1631. Dozens of pamphlets and woodcuts, including this anonymous account, detailed the slaughter of civilians and the devastation of property. It was commonly believed that neither a human nor an animal escaped the destruction.

Focus Questions

What motivated those who destroyed Magdeburg?
What is the writer trying to achieve with this account?

Thus it came about that the city and all its inhabitants fell into the hands of the enemy, whose violence and cruelty were due in part to their common hatred of the adherents of the Augsburg Confession, and in part to their being imbittered by the chain shot which had been fired at them and by the derision and insults that the Magdeburgers had heaped upon them from the ramparts.

Then was there naught but beating and burning, plundering, torture, and murder. Most especially was every one of the enemy bent on securing much booty. When a marauding party entered a house, if its master had anything to give he might thereby purchase respite and protection for himself and his family till the next man, who also wanted something, should come along. . . .

Thus in a single day this noble and famous city, the pride of the whole country, went up in fire and smoke; and the remnant of its citizens, with their wives and children, were taken prisoners and driven away by the enemy with a noise of weeping and wailing that could be heard from afar, while the cinders and ashes from the town were carried by the wind to Wanzleben, Egeln, and still more distant places. . . .

---

aggression and by doing so protect Sweden's Baltic empire. "I seek not my own advantage in this war, nor any gain save the security of my Kingdom," he lectured the reluctant Germans. It was a farsighted strategy. In fact, the only thing he could not foresee when he landed in Germany early in 1630 was how successful his intervention would be.

While Gustavus Adolphus struggled to construct his alliance, imperial forces continued their triumphant progress. In 1631 they besieged, captured, and put to the torch the town of Magdeburg. In a war noted for cruelty between combatants and atrocities against civilians, the destruction of Magdeburg set new standards. Perhaps three-fourths of the 40,000 inhabitants of the town were slaughtered—"in the midst of a horrible din of heart-rending shrieks and cries they were tortured and put to death in so cruel a manner that no words would suffice to describe nor no tears to bewail it," was the report in one pamphlet. The sack of Magdeburg marked a turning point in Protestant fortunes. It gave the international Protestant community a unifying symbol that enhanced Gustavus's military efforts. Hundreds of pamphlets, woodcuts, and newspaper accounts brought the horror of Magdeburg home to Protestants throughout the Continent. Brandenburg and Saxony joined Gustavus Adolphus, not only enlarging his forces, but allowing him to open a second front in Bohemia. He would soon have 140,000 men under his command, only 13,000 of whom were Swedish. In the autumn of 1631, the combination overwhelmed the imperial armies. Gustavus won a decisive triumph at Breitenfeld, while the Saxons occupied Prague. For the first time since 1618, Protestant forces were ascendant, and they brought the war into the Catholic heartland of the empire.

Gustavus Adolphus lost no time in pressing his advantage. The Swedes marched west to the Rhine, easily conquering the richest of the Catholic cities and retaking the Lower Palatinate. In early 1632, Protestant forces plundered Bavaria. It was the Bavarian ruler Maximilian who had gained most from the years of war. His troops had occupied the Upper Palatinate, and he had received Frederick's rights as imperial elector in return for support of Ferdinand. Moreover, Maximilian had played a double game of negotiating with the French for neutrality and with the emperor for the spoils of victory. So there was poetic justice when Maximilian's state was invaded, his castles looted, and his lands plundered. But there was no justice at all for the wretched inhabitants of that stronghold of German Catholicism. Town and countryside were laid waste. Not until the winter of 1632 did the armies of Gustavus and Wallenstein finally meet. At the battle of Lützen the Swedes won the field but lost their beloved king. Wounded in the leg, the back, and the head, Gustavus Adolphus died. In less than two years he had decisively transformed the course of the war and the course of Europe's future. Protestant forces now occupied most of central and northern Germany. Ferdinand's ability to redraw the religious map of the empire was at an end.

MAP DISCOVERY

Percentage Loss:

| No Change | Up to 10 | 11–20 | 21–30 | 31–40 | 41–50 | Over 50 |

Population Loss in Germany During the Thirty Years' War

Notice the pattern of population loss during the war. Where was it heaviest? Where was it lightest? Based on the chapter discussion, how might the intervention of Sweden into the War help explain this pattern?

of the war involved the resumption of the century-old struggle between France and Spain. When the Twelve Years' Truce expired in 1621, Spain again declared war upon the Dutch. Philip III's hopes of concentrating all his resources against Holland had been disappointed by the outbreak of war in central Europe. Not until after the Bohemian revolt had been repressed did the Spanish army begin the long, laborious process of besieging the well-fortified and well-defended towns of the Netherlands. The resumption of war in the Netherlands, combined with the continued successes of Habsburg forces in central Europe, convinced Louis XIII and his chief minister, Cardinal Richelieu, that the time for active French involvement in European affairs was at hand. Throughout the early stages of the war, France had secretly aided anti-Habsburg forces. The time had come to take an open stand. In 1635, France declared war on Spain.

Neither country was prepared for large-scale military action, and neither could afford it. The war resembled nothing so much as two punch-drunk fighters pounding each other, both receiving as much punishment as they inflicted. France took the offensive first, invading the Spanish Netherlands. In 1636, a Spanish army struck back, pushing to within 25 miles of Paris before it was repelled. Both sides soon began to search for a settlement, but pride prevented them from laying down their gloves. Spain toppled first. Its economy in shambles and its citizens in revolt over high prices and higher taxes, it could no longer maintain its many-fronted war. The Swedes again defeated imperial forces in Germany, the Dutch destroyed much of Spain's Atlantic fleet in 1639, and the Portuguese rose up against the union of crowns that had brought them nothing

The Long Quest for Peace

The Thirty Years' War was barely half over when Gustavus Adolphus fell at Lützen. But from that time forward, its central European phase receded in importance. The final stages

■ This painting by Jan Brueghel (1568–1625) and Sebastien Vranx (1573–1647) evokes the ravaging of the country-side by the belligerent armies between battles in the Thirty Years' War.

but expense and the loss of crucial portions of their empire. In 1640, the Portuguese regained their independence. In 1643, Spain gambled once more on a knockout blow against the French. But at the battle of Rocroi, exhausted French troops held out and the Spanish invasion failed.

By then the desire for peace was universal. Most of the main combatants had long since perished: Philip III, ever optimistic, in 1621; Frederick V, an exile to the end, in 1632; Gustavus Adolphus, killed at Lützen in the same year; Wallenstein, murdered by order of Ferdinand II in 1634; Ferdinand himself in 1637; and Louis XIII in 1643, five days before the French triumph at Rocroi. Those who succeeded them had not the same passions, and after so many decades the longing for peace was the strongest emotion on the Continent. At the beginning of 1648, Spain and the Netherlands concluded their 80 years of fighting. The bilateral agreement broke the logjam. One by one, the combatants agreed to end their hostilities with one another, and soon the stage was set for a Continentwide settlement.

A series of agreements, collectively known as the Peace of Westphalia, established the outlines of the political geography of Europe for the next century. Its focus was on the Holy Roman Empire, and it reflected Protestant successes in the final two decades of war. Sweden gained further territories on the Baltic, making it master of the north German ports. France, too, gained in territory and prestige. It kept the vital towns in the Lower Palatinate through which Spanish men and material had moved, and though it did not agree to come to terms with Spain immediately, France's fear of encirclement was at an end. The Dutch gained statehood

through official recognition by Spain and through the power they had displayed in building and maintaining an overseas empire.

Territorial boundaries were reestablished as they had existed in 1624, giving the Habsburgs control of both Bohemia and Hungary. The independence of the Swiss cantons was now officially recognized, as were the rights of Calvinists to the protection of the Peace of Augsburg, which again was to govern the religious affairs of the empire. Two of the larger German states were strengthened to balance the emperor's power. Bavaria was allowed to retain the Upper Palatinate, and Brandenburg, which ceded some of its coastal territory to Sweden, gained extensive territories in the east.

The emperor's political control over the German states was also weakened. German rulers were given independent authority over their states, and the imperial Diet, rather than the emperor, was empowered to settle disputes. Thus weakened, future emperors ruled in the Habsburg territorial lands with little ability to control, influence, or even arbitrate German affairs. The judgment that the Holy Roman Empire was neither holy, nor Roman, nor an empire was now irrevocably true.

Conclusion

The Peace of Westphalia put the pieces of the map of European states back together. Protestantism and Catholicism now coexisted and there was to be little further change in the geography of religion. The northwest of Europe—England, Holland, Scandinavia, and the north German states—was

■ The Peace of Westphalia, 1648. The agreement recognized the new boundaries of European states that included an independent Portugal and the United Netherlands. It also recognized the growth of the Ottoman Empire into the Balkans.

Protestant, while the south was Catholic. The empire of the German peoples was at an end, the Austro-Hungarian Empire at a beginning. Holland and Sweden had become international powers; Spain and Denmark faded from prominence. Muscovy began a long period of isolation from the west, attempting to restore a semblance of government to its people. But if the negotiators at Westphalia could resolve the political and religious ambitions that gave rise to a century of nearly continuous warfare, they could do nothing to eradicate the effects of war itself. The devastation of humanity in the name of God with which the reform of religion had begun was

exhausted. The costs were horrific. The population of Germany fell from 15 million in 1600 to 11 million in 1650. The armies brought destruction of all kinds in their wake. Plague again raged in Europe—the town of Augsburg lost 18,000 inhabitants in the early 1630s. Famine, too, returned to a continent that 50 years earlier had been self-sufficient in grain. The war played havoc with all of the economies that it touched. Inflation, devaluation of coinage, and huge public and private debts were all directly attributable to the years of fighting. And the toll taken on the spirit of those generations that never knew peace is incalculable.

QUESTIONS FOR REVIEW

1. How was Henry IV able to bring peace to France after decades of civil war?
2. What were the political and religious connections between the Armada launched against England by Philip II and the revolt of the Netherlands?
3. How did Sweden rise to become one of Europe's great powers in the first half of the seventeenth century?
4. How did religion help spark and spread the Thirty Years' War?
5. What were the effects of the Peace of Westphalia on political arrangements in the heart of Europe?

KEY TERMS

Edict of Nantes, *p. 429*

French wars of religion, *p. 422*

Huguenots, *p. 426*

politiques, *p. 427*

Spanish Armada, *p. 430*

Thirty Years' War, *p. 440*

Time of Troubles, *p. 437*

DISCOVERING WESTERN CIVILIZATION ONLINE

You can obtain more information about Europe at war at the Websites listed below. See also the Companion Website that accompanies this text, www.ablongman.com/kishlansky, which contains an online study guide and additional resources.

The Crises of the Western States

Internet Modern History Sourcebook: Early Modern West

www.fordham.edu/halsall/mod/modsbook1.html#Conflict
Links to documents on the French wars of religion, the invasion of the Spanish Armada, and the Thirty Years' War.

WebMuseum: The Northern Renaissance (1500–1615)

www.ibiblio.org/wm/paint/tl/north-ren/
Links to pictures and portraits from the late sixteenth and early seventeenth centuries.

Pieter Bruegel the Elder: *The Triumph of Death*

www.ibiblio.org/wm/paint/auth/bruegel/death.jpg
A Web page depicting Peter Brueghel's *Triumph of Death*, one of the most evocative paintings of the destruction wrought by warfare in early modern Europe.

The Thirty Years' War, 1618–1648

The Avalon Project: Treaty of Westphalia

www.yale.edu/lawweb/avalon/westphal.htm
The full text of the Treaty of Westphalia that ended the Thirty Years' War.

SUGGESTIONS FOR FURTHER READING

General Reading

M. S. Anderson, *The Origins of the Modern European State System, 1494–1618* (London: Longman, 1998). A survey of developments stressing war and diplomacy across all of Europe.

Jan de Vries, *The European Economy in an Age of Crisis* (Cambridge: Cambridge University Press, 1976). A comprehensive study of economic development, including long-distance trade and commercial change.

J. H. Elliott, *Europe Divided, 1559–1598* (New York: Harper & Row, 1968). An outstanding synthesis of European politics in the second half of the sixteenth century.

Geoffrey Parker, *Europe in Crisis, 1598–1648* (London: William Collins and Sons, 1979). Compelling study of European states in the early seventeenth century.

The Crises of the Western States

Susan Brigden, *New Worlds, Lost Worlds: The Rule of the Tudors, 1485–1603* (New York: Viking, 2001). The latest volume in the new Penguin History of Britain series.

J. A. Guy, *Tudor England* (Oxford: Oxford University Press, 1988). A magisterial survey by the leading scholar of Tudor England.

Henry Kamen, *Spain, 1469–1714* (London: Longman, 1983). A thorough survey with valuable interpretations.

Robert Kingdon, *Myths about the St. Bartholomew's Day Massacres, 1572–76* (Cambridge, MA: Harvard University Press, 1988). A study of the impact of a central event in the history of France.

R. J. Knecht, *The French Civil Wars, 1562–1598* (New York: Pearson Education, 2000). A compact survey of the religious, social, and political dimensions of the conflicts that raged in France through the second half of the sixteenth century.

John Lynch, *Spain, 1516–1598: From Nation State to World Empire* (Cambridge, MA: Blackwell, 1994). An up-to-date survey.

Garrett Mattingly, *The Armada* (Boston: Houghton Mifflin, 1959). Still the classic account, despite recent reinterpretations.

Geoffrey Parker, *The Dutch Revolt* (London: Penguin Books, 1977). An outstanding account of the tangle of events that comprised the revolts of the Netherlands.

Geoffrey Parker, *Philip II* (Boston: Little, Brown, 1978). The best introduction.

Michael Roberts, *Gustavus Adolphus and the Rise of Sweden* (London: English Universities Press, 1973). A highly readable account of Sweden's rise to power.

C. V. Wedgwood, *William the Silent, William of Nassau, Prince of Orange, 1533–1584* (New York: Norton, 1968). A stylish biography.

Alison Weir, *Elizabeth the Queen* (London: J. Cape, 1998). A lively biography of the great queen.

The Struggles in Eastern Europe

David Kirby, *Northern Europe in the Early Modern Period: The Baltic World, 1492–1772* (London: Longman, 1990). The best single volume on Baltic politics.

S. F. Platonov, *The Time of Troubles* (Lawrence: University Press of Kansas, 1970). A good narrative of the disintegration of the Muscovite state.

Michael Roberts, *The Swedish Imperial Experience* (Cambridge: Cambridge University Press, 1979). Reflections on Swedish history by the preeminent historian of early modern Sweden.

The Thirty Years' War

J. H. Elliott, *Richelieu and Olivares* (Cambridge: Cambridge University Press, 1984). A comparison of statesmen and statesmanship in the early seventeenth century.

Peter Limm, *The Thirty Years' War* (London: Longman, 1984). An excellent brief survey with documents.

Geoffrey Parker, ed., *The Thirty Years' War*, 2d ed. (London: Routledge, 1997). A revised edition of the standard survey of the conflict.

For a list of additional titles related to this chapter's topics, please see http://www.ablongman.com/kishlansky.

Chapter **15**

THE EXPERIENCES OF LIFE IN EARLY MODERN EUROPE, 1500–1650

Chapter Outline

Ordinary people were rarely the subject of artistic work in the early modern era since most works of art were commissioned by the wealthy. But artist Pieter Brueghel was fascinated by the common folk and depicted them performing many different activities. Turn the page to catch a glimpse of real life during the sixteenth century in The Visual Record. ➤

HAYMAKING

Agriculture in a European Community

It is summer in the Low Countries. The trees are full, the meadows green; flowers rise in clumps and bushes hang heavy with fruit. The day has dawned brightly for haymaking. Yesterday the long meadow was mowed, and today the hay will be gathered and the first fruits and vegetables of the season harvested. From throughout the village families come together to labor. Twice each summer the grass is cut, dried, and stacked. Some of it will be left in the fields for the animals until autumn; some will be carried into large lofts and stored for the winter.

The scene of communal farming shown here was repeated with little variation throughout Europe in the early modern era. The village pictured is fairly prosperous with at least three horses and a large wheeled cart in view. Horses were still a luxury for farmers; they could be used for transportation as well as labor, but they were weaker than oxen and had to be fed grain rather than grass. The houses of the village also suggest comfort. The one at the far right is typical. It contains one floor for living and a loft for storage. The chimney separates a kitchen in the back from the long hall where the family works, sleeps, and entertains itself. The bed—it was not uncommon for there to be only one for the whole family—would be near the fireplace, and would be restuffed with straw after the harvest. The long end of the hall, farthest from heat and light, would be home to the family's animals once winter set in. But in summer it was a luxurious space where children could play or parents could claim a little privacy.

The church is easily distinguished by its steeple and is made of brick. The steeple has 16 windows, probably all set with expensive glass and even some stained glass. The church would have been built over several generations at considerable cost to the villagers. Even the most prosperous houses in the far meadow are made of timber and thatch. The layout of the buildings shows how the village must have grown. The original settlement was all on the rise above the church. The houses nearer the center of the picture were added later, perhaps to allow the sons of the more prosperous village farmers to begin their own families before their parents' deaths.

In the center of the scene are a large number of laborers. Four men with pitchforks load the cart while two women sweep the hay that falls back into new piles. Throughout the field, men and women, distinguished only by their clothing, rake hay into large stacks for successive loadings of the cart. At least 25 individuals work at these tasks. Men perform the heaviest work of loading the haycart and hammering the scythes while men and women share all the other work. Although no children appear in the scene, some are undoubtedly at work picking berries and beans.

■ Detail of women laborers.

■ *Haymaking* (ca. 1565) by Pieter Brueghel.

The scenes of physical labor remind us that the life of ordinary people in the early modern period was neither romantic nor despondent, neither quaint nor primitive. It had its own joys and sorrows, its own triumphs and failures, its own measures of progress and decay. By today's standards, a sixteenth-century prince endured greater material hardships than a twentieth-century welfare recipient. There was no running water, no central heating, no lavatories, no electricity. There was no relief for toothache, headache, or numbing pain. Travel was dangerous and exhausting. There was no protection from the open air, and many nights were spent on the bare ground. Waiting for winds to sail was more tedious than waiting to board a plane. Entertainment was sparse, and the court jester would have been little match for stereo and video. Though we cannot help but be struck by the differences, we will not understand very much about the experience of life in sixteenth-century Europe if we judge it by our own standard of living.

Looking Ahead

In this chapter, we will examine the social and economic conditions of early modern European society, dominated as it was by extreme change, and often, hardship. We will see how population growth put pressure on the European economy and how the rich became richer as food prices rose. We will also see how European governments were overwhelmed by changes they could only dimly perceive. ➤

ECONOMIC LIFE

There was no typical sixteenth-century European. Travelers' accounts and ambassadors' reports indicate that contemporaries were constantly surprised by the habits and possessions of other Europeans. Language, custom, geography, and material conditions separated peoples in one place from those in another. Contrasts between social groups were more striking still. A Muscovite boyar had more in common with an English nobleman than either had with his country's peasants. A Spanish goldsmith and a German brass maker lived remarkably similar lives when compared to that of a shepherd anywhere in Europe. No matter how carefully historians attempt to distinguish between country and town life, between social or occupational groups, or between men and women, they are still smoothing out edges that are very rough, still turning individuals into aggregates, still sacrificing the particular for the general. No French peasant family ever had 3.5 children even if, on average, they all did. There was no typical sixteenth-century European.

But there were experiences that most Europeans shared and common structures through which their activities were channeled that separated them from their predecessors and their successors. There was a distinctive sixteenth-century experience that we can easily discern and that they could dimly perceive. Much of it was a natural progression in which one generation improved upon the situation of another. Agriculture increased: more land was cleared, more crops were grown, and better tools were crafted. Some of the experience was natural regression. Irreplaceable resources were lost: more trees were felled, more soil was eroded, and more fresh water was polluted. But some of what was distinctive about sixteenth-century life resulted from dynamic changes in economic and social conditions. The century-long population explosion and increase in commodity prices fundamentally altered people's lives. Not since the Black Death had Europe experienced so thorough a transformation in its economic development and its social organization. Change and reactions to change became dominant themes of everyday life.

Rural Life

In the early modern era, as much as 90 percent of the European population lived on farms or in small towns in which farming was the principal occupation. Villages were small and relatively isolated, even in densely populated regions such as Italy and the Low Countries. They might range in size from 100 families, as was common in France and Spain, to fewer than 20 families, which was the average size of Hungarian villages. The villages, large or small, prosperous or poor, were the bedrock of the sixteenth-century state. A surplus peasant population fed the insatiable appetite of towns for laborers and of crowns for soldiers. The manor, the parish, and the rural administrative district were the institutional infrastructures of Europe. Each organized the peasantry for its own purposes. Manorial rents supported the lifestyle of the nobility; parish tithes supported the works of the Church; local taxes supported the power of the state. Rents, tithes, and taxes easily absorbed more than half of the wealth produced by the land. From the remaining half, the peasants had to make provisions for their present and their future.

To survive, the village community had to be self-sufficient. In good times there was enough to eat and some to save for the future. Hard times meant hunger and starvation. Both conditions were accepted as part of the natural order, and both occurred regularly. One in every three harvests was bad; one in every five was disastrous. Bad harvests came in succession. Depending upon the soil and crop, between one-fifth and one-half of the grain harvested had to be saved as seed for the next planting season. When hunger was worst, people faced the agonizing choice of eating or saving their seed corn.

The Sixteenth-Century Household.   Hunger and cold were the constant companions of the average European. In Scandinavia and Muscovy, winter posed as great a threat to survival as did starvation. There the stove and garments made from animal fur were essential requirements, as were the hearth and the woolen tunic in the south. Everywhere in Europe, homes were inadequate shelter against the cold and damp. Most were built of wood and roofed in thatch. Inside walls were patched with dried mud and sometimes covered with bark or animal skins. Windows were few and narrow. Piled leaves or straw, which could easily be replaced, covered the ground and acted as insulation. The typical house was one long room with a stone hearth at the end. The hearth provided both heat and light and belched forth soot and smoke through a brick chimney.

People had relatively few household possessions. The essential piece of furniture was the wooden chest, which was used for storage. A typical family could keep all of its belongings in the chest, which could then be buried or carried away in times of danger. The chest could also serve as a table or bench or as a sideboard on which food could be placed. Tables and stools were becoming more common during the sixteenth century, though chairs were still a great luxury. Most domestic activities, of which cooking, eating, and sleeping were dominant, took place close to the ground, and squatting, kneeling, and sitting were the usual postures of family members. All other family possessions related to food production. Iron spits and pots, or at least metal rings and clamps for wooden ones, were treasured goods that were passed from generation to generation. Most other implements were wooden. Long-handled spoons; boards known as trenchers, which were used for cutting and eating; and one large cup and bowl were the basic stock of the kitchen. The family ate from the long trencher and passed the bowl and cup. Knives were essential farm tools that doubled for kitchen and mealtime duty, but forks were still a curiosity.

The scale of life was small, and its pace was controlled by the limits that nature imposed. It was a civilization of daylight—up at dawn, asleep at dusk; long working hours in summer, short ones in winter. For most people, the world was bounded by the distance that could be traveled on foot. Those who stayed all their lives in their rural villages may never have seen more than a hundred other people at once or have heard any noise louder than a human voice and terrifying thunder. Their wisdom—hard won and carefully preserved—was of the practical experience necessary to survive the struggle with nature. That was the most important legacy that parents left their children.

Reliance on Agriculture.   Peasant life centered on agriculture. Technology and technique varied little across the continent, but there were significant differences depending upon climate and soil. The lives of those who grew crops contrasted with the experiences of those who raised animals. Across the great plain, the breadbasket that stretched from the Low Countries to Poland-Lithuania, the most common form of crop growing was still the three-field rotation system. In that method, winter crops such as wheat or rye were planted in one field; spring crops such as barley, peas, or beans were planted in another; and the third field was left fallow. More than 80 percent of what was grown on the farm was consumed on the farm. Most of the grain was baked into the coarse black bread that was the monotonous fare of the peasant diet. Two to three pounds a day for an adult male was an average allotment when grain was readily available. Beer and gruels of grain and skimmed milk or water flavored with fruit juice supplemented peasant fare. In one form or another, grain provided more than 75 percent of the calories in a typical diet.

The warm climate and dry weather of Mediterranean Europe favored a two-crop rotation system. With less water and stronger sunlight, half the land had to be left fallow each year to restore its nutrients. There fruit, especially grapes and olives, was an essential supplement to diet. With smaller cereal crops, wine replaced beer as a nutritious beverage. The fermentation of grapes and grain into wine and beer also provided convenient ways of storing foodstuffs, a constant problem during the winter and early spring. Wine and olive oil were also luxury products and were most commonly exchanged for meat, which was less plentiful on southern European farms.

Animal husbandry was the main occupation in the third agricultural area of Europe, the mountainous and hilly regions. Sheep were the most common animal that Europeans raised. Sheep provided the raw material for almost all clothing, their skins were used for parchment and as window coverings, and they were a ready source of inexpensive meat. They were bred in hundreds of thousands, migrating across large areas of grazing land, especially in western Europe, where their wool was the main export of both England and Spain. Pigs were domestic animals prevalent in woodland settlements. They foraged for food and were kept, like poultry, for slaughter. Cattle, on the other hand, were essential farm animals. "The fundamentals of the home," wrote the Spanish poet Luis de Leon (1527–1591), "are the woman and the ox, the ox to plow and the woman to manage things." In the dairying areas of Europe, cattle produced milk, cheese, and butter; in Hungary and Bohemia, the great breeding center of the Continent, they were raised for export; and most everywhere else they were used as beasts of burden.

Because agriculture was the principal occupation of Europeans, land was the principal resource. Most land was

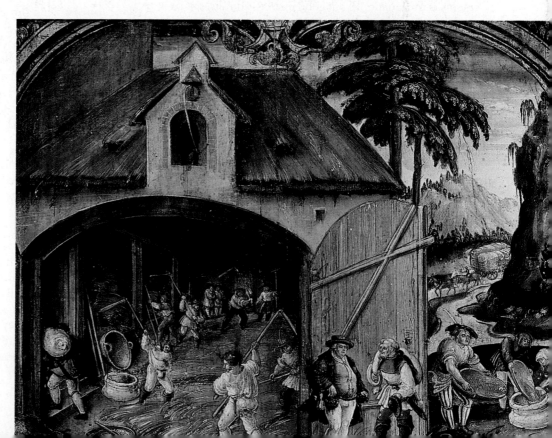

■ This picture, painted in 1530, shows farmworkers threshing grain. The figure at the door seems to be an overseer. He has just sold a sack of grain, indicating the transition from a system of self-sufficient manors to a market economy.

LIVING BY ONE'S WITS

The Life of Lazarillo des Tormes (1554) is among the first modern novels, one of a variety of sixteenth-century Spanish stories that are called picaresque *after the wandering beggars that are their heroes. Although the picaresque novel was a fictional account, much of the descriptive detail accurately portrays the social conditions for the vast majority of the Spanish population in the so-called Golden Age.*

Focus Questions

Why is it so important for Lazarillo to use his cunning? Why is the reader encouraged to sympathize with the narrator?

We began our journey, and in a few days he taught me thieves' jargon, and when he saw me to be of a good wit, was well pleased, and used to say: "Gold or silver I cannot give thee, but I will show thee many pointers about life." And it was so; for after God this man gave me my life, and although blind lighted and guided me in the career of living.

He used to carry bread and everything else in a linen sack which closed at the mouth with an iron ring and a padlock and key, and when he put things in and took them out, it was with so much attention, so well counted, that the whole world wouldn't have been equal to making it a crumb less. But I would take what stingy bit he gave me, and finish it in less than two mouthfuls. After he had fastened the lock and stopped worrying about it, thinking me to be engaged in other things, by a little seam, which I unsewed and sewed up again many times in the side of the sack, I used to bleed the miserly sack, taking out bread—not measured quantities but good pieces—and slices of bacon and sausage; and thus would seek a convenient time to make good the devilish state of want which the wicked blind man left me in.

When we ate he used to put a little jug of wine near him. I would quickly seize it and give it a couple of silent kisses and return it to its place; but this plan didn't work long, for he noticed the deficiency in his draughts, and in order to keep his wine safe, he never after let go the jug, but kept hold of the handle. But there is no lode-stone that draws things to it so strongly as I with a long rye straw, which I had prepared for that purpose, and placing which in the mouth of the jug, I would suck up the wine to a fare-ye-well. But the villain was so clever that I think he heard me; and from then on he changed procedure and set his jug between his legs and covered it with his hand, and thus drank secure.

We were at Escalona, town of the Duke of that ilk, in an inn, and he gave me a piece of sausage to roast. When he had basted the sausage and eaten the basting, he took a maravedi from his purse and bade me fetch wine from the tavern. The devil put the occasion before my eyes, which, as the saying is, makes the thief; and it was this: there lay by the fire a small turnip, rather long and bad, and which must have been thrown there because it was not fit for the stew. And as nobody was there at the time but him and me alone, as I had an appetite whetted by having got the toothsome odour of the sausage inside me (the only part, as I knew, that I had to enjoy myself with), not considering what might follow, all fear set aside in order to comply with desire—while the blind man was taking the money out of his purse, I took the sausage, and quickly put the above-mentioned turnip on the spit, which my master grasped, when he had given me the money for the wine, and began to turn before the fire, trying to roast what through its demerit had escaped being boiled. I went for the wine, and on the way did not delay in despatching the sausage, and when I came back I found the sinner of a blind man holding the turnip ready between two slices of bread, for he had not yet recognized it, because he had not tried it with his hand. When he took the slices of bread and bit into them, thinking to get part of the sausage too, he found himself chilled by the chilly turnip.

From *Lazarillo des Tormes.*

owned, not by those who worked it, but by lords who let it out in various ways. The land was still divided into manors, and the manor lord, or **seigneur,** was still responsible for maintaining order, administering justice, and arbitrating disputes. Although the personal bonds between lords and tenants were gradually loosening, political and economic ties were as strong as ever. In western Europe, peasants generally owned between a third and a half of the land they worked, while eastern European peasants owned little if any land. But by the sixteenth century, almost all peasants enjoyed security of tenure on the land they worked. In return for various forms of rents, they used the land as they saw fit and could hand it down to their children. Rents were only occasionally paid in coin, although money rents became more common as the century progressed. More frequently, the lord received a fixed proportion of the yield of the land or received labor from the peasant. Labor service was being replaced by monetary payments in northern and western Europe, but it continued in the east, where it was known as the **robot**. German and Hungarian peasants normally owed two or three days' labor on the lord's estate each week, while Polish peasants might owe as many as four days. Labor service tied the peasants to the land they worked. Eastern European peasants were less mobile than peasants in the west, and as a result towns were fewer and smaller in the east.

Although the land in each village was set out in large fields so that crops could be rotated, families owned their own pieces within the field, usually in scattered strips that they plowed, manured, and planted individually. There were also large common fields used as pasture, as well as common woodlands where animals foraged, fuel was gathered, and game hunted. Even the common fields and woodlands were not shared equally. Those who held the most land in the fields possessed greater shares of the commons. Villagers disputed frequently over rights to sticks and branches of trees and over the number of sheep or cows that could be grazed in the meadows, especially when resources were scarce.

Farm work was ceaseless toil. Six or seven times a year farmers tilled the fields to spread animal manure below the surface of the soil. While most villages possessed metal plows, the team of draught animals was the single essential component for farming. The births of foals and calves were more celebrated events than the births of children; the death of an ox or horse was a catastrophe that could drive a family into debt or from the land entirely. Calamities lurked everywhere, from rain and drought to locusts and crows. Most farms could support only one family at subsistence level, and excess sons and daughters had to fend for themselves, either through marriage in the village or by migration to a town.

Town Life

In the country, men and women worked to the natural rhythm of the day: up at the cock's crow, at work in the cooler hours, at rest in the hotter ones. Rain and cold kept them idle; sunlight kept them busy. Each season brought its own activity. In the town the bell tolled every hour. In the summer the laborers gathered at the town gates at four in the morning, in the winter at seven. The bell signaled the time for morning and afternoon meals as well as the hour to lay down tools and return home. Wages were paid for hours worked: 7 in winter, as many as 16 in June and July.

The Heart of Commerce. In all towns there was an official guild structure that organized and regulated labor. Rules laid down the requirements for training, the standards for quality, and the conditions for exchange. Only those officially sanctioned could work in trades, and each trade could perform only specified tasks. In the German town of Nuremberg, a sword maker could not make knives nor could a pin maker make thimbles. Specialization went even further in London, Paris, and other large cities.

While the life of the peasant community turned on self-sufficiency, that of the town turned on interdependence. Exchange was the medium that transformed labor and skill into food and shelter. The town was one large marketplace in which the circulation of goods dictated the survival of the residents. Men and women in towns worked as hard as did those on farms, but town dwellers received a more varied and more comfortable life in return. However, that did not mean that hunger and hardship were unknown in towns. Urban poverty was endemic and

■ Painting of a town market by Italian painter Leandro da Ponte Bassano (1557–1622). In sixteenth-century Europe, towns were centers of commercial activity, and such scenes of bartering and buying goods were common.

grew worse as the century wore on. In most towns, as much as a quarter of the entire population might be destitute, living from casual day labor, charity, or crime. But even for those people, food was more readily available in greater varieties than in the countryside, and the institutional network of support for the poor and homeless was stronger. In Lyon, the overseers of the poor distributed a daily ration of a pound and a half of bread, more than half of what a farm laborer would consume. The urban poor more often fell victim to disease than to starvation.

Towns were distinguished by the variety of occupations that existed within them. The preparation and exchange of food dominated small market towns. Peasants would bring in their finest produce for sale and exchange it for vital manufactured goods such as iron spits and pots for cooking or metal and leather tools for farm work. In smaller towns, there was as much barter as sale; in larger places, money was exchanged for commodities. Women dominated the food trades in most market towns, trading, buying, and selling in the shop fronts that occupied the bottom story of their houses. Because of their skills in food preparation, they were better able to obtain the best prices and advantageously display the best goods.

The Work Force. In larger towns, the specialization of labor was more intense and wage earning more essential. Large traders dominated the major occupations such as baking, brewing, and cloth manufacture, leaving distribution in the hands of the family economy, where there might still be a significant element of bartering. Piecework handicrafts became the staple for less prosperous town families, who prepared raw materials for the large manufacturers or finished products before their sale. Occupations were usually organized geographically, with metal or glassworking taking place in one quarter of the town, brewing or baking in another. There was a strong family and kin network to the occupations, as each craft required long years of technical training, which was handed down from parents to children.

In large towns there were also specialized trades performed by women. There were 55 midwives in Nuremberg in the middle of the sixteenth century, and a board of women chosen from among the leading families of the town supervised their work. Nursing the sick was a logical extension of those services and also appears to have been an exclusively female occupation. So, too, was prostitution, which was an officially sanctioned occupation in most large towns in the early modern era. There were town brothels, situated in specified districts, subject to taxation and government control. Public bathhouses, which employed skilled women workers, served as unofficial brothels for the upper ranks of urban society. They too were regulated, especially after the first great epidemic of venereal disease in the early sixteenth century.

Most town dwellers, however, lived by unskilled labor. The most lucrative occupations were strictly controlled, so those who flocked to towns in search of employment usually hired themselves out as day laborers, hauling and lifting goods onto carts or boats, stacking materials at building sites, or delivering water and food. After the first decades of the century, the supply of laborers exceeded the amount of work to occupy them, and town authorities were constantly attempting to expel them. The most fortunate might succeed in becoming servants.

Domestic service was a critical source of household labor. Even families on the margins of subsistence employed servants

■ Van Schwanerburg (1537–1614), *The Spinners*. Workers spinning and weaving wool. Labor in large towns was often specialized into occupations such as baking, brewing, and cloth manufacture.

MAP DISCOVERY

Grain Supply and Trade in Sixteenth-Century Europe

Where were the breadbaskets of Europe located? What was the relationship between urban areas and grain supply? How did grain move from suppliers to consumers?

Just as towns grew by the influx of surplus rural population, they sustained themselves by the import of surplus agricultural production. Most towns owned tracts of land, which they leased to peasants or farmed by hired labor. The town of Nuremberg controlled 25 square miles of forest and farmlands, while the region around Toledo was inhabited by thousands of peasants who paid taxes and rents to city landlords. Agriculture was the fourth largest occupation in the Spanish city of Barcelona, which had a population of more than 35,000 in the early sixteenth century. All towns had municipal storehouses of grain to preserve their inhabitants from famine during harvest failures. Grain prices were strictly regulated and frequently subsidized to ensure that laborers were adequately fed. The diet of even a casual laborer would have been envied by an average peasant. Male grape pickers in Stuttgart received meat, soup, vegetables, wine, and beer; females received soup, vegetables, milk, and bread. In addition they received their wages. It is hardly surprising that towns were enclosed by thick walls and defended by armed guards.

Economic Change

Over the course of the sixteenth century, the European population increased by about a third, with much of the growth taking place in the first 50 years. Rough estimates suggest the rise to have been from about 80 to 105 million. Patterns of growth varied by region. The population of the eastern part of Europe seems to have increased more steadily across the century, while western Europe experienced a population explosion in the early decades. The population of France may have doubled between 1450 and 1550, from 10 to 20 million. The population of England nearly doubled between 1500 and 1600, from more than 2 million to more than 4 million. Castile, the largest region in Spain, grew 50 percent in 50 years. Europe had finally recovered from the devastation of

to undertake the innumerable household tasks, which allowed parents to pursue their primary occupations. Everything was done by hand and on foot, and extra pairs of each were essential. In Münster at mid-century, there were 400 servants for 1000 households. Domestics were not apprentices, though they might aspire to become apprentices to the trade followed in the family with whom they lived. If they had kinship bonds in the town, apprenticeship was a likely outcome. But more commonly, domestics remained household servants, frequently changing employers in hope of more comfortable housing and better food.

MAP DISCOVERY

People per square mile

- Over 60
- 30 to 60
- 10 to 30
- Under 10

Population Density in Europe, ca. 1600

Which were the most populated parts of Europe at the beginning of the seventeenth century? Which were the least populated? What was the relationship between population and access to water routes?

the Black Death, and by 1600 its population was greater than it had ever been. Demographic growth was even more dramatic in the cities. In 1500, only four cities had populations greater than 100,000; in 1600, there were eight. Naples grew from 150,000 to 280,000, and both Paris and London to more than 200,000 inhabitants. Fifteen large cities more than doubled their populations, with London experiencing a phenomenal 400 percent increase.

The rise in population dramatically affected the lives of ordinary Europeans. In the early part of the century, the first phase of growth brought prosperity. The land was still not farmed to capacity, and extra hands meant increased productivity. As there was uncultivated land that could be plowed, convenient room for new housing, and enough commons and woodlands to be shared, the population increase was a welcome development. Even when rural communities began to reach their natural limits as people's needs pressed against nature's resources, opportunity still existed in the burgeoning towns and cities. At first the cycle was beneficial. Surplus on the farms led to economic growth in the towns. Growth in the towns meant more opportunities for those on the farms. More food supported more workers, and more workers produced more goods and services, which were exchanged for more food.

The first waves of migrants to the towns found opportunity everywhere. Even the most lucrative textile and provisioning trades were recruiting new members, and apprenticeships were easy to find. A shortage of casual labor kept wages at a decent rate. Successful migrants encouraged kin from their villages to move to the towns and sponsored their start in trade or service. For a while, rural families did not have to make elaborate preparations to provide for their younger sons and daughters: they could be sent to the towns. Instead of saving every extra penny to give their children a start in life, farmers could purchase some luxury goods or expand their landholdings.

European Population Density, c. 1600

Such an opportunity could not last. With more mouths to feed, more crops had to be planted. Since the most productive land was already under the plow, new fields were carved from less fertile areas. In some villages, land was taken from the common waste, the woodlands or scrublands that were used for animal forage and domestic fuel. The land was less suitable for crops, and it became unavailable for other important uses.

By midcentury there was a natural limit to the number of workers who could profitably engage in any given trade, and

■ The new money economy inspired this satirical portrait by Quentin Massys. It shows a moneylender counting his receipts while his wife is distracted from her Bible by the pile of coins. Many such merchants won fame and power and even titles.

those safely in were pulling the ladder up behind them. Town governments came under pressure from the guilds to enforce apprenticeship requirements that had been relaxed during the period of growth. Guilds raised fees for new entrants and designated only a small number of places where their goods could be purchased. Most apprenticeships were limited to patrimony: one son for each full member. Such restrictions meant that newly arrived immigrants could enter only into the less profitable small crafts.

As workers continued to flood into the towns, real wages began to fall, not only among the unskilled but throughout the work force. A black market in labor developed to take advantage of the surplus population. In terms of purchasing power, the wages of a craftsman in the building trade in England fell by one-half during the sixteenth century. A French stonemason, a highly paid skilled laborer, could buy 33 pounds of bread with his daily wage in 1480; by 1550 he could buy fewer than 10. Peasants in the French region of Languedoc who hired out for farm labor lost 56 percent of their purchasing power during the century. Only reapers, who were the physically strongest agricultural laborers, appear to have kept pace with inflation; grape pickers, among the least skilled, endured declines of up to 300 or 400 percent.

The fall in real wages took place against a backdrop of inflation that has come to be called the **Price Revolution.** Between 1500 and 1650, cereal prices increased between five- and sixfold, manufactured goods between two- and threefold. Most of the rapid increase came in the second half of the sixteenth century, a result of both population growth and the import of precious metals from the New World. Sixteenth-century governments understood little about the relationship between money supply and prices. Gold and silver from America flooded the international economy, raising commodity prices. As prices rose so did the deficits of the state, which was the largest purchaser of both agricultural and manufactured goods. With huge deficits, states began to devalue their coins in the mistaken belief that this would lower their debt. But debased coinage resulted in still higher prices, and higher prices resulted in greater debt. The Price Revolution was felt throughout the Continent and played havoc with government finances, international trade, and the lives of ordinary people.

A 500 percent inflation in agricultural products over a century is not much by modern standards. Compounded, the rate averages less than 2 percent a year. But the Price Revolution did not take place in a modern society or within a modern market economy. In the sixteenth century, that level of rising prices disrupted everything. In the Spanish town of Seville, almost all buildings were rented on 99-year leases to the families who lived and worked in them. That was a fairly common practice throughout Europe. It meant that a landlord who rented a butcher shop and living quarters in 1501 could not raise the rent until 1600! Similarly, lords frequently held the right to purchase agricultural produce at specified prices. That system, similar to today's commodity market, helped both lords and peasants plan ahead. It assured the lord a steady supply and the peasant a steady market. But it assumed steady prices. Until the middle of the seventeenth century, the king of England had the right to purchase wheat at prices set 300 years earlier.

Thus an enduring increase in prices created profound social dislocation. Some people became destitute; others became rich beyond their dreams. The towns were particularly hard hit, for they exchanged manufactured goods for food and thus suffered when grain prices rose faster than those of other commodities. Landholders who derived their income from rents were squeezed; those who received payment in kind reaped a windfall of more valuable agricultural goods. Peasants were largely protected from the rise in food prices, but they were not insulated from its consequences. As long as they consumed what they raised, the nominal value of commodities was of no great matter. But if some part of their subsistence had to be obtained by labor, they were in grave peril.

There was now an enormous incentive to produce a surplus for market and to begin to specialize in particular grains that were in high demand. Every small scrap of land that individual peasant families could bring under cultivation would now yield foodstuffs that could be exchanged for manufactured luxury goods. The tendency for all peasants to hold roughly equivalent amounts of land abruptly ceased. The fortunate could become prosperous by selling their surplus. The unfortunate found ready purchasers for their strips and common rights. Villagers began to be divided into those who held large amounts of land and sold their surplus at a profit and those who held small amounts of land and hired out as laborers to their more fortunate neighbors.

The beneficial cycle now turned vicious. Those who had sold out and left the land looking for prosperity in the towns were forced to return to the land as agrarian laborers. In western Europe, they became the landless poor, seasonal migrants without the safety net of rooted communal life. In eastern Europe, labor service enriched the landed nobility, who were able to sell stores of grain in the export market. They used the law to tie the peasants to the land in order to ensure that grain would be cultivated for the market. Poland-Lithuania became a major supplier of cereals to northern Europe, and Gdansk became the most important agricultural seaport in the world. But agricultural surplus from the east could not make up for the great shortfall in the west. By the beginning of the seventeenth century, the western European states faced a crisis of subsistence. Everyone was hungry; many were starving.

SOCIAL LIFE

Social organization combines elements of tradition, belief, and function, but the elements are so fused together that it is impossible to determine where one ends and the other begins. Society is a human construct, subject to the strengths and frailties of its creators. The basic assumption of sixteenth-century European society was inequality, and its basic form of social organization was stratification. The group, rather than the individual, was the predominant unit in society. The first level of the social order was the family and the household; then came the village or town community; and finally the gradations of ranks and orders of society at large. Elaborate rituals helped define membership in each of the groups, from the marriage ceremony to the initiation rites of citizens and to the processions and ceremonial displays of the nobility. All stressed the significance of the rights and obligations of different levels of society. Each group had its own place in the social order and each performed its own essential function. Society was the sum of its parts.

The traditional social organization was severely tested over the course of the early modern period. Economic change reshaped ideas of mobility and drew sharper distinctions between rural and urban life. The growth of towns and their domination of the countryside around them challenged beliefs about the primacy of agricultural production and the subordinate nature of trade and commerce. The rise to new wealth and prominence of some social groups challenged traditional elites' hold on power and prestige. The transformation of landholding patterns in the villages challenged the stability of rural communities. The rising numbers of both urban and rural poor challenged the institutions of charitable relief and posed the threat of crime and disorder. Eventually those developments led to bloody confrontations between social groups.

Social Constructs

Hierarchy was the dominant principle of social organization in the early modern era. Hierarchy existed at every level, from the basic distinction between lords and commoners to the fastidious complexity of the ranks of the nobility. The hierarchy of masters, journeymen, and apprentices dominated trades; trades themselves existed in a hierarchy. In the hierarchy of civic government, each official held a place in an ascending order, up to the elite of councillors and mayors. On the land was the hierarchy of freeholder, laborer, and leaseholder among the peasants. The family itself was hierarchically organized, with the wife subordinate to her husband, the children to their parents, and the apprentices and servants to their master and mistress. "All things observe degree, priority and place," Shakespeare wrote of both natural and human order in *Troilus and Cressida* (1601–1602). "Take but degree away, untune that string, and hark what discord follows."

Hierarchy was a principle of orderliness that helped govern social relations. It is tempting to approach hierarchy through wealth, to divide groups and individuals into rich and poor. Many gradations in the sixteenth-century social hierarchy corresponded to levels of wealth, but they were threshold levels rather than absolute levels. Lords, by definition, did not engage in manual labor. They were wealthier than peasants. The governing elites of towns needed sufficient wealth to neglect their own affairs while occupied in public service. They were wealthier than wage earners. But the ranks of the nobility cannot be explained by gradations of wealth among nobles, and there

■ Joris Hoefnagel, *Wedding Feast at Bermondsey* (ca. 1590). In this painting of an Elizabethan wedding feast, as depicted by the Flemish painter Joris Hoefnagel, bakers and violinists usher in the wedding party to the feast. In the background in the left of the picture is the imposing Tower of London.

were many rich town dwellers who were not members of the governing elite.

Status, rather than wealth, determined the social hierarchy. It conferred privileges and exacted responsibilities according to rank. Status was everywhere apparent. It was confirmed in social conventions such as bowing and hat doffing. In towns and cities the clothing that people were allowed to wear—even the foods that they were allowed to eat—reflected status. Status was signified in titles: not just in the ranks of the nobility or between nobles and commoners, but even in ordinary communities masters and mistresses, goodmen and goodwives, squires and ladies, adopted the English equivalents of European titles. The acceptance of status was an everyday, uncomplicated, unreflective act, similar to stopping at a red light. Inequality was a fact of European social life that was as unquestioned as it was unquestionable.

Images that people used to describe both the natural world and their social world reinforced the functional nature of hierarchy. The first, and most elaborate image, was that of the **Great Chain of Being.** The Great Chain was a description of the universe in which everything had a place, from God at the top of the chain to inanimate objects like rocks at the bottom. Complex accounts of the chain listed the seven orders of angels, the multiple ranks of humans, even the degrees of animals and plants, from which lions emerged as kings of the jungle. Spanish botanists were dispatched to the New World to help identify the unknown flora and fauna in terms of their places in the chain. Native Americans were first thought to be the lost tribes of Israel, as they were the only humans missing from traditional accounts of the chain. For ordinary people, the Great Chain of Being expressed the belief that all life was interconnected, that every link was a part of a divinely ordered universe and was as necessary as every other.

The second metaphor used to describe society stressed the notion of interdependency even more strongly. This was the image of the Body Politic, in which the head ruled, the arms protected, the stomach nourished, and the feet labored. The image described a small community as well as a large state. In the state, the king was the head, the Church the soul, the nobles the arms, the artisans the hands, and the peasants the feet. Each performed its own function, and each function was essential to the health of the body. Like the Great Chain of Being, the Body Politic was a profoundly conservative concept of social organization. Taken literally, it precluded the idea of social mobility, of people rising or falling from one group to another.

Social Structure

The Great Chain of Being and the Body Politic were static concepts of social organization. But in the early modern era, European society was in a state of dynamic change. Fundamentally, all European societies were divided into nobles and commoners. That basic distinction existed throughout the Continent, although relationships between the two orders differed from place to place.

The Nobles. Nobility was a legal status that conferred certain privileges upon its holders. The first was rank and title, a well-defined place at the top of the social order that was passed from one generation to the next. Each rank had its own privileges and each was clearly demarcated from the next by behavior, dress, and title. The escutcheon—the coat of arms—was a universally recognized symbol of rank and family connection. The coat of arms was woven in garments; emblazoned on windows, carriages, and household goods; and displayed on banners during formal processions. Although there were various systems of title in use across the Continent and the nobility of one state could not claim noble privileges in another state, the hierarchy of prince, duke, earl, count, and baron was roughly standard.

Because rulers conferred the titles on individuals, elevating some to higher ranks and others from commoner to noble, the nobility was a political order as well as a social one. Political privileges were among the nobility's most important attributes. In many countries, the highest offices of the state and the military were reserved for members of the nobility. In Poland, for example, all offices were held by noblemen. It was a privilege that could work both ways, either restricting officeholders to those already ennobled or, as in town councils in France and Spain, ennobling those who achieved certain offices. The nobility was also granted rights of political participation in the deliberative bodies of the state. In England, the peerage was defined as all those who were summoned to the House of Lords. In most parts of central Europe, the nobility alone composed the diets that advised the monarch. In the Holy Roman Empire, the rank of imperial free knights allowed the nobility to separate itself entirely from the jurisdiction of towns or individual principalities.

Finally, members of the nobility held economic privileges, a result both of their rank and of their role as lords on the lands they owned. In almost every state, the nobility was exempt from most taxation. That was an area in which the interests of the nobles conflicted directly with those of the ruler. The larger the number of tax exemptions for the nobility, the stronger was its power in relation to the monarch. Tax exemptions of the nobility were most extensive in eastern and central Europe. There the crowns were elective rather than hereditary, allowing the nobles to bargain their support. The Polish nobility was exempt from the salt tax, the alcohol tax, and all internal tolls and customs. As Polish agriculture developed into an export industry, exemption from tolls gave the nobility a competitive advantage over merchants in the marketing of goods. The Hungarian nobility was exempt from all direct taxes, including the land tax. The nobility in western Europe enjoyed fewer immunities but not necessarily less valuable ones. French nobles were exempt from the taille, Spanish nobles from the hearth tax.

Privileges implied obligations. Initially the nobility was the warrior caste of the state and its primary obligations were to raise, equip, and lead troops into battle. Much of the great wealth that nobles possessed was at the service of the ruler during times of war, and war was a perpetual activity. By the sixteenth century, the military needs of the state had far surpassed the military power of its nobility. Warfare had become a national enterprise that required central coordination. Nobles became administrators as much as warriors, though it is fair to say that many did both. The French nobility came to be divided into the nobility of the sword and the nobility of the robe—that is, warriors and officeholders. The old military nobility could hardly understand the new service nobility. "I have continually been astounded," one of them remarked, "that so many young men could thus amuse themselves in a law court, since ordinarily youthful blood is boiling." A glorious battlefield death was still an ideal for most of Europe's noblemen.

Nobles also had the obligation of governing at both the national and the local level. At the discretion of the ruler, they could be called to engage in any necessary occupation, no matter how disruptive to their economic or family affairs. On their land, they administered their estates and settled the disputes of their tenants. In times of want they were expected to provide for the needy, in times of dearth for the hungry. There was an obligation of good lordship that was implicitly understood, if not always explicitly carried out, between lord and peasant.

Town Elite and Gentry. The principal distinction in sixteenth-century society was between lord and commoners, but it was not the only one. In both town and countryside a new social group was emerging. It had neither the legal nor the social privileges of nobility, but it performed many of the same functions. Over the course of the century the group carved out a place that was clearly distinct from that of the commoners, even if it was not clearly identical to the lords. It was most evident in the towns, for the towns remained a separate unit of social organization in most states. Towns enjoyed many of the same political and economic privileges as the nobility. In many states, the towns sent representatives to meet with the nobles and the king and were the most important part of national deliberative assemblies such as the English Parliament, the French Estates, or the Spanish Cortes. Towns were granted legal rights to govern their own citizens, to engage in trade, and to defend themselves by raising and storing arms. Although

■ Georges de La Tour, *The Fortune Teller*. In the painting, which serves as a warning to the naive about the wicked ways of the world, a fashionably dressed young innocent is drawn into the snare of the wily fortune teller.

they paid a large share of most taxes, towns also received large tax concessions.

Yet, as individuals, members of the town elite held no special status in society at large. Some were among the richest people in the state—great bankers and merchants who were wealthier than dukes—but they had to devise their own systems of honor and prestige. In Venice, the *Book of Gold* distinguished the local elite from the ranks of ordinary citizens. Members of the "Old Families," who monopolized the highest civic offices, ruled Nuremberg. In France and Spain, some of the highest officers of leading towns were granted noble status, such as the "honored citizens" of Barcelona who were ennobled by King Ferdinand of Aragon. German burghers, as prosperous townsmen were called, remained caught in a state between noble and common, despised from above because they worked with their hands, envied from below for their wealth and comfort. In Münster, many withdrew from urban affairs and sought the privileges of the lower nobility.

In rural society, the transformation of agricultural holdings in many places also created a group that fit uncomfortably between lords and commoners. The accumulation of larger and larger estates through purchase from the nobility, the state, or the Church made lords—in the sense of landowners with tenants—out of many who were not lords in rank. They received rents and dues from their tenants, administered their estates, and preserved the so-called moral economy that sustained the peasants during hard times. In England, the group came to be known as the gentry, and there were parallel groups in Spain, France, and the empire. The

gentry aspired to the privileges of the nobility. In England, members of the gentry had the right to have a coat of arms and could be knighted. But knighthoods were not hereditary and did not confer membership in the House of Lords. In Spain, the caballeros and hidalgos gained noble privileges but were still of lower status than the grandees. The gentry aped the habits of the nobility, often outdoing nobles in lavish displays of wealth and spending.

Social stratification did not only apply to the wealthy groups within European societies. Although it is more difficult to reconstruct the principles upon which rural communities based their complicated systems of status and order, there can be no doubt that systems existed and that they helped create the bonds that tied communities together. In many German villages, a principal distinction was between those who held land in the ancient part of the settlement—the *Esch*—and those who held land in those areas into which the village had expanded. The *Esch* was normally the best land, and thus the distinction was likely to correlate with the relative wealth of the two groups. But interestingly, the holders of the *Esch* were tied to the lord of the estate, while holders of the less desirable lands were free peasants. Their freedom to move from place to place was less valued than the right to live in the heart of the village.

Just the opposite set of values prevailed in English villages, where freeholders were in the most enviable position. They led the movements to break up the common fields for planting and were able to initiate legal actions against their lord. They might not have the best lands in the village, but whenever village land

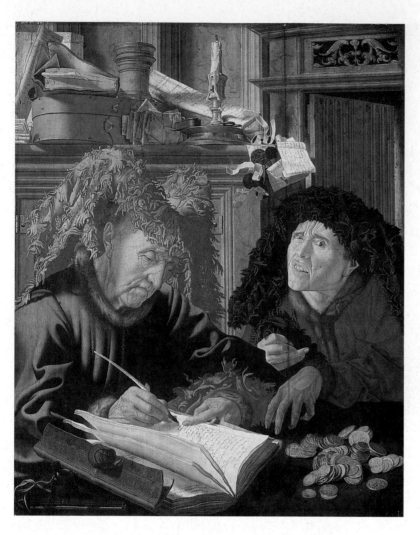

■ Marinus van Reymerswaele, *The Two Tax Gatherers*. The figure on the left is a city treasurer who is posting in the book an account of the city's revenues from taxes on wine, beer, fish, and other commodities. The painting is probably a satirical composition intended to expose the iniquity of covetousness, usury, or extortion.

was converted to freehold, unfree tenants would go into debt to buy it. Increasingly, French peasants came to own the land that they farmed. They protested against the very title of *villein*, claiming that its older association with serfdom discouraged others from trading with those so labeled. The relationship of free and unfree went even further in Muscovy, where thousands of starving laborers sold themselves into slavery. Perhaps as much as 10 percent of the population of Muscovy accepted their loss of freedom and became domestic slaves of the military and noble orders.

In towns, the order of rank below the elite pertained as much to the kind of work that one performed as it did to the level at which it was undertaken. The critical division in town life was between those who had the freedom of the city—citizens—and those who did not. Citizenship was restricted to membership in certain occupations and was closely regulated. It could be purchased, especially by members of learned professions whose services were becoming vital in the early modern era, but most citizenship was earned by becoming a master in one of the guilds after a long period of apprenticeship and training. Only males could be citizens. In Germany, the feminine equivalent for the word used to denote a male citizen in good standing meant "prostitute"! But women who

were married to citizens enjoyed their husbands' privileges, and widows of citizens could pass the privileges to their new husbands when they remarried. In both town and countryside, the privileges and obligations of each social group were the glue that held communities together.

Social Change

In the sixteenth century, social commentators believed that change was transforming the world in which they lived. In 1600, a Spanish observer blamed the rise of the rich commoners for the ills of the world: "They have obtained a particular status, that of a self-made group; and since they belong neither to the rich nor to the poor nor to the middle, they have thrown the state into the confusion we now see it in." An Englishman commenting on the rise of the gentry could give no better definition of its status than to say that a gentleman was one who lived like a gentleman. The challenge that the new nobility of the robe posed to the old nobility of the sword poisoned relations between the two segments of the French ruling elite. The military service class in Muscovy, who were of more use to the Muscovite princes than were the traditional landed nobility, posed an even greater threat to the privileges of the boyars.

The New Rich.   Pressures on the ruling elites of European society came from above as well as below. The expansion of the state and the power of the prince frequently came as a result of direct conflict with the nobility. Only in east-central Europe—in Hungary, Bohemia, and Poland-Lithuania, where towns were small and urban elites weak—did the consolidation of the state actually enhance the privileges of the traditional noble orders.

There were many reasons why the traditional European social hierarchy was transformed during the course of the early modern era. In the first place, population increase necessitated an expansion of the ruling orders. With more people to govern, there had to be more governors who could perform the military, political, and social functions of the state. The traditional nobility grew slowly, as titles could be passed to only one son and intermarriage within the group was very high. Second, opportunities to accumulate wealth expanded dramatically with the Price Revolution. Traditionally, wealth was calculated in land and tenants rather than in the possession of liquid assets such as gold and silver. But with the increase in commodity prices, surplus producers could rapidly improve their economic position. What previously might have taken a generation or two of good fortune to amass could now be gathered seemingly overnight. Moreover, state service became a source of unlimited riches. The profits to be made from tax collecting, officeholding, or administering the law could easily surpass those to be made from landholding, especially after the economic downturn at the end of the century. The newly rich clamored for privileges, and many were in a position to lobby rulers effectively for them. Across European society the nobility grew, fed from fortunes made on the land, in trade, and in office.

The New Poor.   Social change was equally apparent at the bottom of the social scale, but there it could not be so easily absorbed. The continuous population growth created a group of landless poor who squatted in villages and clogged the streets of towns and cities. Although poverty was not a new development of the early modern era, its growth created new problems. Rough estimates suggest that as many as a quarter of all Europeans were destitute. That was a staggering figure in great cities. There were tens of thousands of destitute people in London or Paris, where, it was observed, "the crowds of poor were so great that one could not pass through the streets."

Traditionally, local communities cared for their poor. Widows, orphans, and the handicapped, who would normally constitute more than half the poor in a village or town, were viewed as the "deserving poor," worthy of the care of the community through the Church or through private almsgiving. Catholic communities such as Venice created a system of private charity that paralleled the institutions of the Church. Although Protestant communities took charity out of the control of the church, they were no less concerned about the plight of the deserving poor. In England, a special tax, the poor rate, supported the poor and provided them with subsistence until they remarried or

■ *Feeding the Hungry* by Cornelius Buys, 1504. A maidservant is doling out small loaves to the poor and the lame at the door of a wealthy person's home. The poor who flocked to the towns were often forced to rely on charity to survive.

found employment. Perhaps the most elaborate system of all existed in the French town of Lyon where all the poor were registered and given identity cards. Each Sunday they would receive a week's worth of food and money. Young girls were provided with dowries, and young boys were taught crafts. Vagrants from the surrounding countryside were given one week's allotment to enable them to travel on. But Lyon's enlightened system was only for the deserving poor, and as the century progressed it was overwhelmed.

Charity was an obligation of the community, but as the sixteenth century progressed, the number of people who lived on the margins of subsistence grew beyond the ability of the local community to care for them. Perhaps more importantly, many of those who now begged for alms fell outside the traditional categories of the deserving poor. In England, they were called the sturdy beggars, men and women capable of working but incapable of finding more than occasional labor. To support themselves and their families, they left their native communities in search of employment and thus forfeited their claims on local charity. Most wound up in the towns and cities, where they slept and begged in the streets. Some disfigured themselves to enhance their abilities as beggars. As strangers they had no claim on local charity; as able-bodied workers they had no claim on local sympathy. Poor mothers abandoned their newborn infants on the steps of foundling hospitals or the houses of the rich. It is estimated that 10 percent of all newborn babies in the Spanish city of Valladolid were abandoned.

The problem of crime complicated the problems of poverty and vagrancy. Increasing population and increasing wealth equaled increasing crime; the addition of the poor to the equation aggravated the situation. The poor, destitute outsiders to the community, without visible means of support, were the easiest targets of official retribution. Throughout the century, numerous European states passed vagrancy laws in an effort to alleviate the problem of the wandering poor. In England, the poor were whipped from village to village until they were returned home. The sturdy beggars were branded with the letter *V* on their chests to identify them as vagrants, and therefore as potential criminals. Both Venetian and Dutch vagrants were regularly rounded up for galley service, while vagrants in Hungary were sold into slavery. Physical mutilation was used as an ineffective method of deterrence; thieves had fingers chopped off—which made it impossible for them to perform manual labor, and thus likely to steal again. Sexual offenses were criminalized—especially bastardy, since the birth of illegitimate children placed an immediate burden on the community. Prostitutes, who had long been tolerated and regulated in towns, were now persecuted. Rape increased. Capital punishment was reserved for the worst crimes—murder, incest, and grand larceny being most common—but, not surprisingly, executions were carried out mostly on outsiders to the community, with single women, the poor, and the vagrant being the most frequent victims.

Peasant Revolts

The economic and social changes of the sixteenth century bore serious consequences. Most telling was the upswing of violent confrontations between peasants and their lords. There was more than one difference between rich and poor in sixteenth-century society, but when conflict arose between them the important difference was that the wealthy controlled the means of coercion: the military and the law. Across Europe, and with alarming regularity, peasants took up arms to defend themselves from what they saw as violations of traditional rights and obligations. Peasant revolts were not

hunger riots. Although they frequently occurred in periods of want, after bad harvests or marauding armies had impoverished villages, peasant revolts were not desperate attacks against warehouses or grain silos. Nor did those who took part in them form undisciplined mobs. Most revolts chose leaders, drew up petitions of grievances, and organized the rank and file into a semblance of military order. Leaders were literate—usually drawn from the lower clergy or minor gentry rather than from the peasantry—political demands were moderate, and tactics were sophisticated. But peasant revolts so profoundly threatened the social order that they were met with the severest repression. Confronted with the execution of their estate agents, rent strikes, and confiscation of their property, lords responded as if they were at war. Veteran soldiers and trained mercenaries were called out to fight peasant armies composed mostly of raw recruits. The results were horrifying.

Agrarian Changes. It is essential to realize that while peasants revolted against their lords, fundamentally their anger and frustration were products of agrarian changes that could be neither controlled nor understood. As population increased and market production expanded, many of the traditional rights and obligations of lords and peasants became oppressive. One example is that of forest rights. On most estates, the forests surrounding a village belonged to the lord. Commonly the village had its own woodlands in which animals foraged and fuel and building material were available. As the population increased, more farms came into existence. New land was put under the plow, and grain fields pressed up against the forest. There were more animals in the village, and some of them were let loose to consume the young sprouts and saplings. Soon there was not enough food for the wild game that was among the lord's most valuable property. So the game began to feed on the peasants' crops, which were now placed so appetizingly close to the forests. It was a capital crime for a peasant to kill wild game, but peasants couldn't allow the game to consume their crops.

A similar conflict arose over enclosing crop fields. An **enclosure** was a device—normally a fence or hedge that surrounded an area—to keep a parcel of land separate from the planted strips of land owned by the villagers. The parcel could be used for grazing animals or raising a specialty crop for the market. But an enclosure destroyed the traditional form of village agriculture, whereby decisions on which crops to plant were made communally. It became one of the chief grievances of the English peasants. But while enclosures broke up the old field system in many villages, they were a logical response to the transformation of land ownership that had already taken place. As more land was accumulated by fewer families, it made less sense for them to work widely scattered strips all over the village. If a family could consolidate its holdings by swaps and sales, it could gain an estate large enough to be used for both crops and grazing. An enclosed estate allowed wealthy farmers to grow more luxury crops for market or to raise only sheep on a field that had once been used for grain.

Enclosure was a process that both lord and rich peasant undertook, but it drove the smallholders from the land and was thus a source of bitter resentment for the poorer peasants. It was easy to protest the greed of the lords who, owning the most land, were the most successful enclosers. But enclosures were more a result of the process in which villages came to be characterized by a very small elite of large landholders and a very large mass of smallholders and landless poor. They were an effect rather than a cause.

From Hungary to England, peasant revolts brought social and economic change into sharp relief. A call for a crusade against Ottoman advances in 1514 provided the opportunity for Hungarian peasants to revolt against their noble landlords. Thousands dropped their plowshares and grasped the sword of a holy war. However, in fact, war against the Ottomans did not materialize. Instead, the mobilized peasants, under the leadership of disaffected army officers and clergymen, issued grievances against the labor service that they owed to their lords as well as numerous violations of customary agricultural practices. Their revolt turned into a civil war that was crushed with great brutality. In England, severe economic conditions led to a series of revolts in 1549. Participants in the Western Rising, who succeeded in storming the town of Exeter, also combined religious and economic grievances. Cornish rebels added a social dimension with their slogan "Kill the gentlemen." In eastern England, Ket's Rebellion arose from peasant opposition to enclosure. The rebels occupied Norwich, the second largest city in the realm, but their aspirations were for reform rather than revolution. They, like the Hungarian peasants, were crushed by well-trained forces.

Uprising in Germany.   The complexity of the peasants' problems is perhaps best revealed in the series of uprisings that are known collectively as the German Peasants' War. It was by far the most widespread peasant revolt of the sixteenth century, involving tens of thousands of peasants, and it combined a whole series of agrarian grievances with an awareness of the new religious spirit preached by Martin Luther. Luther condemned both lords and peasants: the lords for their rapaciousness, the peasants for their rebelliousness. Although he had a large following among the peasants, his advice that earthly oppression be passively accepted was not followed. The Peasants' War was directed against secular and ecclesiastical lords, and the rebels attacked both economic and religious abuses. Their combination of demands, such as the community's right to select its own minister and the community's right to cut wood freely, attracted a wide following in the villages and small towns of southern and central Germany. The printed demands of the peasantry, the most famous of which was the Twelve Articles of the Peasants of Swabia (1525), helped spread the movement far beyond its original bounds. The peasants organized themselves into large armies led by experienced soldiers. Initially they were able to besiege castles

THE PEASANTS' REVOLT

In 1524 and 1525, a series of local protests over economic conditions coalesced into one of the largest concerted peasant uprisings in German history. The Peasants' Revolt was not a disorganized uprising of the hungry and dispossessed, but rather a carefully coordinated movement that attempted to win widespread social reforms. The Twelve Articles of the Peasants of Swabia show both the nature of the peasants' grievances and their ability to articulate them.

Focus Questions

On what grounds do the peasants base their pleas? Why are religious and economic issues so intertwined for these peasants?

The First Article. First, it is our humble petition and desire, as also our will and resolution, that in the future we should have power and authority so that each community should choose and appoint a pastor, and that we should have the right to depose him should he conduct himself improperly. The pastor thus chosen should teach us the gospel pure and simple, without any addition, doctrine, or ordinance of man.

The Second Article. According as the just tithe is established by the Old Testament and fulfilled in the New, we are ready and willing to pay the fair tithe of grain. . . . We will that for the future our church provost, whomsoever the community may appoint, shall gather and receive this tithe. . . .

The Tenth Article. In the tenth place, we are aggrieved by the appropriation by individuals of meadows and fields which at one time belonged to a community. These we will take again into our own hands. . . .

Conclusion. In the twelfth place, it is our conclusion and final resolution that if any one or more of the articles here set forth should not be in agreement with the word of God, as we think they are, such article we will willingly retract if it is proved really to be against the word of God by a clear explanation of the Scripture.

From the Twelve Articles of the Peasants of Swabia.

and abbeys and plunder lords' estates. Ultimately, those movements that refused compromise were ruthlessly crushed. By conservative estimates, more than 100,000 peasants were slaughtered during and after the war, many to serve as warning against future uprisings.

At base, the demands of the peasantry addressed the agrarian changes that were transforming German villages. Population growth was creating more poor villagers who could only hire out as laborers but who demanded a share of common grazing and woodlands. Because the presence of the poor increased the taxable wealth of the village, they were advantageous to the lord. But the strain they placed on resources was felt by both the subsistence and the surplus farmers. Tensions within the village were all the greater because the landless members were the kin of the landed—sons and daughters, brothers and sisters. If they were to be settled properly on the land, then the lord would have to let the village expand. If they were to be kept on the margins of subsistence, then the more prosperous villagers would have to be able to control their numbers and their conduct. In either case, the peasants needed more direct responsibility for governing the village than existed in their traditional relationship with their lord. Thus the grievances of the peasants of Swabia demanded release of the village peasantry from the status of serfs. They wanted to be allowed to move off the land, to marry out of the village without penalty, and to be free of the death taxes that further impoverished their children. The concessions would make it easier for the excess population to adjust to new conditions. They also wanted stable rents fixed at fair rates, a limit placed on labor service, and a return to the ancient customs that governed relations between lords and peasants. All the proposals were backed by an appeal to Christian principles of love and charity. They were profoundly conservative.

The demands of the German peasants reflected a traditional order that no longer existed. In many places, the rents and tithes that the peasants wanted to control no longer belonged to the lords of the estates. They had been sold to town corporations or wealthy individuals who purchased them as an investment and expected to realize a fair return. Most tenants did enjoy stable and fixed rents, but only on their traditional lands. As they increased their holdings, perhaps to keep another son in the village or to expand production for the market, they were faced with the fact that rents were higher and land more expensive than it had been before. Marriage fines, death duties, and labor service were oppressive, but they balanced the fact that traditional rents were very low. In many east German villages, peasants willingly increased their labor service for a reduction in their money rents. It was hardly likely that they could have both. If the peasants were being squeezed, and there can be little doubt that they were, it was not only the lords who were doing the squeezing. The Church took its tenth, the state increased its exactions, and the competition for survival and prosperity among the peasants themselves was ferocious. Peasants were caught between the jaws of an expanding state and a changing economy. When they rebelled, the jaws snapped shut.

PRIVATE AND COMMUNITY LIFE

The great events of the sixteenth century—the discovery of the New World, the consolidation of states, the increasing incidence and ferocity of war, the reform of religion—all had profound impact on the lives of ordinary people. However slowly and intermittently these developments penetrated to isolated village communities, they were inextricably bound up with the experiences and the worldview of all Europeans. The states offered more protection and demanded more resources. Taxes increased, and tax collecting became more efficient. Wars took village boys and made them soldiers. Armies brought devastation to thousands of communities. The New World offered new opportunities, brought new products, and increased the wealth of the Continent. Religious reform, both Protestant and Catholic, penetrated into popular beliefs and personal piety. All the sweeping changes blurred the distinction between public and private life.

Still, the transformations wrought by political and intellectual developments were not necessarily the most important ones in people's lives. The lives of most Europeans centered on births and deaths, on the harvest, and on the social relations in their communities. For them, great events were the successful crop, the marriage of an heir, or the festivals that marked the progress of the year. Their beliefs were based as much on the customs they learned as children as on the religion they learned at church. Their strongest loyalties were to family and community rather than to church or state.

The Family

Sixteenth-century life centered on the family. The family was a crucial organizing principle for Europeans of all social ranks, and it served a variety of functions. In the most obvious sense, the family was the primary kin group. European families were predominantly nuclear, composed of a married couple and their children. In western Europe, a small number of families contained the adult siblings of the family head, uncles and aunts who had not yet established their own families. That pattern was more common in the east, especially in Hungary and Muscovy, where taxation was based on households and thus encouraged extended families. There, several nuclear families might live under the same roof. Yet however families were composed, kinship had a wider orbit than just parents and children. In-laws, step-relations, and cousins were considered part of the kin group and could be called upon for support in a variety of contexts, from charity to employment and business partnerships. In towns, such family connections created large and powerful clans.

In a different sense, family was lineage, the connections between preceding and succeeding generations. That was an important concept among the upper ranks of society, where ancient lineage, genuine or fabricated, was a valued component of nobility. That concept of family imparted a sense of stability and longevity in a world in which individual life was short. Even in peasant communities, however, lineage existed in the form of the family farm, that is, the strips in the field that were passed from generation to generation and named for the family that owned them. The village's fields and landmarks also bore the names of individual families, and membership in one of the ancient families of the village was a mark of social distinction.

The family was also an economic unit. In this sense, family overlapped with the household—all those who lived under the same roof, including servants and apprentices. In its economic functions, the family was the basic unit for the production, accumulation, and transmission of wealth. Occupation determined the organization of the economic family. Every member of the household had his or her own functions that were essential to the survival of the unit. Tasks were divided by gender and by age, but there was far more intermixture than is traditionally assumed. On farms, women worked at nearly every occupation with the exception of mowing and plowing. In towns, they were vital to the success of shops and trades, though they were denied training in the skilled crafts. As laborers, they worked in the town fields— for little more than half the wages of men performing the same tasks—and in carrying and delivering goods and materials. Children contributed to the economic vitality of the household from an early age.

Finally, the family was the primary unit of social organization. In the family, children were educated and the social values of hierarchy and discipline were taught. Authority in the family was strictly organized in a set of three overlapping categories. At the top was the husband, head of the household, who ruled over his wife, children, and servants. All members of the family owed obedience to the head. The family was like "a little commonwealth," as English writers put it, in which the adult male was the governor and all others the governed. But two other categories of relationships in the family dispersed the authority. Children owed obedience to their parents, male or female. In this role, the wife and mother was governor as well as governed. Similarly, servants owed obedience to both master and mistress. Male apprentices were under the authority of the wife, mother, and mistress of the household. The importance of the family as a social unit was underscored by the fact that people unattached to families attracted suspicion in sixteenth-century society. Single men were often viewed as potential criminals; single women as potential prostitutes. Both lived outside the discipline and social control of families.

Although the population of Europe was increasing in the early modern era, families were not large. Throughout northern and western Europe, the size of the typical family was two adults and three or four children. Late marriages and breastfeeding helped control family size: the former restricted the number of childbearing years while the latter increased the space between pregnancies. Women married around age 25,

■ Jan Vermeer's *The Milkmaid* (1658–1660) shows a domestic servant absorbed in her household tasks. Homes were sparsely furnished, though this family was rich enough to possess a table, an earthenware bowl and jug, and a footstove that held hot coals (seen on the floor behind the maid).

A FEMININE PERSPECTIVE

Arcangela Tarabotti was born in Venice in the early seventeenth century. Her family did not have the means to provide her with a sufficient dowry, so she was sent to live in a Catholic convent, where she unhappily remained for the rest of her life. She wrote two major works. The first, Monastic Hell, *gives the flavor of her attitude toward her fate. The second was* Innocence Undone, *from which the following excerpt is taken.*

Focus Questions

What does Tarabotti point to as evidence of female superiority? Why do you think Tarabotti concentrates on the biblical account of the Creation?

Since woman is the epitome of all perfections, she is the last of the works of God, as far as material creation is concerned, but otherwise she dates from the beginning, and is the first-generated of all creatures, generated by the breath of God himself, as the Holy Spirit inferred, through the mouth of Solomon in the Ecclesiastes where he introduces the Most Holy Virgin to sing of herself: *The Lord possessed me in the beginning of his ways, before he made any thing from the beginning.*

This creature, although a woman, did not need to be made with a rib taken from man, because, so to speak, she was born before the beginning of time as well as before men, who, blinded by their ambition to dominate the world alone, astutely fail to mention this infallible truth, that the woman has existed in the Divine mind from the beginning. *I was set up from eternity, and of old before the earth was made. The depths were not as yet, and I was already conceived.*

They cannot deny the fact, although their malice prevents them from speaking it openly; but let us try to make them admit, in accordance with the Holy Scriptures rather than with some ill-informed preachers, that the woman made the man perfect and not vice versa.

After the Supreme Being created the world and all the animals (as I have said before), the text says *And God saw all the things that he had made; and they were very good.* Foreseeing that the man without woman would be the compendium of all imperfections, God said: *It is not good for man to be alone: let us make him a help like unto himself.* And therefore he created a companion for him that would be the universal glory of humanity and make him rich with merits.

Almighty God, having kept the creation of the woman as the last act of his wonderful work, desired to bestow privileges upon her, reinforce her graces and gladden the whole world with her splendour. If the supreme Architect's greatness, wisdom and love towards us shone brightly in his other works, he planned to make the woman, this excellent last addition to his splendid construction, capable of filling with wonder whoever looked at her. He therefore gave her the strength to subdue and dominate the proudest and wildest hearts and hold them in sweet captivity by a mere glance or else by the power of her pure modesty. God formed Man, who is so proud, in the field of Damascus; and from one of his ribs he formed woman in the garden of Eden.

If I were not a female, I would deduce from this that the woman, both because of her composition and because of the place in which she was created, is nobler, gentler, stronger and worthier than the man.

What is true strength anyway, if not domination over one's feelings and mastery over one's passions? And who is better at this than the female sex, always virtuous and capable of resisting every temptation to commit or even think evil things? Is there anything more fragile than your head? Compare it to the strength of a rib, the hard bone that is the material from which we were created, and you will be disappointed. Anyone knows that women show more strength than men when they conceive and give birth, by tirelessly carrying all that weight around for nine months.

But you cruel men, who always go around preaching evil for good and good for evil, you pride yourselves in your strength because, like the inhuman creatures you are, you fight and kill each other like wild beasts. . . . Thus, if strength is the ability to bear misfortunes and insults, how can you call yourselves strong when you shed other people's blood sometimes for no reason at all and take the life of innocent creatures at the slightest provocation of a word or a suspicion?

Strength is not mere violence; it requires an indomitable soul, steadfast and constant in Christian fortitude. How can you, o most inconstant ones, ever boast of such virtù? Improperly and deceitfully you have called yourselves virtuous, because only those who fill the world with people and virtù can be called strong.

And those are women. Listen to Solomon, whose words about women reinforce my argument: *Strength and dignity are her clothing.*

From Tarabotti, *Innocence Undone.*

men slightly later. A woman could expect about 15 fertile years and seven or eight pregnancies if neither she nor her husband died in the interim. Only three or four children were likely to survive beyond the age of ten. In her fertile years, a woman was constantly occupied with infants. She was either about to give birth or about to become pregnant. If she used a

■ In an age of high infant mortality and short life expectancy, women were expected to bear many children to ensure family continuity. This embroidery depicts a mother with her thirteen daughters.

wet nurse rather than feed her own babies, as many women in the upper ranks of society did, then she was likely to have 10 or 12 pregnancies during her fertile years and correspondingly more surviving children.

Constant pregnancy and child care may help explain some of the gender roles that men and women assumed in the early modern era. Biblical injunctions and traditional stereotypes help explain others. Pregnant or not, women's labor was a vital part of the domestic economy, especially until the first surviving children were strong enough to assume their share. The woman's sphere was the household. On the farm, she was in charge of the preparation of food, the care of domestic animals, the care and education of children, and the manufacture and cleaning of the family's clothing. In towns, women supervised the shop that was part of the household. They sold goods, kept accounts, and directed the work of domestics or apprentices. Mothers trained their daughters to perform the tasks in the same way that fathers trained their sons to work the fields or ply their craft.

CASE STUDY
The Ideal Wife

The man's sphere was public—the fields in rural areas, the streets in towns. Men plowed, planted, and did the heavy reaping work of farming. They made and maintained essential farm equipment and had charge of the large farm animals. They marketed surplus produce and made the few purchases of equipment or luxury goods. Men performed the labor service that was normally due the lord of the estate, attended the local courts in various capacities, and organized the affairs of the village. In towns, men engaged in heavy labor, procured materials for craft work, and marketed their product if it was not sold in the household shop. Only men could be citizens of the towns or full members of most craft guilds, and only men were involved in civic government.

The separation of men and women into the public and the domestic spheres meant that marriage was a blending of complementary skills. Each partner brought to the marriage essential knowledge and abilities that were fundamental to the economic success of the union. Except in the largest towns, nearly everyone was married for at least a part of his or her life. Remarriage was more common for men than women, however, because a man continued to control the family's property after the death of his wife, whereas a widow might have only a share of it after bequests to children and provisions for apprentices. In the French town of Nantes, a quarter of the annual weddings were remarriages.

While male roles were constant throughout the life cycle, as men trained for and performed the same occupations from childhood to death, female roles varied greatly depending upon the situation. While under the care of fathers, masters, or husbands, women worked in the domestic sphere; once widowed, they assumed the public functions of head of household. Many women inherited shops or farmland; most became responsible for the placement and training of their children. But because of the division of labor upon which the family depended and because of the inherent social and economic prejudices that segregated public and domestic roles, widows were particularly disadvantaged. The most fortunate among them remarried—"The widow weeps with one eye and casts glances with the other," an English proverb held. Their financial and personal independence from men, prized today, was a millstone in the early modern world.

Communities

Despite its central place in all aspects of sixteenth-century life, the family was a fragile and impermanent institution. Even without divorce—permitted in Protestant communities, though never very common—marriages were short. The early death of one of the partners abbreviated the life of the natural family. New marriage partners or social welfare to aid the indigent was sought from within the wider community. On the farm, that community was the rural village; in the town, it was the ward, quarter, or parish in which the family lived. Community life must not be romanticized. Interpersonal violence, lawsuits, and feuds were extraordinarily common in both rural and urban communities. The community was not an idyllic haven of charity and love, where everyone knew and respected neighbors and worked toward a common goal. Like every other aspect of society, the community was socially and economically stratified, gender roles were segregated, and resources were inequitably divided. But the community was the place where people found their social identity. It provided marriage partners for its families, charity for its poor, and a local culture for all of its inhabitants.

Identities and Customs. The two basic forces that tied the rural community together were the lord and the priest. The lord set conditions for work and property ownership that necessitated common decision making on the part of the village farmers. The lord's presence, commonly in the form of an agent, could be both a positive and a negative force for community solidarity. Use of the common lands, the rotation of labor service, and the form in which rents in kind were paid were all decisions that had to be made collectively. Village leadership remained informal, though in some villages headmen or elders bargained with the lord's agent or resolved petty disputes among the villagers. Communal agreement was also expressed in communal resistance to violations of custom or threats to the moral economy. All those forms of negotiation fused individual families into a community. So, too, in a different way did the presence of the parish priest or minister, who attended all the pivotal events of life—birth, marriage, and death. The church was the only common building of the community; it was the only space that was not owned outright by the lord or an individual family. The scene of village meetings and ceremonies, it was the center of both spiritual and social life. The parish priest served as a conduit for all the news of the community and the focal point for the village's festive life. In rural communities, the church was the only organization to which people belonged.

Communities were bound together by the authorities who ruled them and by their common activities. But they were also bound together by their own social customs. Early modern communities used a number of ceremonial occasions as opportunities for expressing solidarity and confirming, in one way or another, the values to which they adhered. In rural parishes there was the annual perambulation, a walk around the village fields that usually occurred before planting began. It was led by the priest, who carried with him any particularly sacred objects that the parish possessed. Behind him followed the village farmers, in some places all members of the village who were capable of walking the distance. The perambulation had many purposes. The priest blessed the fields and prayed for a bountiful crop; the farmers surveyed their own strips and any damage that had been done to the fields during the winter; the community defined its geographical space in distinction to the space of others; and all the individuals who took part reaffirmed their shared identity with others in the village.

In towns, ceremonial processions were far more elaborate. Processions might take place on saints' days in Catholic communities or on anniversaries of town liberties. The order of the march, the clothing worn by the participants, and the objects displayed reflected the strict hierarchies of the town's local organizations. In Catholic towns, the religious orders led the town governors in their robes of office. Following the governors were the members of guilds, each guild placed according to its rank of importance and each organized by masters, journeymen, and apprentices. In some towns, the wives of citizens marched in procession; in others, they were accorded special places from which to view the ceremony. Village and civic ceremonies normally ended with communal feasting and dancing, which were the most popular forms of recreation.

Weddings and Festivals. Not all ceremonial occasions were so formal. The most common ceremony was the wedding, a rite of passage that was simultaneously significant to the individual, the family, and the community. The wedding was a public event that combined a religious ceremony and a community procession with feasting and festivity. It took different forms in different parts of Europe and in different social groups. But whether eastern or western, noble or common, the wedding was celebrated as the moment when the couple entered fully into the community. Marriage involved more than just the union of bride and groom. Parents were a central feature in the event, both in arranging the economic aspects of the union—dowry and inheritance—and in approving the occasion. Many couples were engaged long before they were married, and in many places it was the engagement that was most important to the individuals and the wedding that was most important to the community. One German townsman described how he "had taken a wife but they have not held the wedding yet."

Traditional weddings involved the formal transfer of property, an important event in rural communities, where the ownership of strips of land or common rights concerned everyone. The bridal dowry and the groom's inheritance were formally exchanged during the wedding, even if both were small. The public procession—"the marriage in the streets" as it was sometimes called in towns—proclaimed the union throughout the community and was considered to be as important as the

■ Jan van Eyck, *The Marriage of Giovanni Arnolfini and Giovanna Cenami.* This outstanding fifteenth-century painting of a nuptial scene teems with symbols, including the religious symbols of the rosary, the roundels on the mirror frame, and the post of the chair. The little dog in the foreground may represent fidelity, and the candles in the chandelier may be a symbol of marriage. The mirror reflects the image of two witnesses, who would have been standing where spectators viewing the picture would stand. The inscription on the wall, "Jan van Eyck was here, 1434," suggests that one of the figures is a self-portrait of the artist.

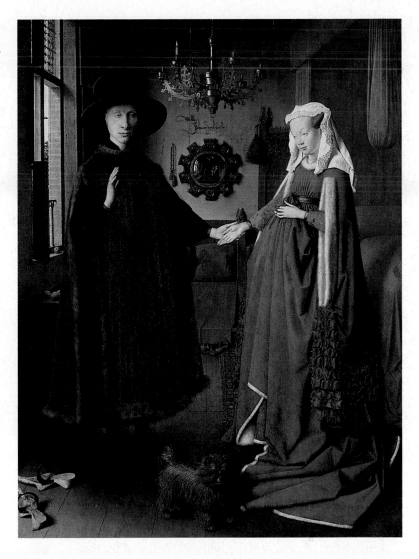

religious ceremony. It was followed by a feast as abundant as the families of bride and groom could afford. In peasant communities, gifts of food for the feast were as common as were gifts to the couple. There were always provisions made that excess food should be sent to the poor or unfortunate after the wedding.

Weddings also legitimated sexual relations. Many of the dances and ceremonies that followed the feast symbolized the sexual congress. Among German burghers it was traditional for the bride to bring the bed to her new home, and bridal beds were passed from mothers to daughters. Among the nobility, the consummation of the marriage was a vital part of the wedding, for without it the union could be annulled. Finally, the marriage inaugurated both bride and groom into new roles in the community. Their place at the wedding table next to their parents elevated them to the status of adults.

Other ceremonies were equally important in creating a shared sense of identity within the community. In both town and countryside, the year was divided by a number of festivals that defined the rhythm of toil and rest. They coincided with both the seasonal divisions of agricultural life and the central events of the Christian calendar. There was no essential difference between the popular and Christian elements in festivals, however strongly the official church insisted upon one. Christmas and Easter were probably the most widely observed Christian holidays, but **Carnival,** which preceded Lent, was a frenzied round of feasts and parties that resulted in a disproportionate number of births nine months later. The Twelve Days of Christmas, which inaugurated the slow, short days of winter, were only loosely attached to the birth of Jesus and were even abolished by some Protestant churches. The rites of May, which celebrated the rebirth of spring, were filled with sexual play among the young adults of the community. Youth groups went "a-Maying" by placing flowers at the homes of marriageable girls, electing a Queen of the May, and dancing and reveling before the hard work of planting. All Hallows' Eve was a celebration for the community's dead, whose spirits were believed to have wandered the village on that night, visiting kin and neighbors.

Festivals helped maintain the sense of community that might be weakened during the long months of increased work or enforced indoor activity. They were first and foremost celebrations in which feasting, dancing, and play were central. But they also

■ Carnivals were occasions for games and feasting. In this painting, *Struggle Between Carnival and Lent*, Pieter Brueghel the Elder depicts a contest between the fasting and other forms of self-denial during Lent (the period of fasting and penitence before Easter) and the tempting attractions of Carnival.

served as safety valves for the pressures and conflicts that built up over the year. There were frequently group and individual sports, such as soccer or wrestling, which served to channel aggressions. Village elders would arbitrate disputes, and marriage alliances or property transactions would be arranged.

Festivals further cemented the political cohesion of the community. Seating arrangements reflected the hierarchy of the community, and public punishment of offenders reinforced deference and social and sexual mores. Youth groups, or even the village women, might band together to shame a promiscuous woman or to place horns on the head of a cuckolded husband. Sometimes a man who had been beaten or abused by his wife, or who had simply failed to enforce obedience from her, was forced to ride backward on a horse or donkey to symbolize the misrule in his family. At such processions, which the French called *charivaris* and the English *skimmingtons*, rough music was played and the offense of the individual or couple was elaborately recreated. (See "A Closer Look: Sex and the Married Man," pp. 476–477.) Such forms of community ritual worked not only to punish offenders but also to reinforce the social and sexual values of the village as a whole.

Popular Beliefs and the Persecution of Witches

Ceremony and festival are reminders that sixteenth-century Europe was still a preliterate society. Despite the introduction of printing and the millions of books that were produced

during the period, the vast majority of Europeans conducted their affairs without the benefit of literacy. Their culture was oral and visual. They had need of an exact memory, and they developed a shorthand of adages, charms, and spells that helped them organize their activities and pass down their knowledge. It is difficult for us to recreate that mental world, in which almost all natural events were unpredictable and in which there was little certainty. Outside a small circle of intellectuals, there was little effective knowledge about either human or celestial bodies. The mysteries of the sun, moon, and stars were as deep as those of health and sickness. But ordinary people did not live in a constant state of terror and anxiety. They used the knowledge they did have to form a view of the universe that conformed to their experiences and that responded to their hopes. Although many of their beliefs seem mere superstitions, they allowed people to form a coherent explanation of the natural world and of their relationship to it.

Magical Practices. The people's beliefs blended Christian teaching and folk wisdom with a strong strain of magic. Popular belief in magic could be found everywhere in Europe, and it operated in much the same way as science does today. Only skilled practitioners could perform magic. It was a technical subject that combined expertise in the properties of plants and animals with theories about the composition of human and heavenly bodies. It had its own language, a mixture of ancient words and sounds with significant numbers and catchphrases. Magicians specialized: some concentrated on herbs and plants, others on the diseases of the body. Alchemists worked with rocks and minerals, astrologers with the movement of the stars. Witches were thought to understand the properties of animals especially well. The witches of Shakespeare's *Macbeth* chanted their exotic recipe for witch's gruel:

> *Eye of newt and toe of frog,*
> *Wool of bat and tongue of dog,*
> *Adder's fork and blindworm's sting,*
> *Lizard's leg and owlet's wing,*
> *For a charm of powerful trouble,*
> *Like a hell-broth boil and bubble.*

Magical practices appealed to people at all levels of society. The wealthy favored astrology and paid handsomely to discover which days and months were the most auspicious for marriages and investments. So-called cunning men predicted the future for those of the lower orders who would not be able to give an astrologer such vital information as the date of their birth or to pay exorbitant fees. The poorest villagers sought the aid of herbalists to help control the constant aches and pains of daily life. Sorcerers and wizards were called upon in more extreme circumstances, such as a threatened harvest or matters of life and death. The magicians competed with the remedies offered by the Church. Special prayers and visits to

THE DEVIL'S DUE

Evidence of the supernatural world abounded for the people of premodern Europe. Natural disasters such as plague and human disasters such as war promoted fear of witchcraft. When the world seemed out of balance and the forces of good retreated before the forces of evil, people sought someone to blame for their troubles. Witches were an obvious choice. Accused witches were most commonly women on the margins of society. Once brought before the authorities, many admitted their traffic with Satan, especially under torture. The Witch Hammer is a set of detailed instructions for the rooting out of witches, including procedures to induce their confessions.

Focus Questions

What is the point of torture, punishment, or investigation? Is the suspected witch seen as being in control of his or her magic?

The method of beginning an examination by torture is as follows: First, the jailers prepare the implements of torture, then they strip the prisoner (if it be a woman, she has already been stripped by other women, upright and of good report). This stripping is lest some means of witchcraft may have been sewed into the clothing—such as often, taught by the Devil, they prepare from the bodies of unbaptized infants, [murdered] that they may forfeit salvation. And when the implements of torture have been prepared, the judge, both in person and through other good men zealous in the faith, tries to persuade the prisoner to confess the truth freely; but, if he will not confess, he bids attendants make the prisoner fast to the strappado or some other implement of torture. The attendants obey forthwith, yet with feigned agitation. Then, at the prayer of some of those present, the prisoner is loosed again and is taken aside and once more persuaded to confess, being led to believe that he will in that case not be put to death.

But if, neither by threats nor by promises such as these, the witch cannot be induced to speak the truth, then the jailers must carry out the sentence, and torture the prisoner according to the accepted methods, with more or less of severity as the delinquent's crime may demand. And,

while he is being tortured, he must be questioned on the articles of accusation, and this frequently and persistently, beginning with the lighter charges—for he will more readily confess the lighter than the heavier. And, while this is being done, the notary must write down everything in his record of the trial—how the prisoner is tortured, on what points he is questioned, and how he answers.

And note that, if he confesses under the torture, he must afterward be conducted to another place, that he may confirm it and certify that it was not due alone to the force of the torture.

But, if the prisoner will not confess the truth satisfactorily, other sorts of tortures must be placed before him, with the statement that, unless he will confess the truth, he must endure these also. But, if not even thus he can be brought into terror and to the truth, then the next day or the next but one is to be set for a *continuation* of the tortures—not a *repetition*, for they must not be repeated unless new evidence be produced. . . .

And during the interval, before the day assigned, the judge, in person or through approved men, must in the manner above described try to persuade the prisoner to confess, promising her (if there is aught to be gained by this promise) that her life shall be spared.

The judge shall see to it, moreover, that throughout this interval guards are constantly with the prisoner, so that she may not be left alone; because she will be visited by the Devil and tempted into suicide.

From *The Witch Hammer.*

A Closer Look
Sex and the Married Man

On 27 May 1618 the peace of the small hamlet of Quemerford, in the west of England, was shattered by the appearance of a large crowd from the neighboring market town of Calne. Men marched with fowling pieces and muskets to a cacophony of drums, clanging pots, whistles, and shouts. Among them, on a red horse, rode an outlandishly costumed man—a smock covering his body; on his head a nightcap with two long shoehorns tied to his ears; and on his face a false beard made from a deer's tail. The crowd escorted the rider to the home of Thomas Mills, who worked in Calne as a cutler. There they stopped. Guns were discharged into the air; an even greater clamor of rough music arose from drums, pipes, and metal objects; and when Mills opened his door, members of the crowd waved aloft the horns of goats or rams mounted on sticks. Then a few strong men entered the house; seized hold of his wife, Agnes; and dragged her to a village mud hole where she was ducked and covered in filth. She was rescued from being set on the horse and ridden to Calne.

That event, known as a skimmington in the west of England and a charivari in France, was a shaming ritual. It was an element of popular culture that took place against the wishes of local authorities and without their connivance. Its purpose was twofold: to identify and punish sexual misconduct and to maintain the male-dominated gender system. The shaming rituals resulted from conduct that the male members of the community believed threatened local order (few women are known to have taken part in the events). In France,

most charivaris were conducted against husbands who were beaten by their wives; in England, many skimmingtons were directed against husbands whose wives had been unfaithful. In both they were designed to shame men into disciplining women and to warn women to remain obedient.

Although skimmingtons and charivaris differed from place to place, all contained similar elements which were designed to invert normal behavior in one way or another. The rough music symbolized the disharmony of a household in which the woman dominated, either by her physical conduct—adultery or husband beating—or her verbal conduct—cursing or abusing her husband or other men. The music was made with everyday objects rather than instruments, and pots and pans were universally present. The "riding" of the husband was another common feature. In many rituals, the "husband," played by a neighbor, was placed facing the tail of the horse or donkey to symbolize the backwardness of his behavior. In some, a "wife," also acted by a neighbor, rode behind the man and beat him with a stick or, in England, with the long-handled ladle used to skim cream that was known as a skimmington. In the end, the real husband or wife was captured, the man to ride in shame throughout the town, the woman to be sat on a cucking stool and dunked in water.

The presence of horns on the male riding the horse and on sticks carried by members of the crowd or worn atop their heads was the universal symbol of adultery. The cuckold—a word derived from the name of a promiscuous female

bird—was an object of derision throughout European society. Codes of conduct from noble to peasant stressed the importance of female sexual fidelity in maintaining the purity of bloodlines and the order of the household. The cuckold was shorn of his masculinity; he had lost his "horns," in common parlance. His personal indignity was a cause for jest and insult, but the disorderliness implicit in the conduct of his wife was a cause for community concern. In local society, reputation was equated with personal worth, and no one had less reputation than the cuckold. Among the nobility, duels were fought over the slightest suggestion of a wife's unfaithfulness, while among ordinary folks the raising of the forefinger and pinkie—the sign of horns—initiated brawls.

The skimmington or charivari combined festive play with the enforcement of social norms. It was rough justice, as the objects of shame were allowed neither explanation nor defense. They were guilty by common fame, that is, by the report of their neighbors and the gossip of the local alehouse rather than by any examination of evidence. Women who yelled at their husbands were sometimes assumed to have beaten them; women who had beaten their husbands were assumed to have cuckolded them. The crimes were all interrelated, and protestations of innocence were useless. The crowds that gathered to perform the ceremony usually had bolstered their courage at the local tavern, and among them were village toughs and those who held grudges against the targeted family. Assault, property damage, and theft occasionally accompanied a skimmington.

■ Scene of a shaming ritual, with the object of derision wearing horns and riding a donkey.

But most of the crowd was there to have a bit of sport and revel in the discomfort of the victims. Their conduct was the inverse of a legal procedure, as disorderly as the conduct of those to be punished. However, their purpose was not to turn the world upside down, but to set it right side up again by restoring the dominance of husbands over wives.

While shaming rituals like the charivari and the skimmington had a long history in Europe, they seem to have exploded into prominence in the late sixteenth and early seventeenth centuries. Population pressures and economic hardship are two conventional explanations for why there were greater local tensions during that period. Skimmingtons and charivaris frequently had rough edges, with some participants motivated by hatred or revenge. But it is also likely that there were more inversion rituals because there was more inversion. Women were taking a larger role in economic affairs and were becoming increasingly literate and active in religion, especially in Protestant countries. Assertive, independent women threatened the male-dominated social order as much as demographic and social change. That the threats were most identified with sexual misconduct and with the stripping of a husband's masculinity was hardly surprising. The image of the obedient female was conventionally the image of chastity. Thus the image of the independent female had to become one of promiscuity. Through the use of skimmingtons and charivaris, men attempted to restore norms of sexual conduct and gender relations that were increasingly under attack. As one English poet put it:

Ill fares the hapless family that shows
A cock that's silent, and a Hen that crows.
I know not which live more unnatural lives,
Obedient husbands, or commanding wives.

the shrines of particular saints were believed to have similar curative value. Magical and Christian beliefs did not oppose each other; they existed on a continuum and were practiced simultaneously. In some French villages, for example, four-leaf clovers were considered especially powerful if they were found on a particular saint's day. It was not until the end of the century, when Protestant and Catholic leaders condemned magical practices and began a campaign to root them out, that magic and religion came into conflict.

Magical practices served a variety of purposes. Healing was the most common, and many "magical" brews were effective remedies of the minor ailments for which they were prescribed. Most village magicians were women because it was believed that women had unique knowledge and understanding of the body. Women were also familiar with the properties of the herbs from which most remedies were derived. Magic was also used for predictive purposes. Certain charms and rituals were believed to have the power to affect the weather, the crops, and even human events. As always, affairs of the heart were as important as those of the stomach. Magicians advised the lovesick on potions and spells that would gain them the object of their desires. Cats were particularly associated with love spells, as were the petals of certain flowers. "He loves me, he loves me not" was more than a child's game. Magic was believed to have the power to alter the course of nature, and it could be used for both good and evil purposes.

The Witch Craze. Magic for evil was black magic, or witchcraft, which utilized beliefs in the presence of spiritual forces in nature. Witches were believed to possess special powers that put them into contact with the devil and the forces of evil, which they could then use for their own purposes. Belief in the prevalence of good and evil spirits was Christian as well as magical. But the Church had gradually consigned the operation of the devil to the afterlife and removed his direct agency from earthly affairs. Beginning in the late fifteenth century, Church authorities began to prosecute large numbers of suspected witches. By the end of the sixteenth century, there was a continentwide witchcraze. Unexplained misfortune or simple malice could set off accusations that might include dozens or even hundreds of suspected witches. Confessions were obtained under torture, as were further accusations. In the period from 1550 to 1650, there were more than 30,000 prosecutions in Germany alone.

Witches were usually women, most often those unmarried or widowed. Although male sorcerers and wizards were thought to have powers over evil spirits, by the sixteenth century it was females who served as the mediators between humans and the diabolical. In a sample of more than 7000 cases of witchcraft prosecuted in early modern Europe, more than 80 percent of the defendants were women. There is no clear explanation why women fulfilled this important and powerful role. Belief in women's special powers over the body through their singular ability to give birth is certainly one part of the

■ This image from Germany depicts events in the imagined lives of witches, who were believed to worship Satan. On the left, two witches dance with demons, while another demon is busy preparing a feast. On the right, three witches are burned alive on a pyre.

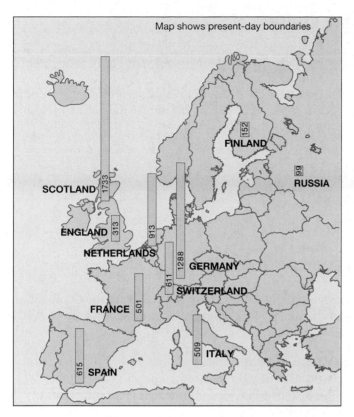

Map shows present-day boundaries

■ Witchcraft Persecutions. There were more trials for witchcraft in Calvinist Scotland than in all of Spain and France combined.

But as the century progressed, more and more notice was taken of black magic. Misfortunes that befell particular families or social groups were blamed upon the activities of witches. The campaign of the established churches to root out magic was largely directed against witches. The churches transposed witches' supposed abilities to communicate with the devil into the charge that they worshipped the devil. Because there was such widespread belief in the presence of diabolical spirits and in the capabilities of witches to control them, Protestant and Catholic church courts could easily find witnesses to testify in support of the charges against individual witches. Yet wherever sufficient evidence exists to understand the circumstances of witchcraft prosecutions, it is clear that the community itself was under some form of social or economic stress. Sacrificing a marginal member of the community might have been the means to restore village solidarity.

CONCLUSION

Population growth, economic diversification, and social change characterized life in early modern Europe. It was a century of extremes. The poor were getting poorer and the rich were getting richer. The early part of the century has been called the golden age of the peasantry; the later part has been called the crisis of subsistence. At all levels of the social scale, the lives of grandparents and grandchildren were dramatically different. For surplus producers, the quality of life improved throughout the century. The market economy expanded. Agricultural surplus was exchanged for more land and a wider variety of consumer goods. Children could be provided with an education, and domestic and agricultural labor was cheap and plentiful. For subsistence producers, the quality of life eroded. In the first half of the century, their diet contained more meat than it would for the next 300 years. Their children could be absorbed on new farms or sent to towns where there was a shortage of both skilled and unskilled labor. But gradually the outlook turned bleak. The land could support no more new families, and the towns needed no more labor. As wages fell and prices rose, peasants in western Europe were caught between the crushing burdens of taxation from lord, state, and church and the all-too-frequent catastrophes of poor harvests, epidemic disease, and warfare. In eastern Europe, the peasantry was tied to the land in a new serfdom that provided minimum subsistence in return for the loss of freedom and opportunity. When peasants anywhere rose up against those conditions, they were cut down and swept away like new-mown hay.

explanation, for many stories about the origins of witches suggest that they were children fathered by the devil and left to be raised by women. The sexual element of union with the devil and the common belief that older women were sexually aggressive combined to threaten male sexual dominance. Witches were also believed to have peculiar physical characteristics. A group of Italian witches, male and female, were distinguished by having been born with a caul (a membrane around their heads that was removed after birth). Accused witches were strip-searched to find the devil's mark, which might be any bodily blemish. Another strand of explanation lies in the fact that single women existed on the fringes of society, isolated and exploited by the community at large. Their occult abilities thus became a protective mechanism that gave them a function within the community while they remained outside it.

It is difficult to know how important black magical beliefs were in ordinary communities. Most of the daily magic that was practiced was the mixture of charms, potions, and prayers that mingled magical, medical, and Christian beliefs.

QUESTIONS FOR REVIEW

1. What physical forces and social customs shaped the everyday life of Europe's rural population?
2. What was the nature of demographic change in the sixteenth century, and what was its impact on the European economy?
3. How are the terms "stratification," "hierarchy," and "status" useful for understanding social relations in early modern Europe?
4. How were the different roles of men and women within the family reflected in the different lives of men and women in the wider community?

KEY TERMS

Carnival, *p. 473*

enclosure, *p. 466*

Great Chain of Being, *p. 461*

Price Revolution, *p. 459*

seigneur, *p. 454*

robot, p. 455

DISCOVERING WESTERN CIVILIZATION ONLINE

You can obtain more information about life in early modern Europe at the Websites listed below. See also the Companion Website that accompanies this text, www.ablongman.com/kishlansky, which contains an online study guide and additional resources.

Social Life

Internet Modern History Sourcebook: Everyday Life in Premodern Europe

www.fordham.edu/halsall/mod/modsbook04.html

A site with links to sources, pictures, and accounts of everyday life in early modern Europe. A good place to start.

Modern History Sourcebook: Social Conditions in 17th Century France

www.fordham.edu/halsall/mod/17france-soc.html

Documents illustrating social conditions in early modern France.

Private Life

Witchcraft

www2.kenyon.edu/projects/margin/witch.htm

A site with links to sources concerning European witchcraft. Also includes suggestions for further reading and a brief overview of the subject.

Witches and Witchcraft

Womenshistory.about.com/cs/witches

This site offers historical information about witches and witchcraft in Europe and America and includes links to related sites.

Life in Tudor England

englishhistory.net/tudor/tudorlife.html

Part of a comprehensive site on Tudor England, this section on life in Tudor England offers information on topics including food and drink, pastimes and entertainment, and mental illness.

SUGGESTIONS FOR FURTHER READING

General Reading

Peter Burke, *Popular Culture in Early Modern Europe* (New York: Harper & Row, 1978). A lively survey of cultural activities among the European populace.

Henry Kamen, *European Society, 1500–1700* (London: Hutchinson, 2000). A general survey of European social history.

Peter Laslett, *The World We Have Lost: Further Explored* (New York: Scribners, 1984). One of the pioneering works on the family and population history of England.

Economic Life

Judith Bennett, *Ale, Beer, and Brewsters: Women's Work in a Changing World* (Oxford: Oxford University Press, 1996). An important study of the role of women in one of the most traditional trades.

Fernand Braudel, *Civilization and Capitalism: The Structures of Everyday Life* (New York: Harper & Row, 1981). Part of a larger work filled with fascinating detail about the social behavior of humankind during the early modern period.

Emmanuel Le Roy Ladurie, *The French Peasantry, 1450–1660* (London: Scholar Press, 1987). A complex study of the lives of the French peasantry.

Peter Musgrave, *The Early Modern European Economy* (New York: St. Martin's Press, 1999). A multidimensional survey of economic life.

Social Life

Yves-Marie Bercé, *Revolt and Revolution in Early Modern Europe* (New York: St. Martin's Press, 1987). A study of the structure of uprisings throughout Europe by a leading French historian.

Natalie Zemon Davis, *Women on the Margins: Three Seventeenth-Century Lives* (Cambridge, MA: Harvard University Press, 1995). Three short and stimulating biographies of early modern European women by a leading historian of popular culture.

Jonathan Dewald, *The European Nobility 1400–1800* (Cambridge: Cambridge University Press, 1996). An outstanding survey based on a wide range of sources.

Edward Muir, *Ritual in Early Modern Europe* (Cambridge: Cambridge University Press, 1997). A fascinating account of the transformations in concepts of time and the body in early modern Europe.

Barry Reay, *Popular Cultures in England, 1550–1750* (New York: Addison Wesley Longman, 1998). A sound and insightful thematic survey.

E. M. W. Tillyard, *The Elizabethan World Picture* (New York: Harper & Row, 1960). The classic account of the social constructs of English society.

Private Life

Roger Chartier, ed., *A History of Private Life, Vol. 3, Passions of the Renaissance* (Cambridge, MA: Harvard University Press, 1989). A lavishly illustrated study of the habits, mores, and structures of private life from the fifteenth to the eighteenth centuries.

Stuart Clark, *Thinking with Demons: The Idea of Witchcraft in Early Modern Europe* (Oxford: Oxford University Press, 1997). A sensitive reading of the sources for the study of witchcraft.

Beatrice Gottlieb, *The Family in the Western World from the Black Death to the Industrial Age* (Oxford: Oxford University Press, 1994). An outstanding introduction to the transformations in the lives of families.

R. A. Houston, *Literacy in Early Modern Europe* (London: Longman, 1988). How literacy and education became part of popular culture from 1500 to 1800.

Brian Levack, *The Witch-Hunt in Early Modern Europe* (London: Longman, 1987). A study of the causes and meaning of the persecution of European witches in the sixteenth and seventeenth centuries.

R. Muchembled, *Popular Culture and Elite Culture in France, 1400–1750* (Baton Rouge: Louisiana State University Press, 1985). A detailed treatment of the practices of two conflicting cultures.

Steven Ozment, *Ancestors: The Loving Family in Old Europe* (Cambridge, MA: Harvard University Press, 2001). A brief and accessible survey by a leading historian, making a spirited defense of early modern family life against historians who have portrayed the premodern family in grim terms.

D. Underdown, *Revel, Riot, and Rebellion* (Oxford: Oxford University Press, 1985). An engaging study of popular culture and its relationship to social and economic structures in England.

Merry E. Wiesner, *Women and Gender in Early Modern Europe* (Cambridge: Cambridge University Press, 1993). The best introduction to European women's history.

For a list of additional titles related to this chapter's topics, please see http://www.ablongman.com/kishlansky.

Chapter 16

THE ROYAL STATE IN THE SEVENTEENTH CENTURY

Chapter Outline

Much of the wealth of seventeenth century societies was invested in building. The wealthiest nobles built the greatest palaces, and kings were the wealthiest nobles. But no one ever built more lavishly than did Louis XIV of France. In The Visual Record, you will behold the palace of all palaces. ➤

FIT FOR A KING
The Grandeur of the European Monarchy

Behold Versailles: the greatest palace of the greatest king of the greatest state in seventeenth-century Europe. Everything about it was stupendous, a reflection of the grandeur of Louis XIV and of France. Sculptured gardens in dazzling geometric forms stretched for acres, scenting the air with exotic perfumes. Nearly as beautiful as the grounds were the 1400 fountains, especially the circular basins of Apollo and Latona, the sun god and his mother. The hundreds of water jets that sprayed at Versailles defied nature as well as the senses, for the locale was not well irrigated and water had to be pumped through elaborate mechanical works all the way from the Seine. Gardens and fountains provided the setting for the enormous palace with its hundreds of rooms for both use and show. Five thousand people, a tenth of whom served the king alone, inhabited the palace. Thousands of others flocked there daily. Most lived in the adjacent town, which had grown from a few hundred people to more than 40,000 in a single generation. The royal stables quartered 12,000 horses and hundreds of carriages. The cost of all that magnificence was equally astounding. Fragmentary accounts indicate that construction costs were more than 100 million French pounds. Louis XIV ordered the official receipts burned.

Like the marble of the palace, nature itself was chiseled to the requirements of the king. Forests were pared to make leafy avenues or trimmed to conform to the geometric patterns of the gardens. In spring and summer, groves of orange trees grown in tubs were everywhere; in winter and fall they were housed indoors at great expense. Life-size statues and giant carved urns lined the carefully planned walkways that led to breathtaking views or sheltered grottoes. A cross-shaped artificial canal, more than a mile long, dominated the western end of the park. Italian gondolas skimmed along its surface, carrying visitors to the zoo and aviary on one side or to the king's private chateau on the other.

But that great pile of bricks and stone, of marble and precious metals, expressed the contradictions of its age as well as its grandeur. The seventeenth century was an era when the rich got richer and the poor got poorer. It was a time when the monarchical state expanded its power and prestige even as it faced grave challenges to its very existence. It was an epoch of unrelenting war amid a nearly universal desire for lasting peace. Thus it was fitting that the prodigious monument was uncomfortable to live in, so unpleasant that Louis had a separate chateau built on the grounds as a quiet retreat. His wife and his mistresses complained constantly of accommodations in which all interior comforts had been subordinated to the external facade of the building. Versailles was a seat of state as well as the home of the monarch, and it is revealing that the private was sacrificed to the public.

The duc de Saint-Simon, who passed much of his time at Versailles, was well aware of the contradictions: "The beautiful and the ugly were sown together, the vast and the constricted." Soldiers, artisans, and the merely curious clogged the three great avenues that led from Paris to the palace. When the king dined in public, hordes of Parisians drove out for the spectacle, filing past the monarch as if he were an exhibit at a museum. The site itself was poorly drained. "Its mud is black and stinking with a stench so penetrating that you can smell it for several leagues around." The orange groves and the stone urns filled with flower petals were more practical than beautiful: they masked the stench of sewage that was particularly noxious in the heat and the rain. Even the gardens were too vast to be enjoyed. In the planted areas, the smell of flowers was overpowering while the acres of mown lawn proved unattractive to an aristocracy little given to physical exercise. "The gardens were admired and avoided," Saint-Simon observed acidly. In those contrasts of failure amid achievement, Versailles stands as an apt symbol of its age: a gaudy mask to hide the wrinkles of the royal state.

Looking Ahead

The great palaces of European absolute monarchs were designed to intimidate those who visited them. They were the representation of royal power at its apex. As we will learn in this chapter, not since Rome's emperors were at the height of their glory had power been more concentrated in the hands of rulers, and what they had consolidated over centuries they now had to protect against competing dynasties or rebellious subjects. ➤

■ Pierre Patel the Elder, *View of Versailles,* 1668.

THE RISE OF THE ROYAL STATE

The religious and dynastic wars that dominated the early part of the seventeenth century had a profound impact upon the western European states. Not only did they cause terrible suffering and deprivation, but they also demanded efficient and better centralized states to conduct them. War was both a product of the European state system and a cause of its continued development. As armies grew in size, the resources necessary to maintain them grew in volume. As the battlefield spread from state to state, defense became government's most important function. More and more power was absorbed by the monarch and his chief advisers; more and more of the traditional privileges of aristocracy and towns were eroded. At the center of the rising states, particularly in western Europe, were the king and his court. In the provinces were tax collectors and military recruiters.

Divine Kings

"There is a divinity that doth hedge a king," wrote Shakespeare. Never was that hedge more luxuriant than in the seventeenth century. In the early sixteenth century, monarchs treated their states and their subjects as personal property. Correspondingly, rulers were praised in personal terms: for their virtue, wisdom, or strength. By the early seventeenth century, the monarchy had been transformed into an office of state. Now rulers embodied their nation and, no matter what their personal characteristics, they were held in awe because they were monarchs.

Thus, as rulers lost direct personal control over their patrimony, they gained indirect symbolic control over their nation. The symbolic power was to be seen everywhere. By the beginning of the seventeenth century, monarchs had set permanent seats of government attended by vast courts of officials, place seekers, and servants. The idea of the capital city emerged, with Madrid, London, Paris, and Vienna as the models. There the grandiose style of the ruler stood proxy for the wealth and glory of the nation. Great display bespoke great pride, and great pride was translated into great strength.

Portraits of rulers in action and repose conveyed the central message. Elizabeth I was depicted bestriding a map of England or clutching a rainbow and wearing a gown woven of eyes and ears to signify her power to see and hear her subjects. The Flemish painter Sir Anthony Van Dyck (1599–1641) created powerful images of three generations of Stuart kings of England. He was court painter to Charles I, whose qualities he portrayed with great sympathy and not a little exaggeration. Diego Velázquez (1599–1660) was court painter to Philip IV of Spain. His series of equestrian portraits of the Habsburgs—kings, queens, princes, and princesses—exude the spirit of the seventeenth-century monarchy, the grandeur and pomp, the power and self-assurance. Peter Paul Rubens (1577–1640) represented 21 separate episodes in the life of Marie de Médicis, queen regent of France.

The themes of writers were no different than those of artists. Monarchy was glorified in a variety of forms of literary representation. National history, particularly of recent events, enjoyed wide popularity. Its avowed purpose was to draw the connection between the past and the present glories of the state. One of the most popular French histories of the period was entitled *On the Excellence of the Kings and the Kingdom of France*. Francis Bacon (1561–1626), who is remembered more as a philosopher and scientist, wrote a laudatory history of Henry VII, founder of the Tudor dynasty.

■ Queen Elizabeth I of England. This portrait was commissioned by Sir Henry Lee to commemorate the queen's visit to his estate at Ditchley. Here the queen, shown standing on a map of England, is the very image of Gloriana—ageless and indomitable.

In England it was a period of renaissance. Poets, playwrights, historians, and philosophers by the dozens gravitated to the English court. One of the most remarkable of them was Ben Jonson (1572–1637). He began life as a bricklayer, fought against the Spanish in Flanders, and then turned to acting and writing. His wit and talent brought him to court, where he made his mark by writing and staging masques, light entertainment that included music, dance, pantomime, and acting. Jonson's masques were distinguished by their lavish productions and exotic costumes and the inventive set designs of the great architect Inigo Jones (1573–1652). They were frequently staged at Christmastime and starred members of the court as players. The masques took the grandeur of England and its rulers for their themes.

Shakespeare and Kingship. The role of William Shakespeare (1564–1616) in the celebration of monarchy was more ambiguous. Like Jonson, Shakespeare came from an ordinary family, had little formal education, and began his astonishing career as an actor and producer of theater. He soon began to write as well as direct his plays, and his company, the King's Players, received royal patronage. He set many of his plays at the courts of princes, and even comedies such as *The Tempest* (1611) and *Measure for Measure* (1604) centered on the power of the ruler to dispense justice and to bring peace to his subjects. Both plays were staged at court.

Shakespeare's history plays focused entirely on the character of kings. In *Richard II* (1597) and *Henry VI* (three parts, 1591–1594) Shakespeare exposed the harm that weak rulers inflicted on their states, while in *Henry IV* (two parts, 1598–1600) and *Henry V* (1599) he highlighted the benefits to be derived from strong rulers.

Shakespeare's tragedies made the point in a different way. The tragic flaw in the personality of rulers exposed the world around them to ruin. In *Macbeth* (1606), the flaw was ambition. Macbeth killed to become a king and had to keep on killing to remain one. In *Hamlet* (1602), the tragic flaw was irresolution. The inability of the Prince of Denmark to act decisively and reclaim the crown that was his by right brought his state to the brink of collapse. Shakespeare's plays were viewed in London theaters by members of all social classes, and his concentration on the affairs of rulers helped reinforce their dominating importance in the lives of all of their subjects.

Monarchy and Law. The political theory of the **divine right of kings** further enhanced the importance of monarchs. The theory held that the institution of monarchy had been created by God and that the monarch functioned as God's representative on earth. One clear statement of divine right theory was actually written by a king, James VI of Scotland, who later became James I of England (1603–1625). In *The True Law of*

DOCUMENT

James I on Divine Right of Kings

A GLIMPSE OF A KING

Louis de Rouvroy, duc de Saint-Simon, spent much of his career at the court of Louis XIV. His Memoires *provide a fascinating study of life at Versailles, as well as poison pen portraits of the king and his courtiers. Here he describes some habits of the king.*

Focus Questions

How does the king maintain his power over the nobles? Why does so much in this political system depend on personal skills and self-presentation?

He always took great pains to find out what was going on in public places, in society, in private houses, even family secrets, and maintained an immense number of spies and tale-bearers. These were of all sorts; some did not know that their reports were carried to him; others did know it; there were others, again, who used to write to him directly, through channels which he prescribed; others who were admitted by the backstairs and saw him in his private room. Many a man in all ranks of life was ruined by these methods, often very unjustly, without ever being able to discover the reason; and when the King had once taken a prejudice against a man, he hardly ever got over it. . . .

No one understood better than Louis XIV the art of enhancing the value of a favour by his manner of bestowing it; he knew how to make the most of a word, a smile, even of a glance. If he addressed any one, were it but to ask a trifling question or make some commonplace remark, all eyes were turned on the person so honored; it was a mark of favour which always gave rise to comment. . . .

He loved splendour, magnificence, and profusion in all things, and encouraged similar tastes in his Court; to spend money freely on equipages and buildings, on feasting and at cards, was a sure way to gain his favour, perhaps to obtain the honour of a word from him. Motives of policy had something to do with this; by making expensive habits the fashion, and, for people in a certain position, a necessity, he compelled his courtiers to live beyond their income, and gradually reduced them to depend on his bounty for the means of subsistence.

From duc de Saint-Simon, *Memoires.*

Free Monarchies (1598), James reasoned that God had placed kings on earth to rule and that he would judge them in heaven for their transgressions.

The idea of the divine origin of monarchy was uncontroversial, and it was espoused not only by kings. One of the few things that the French Estates-General actually agreed upon during its meeting in 1614—the last for more than 175 years—was the statement: "The king is sovereign in France and holds his crown from God only." That sentiment echoed the commonplace view of French political theorists. The greatest writer on the subject, Jean Bodin (1530–1596), called the king "God's image on earth." In *The Six Books of the Commonwealth* (1576), Bodin defined the essence of the monarch's power: "The principal mark of sovereign majesty is essentially the right to impose laws on subjects generally without their consent."

Although at first glance the theory of the divine right of kings appears to be a blueprint for arbitrary rule, in fact it was yoked together with a number of principles that restrained the conduct of the monarch. As James I pointed out, God had charged kings with obligations: "to minister justice; to establish good laws; and to procure peace."

The Court and the Courtiers

For all of the bravura of divine right theory, far more was expected of kings than they could possibly deliver. The day-to-day affairs of government had grown beyond the capacity of any monarch to handle them. The expansion in the powers of the western states absorbed more officials than ever. At the beginning of the sixteenth century, the French court of Francis I employed 622 officers; at the beginning of the seventeenth century, the court of Henry IV employed more than 1500. Yet the difference was not only in size. Members of the seventeenth-century court were becoming servants of the state as well as of the monarch.

Expanding the court was one way in which monarchs coopted potential rivals within the aristocracy. In return, those who were favored enhanced their power by royal grants of titles, lands, and income. As the court expanded, so did the political power of courtiers. Royal councils—a small group of leading officeholders who advised the monarch on state business—grew in significance. Not only did the council assume the management of government, it also began to advocate policies for the monarch to adopt.

Yet, like everything else in seventeenth-century government, the court revolved around the monarch. The monarch appointed, promoted, and dismissed officeholders at will. As befit that type of personal government, most monarchs chose a single individual to act as a funnel for private and public business. That person was the "favorite," whose role combined varying proportions of best friend, right-hand man, and hired gun. Some favorites, such as Cardinal Richelieu of France and Spain's Count-Duke Olivares, were able to transform themselves into chief ministers with a political philosophy and a vision of government. Others, like the English duke of

Buckingham, simply remained royal companions. Favorites walked a not very tight rope. They could retain their balance only as long as they retained their influence with the monarch. Richelieu claimed that it was "more difficult to dominate the four square feet of the king's study than the affairs of Europe." The parallel careers of Richelieu, Olivares, and Buckingham neatly illustrate the dangers and opportunities of the office.

Cardinal Richelieu (1585–1642) was born into a French noble family of minor importance. A younger son, he trained for the law and then for a position that his family owned in the Church; he was made a cardinal in 1622. After skillful participation in the meeting of the Estates-General of 1614, Richelieu was given a court post through the patronage of Queen Marie de Médicis, mother of Louis XIII. The two men

■ This portrait of Richelieu by Philippe de Champaigne shows the cardinal's intellectual power and controlled determination.

Olivares used his closeness to the monarch to gain court appointments for his relatives and political supporters, but he was more interested in establishing political policy than in building a court faction. His objective was to maintain the greatness of Spain, whose fortunes, like his moods, waxed and waned. Like Richelieu, Olivares attempted to further the process of centralizing royal power, which was not very advanced in Spain. Olivares's plans for a nationally recruited and financed army ended in disaster. His efforts at tax reform went unrewarded. He advocated the aggressive foreign policy that mired Spain in the Thirty Years' War and 80 years of war in the Netherlands. As domestic and foreign crises mounted, Philip IV could not resist the pressure to dismiss his chief minister. In 1643, Olivares was removed from office

■ George Villiers, duke of Buckingham. The royal favorite virtually ruled England between 1618 and 1628. The general rejoicing at his death embittered the king and helped bring about the 11 years' rule without Parliament.

■ The Spanish master Diego Velázquez painted this portrait of the Count-Duke Olivares.

made a good match. Louis XIII hated the work of ruling and Richelieu loved little else.

Although Richelieu received great favor from the king—he became a duke and amassed the largest private fortune in France—his position rested on his managerial abilities. Richelieu never enjoyed a close personal relationship with his monarch, and he never felt that his position was secure. In 1630, Marie de Médicis turned against him and he very nearly was ousted from office. His last years were filled with suppressing plots to undermine his power or to take his life.

Count-Duke Olivares (1587–1645) was a younger son of a lesser branch of a great Spanish noble family. By the time he was 20 he had become a courtier with a title, a large fortune, and, most unusually, a university education. Olivares became the favorite of King Philip IV (1621–1665). He was elevated to the highest rank of the nobility and lost no time consolidating his position.

and two years later, physically exhausted and mentally deranged, he died.

The duke of Buckingham (1592–1628) was also a younger son, but not of the English nobility. He received the aimless education of a country gentleman, spending several years in France learning the graces of fashion and dancing. Reputedly one of the most handsome men in Europe, Buckingham hung about the fringes of the English court until his looks and charm brought him to the attention of Queen Anne, James I's wife. She recommended him for a minor office that gave him frequent access to the king. Buckingham quickly caught the eye of James I, and his rise was meteoric. In less than seven years he went from commoner to duke, the highest rank of the English nobility.

Along with his titles, Buckingham acquired political power. He assumed a large number of royal offices, among them Admiral of the Navy, and placed his relatives and dependents in many others. Buckingham took his obligations seriously. He began a reform of naval administration, for example, but his rise to power had been so sudden that he found enemies at every turn. Those increased dramatically when James I died in 1625. But Buckingham succeeded where so many others had failed by becoming the favorite and chief minister of the new king, Charles I (1625–1649). His accumulation of power and patronage proceeded unabated, as did the enmity he aroused. But Charles I stood firmly behind him. In 1628, a discontented naval officer finally accomplished what the most powerful men in England could not: Buckingham was assassinated. While Charles I wept inconsolably at the news, ordinary Londoners drank to the health of his killer.

The Drive to Centralize Government

Richelieu, Olivares, and Buckingham met very different ends. Yet in their own ways they shared a common goal: to extend the authority of the monarch over his state and to centralize his control over the machinery of governance.

One of the chief means by which kings and councillors attempted to expand the authority of the state was through the legal system. Administering justice was one of the sacred duties of the monarchy. The complexities of ecclesiastical, civil, and customary law gave trained lawyers an essential role in government. As legal experts and the demands for legal services increased, royal law courts multiplied and expanded. In France, the Parlement of Paris, the main law court of the state, became a powerful institution that contested with courtiers for the right to advise the monarch. The number of regional **parlements** increased, bringing royal justice to the farthest reaches of the realm. Members of the Parlement of Paris and of the expanding provincial parlements were known as nobility of the robe, because of the long gowns lawyers and judges wore.

In Spain, the *letrados*—university-trained lawyers who were usually members of the nobility—were the backbone of royal government. Formal legal training was a requirement for many of the administrative posts in the state. In Castile, members of all social classes frequently used the royal courts

to settle personal disputes. The expansion of a centralized system of justice thus joined the interests of subjects and the monarchy.

In England, the legal system expanded differently. Central courts, situated in the royal palace of Westminster, grew and the lawyers and judges who practiced in them became powerful. They were especially active in the House of Commons of the English Parliament, which, along with the House of Lords, had extensive advisory and legislative powers. More important than the rise of the central courts, however, was the rise of the local courts. The English Crown extended royal justice to the counties by granting legal authority to members of the local social elite. The justices of the peace, as they were known, became agents of the crown in their own localities. Justices were given power to hear and settle minor cases and to imprison those who had committed serious offenses until the assizes, the semiannual sessions of the county court.

Assizes combined the ceremony of rule with its process. Royal authority was displayed in a great procession to the courthouse that was led by the judge and the county justices, followed by the grand and petty juries of local citizens who would hear the cases, and finally by the carts carrying the prisoners to trial. Along with the legal business that was performed, assizes were occasions for edifying sermons, typically on the theme of obedience. Their solemnity—marked by the black robes of the judge, the Latin of the legal proceedings, and the public executions with which assizes invariably ended—all served to instill a sense of the power of the state in the throngs of ordinary people who witnessed them.

Efforts to integrate center and locality extended to more than the exercise of justice. The monarch also needed officials who could enforce royal policy in those localities where the special privileges of groups and individuals remained strong. The best strategy was to appoint local leaders to royal office. But with so much of the aristocracy resident at court, that was not always an effective course. In France, the provincial governors were traditionally members of the ancient nobility who enjoyed wide powers in matters of military recruitment, revenue collection, and judicial administration. But many governors spent far more time in Paris than in the locality that they were to administer and often opposed the exactions demanded by the monarch. By the beginning of the seventeenth century, the French monarchy began to rely on new central officials known as **intendants** to perform many of the tasks of the provincial governors. Cardinal Richelieu expanded the use of the intendants, and by the middle of the century they had become a vital part of royal government.

Efforts to centralize the affairs of the Spanish monarchy could not proceed so easily. The separate regions over which the king ruled maintained their own laws and privileges. Attempts to apply Castilian rules or implant Castilian officials always drew opposition from other regions. Olivares frequently complained that Philip IV was the king of Castile only and nothing but a thorough plan of unification would make him the king of Spain. He proposed such a plan in 1625 to attempt to solve the dual problems of military manpower and military finance. After 1621, Spain was again deeply involved in European warfare. Fighting in the Netherlands and in Germany demanded large armies and larger sums of money. Olivares launched a plan for a Union of Arms to which all the separate regions of the empire—including Mexico and Peru in the west, Italy in the east, and the separate regions in Iberia—would contribute. He envisioned an army of 140,000 but soon lowered his sights. Not all of the Iberian provinces were persuaded to contribute: Catalonia stood upon its ancient privileges and refused to grant either troops or funds. But Olivares was able to establish at least the principle of unified cooperation.

The Taxing Demands of War

More than anything else, war propelled the consolidation of the state. Whether offensive or defensive, continuous or intermittent, successful or calamitous, war was the irresistible force of the seventeenth-century monarchy. War taxation was its immovable object. Perhaps half of all revenue of the western states went to finance war. To maintain its armies and navies, its fortresses and outposts, the state had to squeeze every penny from its subjects. Old taxes had to be collected more efficiently; new taxes had to be introduced and enforced. As one Spanish jurist observed, in a familiar refrain, "There can be no peace without arms, no arms without money, and no money without taxation." However, the unprecedented demands for money by the state were always resisted. The privileged challenged the legality of levying taxes; the unprivileged did whatever they could to avoid paying them.

The claims and counterclaims of subjects and sovereigns were very strong. Armies had grown bigger and more expensive. In 1625, Philip IV had nearly 300,000 men in arms throughout his empire. The expense of maintaining Spanish fortresses alone had quintupled since the time of Philip II. Not only were there more men to pay, equip, and supply, but the cost of war materials continued to rise with inflation. Similarly, the cost of food and fodder rose. Marauding armies might be able to plunder sufficient grain during the spring and autumn, but they still consumed massive amounts of meat and drink that could not be supplied locally.

In fact, the inability of the lower orders of European society to finance a century of warfare was clear from the beginning. In Spain and France, the principal problem was that so much of the wealth of the nation was beyond the reach of traditional royal taxation. The nobility and many of the most important towns had long achieved exemption from basic taxes on consumption and wealth. European taxation was regressive, falling most heavily on those least able to pay. Rulers and subjects alike recognized the inequities of the system. Regime after regime began with plans to overhaul the national system of taxation before settling for propping up new emergency levies against the rotting foundations of the old structure. Nevertheless, the fiscal crisis that the European wars provoked did result in an expansion of state taxation.

Fiscal Expedients. In France, for example, royal expenditures rose 60 percent during the first two decades of the seventeenth century, while the yield from the *taille,* the crown's basic commodity tax, remained constant. Thus the crown was forced to search for new revenues, the most important of which was the *paulette,* a tax on officeholding. To raise money, especially in emergencies, the crown had been forced to sell government offices, until by the seventeenth century a majority of offices had been obtained by direct purchase. The sale of an office provided a one-time windfall for the crown, but after that the cost of salaries and benefits was a perpetual drain. Draining, too, were the administrative costs of potentially inefficient officeholders. Many purchased their posts as an investment and treated them as personal property. For an annual payment of one-sixtieth of the value of the office, the paulette allowed the current holder to sell or bequeath it as desired. Henry IV instituted the paulette in 1604, and it became a vital source of royal revenue as well as an acute source of aristocratic and legal complaint. In the early 1620s, revenue from the sale of offices amounted to one-third of the crown's income.

The purchase of office was inherently corrupt, but it was not necessarily inefficient. Sons who were to inherit offices could be trained for their posts, if for no other reason than to operate them profitably. The crown received money from classes in society that were generally beyond the reach of taxation, while members of those classes received power, prestige, and experience in public service. As long as profit and efficiency went hand in hand, both officeholder and monarch might be well served. Unfortunately, it was the king rather than his officers who had the greatest incentive to manipulate the system. The more offices that could be created, the larger the income from the paulette. During fiscal emergencies it was a temptation to which all French monarchs succumbed.

"Fiscal emergency" was just another name for the routine problems of the Spanish monarchy. As the greatest military power in Europe, Spain necessarily had the greatest military budget, and thus the most extensive system of taxation. The crown taxed both domestic and imperial trade and took a healthy share of the gold and silver that continued to be mined in America. But all the revenues fell short of the state's needs. In the 1590s, Philip II established an important new source of internal taxation. In an agreement with the Cortes of Castile, he introduced the *milliones,* a tax on consumption that was to yield millions of ducats a year for war costs. An extremely regressive measure, the milliones taxed the sale of meat, wine, and oil—the basic elements of diet. The tax, which hit urban areas particularly hard, was originally designed to last only six years. But the crises that the crown pleaded in the 1590s were even deeper at the turn of the century. The milliones became a permanent tax and a permanent grievance throughout Castile.

Taxation in England. By contrast, the English crown was never able to persuade Parliament to grant permanent additional revenues. Although uninvolved in European conflicts, England was not immune from military spending. War with

■ Charles I by Daniel Myrtens. The antagonism between Charles and Parliament sparked a civil war in England.

Ireland in the 1590s and with Spain between 1588 and 1604 depleted the reserves that the crown had obtained when Henry VIII dissolved the monasteries. Disastrous wars against France and Spain in the 1620s provoked fiscal crisis for a monarchy that had few direct sources of revenue. While the great wealth of the kingdom was in land, the chief sources of revenue for the crown were in trade. In the early seventeenth century, customs duties, or *impositions,* became a lucrative source of income when the judges ruled that the king could determine which commodities could be taxed and at what rate. Impositions fell heavily upon the merchant classes and urban consumers, but unlike the milliones, impositions were placed on luxury import goods rather than on basic commodities.

Because so much of the crown's revenues derived from commerce and because foreign invasion could only come from the sea, the most pressing military need of the English monarchy was for naval defense. Even during the Armada crisis, the largest part of the English fleet had been made up of private merchant ships pressed into service through the emergency tax of Ship Money, which was a tax on each port town to hire a merchant ship and fit it out for war. In the 1630s, Charles I revived Ship Money and extended it to all English localities. His innovation aroused much opposition from the gentry, especially after his refusal to call Parliament into session to have the tax confirmed.

Still, no matter how much new revenue was provided for war finance, more was needed. New taxes and increased rates of traditional taxation created suffering and a sense of grievance throughout the western European states. Opposition to taxation was not based on greed: the state's right to tax was not yet an established principle. Monarchs received certain forms of revenue in return for grants of immunities and privileges to powerful groups in their state. The state's efforts to go beyond the restricted grants were viewed as theft of private property. In the case of Ship Money, challengers argued that the king had no right to what belonged to his subjects except in a case of national emergency. That was a claim that the king accepted, arguing that such an emergency existed in the presence of pirates who were attacking English shipping. But if Charles I did not make a convincing claim for national emergency, the monarchs of France and Spain, the princes of Germany, and the rulers of the states of eastern Europe all did.

Throughout the seventeenth century, monarchy solidified itself as a form of government. The king's authority came from God, but his power came from his people. By administering justice, assembling armies, and extracting resources through taxation, the monarch ruled as well as governed. The richer the king and the more powerful his might, the more potent was his state. Europeans began to identify themselves as citizens of a nation and to see themselves in distinction to other nations.

THE CRISES OF THE ROYAL STATE

The expansion of the functions, duties, and powers of the state in the early seventeenth century was not universally welcomed in European societies. The growth of central government came at the expense of local rights and privileges held by corporate bodies such as the Church and the towns or by individuals such as provincial officials and aristocrats. The state proved a powerful competitor, especially in the contest for the meager surplus produced on the land. As rents and prices stabilized in the early seventeenth century after a long period of inflation, taxation increased, slowly at first and then at a pace with the gathering momentum of the Thirty Years' War. State exactions burdened all segments of society. Peasants lost the small benefit that rising prices had conferred on producers. The surplus that parents had once passed on to children was now taken by the state. Local officials, never altogether popular, came to be seen as parasites and were easy targets for peasant rebellions. Larger landholders, whose prosperity depended on rents and services from an increasingly impoverished peasantry, suffered along with their tenants. Even the great magnates were appalled by the state's insatiable appetite.

EUROPEAN POPULATION DATA (IN MILLIONS)

Year	1550	1575	1600	1625	1650	1675	1700
England	3.0	—	4.0	4.5	—	5.8	5.8
France	—	20.0	—	—	—	—	19.3
Italy	11.0	13.0	13.0	13.0	12.0	11.5	12.5
Russia	9.0	—	11.0	8.0	9.5	13.0	16.0
Spain	6.3	—	7.6	—	5.2	—	7.0
All Europe	85.0	95.0	100.0	100.0	80.0	90.0	100.0

Taxation was not the only thing that aroused opposition. Social and economic regulation meant more laws. More laws meant more lawyers and agents of enforcement. State regulation may have been more efficient (though many believed it was more efficient only for the state) but it was certainly disruptive. It was also expensive at a time when the fragile European economy was in a phase of decline. The early seventeenth century was a time of hunger in most of western Europe. Subtle changes in climate reduced the length of growing seasons and the size of crops. Bad harvests in the 1620s and 1640s left disease and starvation in their wake. And the wars ground on.

By the middle of the seventeenth century, a European crisis was taking shape, though its timing and forms differed from place to place. Rural protests, such as grain riots and mob assaults on local institutions, had a long history in all of the European states. Popular revolt was not the product of mindless despair, but rather the natural form of political action for those who fell outside the institutionalized political process. Bread riots and tax revolts became increasingly common in the early seventeenth century. More significantly, as the focus of discontent moved from local institutions to the state, the forms of revolt changed. So, too, did the participants. Members of the political elite began to formulate their own grievances against the expansion of state power. A theory of resistance, first developed in the French wars of religion, came to be applied to political tyranny and posed a direct challenge to the idea of the divine right of kings. By the 1640s, all those forces had converged, and rebellion exploded across the Continent. In Spain, the ancient kingdoms of Catalonia and Portugal asserted their independence from Castilian rule; in France, members of the aristocracy rose against a child monarch and his regent. In Italy, revolts rocked Naples and Sicily. In England, a constitutional crisis gave way to civil war, and then to the first political revolution in European history.

The Need to Resist

Europeans lived more precariously in the seventeenth century than in any period since the Black Death. One benchmark of crisis was population decline. In the Mediterranean, Spain's population fell from 8.5 to 7 million and Italy's population from 13 to 11 million. The ravages of the Thirty Years' War were most clearly felt in central Europe: Germany lost nearly a third of its people, Bohemia nearly half. Northwestern Europe—England, the Netherlands, and France—was hardest hit in the first half of the century and only gradually recovered by 1700. Population decline had many causes and, rather remarkably, direct casualties from warfare were a very small component. The indirect effects of war—the disruption of agriculture and the spread of disease—were far more devastating. Spain alone lost a half million people at the turn of the century and another half million between 1647 and 1652. Severe outbreaks of plague in 1625 and in 1665 hit England, while France endured three consecutive years of epidemics, from 1629 to 1631.

All sectors of the European economy, from agriculture to trade, stagnated or declined in the early seventeenth century. Not surprisingly, peasants were hardest hit. The surplus from good harvests did not remain in rural communities to act as a buffer for bad ones. Tens of thousands died during the two great subsistence crises in the late 1620s and the late 1640s. Predictably, acute economic crisis led to rural revolt. As the French peasants reeled from visitations of plague, frost, and floods, the French state was raising the taille, the tax that fell most heavily on the lower orders. A series of French rural revolts in the late 1630s focused on opposition to tax increases. The Nu-Pieds—"the barefooted"—rose against changes in the salt tax; others rose against new levies on wine. The revolts began in the same way: with the murder of a local tax official, the organization of a peasant militia, and the recruitment of local clergy and notables. The rebels forced temporary concessions from local authorities, but they never achieved lasting reforms. Each revolt ended with the reimposition of order by the state. In England, the largest rural protests, like the Midland Revolt of 1607, centered on opposition to the enclosure of grain fields and their conversion to pasture.

The most spectacular popular uprisings occurred in Spanish-occupied Italy. In the spring of 1647, the Sicilian city of Palermo exploded under the pressure of a disastrous harvest,

■ War, famine, and disease all contributed to population decline in the seventeenth century. This broadsheet shows the weekly burial of plague victims in London during a severe outbreak in 1665.

rising food prices, and relentless taxation. A city of 130,000 inhabitants, Palermo imported nearly all of its foodstuffs. As grain prices rose, the city government subsidized the price of bread, running up huge debts in the process. When the town governors could no longer afford the subsidies, they decided to reduce the size of the loaf rather than increase its price. This did not fool the women of the city, who rioted when the first undersized loaves were placed on sale. Soon the entire city was in revolt. "Long live the king and down with taxes!" became the rebel slogan. Commoners who were not part of the urban power structure led the revolt in Palermo. For a time they achieved the abolition of Spanish taxes on basic foodstuffs. Their success provided the model for a similar uprising in Naples, the largest city in Europe. The Neapolitan revolt began in 1647 after the Spanish placed a tax on fruit. A crowd gathered to protest the new imposition, burned the customs house, and murdered several local officials. The protesters were led first by a fisherman and then by a blacksmith, and again the rebels achieved the temporary suspension of Spanish taxation. But neither of the Italian urban revolts could attract support from the local governors or the nobility. Both uprisings were eventually crushed.

The Right to Resist

Rural and urban revolts by members of the lower orders of European society were doomed to failure. Not only did the state control vast military resources, but it could count on the loyalty of the governing classes to suppress local disorder. It was only when local elites rebelled and joined their social and political discontent to the economic grievances of the peasants that the state faced a genuine crisis. Traditionally, aristocratic rebellion focused on the legitimacy rather than the power of the state.

Claimants to the throne initiated civil wars for the prize of the crown. By the early seventeenth century, however, hereditary monarchy was too firmly entrenched to be threatened by aristocratic rebellions. When Elizabeth I of England died without an heir, the throne passed to her cousin, James I, without even a murmur of discontent. The assassination of Henry IV in 1610 left a child on the French throne, yet it provoked little more than intrigue over which aristocratic faction would advise him. The principles of hereditary monarchy and the divine right of kings laid an unshakable foundation for royal legitimacy. But if the monarch's right to rule could no longer be challenged, was the method of rule equally unassailable? Were subjects bound to their sovereign in all cases whatsoever?

Resistance Theory.   Luther and Calvin had preached a doctrine of passive obedience. Magistrates ruled by divine will and had to be obeyed in all things, they argued. Both left a tiny crack in the door of absolute submission, however, by recognizing the right of lesser magistrates to resist their superiors if divine law was violated. It was during the French civil wars that a broader theory of resistance began to develop. In attempting to defend themselves from accusations that they were rebels, a number of Huguenot writers responded with an argument that accepted the divine right of kings but limited royal power. They claimed that kings were placed on earth by God to uphold piety and justice. When they failed to do so, lesser magistrates were obliged to resist them. As God would not institute tyranny, oppressive monarchs could not be acting by divine right. Therefore, the king who violated divine law could be punished. In the most influential of such writings, *A Defense of Liberty Against Tyrants* (1579), Philippe Duplessis-Mornay (1549–1623) took the critical next step and argued that the king who violated the law of the land could also be resisted.

In the writings of both Huguenot and Dutch Protestants there remained strict limits to the right to resist. Those authors accepted all the premises of divine right theory and restricted resistance to other divinely ordained magistrates. Obedience tied society together at all levels, and loosening any of the knots might unravel everything. In fact, one crucial binding had already come loose when the arguments used to justify resistance in matters of religion came to be applied to matters of state. Logic soon drove the argument further. If it was the duty of lesser magistrates to resist monarchical tyranny, why was it not the duty of all citizens to do so? That was a question posed not by a Protestant rebel, but by a Jesuit professor, Juan de Mariana (1536–1624). In *The King and the Education of the King* (1598), Mariana described how human government developed from the need of individuals to have leaders to act for their convenience and well-being. The magistrates were established by the people and then legitimated by God. Magistrates were nothing other than the people's representatives, and if it was the duty of magistrates to resist the tyranny of monarchs, then it must also be the duty of every individual citizen. "If the sacred fatherland is falling into ruins, he who tries to kill the tyrant will be acting in no ways unjustly."

There remained one more vital link in the chain, which was supplied by the great English poet John Milton (1608–1674) in his defense of the English Revolution. Milton built upon traditional resistance theory as it had developed over the previous 50 years. Kings were instituted by the people to uphold piety and justice. Lesser magistrates had the right to resist monarchs. An unjust king forfeited his divine right and was to be punished as any ordinary citizen. In *The Tenure of Kings and Magistrates* (1649), Milton expanded upon the conventional idea that society was formed by a covenant, or contract, between ruler and ruled. The king in his coronation oath promised to uphold the laws of the land and rule for the benefit of his subjects. The subjects promised to obey. Failure by either side to meet obligations broke the contract.

Resistance and Rebellion.   By the middle of the seventeenth century, resistance theory provided the intellectual justification for a number of different attacks on monarchical authority. In 1640, simultaneous rebellions in the ancient kingdoms of Portugal and Catalonia threatened the Spanish monarchy. The Portuguese successfully dissolved the rather artificial bonds that had been created by Philip II and resumed their separate national identity. Catalonia, the easternmost province of Spain, which Ferdinand of Aragon had brought to the union of crowns in the fifteenth century, presented a more serious challenge. Throughout the 1620s, Catalonia, with its rich Mediterranean city of Barcelona, had consistently rebuffed Olivares's attempts to consolidate the Spanish provinces. The Catalonian Cortes—the representative institution of the towns—refused to make even small contributions to the Union of Arms or to successive appeals for emergency tax increases. Catalonian leaders feared that the demands were only the thin edge of the wedge. They did not want their province to go the way of Castile, where taxation was as much an epidemic as plague.

Catalonia relied on its ancient laws to fend off demands for contributions to the Spanish military effort. But soon the province was embroiled in the French war, and Olivares was forced to bring troops into Catalonia. The presence of the soldiers and their conduct inflamed the local population. In the spring of 1640 an unconnected series of peasant uprisings took place. Soldiers and royal officials were slain, and the Spanish viceroy of the province was murdered. But the violence was not directed only against outsiders. Attacks on wealthy citizens raised the specter of social revolt.

At that point a peasant uprising broadened into a provincial rebellion. The political leaders of Barcelona not only decided to approve the rebellion but decided to lead it. They declared that Philip IV had violated the fundamental laws of Catalonia and that as a consequence their allegiance to the crown of Spain was dissolved. They turned to Louis XIII of France, offering him sovereignty if he would preserve their liberties. In fact, the Catalonians simply exchanged a devil they knew for one they did not. The French happily sent troops into Barcelona to repel a Spanish attempt to crush the rebellion, and then two armies occupied Catalonia. The Catalonian rebellion lasted for 12 years. When the Spanish finally took Barcelona in 1652, both rebels and ruler were exhausted from the struggle.

The revolt of the Catalonians posed a greater external threat to the Spanish monarchy than it did an internal one. In contrast, the French **Fronde,** an aristocratic rebellion that began in 1648, was more directly a challenge to the underlying authority of the state. It too began in response to fiscal crises brought on by war. Throughout the 1640s the French state had tottered on the edge of bankruptcy. It had used every means of creative financing that its ministers could devise, mortgaging as much of the future as anyone would buy. Still, it was necessary to raise traditional taxes and institute new ones. The first tactic revived peasant revolts, especially in the early years of the decade; the second led to the Fronde.

The Fronde was a rebellion against the regency government of Louis XIV (1643–1715), who was only four years old when he inherited the French throne. His mother, Anne of Austria (1601–1666), ruled as regent with the help of her Italian adviser, Cardinal Mazarin (1602–1661). In the circumstances of war, agricultural crisis, and financial stringency, no regency government was popular, but Anne and Mazarin made the worst of a bad situation. They initiated new taxes on officeholders, Parisian landowners, and the nobility. Soon all three united against them, led by the Parlement of Paris, the highest court in the land, in which new decrees of taxation had to be registered. When the Parlement refused to register a number of the new taxes proposed by the government and soon insisted on the right to control the crown's financial policy, Anne and Mazarin struck back by arresting a number of leading members of the Parlement. But in 1648 barricades went up in Paris, and the court, along with the nine-year-old king, fled the capital. Quickly the Fronde—which took its name from the slingshots that children used to hurl stones at carriages—became an aristocratic revolt aimed not at the king, but at his advisers. Demands for Mazarin's resignation,

■ Anne of Austria acted as a regent during her son's minority, though in practice she delegated most power to her adviser Cardinal Mazarin. This painting emphasizes the piety of the royal family, as Anne, Louis, and his younger brother Philippe kneel in prayer against a backdrop of God, Jesus, and their heavenly and worldly servants.

the removal of the new taxes, and greater participation in government by nobles and Parlement were coupled with profuse statements of loyalty to the king.

The duc de Condé, leader of the Parisian insurgents, courted Spanish aid against Mazarin's forces, and the cardinal was forced to make concessions in order to prevent a Spanish invasion of France. The leaders of the Fronde agreed that the crown must overhaul its finances and recognize the rights of the administrative nobility to participate in formulating royal policy, but they had no concrete proposals to accomplish either aim. Nor could they control the deteriorating political situation in Paris and a number of provincial capitals where urban and rural riots followed the upper-class attack upon the state. The catastrophic winter of 1652, with its combination of harvest failure, intense cold, and epidemic disease, brought the crisis to a head. Louis XIV was declared old enough to rule and his forces recaptured Paris, where he was welcomed as a savior. Born of frustration, fear, and greed, the Fronde accomplished little. It demonstrated only that the French aristocracy remained an independent force in politics. Like the Catalonian revolt, it revealed the fragility of the absolute state on the one hand, yet its underlying stability on the other.

The English Civil War

On the surface, it is difficult to understand why the most profound challenge to monarchical authority took place in England. Among the nations of Europe, England alone enjoyed peace in the early seventeenth century. Except for a brief period around 1620, the English economy sputtered along. The monarchy itself was stable. James I had succeeded his cousin Elizabeth I without challenge and already had as many children as the Tudors had produced in nearly a century.

James I.   James I was not a lovable monarch, but he was capable, astute, and generous. In the eyes of his critics he had two great faults: he succeeded a legend and he was Scottish. There was little he could do about either. Elizabeth I had ruled England successfully for more than 40 years. As the economy soured and the state tilted toward bankruptcy in the 1590s, the queen remained above criticism. She sold off royal lands worth thousands of pounds and ran up huge debts at the turn of the century, yet the gleaming myth of the glorious virgin queen tarnished not the least bit. When she died, the general population wept openly and the governing elite breathed a collective sigh of relief. There was so much to be done to set things right.

At first, James I endeared himself to the English gentry and aristocracy by showering them with the gift of social elevation. On his way to London from Scotland, the first of the Stuart kings knighted thousands of gentlemen who had waited in vain for favor from the queen. He promoted peers and created new titles to meet the pent-up demands of decades of stinginess. But he showered favor equally on his own countrymen, members of his royal Scottish court who accompanied him to England. A strong strain of ethnic prejudice combined with the disappointed hopes of English courtiers to generate immediate hostility to the new regime. If Elizabeth could do no wrong, James could do little right. Although he relied upon Elizabeth's most trusted ministers to guide state business, James was soon plunged into financial and political difficulties. He never escaped from either.

Charles I. James's financial problems resulted directly from the fact that the tax base of the English monarchy was undervalued. For decades the monarchy had staved off a crisis by selling lands that had been confiscated from the Church in the mid-sixteenth century. But that solution reduced the crown's long-term revenues and made it dependent on extraordinary grants of taxation from Parliament. Royal demands for money were met by parliamentary demands for political reform, and the differing objectives provoked unintentional political controversies in the 1620s. The most significant, in 1628, during the reign of Charles I, led to the formulation of the Petition of Right, which restated the traditional English freedoms from arbitrary arrest and imprisonment (habeas corpus), nonparliamentary taxation, and the confiscation of property by martial law.

Religious problems mounted on top of economic and political difficulties. Demands were made for thoroughgoing church reforms by groups and individuals who had little in common apart from the name given to them by their detractors: **Puritans.** One of the most contentious issues raised by Puritans was the survival in the Anglican church of the Catholic hierarchy of archbishops and bishops. They demanded the abolition of this episcopal form of government and its replacement with a presbyterial system similar to that in Scotland, in which congregations nominated their own representatives to a national assembly. As the king was the supreme head of the English church, an attack upon church structure was an attack upon the monarchy. "No bishop, no king," James I declared as he rejected the first formal attempts at reform. But neither James I nor his son, Charles I, opposed religious reform. They, too, wanted a better educated clergy, a plain and decorous worship service, and godly citizens. But to achieve their reforms they strengthened episcopal power. In the 1620s, Archbishop William Laud (1573–1645)

A SHORT, SHARP SHOCK

Charles I was executed at Westminster on a bitter January afternoon in 1649. This excerpt comes from an eyewitness account of his last moments. Charles, who was accompanied on the scaffold by the bishop of London, discovered that the chopping block was very short so that he could be held down if he resisted.

Focus Questions
Is Charles resigned to his execution? In what ways is the divine right of kings commented upon in this passage?

And to the executioner he said, "I shall say but very short prayers, and when I thrust out my hands—"

Then he called to the bishop for his cap, and having put it on, asked the executioner, "Does my hair trouble you?" who desired him to put it all under his cap; which, as he was doing by the help of the bishop and the executioner, he turned to the bishop, and said, "I have a good cause, and a gracious God on my side."

The bishop said, "There is but one stage more, which, though turbulent and troublesome, yet is a very short one. You may consider it will soon carry you a very great way; it will carry you from earth to heaven; and there you shall find to your great joy the prize you hasten to, a crown of glory."

The king adjoins, "I go from a corruptible to an incorruptible crown; where no disturbance can be, no disturbance in the world."

The bishop. "You are exchanged from a temporal to an eternal crown—a good exchange."

Then the king asked the executioner, "Is my hair well?" . . . and looking upon the block, said . . . "You must set it fast."

The executioner. "It is fast, sir."

King. "It might have been a little higher."

Executioner. "It can be no higher, sir."

King. "When I put out my hands this way, then—"

Then having said a few words to himself, as he stood, with hands and eyes lifted up, immediately stooping down he laid his neck upon the block; and the executioner, again putting his hair under his cap, his Majesty, thinking he had been going to strike, bade him, "Stay for the sign."

Executioner. "Yes, I will, and it please your Majesty."

After a very short pause, his Majesty stretching forth his hands, the executioner at one blow severed his head from his body; which, being held up and showed to the people, was with his body put into a coffin covered with black velvet and carried into his lodging.

His blood was taken up by divers persons for different ends: by some as trophies of their villainy; by others as relics of a martyr; and in some hath had the same effect, by the blessing of God, which was often found in his sacred touch when living.

rose to power in the English church by espousing a Calvinism so moderate that many denied it was Calvinism at all. Laud preached the beauty of holiness and strove to reintroduce decoration in the church and a formal decorum in the service. One of Laud's first projects after he was appointed archbishop of Canterbury was to establish a consistent divine service in England and Scotland by creating new prayer books.

It fell to the unfortunate dean of St. Giles Cathedral in Edinburgh to introduce the new Scottish prayer book in 1637. The reaction was immediate: someone threw a stool at his head and dozens of women screamed that "popery" was being brought to Scotland. There were riots by citizens and resistance to the use of the new prayer book by clergy and the nobility. To Charles I the opposition was rebellion, and he began to raise forces to suppress it. But Scottish soldiers were far more determined to preserve their religious practice than were English soldiers to impose the king's. By the end of 1640, a Scottish army had successfully invaded England.

Now the fiscal and political problems of the Stuart monarchs came into play. For 11 years, Charles I had managed to do what he was in theory supposed to do: live from his own revenues. He had accomplished that by a combination of economy and the revival of ancient feudal rights that struck hard at the governing classes. He levied fines for unheard-of offenses, expanded traditional taxes, and added a brutal efficiency to the collection of revenue. While these expedients sufficed during peacetime, they could not support an army and war. Charles I was again dependent on grants from Parliament, which he reluctantly summoned in 1640.

The Long Parliament.   The **Long Parliament,** which met in November 1640 and sat for 13 years, saw little urgency in levying taxes to repel the Scots. After all, the Scots were resisting Laud's religious innovations, and there were many Englishmen who believed that they should be resisted. More to the point, members of Parliament had a host of political grievances to be redressed before they granted the king his money. Parliament proposed a number of constitutional reforms that Charles I reluctantly accepted. The Long Parliament would not be dismissed without its own consent. In the future, Parliaments would be summoned once every three years. Due process in common law would be observed, and the ancient taxes that the crown had revived would be abolished. To show its seriousness of purpose, Parliament, as the highest court in the land, tried and executed Charles's leading political adviser, the Earl of Strafford, and imprisoned Archbishop Laud.

At first Charles I could do nothing but bide his time and accept the assaults on his power and authority, believing that once he had crushed the Scots he would be able to bargain from a position of strength. But as the months passed, it became clear that Parliament had no intention of providing him with money or forces. Rather, the members sought to negotiate with the Scots themselves and to continue to demand concessions from the king as long as the Scottish threat remained. By the end of 1641, Charles's patience had worn thin. He bungled an attempt to arrest the leaders of the House of Commons, but he successfully spirited his wife and children out of London. Then he too left the capital and headed north

MAP DISCOVERY

Areas controlled by Royalists
Areas controlled by Parliamentarians
★ Major battles
0   200 Miles
0   200 Kilometers

December 1642 — SCOTLAND, IRELAND, North Sea, ★ Edge Hill Oct. 1642, London, English Channel

December 1643 — SCOTLAND, IRELAND, North Sea, Adwalton Moor June 1643 ★, London, English Channel

December 1644 — SCOTLAND, IRELAND, North Sea, Marston Moor July 1644 ★, London, English Channel

December 1645 — SCOTLAND, IRELAND, North Sea, Naseby June 1645 ★, London, English Channel

English Civil War

How would you describe the geographical divisions at the beginning of the war in 1642? Who appears to have been winning the war by December 1643? How did the war progress between 1644 and 1645?

■ Print of the 1649 execution of Charles I, who was tried and found guilty of treason. As the ax fell, one witness recorded, "such a groan as I never heard before and hope never to hear again" broke forth from the crowd. With the king's execution, England was declared to be a commonwealth, and the monarchy was abolished.

where, in the summer of 1642, he raised the royal standard and declared the leaders of Parliament rebels and traitors. England was plunged into civil war.

Parliament had finally pushed too hard, and its members now found themselves in the unprecedented situation of having to fight a war against their sovereign, a war that few of them wanted and that hardly anyone believed they could win. One of the Parliament's generals summed up the futility of the situation: "If we defeat the king ninety-nine times, yet still he is king. But if he defeat us once we will all be hanged as traitors." Nevertheless, there were strong passions on both sides. Parliamentarians believed that they were fighting to defend their religion, their liberties, and the rule of law. Royalists believed they were fighting to defend their monarch, their church, and social stability. After nearly three years of inconclusive fighting, in June 1645 Parliament won a decisive victory at Naseby and brought the war to an end the following summer. The king was in captivity, bishops had been abolished, a Presbyterian church had been established, and limitations were placed on royal power. All that remained necessary to end three years of civil war was the king's agreement to abide by the judgment of battle.

But Charles I had no intention of surrendering either his religion or his authority. Despite the rebels' successes, they could not rule without him, and he would concede nothing as long as opportunities to maneuver remained. In 1647 there

were opportunities galore. The war had proved ruinously expensive to Parliament. It owed enormous sums to the Scots, to its own soldiers, and to the governors of London. Each of those elements had its own objectives in a final settlement of the war, and they were not altogether compatible. London feared the parliamentary army, unpaid and camped dangerously close to the capital. The Scots and the English Presbyterians in Parliament feared that the religious settlement already made would be sacrificed by those known as Independents, who desired a more decentralized church. The Independents feared that they would be persecuted just as harshly by the Presbyterians as they had been by the king. In fact, the war had settled nothing.

The English Revolutions

Charles I happily played both ends against the middle until the army decisively ended the game. In June 1647, soldiers kidnapped the king and demanded that Parliament pay their arrears, protect them from legal retribution, and recognize their service to the nation. Those in Parliament who opposed the army's intervention were impeached, and when London Presbyterians rose up against the army's show of force, troops moved in to occupy the city. The civil war, which had come so close to resolution in 1647, had now become a military revolution. Religious and political radicals flocked to the army and encouraged the soldiers to support their programs and resist disbandment. New fighting broke out in 1648 as Charles encouraged his supporters to resume the war. But forces under the command of Sir Thomas Fairfax (1612–1671) and Oliver Cromwell (1599–1658) easily crushed the royalist uprisings in England and Scotland. The army then demanded that Charles I be brought to justice for his treacherous conduct both before and during the war. When the majority in Parliament refused, still hoping against hope to reach an accommodation with the king, the soldiers again acted decisively. In December 1648, army regiments were sent to London to purge the two houses of Parliament of those who opposed the army's demands. The remaining members, contemptuously called the Rump Parliament, voted to bring the king to trial for his crimes against the liberties of his subjects. On 30 January 1649, Charles I was executed and England was declared to be a commonwealth. The monarchy and the House of Lords were abolished, and the nation was to be governed by what was left of the membership of the House of Commons.

Oliver Cromwell. For four years, the members of the Rump Parliament struggled with proposals for a new constitution while balancing the demands of moderate and radical reformers and an increasingly hostile army. It achieved little other than to raise the level of frustration. In 1653, Oliver Cromwell, with the support of the army's senior officers, forcibly dissolved the Rump and became the leader of the revolutionary government. At first he ruled along with a Parliament hand-picked from among the supporters of the commonwealth. When Cromwell's Parliament proved no more capable of governing than had the Rump, a written constitution, The Instrument of Government (1653), established a new polity. Cromwell was given the title Lord Protector, and he was to rule along with a freely elected Parliament and an administrative body known as the Council of State.

DOCUMENT

Cromwell Abolishes Monarchy

Cromwell was able to hold the revolutionary cause together through the force of his own personality. A member of the lesser landed elite who had opposed the arbitrary policies of Charles I, he was a devout Puritan who believed in a large measure of religious toleration for Christians. As both a member of Parliament and a senior officer in the army, he had been able to temper the claims of each when they conflicted. Cromwell saw God's hand directing England toward a more glorious future, and he believed that his own actions were divinely ordained: "No man climbs higher than he that knows not whither he goes." Although many urged him to accept the crown of England and begin a new monarchy, Cromwell steadfastly held out for a government in which fundamental authority resided in Parliament. Until his death he defended the achievements of the revolution and held its conflicting constituents together.

But a sense that only a single person could effectively rule a state remained too strong for the reforms of the revolutionary regimes to have much chance of success. When Cromwell died in 1658 it was only natural that his eldest son, Richard, should

■ Allegorical view of Cromwell as savior of England. Babylon and Error are trampled under his feet. On the pillar at the right, England, Scotland, and Ireland pay him homage, and the left pillar enumerates the legal bases of his power.

be proposed as the new Lord Protector despite the fact that Richard had very little experience in either military or civil affairs. Nor did he have the sense of purpose that was his father's greatest source of strength. Without an individual to hold the movement together, the revolution fell apart. In 1659, the army again intervened in civil affairs, dismissing the recently elected Parliament and calling for the restoration of the monarchy to provide stability to the state. After a period of negotiation in which the king agreed to a general amnesty with only a few exceptions, the Stuarts were restored when Charles II (1649–1685) took the throne in 1660.

Twenty years of civil war and revolution had had their effect. Parliament became a permanent part of civil government and now had to be managed rather than ignored. Royal power over taxation and religion was curtailed, although in fact Parliament proved more vigorous in suppressing religious

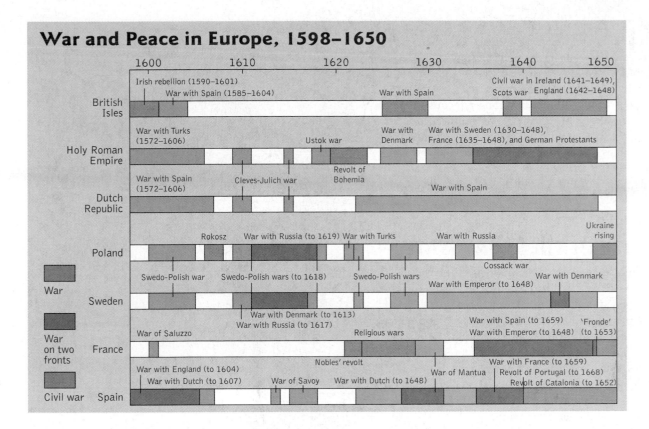

War and Peace in Europe, 1598–1650

	1600	1610	1620	1630	1640	1650

British Isles
Irish rebellion (1590–1601)
War with Spain (1585–1604)
War with Spain
Civil war in Ireland (1641–1649),
Scots war   England (1642–1648)

Holy Roman Empire
War with Turks (1572–1606)
Ustok war
War with Denmark
War with Sweden (1630–1648), France (1635–1648), and German Protestants

Dutch Republic
War with Spain (1572–1606)
Cleves-Julich war
Revolt of Bohemia
War with Spain

Poland
Rokosz
War with Russia (to 1619)   War with Turks
War with Russia
Ukraine rising

Sweden
Swedo-Polish war
Swedo-Polish wars (to 1618)
Swedo-Polish wars
War with Emperor (to 1648)
Cossack war
War with Denmark

France
War with Denmark (to 1613)
War with Russia (to 1617)
War of Saluzzo
Religious wars
Nobles' revolt
War with Spain (to 1659)
War with Emperor (to 1648)
'Fronde' (to 1653)

Spain
War with England (to 1604)
War with Dutch (to 1607)
War of Savoy
War with Dutch (to 1648)
War of Mantua
War with France (to 1659)
Revolt of Portugal (to 1668)
Revolt of Catalonia (to 1652)

Legend:
War
War on two fronts
Civil war

dissent than the monarchy ever had. England was to be a reformed Protestant state, although there remained much dispute about what constituted reform. Absolute monarchy had become constitutional monarchy, with the threat of revolution behind the power of Parliament and the threat of anarchy behind the power of the crown.

The "Glorious Revolution."

The threats of revolution and of anarchy proved potent in 1685 when James II (1685–1688) came to the throne. A declared Catholic, James attempted to use his power of appointment to foil the constraints that Parliament imposed on him. He elevated Catholics to leading posts in the military and in the central government and began a campaign to pack a new Parliament with his supporters. That proved too much for the governing classes, who entered into negotiations with William, Prince of Orange, husband of Mary Stuart, James's eldest daughter. In 1688, William landed in England with a small force. Without support, James II fled to France, the English throne was declared vacant, and William and Mary were proclaimed king and queen of England. There was little bloodshed in England and little threat of social disorder, and the event soon came to be called the **Glorious Revolution.** Its achievements were set down in the Declaration of Rights (1689), which was presented to William and Mary before they took the throne. The Declaration reasserted the fundamental principles of constitutional monarchy as they had developed over the previous half century. Security of property and the regularity of

DOCUMENT
English Bill of Rights

Parliaments were guaranteed. The Toleration Act (1689) granted religious freedom to nearly all groups of Protestants. The liberties of the subject and the rights of the sovereign were to be in balance.

The events of 1688 in England reversed a trend toward increasing power on the part of the Stuarts and resulted in the development of a unique form of government that a century later would spawn dozens of imitators. John Locke (1632–1704) was the theorist of the Revolution of 1689. He was heir to the century-old debate on resistance, and he carried the doctrine to a new plateau. In *Two Treatises on Civil Government* (1690), Locke developed the contract theory of government. Political society was a compact that individuals entered into freely for their own well-being. It was designed to maintain each person's natural rights—life, liberty, and property. Natural rights were inherent in individuals; they could not be given away. The contract between rulers and subjects was an agreement for the protection of natural rights. "Arbitrary power cannot consist with the ends of society and government. Men would not quit the freedom of the state of nature were it not to preserve their lives, liberties, and fortunes and by stated rules to secure their peace and happiness." When rulers acted arbitrarily, they were to be deposed by their subjects, preferably in the relatively peaceful manner in which James II had been replaced by William III.

The efforts of European monarchies to centralize their power came at the expense of the Church, the aristocracy, and the localities. It was a struggle that took place over decades and was not accomplished easily. In France, the Fronde was an aristocratic backlash; in Spain, the revolt of the Catalonians pitted the Castilian crown against a proud ethnic province. In England, a civil war fought to prevent the encroachments of the crown against the rights of the community gave way to a bloody revolution that combined religious and constitutional grievances—the excesses of monarchy were succeeded by the excesses of parliamentary rule. But the lesson learned by the English ruling elites was that for a nation to enjoy the benefits of a powerful central authority, it was necessary to restrain that authority. The Glorious Revolution of 1689 helped create a constitutional balance between ruler and ruled.

THE ZENITH OF THE ROYAL STATE

The crises of midcentury tested the mettle of the royal states. Over the long term, the crises had two different consequences. First, they provided a check to the exercise of royal power. Fear of recurring rebellions had a chilling effect upon policy, especially taxation. Reforms of financial administration, long overdue, were one of the themes of the later seventeenth century. Even as royal government strengthened itself, it remained concerned about the impact of its policies. Second, the memory of rebellion served to control the ambitions of factious noblemen and town oligarchs.

If nothing else, the episodes of opposition to the rising royal states made clear the universal desire for stable government, which was seen as the responsibility of both subjects and rulers. By the second half of the seventeenth century, effective government was the byword of the royal state. As Louis XIV proclaimed, rule was a trade that had to be constantly studied and practiced. The natural advantages of monarchy had to be merged with the interests of the state's citizens and their desires for wealth, safety, and honor. After so much chaos and instability, the monarchy had to be elevated above the fray of day-to-day politics; it had to become a symbol of the power and glory of the nation. Control no longer meant the greedy grasp of royal officials but rather their practiced guidance of affairs.

In England, Holland, and Sweden, a form of constitutional monarchy developed in which rulers shared power, in varying degrees, with other institutions of state. In England it was Parliament, in Holland the town oligarchies, and in Sweden the nobility. But in most other states in Europe there developed a pure form of royal government known as **absolutism.** Absolute monarchy revived the divine right theories of kingship and added to them a cult of the personality of the ruler. Absolutism was practiced in states as dissimilar as Denmark, Brandenburg-Prussia, and Russia. It reached its zenith in France under Louis XIV, the most powerful of the seventeenth-century monarchs.

The Nature of Absolute Monarchy

Locke's theory of contract provided one solution to the central problem of seventeenth-century government: how to

■ The title page of the first edition of Thomas Hobbes's *Leviathan*, published in 1651. The huge figure, composed of many tiny human beings, symbolizes the surrender of individual human rights to those of the state.

balance the monarch's right to command and the subjects' duty to obey. By establishing a constitutional monarchy in which power was shared between the ruler and a representative assembly of subjects, England found one path out of this thicket. But it was not a path that many others could follow. The English solution was most suited to a state that was largely immune from invasion and land war. Constitutional government required a higher level of political participation of citizens than did an absolute monarchical one. Greater participation in turn meant greater freedom of expression, greater toleration of religious minorities, and greater openness in the institutions of government. All were dangerous. The price that England paid was a half century of governmental instability.

The alternative to constitutional monarchy was absolute monarchy. It too found its greatest theorist in England. Thomas Hobbes (1588–1679) was one of many Englishmen who went into exile in France during the course of the English

THE NATURE OF MAN

Thomas Hobbes's Leviathan *(1651) is one of the classic works of political theory in Western history. Hobbes describes the state of nature as a state of perpetual insecurity from which mankind emerged by surrendering power to a sovereign and thereby creating a political society. Writing in the context of both the English and French civil wars, Hobbes's sovereign held absolute power over life and property which he used to protect and defend his subjects.*

Focus Questions

What is the importance of security to a civilized state? What is Hobbes's view of the nature of man without government?

Whatsoever therefore is consequent to a time of war, where every man is enemy to every man, the same consequent to the time wherein men live without other security than what their own strength and their own invention shall furnish them withal. In such condition there is no place for industry, because the fruit thereof is uncertain: and consequently no culture of the earth; no navigation, nor use of the commodities that may be imported by sea; no commodious building; no instruments of moving and removing such things as require much force; no knowledge of the face of the earth; no account of time; no arts; no letters; no society; and which is worst of all, continual fear, and danger of violent death; and the life of man, solitary, poor, nasty, brutish, and short.

To this war of every man against every man, this also is consequent; that nothing can be unjust. The notions of right and wrong, justice and injustice, have there no place. Where there is no common power, there is no law; where no law, no injustice. Force and fraud are in war the two cardinal virtues. Justice and injustice are none of the faculties neither of the body nor mind. If they were, they might be in a man that were alone in the world, as well as his senses and passions. They are qualities that relate to men in society, not in solitude. It is consequent also to the same condition that there be no propriety, no dominion, no mine and thine distinct; but only that to be every man's that he can get, and for so long as he can keep it. And thus much for the ill condition which man by mere nature is actually placed in; though with a possibility to come out of it, consisting partly in the passions, partly in his reason.

From Thomas Hobbes, *Leviathan.*

civil wars. In his greatest work, *Leviathan* (1651), Hobbes argued that before civil society had been formed, humans lived in a savage state of nature, "in a war of every man against every man." That was a ghastly condition without morality or law—"the notions of right and wrong, of justice and injustice have there no place." People came together to form a government for the most basic of all purposes: self-preservation. Without government they were condemned to a life that was "solitary, poor, nasty, brutish, and short." To escape the state of nature, individuals pooled their power and granted it to a ruler. The terms of the Hobbesian contract were simple. Rulers agreed to rule; subjects agreed to obey. When the contract was intact, people ceased to live in a state of nature. When it was broken, they returned to it. With revolts, rebellions, and revolutions erupting in all parts of Europe, Hobbes's state of nature never seemed very far away.

For most states of Europe in the later seventeenth century, absolute monarchy became not only a necessity but an ideal. The consolidation of power in the hands of the divinely ordained monarch who nevertheless ruled according to principles of law and justice was seen as the perfect form of government. Absolutism was an expression of control rather than of power. If the state was sometimes pictured as a horse, the absolute monarch gripped the reins more tightly than the whip. "Many writers have tried to confound absolute government with arbitrary government. But no two things could be more unlike," wrote Bishop Jacques Bossuet (1627–1704), who extolled absolutism in France. The absolute ruler ruled in the interests of his people: "The prince is the public person, the whole state is included in him, the will of all the people is enclosed within his own."

The main features of absolute monarchy were designed to extend royal control. As in the early seventeenth century, the person of the monarch was revered. Courts grew larger and more lavish in an effort to enhance the glory of the monarchy, and thereby of the state. "L'état, c'est moi"—"I am the state"—Louis XIV was supposed to have said. No idea better expresses absolutism's connection between governor and governed. As the king grew in stature, his competitors for power all shrank. Large numbers of nobles were herded together at court under the watchful eye of monarchs who now ruled rather than reigned. The king shed the cloak of his favorites and rolled up his own sleeves to manage state affairs. Representative institutions, especially those that laid claim to control over taxation, were weakened or cast aside for obstructing efficient government and endangering the welfare of the state. Monarchs needed standing armies, permanent forces that could be drilled and trained in the increasingly sophisticated arts of war. Thus the military was expanded and made an integral part of the machinery of government. The military profession developed within nations, gradually replacing mercenary adventurers who had fought for booty rather than for duty.

Yet the absolute state was never as powerful in practice as it was in theory, nor did it ever exist in its ideal shape. Absolutism was always in the making, never quite made. Its success depended upon a strong monarch who knew his own will and could enforce it. It depended upon unity within the state and the absence or ruthless suppression of religious or political minorities. The absolute ruler needed to control information and ideas, to limit criticism of state policy. Ultimately, the absolute state rested upon the will of its citizens to support it.

Absolutism in the East

Frederick William, the Great Elector of Brandenburg-Prussia (1640–1688), was one of the European princes who made the most effective use of the techniques of absolutism. In 1640, he inherited a scattered and ungovernable collection of territories that had been devastated by the Thirty Years' War. Brandenburg, the richest of his possessions, had lost nearly half of its population. The war had a lasting impact on Frederick William's character. As a child, he had hidden in the woods to escape bands of marauding soldiers; as a teenager, he had followed to its burial the corpse of Gustavus Adolphus, the man he most admired and wished to emulate. A long stay in Holland during the final stages of the Dutch Revolt impressed on him the importance of a strong army and a strong base of revenue to support it.

Frederick William had neither. In 1640, his forces totaled no more than 2500 men, most of them, including the officers, the dregs of German society. Despite the fact that he was surrounded by powerful neighbors—Sweden and Poland both claimed sovereignty over parts of his inheritance—the territories under his control had no tradition of military taxation. The nobility, known as the Junker, enjoyed immunity from almost all forms of direct taxation, and the towns had no obligation to furnish either men or supplies for military operations beyond their walls. When Frederick William attempted to introduce an excise—the kind of commodity tax on consumption that had so successfully financed the Dutch Revolt and the English Revolution—he was initially rebuffed. But military emergency overcame legal precedents. By the 1650s Frederick William had established the excise in the towns, though not on the land.

With the excise as a steady source of revenue, the Great Elector could now create one of the most capable standing armies of the age. The strictest discipline was maintained in the new army, and the Prussian army developed into a feared and efficient fighting machine. Frederick William organized one of the first departments of war to oversee all of the details

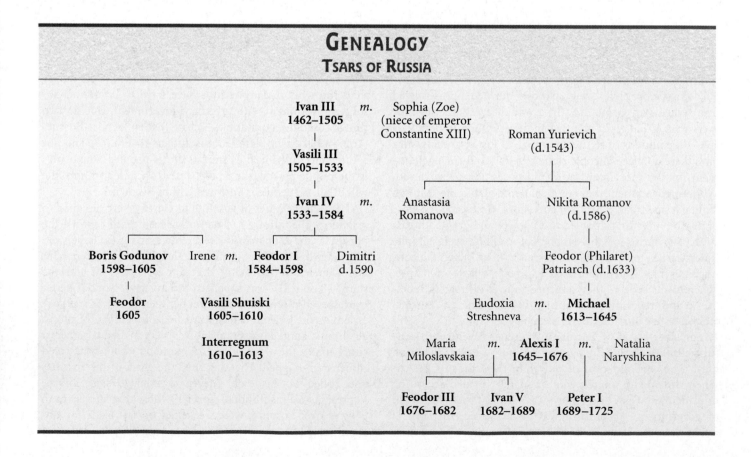

GENEALOGY
TSARS OF RUSSIA

Ivan III 1462–1505	*m.*	Sophia (Zoe) (niece of emperor Constantine XIII)

Roman Yurievich (d.1543)

Vasili III 1505–1533

Ivan IV 1533–1584   *m.*   Anastasia Romanova   Nikita Romanov (d.1586)

Boris Godunov 1598–1605   Irene *m.* **Feodor I** 1584–1598   Dimitri d.1590

Feodor (Philaret) Patriarch (d.1633)

Feodor 1605   **Vasili Shuiski** 1605–1610

Eudoxia Streshneva   *m.*   **Michael** 1613–1645

Interregnum 1610–1613

Maria Miloslavskaia   *m.*   **Alexis I** 1645–1676   *m.*   Natalia Naryshkina

Feodor III 1676–1682   **Ivan V** 1682–1689   **Peter I** 1689–1725

A Close Shave

Peter the Great made many efforts to westernize Russia after his travels in Holland and England. He reformed the navy, built a great seaport at St. Petersburg, and instituted an array of governmental reforms. But nothing was so prominent as or affected ordinary people more than his edicts on beards and clothing.

Focus Questions

Why would Peter want Russians to look more like western Europeans? In dealing with his subjects, is Peter acting like Louis XIV?

The tsar labored at the reform of fashions, or, more properly speaking, of dress. Until that time the Russians had always worn long beards, which they cherished and preserved with much care, allowing them to hang down on their bosoms, without even cutting the moustache. With these long beards they wore the hair very short, except the ecclesiastics, who, to distinguish themselves, wore it very long. The tsar, in order to reform that custom, ordered that gentlemen, merchants, and other subjects, except priests and peasants, should each pay a tax of one hundred rubles a year if they wished to keep their beard; the commoners had to pay one kopeck each. Officials were stationed at the gates of the towns to collect that tax, which the Russians regarded as an enormous sin on the part of the tsar and as a thing which tended to the abolition of their religion.

These insinuations, which came from the priests, occasioned the publication of many pamphlets in Moscow, where for that reason alone the tsar was regarded as a tyrant and a pagan; and there were many old Russians who, after having their beards shaved off, saved them preciously, in order to have them placed in their coffins, fearing that they would not be allowed to enter heaven without their beards. As for the young men, they followed the new customs with the more readiness as it made them appear more agreeable to the fair sex.

From the reform in beards we may pass to that of clothes. Their garments, like those of the Orientals, were very long, reaching to the heel. The tsar issued an ordinance abolishing that costume, commanding all the boyars (nobles) and all those who had positions at the court to dress after the French fashion, and likewise to adorn their clothes with gold or silver according to their means. . . .

The same ordinance also provided that in the future women, as well as men, should be invited to entertainments, such as weddings, banquets, and the like, where both sexes should mingle in the same hall, as in Holland and England. It was likewise added that these entertainments should conclude with concerts and dances, but that only those should be admitted who were dressed in English costumes. His Majesty set the example in all these changes.

From "De Missy's Life of Peter."

---

of the creation of his army, from housing and supplies to the training of young officer candidates. The department was also responsible for the collection of taxes. By integrating military and civilian government, Frederick William was able to create an efficient state bureaucracy that was particularly responsive in times of crisis. The creation of the Prussian army was the force that led to the creation of the Prussian state.

The same materials that forged the Prussian state led to the transformation of Russia. Soon after the young tsar Peter I (1682–1725) came to the throne, he realized that he could compete with the western states only by learning to play their game. In 1697, Peter visited the West, ostensibly to build an alliance against the Turks but actually to learn as much as he could about Western military technology. He loved novelty and introduced new agricultural products such as wine and potatoes to his subjects. When he determined that Russians should no longer wear beards, he took a hand in cutting them off. When he was persuaded of the benefits of dentistry, he practiced it himself on his terrified subjects. His campaign to westernize Russia frequently confused the momentous with the inconsequential, but it had an extraordinary impact at all levels of government and society.

Like those of Frederick William, Peter's greatest reforms were military. Peter realized that if Russia were to flourish in a world dominated by war and commerce, it would have to reestablish its hold on the Baltic ports. That meant dislodging the Swedes from the Russian mainland and creating a fleet to protect Russian trade. Neither goal seemed likely. The Swedes were one of the great powers of the age, constant innovators in battlefield tactics and military organization. Peter studied their every campaign. His first wars against the Swedes ended in humiliating defeats, but with each failure came a sharper sense of what was needed to succeed.

First Peter introduced a system of conscription that resulted in the creation of a standing army. Conscripts were branded to inhibit desertion, and a strict discipline was introduced to prepare the soldiers for battle. Peter unified the military command at the top and stratified it in the field. He established promotion based on merit. For the first time, Russian officers were given particular responsibilities to fulfill

MAP DISCOVERY

Expansion of Russia Under Peter the Great

Notice the extent of the Russian Empire in 1689 and territory added by Peter the Great. What was important about the new territory? What was the role of the battle of Poltava in expanding the empire? The route of Peter's trip to western Europe is marked here. Why did he travel where he did? Based on the chapter discussion, what impact did his trip have on the way he ruled his empire?

during both training and battle. Peter created military schools to train cadets for the next generation of officers.

Finally, in 1709, Peter realized his ambitions. At the battle of Poltava, the Russian army routed the Swedes, wounding King Charles XII, annihilating his infantry, and capturing dozens of his leading officers. That night Peter toasted the captured Swedish generals. He claimed that everything he knew about warfare he had learned from them, and he congratulated them on their success as teachers. After the battle of Poltava, Russia gradually replaced Sweden as the dominant power in the Baltic.

Like everything else about him, Peter the Great's absolutism was uniquely his own. But though Peter's power was unlimited, it was not uncontested. He secularized the Russian Orthodox Church, subjecting it to the control of state power and confiscating much of its wealth in the process. He broke the old military service class, which attempted a coup d'état when Peter was abroad in the 1690s.

By the end of his reign, the Russian monarchy was among the strongest in Europe.

The Origins of French Absolutism

Nowhere was absolutism as successfully implanted as in France. Louis XIII (1610–1643) was only eight years old when he came to the throne, and he grew slowly into his role under the tutelage of Cardinal Richelieu. It was Richelieu's vision that stabilized French government. As chief minister, Richelieu saw clearly that the prosperity and even the survival of France depended upon strengthening royal power. He preached a doctrine of **raison d'état**—reason of state—in which he placed the needs of the nation above the privileges of its most important groups. Richelieu saw three threats to stable royal government: "The Huguenots shared the state, the nobles conducted themselves as if they were not subjects, and the most powerful governors in the provinces acted as if they were sovereign in their office."

■ The Battle of Poltava (1709) led to the decline of Swedish influence in Europe. Peter the Great is depicted receiving the laurel of victory.

Richelieu took measures to control all three. The power of the nobles was the most difficult to attack. The nobles' long tradition of independence from the crown had been enhanced by the wars of religion. Perhaps more importantly, the ancient aristocracy, the nobility of the sword, believed themselves to be in a particularly vulnerable position. Their world was changing and their traditional roles were becoming obsolete. Professional soldiers replaced them at war, professional administrators at government. Mercantile wealth threatened their economic superiority; the growth of the nobility of the robe—lawyers and state officials—threatened their social standing. They were hardly likely to take orders from a royal minister such as Richelieu, especially when he attacked one of the great symbols of their power, the duel.

To limit the power of local officials, Richelieu used intendants to examine their conduct and to reform their administration. He made careful appointments of local governors and brought more regions under direct royal control. Against the Huguenots, Richelieu's policy was more subtle. He was less interested in challenging their religion than their autonomy. In 1627, when the English sent a force to aid the Huguenots against the government, Richelieu and Louis XIII abolished the Huguenots' privileges altogether. They were allowed to maintain their religion, but not their special status. They would have no privileges other than to be subjects of the king of France.

Richelieu's program was a vital prelude to the development of absolute monarchy in France. But the cardinal was not a king. While it is clear that Richelieu did not act without the full support of Louis XIII and clear that the king initiated many reforms for which the cardinal received credit, there can be no doubt that Richelieu was the power behind the throne. Louis XIII hated the business of government and even neglected his principal responsibility of providing the state with an heir. For years he and his wife slept in separate palaces, and only a freak rainstorm in Paris forced him to spend a night with the queen, Anne of Austria, in 1637. It was the night Louis XIV was conceived. Louis XIII and Richelieu died within six months of each other in 1642 and 1643, and the nation again endured the turmoil of a child king. Richelieu's aggressive policy to curb the nobility and his stringent financial program in the 1630s helped precipitate the Fronde. Louis XIV (1643–1715) was never to forget the terror of the aristocratic rebellion in Paris: how he was forced to flee the capital in the dead of night, how he endured the penury of exile, how he suffered the humiliation of being bossed about by the rebels. He would never forget, and he would have a long time to remember.

Louis le Grand

Not quite five years old when he came to the throne, Louis XIV was tutored by Cardinal Jules Mazarin (1602–1661), Richelieu's successor as chief minister. If anything, Mazarin was more ruthless and less popular than his predecessor. An Italian from a modest background, Mazarin won the money to launch his career at the gaming table. Good fortune seemed to follow him everywhere. He gambled with his life and his career, and each time he raked in the stakes. He died with the largest private fortune that had ever been accumulated by a French citizen, easily surpassing the fortune of Richelieu. Like Richelieu, whom he emulated, Mazarin was an excellent administrator who had learned well the lessons of raison d'état. At the conclusion of the Thirty Years' War, for example, Mazarin refused to make peace with Spain, believing that the time was ripe to deliver a knockout blow to the Spanish Habsburgs.

The King and His Ministers.   In order to pacify the rebellious nobility of the Fronde, who opposed Mazarin's power, Louis XIV was declared to have reached his majority at the age of 13. But it was not until Mazarin died ten years later in 1661 that the king began to rule. Louis was blessed with able and energetic ministers. The two central props of his state—money and might—were in the hands of dynamic men, Jean-Baptiste Colbert (1619–1683) and the Marquis de Louvois (1639–1691). Colbert—to whom credit belongs for the building of the French navy, the reform of French legal codes, and the establishment of national academies of culture—was Louis's chief

■ This Hyacinthe Rigaud portrait of Loius XIV in his coronation robes shows the splendor of *Le Roi Soleil* (the Sun King), who believed himself to be the center of France as the sun is the center of the solar system.

merit rather than purchase. He also solved one of the most serious logistical problems of the age by establishing storehouses of arms and ammunition throughout the realm. The greatest achievements of the reign were built on the backs of fiscal and military reforms, which were themselves a product of the continuing sophistication of French administration.

Louis XIV furthered the practice of relying on professional administrators to supervise the main departments of state and offer advice on matters of policy. He created a separation between courtiers and officeholders and largely excluded the nobility of the sword from the inner circles of government, which were composed of ministers of departments and small councils that handled routine affairs. The councils were connected to the central advisory body of government, the secret council of the king. Within each department, ministers furthered the process of professionalization that led to the advancement of talented clerks, secretaries, and administrators. Although there still remained a large gulf between the promulgation of policy at Versailles and its enforcement in the provinces, it was now a gulf that could be measured and ultimately bridged. Louis XIV built on the institution of the intendant that Richelieu had developed with so much success. Intendants were now a permanent part of government, and their duties expanded from their early responsibilities as coordinators and mediators into areas of policing and tax collection. It was through the intendants that the wishes of central government were made known in the provinces.

The Court of Versailles. Although Louis XIV was well served, it was the king himself who set the tone for French absolutism. "If he was not the greatest king, he was the best actor of majesty that ever filled the throne," wrote an English observer. The acting of majesty was central to Louis's rule. His residence at Versailles was the most glittering court of Europe, renowned for its beauty and splendor. It was built on a scale never before seen, and Louis took a personal interest in making sure it was fit for a king. When the court and king moved there permanently in 1682, Versailles became the envy of the Continent. But behind the imposing facade of Versailles stood a well-thought-out plan for domestic and international rule.

Louis XIV attempted to tame the French nobles by requiring their attendance at his court. Louis established a system of court etiquette so complex that constant study was necessary to prevent humiliation. While the nobility studied decorum they could not plot rebellion. At Versailles one never knocked on a door; one scratched with a fingernail. That insignificant custom had to be learned and remembered—it was useless anywhere else—and practiced if one hoped for the favor of the king. Leading noblemen of France rose at dawn so that they could watch Louis be awakened and hear him speak his first words. Dozens followed him from hall to gallery and from gallery to chamber as he washed, dressed, prayed, and ate.

That aura of court culture was equally successful in the royal art of diplomacy. During Louis's reign, France replaced Spain as the greatest nation in Europe. Massive royal patronage of art, science, and thought brought French culture to new heights.

minister for finance. Colbert's fiscal reforms were so successful that in less than six years a debt of 22 million French pounds had become a surplus of 29 million. Colbert achieved that astonishing feat not by raising taxes but by increasing the efficiency of their collection. Until Louis embarked on his wars, the French state was solvent.

To Louvois, Louis's minister of war, fell the task of reforming the French army. During the Fronde, royal troops were barely capable of defeating the makeshift forces of the nobility. By the end of the reign, the army had grown to 400,000 and its organization had thoroughly been reformed. Louvois introduced new ranks for the field officers who actually led their men into battle, and promotions were distributed by

The French language replaced Latin as the universal European tongue. France was the richest and most populous European state, and Louis's absolute rule finally harnessed the resources to a single purpose. France became a commercial power rivaling the Netherlands, a naval power rivaling England, and a military power without peer. It was not only for effect that Louis took the image of the sun as his own. In court, in the nation, and throughout Europe, everything revolved around him.

France's rise to preeminence in Europe was undoubtedly the greatest accomplishment of the absolute monarchy of Louis XIV. But it did not come without costs. Louis XIV made his share of mistakes, which were magnified by the awe in which his opinions were held. His aggressive foreign policy ultimately bankrupted the crown. But without doubt his greatest error was to persecute the Huguenots. As an absolute ruler, Louis believed that it was necessary to have absolute conformity and obedience. The existence of the Huguenots, with their separate communities and distinct forms of worship, seemed an affront to his authority. Almost from the beginning, Louis allowed the persecution of Protestants, despite the protection provided by the Edict of Nantes. Protestant churches were pulled down, conversions to Catholicism were bought with the lure of immunities from taxation, and children were separated from their families to be brought up in Catholic schools. Finally, in 1685 Louis XIV revoked the Edict of Nantes. All forms of Protestant worship were outlawed, and the ministers who were not hunted down and killed were forced into exile. Despite a ban on Protestant emigration, more than 200,000 Huguenots fled the country, many of them carrying irreplaceable skills with them to Holland and England in the west and Brandenburg in the east.

Supporters of the monarchy celebrated the revocation of the Edict of Nantes as an act of piety. Religious toleration in seventeenth-century Europe was still a policy of expediency rather than of principle. Even the English, who prided themselves on developing the concept of toleration, and the Dutch, who welcomed Jews to Amsterdam, would not officially tolerate Catholics. But the persecution of the Huguenots was a social and political disaster for France. Those who fled to other Protestant states spread the stories of atrocities that stiffened European resolve against Louis. Those who remained became an embittered minority who pulled at the fabric of the state at every chance. Nor did the official abolition of Protestantism have much effect upon its existence. Against the policies, the Huguenots held firm to their beliefs. There were well more than a million French Protestants, undoubtedly the largest religious minority in any state. Huguenots simply went underground, practicing their religion secretly and gradually replacing their numbers. No absolutism, however powerful, could succeed in eradicating religious beliefs.

CONCLUSION

Louis XIV gave his name to the age that he and his nation dominated, but he was not its only towering figure. The

LE ROY DE FRANCE.
l'Home immortel Chef de la S.te Ligue.

Mon soleil parsa force eclaira l'heretique.
Il chassa tout d'un coup les brouillards de Calvin:
Non pas par un Zele divin,
Mais afin de cacher ma fine Politique.

■ A symbolic drawing shows how heretics will be driven from France by the Sun King. Such a policy proved shortsighted, however, as thousands of Huguenot émigrés enriched Louis's potential enemies with their valuable skills.

Great Elector, Peter the Great, Louis the Great—so they were judged by posterity, kings who had forged nations for a new age. Their style of rule showed the royal state at its height, still revolving around the king but more and more dependent upon permanent institutions of government that followed their own imperatives. The absolute state harnessed the economic and intellectual resources of the nation to the political will of the monarch. It did so to ensure survival in a dangerous world. But while monarchs ruled as well as reigned, they did so by incorporating vital elements of the state into the process of government. In England, the importance of the landholding classes was recognized in the constitutional powers of Parliament. In Prussia, the military power of the Junker was asserted through command in the army, the most important institution of the state. In France, Louis XIV co-opted many nobles at his court while making use of a talented pool of lawyers, clergymen, and administrators in his government. A delicate balance existed between the will of the king and the will of the state, a balance that would soon lead the continental powers into economic competition and military confrontation.

QUESTIONS FOR REVIEW

1. How did war in the seventeenth century contribute to the creation of more powerful monarchical states?
2. What religious and political ideas were developed to justify resistance to monarchical authority?
3. What political and religious problems combined to bring England to civil war, and what results did the conflict produce in English government?
4. How did rulers such as Frederick William of Brandenburg, Peter the Great, and Louis XIV and theorists such as Hobbes and Bossuet justify absolute monarchical power?

KEY TERMS

absolutism, *p. 502*

divine right of kings, *p. 487*

Fronde, *p. 495*

Glorious Revolution, *p. 501*

intendants, *p. 490*

Long Parliament, *p. 498*

parlements, *p. 490*

Puritans, *p. 497*

raison d'état, *p. 506*

DISCOVERING WESTERN CIVILIZATION ONLINE

You can obtain more information about the royal state in the seventeenth century at the Websites listed below. See also the Companion Website that accompanies this text, www.ablongman.com/kishlansky, which contains an online study guide and additional resources.

The Crises of the Royal State

Internet Modern History Sourcebook: Constitutional States

www.fordham.edu/halsall/mod/modsbook06.html

Links to sources relating to the reign of Charles I and the revolution against him.

The Execution of Charles I

www.baylor.edu/BIC/WCIII/Essays/charles.1.html

Excerpts from primary sources describing the execution of Charles I.

The Zenith of the Royal State

Baroque Living History Society: L'Age d'Or & Kirke's Lambs

www.kipar.org/

A site on the Golden Age of France in the seventeenth century but with extensive links to English and Dutch materials on a variety of subjects.

Chateau de Versailles

www.chateauversailles.fr/en

The Website of Versailles, with views of the gardens and rooms inside the palace. (Version of site in English.)

Creating French Culture

www.loc.gov/exhibits/bnf/bnf0005.html

The Library of Congress's exhibition on the Age of Absolutism shows manuscripts, medals, and portraits of leading figures at the French court.

SUGGESTIONS FOR FURTHER READING

General Reading

Perry Anderson, *Lineages of the Absolutist State* (London: NLB Books, 1974). A sociological study of the role of absolutism in the development of the Western world.

Euan Cameron, ed., *Early Modern Europe: An Oxford History* (Oxford, New York: Oxford University Press, 1999). Up-to-date essays by leading historians with well-chosen topics and illustrations.

Thomas Munck, *Seventeenth-Century Europe, 1598–1700* (New York: St. Martin's Press, 1990). An up-to-date survey.

David Sturdy, *Fractured Europe 1600–1721* (Oxford: Blackwell, 2002). A thorough survey of the complex military and political events of the long seventeenth century.

The Rise of the Royal State

Yves-Marie Bercé, *The Birth of Absolutism* (London: Macmillan, 1996). A history of France from the reign of Louis XIV to the eve of the Revolution by a leading historian of France.

J. H. Elliott, *Richelieu and Olivares* (Cambridge: Cambridge University Press, 1984). A brilliant dual portrait.

J. H. Elliott and Jonathan Brown, *A Palace for a King* (New Haven, CT: Yale University Press, 1980). An outstanding work on the building and decorating of a Spanish palace.

Graham Parry, *The Golden Age Restor'd* (New York: St. Martin's Press, 1981). A study of English court culture in the reigns of James I and Charles I.

The Crises of the Royal State

Jonathan Israel, ed., *The Anglo-Dutch Moment* (Cambridge: Cambridge University Press, 1991). Essays by an international team of scholars on the European dimensions of the Revolution of 1688.

M. A. Kishlansky, *A Monarchy Transformed* (London: Penguin Books, 1996). The most recent survey of a remarkable era.

G. Parker and L. Smith, eds., *The General Crisis of the Seventeenth Century* (London: Routledge & Kegan Paul, 1978). A collection of essays on the problem of the general crisis.

Quentin Skinner, *The Foundations of Modern Political Thought,* 2 vols. (Cambridge: Cambridge University Press, 1978). A seminal work on the history of ideas from Machiavelli to Calvin.

W. A. Speck, *The Revolution of 1688* (Oxford: Oxford University Press, 1988). The best single volume on the event that transformed England into a global power.

Lawrence Stone, *The Causes of the English Revolution* (New York: Harper & Row, 1972). A vigorously argued explanation of why England experienced a revolution in the mid-seventeenth century.

The Zenith of the Royal State

Joseph Bergin, *The Rise of Richelieu* (New Haven, CT: Yale University Press, 1991). A fascinating portrait of a consummate politician.

Peter Burke, *The Fabrication of Louis XIV* (New Haven, CT: Yale University Press, 1992). A compelling account of a man and a myth.

Paul Dukes, *The Making of Russian Absolutism* (London: Longman, 1982). A thorough survey of Russian history in the seventeenth and eighteenth centuries.

Nicholas Henshall, *The Myth of Absolutism: Change and Continuity in Early Modern European Monarchy* (London: Longman, 1992). A searching examination of the problem of absolutism in the western European states.

Vasili Klyuchevsky, *Peter the Great* (London: Random House, 1958). A classic work, still the best study of Peter.

H. W. Koch, *A History of Prussia* (London: Longman, 1978). A comprehensive study of Prussian history, with an excellent chapter on the Great Elector.

Geoffrey Parker, *The Military Revolution* (Cambridge: Cambridge University Press, 1988). A lucid discussion of how power was organized and deployed in the early modern state.

John Wolf, *Louis XIV* (New York: Norton, 1968). An outstanding biography of the Sun King.

For a list of additional titles related to this chapter's topics, please see http://www.ablongman.com/kishlansky.

Chapter **17**

SCIENCE AND COMMERCE IN EARLY MODERN EUROPE

Chapter Outline

There was never another artist like Rembrandt. He studied anatomy like a surgeon and was famous for his group portraits, for his dramatic representations, and for the way in which he used light and shadow to approximate reality. In the growing market for works of art, his paintings fetched the highest prices. His name has come down through the centuries as the personification of the artistic master. Turn the page to The Visual Record to see why. ➤

REMBRANDT'S LESSONS
Anatomy and the New Science

By the early seventeenth century, interest in scientific investigation had spread out from narrow circles of specialists to embrace educated men and women. One of the more spectacular demonstrations of new knowledge was public dissection, by law performed only on the corpses of criminals. There the secrets of the human body were revealed both for those who were training to be physicians and those who had the requisite fee and strong stomach. Curiosity about the human body was becoming a mark of education. New publications, both scientific and popular, spread ancient wisdom as well as the controversial findings of the moderns. Pictures drawn on the basis of dissections filled the new medical texts, such as the one shown in the photo on the stand at the feet of the corpse in *The Anatomy Lesson of Dr. Nicolaes Tulp* (1632) by Rembrandt van Rijn (1606–1669).

Dr. Tulp's anatomy lesson was not meant for the public. In fact, those gathered around him in various poses of concentration were not students at all. They were members of the Amsterdam company of surgeons, the physicians' guild of the early seventeenth century. The sitters had commissioned the picture, which was a celebration of themselves as well as of the noted Professor Tulp. They hired the young Rembrandt to compose the picture with the assurance that each of the sitters (whose names are written on the paper one of them holds in his hand) would appear as if he alone were the subject of a portrait. Rembrandt succeeded beyond expectation. Each individual was given his due. The expressions on their faces as much as their physical characteristics mark each one out from the group. Yet the portraits were only one part of the painting. The scene that Rembrandt depicted unified them. They became a group by their participation in the anatomy lesson. Rembrandt has chosen a moment of drama to stop the action. Dr. Tulp is demonstrating

how the gesture he is making with his left hand would be made by the tendons in the arm of the gruesome cadaver. The central figures of the group are rapt in attention, although only one of them is actually observing the procedure of the dissection. Each listens to Tulp, comparing his own experience and knowledge to that of the professor and the text that stands open.

The Anatomy Lesson established the 25-year-old Rembrandt as one of the most gifted and fashionable painters in Amsterdam. If any people could be said to be consumers of art in seventeenth-century Europe, it was the Dutch. Artists flourished and pictures abounded. Travelers were struck by the presence of artwork in both public and private places and in the homes of even moderately prosperous people. The group portrait, which Rembrandt brought to new levels of expression, was becoming a favorite genre. It was used to celebrate the leaders of Dutch society, who—unlike the leaders of most other European states—were not princes and aristocrats, but rather merchants, guild officials, and professionals. Rembrandt captured a spirit of civic pride in his group portraits. Then it was the surgeons' guild; later it would be the leaders of the cloth merchants' guild, another time a militia company.

Like the leaders of the surgeons' guild, who hung their commissioned portraits in their company's hall, the Dutch Republic swelled with pride in the seventeenth century. Its long war with Spain was finally drawing to a close, and it was time to celebrate the birth of a new state. The Dutch were a trading people, and their trade flourished as much in times of war as in times of peace. Their ships traveled to all parts of the globe, and they dominated the great luxury trades of the age. Bankers and merchants were the backbone of the Dutch Republic. Yet that republic of merchants was also one

■ Rembrandt van Rijn, *The Anatomy Lesson of Dr. Nicolaes Tulp* (1632).

of the great cultural centers of the Continent. Intellectual creativity was cultivated in the same manner as was a trading partner. In the burgeoning port of Amsterdam, the fastest-growing city in Europe, artists, philosophers, and mathematicians lived cheek by jowl. The free exchange of ideas made Amsterdam home to those exiled for their beliefs. The Dutch practiced religious toleration as did no one else. Catholics, Protestants, and Jews all were welcomed to the Dutch Republic and found that they could pursue their own paths without persecution.

Looking Ahead

Freedom of thought and freedom of expression helped develop a new spirit of scientific inquiry, like that portrayed in The Anatomy Lesson of Dr. Nicolaes Tulp. *As this chapter will show, maritime nations such as Holland and England took full advantage of scientific and technological discovery to expand their overseas trade and enrich their citizens. Although much of the new science was seemingly abstract, its practical applications ultimately fueled a new commercial spirit and a new European economy.* ➤

THE NEW SCIENCE

And new Philosophy calls all in doubt,
The element of fire is quite put out;
The sun is lost and the earth, and no man's wit
Can well direct him where to look for it.

So wrote the English poet John Donne (1572–1631) about one of the most astonishing yet perplexing moments in the history of Western thought: the emergence of the new science. It was astonishing because it seemed truly new. The discoveries of the stargazers, like those of the sea explorers, challenged people's most basic assumptions and beliefs. Men dropping balls from towers or peering at the skies through a glass claimed that they had disproved thousands of years of certainty about the nature of the universe: "And new Philosophy calls all in doubt." But the new science was perplexing because it seemed to loosen the moorings of everything that educated people thought they knew about their world. Nothing could be more disorienting than to challenge common sense. People needed to do little more than wake up in the morning to know that the sun moved from east to west while the earth stood still. But mathematics, experimentation, and deduction were needed to understand that the earth was in constant motion and that it revolved around the sun—"And no man's wit/ Can well direct him where to look for it."

The **scientific revolution** was the opening of a new era in European history. After two centuries of classical revival, European thinkers had finally come against the limits of ancient knowledge. Ancient wisdom had served Europeans well, and it was not to be discarded lightly. But one by one, the certainties of the past were being called into question. The explanations of the universe and the natural world that had been advanced by Aristotle and codified by his followers no longer seemed adequate. There were too many contradictions between theory and observation, too many things that did not fit. Yet breaking the hold of Aristotelianism was no easy task. A full century was to pass before even learned people would accept the proofs that the earth revolved around the sun. Even then, the most famous of them—Galileo—had to recant those views or be condemned as a heretic.

The two essential characteristics of the new science were that it was materialistic and mathematical. Its materialism was contained in the realization that the universe is composed of matter in motion. That meant that the stars and planets were not made of some perfect ethereal substance but of the same matter that was found on earth. They were thus subject to the same rules of motion as were earthly objects. The mathematics of the new science was contained in the realization that calculation had to replace common sense as the basis for understanding the universe. Mathematics itself was transformed with the invention of logarithms, analytic geometry, and calculus. More importantly, scientific experimentation took the form of measuring repeatable phenomena. When Galileo attempted to develop a theory of acceleration, he rolled a brass ball down an inclined plane and recorded the time and

DOCUMENT

Galileo, Letter to Grand Duchess Christina

distance of its descent 100 times before he was satisfied with his results.

The new science was also a Europewide movement. The spirit of scientific inquiry flourished everywhere. The main contributors to astronomy were a Pole, a Dane, a German, and an Italian. The founder of medical chemistry was Swiss; the best anatomist was Belgian. England contributed most of all—the founders of modern chemistry, biology, and physics. By and large, the scientists operated outside the traditional seats of learning at the universities. Although most were university trained and not a few taught the traditional Aristotelian subjects, theirs was not an academic movement. Rather, it was a public one made possible by the printing press. Once published, findings became building blocks for scientists throughout the Continent and from one generation to the next. Many discoveries were made in the search for practical solutions to ordinary problems, and what was learned fueled advances in technology and the natural sciences. The new science gave seventeenth-century Europeans a sense that they might finally master the forces of nature.

Heavenly Revolutions

There was much to be said for Aristotle's understanding of the world, for his cosmology. For one thing, it was harmonious. It incorporated a view of the physical world that coincided with a view of the spiritual and moral one. The heavens were unchangeable, and therefore they were better than the earth. The sun, moon, and planets were all faultless spheres, unblemished and immune from decay. Their motion was circular because the circle was the perfect form of motion. The earth was at the center of the universe because it was the heaviest planet and because it was at the center of the Great Chain of Being, between the underworld of spirits and the upper world of gods. The second advantage to the Aristotelian world view was that it was easily incorporated into Christianity. Aristotle's description of the heavens as being composed of a closed system of crystalline rings that held the sun, moon, and planets in their circular orbits around the earth left room for God and the angels to reside just beyond the last ring.

There were, of course, problems with Aristotle's explanation of the universe as it was preserved in the work of Ptolemy, the greatest of the Greek astronomers. For one thing, if the sun revolved in a perfect circle around the earth, then why were the seasons not perfectly equal? If the planets all revolved around the earth in circles, then why did they look nearer or farther, brighter or darker at different times of year? To solve those problems, a host of ingenious hypotheses were advanced. Perhaps the sun revolved around the earth in an eccentric circle, that is, a circle not centered on the earth. That would account for the differing lengths of seasons. Perhaps the planets revolved in circles that rested on a circle around the earth. Then, when the planet revolved within the larger circle, it would seem nearer and brighter, and when it revolved outside it, it would seem farther away and darker. That was the theory of epicycles. Yet to account for the observable

■ Andreas Cellarius created this artistic depiction of the solar system in the late seventeenth century. This chart portrays the heliocentric universe described by Copernicus and Galileo and the elliptical orbits of the planets posited by Kepler. An outsized earth is shown in four different positions as it orbits the sun.

movement of all the known planets, there had to be 55 epicycles. As ingeniously complex as they were, the modifications of Aristotle's views made by the theories of eccentric circles and epicycles had one great virtue: they accurately predicted the movements of the planets. Although they were completely hypothetical, they answered the most troubling questions about the Aristotelian system.

Epicycle and Eccentric Circles

EPICYCLE

Planetary orbit

Planet

Circle around earth

Earth

ECCENTRIC CIRCLE

Sun's orbit

Sun

Circle around earth

Earth

Copernicus. During the 1490s, Nicolaus Copernicus (1473–1543) came to the Polish University of Krakow, which had one of the leading mathematical faculties in Europe. There they taught the latest astronomical theories and vigorously debated the existence of eccentric circles and epicycles. Copernicus came to Krakow for a liberal arts education before pursuing a degree in Church law. He became fascinated by astronomy and puzzled by the debate over planetary motion. Copernicus believed, like Aristotle, that the simplest explanations were the best. If the sun was at the center of the universe and the earth simply another planet in orbit, then many of the most elaborate explanations of planetary motion were unnecessary. "At rest, in the middle of everything is the sun," Copernicus wrote in *On the Revolutions of the Heavenly Spheres* (1543). "For in this most beautiful temple who would place this lamp in another or better position than that from which it can light up the whole thing at the same time?" Because Copernicus accepted most of the rest of the traditional Aristotelian explanation, especially the belief that the planets moved in circles, his sun-centered universe was only slightly better at predicting the

DOCUMENT

Copernicus, *On the Revolution of the Heavenly Spheres*

STARGAZING

Nicolaus Copernicus was born in Poland and educated at the University of Krakow, which had one of the greatest mathematics faculties of the age. He prepared for a career in the Church, but his abiding interest was the study of astronomy. Through observation and calculation, Copernicus worked out a heliocentric view of the universe in which the earth revolved on an axis and orbited the sun. His pathbreaking work was not published until the year of his death, although he was fully aware of the implications of his discovery.

Focus Questions

What is the problem Copernicus is trying to solve by focusing on the movements of the Earth? In what ways is this passage consistent with the established theories of cosmology?

For, first, the mathematicians are so unsure of the movements of the Sun and Moon that they cannot even explain or observe the constant length of the seasonal year. Secondly, in determining the motions of these and of the other five planets, they use neither the same principles and hypotheses nor the same demonstrations of the apparent motions and revolutions. . . . Nor have they been able thereby to discern or deduce the principal thing—namely the shape of the Universe and the unchangeable symmetry of its parts. . . .

Thus assuming motions, which in my work I ascribe to the Earth, by long and frequent observations I have at last discovered that, if the motions of the rest of the planets be brought into relation with the circulation of the Earth and be reckoned in proportion to the circles of each planet, not only do their phenomena presently ensue, but the orders and magnitudes of all stars and spheres, nay the heavens themselves, become so bound together that nothing in any part thereof could be moved from its place without producing confusion of all the other parts of the Universe as a whole.

From Copernicus, *On the Revolutions of Heavenly Spheres* (1543).

position of the planets than the traditional earth-centered one, but Copernicus's idea stimulated other astronomers to make new calculations.

Brahe and Kepler.   Under the patronage of the king of Denmark, Tycho Brahe (1546–1601) built a large observatory to study planetary motion. In 1572, Brahe discovered a nova, a brightly burning star that was previously unknown. The discovery challenged the idea of an immutable universe composed of crystalline rings. In 1577, the appearance of a comet cutting through the supposedly impenetrable rings punched another hole into the old cosmology. Brahe's own views were a hybrid of old and new. He believed that all planets but the earth revolved around the sun and that the sun and the planets revolved around a fixed earth. To demonstrate his theory, Brahe and his students compiled the largest and most accurate mathematical tables of planetary motion yet known. From this research, Brahe's pupil Johannes Kepler (1571–1630), one of the great mathematicians of the age, formulated laws of planetary motion. Kepler discovered that planets orbited the sun in an elliptical rather than a circular path, which accounted for their movements nearer and farther from the earth. More importantly, he demonstrated that there was a precise mathematical relationship between the speed with which a planet revolved and its distance from the sun. Kepler's findings supported the view that the galaxy was heliocentric and that the heavens, like the earth, were made of matter that was subject to physical laws.

Galileo.   What Kepler demonstrated mathematically, the Italian astronomer Galileo Galilei (1564–1642) confirmed by observation. Creating a telescope by using magnifying lenses and a long tube, Galileo saw parts of the heavens that had never been dreamed of before. In 1610, he discovered four moons of Jupiter, proving conclusively that all heavenly bodies did not revolve around the earth. He observed the landscape of the earth's moon and described it as full of mountains, valleys, and rivers. It was of the same imperfect form as the earth itself. He even found spots on the sun, which suggested that it, too, was composed of ordinary matter. Through the telescope, Galileo gazed upon an unimaginable universe: "The Galaxy is nothing else but a mass of innumerable stars," he wrote. Galileo's greatest scientific discoveries had to do with motion—he was the first to posit a law of inertia—but his greatest contribution to the new science was his popularization of the Copernican theory. He took the debate over the structure of the universe to the public, popularizing the discoveries of scientists in his vigorous Italian tracts.

As news of his experiments and discoveries spread, Galileo became famous throughout the Continent, and his support for heliocentrism became a celebrated cause. In 1616, the Roman Catholic Church cautioned him against promoting his views. In 1633, a year after publishing his *A Dialogue Between the Two Great Systems of the World,* Galileo was tried by the Inquisition and forced specifically to recant the idea that the earth moves. He spent the rest of his life under house

■ Tycho Brahe designed and built this observatory, much of which was constructed underground. In each of the large cupolas were instruments through which Brahe and his collaborators could make their celestial observations. Astronomers could also view the heavens through apertures in the flat roofs of the underground chambers.

arrest. Galileo insisted that there was nothing in the new science that was anti-Christian. He rejected the view that his discoveries refuted the Bible, arguing that the words of the Bible were often difficult to interpret and that nature was another way in which God revealed himself. In fact, Galileo feared that the Church's opposition to what he deemed as scientific truth could only bring the Church into disrepute.

The Natural World

The new science originated from a number of traditions that were anything but scientific. Inquiry into nature and the environment grew out of the discipline of natural philosophy and was nurtured by spiritual and mystical traditions. Much of the most useful medical knowledge had come from the studies of herbalists; the most reliable calculations of planetary motion had come from astrologers. Although the first laboratories and observatories were developed in aid of the new science, practice in them was as much magical as experimental. For those attempting to unlock the mysteries of the universe, there was no separation between magic and science. Some of the most characteristic features of modern science, such as the stress on experimentation and empirical observation, developed only gradually. What was new about the new science was the determination to develop systems of thought that could help humans understand and control their environment. Thus there was a greater openness and spirit of cooperation about discoveries than in the past, when experiments were conducted secretly and results were kept hidden away.

DOCUMENT

Bacon,
*Novum
Organum*

Neoplatonism and the New Scientists. Aristotelianism was not the only philosophical system to explain the nature and composition of the universe. During the Renaissance the writings of Plato had attracted a number of Italian humanists, most notably Marsilio Ficino (1433–1499) and Pico della Mirandola (1463–1494). Those Neoplatonic humanists taught Plato's theory that the world was composed of ideas and forms that were hidden by the physical properties of objects. They believed that the architect of the universe possessed the spirit of a geometrician and that the perfect disciplines were music and mathematics. Those elements of **Neoplatonism** created an impetus for the mathematically based studies of the new scientists. They were especially important among the astronomers, who used both calculation and geometry in exploring the heavens. But they also served to bolster the sciences of alchemy and astrology. **Alchemy** was the use of fire in the study of metals, an effort to find the essence of things through their purification. While medieval alchemists mostly attempted to find gold and silver as the essence of lead and iron, the new experimentation focused on the properties of metals in general. Astrology was the study of the influence of the stars on human behavior, calculated by planetary motion and the harmony of the heavenly spheres. Astrologers made careful calculations based on the movement of the planets and were deeply involved in the new astronomy. The Neoplatonic emphasis on mathematics also accorded support for a variety of mystical sciences based on numerology. Those were efforts to predict events from the combination of particular numbers.

The most influential of the mystical traditions was that associated with Hermes Trismegistus ("Thrice Greatest"), an

THE TELESCOPE

No single individual is as much associated with the scientific revolution as Galileo Galilei. He made formative contributions to mathematics, physics, and astronomy, but he also served as a lightning rod for the dissemination of the newest ideas. He popularized the work of Copernicus and was condemned by the Catholic Church for his views and publications. He ended his life under house arrest. Among his other accomplishments, Galileo was the first to use a telescope to make scientific observations.

Focus Questions

How does Galileo get the idea for building a telescope, and why is that significant? What significance did Galileo's observations about the moon have for contemporary theories of the nature of the universe?

About ten months ago a report reached my ears that a certain Fleming had constructed a spyglass by means of which visible objects, though very distant from the eye of the observer, were distinctly seen as if nearby. Of this truly remarkable effect several experiences were related, to which some persons gave credence while others denied them. A few days later the report was confirmed to me in a letter from a noble Frenchman at Paris, Jacques Badovere, which caused me to apply myself wholeheartedly to inquire into the means by which I might arrive at the invention of a similar instrument. This I did shortly afterwards, my basis being the theory of refraction. First I prepared a tube of lead, at the ends of which I fitted two glass lenses, both plane on one side while on the other side one was spherically convex and the other concave. Then placing my eye near the concave lens I perceived objects satisfactorily large and near, for they appeared three times closer and nine times larger than when seen with the naked eye alone. Next I constructed another

one, more accurate, which represented objects as enlarged more than sixty times. Finally, sparing neither labor nor expense, I succeeded in constructing for myself so excellent an instrument that objects seen by means of it appeared nearly one thousand times larger and over thirty times closer than when regarded with our natural vision.

It would be superfluous to enumerate the number and importance of the advantages of such an instrument at sea as well as on land. But forsaking terrestrial observations, I turned to celestial ones, and first I saw the moon from as near at hand as if it were scarcely two terrestrial radii. . . .

. . . Let us speak first of that surface of the moon which faces us. For greater clarity I distinguish two parts of this surface, a lighter and a darker; the lighter part seems to surround and to pervade the whole hemisphere, while the darker part discolors the moon's surface like a kind of cloud, and makes it appear covered with spots. . . . From observation of these spots repeated many times I have been led to the opinion and conviction that the surface of the moon is not smooth, uniform, and precisely spherical as a great number of philosophers believe it (and the other heavenly bodies) to be, but is uneven, rough, and full of cavities and prominences, being not unlike the face of the earth, relieved by chains of mountains and deep valleys.

From Galileo, *The Starry Messenger* (1610).

Egyptian who was reputed to have lived in the second century C.E. and to have known the secrets of the universe. A body of writings mistakenly attributed to Hermes was discovered during the Renaissance and formed the basis of a Hermetic tradition. The core of Hermetic thinking was belief in a universal spirit that was present in all objects and that spontaneously revealed itself. Kepler was one of many of the new scientists influenced by Hermeticism. His efforts to understand planetary motion derived from his search for a unifying spirit.

Paracelsus. A combination of Neoplatonic and Hermetic traditions was central to the work of one of the most curious of the new scientists, the Swiss alchemist Paracelsus (1493–1541). Paracelsus studied with a leading German alchemist before following in his father's footsteps by becoming a physician. Although he worked as a doctor, his true vocation was alchemy, and he conducted innumerable

experiments designed to extract the essence of particular metals. Paracelsus taught that all matter was composed of combinations of three principles: salt, sulfur, and mercury. That view replaced the traditional belief in the four elements of earth, water, fire, and air.

Although the Paracelsian system was peculiar, it transformed ideas about chemistry and medicine. Paracelsus rejected the theory that disease was caused by an imbalance in the humors of the body—the standard view of Galen, the great Greek physician of the second century C.E. Instead, Paracelsus argued that each disease had its own cause, which could be diagnosed and remedied. Where traditional doctors treated disease by bloodletting or sweating to correct the patient's imbalance of humors, Paracelsus prescribed the ingestion of particular chemicals—especially distilled metals such as mercury, arsenic, and antimony—and he favored administering them at propitious astrological moments.

relationship between the volume and pressure of a gas (Boyle's law) and invented the air pump.

Medical Science.   The new spirit of scientific inquiry also affected medical studies. The study of anatomy through dissection had helped the new scientists reject many of the descriptive errors in Galen's texts. The Belgian doctor Andreas Vesalius (1514–1564), who was physician to the emperor Charles V, published the first modern set of anatomical drawings in 1543, the same year that Copernicus published his work. But accurate knowledge of the composition of the body did not also mean better understanding of its operation. Dead bodies didn't easily yield the secrets of life. Much of what was known about matters as common as reproduction was a combination of ancient wisdom and the

■ Tenth "Muscle Plate" from Andreas Vesalius's *De Humani Corporis Fabrica (Concerning the Fabric of the Human Body)*, published in 1543. The muscles of the back of the body are laid bare.

■ Paracelsus was a physician and philosopher who rejected Galen's theory that disease was caused by an imbalance of humors in the body. Instead, he argued that diseases each had their own causes and remedies.

Paracelsus's experimentation with metals and his practice of diagnostic medicine gave a practical turn to the study of alchemy. Efforts to cure new diseases such as syphilis led to the continued study of the chemical properties of substances and to a new confidence about medical science.

Boyle and Chemistry.   Although established physicians and medical faculties rejected Paracelsian cures and methods, his influence spread among ordinary practitioners. It ultimately had a profound impact on the studies of Robert Boyle (1627–1691), an Englishman who helped establish the basis of the science of chemistry. Boyle devoted his energies to raising the study of medical chemistry above that of merely providing recipes for the cure of disease. He worked carefully and recorded each step in his experiments. Boyle's first important work, *The Sceptical Chymist* (1661), attacked both Aristotelian and Paracelsian views of the basic components of the natural world. Boyle rejected both the four humors and the three principles. Instead he favored an atomic explanation in which matter "consisted of little particles of all sizes and shapes." Changes in the particles, which would later be identified as the chemical elements, resulted in changes in matter. Boyle's most important experiments were with gases—a word invented by Paracelsus. He formulated the practical experiences of midwives and doctors. Both were woefully inadequate.

One of the greatest mysteries was the method by which blood moved through the vital organs. It was generally believed that the blood originated in the liver, traveled to the right side of the heart, and then passed to the left side through invisible pores. Anatomical investigation proved beyond doubt that there was blood in both sides of the heart, but no one could discover the pores through which it passed. William Harvey (1578–1657), an Englishman who had received his medical education in Italy, offered an entirely different explanation. Harvey was employed as royal physician to both James I and Charles I and had one of the most lucrative medical practices in Europe. His real interest, however, was in studying the anatomy of the heart. Harvey examined hearts in more than 40 species before concluding that the heart worked like a pump or, as he put it, a water bellows. Harvey observed that the valves of the heart's chambers allowed the blood to flow in only one direction. He thus concluded that the blood was pumped by the heart and circulated throughout the entire body.

But Harvey's theory could not explain how the blood in the heart moved from the arteries to the veins. The explanation was uncovered by Marcello Malpighi using a primitive microscope. Studying the lungs of a frog, Malpighi was able to see a network of tiny blood vessels, the capillaries. The microscope served to advance medical science in a number of areas. While it had probably been invented in Holland, it was Galileo who was able to improve its function so that it could be used for experimentation. Like the telescope, the microscope encouraged precise observation and measurement and thus continued the transformation to experimental science. It was popularized by Robert Hooke whose 1665 book *Micrographia* was internationally acclaimed. Among the most important discoveries made possible by use of the microscope was the existence of bacteria. This observation was the work of Antony van Leeuwenhoek, the greatest of all Dutch scientists of the seventeenth century who also first observed blood cells in human tissue. Although Leeuwenhoek, who spent much of his life as a merchant, had no formal training or education, he learned to grind lenses and developed a small single lens microscope that magnified images over two hundred times. He discovered bacteria by examining the plaque between his own teeth. He found, he wrote to the Royal Society in London, "an unbelievably great company of living animalcules, a-swimming more nimbly than any I had ever seen." Though it would be a long time before scientists made the connection between bacteria and disease, the new experimental scientists took the first step.

Sir Isaac Newton.

The greatest of all English scientists was the mathematician and physicist Sir Isaac Newton (1642–1727). It was Newton who brought together the various strands of the new science. He merged the materialists and Hermeticists, the astronomers and astrologers, the chemists and alchemists. He made stunning contributions to the sciences of optics, physics, astronomy, and mathematics, and his

■ Sir Isaac Newton provided a clear and comprehensive explanation of the physical universe in mathematical terms. He established the theory of gravity and invented a new kind of mathematics: calculus.

magnum opus, *Mathematical Principles of Natural Philosophy* (1687), is one of a handful of the most important scientific works ever composed. Most important, Newton solved the single most perplexing problem: If the world was composed of matter in motion, what was motion?

Newton came from a moderately prosperous background and was trained at a local grammar school before entering Cambridge University. There was little in his background or education to suggest his unique talents, and in fact his most important discoveries were not appreciated until years after he had made them. Newton was the first to understand the composition of light, the first to develop a calculus, and the first to build a reflecting telescope. Newton became a professor at Cambridge, but he spent much of his time alone. He made a great study of Hermetic writings and from them revived the mystical notions of attraction and repulsion.

Although Galileo had developed a *theory of inertia*, the idea that a body at rest stays at rest, most materialists believed that motion was inherent in objects. In contrast, Newton believed that motion was the result of the interaction of objects and that it could be calculated mathematically. From his experiments he formulated the concept of force and his famous laws of motion:

(1) that objects at rest or of uniform linear motion remain in such a state unless acted upon by an external force; (2) that changes in motion are proportional to force; and (3) that for every action there is an equal and opposite reaction. From the laws of motion, Newton advanced one step further. If the world was no more than matter in motion and if all motion was subject to the same laws, then the movement of the planets could be explained in the same way as the movement of an apple falling from a tree. There was a mathematical relationship between attraction and repulsion—a universal gravitation, as Newton called it—that governed the movement of all objects. Newton's theory of gravity joined together Kepler's astronomy and Galileo's physics. The mathematical, materialistic world of the new science was now complete.

Science Enthroned

By the middle of the seventeenth century, the new science was firmly established throughout Europe. Royal and noble patrons supported the enterprise by paying some of the costs of equipment and experimentation. Royal observatories were created for astronomers, colleges of physicians for doctors, and laboratories for chemists. Both England and France established royal societies of learned scientists to meet together and discuss their discoveries. The French Academie des Sciences (1666) was composed of 20 salaried scientists and an equal number of students, representing the different branches of scientific learning. They met twice weekly throughout the year, and each member worked on a project of his own devising. The English Royal Society (1662) boasted some of the greatest minds of the age. It was there that Newton first made public his most important discoveries. Scientific bodies were also formed outside the traditional universities. Those were the so-called mechanics colleges, such as Gresham College in London, where the practical applications of mathematics and physics were studied and taught. Navigation was a particular concern of the college, and the faculty established close ties with the Royal Navy and with London merchants.

The establishment of learned scientific societies and practical colleges fulfilled part of the program advocated by Sir Francis Bacon (1561–1626), one of the leading supporters of scientific research in England. In *The Advancement of Learning* (1605), Bacon had proposed a scientific method through inductive empirical experimentation. Bacon believed that experiments should be carefully recorded so that results were both reliable and repeatable. He advocated the open world of the scientist over the secret world of the magician. In his numerous writings, he stressed the practical impact of scientific discovery and even wrote a utopian work in which science appeared as the savior of humanity. Although he was not himself a scientific investigator, Bacon used his considerable influence to support scientific projects in England.

Bacon's support for the new science contrasts markedly with the stance taken by the Roman Catholic Church. Embattled by the Reformation and the wars of religion, the Church had taken the offensive in preserving the core of its

heritage. By the early seventeenth century, the missionary work of the Jesuits had won many reconversions and had halted the advance of Protestantism. Now the new science appeared to be another heresy. Not only did it confound ancient wisdom and contradict Church teachings, but it was also a lay movement that was neither directed nor controlled from Rome. The trial of Galileo slowed the momentum of scientific investigation in Catholic countries and starkly posed the conflict between authority and knowledge. But the stand taken by the Church was based on more than narrow self-interest. Ever since Copernicus had published his views, a new skepticism had emerged among European intellectuals. Every year new theories competed with old ones, and dozens of contradictory explanations for the most common phenomena were advanced and debated. The skeptics concluded that nothing was known and nothing was knowable. Their position led inevitably to the most shocking of all possible views: atheism.

There was no necessary link between the new science and an attack upon established religion: so Galileo had argued all along. Few of the leading scientists ever saw a contradiction between their studies and their faith. Sir Robert Boyle endowed a

■ The new philosophers attracted the attention of governments as well as scholars. René Descartes traveled to Sweden at the invitation of Queen Christina with whom he is shown conversing.

lectureship for the advancement of Christian doctrine and contributed money for the translation of the New Testament into Turkish. Still, by the middle of the century attacks on the Church were increasing, and some blamed the new science for them. Thus it was altogether fitting that one of the leading mathematicians of the day should also provide the method for harmonizing faith and reason.

René Descartes (1596–1650) was the son of a provincial lawyer and judge. He was trained in one of the best Jesuit schools in France before taking a law degree in 1616. While it was his father's intention that his son practice law, it was René's intention that he become educated in "the school of life." He entered military service in the Dutch Republic, and after the outbreak of the Thirty Years' War served in the Duke of Bavaria's army. Descartes was keenly interested in mathematics, and during his military travels he met and was tutored by a leading Dutch mathematician. For the first time he learned of the new scientific discoveries and of the advances made in mathematics. In 1619, he dreamed that he had discovered the scientific principles of universal knowledge. After the dream, Descartes returned to Holland and began to develop his system. He was on the verge of publishing his views when he learned of the Church's condemnation of Galileo. Reading Galileo's *Dialogue Between the Two Great Systems of the World,* Descartes discovered that he shared many of the same opinions and had worked out mathematical proofs for them. He refrained from publishing until 1637 when he brought out his *Discourse on Method.*

In the *Discourse on Method,* Descartes demonstrated how skepticism could be used to produce certainty. He began by declaring that he would reject everything that could not be clearly proved beyond doubt. Thus he rejected his perception of the material world, the testimony of his senses—all known or imagined opinions. He was left only with doubt. But what was doubt, if not thought, and what was thought, if not the workings of his mind? The only thing of which he could be certain, then, was that he had a mind. Thus his famous formulation: "I think, therefore I am." From this first certainty came another: the knowledge of perfectibility. He knew that he was imperfect and that a perfect being had to have placed that knowledge within him. Therefore, a perfect being—God—existed.

Descartes's philosophy, known as **Cartesianism,** rested on the dual existence of matter and mind. Matter was the material world, subject to the incontrovertible laws of mathematics. Mind was the spirit of the creator. Descartes was one of the leading mechanistic philosophers, believing that all objects operated in accord with natural laws. He invented analytic geometry and made important contributions to the sciences of optics and physics on which Newton would later build. Yet it was in his proof that the new science could be harmonized with the old religion that Descartes made his greatest contribution to the advancement of learning. Despite the fact that his later work was condemned by the Catholic Church and that he preferred the safety of Protestant Holland to the uncertainty of his Catholic homeland, Cartesianism became the basis for the unification of science and religion.

"I shall attempt to make myself intelligible to everyone," Descartes wrote. Like many of the new scientists, he preferred the use of vernacular languages to elite Latin, hoping that his

DESCARTES EXPERIMENTS

René Descartes contributed new observations and theories to the emerging scientific community of the seventeenth century. Published in 1637, his Discourse on Method *presents a system that combines mathematical reasoning with central problems of moral philosophy. The passage here is from the final section of* Discourse, *in which Descartes puts forth his reasons for writing and his ideas for advancing the scientific investigation of nature.*

Focus Questions

According to Descartes, what is the obligation of the scientist to humankind? What kind of philosophy does Descartes oppose?

I have never attributed great significance to what came from my own mind. . . . However, I soon acquired some general notion about physics; and when I began to test them in relation to specific problems and noticed where they can lead and how much they differ from the principles that had been used up to now, I thought I could not keep them hidden without sinning greatly against the law that obliges us to realize, as much as we can, the general welfare of all people. For they made me see that it was possible to achieve knowledge which would be very useful for life and that, in place of the speculative philosophy by which, knowing the force and actions of fire, water, air, the stars, the heavens and all the other bodies that surround us, as distinctly as we know the various crafts of our artisans, we would be able to use them in the same way for all the applications for which they are appropriate, and thereby make ourselves, as it were, the lords and masters of nature.

René Descartes, *Discourse on Method and Related Writings* (translated by Desmond M. Clarke, Penguin 1999).

work would reach beyond the narrow bounds of high culture. Descartes was one of many new scientists who saw the practical import of what they had learned and who hoped to bring that knowledge to the aid of the material well-being of their contemporaries. John Dee (1527–1608) translated the Greek geometrician Euclid into English so that ordinary people might "find out and devise new works, strange engines and instruments for sundry purposes in the commonwealth." Although many of the breakthrough discoveries of the new scientists would not find practical use for centuries, the spirit of discovery was to have great impact in an age of commerce and capital. The quest for mathematical certainty led directly to improvements in agriculture, mining, navigation, and industrial activity. It also brought with it a sense of control over the material world that provided a new optimism for generations of Europeans.

EMPIRES OF GOODS

Under the watchful eye of the European states, a worldwide marketplace for the exchange of commodities had been created. First the Dutch and then the English had established monopoly companies to engage in exotic trades in the East. First the Spanish and Portuguese, then the English and French, had established colonial dependencies in the Atlantic that they carefully nurtured in hope of economic gain. Protected trade had flourished beyond the wildest dreams of its promoters. Luxury commodities became staples; new commodities became luxuries. Trade enhanced the material life of all Europeans, although it came at great cost to the Asians, Africans, and Latin Americans whose labor and raw materials were converted into the new crazes of consumption.

While long-distance trade was never as important to the European economy as inland and intracontinental trade, its development in the seventeenth and eighteenth centuries had a profound impact on lifestyles, economic policy, and, ultimately, warfare. The Dutch became the first great commercial power. Their achievements were based on innovative techniques, rational management, and a social and cultural environment that supported mercantile activities. Dutch society was freer than any other; it was open to new capital, new ventures, and new ideas. The Dutch improved the organization of trade by developing the concept of the **entrepôt,** a place where goods were brought for storage before being exchanged. They pioneered in finance by establishing the Bank of Amsterdam. They led in shipbuilding by developing the flyboat, a long, flat-hulled vessel designed specifically to carry bulky cargoes like grain. They traded around the globe with the largest mercantile fleet yet known. It was not until the end of the seventeenth century that England and France surpassed the Dutch. That reversal owed less to new innovations than it did to restrictions on trade. Because the Dutch dominated the European economy, the French and English began to pass laws to eliminate Dutch competition. The English banned imports carried in Dutch ships; the French banned Dutch products. Both policies cut heavily into the Dutch superiority, and both ultimately resulted in commercial warfare.

The Marketplace of the World

By the sixteenth century, all the major trading routes had already been opened. The Spanish moved back and forth across the Atlantic; the Dutch and Portuguese sailed around the tip of Africa to the Indian Ocean. The Baltic trade connected the eastern and western parts of Europe as Danes, Swedes, and Dutch exchanged Polish and Russian raw materials for English and French manufactured goods. The Mediterranean, which had dominated world trade for centuries, was still a vital artery of intercontinental trade, but its role was diminishing. In 1600, almost three-quarters of the Asian trade was still land based, much of it carried through the Middle East to the Mediterranean. A century later, nearly all Asian trade was carried directly to western Europe by Dutch and English vessels. Commercial power was shifting to the northern European states just as dramatically as military and political power.

■ *The Geographer* by Jan Vermeer van Delft, 1669. A Dutch cartographer, holding dividers, is shown surrounded by charts, a globe, and other paraphernalia of his craft. Such cartographers combined the skills of artist and mathematician.

The Evolution of Long-Distance Travel. The technology associated with commerce achieved no breakthroughs to compare with the great transformations of the fifteenth century, when new techniques of navigation made transatlantic travel possible. It is certainly true that there continued to be improvements. The astronomical findings of the new science were a direct aid to navigation, as were the recorded experiences of so many practiced sea travelers. The materials used to make and maintain ships improved with the importation of pitch and tar from the East and with the greater availability of iron and copper from Scandinavia. It was the Dutch who made the single most important innovation in shipbuilding. To gain maximum profit from their journeys to the Baltic, the Dutch designed the so-called flyboats. Flyboats sacrificed speed and maneuverability, but they were cheap to build and could be manned by small crews. They carried no heavy armaments and were thus well adapted to the serene Baltic trade.

It was unspectacular developments such as the flyboat that had such an impact on seventeenth- and eighteenth-century transcontinental trade. Innovation, organization, and efficient management were the principal elements of what historians have called the commercial revolution. Concerted efforts to maximize opportunities and advantages accounted for the phenomenal growth in the volume and value of commercial exchange. One of the least spectacular and most effective breakthroughs was the replacement of bilateral with **triangular trade.** In bilateral trade, the surplus commodities of one community were exchanged for those of another. The method, of course, restricted the range of trading partners to those with mutually desirable surplus production: England and Italy were unlikely to swap woolens or Sicily and Poland to trade grain. For those with few desirable commodities, bilateral trade meant the exchange of precious metals for goods, and throughout much of the sixteenth and early seventeenth

MAP DISCOVERY

Dutch Trade Routes, ca. 1650

The Dutch were the greatest commercial nation of the seventeenth century. According to the trade routes shown here, how would you describe the extent of Dutch trade? Why are there so many trading centers in the East? Based on information provided in the chapter, what were some of the major goods exchanged in the various trade regions? Why did the Dutch not secure major colonial possessions (orange shaded areas) in the East?

centuries, bullion was by far the most often traded commodity. Triangular trade created a larger pool of desirable goods. British manufactured goods could be traded to Africa for slaves, the slaves could be traded in the West Indies for sugar, and the sugar could be consumed in Britain. Moreover, the merchants involved in shifting the goods from place to place could achieve profits on each exchange. Indeed, their motive in trading could now change from dumping surplus commodities to matching supply and demand.

The New Forms of Banking.
Equally important were the changes made in the way trade was financed. As states, cities, and even individuals could stamp their own precious metal, there were hundreds of different European coins with different nominal and metallic values. The influx of American silver further destabilized an already unstable system of exchange. The Bank of Amsterdam was created in 1609 to establish a uniform rate of exchange for the various currencies traded in that city. From that useful function a second developed—transfer, or giro, banking, a system that had been invented in Italy. In giro banking, various merchant firms held money on account and issued bills of transfer from one to another. The transfer system meant that merchants in different cities did not have to transport their precious metals or endure long delays in having their accounts settled.

Giro banking also aided the development of bills of exchange, an early form of checking. Bills of exchange were especially important in international trade, as they made large-scale shipments of precious metals to settle trade deficits unnecessary. By the end of the seventeenth century, bills of exchange had become negotiable; that is, they could pass from one merchant to another without being redeemed. There were two disadvantages to the system: ultimately the bill had to return for redemption; when it did, the account on which it was drawn might be empty. The establishment of the Bank of England in 1694 overcame such difficulties. The Bank of England was licensed to issue its own bills of exchange, or bank notes, which were backed by the revenue from specific English taxes. That security of payment was widely sought after, and the Bank of England soon became a clearinghouse for all kinds of bills of exchange. The Bank would buy in bills at a discount, paying less than their face value, and pay out precious metal or its own notes in exchange.

The effects of those and many other small-scale changes in business practice helped fuel prolonged growth in European commerce. It was the European merchant who made that growth possible by accepting the risks of each individual transaction and building up small pools of capital from which successive transactions could take place. Most mercantile ventures were conducted by individuals or families and were based on the specialized trade of a single commodity. Trade offered high returns because it entailed high risks. The long delays in moving goods and their uncertain arrival; the unreliability of agents and the unscrupulousness of other traders; and the inefficiencies in transport and communication all weighed heavily against success. Those who succeeded did so

less by luck than by hard work. They used family members to receive shipments. They lowered shipping costs by careful packaging. They lowered protection costs by securing their trade routes. Financial publications lowered the costs of information. Ultimately, lower costs meant lower prices. For centuries luxury goods had dominated intercontinental trade. But by the eighteenth century, European merchants had created a world marketplace in which the luxuries of the past were the common fare of the present.

Consumption Choices

As long-distance trade became more sophisticated, merchants became more sensitive to consumer tastes. Low-volume, high-quality goods such as spices and silks could not support the growing merchant communities in the European states. Those goods were the preserve of the largest trading companies and, more importantly, they had reached saturation levels by the early seventeenth century. The price of pepper, the most used of all spices, fell nearly continuously after 1650. Moreover, triangular trade allowed merchants to provide a better match of supplies and demands. The result was the rise to prominence of a vast array of new commodities, which not only continued the expansion of trade but also reshaped diet, lifestyles, and patterns of consumption. New products came from both East and West. Dutch and English incursions into the Asian trade provoked competition with the Portuguese and expanded the range of commodities that were shipped back to Europe. An aggressive Asian triangle was created in which European bullion bought Indonesian spices that were exchanged for Persian silk and Chinese and Japanese finished goods. In the Atlantic, the English were quick to develop both home and export markets for a variety of new or newly available products.

Commodities from the East.
European trade with Asia had always been designed to satisfy consumer demand rather than to exchange surplus goods. Europeans manufactured little that was desired in Asia, and neither merchants nor governments saw fit to attempt to influence Asian tastes in the way they did those of Europeans. The chief commodity imported to the East was bullion: tons of South American silver, perhaps a third of all that was produced. In return came spices, silk, coffee, jewels, jade, porcelain, dyes, and a wide variety of other exotic goods. By the middle of the seventeenth century, the Dutch dominated the spice trade, obtaining a virtual monopoly over cinnamon, cloves, nutmeg, and mace and carrying the largest share of pepper. Each year, Europeans consumed perhaps a million pounds of the four great spices and seven million pounds of pepper. Both the Dutch and the English competed for preeminence in the silk trade. The Dutch concentrated on Chinese silk, which they used mostly in trade with Japan. The English established an interest in lower-quality Indian silk spun in Bengal and even hired Italian silk masters to try to teach European techniques to the Indian spinners.

The most important manufactured articles imported from the East to Europe were the lightweight, brightly colored

■ Detail of an Indian textile from the Madras region (ca. 1650). Calicut gave its name to the cotton cloth called calico. This is an example of a "painted Calicut," a wall hanging that shows richly dressed Indian women. (Photograph © 1980 The Metropolitan Museum of Art.)

Indian cottons known as calicoes. The Dutch first realized the potential of the cotton market. Until the middle of the seventeenth century, cotton and cotton blended with silk were used in Europe only for wall hangings and table coverings. Colorful Asian chintz contained floral patterns that Europeans still considered exotic. But the material was also soft and smooth to the touch, and it soon replaced linen for use as underwear and close-fitting garments among the well-to-do. The fashion quickly caught on, and the Dutch began exporting calicoes throughout the Continent. The English and French followed suit, establishing their own trading houses in India and bringing European patterns and designs with them for the Asians to copy. The calico trade was especially lucrative because the piece goods were easy to pack and ship and, unlike consumables, could be stored indefinitely. When the English finally came to dominate the trade in the middle of the eighteenth century, they were shipping more than a million cloths a year into London. The craze for calicoes was so great that both the English and French governments attempted to ban their import to protect their own clothing industries.

Along with the new apparel from the East came new beverages. Coffee, which was first drunk in northern Europe in the early seventeenth century, had become a fashionable drink by the end of the century. Coffeehouses sprang up in the major urban areas of northern Europe. There political and intellectual conversation was as heady as the strong Middle Eastern brew that was served. The Dutch and English both established themselves in the coffee trade, which was centered in the Middle Eastern seaport of Mocha. By the beginning of the eighteenth century, the Dutch had begun to grow their own coffee for export from their island colony of Java, and the two different types of coffee competed for favor.

As popular as coffee became among the European elites, it paled in comparison to the importance of tea as both an import commodity and a basic beverage. While coffee drinking remained the preserve of the wealthy, tea consumption spread throughout European society. It was probably most prevalent in England, where the combination of Chinese tea and West Indian sugar created a virtual revolution in nutrition. The growth in tea consumption was phenomenal. In 1706, England imported 100,000 pounds of tea. By the end of the century, the number had risen to more than 15 million pounds. The English imported most of the tea directly from China, where an open port had been established at Canton. Originally just one of a number of commodities that were carried on an Asian voyage, tea soon became the dominant cargo of the large English merchant ships. Some manufactured goods would be brought to India on the outward voyage in order to fill as much cargo space as possible, but once the ships had loaded the green and black teas, they sailed directly home. Almost all tea was purchased with

■ *An English Family at Tea* by Joseph Van Aken, ca. 1720. In the eighteenth century, tea imports from China soared as tea-drinking became a domestic ritual in Europe. The enormous popularity of tea also resulted in an increased demand for goods related to its consumption, such as tea tables, porcelain dishes, and silver serving sets.

■ Based on a 1667 drawing, this engraving of a sugar plantation in Barbados depicts slaves performing various tasks in the harvesting and production of sugar.

bullion, as the Chinese had even less use for European goods than did other Asians. It was not until the discovery that the Chinese consumed large quantities of opium, which was grown in India and Southeast Asia, that a triangular trade developed.

Colonial Trade: The Demand for Sugar.

The success of tea was linked to the explosive growth in the development of sugar in Europe's Atlantic colonies. The Portuguese had attempted to cultivate sugar in the Azores at the end of the fifteenth century, but it was not until the settlement of Brazil, whose hot, humid climate was a natural habitat for the cane plants, that widespread cultivation began. The island of Barbados became the first English sugar colony. Barbados turned to sugar production accidentally, when its first attempts to market tobacco failed. The planters modeled their methods on those of Brazil, where African slaves were used to plant, tend, and cut the giant canes from which the sugar was extracted. For reasons that will never be fully understood, the English had an insatiable appetite for sugar's sweetness. It was taken plain, like candy; used in small quantities in almost all types of recipes; and diluted in ever-increasing quantities of tea. Hot, sweet tea became a meal for the lower orders of English society, a meal which—unlike beer—provided a quick burst of energy. By 1700, the English were sending home more than 50 million pounds of sugar besides what they were shipping directly to the North American colonies. The quantity doubled by 1730, and still there was no slackening of demand. What might have become a valuable raw material in English trade instead became a staple of consumption.

The African Slave Trade.

The triangular trade of manufactures—largely reexported calicoes—to Africa for slaves, who were exchanged in the West Indies for sugar, became the dominant form of English overseas trade. Colonial production depended upon the enforced labor of hundreds of thousands of Africans. Gold and silver, tobacco, sugar, rice, and indigo were all slave crops. Africans were enslaved by other Africans and then sold to Europeans to be used in the colonies. More than six million black slaves were imported into the Americas during the course of the eighteenth century. While rum and calicoes were the main commodities exchanged for slaves, the African tribes that dominated the slave trade organized a highly competitive market. Every colonial power participated in the lucrative trade. More than three million slaves were imported into the Portuguese colony of Brazil; by the end of the eighteenth century, there were 500,000 slaves and only 35,000 French inhabitants on the sugar island of Saint Domingue. But it was the English, with their sugar colonies of Barbados and Jamaica and their tobacco colonies of Virginia and Maryland, who ultimately came to control the slave trade. The prosperity of Newport, Rhode Island, in North America and the port of Liverpool in Lancashire was built entirely on the slave trade, as were hundreds of plantation fortunes. The sweet tooth of Europe was fed by the sweat of black Africans.

The new commodities flooded into Europe from all parts of the globe. By the middle of the eighteenth century, tea, coffee, cocoa, gin, and rum were among the most popular beverages. All were products that had largely been unknown a century earlier. Among the wealthy, tea was served from porcelain pots imported from China; among all classes it was drunk with

■ This diagram shows how slaves were packed into cargo holds for the notorious Middle Passage to the Americas. The plan was a model of efficiency, for slave traders sought to maximize profits.

Scale of Feet

PLAN OF A SLAVE VESSEL.

THE SLAVE TRADE.

THE motion in the House of Lords made by Lord Denman, on Tuesday night, has naturally revived the interest of the measures for the extinction of this vile traffic of " man-selling and man-stealing." The close of the session is marked by these humane exertions, as was its commencement, in the comprehensive speech of Lord George Bentinck, in the House of Commons, on February 3. His Lordship then held in his hand a communication from Captain Pilkington, of the Royal Navy, on the subject of the slave-trade, accompanied with a plan of one of the slave vessels (which we now Engrave). They were sit-

Water Line

entertainment enlivened by some most exquisite performances on the national instrument, the harp, much to the delight of all assembled. From the dinner-table the company retired at an early hour to the School-rooms, where the *conversazioni* were held.

WEDNESDAY.

On Wednesday, as the Geological and Natural History Sections were unable to finish the business before them, they each held meetings; but as a great number of members had left Swansea that morning by the *Lord Beresford* steamer, and others were examining the works in the neighbourhood, the Sections were very slightly attended, and the papers communicated were of small general interest.

A dinner, given by Lewis W. Dillwyn, Esq., who is himself one of the oldest members of the Royal Society, may be regarded as the close of the proceedings.

The last General Meeting was held in the afternoon, when it appeared, that, notwithstanding the inferiority of Swansea as respects population, this meeting has added considerably to the funds of the Association.

In concluding our notice of an Association which numbers among its members all the most eminent men in every department of physical and natural science, we cannot but express our satisfaction at the business-like character of this meeting. It is true that it has not startled the world by the announcement of any great discovery; but it will be found, upon examination, to present a fair average rate of progress. The vulnerable points have been less apparent than hitherto; and by the exclusion from the sections of all subjects which were not purely scientific, and by particularly avoiding those communications which have frequently been introduced as mere trading advertisements, of which we witnessed but one, that on gutta percha, which in our opinion should not have

---

sugar imported from America. Beaver hats and Persian silks were fashionable in the upper reaches of society, rabbit caps and calico prints in the lower. New habits were created as new demands were satisfied. Tea and sugar passed from luxury to staple in little more than a generation, and the demand for both products continued to increase. To meet it, the European trading powers needed to create and maintain a powerful and efficient mercantile system.

Dutch Masters

For the nearly 80 years between 1565 and 1648 that the Dutch were at war, they grew ever more prosperous. While the economies of most other European nations were sapped by warfare, the Dutch seemed to draw strength from their interminable conflict with the Spanish Empire. They had the advantage of fighting defensively on land and offensively on sea. Land war was terribly costly to the aggressor, who had to raise large armies, transport them to the site of battles or sieges, and feed them while they were there. The defender simply had to fortify strong places, keep its water routes open to secure supplies, and wait for the weather to change. Sea war—or piracy, depending on one's viewpoint—required much smaller outlays for men and material and promised the rewards of captured prizes. The Dutch became expert at attacking the Spanish silver fleets, hunting like a lion against a herd by singling out the slower and smaller vessels for capture. The Dutch also benefited from the massive immigration into their provinces of Protestants who had lived and worked in the southern provinces. The immigrants brought with them vital skills in manufacturing and large reserves of capital for investment in Dutch commerce.

The Dutch grounded their prosperity on commerce. Excellent craftsmen, they took the lead in the skilled occupations necessary for finishing cloth, refining raw materials, and decorating consumer goods. They were also successful farmers, especially given the small amounts of land with which they had to work and the difficult ecological conditions in which they worked it. But their greatest abilities were in trade.

Although the Dutch Republic comprised seven separate political entities, with a total population of about two million, the province of Holland was preeminent among them. Holland contained more than a quarter of that population, and its trading port of Amsterdam was one of the great cities of Europe. The city had risen dramatically in the seventeenth century, growing from a midsized urban community of 65,000 in 1600 to a metropolis of 170,000 fifty years later. The port was one of the busiest in the world, for it was built to be an entrepôt. Vast warehouses and docks lined its canals. Visitors were impressed by the bustle, the cleanliness, and the businesslike appearance of Amsterdam. There were no great public squares and few recognizable monuments. The central buildings were the Bank and the Exchange, testimony to the dominant activities of the residents.

The Dutch dominated all types of European trade. They carried more English coal than England, more French wine than France, more Swedish iron than Sweden. Dutch ships outnumbered all others in every important port of Europe. Goods were brought to Amsterdam to be redistributed throughout the world. Dutch prosperity rested first upon the Baltic trade. Even after it ceased to expand in the middle of the seventeenth century, the Baltic trade composed more than one-quarter of all of

■ The Old Stock Exchange in
Amsterdam was a center of mercantile activity and religious and
intellectual interactions.

Trade Routes
to Asia

Holland's commercial enterprise. The Dutch also were the leaders in the East Indian trade throughout the seventeenth century. They held a virtual monopoly on the sale of exotic spices and the largest share of the pepper trade.
Their imports of cottons, and especially of porcelain,
began new consumer fads that soon resulted in the
development of European industries. Dutch potteries
began to produce china, as lower-quality ceramic
goods came to be known. Dutch trade in the Atlantic was of less
importance, but the Dutch did have a colonial presence in the
New World, controlling a number of small islands and the
rapidly growing mainland settlement of New Netherland. Yet
the Dutch still dominated the secondary market in tobacco and
sugar, becoming the largest processor and refiner of those important commodities. (See "A Closer Look: The Dutch Tulip
Mania of the Seventeenth Century," pp. 532–533.)

In all of the activities the Dutch acted as merchants rather
than as consumers. Unlike most other Europeans, they regarded precious metal as a commodity like any other and
took no interest in accumulating it for its own sake. That attitude enabled them to pioneer triangular trading and develop
the crucial financial institutions necessary to expand their
overseas commerce. The Dutch were not so much inventors as
improvers. They saw the practical value in Italian accounting
and banking methods and raised them to new levels of efficiency. They made use of marine insurance to help diminish

the risks of mercantile activity. Their legal system favored the
creation of small trading companies by protecting individual
investments. The European stock and commodity markets
were centered in Amsterdam. By the 1670s, more than 500
commodities were traded on the Amsterdam exchange, and
even a primitive futures market had evolved for those who
wanted to speculate.

There were many explanations for the unparalleled growth
of the small maritime state into one of the greatest of European
trading empires. Geography and climate provided one impetus,
the lack of sufficient foodstuffs another. Yet there were cultural
characteristics as well. One was the openness of Dutch society.
Even before the struggle with Spain, the northern provinces
had shown a greater inclination toward religious toleration
than had most parts of Europe. Amsterdam became a unique
center for religious and intellectual exchange. European Jews
flocked there, as did Catholic dissidents like Descartes. Those
people brought with them a wide range of skills and knowledge, along with capital that could be invested in trade. There
was no real nobility among the Dutch, and certainly no set of
values that prized investment in land over investment in trade.
The French and Spanish nobility looked with scorn upon their
mercantile classes and shunned any form of commercial investment; the English, though more open to industry and trade,
sank as much of their capital as possible into landed estates and
country houses. The Dutch economic elite invested in trade. By

A Closer Look
The Dutch Tulip Mania of the Seventeenth Century

The Semper Augustus was believed to be the most beautiful tulip in the world. On the inside of its silken white petals shot flames of crimson; on the outside the color was finely mottled. Like all two-toned tulips, it had simply appeared one year from the bulb of a solid flower. In 1637, only a dozen bulbs were known to exist, and just one of them cost more than the finest house on the central canal of Amsterdam.

No one will ever know for certain why a tulip mania struck amongst the solid burghers and tradesmen of the Dutch Republic in the 1630s, or why the techniques developed to trade the goods of the burgeoning Dutch Empire were suddenly applied to the exchange of flower bulbs. But for a few brief years, nearly everyone in the republic was mad about tulips and desperate to purchase them. Perhaps it was an embarrassment of riches as the products of the East and the West flooded into the small northern communities where every investment in overseas trade seemed to yield a windfall. Perhaps it was release after two devastating bouts of bubonic plague swept indiscriminately through the United Provinces leaving in their wake misery and relief in equal parts. For those who survived that lottery of life and death, a lottery of risk and reward over flower bulbs was hardly terrifying. Perhaps it was irrational exuberance brought on by the sudden turn of Protestant fortune in the Thirty Years' War. After a decade of defeat and ominous threat, the triumphs of Gustavas Adolphus no less than French intervention against the Habsburgs, mortal enemies to the Dutch, allowed for a gamble

on getting rich quick. But whatever it was, the mania hit quickly. No one seemed immune and, despite the diatribes of moralists, no one stood aloof. Everyone had to have a tulip or rather a tulip bulb, or rather a weight of tulip bulb that might come to exist.

The tulip had first come to Europe from Constantinople in the sixteenth century, most likely imported by a Frenchman. But it flourished in the watery fields of the Dutch towns where its graceful shape, sturdy stem, and delicate flower were prized more than in any other European nation. The ceramic tile industry began using decorative tulips on its products only two decades after they were first cultivated in Holland. Dutch painters, attracted to still lifes of the new products of empire—lobsters, porcelains, and fine Persian carpets—were soon incorporating tulips into their pictures in every conceivable way. Their work was purchased not only by the rich and powerful, but by ordinary citizens who adorned their walls with seascapes, landscapes, and now floral celebrations. Horticulturists had their prized varietals named not only in formal botany Latin but as if they were heroic figures such as Admiral Van Hoorn or General Bol. Thus before they achieved their astounding monetary value, tulips already had acquired significant symbolic value.

The Dutch had already perfected the art of commodity exchange. On the Amsterdam stock exchange shares of the Dutch East India Company changed hands at prices listed in inns, and speculators dumped their holdings on every rumor of storms or pirates

and increased them on every sighting of a sail. Until the tulip mania, share trading was considered a highly technical activity and moralists warned that a fool and his gold would soon be parted in what was considered by many to be little more than legalized gambling. But tulips were good commodities for speculation. First of all, they were grown in the United Provinces themselves, which removed the considerable risks of overseas trade. The purchase of flowers planted in Harlaam or Delft was a far safer investment than the purchase of porcelain that had to be carried from China. And tulips were rare. It took seven years for a seedling to become a bulb, thereby limiting supply and keeping the overall stock scarce. Finally, and this was the greatest attraction of all, the "breaks" that turned solid colored tulips into polychromes were a naturally occurring phenomenon—actually the result of a virus—and, for all anyone knew in the seventeenth century, entirely random. Thus for the uninitiated every purchase had the qualities of both a sure thing and a long shot. There was the highest probability that you would get the tulip you paid for and at least a chance that you would get one far more valuable.

Things began to go wrong in tulip exchange almost at once. There would have been neither speculative fever nor profit gouging if people simply bought tulips once they had flowered. But it was the bulbs that came to be bought and sold so that investors were quite literally in the dark as to what they owned. In the language of sophisticated modern investors, they were buying futures. At first, one could buy title to a specific bulb in a specific field, but as the market expanded and more people clambered to purchase that became too cumbersome. Instead, one came to purchase a weight of a bulb of a certain variety, the weight expressed in *azens*. The planted fields were auctioned in lots with the grower selling the weight of the bulbs he was cultivating. Responsible growers knew that early in their lives tulip bulbs gained in weight but that eventually they stopped producing flowers. Therefore, selling the planted bulb weight ensured that there was some rough equilibrium between growth and decay and that the weight of bulbs sold would roughly match either the weight of bulbs delivered or the production of actual tulips. But, such a system left plenty of room for unscrupulous growers, especially as demand for *azens* of tulip bulbs increased.

Along with a lack of checks on growers was a lack of restraint on sellers. Between 1634 and 1637 the mania reached its height. No longer were speculators buying and selling tulips, or even tulip bulbs. All anyone was selling was *azens*, what today would be known among sophisticated investors as derivatives, and as long as people were willing to buy and sell *azens* there seemed little reason to worry about the fact that more *azens* were being sold than were being planted. By 1637 more *azens* were being traded than probably could ever have been planted. But no one cared. It was the contracts rather than the tulips which now held the value. Lots that had traded for less than $100 in the 1620s now changed hands for thousands. In just three years, the price of pale yellow Switzers, by no means the most sought after variety, rose an astounding 3000 percent. A single trade of a Semper Augustus took place for more than

■ Illustration of a highly valued multicolored tulip by Bartholomeus Asseytn (1607–1667).

$100,000, while an auction of 99 lots of polychromes was won for $10,000,000 by a syndicate that believed it could more than double its investment in a year. The demand for tulip shares was insatiable and the bubble of speculation grew bigger and bigger until it inevitably burst. In 1637, after the market hit its peak, growers began to renege on their contracts. There was nowhere near enough productive capacity to supply all of the *azens* of tulip bulbs that now began to trade as devalued currency. The inevitable government investigation followed, and there was more than enough blame to go around.

The tulip mania was the first of a series of speculative bubbles by which the system of financial capitalism gradually developed procedures and controls. No one could have foreseen the confluence of circumstances that would turn a decorative plant into the most sought after commodity in Holland, but buyers, sellers, and government officials could all learn from the consequences of the bubble. Tulip mania revealed the dangers of both a market in futures and the buying and selling of derivatives. It would take centuries before either could be safely traded; even today those who warn of irrational exuberance remember the Dutch tulip mania of the seventeenth century.

the middle of the seventeenth century, the Dutch Republic enjoyed a reputation for cultural creativity that was the envy of the Continent. A truly extraordinary school of Dutch artists led by Rembrandt celebrated the new state born of commerce with vivid portrayals of its people and its prosperity.

Mercantile Organization

Elsewhere in Europe, trade was the king's business. The wealth of the nation was part of the prestige of the monarch, and its rise or fall part of the crown's power. Power and prestige were far more important to absolute rulers than was the profit of merchants. Indeed, in all European states except the Dutch Republic, the activities of merchants were scorned by both the landed elite and the salaried bureaucrats. Leisure was valued by the one and royal service by the other. The pursuit of wealth by buying and selling somehow lacked dignity, yet the activities of the mercantile classes took on increasing importance for the state for two reasons. First, imported goods, especially luxuries, were a noncontroversial target for taxation. Customs duties and excise taxes proliferated all over Europe. Representative assemblies composed of landed elites were usually happy to grant them to the monarch, and merchants could pass them on to consumers in higher prices. Second, the competition for trade was seen as a competition between states rather than individual merchants. Trading privileges involved special arrangements with foreign powers, arrangements that recognized the sovereign power of European monarchs. In this way, trade could bring glory to the state.

Mercantilism. The competition for power and glory derived from the theory of **mercantilism,** a set of assumptions about economic activity that were commonly held throughout Europe and that guided the policies of almost every government. There were two interrelated ideas. One was that the wealth of a nation resided in its stock of precious metal, and the other was that economic activity was a zero-sum game. There was thought to be a fixed amount of money, a fixed number of commodities, and a fixed amount of consumption. Thus, what one country gained, another lost. If England bought wine from France and paid £100,000 in precious metal for it, then England was £100,000 poorer and France £100,000 richer. If one was to trade profitably, it was absolutely necessary to wind up with a surplus of precious metal. Therefore, it was imperative that governments regulate trade so that the stocks of precious metal were protected from the greed of the merchants. The first and most obvious measure of protection, then, was to prohibit the export of coin except by license, a prohibition that was absolutely unenforceable and was violated more often by government officials than by merchants.

Those ideas about economic activity led to a variety of forms of economic regulation. The most common was the **monopoly,** a grant of special privileges in return for both financial considerations and an agreement to abide by the rules set out by the state. In the context of the seventeenth-century economy, there were a number of advantages to monopolies. First, of course, were those that accrued to the crown. There were direct and indirect revenues: monopolists usually paid considerable fees for their rights, and their activities were easy to monitor for purposes of taxation. The crown could use the grant of monopoly to reward past favors or to purchase future support from powerful individuals. There were also advantages for the monopolists. They could make capital investments with the expectation of long-term gains. That advantage was especially important in attracting investors for risky and expensive ventures such as long-distance trade. Indeed, there were even benefits for the economy as a whole, as monopolies increased productive investment at a time when most capital was being used to purchase land, luxury goods, or offices.

The East India Companies. Two monopoly companies, the English and the Dutch East India companies, dominated the Asian trade. The English East India Company, founded in 1600 with capital of £30,000, was given the exclusive right to the Asian trade and immediately established itself throughout the Indian Ocean. The Dutch East India Company was formed two years later with ten times the capital of its English counterpart. By the end of the century, the Dutch company employed more than 12,000 people. Both companies were known as **joint-stock companies,** an innovation in the way in which businesses were organized. Subscribers owned a percentage of the total value of the company, based on the number of shares they bought, and were entitled to a distribution of profits on the same basis. Initially, the English company determined profits on single voyages and was supposed to distribute all of its assets to its shareholders after a given period. But changes in legal practice gave the company an identity separate from the individuals that held the shares. Now shares could be exchanged without the breakup of the company as a whole. Both Amsterdam and London soon developed stock markets to trade the shares of monopoly companies.

Both East India companies were remarkably good investments. The Dutch East India Company paid an average dividend of 18 percent for more than 200 years. The value of English East India Company shares rose fivefold in the second half of the seventeenth century alone. Few other monopoly companies achieved a record comparable to that of the East India companies. The English Royal African Company, founded in 1672 to provide slaves for the Spanish colonies, barely recouped costs and was soon superseded by private trade. Even the French East Indian and African companies, which were modeled on the Dutch and English, were forced to abandon their monopolies. The Dutch and English companies were successful not because of their special privileges but because they were able to lower the costs of protecting their ships and cargoes.

Protective Trade Regulations. Monopolies were not the only form of regulation in which seventeenth-century government engaged. For those states with Atlantic colonies, regula-

■ The Dutch East India Company's trading station on the Hooghly River in Bengal, 1665. The station was one of a network of bases the company established throughout its Eastern trading empire.

tion took the form of restricting markets rather than traders. In the 1660s, the English government, alarmed at the growth of Dutch mercantile activity in the New World, passed a series of **Navigation Acts** designed to protect English shipping. Colonial goods—primarily tobacco and sugar—could be shipped to and from England only in English boats. If the French wanted to purchase West Indian sugar, they could not simply send a ship to the English colony of Barbados loaded with French goods and exchange them for sugar. Rather, they had to make their purchases from an English import-export merchant and the goods had to be unloaded in an English port before they could be reloaded to be shipped to France. As a result, the English reexport trade skyrocketed. In the year 1700, reexports amounted to nearly 40 percent of all English commerce. With such a dramatic increase in trading, all moved in English ships, shipbuilding boomed. English coastal towns enjoyed heightened prosperity, as did the great colonial ports of Bristol and Liverpool. For a time, colonial protection proved effective.

French protectionism was as much internal as colonial. The French entered the intercontinental trade later than their North Atlantic rivals, and they were less dependent on trade for their subsistence. Of all the states of Europe, only France could satisfy its needs from its own resources. But to achieve such self-sufficiency required coordination and leadership. In the 1670s, Louis XIV's finance minister, Jean-Baptiste Colbert (1619–1683), developed a plan to bolster the French economy by protecting it against European imports. First Colbert followed the English example of restricting the reexport trade by requiring that imports come to France either in French ships or in the ships of the country from which the goods originated. In addition, he used tariffs to make imported goods unattractive in France. He sponsored a drive to increase French manufacturing, especially of textiles, tapestries, linens, glass, and furniture. To protect the investments in French manufacturing, enormous duties were placed on the import of similar goods manufactured elsewhere. The Venetian glass industry, for example, suffered a serious blow from Colbert's tariffs. English woolen manufacturers were also damaged, and the English sought retaliatory measures. But in fact, the English had already begun to imitate that form of protection. In the early eighteenth century, England attempted to limit the importation of cotton goods from India to prevent the collapse of the domestic clothing industry.

The Navigation Acts and Colbert's program of protective tariffs were directed specifically against Dutch reexporters. The Dutch were the acknowledged leaders in all branches of commerce in the seventeenth century. There were many summers when there were more Dutch vessels in London Harbor than there were English ships. In the 1670s, the Dutch merchant fleet was probably larger than the English, French, Spanish, Portuguese, and German fleets combined! Restrictive navigation practices were one way to combat an advantage that the Dutch had built through heavy capital investment and by breaking away from the prevailing theories about the relationship between wealth and precious metals. The English and French Navigation Acts cut heavily into the Dutch trade, and ultimately both the English and French overtook them. But protectionism had its price. Just as the dynastic wars were succeeded by the wars of religion, so the wars of religion were succeeded by the wars of commerce.

■ Rembrandt, *The Syndics of the Cloth Guild* (1662). This work was painted for the Drapers' or Cloth Guild and installed at the Guild's headquarters in Amsterdam. The five hatted Syndics look as though they have been caught in a momentary interruption of business. The bareheaded figure in the background is the valet, who unlike the Syndics, was not required to pay for his portrait.

"The discovery of America and that of a passage to the East Indies by the Cape of Good Hope are the two greatest and most important events in the history of mankind." So wrote the great Scottish economist Adam Smith (1723–1790) in *The Wealth of Nations* (1776). For Smith and his generation, the first great age of commerce was coming to an end. The innovations of the Dutch had given way to a settled pattern of international long-distance trade. States now viewed commerce as a part of their national self-interest. They developed overseas empires, which they protected as markets for their goods and sources for their raw materials. The empires were justified by the theory of mercantilism and the demands of a generation of consumers who saw the luxuries of the past as the necessities of the present.

THE WARS OF COMMERCE

The belief that there was a fixed amount of trade in the world was still strong in the late seventeenth century. One country's gains in trade were another's losses. There was not more than enough to go around, and it could not be easily understood how the expansion of one country's trade could benefit all countries. Competition for trade was the same as competition for territory or subjects, part of the struggle by which the state grew powerful. It was not inevitable that economic competition would lead to warfare, only that restrictive competition would.

Thus the scramble for colonies in the seventeenth century led to commercial warfare in the eighteenth. As the English gradually replaced the Dutch as the leading commercial nation,

so the French replaced the English as the leading competitor. Hostility between the English and the French had existed for centuries, and it was not without cause that the commercial wars of the eighteenth century should be likened to the territorial wars of the Middle Ages. The greed of merchants and the glory of princes fueled a struggle for the dominance of world markets that brought European warfare to every corner of the globe.

The Mercantile Wars

Commercial warfare in Europe began between the English and the Dutch in the middle of the seventeenth century. Both had established aggressive overseas trading companies in the Atlantic and in Asia. In the early seventeenth century, the Dutch were the undisputed leaders, their carrying capacity and trade monopolies the greatest in the world. But the English were rising quickly. Their Atlantic colonies began to produce valuable new commodities such as tobacco and sugar, and their Asian trade was expanding decade after decade. Conflict was inevitable, and the result was a series of three naval wars fought between 1652 and 1674. (See "The West and the Wider World: The Nutmeg Wars," pp. 538–539.)

The Dutch had little choice but to strike out against English policy, but they also had little chance of overall success. Their spectacular naval victory in 1667, when the Dutch fleet surprised many English warships at port and burned both ships and docks at Chatham, obscured the fact that Dutch commercial superiority was slipping. In 1664, the English conquered New Netherland on the North American

DEFINING COMMERCE

Adam Smith was a Scottish political theorist whose work The Wealth of Nations *(1776) was the first great work of economic analysis in European history. Smith had wide-ranging interests and wrote with equal authority about manufacturing, population, and trade. He was the first to develop the doctrine of free trade, which he called* laissez-faire. *Smith argued that the government that governed least governed best, and he was an early critic of protective tariffs and monopolies.*

Focus Questions

According to Smith, why are tariffs and monopolies damaging? Why should commerce be a bond rather than a division between nations?

Every individual necessarily labours to render the annual revenue of the society as great as he can. He generally, indeed, neither intends to promote the public interest, nor knows how much he is promoting it. By preferring the support of domestic to that of foreign industry, he intends only his own security; and by directing that industry in such a manner as its produce may be of the greatest value, he intends only his own gain, and he is in this, as in many other cases, led by an invisible hand to promote an end which was no part of his intention. Nor is it always the worse for the society that it was no part of it. By pursuing his own interest he frequently promotes that of the society more effectually than when he really intends to promote it. I have never known much good done by those who affected to trade for the public good. . . .

. . . Each nation has been made to look with an invidious eye upon the prosperity of all the nations with which it trades, and to consider their gain as its own loss. Commerce, which ought naturally to be, among nations as among individuals, a bond of union and friendship, has become the most fertile source of discord and animosity. The capricious ambition of kings and ministers has not, during the present and the preceding century, been more fatal to the repose of Europe, than the impertinent jealousy of merchants and manufacturers. The violence and injustice of the rulers of mankind is an ancient evil, for which, I am afraid, the nature of human affairs can scarce admit of a remedy. But the mean rapacity, the monopolizing spirit of merchants and manufacturers, who neither are, nor ought to be, the rulers of mankind, though it cannot perhaps be corrected, may very easily be prevented from disturbing the tranquility of anybody but themselves. . . .

The natural advantages which one country has over another in producing particular commodities are sometimes so great, that it is acknowledged by all the world to be in vain to struggle with them. . . . Very good grapes can be raised in Scotland, and very good wine too can be made of them at about thirty times the expense for which at least equally good can be brought from foreign countries. Would it be a reasonable law to prohibit the importation of all foreign wines merely to encourage the making of claret and burgundy in Scotland?

From Adam Smith, *The Wealth of Nations* (1776).

---

mainland and renamed it New York. With that defeat, the Dutch lost their largest colonial possession. The wars were costly to both states, nearly bankrupting the English Crown in 1672. Anglo-Dutch rivalry was finally laid to rest after 1688, when William of Orange, stadtholder of Holland, became William III (1689–1702), king of England.

The Anglo-Dutch commercial wars were just one part of a larger European conflict. Dutch commerce was as threatening to France as it was to England, though in a different way. Under Colbert, France pursued a policy of economic independence. The state supported internal industrial activity through the financing of large workshops and the encouragement of new manufacturing techniques. To protect French products, Colbert levied a series of punitive tariffs on Dutch imports, which severely depressed both trade and manufacture in Holland. Although the Dutch retaliated with restrictive tariffs of their own—in 1672 they banned the import of all French goods for an entire year—the Dutch economy depended on free trade. The Dutch had much more to lose than did France in a battle of protective tariffs.

But the battle that Louis XIV had in mind was to be more deadly than one of tariffs. Greedily he eyed the Spanish Netherlands—to which he had a weak claim through his Habsburg wife—believing that the Dutch stood in the way of his plans. The Dutch had entered into an alliance with the English and Swedes in 1668 to counter French policy, and Louis was determined to crush them in retaliation. He successfully bought off both of Holland's supposed allies, providing cash pensions to the kings of England and Sweden in return for England's active participation and Sweden's passive neutrality in the impending war. In 1672, Louis's army, more than 100,000 strong, invaded the Low Countries and swept all before them. Only the opening of the dikes prevented the French from entering the province of Holland itself.

The West and the Wider World
THE NUTMEG WARS

A seed about the size of an acorn connected Portugal, Holland, and England to a small string of islands in the Pacific Ocean and to the eastern seaboard of North America. It created a series of trading wars among the European powers in the seventeenth century and resulted in a number of trade treaties with the leaders of the Banda Islands, in what is now Indonesia. East and West became linked as great European sailing ships made port at the juncture of the Indian and Pacific Oceans in search of the seeds of the tree *Myristica Fragrans*, which grew only on the Banda Islands and which had the singular virtue of producing two rare spices greatly prized by Europeans: mace and, especially, nutmeg.

Flimsy in appearance, the seeds of the *Myristica Fagrans* could be harvested with no greater effort than the shaking of its branches. The husk of the seed pod yielded the delicate spice mace that was used in cookery and as a base for fragrances. The pod itself after husking, drying, and cracking yielded the nutmeg, a versatile spice (some think it is the distinctive ingredient in Coca Cola) that experienced a craze in the first decades of the seventeenth century. Its use as a flavoring was long known in China and South Asia and it had entered the Mediterranean in small quantities through the efforts of Muslim traders. But once the Portuguese started importing it in bulk, around twenty tons a year by the middle of the sixteenth century, merchants and apothecaries began to tout its other virtues. Its fragrance was a desirable mask for the acrid odors of ordinary life when applied either to the skin or a piece of linen. Its exotic origins

suggested mystical power. By the end of the century, when the Dutch entered the trade and annual imports grew toward 100 tons, nutmeg was widely believed to be an aphrodisiac, and since aphrodisiacs work on the mind rather than the body, what was believed was all that

■ Engraving of the Banda Islands, based on a sixteenth-century map by Theodore de Bry.

mattered. Demand rose and supply fell. By the beginning of the seventeenth century, when the English contested Dutch supremacy in global trade, the two nations were bringing back a staggering 200–250 tons from the Bandas. By then nutmeg was a wonder drug indeed, believed capable of curing ailments from headache to the sweating sickness associated with plague. What cost a tenth of a penny a pound on the island docks of the South Seas sold in a London or Amsterdam shop for 7000 times that amount. Small wonder that the greatest trading companies in the world were pooling resources to outfit ships to sail for nutmeg.

Indeed, nutmeg was so valuable to Europeans in the seventeenth century

that their quest to obtain it led three nations to dispatch their merchants on eighteen-month journeys from which most never returned. If they did not perish during the long sea voyage around the horn of Africa, along the Coromandel Coast of India, and past the great pepper island of Java, they were imperiled by barely submerged razor-sharp volcanic rocks that guarded the Banda Islands on which the trees flourished. Shifting trade winds also made the islands inaccessible six months a year. Only those with good guides or good luck laid anchor there. If the merchants survived the dangers of nature, then they faced those of man. Every European captain claimed his nation held exclusive trading rights to these miraculous seeds, and in the open waters of the Pacific Ocean might made right. More than one great sailing ship had its hull punctured by cannon balls, its mast burned by flaming arrows, its crew killed or scuttled by rival merchants.

Even to reach an island port in safety was no guarantee of success. The indigenous peoples were fierce, capable, and resolutely independent. As one Englishman described them, the Bandanese were "men warlike and agile, strong and valiant . . . courteous and affable . . . full of contention amongst themselves, but generally united against the common enemy." Though the islands were small, they were not unified politically. Each village contained its own governing council, which meant that trade was very much a local affair. The Bandanese granted "exclusive" trading rights as often as possible and placidly watched the Europeans squabble over them. In the long months during which the traders waited for the winds to shift so they could depart, misunderstandings and misdeeds were resolved lethally.

The growing popularity of nutmeg in the West and the evolution of trade with European merchants had an enormous impact on the Banda Islands. Though the Bandanese used nutmeg in their cooking, the abundant resource was hardly considered a prized commodity. Until the Portuguese arrived, most nutmeg was carried off the islands in small boats and bartered for ceramics, metalwork, and agricultural products. The Portuguese attempted to control the nutmeg trade as well as to convert local leaders, many of whom were Muslim, to Christianity. While the Portuguese greatly increased the amount of nutmeg that was gathered and shipped, their attempts to prevent the traditional barter trade and to win religious converts led to near constant conflict with the locals. Thus, when the Dutch arrived in 1599 and dispersed the Portuguese fleet, they were welcomed by the Bandanese and were allowed to build a fort where they could store bags of seed and await return voyages.

The Bandanese soon tired of the Dutch as well. By now the islanders had become more sophisticated traders, securing guns, powder, and shot in return for bags of nutmeg, and their conflicts with the Dutch occasionally turned into pitched battles. In 1609, the Bandanese massacred 46 Dutchman; in 1616 the Dutch invaded Ay Island and slaughtered hundreds of indigenous people. In this environment of conflict, the arrival of the English seemed the answer to a prayer, and local Bandanese leaders entered into contracts to provide these new European visitors with as much nutmeg as they could carry away in exchange for weapons. Just as the leaders had hoped, the Dutch and the English

■ Engraving of a massacre of Dutch soldiers by the Bandanese.

began to fight each other, the English insisting that the commerce of the seas was open to everyone, the Dutch that they held monopoly rights to nutmeg.

The Dutch were the greater power, and they soon drove the English from all but one of the Banda islands, the small island of Rhun. In 1619 the European nations signed a treaty granting each the territory they held but it had little effect in Banda. The Dutch began a systematic depopulation of the smaller islands, invaded Rhun, and cut down all of its nutmeg trees. In 1621 they assaulted the English fort that was now inhabited by the Bandanese and killed anyone who did not flee into the mountains. Most of the islanders were captured and sold into slavery, replaced in turn by other South Asian slaves.

Not only had the Dutch gained control of the nutmeg trade, they now controlled the nutmegs as well. They offered land on the islands to any Dutch trader who would settle there. Again, in violation of their treaty with the English, they invaded Rhun and destroyed whatever new growth had occurred there. In retaliation, the English attacked a Dutch island outpost half a world away, the settlement of New Amsterdam. In 1667

the two European powers settled their differences with an exchange. The English turned over the Banda island of Rhun, the Dutch the American island of Manhattan. Wily Dutch traders had once purchased it for the derisory sum of $24 worth of trinkets. Now their government traded it away for a volcanic rock where nutmeg would no longer grow, and they were convinced they had gotten the better of the deal. The linking of East and West in seventeenth-century global trade networks had enormous consequences. In the case of nutmeg, the search for seeds had led to half a century of fighting among the Europeans, the decimation of the population of Banda, and Dutch domination of the spice.

▧ QUESTIONS FOR DISCUSSION

Why did Europeans come to the Pacific Islands? How did the organization of Bandanese society create conflict for the Portuguese and Dutch? How did the Bandanese manage to maintain their freedom for half a century after the first Europeans arrived? What was the Dutch solution to threats to their nutmeg monopoly?

The French invasion coincided with the third Anglo-Dutch war, and the United Provinces found themselves besieged on land and sea. Their international trade was disrupted, their manufacturing industries were in ruins, and their military budget skyrocketed. Only able diplomacy and skillful military leadership prevented total Dutch demise. A separate peace was made with England, and Spain, whose sovereign territory had been invaded, entered the war on the side of the Dutch, as did a number of German states. Louis's hope for a lightning victory faded, and the war settled into a series of interminable sieges and reliefs of fortified towns. The Dutch finally persuaded France to come to terms in the Treaty of Nijmegen (1678–1679). While Louis XIV retained a number of the territories he had taken from Spain, his armies withdrew from the United Provinces, and he agreed to lift most of the commercial sanctions against Dutch goods. The first phase of mercantile warfare was over.

The Wars of Louis XIV

It was Louis XIV's ambition to restore the ancient Burgundian territories to the French crown and to provide secure northern and eastern borders for his state. Pursuit of those aims involved him in conflicts with nearly every other European state. Spain had fought for 80 years to preserve the Burgundian inheritance in the Low Countries. By the Peace of Westphalia (1648), the northern portion of the territory became the United Provinces,

■ France Under Louis XIV. France gained vital territories in the north and east including Alsace and Lorraine, which would become a source of friction for centuries.

while the southern portion remained loyal to the crown and became the Spanish Netherlands. That territory provided a barrier between Holland and France that both states attempted to strengthen by establishing fortresses and bridgeheads at strategic places. In the east, Louis eyed the duchies of Lorraine and Alsace and the large swath of territory farther south known as Franche-Comté. The Peace of Westphalia had granted France control of a number of imperial cities in the duchies, and Louis aimed to link them together. All the territories were ruled by Habsburgs: Alsace and Lorraine by the Austrian Holy Roman Emperor, Franche-Comté by the Spanish king.

The Balance of Power. In the late seventeenth century, ambassadors and ministers of state began to develop the theory of a **balance of power** in Europe. It was a belief that no state or combination of states should be allowed to become so powerful that its existence threatened the peace of the others. Behind the purely political idea of the balance of power lay a theory of collective security that knit together the European state system. French expansion in either direction not only threatened the other states directly involved but also posed a threat to European security in general.

Louis showed his hand clearly enough in the Franco-Dutch war that had ended in 1679. Although he withdrew his forces from the United Provinces and evacuated most of the territories he had conquered, France absorbed Franche-Comté by the Treaty of Nijmegen, as well as portions of the Spanish Netherlands. Louis began plotting his next adventure almost as soon as the treaty was signed. During the next several years, French troops advanced steadily into Alsace, ultimately forcing the city of Strasbourg, a vital bridgehead on the Rhine, to recognize French sovereignty. Expansion into northern Italy was similarly calculated. Everywhere Louis looked, French engineers rushed to construct fortresses and magazines in preparation for another war.

War finally came in 1688 when French troops poured across the Rhine to seize Cologne. A united German empire led by Leopold I, archduke of Austria, combined with the maritime powers of England and Holland, led by William III, to form the Grand Alliance, the first of the great balance-of-power coalitions. In fact, the two sides proved so evenly matched that the Nine Years' War (1688–1697) settled very little, but it demonstrated that a successful European coalition could be formed against France. It also signified the permanent shift in alliances that resulted from the Revolution of 1688 in England. Although the English had allied with France against the Dutch in 1672, after William became king he persuaded the English Parliament that the real enemy was France. Louis's greatest objective, to secure the borders of his state, had withstood its greatest test. He might have rested satisfied but for the vagaries of births, marriages, and deaths.

Like his father, Louis XIV had married a daughter of the king of Spain. Philip IV had married his eldest daughter to Louis XIV and a younger one to Leopold I of Austria, who subsequently became the Holy Roman Emperor (1658–1705). Before he died, Philip finally fathered a son, Charles II

■ The ratification of the Treaty of Münster (1648). Under the treaty, Spain finally recognized Dutch independence.

(1665–1700), who attained the Spanish crown at the age of four but was mentally and physically incapable of ruling his vast empire. For decades it was apparent that there would be no direct Habsburg successor to an empire that, despite its recent losses, still contained Spain, South America, the Spanish Netherlands, and most of Italy. Louis XIV and Leopold I both had legitimate claims to an inheritance that would have irreversibly tipped the European balance of power.

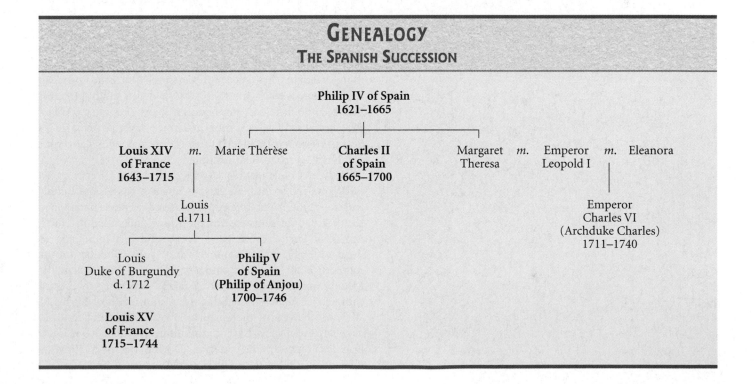

GENEALOGY
THE SPANISH SUCCESSION

Philip IV of Spain
1621–1665

Louis XIV   *m.*   Marie Thérèse   **Charles II**   Margaret   *m.*   Emperor   *m.*   Eleanora
of France   **of Spain**   Theresa   Leopold I
1643–1715   **1665–1700**

Louis
d.1711   Emperor
Charles VI
(Archduke Charles)
1711–1740

Louis   **Philip V**
Duke of Burgundy   **of Spain**
d. 1712   **(Philip of Anjou)**
1700–1746

Louis XV
of France
1715–1744

The War of the Spanish Succession. As Charles II grew increasingly feeble, efforts to find a suitable compromise to the problem of the Spanish succession were led by William III, who, as stadtholder of Holland, was vitally interested in the fate of the Spanish Netherlands and, as king of England, in the fate of the Spanish American colonies. In the 1690s, two treaties of partition were drawn up. The first achieved near universal agreement but was nullified by the death of the German prince who was to inherit the Spanish crown. The second, which would have given Italy to Louis's son and everything else to Leopold's son, was opposed by Leopold, who had neither naval nor commercial interests and who claimed most of the Italian territories as imperial fiefs.

All the plans had been made without consulting the Spanish. If it was the aim of the European powers to partition the Spanish Empire in order to prevent any one state from inheriting too much of it, it was the aim of the Spanish to maintain their empire intact. To this end, they devised a brilliant plan. Charles II bequeathed his entire empire to Philip of Anjou, the younger grandson of Louis XIV, with two stipulations: first, that Philip renounce his claim to the French throne; and second, that he accept the empire intact, without partition. If he—or more to the point, if his grandfather Louis XIV—did not accept the conditions, then the empire would pass to Archduke Charles, the younger son of Leopold I. Such provisions virtually assured war between France and the empire unless compromise between the two powers could be reached. But before terms could even be suggested, Charles II died and Philip V (1700–1746) was proclaimed king of Spain and its empire.

Thus the eighteenth century opened with the War of the Spanish Succession (1702–1714). Emperor Leopold rejected the provisions of Charles's will and sent his troops to occupy Italy. Louis XIV confirmed the worst fears of William III when he provided his grandson with French troops to "defend" the Spanish Netherlands. William III revived the Grand Alliance and initiated a massive land war against the combined might of France and Spain. The allied objectives were twofold: to prevent the unification of the French and Spanish thrones and to partition the Spanish Empire so that both Italy and the Netherlands were ceded to Austria. The objective of Louis XIV was simply to preserve as much as possible of the Spanish inheritance for the house of Bourbon.

William III died in 1702 and was succeeded by Anne (1702–1714). John Churchill (1650–1722), duke of Marlborough and commander in chief of the army, continued William's policy. England and Holland again provided most of the finance and sea power, but, in addition, the English also provided a land army nearly 70,000 strong. Prussia joined the Grand Alliance, and disciplined Prussian troops helped offset the addition of the Spanish army to Louis's forces. In 1704, Churchill defeated French forces at Blenheim in Germany, and in 1706 at Ramillies in the Spanish Netherlands. France's military ascendancy was over.

Efforts to negotiate a peace settlement took longer than the war itself. The Austrians had taken control of Italy, the English and Dutch had secured the Spanish Netherlands, and the French had been driven back beyond the Rhine. The Allies believed that they could now enforce any treaty they pleased on Louis XIV and, along with concessions from France, attempted to oust his grandson, Philip V, from the Spanish throne. That proved impossible to achieve, though it took more than five years to learn the lesson. By then the European situation had taken another strange twist. Both Emperor Leopold and his eldest son had died. Now Leopold's younger son, Archduke Charles, inherited the empire as Charles VI (1711–1740) and raised the prospect of an equally dangerous combined Austrian-Spanish state.

Between 1713 and 1714, a series of treaties at Utrecht settled the War of the Spanish Succession. Spanish possessions in Italy and the Netherlands were ceded to Austria; France abandoned all its territorial gains east of the Rhine and ceded its North American territories of Nova Scotia and Newfoundland to England. England also acquired from Spain Gibraltar, on the southern coast of Spain, and the island of Minorca in the Mediterranean. Both were strategically important to English commercial interests. English intervention in the Nine Years' War and the War of the Spanish Succession did not result in large territorial gains, but it did result in an enormous increase in English power and prestige. During the next 30 years England would assert its own imperial claims.

■ War of the Spanish Succession. The great British victories in this war were in the Spanish Netherlands and the Holy Roman Empire, establishing Britain as a great power.

MAP DISCOVERY

The Treaty of Utrecht

What critical gains did Britain make as a result of the 1714 Treaty of Utrecht? Notice the extent of Austria after the treaty. What problems were the Austrian government most likely to face? What did Savoy gain?

The Colonial Wars

The Treaty of Utrecht (1713–1714) ushered in almost a quarter century of peace in western Europe. Austrian rule in the Netherlands and Italy remained a major irritant to the Spanish, but Spain was too weak to do more than sulk and snarl. The death of Louis XIV in 1715 quelled French ambitions for a time and even led to an Anglo-French accord that guaranteed the preservation of the settlement reached at Utrecht. Peace allowed Europe to rebuild its shattered economy and resume the international trade that had been so severely disrupted during the last 40 years. The Treaty of Utrecht had resolved a number of important trading issues, all in favor of Great Britain (as England was known after its union with Scotland in 1707). In addition to receiving Gibraltar and Minorca from Spain, Britain was also granted the monopoly to provide slaves to the Spanish American colonies and the right to send one trading ship a year to them.

In east and west, Britain was becoming the dominant commercial power in the world.

At least some of the reason for Britain's preeminence was the remarkable growth of the Atlantic colonies. The colonial economy was booming, and consumer goods that were in demand in London, Paris, and Amsterdam were also in demand in Boston, Philadelphia, and New York. Like every other colonial power, the British held a monopoly on their colonial trade. They were far less successful than the Spanish and French in enforcing the notion that colonies existed only for the benefit of the parent country, but the English Parliament continued to pass legislation aimed at restricting colonial trade with other nations and other nations' colonies. Like almost all other mercantile restrictions, the efforts were stronger in theory than in practice. Tariffs on imports and customs duties on British goods provided a double incentive for smuggling.

France emerged as Britain's true colonial rival. In the Caribbean, the French had the largest and most profitable of the West Indian sugar islands, Saint Domingue (modern-day Haiti). In North America, France not only held Canada but laid claim to the entire continent west of the Ohio River. The French did not so much settle their colonial territory as occupy it. They surveyed the land, established trading relations with the Native Americans, and built forts at strategic locations. The English, in contrast, had developed fixed communities, which grew larger and more prosperous by the decade. France determined to defend its colonies by establishing an overseas military presence. Regular French troops were shipped to Canada and installed in Louisbourg, Montreal, and Quebec. The British responded with troops of their own and sent an expeditionary force to clear the French from the Ohio River Valley. That action was the immediate cause of the Seven Years' War (1756–1763).

Although the Seven Years' War had a bitter Continental phase, it was essentially a war for empire between the English and the French. There were three main theaters: the North American mainland, the West Indian sugar plantations, and the eastern coast of India. All over the globe, the British won smashing victories. The British navy blockaded the water route to Canada, inflicting severe hardship on French settlers in Montreal and Quebec. British forces ultimately captured both towns. After some initial successes, the French were driven back west across the Mississippi River, and their line of fortresses in the Ohio Valley fell into English hands. The English also succeeded in taking all the French sugar islands except Saint Domingue. British success in India was equally complete. The French were chased from their major trading zone and English dominance was secured.

By the end of the Seven Years' War, Britain had become a global imperial power. In the Peace of Paris (1763), France ceded all of Canada in exchange for the return of its West Indian islands. British dominion in the East Indian trade was recognized and led ultimately to British dominion of India itself. In less than a century, the ascendancy of France was broken and Europe's first modern imperial power had been created.

MAP DISCOVERY

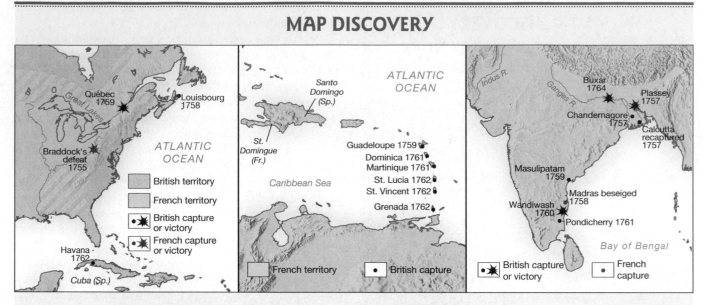

The Seven Years' War

This war was fought all around the globe between Britain and France for imperial supremacy. In North America, it was called the French and Indian War. Who controlled most of North America at the beginning of the Seven Years' War? What was British strategy in the Caribbean? Who won India?

CONCLUSION

European commercial expansion was the first step in a long process that would ultimately transform the material life of all human beings. The quest for new commodities led to increased sophistication in transportation, marketing, and distribution—all vital developments for agricultural changes in the future. The ability to move large quantities of goods from place to place and to exchange them between different parts of the globe laid the foundation for organized manufacturing. The practical impact of scientific discovery, as yet only dimly glimpsed, would soon spur the transformation of handicrafts into industries. In the eighteenth century, the material world was still being conquered, and the most unattractive features of that conquest were all too plainly visible. Luxuries for the rich were won by the labors of the poor. The pleasures of sugar and tobacco were purchased at the price of slavery for millions of Africans. The greed of merchants and the glory of princes was an unholy alliance that resulted in warfare around the globe. But it was a shrinking globe, one whose peoples were becoming increasingly interdependent, tied together by the goods and services that they could provide to each other.

QUESTIONS FOR REVIEW

1. What was new about the methods and ideas of Copernicus, Brahe, Kepler, and Galileo, and why were they threatening to Roman Catholic doctrine?
2. In what ways did the new science build upon traditional ideas associated with alchemy, astrology, and Hermetic thinking? In what ways was it a departure?
3. What new technologies, trading practices, and financial devices assisted the expansion of long-distance trading?
4. Why were the Dutch especially well suited to participate in the worldwide expansion of European commerce?
5. How did the governments of the various European nations promote their own commercial interests?

KEY TERMS

alchemy, *p. 519*

balance of power, *p. 540*

Cartesiansim, *p. 524*

entrepôt, *p. 525*

joint-stock companies, *p. 534*

mercantilism, *p. 534*

monopoly, *p. 534*

Navigation Acts, *p. 535*

Neoplatonism, *p. 519*

scientific revolution, *p. 516*

triangular trade, *p. 526*

DISCOVERING WESTERN CIVILIZATION ONLINE

You can obtain more information about science and commerce in early modern Europe at the Websites listed below. See also the Companion Website that accompanies this text, www.ablongman.com/kishlansky, which contains an online study guide and additional resources.

The New Science

Internet Modern History Sourcebook: Scientific Revolution

www.fordham.edu/halsall/mod/modsbook09.html

Links to sources and other sites dealing with the scientific revolution.

The Art of Renaissance Science

www.crs4.it/Ars/arshtml/arstoc.html

An interesting site dealing with the relations between Renaissance art and early modern science.

Sir Isaac Newton

www-gap.dcs.st-and.ac.uk/~history/Mathematicians/Newton.html

A miscellany of material on Sir Isaac Newton.

The Galileo Project

es.rice.edu/ES/humsoc/Galileo/

A site devoted to Galileo that contains pictures of his instruments and guides to his experiments.

Empires of Goods

Trade Products in Early Modern History

www.bell.lib.umn.edu/Products/Products.html

A site describing the new products introduced to Europe during the period of global expansion.

Holland Museums

www.hollandmuseums.nl/

An online gallery of Dutch art, with text available in English.

History House: Tulipomania

www.historyhouse.com/in_history/tulip/

The story of Tulip mania in seventeenth-century Holland.

SUGGESTIONS FOR FURTHER READING

General Reading

Jeremy Black, *The Rise of the European Powers, 1679–1793* (New York: Edward Arnold, 1990). A look at diplomatic history from an English point of view.

Jan de Vries, *The European Economy in an Age of Crisis* (Cambridge: Cambridge University Press, 1976). A comprehensive study of economic development, including long-distance trade and commercial change.

K. H. D. Haley, *The Dutch in the Seventeenth Century* (London: Thames and Hudson, 1972). A well-written and well-illustrated history of the golden age of Holland.

A. Rupert Hall, *The Revolution in Science, 1500–1750* (London: Longman, 1983). The best introduction to the varieties of scientific thought in the early modern period. Detailed and complex.

Derek McKay and H. M. Scott, *The Rise of the Great Powers, 1648–1815* (London: Longman, 1983). An outstanding survey of diplomacy and warfare.

The New Science

H. F. Cohen, *The Scientific Revolution* (Chicago: University of Chicago Press, 1994). The history of the idea of the scientific revolution and of the events that comprised it.

Stillman Drake, *Galileo* (New York: Hill and Wang, 1980). A short but engaging study of the great Italian scientist.

Margaret C. Jacob, *The Cultural Meaning of the Scientific Revolution* (New York: Alfred A. Knopf, 1988). Scientific thought portrayed in its social context.

Lisa Jardine, *Ingenious Pursuits: Building the Scientific Revolution* (New York: Anchor Books, 1999). A new study emphasizing the technical contexts of the scientific revolution and interactions between its major figures.

Londa Schiebinger, *The Mind Has No Sex? Women in the Origins of Modern Science* (Cambridge, MA: Harvard University Press, 1990). The role of women in the scientific revolution.

Steven Shapin, *The Scientific Revolution* (Chicago: University of Chicago Press, 1996). An excellent brief introduction.

Richard Westfall, *The Construction of Modern Science: Mechanisms and Mechanics* (Cambridge: Cambridge University Press, 1977). A survey of scientific developments from Kepler to Newton. A good introduction to both mechanics and mathematics.

Richard Westfall, *The Life of Isaac Newton* (Cambridge: Cambridge University Press, 1993). The best short biography.

Empires of Goods

J. N. Ball, *Merchants and Merchandise: The Expansion of Trade in Europe* (London: Croom Helm, 1977). A good overview of European overseas economies.

K. N. Chaudhuri, *The Trading World of Asia and the English East India Company* (Cambridge: Cambridge University Press, 1978). A brilliant account of the impact of the Indian trade on both Europeans and Asians.

Philip Curtin, *The Atlantic Slave Trade* (Madison: University of Wisconsin Press, 1969). A study of the importation of African slaves into the New World, with the best estimates of the numbers of slaves and their destinations.

Ralph Davis, *The Rise of the Atlantic Economies* (Ithaca, NY: Cornell University Press, 1973). A nation-by-nation survey of the colonial powers.

Jonathan Israel, *Dutch Primacy in World Trade, 1585–1740* (Oxford: Oxford University Press, 1989). The triumph of Dutch traders and techniques written by the leading authority.

Joseph Miller, *Way of Death: Merchant Capitalism and the Angolan Slave Trade, 1730–1830* (Madison: University of Wisconsin Press, 1988). An illuminating portrait of the eighteenth-century slave trade, with an unforgettable account of the slave voyages.

Sidney Mintz, *Sweetness and Power* (New York: Viking Press, 1985). An anthropologist explores the lure of sugar and its impact on Western society.

Simon Schama, *The Embarrassment of Riches* (New York: Alfred A. Knopf, 1987). A social history of the Dutch Republic that explores the meaning of commerce in Dutch society.

The Wars of Commerce

Jeremy Black, *A System of Ambition? British Foreign Policy, 1660–1793* (London: Longman, 1991). The best survey of Britain's international relations during the long eighteenth century.

A. C. Carter, *Neutrality or Commitment: The Evolution of Dutch Foreign Policy, 1667–1795* (London: Edward Arnold, 1975). A tightly written study of the objectives and course of Dutch diplomacy.

Paul Langford, *The Eighteenth Century, 1688–1815* (New York: St. Martin's Press, 1976). A reliable guide to the growth of British power.

J. A. Lynn, *The Wars of Louis XIV, 1667–1714* (London: Longman, 1999). A comprehensive study by a leading military historian of France.

Richard Pares, *War and Trade in the West Indies, 1739–1763* (Oxford: Oxford University Press, 1936). A blow-by-blow account of the struggle for colonial supremacy in the sugar islands.

For a list of additional titles related to this chapter's topics, please see http://www.ablongman.com/kishlansky.

Chapter **18**

THE BALANCE OF POWER IN EIGHTEENTH-CENTURY EUROPE

Chapter Outline

Whereas war had been a brutal affair in the seventeenth century, it had become professionalized by the eighteenth century. Gentlemen trained to enter the military service and were proud of their achievements. Even low ranking officers could present themselves to the great portraitists of the day, as you can see in The Visual Record. ➤

A DASHING OFFICER
The Rise of Militarism

From the middle of the seventeenth century Britain was a great sea-faring power. Its navy, built up during the reign of Charles I and the rule of Oliver Cromwell, challenged the Dutch for imperial supremacy in the East and the Spanish for colonial supremacy in the West. Louis XIV actually paid the British government a subsidy to remain neutral in his commercial and territorial wars and even attempted to rent British ships on occasion. The British flag flew on seas worldwide, and it would not be long before Britannia ruled the waves. But beginning at the end of the seventeenth century Great Britain also became a feared landed military power. Under its Dutch king, William III, British armies successfully held the French at bay in the Nine Years' War and inflicted defeat upon them in the brutal War of the Spanish Succession (1702–1714). British generals, such as the Duke of Marlborough, became Europeanwide celebrities, their feats the subject of story, song, and painting.

Britain's rise to military greatness was as swift as it was unexpected, and it lasted for more than one hundred years. The titanic struggle with France dominated the lives of four successive generations and was not finally concluded until the Battle of Waterloo in 1815. Throughout the eighteenth century, the military was present in British society in a way in which it never had been before or would be again. A society that had openly condemned the concept of a standing army now gave way to one in which the presence of uniformed officers was everywhere. Where younger sons had once gone into the church, now they joined the guards. Where the impoverished and luckless had once migrated to London, now they took the King's shilling, as voluntary enlistment was called. The excess agricultural populations of Scotland and Ireland, once doomed to hunger and starvation, now became the raw materials for the greatest fighting men Europe had known.

One indication of the new prominence given soldiers was the painting of their portraits by the most talented artists of the day. This portrait of Captain Robert Orme was painted by Sir Joshua Reynolds, founder and first president of the Royal Academy and one of the greatest portrait artists of the age. Reynolds revived the long tradition of English portrait painting that had reached its height with the Fleming Van Dyck and the Dutch Kneller. But Reynolds was no foreign import. He was born and raised in Devonshire, learned his trade by painting sailors at Plymouth Docks, and even sailed on a naval expedition. Reynolds's military portraits capture that spirit of patriotism, of strength, and of courage that the British expected from their officers. Captain Orme, a member of the prestigious Coldstream Guards, is portrayed in a moment of action, his stead foaming and winded, the message that he carries admitting of no delay. Slaughter rages behind him. In his haste, his hair has come undone and his extended right arm suggests that he is about to mount and gallop away. But in his pause there is a great stillness and confidence. His gaze is suffused with reassurance, the jaw solid, the eyes piercing. This is the image of flesh and blood that carried Britain to its greatness in the wars of the eighteenth century.

Looking Ahead

The balance of power established by the European monarchies in the eighteenth century was achieved on the battlefield. As we shall see in this chapter, in Russia, Prussia, and Austria, noblemen flocked to military service and the military portion of national economies multiplied dramatically. In the east, her neighbors three times carved up Poland. In the west, the continuing struggle between France and Britain resulted in the destabilization of French society that prepared the way for the French Revolution. In the Atlantic, Britain casually lost its North American colonies in a war it fought half-heartedly for a prize it no longer appreciated. ➤

■ Portrait of Captain Robert Orme (1756) by Sir Joshua Reynolds.

GEOGRAPHICAL TOUR
A Grand Tour of Europe in 1714

In the eighteenth century young noblemen from every European nation completed their education by taking a grand tour. Usually in company with a tutor, they would visit the palaces, castles, and churches of their neighboring countries, learn a little of the language, and mingle with others of their class who were engaged in a similar experience. Nobleman were prepared for the grand tour by reading history, studying antiquities—many of them would purchase ancient Roman sculptures to place in their gardens—and viewing great works of art, normally religious decorations in cathedrals and urban churches. The grand tour made them cosmopolitan or at least European. They learned French language, Italian art, German music, and British science. Some even visited more exotic locations such as Prague or Moscow where language, architecture, and music all had an eastern tinge. Nobleman who took the grand tour in the second decade of the century witnessed the redrawing of Europe's political map as well as a new balance of power among the European states.

Within a relatively short span of time at the beginning of the eighteenth century, two treaties brought about a considerable reorganization of the political geography of Europe. The Treaty of Utrecht (1713–1714) created a new Europe in the west. The Treaty of Nystad (1721) created a new Europe in the east. Both agreements reflected the dynamics of change that had taken place over the previous century. The rise of France on the Continent and Britain's colonial empire around the globe were facts that could no longer be ignored. The decline of Sweden and Poland and the emergence of Russia as a great power were the beginning of a long-term process that would continue to dominate European history.

All of that could be seen on a map of Europe in the early eighteenth century (see **Map A**). France's absorption of Alsace and encroachments into Lorraine would be bones of

■ **Map A. Europe in 1714.** Europe as established by the Treaty of Utrecht.

contention between the French and the Germans for two centuries and would ultimately contribute to the outbreak of World Wars I and II. The political footballs of the Spanish Netherlands and Spanish Italy, now temporarily Austrian, continued to be kicked about until the nationalist movements of the nineteenth century gave birth to Belgium, Luxembourg, and a united Italy. The emergence of Brandenburg-Prussia on the north German coast and the gradual decline of the Holy Roman Emperor's power were both vital to the process that created a unified Germany and a separate Austria. In the southeast, the slow but steady reconquest of the Balkans from Ottoman dominion restored the historic southern border of the Continent. The inexorable expansion of Russia was also already apparent.

Expansion of Western Europe

Few noblemen would have traveled to the new outposts of the European empires, and only scholars, missionaries, and adventurers included the colonies among their travels. Yet perhaps the most obvious transformation in the political geography of western Europe was the expansion of European power around the globe.

Colonies in the Americas. In the Atlantic, Spain remained the largest colonial power. Through its vice-royalty system it controlled all of Mexico and Central America; the largest and most numerous of the Caribbean islands; North America from Colorado to California (as well as Florida); and most of South America (see **Map B**). The other major colonial power in the region was Portugal, which shared dominion over the South American continent. In the Portuguese colony of Brazil, production of sugar, dyestuffs, timbers, and exotic commodities amply repaid the meager investment the Portuguese had made.

In North America, the French and British shared the eastern half of the continent (see **Map B**). The French controlled most of it. They had landed first in Canada and then slowly made their way down the Saint Lawrence River. New France, as their colonial empire was called, was a trading territory, and it expanded along the greatest of the waterways: the Great Lakes and the Ohio, Missouri, and Mississippi rivers. French settlements had sprung up as far south as the Gulf of Mexico. France also claimed the territory of Louisiana, named for Louis XIV, which stretched from New Orleans to Montana. The British settlements were all coastal, stretching from Maine to Georgia on the Atlantic seaboard. Unlike the French, the British settled their territory and were only interested in expansion when their population, which was doubling every 25 years, outgrew its resources. By the early eighteenth century, the ports of Boston, New York, Philadelphia, and Charleston were thriving commercial centers.

Colonies in the Far East. Europeans managed their eastern colonial territories differently than they did those in the Atlantic. Initially, the Portuguese and the Dutch had been

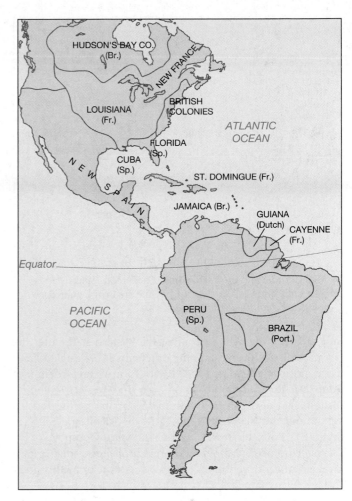

■ **Map B. The Americas.** Much of the American continents was still uncharted with most settlements in the coastal areas.

satisfied with establishing trading factories—coastal fortresses in Africa and Asia that could be used as warehouses and defended against attack. But in the seventeenth century, the European states began to take control of vital ports and lucrative islands (see **Map C**). There the Dutch were the acknowledged leaders, replacing the Portuguese, who had begun the process at the end of the sixteenth century. Holland held by force or in conjunction with local leaders all the Spice Islands in the Pacific. The Dutch also occupied both sides of the Malay Peninsula and nearly all the coastal areas of the islands in the Java Sea. Dutch control of Ceylon was strategically important for its Indian trade. Compared to the Dutch Republic, all other European states had only a minor territorial presence in the East, with the exception of Spain, which still controlled the Philippines. The British had originally limited their eastern outposts to trading establishments, and through those they maintained a significant presence in India. During the eighteenth century, however, the British began to colonize the Indian subcontinent directly (see **Map C**).

Great Britain. Imperial expansion was the most obvious change in the geopolitical boundaries of Europe, but it was

■ **Map C. India and the East Indies.** The famous Spice Islands were still controlled by the Dutch while the British gained footholds on both coasts of India.

not the only one. A brief tour of the western states after the Treaty of Utrecht reveals some others. In 1707, England and Scotland formally joined together to form Great Britain (see **Map D**). In addition to its eastern and western colonies, Britain had also gained control of Gibraltar at the foot of Spain and the island of Minorca in the Mediterranean (see **Map E**). Both territories were strategically important to British commerce. More and more, Europeans visited Britain in the eighteenth century. Though it was a site of neither great

■ **Map D. Great Britain and the Low Countries.** Great Britain and the Low Countries were the two leading European commercial nations.

palaces nor cathedrals, London was acknowledged to be one of the greatest cities in the world.

The Low Countries. Across the English Channel were the Low Countries, now permanently divided between the United Provinces in the north, led by Holland, and those provinces in the south that had remained loyal to the Spanish crown in the sixteenth century (see **Map D**). By 1714 the golden age of the Dutch was over. Although the Dutch continued as a colonial and maritime power, their small numbers and meager natural resources eventually outweighed their abilities as innovators and managers. They lost their eastern empire to Britain and their predominance in European trade to France. What the Dutch gained at Utrecht was the right to maintain their forces in the towns along the border between France and the old Spanish Netherlands. The Spanish Netherlands, the original Burgundian inheritance, was now being slowly dismembered. Since the accession of Louis XIV, France had plucked small pieces from the territories that had been contested between France and Spain since the fifteenth century. Between French aggression and the Dutch occupation of such important places as Ghent and Ypres, the ability of the southern provinces to maintain a separate identity suffered a grave blow. But the blow was not as grave as that delivered at Utrecht, when sovereignty over the territory was assigned to Austria, ostensibly because the emperor was a Habsburg, but really because the balance of power in western Europe demanded it.

France. To the south lay France, still the most powerful nation in Europe despite its losses in the War of the Spanish Succession (see **Map E**). No grand tour was complete without a sight of one of the king's great palaces, either the Louvre in Paris or monstrous Versailles, now considered one of the wonders of the world. Those with imagination could tour grand chateaux or visit vast cathedrals in every part of the nation. By 1714, Louis XIV had broken forever the danger of Spanish encirclement that had been the worry of every French king since Francis I in the early sixteenth century. Louis had methodically set out to occupy those territories that were strategically necessary to defend his state from invasion by the Dutch, the Spanish, the British, or the emperor. In the northeast, he absorbed the Duchy of Bar. In the north, he absorbed a healthy portion of Flanders, including Dunkirk on the English Channel and the prosperous clothing town of Lille. He pushed the eastern boundary of his state to the Rhine by overrunning Alsace and parts of Lorraine (see **Map E**). Strasbourg remained French under the settlement of 1714, testimony to the fact that it was possible to hold France only at the western banks of the Rhine. Finally, farther to the south, Louis had won and held Franche-Comté, once the center of Burgundy. In 1714, France was larger, stronger, and better able to defend its borders than ever before. It was also exhausted.

Spain. As France expanded, so Spain contracted. Less than two centuries earlier, a Spanish king had dreamed of being monarch of all of Europe. Instead, a French Bourbon sat on

■ **Map E. France and Spain.** The War of the Spanish Succession permanently separated France and Spain.

■ **Map F. The Holy Roman Empire.** It was still a conglomeration of towns, principalities, and bishoprics, but increasingly the empire was losing political and administrative control over its lands.

the great Habsburg throne and Spain was slowly being sliced to pieces. By 1714 the European territories of the Spanish empire had been reduced to Iberia itself (see **Map E**). But the loss of its European empire was to prove a blessing in disguise for Spain, which now entered a new and unexpected phase of growth and influence. Grand tourists did not always find Spain a congenial destination; a trek across the Pyrenees and on to an arid plain was a deterrent to reaching Madrid and Toledo, but those who ventured forth were richly rewarded by the sight of great walled castles, Philip II's palace of L'Escorial, and some of the greatest cathedrals on the Continent.

The Empire. The center of Europe remained occupied by the agglomeration of cities, bishoprics, principalities, and small states known collectively as the Holy Roman Empire, but now more accurately called the German Empire (see **Map F**). There were still more than 300 separate jurisdictions, most of them vulnerable to preying neighbors such as Louis XIV. Bavaria in the south and Saxony, Brandenburg, and Hanover in the north were among the most important of the large states, with the added twist that Hanover was now ruled by the king of Great Britain. The emperor, now officially prohibited from interference in the internal administration of the large states, was less dominant in German affairs than he had been before the Thirty Years' War. Grand tourists were welcomed into dozens of palaces occupied by the princes of the empire and while most churches were devoid of the rich decorations to be found in

Catholic countries, German cities were finally recovering from the devastation of the Thirty Years' War.

Increasingly, Habsburg power centered on Austria, Bohemia, and Hungary (see **Map F**). That was especially true during the reign of Leopold I (1655–1705). Withstanding threats on all sides, Leopold was able to expand his state both to the west and to the south and to bring Austria into the ranks of the great European powers. Such an outcome could hardly have been foreseen in the middle of the seventeenth century, when the Ottomans made their last great thrust into the interior of Europe. In 1683, the Ottomans besieged Vienna itself, and only the arrival of 70,000 Polish-led troops saved it from falling. But from that time forward, Austrian forces scored stunning victories. By 1699 almost all of Hungary had been retaken by Austria; with the Treaty of Passarowitz in 1718 Austria gained the rest of Hungary and Serbia. When the Treaty of Utrecht granted Austria control of the Netherlands, Lombardy, and Naples, the Austrian Habsburgs became rulers of a European empire (see **Map F**).

Austria's Italian possessions included the vast southern territories of Naples (including Sicily after 1720) and the rich industrial area surrounding Milan in the north. Alongside the Austrian territories, a number of independent city-states continued to flourish on the Italian peninsula. Both Venice and Genoa remained prosperous and independent. The Grand

Duchy of Tuscany, with its great city of Florence, and the Papal States had both expanded over the course of the seventeenth century, absorbing their smaller neighbors until both were large consolidated territories (see **Map F**). Florence was one of the traditional destinations of those on the grand tour and a place to purchase great works of art from all periods. The palaces of the Medici on both sides of the Arno River were among the most opulent to be seen and the public art of masters such as Leonardo da Vinci and Michelangelo was as popular then as it is now. To the west of the Italian states was the Duchy of Savoy (see **Map F**). Savoy had pursued a flexible foreign policy, pleasing whichever of its powerful neighbors was most dangerous and accepting the patronage of whichever seemed most friendly. As a client of the Spanish, French, and Austrians, Savoy grew and prospered. After the War of the Spanish Succession, Savoy was counted among the victors, though it had fought on both sides. Duke Victor Amadeus II became a king when he received the island of Sicily, which he exchanged with Austria for Sardinia in 1720 (see **Map F**).

Thus the Treaty of Utrecht signaled a new configuration of political power. England, France, Prussia, and Austria were the ascending powers, Holland and Spain the declining ones. Italy and the southern Netherlands were the bones over which the biggest dogs fought, sometimes playfully, sometimes in deadly earnest.

Realignment in Eastern Europe

In eastern Europe, the Treaty of Nystad (1721) ended the Great Northern War (1700–1721) and fixed the political geography in the east. There the emerging powers were Russia and Prussia, while those in decline were Sweden and Poland. The critical factor in eastern European politics remained access to the sea. Outlets to the Baltic Sea in the north and the Black Sea in the south were the vital lifeline for that part of the Continent, and control of those outlets was the central motivation for the long years of war fought among the eastern states.

Russia. The expansion of Russia is one of the central events in European history, and the early eighteenth century is its pivotal period. During the long years of social and eco-

DOCUMENT
Foreign Traveler in Russia

nomic recovery after the death of Ivan the Terrible in 1584, Russia had been easy prey for its powerful neighbors Sweden and Poland. Through a series of wars and political pacts, Russia had ceded most of its Baltic territories to Sweden, while it had relinquished land and population in the west to Poland. Peter the Great (1682–1725) set out to reclaim what had been lost. As a result of the Great Northern War, Russia regained the eastern Baltic coastline from the southeastern end of Finland to Riga in the west (see **Map G**). Russia now controlled all of the vital Baltic ports in the east. Peter built a new capital on the Gulf of Finland. In the new city, named Saint Petersburg, he laid the foundation for the Russian navy. Russia was still an unusual destination for traveling

■ **Map G. Russia and Sweden.** Sweden's age of territorial expansion was over by the beginning of the eighteenth century.

noblemen but there was much curiosity about the new city that Peter and his successors were building. Russian monarchs did all they could to westernize their state, even purchasing some of the greatest works of Italian art for the new royal palace L'Hermitage.

Sweden. What Russia gained, Sweden lost (see **Map G**). At the height of its power in the middle of the seventeenth century, Sweden had dominated the Baltic. It occupied all of Finland, controlled the important eastern coast of Norway, and had gained a foothold in Germany. Most importantly, Sweden had captured the southern tip of its own peninsula from the Danes, making the mainland portion of its state whole. But Sweden's century-long rise to power was followed by a rapid period of decline. The small and relatively poor population could not long succeed in governing an empire. The Great Northern War ended whatever pretensions Sweden still had. It lost all of its German territories: those on the North Sea went to Hanover, those on the Baltic to Prussia. Livonia, Estonia, and the eastern provinces were returned to Russia, but Sweden was able to hold on to its vital gains from the Danes. Sweden had built its own window to the west at Göteborg on the North Sea, and from there it could carry on a direct trade with Britain and the Netherlands (see **Map G**).

Prussia. Since the end of the Thirty Years' War, Brandenburg-Prussia had been growing steadily. A strange

CAPTAIN COOK ENCOUNTERS THE TAHITIANS

The English explorer Captain James Cook, trained as a map maker, was sent by the Royal Navy on an astronomical expedition to the South Pacific. While there he decided to explore islands to the east and discovered Australia and New Zealand. He was the first European to make contact with Pacific islanders. He kept a diary of his experiences. This entry is from April 14, 1769.

Focus Questions

What is Captain Cook's attitude toward the Tahitians? How do chiefs differ from ordinary islanders? What kind of names did Cook bestow upon the Tahitian chiefs? What qualities might they have relected?

This morning we had a great many canoes about the ship, the most of them came from the westward but brought nothing with them but a few Cocoa-nuts. Two that appeared to be chiefs we had on board together with several others for it was a hard matter to keep them out of the ship as they climb like monkeys, but it was still harder to keep them from stealing but every thing that came within their reach. In this they are prodigious expert. I made each of the two chiefs a present of a hatchet, things that they seemed mostly to value. . . .

As soon as we had partly got clear of these people, I took two boats and went to the westward. Here the natives flocked about us in great numbers and in as friendly a manner as we could wish, only that they showed a great inclination to pick our pockets. We were conducted to a chief who for distinction sake we called Hercules. After staying a short time with him and distributing a few presents about us, we proceeded further and came to a chief who I shall call Lycurgus. This man entertained us with broiled fish, breadfruit, cocoa-nuts etc. with a great hospitality, and all the time took great care to tell us to take care of our pockets, as a great number of people had crowded about us.

From *The Journals of Captain Cook* by James Cook. Edited by Philip Edwards (Penguin: 1999), pp. 39–41.

configuration of a state, with its geographical heart in Brandenburg, it was one of the domains of the Holy Roman Empire (see **Map G**). From the capital at Berlin the princes of Brandenburg directed the accumulation of small neighboring German lands: Magdeburg and Halle to the southwest, a piece of Pomerania to the northeast. But while Brandenburg expanded in every direction, it could do little to join itself to the kingdom of Prussia. A huge swath of Poland, cutting between the two, stood in the way. That division of Brandenburg-Prussia was its most important geopolitical feature. In the eighteenth century, the determination to join together dominated Prussian history.

Poland. That aim, of course, meant eventual conflict with Poland. Despite its political weakness, Poland was one of the largest landmasses in Europe (see **Map G**). On its southern border it held back Ottoman expansion; on its eastern border it held back the Russians. Its great port of Gdansk on the Baltic dominated the grain and timber trade with northern Europe as well as local Baltic commerce between Scandinavia and the mainland. Sweden and Russia, the eastern powers, controlled Poland politically, helping nominate its elected kings and ensuring that its decentralized form of aristocratic government kept Poland weak. Poland served as a useful counterweight in the balance of power in eastern Europe. Except for its Baltic territories, Poland was not yet seen as a great prize to be fought over. But by the beginning of the eighteenth century it was a helpless giant ready to be toppled.

Thus a potent Prussia and Russia and a prostrate Poland characterized the realignment of the eastern portion of Europe. Most importantly, the separation between east and west was narrowing. Prussia's German orientation and the Westernization of Russia led to closer ties with the west. More and more grand tourists visited the Prussian palace of Sans Souci or ventured as far east as St. Petersburg or Moscow. More and more they became part of a single European aristocratic culture.

THE RISE OF RUSSIA

At the beginning of the eighteenth century, Russia was scarcely known or cared about in the rest of Europe. Peter the Great changed that. The Treaty of Nystad had confirmed the magnitude of his victory over the Swedes in the Great Northern War, both in territory and prestige. The change created consternation in the courts of Europe. Just a quarter century before, no one had cared very much what the king of Russia called himself. In fact, little was known for sure about the Russian ruler or his state. What little mercantile contact there was between Russia and the West was conducted entirely by westerners. Foreign merchants were allowed to live in Moscow in a separate ghetto called "Germantown." Their letters were the main source of western knowledge about the vast Muscovite empire.

Peter the Great brought Europe to Russia and Russia to Europe. Twice he visited Europe to discover the secrets of western prosperity and might. He arranged marriages between the closest heirs to his throne, including his son Alexis, and the sons and daughters of German princes and dukes. By 1721 he had established 21 separate foreign embassies. The sons of the Russian gentry and nobility were sent west—sometimes forcibly—to further their education and to learn to adapt to western outlooks. Peter recruited Europeans to fill the most important skilled positions in the state: foreign engineers and gunners to serve in the army; foreign architects to build the new capital at Saint Petersburg; foreign scholars to head the new state schools; foreign administrators to oversee the new departments of state. Peter borrowed freely and adapted sensibly. If necessary, he would drag his countrymen kicking and screaming into the modern world.

By 1721, Russia was recognized all over Europe as an emerging power. The military defeat of the seemingly invincible Swedes had made monarchs from Louis XIV to William III sit up and take notice. And the great Russian victory over Sweden at Poltava in 1709 was no fluke. Peter's forces followed it up with several strong campaigns, which proved that Russia could organize, equip, finance, and train an up-to-date military force. Moreover, Peter's absorption of Sweden's Baltic territories made Russia a power in the north. The Russian navy, built mostly by foreigners, was now capable of protecting Russian interests and defending important ports such as Riga and Saint Petersburg. Even the Dutch, who had long plotted the decline of Swedish might, now became nervous. Thus it was unsettling that Peter wanted to be recognized as emperor.

The Reforms of Peter the Great

Peter the Great was not the first Russian tsar to attempt to borrow from western developments. The process had been under way for decades. The opening of the northern port of Archangel in 1584 led to direct contact with British and Dutch

■ *The Apotheosis of Peter the Great* (1710). Here Peter the Great is depicted in all his glory as a lawgiver, military commander, and leader of a new Russia.

traders, who brought with them new ideas and useful products. But Russia was a vast state, and Europe was only one of its neighbors. Russia's religion had come from Byzantium rather than Rome, thus giving Russian Christianity an eastern flavor. Its Asian territories mixed the influence of Mongols and Ottomans; its southern borders met Tatars and Cossacks. While most European states were racially and ethnically homogeneous, Russia was a loose confederation of diverse peoples. Yet the western states posed the greatest threat to Russia in the seventeenth century, and it was to the west that Peter, like his father before him, turned his attention.

It would be wrong to see Peter's westernizing innovation as a systematic program. More to the point, nearly all of his reforms—economic, educational, administrative, social, military—were done to enhance military efficiency rather than civil progress. In his 30 years of active rule there was only one year—1724—during which he was not at war. Vital reforms such as the poll tax (1724), which changed the basis of taxation from the household to the individual adult male, had enormous social consequences. The new policy of taxing individuals officially erased whole social classes. A strict census taken (and retaken) to inhibit tax evasion became the basis for further governmental encroachments on the tsar's subjects. Yet the poll tax was not designed for any of those purposes. It was instituted to increase tax revenue for war. Similarly, compulsory lifetime military service required of the landowning classes (the nobility and gentry) was established to provide officers and state servants for an expanding military machine.

Although Peter's reforms were developed from little other than military necessity, they constituted a fundamental transformation in the life of all Russian people. The creation of a gigantic standing army and an entirely new navy meant conscription of the Russian peasantry on a grand scale. In a ten-year period of the Great Northern War, the army absorbed 330,000 conscripts, most of whom never returned to their homes. Military service was not confined to the peasantry. Traditionally, the rural gentry raised and equipped the local conscript forces and gave them what training they could. Most gentry lived on estates that had been granted to them, along with the resident peasants, as a reward for their military contributions. Peter the Great intensified the obligations of the gentry. Not only were they to serve the state for life, but they were to accompany their regiments to the field and lead them in battle. When too old for active military service, they were to perform administrative service in the new departments of state.

The expansion of military forces necessitated an expansion of military administration as well. Peter's first innovation was the creation of the Senate, a group of nine senior administrators who were to oversee all aspects of military and civil government. The Senate became a permanent institution of government led by an entirely new official, the Procurator-General, who presided over its sessions and could propose legislation as well as oversee administration. From the Senate emanated 500 officials known as the *fiscals,* who traveled throughout the state looking for irregularities in tax assessment and collection. They quickly developed into a hated and feared internal police force.

Peter's efforts to reorganize his government went a step further in 1722, when he issued the **Table of Ranks,** an official hierarchy of the state that established the social position or rank of individuals. It was divided into three categories: military service, civil service, and owners of landed estates. Each category contained 14 ranks, and it was decreed that every person who entered the hierarchy did so at the bottom and worked his way up. The creation of the Table of Ranks demonstrated Peter's continued commitment to merit as a criterion for advancement. This standard had been shown in the military, where officers were promoted on the basis of service and experience rather than birth or background. Equally important was Peter's decision to make the military service

■ St. Petersburg, the new capital city Peter the Great had built, testified to the growing strength of Russia through the eighteenth century.

the highest of the three categories. This reversed the centuries-old position of the landed aristocracy and the military service class. Although the old nobility also served in the military and continued to dominate state service, the Table of Ranks opened the way for the infusion of new elements into the Russian elite.

Many of those who were able to advance in the Table of Ranks did so through attendance at the new institutions of higher learning that Peter founded. His initial educational establishments were created to further the military might of the state. The Colleges of Mathematics, Engineering, and Artillery, which became the training grounds for his army officers, were all founded during the Great Northern War. But Peter was also interested in liberal education, and he had scores of western books translated into Russian. He had a press established in Moscow to print original works, including the first Russian newspaper. He decreed that a new, more westernized alphabet replace the one used by the Russian Orthodox Church and that books be written in the language that the people spoke rather than in the formal literary language of religious writers. He also introduced Arabic numerals into official accounting records.

Peter's reforms of government and society were matched by his efforts to energize the economy. No state in Europe had as many natural resources as did Russia, yet manufacturing barely existed there. As with everything else he did, Peter took a direct hand in establishing factories for the production of textiles, glass, leather, and, most importantly, iron and copper. The state directly owned about half of the establishments, most of them on a larger scale than any known in the west. By 1726, more than half of all Russian exports were manufactured goods and Russia had become the largest producer of iron and copper in the world.

In all those ways and more, Peter the Great transformed Russia, but the changes did not come without cost. The traditions of centuries were not easily broken. Intrigue against Peter led first to confrontation with the old military elite, and later to conflict with his only son, Alexis. It remains unclear whether the plot with which Alexis was connected actually existed or whether it was a figment of Peter's imagination, but it is abundantly clear that Alexis's death from torture plunged the state into a succession crisis in 1725. In the end, the great costs of westernization were paid by the masses of people, who benefited little from the improvement in Russia's international standing or from the social and economic changes that affected the elites.

DOCUMENT

Panegyric to
Peter the Great

Life in Rural Russia

At the beginning of the eighteenth century, nearly 97 percent of the Russian people lived on the land and practiced agriculture. Farming techniques and agrarian lifestyles had changed little for centuries. Most of the country's soil was poor. Harsh climate and low yields characterized Russian agriculture. Thirty-four of the 100 Russian harvests during the eighteenth century can be termed poor or disastrous, yet throughout the century state taxation was making larger and larger demands upon the peasantry. During Peter's reign alone, direct taxation increased by 500 percent.

The theory of the Russian state was one of service, and the role of Russian peasants was to serve their master. Beginning in the mid-seventeenth century, the peasantry had undergone a change in status. The law code of 1649 formalized a process that had been under way for more than a century whereby peasants were turned into the property of their landlords. During the next century, laws curtailed the ability of peasants to move freely from one place to another, eliminated their right to hold private property, and abolished their freedom to petition the tsar against their masters. At the same time that landlords increased their hold over peasants, the state increased its hold over landlords. They were made responsible for the payment of taxes owed by their peasants and for the military service due from them. By the middle of the eighteenth century, more than half of all peasants—6.7 million adult males by 1782—had thus become serfs, the property of their masters, without any significant rights or legal protection.

If serfs made up the bottom half of the Russian peasantry, there were few advantages to being in the top half, among the state peasants. State peasants lived on lands owned by the monarchy itself. Like the serfs, they were subject to the needs of the state for soldiers and workers. The use of forced labor was a feature of each of Peter's grandiose projects. Saint Petersburg was built by the backbreaking labor of peasant conscripts. From 1709, when the project began, perhaps as many as 40,000 laborers a year were forced to work on the various sites. The unhealthy conditions of the swampy environment from which the new capital rose claimed the lives of thousands of the workers, as did the appalling conditions of overwork and undernourishment in which they lived.

Many Russian peasants developed a philosophy of submission and a rich folk culture that valued a stubborn determination to endure. For those who would no longer bend to the knout—the heavy leather whip that was the omnipresent enforcer of obedience—there was only flight or rebellion. Hundreds of thousands of serfs fled to state-owned lands in hope of escaping the cruelties of individual landlords. Although severe penalties were imposed for aiding runaway serfs, in fact most state overseers and many private landlords encouraged runaways to settle on their lands. In their social and economic conditions, eighteenth-century Russian peasants were hardly distinguishable from medieval European serfs.

The Enlightened Empress Catherine

Of all the legacies of Peter the Great, perhaps the one of most immediate consequence was that government could go on without him. During the next 37 years, six tsars ruled Russia, "three women, a boy of twelve, an infant, and a mental weakling," as one commentator acidly observed. More to the point, each succession was contested, as there were no direct male heirs to the throne in this period. Nevertheless, despite turmoil at the top, government continued to function smoothly and Peter's territorial conquests were largely maintained. Russia also experienced a remarkable increase in numbers during this period. Between 1725 and 1762, the population increased from 13 to 19 million, a jump of nearly 50 percent in a single generation. The explosion of people dramatically increased the wealth of the landholding class, who reckoned their status by the number of serfs they owned.

The expansion of the economic resources of the nobility was matched by a rise in legal status and political power. This was the period sarcastically dubbed "the emancipation of the nobility," a phrase that captures not only the irony of the growing gap between rich and poor but also the contrast between the social structures of Russia and those of western Europe. In return for their privileges and status, Peter the Great extended the duties the landowning classes owed to the state. By granting unique rights, such as the ownership of serfs, to the descendants of the old military service class, Peter had forged a Russian nobility. Lifetime service, however, was the price of nobility.

In order to gain and hold the throne, each succeeding tsar had to make concessions to the nobility to gain their loyalty. At first it was a few simple adjustments. The sons of wealthy landowners who completed a course of education at one of the state academies were allowed to enter the Table of Ranks in the middle of the hierarchy rather than at the bottom. Then life service was commuted to a term of 25 years, still a long time in a world of short lives and sudden deaths. But the concessions were not enough.

Twenty-five years of service did not solve the problem of estate management, especially as the tasks of management grew along with the population of serfs. Thus the next capitulation was that a single son could remain on the estate and escape service altogether. The births of younger sons were concealed; owners of multiple estates claimed the exemption of one son for each. Most decisively, the talented remained at home to serve the family while the wastrels were sent to serve the state. Finally, in 1762, the obligation for state service by the nobility was abolished entirely.

Catherine's Accession.   The abolition of compulsory service was not the same as the abolition of service itself. In fact, the end of compulsory service enabled Catherine II, "the Great" (1762–1796), to enact some of the most important reforms of her reign. At first, Catherine's accession seemed nothing more than a continuation of monarchical instability—her first two acts were to have her husband, Peter III, murdered and to lower the salt tax. Each brought her a measure of security.

Catherine was a dynamic personality who alternately captivated and terrified those with whom she came into contact. Her policies were as complex as her personality, influenced on the one hand by the new French ideas of social justice and the nobility of the human race, and on the other hand by the traditional Russian ideas of absolute rule over an enserfed and subhuman population. Catherine handled the contrasting

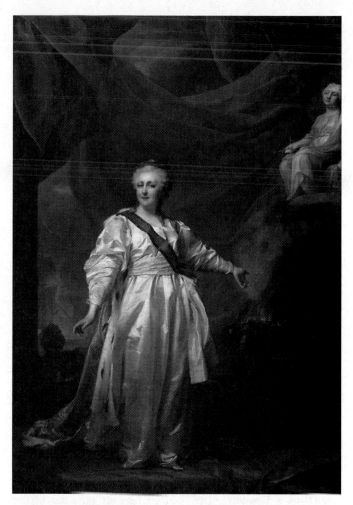

■ Portrait of Catherine II of Russia in the Temple of Justice, ca. 1783.

dimensions of her rule masterfully, gaining abroad the reputation as the most enlightened of European monarchs and at home the sincere devotion of her people.

The most important event in the early years of Catherine's reign was the establishment of a legislative commission to review the laws of Russia. Catherine herself wrote the *Instruction* (1767), by which the elected commissioners were to operate. She borrowed her theory of law from the French jurist Baron de Montesquieu (1689–1755) and her theory of punishment from the Italian reformer Cesare Beccaria (1738–1794). Among other things, Catherine advocated the abolition of capital punishment, torture, serf auctions, and the breakup of serf families by sale. Few of the radical reforms were ever put into practice.

On Corruption of Morals in Russia

But in 1775 Catherine did restructure local government. Russia was divided into 50 provincial districts, each with a population of between 300,000 and 400,000 inhabitants. Each district was to be governed by both a central official and elected local noblemen. The reform was modeled upon the English system of justices of the peace. Previous local reforms had failed because of the absence of a resident local nobility. The abolition of compulsory service finally made possible the establishment of local institutions. In 1785, Catherine issued the Charter of the Nobility, a formal statement of the rights and privileges of the noble class. The Charter incorporated all the gains the nobility had made since the death of Peter the Great, but it also instituted the requirements for local service that had been the basis of Catherine's reforms. District councils with the right to petition directly to the tsar became the centerpiece of Russian provincial government.

To train the local nobility for government service, Catherine introduced educational reforms. Peter had established military schools for the nobility and had staffed them with foreigners. The University of Moscow had been founded in 1755, and its faculty too was dominated by European emigrants. Catherine saw the need to broaden the educational system. Borrowing from the Austrian system, she established provincial elementary schools to train the sons and daughters of the local nobility. To staff the schools, Catherine created teachers' colleges so that the state would have its own educators. Although the program called for the equal education of women, except in Saint Petersburg and Moscow few females attended either elementary or high schools.

Catherine's reforms did little to enhance the lives of the vast majority of her people. She took no effective action either to end serfdom or to soften its rigors. In fact, by grants of state land Catherine gave away 800,000 state peasants, who became serfs. So, too, did millions of Poles who became her subjects after the partition of Poland in 1793 and 1795.

Pugachev's Revolt. The most significant uprising of the century, Pugachev's revolt (1773–1775), took place during Catherine's reign. Emelyan Pugachev (1726–1775) was a Cossack who in his youth had been a military adventurer. Disappointed in his career, he made his way to the Ural Mountains, where he recruited Asian tribesmen and laborers forced to work in the mines. By promising freedom and land ownership, he drew peasants to his cause. In 1773, Pugachev declared himself to be Tsar Peter III, the murdered husband of Catherine II. He began with small raiding parties against local landlords and military outposts and soon had gained the allegiance of tens of thousands of peasants. In 1774, with an army of nearly 20,000, Pugachev took the city of Kazan and threatened to advance on Moscow. It was another year before state forces could effectively control the rebellion. Finally, Pugachev was betrayed by his own followers and sent to Moscow, where he was executed.

During the reigns of Peter and Catherine the Great, Russia was transformed into an international power. Saint Petersburg, a window to the west, was a capital worthy of a potent monarch, and during the course of the eighteenth century it attracted many of Europe's leading luminaries. At court French was spoken, the latest fashions were worn, and the newest ideas for

Russia

economic and educational reform were aired. The Russian nobility mingled comfortably with its European counterparts, while the military service class developed into bureaucrats and administrators. But if life glittered at court, it remained the same dull regimen in the country. Millions of peasants were owned either by the state or by private landlords, and their quality of life was no different at the end of the campaign of westernization than it had been at the beginning.

THE TWO GERMANIES

The Thirty Years' War, which ended in 1648, initiated a profound transformation of the Holy Roman Empire. Warfare had devastated imperial territory. It was decades before the rich imperial lands recovered, and then the political consequences of the war had taken effect. There were now two empires, a German and an Austrian, though both were ruled by the same person. In the German territories, whether Catholic or Protestant, the Holy Roman Emperor was more a constitutional monarch than the absolute ruler he was in Austria. The larger states such as Saxony, Bavaria, and Hanover made their own political alliances despite the jurisdictional control that the emperor claimed to exercise. Most decisively, so did Brandenburg-Prussia. By the beginning of the eighteenth century, the electors of Brandenburg had become the kings of Prussia, and Prussia's military power and efficient administrative structure became the envy of its German neighbors.

The Austrian Empire was composed of Austria and Bohemia, the Habsburg hereditary lands, and as much of Hungary as could be controlled. In Austria, the Habsburgs clung tightly to their power. For decades, Austria was the center of the still-flourishing Counter-Reformation, and the power and influence of the Jesuits was as strong there as it was in Spain. The War of the Spanish Succession, which gave the Habsburgs control of the southern Netherlands and parts of Italy, brought Austria an enhanced role in European affairs. Austria remained one of the great powers of Europe and the leading power in the Holy Roman Empire despite the rise of Prussia. Indeed, from the middle of the eighteenth century, the conflict between Prussia and Austria was the defining characteristic of central European politics.

The Rise of Prussia

The transformation of Brandenburg-Prussia from a petty German principality to a great European power was one of the most significant and least expected developments of the eighteenth century. Frederick William, the Great Elector (1640–1688), had begun the process of forging Brandenburg-Prussia into a power in its own right by building a large and efficient military machine. At the beginning of the eighteenth century, Prussia was on the winning side in both the War of the Spanish Succession and the Great Northern War. When the battlefield dust had settled, Prussia found itself in possession of Pomerania and the Baltic port of Stettin. It was now a recognized power in eastern Europe.

Frederick William I.   Frederick William I (1713–1740) and his son Frederick II, "the Great" (1740–1786), turned the promising beginning into an astounding success. A devout Calvinist, Frederick William I deplored waste and display as much on moral as on fiscal grounds. The reforms he initiated were intended to subordinate both aristocracy and peasantry to the needs of the state and to subordinate the needs of the state to the demands of the military.

Because of its geographical position, Prussia's major problem was to maintain an efficient and well-trained army during peacetime. Defense of its exposed territories required a constant state of military preparedness, yet the relaxation of military discipline and the desertion of troops to their homes inevitably followed the cessation of hostilities. Frederick William I solved the problem by integrating the economic and military structures of his state. First he appointed only German officers to command his troops, eliminating the mercenaries who sold their services to the highest bidders. Then he placed the noblemen at the head of locally recruited regiments. Each adult male in every district was required to register for military service in the regiment of the local landlord. The reforms dramatically increased the effectiveness of the army by shifting the burden of recruitment and training to the localities.

Yet despite all the attention that Frederick William I lavished on the military—by the end of his reign nearly 70 percent of state expenditures went to the army—his foreign policy was largely pacific. In fact, his greatest achievements were in civil affairs, reforming the bureaucracy, establishing a sound economy, and raising state revenues. Through generous settlement schemes and by welcoming Protestant and Jewish refugees, Frederick William was able to expand the economic potential of the eastern territories. Frederick William I pursued an aggressive policy of land purchase to expand the royal domain, and the addition of so many new inhabitants in Prussia further increased his wealth. While

MAP DISCOVERY

The Expansion of Prussia

Notice how Brandenburg-Prussia grew in its first phase to 1618. How did its acquisitions made between 1618 and 1740 differ from its earlier growth? Notice how the acquisition of Silesia made Prussia an inland power in control of most of the Oder River. Why was the acquisition of West Prussia strategically important?

the major western European powers were discovering deficit financing and the national debt, Prussia was running a surplus.

Frederick the Great.   Financial security was vital to the success of Frederick the Great. Father and son had quarreled bitterly throughout Frederick's youth—not only about music—and most observers expected that out of spite Frederick would tear down all that his father had built up. In fact, father and son were cast in the same mold, with the unexpected difference that the son was more ruthless and ambitious. With his throne, Frederick II inherited the fourth-largest army in Europe and the richest treasury. He wasted no time in putting both to use. His two objectives were to acquire the Polish corridor of West Prussia that separated his German and Prussian territories and to acquire the agriculturally and industrially rich Austrian province of Silesia to the southeast of Berlin. Just months after

his coronation, Frederick conquered Silesia, increasing the size of Prussia by nearly a quarter. Within a decade, the province dominated the Prussian economy, outproducing and outconsuming all other areas of Frederick's state.

It was Frederick's military prowess that earned him the title "the Great." But that was only a part of his achievement. More than his father, Frederick II forged an alliance with the Prussian nobility, integrating them into a unified state. A tightly organized central administration, which depended upon the cooperation of the local nobility, directed both military and bureaucratic affairs. At the center, Frederick worked tirelessly to oversee his government. Where Louis XIV had proclaimed, "I am the state," Frederick the Great announced, "I am the first servant of the state." He codified the laws of Prussia, abolished torture and capital punishment, and instituted agricultural techniques imported from the states of western Europe. By the end of Frederick's reign,

■ Prussian infantry officers display their uniforms in this painting from the late eighteenth century. Distinctive, colorful, and elaborate uniforms, different for each regiment, were common in European armies before the field-gray and khaki era of the twentieth century.

A KING'S-EYE VIEW

Frederick the Great wrote philosophical and military tracts as well as composing dozens of compositions for the flute. Here is his definition of the enlightened despot.

Focus Questions

What is the relation of the sovereign to the state and its people? What is enlightened about an enlightened despot?

The sovereign is attached by indissoluble ties to the body of the state; hence it follows that he, by repercussion, is sensible to all the ills which afflict his subjects; and the people, in like manner, suffer from the misfortunes which affect their sovereign. There is but one general good, which is that of the state. . . . The sovereign represents the state; he and his people form but one body, which can only be happy as far as united by concord. The prince is to the nation he governs what the head is to the man; it is his duty to see, to think, and act for the whole community, so that he may procure it every advantage of which it is capable. . . . Such are in general the duties imposed upon a prince, from which, in order that he may never depart, he ought often to recollect that he himself is but a man, like the least of his subjects. If he be the first general, the first minister of the realm, it is not so that he should shelter in the shadow of authority, but that he should fulfill the duties of such titles. He is only the first servant of the state, who is obliged to act with probity and prudence; and to remain as totally disinterested as if he were each moment liable to render an account of his administration to his fellow citizens.

From Frederick the Great, *An Essay on Forms of Government.*

Prussia had become a model for bureaucratic organization, military reform, and enlightened rule.

Austria Survives

Austria was the great territorial victor in the War of the Spanish Succession, acquiring both the Netherlands and parts of Italy. Austrian forces recaptured a large part of Hungary from the Turks, thereby expanding their territory to the south and the east. As hereditary ruler of Austria and Bohemia, king of Hungary, and Holy Roman Emperor of the German nation, Charles VI (1711–1740) was recognized as one of Europe's most potent rulers. But appearances were deceptive. The apex of Austrian power and prestige had already passed. Austria had benefited from balance-of-power politics, not so much from its own strength as from the leverage it could give to others. With the rise of Russia and Prussia, there was now more than one fulcrum to power in eastern Europe.

Decentralized Rule. The difficulties facing Austria ran deep. The Thirty Years' War had made the emperor more an Austrian monarch than an imperial German ruler. On the Austrian hereditary estates, the Catholic Counter-Reformation continued unabated, bringing with it the benefits of Jesuit education, cultural revival, and the religious unity necessary to motivate warfare against the Ottomans. But the benefits came at a price. Perhaps as many as 200,000 Protestants fled Austria and Bohemia, taking with them their skills and capital. For centuries, the vision of empire had dominated Habsburg rule. That meant that the Austrian monarchy was a multiethnic confederation of lands loosely tied together by loyalty to a single head. The components preserved a high degree of autonomy: Hungary elected the Habsburg emperor its king in a separate ceremony. Local autonomy continually restricted the imposition of central policy, and never were the localities more autonomous than in the matter of taxation. Thus it was hard for Austria to centralize in the same way as had Prussia.

Lack of finance, human resources, and governmental control were the underlying problems of Austria, but they were not the most immediate difficulties facing Charles VI. With no sons to succeed him, Charles feared that his hereditary and elective states would go their separate ways after his death and that the great Habsburg monarchy would end. For 20 years, his abiding ambition was to gain recognition for the principle that his empire would pass intact to his daughter, Maria Theresa. He expressed the principle in a document known as the **Pragmatic Sanction,** which stated that all Habsburg lands would pass intact to the eldest heir, male or female. Charles VI made concession after concession to gain acceptance of the Pragmatic Sanction. But the leaders of Europe licked their lips at the prospect of a dismembered Austrian Empire.

Maria Theresa. Maria Theresa (1740–1780) inherited the imperial throne in 1740 and quickly discovered what it was like to be a woman in a man's world. In 1740, Frederick of Prussia invaded the rich Austrian province of Silesia and attracted allies for an assault upon Vienna. Faced with Bavarian, Saxon, and Prussian armies, Maria Theresa might

MILITARY DISCIPLINE

Herman Maurice de Saxe was the illegitimate son of the king of Poland. He had extensive military experience in both eastern and western Europe. He ultimately achieved the office of Marshal of France, where he was celebrated as a military reformer. He modeled many of his reforms on the Prussian army.

Focus Questions

Why would it be desirable for men in their twenties to have to perform military service? What would be the consequences of requiring men from all levels of the social hierarchy to serve in the military?

Would it not be much better to establish a law obliging men of all conditions of life to serve their king and country for the space of five years? A law, which could not reasonably be objected against, as it is both natural and just for people to be engaged in the defense of that state of which they constitute a part, and in choosing them between the years of twenty and thirty, no manner of inconvenience can possibly be the result; for those are years devoted, as it were, to libertinism; which are spent in adventures and travels, and, in general, productive of but small comfort to parents. An expedient of this kind could not come under the denomination of a public calamity, because every man, at the expiration of his five years service, would be discharged. It would also create an inexhaustible fund of good recruits, and such as would not be subject to desertion. In course of time, everyone would regard it as an honor rather than a duty to perform his task; but to produce this effect upon a people, it is necessary that no sort of distinction should be admitted, no rank or degree whatsoever excluded, and the nobles and rich rendered, in a principal manner, subservient to it. This would effectually prevent all murmur and repining, for those who had served their time, would look upon such, as betrayed any reluctance, or dissatisfaction at it, with contempt; by which means, the grievance would vanish insensibly, and every man at length esteem it an honor to serve his term. The poor would be comforted by the example of the rich; and the rich could not with decency complain, seeing themselves on a footing with the nobles.

From Marshal de Saxe, *Memoirs on the Art of War* (1757).

---

well have lost her inheritance had she not shown her remarkable capacities so early in her reign. She appeared before the Hungarian estates, accepted their crown, and persuaded them to provide her with an army capable of halting the allied advance. Although she was unable to reconquer Silesia, Hungarian aid helped her hold the line against her enemies.

The loss of Silesia, the most prosperous part of the Austrian domains, signaled the need for fundamental reform. The new eighteenth-century idea of building a state replaced the traditional Habsburg concern with maintaining an empire. Maria Theresa and her son Joseph II (1780–1790) began the process of transformation. For Austria, state building meant first the reorganization of the military and civil bureaucracy to clear the way for fiscal reform. As in Prussia, a central directory was created to oversee the collection of taxes and the disbursement of funds. Maria Theresa personally persuaded her provincial estates both to increase taxation and to extend it to the nobles and the clergy. While her success was limited, she finally established royal control over the raising and collection of taxes.

The second element in Maria Theresa's reform program involved the condition of the Austrian peasantry. Maria Theresa established the doctrine that "the peasant must be able to support himself and his family and pay his taxes in time of peace and war." She limited labor service to two days per week and abolished the most burdensome feudal dues. Joseph II ended serfdom altogether. The new Austrian law codes guaranteed peasants' legal rights and established their ability to seek redress through the law. Joseph II hoped to extend reform even further. In the last years of his life, he abolished obligatory labor service and ensured that all peasants kept one-half of their income before paying local and state taxes. Such a radical reform met a storm of opposition and was ultimately abandoned at the end of the reign.

The reorganization of the bureaucracy, the increase in taxation, and the social reforms that created a more productive peasantry revitalized the Austrian state. The efforts of Maria Theresa and Joseph II to overcome provincial autonomy worked better in Austria and Bohemia than in Hungary. The Hungarians declined to contribute at all to state revenues, and Joseph II took the unusual step of refusing to be crowned king of Hungary so that he would not have to make any concessions to Hungarian autonomy. He even imposed a tariff on Hungarian goods sold in Austria. More seriously, parts of the empire already had been lost before the process of reform could begin. Prussia's seizure of Silesia was the hardest blow of all. Yet in 1740, when Frederick the Great and his allies swept down from the north, few would have predicted that Austria would survive.

■ Maria Theresa and her family. Eleven of Maria Theresa's 16 children are posed with the empress and her husband, Francis of Lorraine. Standing next to his mother is the future emperor Joseph II.

The Politics of Power

Frederick the Great's invasion of Silesia in 1740 was callous and cynical. Since the Pragmatic Sanction bound him to recognize Maria Theresa's succession, Frederick cynically offered her a defensive alliance in return for which she would simply hand over Silesia. It was an offer she should not have refused. Although Frederick's action initiated the War of the Austrian Succession, he was not alone in his desire to shake loose parts of Austria's territory. Soon nearly the entire Continent became embroiled in the conflict.

The War of the Austrian Succession.   The War of the Austrian Succession (1740–1748) resembled a pack of wolves stalking its injured prey. It quickly became a major international conflict, involving Prussia, France, and Spain on one side and Austria, Britain, and Holland on the other. Spain joined the fighting to recover its Italian possessions, Saxony claimed Moravia, France entered Bohemia, and the Bavarians moved into Austria from the south. With France and Prussia

allied, it was vital that Britain join with Austria to maintain the balance of power. Initially, the British did little more than subsidize Maria Theresa's forces, but once France renewed its efforts to conquer the Netherlands, both Britain and the Dutch Republic joined in the fray.

That the British cared little about the fate of the Habsburg Empire was clear from the terms of the treaty that they dictated at Aix-la-Chapelle (Aachen) in 1748. Austria recognized Frederick's conquest of Silesia, as well as the loss of parts of its Italian territories to Spain. France, which the British had always regarded as the real enemy, withdrew from the Netherlands in return for the restoration of a number of colonial possessions. The War of the Austrian Succession made Austria and Prussia permanent enemies and gave Maria Theresa a crash course in international diplomacy. She learned firsthand that self-interest rather than loyalty underlay power politics.

The Seven Years' War.   That lesson was reinforced in 1756 when Britain and Prussia entered into a military accord at the beginning of the Seven Years' War (1756–1763). Prussian expansion and duplicity had already alarmed both Russia and France, and Frederick II feared that he would be squeezed from east and west. He could hardly expect help from Maria Theresa, so he extended overtures to the British, whose interests in protecting Hanover, the hereditary estates of their German-born king, outweighed their prior commitments to Austria. Frederick's actions drove France into the arms of both the Austrians and the Russians, and an alliance that included the German state of Saxony was formed in defense. Thus was initiated a diplomatic revolution in which France and Austria became allies after 300 years as enemies.

Once again Frederick the Great took the offensive. His attack on Saxony and Austria in 1756 brought a vigorous response from the Russians, who interceded on Austria's behalf with a massive army. Three years later, at the battle of Kunersdorf, Frederick suffered the worst military defeat of his career when the Russians shattered his armies. In 1760, his forces were barely a third of the size of those massed by his opponents, and it was only a matter of time before he was fighting defensively from within Prussia.

In 1762 Empress Elizabeth of Russia died. She was succeeded by her nephew, the childlike Peter III, a German by birth who worshipped Frederick the Great. When Peter came to the throne, he immediately negotiated peace with Frederick, abandoning not only his allies but also the substantial territorial gains that the Russian forces had made within Prussia. It was small wonder that the Russian military leadership joined in the coup d'état that brought Peter's wife, Catherine, to the throne in 1762. With Russia out of the war, Frederick was able to fend off further Austrian offensives and to emerge with his state, including Silesia, intact.

The Seven Years' War did little to change the boundaries of the German states, but it had two important political results. The first was to establish beyond doubt the status of Prussia as

■ This painting by Pierre L'Enfant (1704–1787) depicts the Battle of Fontenoy (1745), an important engagement in the War of the Austrian Succession. The French won a victory over the English army that was defending Austrian territory in the Netherlands.

a major power and a counterbalance to Austria in central Europe. The existence of the dual Germanies, one led by Prussia and the other by Austria, was to have serious consequences for German unification in the nineteenth century and for the two world wars in the twentieth century. The second result of the Seven Years' War was to initiate a long period of peace in eastern Europe. Both Prussia and Austria were financially exhausted from two decades of fighting. Both states needed a breathing spell to initiate administrative and economic improvements, and the period following the Seven Years' War witnessed the sustained programs of internal reforms for which Frederick the Great, Maria Theresa, and Joseph II were famous in the decades following 1763.

The Partitions of Poland. Peace among the eastern European powers did not mean that they abandoned their territorial ambitions. All over Europe, absolute rulers reformed their bureaucracies, streamlined their administrations, increased their sources of revenue, and built enormous standing armies. All over Europe, except in Poland. There the autonomous power of the nobility remained as strong as

ever. No monarchical dynasty was ever established, and each elected ruler not only confirmed the privileges of the nobility but usually was forced to extend them. In the Diet, the Polish representative assembly, small special-interest groups could bring legislative business to a halt by exercising their veto power. Given the size of Poland's borders, its army was pathetically inadequate for the task it had to face. The Polish monarchy was helpless to defend its subjects from the destruction on all sides.

In 1764, Catherine the Great and Frederick the Great joined to place one of Catherine's former lovers on the Polish throne and to turn Poland into a weak dependent. Russia and Prussia had different interests in Poland's fate. For Russia, Poland represented a vast buffer state that kept the German powers at a distance from Russia's borders. It was more in Russia's interest to dominate Polish foreign policy than to conquer its territory. For Prussia, Poland looked like another helpless flower, "to be picked off leaf by leaf," as Frederick observed. Poland seemed especially appealing because Polish territory, including the Baltic port of Gdansk, separated the Prussian and Brandenburg portions of Frederick's state.

■ This engraving by Le Mire is called *The Cake of the Kings: First Partition of Poland, 1773*. The monarchs of Russia, Austria, and Prussia join in carving up Poland. The Polish king is clutching his tottering crown.

Poland made it a single geographical entity, as well as a great economic and military power. Austria, despite its lost territory, proved capable of surviving the accession of a female ruler and of fighting off an attempt to dismember its empire. Its participation in the partition of Poland strengthened its role in the politics of the eastern powers, while its alliance with France fortified its role in the west. From one empire there were now two states, and the relationship between Prussia and Austria would dominate central Europe for the next century.

THE GREATNESS OF GREAT BRITAIN

By the middle of the eighteenth century, Great Britain had become the leading power of Europe. It had won its spurs in Continental and colonial wars. Britain was unsurpassed as a naval power, able to protect its far-flung trading empire and to make a show of force in almost any part of the world. Perhaps more impressively for a nation that did not support a large standing army, British soldiers had won decisive victories in the European land wars. Until the American Revolution, Britain came up a winner in every military venture it undertook. But might was only one part of British success. Economic preeminence was every bit as important. British colonial possessions in the Atlantic and Indian Oceans poured consumer products into Britain for export to the European marketplaces. (See "The West and the Wider World: The British Raj in India," pp. 570–571.) Growth in overseas trade was matched by growth in home production. British advances in agricultural technique had transformed Britain from an importer to an exporter of grain. The manufacturing industries that other European states attempted to create with huge government subsidies flourished in Britain through private enterprise.

British military and economic power was supported by a unique system of government. In Britain, the nobility served the state through government. The British constitutional system, devised in the seventeenth century and refined in the eighteenth, shared power between the monarchy and the ruling elite through the institution of Parliament. Central government integrated monarch and ministers with chosen representatives from the localities. Such integration not only provided the Crown with the vital information necessary to formulate national policy, but it eased acceptance and enforcement of government decisions. Government was seen as the rule of law that, however imperfect, was believed to operate for the benefit of all.

The parliamentary system gave Britain some of its particular strengths, but they came at a cost. Politics was a national pastime rather than the business of an elite group of administrators and state servants. Decentralization of decision making led to half-measures designed to placate competing interests. Appeals to public opinion, especially by candidates for Parliament, often played upon fears and prejudices that divided rather than united the nation. Moreover, the relative openness of the British system hindered diplomatic and

By the 1770s the idea of carving up Poland was being actively discussed in Berlin, Saint Petersburg, and Vienna. Austria, too, had an interest in a Polish partition, especially to maintain its power and status with the other two states, and perhaps to use Polish territory as a potential bargaining chip for the return of Silesia. Finally, in 1772, the three great eastern powers struck a deal. Russia would take a large swath of the grain fields of northeast Poland, which included more than one million people, while Frederick would unite his lands by seizing West Prussia. Austria gained both the largest territories, including Galicia, and the greatest number of people, nearly two million Polish subjects.

In a half century, the balance of power in central Europe had shifted decisively. Prussia's absorption of Silesia and parts of

MAP DISCOVERY

First Partition 1772
- To Prussia
- To Russia
- To Austria
- – – Poland in 1772

Second Partition 1793
- To Prussia
- To Russia
- Poland in 1793

Third Partition 1795
- To Prussia
- To Russia
- To Austria

0   200 Miles
0   200 Kilometers

The Partitions of Poland

Three successive partitions broke apart Poland, which had once been one of the largest states in Europe. Which of the partitions of Poland cede the most land? Notice how Poland's access to the sea was eroded during the partitions. Which country gained the most land overall? In "Map Discovery: The Expansion of Prussia" on p. 561, we examined the growth of Prussia to 1786. What additional territory did Prussia gain in the partitioning of Poland?

colonial affairs, in which secrecy and rapid changes of direction were often the monarch's most potent weapons. The weaknesses came to light most dramatically during the struggle for independence waged by Britain's North American colonists. There the clash of principle and power was most extreme and the strengths and weaknesses of parliamentary rule were ruthlessly exposed.

The British Constitution

The British Constitution was a patchwork of laws and customs that was gradually sewn together to form a workable system of government. At the apex of the government stood the king, not an absolute monarch like his European counterparts, but not necessarily less powerful for having less arbitrary power. The British people revered monarchy and the monarch. The theory of mixed government depended upon the balance of interests represented by the monarchy in the Crown, the aristocracy in the House of Lords, and the people in the House of Commons. Less abstractly, the monarch was still regarded as divinely ordained and a special gift to the nation. The monarch was the actual and symbolic leader of the nation as well as the Supreme Head of the Church of England. Allegiance to the Anglican Church, whether as a political creed among the elite or as a simple matter of devotion among the populace, intensified allegiance to the king.

The partnership between Crown and representative body was best expressed in the idea that the British government was composed of King-in-Parliament. Parliament consisted of three separate organs: monarch, lords, and commons. Although each existed separately as a check upon the potential excesses of the others, it was only when the three functioned together that parliamentary government could operate. The king was charged with selecting ministers, initiating policy, and supervising administration. The two houses of Parliament were charged with raising revenue, making laws, and presenting the grievances of subjects to the Crown.

There were 558 members of the House of Commons after the union with Scotland in 1707. Most members of the lower house were nominated to their seats. The largest number of seats were located in small towns where a local oligarchy, or neighboring patron, had a customary right to make nominations that were invariably accepted by the electorate. Even in the largest cities, influential citizens made arrangements for nominating members in order to avoid the cost and confusion of an actual election. Campaigns were ruinously expensive for the candidates—an election in 1754 cost the losing candidates £40,000—and potentially dangerous to the local community, where bitter social and political divisions boiled just below the surface.

The British gentry dominated the Commons, occupying more than 80 percent of the seats in any session. Most of the members also served as unpaid local officials in the counties, as justices of the peace, captains of the local militias, or collectors of local taxes. They came to Parliament not only as representatives of the interests of their class, but as experienced local governors who understood the needs of both Crown and subject.

Nevertheless, the Crown had to develop methods to coordinate the work of the two houses of Parliament and facilitate the passage of governmental programs. The king and his ministers began to use the deep royal pockets of offices and favors to bolster their friends in Parliament. Despite its potential for abuse, it was a political process that integrated center and locality, and at first it worked rather well. Those with local standing were brought into central offices, where they could influence central policy making while protecting their local constituents. The officeholders, who came to be called *placemen,* never constituted a majority of the members of Parliament. They formed the core around which eighteenth-century governments operated, but it was a core that needed direction and cohesion. It was such leadership and organization that was the essential contribution of eighteenth-century politics to the British Constitution.

Parties and Ministers

Although parliamentary management was vital to the British Crown, it was not the Crown that developed the basic tools of management. Rather, those techniques originated within the political community itself, and their usefulness was only slowly grasped by the monarchy. The first and, in the long term, most important tool was the party system.

Political **parties** initially developed in the late seventeenth century around the issue of the Protestant succession. Those who opposed James II because he was a Catholic attempted to exclude him from inheriting the crown. They came to be called by their opponents **Whigs,** which had come to mean "horse thieves" (the term originally derived from *Wiggamore,* a name for Western Isle Scots who cried "Whig, whig!" to spur their horses on). Those who supported James's hereditary rights but who also supported the Anglican Church came to be called by their opponents **Tories,** which in Gaelic meant "cattle rustlers."

The Tories cooperated in the Revolution of 1688 that placed William and Mary on the throne because James had threatened the Anglican Church by tolerating Catholics and because Mary had a legitimate hereditary right to be queen. After the death of Queen Anne in 1714, the Tories supported the succession of James III, James II's Catholic son, who had been raised in France, rather than of George I (1714–1727), prince of Hanover and Protestant great-grandson of James I. An unsuccessful rebellion to place James III on the throne in 1715 discredited the leadership of the Tory party but did not weaken its importance in both local and parliamentary politics.

The Whigs supported the Protestant succession and a broad-based Protestantism. They attracted the allegiance of large numbers of dissenters, heirs to the Puritans of the seventeenth century who practiced forms of Protestantism different from that of the Anglican Church. The struggle between Whigs and Tories was less a struggle for power than it was for loyalty to their opposing viewpoints. As the Tories opposed the Hanoverian succession and the Whigs supported it, it was no mystery which party would find favor with George I. Moreover, as long as there was a pretender to the British throne—another rebellion took place in Scotland in 1745 led by the grandson of James II—the Tories continued to be tarred with the brush of disloyalty.

The division of political sympathies between Whigs and Tories helped create a set of groupings to which parliamentary leadership could be applied. A national rather than a local or regional outlook could be used to organize support for royal policy as long as royal policy conformed to that national outlook. The ascendancy of the Whigs enabled George I and his son George II (1727–1760) to govern effectively through Parliament, but at the price of dependence upon the Whig leaders. Although the monarch had the constitutional freedom to choose his ministers, realistically he could choose only Whigs, and practically none but the Whig leaders of the House of Commons. Happily for the first two Georges, they found Sir Robert Walpole, who was able to manage Parliament but desired only to serve the Crown.

Sir Robert Walpole (1676–1745) came from a long-established gentry family in Norfolk. Walpole was an early supporter of the Hanoverian succession and an early victim of

The West and the Wider World
THE BRITISH RAJ IN INDIA

In the middle of the eighteenth century, the focus of the British Empire shifted from west to east. Up to that point, Britain had only been a bit player in the scramble for the spice trade and had lost the competition for nearly all of the Caribbean and South American commodities, but it had managed to claim much of the Atlantic seaboard of the inhospitable North American continent. There, English, Scots, and Irish settled colonies and built villages and towns. Thousands and then tens of thousands of Britons had made the transatlantic journey throughout the seventeenth century seeking their fortunes in the wilderness. By the middle of the eighteenth century, British North America was a flourishing society that provided a ready market for manufactured and luxury commodities. Over 25 percent of all British exports went to North America, nearly £1 million by 1740.

By contrast, English ventures in the East had resulted in only one success: the right of the East India Company to trade in India. The Mughal emperors granted this right in the early seventeenth century, as much a slight to the Portuguese as a favor to the English. Here, a classic mercantile venture was established. A few hundred Englishmen were placed in forts that contained warehouses for the accumulation of Asian goods and that kept the Westerners largely segregated from the indigenous population. English trade in India grew slowly. Each year the Company would send its fleet of ships to be laden with the merchandise that had been collected from the hinterland. Purchases were made mostly with bullion that was carried to India by the Company's expedition. Brightly colored cottons called

chintzes, porcelain, woven carpets, spices, and tea were the most highly prized goods, with tea becoming the most profitable by the beginning of the eighteenth century. The English had taken up residence on the east coast of India where they established their largest base at Calcutta, and it was not

■ Oudh watercolor (1782) of British colonial administrator Warren Hastings with a servant. Hastings was the first governor-general of all India, 1773–1784.

long before those who stayed behind became involved in the lucrative trans-Asian trade, especially with China.

Company employees supplemented their meager wages by using their privileged position to exchange Indian goods for Chinese goods. The Indian commodity most prized in China was the drug opium because its production was illegal in China. Other Company members traded with Persia, the great Middle Eastern Empire whose contacts with India went back centuries. In this way, British products like North American tobacco made their way around the globe. Trading on their own accounts while awaiting the arrival of the Company's annual fleet, English merchants in India could make enormous fortunes. If they were lucky enough to survive the perils of Eastern climes and diseases they could return to Britain as wealthy men, "nabobs" in eighteenth-century parlance, belittled for the source of their wealth but tolerated for its quantity.

The British went to India to trade and stayed to rule. The Raj (a Hindi word for kingdom) came about accidentally and by degrees. At the beginning no one would have thought that India could have been conquered and few thought that it could be ruled. It was governed throughout the seventeenth century by the Mughals, Persians who had fled marauding Afghans and who had slowly expanded their power until they established a capital at Agra, where one of their emperors built a palace for his wife known ever after as the Taj Mahal. The Mughals created a magnificent court and were protected by an efficiently trained army. In the areas that they controlled directly they extracted a tax on land—the dirwani—from the entire peasant population. But their hold over the South Asian subcontinent was precarious and ever shifting. Most of India was ruled by independent princes known as nawabs. They paid a cash tribute to the Mughals when they had to but otherwise fiercely guarded their independence. The East India Company was treated similarly. They had been granted trading rights in return for an annual payment, but unlike the nawabs they had no incentive to weaken Mughal power.

This arrangement worked smoothly until the 1760s. By then the India trade had become essential to the English economy and the number of Englishmen living in Company forts in Bengal had grown to number in the thousands. To protect their large investment and their teeming warehouses, the Company employed former British military officers and soldiers and equipped them with the latest armaments. Not surprisingly, Company leaders were drawn into local disputes where their power was often decisive. As Mughal influence declined, British prestige rose and inevitably a clash occurred. It began not between the British and the Indians, but between the British and the French, the other European nation with a strong presence in India. Wars in Europe that pitted Britain against France expanded to become world wars throughout their colonial empires.

In India it was the military brilliance of a young cavalry officer, Robert Clive, that eventually led to British dominance and the expulsion of the French in the 1760s. Clive was simply an employee of the East India Company and not an agent of the British government. His actions were designed to protect the Company's trading factories—the French had captured Madras in the 1740s—and defend its employees. But British successes made the Mughals wary. In 1756 Mughal forces besieged and captured Calcutta, the most important British trading settlement. The city's governor fled the town and those officials captured by the Mughals were imprisoned in the local jail known descriptively as the Black Hole. The imprisonment of Englishmen in the Black Hole of Calcutta demanded retribution, and Clive inflicted it. Not only did his

■ In this painting by Edward Penny (1773), Robert Clive is shown receiving a grant from a nawab of Bengal.

forces recapture Calcutta, but Clive also connived to oust the Mughal emperor and have him replaced by a rival willing to reconfirm all of Britain's trading rights and also to grant it political control over the province of Bengal. As if he were a local ruler, Clive was offered the dirwani—the right to collect local taxes from the entire population. It was an offer he could not refuse.

It was also the most poisoned of all chalices for the British. Quickly and inevitably the East India Company was drawn into governing Bengal and soon other provinces of India as well. The yield from the dirwani changed the balance of trade in Asia dramatically. Now it was the British who were exporting bullion and creating a drain on the local Indian economy. On the other hand, the Company needed to send thousands of

administrators east to protect their rights and to offer government to the tangle of feuding religious, ethnic, and class interests. Shares of the Company's stock declined while the cost of administering an Empire rose. After the American War of Independence, it was in India that British imperial interest and efforts were focused, forging a relationship quite different than the trading partnership with which it had begun.

QUESTIONS FOR DISCUSSION

What was Britain's initial interest in India? What European nation challenged this interest? How did the British East India Company come to rule the province of Bengal and other Indian provinces? How did these developments change Britain's relationship with India?

571

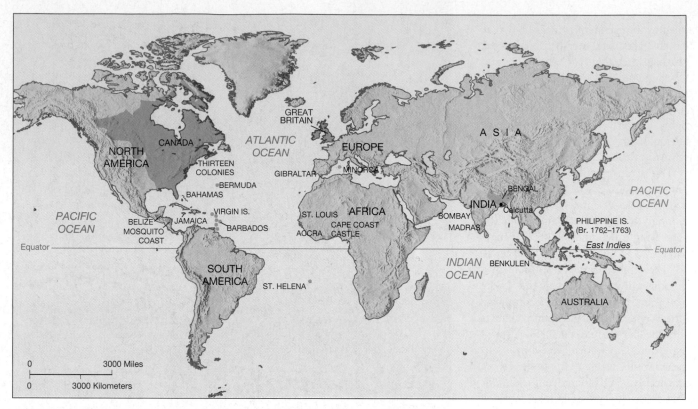

■ The First British Empire (ca. 1763). The empire was the result of commercial enterprise and Britain's military successes.

party warfare. But once George I was securely on the throne, Walpole became an indispensable leader of the House of Commons. His success rested upon his extraordinary abilities: he was an excellent public speaker, he relished long working days and the details of government, and he understood better than anyone else the intricacies of state finance. Walpole became First Lord of the Treasury, a post that he transformed into first minister of state. From his treasury post, Walpole assiduously built a Whig parliamentary party. He carefully dispensed jobs and offices, using them as bait to lure parliamentary supporters. Walpole's organization paid off both in the passage of legislation desired by the Crown and at the polls, where Whigs were returned to Parliament time and again.

From 1721 to 1742, Walpole was the most powerful man in the British government. He refused an offer of a peerage so that he could continue to lead the House of Commons. He brought a measure of fiscal responsibility to government by establishing a fund to pay off the national debt. In foreign policy he pursued peace with the same fervor that both his predecessors and successors pursued war. The long years of peace brought prosperity to both the landed and merchant classes, but they also brought criticism of Walpole's methods. The way in which he used government patronage to build his parliamentary party was attacked as corruption. So, too, were the ways in which the pockets of Whig officeholders were lined. During his last decade in office, Walpole struggled to survive. His attempt to extend the excise tax on colonial goods nearly led to his loss of office in 1733. His refusal to respond to the clamor for continued war with Spain in 1741 finally led to his downfall.

Walpole's 20-year rule established the pattern of parliamentary government. The Crown needed a "prime" minister who was able to steer legislation through the House of Commons. It also needed a patronage broker who could take control of the treasury and dispense its largess in return for parliamentary backing. Walpole's personality and talents had combined the two roles. Thereafter they were divided. Those who had grown up under Walpole had learned their lessons well. The Whig monopoly of power continued unchallenged for nearly another 20 years. The patronage network Walpole had created was vastly extended by his Whig successors. Even minor posts in the customs or the excise offices were now exchanged for political favor, and only those approved by the Whig leadership could claim them. The cries of corruption grew louder not only in the country houses of the long-disfranchised Tories, but in the streets of London, where a popular radicalism developed in opposition to the Whig oligarchy. They were taken up as well in the North American colonies, where two million British subjects champed at the bit of imperial rule.

America Revolts

Britain's triumph in the Seven Years' War (1756–1763) had come at great financial cost to the nation. At the beginning of the eighteenth century, the national debt stood at £14 million; by 1763, it had risen to £130 million, despite the fact that Walpole's government had been paying off some of it. Then, as now, the cost of world domination was staggering. George III (1760–1820) came to the throne with a taste for reform and a desire to break the Whig stranglehold on government. He was to have limited success on both counts, though not for want of trying. In 1763, the king and his ministers agreed that reform of colonial administration was long overdue. Such reform would have the twin benefit of shifting part of the burden of taxation from Britain to North America and of making the commercial side of colonization pay.

That was sound thinking all around, and in due course Parliament passed a series of duties on goods imported into the colonies, including glass, wine, coffee, tea, and, most notably, sugar. The so-called Sugar Act (1764) was followed by the Stamp Act (1765), a tax on printed papers such as newspapers, deeds,

■ In Britain's North American colonies, public sentiment against the importation of tea and other taxed British goods often found expression in a coat of tar and feathers applied to the bare skin of the offending importer. Note the symbols in *The Bostonians Paying the Excise-Man:* the Liberty Tree from which dangles a hangman's noose and the overturned copy of the Stamp Act. In the background, Bostonians dump chests of tea into the harbor.

The BOSTONIAN'S Paying the EXCISE-MAN, or TARRING & FEATHERING

CHRONOLOGY
THE NEW EUROPEAN POWERS

1707	England and Scotland unite to form Great Britain
1713–1714	Peace of Utrecht ends War of the Spanish Succession (1702–1714)
1714	British crown passes to House of Hanover
1721	Treaty of Nystad ends Great Northern War (1700–1721)
1721–1742	Sir Robert Walpole leads British House of Commons
1722	Peter the Great of Russia creates Table of Ranks
1740	Frederick the Great of Prussia invades Austrian province of Silesia
1748	Treaty of Aix-la-Chapelle ends War of the Austrian Succession (1740–1748)
1756–1763	Seven Years' War pits Prussia and Britain against Austria, France, and Russia
1773–1775	Pugachev's revolt in Russia
1774	Boston Tea Party
1775	American Revolution begins
1785	Catherine the Great of Russia issues Charter of the Nobility

and court documents. Both acts imposed taxes in the colonies similar to those that already existed in Britain. Accompanying the acts were administrative orders designed to cut into the lucrative black market trade. The government instituted new rules for searching ships and transferred authority over smuggling from the local colonial courts to Britain's Admiralty courts. Although British officials could only guess at the value of the new duties imposed, it was believed that with effective enforcement £150,000 would be raised. All that would go to pay the vastly greater costs of colonial administration and security.

British officials were more than perplexed when the mild measures met with a ferocious response. Assemblies of nearly every colony officially protested the Sugar Act. They sent petitions to Parliament begging for repeal and warning of dire economic and political consequences. Riots followed passage of the Stamp Act. Tax collectors were hounded out of office, their resignations precipitated by threats and acts of physical violence. In Massachusetts, mobs that included political leaders in

UNALIENABLE RIGHTS

The Declaration of Independence, written by Thomas Jefferson (1776), succinctly summarized the principles on which the American colonists were to build a new form of democratic government.

Focus Questions
Why is it a "duty" to oppose an oppressive government?
What is the purpose of government?

We hold these truths to be self-evident, that all men are created equal, that they are endowed by their Creator with certain unalienable Rights, that among these are Life, Liberty, and the pursuit of Happiness. That to secure these rights, Governments are instituted among Men, deriving their just powers from the consent of the governed. That whenever any Form of Government becomes destructive of these ends, it is the Right of the People to alter or to abolish it, and to institute new Government, laying its foundation on such principles and organizing its powers in such form, as to them shall seem most likely to effect their Saftey and Happiness. Prudence, indeed, will dictate that Governments long established should not be changed for light and transient causes; and accordingly all experience hath shown that mankind are more disposed to suffer, while evils are sufferable, that to right themselves by abolishing the forms to which they evinces a design to reduce them under absolute Despotism, it is their right, it is their duty, to throw off such Government, and to provide new Guards for their future security

From The Declaration of Independence

---

the colony razed the homes of the collector and the lieutenant-governor. However much the colonists might have regretted the violence that was done, they believed that an essential political principle was at stake. It was a principle of the freedom of an Englishman.

At their core, the protests of the American colonists underscored the vitality of the British political system. The Americans argued that they could not be taxed without their consent and that their consent could come only through representation in Parliament. Since there were no colonists in Parliament, Parliament had no jurisdiction over the property of the colonists. Taxation without representation was tyranny. There were a number of subtleties to the argument that were quickly lost as political rhetoric and political action heated up. In the first place, the colonists did tax themselves through their own legislatures, and much of that money paid the costs of administration and defense. Second, as a number of pamphleteers pointed out, no one in the colonies had asked the British government to send regiments of the army into North America. The colonists had little reason to put their faith in British protection. Hard-fought colonial victories were tossed away at European negotiating tables, while the British policy of defending Indian rights in the Ohio Valley ran counter to the interests of the settlers. When defense was necessary, the colonists had proved themselves both able and cooperative in providing it. A permanent tax meant a permanent army, and a standing army was as loathed in Britain as it was in the colonies.

In opposing the Stamp Act, colonists also tried to draw a distinction between internal and external taxation. They deemed regulation of overseas commerce a legitimate power of Parliament but argued that the regulation of internal exchange was not. But that distinction was lost once the issue of parliamentary representation was raised. If the colonists had not consented to British taxation, then it made no difference whether taxation was internal or external. The passion generated in the colonies was probably no greater than that generated in Britain. The British government also saw the confrontation as a matter of principle, but for Britain the principle was parliamentary sovereignty. That, above all, was the rock upon which the British Constitution had been built over the previous century. Parliament had entered into a partnership with the Crown. The Crown had surrendered—willingly or not—many of its prerogatives. In return, Parliament had bound the people to obedience. There were well-established means by which British subjects could petition Parliament for redress of grievances against the monarch, but there were no channels by which they could question the sovereignty of Parliament.

Once the terms of debate had been so defined, it was difficult for either side to find a middle ground. Parliamentary moderates managed repeal of the Stamp Act and most of the clauses of the Sugar Act, but they also joined in passing the **Declaratory Act** (1766), which stated unequivocally that Parliament held sovereign jurisdiction over the colonies "in all cases whatsoever." That was a claim that became more and more difficult to sustain as colonial leaders began to cite the elements of resistance theory that had justified the Revolution of 1688. Then the protest had been against the tyranny of the king; the new protest was against the tyranny of Parliament. American propagandists claimed that a conspiracy existed to deprive the colonists of their property and rights and to enslave them for the benefit of special interests and corrupt politicians.

The techniques of London radicals who opposed parliamentary policy were imported into the colonies. Newspapers were used to whip up public support; boycotts brought ordinary people into the political arena; public demonstrations such as the Boston Tea Party (1774) were carefully designed to intimidate; mobs were occasionally given free rein. Although the government had faced down those tactics when they were used in London to support John Wilkes (1725–1797), an ardent critic of royal policy, they were less successful when the crisis lay an ocean away. When, in 1770, British troops fired on a Boston mob, American propagandists were provided with empirical evidence that Britain intended to enslave the colonies. Violence was met by violence, passion by passion. In 1775, full-scale fighting was under way. Eight years later, Britain withdrew from a war it could not win, and the American colonies were left to govern themselves.

CONCLUSION

By the end of the third quarter of the eighteenth century, Europe had a new political configuration. A continent once dominated by a single power—Spain in the sixteenth century and France in the seventeenth—was now dominated by a state system in which alliances among several great powers held the balance. Despite the loss of its American colonies, Great Britain had proved the most potent of the states. Its victories over the French in the Seven Years' War and over France and Prussia in the War of the Austrian Succession secured its position. But it was a position that could be maintained only through alliances with the German states, with either Prussia or Austria. The rise of Prussia provided a counterweight to French domination of the Continent. Although those two states became allies in the middle of the century, the ambitions of their rulers made them natural enemies, and it would not be long before French and Prussian armies were again pitted against each other. France, still the wealthiest and most populous of European states, had slumbered through the eighteenth-century reorganization. The legacies of Louis XIV took a long time to reach fruition. He had claimed glory for his state, giving the French people a sense of national identity and national destiny, but making them pay an enormous price in social and economic dislocation. Thus the mid-eighteenth century was to be an age of the greatest literary and philosophical achievement for France, but the late eighteenth century was to be an age of the greatest social upheaval that Europe had ever known.

QUESTIONS FOR REVIEW

1. What were the great powers of Europe in the eighteenth century, and in what ways was there a "balance of power" among them?
2. What did Peter I and Catherine II of Russia accomplish during their reigns that justifies the title "the great"?
3. How was the tiny state of Brandenburg-Prussia able to make itself into one of Europe's major powers, and what did that mean for the Austrian Empire?
4. How did Britain's theory of mixed government and its parliamentary party system assist its rise to become Europe's great imperial power?
5. How and why did the "balance of power" shift during the eighteenth century?

KEY TERMS

Declaratory Act, *p. 574*

parties, *p. 569*

Pragmatic Sanction, *p. 563*

Table of Ranks, *p. 557*

Tories, *p. 569*

Whigs, *p. 569*

DISCOVERING WESTERN CIVILIZATION ONLINE

You can obtain more information about the balance of power in eighteenth-century Europe at the Websites listed below. See also the Companion Website that accompanies this text, www.ablongman.com/kishlansky, which contains an online study guide and additional resources.

The Rise of Russia

Russia

www.english.upenn.edu/~jlynch/FrankenDemo/Places/russia.html
A site detailing the history of Russia from the time of Peter the Great. Links to the building of St. Petersburg.

Modern History Sourcebook: Catherine the Great
www.fordham.edu/halsall/mod/18catherine.html
Sources from the reign of Catherine the Great.

The Two Germanies

Friedrich II, the Great (1712–1786)

www.hfac.uh.edu/gbrown/philosophers/leibniz/Friedrich Great/FriedrichGreat.html
A hyper-linked biographical essay on Frederick the Great of Prussia.

The Greatness of Great Britain

The American Revolution
www.revolution.h-net.msu.edu/
A site with extensive links to all aspects of the American Revolution.

Declaring Independence: Drafting the Documents
www.loc.gov/exhibits/declara/declara1.html
An online exhibit at the Library of Congress on the drafting of the Declaration of Independence.

SUGGESTIONS FOR FURTHER READING

General Reading

M. S. Anderson, *Europe in the Eighteenth Century, 1713–1783*, 3d ed. (London: Longman, 1987). A country-by-country survey of political developments.

Jeremy Black, *Europe and the World 1650–1830* (New York: Routledge, 2002). An intelligent survey of Europe in a wider perspective.

David Kirby, *Northern Europe in the Early Modern Period* (London: Longman, 1991). Political history from a Baltic perspective, with excellent chapters on Sweden and Russia.

Nicholas Riasanovsky, *A History of Russia* (New York: Oxford University Press, 1993). The best one-volume history of Russia.

Geographical Tour: Europe in 1714

Derek McKay and H. M. Scott, *The Rise of the Great Powers* (London: Longman, 1983). An outstanding survey of diplomacy and warfare.

The Rise of Russia

John T. Alexander, *Catherine the Great: Life and Legend* (Oxford: Oxford University Press, 1989). A lively account of the public and private life of the Russian Empress.

M. S. Anderson, *Peter the Great* (London: Thames and Hudson, 1978). A well-constructed, comprehensive biography.

Paul Dukes, *The Making of Russian Absolutism, 1613–1801* (London: Longman, 1982). An extensive survey of the Russian monarchy in its greatest period.

Lindsey Hughes, *Russia in the Age of Peter the Great* (New Haven: Yale University Press, 1998). A detailed, thematically organized reappraisal of Russia in the era of Peter's reign.

The Two Germanies

Reed S. Browning, *The War of the Austrian Succession* (London: Macmillan, 1995). A comprehensive history of a complicated event.

David Fraser, *Frederick the Great: King of Prussia* (New York: Allen Lane, 2001). The latest biography.

J. Gagliardo, *Germany Under the Old Regime* (London: Longman, 1991). The best single-volume history.

H. W. Koch, *A History of Prussia* (London: Longman, 1978). A study of the factors that led to Prussian dominance of Germany.

C. A. Macartney, *Maria Theresa and the House of Austria* (Mystic, CT: Verry Inc., 1969). Still the best introductory study.

The Greatness of Great Britain

Bernard Bailyn, *The Ideological Origins of the American Revolution* (Cambridge, MA: Harvard University Press, 1967). A brilliant interpretation of the underlying causes of the break between Britain and the North American colonies.

Jeremy Black, *Britain as a Military Power* (London: UCL Press, 1999). A reliable survey of military developments in Britain.

John Brewer, *The Sinews of Power: War, Money, and the English State, 1688–1783* (Cambridge, MA: Harvard University Press, 1990). An influential and clearly written book on the fiscal and military innovations that underwrote English power in the eighteenth century.

J. C. D. Clark, *English Society, 1688–1832* (Cambridge: Cambridge University Press, 1985). A bold reinterpretation of the most important features of English society.

Linda Colley, *Britons* (New Haven, CT: Yale University Press, 1992). A lively account of how a nation was forged from Welsh, Scots, and English and how unity and diversity intermixed.

Paul Langford, *A Polite and Commercial People: England 1727–1783* (Oxford: Oxford University Press, 1989). The standard survey in the Oxford history series.

Gordon Wood, *The Radicalism of the American Revolution* (New York: Alfred A. Knopf, 1992). How the ideals of the American Revolution shaped an emerging nation.

For a list of additional titles related to this chapter's topics, please see http://www.ablongman.com/kishlansky.

Chapter 19

CULTURE AND SOCIETY IN EIGHTEENTH-CENTURY EUROPE

Chapter Outline

The middle classes, the *bourgeoisie* in French, emerged in the eighteenth century. Many shared the enlightened ideas of the upper classes and participated in public debate. But they valued their domestic life as much as their public achievements. Sentiment, politeness, and romance were the watchwords of the day. Turn the page to The Visual Record to see a painting that captures such feelings. ➤

HAPPY FAMILIES

An Enlightenment Institution

"Happy families are all alike," wrote Lev Tolstoy in the nineteenth century when the idea of a happy family was already a cliché. Such an idea would never have occurred to his eighteenth-century forebears. For them the happy family was new. Personal happiness was an invention of the Enlightenment, the result of novel attitudes about human aspirations and human capabilities. "Happiness is a new idea in Europe," wrote Louis de Saint-Just (1767–1794). It emerged in response to the belief that what was good brought pleasure and what was evil brought pain. Happiness, both individual and collective, became the yardstick by which life was measured. That meant a reorientation in personal conduct and, most of all, a reorientation of family life. Especially for those with an economic cushion, a pleasurable family life became essential. Husbands and wives were to be companions, filled with romantic love for each other and devoted to domestic bliss. Children, the product of their affection, were to be doted on, treated not as miniature adults to be lectured and beaten, but as unfilled vessels into which was poured all that was good.

Were ever a couple more in love than the husband and wife depicted in *A Visit to the Wet Nurse* by Jean-Honoré Fragonard (1732–1806)? In the painting, the man clasps his wife's arm to his cheek, she lays her hand on his shoulder. Their sighs are almost audible! Together they admire the fruit of their love, the baby asleep in the cradle. It is hard to guess which parent dotes more, the mother with her rapturous expression or the father with his intensity as he kneels on a cushion in almost religious devotion, his hands folded as if in prayer. Who would doubt their companionship or their love for their babe? They have come together to see how the wet nurse is caring for their child.

At the beginning of the eighteenth century, the use of a wet nurse was still common among the families of the French bourgeoisie, the class to which the couple pictured belonged. As time passed, however, more and more families began to keep their children at home and more mothers began to nurse their babies themselves. In part this change was a response to the higher mortality rate among infants sent out to wet nurses. But a wet nurse who could be supervised, that is, one who lived near enough to be visited, but far enough away from the town

to enjoy wholesome air, might be the best of both worlds. That is just what the couple here found, and in the picture they come, with their other child (the boy in the hat), to see their baby sleeping peacefully, the wet nurse sitting attentively at the infant's side.

But there are two families in this picture, and they are hardly alike. At first glance, the wet nurse looks like an old woman, perhaps even an aging nanny. She sits with her distaff in her hand, for the arrival of her clients has interrupted her spinning. It is shocking to realize that she cannot be much older than 30, an age beyond which wealthy families would not hire her for fear either that she would not have much milk or that it would be sour. The two younger children on the far right are undoubtedly hers, the youngest probably just weaned so that all of the milk would go to the baby. No adoring husband sits beside the wet nurse. Her husband, if he is still alive, is hard at work with no leisure time for visits to the country. Not only does the wet nurse have to sell her milk, but she also spins, to keep her family clothed and to earn a little extra to put away for hard times.

The newest fads of the age have passed her family by. While the child in the cradle will be spoiled by toys manufactured especially for children—puzzles, games, rocking horses, and balls—the children of the wet nurse must make do with household objects and their own imaginations. A ball of yarn thrown to the cat helps the elder child while away the hours.

Looking Ahead

Like much else in the eighteenth century, the world of the family was divided between high and low. As we shall see in this chapter, it was developments in the middle that were most characteristic of eighteenth-century social and cultural developments. The spirit of Enlightenment was spreading from the elites throughout all social ranks, improving education, health, and social welfare. The rapid growth of the bourgeoisie, or the middle class, enhanced the quality of life for tens of thousands and transformed values in the most basic institutions of society. ➤

■ Jean-Honoré Fragonard, *A Visit to the Wet Nurse.*

EIGHTEENTH-CENTURY CULTURE

The eighteenth century spawned a rich and costly culture. Decorative architecture, especially interior design, reflected the increasing sociability of the aristocracy. Entertainment became a central part of aristocratic life, losing its previous formality. Music became a cultural passion. The string quartet made its first appearance in the eighteenth century, and chamber music enjoyed unparalleled popularity. Only the wealthiest could afford to stage private operas, the other musical passion of the age. The Esterhazys of Hungary employed 22 musicians and a conductor, who for most of the late eighteenth century was Joseph Haydn (1732–1809), the father of the modern symphony. Haydn's post was not an honorary one. In addition to hiring and managing the orchestra, he was expected to direct two operas and two concerts a week, as well as the music for Sunday services. An aristocratic patron was essential for the aspiring composer. If he could not find one or if, like Wolfgang Amadeus Mozart (1756–1791), he could not bend his will to one, he could not flourish. While Haydn lived comfortably in a palace, Mozart, probably the greatest musical genius in Western history, lived impoverished in a garret and died at age 35 from lack of medical attention.

Musical entertainments in European country houses were matched by the literary and philosophical entertainments of the urban **salons.** Papers on scientific and literary subjects were read at gala dinner parties and discussed with great seriousness in drawing rooms. In the salons, most of which were organized by the wives and daughters of the nobility, were to be found the most influential thinkers of the day presenting the ideas of the **Enlightenment,** a new European outlook on religion, society, and politics.

The Enlightenment

The Enlightenment was less a set of ideas than it was a set of attitudes. At its core was criticism, a questioning of traditional institutions, customs, and morals. In 1762, the French philosopher Jean-Jacques Rousseau (1712–1778) published one of the most important works on social theory, *The Social Contract,* which opened with the gripping maxim, "Man is born free and everywhere he is in chains." But most of the great thinkers of the Enlightenment were not so much philosophers as savants, knowledgeable popularizers whose skills were in simplifying and publicizing a hodgepodge of new views.

In France, Enlightenment intellectuals were called **philosophes** and claimed all the arts and sciences as their purview. The *Encyclopedia* (35 volumes, 1751–1780), edited by Denis Diderot (1713–1784), was one of the greatest achievements of the age. Titled *Systematic Dictionary of the Sciences, Arts, and Crafts,* it attempted to summarize all acquired knowledge and to dispel all imposed superstitions. There was no better definition of a philosophe than that given them by one of their enemies: "Just what is a philosophe? A kind of monster in society who feels under no obligation towards its manners and morals, its proprieties, its politics, or its religion. One may expect anything from men of their ilk."

The influence of French counterculture on enlightened thought was great, but the Enlightenment was by no means a strictly French phenomenon. Its greatest figures included the

■ Painting of the Mozart family by Johann Nepomuk della Croce, ca. 1781. Wolfgang Amadeus Mozart plays the harpsichord, accompanied by his father Leopold and his sister Nannerl. As a boy, Mozart won great ovations on concert tours throughout Europe and persistently challenged authority.

■ During the Enlightenment, salons showcased the most influential thinkers of the day. Here, a lecture is being given at the house of Madame Geoffrin.

THE ALL-KNOWING

The Encyclopedia *was one of the great collaborative ventures of the new spirit of reason that so characterized the Enlightenment. Following is the* Encyclopedia's *entry on itself, the purpose of compiling human knowledge in book form.*

Focus Questions

What is the purpose of an encyclopedia according to Diderot? Why can an encyclopedia only be attempted in a "philosophical" age, and what kind of age is that?

Encyclopedia . . . in truth, the aim of an *encyclopedia* is to collect all the knowledge scattered over the face of the earth, to present its general outlines and structure to the men with whom we live, and to transmit this to those who will come after us, so that the work of past centuries may be useful to the following centuries, that our children, by becoming more educated, may at the same time become more virtuous and happier, and that we may not die without having deserved well of the human race. . . .

I have said that it could only belong to a philosophical age to attempt an *encyclopedia;* and I have said this because such a work constantly demands more intellectual daring than is commonly found in [less courageous periods]. All things must be examined, debated, investigated without exception and without regard for anyone's feelings. . . . We must ride roughshod over all these ancient puerilities, overturn the barriers that reason never erected, give back to the arts and sciences the liberty that is so precious to them. . . . We have for quite some time needed a reasoning age when men would no longer seek the rules in classical authors but in nature. . . .

From Denis Diderot, *Encyclopedia* (1751–1772).

Scottish economist Adam Smith (1723–1790), the Italian legal reformer Cesare Beccaria (1738–1794), and the German philosopher Immanuel Kant (1724–1804). In France, it began among anti-establishment critics; in Scotland and the German states, it flourished in the universities; in Prussia, Austria, and Russia, it was propagated by the monarchy. The Enlightenment began in the 1730s and was still going strong a half century later when its attitudes had been absorbed into the mainstream of European thought.

DOCUMENT

Kant, *What Is Enlightenment*

No brief summary can do justice to the diversity of enlightened thought in eighteenth-century Europe. Because it was an attitude of mind rather than a set of shared beliefs, there are many contradictory strains to follow. In his famous essay *What Is Enlightenment?* (1784), Immanuel Kant described it simply as freedom to use one's own intelligence. "I hear people clamor on all sides: Don't argue! The officer says: Don't argue, drill! The tax collector says: Don't argue, pay. The pastor says: Don't argue, believe." To all of them Kant replied: "Dare to know! Have the courage to use your own intelligence."

The Spirit of the Enlightenment

In 1734, there appeared in France a small book titled *Philosophical Letters Concerning the English Nation*. Its author, Voltaire (1694–1778), had spent two years in Britain, and while there he had made it his business to study the differences between the peoples of the two nations. In a simple but forceful style, Voltaire demonstrated time and again the superiority of the British. They practiced religious toleration and were not held under the sway of a venal clergy. They valued people for their merits rather than their birth. Their political constitution

was a marvel: "The English nation is the only one on earth that has succeeded in controlling the power of kings by resisting them." They made national heroes of their scientists, poets, and philosophers. In all of this, Voltaire contrasted British virtue with French vice. He attacked the French clergy and nobility directly, the French monarchy implicitly. Not only did he praise the genius and accomplishments of Sir Isaac Newton above those of René Descartes, but he also graphically contrasted the Catholic Church's persecution of Descartes with the British state's celebration of Newton. "England, where men think free and noble thoughts," Voltaire enthused.

Voltaire.   It is difficult to recapture the psychological impact that the *Philosophical Letters* had on the generation of educated Frenchmen who first read them. The book was officially banned and publicly burned, and a warrant was issued for Voltaire's arrest. The *Letters* dropped like a bombshell upon the moribund intellectual culture of the Church and the universities and burst open the complacent, self-satisfied Cartesian worldview. The book ignited in France a movement that would soon be found in nearly every corner of Europe.

DOCUMENT

Voltaire on Relations Between Church and State

Born in Paris in 1694 into a bourgeois family with court office, François-Marie Arouet, who later took the pen name Voltaire, was educated by the Jesuits, who encouraged his poetic talents and instilled in him an enduring love of literature. He was a difficult student, especially as he had already rejected the core of the Jesuits' religious doctrine. He was no less difficult as he grew older and began a career as a poet and playwright. It was not long before he was imprisoned in the Bastille for penning verses that maligned the honor of the regent of France. Released from prison, he insulted a nobleman,

---

THE HUMAN CONDITION

More than anyone else, Voltaire symbolized the new thinking of the Enlightenment. Witty, ironic, irreverent, and penetrating, his writings provoked howls of protest and squeals of delight. Among the most widely read was his philosophical dictionary, from which this definition of evil is drawn.

Focus Questions

How does Voltaire prove that humans are not born evil? What implications could Voltaire's opinions have for contemporary religious and political beliefs?

People clamor that human nature is essentially perverse, that man is born the child of the devil, and of evil. Nothing is more ill-advised; for, my friend, in preaching at me that everybody is born perverse, you warn me that you were born that way, that I must distrust you as I would a fox or a crocodile. . . . It would be much more reasonable, much nobler, to say to me: "You were all born good; see how

frightful it would be to corrupt the purity of your being." We should treat mankind as we should treat all men individually. . . .

Man is not born evil; he becomes evil, as he becomes sick. . . . Gather together all the children of the universe; you will see in them nothing but innocence, gentleness, and fear. . . .

If men were essentially evil, if they were all born the subjects of a being as malevolent as it is unhappy, who inspired them with all this frenzy to avenge his own torment, we would see husbands murdered by their wives, and fathers by their children every morning. . . .

From Voltaire, *The Philosophical Dictionary* (1764).

F. M. AROUET DE VOLTAIRE.

■ Decorative portrait of Voltaire. The most famous of the *philosophes*, Voltaire sought to reinvent the universe of knowledge.

she undertook the immense challenge of translating Newton into French, Voltaire worked on innumerable projects: poems, plays, philosophical and antireligious tracts (which she wisely kept him from publishing), and histories. It was one of the most productive periods of his life, and when the Marquise du Châtelet died in 1749, Voltaire was crushed.

Then older than 50, Voltaire began his travels. He was invited to Berlin by Frederick the Great, who admired him most of all the intellectuals of the age. The relationship between the two great egotists was predictably stormy and resulted in Voltaire's arrest in Frankfurt. Finally allowed to leave Prussia, Voltaire eventually settled in Geneva, where he quickly became embroiled in local politics and was none too politely asked to leave. He was tired of wandering and tired of being chased. His youthful gaiety and high spirits, which remained in Voltaire long past youth, were dealt a serious blow by the tragic earthquake in Lisbon in 1755, when thousands of people attending church services were killed.

Optimism in the face of such a senseless tragedy was no longer possible. His black mood was revealed in *Candide* (1759), which was to become his enduring legacy. *Candide* introduced the ivory-tower intellectual Dr. Pangloss, the overly optimistic Candide, and the very practical philosophy, "We must cultivate our own garden." It was Voltaire's capacity to challenge all authority that was probably his greatest contribution to Enlightenment attitudes. He held nothing sacred. He questioned his own paternity and the morals of his mother; he lived openly with the Marquise du Châtelet and her husband; and he spoke as slightingly of kings and aristocrats as he did of his numerous critics. At the height of the French Revolution, Voltaire's body was removed from its resting place in Champagne and taken in great pomp to Paris, where it was interred in the Panthéon, where the heroes of the nation were put to rest. "Voltaire taught us to be free" was the slogan that the Parisian masses chanted during the funeral procession. It was an ending perhaps too solemn and conventional for one as irreverent as Voltaire. When the monarchy was restored after 1815, his bones were unceremoniously dumped into a lime pit.

Hume.   Some enlightened thinkers based their critical outlook on skepticism, the belief that nothing could be known for certain. When the Scottish philosopher David Hume (1711–1776) was accused of being an atheist, he countered the charge by saying he was too skeptical to be certain that God did not exist. Hume's first major philosophical work, *A Treatise of Human Nature* (1739), made absolutely no impression upon his contemporaries. For a time he took a post as a merchant's clerk, then he served as a tutor, and finally he found a position as a private secretary. During the course of his various employments he continued to write, publishing a series of essays on the subject of morality and rewriting his treatise into *An Enquiry Concerning Human Understanding* (1748), his greatest philosophical work.

Hume made two seminal contributions to Enlightenment thought. He exploded the synthesis of Descartes by arguing

who retaliated by having his servants publicly beat Voltaire. Voltaire issued a challenge for a duel, a greater insult than the first, given his low birth. Again he was sent to the Bastille and was only released on the promise that he would leave the country immediately.

Thus Voltaire found himself in Britain, where he spent two years learning English, writing plays, and enjoying his celebrity free from the dangers that celebrity entailed in France. When he returned to Paris in 1728, it was with the intention of popularizing Britain to Frenchmen. He wrote and produced a number of plays and began writing the *Philosophical Letters,* a work that not only secured his reputation but also forced him into exile at the village of Cirey, where he moved in with the Marquise du Châtelet (1706–1749).

The Marquise du Châtelet, though only 27 at the time of her liaison with Voltaire, was one of the leading advocates of Newtonian science in France. She built a laboratory in her home and introduced Voltaire to experimental science. While

■ Scottish philosopher David Hume argued that neither matter nor mind could be proved to exist with any certainty.

that neither matter nor mind could be proved to exist with any certainty. He believed that only perceptions existed, either as impressions of material objects or as ideas and if human understanding was based on sensory perception rather than on reason, then there could be no certainty in the universe. Hume's second point launched a frontal attack upon established religion: if there could be no certainty, then the revealed truths of Christian religion could have no basis. In his historical analysis of the origins of religion, Hume argued that "religion grows out of hope or fear." He attacked the core of Christian explanations based on either Providence or miracles by arguing that to anyone who understood the basis of human perception it would take a miracle to believe in miracles.

Montesquieu.   In 1749, Hume received in the mail a work from an admiring Frenchman, titled *The Spirit of the Laws.* The sender was Charles-Louis de Secondat, Baron Montesquieu (1689–1755). Born in Bordeaux, he ultimately inherited both a large landed estate and the office of president of the Parlement of Bordeaux. His novel *Persian Letters* (1721)

was a brilliant satire of Parisian morals, French society, and European religion all bound together by the story of a Persian despot who leaves his harem to learn about the ways of the world. The use of the Persian outsider allowed Montesquieu to comment on the absurdity of European customs in general and French practices in particular. The device of the harem allowed him to titillate his audience with exotic sexuality.

After that success, Montesquieu decided to sell his office and make the grand tour. He spent nearly two years in England, for which, like Voltaire, he came to have the greatest admiration. Back in Bordeaux, Montesquieu began to assemble his thoughts for what he believed would be a great work of political theory. The two societies that he most admired were ancient Rome and the then present-day Britain, and he studied the forms of their government and the principles that animated them. *The Spirit of the Laws* was published in 1748, and despite its gargantuan size and densely packed examples, it was immediately recognized as a masterpiece. Catherine the Great of Russia kept it at her bedside, and it was the single most influential work for the framers of the United States Constitution.

In both *Persian Letters* and *The Spirit of the Laws* Montesquieu explored how liberty could be achieved and despotism avoided. He divided all forms of government into republics, monarchies, and despotisms. Each form had its own peculiar spirit: virtue and moderation in republics, honor in monarchies, and fear in despotisms. Like each form, each spirit was prone to abuse and had to be restrained if republics were not to give way to vice and excess, monarchies to corruption, and despotisms to repression. Montesquieu classified regimes as either moderate or immoderate, and through the use of extensive historical examples attempted to demonstrate how moderation could be maintained through rules and restraints, through the spirit of the law.

For Montesquieu, a successful government was one in which powers were separated and checks and balances existed within the institutions of the state. As befit a provincial magistrate, he insisted on the absolute separation of the judiciary from all other branches of government. The law needed to be independent and impartial, and it needed to be just. Montesquieu advocated that law codes be reformed and reduced mainly to regulate crimes against persons and property. Punishment should fit the crime but should be humane. Montesquieu was one of the first to advocate the abolition of torture. Like most Europeans of his age, he saw monarchy as the only realistic form of government, but he argued that for a monarchy to be successful, it needed a strong and independent aristocracy to restrain its tendency toward corruption and despotism. He based his arguments on what he believed was the case in Britain, which he praised as the only state in Europe in which liberty resided.

Enlightened Education and Social Reform.   Enlightened thinkers attacked established institutions, above all the Church. Most were deists who believed in the existence of God on rational grounds only. Following the materialistic ideas of experience. For Locke, as for a host of thinkers after him, good and evil were defined as pleasure and pain: people did good because it was pleasurable and avoided evil because it was painful. Morality was a sense experience rather than a theological experience. It was also relative rather than absolute, an observation that derived from increased interest in non-European cultures. The *Persian Letters* of Baron Montesquieu was the most popular of a genre describing non-European societies that knew nothing of Christian morality.

By the middle of the eighteenth century, the pleasure/pain principle enunciated by Locke had come to be applied to the foundations of social organization. If personal good was pleasure, then social good was happiness. The object of government, in the words of the Scottish moral philosopher Francis Hutcheson (1694–1746), was "the greatest happiness of the greatest number." The principle was at the core of *Crimes and Punishments* (1764), Cesare Beccaria's pioneering work of legal reform. Laws were instituted to promote happiness within society. They had to be formulated equitably for both criminal and victim. Punishment was to act as a deterrent to crime rather than as retribution. Therefore, Beccaria advocated the abolition of torture to gain confessions, the end of capital punishment, and the rehabilitation of criminals through the improvement of penal institutions. By 1776, happiness was established as one of the basic rights of man, enshrined in the American Declaration of Independence as "life, liberty, and the pursuit of happiness."

It was in refashioning the world through education and social reform that the Enlightenment revealed its orientation toward the future. *Optimism* was a word invented in the eighteenth century to express the feeling of liberation from the weight of centuries of traditions. "This is the best of all possible worlds and all things turn out for the best," was the satirical slogan of Voltaire's *Candide*. But if Voltaire believed that enlightened thinkers had taken optimism too far, others believed that it had to be taken further still.

Progress, an idea that not all enlightened thinkers shared, was another invention of the age. It was expressed most cogently by the French philosopher the Marquis de Condorcet (1743–1794) in *The Progress of the Human Mind* (1795), in which he developed an almost evolutionary view of human development from a savage state of nature to a future of harmony and international peace.

The Impact of the Enlightenment

As there was no single set of Enlightenment beliefs, so there was no single impact of the Enlightenment. Its general influence was felt everywhere, even seeping to the lowest strata of society. Its specific influence is harder to gauge. Paradoxically, enlightened political reform took firmer root in eastern Europe, where the ideas were imported, than in western Europe, where they originated. It was absolute rulers who were most successful in borrowing Enlightenment reforms.

It is impossible to determine what part enlightened ideas and what part practical necessities played in the eastern

■ Jean-Jacques Rousseau produced one of the greatest works of the Enlightenment, *The Social Contract* (1762), in which he envisioned a society capable of controlling evil. This portrait was painted by Maurice Quentin around 1740.

the new science, **deists** believed that nature conformed to its own material laws and operated without divine intervention. God, in a popular Enlightenment image, was like a clockmaker who constructed the elaborate mechanism, wound it, and gave the pendulum its first swing. After that the clock worked by itself. Deists were accused of being anti-Christian, and they certainly opposed the ritual forms of both Catholic and Protestant worship. They also opposed the role of the Church in education, for education was the key to an enlightened view of the future. That meant, above all, conflict with the Jesuits. "Let's eat a Jesuit," was Voltaire's half-facetious comment.

Jean-Jacques Rousseau attacked the educational system. His tract on education, disguised as the romantic novel *Émile* (1762), argued that children should be taught by appealing to their interests rather than with strict discipline. Education was crucial because the Enlightenment was dominated by the idea of the British philosopher John Locke (1632–1704) that the mind was blank at birth, a *tabula rasa*—"white paper void of all characters"—and that it was filled up by experience. Contrary to the arguments of Descartes, Locke wrote in *An Essay Concerning Human Understanding* (1690) that there were no innate ideas and no good or evil that was not conditioned by

THE GOOD OF ALL

The Social Contract (1762) was one of the greatest visionary tracts of the eighteenth century. In it Jean-Jacques Rousseau envisioned a harmonious society capable of eliminating want and controlling evil. Here he discusses his famous idea of the general will.

Focus Questions

What benefits flow from unity and simplicity? How large a "state" do you think could be effectively organized in the way Rousseau sets out here?

As long as men united together look upon themselves as a single body, they have but one will relating to the common preservation and general welfare. Then all the energies of the state are vigorous and simple: its maxims are clear and luminous; there are no mixed contradictory interests; the common prosperity shows itself everywhere, and requires only good sense to be appreciated. Peace, union, and equality are enemies of political subtleties. Upright, honest men are difficult to deceive, because of their simplicity: decoys and pretexts do not impose upon them, they are not cunning enough to be dupes. When we see among the happiest people in the world troops of peasants regulating the affairs of state under an oak, and conducting themselves wisely, can we help despising the refinements of other nations, who make themselves illustrious and miserable with so much art and mystery?

From Jean-Jacques Rousseau, *The Social Contract.*

European reform movement that began around midcentury. In at least three areas, the coincidence between ideas and actions was especially strong: law, education, and the extension of religious toleration. Law was the basis of Enlightenment views of social interaction, and the influence of Montesquieu and Beccaria spread quickly. In Prussia and Russia, the movement to codify and simplify the legal system did not reach fruition in the eighteenth century, but in both places it was well under way. The Prussian jurist Samuel von Cocceji (1679–1755) initiated the reform of Prussian law and legal administration. Cocceji's project was to make the enforcement of law uniform throughout the realm, to prevent judicial corruption, and to produce a single code of Prussian law. The code, finally completed in the 1790s, reflected the principles of criminal justice articulated by Beccaria. In Russia, the Law Commission summoned by Catherine the Great in 1767 never completed its work. Nevertheless, profoundly influenced by Montesquieu, Catherine attempted to abolish torture and to introduce the Beccarian principle that the accused was innocent until proved guilty. In Austria, Joseph II presided over a wholesale reorganization of the legal system. Courts were centralized, laws codified, and torture and capital punishment abolished.

Enlightenment ideas also underlay the efforts to improve education in eastern Europe. The religious orders, especially the Jesuits, were the most influential educators of the age, and the Enlightenment attack upon them created a void that had to be filled by the state. Efforts at compulsory education were first undertaken in Russia under Peter the Great, but those were aimed at the compulsory education of the nobility. It was Catherine who extended the effort to the provinces, attempting to educate a generation of Russian teachers. She was especially eager that women receive primary schooling, although the prejudice against educating women was too strong to overcome. Austrian and Prussian reforms were more successful in extending the reach of primary education, even if its content remained weak.

Religious toleration was the area in which the Enlightenment had its greatest impact in Europe, though again it was in the eastern countries that it was most visible. Freedom of worship for Catholics was barely whispered about in Britain, while neither France nor Spain were moved to tolerate Protestants. Nevertheless, within those parameters there were some important changes in the religious makeup of the western European states. In Britain, Protestant dissenters were no longer persecuted for their beliefs. By the end of the eighteenth century, the number of Protestants outside the Church of England was growing; and by the early nineteenth century discrimination against Protestants was all but eliminated. In France and Spain, relations between the national church and the papacy were undergoing a reorientation. Both states were asserting more independence—both theologically and financially—from Rome. The shift was symbolized by disputes over the role of the Jesuits, who were finally expelled from France in 1764 and from Spain in 1767.

In eastern Europe, enlightened ideas about religious toleration did take effect. Catherine the Great abandoned persecution of a Russian Orthodox sect known as the Old Believers. Prussia had always tolerated various Protestant groups, and with the conquest of Silesia it acquired a large Catholic population. Catholics were guaranteed freedom of worship, and Frederick the Great even built a Catholic church in Berlin to symbolize the policy. Austria extended enlightened ideas about toleration the furthest. Maria Theresa was a devout Catholic

CHRONOLOGY
MAJOR WORKS OF THE ENLIGHTENMENT

1690	*An Essay Concerning Human Understanding* (Locke)
1721	*Persian Letters* (Baron Montesquieu)
1734	*Philosophical Letters Concerning the English Nation* (Voltaire)
1739	*A Treatise of Human Nature* (Hume)
1740	*Pamela* (Richardson)
1748	*An Enquiry Concerning Human Understanding* (Hume); *The Spirit of the Laws* (Baron Montesquieu)
1751–1780	*Encyclopedia* (Diderot)
1759	*Candide* (Voltaire)
1762	*Émile; The Social Contract* (Rousseau)
1764	*Crimes and Punishments* (Beccaria)
1784	*What Is Enlightenment?* (Kant)
1795	*The Progress of the Human Mind* (Marquis de Condorcet)
1798	*An Essay on the Principles of Population* (Malthus)

and had actually increased religious persecution in her realm, but Joseph II rejected his mother's dogmatic position. In 1781, he issued the **Patent of Toleration,** which granted freedom of worship to Protestants and members of the Eastern Orthodox Church. The following year he extended the toleration to Jews. Joseph's attitude toward toleration was as practical as it was enlightened. He believed that the revocation of the Edict of Nantes—which had granted limited toleration to Protestants— at the end of the seventeenth century had been an economic disaster for France, and he encouraged religious toleration as a means to economic progress.

A science of economics was first articulated during the Enlightenment. A group of French thinkers known as the **Physiocrats** subscribed to the view that land was wealth and thus argued that agricultural activity, especially improved means of farming and livestock breeding, should take first priority in state reforms. As wealth came from land, taxation should be based only on land ownership, a principle that was coming into increased prominence despite the opposition of the landowning class. Physiocratic ideas combined a belief in the sanctity of private property with the need for the state to increase agricultural output. Ultimately the Physiocrats, like the great Scottish economic theorist Adam Smith, came to believe that government should cease to interfere with private economic activity. They articulated the doctrine *Laissez faire, laissez passer*—"Let it be, let it go." The ideas of Adam Smith and the Physiocrats, particularly the **laissez faire** doctrine, ultimately formed the basis for nineteenth-century economic reform.

If the Enlightenment did not initiate a new era, it did offer a new vision, whether in Hume's psychology, Montesquieu's political science, Rousseau's sociology, or Smith's economic theory. All of the subjects, which have such a powerful impact on contemporary life, had their modern origins in the Enlightenment. As the British poet Alexander Pope (1688–1744) put it: "Know then thyself, presume not God to scan/ The proper study of mankind is man." Enlightened thinkers challenged existing ideas and existing institutions. A new emphasis on self and on pleasure led to a new emphasis on happiness. All three fed into the distinctively Enlightenment idea of self-interest. Happiness and self-interest were values that would inevitably corrode the old social order, which was based upon principles of self-sacrifice and corporate identity. It was only a matter of time.

EIGHTEENTH-CENTURY SOCIETY

Eighteenth-century society was a hybrid of old and new. It remained highly stratified socially, politically, and economically. Birth and occupation determined wealth, privilege, and quality of life as much as they had in the past. But in the eighteenth century the gulf between top and bottom was being filled by a thriving middle class, a **bourgeoisie,** as they were called in France. There were now more paths toward the middle and upper classes, more wealth to be distributed among those above the level of subsistence. It was bourgeois culture and bourgeois values that were new in the eighteenth century. At the bottom of society, poverty still gripped the mass of European people. Changes in agriculture allowed more to survive than ever before, but their survival was still perilous, dependent upon chance rather than effort.

The Nobility

Nobles were defined by their legal rights. They had the right to bear arms, the right to special judicial treatment, the right to tax exemptions. In Russia, only nobles could own serfs; in Poland, only nobles could hold government office. In France and Britain, the highest court positions were always reserved for noblemen. Nobles dominated the Prussian army. In 1786, out of nearly 700 senior officers only 22 were not noblemen. The Spanish nobility claimed the right to live idly. Rich or poor, they shunned all labor as a right of their heritage. Swedish and Hungarian noblemen had their own legislative chambers, just as the British had the House of Lords. Noble privilege was as vibrant as ever.

Although all who enjoyed the special rights were noble, not all nobles were equal. In many states, the noble order was subdivided into easily identifiable groups. The Spanish grandees, the upper nobility, numbered in the thousands; the Spanish hidalgos, the lower nobility, in the hundreds of thousands. In Hungary, out of 400,000 noblemen only about 15,000 belonged to the landed nobility, who held titles and were exempt from taxes. The landed nobility were personally members of the upper chamber of the Hungarian Diet, while the lesser nobility sent representatives to the lower chamber.

The situation was similar in England, where the elite class was divided between the peerage and the gentry. The peerage held titles, were members of the House of Lords, and had a limited range of judicial and fiscal privileges. In the mid-eighteenth century, there were only 190 British peers. The gentry, which numbered more than 20,000, dominated the House of Commons and local legal offices but were not strictly members of the nobility. The French nobility was informally distinguished among the small group of peers known as the Grandes, whose ancient lineage, wealth, and power set them apart from all others; a rather larger service nobility whose privileges derived in one way or another from municipal or judicial service; and what might be called the country nobility, whose small estates and local outlook made their fiscal immunities vital to their survival.

The distinctions among the nobilities of the European states masked a more important one: wealth. As the saying went, "All who were truly noble were not wealthy, but all who were truly wealthy were noble." In the eighteenth century, despite the phenomenal increase in mercantile activity, wealth was still calculated in profits from the ownership of land, and it was the wealthy landed nobility who set the tone of elite life in Europe.

Maintaining Wealth. Eighteenth-century Europe was a society of orders gradually transforming itself into a society of classes. At the top, as vigorous as ever, was the nobility, the privileged order in every European state. In different parts of Europe the nobility used different methods to maintain their land-based wealth. In places such as Britain, Spain, Austria, and Hungary, forms of entail were the rule. In simple terms, an entail was a restriction prohibiting the breakup of a landed estate either through sale or inheritance. The owner of the estate was merely a caretaker for his heir, and while he could add land, he could not easily subtract any. Entailed estates grew larger and larger and, like magnets, attracted other entailed estates through marriage. In Britain, where primogeniture—inheritance by the eldest son—accompanied entail, 400 families owned one-quarter of the entire country. Yet the concentration of landed wealth paled into insignificance when compared to the situation in Spain, where just four families owned one-third of all the cultivable land. In the east, where land was plentiful, the Esterhazys of Hungary and the Radziwills of Poland owned millions of acres.

The second method by which the European nobility ensured that the wealthy would be noble was by absorption. There were several avenues to upward mobility, but by the eighteenth century the holding of state offices was the most common. In France, for example, a large number of offices were reserved for the nobility. Many of those were owned by their holders and passed on to their children, but occasionally an office was sold on the market and the new holder was automatically ennobled. The office of royal secretary was one of the most common routes to noble status. The number of secretaries increased from 300 to 900 during the course of the eighteenth century, yet despite the dilution the value of the offices continued to skyrocket. An office that was worth 70,000 French pounds at the beginning of the century was worth 300,000 by the 1780s. In fact, in most European societies there was more room for new nobles than there were aspiring candidates because of the costs that maintaining the new status imposed. In Britain, anyone who could live like a gentleman was accounted one. But the practice of entail made it very difficult for a newcomer to purchase the requisite amount of land. Philip V increased the number of Spanish grandees in an effort to dilute their power, yet when he placed a tax on entrance into the lower nobility, the number of hidalgos dropped precipitously.

Increased Consumption. For the wealthy, aristocracy was becoming an international status. The influence of Louis XIV and the court of Versailles lasted for more than a century and spread to town and country life. Most nobles maintained multiple residences. The new style of aristocratic entertainment required more public space on the first floor, while the increasing demand for personal and familial privacy necessitated more space in the upper stories. The result was larger and more opulent homes. There the British elite led all others. More than 150 country houses were built in the early eighteenth century alone, including Blenheim Palace, which was built for John Churchill, duke of Marlborough, at a cost of £300,000. To the expense of architecture was added the expense of decoration. New materials such as West Indian mahogany occasioned new styles, and both drove up costs. The high-quality woodwork and plastering made fashionable by the English Adam brothers was quickly imitated on the Continent. Only the Spanish nobility shunned country estates, preferring to reside permanently in towns.

The building of country houses was only one part of the conspicuous consumption of the privileged orders. Improvements in travel, both in transport and roads, permitted increased contact between members of the national elites. The stagecoach linked towns, and canals linked waterways. Both made travel quicker and more enjoyable. The grand tour of historical sites continued to be used as a substitute for formal education. Young men would pass from country house to country house buying up antiquities, paintings, and books along the way. The grand tour was a means of introducing the European aristocracies to each other, and also a means of communicating taste and fashion among them. Whether it was a Russian noble in Germany, a Swede in Italy, or a Briton in Prussia, all spoke French and shared a cultural outlook.

The Salons. Much of that outlook was cultivated in the salons, a social institution begun in the seventeenth century

■ This dining room from Lansdowne House in London is one of the finest examples of Robert Adam's style. Characteristic of Adam's style are the vases, trophies of arms, leaf garlands, sprays, rosettes, scrolls, and fan-shaped motifs cast in plaster adorning the room.

by French women that gradually spread throughout the Continent. In the salons, especially those in Paris, the aristocracy and bourgeoisie mingled with the leading intellectuals of the age. There wit and insight replaced polite conversation. At formal meetings, papers on scientific or philosophical topics were read and discussed. At informal gatherings, new ideas were examined and exchanged. The British ambassador to Spain was appalled to discover that men and women were still kept separate in the salons of Madrid and that there was no serious conversation during evenings out. It was in the salons that the impact of the Enlightenment first made itself felt.

The Bourgeoisie

Bourgeois is a French word, and it carried the same tone of derision in the eighteenth century that it does today. The bourgeois was a man on the make, scrambling after money or office or title. He was neither well-born nor well-bred, or so said the nobility. Yet the bourgeoisie served vital functions in all European societies. They dominated trade, both nationally and internationally. They made their homes in cities and did much to improve the quality of urban life. They were the civilizing influence in urban culture, for unlike the nobility, they were the city's permanent denizens. Perhaps most importantly, the bourgeoisie provided the safety valve between the nobility and those who were acquiring wealth and power but lacked the advantages of birth and position. By developing their own culture and class identity, the bourgeoisie provided successful

individuals with their own sense of pride and achievement and eased the explosive buildup of social resentments.

During the eighteenth century, the bourgeoisie grew both in numbers and importance. An active commercial and urban life gave many members of the group new social and political opportunities, and many of them passed into the nobility through the purchase of land or office. But for those whose aspirations or abilities were different, the social group began to define its own values, which centered on the family and the home. A new interest in domestic affairs touched both men and women of the European bourgeoisie. Their homes became social centers for kin and neighbors, and their outlook on family life reflected new personal relationships. Marriages were made for companionship as much as for economic advantage. Romantic love between husbands and wives was newly valued. So were children, whose futures came to dominate familial concern. Childhood was recognized as a separate stage of life and the education of children as one of the most important of all parental responsibilities. The image of the affectionate father replaced that of the hard-bitten businessman; the image of the doting mother replaced that of the domestic drudge.

Urban Elites.   In the society of orders, nobility was the acid test. The world was divided into the small number of those who had it and the large number of those who did not. At the apex of the non-noble pyramid was the bourgeoisie, the elites of urban Europe whose place in the society of orders was ambiguous. *Bourgeois,* or *burgher,* simply meant "town

■ William Hogarth was famous for his satirical series paintings. *Marriage à la Mode,* ca. 1743, depicts the complicated negotiations between a wealthy merchant and an aristocrat for a marriage between their families and shows the progress of the arranged match to its end. In this scene of domestic disarray, second in the series, the marriage quickly proves to be a disaster.

dweller," but as a social group it had come to mean wealthy town dweller. The bourgeoisie was strongest where towns were strongest: in western rather than in eastern Europe and in northern rather than southern Europe, with the notable exception of Italy. Holland was the exemplar of a bourgeois republic. More than half of the Dutch population lived in towns, and there was no significant aristocratic class to compete for power. The Regents of Amsterdam were the equivalent of a European court nobility in wealth, power, and prestige, though not in the way in which they had accumulated their fortunes. The size of the bourgeoisie in various European states cannot be determined absolutely. At the end of the eighteenth century, the British middle classes probably constituted around 15 percent of the population, the French bourgeoisie less than 10 percent. By contrast, the Russian or Hungarian urban elites were less than 2 percent of the population in those states.

Like the nobility, the bourgeoisie constituted a diverse group. At the top were great commercial families engaged in the expanding international marketplace and reaping the profits of trade. In wealth and power they were barely distinguishable from the nobility. At the bottom were the so-called petite bourgeoisie: shopkeepers, artisans, and small manufacturers. The solid core of the bourgeoisie was employed in trade, exchange, and service. Most were engaged in local or national commerce. Trade was the lifeblood of the city, for by itself the city could neither feed nor clothe its inhabitants. Most bourgeois fortunes were first acquired in trade. Finance was the natural outgrowth of commerce, and another segment of the bourgeoisie accumulated or preserved their capital through the sophisticated financial instruments of the eighteenth century. While the very wealthy loaned directly to the central government or bought shares in overseas trading companies, most bourgeois participated in government credit markets. They purchased state bonds or lifetime annuities and lived on the interest. The costs of war flooded the urban credit markets with high-yielding and generally stable financial instruments. Finally, the bourgeoisie were members of the burgeoning professions that provided services for the rich. Medicine, law, education, and the state bureaucracy were all bourgeois professions, for the cost of acquiring the necessary skills could be borne only by those already wealthy.

During the course of the eighteenth century, the combination of occupational groups was expanding, both in numbers and in importance, all over Europe. So was the bourgeois habitat. The urbanization of Europe continued steadily throughout the eighteenth century. A greater percentage of the European population were living in towns, and a greater percentage were living in large towns of more than 10,000 inhabitants, which, of necessity, were developing complex socioeconomic structures. In France alone there were probably more than a hundred such towns, each requiring the services of the bourgeoisie and providing opportunities for their expansion. And the larger the metropolis, the greater the need. In 1600, only 20 European cities contained as many as 50,000 people; in 1700, that number had risen to 32, and by 1800 it reached 48. During the course of the eighteenth century, the number of cities with 75,000 inhabitants doubled. London, the largest city, had grown to 865,000, a remarkable feat considering that in 1665 more than one-quarter of the London population had died in the Great Plague. In such cities, the demand for lawyers, doctors, merchants, and shopkeepers was almost insatiable.

Besides wealth, the urban bourgeoisie shared another characteristic: mobility. The aspiration of the bourgeoisie was to become noble, either through office or by acquiring rural estates. In Britain, a gentleman was still defined by lifestyle: "All are accounted gentlemen in England who maintain themselves without manual labor." Many trading families left their wharves and countinghouses to acquire rural estates, live off rents, and practice the openhanded hospitality of gentlemen. In France and Spain, nobility could still be purchased, though the price was constantly going up. For the greater bourgeoisie, the transition was easy; for the lesser, the failure to move up was all the more frustrating for being just beyond their grasp. The bourgeoisie did not only imagine their discomfort, they were made to feel it at every turn. They were the butt of jokes, theater, and popular songs. They were the first victims in the shady financial dealings of crown and court, the first casualties in urban riots. Despised from above and envied from below, the bourgeoisie were uncomfortable with their present yet profoundly conservative about their future. The one consolation to their perpetual misery was that as a group they became richer and richer. And as a group they began to develop a distinctive culture that reflected their qualities and aspirations.

Bourgeois Values.   Many bourgeoisie viewed their condition as temporary and accepted the pejorative connotations of the word *bourgeois*. They had little desire to defend a social group out of which they fervently longed to pass. Others, whose aspirations were lower, were nevertheless uncomfortable with the status that they had already achieved. They had no ambition to wear the silks and furs reserved for the nobility or to attend the opening night at the opera decked in jewels and finery. In fact, such ostentation was alien to their existence and to the success that they had achieved. There was a real tension between the values of noble and bourgeois. The ideal noble was idle, wasteful, and ostentatious; the ideal bourgeois was industrious, frugal, and sober. Voltaire, who made his fortune as a financial speculator rather than as a man of letters, aped the lifestyle of the nobility. But he could never allow himself to be cheated by a tradesman, a mark of his origins. When Louis XVI tried to make household economies in the wake of a financial crisis, critics said that he acted "like a bourgeois."

Even if the bourgeoisie did not constitute a class, they did share certain attitudes that constituted a culture. The wealthy among them participated in the new world of consumption, whether they did so lavishly or frugally. For those who aspired to more than their birth allowed, there was a loosening of the strict codes of dress that reserved certain fabrics, decorative materials, and styles to the nobility. Merchants and bankers could now be seen in colored suits or with piping made of cloth of gold; their wives could be seen in furs and silks. They might acquire silverware, even if they did not go so far as the nobility and have a coat of arms engraved upon it. Coaches and carriages were also becoming common among the bourgeoisie, to take them on the Sunday rides through the town gardens or to their weekend retreats in the suburbs. Parisian merchants, even master craftsmen such as clockmakers, were acquiring suburban homes, although they could not afford to retire to them for the summer months.

But more and more, the bourgeoisie was beginning to travel. In Britain, whole towns were established to cater to leisure travelers. The southwestern town of Bath, which was rebuilt in the eighteenth century, was the most popular of all European resort towns, famous since Roman times for the soothing qualities of its waters. Bath was soon a social center as notable for its marriage market as for its recreations. Brighton, a seaside resort on the south coast, quadrupled in size in the second half of the eighteenth century. Bathing—what we would call swimming—either for health or recreation, became a middle-class fad, displacing traditional fear of the sea.

Leisure and Entertainment.   The leisure that wealth bestowed on the bourgeoisie, in good bourgeois fashion, quickly became commercialized. Theater and music halls for both light and serious productions proliferated. By the 1760s, an actual theater district had arisen in London and was attracting audiences of more than 20,000 a week. London was unusual, both for its size and for the number of well-to-do visitors who patronized its cultural events. The size of the London audiences enabled the German-born composer Georg Friedrich Handel (1685–1759) to earn a handsome living by performing and directing concerts. He was one of the few musicians in the eighteenth century to live without noble patronage. But it was not only in Britain that theater and music flourished. Voltaire's plays were performed before packed houses in Paris, with the author himself frequently in attendance to bask in the adulation of the largely bourgeois audiences who attended them. In Venice, it was estimated that more than 1200 operas were produced in the eighteenth century. Rome and Milan were even better known, and Naples was the center for Italian opera. Public concerts were a mark of bourgeois culture, for the court nobility was entertained at the royal palaces or great country houses. Public concerts began in Hamburg in the 1720s, and Frederick the Great helped establish the Berlin Opera House some decades later.

Theater and concert going were part of the new attitude toward socializing that was one of the greatest contributions of the Enlightenment. Enlightened thinkers spread their views in the salons, and the salons soon spawned the academies, local scientific societies that, though led and patronized by provincial nobles, included large numbers of bourgeois members. The academies sponsored essay competitions, built up libraries, and became the local centers for intellectual interchange. A less structured form of sociability took place in the coffeehouses and tearooms that came to be a feature of even small provincial towns. In the early eighteenth century, there were more than 2000 London coffee shops where men—for the coffeehouse was largely a male preserve—could talk politics, read the latest

■ This scene shows activity at a London coffeehouse. Coffeehouses became increasingly popular in European cities in the eighteenth century. As a forum for discussion and for reading newspapers, they have been seen as important sites for the dissemination of Enlightenment ideas.

newspapers and magazines, and indulge their taste for this still-exotic beverage. More exclusive clubs were also a form of middle-class sociability, some centering on political issues, some (such as the chambers of commerce) centering on professional interests. Parisian clubs, called *sociétés,* covered a multitude of diverse interests. Literary *sociétés* were the most popular, maintaining their purpose by forbidding drinking, eating, and gambling on their premises.

Above all, bourgeois culture was literate culture. Wealth and leisure led to mental pursuits—if not always to intellectual ones. The proliferation of relatively cheap printed material had an enormous impact on the lives of those who were able to afford it. Holland and Britain were the most literate European societies and also, because of the absence of censorship, the centers of European printing.

It was the first great period of the newspaper and the magazine. The first daily newspaper appeared in London in 1702; 80 years later, 37 provincial towns had their own newspapers, while the London papers were read all over Britain. Then as now, the newspaper was as much a vehicle for advertisement as for news. News reports tended to be bland, avoiding controversy and concentrating on general national and international events. Advertising, on the other hand, tended to be lurid, promising cures for incurable ills and the most exquisite commodities at the most reasonable prices.

For entertainment and serious political commentary, the British reading public turned to magazines, of which there were more than 150 separate titles by the 1780s. The most famous were *The Spectator,* which ran in the early part of the century and did much to set the tone for a cultured middle-class life, and *The Gentleman's Magazine,* which ran in mid-century and was said to have had a circulation of nearly 15,000. The longest-lived of all British magazines was *The*

Ladies' Diary, which continued in existence from 1704 to 1871 and doled out self-improvement, practical advice, and fictional romances in equal proportion.

The Ladies' Diary was not the only literature aimed at the growing number of leisured and lettered bourgeois women. Although enlightened thinkers could be ambivalent about the place of women in the new social order, they generally stressed the importance of female education and welcomed women's participation in intellectual pursuits. Whether it was new ideas about women or simply the fact that more women had leisure, a growing body of both domestic literature and light entertainment was available to them. The literature included a vast number of teach-yourself books aimed at instructing women how best to organize domestic life and how to navigate the perils of polite society. Moral instruction, particularly on the themes of obedience and sexual fidelity, was also popular. But the greatest output directed toward women was in the form of fanciful romances, from which a new genre emerged. The novel first appeared in its modern form in the 1740s. Samuel Richardson (1689–1761) wrote *Pamela* (1740), the story of a servant girl who successfully resisted the advances of her master until he finally married her. It was composed in long episodes, or chapters, that developed Pamela's character and told her story at the expense of the overt moral message that was Richardson's original intention. Richardson's novels were printed in installments and helped to drive up the circulation of national magazines.

Family Life and Companionate Marriage. While the public life of the bourgeoisie can be measured in the sociability of the coffeehouse and the academy, private life must be measured in the home. There a remarkable transformation was under way, one that the bourgeoisie shared with the nobility. In the pursuit of happiness encouraged by the Enlightenment, one of the newest joys was domesticity. The image—and sometimes the reality—of the happy home, where love was the bond between husband and wife and care the bond between parents and children, came to dominate both the literary and visual arts. Only those wealthy enough to afford to dispense with women's work could partake of the new domesticity; only those touched by Enlightenment ideas could attempt to make the change. But where it occurred, the transformation in the nature of family life was one of the most profound alterations in eighteenth-century culture.

The first step toward the transformation of family relationships was in centering the conjugal family in the home. In the past, the family was a less important structure for most people than the social groups to which they belonged or the neighborhood in which they lived. Marriage was an economic partnership and a means to carry on lineage. Individual fulfillment was not an object of marriage, and that attitude could be seen among the elites in the great number of arranged marriages, the speed with which surviving spouses remarried, and the formal and often brutal personal relationships between husbands and wives.

Patriarchy was the dominant value within the family. Husbands ruled over wives and children, making all of the crucial decisions that affected both the quality of their lives and their futures. As late as the middle of the eighteenth century, a British judge established the "rule of thumb," which asserted that a husband had a legal right to beat his wife with a stick, but the stick should be no thicker than a man's thumb. It was believed that children were stained with the sin of Adam at birth and that only the severest upbringing could clean some of it away. In nearly 200 child-rearing advice books published in England before the middle of the eighteenth century, only three did not advise the beating of children. John Wesley (1703–1791), the founder of Methodism, remembered his own mother's dictum that "children should learn to fear the rod and cry softly." Children were sent out first for wet-nursing; then at around the age of seven for boarding, either at school or in a trade; and finally into their own marriages.

There can be no doubt that the profile of family life began to change, especially in western Europe, during the second half of the eighteenth century. Although the economic elements of marriage remained strong—newspapers actually advertised the availability of partners and the dowries or annual income that they would bring to the marriage—other elements appeared. Fed by an unending stream of stories and novels and a new desire for individual happiness, romantic and sexual attraction developed into a factor in marriage. Potential marriage partners were no longer kept away from each other or smothered by chaperons. The social season of polite society, in which prospective partners could dance, dine, and converse with each other to determine compatibility, gave greater latitude to courtship. Perhaps more importantly, the role of potential spouses in choosing a partner appears to have increased. That was a subtle matter, for even in earlier centuries parents did not simply assign a spouse to their children. But by the eighteenth century, adolescents

■ *The Snatched Kiss,* or *The Stolen Kiss* (1750s), by Jean-Honoré Fragonard, was one of the "series paintings" popular in the late eighteenth century. A later canvas entitled *The Marriage Contract* shows the next step in the lives of the lovers.

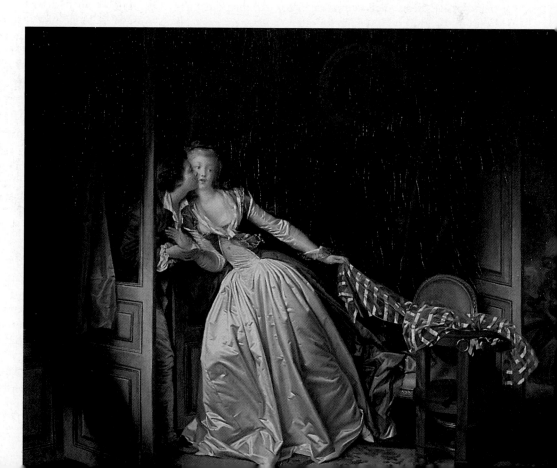

LOVE AND MARRIAGE

Frances Brooke (1724–1789) was one of the earliest women novelists in Britain, publishing her first novel, The History of Lady Julia Mandeville, *in 1763. Orphaned at an early age, she settled in London and earned her living as a translator, writer, and editor. Brooke also participated in the thriving magazine culture of mid-eighteenth-century London. In her essay periodical,* The Old Maid, *she addressed domestic and public issues through the voice of a fictional mouthpiece, "Mary Singleton, Spinster." In this excerpt from the first issue of the magazine, the "Old Maid" reflects on her personal history and the circumstances that led to her unmarried state.*

Focus Questions

How does the passage of time affect the Old Maid's recollections about her past? According to this selection, how do parents control the destiny of their children and heirs? What appears to be the role of love in eighteenth-century marriages?

I was born in the north of England, being the eldest daughter of an honest country justice, who having no children but me and a younger sister, proposed leaving his estate, a clear eight hundred a year, betwixt us. My sister married a neighboring gentleman, and I might perhaps have followed her example, having very good offers (upon my word it's true, I have several love letters by me, which I read once a year, on my birthday, by the help of spectacles) but unluckily, at the age of twenty three, I was addressed by a gentleman so very agreeable, and so passionately fond of me, that though he had not a shilling, I unknown to any body, partly from inclination, partly for fear the poor man should hang himself, which he often threatened, engaged myself to him. As it was impossible to get my father's consent, we agreed to wait till his death; and my lover, who was bred to no employment, went in the meantime to reside with an old relation, in a distant country, who had a good estate, and whose son had a friendship for him. After two years of expectation, during which my faithful admirer, who contrived to see me as often as the distance of the place, and his dependent situation would permit, had frequently pressed me to marry him privately, my father died. Though my concern for his death was real, love soon dried up my tears: no one who is not as romantic as I then was can imagine the joy I felt at being able to give my lover such a proof of the disinterestedness of my passion: I sent a servant post with a letter full of fine sentimental rhapsodies which I am now convinced were very foolish, and received the following answer,

MADAM,

I am sorry for your loss: I have also been so unhappy as to lose my uncle and cousin, who both died of the smallpox within this week: the excess of my grief, and the multiplicity of business I am at present engaged in, by being left heir to my uncle's estate, render it impossible for me to wait upon you. I am much obliged to you for the expressions of regard in your's [sic], and am sorry to tell you, my uncle when dying, insisted on my promise to marry Miss Wealthy, who was intended for my cousin. The will of the dead ought to be sacred therefore it is impossible for me to fulfill the engagement into which we, perhaps imprudently, entered. I expect from your known candor that you will do me the justice to believe no motive but the gratitude and respect I own to the memory of this dear relation, to whose generosity I am so much obliged, could make me give up the hope of being yours. I doubt not your good sense and religion will enable you to bear with becoming fortitude, a shock, which I have need of all the strength of manly reason to support. I sincerely wish you every happiness, and that you may whenever you marry, meet with a man more worthy of you . . .
—J.C.

From *The Old Maid*, Number 1 (November 15, 1755).

themselves searched for their own marriage partners and exercised a strong negative voice in identifying unsuitable ones.

The quest for compatibility, no less than the quest for romantic love, led to a change in personal relationships between spouses. The extreme formality of the past was gradually breaking down. Husbands and wives began spending more time with each other, developing common interests and pastimes. Their personal life began to change. For the first time, houses were built to afford a couple privacy from their children, servants, and guests. Rooms were designed for specific functions and were set off by hallways. Corridors were an important innovation in creating privacy. In earlier architecture, one walked through a room to the next one behind it. In new design, rooms were separated and doors could be closed, which allowed for an intimate life that earlier generations did not find necessary and that they could not, in any case, have put into practice.

Couples had more time for each other because they were beginning to limit the size of their families. There were a number of reasons for that development, which again pertained only to the upper classes. For one thing, child mortality rates were declining among wealthy social groups. Virulent epidemic diseases such as the plague, which knew no class lines, were gradually disappearing. Moreover, though there were few medical breakthroughs in the period, sanitation was improving. Bearing fewer children had an enormous impact on the lives of women, reducing the danger of death and disablement in childbirth and giving them leisure time to pursue domestic tasks. However, that did not mean that the early part of a woman's marriage was not dominated by children; in fact, because of new attitudes toward child-rearing it may have been dominated more than ever by children. Many couples appear to have made a conscious decision to space births, though success was limited by the fact that the most common technique of birth control was coitus interruptus, or withdrawal.

New Attitudes Toward Children. The transformation in the quality of relationships between spouses was mirrored by an even greater transformation in attitudes toward children. There were many reasons why childhood now took on a new importance. Decline in mortality rates had a profound psychological impact. Parents could feel that their emotional investment in their children had a greater chance of fulfillment. But equally important were the new ideas about education, especially Locke's belief that the child enters the world a blank slate whose personality is created through early education. That view not only placed a new responsibility on parents but also gave them the concept of childhood as a stage through which individuals passed. The idea could be seen in the commercial sphere as well as in any other. In 1700, there was not a single shop in London

■ English wax doll with silk gown, 1757. The eighteenth century saw a transformation in family life, including new attitudes toward children that created a market for new products such as books, toys, and games.

that sold children's toys exclusively; by the 1780s, there were toy shops everywhere, three of which sold nothing but rocking horses. Children's toys abounded: soldiers and forts, dolls and dollhouses. The jigsaw puzzle was invented in the 1760s as a way to teach children geography. There were also shops that sold nothing but clothes specifically designed for children, no longer simply adult clothes in miniature.

Most important of all was the development of materials for the education of children, which took place in two stages. At first, so-called children's books were books whose purpose was to help adults teach children. Later came books directed at children themselves, with large print, entertaining illustrations, and nonsensical characters, usually animals who taught moral lessons. In Britain, the Little Pretty Pocket Book series, created by John Newbery (1713–1767), not only encompassed educational primers but also included books for the entertainment of the child. Newbery published a Mother Goose book of nursery rhymes and created the immortal character of Miss Goody Two-Shoes. Instruction and entertainment also lay behind the development of children's playing cards, in which the French specialized. Dice games, such as one in which a child made a journey across Europe, combined geographical instruction with the amusement of competition.

The commercialization of childhood was, of course, directed at adults. The new books and games that were designed to enhance a child's education not only had to be purchased by parents but had to be used by them as well. More and more mothers were devoting their time to their children. Among the upper classes, the practice of wet-nursing began to decline. Mothers wanted to nurture their infants—both literally, by breast feeding, and figuratively, by teaching them. Children became companions to be taken on outings to the increasing number of museums or shows of curiosities, which began to discount children's tickets by the middle of the century.

The preconditions of the transformation of family life could not be shared by the population at large. Working women could afford neither the cost of instructional materials for their children nor the time to use them. Ironically, they now began using wet nurses, once the privilege of the wealthy, for increasingly a working woman's labor was the margin of survival for her family. Working women enjoyed no privacy in the hovels in which they lived, with large families in single rooms. Wives and children were still beaten by husbands and fathers and were unacquainted with enlightened ideas of the worth of the individual and the innocence of the child. By the end of the eighteenth century, two distinct family cultures coexisted in Europe: one based on companionate marriage and the affective bonds of parents and children; the other based on patriarchal dominance and the family as an economic unit.

The Masses

Although more Europeans were surviving than ever before, with more food, more housing, better sanitation, and even better charities, there was also more misery. Those who would have succumbed to disease or starvation a century before now survived from day to day, beneficiaries—or victims—of increased farm production and improved agricultural marketing. The market economy organized a more effective use of land, but it created a widespread social problem. The landless agrarian laborer of the eighteenth century was the counterpart of the sturdy sixteenth-century beggar, capable of working but incapable of finding work. In the cities, the plight of the poor was as desperate as ever. Even the most openhearted charitable institutions were unable to cope with the massive increase in the poor. Thousands of mothers abandoned their children to the foundling hospitals, hoping that they would have a better chance of survival, even though hospital death rates were nearly 80 percent.

Despite widespread poverty, many members of the lower orders were able to gain some benefit from existing conditions. The richness of popular culture, signified by a spread of literacy into the lower reaches of European society, was one indication of the change. So, too, were the reforms urged by enlightened thinkers to improve basic education and the quality of life in the cities. For the segment of the lower orders that could keep its head above water, the eighteenth century offered new opportunities and new challenges.

Breaking the Cycle.   Of all the legacies of the eighteenth century, none was more fundamental than the steady increase in European population that began around 1740. It was not the first time that Europe had experienced sustained population growth, but it was the first time that such growth was not checked by a demographic crisis. Breaking the cycle of population growth and crisis was a momentous event in European history, despite the fact that it went unrecorded at the time and unappreciated for centuries after.

The figures tell one part of the story. In 1700, European population is estimated to have been 120 million. By 1800, it had grown 50 percent, to more than 180 million. And the aggregate hides significant regional variations. While populations in France, Spain, and Italy expanded between 30 and 40 percent, the population of Prussia doubled and those of Russia and Hungary may have tripled in number. Britain's population increased by 80 percent, from about 5 to 9 million, but the rate of growth was accelerating. In 1695, the English population stood at 5 million. It took 62 years to add the next million and 24 years to add the million after that. In 1781, the population was 7 million, but it took only 13 years to reach 8 million and only 10 more years to reach 9 million. Steady population growth had continued without significant checks for more than a half century.

Ironically, the traditional pattern of European population found its theorist at the very moment that it was about to disappear. In 1798, Thomas Malthus (1766–1834) published *An Essay on the Principles of Population*. Reflecting on the history of European population, Malthus observed the cyclical pattern by which growth over one or two generations was

checked by a crisis that significantly reduced population. From the lower levels new growth began until it was checked and the cycle repeated itself. Because people increased more quickly than did food supplies, the land could only sustain a certain level of population. When that level was near, population became prone to a demographic check. Malthus divided population checks into two categories: positive and preventive. Positive checks were famine, war, and disease, all of which Malthus believed were natural, although brutal, means of population control. Famine was the obvious result of the failure of food supplies to keep pace with demand; war was the competition for scarce resources; disease often accompanied both. It was preventive checks that most interested Malthus. Those were the means by which societies could limit their growth to avoid the devastating consequences of positive checks. Celibacy, late marriages, and sexual abstinence were among the choices that Malthus approved, although abortion, infanticide, and contraception were also commonly practiced.

DOCUMENT

Malthus, Laws of Population Growth

Patterns of Population.   In the sixteenth and seventeenth centuries, the dominant pattern of the life cycle was high infant and child mortality, late marriages, and early death. All controlled population growth. Infant and child mortality rates were staggering: only half of all those born reached the age of ten. Late marriage was the only effective form of birth control—given the strong social taboos against sexual relations outside marriage—for a late marriage reduced a woman's childbearing years. Women in western Europe generally married between the ages of 24 and 26; they normally ceased bearing children at the age of 40. But not all marriages lasted that 14- or 16-year span, as one or the other partner died. On average, the childbearing period for most women was between 10 and 12 years, long enough to endure six pregnancies, which would result in three surviving children. (See "A Closer Look: Giving Birth in the Eighteenth Century," pp. 598–599.)

Three surviving children for every two adults would, of course, have resulted in a 50 percent rise in population in every generation. Celibacy was one limiting factor; cities were another. Perhaps as much as 15 percent of the population in western Europe remained celibate, either by entering religious orders that imposed celibacy or by lacking the personal or financial attributes necessary to make a match. Religious orders that enforced celibacy were still central features of Catholic societies, and spinsters, as unmarried women were labeled, were increasing everywhere. Cities were like sticky webs, trapping the surplus rural population for the spiders of disease, famine, and exposure to devour. Throughout the early modern period, urban areas grew through migration. Settled town dwellers might have been able to sustain their own numbers despite the unsanitary conditions of cities, but it was migrants who brought about the cities' explosive growth. Rural migrants accounted for the appallingly high urban death rates. The largest European cities were continuously growing—London from 200,000 in 1600 to 675,000 in 1750; Paris from

220,000 to 576,000; Rome from 105,000 to 156,000; Madrid from 49,000 to 109,000; Vienna from 50,000 to 175,000—and many countless thousands of immigrants perished before marriage. If urban perils were not enough, there were still the so-called positive checks. Plagues carried away hundreds of thousands, wars halved populations of places in their path, and famine overwhelmed the weak and the poor. The worst famine in European history came as late as 1697, when one-third of the population of Finland starved to death.

The late seventeenth and early eighteenth centuries was a period of population stagnation, if not actual decline. It was not until the third or fourth decade of the eighteenth century that another growth cycle began. It rapidly gained momentum throughout the Continent and showed no signs of abating after two full generations. More important, the upward cycle revealed unusual characteristics. In the first place, fertility was increasing, for several reasons. In a few areas, most notably in Britain, women were marrying younger, thereby increasing their childbearing years. That pattern was also true in eastern Europe, where women traditionally married younger. In the late eighteenth century, the average age at marriage for Hungarian women had dropped to 18.6 years. Elsewhere, most notably in France, the practice of wet-nursing was becoming more common among the masses. As working women increasingly took jobs outside the house, they were less able to nurse their own children. Finally, sexual activity outside marriage was rising. Illegitimacy rates, especially in the last decades of the century, were spurting everywhere. Over the course of the century, they rose by 60 percent in France, more than doubled in England, and nearly quadrupled in Germany. So, too, were the rates of premarital pregnancy on the rise. The number of couples rushed to the altar in 1800 was nearly double that before 1750 in most of western Europe.

But increasing fertility was only part of the picture. More significant was decreasing mortality. The positive checks of the past were no longer as potent. European warfare not only diminished in scale after the middle of the century, it changed location as well. Rivalry for colonial empires removed the theater of conflict from European communities. So did the increase in naval warfare. The damage caused by war had always been more by aftershock than by actual fighting. The destruction and pillage of crops and the wholesale slaughter of livestock created food shortages that weakened local populations for the diseases that came in train with the armies. As the virulence of warfare abated, so did that of epidemic disease. The plague had all but disappeared from western Europe by the middle of the eighteenth century. The widespread practice of quarantine—especially in Hungary, which had been the crucial bridge between eastern and western epidemics—went far to eradicate the scourge of centuries.

Public health improvements also played a role in population increases. Urban sanitation, at least for permanent city dwellers, was becoming more effective. Clean water supplies, organized waste and sewage disposal, and strict quarantines were increasingly part of urban regulations. The use of doctors and trained midwives helped lower the incidence of stillbirth and decreased the number of women who died in childbirth. Almost everywhere levels of infant and child mortality were decreasing. More people were being born, more were surviving the first ten dangerous years, and thus more were marrying and reproducing. Increased fertility and decreased mortality could have only one result: renewed population growth. No wonder Malthus was worried.

Agricultural Improvements.   In the past, if warfare or epidemic diseases failed to check population growth, famine would have done the job. How the European economy conquered famine in the eighteenth century is a complicated story. There was no single breakthrough that accounts for the ability to feed the tens of millions of additional people who inhabited the Continent. Holland and Britain, at the cutting edge of agricultural improvement, employed dynamic new techniques that would ultimately provide the means to support continued growth, but most European agriculture was still mired in the time-honored practices that had endured for centuries. Thus, not everyone could be fed or fed adequately. Widespread famine might have disappeared, but slow starvation and chronic undernourishment had not. Hunger was more common at the end of the eighteenth century than at the beginning, and the nutritional content of a typical diet might have reached its lowest point in European history.

Nevertheless, the capacity to sustain rising levels of population can only be explained in terms of agricultural improvement. Quite simply, European farmers were now producing more food and marketing it better. In the most advanced societies, that was a result of conscious efforts to make agriculture more efficient. In traditional open-field agriculture, communities quickly ran up against insurmountable obstacles to growth. The three-field crop rotation system left a significant proportion of land fallow each year, while the concentration on subsistence cereal crops progressively eroded the land that was in production. Common farming was only as strong as the weakest member of the community. There was little incentive for successful individuals to plow profits back into the land, either through the purchase of equipment or the increase of livestock. Livestock was a crucial variable in agricultural improvement. As long as there was only enough food for humans to eat, only essential livestock could be kept alive over the winter. Oxen, which were still the ordinary beasts of burden, and pigs and poultry, which required only minimal feed, were the most commonly kept livestock. But few animals meant little manure, and without manure the soil could not easily be regenerated.

It was not until the middle of the seventeenth century that solutions to those problems began to appear. The first change was consolidation of landholdings so that traditional crop rotations could be abandoned. A second innovation was the introduction of **fodder crops,** some of which—such as clover—added nutrients to the soil, while others—such as turnips—were used to feed livestock. Better grazing and better

A Closer Look
Giving Birth in the Eighteenth Century

"In sorrow thou shalt bring forth children." Such was Eve's punishment for eating of the forbidden tree, and that sorrow continued for numberless generations. Childbirth was painful, dangerous, and all too often deadly. Although successful childbirth needed no outside intervention, without the accumulated wisdom of the ages, babies and mothers routinely perished. The wisdom was passed from mother to daughter and finally was collected by skilled women who practiced the craft of midwifery. Every village, no matter how small, had women who were capable of assisting others in childbirth. Midwives' skills ranged widely, from the use of herbal potions and strong drink to ease the pain of labor to a rudimentary understanding of how to assist a complicated delivery when the fetus was not in the proper position.

Midwives, who until the late seventeenth century were always women, were part of the support group that attended a woman during her labor. Typically, childbirth was a social occasion. Along with the midwife would be a wet nurse and female kin and neighbors, who would offer encouragement, bring refreshments, and tend to the chores that the pregnant woman would have performed herself. Without chemicals to induce contractions and without the ability to intervene in the delivery, labor was usually long. Ordinarily, it did not take place in bed, but rather in a room or a part of a room that had been set aside for the occasion. By the eighteenth century, at least in larger urban areas, poor women who had no separate space for labor could give birth in lying-in hospitals. Within the birthing room, the conclave of women was much like a social gathering. The pregnant woman was advised to adopt any position that made her feel comfortable; standing and walking were favored in the belief that the effects of gravity helped the baby move downward. The woman might sit on a neighbor's lap or on a birthing stool, a chair open at the bottom, during contractions and delivery.

Most midwives subscribed to the philosophy of letting nature take its course. Because the difficulties and length of labor differed markedly from woman to woman, the midwife's most important contribution was to offer comfort and reassurance based on her long experience. By the seventeenth century, manuals for midwives were being published, some of them written by women, but most by male doctors with surgical experience. Midwives and doctors were always at daggers drawn. Trained physicians increasingly saw childbirth as a process that could be improved by the application of new medical knowledge, but as childbirth was a female experience, midwives jealously guarded their role in it. No matter how skilled they were, they were denied access to medical training that might have enabled them to develop lucrative practices on their own. Thus they had no intention of letting male doctors into their trade. For a time, the compromise was the handbooks, which contained guides to anatomy, descriptions of the most common complications, and the direst warnings to call trained physicians when serious problems arose.

By the beginning of the eighteenth century, the "man-midwife" had made his appearance in western Europe. Medically trained and usually experienced in other forms of surgery, the emergence of the man-midwife led to a number of breakthroughs in increasing the safety of childbirth. There can be no question that more mothers and children survived as a result of the man-midwives' knowledge and skills. But at the same time, the social experience of childbirth changed dramatically. What had been a female rite of passage, experienced by and with other women, now became a private event experienced by an individual woman and her male doctor. As female midwives were still excluded from medical

■ Early application of forceps.

training and licensing, their ability to practice their trade eroded in the face of new techniques and information to which they were denied access.

Although most man-midwives trained in hospitals where the poor came to give birth, they practiced among the rich. New attitudes toward marriage and children made the pain and danger of childbirth less acceptable to husbands, who sought every remedy they could afford. British and French man-midwives made fortunes practicing their trade. Their first task was to ascertain that the fetus was in the proper position to descend. In order to do this, however, they had to make an examination that was socially objectionable. Although advanced thinkers could face their man-midwife with the attitude that shame was better than death—"I considered that through modesty I was not to give up my life," as one English noblewoman reasoned— many women and more husbands were unprepared for the actual practice of a man. Thus students were taught as much about bedside manner as about medicine. They were not to examine the patient unless there was another person present in the room, they were not to ask direct questions, and they were not to face the patient during any of their procedures. They were taught to keep a linen cloth on top of the woman's abdomen and to make the examination only by touch—incredulous students were reminded that the most famous French man-midwife was blind! If the fetus was in the correct position, nothing further would be done until the delivery itself. It was only when the fetus was in what was labeled an "unnatural" position that the skill of the physician came into play.

For the most part, a child that could not be delivered head first, face down was in serious risk of being stillborn and the mother in serious risk of dying in labor. That was the problem to which the physicians addressed themselves in the eighteenth century and for which they found remarkable solutions. Most answers came from better understanding of female anatomy and a better visualization of the way in which the fetus moved during labor. The first advance was the realization that the fetus could be turned while still in the womb. Pressure applied on the outside of the stomach, especially in early stages of labor, could help the fetus drop down correctly. A baby who emerged feet first had to be turned face down before it was pulled through the birth canal.

For babies who could not be manually manipulated, the greatest advance of the eighteenth century was the invention of the forceps, or the *tire-tête*, as the French called them. With forceps, the physician could pull the baby by force when the mother was incapable of delivery. Forceps were used mostly in

■ Childbirth with assistance from a man-midwife seated in a chair.

breech births but were also a vital tool when the baby was too large to pass through the cervix by contraction. The forceps were invented in Britain in the middle of the seventeenth century but were kept secret for more than 50 years. During that time they were used by three generations of a single family of man-midwives. In the eighteenth century, they came into general use when the Scotsman William Smellie (1697–1765) developed a short, leather-covered instrument that enabled the physician to do as little damage as possible to either mother or child. Obstetrics now emerged as a specialized branch of medical practice. If neither the pain nor the sorrow of childbirth could be eliminated, its dangers could be lessened.

winter feed increased the size of herds, while new techniques of animal husbandry, particularly crossbreeding, produced hardier strains. It was quite clear that the key to increased production lay in better fertilization, and by the eighteenth century some European farmers had broken through the "manure barrier." Larger herds, the introduction of clover crops, the use of human waste from towns, and even the first experiments with lime as an artificial fertilizer were all part of the new agricultural methods. The impact of new farming techniques was readily apparent. In Britain and Holland, where they were used most extensively, grain yields exceeded ten kernels harvested for each one planted, while in eastern Europe, where the techniques were hardly known, yields were less than five to one.

The New Staples.   Along with the new crops that helped nourish both soil and animals came new crops that helped nourish people. Indian corn, or maize, was a staple crop for Native Americans and gradually came to be grown in most parts of western Europe. Maize not only had higher nutritional value than most other cereals, it also yielded more food per acre than traditional grains, reaching levels as high as 40 to 1. So, too, did the potato, which also entered the European diet from the New World. The potato grew in poor soil, required less labor, and yielded an abundant and nutritious harvest. It rapidly took hold in Ireland and parts of Prussia, from where it spread into eastern Europe. French and Spanish peasants reluctantly introduced it into their diet. Wherever it took root, the potato quickly established itself as survival food. It allowed families to subsist on smaller amounts of land and with less capital outlay. As a result, potato cultivation enabled people in some parts of Europe to marry younger, and thus to produce more children.

However, the new developments involved only a very narrow range of producers. The new techniques were expensive, and knowledge of the new crops spread slowly. Change had to overcome both inertia and intransigence. With more mouths to feed, profits from agriculture soared without landowners having to lift a finger. Only the most ambitious were interested in improvement. At the other end, peasant farmers were more concerned with failure than success. An experiment that did not work could devastate a community; one that did work

MAP DISCOVERY

Wheat

Oats

Rye

Winter Barley

Barley

Cereal Crops in Europe

Soil, climate, and agricultural techniques all combined to determine the diet of Europeans in different parts of the Continent. What were the predominant cereal crops in eastern Europe? Where were the heaviest concentrations of grain grown? If wheat was the most expensive cereal crop, which do you think were the richest parts of Europe?

only meant higher taxes. Thus the most important improvements in agricultural production were more traditional ones. Basically, there was an increase in the amount of land that was utilized for growing. In most of western Europe there was little room for agricultural expansion, but in the east there remained great tracts of uncultivated land. In Russia, Prussia, and Hungary, hundreds of thousands of new acres came under the plow, although some of it simply went to replace land that had been wastefully exhausted in previous generations. In one German province, nearly 75 percent more land was in cultivation at the end of the eighteenth century than had been at the beginning. Even in the west, drainage schemes and forest clearance expanded productive capacity.

There was also an upswing in the efficiency with which agricultural products were marketed. From the seventeenth century onward, market agriculture was gradually replacing subsistence agriculture in most parts of Europe. Market agriculture had the advantage of allowing specialization on farms. Single-crop farming enabled farmers to benefit from the peculiarities of their own soil and climate. They could then exchange their surplus for the range of crops they needed to subsist. Market exchange was facilitated by improved transportation and communication, and above all by the increase in the population of towns, which provided demand. On a larger scale, market agriculture was able to respond to regional harvest failures in a way that subsistence agriculture could not. The most hated figure in the eighteenth century was the grain engrosser, a middleman who bought up local surplus and shipped it away. Engrossers were accused of driving up prices—which they did—and of creating famines—which they did not. In fact, the national and international trade in large quantities of grain evened out regional variations in harvests and went a long way toward reducing local grain shortages. The upkeep of roads, the building of canals, and the clearing of waterways created a national lifeline for the movement of grain.

Finally, the increase in agricultural productivity may have owed something to a change in climate that took place in the late eighteenth century. It is thought that the annual ring of growth inside tree trunks is an indicator of changes in climate. Hot years produce markedly different rings than cold ones; wet years are etched differently than dry ones. Examination of trees that are centuries old seems to indicate that the European climate was unusually cold and wet during the seventeenth century—some have even called it a little ice age—and that it gradually warmed during the eighteenth century. Even moderate climatic change, when combined with new techniques, new crops, expanded cultivation, and improved marketing, would go a long way toward explaining how so many more people were being fed at the end of the eighteenth century.

The Plight of the Poor.   "Of every ten men one is a beggar, five are too poor to give him alms, three more are ill at ease, embarrassed by debts and lawsuits, and the tenth does not represent a hundred thousand families." So observed an eighteenth-century Frenchman about the distribution of wealth in his country. There can be no doubt that the most

serious social problem of the eighteenth century was the explosion of poor people throughout Europe. There was grim irony in the fact that advances in the production and distribution of food and the retreat of war and plague allowed more people to survive hand-to-mouth than ever before. Whereas their ancestors had succumbed to quick death from disease or starvation, they eked out a miserable existence of constant hunger and chronic pain, with death at the end of a seemingly endless corridor.

It is impossible to gauge the number of European poor or to separate them into categories of greater and greatest misery. The truly indigent, the starving poor, probably composed 10 to 15 percent of most societies, perhaps as many as 20 million people throughout the Continent. They were most prevalent in towns but were an increasing burden on the countryside, where they wandered in search of agricultural employment. The wandering poor had no counterpart in the

■ *Return from Market* (1739) by French painter Jean-Baptiste-Siméon Chardin. Domestic service was the most common form of employment for girls, who spent their days cooking, carrying, and cleaning.

east, where serfdom kept everyone tied to the land, but the hungry and unsheltered certainly did. Yet the problem of poverty was not only to be seen among the destitute. In fact, the uniqueness of the poor in the eighteenth century was that they were drawn from social groups that even in the hungry times of the early seventeenth century had been successful subsistence producers. Perhaps another 40 percent of the population in western Europe was described by contemporaries as those without a fixed interest: in the country, those without land; in the towns, those without steady jobs.

It was easy to see why poverty was increasing. The relentless advance of population drove up the price of food and drove down the price of wages. In the second half of the eighteenth century, the cost of living in France rose by more than 60 percent while wages rose only by 25 percent. In Spain, the cost of living increased by 100 percent while wages rose only 20 percent. Only in Britain did wages nearly keep pace with prices. Rising prices made land more valuable. At the beginning of the eighteenth century, as the first wave of population expansion hit western Europe, small holdings began to decrease in size. The custom of partible inheritance, by which each son received a share of land, shrank the average size of a peasant holding below that necessary to sustain an average-size family, much less one that was growing larger. In one part of France it was estimated that 30 acres was a survival plot of land in good times. At the end of the seventeenth century, 80 percent of the peasants there owned less than 25 acres.

As holdings contracted, the portion of the family income derived from wage labor expanded. In such circumstances, males were more valuable than females, both as farmers and laborers, and there is incontrovertible evidence that European rural communities practiced female infanticide. In the end, however, it became increasingly difficult for the peasant family to remain on the land. Mediterranean sharecroppers fell further and further into debt until they finally lost their land entirely. Small freeholders were forced to borrow against future crops until a bad harvest led to foreclosure. Many were allowed to lease back their own lands, on short terms and at high rents, but most swelled the ranks of agricultural laborers, migrating during the planting and harvest seasons and suffering cruelly during winter and summer. In Britain, the rural landless outnumbered the landed by two to one. In France, there were as many as 8 million peasants who no longer owned their own land.

Emigration was the first logical consequence of poverty. In places where rural misery was greatest, such as Ireland, whole communities pulled up stakes and moved to America. Frederick the Great attracted hundreds of thousands of emigrants to Prussia by offering them land. But most rural migrants did not move to new rural environments. Rather, they followed the well-trodden paths to the cities. Many traditional domestic crafts were evolving into industrial activities. In the past, peasants had supplemented their family income by processing raw materials in the home. Spinning, weaving, and sewing were common cottage industries in which the workers took in the work, supplied their own equipment, and were paid by the piece. Now, especially in the cloth trades, a new form of industrial activity was being organized. Factories, usually located in towns or larger villages, assembled workers together, set them at larger and more efficient machines, and paid them for their time rather than for their output. Families unable to support themselves from the land had no choice but to follow the movement of jobs.

Caring for the Poor.   Urban poverty seemed more extreme to observers because there were more poor to observe. They crowded into towns in search of work or charity, though they were unlikely to find much of either. Urban areas were better equipped to assist the poor than were the rural communities from which they came, but the likelihood of finding aid only attracted more and more poor, straining and finally breaking the capacities of urban institutions. The death rate of the migrants and their children was staggering. It is perhaps best typified by the dramatic increase in the numbers of abandoned babies throughout western European cities. The existence of foundling hospitals in cities meant that unwed or poor mothers could leave their children in the hope that they would receive better care than the mother herself could provide. In fact, that was rarely the case. In the largest foundling hospital in Paris, only 15 percent of the children survived their first year of "care." But that did little to deter abandonment. In 1772, more than 7500 babies were left at that charnel house, representing 40 percent of all the children born in Paris that year. The normal rates of abandonment of between 10 and 15 percent of all children born in cities as diverse as Madrid and Brussels were little better.

Neither state nor private charities could cope with the flood of poor immigrants. Although the English pundit Samuel Johnson (1709–1784) opined that "a decent provision for the poor is the true test of civilization," what he meant was provision for the deserving poor, those unfortunates who were physically or mentally unable to support themselves. The distinction between the worthy and unworthy poor was one involved with changing definitions of charity itself. In earlier times, charity was believed to benefit the soul of the giver as much as the body of the recipient. Thus the poor were socially useful, providing the rich with the opportunity to do good works. But the poor were coming to be viewed as a problem of social administration. Hospitals, workhouses, and, more ominously, prisons were established or expanded to deal with them.

Hospitals were residential asylums rather than places for health care. They took in the old, the incapacitated, and, increasingly, the orphaned young. Those in France were aptly named "Hotels of God," considering their staggering death rates. "There children dwell who know no parents' care/Parents who know no children's care dwell there," one poet lamented. Workhouses existed for those who were capable of work but incapable of finding it. They were supposed to improve the values of the idle by keeping them busy, though in most places they served only to improve the profits of the industrialists, who rented out workhouse inmates at below-market wages. Prisons grew with crime. There were spectacular increases in crimes against property in all eighteenth-century cities, and despite severe penalties that could include hanging for petty theft, more criminals were incarcerated than executed. Enlightened arguments for the reform of prisons and punishment tacitly acknowledged the social basis of most crime. As always, the victims of crime were mostly drawn from the same social backgrounds as the perpetrators. Along with all of their other troubles, it was the poor who were most commonly robbed, beaten, and abused.

Popular Culture.   However depressing the story of the unrelieved misery of the poor is, the masses of eighteenth-century society were not only the downtrodden victims of social and economic forces beyond their control. For the peasant farmer about to lose his land or the urban artisan without a job, security was an overwhelming concern. But while many were to endure such fates, many others lived comfortably by the standards of the age, and almost everyone believed that things were better than they had ever been before. Popular culture was a rich mixture of family and community activities that provided outlets from the pressures of work and the vagaries of fortune. It was no less sustaining to the population at large than was the purely literate culture of the elite, no less vital as a means of explanation for everyday events than the theories of the philosophers or the programs of the philosophes.

In fact, the line between elite and popular culture in the eighteenth century is a thin one. For one thing, there was still much mixing of social classes in both rural and urban environments. Occasions of display such as festivals, village fairs, and religious holidays brought entire communities together and reinforced their collective identities. Moreover, there were many shared elements between the two cultures. All over Europe, literacy was increasing, the result of primary education, of new business techniques, and of the millions of books that were available in editions tailored to even the most modest purse. Nearly half of the inhabitants of France were literate by the end of the eighteenth century, perhaps 60 percent of those in Britain. Men were more likely to have learned to read than women, as were those who lived in urban areas. More than a quarter of French women could read, a number that had doubled over the century. As the rates of female literacy rose, so did overall rates, for women took the lead in teaching children.

Popular literacy spawned popular literature in remarkable variety. Religious works remained the most important, but they were followed by almanacs, romances, and (perhaps surprisingly) chivalric fiction. Religious tracts aimed at the populace were found throughout Europe. They contained stories of the saints in Catholic countries and of the martyrs in Protestant ones, proverbs intended to increase spirituality, and prayers to be offered for all occasions. Almanacs combined prophecies, home remedies, astrological tables, predictions about the weather, and advice on all varieties of agricultural and industrial activities. In the middle of the

■ A 1781 colored mezzotint by J. R. Smith shows a lady leaving a lending library with a book.

century, just one of the dozens of British almanacs was selling more than 80,000 copies a year. Romances were the staple of lending libraries, which were also becoming a common feature of even small towns. The books were usually published in inexpensive installments spaced according to the time working families needed to save the pennies to purchase them. Written by middle-class authors, popular romances had a strong moral streak, promoting chastity for women and sobriety for men. Yet the best-selling popular fiction, at least in western Europe, was melodramatic tales of knights and ladies from the age of chivalry. The themes had seeped into popular consciousness after having fallen out of favor among the elites. But cultural tastes did not only trickle down. The masses kept the chivalric tradition alive during the eighteenth century; it would percolate up into elite culture in the nineteenth.

■ The poverty of eighteenth-century London slums was a favorite subject of the English artist William Hogarth. *Gin Lane* depicts the London poor in alcoholic delirium, their only escape from the misery of their daily lives.

Nevertheless, literate culture was not the dominant form of popular culture. Traditional social activities continued to reflect the violent and even brutal nature of day-to-day existence. Many holidays were celebrated by sporting events that pitted the inhabitants of one village against those of another. The events almost always turned into free-for-alls in which broken bones were common and deaths not unknown. In fact, the frequent breakdown of sporting activities into gang wars was the principal cause for the development of rules for soccer, as well as more esoteric games such as cricket in Britain. Well-organized matches soon became forms of popular entertainment. More than 20,000 spectators attended one eighteenth-century cricket match, and soccer and cricket soon became as popular for gambling as horse racing was among the wealthy.

Even more popular were the so-called blood sports, which continued to be the most common form of popular recreation.

Those were brutal competitions in which, in one way or another, animals were maimed or slaughtered. Dogfighting and cockfighting were among those that survive today. Less attractive to the modern mind were blood sports such as bearbaiting or bull running, in which the object was the slaughter of a large beast over a prolonged period of time. Blood sports were certainly not confined to the masses—foxhunting and bullfighting were pastimes for the very rich—but they formed a significant part of local social activity.

The local tavern or alehouse also became a significant part of social activity, and in town or country was the site for local communication and recreation. There women and men gossiped and gambled to while away the hours between sundown and bedtime. Discussions and games became animated as the evening wore on, for staggering amounts of alcohol were consumed. "Drunk for a penny, dead drunk for two pennies, straw for nothing," advertised one of the thousands of British gin mills that dominated the poorer quarters of towns. The increased use of spirits—gin, brandy, rum, and vodka—changed the nature of alcohol consumption in Europe. Wine and beer had always been drunk in quantities that we would find astounding, but those beverages were also an important part of diet. The nutritional content of spirits was negligible. People drank spirits to get drunk. The British reformer Francis Place (1771–1854), who grew up in a working-class family, commented that the British masses had only two pleasures, "sex and drinking. And drunkenness is by far the most desired." The level to which it rose in the eighteenth century speaks volumes about the changes in social and economic life that the masses of European society were then experiencing.

CONCLUSION

Eighteenth-century society was a hybrid of old and new. It remained highly stratified. Birth and occupation determined wealth, privilege, and quality of life as much as they had in the past, but there were now more paths toward the middle and upper classes, more wealth to be distributed among those above the level of subsistence. Opulence and poverty increased in step as the fruits of commerce and land enriched the upper orders while rising population impoverished the lower ones. Enlightenment ideas highlighted the contradictions. The attack on traditional authority, especially the Roman Catholic Church, was an attack on a conservative, static world view. Enlightenment thinkers looked to the future, to a new world shaped by reason and knowledge, a world ruled benevolently for the benefit of all human beings. Government, society, the individual—all could be improved if only the rubble of the past was cleared away. Those thinkers could hardly imagine how potent their vision would become.

QUESTIONS FOR REVIEW

1. What were the main elements of Enlightenment thought?
2. What social, moral, and religious traditions were challenged by the ideas of thinkers such as Voltaire, Hume, Montesquieu, and Rousseau?
3. How did the European nobility maintain its social eminence in the face of a new bourgeois culture created by an expanding middle class?
4. Why did Europe's population begin to grow so dramatically in the eighteenth century, and how did society respond to the challenges that posed?

KEY TERMS

bourgeoisie, *p. 587*

deists, *p. 585*

Enlightenment, *p. 580*

fodder crops, *p. 597*

laissez-faire, p. 587

Patent of Toleration, *p. 587*

philosophes, *p. 580*

Physiocrats, *p. 587*

salons, *p. 580*

DISCOVERING WESTERN CIVILIZATION ONLINE

You can obtain more information about culture and society in eighteenth-century Europe at the Websites listed below. See also the Companion Website that accompanies this text, www.ablongman.com/kishlansky, which contains an online study guide and additional resources.

Eighteenth-Century Culture

NM's Creative Impulse: Enlightenment

www.history.evansville.net/enlighte.html

The best starting point for the culture and history of the age of Enlightenment.

Eighteenth-Century Resources

andromeda.rutgers.edu/~jlynch/18th/

A gateway to a wealth of sources on many different aspects of eighteenth-century culture.

Eighteenth-Century Studies

eserver.org/18th/

A list of links to a wide range of material relating to eighteenth-century literature and culture.

Internet Modern History Sourcebook: The Enlightenment

www.fordham.edu/halsall/mod/modsbook10.html

An outstanding collection of texts of Enlightenment writers.

Eighteenth-Century Society

The New Child: British Art and the Origins of Modern Childhood

www.bampfa.berkeley.edu/exhibits/newchild/

A site devoted to the nature of childhood in eighteenth-century Britain.

Voice of the Shuttle: Restoration and 18th Century

vos.ucsb.edu/browse.asp?id=2738

An inclusive page of links and resources for the study of English literature in the eighteenth century.

SUGGESTIONS FOR FURTHER READING

General Reading

T. C. W. Blanning, *The Culture of Power and the Power of Culture: Old Regime Europe 1660–1789* (New York: Oxford University Press, 2002). An outstanding example of the new cultural history.

William Doyle, *The Old European Order, 1660–1800,* 2d ed. (Oxford: Oxford University Press, 1992). An important essay on the structure of European societies and the ways in which they held together.

Henry Kamen, *Early Modern European Society* (New York: Routledge, 2000). A concise social history by a leading historian.

Eighteenth-Century Culture

A. J. Ayer, *Voltaire* (New York: Random House, 1986). A brief and vibrant study.

Robert Darnton, *The Forbidden Best-Sellers of Pre-Revolutionary France* (New York: W. W. Norton, 1995). A look at the underbelly of the Enlightenment that both provides gripping reading and makes us think about the Enlightenment in new ways.

John G. Gagliardo, *Enlightened Despotism* (New York: Thomas Y. Crowell, 1967). A sound exploration of the impact of Enlightenment ideas on the rulers of Europe, with emphasis on the east.

Norman Hampson, *The Enlightenment* (London: Penguin Books, 1982). The best one-volume survey.

Patrick Mauries, *Cabinets of Curiosities* (London: Thames and Hudson 2002). A fascinating account of collectors and collecting.

Daniel Roche, *France in the Enlightenment* (Cambridge, MA: Harvard University Press, 1998). A wide-ranging survey of everything from politics to popular culture.

Judith Sklar, *Montesquieu* (Oxford: Oxford University Press, 1987). A concise, readable study of the man and his work.

Eighteenth-Century Society: The Nobility

Jonathan Dewald, *The European Nobility, 1400–1800* (Cambridge: Cambridge University Press, 1996). An insightful survey.

Jerzy Lukowski, *The European Nobility in the Eighteenth Century* (New York: Palgrave MacMillan, 2003). Especially valuable for its treatment of eastern Europe.

Eighteenth-Century Society: The Bourgeoisie

John Brewer, *The Pleasures of the Imagination: English Culture in the Eighteenth Century* (London: HarperCollins, 1997). A fascinating study of the making of high culture in England.

Peter Earle, *The Making of the English Middle Class* (London: Methuen, 1989). The manners, mores, and mindset of the group that would come to dominate nineteenth-century Britain.

Jean-Louis Flandrin, *Families in Former Times* (Cambridge: Cambridge University Press, 1979). Strong on family and household organization.

Olwen Hufton, *The Prospect Before Her: A History of Women in Western Europe* (New York: Alfred Knopf, 1996). A survey of women's history that is particularly strong on the eighteenth century.

Simon Shama, *The Embarrassment of Riches* (Berkeley: University of California Press, 1987). The social life of Dutch burghers, richly portrayed.

Lawrence Stone, *The Family, Sex and Marriage in England, 1500–1800* (New York: Harper & Row, 1979). A controversial but extremely important argument about the changing nature of family life.

Eighteenth-Century Society: The Masses

Peter Burke, *Popular Culture in Early Modern Europe* (New York: Harper & Row, 1978). A wide survey of practices throughout the Continent.

Olwen Hufton, *The Poor in Eighteenth-Century France* (Oxford: Oxford University Press, 1974). A compelling study of the life of the poor.

E. A. Wrigley and R. S. Schofield, *The Population History of England* (Cambridge, MA: Harvard University Press, 1981). The most important reconstruction of a national population, by a team of researchers.

For a list of additional titles related to this chapter's topics, please see http://www.ablongman.com/kishlansky.

Chapter 20

THE FRENCH REVOLUTION AND THE NAPOLEONIC ERA, 1789–1815

Chapter Outline

INDÉPENDANCE DES ÉTATS-UNIS.

The eighteenth century was a time of revolution on both sides of the Atlantic. The tremendous struggle for independence was a powerful subject for writers and artists of this period. How might an artist in one country depict the revolution in another? Turn to The Visual Record to see how one French artist imagined the American Revolution. ➤

EIGHTEENTH-CENTURY REVOLUTION

In the second half of the eighteenth century, two separate revolutions toppled regimes on both sides of the Atlantic. In the first of the two great upheavals, the American Revolution, which lasted from 1775 to 1783, the thirteen British colonies located along the Atlantic seaboard secured their independence from Great Britain. They formed themselves into the United States, a democratic republic with its own Declaration of Independence and Constitution. While the American Revolution was challenging British hegemony in the New World, France appeared to be ruled by a stable and powerful monarchy, one so secure in its reign that it was able to lend a helping hand to those colonists opposing England's king George III.

In the image shown here, entitled "Independence of the United States," the unknown artist is glorifying both the king of France, Louis XVI (1774–1791) and the American Revolution. More dramatically still, the inscription on the base of the pedestal acknowledges Louis as the "Liberator" of America and the seas, an assertion that would have come as a surprise to the colonists struggling to cast off the British yoke. King Louis XVI is commemorated in the painting as a great man of revolution, more important by virtue of his position on the monument than even George Washington and Benjamin Franklin, whose medallions surrounded by laurels serve as a base for Louis's image. Washington, whose name is misspelled above his likeness as "Waginston," is not memorialized as father of his country. Instead, it is Louis XVI who is described as America's savior. The memorial column itself is topped by images of the French monarchy including a globe with three fleurs-de-lis and the rooster of the French nation.

Next to the monument and commanding equal interest is the figure of America. America is not symbolized by a minuteman, a colonial militiaman, or a farmer typical of those who fought the American Revolution. Instead, America appears half naked as a "noble savage" draped in animal skins and feathers.

In his right hand America holds the scepter of power and in his left hand a pole surmounted by a Phrygian cap of ancient Roman origins, which became popular in the French Revolution as the symbol of liberty. Under his left foot, America is trampling the British lion, a sorry sight lying next to the broken British trident symbolizing British failure both as a land and sea power.

The landscape of the scene is not a New England scene at all, but a tropical one with palm trees swaying. One of the trees is wrapped in a banner proclaiming, "In raising myself up, I make myself beautiful." The aura of the New World as an uncharted territory as different from Europe and the French countryside as could be imagined served both to idealize the American continent and to distance its revolution from the political experience of the French. In an exotic terrain, Louis XVI could appear as a "liberator," as unearned as the designation might be.

The American Revolution was popular in France and attracted supporters including the French aristocrat and military man, the Marquis de Lafayette. Lafayette was so enthusiastic about the American Revolution that he packed his bags in 1777 and embarked for the New World to fight for the cause. He stood beside General Washington at Valley Forge, was appointed a major general in the American revolutionary army, and was given his own command. It was Lafayette who persuaded the French government to provide financial aid to the American cause. Lafayette was so enamored of the American Revolution and respectful of its leader that he named his first son George Washington. Lafayette's respectful sentiments are shared by the artist of "L'Indépendance des États-Unis." In grouping the images of Louis XVI, Franklin, and Washington, he shows these American and French leaders as partners in the struggle for independence. The artist could not know that the king he commemorated as a liberator would be guillotined as a traitor to the French Revolution in 1793.

INDÉPENDANCE DES ÉTATS-UNIS.

■ L 'Independance des États-Unis.

Looking Ahead

The French Revolution began six years after the American War of Independence ended, and lasted for a decade. The French revolutionaries of 1789 shared many elements in common with their American counterparts, including an awareness of the writings of the same philosophers and intellectuals on both sides of the Atlantic whose works questioned existing institutions and traditions in favor of democracy, liberty, and equality. Yet to understand the Revolution in France, which, like its American predecessor, also embodied new ideas about government and citizenship, one must understand the distinctive nature of French society, economy, and politics in the 50 years preceding 1789 and the crisis in the Old Regime. In their revolution the French experimented with parliamentary government and representative and participatory democracy, all the while contending with internal violence and foreign wars. The French Revolution ended with the coming to power of Napoleon, who was able to consolidate the French state through reform at home and victory abroad, and in so doing was both the heir of the Revolution and its destroyer. ➤*

THE FRENCH REVOLUTION AND THE FALL OF THE MONARCHY

Those who lived through it were sure that there had never been a time like it before. The French Revolution, or the Great Revolution, as it was known to people alive at the time, was a period of creation and discovery. The ten years from 1789 to 1799 were punctuated by genuine euphoria and democratic transformations. But the French Revolution was also a time of violence and destruction. From the privileged elites who initiated the overthrow of the existing order to the peasants and workers, men and women, who railed against tyranny, the revolution touched every segment of society.

The revolution achieved most in the area of politics. The overthrow of absolutist monarchy brought with it new social theories, new symbols, and new behavior. The excitement of anarchy was matched by the terror of repression. In the search for a new order, competing political forms followed one after the other in rapid succession: constitutional monarchy, republic, oligarchy, and dictatorship.

At the end of the eighteenth century France was a state in trouble, but it was not alone. Revolutionary incidents flared up throughout Europe in the second half of the eighteenth century in the Netherlands, Belgium, and Ireland. Absolute authority was challenged and sometimes modified. Across the Atlantic, American colonists concerned with the principle of self-rule had thrown off the yoke of the British in the War of Independence. But none of the events, including the American Revolution, was so violent in breaking with the old order, so extensive in involving millions of men and women in political action, and so consequential for the political futures of other European states as was the French Revolution. The triumphs and contradictions of the revolutionary experiment in democracy mark the end of the old order and the beginning of modern history. Politics would never be the same again.

The Political and Fiscal Crisis of Eighteenth-Century France

The French monarchy was in a state of perpetual financial crisis across the eighteenth century. Louis XV, like his great-grandfather Louis XIV, ruled as an absolute monarch; but he lacked sufficient funds to run the state. He sought loans to meet his needs as well as to pay the interest on existing debts. Borrowing at high rates required the government to pay out huge sums in interest and service fees on the loans that were keeping it afloat. The outlays in turn piled the state's indebtedness ever higher, requiring more loans, and threatening to topple the whole financial structure of the state and the regime itself. The monarchy tried to reduce expenditures, but such attempts were limited by the necessity of maintaining an effective and costly army and navy because of wars on both the Continent and in the colonies.

The nadir of Louis XV's reign came in 1763, with the French defeat in the Seven Years' War. The defeat not only left France barren of funds, it also promoted further expenditures for strengthening the French navy against the superior British fleet. The king saw taxation as the only way out of the financial trap in which he now found himself.

But raising taxes was far from an easy undertaking, and it was one that required the support of the aristocracy. The heightened tensions between the monarch and the aristocracy found expression in various institutions, especially the parlements, which were the 13 sovereign courts in the French judicial system, with their seats in Paris and a dozen provincial centers. The magistrates of each parlement were members of the aristocracy, some of them nobles of recent origin and others of long standing, depending on the locale. Following the costly Seven Years' War, the parlements chose to exercise the power of refusal by blocking a proportional tax to be imposed on nobles and commoners alike. The magistrates resisted taxation, arguing that the king was attacking the liberty of his subjects by attempting to tax those who were exempt by virtue of their privileged status.

By challenging the king, the parlements became a battleground between the elite, who claimed that they represented the nation, and the king, who said the nation was himself. The king repeatedly attempted to neutralize the power of the parlements by relying instead on his own state bureaucracy, which was too weak for the task. The king's agents in the provinces, called intendants, were accountable directly to the central government. The intendants, as the king's men, and the magistrates who presided in the parlements represented contradictory claims to power. As the king's needs increased in the second half of the eighteenth century, the situation was becoming intolerable for those exercising power and those aspiring to rule in the name and for the good of the nation. The financial crisis provided the elite of notables, made up of both aristocrats and bourgeois, with the basis for asserting their own ascendancy to political power. Louis XV, who is often remembered for his cavalier prediction, "*Après moi, la déluge,*" ("After me comes the flood,") indeed left a debt that swamped his grandson and successor Louis XVI. This tension between a growing debt that was undermining the monarchy and the increased ascendancy of an elite of nobles and bourgeois came to characterize the **Old Regime** in France.

When Louis XVI assumed the French throne in 1774, he was only 20 years old. He inherited a monarchy in a state of perpetual financial crisis. Not only did he inherit a trouble-ridden fiscal structure, but Louis XVI also made his own contributions to it, increasing the debt greatly by his involvement in the War of American Independence (1775–1783). Following the advice of a series of ministers, Louis sought structural solutions to the debt through a reformed fiscal policy, taxation, and other new sources of revenue, but each set of reforms offended different established interests. In the end he resorted to an unusual but available step—the convening of the **Estates-General**—as a means of achieving reforms and providing financial stability for the state.

Historically, the Estates-General was the representative body of the three "estates," or social groups, of France—the clergy (the First Estate), the nobility (the Second Estate), and the commoners (the Third Estate). The **Third Estate** was composed of all those members of the realm who enjoyed no special privilege—28 million French people. The Estates-General had not been convened since 1614. Through this body and its duly chosen representatives, Louis XVI sought the consent of the nation to levy taxes. In the political organizing that took place in the winter of 1788–1789 the seeds of revolution were sown.

Convening the Estates-General

When Louis XVI announced in August 1788 that the Estates-General would meet at Versailles in May 1789, people from all walks of life hoped for some redress of their miseries. The king hoped that the clergy, nobility, and commoners would solve his fiscal problems. Every social group, from the nobles to the poorest laborers, had its own agenda and its own ideas about justice, social status, and economic well-being.

One in four nobles had moved from the bourgeoisie to the aristocratic ranks in the eighteenth century; two out of every three had been ennobled during the seventeenth or eighteenth centuries. Nobles had succeeded in expanding their economic and social power and they now sought to preserve it. Furthermore, a growing segment of the nobility, influenced by Enlightenment ideas and the example of English institutions, was intent on increasing the political dominance of the aristocracy.

Members of the Third Estate, traditionally excluded from political and social power, were presented with the opportunity of expressing their opinions on the state of government and society. As commoners in the Third Estate, the bourgeoisie embraced within it a variety of professions, from bankers and financiers to businessmen, merchants, entrepreneurs, lawyers, shopkeepers, and artisans. Those who could not read stood in marketplaces and city squares or sat around evening fires and had the political literature read to them. Farmhands and urban laborers realized that they were participating in the same process as their social betters, and they believed they had a right to speak and be heard.

It was a time of great hope, especially for workers and peasants who had been buffeted by the rise in prices, decline in real wages, and the hunger that followed crop failures and poor harvests. There was new promise of a respite and a solution. Taxes could be discussed and changed, the state bureaucracy could be reformed—or better, abolished. Intellectuals discussed political alternatives in the salons of the wealthy. Nobles and bourgeois met in philosophical societies dedicated to enlightened thought. Commoners gathered in cafes to drink and debate. Although the poor often fell outside of the network of communication, they were not immune to the ideas that emerged. In the end, people of all classes had opinions and were more certain than ever of their right to express their ideas. Absolutism was in trouble, though Louis XVI did not know it, as people began to forge a collectively shared idea of politics. People now had a forum—the Estates-General—and a focus—the politics of taxation.

■ This cartoon depicts the plight of the French peasants. An old farmer is bowed down under the weight of the privileged aristocracy and clergy while birds and rabbits, protected by unfair game laws, eat his crops.

"If Only the King Knew." In conjunction with the political activity and in scheduled meetings, members of all three estates drew up lists of their problems. This process took place in a variety of forums, including guilds and village and town meetings. The people of France drew up grievance lists—known as *cahiers de doléances*—that were then carried to Versailles by the deputies elected to the Estates-General. The grievance lists contained the collective outpouring of problems of each estate and are important for two major reasons. First, they made clear the similarity of grievances shared throughout France. Second, they indicated the extent to which a common political culture, based on a concern with political reform, had permeated different levels of French society. Both the privileged and the nonprivileged identified a common enemy in the system of state bureaucracy to which the monarch was so strongly tied. Although the king was still addressed with respect, new concerns with liberty, equality, property, and the rule of law were voiced.

"If only the king knew!" In that phrase, French men and women had for generations expressed their belief in the inevitability of their fate and the benevolence of their king. They saw the king as a loving and wise father who would not tolerate the injustices visited on his subjects if only he knew what was really happening. In 1789, peasants and workers

ABUS À SUPPRIMÉ

Présentée a l'Assemblée Nationale par le Tiers Etat, Année 1789

■ "Abuses to Suppress." This cartoon depicts the Third Estate—represented here by the peasant following the carriage, the worker leading the horses, and the merchant driving—delivering a petition of "abuses" to be remedied by the National Assembly.

were questioning why their lives could not be better, but they continued to express their trust in the king. Combined with their old faith was a new hope. The peasants in the little town of Saintes recorded their newly formed expectations:

> Our king, the best of kings and father of a great and wise family, will soon know everything. All vices will be destroyed. All the great virtues of industriousness, honesty, modesty, honor, patriotism, meekness, friendliness, equality, concord, pity, and thrift will prevail and wisdom will rule supreme.

Those who opposed the revolution later alleged that the grievance lists proved the existence of a highly coordinated plot on the part of secret societies out to destroy the regime. They were wrong. Similarities in complaints, demands, and language proved the forging of a new political consciousness, not a conspiracy. Societies and clubs circulated "model" grievance lists among themselves, resulting in the use of similar forms and vocabulary. People were questioning their traditional roles and now had elected deputies who would represent them before the king. In the spring of 1789, a severe economic crisis that heightened political uncertainty swept through France. For a king expected to save the situation, time was running out.

The elected deputies arrived at Versailles at the beginning of May 1789 carrying in their valises and trunks the grievances of their estates. The opening session of the Estates-General took place in a great hall especially constructed for the event. The 1248 deputies presented a grand spectacle as they filed to their assigned places to hear speeches by the king and his ministers. Contrasts among the participants were immediately apparent. Seated on a raised throne under a canopy at one end of the hall, Louis XVI was vested in full kingly regalia. On his right sat the archbishops and cardinals of the First Estate, strikingly clad in the pinks and purples of their offices. On his left were the richly and decorously attired nobility of the Second Estate. Facing the stage sat the 648 deputies of the Third Estate, dressed in plain black suits, stark against the colorful and costly costumes of the privileged. Members of the Third Estate had announced beforehand that they would not follow the ancient custom for commoners of kneeling at the king's entrance. Fired by the hope of equal treatment and an equal share of power, they had come to Versailles to make a constitution. The opening ceremony degenerated into a moment of confusion over whether members of the Third Estate should be able to wear their hats in the presence of the king. Many saw in the politics of clothing a tense beginning to their task.

The Crisis in Voting by Estate.   The tension between commoners and the privileged was aggravated by the unresolved issue of how the voting was to proceed. Traditionally, each of the three orders was equally weighted. The arrangement favored the nobility, who controlled the first two estates, since the clergy themselves were often noble.

The Third Estate was adamant in its demand for vote by head. The privileged orders were equally firm in insisting on vote by order. Paralysis set in, as days dragged into weeks and the Estates were unable to act. The body that was to save France from fiscal collapse was hopelessly deadlocked.

Abbé Emmanuel Joseph Sieyès (1748–1836), a member of the clergy, emerged as the critical leader of the Third Estate. Sieyès had already established his reputation as a firebrand reformer with his eloquent pamphlet, "What Is the Third Estate?" published in January 1789. (See document on the next page.) He understood that although eighteenth-century French society continued to be divided by law and custom into a pyramid of three tiers, these orders or estates were obsolete in representing social realities. The base of the pyramid was formed by the largest of the three estates, those who worked—the bourgeoisie, the peasantry, and urban and rural workers—and produced the nation's wealth. He argued that as long as the First and Second Estates did not share

"WHAT IS THE THIRD ESTATE?"

As an ambitious clergyman from Chartres, Abbé Emmanuel Joseph Sieyès was a member of the First Estate. Yet Sieyès was elected deputy to the Estates-General for the Third Estate on the basis of his attacks on aristocratic privilege. He participated in the writing and editing of the great documents of the early revolution: the Oath of the Tennis Court and the Declaration of the Rights of Man and Citizen. The pamphlet for which he is immortalized in revolutionary lore was his daring "What Is the Third Estate?" Written in January 1789, it boldly confronted the bankruptcy of the system of privilege of the Old Regime and threw down the gauntlet to those who ruled France. In this document the revolution found its rallying point.

Focus Questions

Why does Sieyès claim that nothing in the nation can "progress" without the Third Estate? When he states that "the nobility does not belong to the social organization at all," what point is he making about the social utility of privilege?

1st. What is the Third Estate? Everything.

2nd. What has it been heretofore in the political order? Nothing.

3rd. What does it demand? To become something therein. . . .

Who, then, would dare to say that the Third Estate has not within itself all that is necessary to constitute a complete nation? It is the strong and robust man whose one arm remains enchained. If the privileged order were abolished, the nation would not be something less but something more. Thus, what is the Third Estate? Everything; but an everything shackled and oppressed. What would it be without the privileged order? Everything; but an everything free and flourishing. Nothing can progress without it; everything would proceed infinitely better without the others. It is not sufficient to have demonstrated that the privileged classes, far from being useful to the nation, can only enfeeble and injure it; it is necessary, moreover, to prove that the nobility does not belong to the social organization at all; that, indeed, it may be a *burden* upon the nation, but that it would not know how to constitute a part thereof.

The Third Estate, then, comprises everything appertaining to the nation; and whatever is not the Third Estate may not be regarded as being of the nation. What is the Third Estate? Everything!

---

their privileges and rights, they were not a part of the French nation.

Under the influence of Sieyès and the reformist consensus that characterized their ranks, the delegates of the Third Estate decided to proceed with their own meetings. On 17 June 1789, joined by some sympathetic clergy, the Third Estate changed its name to the National Assembly as an assertion of its true representation of the French nation. Three days later, members of the new National Assembly found themselves locked out of their regular meeting room by the king's guard. Outraged by the insult, they moved to a nearby indoor tennis court, where they vowed to stay together for the purpose of writing a constitution. The event, known as the Oath of the Tennis Court, marked the end of the absolutist monarchy and the beginning of a new concept of the state that power resided in the people. The revolution had begun.

The Importance of Public Opinion. The drama of Versailles, a staged play of gestures, manners, oaths, and attire, also marked the beginning of a far-reaching political revolution. Although it was a drama that took place behind closed doors, it was not one unknown to the general public. Throughout May and June 1789, Parisians trekked to Versailles to watch the deliberations and then they brought the news back to the capital. Deputies wrote home to their constituents to keep them abreast of events. Newspapers that reported daily on the wranglings and pamphleteers who analyzed them spread the news throughout the nation. Information, often conflicting, stirred up anxiety; news of conflict encouraged action.

The frustration and stalemate of the Estates-General threatened to put the spark to the kindling of urban unrest. The people of Paris had suffered through a harsh winter and spring under the burdens of high prices (especially of bread), limited supplies, and relentless tax demands. The rioting of the spring had for the moment ceased as people waited for their problems to be solved by the deputies of the Estates-General. The suffering of the urban poor was not new, but their ability to connect economic hardships with the politics at Versailles and to blame the government was. As hopes began to dim with the news of political stalemate, news broke of the creation of the National Assembly. It was greeted with new anticipation.

The Outbreak of Revolutionary Action in 1789

The king, who had temporarily withdrawn from sight following the death of his son at the beginning of June, reemerged to meet with the representatives of each of the three estates and propose reforms, including a constitutional monarchy. But Louis XVI refused to accept the now popularly supported National Assembly as a legitimate body, insisting instead that he must rely on the three estates for advice. He simply did not understand that the choice was no longer his to make. He summoned troops to Versailles and began concentrating soldiers in Paris. Civilians continually clashed with members of the military, whom they jostled and jeered. The urban crowds recognized the threat of repression that the troops represented. People decided to meet force with force. To do so, they needed arms themselves—and they knew where to get them.

The Storming of the Bastille.

On 14 July 1789, the irate citizens of Paris stormed the Bastille, a royal armory that also served as a prison for a handful of debtors. The storming of the Bastille became the great symbol in the revolutionary legend of the overthrow of the tyranny and oppression of the Old Regime. But it is significant for another reason. It was an expression of the power of the people to take politics into their own hands. Parisians were following the lead of their deputies in Versailles. They had formed a citizen militia known as the National Guard, and they were prepared to defend their concept of justice and law.

The people who stormed the Bastille were not the poor, the unemployed, the criminals, or the urban rabble, as their detractors portrayed them. They were petty tradesmen, shopkeepers, and wage-earners, who considered it their right to seize arms in order to protect their interests. The Marquis de Lafayette (1757–1834), a noble beloved of the people because of his participation in the American Revolution, helped organize the National Guard. Under his direction, the militia

adopted the tricolor flag as its standard. The tricolor combined the red and blue colors of the city of Paris with the white of the Bourbon royal family. It became the flag of the revolution, replacing the fleur-de-lis of the Bourbons. It is the national flag of France today.

The king could no longer dictate the terms of the constitution. By their actions, the people in arms had ratified the National Assembly. Louis XVI was forced to yield. The events in Paris set off similar uprisings in cities and towns throughout France. National guards in provincial cities modeled themselves after the Parisian militia. Government officials fled their posts and abandoned their responsibilities. Commoners stood ready to fill the power vacuum. But the revolution was not just an urban phenomenon: the peasantry had their own grievances and their own way of making a revolution.

Peasant Fear of an Aristocratic Plot.

The precariousness of rural life and the increase in population in the countryside contributed to the permanent displacement and destitution of a growing sector of rural society. Without savings and destroyed by poor harvests, impoverished rural inhabitants wandered the countryside looking for odd jobs and eventually begging to survive. All peasants endured common obligations placed on them by the crown and the privileged classes. A bewildering array of taxes afflicted peasants: they owed the tithe to the Church, land taxes to the state, and seigneurial dues and rents to the landlord. In some areas, peasants repaired roads and drew lots for military service. Dues affected almost every aspect of rural life. The labor of women was essential to the survival of the rural family. Peasant women sought employment in towns and cities as seamstresses and

■ This lively amateur painting of the fall of the Bastille is by Claude Cholat, one of the attackers. Tradition has it that Cholat is manning the cannon in the background. The inscription proclaims that the painting is by one of the "conquerors of the Bastille."

MAP DISCOVERY

Boundaries, 1789

★ **Revolutionary centers**

Areas of the Great Fear, July – Aug. 1789

French boundaries, 1793

Counterrevolutionary activity

• **Centers of counter-revoluntionary activity**

Areas of insurrection

0   200 Miles

0   200 Kilometers

Revolutionary France

The French Revolution was not merely a Parisian phenomenon, as this map shows. Locate the revolutionary centers on the map. What feature is common to all of these centers? How do you explain their distribution throughout France? Pockets of insurrection and counter-Revolution were scattered for the most part in the southeast and west. What did they have in common? What territories did France gain between 1789 and 1793 and why did it expand?

servants in order to send money back home to struggling relatives. Children, too, added their earnings to the family pot. In spite of various strategies for survival, the lives of more and more peasant families were disrupted by the end of the eighteenth century as they were displaced from the land.

News of the events of Versailles and then of the revolutionary action in Paris did not reassure rural inhabitants. By the end of June the hope of deliverance from crippling taxes and dues was rapidly fading. The news of the Oath of the Tennis Court and the storming of the Bastille terrified country folk, who saw the actions as evidence of an aristocratic plot that threatened sorely needed reforms. As information moved along postal routes in letters from delegates to their supporters, and as news was repeated in the Sunday market gatherings, distortions and exaggerations crept in. It seemed to rural inhabitants that their world was falling apart. Some peasants believed that Paris was in the hands of brigands and that the king and the Estates-General were victims of an aristocratic plot. Rural vision, fueled by empty stomachs, was apocalyptic.

That state of affairs was aggravated as increasing numbers of peasants were pushed off the land to seek employment as transient farm laborers, moving from one area to another with the cycles of sowing and harvesting. Throughout the 1780s, the number of peasants without land was increasing steadily. Starving men, women, and children, filthy and poorly dressed, were frightening figures to villagers who feared that the same fate would befall them with the next bad harvest. As one landowner lamented, "We cannot lie down without fear, the nighttime paupers have tormented us greatly, to say nothing of the daytime ones, whose numbers are considerable."

Most peasants had lived in the same place for generations and knew only the confines of their own villages. They were uneasy about what existed beyond the horizon. Transients, often speaking strange dialects, disrupted and threatened the social universe of the village. In order to survive, wanderers often resorted to petty theft, stealing fruit from trees or food from unwatched hearths. Often traveling in groups, hordes of vagabonds struck fear into the hearts of farm workers, trampling crops and sleeping in open fields. Peasants were sure that the unfortunate souls were brigands paid by the local aristocracy to persecute a peasantry already stretched to the breaking point.

The Peasant Revolt. Hope gave way to fear. Beginning on 20 July 1789, peasants in different areas of France reacted collectively throughout France, spreading false rumors of a great conspiracy. Fear gripped whole villages and in some areas spawned revolt. Just as urban workers had connected their economic hardships to politics, so too did desperate peasants see their plight in political terms. They banded together and marched to the residences of the local nobility, breaking into chateaux with a single mission in mind: to destroy all legal documents by which nobles claimed payments, dues, and services from local peasants. They drove out the lords and in some cases burned their chateaux, putting an end to the tyranny of the privileged over the countryside. The peasants had taken matters into their own hands. They intended to consign the last vestiges of aristocratic privilege to the bonfires of aristocratic documents.

The overthrow of privileges rooted in a feudal past was not as easy as that. Members of the National Assembly were aghast at the eruption of rural violence. They knew that to stay in power they had to maintain peace. They also knew that to be credible they had to protect property. Peasant destruction of seigneurial claims posed a real dilemma for the bourgeois deputies directing the revolution. If they gave in to peasant demands, they risked losing aristocratic support and undermining their own ability to control events. If they gave in to the aristocracy, they risked a social revolution in the countryside, which they could not police or repress. Liberal members of the aristocracy cooperated with the bourgeois leaders in finding a solution.

In a dramatic meeting that lasted through the night of 4 August 1789, the National Assembly agreed to abolish the principle of privilege. The peasants had won—or thought

■ A contemporary print of the women of Paris advancing on Versailles. The determined marchers are shown waving pikes and dragging an artillery piece. The women were hailed as heroines of the revolution.

Depart des Heroines de Paris pour Versailles le 5 Octobre 1789.

they had. In the weeks and months ahead, rural people learned that they had lost their own prerogatives—the rights to common grazing and gathering—and were expected to buy their way out of their feudal services. In the meantime, parliamentary action had saved the day: the deputies stabilized the situation through legislating compromise.

Women on the March.   Women participated with men in both urban and rural revolutionary actions. Acting on their own, women were responsible for one of the most dramatic events of the early years of the revolution: in October 1789 they forced the king and the royal family to leave Versailles for Paris to deal in person with the problems of bread supply, high prices, and starvation. Women milling about in the marketplaces of Paris on the morning of 5 October were complaining bitterly about the high cost and shortages of bread. The National Assembly was in session, and the National Guards were patrolling the streets of Paris. But the trappings of political change had no impact on the brutal realities of the marketplace.

Women were in charge of buying the food for their families. Every morning they stood in lines with their neighbors reenacting the familiar ritual. Some mornings they were turned away, told by the baker or his assistants that there was no bread. On other days they did not have enough coins in their purses to buy the staple of their diet. Women responsible for managing the consumption of the household were most directly in touch with the state of provisioning the capital. When they were unable to feed their families, the situation became intolerable.

So it was, on the morning of 5 October 1789, that 6000 Parisian women marched out of the city and toward Versailles. They were taking their problem to the king with the demand that he solve it. Later in the day, Lafayette led the Parisian National Guard to Versailles to mediate events. The women were armed with pikes, the simple weapon available to the poorest defender of the revolution, and they were prepared to use them. The battle came early the next morning, when the women, now accompanied by revolutionary men, tired and cold from waiting all night at the gates of the palace, invaded the royal apartments and chased Marie Antoinette from her bedroom. Several members of the royal guards, hated by the people of Paris for alleged insults against the tricolor cockade, were killed by the angry crowd, who decapitated them and mounted their heads on pikes. A shocked Louis XVI agreed to return with the crowd to Paris. The crowd cheered Louis's decision, which briefly reestablished his personal popularity. But as monarch, he had been humiliated at the hands of women of the capital. Reduced to the roles of "the baker, the baker's wife, and the baker's son" by jeering crowds, the royal family was forced to return to Paris that very day. Louis XVI was now captive to the revolution, whose efforts to form a constitutional monarchy he purported to support.

Declaring Political Rights

"Liberty consists in the ability to do whatever does not harm another." So wrote the revolutionary deputies of 1789. Sounding a refrain similar to that of the American Declaration of Independence, the Declaration of the Rights of Man and Citizen appeared on 26 August 1789. The document amalgamated a variety of Enlightenment ideas drawn from the works of political philosophy, including those of Locke and Montesquieu. "Men are born and remain free and equal in rights. Social distinctions may be based only on common utility." Perhaps most significant of all was the attention given to property, which was declared a "sacred and inviolable," "natural," and "imprescriptible" right of man.

In the year of tranquility that followed the violent summer of 1789, the new politicians set themselves the task of creating institutions based on the principle of liberty and others embodied in the Declaration of the Rights of Man and Citizen. The result was the Constitution of 1791, a statement of faith in a progressive constitutional monarchy. A king accountable to an elected parliamentary body would lead France into a prosperous and just age. The constitution acknowledged the

■ Slaves revolting against the French in Saint Domingue in 1791. Napoleon sent an army to restore colonial rule in 1799, but yellow fever decimated the French soldiers, and the rebels defeated the weakened French army in 1803.

DECLARATION OF THE RIGHTS OF MAN AND CITIZEN

Sounding a refrain similar to that of the American Declaration of Independence (1776), the Declaration of the Rights of Man and Citizen was adopted by the French National Assembly on 26 August 1789. The document amalgamated a variety of Enlightenment ideas, including those of Locke and Montesquieu. The attention to property, which was defined as "sacred and inviolable," rivaled that given to liberty as a "natural" and "imprescriptible" right of man.

Focus Questions

How are individual rights defined in relation to the rights of "society" and the "nation"? What is the role of law in protecting rights?

1. Men are born and remain free and equal in rights. Social distinctions may be founded only upon the general good.

2. The aim of all political association is the preservation of the natural and imprescriptible rights of man. These rights are liberty, property, security, and resistance to oppression.

3. The principle of all sovereignty resides essentially in the nation. No body nor individual may exercise any authority which does not proceed directly from the nation.

4. Liberty consists in the freedom to do everything which injures no one else; hence the exercise of the natural rights of each man has no limits except those which assure to the other members of the society the enjoyment of the same rights. These limits can only be determined by law.

5. Law can only prohibit such actions as are hurtful to society. Nothing may be prevented which is not forbidden by law, and no one may be forced to do anything not provided for by law.

6. Law is the expression of the general will. Every citizen has a right to participate personally, or through his representative, in its formation. It must be the same for all, whether it protects or punishes. All citizens, being equal in the eyes of the law, are equally eligible to all dignities and to all public positions and occupations, according to their abilities, and without distinction except that of their virtues and talents.

7. No person shall be accused, arrested, or imprisoned except in the cases and according to the forms prescribed by law. Any one soliciting, transmitting, executing, or causing to be executed, any arbitrary order, shall be punished. But any citizen summoned or arrested in virtue of the law shall submit without delay, as resistance constitutes an offense.

8. The law shall provide for such punishments only as are strictly and obviously necessary. . . .

9. As all persons are held innocent until they shall have been declared guilty, if arrest shall be deemed indispensable, all harshness not essential to the securing of the prisoner's person shall be severely repressed by law.

10. No one shall be disquieted on account of his opinions, including his religious views, provided their manifestation does not disturb the public order established by law.

11. The free communication of ideas and opinions is one of the most precious of the rights of man. Every citizen may, accordingly, speak, write, and print with freedom, but shall be responsible for such abuses of this freedom as shall be defined by law.

12. The security of the rights of man and of the citizen requires public military forces. These forces are, therefore, established for the good of all and not for the personal advantage of those to whom they shall be entrusted.

13. A common contribution is essential for the maintenance of the public forces and for the cost of administration. This should be equitably distributed among all the citizens in proportion to their means.

14. All the citizens have a right to decide, either personally or by their representatives, as to the necessity of the public contribution; to grant this freely; to know to what uses it is put; and to fix the proportion, the mode of assessment and of collection and the duration of the taxes.

15. Society has the right to require of every public agent an account of his administration.

16. A society in which the observance of the law is not assured, nor the separation of powers defined, has no constitution at all.

17. Since property is an inviolable and sacred right, no one shall be deprived thereof except where public necessity, legally determined, shall clearly demand it, and then only on condition that the owner shall have been previously and equitably indemnified.

DECLARATION OF THE RIGHTS OF WOMAN AND CITIZEN

"Woman, wake up!" Thus did Olympe de Gouges (d. 1793), a self-educated playwright, address French women in 1791. Aware that women were being denied the new rights of liberty and property extended to all men by the Declaration of the Rights of Man and Citizen, Gouges composed her own Declaration of the Rights of Woman and Citizen, modeled on the 1789 document. Persecuted for her political beliefs, she foreshadowed her own demise at the hands of revolutionary justice in Article 10 of her declaration. The Declaration of the Rights of Woman and Citizen became an important document in women's demands for political rights in the nineteenth century, and Gouges herself became a feminist hero.

Focus Questions

Why was a separate declaration of rights necessary for women? How does this declaration differ from the "Declaration of the Rights of Man and Citizen"?

Article I Woman is born free and lives equal to man in her rights. Social distinctions can be based only on the common utility.

Article II The purpose of any political association is the conservation of the natural and imprescriptible rights of woman and man; these rights are liberty, property, security, and especially resistance to oppression.

Article III The principle of all sovereignty rests essentially with the nation, which is nothing but the union of woman and man; no body and no individual can exercise any authority which does not come expressly from it [the nation].

Article IV Liberty and justice consist of restoring all that belongs to others; thus, the only limits on the exercise of the natural rights of woman are perpetual male tyranny; these limits are to be reformed by the laws of nature and reason.

Article V Laws of nature and reason proscribe all acts harmful to society; everything which is not prohibited by these wise and divine laws cannot be prevented, and no one can be constrained to do what they do not command.

Article VI The law must be the expression of the general will; all female and male citizens must contribute either personally or through their representatives to its formation; it must be the same for all: male and female citizens, being equal in the eyes of the law, must be equally admitted to all honors, positions, and public employment according to their capacity and without other distinctions besides those of their virtues and talents.

Article VII No woman is an exception; she is accused, arrested, and detained in cases determined by law. Women, like men, obey this rigorous law.

Article VIII The law must establish only those penalties that are strictly and obviously necessary. . . .

Article IX Once any woman is declared guilty, complete rigor is [to be] exercised by the law.

Article X No one is to be disquieted for his very basic opinions; woman has the right to mount the scaffold; she must equally have the right to mount the rostrum, provided that her demonstrations do not disturb the legally established public order.

Article XI The free communication of thoughts and opinions is one of the most precious rights of woman, since that liberty assures the recognition of children by their fathers. Any female citizen thus may say freely, I am the mother of a child which belongs to you, without being forced by a barbarous prejudice to hide the truth; [an exception may be made] to respond to the abuse of this liberty in cases determined by the law.

Article XII The guarantee of the rights of woman and the female citizen implies a major benefit; this guarantee must be instituted for the advantage of all, and not for the particular benefit of those to whom it is entrusted.

Article XIII For the support of the public force and the expenses of administration, the contributions of woman and man are equal; she shares all the duties [*corvées*] and all the painful tasks; therefore, she must have the same share in the distribution of positions, employment, offices, honors and jobs [*industrie*].

Article XIV Female and male citizens have the right to verify, either by themselves or through their representatives, the necessity of the public contribution. This can only apply to women if they are granted an equal share, not only of wealth, but also of public administration, and in the determination of the proportion, the base, the collection, and the duration of the tax.

Article XV The collectivity of women, joined for tax purposes to the aggregate of men, has the right to demand an accounting of his administration from any public agent.

Article XVI No society has a constitution without the guarantee of rights and the separation of powers: the constitution is null if the majority of individuals comprising the nation have not cooperated in drafting it.

Article XVII Property belongs to both sexes whether united or separate; for each it is an inviolable and sacred right; no one can be deprived of it, since it is the true patrimony of nature, unless the legally determined public need obviously dictates it, and then only with a just and prior indemnity.

people's sovereignty as the source of political power. It also enshrined the principle of property by making voting rights dependent on property ownership. All men might be equal before the law, but by the Constitution of 1791 only wealthy men had the right to vote for representatives and hold office.

Civil Liberties. All titles of nobility were abolished. In the early period of the revolution, civil liberties were extended to Protestants and Jews, who had been persecuted under the Old Regime. Previously excluded groups were granted freedom of thought, worship, and full civil liberties. More reluctantly, deputies outlawed slavery in the colonies in 1794. Slave unrest in Saint Domingue (modern-day Haiti) had coincided with the political conflicts of the revolution and exploded in rebellion in 1791, driving the revolutionaries in Paris to support black independence although it was at odds with French colonial interests. Led by Toussaint L'Ouverture (1743–1803), black rebels worked to found an independent Haitian state, which was declared in 1804. But the concept of equality with regard to race remained incompletely integrated with revolutionary principles, and slavery was reestablished in the French colonies in 1802.

Women's Rights. Men were the subject of the newly defined rights. No references to women or their rights appear in the constitutions or the official Declarations of Rights. Women's organizations agitated for an equitable divorce law, and divorce was legalized in September 1792. Women were critical actors in the revolution from its very inception, and their presence shaped and directed the outcome of events, as the women's march to Versailles in 1789 made clear. The Marquis de Condorcet (1743–1794), elected to the Legislative Assembly in 1791, was one of the first to chastise the revolutionaries for overlooking the political rights of women who, he pointedly observed, were half of the human race. "Either no individual of the human race has genuine rights, or else all have the same; and he who votes against the right of another, whatever the religion, color, or sex of that other, has henceforth abjured his own." Condorcet argued forcefully but unsuccessfully for the right of women to be educated.

The revolutionaries had declared that liberty was a natural and inalienable right, a universal right that was extended to all with the overthrow of a despotic monarch and a privileged elite. The principle triumphed in religious toleration. Yet the revolutionary concept of liberty foundered on the divergent claims of excluded groups—workers, women, and slaves—who demanded full participation in the world of politics. In 1792, revolutionaries confronted the contradictions inherent in their political beliefs of liberty and equality that were being challenged in the midst of social upheaval and foreign war. In response, the revolution turned to more radical measures to survive.

The Trials of Constitutional Monarchy

The disciplined deliberations of committees intent on fashioning a constitutional monarchy replaced the passion and fervor of revolutionary oratory. The National, or Constituent, Assembly divided France into new administrative units—*départements*—for the purpose of establishing better control over municipal governments. Along with new administrative trappings, the government promoted its own rituals. On 14 July 1790, militias from each of the newly created 83 départements of France came together in Paris to celebrate the first anniversary of the storming of the Bastille. A new national holiday was born and with it a sense of devotion and patriotism for the new France liberated by the revolution. In spite of the unifying elements, however, the newly achieved revolutionary consensus began to show signs of breaking down.

The Counterrevolution. In February 1790, legislation dissolved all monasteries and convents, except for those that provided aid to the poor or that served as educational institutions. As the French church was stripped of its lands, Pope Pius VI (1775–1799) denounced the principles of the revolution. In July 1790, the government approved the Civil Constitution of the Clergy: priests now became the equivalent of paid agents of the state. By requiring an oath of loyalty to the state from all practicing priests, the National Assembly created a new arena for dissent. Catholics were forced to choose to embrace or reject the revolution. Many "nonjuring" priests who refused to take the oath went into hiding. The wedge driven between the Catholic Church and revolutionary France allowed a mass-based counterrevolution to emerge. Aristocratic émigrés who had fled the country because of their opposition to the revolution were languishing for lack of a popular base. From his headquarters in Turin, the king's younger brother, the comte d'Artois, was attempting to incite a civil war in France. When the revolutionaries decided to attack the Church not just as a landed and privileged institution but also as a religious one, the counterrevolution rapidly expanded.

Late one night in June 1791, Louis XVI, Marie Antoinette, and their children disguised themselves as commoners, crept out of the royal apartments in the Tuileries Palace, and fled Paris. Louis intended to leave France to join royalist forces opposing the revolution at Metz. He got as far as Varennes, where he was captured by soldiers of the National Guard and brought back to a shocked Paris. The king had abandoned the revolution. Although he was not put to death for another year and a half, he was more than ever a prisoner of the revolution.

The Fiscal Crisis. The defection of the king was certainly serious, but it was not the only problem facing the revolutionaries. Other problems plagued the revolutionary government, notably foreign war and the fiscal crisis, coupled with inflation. In order to establish its seriousness and legitimacy, the National Assembly had been willing in 1789 to absorb the debts of the Old Regime. The new government could not sell titles and offices, as the king had done to deal with financial problems, but it did confiscate Church property. In addition, it issued treasury bonds in the form of assignats in order to raise money. The assignats soon assumed the status of bank notes, and by the spring of 1790 they had become compulsory legal tender.

Initially they were to be backed by land confiscated from the Church and sold by the state. But the need for money soon outran the value of the land available, and the government continued to print assignats according to its needs. Depreciation of French currency in international markets and inflation at home resulted. The revolutionary government found itself in a situation which in certain respects was worse than that experienced by Louis XVI before the calling of the Estates-General. Assignat-induced inflation produced a sharp decline in the fortunes of bourgeois investors living on fixed incomes. Rising prices meant increased misery for workers and peasants.

New counterrevolutionary groups were becoming frustrated with revolutionary policies. Throughout the winter and spring of 1791–1792, people rioted and demanded that prices be fixed, while the assignat dropped to less than half its face value. Peasants refused to sell crops for the worthless paper. Hoarding further drove up prices. Angry crowds turned to pillaging, rioting, and murder, which became more frequent as the value of the currency declined and prices rose.

Foreign war beginning in the fall of 1791 also challenged stability. Some moderate political leaders welcomed war as a blessing in disguise, since it could divert the attention of the masses away from problems at home and promote loyalty to the revolution. Others envisioned war as a great crusade to bring revolutionary principles to oppressed peoples throughout Europe. The king and queen, trapped by the revolution, saw war as their only hope of liberation. Louis XVI could be rightfully restored as the leader of a France defeated by the sovereigns of Europe. Some who opposed the war believed it would destabilize the revolution. France must solve its problems at home, they argued, before fighting a foreign enemy. Louis, however, encouraged those ministers and advisers eager for battle. In April 1792, France declared war against Austria.

Individuals, events, economic realities, and the nature of politics conspired against the success of the first constitutional experiment. The king's attempt to flee France in the summer of 1791 seriously wounded the attempt at compromise. Many feared that the goals of the revolution could not be preserved in a country at war and with a king of dubious loyalties.

EXPERIMENTING WITH DEMOCRACY, 1792–1799

The Revolution was a school for the French nation. A political universe populated by individual citizens replaced the eighteenth-century world of subjects loyal to their king. The new construction of politics, in which all individuals were equal, ran counter to prevailing ideas about collective identities defined in guilds and orders. People on all levels of society learned politics by doing it. In the beginning, experience helped. The elites, both noble and bourgeois, had served in government and administration. But the rules of the game under the Old Regime had been very different, with birth and wealth determining power.

After 1789, all men were declared free and equal, in opportunity if not in rights. Men of ability and talent, who had served as middlemen for the privileged elite under the Old Regime, now claimed power as their due. Many of them were lawyers, educated in the rules and regulations of the society of orders. They experienced firsthand the problems of the exercise of power in the Old Regime, and they had their own ideas about reform. But the school of the revolution did not remain the domain of a special class. Women demanded their places but continued to be excluded from the political arena, though the importance of their participation in the revolution was indisputable. Workers talked of seizing their rights, but because of the inherent contradictions of representation and participation, experimenting with democracy led to outcomes that did not look very democratic at all.

The Revolution of the People

The first stage of the French Revolution, lasting from 1789 through the beginning of 1792, was based on liberty—the liberty to compete, to own, and to succeed. The second stage of the French Revolution, which began in 1792, took equality as its rallying cry. It was the revolution of the working people of French cities. The popular movement that spearheaded political action in 1792 was committed to equality of rights in a way not characteristic of the leaders of the revolution of 1789. Urban workers were not benefiting from the revolution, but they had come to believe in their own power as political beings. Organized on the local level into sections, artisans in cities identified themselves as **sans-culottes**—literally, those trousered citizens who did not wear knee breeches (*culottes*)—to distinguish themselves from the privileged elite.

Who constituted the popular movement? The self-designated sans-culottes were the working men and women of Paris. Some were wealthier than others, some were wage earners, but all shared a common identity as consumers in the marketplace. They hated the privileged (*les gros*), who appeared to be profiting at the expense of the people. The sans-culottes wanted government power to be decentralized, with neighborhoods ruling themselves through sectional organizations. As the have-nots, they were increasingly intent on pulling down the haves, and they translated the sense of vengeance into a new revolutionary justice. On 10 August 1792, the people of Paris stormed the Tuileries, chanting their demands for "Equality!" and "Nation!" The people tramped across the silk sheets of the king's bed and broke his fine furniture, reveling in the private chambers of the royal family. Love and respect for the king had vanished. What the people of Paris demanded was the right to vote and participate in a popular democracy. Working people were acting independently of other factions, and the bourgeois political leadership became quickly aware of the need to scramble to maintain order. When they invaded the Tuileries Palace on the morning of 10 August, the sans-culottes did so in the name of the people. They saw themselves as patriots whose duty it was to brush the monarchy aside. The people were now a force to be reckoned with and feared.

A Closer Look
The Guillotine and Revolutionary Justice

In the sultry summer days of 1792, Parisians found a new way to entertain themselves. They attended executions. French men, women, and children were long accustomed to watching criminals being tortured and put to death in public view. During the Old Regime, spectators could enjoy a variety of methods: drawing and quartering, strangling, or hanging. Decapitation, reputedly a less painful death, was a privilege reserved for nobles sentenced for capital crimes. The French Revolution extended that formerly aristocratic privilege to all criminals condemned to death. What especially attracted people to public squares in the third year of the revolution was the introduction of a novel method of decapitation. In 1792, the new instrument of death, the guillotine, became the center of the spectacle of revolutionary justice.

The guillotine promised to eliminate the suffering of its victims. Axes, swords, and sabers—the traditional tools of decapitation and dismemberment—were messy and undependable, producing slow and bloody ordeals when inept or drunken executioners missed their mark or victims flinched at the fatal moment. The design of the guillotine took all of that into account. On its easel-like wooden structure, victims, lying on their stomachs, were held in place with straps and a pillory. Heavy pulleys guaranteed that the sharp blade would fall efficiently from its great height. A basket was placed at the base of the blade to catch the severed head; another was used to slide the headless body through the base of the scaffolding for removal. In place of unintended torture and gore, the guillotine was devised as a humanitarian instrument to guarantee swift and painless death.

It should have been called the Louisette, after its inventor, Dr. Antoine Louis. In what now seems a dubious honor, the new machine was named instead after its greatest supporter, Dr. Joseph Ignace Guillotin, a delegate to the National Assembly. Both Guillotin and Louis were medical doctors, men of science influenced by Enlightenment ideas and committed to the revolution's elimination of the cruelty of older forms of punishment. In the spirit of scientific experimentation, Louis's invention was tested on sheep, cadavers, and then convicted thieves. In 1792, it was used for the first time against another class of offenders: political prisoners.

Early in the revolution, the Marquis de Condorcet, philosophe and mathematician, had opposed capital punishment with the argument that the state did not have the right to take life. Ironically, Maximilien Robespierre, future architect of the Reign of Terror, was one of the few revolutionaries who agreed with Condorcet. Those who favored justice by execution of the state's enemies prevailed. The revolutionary hero and associate of the radical Jacobins Jean-Paul Marat (1743–1793), who was himself stabbed to death in his bathtub, advocated the state's use of violence against its enemies: "In order to ensure public tranquility, 200,000

■ Execution of Louis XVI on 21 January 1793.

heads must be cut off." By the end of 1792, as revolution and civil war swept over France, 83 identical guillotines were constructed and installed in each of the départements of France. For the next two years, the guillotine's great blade was rhythmically raised and lowered daily in public squares all over France. In the name of the revolution, the "axe of the people" dispatched over 50,000 victims.

Although intended as a humanitarian instrument, the guillotine became the symbol of all that was arbitrary and repressive about a revolution run amok. Day and night, the Revolutionary Tribunal in Paris delivered the death sentence to the "enemies of the people." Most of those executed were members of what had been the Third Estate: members of the bourgeoisie, workers, and peasants. Only 15 percent of the condemned were nobles and priests. During the Terror, the guillotine could be used to settle old scores. Sans-culottes turned in their neighbors, sometimes over long-standing grievances that owed more to spite than politics. The most fanatical revolutionaries had fantasies that guillotines were about to be erected on every street corner to dispense with hoarders and traitors. Others suggested that guillotines be made portable so that by putting justice on wheels, it could be taken directly to the people.

As usual, Paris set the style. The most famous of the guillotines stood on the Place du Carrousel, deliberately placed in front of the royal palace of the Tuileries. It was eventually moved to the larger Place de la Révolution in order to accommodate the growing numbers of spectators. Famous victims drew especially large crowds. The revolutionary drama took on the trappings of a spectacle as hawkers sold toy guillotines, miniature pikes, and liberty caps as souvenirs, along with the usual food and drink. Troops attended the events, but not to control the crowd. Members of the National Guard in formation, their backs to the people, faced the stage of the scaffold. They, like the citizenry, were there to witness the birth of a new nation and, by their presence, to give legitimacy to the event. The crowd entered into the ritual, cheering the victim's last words and demanding that the executioner hold high the severed head. In the new political culture, death was a festival.

For two centuries, Western societies have debated the legitimacy of the death sentence and have periodically considered the relative merits of the guillotine, the gas chamber, and the electric chair. For the French, the controversy temporarily ceased in 1794, when people were convinced that justice had gotten out of hand and that they had had enough. The guillotine would return, but for the time being, the government put an end to capital punishment. At the height of its use, between 1792 and 1794, it had played a unique role in forging a new system of justice: the guillotine had been the great leveler. In the ideology of democracy, people were equal—in death as well as in life. The guillotine came to be popularly known as the "scythe of equality." It killed king and commoner alike.

(La Scène se passe sur la place de la Révolution
Admirez de Samson l'intelligence extrême
Par le couteau fatal, il a tout fait périr.
Dans cet affreux état que va t'il devenir?
Il se guillotine lui même.

■ This frontispiece from the anti-Robespierre work *Almanach des Prisons* illustrates the results of the Reign of Terror under Robespierre's leadership and the guillotine's blade.

"Terror Is the Order of the Day"

Political factions characterized revolutionary politics from the start. The terms *Left* and *Right*, which came to represent opposite ends of the political spectrum, originated in a description of where people sat in the Assembly in relation to the podium. Political designations were refined in successive parliamentary bodies. The Convention was the legislative body elected in September 1792 that succeeded the Legislative Assembly and had as its charge determining the best form of government after the collapse of the monarchy. On 21 September 1792, the monarchy was abolished in France; on the following day the Republic, France's first, came into being. Members of the Convention conducted the trial of Louis XVI for treason and pronounced his sentence: execution by the guillotine in January 1793.

The various political factions of the Convention were described in terms borrowed from geography. The Mountain, sitting on the upper benches on the left, was made up of members of the Jacobin Club (named for its meeting place in an abandoned monastery). The **Jacobins** were the most radical element in the National Convention, supporting democratic solutions and speaking in favor of the cause of people in the streets.

Jacobin Ascendancy. Both **Girondins**, the more moderate revolutionary faction, and Jacobins were from the middle ranks of the bourgeoisie, and both groups were dedicated to the principles of the revolution. Although they controlled the ministries, the Girondins began to lose their hold on the revolution and the war. The renewed European war fragmented the democratic movement, and the Girondins, unable to control violence at home, saw political control slipping away. They became prisoners of the revolution when 80,000 armed Parisians surrounded the National Convention in June 1793.

Girondin power had been eroding in the critical months between August 1792 and June 1793. A new leader was working quietly and effectively behind the scenes to weld a partnership between the popular movement of sans-culottes and the Jacobins. He was Maximilien Robespierre (1758–1794), leader of the Mountain and the Jacobin Club. Robespierre was typical of the new breed of revolutionary politician. Only 31 years old in 1789, he wrote mediocre poems and attended the local provincial academy to discuss the new ideas when he was not practicing law in his hometown of Arras. Elected to the Estates-General, he joined the Jacobin Club and quickly rose to become its leader. He was willing to take controversial stands on issues: unlike most of his fellow members of the Mountain—including his rival, the popular orator Georges-Jacques Danton (1759–1794)—he opposed the war in 1792. Although neither an original thinker nor a compelling orator, Robespierre discovered with the revolution that he was an adroit political tactician. He gained a following and learned how to manipulate it. It was he who engineered the Jacobins' replacement of the Girondins as leaders of the government.

Robespierre and the Reign of Terror. Robespierre's chance for real power came when he assumed leadership of the Committee of Public Safety in July 1793. Faced with the threat of internal anarchy and external war, the elected body, the National Convention, yielded political control to the 12-man Committee of Public Safety that ruled dictatorially under Robespierre's direction. The Great Committee, as it was known at the time, orchestrated the **Reign of Terror** (1793–1794), a period of systematic state repression that meted out justice in the people's name. Summary trials by specially created revolutionary tribunals were followed by the swift execution of the guilty under the blade of the guillotine.

Influenced by *The Social Contract* (1762) and other writings of Jean-Jacques Rousseau, Robespierre believed that sovereignty resided with the people. For him, individual wills and even individual rights did not matter when weighed against the will of the nation. The king was dead; the people were the new source of political power. Robespierre saw himself in the all-important role of interpreting and shaping the people's will. His own task was to guide the people "to the summit of its destinies." As he explained to his critics, "I am defending not my own cause but the public cause." As head of the Great Committee, Robespierre oversaw a revolutionary machinery dedicated to economic regulation, massive military mobilization, and a punitive system of revolutionary justice characterized by the slogan, "Terror Is the Order of the Day." Militant revolutionary committees and revolutionary tribunals were established throughout France to identify traitors and to mete out the harsh justice that struck hardest against those members of the bourgeoisie perceived as opponents of the government.

The guillotine became the symbol of revolutionary justice, but it was not the only means of execution. (See "A Closer Look: The Guillotine and Revolutionary Justice," pp. 622–623.) In Lyon, officials of the Reign of Terror had prisoners tied to stakes in open fields and fired on with cannons. In Nantes, a Parisian administrator of the new justice had enemies of the revolution chained to barges and drowned in the estuary of the Loire. The civil war, which raged most violently in the Vendée in the west of France, consisted often of primitive massacres that sent an estimated quarter of a million people to their deaths. The bureaucratized Reign of Terror was responsible for about 40,000 executions in a nine-month period, resulting in the image of the republicans as "drinkers of blood."

The Cult of the Supreme Being, a civic religion without priests or churches and influenced by Rousseau's ideas about nature, followed de-Christianization. The cathedral of Notre Dame de Paris was turned into the Temple of Reason, and the new religion established its own festivals to undermine the persistence of Catholicism. The cult was one indication of the Reign of Terror's attempt to create a new moral universe of revolutionary values.

Women Excluded. Women remained conspicuously absent from the summit of political power. After 1793, Jacobin revolutionaries, who had been willing to empower the popular movement of workers, turned against women's participation and denounced it. Women's associations were outlawed and the Society of Revolutionary Republican Women was disbanded. Olympe de Gouges, revolutionary author of the Declaration of the Rights of Woman and Citizen (see p. 619), was guillotined. Women were declared unfit for political participation, according to the Jacobins, because of their biological functions of reproduction and child-rearing. Rousseau's ideas about family policy were probably more influential than his political doctrines. His best-selling books, *La Nouvelle Héloïse* (1761) and *Émile* (1762), which combined went into 72 editions before 1789, were moral works that transformed people's ideas about family life. Under his influence, the reading public came to value a separate and private sphere of domestic and conjugal values. Following Rousseau's lead, Robespierre and the Jacobins insisted that the role of women as mothers was incompatible with women's participation in the political realm.

The Thermidorian Reaction. By attacking his critics on both the Left and the Right, Robespierre undermined the support he needed to stay in power. He abandoned the alliance with the popular movement that had been so important in bringing him to power. Robespierre's enemies—and he had many—were able to break the identification between political power and the will of the people that Robespierre had established. As a result, he was branded a traitor by the same process that he had used against many of his own enemies. He saved France from foreign occupation and internal collapse, but he could not save democracy through terror. In the summer of 1794, Robespierre was guillotined. The Reign of Terror ceased with his death in the revolutionary month of Thermidor 1794.

The revolution did not end with the **Thermidorian Reaction,** as the fall of Robespierre came to be known, but his execution initiated a new phase. For some, democracy lost its legitimacy. The popular movement was reviled, and sans-culotte became a term of derision. Jacobins were forced underground. Price controls were abolished, resulting in extreme hardship for most urban residents. Out of desperation, in April 1795 the Jacobins and the sans-culottes renewed their alliance and united to demand "bread and the Constitution of 1793." The politics of bread had never been more accurately captured in slogan. Those who took to the streets in 1795 saw the universal manhood suffrage of the unimplemented 1793 constitution as the way to solve their economic problems. But their demands went unheeded; the popular revolution had failed.

The End of the Revolution

In the four years after Robespierre's fall, a new government by committee, called the Directory, appeared to offer mediocrity, caution, and opportunism in place of the idealism and action of the early years of the revolution. No successor to Robespierre stepped forward to command center stage. There were no heroes like Lafayette or the great Jacobin orator Georges-Jacques Danton to inspire patriotic fervor. Nor were there women like Olympe de Gouges to demand in the public arena equal rights for women. Most people, numbed after

CHRONOLOGY	
THE FRENCH REVOLUTION	
August 1788	Louis XVI announces meeting of Estates-General to be held May 1789
5 May 1789	Estates-General convenes
17 June 1789	Third Estate declares itself the National Assembly
20 June 1789	Oath of the Tennis Court
14 July 1789	Storming of the Bastille
20 July 1789	Revolution of peasantry begins
26 August 1789	Declaration of the Rights of Man and Citizen
5 October 1789	Parisian women march to Versailles; force Louis XVI to return to Paris
February 1790	Monasteries, convents dissolved
July 1790	Civil Constitution of the Clergy
June 1791	Louis XVI and family attempt to flee Paris; are captured and returned
September 1791	France's first Constitution
April 1792	France declares war on Austria
10 August 1792	Storming of the Tuileries
22 September 1792	Revolutionary calendar implemented
January 1793	Louis XVI executed
July 1793	Robespierre assumes leadership of Committee of Public Safety
1793–1794	Reign of Terror
1794	Robespierre guillotined
1795	Directory rules France
1799	Napoleon overthrows the Directory and seizes power

years of change, barely noticed that the revolution was over. Ordinary men in parliamentary institutions effectively did the day-to-day job of running the government. They tried to steer a middle path between royalist resurgence and popular insurrection. This nearly forgotten period in the history of the French Revolution was the fulfillment of the liberal hopes of 1789 for a stable constitutional rule.

The Directory, however, continued to be dogged by European war. A mass army of conscripts and volunteers had successfully extended France's power and frontiers. France expelled foreign invaders and annexed territories, including

Belgium, while increasing its control in Holland, Switzerland, and Italy. But the expansion of revolutionary France was expensive and increasingly unpopular. Military defeats and the corruption of the Directory undermined government control. The Directory might have succeeded in the slow accretion of a parliamentary tradition, but reinstatement of **conscription** in 1798 met with widespread protest and resistance. No matter what their political leanings, people were weary. They turned to those who promised stability and peace.

In the democratic experiment at the heart of the second stage of the French Revolution, the sovereign will of the people permanently replaced the monarch's claim to divine right to rule. Yet with democracy came tyranny. The severe repression of the terror revealed the pressures that external war and civil unrest created for the new Republic. The Thermidorian Reaction and the elimination of Robespierre as the legitimate interpreter of the people's will ushered in a period of conciliation, opportunism, and a search for stability. Ironically, the savior that France found to answer its needs for peace and a just government was a man of war and a dictator.

THE REIGN OF NAPOLEON, 1799–1815

The great debate that rages to this day about Napoleon revolves around the question of whether he fulfilled the aims of the revolution or perverted them. In his return to a monarchical model, Napoleon resembled the enlightened despots of eighteenth-century Europe. In a modern sense, he was also a dictator, manipulating the French population through a highly centralized administrative apparatus. He locked French society into a program of military expansion that depleted its human and material resources. Yet, in spite of destruction and war, he dedicated his reign to building a French state according to the principles of the Revolution. Napoleon is one of those individuals about whom one can say that if he had not lived, history would have been different. He left his mark on an age and a continent.

Bonaparte Seizes Power

In Paris in 1795 a young, penniless, and unknown military officer moved among the wealthy and the beautiful of Parisian society and longed for fame. Already nicknamed at school "the Little Corporal" on account of his short stature, he was snubbed because of his background and ridiculed for his foreign accent. His story is typical of all stories of thwarted ambition. Yet the outcome of his story is unique: within four years, that young man would become ruler of France. The story of his ascent to power is also a story of the demise of the revolution.

Napoleon's Training and Experience.   Napoleon Bonaparte (1769–1821) was a true child of the eighteenth century. He shared the philosophes' belief in a rational and progressive world. Born in Corsica, which until a few months before his birth was part of the Republic of Genoa, he received his training in French military schools. As a youth, he was arrogant and ambitious. But he could have never aspired to a position of leadership in the army during the Old Regime because he lacked the noble birth necessary for advancement. The highest rank Napoleon could hope to achieve was that of captain or major.

DOCUMENT

The Rise of Napoleon

The revolution changed everything for him. First, it opened up careers previously restricted by birth, including those in the military, to those with talent. Second, the revolution made new posts available when aristocratic generals defected and crossed over to the enemy side, both before and after the execution of the king. Finally, the revolution created great opportunities for military men to test their mettle.

Foreign war and civil war required military leaders devoted to the revolution. Forced to flee Corsica because he had sided with the Jacobins, Napoleon and his troops were given the task of crushing Parisian protesters who rioted against the Directory in 1795. His victories in the Italian campaign in 1796–1797 launched his political career. As he extended French rule into central Italy, he became the embodiment of revolutionary values and energy.

The revolutionary wars had begun as wars to liberate humanity in the name of liberty, equality, and fraternity. Yet concerns for power, territory, and riches soon replaced earlier concerns with defense of the nation and of the revolution. The aggrandizement was nowhere more evident than in the Egyptian campaign of 1798, in which Napoleon Bonaparte headed an expedition whose goal was to enrich France by hastening the collapse of the Turkish Empire, crippling British trade routes, and handicapping Russian interests in the region. With Napoleon's highly publicized campaigns in Egypt and Syria, the war left the European theater and moved to the East, leaving behind its original revolutionary ideals. The Egyptian campaign, which was in reality a disaster, made Napoleon a hero at home.

Napoleon as First Consul.   In 1799, Napoleon Bonaparte readily joined a conspiracy that pulled down the Directory, the government he had earlier preserved, and became the First Consul of a triumvirate of consuls. Napoleon set out to secure his position of power by eliminating his enemies on the Left and weakening those on the Right. He guaranteed the security of property acquired in the revolution, a move that undercut royalists who wanted to return property to its original owners. Through policing forces and special criminal courts, law and order prevailed and civil war subsided. The First Consul promised a balanced budget and appeared to deliver it. Bonaparte spoke of healing the nation's wounds, especially those opened by de-Christianization during the revolution. Realizing the importance of religion in maintaining domestic peace, Napoleon reestablished relations with the pope in 1801 by the Concordat, which recognized Catholicism as the religion of the French and restored the Roman Catholic hierarchy.

Napoleon's popularity as First Consul flowed from his military and political successes and his religious reconciliation. He had come to power in 1799 by appealing for the support of the army. In 1802, Napoleon decided to extend his power by calling for a plebiscite in which he asked the electorate to vote him First Consul for life. Public support was overwhelming. An electoral landslide gave Napoleon greater political power than any of his Bourbon predecessors. Using revolutionary mechanisms, Napoleon laid the foundation for a new dynasty.

Napoleon at War with the European Powers

Napoleon was either at war or preparing for war during his entire reign. He certainly seemed up to the task of defeating the European powers. His military successes before 1799, real and apparent, had been crucial in his bid for political power. By 1802, he had signed favorable treaties with both Austria and Great Britain. He appeared to deliver a lasting peace and to establish France as the dominant power in Europe. But the peace was short-lived. In 1803, France embarked on an 11-year period of continuous war. Under Napoleon's command, the French army delivered defeat after defeat to the European powers. Austria fell in 1805, Prussia in 1806, and the Russian armies of Alexander I were defeated at Friedland in 1807. In 1808, Napoleon invaded Spain to drive out British expeditionary forces intent on

invading France. The great painter of the Spanish court, Francisco Goya (1746–1828), produced a series of etchings, *The Disasters of War,* that depicted the atrocities accompanying the Napoleonic invasion. Spain became a satellite kingdom of France, though the conflict continued.

Britain was the one exception to the string of Napoleonic victories. Napoleon initially considered sending a French fleet to invade the island nation. Lacking the strength necessary to achieve that, he turned to economic warfare, blockading European ports against British trade. Beginning in 1806, the **Continental System,** as the blockade was known, erected a structure of protection for French manufactures in all continental European markets. The British responded to the tariff walls and boycotts with a naval blockade that succeeded in cutting French commerce off from its Atlantic markets. The Continental System did not prove to be the decisive policy that Napoleon had planned: the British economy was not broken and the French economy did not flourish when faced with restricted resources and the persistence of a black market in smuggled goods.

Still, by 1810 the French leader was master of the Continent. French armies had extended revolutionary reforms and legal codes outside France and brought with them civil equality and religious toleration. They had also drained defeated countries of their resources and had inflicted the horrors of war with armies of occupation, forced billeting, and pillage. Napoleon's empire extended across Europe, with

■ This engraving, from the series *Disasters of War* by Francisco Goya, depicts the horrors of war. The series was inspired by Napoleon's invasion and occupation of Spain from 1808 to 1814.

only a diminished Austria, Prussia, and Russia remaining independent. He placed his relatives and friends on the thrones of the new satellite kingdoms of Italy, Naples, Westphalia, Holland, and Spain. It was a fine empire, Napoleon later recalled in the loneliness of exile. Napoleon's empire did not endure, but at its acme, it seemed as though it would never fall.

The First Empire and Domestic Reforms

Napoleon measured domestic prosperity in terms of the stability of his reign. Through the 1802 plebiscite that voted him First Consul for life, he maintained the charade of constitutional rule while he ruled as virtual dictator. In 1804, he abandoned all pretense and had himself proclaimed emperor of the French. Mimicking the rituals of kingship, he staged his own coronation and that of his wife Josephine at the cathedral of Notre Dame de Paris. Breaking the tradition set by Charlemagne, Napoleon took the crown from the hands of Pope Pius VII (1800–1823) and placed it on his own head.

The Importance of Science and Economic Reforms. Secure in his regime, surrounded by a new nobility that he created based on military achievement and talent and that he rewarded with honors, Napoleon set about implementing sweeping reforms in every area of government. Like many of the men of the revolutionary assemblies who had received scientific educations in their youth, he recognized the importance of science for both industry and war. The revolution had removed an impediment to the development of a national market by creating a uniform system of weights and measures. The metric system was established by 1799. But Napoleon felt the need to go further: France must be first in scientific research and application. To assure French predominance, Napoleon became a patron of science, supporting important work in the areas of physics and chemistry. Building for the future, Napoleon made science a pillar in the new structure of higher education.

The Directory had restored French prosperity through stabilization of the currency, fiscal reform, and support of industry. Napoleon's contribution to the French economy was the much needed reform of the tax system. He authorized the creation of a central banking system. French industries flourished under the protection of the state. The blockade forced the development of new domestic crops such as sugar beets and indigo, which became

MAP DISCOVERY

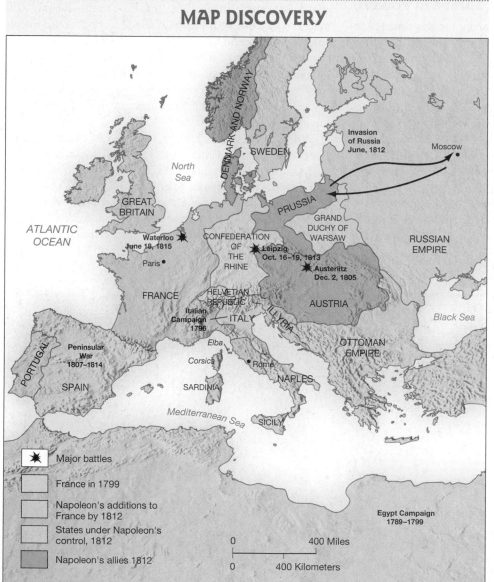

Napoleon's Empire

Note the expansion of France under Napoleon's rule. How much of western and central Europe did Napoleon control by 1812? Why did Great Britain remain outside of Napoleon's influence? Why were Prussia, Austria, and Denmark and Norway allies of France in 1812?

THE CIVIL CODE OF THE CODE NAPOLÉON (1804)

While still First Consul, Bonaparte assembled a group of the country's leading legal specialists to replace the vast agglomeration of feudal, customary, and canon laws, all with their own courts and procedures, with a unified system based on Roman law. The Civil Code, along with the Criminal Code, made up the Code Napoléon, and consisted of 2281 articles intended to cover all aspects of civil life from birth to death, all civic aspects relating to family and property, contractual responsibilities, and civil liberties. A unified legal system became the basis for economic development and was arguably Napoleon's greatest achievement as ruler of France. The Civil Code replaced the Roman Catholic Church as having authority over marriage, and although divorce was permitted in the Code, it was outlawed in 1816 and not permitted again until 1884.

Focus Questions

What rights do men enjoy in this passage that women do not? What are you able to conclude about the rights of married women who work?

Of the respective rights and duties of parent and children

212. Husband and wife owe each other fidelity, support, and assistance.
213. A husband owes protection to his wife; a wife owes obedience to her husband.
214. A wife is bound to live with her husband and to follow him wherever he deems proper to reside. The husband is bound to receive her, and to supply her with whatever is necessary for the wants of life, according to his means and condition.
215. A wife cannot sue in court without the consent of her husband, even if she is a public tradeswoman or if there is no community or she is separated as to property.
216. The husband's consent is not necessary when the wife is prosecuted criminally or in a police matter.
217. A wife, even when there is no community, or when she is separated as to property, cannot give, convey, mortgage, or acquire property, with or without consideration, without the husband joining in the instrument or giving his written consent.
218. If a husband refuses to allow his wife to sue in court, the Judge may grant the authorization.
219. If a husband refuses to allow his wife to execute an instrument, the wife can cause her husband to be summoned directly before the Tribunal of the First Instance of the common domicile, and such Tribunal shall grant or refuse its consent in the Judges' room after the husband has been heard or has been duly summoned.
220. A wife may, if she is a public tradeswoman, bind herself without the husband's consent with respect to what relates to her trade, and in that case she also binds her husband if there is a community of property between them. She is not considered a public tradeswoman if she merely retails the goods of her husband's business, but only when she has a separate business.
221. When a sentence has been passed upon a husband which carries with it a degrading corporal punishment, even if it has been passed by default, a wife, even of full age, cannot, during the continuance of the punishment, sue in court nor bind herself, unless she has been authorized by the Judge, who may in such cases grant the consent without the husband having been heard or summoned.
222. If a husband has been interdicted or is absent, the Judge may with proper knowledge of the case, authorize the wife to sue in court or to bind herself.
223. Any general authorization, even given by marriage contract, is only valid as to the management of the wife's property.
224. If the husband is a minor, the authorization of the Judge is necessary to the wife, either to sue in court or to bind herself.
225. A nullity based on the want of authorization can only be set up by the wife, the husband, or the heirs.
226. A wife can make a will without her husband's consent.

substitutes for colonial products. Napoleon extended the infrastructure of roads necessary for the expansion of national and European markets.

The New Legal System.   Perhaps his greatest achievement was the codification of law, a task begun under the revolution. Many of the new articles of the **Napoleonic Code**

were hammered out in Napoleon's presence, as he presided regularly over meetings with legal reformers. Combined with economic reforms, the Napoleonic Code facilitated trade and the development of commerce by regularizing contractual relations and protecting property rights and equality before the law.

The civil laws of the new code carved out a family policy characterized by hierarchy and subordination. Married women were neither independent nor equal to men in ownership of property, custody of children, or access to divorce. Women also lacked political rights. In the Napoleonic Code, women, like children, were subjected to paternal authority. The Napoleonic philosophy of woman's place is well captured in an anecdote told by Madame Germaine de Staël (1766–1817), a leading intellectual of her day. As the daughter of Jacques Necker, a Swiss financier and adviser to Louis XVI at the time of the revolution, she had been taught Enlightenment ideas from an early age. On finding herself seated next to Napoleon at a dinner party, she asked him what was very likely a self-interested question: Whom did he consider the greatest woman, alive or dead? Napoleon had no name to give her but responded, without pausing: "The one who has had the most children."

Napoleon turned his prodigious energies to every aspect of French life. He encouraged the arts while creating a police force. He had monuments built but did not forget about sewers. He organized French administrative life in a fashion that has endured. In place of the popular democratic movement, he offered his own singular authority. In place of elections, clubs, and free associations, he gave France plebiscites and army service. To be sure, Napoleon believed in constitutions, but he thought they should be "short and obscure." For Napoleon, the great problem of democracy was its unpredictability. His regime solved that problem by eliminating choices.

Decline and Fall

Militarily, Napoleon went too far. The first cracks in the French facade began to show in the Peninsular War (1808–1814) with Spain, in which Spanish guerrilla tactics proved costly for French troops. Napoleon's biggest mistake, the one that shattered the myth of his invincibility, occurred when he decided to invade Russia in June 1812.

The Invasion of Russia and the Battle of Nations.

Having decisively defeated Russian forces in 1807, Napoleon had entered into a peace treaty with Tsar Alexander I that guaranteed Russian allegiance to French policies. Alexander repudiated the Continental System in 1810 and appeared to be preparing for his own war against France. Napoleon seized the initiative, sure that he could defeat Russian forces once again. With an army of 500,000 men, Napoleon moved deep into Russia in the summer of 1812. The tsar's troops fell back in retreat. It was a strange war, one that pulled the French army to Moscow like a bird following bread crumbs. When Napoleon and his men entered Moscow in September, they found a city in flames. The people of Moscow had destroyed their own city to deprive the French troops of winter quarters.

Winter came early in Moscow, Napoleon's men discovered. They had left France basking in the warmth of summer and sure of certain and early victory. They then found themselves facing a severe Russian winter without overcoats, supplies, or food. Russia's strategy has become legendary. The Russians destroyed grain and shelter that might be of use to the French. Napoleon and his starving and frostbitten troops were forced into retreat. The horses of the French cavalry died because they were not properly shod for cold weather. The French army was decimated. Fewer than 100,000 men made it back to France.

■ This 1835 painting by De Boisdenier depicts the suffering of Napoleon's Grand Army on the retreat from Moscow. The Germans were to meet a similar fate more than 100 years later when they invaded Russia without adequate supplies for the harsh winter.

CHRONOLOGY
THE REIGN OF NAPOLEON

1799	Napoleon establishes consulate, becomes First Consul
1801	Napoleon reestablishes relations with pope, restores Roman Catholic hierarchy
1802	Plebiscite declares Napoleon First Consul for life
1804	Napoleon proclaims himself Emperor of the French
1806	Continental System implemented
1808–1814	France engaged in Peninsular War with Spain
June 1812	Napoleon invades Russia
September 1812	French army reaches Moscow; trapped by Russian winter
1813	Napoleon defeated at Battle of Nations at Leipzig
March 1814	Napoleon abdicates and goes into exile on island of Elba
March 1815	Napoleon escapes Elba and attempts to reclaim power
15 June 1815	Napoleon is defeated at Waterloo and exiled to island of Saint Helena

Britain, unbowed by the Continental System, remained Napoleon's sworn enemy. Prussia joined Great Britain, Sweden, Russia, and Austria in opposing France anew. In the Battle of Nations at Leipzig in October 1813, France was forced to retreat. Napoleon refused a negotiated peace and fought on until the following March, when the victorious allies marched down the streets of Paris and occupied the French capital. Only then did Napoleon abdicate in favor of his young son, François, the titular king of Rome (1811–1832). Napoleon was exiled to the Mediterranean island of Elba.

The allies refused to accept the young "Napoleon II" and supported instead the Bourbon claimant to the throne, the brother of the guillotined Louis XVI. Naming himself Louis XVIII (skipping "XVII" in deference to his nephew dead at the hands of the Revolution), the new king claimed to rule over a "restored" France.

Napoleon's Final Defeat: Waterloo.   Still it was not quite the end for Napoleon. While the European heads of state sat in Vienna trying to determine the future of Europe and France's place in it, Napoleon returned from his exile on the Mediterranean island of Elba to reclaim leadership of France. On 15 June 1815, Napoleon once again, and for the final time, confronted the European powers in one of the most famous military campaigns in history. With 125,000 loyal French forces, Napoleon seemed within hours of reestablishing the French Empire in Europe.

But he had underestimated his opponents. The defeat of Napoleon's forces at Waterloo was decisive. Napoleon later explained, "Everything failed me just when everything had succeeded!" He had met his Waterloo, and with his defeat a new expression entered the language to describe devastating, permanent, irreversible downfall. Napoleon's return proved brief—it lasted only 100 days. An era had come

DOCUMENT

Napoleon's Exile to St. Helena

■ "The Song of the End." Napoleon is depicted in flight with the whole world chasing him as he stumbles through a graveyard of bones and fallen symbols of power. Behind the globe is the masonic symbol of Providence, a shining eye within a triangle, a symbol also used by the American founding fathers on the Great Seal.

to an end. Napoleon was exiled to the inhospitable island of Saint Helena in the South Atlantic. For the next six years, Napoleon wrote his memoirs under the watchful eyes of his British jailers. He died a painful death on 5 May 1821 from what today is believed to have been cancer.

CONCLUSION

The period of revolution and empire from 1789 to 1815 radically changed the face of France. A new, more cohesive elite of bourgeois and nobles emerged, sharing power based on wealth and status. Ownership of land remained a defining characteristic of both old and new elites. A new state bureaucracy, built on the foundations of the old, expanded and centralized state power.

The people as sovereign now legitimated political power. Napoleon at his most imperial never doubted that he owed his existence to the people. In this sense, Napoleon was the king of the revolution—an apparently contradictory fusion of old forms and new ideology. Napoleon channeled democratic forces into enthusiasm for empire. He learned his lessons from the failure of the Bourbon monarchy and the politicians of the revolution. For 16 years, Napoleon successfully reconciled the Old Regime with the new France. Yet he could not resolve the essential problem of democracy: the relationship between the will of the people and the exercise of political power. The picture in 1815 was not dramatically different from the situation in 1789. The revolution might have been over, but changes fueled by the revolutionary tradition were just beginning. The struggle for a workable democratic government continued in France for another century and elsewhere in Europe throughout the twentieth century.

QUESTIONS FOR REVIEW

1. To what extent was the French nobility responsible for the crisis that destroyed the Old Regime?
2. How did commoners, men and women, transform a crisis of government into a revolution?
3. Why did the leaders of the Revolution resort to a "reign of terror," and what effect did that have on the Revolution?
4. What problems in France and beyond contributed to the rise of Napoleon?
5. What did Napoleon accomplish in France, and what brought about his fall?

KEY TERMS

cahiers de doléances, p. 611

conscription, p. 626

Continental System, p. 627

Estates-General, p. 610

Girondins, p. 624

Jacobins, p. 624

Napoleonic Code, p. 629

Old Regime, p. 610

Reign of Terror, p. 624

sans-culottes, p. 621

Thermidorian Reaction, p. 625

Third Estate, p. 611

DISCOVERING WESTERN CIVILIZATION ONLINE

You can obtain more information about the French Revolution and the Napoleonic Era at the Websites listed below. See also the Companion Website that accompanies this text, www.ablongman.com/kishlansky, which contains an online study guide and additional resources.

The French Revolution and the Fall of the Monarchy

Creating French Culture
www.loc.gov/exhibits/bnf/bnf0001.html
Different aspects of French culture as a form of elite power from Charlemagne to Charles de Gaulle are presented by the Library of Congress. Most of the material is from the collections of the Bibliothèque Nationale de France.

Liberty, Equality, Fraternity: Explaining the French Revolution
Chnm.gmu.edu/revolution/
This site contains an extraordinary archive of key images, maps, songs, timelines, and texts from the French Revolution. The site is authored by Professors Lynn Hunt and Jack Censer, leading scholars in the field of French revolutionary history.

Château de Versailles

www.chateauversailles.fr/en/

Devoted to the history and images of Versailles, this site provides brief essays about the people and events significant to court culture during the seventeenth and eighteenth centuries. It also explores the role of Versailles in French culture after the French Revolution.

Experimenting with Democracy, 1789–1792

St. Just

history.hanover.edu/texts/stjust.html

Texts by St. Just, a close colleague of Robespierre and a member of the Committee of Public Safety, which orchestrated the Reign of Terror.

Modern History Sourcebook: Robespierre: The Supreme Being

www.fordham.edu/halsall/mod/robespierre-supreme.html

This site contains Robespierre's words on The Cult of the Supreme Being and links to other sites.

The Reign of Napoleon, 1799–1815

Internet Modern History Sourcebook: French Revolution

www.fordham.edu/halsall/mod/modsbook13.html

This site will direct students to the Modern History Sourcebook section of documents on the French Revolution, Napoleon, and the Napoleonic Wars.

Napoleon

www.napoleon.org/en/home.asp

Sponsored by the Foundation Napoleon for "the furtherance of study and research into the civil and military achievements of the First and Second Empires," this site is aimed at a nonacademic audience providing chronologies, essays, images and videos, and links to other sites on Napoleon.

SUGGESTIONS FOR FURTHER READING

The French Revolution and the Fall of the Monarchy

Keith Michael Baker, *Inventing the French Revolution* (Cambridge: Cambridge University Press, 1992). The author views the French Revolution as a basically political event that can only be understood in the context of the changing political culture of the eighteenth century, with special attention to the use of language and the role of public opinion as a political invention.

Roger Chartier, *The Cultural Origins of the French Revolution,* tr. Lydia G. Cochrane (Durham, NC: Duke University Press, 1991). Argues for the importance of the rise of critical modes of thinking in the public sphere in the eighteenth century and of long-term de-Christianization in shaping the desire for change in French society and politics.

William Doyle, *Origins of the French Revolution* (Oxford: Oxford University Press, 1988). An excellent introduction devoted to the historiography of the Revolution since 1939, followed by an analysis of the breakdown of the Old Regime and the struggle for power.

François Furet and Denis Richet, *The French Revolution* (New York: Macmillan, 1970). Two experts on the French Revolution present a detailed overview of the period from 1789 to 1798.

Georges Lefebvre, *The Great Fear of 1789* (New York: Pantheon Books, 1973). This classic study analyzes the rural panic that swept through parts of France in the summer of 1789 as a distinct episode in the opening months of the Revolution with its own internal logic.

Colin Lucas, ed., *Rewriting the French Revolution* (Oxford: Clarendon Press, 1991). Eight scholars present interpretations in the areas of social development, ideas, politics, and religion.

Daniel Roche, *The People of Paris* (Berkeley: University of California Press, 1987). An essay on popular culture in the eighteenth century in which the author surveys the lives of the Parisian popular classes—servants, laborers, and artisans—and examines their housing, furnishings, dress, and leisure activities.

D. M. G. Sutherland, *France, 1789–1815: Revolution and Counter-Revolution* (New York: Oxford University Press, 1986). An interpretation of the revolutionary period that stresses the struggle against counterrevolution and presents the Revolution as a complex and contradictory process of social and political conflict over incompatible rights and privileges enjoyed by significant portions of the population.

Timothy Tackett, *Becoming a Revolutionary: The Deputies of the French National Assembly and the Emergence of a Revolutionary Culture* (Princeton: Princeton University Press, 1996). This collective biography of the cohort of deputies to the National Assembly demonstrates that their practical experience was distinct from that of the nobility.

Michel Vovelle, *The Fall of the French Monarchy* (Cambridge: Cambridge University Press, 1984). A social history of the origins and early years of the Revolution, beginning with a brief examination of the Old Regime and paying special attention to social and economic changes initiated by the Revolution, the role of the popular classes, and the creation of revolutionary culture.

Experimenting with Democracy, 1792–1799

Jack Censer and Lynn Hunt, *Liberty, Equality, Fraternity: Exploring the French Revolution* (University Park: Pennsylvania State University Press, 2001). This book is accompanied by a CD-ROM and provides a unique multimedia introduction to the French Revolution.

François Furet, *Interpreting the French Revolution* (Cambridge: Cambridge University Press, 1981). A series of essays challenging many of the assumptions about the causes and outcome of the Revolution and reviewing its historiography.

Dominique Godineau, *The Women of Paris and Their French Revolution* (Berkeley: University of California Press, 1998). A compelling account on the lives of women revolutionaries. Godineau presents women's protests as a mass movement within the Revolution.

Patrice Higonnet, *Goodness Beyond Virtue: Jacobins During the French Revolution* (Cambridge: Harvard University Press, 1998). The author considers the Jacobin politics as a model for modern democrats, not to be reduced to the tragedy of the Terror.

Michael L. Kennedy, *The Jacobin Clubs in the French Revolution, 1793–1795* (New York: Berghahn Books, 2000). The final volume of Kennedy's three-volume history of the Jacobin Club focusing on the period between May 1793 and August 1795.

Sara E. Melzer and Leslie Rabine, eds., *Rebel Daughters: Women and the French Revolution* (New York: Oxford University Press, 1992). Contributors from a variety of disciplines examine the importance of women in the French Revolution, with special attention to the exclusion of women from the new politics.

Albert Soboul, *The Sans-Culottes* (New York: Anchor, 1972). A study of the artisans who composed the core of popular political activism in revolutionary Paris.

The Reign of Napoleon, 1799–1815

Louis Bergeron, *France Under Napoleon* (Princeton, NJ: Princeton University Press, 1981). An analysis of the structure of Napoleon's regime, its social bases of support, and its opponents.

Jean Tulard, *Napoleon: The Myth of the Saviour* (London: Weidenfeld and Nicolson, 1984). In this biography of Napoleon, the Napoleonic Empire is presented as a creation of the bourgeoisie, who desired to end the Revolution and consolidate their gains and control over the lower classes.

Isser Woloch, *Napoleon and His Collaborators: The Making of a Dictatorship* (New York: Norton, 2001). Woloch explains the success of Napoleon's regime in terms of the support of his civilian collaborators.

Isser Woloch, *The New Regime: Transformations of the French Civic Order* (New York: Norton, 1994). Woloch's study emphasizes the break of the new regime from the old, placing the institutions created or revamped after 1789 in the context of a new civic order and citizenship.

For a list of additional titles related to this chapter's topics, please see http://www.ablongman.com/kishlansky.

Chapter 21
INDUSTRIAL EUROPE

Chapter Outline

Work was the watchword of the new industrial economy that emerged in Europe in the late eighteenth century. New technologies made men and women more efficient workers and created vast amounts of new wealth for those fortunate enough to own the machines and factories. In The Visual Record, old and new economies meet in a blacksmith's shop. ➤

AN IRON FORGE

Machinery and Industrialization

The key to industrialization was the replacement of muscle with machine. This demanded ingenuity on the part of inventors, capital on the part of investors, and adaptability on the part of workers. Whether in the cotton mills, where water-powered jennies allowed one worker to spin more than one hundred had before, or in the pits, where engines allowed water to be drained and miners to dig deeper, machinery changed the nature of production and productivity. Technological innovation transformed the nature of work in Britain.

Although we think of industry in terms of factories, labor forces, and mass output, early industry developed within the context of individual producers. Families worked in cottages to spin and weave, iron was refined and shaped by the village smith. The initial stages of the Industrial Revolution involved changing the ways in which these small producers worked. Joseph Wright's depiction of *An Iron Forge* is a case in point, a family portrait that almost resembles a nativity scene except that the birth being celebrated is the machine forging of iron, the miracle product of the age.

Joseph Wright of Derby was born and bred in the English Midlands where the Industrial Revolution first began. He was fascinated by the scientific developments of his age and specialized in paintings that were technically accurate. *An Iron Forge* was one of a number of industrial scenes that Wright painted in the 1770s when advances in technology were changing the face of rural life. The small shop must have once been that of an ordinary blacksmith, but now it has been transformed into a forge. Outside of the picture a giant water wheel turns a rod that is attached to the drum in the bottom left-hand corner of the painting. The drum turns a shaft which lifts the heavy tilting hammer until it strikes the wooden beam above it. The hammer then falls with the force of its weight to strike the bar of iron that is held in place on the anvil by the iron forger's assistant. No human could swing so heavy a hammer or shape so large a bar of iron so easily.

Every detail is precise, in imitation of the mechanical process. For example, the anvil sits in a pan filled with wooden chips which act as a cushion to absorb the shock of the hammer blows. The tiled floor and bricked walls absorb the flying sparks as the red hot metal is molded into bars.

While the machinery is drawn precisely and the technology of the forge is represented accurately, it is the artist's imagination that creates the scene. Though the iron forger who gazes proudly upon his family is portrayed with huge, muscular arms and a powerful torso, he is not engaged in toil. He represents enlightened industry, able to stand above the backbreaking work that had previously been associated with smithing. Indeed, of the three workmen in the picture, only one is actually laboring and he is simply holding the tongs, which keep the iron in place. It is the machine that labors—the drum turning, the cam lifting, the hammer falling—and the people who benefit—proud parents, healthy and happy children. All the product, the artist seems to be saying, of the new industrialization.

Looking Ahead

As this chapter will discuss, industrialization began in Great Britain around forges like the one portrayed by Joseph Wright. It was the result of changes in agricultural practices that allowed for a larger population to be supported by fewer farmers. It was powered first by coal and its use in the production of iron and then by steam which allowed for powerful engines to mechanize production. The steam engine also allowed for a revolution in transportation with the development of the railroads. Industrialization transformed every aspect of the British economy and soon spread throughout Europe. ➤

■ Joseph Wright of Derby, *An Iron Forge* (1772).

THE TRADITIONAL ECONOMY

The curse of Adam and Eve was that they would earn their daily bread by the sweat of their brows. For generation after generation, age after age, economic life was dominated by toil. Man, woman, and child labored to secure their supply of food against the caprice of nature. There was nothing even vaguely romantic about the backbreaking exertion needed to crack open the hard ground, plant seeds in it, and protect the crops from the ravages of insects, birds, and animals long enough to be harvested. Every activity was labor-intensive. Wood for shelter or fuel was chopped with thick, blunt axes. Water was drawn from deep wells by the long, slow turn of a crank or dragged in buckets from the nearest stream. Everything that was consumed was pulled or pushed or lifted. French women carried soil and water up steep terraces in journeys that could take as long as seven hours. "The women seemed from their persons and features to be harder worked than horses," Arthur Young (1741–1820), the English agricultural expert, observed with a combination of admiration and disgust. The capital that was invested in the traditional economy was human capital, and by the middle of the eighteenth century nearly eight out of every ten Europeans still tilled the soil, earning their bread by the sweat of their brow.

Although the traditional economy was dominated by agriculture, an increasing amount of labor was devoted to manufacture. The development of a secure and expanding overseas trade created a worldwide demand for consumer goods. In the countryside, small domestic textile industries grew up. Families would take in wool for spinning and weaving to supplement their income from agriculture. When times were good, they would expend proportionately less effort in manufacturing; when times were bad, they would expend more. Their tasks were set by an entrepreneur who provided raw materials and paid the workers by the piece. Wages paid to rural workers were lower than those paid to urban laborers because they were not subject to guild restrictions and because the wages supplemented farm income. Thus entrepreneurs could profit from lower costs, although they had to bear the risk that the goods produced in that fashion would be of lesser quality or that markets would dry up in the interval. Although domestic industry increased the supply of manufactured commodities, it demanded even more labor from an already overworked sector of the traditional economy.

Throughout the traditional economy, the limits on progress were set by nature. Good harvests brought prosperity, bad harvests despair. Over the long run, the traditional economy ran in all-too-predictable cycles. Sadly, the adage, "Eat, drink, and be merry, for tomorrow we may die," was good advice. Prosperity was sure to bring misery in its train. The good fortune of one generation was the hard luck of the next, as more people competed for a relatively fixed quantity of food. No amount of sweat and muscle and, as yet, ingenuity could rescue the traditional economy from its pendulum swings of boom and bust.

By the eighteenth century, the process that would ultimately transform the traditional economy was already under way. It began with the **agricultural revolution,** one of the great turning points in human history. Before it occurred, the life of every community and of every citizen was always held hostage to nature. The struggle to secure an adequate food supply was the dominant fact of life to which nearly all productive labor was dedicated. After the agricultural revolution, an inadequate food supply was a political rather than an economic fact of life. Fewer and fewer farmers were required to feed more and more people. In Britain, where nearly 70 percent of the population was engaged in agriculture at the end of the seventeenth century, fewer than 2 percent today work on farms. By the middle of the nineteenth century, the most advanced economies were capable of producing vast surpluses of basic commodities. The agricultural revolution was not an event, and it did not happen suddenly. It would not deserve the label "revolution" at all were it not for its momentous consequences: Europe's escape from the shackles of the traditional economy.

Farming Families

Over most of Europe, agricultural activity in the eighteenth century followed methods of crop rotation that had been in place for more than a thousand years. Fields were divided into strips of land, and each family "owned" a certain number of strips, which they cultivated for their livelihood. Between one-half and one-third of village land lay fallow each year so that its nutrients could be restored. Open-field farming, as the system was called, was communal rather than individual. Decisions about which crops to grow in the productive fields, where animals would be pastured, or how much wood could be cut from the common wastes affected everyone. Moreover, many activities, such as plowing, gleaning, and manuring, could not conveniently observe the distinctions of ownership of separate strips. Nor, given the realities of nature, could individual families be self-sustaining without the services of a village tanner or milkmaid or hog minder drawn from the closely intertwined group of kin and neighbors that constituted the community. Communal agriculture was effective, but it also limited the number of people that could survive on the produce from a given amount of land.

Agriculture was a profoundly conservative occupation, for the risk of experimentation was nothing less than survival. Lords and peasants both practiced defensive innovation, introducing change only after its practical benefits were easily demonstrable. For example, in the mid-seventeenth century two French provincial parlements banned the cultivation of potatoes in the mistaken belief that they caused leprosy. Yet both potatoes and corn became peasant crops and spread rapidly throughout southern Europe, not least because as new commodities they were untaxed. Peasants bartered their surplus, hoarded their profits, and took what few advantages they could out of a system in which the deck was stacked against them.

As the European population entered a new cycle of growth in the second quarter of the eighteenth century, the traditional economy began to increase agricultural productivity in

MAP DISCOVERY

Percentage increase

- Over 80
- 60 – 79
- 40 – 59
- 20 – 39
- Under 20

Population Growth in Europe, 1800–1850

Notice which parts of Europe experienced the largest growth in population in the first half of the nineteenth century. Compare the rate of population growth in Spain and Norway and Sweden. Which grew faster? In which parts of Europe did the population increase the most during this period? What impact would you expect such growth to have on the agricultural economy? On the rate of industrialization?

an increase in productivity. For a time, more able-bodied workers produced more food. In the half century that ended in the 1770s, French peasants increased agricultural production by nearly 60 percent. The intensification of traditional methods rather than innovation accounted for the increase. The number of strips held by each family declined, but each strip was more carefully cultivated.

By the end of the eighteenth century, the European population was reaching the point at which another check on its growth might be expected. Between 1700 and 1800, total European population had increased by nearly 50 percent, and the rate of growth was continuing to accelerate. The vast expansion of rural population placed a grave strain on agricultural production. Decade by decade, more families attempted to eke out an existence from the same amount of land. The gains made by intensive cultivation were now lost to overpopulation. In areas that practiced partible inheritance, farms were subdivided into units too small to provide subsistence. Competition for the "morsels" of land, as the French called them, was intense. Older sons bought out younger brothers; better-off families purchased whatever came on the market to prevent their children from slipping into poverty. Even in areas in which primogeniture was the rule, portions for younger sons and daughters ate into the meager inheritance of the eldest son. Over much of Europe, it was becoming increasingly difficult to live by bread alone.

Rural Manufacture

The crisis of overpopulation meant that not only were there more mouths to feed, there were more bodies to clothe. That increased the need for spun and woven cloth, and thus for spinners and weavers. Traditionally, commercial cloth production

traditional ways. In the east, new lands were colonized and slowly brought under cultivation. Frederick the Great welcomed immigrants to Prussia, where land was plentiful, if not very fertile. In settled communities, less productive land, which had provided fodder for animals at the end of the seventeenth century, now had to provide food for humans. Scrubland was cleared and hillsides terraced. Dry ground was irrigated manually by women and children working in bucket brigades. As always, an increase in population initially meant

■ The European Linen Industry. By the eighteenth century, linen production was dominated by the Low Countries and the north German principalities where skilled labor could still be found for the complicated process of linen weaving.

was the work of urban artisans, but the expansion of the marketplace and the introduction of new fabrics, especially cotton and silk, had eroded the monopoly of most of the clothing guilds. Merchants could sell as much finished product as they could find, and the teeming rural population provided a tempting pool of inexpensive labor for anyone willing to risk the capital to purchase raw materials. Initially, farming families took manufacturing work into their homes to supplement their income. Spinning and weaving were the most common occupations, and they were treated as occasional work, reserved for the slow times in the agricultural cycle. This was known as cottage industry. It was side-employment, less important and less valuable than the vital agricultural labor that all members of the family undertook.

But by the middle of the eighteenth century, cottage industry was developing in a new direction. As landholdings grew smaller, even good harvests did not promise subsistence to many families. The oversupply of labor was soon organized into the **putting-out system,** which mobilized the resources of the rural labor force for commercial production of large quantities of manufactured goods. The characteristics of the putting-out system were similar throughout Europe, whether it was undertaken by individual entrepreneurs or lords of the manor, or even sponsored by the state. The process began with the capital of the entrepreneur, which was used to purchase

raw materials. The materials were "put out" to the homes of workers where the manufacture, most commonly spinning or weaving, took place. The finished goods were returned to the entrepreneur, who sold them at a profit, with which he bought raw materials to begin the process anew.

The simplicity of the putting-out system was one of its most valuable features. All of its essential elements were already present in rural communities. The small nest egg of a prosperous farmer or small trader was all the money needed to make the first purchase of raw materials. The raw materials could be put out to his kin or closest neighbors and the finished goods then delivered to market along with surplus crops. Not only could a small amount of cash begin the cycle of putting-out, but that capital continued to circulate to keep the process in motion.

The small scale of the initial enterprise can be seen in the fact that many entrepreneurs had themselves begun as workers. In Bohemia, for example, some of the largest putting-out operations were run by serfs who paid their lords fees for the right to engage in trade. At the end of the eighteenth century, there were more than one-quarter million spinners in the Bohemian linen industry alone, most of them organized into small groups around a single entrepreneur, though one monastery employed more than 650 women spinners. Putting-out also required only a low level of skill and common, inexpensive tools. Rural families did their own spinning and rural villages their own weaving. Thus, putting-out demanded little investment, either in plant, equipment, or education. Nor did it inevitably disrupt traditional gender-based tasks in the family economy. In most places spinning was women's work, weaving was done by men, and children helped at whichever task was under way. In fact, certain occupations, such as lacemaking in France, were so gender-based that men would not even act as entrepreneurs. In Austria, lacemaking was considered less honorable than other forms of clothmaking because of its association with women and household-based production. Performed at home, rural manufacture remained a traditional family-oriented occupation.

Gradually, the putting-out system came to dominate the lives of many rural families. From small networks of isolated villages, domestic manufacture grew to cover entire regions. Perhaps as many as one-quarter of the inhabitants of the Irish province of Ulster were engaged in manufacturing linen by the end of the eighteenth century. Spinning and weaving became full-time occupations for families that kept no more than a small garden. But without agricultural earnings, piecework rates became starvation wages, and families unable to purchase their subsistence were forced to rely upon loans from the entrepreneurs who set them at work. Long hours in dank cottages performing endlessly repetitive tasks became the lot of millions of rural inhabitants, and their numbers increased annually. While the sons of farmers waited to inherit land before they formed their families, the sons of cottage weavers needed only a loom to begin theirs. They could afford to marry younger and to have more children, for children could contribute to manufacturing from an early age.

■ This 1783 engraving shows women engaged in typical tasks of eighteenth-century cottage industry: spinning, reeling with the clock reel, and boiling the yarn.

Consequently, the expansion of the putting-out system, like the expansion of traditional agriculture, fueled the continued growth of population. Like traditional agriculture, putting-out contained a number of structural inefficiencies. Both entrepreneur and worker were potential victims of unscrupulousness. Embezzlement of raw materials was a problem for the entrepreneur, arbitrary wage cuts for the laborers. Because the tasks were performed at home, the entrepreneur could not supervise the work. Most disputes in domestic manufacturing arose over specifications of quality. Workers would not receive full pay for poorly produced goods that could not be sold for full value. Inexperienced, aged, or infirm workers could easily spoil costly raw materials. One Bohemian nobleman created village spinning rooms on his estates so that young girls could be given four weeks of training before they set up on their own. Finally, the putting-out system was labor- rather than capital-intensive. As long as there were ready hands to employ, there was little incentive to seek better methods or more efficient techniques.

The Agricultural Revolution

The continued growth of Europe's population necessitated an expansion of agricultural output. In most places that was achieved by intensifying traditional practices, bringing more land into production and more labor to work the land. But in the most advanced European economies, first in Holland and then in England, traditional agriculture underwent a long but dynamic transformation, an agricultural revolution. It was a revolution of technique rather than technology. Humans were not replaced by machines nor were new forms of energy substituted for human and animal muscle. Indeed, many of the methods that were to increase crop yields had been known for centuries and practiced during periods of population pressure. But they had never been practiced as systematically as they came to be from the seventeenth century onward, and they were never combined with a commercial attitude toward farming. It was the willingness and ability of owners to invest capital in their land that transformed subsistence farming into commercial agriculture.

Enclosures. As long as farming was practiced in open fields, there was little incentive for individual landowners to invest in improvements to their scattered strips. While the community as a whole could enclose a small field or plant some fodder crops for the animals, its ability to change traditional practice was limited. In farming villages, even the smallest landholder had rights in common lands, which were jealously guarded. Rights in commons meant a place in the community itself. Commercial agriculture was more suited to large rather than small estates and was more successful when the land could be utilized in response to market conditions rather than the necessities of subsistence.

The consolidation of estates along with the enclosure of fields was thus the initial step toward change. It was a long-term process that took many forms. In England, where it was to become most advanced, enclosure was already under way in the sixteenth century. Prosperous families had long been consolidating their strips in the open fields, and at some point the lord of the manor and the members of the community agreed to carve up the common fields and make the necessary exchanges to consolidate everyone's lands. Perhaps as much as three-quarters of the arable land in England was enclosed by agreement before 1760. Enclosure by agreement did not mean that the breakup of the open-field community was necessarily a harmonious process. Riots preceding or following agreed enclosures were not uncommon.

Paradoxically, it was the middling rather than the poorest villagers who had the most to lose. The breakup of the commons initially gave the poor more arable land from which to eke out their subsistence, and few of them could afford to sacrifice present gain for future loss. The smallholders were quickly bought out. It was the middle-size holders who were squeezed hardest. Although prosperous in communal farming, those families did not have access to the capital necessary to make agricultural improvements such as converting grass to grain land or purchasing large amounts of fertilizer. They could not compete in producing for the market, and gradually they, too, disappeared from the enclosed village. Their opposition to enclosure by agreement led, in the eighteenth century, to enclosure by act of Parliament. Parliamentary enclosure was legislated by government, a government composed for the most part of large landowners. A commission would view the community's lands and divide them, usually by a prescribed formula. Between 1760 and 1815, more than 1.5 million acres of farmland were enclosed by act of Parliament. During the late eighteenth century, the Prussian and French

■ Surveyors measure a field for land enclosure. The enclosure movement eliminated large areas of what had formerly been communal land.

governments emulated the practice by ordering large tracts of land enclosed.

The enclosure of millions of acres of land was one of the largest expenses of the new commercial agriculture. Hedging or fencing off the land and plowing up the commons required extra labor beyond that necessary for basic agrarian activities. Thus many who sold the small estates that they received on the breakup of the commons remained in villages as agricultural laborers or leaseholders. But they practiced a different form of farming. More and more agricultural activity became market-oriented. Single crops were sown in large enclosed fields and exchanged at market for the mixture of goods that previously had been grown in the village. Market production turned attention from producing a balance of commodities to increasing the yield of a single one.

Agricultural Innovations.   The first innovation was the widespread cultivation of fodder crops such as clover and turnips. Crops like clover restore nutrients to the soil as they grow, shortening the period in which land has to lie fallow. Moreover, farm animals grazing on clover or feeding on turnips return more manure to the land, further increasing its productivity. Turnip cultivation had begun in Holland and was brought to England in the sixteenth century. But it was not until the late seventeenth century that Viscount Charles "Turnip" Townsend (1675–1738) made turnip cultivation popular. Townsend and other large Norfolk landowners developed a new system of planting known as the four-crop rotation, in which wheat, turnips, barley, and clover succeeded one another. The method kept the land in productive use, and both the turnip and clover crops were used to feed larger herds of animals.

The ability of farmers to increase their livestock was as important as their ability to grow more grain. Not only were horses and oxen more productive than humans—a horse could perform seven times the labor of a man while consuming only five times the food—but the animals also refertilized the land as they worked. Light fertilization of a single acre of arable land required an average of 25,000 pounds of manure. But animals competed with humans for food, especially during the winter months when little grazing was possible. To conserve grain for human consumption, lambs were led to the slaughter and the fatted calf was killed in the autumn. Thus the development of the technique of meadow floating was a remarkable breakthrough. By flooding low-lying land near streams in the winter, English and Dutch farmers could prevent the ground from freezing during their generally mild winters. When the water was drained, the land beneath it would produce an early grass crop on which the beasts could graze. That meant that more animals could be kept alive during the winter.

The relationship between animal husbandry and grain growing became another feature of commercial agriculture. In many areas farmers could choose between growing grain and pasturing animals. When prices for wool or meat were relatively higher than those for grain, fields could be left in grass for grazing. When grain prices rose, the same fields could be plowed. Consolidated enclosed estates made convertible husbandry possible. The decision to hire field-workers or shepherds could be taken only by large agricultural employers. Whatever the relative price of grain, the open-field village continued to produce grain as its primary crop. Farmers who could convert their production in tune to the market not only could maximize their profits but also could

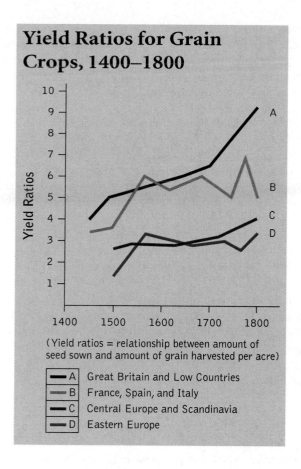

Yield Ratios for Grain Crops, 1400–1800

(Yield ratios = relationship between amount of seed sown and amount of grain harvested per acre)

A	Great Britain and Low Countries
B	France, Spain, and Italy
C	Central Europe and Scandinavia
D	Eastern Europe

each person engaged in farming in England produced enough food for 1.7 people; in 1800, each produced enough for 2.5 people. Cheaper food allowed more discretionary spending, which fueled the demand for consumer goods, which in turn employed more rural manufacturers. But there also were costs. The transformation of agriculture was also a transformation in a way of life. The open-field village was a community; the enclosed estate was a business. The plight of the rural poor was tragic enough in villages of kin and neighbors, where face-to-face charity might be returned from one generation to the next. With their scrap of land and their common rights, even the poorest villagers laid claim to a place of their own. But as landless laborers, either on farms or in rural manufacturing, they could no longer make that claim and many soon became fodder for the factories, the "dark satanic mills" that came to disfigure the land once tilled in open-field villages. For the destitute, charity was now visited upon them in anonymous parish workhouses or in the good works of the comfortable middle class. In all of those ways the agricultural revolution changed the face of Europe.

THE INDUSTRIAL REVOLUTION IN BRITAIN

Like the changes in agriculture, the changes in manufacturing that began in Britain during the eighteenth century were more revolutionary in consequence than in development. But their consequences were revolutionary indeed. A work force that was predominantly agricultural in 1750 had become predominantly industrial a century later. A population that for centuries had centered on the south and east was now concentrated in the north and west. Liverpool, Manchester, Glasgow, and Birmingham mushroomed into giant cities. While the population of England grew by 100 percent between 1801 and 1851, from about 8.5 million people to more than 17 million, the populations of Liverpool and Manchester grew by more than 1000 percent.

It was the replacement of animal muscle by hydraulic and mineral energy that made the continued population growth possible. Water and coal drove machinery that dramatically increased human productivity. In 1812, one woman could spin as much thread as 200 women had in 1770. What was most revolutionary about the Industrial Revolution was the wave after wave of technological innovation, a constant tinkering and improving of the ways in which things were made, which could have the simultaneous effects of cutting costs and improving quality. It was not just the great breakthrough inventions such as the steam engine, the smelting of iron with coke, and the spinning jenny that were important, but also the hundreds of adjustments in technique that applied new ideas in one industry to another, opened bottlenecks, and solved problems. Ingenuity rather than genius was at the root of the **Industrial Revolution** in Britain.

The Industrial Revolution was a sustained period of economic growth and change brought about by the application

prevent shortages of raw materials for domestic manufacturers or of foodstuffs for urban and rural workers.

Convertible husbandry was but the first step in the development of a true system of regional specialization in agriculture. Different soils and climates favored different use of the land. In southern and eastern England the soil was thin and easily depleted by grain growing. Traditionally, the light soil areas had been used almost exclusively for sheep rearing. On the other hand, the clay soils of central England, though poorly drained and hard to work, were more suited to grain growing. The new agricultural techniques reversed the pattern. The introduction of fodder crops and increased fertilization rejuvenated thin soils, and southeastern England became the nation's breadbasket. Large enclosed estates provided a surplus of grain throughout the eighteenth century. By the 1760s, England was exporting enough grain to feed more than a half million people. Similarly, the midland clays became the location of great sheep runs and cattle herds. Experiments in herd management, crossbreeding, and fattening all resulted in increased production of wool, milk, meat, leather, soap, and tallow for candles.

There can be no doubt about the benefits of the transformation of agricultural practices that began in Holland and England in the seventeenth century and spread slowly to all corners of the Continent over the next 200 years. Millions more mouths were fed at lower cost than ever before. In 1700, of mineral energy and technological innovations to the process of manufacturing. It took place during the century between 1750 and 1850, though different industries moved at different paces and sustained economic growth continued in Britain until the First World War. It is difficult to define the timing of the Industrial Revolution with any great precision because, unlike a political event, an economic transformation does not happen all at once. Nor are new systems and inventions ever really new. Coal miners had been using rails and wheeled carriages to move ore since the seventeenth century. In the sixteenth century, "Jack of Newbury" had housed his cloth workers in a large shed. The one was the precursor of the railroad and the other the precursor of the factory, but each preceded the Industrial Revolution by more than a century. Before 1750, innovations made their way slowly into general use, and after 1850 the pace of growth slowed appreciably. By then, Britain had a manufacturing economy: fewer than one-quarter of its labor force engaged in agriculture and nearly 60 percent were involved in industry, trade, and transport.

Britain First

The Industrial Revolution occurred first in Britain, but even in Britain **industrialization** was a regional rather than a national phenomenon. There were many areas of Britain that remained untouched by innovations in manufacturing methods and agricultural techniques, although no one remained unaffected by the prosperity that industrialization brought. That was the result of both national conditions and historical developments. When industrialization spread to the Continent, it took hold—as it had in Britain—in regions where mineral resources were abundant or where domestic manufacturing was a traditional activity. There was no single model for European industrialization, however often contemporaries looked toward Britain for the key to unlock the power of economic growth. There was as much technological innovation in France, as much capital for investment in Holland. Belgium was rich in coal, while eastern Europe enjoyed an agricultural surplus that sustained an increase in population. The finest cotton in the world was made in India; the best iron was made in Sweden. Each of those factors was in some way a precondition for industrialization, but none by itself proved sufficient. Only in Britain did those circumstances meld together.

Water and Coal.　Among Britain's blessings, water was foremost. Water was its best defense, protecting the island from foreign invasion and making it unnecessary to invest in a costly standing army. Rather, Britain invested heavily in its navy to maintain its commercial preeminence around the globe. The navy protected British interests in times of war and transported British wares in times of peace. Britain's position in the Asian trade made it the leading importer of cottons, ceramics, and teas. Its colonies, especially in North America, not only provided sugar and tobacco but also formed a rich market for British manufacturing.

But the commercial advantages that water brought were not confined to oceanic trade. Britain was favored by an internal water system that tied inland communities together. In the eighteenth century, no place in Britain was more than 70 miles from the sea or more than 30 miles from a navigable river. Water transport was far cheaper than hauling goods overland; a packhorse could carry 250 pounds of goods on its back but could move 100,000 pounds by walking alongside a river and pulling a barge. Small wonder that river transport was one of the principal interests of merchants and traders. Beginning in the 1760s, private concerns began to invest in the construction of canals, first to move coal from inland locations to major arteries and then to connect the great rivers themselves. Over the next 50 years several hundred miles of canals were built by authority of Navigation Acts, which allowed for the sale of shares to raise capital. In 1760, the Duke of Bridgewater (1736–1803) lived up to his name by completing the first great canal. It brought coal to Manchester and ultimately to Liverpool. It cost more than £250,000 and took 14 years of labor to build, but it repaid the duke and his investors many times over by bringing an uneconomical coal field into production. Not the least of the beneficiaries were the people of Manchester, where the price of coal was halved.

Coal was the second of Britain's natural blessings on which it improved. Britain's reserves of wood were nearly depleted by the eighteenth century, especially those near centers of population. Coal had been in use as a fuel for several centuries, and the coal trade between London and the northern coal pits had been essential to the growth of the capital. Coal was abundant, much of it almost at surface level along the northeastern coast, and easily transported on water. The location of large coalfields along waterways was a vital condition of its early use. As canals and roadways improved, more inland coal was brought into production for domestic use. Yet it was in industry rather than in the home that coal was put to its greatest use. There again Britain was favored, for large seams of coal were also located near large seams of iron. At first, the coincidence was of little consequence, since iron was smelted by charcoal made from wood and iron foundries were located deep in forests. But ultimately ironmakers learned to use coal for fuel, and then the natural economies of having mineral, fuel, and transport in the same vicinity were given full play.

Economic Infrastructure.　The factors that contributed to Britain's early industrialization were not only those of natural advantage. Over the course of years, Britain had developed an infrastructure for economic advancement. The transformation of domestic handicrafts to industrial production depended as much on the abilities of merchants as on those of manufacturers. The markets for domestic manufacturing had largely been overseas, where British merchants built up relationships over generations. Export markets were vital to the success of industrialization as production grew dynamically and most ventures needed a quick turnaround of sales to reinvest the profits in continued growth. The flexibility of English trading houses would be seen in their ability to shift from reexporting Eastern and North American goods to exporting British manufactures. Equally important, increased production meant increased demand for raw materials: Swedish bar iron for casting, Egyptian and American cotton for textiles, and Oriental silk for luxuries. The expansion of shipping mirrored the expansion of the economy, tripling during the eighteenth century to more than one million tons of cargo capacity.

The expansion of shipping, agriculture, and investment in machines, plant, and raw material all required capital. Not only did capital have to exist, but it had to be made productive. Profits in agriculture, especially in the south and east, somehow had to be shifted to investment in industry in the north and west. The wealth of merchants, which flowed into London, had to be redistributed throughout the economy.

MAP DISCOVERY

Great Britain: Canals and Natural Resources

Examine the locations of canals, navigable rivers, and coal and iron ore deposits in Great Britain. Which parts of Great Britain did not develop canals? Why? Where are the canals concentrated? What is the relationship between canals and major navigable rivers? What about the relationship between the canals and the coal and iron ore deposits? Where would you expect railroads to be built?

More importantly, short-term investments had to give way to long-term financing. At the end of the seventeenth century, the creation of the Bank of England had begun the process of constructing a reliable banking system. The Bank of England dealt almost entirely with government securities, but it also served as a bill broker. It bought the debts of reputable merchants at a discount in exchange for Bank of England notes; Bank of England notes could then be exchanged between merchants, which increased the liquidity of the English economy, especially in London. It also became the model for provincial banking by the middle of the eighteenth century.

Private family banks also grew in importance in London, handling the accounts of merchants and buying shares in profitable enterprises, of which the canals were a favorite. Regional banks, smaller and less capitalized, began to use the private London banks as correspondents, that is, as extensions of their own banks in the city. That allowed local manufacturers and city merchants to do business with one another. The connections between the regional banks and London facilitated the flow of capital from one section of the nation to the other. In 1700, there were just 12 provincial banks; by 1790, there were nearly 300. Banks remained reluctant to invest for the long term, preferring to discount bills for a few months, but after they developed a relationship with a particular firm, they were usually willing to continue to roll the debt over. Although the banking system was vital to large enterprises, in fact the capital for most industry was raised locally, from kin and neighbors, and grew by plowing back profits into the business. At least at the beginning, manufacturers were willing to take risks and to work for small returns to ensure the survival and growth of their business.

Minerals and Metals

There could have been no Industrial Revolution without coal. It was the black gold of the eighteenth century, the fuel that fed the furnaces and turned the engines of industrial expansion. The coal produced by one miner generated as much energy as 20 horses. Coal was the first capital-intensive industry in Britain, already well developed by the seventeenth century. Owners paid the costs of sinking shafts, building roads, and erecting winding machines. Miners were brought to a pit and paid piecework for their labor. Only the very wealthy could afford to invest in coal mining, and it was by chance that British law vested mineral rights in owners rather than users of the land, as was the case on the Continent. That meant that the largest English coalfields were owned by landed families of means who were able to invest agricultural profits in mining. Britain's traditional elites thus played a crucial role in the industrial transformation of the agrarian economy from which their wealth and social standing had derived.

Early Coal Mining.   The technical problems of coal mining grew with demand. As surface seams were exhausted it became necessary to dig deeper shafts, to lower miners farther underground, and to raise the coal greater heights to the surface.

Men loosened the coal from the seam; women and children hauled it to the shaft. They also cleared the tons of debris that came loose with the coal. Underground mining was extremely dangerous. In addition to all-too-frequent cave-ins, miners struggled against inadequate ventilation and light. Better ventilation was achieved by the expensive method of sinking second and third shafts into the same seam, allowing for cross breezes. Candles and sparks created by flint wheels addressed the problem of light, though both methods suffered from the disadvantage that most pits contained combustible gases. Even after a fireman walked through the mine exploding gas with a long lighted stick, many miners preferred to work in total darkness, feeling the edges of the seam.

But by far the most difficult mining problem was water. As pits were sunk deeper they reached pools of groundwater, which enlarged as the coal was stripped away from the earth. Dripping water increased the difficulty of hewing, standing water the difficulty of hauling. The pit acted like a riverbed and filled quickly. Water drainage presented the greatest obstacle to deep-shaft mining. Women and children could carry the water out in large skin-lined baskets, which were attached to a winding wheel and pulled up by horses. Primitive pumps, also horse-powered, had been devised for the same purpose. Neither method was efficient or effective when shafts sank deeper. In 1709, Thomas Newcomen (1663–1729) introduced a steam-driven pump that enabled water to be sucked through a pipe directly from the pit bottom to the surface. Although the engine was expensive to build and needed tons of coal to create the steam, it could raise the same amount of water in a day as 2500 humans. Such economies of labor were enormous, and within 20 years of its introduction there were 78 engines draining coal and metal mines in England.

Innovations such as Newcomen's engine helped increase output of coal at just the time that it became needed as an industrial fuel. Between 1700 and 1830, coal production increased tenfold despite the fact that deeper and more difficult seams were being worked. Eventually, the largest demand for coal came from the iron industry. In 1793, just two ironworks consumed as much coal as the entire population of Edinburgh. Like mining coal, making iron was both capital- and labor-intensive, requiring expensive furnaces, water-powered bellows, and mills in which forged iron could be slit into rods or rolled into sheets. Ironmaking depended upon an abundance of wood, for it took the charcoal derived from 10 acres of trees to refine 1 ton of iron ore. After the ore was mined, it was smelted into pig iron, a low-grade, brittle metal. Pig iron was converted to higher-quality bar iron in charcoal-powered forges that burned off some of its impurities. From bar iron came the rods and sheets used in casting household items such as pots and nails or in making finer wrought iron products such as plows and armaments. Because each process in the making of iron was separate, furnaces, forges, and mills were located near their own supplies of wood. The shipping of the bulky ore, pig iron, and bar iron added substantially to its cost, and it was cheaper to import bars from Sweden than to carry them 20 miles overland.

The great innovations in the production of iron came with the development of techniques that allowed for the use of coal rather than wood charcoal in smelting and forging. As early as 1709, Abraham Darby (ca. 1678–1717), a Quaker nail maker, experimented with smelting iron ore with coke, coal from which most of the gas has been burned off. Iron coking greatly reduced the cost of fuel in the first stages of production, but because most ironworks were located in woodlands rather than near coal pits, the method was not widely adopted. Moreover, although coke made from coal was cheaper than charcoal made from wood, coke added its own impurities to the iron ore. Nor could it provide the intense

■ Britain's ample coal deposits were one of the country's assets as it industrialized. This painting of the pithead of an eighteenth-century coal mine shows the coexistence of the new steam technology with aspects of older forms of production, such as the use of beasts of burden.

heat needed for smelting without a large bellows. The cost of the bellows offset the savings from the coke until James Watt (1736–1819) invented a new form of steam engine in 1775.

The Steam Engine.   Like most innovations of the Industrial Revolution, James Watt's steam engine was an adaptation of existing technology made possible by the sophistication of techniques in a variety of fields. Although Watt is credited with the invention of the condensing steam engine, one of the seminal creations in human history, the success of his work depended upon the achievements of numerous others. Watt's introduction to the steam engine was accidental. An instrument maker in Glasgow, he was asked to repair a model of a Newcomen engine and immediately realized that it would work more efficiently if there were a separate chamber for the condensation of the steam. Although his idea was sound, Watt spent years attempting to implement it. He was continually frustrated that poor-quality valves and cylinders never fit well enough together to prevent steam from escaping from the engine.

Watt was unable to translate his idea into a practical invention until he became partners with the Birmingham ironmaker and manufacturer Matthew Boulton (1728–1809). At Boulton's works, Watt found craftsmen who could make precision engine valves, and at the foundries of John Wilkinson (1728–1808) he found workers who could bore the cylinders of his engine to exact specifications. Watt's partnership with Boulton and Wilkinson was vital to the success of the steam engine. But Watt himself possessed the qualities necessary to ensure that his ideas were transformed into reality. He persevered through

■ James Watt's rotary beam steam engine. This model was built in 1788 to provide rotary power to the lapping and polishing machines at Matthew Boulton's Soho Engineering Works in Birmingham, England, where Watt and Boulton manufactured steam engines from 1775 to 1810.

years of unsuccessful experimentation and searched out partners to provide capital and expertise. He saw beyond bare mechanics, realizing the practical utility of his invention long before it was perfected. Watt designed the mechanism to convert the traditional up-and-down motion of the pumping engine into rotary motion, which could be used for machines and ultimately for locomotion.

Watt's engine received its first practical application in the iron industry. Wilkinson became one of the largest customers for steam engines, using them for pumping, moving wheels, and ultimately increasing the power of the blast of air in the forge. Increasing the heat provided by coke in the smelting and forging of iron led to the transformation of the industry. In the 1780s, Henry Cort (1740–1800), a naval contractor, experimented with a technique for using coke as fuel in removing the impurities from pig iron. The iron was melted into puddles and stirred with rods. The gaseous carbon that was brought to the surface burned off, leaving a purer and more malleable iron than even charcoal could produce. Because the iron had been purified in a molten state, Cort reasoned that it could be rolled directly into sheets rather than first made into bars. He erected a rolling mill adjacent to his forge and combined two separate processes into one.

Puddling and rolling had an immediate impact upon iron production. There was no longer any need to use charcoal in the stages of forging and rolling. From mineral to workable sheets, iron could be made entirely with coke. Ironworks moved to the coalfields, where the economies of transporting fuel and finished product were great. Moreover, the distinct stages of production were eliminated. Rather than separate smelting, forging, and finishing industries, one consolidated manufacturing process had been created. Forges, furnaces, and rolling machines were brought together and powered by steam engines. Cort's rolling technique alone increased output 15 times. By 1808, output of pig iron had grown from 68,000 to 250,000 tons and of bar iron from 32,000 to 100,000 tons.

Cotton Is King

Traditionally, British commerce had been dominated by the woolen cloth trade, in which techniques of production had not changed for hundreds of years. Running water was used for cleaning and separating fleece; crude wooden wheels spun the thread; simple handlooms wove together the long warp threads and the short weft ones. It took nearly four female spinners to provide the materials for one male weaver, the tasks having long been gender-specific. During the course of the seventeenth century, new fabrics appeared on the domestic market, particularly linen, silk, and cotton. It was cotton that captured the imagination of the eighteenth-century consumer, especially brightly colored, finely spun Indian cotton.

Domestic Industries.   Spinning and weaving were organized as domestic industries. Work was done in the home on small, inexpensive machines to supplement the income from farming. Putters-out were especially frustrated by the difficulty in

■ In the eighteenth century, a number of British inventors patented new machines that transformed the British textile industry and marked the beginning of the Industrial Revolution. Among the inventions was the spinning jenny, invented by James Hargreaves in 1764, and named for his daughter. The jenny, which permitted the spinning of a number of threads at the same time, made possible the automatic production of cotton thread.

obtaining yarn for weaving in the autumn, when female laborers were needed for the harvest. Even the widespread development of full-time domestic manufacturers did not satisfy the increased demand for cloth. Limited output and variable quality characterized British textile production throughout the early part of the eighteenth century. The breakthrough came with technological innovation. Beginning in the mid-eighteenth century, a series of new machines dramatically increased output and, for the first time, allowed English textiles to compete with Indian imports.

The first innovation was the flying shuttle, invented by John Kay (1704–1764) in the 1730s. A series of hammers drove the shuttle, which held the weft, through the stretched warp on the loom. The flying shuttle allowed weavers to work alone rather than in pairs, but it was adopted slowly because it increased the demand for spun thread, which was already in short supply. The spinning bottleneck was opened by James Hargreaves (d. 1778), who devised a machine known as the jenny. The jenny was a wooden frame containing a number of spindles around which thread was drawn by means of a hand-turned wheel. The first jennies allowed for the spinning of eight threads at once, and improvements brought the number to more than 100. Jennies replaced spinning wheels by the tens of thousands. The jenny was a crucial breakthrough in redressing the balance between spinning and weaving, though

it did not solve all problems. Jenny-spun thread was not strong enough to be used as warp, which continued to be wheel spun. But the jenny could spin cotton in unimaginable quantities.

As is often the case with technological change, one innovation followed another. The problem set by improvements in weaving gave rise to solutions for increasing the output of spinners. The need to provide stronger warp threads posed by the introduction of the jenny was ultimately solved by the development of the water frame. It was created in 1769 by Richard Arkwright (1732–1792), whose name was also to be associated with the founding of the modern factory system. Arkwright's frame consisted of a series of water-driven rollers that stretched the cotton before spinning. The stronger fibers could be spun into threads suitable for warp, and English manufacturers could finally produce an all-cotton fabric. It was not long before another innovator realized that the water frame and the jenny could be combined into a single machine, one that would produce an even finer cotton yarn than that made in India. The mule, so named because it was a cross between a frame and a jenny, was invented by Samuel Crompton (1753–1827), who sold its rights for only £60. It was the decisive innovation in cotton production. By 1811, ten times as many threads were being spun on mules as on water frames and jennies combined.

▲	Cotton
▲	Linen
■	Silk
■	Wool

North Sea

SCOTLAND

IRELAND

Irish Sea

WALES

ENGLAND

Celtic Sea

■ Great Britain: Textile Centers. Textiles had been the traditional industrial activity in Britain and almost every part of the state had organized textile production.

The original mules were small machines that, like the jennies, could be used for domestic manufactures. But increasingly the mule followed the water frame into purposely built factories, where it became larger and more expensive. The need for large rooms to house the equipment and for a ready source of running water to power it provided an incentive for the creation of factories, but secrecy provided a greater one. The original factories were called "safe-boxes," and whether they were established for the manufacture of silk or cotton, their purpose was to protect trade secrets. Innovators took out patents to prevent their inventions from being copied and fought long lawsuits to prevent their machines from being used. Workers were sworn to secrecy about the techniques they were taught. Imitators practiced industrial espionage as sophisticated as the age would allow: enticing knowledgeable workers; employing spies; copying inventions. Although the factory was designed to protect secrets, its other benefits were quickly realized. Manufacturers could maintain control over the quality of products through strict supervision of the work force. Moreover, workers in shifts could keep the costly machines in continuous use.

Cotton Factories.   Richard Arkwright constructed the first cotton factories in Britain, all of which were designed to house water frames. The first was established in 1769 at Cromford

near Nottingham, which was the center of stocking manufacture. The site was chosen for its isolation, since stockings were an article of fashion in which secrecy was most important. The Cromford mill was a four-story building that ultimately employed more than 800 workers. During the next quarter century, Arkwright built more than a dozen other mills, most in partnership with wealthy manufacturers. Arkwright's genius lay in industrial management rather than mechanical innovation. As others switched from frames to mules, Arkwright stubbornly stuck to his own invention. When steam power began to replace water, he failed to make the shift. But his methods of constructing and financing factories were undeniably successful. From a modest beginning as a traveling salesman of wigs, Sir Richard Arkwright died in possession of a fortune worth more than £500,000.

The organization of the cotton industry into factories was one of the pivotal transformations in economic life. Domestic spinning and weaving took place in agricultural villages; factory production took place in mill towns. The location of the factory determined movements of population, and from the first quarter of the eighteenth century onward a great shift toward northeast England was under way. Moreover, the character of the work itself changed. The operation of heavy machinery reversed the traditional gender-based tasks. Mule spinning became men's work, while handloom weaving was taken over by women. The mechanization of weaving took longer than that of spinning, both because of difficulties in perfecting a power loom and because of opposition to its introduction by workers known as Luddites, who organized machine-breaking riots in the 1810s. The Luddites attempted to maintain the traditional organization of their industry and the independence of their labor. For a time, handloom weavers managed to survive by accepting lower and lower piece rates. But their competition was like that of a horse against an automobile. In 1820, there were more than 250,000 handloom weavers in Britain; by 1850, the number was less than 50,000. Weaving as well as spinning became factory work.

DOCUMENT

Industrial Society and Factory Conditions

The transformation of cotton manufacture had a profound effect on the overall growth of the British economy. It increased shipping because the raw material had to be imported, first from the Mediterranean and then from America. American cotton—especially after 1794, when American inventor Eli Whitney (1765–1825) patented his cotton gin—fed a nearly insatiable demand. This appetite was met primarily because American cotton plantations used slave labor to plant and harvest their crop. In 1750, Britain imported less than 5 million pounds of raw cotton; a century later the volume had grown to 588 million pounds. And to each pound of raw cotton, British manufacturers added the value of their technology and their labor. By the mid-nineteenth century, nearly a half million people earned their living from cotton, which alone accounted for more than 40 percent of the value of all British exports. Cotton was undeniably the king of manufactured goods.

THE WEALTH OF BRITAIN

Cotton was the first of the new industries that led to British economic domination in the nineteenth century. In producing cotton, new inventions such as the spinning jenny and the water frame revolutionized manufacture and the factory system was born. Britain's domination of cotton production impressed contemporaries. In this excerpt, a contemporary tries to explain why Britain took the lead in industrialization.

Focus Questions

How important does the author think geography and natural resources have been to Britain's industrial success? What is the relation between industrialization and forms of government?

In comparing the advantages of England for manufactures with those of other countries, we can by no means overlook the excellent commercial position of the country—intermediate between the north and south of Europe; and its insular situation, which, combined with the command of the seas, secures our territory from invasion or annoyance. The German ocean, the Baltic, and the Mediterranean are the regular highways for our ships; and our western ports command an unobstructed passage to the Atlantic, and to every quarter of the world.

A temperate climate, and a hardy race of men, have also greatly contributed to promote the manufacturing industry of England.

The political and moral advantages of this country, as a seat of manufactures, are not less remarkable than its physical advantages. The arts are the daughters of peace and liberty. In no country have these blessings been enjoyed in so high a degree, or for so long a continuance, as in England. Under the reign of just laws, personal liberty and property have been secure; mercantile enterprise has been allowed to reap its reward; capital has accumulated in safety; the workman has "gone forth to his work and to his labour until the evening"; and, thus protected and favoured, the manufacturing prosperity of the country has struck its roots deep, and spread forth its branches to the ends of the earth.

England has also gained by the calamities of other countries, and the intolerance of other governments. At different periods, the Flemish and French protestants, expelled from their native lands, have taken refuge in England, and have repaid the protection given them by practising and teaching branches of industry, in which the English were then less expert than their neighbours.

From Edward Baines, *The History of the Cotton Manufacture in Great Britain* (1835).

The Iron Horse

The first stage of the Industrial Revolution in Britain was driven by the production of consumer goods. Pottery, cast-iron tools, clocks, toys, and textiles, especially cottons—all were manufactured in quantities unknown in the early eighteenth century. The products fed a ravenous market at home and abroad. The greatest complaint of industrialists was that they could not get enough raw materials or fuel, nor could they ship their finished products fast enough to keep up with demand. Transportation was becoming a serious stumbling block to continued economic growth. Even with the completion of the canal network that linked the major rivers and improvement in highways and tollways, raw materials and finished goods moved slowly and uncertainly. It was said that it took as long to ship goods from Manchester to Liverpool on the Duke of Bridgewater's canal as it did to sail from New York to Liverpool on the Atlantic Ocean. Furthermore, once the canals had a monopoly on bulk cargo, transportation costs began to rise.

It was the need to ship increasing amounts of coal to foundries and factories that provided the spur for the development of a new form of transportation. Ever since the seventeenth century, coal had been moved from the seam to the pit on rails, first constructed of wood and later of iron. Broad-wheeled carts hitched to horses were as much dragged as rolled, but that still represented the most efficient form of hauling, and those railways ultimately ran from the seam to the dock. By 1800, there was perhaps as much as 300 miles of iron rail in British mines.

In the same year, Watt's patent on the steam engine expired, and inventors began to apply the engine to a variety of mechanical tasks. Richard Trevithick (1771–1833), whose father managed a tin mine in Cornwall, was the first to experiment with a steam-driven carriage. George Stephenson (1781–1848), who is generally recognized as the father of the modern railroad, made two crucial improvements. In mine railways the wheels of the cart were smooth and the rail was grooved. Stephenson reversed the construction to provide

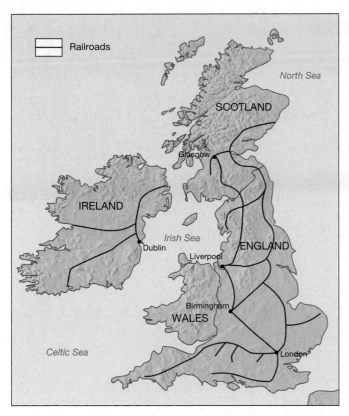

■ Great Britain: Railroads (ca. 1850). All rails led to London as the major lines were built to transport passengers as well as goods.

psychologically prepared for the benefits of technological innovation. By 1835, Parliament had passed 54 separate acts to establish more than 750 miles of railways. Ten years later, more than 6000 miles had been sanctioned and more than 2500 miles built; by 1852, more than 7500 miles of track were in use. The railways were built on the model of the canals. Private bills passed through Parliament, which allowed a company to raise money through the sale of stock. Most railways were trunk lines, connecting one town to another or joining two longer lines together. They were run by small companies, and few ultimately proved profitable. Only because of the dominant influence of George Stephenson and his son Robert (1803–1859) was there an attempt to establish a standard gauge for tracks and engines. Britain was the only country in which the government did not take a leading role in building the railways. Hundreds of millions of pounds were raised privately, and in the end it is calculated that the railroads cost £40,000 a mile to build, more than three times the cost per mile of railroads on the Continent and in the United States.

From Goods to Passengers.   Nevertheless, the investment paid huge dividends. By the 1850s, the original purpose of the railways was being realized as freight revenues finally surpassed passenger revenues. Coal was the dominant cargo shipped by rail, and the speedy, efficient service continued to drive down prices. The iron and steel industries were modernized on the back of demand for rails, engines, and cast-iron seats and fittings. In peak periods—and railway building was a boom-and-bust affair—as much as a quarter of the output of the rolling mills went into domestic railroads, and much more into Continental systems. The railways were also a massive consumer of bricks for beddings, sidings, and especially bridges, tunnels, and stations. Finally, the railways were a leading employer of labor, surpassing the textile mills in peak periods. Hundreds of thousands worked in tasks as varied as engineering and ditch digging, for even in that most advanced industry, sophisticated mechanized production went hand in hand with traditional drudgery. More than 60,000 workers were permanently engaged in the industry to run trains, mind stations, and repair track. Countless others were employed in manufacturing engines, carriages, boxcars, and the thousands of components that went into making them.

Most of all, the railroads changed the nature of people's lives. Whole new concepts of time, space, and speed emerged to govern daily activities. As Henry Booth, an early railroad official, observed, "Notions which we have received from our ancestors and verified by our own experience are overthrown in a day. What was slow is now quick; what was distant is now near." Coach travel had ordinarily been limited to those with means, not only because it was expensive, but also because it was time-consuming. Ordinary people could not take off the days necessary to complete relatively short round-trip journeys. When passenger rail service began, there was even a debate over whether provision should be made for third-class passengers, a class unknown on the coaches, where the only choices were riding inside for comfort or outside for savings.

better traction and less wear. Perhaps more importantly, Stephenson made the vital improvement in engine power by increasing the steam pressure in the boiler and exhausting the smoke through a chimney. In 1829, he won a £500 prize with his engine "The Rocket," which pulled a load three times its own weight at a speed of 30 miles per hour and could actually outrun a horse.

The First Railways.   In 1830 the first modern railway, the Manchester-to-Liverpool line, was opened. Like the Duke of Bridgewater's canal, it was designed to move coal and bulk goods, but surprisingly its most important function came to be moving people. In its first year, the Manchester–Liverpool line carried more than 400,000 passengers, which generated double the revenue derived from freight. The railway was quicker, more comfortable, and ultimately cheaper than the coach. Investors in the Manchester–Liverpool line, who pocketed a comfortable 9.5 percent when government securities were paying 3.5 percent, learned quickly that links between population centers were as important as those between industrial sites. The London–Birmingham and London–Bristol lines were both designed with passenger traffic in mind.

Railway building was one of the great boom activities of British industrialization. Since it came toward the end of the mechanization of factories, investors and industrialists were

■ Honoré Daumier (1808–1879), *The Third-Class Carriage.* Daumier captured a human condition peculiar to the modern era: "the lonely crowd."

Third-class passengers quickly became the staple of railroad service. The cheap excursion was born to provide short holidays or even day trips. The career of Thomas Cook (1808–1892), who became the world's first travel agent, began after he took a short excursion. More than six million people visited London by train to view the Crystal Palace exhibition in 1851, a number equivalent to one-third of the population of England and Wales. The railways did more than link places; they brought people together and helped develop a sense of national identity by speeding up all forms of communication.

Entrepreneurs and Managers

The Industrial Revolution in Britain was not simply invented. Too much credit is given to a few breakthroughs and too little to the ways in which they were improved and dispersed. The Industrial Revolution was an age of gadgets when people believed that new was better than old and that there was always room for improvement. "The age is running mad after innovation," the English moralist Dr. Johnson wrote. "All the business

of the world is done in a new way; men are hanged in a new way." Societies for the advancement of knowledge sprang up all over Britain. Journals and magazines promoted new ideas and techniques. Competitions were held for the best invention of the year; prizes were awarded for agricultural achievements. Practical rather than pure science was the hallmark of industrial development.

Yet technological innovation was not the same as industrialization. A vital change in economic activity took place in the organization of industry. Putters-out with their circulating capital and hired laborers could never make the economies necessary to increase output and quality while simultaneously lowering costs. That was the achievement of industrialists, producers who owned workplace, machinery, and raw materials and invested fixed capital by plowing back their profits. Industrial enterprises came in all sizes and shapes. A cotton mill could be started with as little as £300 or as much as £10,000. As late as 1840, fewer than 10 percent of the mills employed more than 500 workers. Most were family concerns with less than 100 employees, and many of them failed. For every story with a happy ending, there was another with a sad one. When Major Edmund Cartwright (1740–1824) erected a cotton mill, he was offered a Watt steam engine built for a distiller who had gone bankrupt. He acquired his machinery at the auction of another bankrupt mill. Cartwright's mill, engine, and machinery ended on the auction block less than three years later. There were more than 30,000 bankruptcies in the eighteenth century, testimony both to the risks of business and to the willingness of entrepreneurs to take them.

To survive against the odds, successful industrialists had to be both entrepreneur and manager. As entrepreneurs, they raised capital, almost always locally from relatives, friends, or members of their church. Quakers were especially active in financing each other's enterprises. The industrial entrepreneur also had to understand the latest methods for building and powering machinery and the most up-to-date techniques for performing the work. One early manufacturer claimed "a practical knowledge of every process from the cotton-bag to the piece of cloth." Finally, entrepreneurs had to know how to market their goods. In those functions, industrial entrepreneurs developed logically from putters-out.

But industrialists also had to be managers. The most difficult task was organization of the workplace. Most gains in productivity were achieved through the specialization of function. The processes of production were divided and subdivided until workers performed a basic task over and over. The education of the work force was the industrial manager's greatest challenge. Workers had to be taught how to use and maintain their machines and disciplined to apply themselves continuously. At least at the beginning, it was difficult to staff the factories. Many employed children as young as seven from workhouses or orphanages, who, though cheap to pay, were difficult to train and discipline. It was the task of the manager to break old habits of intermittent work, indifference to quality, and petty theft of materials. Families were preferred to individuals, for then parents could instruct and supervise their children. There is no reason to believe that industrial managers were more brutal masters than farmers or that children were treated better in workhouses than in mills. Labor was a business asset, what was sometimes called "living machinery," and its control with carrots and sticks was the chief concern of the industrial manager.

Who were the industrialists who transformed the traditional economy? Because British society was relatively open, they came from every conceivable background: dukes and orphans, merchants and salesmen, inventors and improvers. Although some went from rags to riches—such as Richard Arkwright, who was the thirteenth child of a poor barber—it was extremely difficult for a laborer to acquire the capital necessary to set up a business. Wealthy landowners were prominent in capital-intensive aspects of industries—for example, owning ironworks and mines—but few established factories. Most industrialists came from the middle classes, which, while comprising one-third of the British population, provided as much as two-thirds of the first generation of industrialists. That first generation included lawyers, bankers, merchants,

and those already engaged in manufacturing, as well as tradesmen, shopkeepers, and self-employed artisans. The career of every industrialist was different, as a look at two—Josiah Wedgwood and Robert Owen—will show.

Josiah Wedgwood. Josiah Wedgwood (1730–1795) was the thirteenth child of a long-established English potting family. He worked in the potteries from childhood, but a deformed leg made it difficult for him to turn the wheel. Instead he studied the structure of the business. His head teemed with ideas for improving ceramic manufacturing, but it was not until he was 30 that he could set up on his own and introduce his innovations, which encompassed both technique and organization, the entrepreneurial and managerial sides of his business.

Wedgwood developed new mixtures of clays that took brilliant colors in the kiln and new glazes for both useful and ornamental ware. His technical innovations were all the more remarkable in that he had little education in mineral chemistry and made his discoveries by simple trial and error. But there was nothing of either luck or good fortune in

■ Jasperware copy of the Portland vase by Josiah Wedgwood. The Portland vase is one of the most famous ancient vases. It was found near Rome in the seventeenth century in a tomb believed to be that of Alexander Severus.

Wedgwood's managerial innovations. He was repelled by the disorder of the traditional pottery, with its waste of materials, uneven quality, and slow output. When he began his first works, he divided the making of pottery into distinct tasks and assigned separate workers to them. One group did nothing but throw the pots on the wheel; another painted designs; a third glazed. To achieve the division of function, Wedgwood had to train his own workers almost from childhood. Traditional potters performed every task from molding to glazing and prized the fact that no two pieces were ever alike. Wedgwood wanted each piece to replicate another, and he stalked the works breaking defective wares on his wooden leg. He invested in schools to help train young artists, in canals to transport his products, and in London shops to sell them. Wedgwood was a marketing genius. He named his famed cream-colored pottery Queen's Ware and made special coffee and tea services for leading aristocratic families. He would then sell replicas by the thousands. In less than 20 years, Wedgwood pottery was prized all over Europe and Wedgwood's potting works were the standard of the industry.

Robert Owen.　Robert Owen (1771–1858) did not have a family business to develop. The son of a small tradesman, he was apprenticed to a clothier at the age of 10. As a teenager he worked as a shop assistant in Manchester, where he audaciously applied for a job as a manager of a cotton mill. At 19, he was supervising 500 workers and learning the cotton trade. Owen was immediately successful, increasing the output of his workers and introducing new materials to the mill. In 1816, he entered a partnership to purchase the New Lanark mill in Scotland. Owen found conditions in Scotland much worse than those in Manchester. More than 500 workhouse children were employed at New Lanark, where drunkenness and theft were endemic. Owen believed that to improve the quality of work one had to improve the quality of the workplace. He replaced old machinery with new, reduced working hours, and instituted a monitoring system to check theft. To enhance life outside the factory, he established a high-quality company-run store, which plowed its profits into a school for village children.

Owen was struck by the irony that in the mills, machines were better cared for than were humans. He thought that with the same attention to detail that had so improved the quality of commodities he could make even greater improvements in the quality of life. He prohibited children under 10 from mill work and instituted a 10-hour day for child labor. His local school took infants from one year old, freeing women to work and ensuring each child an education. Owen instituted old-age and disability pensions, funded by mandatory contributions from workers' wages. Taverns were closed and workers were fined for drunkenness and sexual offenses. In the factory and the village, Owen established a principle of communal regulation to improve both the work and the character of his employees. New Lanark became the model of the world of the future, and each year thousands made an industrial pilgrimage to visit it.

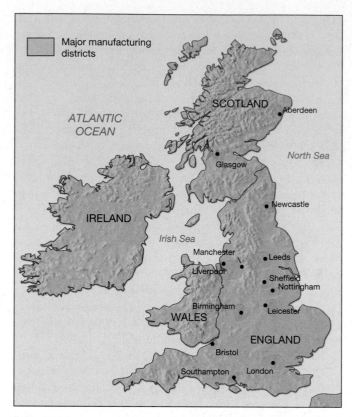

■ Great Britain: Manufacturing Centers. The growth of manufacturers in the midlands led to a massive population shift and the development of major urban areas such as Manchester.

The Wages of Progress

Robert Owen ended his life as a social reformer. His efforts to improve the lot of his workers at New Lanark led to experiments to create ideal industrial communities throughout the world. He founded cooperative societies, in which all members shared in the profits of the business, and supported trade unions in which workers could better their lives. His followers planted colonies where goods were held in common and the fruits of labor belonged to the laborers. Owen's agitation for social reform was part of a movement that produced results of lasting consequence. The **Factory Act (1833)** prohibited factory work by children under nine, provided two hours of daily education, and effectively created a 12-hour day in the mills until the Ten Hours Act (1847). The Mines Act (1842) prohibited women and children from working underground.

Nor was Owen alone in dedicating time and money to the improvement of workers' lives. The rapid growth of unplanned cities exacerbated the plight of those too poor and overworked to help themselves. Conditions of housing and sanitation were appalling even by nineteenth-century standards. The *Report on the Sanitary Condition of the Laboring Population in Britain* (1842), written by Edwin Chadwick (1800–1890), so shocked Parliament and the nation that it helped to shift the burden of social reform to government. The Public Health Act (1848) established boards of health and the office of medical examiner, while the Vaccination Act

THE SIN OF WAGES

Robert Owen was both a successful manufacturer and a leading philanthropist. He believed that economic advance had to take place in step with the improvement of the moral and physical well-being of the workers. He organized schools, company shops, and ultimately utopian communities in an effort to improve the lives of industrial laborers. Owen was one of the first social commentators to argue that industrialism threatened the fabric of family and community life.

Focus Questions

What effect does the luxury market have on "the lower orders"? Why are commercial competition and its effects becoming more intense?

The acquisition of wealth, and the desire which it naturally creates for a continued increase, have introduced a fondness for essentially injurious luxuries among a numerous class of individuals who formerly never thought of them, and they have also generated a disposition which strongly impels its possessors to sacrifice the best feelings of human nature to this love of accumulation. To succeed in this career, the industry of the lower orders, from whose labour this wealth is now drawn, has been carried by new competitors striving against those of longer standing, to a point of real oppression, reducing them by successive changes, as the spirit of competition increased and the ease of acquiring wealth diminished, to a state more wretched than can be imagined by those who have not attentively observed the changes as they have gradually occurred. In consequence, they are at present in a situation infinitely more degraded and miserable than they were before the introduction of these manufactories, upon the success of which their bare subsistence now depends. . . .

The inhabitants of every country are trained and formed by its great leading existing circumstances, and the character of the lower orders in Britain is now formed chiefly by circumstances arising from trade, manufactures, and commerce; and the governing principle of trade, manufactures, and commerce is immediate pecuniary gain, to which on the great scale every other is made to give way. All are sedulously trained to buy cheap and to sell dear; and to succeed in this art, the parties must be taught to acquire strong powers of deception; and thus a spirit is generated through every class of traders, destructive of that open, honest sincerity, without which man cannot make others happy, nor enjoy happiness himself.

From Robert Owen, *Observations on the Effect of the Manufacturing System* (1815).

(1853) and the Contagious Diseases Act (1864) attempted to control epidemics. (See "A Closer Look: Industry and the Environment," pp. 656–657.)

The movement for social reform began almost as soon as industrialization. The Industrial Revolution initiated profound changes in the organization of British society. Cities sprang up from grain fields almost overnight. The lure of steady work and high wages prompted an exodus from rural Britain and spurred an unremitting boom in population. In the first half of the nineteenth century, the population of England doubled from 9 to 18 million, with growth most rapid in the newly urban north and west. In 1750, about 15 percent of the population lived in urban areas; by 1850, about 60 percent did. Industrial workers married younger and produced more children than their agricultural counterparts. For centuries, women had married in their middle twenties, but by 1800, age at first marriage had dropped to 23 for the female population as a whole and to nearly 20 in the industrial areas. That was in part because factory hands did not have to wait until they inherited land or money, and in part because they did not have to serve an apprenticeship. But early marriage and large families were also a bet on the future, a belief that things were better now and would be even better soon, that the new mouths would be fed and the new bodies clothed. It was an investment on the part of ordinary people similar to that made by bankers and entrepreneurs when they risked their capital in new businesses. Was it an investment that paid off?

Expansion of Wealth. It is difficult to calculate the benefits of the Industrial Revolution or to weigh them against the costs. What is certain is that there was a vast expansion of wealth as well as a vast expansion of people to share it. Agricultural and industrial change made it possible to support comfortably a population more than three times larger than that of the seventeenth century, when it was widely believed that England had reached the limits of expansion. Despite the fact that population doubled between 1801 and 1851, per capita income rose by 75 percent. Had the population remained stable, per capita income would have increased by a staggering 350 percent. At the same time, untold millions of pounds had been sunk into canals, roads, railways, factories, mines, and mills.

But the expansion of wealth is not the same as the improvement in the quality of life, for wealth is not equally distributed. An increase in the level of wealth may mean only that the rich are getting richer more quickly than the poor are

A Closer Look
Industry and the Environment

The Industrial Revolution changed the landscape of Britain. Small villages grew into vast metropolises seemingly overnight. The rates of growth were absolutely staggering: in 1801, there were 75,000 people in Manchester; by 1851, the number had more than quadrupled. The unremitting boom in population did more than strain the resources of local authorities: it broke them apart. It was not that the new industrial cities were unplanned; they were beyond the capacity of planning. Every essential requirement for human survival became scarce and expensive. Shortages of food, water, and basic accommodation were commonplace.

Shantytowns sprang up wherever space would allow, making the flimsily built habitations of construction profiteers seem like palaces. There was loud complaint about those nineteenth-century rip-off artists, but in truth the need for housing was so desperate that people willingly lived anywhere that provided shelter. Houses were built back to back and side by side, with only narrow alleyways to provide sunlight and air. In Edinburgh, one could step through the window of one house into the window of the adjoining one. Whole families occupied single rooms where members slept as they worked, in shifts. In Liverpool, more than 38,000 people were estimated to be living in cellars—windowless underground accommodations that flooded with the rains and the tides.

Most cities lacked both running water and toilet facilities. Districts were provided with either pumps or capped pipes through which private companies ran water for a few hours each day. The water was collected in buckets and brought to the home, where it would stand for the rest of the day and serve indifferently for washing, drinking, and cooking. Outhouse toilets were an extravagant luxury; in one Manchester district, 33 outhouses had to accommodate 7095 people. They were a mixed blessing even in the middle-class districts where they were more plentiful, as there was no system of drainage to flush away the waste. It simply accumulated in cesspools, which were emptied manually about every two years. The thing that most impressed visitors as they approached an industrial city was the smoke; what impressed them most when they arrived was the smell.

The quality of life experienced by most of the urban poor who lived in the squalid conditions has been recorded by a number of contemporary observers. Friedrich Engels was a German socialist who was sent to England to learn the cotton trade. He lived in Manchester for two years and spent much of his time exploring the working-class areas of the city. "In this district I found a man, apparently about sixty years old, living in a cow stable," Engels recounted from one of his walking tours in *The Condition of the Working Class in England in 1844.* "He had constructed a sort of chimney for his square pen, which had neither windows, floor, nor ceiling, had obtained a bedstead and lived there, though the rain dripped through his rotten roof. This man was too old and weak for regular work, and supported himself by removing manure with a hand-cart; the dung-heaps lay next door to his palace!" From his own observations Engels concluded that "in such dwellings only a physically degenerate race, robbed of all humanity, degraded, reduced morally and physically to bestiality, could feel comfortable and at home." And as he was quick to point out, his own observations were no different from those of parliamentary commissioners, medical officers, or civic authorities who had seen the conditions firsthand.

Among the observers, the most influential by far was Sir Edwin Chadwick, who began his government career as a commissioner for the poor law and ended it as the founder of a national system of public health. Chadwick wrote the report of a parliamentary commission, *The Sanitary Condition of the Laboring Population of Britain* (1842), which caused a sensation among the governing classes. Building on the work of physicians, overseers of the poor, and the most technical scholarship available, Chadwick not only painted the same grim picture of urban life as Engels did, he proposed a comprehensive solution to one of its greatest problems, waste management.

Chadwick was a civil servant, and he believed that problems were solved by government on the basis of conclusions of experts. He had heard doctors argue their theories about the causes of disease, some believing in fluxes that resulted from combinations of foul air, water, and refuse; others believing disease was spread by the diseased, in this case Irish immigrants who settled in the poorest parts of English industrial towns. Although medical research had not yet detected the existence of germs, it was widely held that lack of ventilation, stagnant pools of water, and the accumulation of human and animal waste in proximity to people's dwellings all contributed to the increasing incidence of disease. Chadwick fixed upon

■ Drawings of workers constructing London's sanitation system.

the last element as crucial. Not even in middle-class districts was there any effective system for the removal of waste. Chamber pots and primitive toilets were emptied into ditches, which were used to drain rain off into local waterways. The few underground sewers that existed were square containers without outlets that were simply emptied once filled. Chadwick's vision was for a sanitation system, one that would carry waste out of the city quickly and deposit it in outlying fields where it could be used as fertilizer.

Chadwick realized that the key to disposing of waste was a constant supply of running water piped through the system. Traditionally, only heavy

rainstorms cleared the waste ditches in most cities, and those were too infrequent to be effective. The river had to be the beginning of the sewerage system as well as its end. River water had to be pumped through an underground construction of sewage pits that were built to facilitate the water's flow. Civil engineers had already demonstrated that pits with rounded rather than angular edges were far more effective, and Chadwick advocated the construction of a system of oval-shaped tunnels, built on an incline beneath the city. Water pumped from one part of the river would rush through the tunnels, which would empty into pipes that would carry the waste to nearby farms.

Chadwick's vision took years to implement. He had all of the zeal of a reformer and none of the tact of a politician. He offended nearly everyone with whom he came into contact, because he believed that his program was the only workable one and because he believed that it had to be implemented whatever the price. He was uninterested in who was to pay the enormous costs of laying underground tunnels and building pumping stations and insisted only that the work begin immediately. In the end, he won his point. Sanitation systems became one of the first great public-works projects of the industrial age.

■ This 1851 painting of Manchester from a distance by William Wyld (1806–1870) contrasts a rural idyll with the murky outline of the city that stood, for better and for worse, as a symbol of industrial growth.

getting poorer. Similarly, economic growth over a century involved the lives of several generations, each of which experienced different standards of living. One set of parents may have sacrificed for the future of their children; another may have mortgaged it. Moreover, economic activity is cyclical. Trade depressions, such as those induced by the War of 1812 and the American Civil War, which interrupted cotton supplies, could have disastrous short-term effects. The "Great Hunger" of the 1840s was a time of agrarian crisis and industrial slump. The downturn of 1842 threw 60 percent of the factory workers in the town of Bolton out of work at a time when there was neither unemployment insurance nor a welfare system. Finally, quality of life cannot be measured simply in economic terms. People with more money to spend may still be worse off than their ancestors, who may have preferred leisure to wealth or independence to the discipline of the clock.

Thus there are no easy answers to the quality-of-life question. In the first stages of industrialization, it seems clear that only the wealthy benefited economically, though much of their increased wealth was reinvested in expansion. Under the impact of population growth, the Napoleonic wars, and regional harvest failure, real wages seem to have fallen from the levels reached in the 1730s. Industrial workers were not substantially better off than agricultural laborers when the high cost of food and rent is considered. But beginning around 1820, there is a convincing evidence that the real wages of industrial workers were rising despite the fact that more and more work was semi- and unskilled machine-minding and more of it was being done by women, who were generally paid only two-thirds the wages of men. Although the increase in real wages was still subject to trade cycles, such as the Great Hunger of the 1840s, it continued nearly unabated for the rest of the nineteenth century. Thus, in the second half of the Industrial Revolution, both employers and workers saw a bettering of their economic situation, which was one reason why rural workers flocked to the cities and Irish peasants emigrated in the hundreds of thousands to work the lowest paid and least desirable jobs in the factories.

Social Costs.   But economic gain had social costs. The first was the decline of the family as a labor unit. In both agricultural and early industrial activity, families labored together. Workers would not move to mill towns without the guarantee of a job for all members of their families, and initially they could drive a hard bargain. The early factories preferred family labor to workhouse conscripts, and it was traditional for children to work beside their parents, cleaning, fetching, or assisting in minding the machines. Children provided an essential part of family income, and youngest children were the agency of care for infirm parents. Paradoxically, it was agitation for improvement in the conditions of child labor that spelled the end of the family work unit. At first, young children were barred from the factories and older ones allowed to work only a partial adult shift. Although reformers intended that schooling and leisure be substituted for work, the separation of children from parents in the workplace ultimately made possible the substitution of teenagers for adults, especially as machines replaced skilled human labor. The individual worker now became the unit of labor, and during economic downturns it was adult males with their higher salaries who were laid off first.

Exploiting the Young

The condition of child laborers was a concern of English legislators and social reformers from the beginning of industrialization. Most of the attention was given to factory workers, and most legislation attempted to regulate the age at which children could begin work, the number of hours they could be made to work, and the provision of schooling and religious education during their leisure. It was not until the early 1840s that a parliamentary commission was formed to investigate the condition of child labor in the mines. In this extract, the testimony of the child is confirmed by the observations of one of the commissioners.

Focus Questions

How does Mr. Franks's account differ from Ellison Jack's own? Why do you think Ellison offers information about her level of literacy and knowledge of the Bible?

Ellison Jack, 11-years-old girl coal-bearer at Loanhead Colliery, Scotland: I have been working below three years on my father's account; he takes me down at two in the morning, and I come up at one and two next afternoon. I go to bed at six at night to be ready for work next morning: the part of the pit I bear in the seams are much on the edge. I have to bear my burthen up four traps, or ladders, before I get to the main road which leads to the pit bottom. My task is four or five tubs: each tub holds 4G cwt. I fill five tubs in twenty journeys.

I have had the strap when I did not do my bidding. Am very glad when my task is wrought, as it sore fatigues. I can read, and was learning the writing; can do a little; not been at school for two years; go to kirk occasionally, over to Lasswade: don't know much about the Bible, so long since read.

R. H. Franks, Esq., the sub-commissioner: A brief description of this child's place of work will illustrate her evidence. She has first to descend a nine-ladder pit to the first rest, even to which a shaft is sunk, to draw up the baskets or tubs of coals filled by the bearers; she then takes her creel (a basket formed to the back, not unlike a cockle-shell flattened towards the neck, so as to allow lumps of coal to rest on the back of the neck and shoulders), and pursues her journey to the wall-face, or as it is called here, the room of work. She then lays down her basket, into which the coal is rolled, and it is frequently more than one man can do to lift the burden on her back. The tugs or straps are placed over the forehead, and the body bent in a semicircular form, in order to stiffen the arch.

"Child Labor in the Coal Mines," Testimony to the Parliamentary Investigative Committee (1842).

The decline of the family as a labor unit was matched by other changes in living conditions when rural dwellers migrated to cities. Many rural habits were unsuited to both factory work and urban living. The tradition of "Saint Monday," for example, was one that was deeply rooted in the pattern of agricultural life. Little effort was expended at the beginning of the work week and progressively more at the end. Sunday leisure was followed by Monday recovery, a slow start to renewed labor. The factory demanded constant application six days a week. Strict rules were enforced to keep workers at their stations and their minds on their jobs. More than efficiency was at stake. Early machines were not only crude, they were dangerous, with no safety features to cover moving parts. Maiming accidents were common in the early factories, and they were the fault of both workers and machines. Similarly, industrial workers entered a world of the cash economy. Most agricultural workers were used to being paid in kind and to barter exchange. Money was an unusual luxury that was associated with binges of food, drink, and frivolities, which made adjustment to the wage packet as difficult as adjustment to the clock. Cash had to be set aside for provisions, rent, and clothing. On the farm, the time of a bountiful harvest was the time to buy durable goods; in the factory, "harvest time" was always the same.

Such adjustments were not easy, and during the course of the nineteenth century a way of life passed forever from England. For some, its departure caused profound sorrow; for others, it was a matter of rejoicing. A vertically integrated society in which lord of the manor, village worthies, independent farmers, workers, and servants lived together interdependently was replaced by a society of segregated social classes. By the middle decades of the nineteenth century, a class of capitalists and a class of workers had begun to form and had begun to clash. The middle classes abandoned the city centers, building exclusive suburban communities in which to raise their children and insulate their families. Conditions in the cities deteriorated under the pressure of overcrowding, lack of sanitation, and the absence of private investment. The loss of interaction between the different segments of society had profound consequences for the struggle to improve the quality of life for everyone. Leaders of labor saw themselves fighting against profits, greed, and apathy; leaders of capital against

■ *Dudley Street, Seven Dials, London,* by Gustave Doré, depicts life in the London slums of the early nineteenth century.

drunkenness, sloth, and ignorance. Between the two stereotypes there was little middle ground.

THE INDUSTRIALIZATION OF THE CONTINENT

Industrialization in Europe

Although Britain took the first steps along the road to an industrial economy, it was not long before other European nations followed. There was intense interest in "the British miracle," as it was dubbed by contemporaries. European ministers, entrepreneurs, even heads of state visited British factories and mines in hope of learning the key industrial secrets that would unlock the prosperity of a new age. The **Crystal Palace Exhibition** of manufacturing and industry held in London in 1851 was the occasion for a Continentwide celebration of the benefits of technology and a chance for ambitious Europeans to measure themselves against the mighty British. By then many European nations had begun the transformation of their own economies and had entered a period of sustained growth.

There was no single model for the industrialization of the Continental states. Contemporaries continually made comparisons with Britain, but in truth the process of British industrialization was not well suited to any but the coal-rich regions in

Belgium and the Rhineland. Nevertheless, all of Europe benefited from the British experience. No one else had to invent the jenny, the mule, or the steam engine. Although the British government banned the export of technology, none of the pathbreaking inventions remained a secret for long. Britain had demonstrated a way to make cheap, durable goods in factories, and every other state in Europe was able to skip the long stages of discovery and improvement. Thus, while industrialization began later on the Continent, it could progress more quickly. France and Germany were building a railroad system within years of Britain despite the fact that they had to import most of the technology, raw materials, and engineers.

Britain shaped European industrialization in another way. Its head start made it very difficult for follower nations to compete against British commodities in the world market, which meant that European industrialization would be directed first and foremost to home markets, where tariffs and import quotas could protect fledgling industries. Although European states were willing to import vital British products, they placed high duties on British-made consumer goods and encouraged higher-cost domestic production. Britain's competitive advantage demanded that European governments become involved in the industrialization of their countries, financing capital-intensive industries, backing the railroads, and favoring the establishment of factories.

MAP DISCOVERY

Industrial Revolution on the Continent

What were the least industrial parts of Europe outside of Great Britain? In what directions did the major railroads run? How did the progress of industrialization in continental Europe compare with that in Britain? What impact did industrialization have on Spain and Italy?

European industrialization was therefore not the thunderclap it was in Britain. In France, it was a slow, accretive development that took advantage of traditional skills and occupations and gradually modernized the marketplace. In Germany, industrialization had to overcome the political divisions of the empire, the economic isolation of the petty states, and the wide dispersion of vital resources. Regions rather than states industrialized in the early nineteenth century, and parts of Austria, Italy, and Spain imported machinery and techniques and modernized their traditional crafts. But most of the states and most of the eastern part of Europe remained tied to a traditional agrarian-based economy that provided neither labor for industrial production nor purchasing power for industrial goods. The areas quickly became sources for raw materials and primary products for their industrial neighbors.

France: Industrialization Without Revolution

The experience of France in the nineteenth century demonstrates that there was no single path to industrialization.

Each state blended together its natural resources, historical experiences, and forms of economic organization in unique combinations. While some mixtures resulted in explosive growth, as in Britain, others made for steady development, as in France.

French industrialization was keyed to domestic rather than export markets and to the application of new technology to a vast array of traditional crafts. The French profited, as did all of the Continental states, from British inventions, but they also benefited from the distinct features of their own economy. France possessed a pool of highly skilled and highly productive labor, a manufacturing tradition oriented toward the creation of high-quality goods, and consumers who valued taste and fashion over cost and function. Thus while the British dominated the new mass market for inexpensive cottons and cast-iron goods, a market with high sales but low profit margins, the French were producing luxury items whose very scarcity kept both prices and profits high. Two decisive factors determined the nature of French industrialization: population growth and the French Revolution.

Slow Growth. From the early eighteenth to the mid-nineteenth centuries, France grew slowly. In 1700, the French population stood at just less than 20 million; in 1850, it was just less than 36 million, a growth rate of 80 percent. In contrast, Germany grew 135 percent, from 15 to 34 million, and England 300 percent, from 5 to 20 million, during the same period. Nevertheless, France remained the most populous nation in western Europe, second on the Continent only to Russia. There is no simple explanation for France's relatively sluggish population growth. The French had been hit particularly hard by subsistence crises in the seventeenth century, and there is reliable evidence that the rural population consciously attempted to limit family size by methods of birth control as well as by delaying marriages. Moreover, France urbanized slowly at a time when city dwellers were marrying younger and producing larger families. As late as the 1860s, a majority of French workers were farmers. Whatever the cause of the moderate population growth, its consequences were clear. France was not pressured by the force of numbers to abandon its traditional agricultural methods, nor did it face a shortage of traditional supplies of energy. Except during crop failures, French agriculture could produce to meet French needs, and there remained more than enough wood for domestic and industrial use.

The Impact of the French Revolution. The consequences of the French Revolution are less clear. Throughout the eighteenth century, the French economy performed at least as well as the British, and in many areas better. French overseas trade had grown spectacularly until checked by military defeat in the Seven Years' War (1756–1763). French agriculture steadily increased output, while French rural manufactures flourished. A strong guild tradition still dominated urban industries, and although it restricted competition and limited growth, it also helped maintain the standards for the production of high-quality goods that made French commodities highly prized throughout the world. The Revolution disrupted every aspect of economic life. Some of its outcomes were unforeseen and unwelcome. For example, Napoleon's Continental System, which attempted to close European markets to Britain, resulted in a shipping war, which the British won decisively and which eliminated France as a competitor for overseas trade in the mid-nineteenth century. But other outcomes were the result of direct policies, even if their impact could not have been entirely predicted. Urban guilds and corporations were abolished, opening trades to newcomers but destroying the close-knit groups that trained skilled artisans and introduced innovative products. Similarly, the breakup of both feudal and common lands to satisfy the hunger of the peasantry had the effect of maintaining a large rural population for decades.

Despite the efforts of the central government, there had been little change in the techniques used by French farmers over the course of the eighteenth century. French peasants clung tenaciously to traditional rights that gave even the smallest landholder a vital say in community agriculture. Landlords were predominantly absentees, less interested in the organization of their estates than in the dues and taxes that could be extracted from them. Thus the policies of successive revolutionary governments strengthened the hold of small peasants on the land. With the abolition of many feudal dues and with careful family planning, smallholders could survive and pass a meager inheritance on to their children. Even prosperous farmers could not grow into the large-scale proprietors that had enclosed English fields, for little land came on the market, and many parts of France practiced partible inheritance, which, over time, tended to even out the size of holdings. French agriculture continued to be organized in its centuries-old patterns. While it was able to supply the nation's need for food, it could not release large numbers of workers for purely industrial activity.

Stages of Industrial Progress. Thus French industrial growth was constrained on the one hand by the relatively small numbers of workers who could engage in manufacturing and on the other by the fact that a large portion of the population remained subsistence producers, cash-poor, and linked only to small rural markets. Throughout the eighteenth century, the French economy continued to be regionally segregated rather than nationally integrated. The size of the state inhibited a highly organized internal trade, and there was little improvement of the infrastructure of transportation. Although some British-style canals were built, canals in Britain were built to move coal rather than staple goods, and France did not have much coal to move. Manufacturing concerns were still predominantly family businesses whose primary markets were regional rather than international. Roads that connected the short distances between producers and consumers were of greater importance to the producers than arterial routes that served the markets of others. Similarly, there was no national capital market until the mid-nineteenth century, and precious few regional ones. French producers were as thrifty and profit-oriented as any others, but they found it more difficult to raise the large amounts of capital necessary to purchase the most expensive new machinery and build the most up-to-date factories. Ironworks, coal mines, and railroads, the three capital-intensive ventures of industrialization, were financed either by government subsidy or by foreign investment.

All those factors determined the slow, steady pace of French industrialization. Recovery after 1815 came in fits and starts. British inventors, manufacturers, and entrepreneurs were enticed to France to demonstrate new machinery and industrial techniques, but in most places the real engine of growth was skilled workers' steady application of traditional methods. By 1820, only 65 French factories were powered by steam engines, and even water-powered machinery was uncommon. Industrial firms remained small and were frequently a combination of putting-out and factory production. It was not until midcentury that sustained industrial growth became evident. This was largely the result of the construction of railroads on a national plan, financed in large part by the central government. Whereas in Britain the railways took advantage of a national market, in France they created one. They also gave the

■ Pierre-Denis Martin's *Waterworks and Aqueduct at Marly* makes clear the transformation of the landscape wrought by the infrastructure of industry in eighteenth-century France.

essential stimulation to the modernization of the iron industry, in which much refining was still done with charcoal rather than coke; of machine making; and of the capital markets. Imported steel and foreign investment were vital ingredients in a process that took several decades to reach fruition.

The disadvantages of being on the trailing edge of economic change were mitigated for a time by conventional practices of protectionism. Except in specialty goods, agricultural produce, and luxury products, French manufactures could not compete with either British or German commodities. Had France maintained its position as a world trader, the comparative disadvantage would have been devastating. But defeat in the wars of commerce had led to a drawing inward of French economic effort. Marseille and Bordeaux, once bustling centers of European trade, became provincial backwaters in the nineteenth century. But the internal market was still strong enough to support industrial growth, and domestic commodities could be protected by prohibitive tariffs, especially against British textiles, iron, and, ironically, coal. Despite the fact that France had to import more than 40 percent of its meager requirements of coal, it still insisted upon slapping high import duties on British supplies. That was in part to protect French mine owners, who had never integrated their operations with iron production and therefore had no interest in keeping fuel costs low. Moreover, the slow pace of French industrialization allowed for the skipping of intermediate stages of development. France had hardly entered the canal age when it began to build its railways. Ultimately, industry moved from hand power to steam power in one long step.

While France achieved industrialization without an industrial revolution, it also achieved economic growth within the context of its traditional values. Agriculture may not have modernized, but the ancient village communities escaped the devastation modernization would bring. The orderly progression of generations of farming families characterized rural France until the shattering experiences of the Franco-Prussian War (1870) and the First World War (1914–1918). Nor did France experience the mushroom growth of new cities with all of their problems of poverty, squalor, and homelessness. Slow population growth ameliorated the worst of the social diseases of industrialization while traditional rural manufacturing softened the transformation of a way of life. If France did not reap the windfall profits of the Industrial Revolution, neither did it harvest the bitter crop of social, economic, and spiritual impoverishment that was pulled in its train.

Germany: Industrialization and Union

The process of industrialization in Germany was dominated by the historic divisions of the empire of the German peoples. Before 1815, there were more than 300 separate jurisdictional units within the empire, and after 1815 there were still more than 30. Those included large advanced states such as Prussia, Austria, and Saxony as well as small free cities and the personal enclaves of petty nobles who had guessed right during the Napoleonic wars. Political divisions had more than political impact. Each state clung tenaciously to its local laws and customs, which favored its citizens over outsiders. Merchants who lived near the intersection of separate jurisdictions could find themselves liable for several sets of tolls to move their goods and several sets of customs duties for importing and exporting them. The tolls and duties would have to be paid in different currencies at different rates of exchange according to the different regulations of each state. Small wonder that German merchants exhibited an intense localism, preferring to trade with members of their own state and supporting trade barriers against others. Such obstacles had a depressing effect on the economies of all German states but pushed with greatest weight against the manufacturing regions of Saxony, Silesia, and the Rhineland.

Agriculture.   Most of imperial Germany was agricultural land suited to a diversity of uses. The mountainous regions of Bavaria and the Austrian alpine communities practiced animal husbandry; there was a grain belt in Prussia, where the soil was poor but the land plentiful, and one in central Germany in which the soil was fertile and the land densely occupied. The Rhine Valley was one of the richest in all of Europe and was the center of German wine production. The introduction of the potato was the chief innovation of the eighteenth century. While English farmers were turning farms into commercial estates, German peasants were learning how to make do with less land.

Agricultural estates were organized differently in different parts of Germany. In the east, serfdom still prevailed. Peasants were tied to the land and its lord and were responsible for labor service during much of the week. Methods of cultivation were traditional, and neither peasants nor lords had much incentive to adopt new techniques. The vast agricultural domains of the Prussian Junkers, as those landlords were called, were built on the backs of cheap serf labor, and the harvest was destined for the Baltic export trade, where world grain prices rather than local production costs would determine profits. In central Germany, the long process of commuting labor service into rents was nearly completed by the end of the eighteenth century. The peasantry was not yet free, as a series of manorial relationships still tied them to the land, but they were no longer mere serfs. Moreover, western Germany was dominated by free farmers who either owned or leased their lands and who had a purely economic relationship with their landlords. The restriction of peasant mobility in much of Germany posed difficulties for the creation of an industrial work force. As late as 1800, more than 80 percent of the German population was engaged in agriculture, a proportion that would drop slowly over the next half century.

Although Germany was well endowed with natural resources and skilled labor in a number of trades, it had not taken part in the expansion of world trade during the seventeenth century, and the once bustling Hanseatic ports had been far outdistanced by the rise of the Atlantic economies. The principal exported manufacture was linen, which was expertly spun and woven in Saxony and the Prussian province of Silesia. The linen industry was organized traditionally, with a mixture of domestic production managed on the putting-out system and some factory spinning, especially after the introduction of British mechanical innovations. But even the most advanced factories were still being powered by water, and thus they were located in mountainous regions where rapidly running streams could turn the wheels. In the 1840s there were only 22 steam-driven spinning mills in Germany, several of them established by the Prussian government, which imported British machines and technicians to run them. Neither linens nor traditional German metal crafts could compete on the international markets, but they could find a wider market within Germany if only the problems of political division could be resolved.

The Zollverein.   The problems of political division were especially acute for Prussia after the reorganization of European boundaries in 1815 (see Chapter 22). Prussian territory included the coal- and iron-rich Rhineland provinces, but a number of smaller states separated those areas from Prussia's eastern domain. Each small state exacted its own tolls and customs duties whenever Prussian merchants wanted to move goods from one part of Prussia to the other. Such movement became more common in the nineteenth century as German manufacturing began to grow in step with its rising population. Between 1815 and 1865, the population of Germany grew by 60 percent to more than 36 million people. It was an enormous internal market, nearly as large as the population of France, and the Prussians resolved to make it a unified trading zone by creating a series of alliances with smaller states known as the **Zollverein** (1834). The Zollverein was not a free-trade zone, as was the British Empire, but rather a customs union in which member states adopted the liberal Prussian customs regulations. Every state was paid an annual portion of receipts based upon its population, and every state—except Prussia—increased its revenues as a result. The crucial advantage the Prussians received was the ability to move goods and materials from east to west, but Prussia reaped political profits as well. It forced Hanover and Saxony into the Zollverein and kept its powerful rival Austria out. Prussia's economic union soon proved to be the basis for the union of the German states.

The creation of the Zollverein was vital to German industrialization. It permitted the exploitation of natural advantages, such as plentiful supplies of coal and iron, and it provided a basis for the building of railroads. Germany was a follower nation in the process of industrialization. It started late and it self-consciously modeled its success on the British experience. British equipment and engineers were brought to Germany to attempt to plant the seeds of an industrial economy. German manufacturers sent their children to England to learn the latest techniques in industrial management. Friedrich Engels (1820–1895) worked in a Manchester cotton factory, where he observed the appalling conditions of the industrial labor force and wrote *The Condition of the Working Class in England* (1845). Steam engines were installed in coal mines, if not in factories, and the process of puddling revolutionized ironmaking, though most iron was still smelted with charcoal rather than coke. Although coal was plentiful in

THE SLAVERY OF LABOR

Although born in Germany, Friedrich Engels witnessed industrialization in England firsthand. His father owned a factory in Manchester of which Engels was put in charge. By day he oversaw industrial production, and by night he wandered the city streets overwhelmed by the suffering of the working classes. His analysis of industrialization developed from his own observations. He became first a socialist and then, with Karl Marx, a founder of the Communist party.

Focus Questions

Why is capital "the all-important weapon in the class war"? Why does Engels view wage labor as a kind of slavery?

Capital is the all-important weapon in the class war. Power lies in the hands of those who own, directly or indirectly, foodstuffs and the means of production. The poor, having no capital, inevitably bear the consequences of defeat in the struggle. Nobody troubles about the poor as they struggle helplessly in the whirlpool of modern industrial life. The working man may be lucky enough to find employment, if by his labour he can enrich some member of the middle classes. But his wages are so low that they hardly keep body and soul together. If he cannot find work, he can steal, unless he is afraid of the police; or he can go hungry and then the police will see to it that he will die of hunger in such a way as not to disturb the equanimity of the middle classes. . . .

The only difference between the old-fashioned slavery and the new is that while the former was openly acknowledged the latter is disguised. The worker *appears* to be free, because he is not bought and sold outright. He is sold piecemeal by the day, the week, or the year. Moreover he is not sold by one owner to another, but he is forced to sell himself in this fashion. He is not the slave of a single individual, but of the whole capitalist class. As far as the worker is concerned, however, there can be no doubt as to his servile status. It is true that the apparent liberty which the worker enjoys does give him some *real* freedom. Even this genuine freedom has the disadvantage that no one is responsible for providing him with food and shelter. His real masters, the middle-class capitalists, can discard him at any moment and leave him to starve, if they have no further use for his services and no further interest in his survival. . . .

From Friedrich Engels, *The Condition of the Working Class in England in 1844* (1845).

Prussia, it was found at the eastern and western extremities of Germany. Even with the lowering of tolls and duties, it was still too expensive to move over rudimentary roads and an uncompleted system of canals.

Thus the railroads were the key to tapping the industrial potential of Germany. There they were a cause rather than a result of industrialization. The agreements hammered out in the creation of the Zollverein made possible the planning necessary to build single lines across the boundaries of numerous states. Initially, German railroads were financed privately, with much foreign investment. But ultimately governments saw the practical advantages of rail transport and took an active part in both planning and financing the system. More than a quarter of the track constructed in Prussia before 1870 was owned directly by the government, and most of the rest had been indirectly financed by the government, which purchased land and guaranteed interest on stock issues.

Germany imported most of its engines directly from Britain and thus adopted standard British gauge for its system. As early as 1850 there were more than 3500 miles of rail in Germany, with important roads linking the manufacturing districts of Saxony and the coal and iron deposits of the Ruhr. Twenty years later, Germany was second only to Britain in the amount of track that had been laid and opened. By then it was no longer simply a follower. German engineers and machinists, trained in Europe's best schools of technology, were turning out engines and rolling stock second to none. And the railroads transported a host of high-quality manufactures, especially durable metal goods that came to carry the most prestigious trademark of the late nineteenth century: "Made in Germany."

The Lands That Time Forgot

Nothing better demonstrates the point that industrialization was a regional rather than a national process than a survey of those states that did not develop industrial economies by the middle of the nineteenth century. The states ranged from the Netherlands, which was still one of the richest areas in Europe, to Spain and Russia, which were the poorest. Also included were Austria-Hungary, the states of the Italian peninsula, and Poland. In all those nations there was some industrial progress. The Bohemian lands of Austria contained a highly developed spinning industry; the Spanish province of Catalonia produced more cotton than did Belgium, and the Basque region was rich in iron and coal. Northern Italy mechanized its textile production, particularly silk spinning, while in the regions around both Moscow and Saint Petersburg, factories were run on serf labor. Nevertheless, the economies of all the states remained nonindustrial and, with the exception of the Netherlands, dominated by subsistence agriculture.

There were many reasons why the states were unable to develop their industrial potential. Some, such as Naples and Poland, were simply underendowed with resources; others, such as Austria-Hungary and Spain, faced difficulties of transport and communications that could not easily be overcome. Spain's modest resources were located on its northern and eastern edges, while a vast, arid plain dominated the center. To move raw materials and finished products from one end of the country to the other was a daunting task, made more difficult by lack of waterways and the rudimentary condition of Spanish roads. Two-thirds of Austria-Hungary was either mountains or hills, a geographic feature that presented obstacles not even the railroads could easily solve. But there was far more than natural disadvantage behind the failure of those parts of Europe to move in step with the industrializing states. Their social structure, agricultural organization, and commercial policies all hindered the adoption of new methods, machines, and modes of production.

Despite the fact that industrialization created new and largely unmanageable social problems, the follower states were eager for its benefits. All imported the latest products of technology, and the ruling elites in even the most traditional economies lived a material life similar to those in the most advanced. British entrepreneurs and artisans were courted by heads of state and their ministers and were offered riches in exchange for their precious knowledge. British industrialists set up textile factories in Moscow, built spinning machines in Bohemia, and taught Spanish miners how to puddle iron. Railroad pioneer George Stephenson himself surveyed the prospect of creating a passenger rail system in Spain, though he concluded pessimistically, "I have not seen enough people of the right sort to fill a single train." In the later part of the nineteenth century, French, Belgian, and German industrialists served similar roles. There were no traditional economies by choice. Industrialization was seen as a miracle, and the latecomers worshiped avidly at its shrine.

It was work rather than faith that would produce economic salvation. The most common characteristic of the latecomers was a traditional agrarian structure that consumed the lion's share of labor and capital while producing little surplus for any but a small dominant class. In areas as dissimilar as Spain, Italy, and Russia, agriculture was organized in vast estates, which kept the mass of peasants perpetually poor. Sharecropping systems in the west and serfdom in the east differed only in formal organization. Both conditions made it impossible for peasants to accumulate the land necessary to invest in capital improvements or to send their children to towns to engage in industrial occupations. In Hungary, Poland, and Russia, it was illegal for people to change occupations, and serfs who engaged in industrial activity paid their lords for the privilege. Although a number of serfs amassed considerable fortunes in organizing domestic or factory spinning, legal constraints restricted the efforts of potential entrepreneurs.

Similarly, the leaders of traditional economies maintained tariff systems that insulated their own producers from competition. Austrian tariffs were not only artificially high, they were accompanied by import quotas to keep all but the smallest fraction of foreign products from Austrian consumers. The Spanish government prohibited the importation of grain, forcing its eastern provinces to pay huge transport costs for domestic grain despite the fact that cheaper Italian grain was readily available. Such policies sapped much-needed capital from industrial investment. There were many reasons for so-called protective tariffs, and it was not only the follower states

■ A Russian peasant tills a field with a primitive horse-drawn wooden plow. Russian fields produced low yields, partly because of the use of such crude farming methods.

that imposed them. France and the Zollverein protected domestic industry while Britain was converted to free trade only in the 1840s. But protection was sensible only when it protected rather than isolated. Inefficiently produced goods of inferior quality were the chief results of the protectionist policies of the follower nations. Failure to adopt steam-powered machines made traditionally produced linens and silks so expensive that smuggling occurred on an international scale. Although the goods might find buyers in domestic markets, they could not compete in international trade, and one by one the industries of the follower nations atrophied. Such nations became exporters of raw materials and foodstuffs. The export of Russian linen was replaced by the export of Russian flax. Spain, once the largest exporter of woolen cloth in Europe, exported mainly wines and fruits. Those economies that remained traditionally organized came to be exploited for their resources by those that had industrialized.

The international situation was not all that different from the dual system that came into effect within the nonindustrialized states. In Austria-Hungary, for example, it was Hungary that was kept from industrializing, first by the continuation of serf-based agriculture, then by the high internal tariffs that favored Austrian over Hungarian manufactures. In Italy, the division was between north and south. In Lombardy and Tuscany, machine-based manufacturing took hold alongside mining and metallurgy; in 1860, northern Italy contained 98 percent of the railways and 87 percent of the roads that existed on the entire peninsula. In Naples and Sicily, half-starved peasants eked out a miserable existence on once-rich soil that had become depleted from overuse. It was estimated that of the 400,000 people living in Naples, more than 100,000 were destitute beggars. In Spain, Catalonia modernized while Castile stagnated. Until the loss of its Latin American empire in the first half of the nineteenth century, Spain had a ready market for Catalonian textiles and handicrafts. But since Castile remained the cultural and administrative center of the state, it did little to encourage change, and much government policy was actually counterproductive. The chief problem faced by the dual economies was that neither part could sustain the other. Traditional agriculture could not produce the necessary surplus of either labor or capital to support industry, and industry could not economize sufficiently to make manufactured goods cheap enough for a poor peasantry.

Thus the advantages of being a follower were all missed. Technology could not be borrowed or stages skipped because the ground was not prepared for widespread industrial activity to be cultivated. Even by standing still, followers fell behind. While over the course of the nineteenth century male illiteracy dropped dramatically in the industrialized states—to 30 percent in Britain and France and 10 percent in Prussia—it remained at 75 to 80 percent in Spain and Italy and more than 90 percent in Russia. There was more than irony in the fact that one of the first railroads built on the Continent was built in Austria but was built to be powered by horses rather than engines. The first railways in Italy linked royal palaces to capital cities. Those in Spain radiated from Madrid and bypassed most centers of natural resources. In those states, the railroads were built to move the military rather than passengers or goods. They were state-financed, occasionally state-owned, and almost always lost money. They were symbols of the industrial age, but in those states they were symbols without substance.

CONCLUSION

The industrialization of Europe in the eighteenth century was an epochal event in human history. The constraints on daily life imposed by nature were loosened for the first time. No longer did population growth in one generation mean famine in the next; no longer was it necessary for the great majority of people to toil in the fields to earn their daily bread. Manufacture replaced agriculture as humanity's primary activity, though the change was longer and slower than the burst of industrialization that took place in the first half of the nineteenth century. For the leaders, Britain especially, industrialization brought international eminence. British achievements were envied, British inventors celebrated, Britain's constitutional and social organization lauded. A comparatively small island nation had become the greatest economic power in Europe. Industrialization had profound consequences for economic life, but its effects ran deeper than that. The search for new markets would result in the conquest of continents; the power of productivity unleashed by coal and iron would result in the first great arms race. Both would reach fruition in World War I, the first industrial war. For better or worse, the industrial era that began in Britain in the middle of the eighteenth century continues today.

QUESTIONS FOR REVIEW

1. Why did early manufacturing develop in the countryside, and what effect did that have on manufacturing practices and social relations?
2. In what ways were the ideas about organization of manufacturers such as Josiah Wedgwood and Robert Owen as significant as new technology in the development of industry in Britain?
3. How did British society address some of the changes in people's lives that were brought about by industrialization?
4. How did industrialization on the Continent differ from industrialization in England?
5. Why did some nations develop little industry at all?

KEY TERMS

agricultural revolution, *p. 638*

Crystal Palace Exhibition, *p. 660*

Factory Act (1833), *p. 654*

industrialization, *p. 644*

Industrial Revolution, *p. 643*

putting-out system, *p. 640*

Zollverein, *p. 664*

DISCOVERING WESTERN CIVILIZATION ONLINE

You can obtain more information about industrial Europe at the Websites listed below. See also the Companion Website that accompanies this text, www.ablongman.com/kishlansky, which contains an online study guide and additional resources.

The Industrial Revolution in Britain

Reminiscences of James Watt

www.history.rochester.edu/steam/hart/

A nineteenth-century account of the life of James Watt and his role as inventor of the steam engine with links to the history of the steam engine.

Women in World History Curriculum: Industrial Revolution

www.womeninworldhistory.com/lesson7.html

Sponsored by Women in World History Curriculum, this site details the plight of working women in industrial England.

Child Labour in the 19th Century

www.spartacus.schoolnet.co.uk/IRchild.main.htm

This site chronicles child labor in Britain, including life in the factory and first-hand experiences.

The Industrialization of the Continent

Modern History Sourcebook: Tables Illustrating the Spread of Industrialization

www.fordham.edu/halsall/mod/indrevtabs1.html

Charts and statistics about industrialization in Europe.

Internet Modern History Sourcebook: Industrial Revolution

www.fordham.edu/halsall/mod/modsbook14.html

An outstanding collection of documents on the Industrial Age with links.

SUGGESTIONS FOR FURTHER READING

General Reading

T. S. Ashton, *The Industrial Revolution* (Oxford: Oxford University Press, 1997). A compelling brief account of the traditional view of industrialization.

Niall Ferguson, *The Cash Nexus: Money and Power in the Modern World, 1700–2000* (New York: Basic Books, 2001). A transnational history of the role of finance in the making of the modern world.

Jordan Goodman and Katrina Honeyman, *Gainful Pursuits: The Making of Industrial Europe, 1600–1914* (London: Edward Arnold, 1988). A brief overview of the entire process of industrialization.

The Traditional Economy

Richard Brown, *Society and Economy in Modern Britain, 1700–1850* (London: Routledge, 1991). A comprehensive survey.

J. D. Chambers and G. E. Mingay, *The Agricultural Revolution* (London: Batsford, 1966). The classic survey of the changes in British agriculture.

The Industrial Revolution in Britain

N. F. R. Crafts, *British Economic Growth During the Industrial Revolution* (Oxford: Oxford University Press, 1986). A highly quantitative study by a new economic historian arguing the case that economic growth was slow in the early nineteenth century.

François Crouzet, *The First Industrialists* (Cambridge: Cambridge University Press, 1985). An analysis of the social background of the first generation of British entrepreneurs.

Martin Daunton, *Progress and Poverty: An Economic and Social History of Britain, 1700–1850* (Oxford: Oxford University Press, 1995). The best single-volume survey on the Industrial Revolution and its effects on British society.

Phyllis Deane, *The First Industrial Revolution*, 2d ed. (Cambridge: Cambridge University Press, 1979). The best introduction to the technological changes in Britain.

Richard Price, *British Society, 1680–1880: Dynamism, Containment, and Change* (New York: Cambridge University Press, 1999). A new argument about the nature of British society in the age of the Industrial Revolution.

John Rule, *The Vital Century: England's Developing Economy, 1714–1815* (London: Longman, 1992). A comprehensive survey of the British economy.

E. P. Thompson, *The Making of the English Working Class* (New York: Random House, 1966). A brilliant and passionate study of the ways laborers responded to the changes brought about by the industrial economy.

The Industrialization of the Continent

W. O. Henderson, *The Rise of German Industrial Power* (Berkeley: University of California Press, 1975). A chronological study of German industrialization that centers on Prussia.

Tom Kemp, *Industrialization in Nineteenth-Century Europe*, 2d ed. (London: Longman, 1985). Survey of the process of industrialization in the major European states.

Sidney Pollard, *Peaceful Conquest* (Oxford: Oxford University Press, 1981). Argues the regional nature of industrialization throughout western Europe.

Roger Price, *The Economic Transformation of France* (London: Croom Helm, 1975). A study of French society before and during the process of industrialization.

Wolfgang Schivelbusch, *The Railway Journey* (Berkeley: University of California Press, 1986). A social history of the impact of railways, drawn from French and German sources.

Clive Trebilcock, *The Industrialization of the Continental Powers, 1780–1914* (London: Longman, 1981). A complex study of Germany, France, and Russia.

For a list of additional titles related to this chapter's topics, please see http://www.ablongman.com/kishlansky.

Chapter 22

POLITICAL UPHEAVALS AND SOCIAL TRANSFORMATIONS, 1815–1850

Chapter Outline

Political and economic upheaval characterized the first half of the nineteenth century. Social inequities fueled protest and even revolution among the working and middle classes. The problems of Europe's poor, an expanding class, were especially harsh and were compounded by natural disasters and famine. How could one crop affect European society? In The Visual Record, see how one French painter depicted peasant farmers planting the most important food among the poor: the potato. ➤

POTATO POLITICS

The Plight of the Poor in European Societies

Vegetables have histories too. But none has a more interesting history in the West than the humble potato. First introduced to northern Europe from the Andean highlands of South America at the end of the sixteenth century, it rapidly became a staple of peasant diets from Ireland to Russia. The potato's vitamins, minerals, and high carbohydrate content provided a rich source of energy to Europe's rural poor. It was simple to plant, required little or no cultivation, and did well in damp, cool climates. Best of all, it could be grown successfully on the smallest plots of land. One acre could support a peasant family of four for a year. Potato peelings helped sustain the family cow and pig, further supplementing family income.

In *Potato Planters*, shown here, the French painter Jean-François Millet (1814–1875) provided a view of the peasant labor involved in planting potatoes. Millet, the son of a wealthy peasant family, understood well the importance of the potato crop in the peasant diet. The man and woman in the painting plant their potatoes as a reverent act, bowing as field laborers might in prayer. (Laborers actually do pray in Millet's more sentimental work *The Angelus*.) The primitive nature of the process is striking: the man uses a short hoe to scrape at what seems to be unyielding soil. The peasants seem part of the nature that surrounds them, patient as the beast that waits in the shade, bent and gnarled and lovely as the tree that arches in the background.

The fleshy root not only guaranteed health, it also affected social relations. Traditionally, peasants delayed marrying and starting families because of the unavailability of land. The potato changed that behavior. Now the potato allowed peasants with only a little land to marry and have children earlier. Millet's depiction of the man and woman working together in the field resonates with the simple fact that potato cultivation aided in the formation of the couple. Millet's couple are parents whose baby sleeps swaddled in a basket and shaded by the tree. In those peasant homes where family members did putting-out work for local entrepreneurs, potato cultivation drew little labor away from the spinning wheel and loom. It permitted prosperous farmers to devote more land to cash crops, since only a small portion of land was required to feed a family. As the sole item of diet, it provided life-sustaining nutrients and a significant amount of the protein so necessary for heavy labor. The Irish adult male ate an average of 12 to 14 pounds of potatoes a day—a figure that may seem preposterous to us today.

Proverbs warned peasants against putting all their eggs in one basket, but no folk wisdom prepared the Irish, many of whom relied on the potato as a single crop, for the potato disaster that struck them. In 1845, a fungus from America destroyed the new potato crop. Although peasants were certainly accustomed to bad harvests and crop failures, they had no precedent for the years of blight that followed. From 1846 to 1850, famine and the diseases resulting from it—scurvy, dysentery, cholera, and typhus fever—killed more than a million people in what became known as the Great Hunger. Another million people emigrated, many to the United States. Total dependence on the potato reaped its grim harvest, devastating all levels of Irish society. Within five years, the Irish population was reduced by almost 25 percent.

Looking Ahead

The Irish potato famine has been called the "last great European natural disaster," to distinguish it from the man-made horrors of war and revolution. But it was as much a social and political disaster as a natural one. As the wealth of European societies expanded in the nineteenth century, so did the number of those who lived on the edge, poised between unemployment and starvation. The Irish Great Hunger was the most striking example of the problem that plagued all Western societies in the first half of the nineteenth century: what to do with the poor. In this chapter, we shall see that while the boundaries of European nations were redefined following the Napoleonic Wars in order to create stability, the economic hardships of peasants and workers continued to plague and disrupt European societies internally. The new ideologies of the first half of the nineteenth century grappled with the challenge of reshaping state and society. But social inequities continued to fuel protest and revolution between 1815 and 1850 and pulled down governments across Europe. ➤

■ Jean-François Millet, *Potato Planters* (ca. 1861).

GEOGRAPHICAL TOUR
Europe in 1815

Peasants like those depicted by Millet (in this chapter's Visual Record) seldom traveled beyond their own villages. Of course, all of that was different in Napoleon's quest for empire. Napoleon had placed large armies of peasants and workers in motion, crisscrossing the continent, and giving his own troops and Europe a geography lesson. At the heart of that lesson was the fact that no one state had been able to defeat Napoleon and his conscript armies. He had made clear the territorial and political interdependence of the European powers. The lesson was not lost on the leaders of Russia, Austria, Prussia, and France as they sat down to redraw the map of Europe in 1815.

Europe's rulers shared the vision of Europe as a machine that must be kept in running order. Those victorious in defeating Napoleon's Empire looked on the whole of Europe as one entity and conceived of peace in terms of a general European security.

The primary goal of European leaders was to devise the most stable territorial arrangement possible. That goal entailed redrawing the map of Europe (see **Map A**). During the negotiations, traditional claims of the right to rule came head to head with new ideas about stabilization. The equilibrium established in 1815 made possible a century-long European peace. Conflicts erupted, to be sure, but they took on the characteristics of the new system that was constructed at Vienna in 1815.

The Congress of Vienna

In 1814, representatives of the victorious Allies agreed to convene in the Austrian capital of Vienna for the purposes of mopping up the mess created in Europe by French rule and restoring order to European monarchies.

On the surface, the **Congress of Vienna,** which began its deliberations in September 1814, seemed to be no more than

■ **Map A. Europe, 1815.** In a series of treaties following Napoleon's defeat, the European powers redrew the map of Europe to create the most stable territorial arrangement and ensure European security. At the center of Europe stood the German confederation, outlined here in red.

an excuse for endless partying among Europe's royalty. Glittering balls as costly as battles gave critics the impression that statesmen were waltzing their way through treaty arrangements. The survival of an old system of precedence and etiquette hobbled negotiations. Issues of who should sign a treaty first and who should have the preferred places at the dinner table were the subjects of endless debates and fatal duels. But the image of bewigged men arguing over how to determine who would enter a room first belied the reality of the diplomats' serious negotiations as they sought to fashion a lasting peace by redrawing the map of Europe.

The central actors whose personalities dominated the Congress were Austrian minister of foreign affairs Prince Klemens von Metternich (1809–1848), British foreign secretary Viscount Castlereagh (1812–1822), French minister of foreign affairs Charles Maurice de Talleyrand (1814–1815), the Russian tsar Alexander I (1801–1825), and the Prussian king Frederick William III (1797–1840). In spite of personal eccentricities, animosities, and occasional outright hostilities among Europe's leaders, all shared a common concern with reestablishing harmony in Europe.

Settling with France. Because of the concern with establishing harmony at the time of Napoleon's defeat, the peace enforced against France was not a punitive one. After Napoleon's abdication in 1814, the victorious powers of Great Britain, Russia, Prussia, and Austria decided that leniency was the best way to support the restored Bourbon monarchy. After 1793, royalist émigrés referred to the young son of the executed Louis XVI as Louis XVII, although the child died in captivity and never reigned. In 1814, the four powers designated the elder of the two surviving brothers of Louis XVI as the appropriate candidate for the restored monarchy. Because of the circumstances of his restoration, the new king, Louis XVIII (1814–1815; 1815–1824), bore the ignominious image of returning "in the baggage car of the Allies." Every effort was made not to weigh down Louis XVIII with a harsh settlement. The First Peace of Paris, signed by the Allies with France in May 1814, had reestablished the French frontiers at the 1792 boundaries, which included Avignon, Venaissin, parts of Savoy, and German and Flemish territories—none of which had belonged to France in 1789.

Even after the hundred-day return of Napoleon, the "Usurper," the Second Peace of Paris of November 1815 declared French frontiers restricted to the boundaries of 1790 (see **Map B**) and exacted from France an indemnity of 700 million francs. An army of occupation consisting of 150,000 troops was also placed on French soil at French expense but was removed ahead of schedule in 1818. Contrary to the terms of the first treaty, the second treaty also required France to return plundered art treasures to their countries of origin.

New Territorial Arrangements. The dominant partnership of Austria and Britain at the Congress of Vienna resulted in treaty arrangements that served to restrain the ambitions of Russia and Prussia. No country was to receive territory

■ **Map B. France, 1815.** In determining the borders of France, European heads of state were torn between the need to punish and control France and the importance of reconciliation with France for a stable Europe. The Second Peace of Paris of November 1815 permitted France to return to the borders of 1790 and to resume its role as one of the Great Powers.

without giving up something in return, and no one country was to receive enough territory to make it a present or future threat to the peace of Europe. To contain France, some steps taken prior to the Congress were ratified or expanded. In June 1814, the Low Countries had been set up as a unitary state to serve as a buffer against future French expansion on the Continent and a block to the revival of French sea power. The new Kingdom of the Netherlands (see **Map C**), created out of the former Dutch Republic and the Austrian Netherlands, was placed under the rule of William I (1815–1840). The Catholic southern provinces were thus uneasily reunited with the Protestant northern provinces, regions that had been separated since the Peace of Westphalia in 1648. Lest there be any doubt about the intended purpose of the new kingdom, Great Britain gave William I of the Netherlands £2 million to fortify his frontier against France.

A reestablished monarchy that united the island kingdom of Sardinia with Piedmont and included Savoy, Nice, and part of Genoa contained France on its southeast border (see **Map D**). To the east, Prussia was given control of the left bank of the Rhine. Switzerland was reestablished as an independent confederation of cantons. Finally, Bourbon rule was restored in Spain on France's southwestern border.

■ **Map C. Kingdom of the Netherlands.** As a buffer on France's northernmost border, the new Kingdom of the Netherlands was a forced union of two regions with different languages and religions. The union lasted only until 1831 when the southern provinces revolted to form Belgium.

■ **Map D. Italian Peninsula, 1815.** Austria gained major territorial concessions on the Italian peninsula. The Austrian Empire now included Lombardy and Venetia. Austria was also influential throughout the peninsula in the Papal States, the three small duchies (Tuscany, Parma, Modena), and the Kingdom of the Two Sicilies.

Austria's power was firmly established in Italy, either through outright territorial control or influence over independent states (see **Map D**). The Papal States were returned to Pope Pius VII (1800–1823), along with territories that had been Napoleon's Cisalpine Republic and the Kingdom of Italy. The Republic of Venice was absorbed into the Austrian Empire. Lombardy and the Illyrian provinces on the Dalmatian coast were likewise restored to Austria. The Italian duchies of Tuscany, Parma, and Modena were placed under the rule of Habsburg princes.

After the fall of Napoleon, the Allies made no attempt to restore the Holy Roman Empire. Napoleon's Confederation of the Rhine, which organized the majority of German territory under French auspices in 1806, was dissolved. In its place, the lands once divided into 300 petty states in central Europe were reorganized into 38 states in the German Confederation (see **Map E**). The 38 states, along with Austria as the thirty-ninth, were represented in a new Federal Diet at Frankfurt, dominated by Austria. The German Confederation was intended as a bulwark against France, not to serve any nationalist or parliamentary function.

All of the changes were the result of carefully discussed but fairly uncontroversial negotiations. The question of Poland was another matter indeed. Successive partitions by Russia, Austria, and Prussia in 1772, 1793, and 1795 had completely dismembered the land that had been Poland. Napoleon had reconstituted a small portion of Poland as the Grand Duchy of Warsaw. The Congress faced the dilemma of what to do with the Napoleonic creation and with Polish territory in general. Fierce debate over Poland threatened to shatter congressional harmony (see **Map F**).

Tsar Alexander I of Russia argued for a large Poland that he intended to be fully under his influence, thus extending Russian-controlled territories to the banks of the Oder. He also envisioned extending Russian dominance farther into central and eastern Europe. He based his claim on the significant contribution the Russian army had made to Napoleon's defeat. But such thinking conflicted with the Austrian minister Metternich's pursuit of equilibrium. Frederick William III of Prussia contended that if a large Poland was to be created, Prussia would expect compensation by absorbing Saxony (see **Map G**). Both Great Britain and France distrusted Russian and Prussian territorial aims.

Negotiating for the French, Talleyrand was a man who knew something about survival and taking advantage of opportunities. A bishop under the Old Regime, a revolutionary who managed to keep his head, an exile in America during the Terror, Napoleon's chief minister, and then the representative of the restored Bourbon monarchy at the Congress, he was a shrewd and experienced diplomat who managed to convince

■ In this French cartoon satirizing the Congress of Vienna, left to right, Talleyrand is watching and waiting as Castlereagh balks, Metternich leads the "dancing," the king of Saxony clutches his crown in fear, and Genoa jumps up and down on the sidelines.

the Allies to accept France, their defeated enemy, as an equal partner in negotiations. In the midst of the crisis over Poland, he persuaded Britain and Austria to sign a secret treaty with France in order to preserve an independent Polish territory. He then deliberately leaked news of the secret agreement of those powers to go to war, if necessary, to block Russian and Prussian aims. Alexander I and Frederick William III immediately backed down. Talleyrand's private opinion of the other four powers was acidic: "Too frightened to fight each other, too stupid to agree."

But under Talleyrand's manipulation, agree they did. In the final arrangement, Prussia retained the Polish territory of Posen and Austria kept the Polish province of Galicia (see **Map F**). Krakow, with its population of 95,000, was declared a free city. Finally, a kingdom of Poland, nominally independent but in fact under the tutelage of Russia, emerged from what remained of the Grand Duchy of Warsaw. It was a solution that benefited no one in particular and disregarded Polish wishes.

In addition to receiving Polish territories, Prussia gained two-fifths of the kingdom of Saxony (see **Map G**). Prussia also received territory on the left bank of the Rhine, the Duchy of Westphalia, and Swedish Pomerania. With the acquisitions, Prussia doubled its population to around 11 million people. The Junkers, the landed class of east Prussia, reversed many of the reforms of the Napoleonic period. The new territories that Prussia gained were rich in waterways and resources but geographically fragmented. The dispersal of holdings that was intended to contain Prussian power in central Europe spurred Prussia to find new ways of uniting its markets. In the endeavor, Prussia constituted a future threat to Austrian power over the German Confederation.

In Scandinavia, the members of the Congress acknowledged Russia's conquest of Finland, and in return Sweden acquired Norway from Denmark. Unlike Austria, Prussia, and Russia, Great Britain made no claim to territories at the Congress. Having achieved its aim of containing France, its

■ **Map E. German Confederation.** The league of German states created in 1815 replaced the Holy Roman Empire. The 39 states, of which 35 were monarchies and 4 were free cities, existed to ensure the independence of its member states and support in case of external attack. The member states of Austria and Prussia lay partially outside of the Confederation.

■ **Map F. Poland, 1815.** An independent kingdom in name only, Poland was under the influence of Russia. Prussia carved off Posen, and Austria maintained control of Galicia. Krakow was defined by treaty as an independent republic.

■ **Map G. Saxony.** In 1806, Saxony had sided with France against Prussia and remained allies with the French for the remainder of the wars. With Napoleon's defeat in 1815, about 40 percent of Saxony became part of Prussia.

greatest rival for dominance on the seas, Britain returned the French colonies it had seized in war. For the time being, the redrawing of the territorial map of Europe had achieved its pragmatic aim of guaranteeing the peace. It was now left to a system of alliances to preserve that peace.

The Alliance System

Only by joining forces had the European powers been able to defeat Napoleon, and a system of alliances continued to be needed even after the battles were over. Two alliance pacts dominated the post-Napoleonic era: the renewed Quadruple Alliance and the Holy Alliance.

The **Quadruple Alliance** (see **Map H**), signed by the victorious powers of Great Britain, Austria, Russia, and Prussia in November 1815, was intended to protect Europe against future French aggression and to preserve the status quo. In 1818, France, having completed its payment of war indemnities, joined the pact, which now became the **Quintuple Alliance.** The five powers promised to meet periodically over the following 20 years to discuss common problems and to ensure the peace.

The **Holy Alliance** (see **Map H**), very different in tone and intent, was the brainchild of Alexander I and was heavily influenced by his mystical and romantic view of international

politics. In the pact, the monarchs of Prussia, Austria, and Russia agreed to renounce war and to protect the Christian religion. The Holy Alliance spoke of "the bonds of a true and indissoluble brotherhood . . . to protect religion, peace, and justice." Russia was able to give some credibility to the alliance with the sheer size of its army. Career diplomats were aware of its hollowness as a treaty arrangement, but it did indicate the willingness of Europe's three eastern autocracies to intervene in the affairs of other states.

The concept of Europe acting as a whole, through a system of periodic conferences, marked the emergence of a new diplomatic era. Conflict, however, was inherent in the tension between the commitment of parliamentary governments to open consultation and the need for secrecy in diplomacy. Dynastic regimes sought to intervene in smaller states to buoy up despots, as was the case in 1822, when European powers met to consider restoring the Bourbon monarchy in Spain. The British acted as a counterbalance to interventionist tendencies, refused to cooperate, and blocked united action by the Alliance. France took military action on its own in 1823, restored King Ferdinand VII, and abolished the Spanish constitution.

Both in the Congress of Vienna and the system of alliances that succeeded it, European nations aimed to establish a balance of power that recognized legitimate rulers and preserved

Quadruple Alliance

Holy Alliance

■ **Map H. Quadruple Alliance and Holy Alliance.** The Quadruple Alliance grew out of the need of the Great Powers to create a stable Europe, and had as its initial impulse the creation of a buffer against a future French threat. Austria, Great Britain, Prussia, and Russia entered into the agreement as the basis for defining the balance of power in Europe. In the Holy Alliance, Russia, Austria, and Prussia entered an accord to treat each other according to the precepts of the Christian religion. As a counterweight to the Quadruple Alliance, the Holy Alliance served as a justification for repression against dissent.

CHRONOLOGY
THE ALLIANCE SYSTEM

May 1814	First Peace of Paris
23 September 1814– 9 June 1815	Congress of Vienna
26 September 1815	Formation of the Holy Alliance
20 November 1815	Second Peace of Paris; Formation of the Quadruple Alliance
November 1818	Quadruple Alliance expands to include France in Quintuple Alliance
1823	French restoration of Bourbon Monarchy in Spain

the peace. The upheaval of the French Revolution and the revolutionary and Napoleonic wars had made clear the interdependence of one nation on another as a guarantee of survival. By maintaining an international equilibrium, Europe's statesmen hoped—erroneously, as it turned out—that by keeping the peace abroad, domestic peace would follow.

■

THE NEW IDEOLOGIES

After 1815, the world was changing in many ways. As national boundaries were being redefined, the ways in which Europeans regarded their world were also being transformed. Steam-driven mechanical power in production and transportation steadily replaced human and animal power. In deference to what it was replacing, the new mechanical force was measured in units of horsepower. The new technology combined with political changes to challenge old values; new definitions of worth emerged from the increasingly mechanized world of work. The fixed, castelike distinctions of the old aristocratic world were under attack or in disarray. Western intellectuals struggled with the changes as they sought to make sense of the way in which Europeans lived, looked at the world, and defined their place in it.

The political and economic upheavals of the first half of the nineteenth century encouraged a new breed of thinkers to search for ways to explain the transformations of the period. During that period, Europeans witnessed one of the most intellectually fertile periods in the history of the West. The search for understanding during this era gave birth to new ideologies—liberalism, nationalism, romanticism, conservatism, and socialism—that continue to shape the ideas and institutions of the present day.

The New Politics of Preserving Order

European states had been dealing with war for more than two decades. Now they faced the challenge of peace. The Revolution and Napoleon had not only meant military engagements; they had also brought the force of revolutionary ideas to the political arena, and those ideas did not retire from the field after Waterloo. Nor did treaties restore an old order, in spite of claims to doing so. Governments throughout Europe had to find new ways to deal with the tension between state authority and individual liberty. Conservative and liberal thinkers took very different paths in the pursuit of political stability.

Conservatism.   **Conservatism** was not a rejection of political, economic, or social change. Early nineteenth-century conservatism represented a dynamic adaptation to a social system in transition. In place of individualism, conservatives stressed the corporate nature of European society; in place of reason and progress, conservatives saw organic growth and tradition. Liberty, argued British statesman Edmund Burke

(1729–1797) in *Reflections on the Revolution in France* (1790), must emerge out of the gradual development of the old order, and not its destruction. On the Continent, conservatives Louis de Bonald (1754–1840) and Joseph de Maistre (1753–1821) defended the monarchical principle of authority against the onslaught of revolutionary events.

Conservatism took a reactionary turn in the hands of the Austrian statesman Metternich. The Carlsbad decrees of 1819 are a good example of the "Metternich system" of espionage, censorship, and repression in central Europe, which sought to eliminate any constitutional or nationalist sentiments that had arisen during the Napoleonic period. The German Confederation approved decrees against free speech and civil liberties and set up mechanisms to root out "subversive" university students. Students who had taken up arms in the Wars of Liberation (1813–1815) against France had done so in hope of instituting liberal and national reforms. Metternich's system aimed at uprooting those goals. Student fraternities were closed, and police became a regular fixture in the university. Political expression in central Europe was driven underground for at least a decade. Metternich set out to crush any form of democratic government, constitutionalism, and parliamentarianism in central Europe.

Liberalism. The term *liberal* was first used in a narrow political sense to indicate the Spanish party of reform that supported the constitution modeled on the French document of 1791. But the term assumed much broader connotations in the first half of the nineteenth century as its appeal spread among the European middle classes. The two main tenets of belief that underlay **liberalism** were the freedom of the individual and the corruptibility of authority. As a political doctrine, liberalism built on Enlightenment rationalism and embraced the right to vote, civil liberties, legal equality, constitutional government, parliamentary sovereignty, and a free-market economy. Liberals firmly believed that less government was better government and that noninterference would produce a harmonious and well-ordered world. They also believed that human beings were basically good and reasonable and needed freedom in which to flourish. The sole end of government should be to promote that freedom.

No single representative thinker embodied all the tenets of liberal thought, but many shared similar ideas and beliefs. Liberal thinkers tried to make sense of the political conflicts of the revolutionary period and the economic disruptions brought on by industrialization. The Great Revolution at the end of the eighteenth century spawned a vast array of liberal thought in France. Republicans, Bonapartists, and constitutional monarchists cooperated as self-styled "liberals" who shared a desire to preserve the gains of the revolution while ensuring orderly rule. In 1807, British law attempted to eliminate the slave trade with very limited success. William Wilberforce led abolitionists in England who continued to agitate for a parliamentary law that would abolish the slave trade throughout the British Empire. Such a law was finally passed in 1833, and about

■ This cameo, made by Josiah Wedgwood for the Society for the Abolition of Slavery, shows a chained and manacled slave and bears the inscription, "Am I Not a Man and a Brother?" Wedgwood sent a batch of the cameos to Benjamin Franklin for distribution among American abolitionists.

£20 million was paid in compensation to British plantation owners in the Caribbean. Also influenced by liberal ideas were a variety of political movements in the United States, including those demanding the liberation of slaves and the extension of legal and political rights to women. Abolitionists justified their opposition to slavery on humanitarian Christian grounds and on the liberal principles of freedom and equality. American women who were active in antislavery societies extended their liberal crusade against oppression to their own legal and political status.

By the mid-nineteenth century, liberal thinking constituted a dominant strain in British politics. Jeremy Bentham (1748–1832), trained in British law, fashioned himself into a social philosopher. He founded **utilitarianism,** a fundamentally liberal doctrine that argued for "the greatest happiness of the greatest number" in such works as *Introduction to the Principles of Morals and Legislation.* Bentham believed that government could achieve positive ends through limited and "scientific" intervention. Only the pursuit of social harmony justified interference with individual liberty. He found the best testing grounds for his theories in prisons, among convicted criminals. By supporting the reform of penal codes and prison regulations in *Rationale of Punishments and Rewards* (1825), he hoped that rewards and punishments could be meted out to convicts in a measurable "geometry" of pain and pleasure. He was sure that behavior could be improved and that prisoners could be rehabilitated and returned as honest citizens to society. (See "A Closer Look: The Birth of the Prison," pp. 682–683.)

The Scottish philosopher, economist, and historian James Mill (1773–1836) met Jeremy Bentham in 1808 and dedicated the rest of his life to promulgating Bentham's utilitarian philosophy. James Mill's son John Stuart Mill (1806–1873) reacted to his early and intense education in Benthamite ideas by rejecting the tenets of utilitarianism. Forging his own brand of classical liberalism in his treatise *On Liberty* (1859), the younger Mill became the greatest liberal thinker of the age. John Stuart Mill criticized Bentham for ignoring human emotions and for the mass tyranny implicit in his ideas. Mill went beyond existing political analyses by applying economic doctrines to social conditions in *Principles of Political Economy* (1848). With his wife and collaborator Harriet Taylor (d. 1858), he espoused social reform for the poor and championed the equality of women and the necessity of birth control. By 1848, his writings on liberty and equality were questioning the sacredness of private property. In later life, John Stuart Mill came to believe that a more equitable distribution of wealth was both necessary and possible.

DOCUMENT

Mill on Enfranchisement of Women

David Ricardo (1772–1823) was a stockbroker prodigy who by the age of 20 had made his fortune. In *Principles of Political Economy and Taxation* (1817), Ricardo outlined his opposition to government intervention in foreign trade and elaborated his "iron law of wages," which contended that wages would stabilize at the subsistence level. Increased wages would cause the working classes to grow, and the resulting competition in the labor market would drive wages down to the level of subsistence. Other liberals, more concerned with social welfare than Ricardo, argued that state intervention was unavoidable but could be limited.

Romanticism and Change

Unlike liberalism and conservatism, which were fundamentally political ideologies, **romanticism** included a variety of literary and artistic movements throughout Europe that spanned the period from the late eighteenth century to the mid-nineteenth century. One could be a liberal and a romantic just as easily as one could be a conservative and a romantic.

The Romantic World View.   Above all, and in spite of variations, romantics shared similar beliefs and a common view of the world. Among the first romantics were the English poets William Wordsworth (1770–1850) and Samuel Taylor Coleridge (1772–1834), whose collaborative *Lyrical Ballads* (1798) exemplified the iconoclastic romantic idea that poetry was the result of "the spontaneous overflow of powerful feelings" rather than a formal and highly disciplined intellectual exercise. Romantics, in general, rebelled against the confinement of classical forms and refused to accept the supremacy of reason over emotions.

The English gardens designed at the end of the eighteenth century provide one of the best visual examples of the new romanticism. The formal gardens that surrounded the castles and manor houses of Europe's wealthy elite throughout the eighteenth century relied on carefully drawn geometric patterns, minutely trimmed hedges and lawns, and symmetrically arranged flowers planted in rows by size and color to achieve the effect of total mastery of nature. The gardens at the great palace of Versailles are a good example of the formal landscaping chosen by France's kings and emulated by the wealthy everywhere in Europe. The romantic or English garden was, by contrast, a rebellious profusion of color in which the landscaper rejected the carefully drawn geometric patterns then in vogue and set out instead, deliberately and somewhat paradoxically, to imitate nature. The romantic aesthetic, whether in landscape gardening or in literature, recognized the beauty of untamed nature and the inspiration produced by the release of human emotions.

Intellectuals, Artists, and Freedom.   By rooting artistic vision in spontaneity, romantics endorsed a concept of creativity based on the supremacy of human freedom. The artist was valued in a new way as a genius through whose insight and intuition great art was created. Intuition, as opposed to scientific learning, was endorsed as a valid means of knowing. Building on the work of the eighteenth-century philosopher Immanuel Kant (1724–1804), romanticism embraced subjective knowledge. Inspiration and intuition took the place of reason and science in the romantic pantheon of values.

Germaine de Staël (1766–1817), often hailed as the founder of French romanticism, was an extraordinary woman whose writings influenced French liberal political theory after 1815. Madame de Staël's mother had followed the principles of education spelled out by Jean-Jacques Rousseau in *Émile* (1762), according to which the child was allowed to follow his or her own path of intellectual development. De Staël authored histories, novels, literary criticism, and political tracts that opposed what she judged to be the tyranny of Napoleonic rule. She, like many other romantics, was greatly influenced by the writings of Rousseau, and through him she discovered that "the soul's elevation is born of self-consciousness." The recognition of the subjective meant for de Staël that women's vision was as essential as men's for the flowering of European culture.

"It is within oneself that one must look at what lies outside." Following de Staël's lead, Victor Hugo (1802–1885), one of the great French writers of the nineteenth century, identified another essential ingredient in romanticism. The turning "within oneself" so apparent in Hugo's poetry was profoundly influenced by the political events of the French Revolution and its principles of liberty and equality. His greatest novels, including *Notre-Dame de Paris* (1831) and *Les Misérables* (1862), offer bold panoramic sweeps of the social universe of Paris across the ages. Whether in words or in music or on canvas, romanticism conveyed a new way of understanding the world. The supremacy of the emotions over reason found its way into the works of the great romantic composers of the age. Liberation from the forms that dominated the classical era could be heard in the works of French composer Louis Hector Berlioz (1803–1869), who set Faust's damnation to

A Closer Look
The Birth of the Prison

There was once a time when modern prisons, what we call penitentiaries, did not exist. Prisons, like modern hospitals and schools, were one of the great achievements of the age of reform in the first half of the nineteenth century. Thanks to the efforts of humanitarians and social reformers, a new rationale for punishment emerged, one that claimed modern prisons were capable of rehabilitating criminals. Reformers argued that the controlled environment of a new prison system would be able to fashion wrongdoers into upstanding citizens through moral instruction, hard work, constant surveillance, and, in some cases, isolation from human contact.

The principles of the new penal arrangement were silence and separation—total or partial, in order to rehabilitate prisoners through supervised activities, including productive work. In French penitentiaries, prisoners were given an occupation and produced goods for the prison system itself—shoes or mattresses, for example—or for sale on the open market. The belief was that through productive labor, prisoners could be taught to be good workers and good citizens. Idle hands were the devil's workshop, so no moment of the prisoner's day was unoccupied or, in theory, unsupervised.

Some of the "new" prisons were built in the shells of ancient military garrisons, seminaries, convents, and retreat houses. Before the beginning of the nineteenth century, prisons existed but they served as waystations, holding areas for those who were about to face their "real" punishments, which could be death, mutilation, forced labor in prison ships, or banishment. After 1820, however, incarceration became a punishment in itself throughout western Europe, with the goal to deprive prisoners of liberty and freedom of movement.

A typical prisoner in the new penitentiaries was a man convicted of theft serving a sentence of five to seven years. He entered a prison world where every aspect of his life was prescribed and supervised. The experience of the prison was intended to transform the behavior of the prisoner. Prisoners for the first time were required to wear uniforms. In addition to the regimented routine of work, meals, and sleep, the prisoner now also received moral and religious instruction behind bars.

Although populations in the old prisons of the eighteenth century were mixed with women and men, adults and children confined in the same spaces, by contrast, in the nineteenth century convicted women and children were systematically separated from male prisoners and subject to separate rules of confinement. Religious orders and philanthropic groups supervised women and children in prisons and continued to watch them in their lives after prison. Reformers now spoke of the punishment being made to fit the criminal—not the crime.

The most controversial aspect of the new punishment was solitary confinement. Women were usually exempted from the initial isolation experiments, deemed as too "social" or too weak to support total separation. Young boys on the other hand were targeted for the special experimental punishment of solitary isolation, something French observers such as historian and political philosopher Alexis de Tocqueville greatly admired on his travels in the United States. In one particularly brutal period of experimentation, beginning in 1838 French prison officials confined boys between the ages of six and sixteen to their cells day and night where they were expected to follow a strict regime of silence, discipline, religious instruction, and constant occupation. Most of the children were court custody cases committed by their fathers because of unruly behavior. The results were dire. There was no accurate way to measure recidivism, and, worse, the children's mortality rates increased sharply. Children in solitary confinement may have been protected from the "moral depravity" of other inmates, but they became sick and died more frequently than their counterparts in free society and than other kinds of prisoners. What began as a humanitarian advance was soon denounced as a form of torture for juvenile offenders.

Why did penitentiaries come into being in the first half of the nineteenth century? The new punishment was considered attractive because, in an age confronted with industrial and political transformations and revolutionary upheavals, it seemed to be a way of controlling criminal disruptions and social unrest. The middle classes, whether in London or Paris, grew increasingly fearful about potential threats to their property and well-being. Industrial workers crowded into substandard urban housing could face long periods of unemployment, when it was feared that desperate men and women would commit crimes to feed themselves and their families. The fear of the poor as dangerous influenced many of the prison reforms of the early nineteenth century. Great Britain and France created growing bureaucracies of penal, policing, and judicial institutions to guarantee the safety of honest citizens. At the same time that new prisons opened their doors, policemen started walking their neighborhood beats in European capitals.

Almost from the beginning prisons were deemed a failure. Specialists concluded that prisons did not correct criminals but instead served as schools for crime. Statistics—a new scientific practice in itself—proved them right. Recidivism rates rose dramatically, as penal authorities devised new ways—eventually fingerprinting and photography—to follow the activities

■ Vincent Van Gogh, *The Prison Courtyard (1890).* The painting is copied after a wood engraving by Gustave Doré representing Newgate—the Exercise Yard in *London, a Pilgrimage* (1872).

of released prisoners. It is very likely that what was increasing in this era was not criminality but the ability of the state to track it.

The science of the new punishment evolved directly in relation to political and social changes in the first half of the nineteenth century. The three major spurts of prison reform in France, for example, coincided with the revolutionary upheavals of 1789, 1830, and 1848. Social reformers and legislators turned to the prison system as a crucial mechanism in the regulation of civil society. The new prisons were part of the network of institutions created to maintain an orderly working class in the new democratic age.

■ *Liberty Leading the People* (1831) by Eugène Dalacroix captures the spirit of the French romantics, who looked upon revolutionary action as a way to achieve union with the spirit of history.

music; Polish virtuoso Frédéric Chopin (1810–1849), who created lyric compositions for the piano; and Hungarian concert pianist Franz Liszt (1811–1886), who composed symphonic poems and Hungarian rhapsodies.

Artists as different as J. M. W. Turner (1775–1851), the English landscape painter, and Eugène Delacroix (1798–1863), the leader of the French romantic school in painting (see photo above), shared a commitment to their iconoclastic art. Turner's intense and increasingly abstract vision of an often turbulent natural world and Delacroix's epic historical and political masterpieces shared a rebellious experimentation with color and a rejection of classical conventions and forms. Characteristic of a particular strain within romanticism was the political message of Delacroix's art. In the magnificent painting *Liberty Leading the People* (1831), for example, Delacroix immortalized the revolutionary events that swept Paris in 1830 in his moving portrayal of valiant revolutionaries of different social classes led into battle by a female Liberty.

In the postrevolutionary years between 1815 and 1850, romanticism claimed to be no more than an aesthetic stance in art, letters, and music, a posture that had no particular political intent. Yet its validation of the individual as opposed to the caste or the estate was the most revolutionary of doctrines, just as its justification of subjective knowledge threatened to erode the authority of classical learning. Artists did not make revolutions, but they supported them. Some stood by on the sidelines; others mounted the barricades; but all romantics, no matter how political or apolitical, helped shape a new way of looking at the world and helped define a new political consciousness.

Reshaping State and Society

As another legacy of the French Revolution, the concept of the *nation* as a source of collective identity and political allegiance became a political force after 1815. Just as nationalism put the

YOUNG ITALY (1832)

Giuseppe Mazzini, an Italian patriot and revolutionary, was the principal theorist of national revolution in Europe in the first half of the nineteenth century. He claimed that his strong commitment to equality and democratic principles stemmed from his readings on the French Revolution of 1789 and his study of the Latin classics. As a young man, he resolved to dress always in black as a sign of mourning for his country, disunited and under foreign oppressors. In 1832 he founded the secret society Young Italy. The goal of the revolutionary group was the unification of Italy under a republican form of government through direct popular action.

Focus Questions

How is Mazzini's message about Italian nationalism reflective of the romantic world view? What is the significance of Mazzini's stress on the role of youth?

We have beheld Italy—Italy, the purpose, the soul, the consolation of our thoughts, the country chosen of God and oppressed by men, twice queen of the world and twice fallen through the infamy of foreigners and the guilt of her citizens, yet lovely still though she be dust, unmatched by any other nation whatever fortune has decreed; and Genius returns to seek in this dust the word of eternal life, and the spark that creates the future. . . .

Young Italy: but we chose this term because the one term seems to marshal before the youth of Italy the magnitude of its duties and the solemnity of the mission that circumstances have entrusted to it, so that it will be ready when the hour has struck to arise from its slumber to a new life of action and regeneration. And we chose it because we wanted to show ourselves, writing it, as what we are, to do battle with raised visors, to bear our faith before us, as the knights of medieval times bore their faith on their shields. For while we pity men who do not know the truth, we despise men who, though they know the truth, do not dare to speak it.

---

needs of the people at the heart of its political doctrine, so did socialism focus on the needs of society and especially of the poor.

Nationalism.   In its most basic sense, nationalism between 1815 and 1850 was the political doctrine that glorified the people united against the absolutism of kings and the tyranny of foreign oppressors. The success of the French Revolution and the spread of Napoleonic reforms boosted nationalist doctrines. In Germany, Johann Gottfried von Herder (1744–1803) rooted national identity in German folk culture. The *Fairy Tales* (1812–1814) of the brothers Jacob Ludwig Grimm (1785–1863) and Wilhelm Carl Grimm (1786–1859) had a similar national purpose. The brothers painstakingly captured in print the German oral tradition of peasant folklore. The philosophers Johann Fichte (1762–1814) and Georg Wilhelm Friedrich Hegel (1770–1831) emphasized the importance of the state.

Nationalism gave birth to a search for new symbols, just as the tricolor flag replaced the fleur-de-lis and the image of Marianne replaced the monarch as a result of the Great Revolution in France. There was a new concern with history as nationalists sought to revive a common cultural past.

The nationalist yearning for liberation sometimes meshed with the liberal political program of overthrowing tyrannical rule. Giuseppe Mazzini (1805–1872) represented the new breed of liberal nationalist. A less-than-liberal nationalist was political economist Georg Friedrich List (1789–1846), who formulated a statement of economic nationalism to counter the liberal doctrines of David Ricardo. Arguing that free trade worked only for the wealthy and powerful, List advocated a program of protective tariffs for developing German industries. He perceived British free trade as merely economic imperialism in disguise. List was one of the few nationalists who did not wholeheartedly embrace liberal economic doctrines. Beyond ideology and political practices, nationalism began to capture the imagination of groups who resented foreign domination. Expanding state bureaucracies did little to tame the centrifugal forces of nationalist feeling and probably exacerbated a desire for independence in eastern and central Europe, especially in the Habsburg-ruled lands.

Nationalists valued the authenticity of the vernacular and folklore over the language and customs imposed by a foreign ruler. Herder and the brothers Grimm were German examples of the romantic appreciation of the roots of German culture. While French romantics emphasized the glories of their revolutionary heritage, German romantics stressed the importance of history as the source of one's identity. By searching for the self in a historic past, and especially in the Middle Ages, they glorified their collective cultural identity and national origins.

Socialism.   Socialists rejected the world as it was. Socialism, like other ideologies of the first half of the nineteenth century, grew out of changes in the structure of daily life and the

THE COMMUNIST MANIFESTO

The Communist Manifesto is one of the most important documents in world history. Translated into many languages in countless editions, it inspired worker organizations throughout Europe in the second half of the nineteenth century and fired the imagination of Communist leaders in Asia, Latin America, Africa, and Europe well into the twentieth century.

The pamphlet, which in its entirety consists of no more than 12,000 words, was written at the beginning of 1848 by Karl Marx, founder of modern communism, and his collaborator and friend, Friedrich Engels. Their intention was to urge exploited workers throughout Europe to prepare themselves for the coming revolution by uniting across national boundaries. The Communist Manifesto is a concise statement of the basic tenets of Marxism. Although mistaken in most of its predictions about the future development of capitalism, it accurately distilled some of the most salient inequities of industrial economies whose remedies, Marx and Engels asserted, could only be found through the revolutionary overthrow of the capitalist system.

Focus Questions

According to Marx and Engels, how do markets and capitalism promote class struggle? What is the basis of their opposition to private property and their justification of a Communist revolution?

Bourgeois and Proletarians

The history of all hitherto existing society is the history of class struggles.

Freeman and slave, patrician and plebeian, lord and serf, guild-master and journeyman, in a word, oppressor and oppressed, stood in constant opposition to one another, carried on an uninterrupted, now hidden, now open fight, a fight that each time ended, either in a revolutionary reconstitution of society at large, or in the common ruin of the contending classes. . . .

The modern bourgeois society that has sprouted from the ruins of feudal society has not done away with class antagonisms. It has but established new classes, new conditions of oppression, new forms of struggle in place of the old ones.

Our epoch, the epoch of the bourgeoisie, possesses, however, this distinctive feature: it has simplified the class antagonisms. Society as a whole is more and more splitting up into two great hostile camps, into two great classes directly facing each other: Bourgeoisie and Proletariat. . . .

The bourgeoisie cannot exist without constantly revolutionizing the instruments of production, and thereby the relations of production, and with them the whole relations of society. Conservation of the old modes of production in unaltered form, was, on the contrary, the first condition of existence for all earlier industrial classes. Constant revolutionizing of production, uninterrupted disturbance of all

structure of power. There were as many stripes of socialists as there were liberals, nationalists, and conservatives. Socialists as a group shared a concern with "alienation," though they may not all have used the term.

Henri de Saint-Simon (1760–1825) rejected liberal individualism in favor of social organization and, for this reason, has been called the father of French socialism. To Saint-Simon, the accomplishments and potential of industrial development represented the highest stage in history. In a perfect and just society, productive work would be the basis of all prestige and power. The elite of society would be organized according to the hierarchy of its productive members, with industrial leaders at the top. Work was a social duty. The new industrial society that Saint-Simon foresaw would be both efficient and ethical, based on a religion similar to Christianity.

Like Saint-Simon, the French social theorist Pierre-Joseph Proudhon (1809–1865) recognized the social value of work. But unlike Saint-Simon, Proudhon refused to accept the dominance of industrial society. A self-educated typesetter of

peasant origin, Proudhon gained national prominence with his ideas about a just society, free credit, and equitable exchange. In his famous pamphlet *What Is Property?* (1840), Proudhon answered, "Property is theft." That statement was not, however, an argument for the abolition of private ownership. Proudhon reasoned that industrialization had destroyed workers' rights, which included the right to the profits of their own labor. In attacking "property" in the form of profits amassed from the labor of others, Proudhon was arguing for a socialist concept of limited possession—people had the right to own only what they had earned from their own labor. Proudhon, who did not himself participate in political agitation, held a profoundly anarchistic view of society, hated government, and favored instead small self-ruling communities of producers. Proudhon's ideal world would be one of comfort but not great wealth.

At least one socialist believed in luxury. Charles Fourier (1772–1837), an unsuccessful traveling salesman, devoted himself to the study and improvement of society and formulated social conditions, everlasting uncertainty and agitation distinguish the bourgeois epoch from all earlier ones. All fixed, fast-frozen relations, with their train of ancient and venerable prejudices and opinions are swept away, all new-formed ones become antiquated before they can ossify. All that is solid melts into air, all that is holy is profaned, and man is at last compelled to face with sober senses, his real conditions of life, and his relations with his kind.

The need of a constantly expanding market for its products chases the bourgeoisie over the whole surface of the globe. It must nestle everywhere, settle everywhere, establish connections everywhere. . . .

The proletariat goes through various stages of development. With its birth begins its struggle with the bourgeoisie. At first the contest is carried on by individual labourers, then by the work-people of a factory, then by the operatives of one trade, in one locality, against the individual bourgeois who directly exploits them. They direct their attacks not against the bourgeois conditions of production, but against the instruments of production themselves; they destroy imported wares that compete with their labour, they smash to pieces machinery, they set factories ablaze, they seek to restore by force the vanished status of the workman of the Middle Ages.

Proletarians and Communists

In what relation do the Communists stand to the proletarians as a whole?

The Communists do not form a separate part opposed to other working-class parties. They have no interests separate and apart from those of the proletariat as a whole. . . .

You are horrified at our [Communists'] intending to do away with private property. But in your existing society, private property is already done away with for nine-tenths of the population; its existence for the few is solely due to its non-existence in the hands of those nine-tenths. You reproach us, therefore, with intending to do away with a form of property the necessary condition for whose existence is the non-existence of any property for the immense majority of society. . . .

In short, the Communists everywhere support every revolutionary movement against the existing social and political order of things.

In all these movements they bring to the front, as the leading question in each, the property question, no matter what its degree of development at the time.

Finally, they labour everywhere for the union and agreement of the democratic parties of all countries.

The Communists disdain to conceal their views and aims. They openly declare that their ends can be attained only by the forcible overthrow of all existing social conditions. Let the ruling classes tremble at a Communistic revolution. The proletarians have nothing to lose but their chains. They have a world to win.

WORKING MEN OF ALL COUNTRIES, UNITE!

---

*By bourgeoisie is meant the class of modern Capitalists, owners of the means of social production and employers of wage labour. By proletariat, the class of modern wage-labourers who, having no means of production of their own, are reduced to selling their labour power in order to live. [*Note by Engels to the English edition of 1888.*]

---

one of the most trenchant criticisms of industrial capitalism. In numerous writings between 1808 and his death, the eccentric, solitary man put forth his vision of a utopian world organized into units called phalanxes that took into account the social, sexual, and economic needs of their members. With a proper mix of duties, everyone in the phalanx would work only a few hours a day. In Fourier's scheme, work was not naturally abhorrent, but care had to be taken to match temperaments with tasks. Women and men fulfilled themselves and found pleasure and gratification through work. People would be paid according to their contributions in work, capital, and talent. In his vision of a better world, Fourier's phalanxes were always rural and were organized communally, though neither poverty nor property would be eliminated. Education would help alleviate discord, and rich and poor would learn to live together in perfect harmony.

Charles Fourier's work, along with that of Saint-Simon and Proudhon, became part of the tradition of utopian thinking that can be traced back to Thomas More in the sixteenth century. Because he believed in the ability of individuals to shape themselves and their world, Fourier intended his critique of society to be a blueprint for living. Fourier's followers set up communities in his lifetime—40 phalanxes were established in the United States alone—but because of financial problems and petty squabbling, all of them failed.

Women, who were active in demanding their own emancipation, were often joined by men who espoused utopian socialist and liberal views. The issue of increased civil liberties for women, tied as it often was to talk of freeing the slaves, was both a moral and political question for social reformers and utopian thinkers, including Fourier, who put the issue of women's freedom at the center of their plans to redesign society. Saint-Simonians argued for woman's social elevation and searched for a female messiah. Other social reformers joined with conservative thinkers in arguing that women must be kept in their place and that their place was in the home. Proudhon, for example, saw women's only choices as working at home as housewives or working in the streets as prostitutes.

Socialists, along with other ideologues in the decades before the middle of the nineteenth century, were aware of how rapidly their world was changing. Many believed that a revolution that would eliminate poverty and the sufferings of the working class was at hand. Followers of Saint-Simon, Fourier, and Proudhon all hoped that their proposals and ideas would change the world and prevent violent upheaval. Not all social critics were so sanguine.

In January 1848, two young men, one a philosopher living in exile and the other a businessman working for his father, began a collaboration that would last a lifetime with the publication of a short tract entitled *The Communist Manifesto.* Karl Marx (1818–1883) and Friedrich Engels (1820–1895) described the dire situation of the European working classes throughout the 1840s. The growing poverty and alienation of the propertyless workers, the authors promised, would bring to industrialized Europe a class war against the capitalists, the owners of the means of production. Exploited workers were to prepare themselves for the moment of revolution by joining with each other across national boundaries: "Workers of the world unite. You have nothing to lose but your chains." In light of subsequent events, the *Manifesto* appears to be a work of great predictive value. But neither Marx nor Engels realized that the hour of revolution was at hand.

Intellectuals and reformers hoped to reshape the world in which they lived with the force of their ideas. Yet the new ideologies were themselves the consequence of the changing role of government and the changing practices of daily life. The technology of industrial production influenced people's values and required a new way of looking at the world. Liberals, nationalists, romantics, conservatives, and socialists addressed the challenges of a changing economy in a political universe buffeted by democratic ideas. The new ideologies did not provide easy answers, but they did serve to incite their followers to take up arms in protests and revolutions throughout Europe.

PROTEST AND REVOLUTION

For European societies that had remained stable, if not stagnant, for centuries, the changes in the first half of the nineteenth century were undoubtedly startling and disruptive. New factories created the arena for exploitation and misery. More people than ever before lived in cities, and national populations faced the prospect of becoming urban. Urban congestion brought crime and disease; patterns of consumption demonstrated beyond dispute that people were not created equal. A new European society that challenged existing political ideas and demanded new political formulations was in the process of emerging.

Causes of Social Instability

The fabric of stability began unraveling throughout Europe in the 1820s. The forces of order reacted to protest with repression everywhere in Europe. Yet armed force proved inadequate to contain the demands for political participation and the increased political awareness of whole segments of the population. Workers, the middle class, and women's political organizations now demanded, through the vote, the right to govern themselves.

Urban Miseries. In 1800, two of every 100 Europeans lived in a city. By 1850, the number of urban dwellers per hundred had jumped to five and was rising rapidly. In England, the shift was more concentrated than the general European pattern. With one of every two people living in a city, England had become an urban society by mid-century. London was the fastest-growing city in Europe, followed at some distance by Paris and Berlin. The numbers of smaller urban centers were also multiplying.

Massive internal migrations caused most urban growth. People from the same rural areas often lived together in the same urban neighborhoods, and even in the same boarding-houses. Irish emigrants crowded together in the "Little Dublin" section of London. Similarly, districts in other cities were set off by regional accents and native provincial dress. Workers from the same hometowns gravitated to their favorite cafes. The social networks helped make the transition from rural to urban life bearable for the tens of thousands of people who poured into Europe's cities in search of jobs and opportunity. Until mid-century, many migrants returned to their rural homes for the winter when work, especially in the building trades, was scarce in the city. Young migrant women who came to the city to work as servants sent money home to support rural relatives, or worked to save a nest egg—or dowry—with the plan of returning to the village permanently. Before 1850, 20 percent of the workers in London were domestics, and most of them were women.

Despite the support networks that migrants constructed for themselves, the city was not always a hospitable place. Workers were poorly paid, and women workers were more poorly paid than men. When working women were cut free of the support of home and family, uncounted numbers were forced into part-time prostitution to supplement meager incomes. It is conservatively estimated that in 1850 there were 34,000 prostitutes in Paris and 50,000 in London. The phenomenon of prostitution indicated changing mores about sexuality in the first half of the nineteenth century. The "angel" of middle-class households and the "whore" of the streets were subjects of fascination in fiction and nonfiction. Increased prostitution created a veritable epidemic of venereal diseases, especially syphilis, for which there was no known cure until the twentieth century.

Urban crime also grew astronomically, with thefts accounting for the greatest number of crimes. Social reformers identified poverty and urban crowding as causes of the increase in criminal behavior. In 1829, both Paris and London began to create modern urban police forces to deal with the challenges to law and order. Crime assumed the character of disease in the minds of middle-class reformers. Statisticians and social scientists, themselves a new urban phenomenon, produced massive theses on social hygiene, lower-class immorality, and the unworthiness of the poor. The pathology of the city was widely discussed. Always at the center of the issue was the growing problem of what to do with the poor.

The "Social Question."

State-sponsored work relief expanded after 1830 for the deserving poor: the old, the sick, and children. Able-bodied workers who were idle were regarded as undeserving and dangerous, regardless of the causes of their unemployment. Performance of work became an indicator of moral worth as urban and rural workers succumbed to downturns in the economic cycle. Those unable to work sought relief from the state as a last resort. What has been called a "revolution in government" took place in the 1830s and 1840s as legislative bodies increased regulation of everything from factories and mines to prisons and schools.

Poverty was not just an urban problem, although it was both more conspicuous and more feared in urban areas. Politicians, social reformers, religious thinkers, and revolutionaries all had different solutions that followed one of two general orientations. There were those who argued, as in the case of the Irish famine, that the government must do nothing to intervene because the problem would correct itself, as Thomas Malthus had predicted 40 years earlier. Malthus had argued that the "positive" means of famine and death would keep population from outgrowing available resources and food supplies. The Irish population, one of the poorest in Europe, had indeed doubled between 1781 and 1841, and for Malthusians the Irish famine was the fulfillment of their vision that famine was the only way to correct overpopulation.

■ This 1834 engraving from *The Oracle of Health* shows the brutal treatment of children working in an English textile factory. The meager wages of children were often necessary for the survival of their families.

Some insisted that poverty was a social necessity; by interfering with it, governments could only make matters worse.

Others contended that poverty was society's problem, and perhaps society's creation, and not a law of nature. Thus it was the social responsibility of the state to take care of its members. The question of how to treat poverty—or the "social question," as it came to be known among contemporaries—underlay many of the protests and reforms of the two decades before 1850 and fueled the revolutionary movements of 1848. Parliamentary legislation attempted to improve the situation of the poor, especially the working class, during the 1830s and 1840s. In 1833, British reformers turned their attention to the question of child labor. Against the opposition of those who argued for a free market for labor, Parliament passed the Factory Act of 1833, which prohibited the employment of children under nine years of age and restricted the workweek of children aged nine to thirteen to 48 hours. No child in this age group could work more than nine hours a day. Teenagers between 13 and 18 years could work no more than 69 hours a week. By modern standards, the "reformed" workloads present a shocking picture of the heavy reliance on child labor. The British Parliament commissioned investigations, compiled in the "Blue Books," that reported the abusive treatment of men, women, and children in factories. Similar studies existed for French and Belgian industry.

British legislation marked an initial step in state intervention in the workplace. Additional legislation over the next three decades further restricted children's and women's labor in factories and concerned itself with improving conditions in the workplace. Fundamentally, the "social question" was the question of what the state's role and responsibility were in caring for its citizens.

The Revolutions of 1830

Few Europeans alive in 1830 remembered the age of revolution that spanned the period from 1789 to 1799. Yet the legends were kept alive from one generation to the next. Secret political organizations perpetuated Jacobin republicanism. Mutual aid societies and artisans' associations preserved the rituals of democratic culture. A new generation of radicals seemed to be budding in the student riots in Germany and in the revolutionary waves that swept across southern and central Europe in the early 1820s. In August of 1819, a crowd of 80,000 people gathered outside Manchester, England, in St. Peter's Field to hear speeches for parliamentary reform and universal male suffrage. The cavalry swept down on them in a bloody slaughter that came to be known as the **"Peterloo" Massacre,** a bitter reference to the Waterloo victory four years before.

Poor harvests in 1829 followed by a harsh winter left people cold, hungry, and bitter. Misery fueled social protest, and political issues of participation and representation commanded new attention. The convergence of social unrest with long-standing political demands touched off apparently simultaneous revolutions all over Europe. Governmental failure to respond to local grievances sparked the revolutions of

■ "Manchester Heroes," a savage satire of the Peterloo Massacre of 1819. The soldiers are urged on by a voice from the skies telling them to cut down the unarmed crowd members. The soldier with the most kills is promised honor and recognition in song.

1830. Highly diverse groups of workers, students, lawyers, professionals, and peasants rose up spontaneously to demand a voice in the affairs of government.

The French Revolution of 1830.   In France, the late 1820s were a period of increasing political friction. Charles X (1824–1830), the former comte d'Artois, had never resigned himself to the constitutional monarchy accepted by his brother and predecessor, Louis XVIII. When Charles assumed the throne in 1824, he dedicated himself to a true restoration of kingship as it had existed before the Revolution. To this end, he realigned the monarchy with the Catholic Church and undertook several unpopular measures, including approval of the death penalty for those found guilty of sacrilege. The king's bourgeois critics, heavily influenced by liberal ideas about political economy and constitutional rights, sought increased political power through their activities in secret organizations and in public elections. The king responded to his critics by relying on his ultraroyalist supporters to run the government. In May 1830, the king dissolved the Chamber of Deputies and ordered new elections. The elections returned a liberal majority unfavorable to the king. Charles X retaliated with what proved to be his last political act, the Four Ordinances, in which he censored the press, changed the electoral law to favor his own candidates, dissolved the newly elected Chamber, and ordered new elections.

Opposition to Charles X might have remained at the level of political wrangling and journalistic protest, if it had not been for the problems plaguing the people of Paris. A severe winter in France had driven up food prices by 75 percent.

Most urban dwellers were barely subsisting. The king had erred in hoping that France's recent conquest of Algeria in North Africa would keep the populace quiet. He underestimated the extent of hardship and the political volatility of the population. Throughout the spring of 1830, prices continued to rise and Charles continued to blunder. In a spontaneous uprising in the last days of July 1830, workers took to the streets of Paris. The revolution they initiated spread rapidly to towns and the countryside as people throughout France protested the cost of living, hoarding by grain merchants, tax collection, and wage cuts. In "three glorious days," the restored Bourbon regime was pulled down and Charles X fled to England.

The people fighting in the streets demanded a republic, but they lacked organization and political experience. Liberal bourgeois politicians quickly filled the power vacuum. They presented Charles's cousin Louis-Philippe, formerly the duc d'Orléans, as the savior of France and the new constitutional monarch. The July Monarchy, born of a revolution, put an end to the Bourbon Restoration. Louis-Philippe became "king of the French." The charter that he brought with him was, like its predecessor, based on restricted suffrage, with property ownership a requisite for voting. The voting age was lowered from 30 to 25, and the tax requirement was also lowered. The electorate nearly doubled, from 90,000 to 170,000, but nevertheless voting remained restricted to a small fraction of the population.

Unrest in Europe.   Popular disturbances did not always result in revolution. In Britain, rural and town riots erupted over grain prices and distribution, but no revolution followed. German workers broke their machines to protest low wages and loss of control of the workplace, but no prince was displaced. In Switzerland, reformers found strength in the French revolutionary example. Ten Swiss cantons granted liberal constitutions and established universal manhood suffrage, freedom of expression, and legal equality.

In southern Europe, Greece had languished as a subjugated country for centuries. Turkish overlords ruled Greece as part of the Ottoman Empire. The longing for independence smoldered in Greece throughout the 1820s as public pressure to support the Greeks mounted in Europe. Greek insurrections were answered by Turkish retaliations throughout the Ottoman Empire. In 1822, a Turkish fleet captured the island of Chios in the Aegean Sea off the west coast of Turkey and massacred or enslaved the population. The atrocities committed by the Turks against Greeks in Constantinople provoked international reaction in the form of a Philhellenic (literally, "lover of Greece") movement supported by two of Britain's great romantic poets, Lord Byron (1788–1824) and Percy Bysshe Shelley (1792–1822). Byron sailed to the besieged Greek city of Missolonghi in 1824 to help coordinate the military effort, and there he contracted malaria and died. The sultan of Turkey had been able to call upon his vassal, the pasha of Egypt, to subdue Greece. In response, Great Britain, France, and Russia signed the Treaty of London in 1827, pledging intervention on behalf of Greece. In a joint effort, the three powers defeated the Egyptian fleet. Russia declared war on Turkey the following year, seeking territorial concessions from the Ottoman Empire. Following the Russian victory, Great Britain and France joined Russia in declaring Greek independence.

The concerted action of the three powers in favor of Greek independence was neither an endorsement of liberal ideals nor a support of Greek nationalism. The British, French, and Russians were reasserting their commitment made at the Congress of Vienna to territorial stability. Yet beneath the veneer of their commitment, the Russians intervened, hoping for territorial gains in the Ottoman Empire. The British favored Ottoman stability while distrusting Russian ambitions in the area. The Turks had been unable to maintain stability on their own. Finally, the three powers abandoned their policy of propping up the Ottoman Empire and supported instead the movement for Greek independence. But they did so on their own terms by creating a monarchy in Greece and placing a German-born prince on the new throne.

Belgian Independence. The overthrow of the Bourbon monarch in France served as a model for revolution in other parts of Europe. Following the French lead, in the midst of the Greek crisis the Belgian provinces revolted against the Netherlands. The Belgians' desire for their own nation struck at the heart of the Vienna settlement. Provoked by a food crisis similar to that in France, Belgian revolutionaries took to the streets in August 1830. As a symbol of their solidarity with the successful French Revolution, they flew the tricolor in defiance of their Dutch rulers. Belgians protested the deterioration of their economic situation and made demands for their own Catholic religion, their own language, and constitutional rights. Bitter fighting on the barricades in Brussels ensued, and the movement for freedom and independence spread to the countryside.

The Great Powers disagreed on what to do. Russia, Austria, and Prussia were all eager to see the revolution crushed. France, having just established the new regime of the July Monarchy, and Great Britain, fearing the involvement of the central and eastern European powers in an area where Britain had traditionally had interests, were reluctant to intervene. A provisional government in Belgium set about the task of writing a constitution. All five great powers recognized Belgian independence, with the proviso that Belgium was to maintain the status of a neutral state.

Russia, Prussia, and Austria were convinced to accept Belgian independence because they were having their own problems in eastern and southern Europe. Revolution erupted to the east in Warsaw, Poland. Driven by a desire for national independence, Polish army cadets and university students revolted in November 1830, demanding a constitution. Landed aristocrats and gentry helped establish a provisional government but soon split over how radical reforms should be. Polish peasants refused to support either landowning group. Within the year, Russia brought in 180,000 troops to crush the revolution and reassert its rule over Poland. All pretext of constitutional rule ended. Thousands of Poles were executed; others fled to exile in western Europe, including the 5000 who settled in France. Inspired by the poetry of Adam Mickiewicz (1798–1855) and the music of Frédéric Chopin, many of them dedicated themselves to the cause of Polish nationalism and to resurrecting an independent Polish kingdom. The Poles remained a captive people of the Habsburg, Hohenzollern, and Romanov empires until 1918–1919.

DOCUMENT

The Books of the Polish Nation

In February 1831, the Italian states of Modena and Parma rose up to throw off Austrian domination of northern Italy. The revolutionaries were ineffective against Austrian troops. Revolution in the Papal States resulted in French occupation that lasted until 1838 without serious reforms. Nationalist and republican yearnings were driven underground, kept alive there in the Young Italy movement under the leadership of Giuseppe Mazzini.

Although the revolutions of 1830 are called "the forgotten revolutions" of the nineteenth century, they are important for several reasons. First, they made clear to European states how closely tied together were their fates. The events of 1830 were a test of the Great Powers' commitment to stability and a balance of power in Europe. True to the principles of the Vienna settlements of 1815, European leaders preserved the status quo. Revolutions in Poland and Italy were contained by Russia and Austria without interference from the other powers. Where adaptation was necessary, as in Greece and Belgium, the Great Powers were able to compromise on settlements, though the solutions ran counter to previous policies. Heads of state were willing to use the forces of repression to stamp out protest.

Although each revolution followed its own pattern of development, all shared origins in domestic crises unsuccessfully addressed by those in power.

The international significance of the revolutions reveals a second important aspect of the events of 1830: the vulnerability of international politics to domestic instability. No state could practice diplomacy in a vacuum. Grain prices and demands for democratic participation had direct impact on the balance of power of European states. The five Great Powers broke down into two ideological camps. On the one hand were the liberal constitutional states of Great Britain and France, on the other stood the autocratic monarchies of Russia, Austria, and Prussia. Yet ideological differences were always less important than the shared desire for internal stability as a prerequisite for international peace.

Finally, the 1830 revolutions exposed a growing awareness of politics at all levels of European society. If policies in 1830 revealed a shared consciousness of events and shared values among ruling elites, the revolutions disclosed a growing awareness among the lower classes of the importance of politics in their daily lives. The cry for "liberty, equality, and fraternity" transcended national borders and the French language. The demands for constitutions, national identity, and civic equality resounded from the Atlantic to the Urals. In a dangerous combination of circumstances, workers and the lower classes throughout Europe were politicized, yet they continued to be excluded from political power.

Reform in Great Britain

The right to vote had been an issue of contention in the revolutions of 1830 in western Europe. Only the Swiss cantons enforced the principle of "one man, one vote." The July Revolution in France had doubled the electorate, but still only a tiny minority of the population (less than 1 percent) enjoyed the vote. Universal male suffrage had been mandated in 1793 during the Great Revolution but not implemented. The exclusion of the mass of the population from participation in electoral politics was no oversight. Those in power believed that the wealthiest property owners were best qualified to govern, in part because they had the greatest stake in politics and society. One also needed to own property to hold office. Because those who served in parliaments received no salary, only the wealthy had the resources and the leisure to represent the electorate. When confronted by his critics, François Guizot (1787–1874), French prime minister and chief spokesman for the July Monarchy, offered this glib advice to an aspiring electorate: "Get rich!"

The Rule of the Landed. Landowners also ruled Britain. There the dominance of a wealthy elite was strengthened by the geographic redistribution of population resulting from industrialization. Migration to cities had depleted the population of rural areas. Yet the electoral system did not adjust to the changes: large towns had no parliamentary representation, while dwindling county electorates maintained their parliamentary strength. Areas that continued to enjoy representation greater than that justified by their population were dubbed "rotten" or "pocket" boroughs to indicate a corrupt and antiquated electoral system. In general, urban areas were grossly underrepresented and the wealthy few controlled county seats.

Liberal reformers attempted to rectify the electoral inequalities by reassigning parliamentary seats on the basis of density of population, but vested interests balked at attempted reforms and members of Parliament wrangled bitterly. Popular agitation by the lower classes provoked the fear of civil war, which helped break the parliamentary deadlock. The **Great Reform Bill of 1832** proposed a compromise. Although the vast majority of the population still did not have the vote, the new legislation strengthened the industrial and commercial elite in the towns, enfranchised most of the middle class,

'Gentlemen,' says Nicholas I, the bear, to the Polish revolutionaries of 1830, 'I know that you wish to address me; but to spare you from delivering a pack of lies, I desire that you hold your tongues.' The Polish rebellion of 1830–31 was brutally suppressed by the Russians. However, this brutality reinforced Polish national sentiment (the Poles rebelled again in 1863) and engaged the sympathy of the West for the Poles—as this English cartoon shows. (2)

■ This English cartoon of 1832 is titled "The Clemency of the Russian Monster." It shows Nicholas I in the guise of a bear with menacing teeth and claws addressing the Poles after crushing their rebellion against Russian rule.

MAP DISCOVERY

★ Revolutions of 1830s

0 — 800 Miles
0 — 800 Kilometers

Unrest of the 1820s and 1830s: Centers of Revolutionary Action

What geographic and political features were common to the centers of popular unrest and revolutionary action in the 1820s and 1830s? How did the French Revolution of 1830 serve as a model for revolutionary action in the Belgian provinces, Poland, and the northern Italian states? How did political actions in Great Britain differ from those of the Continent in this period?

Men's Association, an organization of craft workers, drew up a document known as the People's Charter. The single most important demand of the charter was that all men must have the vote. In addition, Chartists petitioned for a secret ballot, salaries for parliamentary service, elimination of the requirement that a person must own property in order to run for office, equal electoral districts, and annual elections. The proposal favored direct democracy, guaranteed by frequent elections that would ensure maximum accountability of officials to their constituents.

Chartist appeal was greatest in periods of economic hardship. A violent mood swept through the movement in 1839. The Irish Chartist leader Feargus O'Connor (1794–1855) and the Irish journalist and orator James Bronterre O'Brien (1805–1864) urged an unskilled and poorly organized working class to protest inequities through strikes that on occasion became violent. O'Brien thrilled his working-class listeners by haranguing "the big-bellied, little-brained, numbskull aristocracy." **Chartism** blossomed as a communal phenomenon in working-class towns and appeared to involve all members of the family: "Every kitchen is now a political meeting house; the little children are members of the unions and the good mother is the political teacher," one

opened the way to social reforms, and encouraged the formation of political parties.

Years of bad harvests, unemployment, and depression, coupled with growing dissatisfaction with the government's weak efforts to address social problems, put the spur to a new national reform movement in the 1830s. Radical reformers, disillusioned with the 1832 Reform Bill because it strengthened the power of a wealthy capitalist class, argued that democracy was the only answer to the problems plaguing British society.

The Chartist Movement.   In 1838, a small group of labor leaders, including representatives of the London Working

Chartist organizer boasted. Chartist babies were christened with the names of Chartist heroes. When Mrs. King of Manchester, England, attempted to register the birth of her son, James Feargus O'Connor King, her choice of names was challenged. The registrar demanded, "Is your husband a Chartist?" Mrs. King replied, "I don't know, but his wife is." Women organized Chartist schools and Sunday schools in radical defiance of local church organizations. Many middle-class observers were sure that the moment for class war and revolutionary upheaval had arrived. The government responded with force to the perceived threat of armed rebellion and imprisoned a number of Chartist leaders.

Throughout the 1840s, bad harvests and economic hardships continued to fan the flames of discontent. National petitions signed by millions were submitted to the House of Commons, which stubbornly resisted the idea of universal manhood suffrage. Strikes and attacks on factories spread throughout England, Scotland, and Wales in 1842. Increased violence served to make the Parliament intransigent and caused the movement to splinter and weaken as moderates formed their own factions. The final moment for Chartism occurred in April 1848 when 25,000 Chartist workers, inspired by revolutionary events on the Continent, assembled in London to march on the House of Commons. They carried with them a newly signed petition demanding the enactment of the terms of the People's Charter. In response, the government deputized nearly 200,000 "special" constables in the streets. The deputized private citizens were London property owners and skilled workers intent on holding back a revolutionary rabble. Tired, cold, and rain-soaked, the Chartist demonstrators disbanded. No social revolution took place in Great Britain, and the dilemma of democratic representation was deferred.

Workers Unite

The word **proletariat** entered European languages before the mid-nineteenth century to describe those workers afloat in the labor pool who owned nothing, not even the tools of their labor, and who were becoming "appendages" to the new machines that dominated production. To workers, machines could mean the elimination of jobs or the de-skilling of tasks; almost always machines meant a drop in wages.

Luddism. Mechanization deprived skilled craft workers of control of the workplace. In Great Britain, France, and Germany, groups of textile workers destroyed machines in protest. Workers demanding a fair wage smashed cotton power looms, knitting machines, and wool-carding machines. Sometimes the machines were a bargaining point for workers who used violence against them as a last resort. Machine-breakers tyrannized parts of Great Britain from 1811 to 1816 in an attempt to frighten masters. The movement was known as Luddism after its mythical leader, Ned Ludd. Workers damaged and destroyed property for more control over the work process, but such destruction met with severe repression. From the 1820s to the 1850s, sporadic but intense outbursts of machine-breaking occurred in continental Europe. Suffering weavers in Silesia and Bohemia resorted to destroying their looms in 1844.

Craft production continued to deteriorate with the rise in industrial competition. Skilled workers, fearing that they would be pulled down into the new proletariat because of mechanization and the increased scale of production, began organizing in new ways after 1830 by forming associations to assert their control over the workplace and to demand a voice in politics.

THE REFORM BILL.

■ The Reform Bill of 1832 is praised by a contemporary cartoonist. "Rotten boroughs" and political corruption are put through a meat grinder by Whig leaders, and a triumphant Britannia emerges.

In Britain, skilled craft workers built on a tradition of citizenship. They resisted the encroachments of factory production, and some channeled their political fervor into the Chartist movement. Skilled workers in France also built on a cultural heritage of shared language and values to create a consciousness of themselves as an exploited class. Uprisings and strikes in France, favoring the destruction of the monarchy and the creation of a democratic republic, increased dramatically from 1831 to 1834. Many French craft workers grew conscious of themselves as a class and embraced a socialism heavily influenced by their own traditions and contemporary socialist writings. Republican socialism spread throughout France by means of a network of traveling journeymen and tapped into growing economic hardship and political discontent with the July Monarchy. Government repression drove worker organizations underground in the late 1830s, but secret societies proliferated. Increasingly, workers saw the validity of the slogan of the silk workers of Lyon: "Live Working or Die Fighting!"

Women in the Work Force.   Women were an important part of the work force in the industrializing societies. Working men were keenly aware of the competition with cheaper female labor in the factories. Women formed a salaried work force in the home, too. In order to turn out products cheaply and in large quantities, some manufacturers turned to subcontractors to perform the simpler tasks in the work process. The new middlemen contracted out work such as cutting and sewing to needy women who were often responsible for caring

FLORA TRISTAN AND THE RIGHTS OF WORKING WOMEN

Flora Tristan (1803–1844) was a feminist and socialist who in the 1830s was actively involved in efforts to reintroduce divorce and to abolish the death penalty. She made her greatest political efforts for the creation of an international union of workers. The education of women was, Tristan asserted, essential for the success and prosperity of the working class. She toured slums in England and traveled across France on lecture tours to promote workers' unions and the education of women. The excerpt below is taken from her important book, L'Union Ouvrière, *1843. Tristan's argument for women's education is based not only on the claims of women to basic human rights, but on her assertion that educated women held the key to the betterment of families, the working class, and the whole society.*

Focus Questions

Why is education so important in Tristan's justification of women's rights? Would you describe Tristan as a reformer or a revolutionary?

. . . [I]t is imperative, in order to improve the intellectual, moral, and material condition of the working class, that women of the lower classes be given a rational and solid education, conducive to the development of their good inclinations, so that they may become skillful workers, good mothers, capable of raising and guiding their children, and of tutoring them in their school work, and so that they may act as moralizing agents in the life of the men on whom they exert an influence from the cradle to the grave.

Do you begin to understand, you, men, who cry shame before even looking into the question, why I demand rights for woman? Why I should like her to be placed on a footing of absolute equality with man in society, and that she should be so by virtue of the legal right every human being brings at birth?

I demand rights for women because I am convinced that all the misfortunes in the world result from the neglect and contempt in which woman's natural and inalienable rights have so far been held. I demand rights for woman because it is the only way she will get an education, and because the education of man in general and man of the lower classes in particular depends on the education of woman. I demand rights for woman because it is the only way to obtain her rehabilitation in the Church, the law, and society, and because this preliminary rehabilitation is necessary to achieve the rehabilitation of the workers themselves. All the woes of the working class can be summed up in these two words: poverty and ignorance, ignorance and poverty. Now, I see only one way out of this labyrinth: begin by educating women, because women have the responsibility of educating male and female children. . . .

As soon as the dangerous consequences of the development of the moral and physical faculties of women—dangerous because of women's current slave status—are no longer feared, woman can be taught with great care so as to make the best possible use of her intelligence and work. Then, you, men of the lower classes, will have as mothers skillful workers who earn a decent salary, are educated, well brought up, and quite capable of raising you, of educating you, the workers, as is proper for free men. You will have well brought up and well educated sisters, lovers, wives, friends, with whom daily contacts will be most pleasant for you. Nothing is sweeter or more agreeable to a man's heart than the sensible and gracious conversation of good and well educated women.

for family members in their homes. That kind of subcontracting, called "sweated labor" because of the exertion and long hours involved in working in one's own home, was always poorly paid.

Cheap female labor paid by the piece allowed employers to profit by keeping overhead costs low and by driving down the wages of skilled workers. Trade unions opposed women's work, both in the home and in the factories. Women's talents, union leaders explained, were more properly devoted to domestic chores. Unions argued that their members should earn a family wage "sufficient to support a wife and children." Unions consistently excluded women workers from their ranks.

French labor leader Flora Tristan, speaking not only as a worker but also as a wife and mother, had a very different answer for those who wanted to remove women from the workplace and assign them to their "proper place" in the home. She recognized that working women needed to work in order to support themselves and their families. Tristan told audiences in Europe and Latin America that the emancipation of women from their "slave status" was essential if the working class as a whole was to enjoy a better future. She deplored the economic competition between working men and women and denounced the degradation of women in both the home and the workplace. A working woman earned one-third or less of the average working man's wages, and women's working conditions were often deplorable. In the 1840s, British parliamentary commissions heard the horrifying testimony of one young London dressmaker from the country who was forced to work grueling hours—often 20 hours a day—under unhealthy working conditions that had destroyed her health. She concluded that "no men could endure the work enforced from the dressmakers."

Working women's only hope, according to Tristan, lay in education and unionization. She urged working men and women to join together to lay claim to their natural and inalienable rights. In some cases, working women formed their own organizations, like that of the Parisian seamstresses who joined together to demand improved working conditions. On the whole, however, domestic workers in the home remained isolated from other working women, and many women in factories feared the loss of their jobs if they engaged in political activism. The wages of Europe's working women remained low, often below the level of subsistence. In the absence of a man's income, working women and their children were the poorest of the poor in European society in the middle of the nineteenth century.

For some men and women of the working class, the 1840s were a time of mounting unrest, increased organization, and growing protest. Workers used their unity in associations, unions, and mutual aid societies to press for full political participation and government action in times of economic distress.

Revolutions Across Europe, 1848–1850

Europeans had never experienced a year like 1848. Beginning soon after the ringing in of the New Year, revolutionary fervor swept through nearly every European country. By year's end, regimes had been created and destroyed. France, Italy, the German states, Austria, Hungary, and Bohemia were shaken to their foundations. Switzerland, Denmark, and Romania experienced lesser upheavals. Great Britain had survived reformist agitation, and famine-crippled Ireland had endured a failed insurrection. No one was sure what had happened. Each country's conflict was based on a unique mix of issues, but all were connected in their conscious emulation of a revolutionary tradition.

Hindsight reveals warning signs in the two years before the 1848 cataclysm. Beginning in 1846, a severe famine—the last serious food crisis Europe would experience—racked Europe. Lack of grain drove up prices. An increasing percentage of disposable income was spent on food for survival. Lack of spending power severely damaged markets and forced thousands of industrial workers out of their jobs. The famine hurt everyone—the poor, workers, employers, and investors—as recession paralyzed the economy.

The food crisis took place in a heavily charged political atmosphere. Throughout Europe during the 1840s, the middle and lower classes had intensified their agitation for democracy. Chartists in Great Britain argued for a wider electorate. Bourgeois reformers in France campaigned for universal manhood suffrage. Known as the "banquet" campaign because its leaders attempted to raise money by giving speeches at subscribed dinners, the movement for the vote appeared to be developing a mass following by taking its cause directly to the people. In making demands for political participation, those agitating for suffrage necessarily criticized those in power. Freedom of speech and freedom of assembly were demanded as inalienable rights. The food crisis and political activism provided the ingredients for an incendiary situation.

In addition to a burgeoning democratic culture, growing demands for national autonomy based on linguistic and cultural claims spread through central, southern, and eastern Europe. The revolts in Poland in 1846, though failures, encouraged similar movements for national liberation among Italians and Germans. Even in the relatively homogeneous nation of France, concerns with national mission and national glory grew among the regime's critics. National unity was primarily a middle-class ideal. Liberal lawyers, teachers, and businessmen from Dublin to Budapest to Prague agitated for separation from foreign rule. Austria, with an empire formed of numerous ethnic minorities, had the most to lose. Since 1815, Metternich had been ruthless in stamping out nationalist dissent. However, by the 1840s, national claims were assuming a cultural legitimacy that was difficult to dismiss or ignore.

France Leads the Way.   The events in France in the cold February of 1848 ignited the conflagration that swept Europe. Bourgeois reformers had arranged for their largest banquet to date in support of extension of the vote, to take place in Paris on 22 February. City officials became nervous at the prospect of thousands of workers assembling for political purposes and canceled the scheduled banquet. That was the spark that touched off the powder keg. In a spontaneous uprising, Parisians demonstrated against the government's repressive measures. Skilled workers took to the streets, not only in favor of the banned banquet but also with the hope that the government would recognize the importance of labor to the social order. Shots were fired; a demonstrator was killed. The French Revolution of 1848 had begun.

Events moved quickly. The National Guard, a citizen militia of bourgeois Parisians, defected from Louis-Philippe. Many army troops garrisoned in Paris crossed the barricades to join revolutionary workers. The king attempted some reform, but it was too little and too late. Louis-Philippe fled. The Second Republic was proclaimed at the insistence of the revolutionary crowds on the barricades. The Provisional Government, led by the poet Alphonse de Lamartine (1790–1869), included members of both factions of political reformers of the July Monarchy: moderates who sought constitutional reforms and an extension of the suffrage, and radicals who favored universal manhood suffrage and social programs to deal with poverty and work. Only the threat of popular violence held together the uneasy alliance.

The people fighting in the streets had little in common with the bourgeois reformers who assumed power on 24 February. Workers made a social revolution out of a commitment to their "right to work," which would replace the right to property as the organizing principle of the new society. Only one member of the new Provisional Government was a worker, and he was included as a token symbol of the intentions of the new government. He was known as "Albert, the worker," and was not addressed by his surname, Martin. The government acknowledged the demand of the "right to work" and set up two mechanisms to guarantee workers' relief. First, a commission of workers and employers was created to act as a grievance and bargaining board and settle questions of common concern in the workplace. Headed by the socialist Louis Blanc (1811–1882) and known as the Luxembourg Commission, the worker-employer parliament was an important innovation, but accomplished little other than deflecting workers' attention away from the problems of the Provisional Government. The second measure was the creation of "national workshops" to deal with the problems of unemployment in Paris. Although the name was taken from Blanc's plan for worker control of production, the national workshops were no more than an inefficient charity program that paid men minimal wages. The national workshops quickly proved disastrous. Workers from all over France poured into Paris with the hope of finding jobs. However, the workshops had a residency requirement that even Parisians had difficulty meeting. As a result, unemployment skyrocketed. Furthermore, the government was going bankrupt trying to support the program. The need to raise taxes upset peasants in the provinces. National pressure mounted to repudiate the programs of the revolution.

French workers were too weak to dominate the revolution. The government dissolved the workshops and recalled General Louis Cavaignac (1802–1857) from service in Algeria to maintain order. In a wave of armed insurrection, Parisian workers rebelled in June. Using provincial troops having no identification with the urban population and employing guerrilla techniques he had mastered in Algeria, Cavaignac put down the uprising. The June fighting was the bloodiest that Paris had ever seen. The Second Republic was placed under the military dictatorship of Cavaignac until December, when presidential elections were scheduled.

Revolutions in Central and Eastern Europe.
The overthrow of the July Monarchy at the end of February set off shock waves of protest in central and eastern Europe. Long-suppressed desires for civil liberties and constitutional reforms erupted in widespread popular disturbances throughout Prussia and the German states. Fearing a war with France

■ Club-wielding police break up a radical demonstration in Berlin, the capital of Prussia, in 1848. In March, King Frederick William of Prussia acceded to the demands of liberal reformers. But in November, after uprisings against conservative regimes elsewhere in Europe had been put down, the monarch allowed the Prussian army to regain control of Berlin.

MAP DISCOVERY

The Revolutions of 1848

In less than a generation, a second major wave of revolutions swept across Europe from west to east in 1848. What were the centers of revolutionary action in 1848 and what was their relationship to the seats of political power? How do you explain the timing of the eastern trajectory of successive revolutions? How did the map of Europe change as a result of these revolutions?

and unable to count on Austria or Russia for support, the princes who ruled Baden, Württemberg, Hesse-Darmstadt, Bavaria, Saxony, and Hanover followed the advice of moderate liberals and acceded quickly to revolutionary demands. In Prussia, Kaiser Friedrich Wilhelm IV (1840–1861) preferred to use military force to respond to popular demonstrations. Only in mid-March 1848 did the Prussian king yield to the force of the revolutionary crowds building barricades in Berlin by ordering his troops to leave the city and by promising to create a national Prussian assembly. The king was now a prisoner of the revolution.

Meanwhile, the collapse of absolute monarchy in Prussia gave further impetus to a constitutional movement among the liberal leaders of the German states. The governments of

all the German states were invited to elect delegates to a national parliament in Frankfurt. The Frankfurt Assembly, which was convened in May 1848, had as its dual charge the framing of a constitution and the unification of Germany. It was composed for the most part of members of the middle class, with civil servants, lawyers, and intellectuals predominating. In spite of the principle of universal manhood suffrage, no members of the working class served among the 800 men elected. To most of the delegates, who had been trained in universities and shared a social and cultural identity, nationalism and constitutionalism were inextricably related.

As straightforward as the desire for a German nation appeared to be, it was complicated by two important facts. First, there were non-German minorities living in German states.

What was to be done with the Poles, Czechs, Slovenes, Italians, and Dutch in a newly constituted and autonomous German nation? Second, there were Germans living outside the German states under Habsburg rule in Austria, in Danish Schleswig and Holstein, in Posen (Poznan), in Russian Poland, and in European Russia. How were they to be included within the linguistically and ethnically constituted German nation? No matter how small the circle was drawn, it included non-Germans; no matter how wide, it excluded Germans. After much wrangling over a "small" Germany that excluded Austrian Germans and a "large" Germany that included them, the Frankfurt Assembly opted for the small-Germany solution in March 1849. The crown of the new nation was offered to the unpredictable Friedrich Wilhelm IV of Prussia, head of the largest and most powerful of the German states. Unhappy with his capitulation to the revolutionary crowd in March 1848, the Prussian king refused to accept a "crown from the gutter." He had his own plans to rule over a middle-European bloc, but not at the behest of a liberal parliament. The attempt to create a German nation crumbled with his unwillingness to lead.

Revolution in Austrian-dominated central Europe was concentrated in three places: Vienna, where German-speaking students, workers, and middle-class liberals were agitating for constitutional reform and political participation; Budapest, where the Magyars, the dominant ethnic group in Hungary, led a movement for national autonomy; and Prague, where Czechs were attempting self-rule. By April 1848, Metternich had fallen from power and the Viennese revolutionaries had set up a constituent assembly. In Budapest, the initial steps of the patriot Lajos Kossuth (1802–1894) toward establishing a separate Hungarian state seemed equally solid as the Magyars defeated Habsburg troops. Habsburg armies were more successful in Prague, where they crushed the revolution in June 1848. In December 1848, Emperor Ferdinand I (1835–1848), whose authority had been weakened irreparably by the overthrow of Metternich, abdicated in favor of his 18-year-old nephew, Franz Josef I (1848–1916).

DOCUMENT

Metternich on Revolutions of 1848

Italian Nationalism. The Habsburg Empire was also under siege on the Italian Peninsula, where the Kingdom of the Two Sicilies, Tuscany, and Piedmont declared new constitutions in March 1848. Championed by Charles Albert of Piedmont, Venice and Lombardy rose up against Austria. Italian middle-class intellectuals and professionals championed the idea of national unification and the expulsion of the hated Austrian overlords. Nationalist sentiments had percolated underground in the Young Italy movement, founded in 1831 by Giuseppe Mazzini. A tireless and idealistic patriot, Mazzini favored a democratic revolution. In spite of his reputation as a liberal, Pope Pius IX (1846–1878) lost control of Rome and was forced to flee the city. Mazzini became head of the Republic of Rome, created in February 1849.

The French government decided to intervene to protect the pope's interests and sent in troops to defeat the republicans.

CHRONOLOGY	
PROTEST AND REVOLUTION	
August 1819	Peterloo Massacre
1824	Charles X assumes French throne
1827	Treaty of London to support liberation of Greece
July 1830	Revolution in Paris; creation of July Monarchy under Louis-Philippe
August 1830	Revolution in Belgium
November 1830	Revolution in Poland
1831–1838	Revolutions in Italian states
1831–1834	Labor protests in France
1832	Britain's Great Reform Bill
1838	Drawing up the first People's Charter in Britain
1846	Beginning of food crisis in Europe; revolts in Poland
1846–1848	Europewide movements for national liberation
February 1848	Revolution in France; overthrow of the July Monarchy; proclamation of the French Second Republic and creation of Provisional Government
March 1848	Uprisings in some German states; granting of a constitution in Prussia
March 1848–June 1849	Revolutions in Italy
April 1848	Revolutions in Vienna, Budapest, Prague
May 1848	Frankfurt Assembly
June 1848	Second revolution in Paris, severely repressed by army troops under General Cavaignac
December 1848	Presidential elections in France; Louis Napoleon wins

One of Mazzini's disciples, Giuseppe Garibaldi (1807–1882), returned from exile in South America to undertake the defense of Rome. Garibaldi was a capable soldier who had learned the tactics of guerrilla warfare by joining independence struggles in Brazil and Argentina. Although his legion of poorly armed patriots and soldiers of fortune, known from their attire as the Red Shirts, waged a valiant effort to defend the city from April to June 1849, they were no match for the highly trained French army. French troops restored Pius IX as ruler of the Papal States.

Meanwhile, from August 1848 to the following spring, the Habsburg armies fought and finally defeated each of the revolutions. Austrian success can be explained in part because the various Italian groups of Piedmontese, Tuscans, Venetians, Romans, and Neapolitans continued to identify with their local concerns and lacked coordination and central organization. Both Mazzini and Pius IX had failed to provide the focal point of leadership necessary for a successful national movement. By the fall of 1849, Austria had solved the problems in its own capital and with Italy and Hungary by military repression.

Europe in 1850. In 1850, Austrians threatened the Prussians with war if they did not give up their plans for a unified Germany. In November of that year, Prussian ministers signed an agreement with their Austrian counterparts in the Moravian city of Olmütz. The convention became known as "the humiliation of Olmütz" because Prussia was forced to accept Austrian dominance or go to war. In every case, military force and diplomatic measures prevailed to defeat the national and liberal movements within the German states and the Austrian Empire.

By 1850, a veneer of calm had spread over central Europe. In Prussia, the peasantry were emancipated from feudal dues, and a constitution, albeit conservative and based on a three-class system, was established. Yet beneath the surface, there was the deeper reality of Austrian decline and Prussian challenge. The great Habsburg Empire needed to call on outside help from Russia to defeat its enemies within. The imperial giant was again on its feet, but for how long? In international relations, Austria's dominance in the German Confederation had diminished, while Prussia assumed greater political and economic power.

The 1848 revolutions spelled the end to the concert of Europe as it had been defined in the peace settlement of 1815. The European powers were incapable of united action to defend established territorial interests.

The revolutions of 1848 failed in part because of the irreconcilable split between moderate liberals and radical democrats. The participation of the masses had frightened members of the middle classes, who were committed to moderate reforms that did not threaten property. In France, working-class revolutionaries had attempted to replace property with labor as the highest social value. Property triumphed. In the face of more extreme solutions, members of the middle class were willing to accept the increased authority of existing rule as a bulwark against anarchy. In December 1848, Prince Louis Napoleon, nephew of the former emperor, was elected president of the Second Republic by a wide margin. The first truly modern French politician, Louis Napoleon managed to appeal to everyone—workers, bourgeois, royalists, and peasants—by making promises that he did not keep. Severe repression forced radical protest into hiding. The new Bonaparte bided his time, apparently as an ineffectual ruler, until the moment in 1851 when he seized absolute power.

Similar patterns emerged elsewhere in Europe. In Germany, the bourgeoisie accepted the dominance of the old feudal aristocracy as a guarantee of law and order. Repressive government, businessmen were sure, would restore a strong economy. The attempts in 1848 to create new nations based on ethnic identities were in shambles by 1850.

Nearly everywhere throughout Europe, constitutions had been systematically withdrawn with the recovery of the forces of reaction. With the French and Swiss exceptions, the bid for the extension of the franchise failed. The propertied classes remained in control of political institutions. Radicals willing to use violence to press electoral reforms were arrested, killed, or exiled. The leadership of the revolutionary movements had been decapitated, and there seemed no effective opposition to the rise and consolidation of state power. The 1848 revolutions have been called a turning point at which modern history failed to turn. Contemporaries wondered how so much action could have produced so few lasting results.

CONCLUSION

The perception that nothing had changed was wrong. The revolutions of 1848 and subsequent events galvanized whole societies to political action. Conservatives and radicals alike turned toward a new realism in politics. Everywhere governments were forced to adapt to new social realities. No longer could the state ignore economic upheavals and social dislocations if it wanted to survive. Revolutionaries also learned the lesson of repression. The state wielded powerful forces of violence against which nationalists, socialists, republicans, and liberals had all been proved helpless. Organizing, campaigning, and lobbying were newly learned political skills, as was outreach across class lines—from bourgeoisie to peasantry—around common political causes. In these ways, 1848 was a turning point in the formation of a modern political culture.

QUESTIONS FOR REVIEW

1. What problems did European peacemakers confront at the Congress of Vienna, and how did they attempt to resolve the problems?
2. How did industrialization change European families?
3. In what ways were liberalism and nationalism compatible with each other; how were they in conflict?
4. What are the connections between various ideologies—for instance, liberalism, romanticism, or socialism—and the revolutions of 1830 and 1848?

KEY TERMS

chartism, *p. 693*

The Communist Manifesto, p. 688

Congress of Vienna, *p. 674*

conservatism, *p. 679*

Great Reform Bill of 1832, *p. 692*

Holy Alliance, *p. 678*

liberalism, *p. 680*

Peterloo Massacre, *p. 689*

proletariat *p. 694*

Quadruple Alliance, *p. 678*

Quintuple Alliance, *p. 678*

romanticism, *p. 681*

utilitarianism, *p. 680*

DISCOVERING WESTERN CIVILIZATION ONLINE

You can obtain more information about political upheavals and social transformations between 1815 and 1850 at the Websites listed below. See also the Companion Website that accompanies this text, www.ablongman.com/kishlansky, which contains an online study guide and additional resources.

Geographical Tour: Europe in 1815

Internet Modern History Sourcebook: Conservative Order

www.fordham.edu/halsall/mod/modsbook16.html

The site provides documents, discussions, and bibliographies on the Congress of Vienna and charts the development of conservative thought.

The New Ideologies

McMaster University Archive for the History of Economic Thought

socserv.mcmaster.ca/econ/ugcm/3ll3

A site for texts in modern economic theory.

Internet Modern History Sourcebook: Liberalism

www.fordham.edu/halsall/mod/modsbook18.html

A collection of links to primary documents and bibliographies on liberalism.

Internet Modern History Sourcebook: Nationalism

www.fordham.edu/halsall/mod/modsbook17.html

The Nationalism Project

www.nationalismproject.org/

These sites provide links to primary documents and bibliographies of nationalism.

Internet Modern History Sourcebook: Romanticism

www.fordham.edu/halsall/mod/modsbook15.html

This site provides links to primary texts on romantic philosophy and literature.

Voice of the Shuttle

vos.ucsb.edu/index.asp

This comprehensive database for humanities research provides links to general resources, criticism, and primary texts. Type "Romantics" into the search function for resources on romantic philosophy and literature.

Marxist Internet Archive: Marxist Writers

www.marxists.org/archive/index.htm

The site provides translated texts of Marx and Engels as well as other prominent Social Democrats and Communists.

Protest and Revolution

Child Labour in the 19th Century

www.spartacus.schoolnet.co.uk/IRchild.htm

A collection of biographies of reformers and promoters of child labor laws, electronic texts of major child labor legislation, and excerpts from primary sources concerning child labor in nineteenth-century Britain.

The Emancipation of Women: 1750–1920

www.spartacus.schoolnet.co.uk/women.htm

The site contains links to biographies of major figures, essays on the major organizations and societies, and electronic texts of the women's movement in Britain.

Internet Modern History Sourcebook: 1848

www.fordham.edu/halsall/mod/modsbook19.html

The site provides documents, discussions, bibliographies and other links on the revolutions of 1848.

SUGGESTIONS FOR FURTHER READING

Geographical Tour: Europe in 1815

Tim Chapman, *The Congress of Vienna: Origins, Processes, and Results* (New York: Routledge, 1998). A brief, comprehensive survey of how the European powers victorious against Napoleon redrew Europe's frontiers. It follows the impact of the Settlement to its demise in the twentieth century.

Robert Gildea, *Barricades and Borders, Europe 1800–1914* (Oxford: Oxford University Press, 1996). A synthetic overview of economic, demographic, political, and international trends in European society.

Robin Okey, *The Habsburg Monarchy: From Enlightenment to Eclipse* (New York: St. Martin's Press, 2001). An informative survey of Austrian rule from the mid-eighteenth century to the end of World War I, which contains an annotated bibliography and materials drawn from historiographic material in Magyar, Serbo-Croat, Czech, and other eastern European language sources.

The New Ideologies

Jonathan Beecher, *Charles Fourier: The Visionary and His World* (Berkeley: University of California Press, 1986). An intellectual biography that traces the development of Fourier's theoretical perspective and roots it firmly in the social context of nineteenth-century France.

Craig Calhoun, *The Question of Class Struggle: Social Foundations of Popular Radicalism During the Industrial Revolution* (Chicago: University of Chicago Press, 1982). Presents popular protest of eighteenth- and early nineteenth-century England as the reaction of communities of artisans defending their traditions against encroaching industrialization.

Gareth Stedman Jones, *Languages of Class: Studies in English Working Class History, 1832–1982* (Cambridge: Cambridge University Press, 1983). A series of essays, on topics such as working-class culture and Chartism, that examine the development of class consciousness.

William H. Sewell, Jr., *Work and Revolution in France: The Language of Labor from the Old Regime to 1848* (Cambridge: Cambridge University Press, 1980). Traces nineteenth-century working-class socialism to the corporate culture of Old Regime guilds through traditional values, norms, language, and artisan organizations.

Denis Mack Smith, *Mazzini* (New Haven, CT: Yale University Press, 1994). Mazzini is presented as an important force in legitimizing Italian nationalism by associating it with republicanism and the interests of humanity.

Edward P. Thompson, *The Making of the English Working Class* (New York: Pantheon Books, 1963). A classic in social history that spans the late eighteenth to mid-nineteenth centuries in examining the social, political, and cultural contexts in which workers created their own identity and put forward their own demands.

Protest and Revolution

Maurice Agulhon, *The Republican Experiment, 1848–1852* (Cambridge: Cambridge University Press, 1983). Traces the Revolution of 1848 from its roots to its ultimate failure in 1852 through an analysis of the republican ideologies of workers, peasants, and the bourgeoisie.

Clive Church, *Europe in 1830: Revolution and Political Change* (London: Allen & Unwin, 1983). Considers the origins of the 1830 revolutions within a wider European crisis through a comparative analysis of European regions.

R. J. W. Evans and Hartmut Pogge von Strandmann, eds., *The Revolutions in Europe, 1848–1849: From Reform to Reaction* (Oxford: Oxford University Press, 2000). A focused collection of articles on the mid-nineteenth-century collapse of authority across Europe.

Alan J. Kidd, *State, Society, and the Poor in Nineteenth-Century England* (New York: St. Martin's Press, 1999). This volume is part of the *Social History in Perspective* series; it provides an overview of poverty in industrializing England, the role of the poor laws, public welfare, and charitable organizations in the nineteenth century.

Catherine J. Kudlick, *Cholera in Post-Revolutionary Paris: A Cultural History* (Berkeley: University of California Press, 1996). Examines the cultural values of ruling elites and demonstrates the role disease played in shaping political life and class identity in nineteenth-century France.

Patricia O'Brien, *The Promise of Punishment: Prisons in Nineteenth-Century France* (Princeton: Princeton University Press, 1982). An overview of the creation of the penitentiary system in nineteenth-century France and the rise of the new science of punishment, criminology, and the eventual appearance of alternatives to the penitentiary system.

Redcliffe N. Salaman, *The History and Social Influence of the Potato,* revised impression edited by J. G. Hawkes (Cambridge: Cambridge University Press, 1985). The classic study of the potato. A major portion of the work is devoted to the potato famine.

Jonathan Sperber, *Revolutionary Europe, 1780–1850* (New York: Longman, 2000). Considers the revolutions of 1848 within the context of economic and social changes rooted in Old Regime politics and society and from the perspective of the twenty-first century.

For a list of additional titles related to this chapter's topics, please see http://www.ablongman.com/kishlansky.

Chapter 23

STATE BUILDING AND SOCIAL CHANGE IN EUROPE, 1850–1871

Chapter Outline

Painter Anton von Werner, who accompanied troops in the 1870 Franco-Prussian War as a wartime artist, also captured on canvas one of the major political events that followed the war: the Proclamation of the German Empire. How did he depict the birth of a nation? Turn the page to examine The Visual Record. ➤

703

THE BIRTH OF THE GERMAN EMPIRE

Otto von Bismarck's Role

Secret fancies bubbled in Otto von Bismarck's brain. As he explained in long letters to his wife, he imagined that the Russian king and German princes crowding around him were pregnant women seized by "strange cravings." In the next moment, he imagined himself a midwife assisting at a momentous birth. In spite of his remarkable train of thought, Otto von Bismarck (1815–1898) was not a fanciful man. The birth in his daydream was the **Proclamation of the German Empire** on 21 January 1871. The building was the palace of Versailles outside Paris. As the Prussian statesman stood in the great Hall of Mirrors on that fateful day, surrounded by German aristocrats, he could not forget the years of struggle and planning that had preceded the event. His tension and anticipation provoked his birthing fantasies.

The newly proclaimed Second Reich, successor to the Holy Roman Empire (962–1806), united the German states into a single nation. The unification process had been a precarious pregnancy, with years of foreign wars and a demanding labor of diplomatic maneuverings. The placid, glossy scene painted by Anton von Werner (1843–1915) hardly suggests Bismarck's violent emotions on the momentous day. Bismarck saw his task in terms of the female metaphor of birth. Yet the warrior group was the most masculine of gatherings. The painting shows the richly marbled and mirrored room, the site of the birth, figured as prominently in the tableau as the uniformed princes and aristocrats who, with sabers, helmets, and standards raised, cheer the new emperor. The massive mirrors reflect more than the soldier society standing before the long windows of the opposite wall; they reflect a humiliation. It was, after all, the great hall built by Louis XIV at Versailles, one of Europe's greatest palaces, designed to reflect and glorify the power of absolutist France. There the kings of France had presided over

lavish ceremonies and opulent receptions. There Napoleon I had honored his generals, victorious in conquering central Europe. There, not long before, Napoleon III had danced on the parqueted floors with Queen Victoria of Britain. The choice of the Hall of Mirrors as the meeting place for the German princes, who had successfully combined forces to defeat the French Second Empire in only six weeks of war in the fall of 1870, was intended as an assertion of German superiority in Europe.

The painting shows King Wilhelm I of Prussia on the dais, flanked by his son, Crown Prince Friedrich Wilhelm, and his son-in-law, Friedrich I, the Grand Duke of Baden, whose upraised hand signals a cheer for the new emperor. At the foot of the steps, like a loyal retainer, stands the self-described midwife, Otto von Bismarck, who is singled out in his pure white uniform. Yet there is something amiss. The new German emperor, the person for whom the event has been orchestrated, stands to one side of the canvas. Bismarck commands its center. If the eyes of most of the cheering princes turn to the emperor, the viewer's are pulled to the chancellor of the new Reich. The artist has shown that it was Bismarck's event, for it was Bismarck who crafted a united Germany.

In both hands Bismarck clasps the Proclamation of the German Empire, the document wrested out of endless wrangling among the heads of the 38 German states. Bismarck understood that symbols forge unity. The artist Werner also attends to symbol. Beneath the red-encased document, Bismarck firmly grasps his Prussian military helmet. Military victories had ensured Prussian predominance over a united Germany. To Bismarck's left, in profile facing the emperor, stands Count Helmuth von Moltke (1800–1891), head of the Prussian General Staff and the man responsible for reorganizing the Prussian army with Bismarck's support. Medals for

Anton von Werner, *Proclamation of the German Empire on 18 January 1871.*

bravery and service to his sovereign adorn Moltke's chest. With one foot forward, Moltke is a man of action, almost caught in mid-stride, a man ready to move into the future.

The unification of Germany was not achieved by democratic means. Bismarck understood the new age. As he explained in a speech to the Prussian Diet, "The great questions of the time are not decided by speeches and majority decisions— that was the error of 1848 and 1849—but by iron and blood."

Looking Ahead

In this chapter we will examine the period between 1850 and 1871, when unification of territories was an important part of the process of building a nation in both Germany and Italy. Successful statesmen were diplomats who used alliances to further national interests. They were also realists willing to use force to further national interests. The existing nation-states of France, Great Britain, and Russia, with little in common save their commitment to progress, pursued different paths to state reform and consolidation of national power.

The changing values and force of new ideas so evident in the political realm also characterized the changing world of the home and family. Just as realism was a dominant force in politics, realism in arts and sciences became a means of promoting material progress. With the convergence of these changes in a variety of realms, Europeans witnessed the birth of the modern age in the third quarter of the nineteenth century. ➤

BUILDING NATIONS: THE POLITICS OF UNIFICATION

The revolutions of 1848 had occurred in a period of experimentation from below. Radicals enlisting popular support had tried and failed to reshape European states for their own nationalist, liberal, and socialist ends. Governments in Paris, Vienna, Berlin, and a number of lesser states had been swept away as revolutions created a power vacuum but no durable solutions. To fill that vacuum, a new breed of politician emerged in the 1850s and 1860s, men who understood the importance of the centralized nation-state and saw the need of reforms from above. They shared a new realism about means and ends, and about using foreign policy successes to further domestic programs.

The Crimean War

After 1815 Russia, as the greatest military power in Europe, honored its commitment to preserving the status quo by acting as police officer for the continent. Russia supported Austria against Hungary and Prussia in 1849 and 1850. But Russia sought greater power to the south, in the Balkans. The Bosporus, the narrow strait connecting the Black Sea with the Sea of Marmara, and the strait of the Dardanelles, which connects the Sea of Marmara with the Aegean Sea, were controlled by the Ottoman Empire. Russia hoped to benefit from Ottoman weakness caused by internal conflicts and gain control of the straits, which were the only outlet for the Russian fleet to the warm waters of the Mediterranean, Russia's southern outlet to the world.

The Eastern Question.   Each of the Great Powers—including Russia, Great Britain, Austria, Prussia, and France—hoped to benefit territorially from the collapse of Ottoman control. In 1853, Great Power rivalry over the "**Eastern question**," as the anticipated disintegration of the Ottoman Empire was termed, created an international situation that led to war.

In 1853, the Russian government demanded that the Turkish government recognize Russia's right to protect Greek Orthodox believers in the Ottoman Empire. The Russian action was a response to measures taken by the French government during the previous year, when France had gained from the Turkish government rights for Roman Catholic religious orders in certain sanctuaries in the Holy Land. In making its claims as protector, Russia demanded that the rights granted Roman Catholic orders also be rescinded. The Turkish government refused Russian demands and the Russians, feeling that their prestige had been damaged, ordered troops to enter the Danubian Principalities held by the Turks.

In October 1853, the Turkish government, counting on support from Great Britain and France, declared war on Russia. Russia easily prevailed over its weaker neighbor to the south. In a four-hour battle, a Russian squadron destroyed the Turkish fleet off the coast of Sinope. Tsar Nicholas I (1825–1855) drew up the terms of a settlement with the Ottoman Empire and submitted them to Great Britain and France for review.

The two western European powers, fearing Russian aggrandizement at Turkish expense, responded by declaring war on Russia on 28 March 1854, a date that marked a new phase in the Crimean War. Both Great Britain and France, like Russia, had ambitions in the Balkans and the eastern Mediterranean. Great Britain feared Russian expansion as a threat to its trade and holdings in India and had a vested interest in an independent but weak Turkey presiding over the straits. The French hoped that by entering into a partnership with the British to defeat the Russians, they would be able to lay claim to greater power and status in European international politics. The Italian kingdom of Piedmont-Sardinia joined the war on the side of the western European powers in January 1855, hoping to make its name militarily and win recognition for its aim to unite Italy into a single nation. Although Great Britain, France, and the Italian state of Piedmont-Sardinia did not have explicit economic interests, they were motivated by ambition, prestige, and rivalry in the Balkans.

British and French troops landed in the Crimea, the Russian peninsula extending into the Black Sea, in September 1854, with the intention of capturing Sevastopol, Russia's heavily fortified chief naval base on the Black Sea. In March 1855, Nicholas I died and was succeeded by his son Alexander II (1855–1881), who wanted to bring the war to a speedy end. His attempts to negotiate a peace in the spring of 1855 repeatedly failed. In battle, the Russians continued to resist as the allies laid siege to the fortress at Sevastopol, which fell only after 322 days of battle, on 11 September 1855. The defeated Russians abandoned Sevastopol, blew up their forts, and sank their own ships. Facing the threat of Austrian entry into the war, Russia agreed to preliminary peace terms.

In the Peace of Paris of 1856, Russia relinquished its claim as protector of Christians in Turkey. The British gained the neutralization of the Black Sea. The mouth of the Danube was returned to Turkish control, and an international commission was created to oversee safe navigation on the Danube. The Danubian Principalities were placed under joint guarantee of the powers, and Russia gave up a small portion of Bessarabia. In 1861, the Principalities were united in the independent nation of Romania.

The Human Costs of the War.   The Crimean War had the highest number of casualties of any European war between 1815 and 1914. Three-quarters of a million soldiers—Russian, French, British, and Turkish—died. Because no sanitary practices were observed in caring for the wounded, four out of five succumbed to disease, especially typhus and cholera. The English nurse Florence Nightingale (1820–1910) brought medical reforms to the theater of war, introduced sanitation, and organized barracks hospitals, all of which saved the lives of countless British soldiers. (See "A Closer Look: A Working Woman," pp. 708–709.) Russians suffered disproportionately, claiming two-thirds of all dead and wounded; 450,000 Russian soldiers died. Of those who died in battle, many died

MAP DISCOVERY

Russian Troops

British and French Troops

Turkish Troops

Major battles

The Crimean War

The Crimean War, which was Russia's war against the Ottoman Empire, Great Britain, France, and Sardinia, ended Russia's influence over southeastern Europe. What was the strategic importance of control of the Dardanelles Straits for Russia? Why did Russia fear Turkish control of its access to the Mediterranean Sea? Russia controlled a naval base at Sevastopol and resisted French, British, Turkish, and Sardinian attacks for over 11 months during the Crimean War. In excluding Russian influence from southern Europe, why was defeat in the Crimean War such a catastrophe for Russia? Finally, why did a dispute among Christians in the Holy Land result in a war in the Crimea?

down a narrow valley flanked by Russian guns on the heights on both sides and into the teeth of yet another battery at the head of the valley. The battlefield became known as the Valley of Death and was commemorated in Alfred Tennyson's poem, "The Charge of the Light Brigade." When the dust of the fighting had settled, the battlefield lay strewn with the bodies of nearly two-thirds of the soldiers of the Light Brigade. Their horses, slain too, lay beside them.

It was a war no one really won, a war over obscure disagreements in a faraway peninsula in the Black Sea. Nevertheless, it had dramatic and enduring consequences. Russia ceased playing an active role in European affairs and turned toward expansion in central Asia. Its withdrawal opened up the possibility for a move by Prussia in central Europe. The rules of the game had changed. The concert of Europe so carefully crafted by European statesmen in 1815 came to an end with the Crimean War. With the Peace of Paris of 1856, the hope that goals could be achieved by peaceful means also died. Piedmont-Sardinia, an empty-handed victor, realized that only the force of the cannon could achieve the unification of Italy.

Unifying Italy

Italy had not been a single political entity since the end of the Roman Empire in the West in the fifth century. The movement to reunite Italy culturally and politically was known as the **Risorgimento** (literally, "resurgence") and had its roots in the eighteenth century. Hopes for unification encouraged by reorganization during the Napoleonic era had been repeatedly crushed throughout the first half of the nineteenth century. Revolutionary movements had failed to cast out foreign domination by Austria in 1848.

needlessly, under poorly prepared leaders. A typical example occurred during the battle of Balaklava when 600 troops of the British Light Brigade were ordered into battle by incompetent and confused commanders. British soldiers charged

A Closer Look
A Working Woman

Women have always worked, but how society has valued women's work has changed over time. After 1850, women were expected to retire from the workplace upon marrying. Woman's proper role was that of wife and mother in the home, caring for her husband and family, watching over her children. Young women worked before they married to help their parents and to save for dowries. There is no doubt that many women continued to work for wages because they had to; they were too poor to live by society's norms. But mid-nineteenth-century European culture reinforced the idea that woman's place was in the separate domestic sphere of private pleasures and unpaid labor. To be a "public" man was a valued trait. The same adjective applied to a woman meant that she was a harlot.

Yet it is this culture that immortalized Florence Nightingale, a woman who valued what she called "my work" above home and family. She was a single woman in an age when more and more women were making the choice to remain unmarried; but it was also an age in which spinster was a term of derision and a sign of failure. Miss Nightingale, as she was known, received the British Empire's Order of Merit for her achievements. Queen Victoria, the most maternal and domestic of queens, hailed her as "an example to our sex." Nightingale was widely regarded as the greatest woman

of her age, among the most eminent of Victorians. A highly visible and outspoken reformer, Nightingale deviated from woman's unpaid role as nurturer in the private sphere. How could she be an example to the women of her time?

Florence Nightingale was hailed as a national heroine because of her work during the Crimean War in organizing hospital care at Scutari, a suburb outside Constantinople on the Asiatic side of the Bosporus. In the Crimea, she entered her own field of battle, attacking the mismanagement, corruption, and lack of organization characteristic of medical treatment for British soldiers. She campaigned for better sanitation, hygiene, ventilation, and diet, and in 1855 the death rate plummeted from 42 percent to 2 percent thanks to her efforts. The London *Times* declared, "There is not one of England's proudest and purest daughters who at the moment stands on as high a pinnacle as Florence Nightingale."

It was a pinnacle not easily scaled. Blocked by her family and publicly maligned, Nightingale struggled against prevailing norms to carve out her occupation. She was the daughter of a wealthy gentry family, and from her father she received a man's classical education. Women of her milieu were expected to be educated only in domestic arts. The fashion of the day emphasized woman's confinement to the home:

crinolines, corsets, and trains restricted movement and suggested gentility. That was the life of Nightingale's older sister, a life that "the Angel of the Crimea" fiercely resisted. Nightingale railed at the inequity of married life: "A man gains everything by marriage: he gains a 'helpmate,' but a woman does not." Her memoirs are filled with what she called her "complaints" against the plight of women.

Nightingale was not a typical working woman. She struck out on her career as a rebel. Because of her wealth, she did not need to work, yet she felt driven to be useful. Her choice of nursing much alarmed her family, who considered the occupation to be on a level with domestic service. For them, nursing was worse, in fact, because nurses worked with the naked bodies of the sick. Thus nurses were either shameless or promiscuous, or both. Nightingale shattered those taboos. She visited nursing establishments throughout Europe, traveling alone—another feat unheard of for women in her day—and studied their methods and techniques. She conceived of her own mission to serve God through caring for others.

As with any exceptional individual, character and capabilities must figure in an explanation of achievements. Nightingale was a woman of drive and discipline who refused to accept the limited choices available to Victorian women. She possessed, in her sovereign's words, "a wonderful, clear and comprehensive head." Yet her unique talents are not enough to explain her success. In many ways, Nightingale was not a rebel, but rather an embodiment of the changing values of her age. In 1860, she established a school to train nurses, just as similar institutions were being created to train young women as teachers. Those occupations were extensions of women's roles from the arena of the home into society. In keeping with their domestic roles, women remained nurturers in the classroom and at the sickbed.

Florence Nightingale spent a good part of the last 45 years of her life in a sickbed suffering from what she called "nervous fever." During that period she wrote incessantly and continued to lobby for her programs, benefiting, one of her biographers claimed, from the freedom to think and write provided by her illness. It may well be true that her invalidism protected her from the claims on her time made by her family and by society. It may also be true that she, like many of her middle-class female contemporaries, experienced debilitation or suffered from hypo-chon-dria in direct proportion to the limitations they experienced.

New occupations labeled "women's work" were essential to the expansion of industrial society. A healthy and literate population guaranteed a strong citi-

■ English nursing reformer Florence Nightingale (1820–1910) became the first woman to receive the Order of Merit for her tireless efforts during the Crimean War.

zenry, a strong army, and a strong work force. As helpmates, women entered a new work sector identified by the adjective *service*. Women were accepted as clerical workers, performing the "housekeeping" of business firms and bureaucracies.

After midcentury, gender differences, socially defined virtues for men and women, became more set. Individualism, competition, and militarism were the values of the world of

men. Familial support, nurturance, and healing were female virtues. Those were the separate and unequal worlds created by the factory and the battlefield. The virtues of the private sphere were extended into the public world with the creation of new forms of poorly paid female labor. In that sense, Florence Nightingale was not a rebel. The "Lady with the Lamp," whom fever-ridden soldiers called their mother, was another working woman.

■ Soldiers battle during the Crimean War, ca. 1855. This was the first war to be documented by photographers.

Cavour's Political Realism. Both Giuseppe Mazzini's Young Italy movement and Giuseppe Garibaldi's Red Shirts had as their goal in 1848 a united republican Italy achieved through direct popular action. But both movements had failed. Mazzini had been a moralist; and Garibaldi was a fighter. But Camillo Benso di Cavour (1810–1861) was an opportunistic politician and a realist. He knew that only as a unified nation could Italy lay claim to status as a great power in Europe. And he saw that a united Italy could be achieved only through the manipulation of diplomacy and military victory. He understood that international events could be made to serve national ends.

As premier for Piedmont-Sardinia from 1852 to 1859 and again in 1860–1861, Cavour was well placed to launch his campaign for Italian unity. The kingdom of Piedmont-Sardinia had made itself a focal point for unification efforts. Its king, Carlo-Alberto (1831–1849), had stood alone among Italian rulers in opposing Austrian domination of the Italian peninsula in 1848 and 1849. Severely defeated by the Austrians, he was forced to abdicate. He was succeeded by his son Victor Emmanuel II (1849–1861), who had the good sense to appoint Cavour as his first minister. From the start, Cavour undertook liberal administrative reforms that included tax reform, stabilization of the currency, improvement of the railway system, the creation of a transatlantic steamship system, and the support of private enterprise. With these programs, Cavour created for Piedmont-Sardinia the dynamic image of progressive change. He involved Piedmont-Sardinia in the Crimean War, thereby securing its status among the European powers.

Most important, however, was Cavour's alliance with France against Austria in 1858. Cavour shrewdly secured the French pledge of support, including military aid if necessary, against Austria in the Treaty of Plombières, signed by Napoleon III in 1858. The treaty was quickly followed by an arranged provocation against the Habsburg monarchy. Austria declared war in 1859 and was easily defeated by French forces in the battles of Magenta and Solferino. The peace, signed in November 1859 at Zurich, joined Lombardy to Piedmont-Sardinia. Cavour wielded the electoral weapon of the plebiscite—a method of direct voting that gives to electors the choice of voting for or against an important public question—to unite Tuscany, Parma, and Modena under Piedmont's king.

Cavour's approach was not without its costs. His partnership with a stronger power meant sometimes following France's lead. French bullying provoked fits of rage and forced

The Unification of Italy. By 1860, the majority of the Italian "boot" was under the rule of Piedmont-Sardinia. By 1870, the unification was complete.

took secret steps to block the advance of the Red Shirts and their leader. To seize the initiative, Cavour directed the Piedmontese army into the Papal States. After defeating the pope's troops, Cavour's men crossed into the Neapolitan state and scored important victories against forces loyal to the king of Naples. Cavour proceeded to annex southern Italy for Victor Emmanuel II, using plebiscites to seal the procedure.

A King for a United Italy.

At this point, in 1860, Garibaldi yielded his own conquered territories to the Piedmontese ruler, making possible the declaration of a united Italy under Victor Emmanuel II, who reigned as king of Italy from 1861 to 1878.

The new king of Italy was now poised to acquire Venetia, still under Austrian rule, and Rome, still ruled by Pope Pius IX, and he devoted much of his foreign policy in the 1860s to those ends. In 1866, when Austria lost a war with Prussia, Italy struck a deal with the victor and gained control of Venetia. When Prussia prevailed against France in 1870, Victor Emmanuel II took over Rome. The boot of Italy, from top to toe, was now a single nation. The pope remained in the Vatican, opposed to an Italy united under King Victor Emmanuel II. The new national government sought to impose centralization with a heavy hand and had little interest in

In this British cartoon of 1860, Garibaldi surrenders his power to Victor Emmanuel II, king of Piedmont-Sardinia (soon to be king of a united Italy). The caption reads "Right Leg in the Boot at Last."

Cavour to resign from office temporarily in 1859 over a war ended too early by Napoleon III. The need to solicit French support meant enriching France with territorial gain in the form of Nice and Savoy. However, Piedmont-Sardinia gained more than it gave up. In the summer of 1859, revolutionary assemblies in Tuscany, Modena, Parma, and the Romagna, wanting to eject their Austrian rulers, voted in favor of union with the Piedmontese. By April 1860, those four areas of central Italy were under Victor Emmanuel II's rule. Piedmont-Sardinia had doubled in size to become the dominant power on the Italian peninsula.

Southern Italians took their lead from events in central Italy and in the spring of 1860 initiated disturbances against the rule of King Francis II (1859–1861) of Naples. Uprisings in Sicily inspired Giuseppe Garibaldi to return from his self-imposed exile to organize his own army of Red Shirts, known as the Thousand, with whom he liberated Sicily and crossed to the Italian mainland to expel Francis II from Naples. Garibaldi next turned his attention to the liberation of the Holy City, where a French garrison protected the pope. After his defeat in Rome in 1849, Garibaldi had never lost sight of his mission to free all of Italy from foreign rule, even in the 1850s when he had lived on New York's Staten Island as a candlemaker and had become a naturalized citizen of the United States.

As Garibaldi's popularity as a national hero grew, Cavour became alarmed by his competing effort to unite Italy and preserving regional differences and regional cultures. Cavour's liberal constitutional principles, combined with moderately conservative stands on social issues, produced alienation, especially in southern Italy, among both the peasantry and the nobility.

Cavour did not live to see the united Italy that he had worked so hard to fashion. He had succeeded where poets and revolutionaries had failed in preparing the ground for unification because he understood that the world had changed dramatically in the first half of the nineteenth century. He appreciated the relationship between national and international events and was able to manipulate it for his own ends. Both Cavour and his counterpart in Germany, Otto von Bismarck, considered themselves realists who shared a recognition of diplomacy as an instrument of domestic policy.

Unifying Germany

MAP

The Unification of Germany

Seldom in modern history does an individual emerge as a chess master, overseeing international politics and domestic affairs as if the world were a great board game with movable pieces. Otto von Bismarck was such an individual. He was aware that he was playing a game of high risks and high stakes. His vision was limited to the pragmatic pursuit of preserving the power of his beloved Prussia. For him the empire was not an end in itself but a means of guaranteeing Prussian strength. In an age of realistic politicians, Bismarck emerged as the supreme practitioner of **Realpolitik**, the ruthless pursuit by any means, including illegal and violent ones, to advance the interests of his country.

Bismarck was a Junker, an aristocratic estate owner from east of the Elbe River, who entered politics in 1847. As a member of the United Diet of Prussia, he made his reputation as a reactionary when he rose to speak in favor of hunting privileges for the nobility: "I am a Junker and I want to enjoy the advantages of it." In the 1850s, he became aware of Prussia's future in the center of Europe: he saw that the old elites must be allied with the national movement in order to survive. The problem was that nationalism was the property of the liberals, who had been defeated in 1848. Bismarck appropriated it. Liberals and Junkers shared an interest in unification, but for different political ends. As a politician, Bismarck learned how to exploit their common ground.

Prussia's Seven Weeks' War with Austria. In 1850, Prussia had been forced to accept Austrian dominance in central Europe or go to war. Throughout the following decade, however, Prussia systematically undermined Austrian power by wielding the trade agreements of the Zollverein as a tool to exclude Austria from German economic affairs. In 1862, at the moment of a crisis provoked by the new king, Wilhelm I, over military reorganization, Bismarck became minister-president of the Prussian cabinet as well as foreign minister. He overrode the parliamentary body, the Diet, by reorganizing the Prussian army without a formally approved budget. In 1864, he constructed an alliance between Austria and Prussia for the purpose of invading Schleswig, a predominantly German-speaking territory controlled by the king of Denmark. Within five days of the invasion, Denmark yielded the duchies of Schleswig and Holstein, to be ruled jointly by Austria and Prussia.

Ascertaining that he had a free hand in central Europe, Bismarck skillfully provoked a crisis between Austria and Prussia over management of the territories. Counting on the

■ *Im Etappenquartier vor Paris,* 1871. This 1894 painting by Anton von Werner shows Prussian troops making themselves at home in a French drawing room on their way to victory in Paris. The Prussians occupied the city for only 48 hours.

MAP DISCOVERY

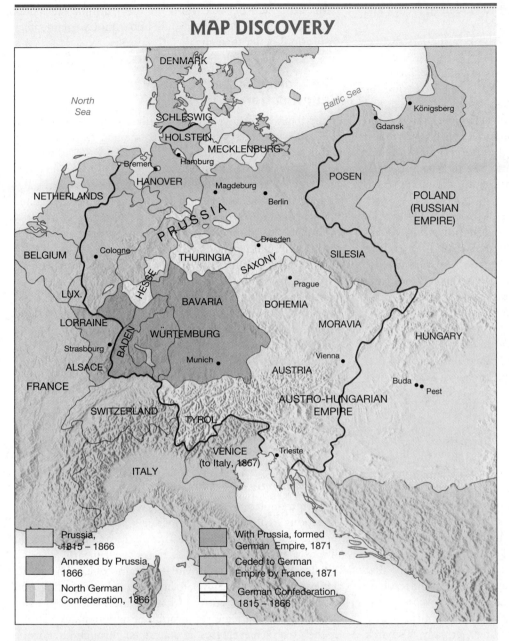

Prussia, 1815 – 1866

Annexed by Prussia, 1866

North German Confederation, 1866

With Prussia, formed German Empire, 1871

Ceded to German Empire by France, 1871

German Confederation, 1815 – 1866

The Unification of Germany

In this map, regard the diversity in size and type of political entities that were combined to form the new state of Germany. What annexation did the War of 1866 make possible? How did the peace settlement with France affect the creation of the German state? Why was the North German Confederation so important in determining the formation of the new German Empire?

---

a united Germany in which Prussia would be the dominant force. Austria's exclusion from Germany forced the Austrian government to deal with its own internal problems of imperial organization. In 1867, in response to pressures from the subject nationalities, the Habsburg Empire transformed itself into a dual monarchy of two independent and equal states under one ruler, who would be both the emperor of Austria and the king of Hungary. In spite of the reorganization, the problem of nationalities persisted, and ethnic groups began to agitate for total independence from imperial rule.

The Franco-Prussian War. Bismarck's biggest obstacle to German unification was laid to rest with Austria's defeat. The south German states, however, continued to resist the idea of Prussian dominance, but growing numbers of people in Baden, Württemberg, Bavaria, and the southern parts of Hesse-Darmstadt recognized the necessity of uniting under Prussian leadership.

Many French observers were troubled by the Prussian victory over Austria and were apprehensive over what a united Germany might portend for the future of French dominance in Europe. Napoleon III attempted unsuccessfully to contain Prussian ambitions through diplomatic maneuverings. Instead, France found itself stranded without important European allies. In the spring of 1870, Bismarck decided to seize the initiative and provoke a crisis with France.

neutrality of France and Great Britain, the support of Piedmont-Sardinia, and good relations with Russia, Bismarck led his country into war with Austria in June 1866. In this Seven Weeks' War, Austrian forces proved to be no match for the better-equipped and better-trained Prussian army. Bismarck dictated the terms of the peace, which demonstrated that he had no desire to cripple Austria, only to exclude it from

Bismarck recognized that war with France could be the dramatic event needed to forge cooperation and unity among all German states. The issue of succession to the Spanish throne gave him the opportunity he sought. Bismarck skillfully created the impression that the French ambassador had insulted the Prussian king, then leaked news of the incident to the press in both countries. Enraged and inflamed French and Prussian publics both demanded war.

As a direct result of this contrived misunderstanding, France declared war on Prussia in July 1870. As Bismarck hoped, the southern German princes immediately sided with the Prussian king. For years before hostilities broke out, the Prussians had been preparing for war. They had been sending Prussian army officers disguised as landscape painters into France to study the terrain of battle. French troops carried maps of Germany but were ignorant of the geography of their own country, where the battles were waged. Sent into battle against the Germans, French troops roamed around in search of their commanders and each other.

The Germans had learned new deployment strategies from studying the use of railroads in the American Civil War of 1861–1865. Unlike the Germans, the French had not coordinated deployment with the new technology of the railroad. Although French troops had the latest equipment, they were sent into battle without instructions on how to use it. Finally, the Prussian-led German army was superior, outnumbering French troops 450,000 to 260,000. All those factors combined to spell disaster for the French. Within a matter of weeks, it was clear that France had lost the Franco-Prussian War, and its eastern territories of Alsace and Lorraine. The path was now clear for the declaration of the German Empire in January 1871.

Prussian Dominance of United Germany. The newly established Second Reich, successor to the Holy Roman Empire, united the German states into a single nation. After years of foreign wars and endless wrangling among the heads of the 38 German states, Bismarck obtained what he wanted: a German Empire under the leadership of the Prussian king. The Proclamation of the German Empire was signed on 21 January 1871 in a ceremony in the French palace of Versailles. Bismarck, always the pragmatist, understood clearly that Europe was not the same place that it had been a decade or two earlier. "Anyone who speaks of Europe is wrong—it is nothing but a set of national expressions." That understanding was the key to his success. In unifying Germany, Bismarck built on the constitution of the North German Confederation formed in 1867, which guaranteed Prussian dominance. Bismarck used the bureaucracy as a mainstay of the emperor. The new **Reichstag**—the national legislative assembly—was to be elected by means of universal male suffrage, a concession to the liberals. Yet the constitution was not a liberal one, since the Reichstag was not sovereign and the chancellor was accountable only to the emperor. Policy was made outside the domain of electoral politics. The federal structure of the constitution, especially with regard to taxation, also kept the central parliament weak. Most liberals supported the constitution, but a minority persisted in a tradition of radical dissent. Critics believed that true constitutional government had been sacrificed to the demands of empire. As one liberal remarked, "Unity without freedom is a unity of slaves." Bismarck spoke in confidence of his aim "to destroy parliamentarianism by parliamentarianism." According to that formula, Bismarck hoped that a weak Reichstag would undermine parliamentary institutions better than any dictatorial ruler.

The United States: Civil War and Reunification

In the 1860s, another crisis in state building was resolved across the Atlantic. The United States cemented political unity through the use of force in its Civil War (1861–1865). The president of the United States, Abraham Lincoln (1809–1865), mobilized the superior resources of the industrial Northern states against the heavily agrarian, slave-owning South. The United States worked to achieve national unity and territorial integrity in another sense through ongoing expansion westward by eliminating and subduing Native American peoples.

With the emancipation of the slaves, republican democracy appeared to triumph in the United States. Newly created European nation-states followed a different path: Plebiscites were manipulated by those in power in Italy, and a neo-absolutism emerged in Germany. Yet the Civil War in the United States and the successful bids for unification in Italy and Germany shared remarkable similarities. In all three countries, wars eventually resulted in a single national market and a single financial system without internal barriers. Unified national economies, particularly in Germany and the United States, paved the way for significant economic growth and the expansion of industrial power.

Nationalism and Force

It is commonplace in the Western historical tradition to speak of nations as if they were individuals possessing emotions, making choices, taking actions, having ideas. "Russia turned inward"; "Germany chose its enemies as well as its friends"; "France vowed revenge"; "Great Britain took pride in its achievements." On one level, to attribute volition, feeling, and insight to an abstract entity such as a nation is nonsense. But on another level, the personification of nation-states was one of the great achievements of statesmen throughout Europe between 1850 and 1870. The language and symbols they put in place created the nation itself, a new political reality whose forms contained a modern political consciousness. The nation-state became an all-knowing being whose rights had to be protected, whose destiny had to be assured.

The nation was above all a creation that minimized or denied real differences in dialect and language, regional loyalties, local traditions, and village identities. The crises in state building in Italy and Germany had been resolved finally by violence. No power was acknowledged to exist above the nation-state. No power could sanction the nation's actions but itself. Force was an acceptable alternative to diplomacy. War was a political act and a political instrument, a continuation of political relations. Violence and nationalism were inextricably linked in the unification of both Italy and Germany in the third quarter of the nineteenth century.

National unification had escaped the grasp of liberals and radicals between 1848 and 1850 with the failure of revolutionary and reform movements. In the 1850s and 1860s, those committed to national transformations worked from within the existing system. The new realists subordinated liberal nationalism to the needs of conservative state building. Military force validated what intellectuals and revolutionaries had not been able to legitimate through ideological claims.

REFORMING EUROPEAN SOCIETY

After the revolutions of 1848, government repression silenced radical movements throughout Europe. But repression could not maintain social harmony and promote growth and prosperity. In the third quarter of the nineteenth century, Europe's leaders recognized that reforms were needed to build dynamic and competitive states. Three different models for social and political reform developed in France, Great Britain, and Russia after 1850. All three sets of reforms took place in unified nation-states. The three societies had little in common with each other ideologically, but all reflected a commitment to progress and an awareness of the state's role and responsibility in achieving it.

The Second Empire in France, 1852–1870

One model was that of France, where the French emperor worked through a highly centralized administrative structure and with a valued elite of specialists to achieve social and economic transformations. The French model was a technocratic one that emphasized the importance of specialized knowledge to achieve material progress. Reform in France relied on both autocratic direction and liberal participation.

Napoleon III. Napoleon III ruled France from the middle of the century until 1870. His apprenticeship for political leadership had been an unusual one. Louis Napoleon (1808–1873) was a nephew of the emperor Napoleon I. The child Louis, born at the peak of French glory, was old enough to remember the devastation of his uncle's defeat in 1815. He dedicated his exiled youth to preparing for his family's restoration as rulers of France. With the death of Napoleon's son, the duc de Reichstadt, in 1832, Louis was aware that the mantle of future power and the family destiny fell to him.

In comparing Louis Napoleon with his uncle, Napoleon I, Karl Marx observed that history happens the first time as tragedy and the second time as farce. There was much that passed as farcical before Louis Napoleon established France's Second Empire in 1852, as one attempt after another to seize power failed. Yet those who viewed Louis Napoleon as a figure of derision were misled: by 1848 he understood the importance of shaping public opinion to suit his own ends. He wielded the Napoleonic legend to play on the dissatisfaction of millions. He understood that to succeed in an electoral system, he had to promise something to everyone. He spoke of

prosperity, order, and the end of poverty, slogans that sent different and incompatible messages to a bourgeoisie who wanted social peace, workers who wanted jobs and social justice, and peasants who wanted land and freedom from taxes. As the dark-horse candidate, he swept the field and in December 1848 became France's first president elected by universal manhood suffrage. The politicians were sure that he could be managed, so insignificant did he seem. They and the rest of France were literally caught sleeping before dawn on 2 December 1851 when the nephew of the great Napoleon seized power in a coup d'état and became dictator of France. Exactly one year later, he proclaimed himself Emperor Napoleon III and set about the tasks of establishing his dynasty and reclaiming French imperial glory.

Napoleon III's regime has been condemned for its decadence and its spectacle. On the surface, the world of the Second Empire glittered like a fancy-dress ball, with men in sparkling uniforms and women in full-skirted, low-necked gowns waltzing to gay tunes. Courtesans in open carriages, parading through the newly landscaped Bois de Boulogne, became as famous as cabinet members. But to judge the empire on superficial criteria alone would be a mistake. The Second Empire achieved significant successes in a variety of areas. Napoleon III supported economic expansion and industrial development. During his reign, the French economy prospered and flourished. The discovery of gold in California and Australia fueled a demand for French products in international markets and initiated a period of sustained economic growth that lasted beyond Napoleon III's reign into the 1880s. A new private banking system, founded in 1852 by financiers and key political figures, enabled the pooling of investors' resources, small and large, to finance industrial expansion. Stable authoritarian government encouraged increased investment in state public works programs.

Napoleon III surrounded himself with advisers who saw in prosperity the answer to all social problems. Between 1852 and 1860, the government supported a massive program of railroad construction. Jobs multiplied and investment increased. Agriculture expanded as railroad lines opened new markets. The rich became richer, but the extreme poverty of the first half of the nineteenth century was diminishing. Brutal misery in city and countryside did not disappear, but on the whole, the standard of living increased as wages rose faster than prices.

Rebuilding Paris. The best single example of the energy and commitment of the imperial regime was the rebuilding of the French capital. As Sir Edwin Chadwick (1800–1890), Britain's leading public health reformer, put it, Napoleon III found Paris stinking and left it sweet. Before midcentury, Paris was one of the most unsanitary, crime-ridden, and politically volatile capitals in Europe. Within 15 years it had been transformed into a city of lights, wide boulevards and avenues, monumental vistas, parks, and gardens. Napoleon III was the architect of the idea for a new Paris, something his uncle never had the time or resources to accomplish. But the real credit for

■ Inauguration of the Boulevard du Prince-Eugenè during the rebuilding of Paris. The renovations were carried out under the direction of Baron Georges Haussmann, who was called "the Attila of the Straight Line" for the ruthless manner in which his pencil cut through city neighborhoods on the map.

carrying through the municipal improvements should be attributed to Baron Georges Haussmann (1809–1891).

As Prefect of the Seine from 1853 to 1870, Baron Haussmann typified the technocrat in power. He was called "the Attila of the Straight Line" for the ruthless manner in which his protractor cut through city neighborhoods, destroying all that lay in his pencil's path. Poor districts were turned into rubble to make way for the elegant apartment buildings of the Parisian bourgeoisie. The new housing was too expensive for workers, who were pushed out of Paris into the suburbs. The boundaries of the city expanded. As workers from all over France migrated to the capital in search of jobs, the population nearly doubled, increasing by just under one million in the 1850s and 1860s. A poor and volatile population encircled the city of monuments and museums. Paris as the radical capital of France was being physically dismantled and a new, more conservative political entity rose in its place as the middle classes took over the heart of the city. The process was very different from the development of other urban areas such as London, where the middle class fled to the suburbs, leaving behind the problems of urban life.

Much has been made of the policing benefits of rebuilding the city of Paris. Wider streets facilitated the movement of troops, which could more easily crush revolutionary disturbances. While the control aspect of urban reconstruction was not lost on Haussmann and Napoleon III, it was not the

primary purpose of the vast public works project that lasted for the whole regime. Napoleon wanted Paris to be the center of Western culture and the envy of the world. Its wide, straight avenues served as the model for other French cities. The new Paris became an international model copied in Mexico City, Brussels, Madrid, Rome, Stockholm, and Barcelona between 1870 and 1900. American city planners of the City Beautiful movement were also influenced by the "Haussmannization" of Paris. In spite of financial scandals that plagued the reconstruction near the end of the regime, few disputed that Napoleon III had transformed Paris into one of the world's most beautiful cities.

The Foreign Policy of the Second Empire. Just as a new Paris would make France the center of culture, Napoleon III intended his blueprint for foreign policy to restore France to its pre-1815 status as the greatest European power. By involving France in both the Crimean War and the war for Italian unification, Napoleon III returned France to adventurous foreign policies. The emperor had undertaken both wars with the hope of further increasing French economic and diplomatic prominence on the Continent. Napoleon III supported Piedmont-Sardinia not out of any sense of altruism, in spite of his claim that he was "doing something for Italy." The accession of Nice and Savoy increased French territory—and reversed the settlements of 1815.

The Italian campaign complicated relations with Great Britain, which feared a resurgent French militarism. French construction of the Suez Canal between the Red Sea and the Mediterranean also created tensions with Great Britain, protective of its own dominance in the Mediterranean and the Near East. Nevertheless, the free-trade agreement between the British and the French in 1860—the Chevalier-Cobden Treaty—was a landmark in overseas policy and a commitment to liberal economic policies.

The Second Empire's involvement in Mexico was a fiasco. The Mexican government had been chronically unable to pay its foreign debts, and France was Mexico's largest creditor. Napoleon III hoped that by intervening in Mexican affairs he could strengthen ties with Great Britain and Spain, to whom the Mexicans also owed money. The emperor planned to turn Mexico into a satellite empire that would be economically profitable to France. The United States, occupied with civil war, did not interfere in 1861 when Napoleon III sent a military expedition to "pacify" the Mexican countryside. With the backing of Mexican conservatives who opposed Mexican president Benito Juárez (1806–1872), Napoleon III supported the Austrian archduke Maximilian (1832–1867) as emperor of Mexico. After he was crowned in 1863, the new Mexican emperor struggled to rule in an enlightened manner, but he was stymied from the beginning by his ineptitude and lack of popular support. Following the recall of the 34,000 French troops that, at considerable expense, were keeping Maximilian's troubled regime in place, Maximilian was captured and executed by a firing squad in the summer of 1867. The Mexican disaster damaged the prestige of Napoleon III's

■ Édouard Manet, *The Execution of the Emperor Maximilian* (1868). The United States pressured France to withdraw support for the Mexican imperial venture, which led to disaster for Maximilian and the reinstatement of Benito Juárez as president of Mexico.

regime in the international arena. Intensely aware of public criticism, the emperor undertook the reorganization of the army and a series of liberal reforms, including increasing parliamentary participation in affairs of state, and granting to trade unions the right of assembly.

The Prussian victory over Austria in the Seven Weeks' War had dramatically changed the situation on the Continent. Pundits in Paris were fond of saying that the Austrian loss really marked the defeat of France. France's position within Europe was threatened, and Napoleon III knew it. In 1870, the humiliatingly rapid defeat of French imperial forces in the Franco-Prussian War brought to an end the experiment in liberal empire.

In 1870, France remained a mixture of old and new. Although industrial production had doubled between 1852 and 1870, France was still an agricultural nation. Foreign trade expanded by 300 percent, growing faster than that of any other nation in Europe. Six times as many miles of railroad track crisscrossed France at the time Napoleon III went into exile as when he came into power. Napoleon III did not create the economic boom from which all of Europe benefited between 1850 and 1880, but he did build on it, using the state to stimulate and enhance prosperity. His policies favored business and initiated a financial revolution of enduring benefits. However, the technocratic model of rule by specialists was not applied to the

army in forcing it to modernize. Nor had foreign policy benefited from the careful calculations employed in domestic administration. The empire had become the victim of its own myth of invincibility.

Victorian Political Reforms

Great Britain provided another model of reform, which was fostered through liberal parliamentary democracy. In government by "amateurs," with local rather than a highly centralized administration, British legislation alternated between a philosophy of freedom and one of protection. But reforms were always hammered out by parliamentary means with the support of a gradually expanding electorate.

Parliamentary Reforms. Contemporaries were aware of two facts of life about Great Britain in 1850: first, that Britain had an enormously productive capitalist economy of sustained growth, and second, that Britain enjoyed apparent social harmony without revolution and without civil war. As revolutions ravaged continental Europe in 1848, the British took pride in a parliamentary system that valued a tradition of freedom. British statesmen were not reluctant to point out to the rest of the world that Great Britain had achieved industrial growth without rending the social fabric.

The political rhetoric of stability and calm was undoubtedly exaggerated. Great Britain at midcentury had its share of serious social problems. British slums rivaled any in Europe. Poverty, disease, and famine ravaged the kingdom. Many feared that British social protests of the 1840s would result in upheavals similar to those in continental Europe. Yet Great Britain avoided a revolution. One explanation for Britain's relative calm lay in the shared political tradition that emphasized liberty as the birthright of English citizens. Building on an established political culture, the British Parliament was able to adapt to the demands of an industrializing society. Adaptation was gradual, but as slow as it seemed, a compromise was achieved among competing social interests. The great compromise of Victorian society was the reconciliation of industrialists' commitment to unimpeded growth with workers' need for the protection of the state. The British political system was democratized slowly after 1832.

The Reform Bill of that year gave increased political power to the industrial and manufacturing bourgeoisie, who joined a landed aristocracy and merchant class. The property qualification meant that only 20 percent of the population was able to vote. The next step toward democracy was not taken for another 35 years. In 1867, under conservative leadership, a second Reform Bill was introduced. Approval of the bill doubled the electorate, giving the vote to a new urban population of shopkeepers, clerks, and workers. In 1884, farm laborers were enfranchised. Women, however, remained disfranchised; they were not granted the vote until after World War I. Through parliamentary cooperation between Liberals and Conservatives, the male franchise was slowly implemented without a revolution.

Gladstone and Disraeli.
The lives and careers of two men, William Ewart Gladstone (1809–1898) and Benjamin Disraeli (1804–1881), exemplify the particular path the British

government followed in maintaining social peace. Rivals and political opponents, both men served as prime ministers and both left their mark on the age. From different political perspectives, they contributed to British reform in the second half of the nineteenth century.

William Gladstone was an example of a British statesman with no counterpart elsewhere in Europe: he was a classical liberal who believed in free enterprise and was opposed to state intervention. Good government, according to Gladstone, should remove obstacles to talent, competition, and individual initiative but should interfere as little as possible in economy and society. Surprisingly, the leader of the Liberal party began his long parliamentary career at the other end of the political spectrum, as a Tory. The son of a successful merchant and slave trader, Gladstone enjoyed the benefits of wealth and attended Eton and Oxford, where he studied classics and mathematics. Discouraged by his father from a career in the Church of England, Gladstone used his connections to launch a parliamentary career in 1832. He gradually left behind his conservative opposition to parliamentary reform and his support of protective tariffs. In 1846, as a member of the government, Gladstone broke with Tory principles and voted in favor of free trade. The best government, he affirmed in true liberal fashion, was the one that governed least.

Those who knew Gladstone in the early years were struck not by his brilliance but by his capacity for hard work and assiduous application to the task at hand. He chopped wood for relaxation. In his spare time he wrote a three-volume study on Homer and the Homeric age. He practiced an overt morality, targeting prostitutes in the hope of convincing them to change their lives. Gladstone was not blind to social problems, but he considered private philanthropy the best way to correct them.

Many of the significant advances of the British liberal state were achieved during Gladstone's first term as prime minister

■ William Gladstone rides in an omnibus in this painting titled *One of the People* by Alfred Morgan. This mode of transport was thought of as a social leveler because all classes of people could afford the fares.

(1868–1874). Taking advantage of British prosperity, Gladstone abolished tariffs, cut defense expenditures, lowered taxes, and sponsored sound budgets. He furthered the liberal agenda by disestablishing the Anglican Church in Ireland in 1869. The Church had been the source of great resentment to the vast majority of Irish Catholics, who had been forced to pay taxes to support the Protestant state church.

Gladstone reformed the army, in disrepute after its poor performance in the Crimea, so that commissions no longer could be purchased. Training and merit would have to justify all future advancements. Similarly, Gladstone reformed the civil service system by separating it from political influence and seniority. A merit system and examinations were intended to ensure the most efficient and effective government administration. The secret ballot was introduced to prevent coercion in voting. Finally, the Liberals stressed the importance of education for an informed electorate and passed an education act that aimed to make elementary schooling available to everyone.

The reforms added up to a liberal philosophy of government. Liberal government was, above all, an attack on privilege. It sought to remove restraints on individual freedom and to foster opportunity and talent. Liberal government sought to protect democracy through education. Voting men must be educated men. As one Liberal put it, "We must educate our masters." Liberals governed in the interests of the bourgeoisie and with the belief that what was good for capitalism was good for society. Tariffs, therefore, were kept low or eliminated to promote British commerce. Gladstone believed that all political questions were moral questions and that fairness and justice could solve political problems. In spite of his moral claims, his programs made him enemies among special interests, including farmers and the Church of England, because his policies undermined their security and privileges.

During those years, another political philosophy also left its mark on British government. It was conservatism. Under the flamboyant leadership of Benjamin Disraeli, the Conservative party supported state intervention and regulation on behalf of the weak and disadvantaged. Disraeli sponsored the Factory Act of 1875, which set a maximum of 56 hours for the factory work week. The Public Health Act established a sanitary code. The Artisans Dwelling Act defined minimum housing standards. Probably the most important conservative legislation was the Trade Union Act, which permitted picketing and other peaceful labor tactics.

Disraeli's personal background and training were very different from Gladstone's and made him unique in British parliamentary politics. He was known primarily as a novelist, social critic, and failed financier before he entered the political arena in 1837. His father was a Jewish merchant descended from a family of Spanish refugees in Venice. The senior Disraeli became a British subject in 1801, three years before Benjamin's birth. In embracing English culture, the senior Disraeli had his children baptized in the Anglican Church.

The split between Disraeli and Gladstone was clearly apparent in 1846 when they, both Tories, disagreed over the issue of free trade versus tariffs. Disraeli moved on to champion protection and throughout the early 1860s consistently opposed Gladstone's financial system. Unlike the Liberals, Disraeli insisted on the importance of traditional institutions including the monarchy, the House of Lords, and the Church of England. Queen Victoria named him the First Earl of Beaconsfield for his strong foreign policy and social reforms. "Dizzy's" real cleverness and contribution to British politics were in an area that few contemporaries appreciated at the time. Disraeli's work in organizing a national party machinery facilitated the adaptation of the parliamentary system to mass politics. His methods of campaigning and building a mass base of support were used by successful politicians regardless of political persuasion.

The terms liberal and conservative hold none of the meaning today that they did for men and women in the nineteenth century. Classical liberalism has little in common with its twenty-first-century counterpart, which favors an active interventionist state. Disraeli is a far more likely candidate for the twenty-first-century liberal label than is Britain's leading nineteenth-century liberal statesman, Gladstone. Disraeli placed value in the ability of the state to correct and protect. Because of his interventionist philosophy, he may be compared with the Continental statesmen Bismarck and Napoleon III.

■ This *Punch* cartoon, "Rival Actors," depicts William Gladstone (left) as popular character William Tell exiting the stage, while Benjamin Disreali (right), as farcical character Jeremy Diddler, sulks in the wings.

In spite of Liberal hopes, Great Britain never had a purely laissez-faire economy. As the intersecting careers of Gladstone and Disraeli demonstrate, the British model combined free enterprise with intervention and regulation. The clear issues and the clear choices of the two great parties—Liberal and Conservative—dominated parliamentary life after mid-century. In polarizing parliamentary politics, the parties also invigorated it.

Reforming Russia

Russia offered a third model for reform in the nineteenth century. Like Britain, Russia had avoided revolution at midcentury. Like Britain, it hoped to preserve social peace. Yet the Russian model for reform stands in dramatic contrast to Britain's. Russia was an unreformed autocracy, a form of government in which the tsar held absolute power. Without a parliament, a constitution, or civil liberties for its subjects, the Russian ruler governed through a bureaucracy and a police force. Russia was a semifeudal agrarian economy with a class of privileged aristocrats supported by serf labor on their estates.

A Serf-Holding Nation. For decades—since the reign of Alexander I (1801–1825)—the tsars and their advisers realized that they were out of step with developments in western Europe. An awareness was growing that serfdom was uncivilized and morally wrong. The remnants of feudalism had been

■ Russian Serfs. Serfdom was created in the sixteenth century as a system of virtual enslavement of Russian peasants. Its greatest density was in areas with a strong presence of landed gentry.

swept away in France in the Great Revolution at the end of the eighteenth century. Prussia had abolished hereditary serfdom beginning in 1806. Among the European powers, only Russia remained a serf-holding nation. Russian serfs were tied to the land and owed dues and labor services in return for the lands they held. Peasant protests mounted, attracting public attention to the plight of the serfs. A Russian aristocrat, Baron N. Wrangel (1847–1920), recounted in his memoirs a story from his childhood in the 1850s, when he was about ten years old, that exemplifies the growing social awareness of the problem:

> One day we were sitting quietly on the terrace listening to the reading aloud of *Uncle Tom's Cabin,* a recently translated book that was then in fashion. My sisters could not get over the horrors of slavery and wept at the sad fate of poor Uncle Tom. "I cannot conceive," said one of them, "how such atrocities can be tolerated. Slavery is horrible." "But," said Bunny, in her shrill little voice, "we have slaves too."

In spite of growing moral concern, there were many reasons to resist the abolition of serfdom. Granting freedom to all serfs was a vastly complicated affair. How were serf-holders to be compensated for the loss of labor power? What was to be the freed serf's relationship to the land? Personal freedom would be worthless without a land allotment. Yet landowners opposed loss of land as strongly as loss of their work force. A landless work force would be a serious social threat, if western European experience could be taken as an example.

Alexander II and the Emancipation of the Serfs. Hesitation about abolition evaporated with the Russian defeat in the Crimean War. The new tsar, Alexander II (1855–1881), viewed Russia's inability to repel an invasion force on its own soil as proof of its backwardness. Russia had no railroads and was forced to transport military supplies by carts to the Crimea. It took Moscow three months to provision troops, whereas the enemy could do so in three weeks. Alexander II believed in taking matters into his own hands. Russia must be reformed. Abolition of serfdom would permit a well-trained reserve army to exist without fear of rebellion. Liberating the serfs would also create a system of free labor so necessary for industrial development. Alexander interpreted rumblings within his own country as the harbinger of future upheavals similar to those that had rocked France and the Austrian Empire. He explained to the Muscovite nobility, "It is better to abolish serfdom from above than to wait until the serfs begin to liberate themselves from below."

In March 1861, the tsar signed the emancipation edict that liberated the serfs. Serfdom was eliminated in Poland three years later. Alexander II, who came to be known as the "Tsar-Liberator," compromised between landlord and serf by allotting land to freed peasants, while requiring from the former serfs redemption payments that were spread out over a period of 49 years. The peasant paid the state in installments; the state reimbursed the landowner in lump sums. To guarantee repayment, the land was not granted directly to individual

THE RUSSIAN EMANCIPATION PROCLAMATION, 1861

Aleksandr Vasilievich Nikitenko, a former serf who had managed through luck and talent to gain an education and a place in the Russian bureaucracy, recorded the joy and excitement he and others felt when Alexander II freed Russia's serfs. Many hoped, and some feared, that the change would revolutionize Russian agriculture and society.

Focus Questions

How do you explain the joy of this state bureaucrat in learning of the emancipation of the serfs? Why was the manor serf who is quoted here indignant about the ongoing obligations of the manor serfs?

5 March. A great day: the emancipation manifesto! I received a copy around noon. I cannot express my joy at reading this precious act which scarcely has its equal in the thousand-year history of the Russian people. I read it aloud to my wife, my children and a friend of ours in my study, under Alexander II's portrait, as we gazed at it with deep reverence and gratitude. I tried to explain to my ten-year-old son as simply as possible the essence of the manifesto and bid him to keep inscribed in his heart forever the date of March 5 and the name of Alexander II, the Liberator.

I couldn't stay at home. I had to wander about the streets and mingle, so to say, with my regenerated fellow citizens. Announcements from the governor-general were posted at all crossways, and knots of people were gathered around them. One would read while the others listened. I encountered happy, but calm faces everywhere. Here and there people were reading the proclamation aloud, and, as I walked, I continually caught phrases like "decree on liberty," "freedom." One fellow who was reading the announcement and reached the place where it said that manor serfs were obligated to their masters for another two years, exclaimed indignantly "The hell with this paper! Two years? I'll do nothing of the sort." The others remained silent. I ran into my friend, Galakhov. "Christ has risen!" I said to him. "He has indeed!" he answered, and we expressed our great joy to each other.

Then I went to see Rebinder. He ordered champagne and we drank a toast to Alexander II.

From Aleksandr Nikitenko, *The Diary of a Russian Censor* (1861).

---

peasants but to the village commune (*mir*), which was responsible for collecting redemption payments.

Emancipation of the serfs, Alexander's greatest achievement, was a reform of unprecedented scale. It affected 52 million peasants, more than 20 million of them enserfed to private landowners. By comparison, Abraham Lincoln's Emancipation Proclamation less than two years later freed four million American slaves. However, beneath the surface of the Russian liberation, peasants soon realized that the repayment schedule increased their burdens and responsibilities. The peasants resented being forced to pay for land they considered rightfully theirs. An old peasant saying reflected that belief: "We are yours"—they acknowledged to the landlords—"but the land is ours." It was not an accident that the mir arrangement prevented mobility; Alexander had no intention of creating a floating proletariat similar to that of western Europe. He wanted his people closely tied to the land, but freed from the servility of feudal obligations.

Russian Serfs

The abolition of serfdom did not solve the problem of Russian backwardness. Farming methods and farming implements remained primitive. Russian agriculture did not become more productive. Nor did emancipation result in a contented and loyal peasantry. Frustrations festered. A large proportion of peasants received too little land to make their redemption payments. Many peasants in the south received smaller plots of land than they had farmed under serfdom. The commune replaced the landowner in a system of peasant bondage. Redemption payments were finally abolished in 1907, but not before exacerbating social tensions in the countryside.

The Great Reforms.   The real winner in the abolition of serfdom was not the landowners, and certainly not the peasantry, but the state. A bureaucratic hierarchy and a financial infrastructure were expanded. Other reforms in the system of credit and banking contributed significantly to rapid economic growth. With the help of foreign—especially French—investment, railway construction increased dramatically, from 660 miles of track in 1855 to 14,000 by 1880. Thanks in large part to the new transportation network, Russia became a world grain supplier during the period, with exports increasing threefold. But development was uneven and remained uncoordinated. The coexistence of the old alongside the new, combined with the speed of change, created friction and promised future unrest.

Alexander II, a man conservative by temperament but aware that Russia must move forward, did not stop there. In 1864, he introduced **zemstvos**, local elected assemblies on the provincial and county levels, to govern local affairs. The three classes of landowners, townspeople, and peasants elected representatives who were responsible for implementing educational, health, and other social welfare reforms. Similar statutes governing towns were passed in 1870. In the spirit of modernization, the state also undertook judicial reforms. New provincial courts were opened in 1866. Corporal punishment was to be eliminated. Separate courts for peasants still endured, however, preserving the impression that peasants were a lower class of citizens subject to different jurisdiction.

With the military triumph of Prussia over France in 1870–1871, the tsar found the excuse he had been looking for in the 1860s to push through fundamental military reforms. Alexander II had admired the Prussian military model since his childhood. In 1874 he used that model to require that all young men upon reaching the age of 20 be eligible for conscription "in defense of the fatherland." Fifteen years of service were specified, but only six were served in active duty. That was a significant reduction from the 25 years of active service that peasant and lower-class conscripts had formerly served. Although length of service was reduced according to educational level, the military reforms were, on the whole, democratizing because they eliminated an important privilege of the wealthy.

In spite of the vast array of "Great Reforms"—emancipating the serfs, creating local parliamentary bodies, reorganizing the judiciary, and modernizing the army—Russia was not sufficiently liberalized or democratized to satisfy the critics of autocracy. Between 1860 and 1870, a young generation of intelligentsia, radical intellectuals who benefited from the democratization of education and were influenced by the rhetoric of revolution in the West, assumed a critical stance in protest against the existing order. Although not itself a class, many members of the intelligentsia shared a similar background as the student sons and daughters of petty officials or priests. Young women, who often sought the education in Switzerland that was denied to them at home, were especially active in supporting ideas of emancipation.

The Populist Movement. In 1873, the imperial government considered the Western liberal and socialist ideas of the intelligentsia so threatening that it ordered Russian students studying in Switzerland to return home. Many returning students combined forces with radical intellectuals in Russia and decided to "go to the people." About 2500 educated young men and women traveled from village to village to educate, to help, and, in some cases, to attempt to radicalize the peasants. The populist crusaders sought to learn from what they considered to be the source of all morality and justice, the Russian peasantry. They paid dearly for what proved to be a fruitless commitment to populism in the mass trials and repression of the late 1870s.

Some of the tsarist regime's critics fled into exile to reemerge as revolutionaries in western Europe, where they continued to oppose the tsarist regime and helped shape the tradition of revolution and dissent in Western countries. Other educated men and women who remained in Russia chose violence as the only effective weapon against absolute rule. Terrorists who called themselves "Will of the People" decided to assassinate the tsar; in the "emperor hunt" that followed, numerous attempts were made on the tsar's life. Miraculously, Alexander II escaped even the bombing of his own living quarters in the Winter Palace. The tsarist state responded with stricter controls, but repression only fanned the flames of discontent.

In response to attempts on his life and the assassination of public officials, which were intended to cripple the central regime, Alexander II put the brakes on reform in the second

■ Russian peasants at a village meeting. With the abolition of serfdom in 1861, village leaders gained considerable power.

half of his reign. The Great Reforms could not be undone, however, and they had set in motion sweeping economic and social changes. The state encouraged capitalist growth and witnessed the rise of a professional middle class and the formation of an embryonic factory proletariat. Serfdom was dead forever. Yet reforms had increased expectations for an equally dramatic political transformation that failed to materialize. In the end, the "Will of the People" movement succeeded in its mission. A terrorist bomb killed Alexander II, the "Tsar-Liberator," in St. Petersburg in 1881.

Growth of Russia to 1914

The Politics of Leadership

Modern politics emerged in Europe only after 1850. Until that time, traditional political categories had prevailed. When faced with revolutionary upheavals, regimes aimed for stability and permanence. Only after 1850 did a new breed of political leader appear who understood the world of politics and directed it to their own ends. Three statesmen typified the new approach to the public world of power: Camillo di Cavour, Otto von Bismarck, and Louis Napoleon.

The Demise of Royal Authority.   In Old Regime Europe, power flowed downward from the monarch, who was perched atop a hierarchically organized social system often depicted as a pyramid. The source of royal power was both timeless and historic. As God's appointed agents, the sovereigns of Europe reinforced their right to rule with the continuity of their dynasties. Men of great political acumen ministered to their royal masters and were legitimated by royal power. In the years between 1789 and 1850, that system was challenged as kings were displaced—sometimes restored to power, sometimes executed. Divine authority was an archaic idea to the growing numbers of those who spoke of democratic principles and rallied to banners that represented new concepts of liberty and equality.

In the first half of the nineteenth century, men and women had learned that those in power could be questioned. The good of the people was the primary justification for government. Power now flowed upward from the citizenry to their appointed and elected representatives. The new power brokers were those who could control and direct the flow, not merely be carried along or swept away by it. The new political men were realists in the same tradition as Machiavelli and reflected the new political culture of the nineteenth century.

Political realists such as Cavour, Bismarck, and Louis Napoleon understood the importance of public opinion. Public opinion had been a central fact of political life from the eighteenth century, but as revolutionary events in France demonstrated, public opinion proved unreliable building material for a stable government. The new political leaders appreciated public opinion for what it was—an unreliable guide for policy making, often a dangerous beast that had to be controlled and tamed. But above all, it was a tool for the shaping of consensus, the molding of support. The new political realists also understood the power of the press. Cavour achieved first prominence

and then power by founding his own newspaper, *Il Risorgimento*. Louis Napoleon ran Europe's first modern political campaign, manipulating the printed word to shape his image and tailor his message to different audiences. Bismarck used public opinion and fashioned an image of German power that served his political ends.

The Supremacy of the Nation-State.   The new political men also shared, to varying degrees, a disregard for traditional morality in decision making. As Bismarck succinctly put it at the end of his long career in public life, "Politics ruins the character." The new political men forged their own standards by which they judged the correctness of decisions and policies.

DOCUMENT

A Letter from Bismarck

The nation-state was the supreme justification for all actions. Cavour, Bismarck, and Louis Napoleon saw struggle as the central fact of life. Nation-states were inherently competitive, with conflicting objectives. Realpolitik meant that statesmen had to think in terms of military capability, technological dominance, and the acceptable use of force. Without a traditional morality of right and wrong, the leaders recognized that there could be no arbiter outside the interests of the nation-state. From exile in England following his military defeat and his abdication, Napoleon III placed the welfare of France above his failed ambitions. At the former emperor's funeral, his son led a cheer, not for the empire but for France.

Modern European statesmen did not, however, share a common ideological outlook. Cavour leaned toward liberal ideas, while Bismarck was unquestionably conservative and Louis Napoleon held a blend of liberal and conservative views. Yet the leaders willingly enacted similar policies and sponsored similar legislation, not from any shared political commitment, but because of their desire to strengthen and promote their nations. In order to maintain power, they adapted to circumstance; they did not insist on principle. As Bismarck explained it, he always had more than one arrow in his quiver.

The new political men were risk takers. They acted without the safety net of tradition or political legitimacy. Bismarck saw himself on a tightrope, but one he felt prepared to walk. Just as Jeremy Bentham, earlier in the century, had figured the relationship between actions and outcomes in terms of profits and losses, the new statesmen were calculators; they weighed levels of risk appropriate for the ends they sought to achieve. Realpolitik was less the invention of a particular statesman and more a characteristic of the new age of gamesmanship in statecraft.

CHANGING VALUES AND THE FORCE OF NEW IDEAS

Like the political world, the material world was changing rapidly after 1850. The world of ideas that explained the place of women and men in the new universe was rapidly changing as well. The railroad journey became the metaphor for the new age. The locomotive hurtling forward signified the strength, power, and progress of materialism. Yet the passenger was strangely dislocated, the landscape between one point and another a blur seen through a carriage window. New points of reference had to be found; new roots had to be put down. In the period between 1850 and 1870, a materialist system of values emerged as behaviors changed. That was as true for the private world of the home as it was for the public world of high politics.

In any age, changes in material life find their way into literature, philosophy, science, and art. Changes in the environment affect the way people look at the world. In turn, intellectuals can have a profound effect on values and behavior. Truly great thinkers not only reflect their times, they also shape them. The third quarter of the nineteenth century was especially rich in both the creativity and critical stance that shaped modern consciousness. Amid the tumult of new ideas in the period after 1850, two titans stand out. Not artists, but scientists—one of biology, the other of society—they sought regularity and predictability in the world they observed and measured. The ideas of Charles Darwin and Karl Marx both reflected and changed the world in which they lived. People alive during the third quarter of the nineteenth century called themselves "modern." They were, indeed, "modern," since in their values and view of the world they were closer to their twentieth-century progeny than they were to their eighteenth-century grandparents.

The Politics of Homemaking

At the Great Exhibition of 1851 in London, the achievements of modern industry were proudly displayed for all the world to see. Engineering marvels and mechanistic wonders dwarfed the thousands of visitors who came to the Crystal Palace to view civilization at its most advanced. In the midst of the machinery of the factory, household items took their place. Modern kitchens with coal-burning stoves were showcased, and the artifacts of the ideal home were carefully displayed. Predictably, mechanical looms, symbols of the new age, were exhibited; but inkstands, artificial flowers, thermostats, and cooking utensils were also enshrined. Visitors did not find strange the juxtaposition of the public world of production with the private world of the home in an exhibition celebrating British superiority.

The world of the home, not immune to changes in society and the economy, was invested with new power and meaning in mid-nineteenth-century Europe. Home was glorified as the locus of shelter and comfort where the harsh outside world could be forgotten. In 1870, an article in a popular Victorian magazine explained that the home functioned as a haven: "Home is emphatically man's place of rest, where his wife is his friend who knows his mind, where he may be himself without fear of offending, and relax the strain that must be kept out of doors: where he may feel himself safe, understood, and at ease."

Throughout Europe, the home served another function, as a symbol of status and achievement. Objects of a proper sort indicated wealth, upward mobility, and taste. In the belief that the more objects that could be displayed the better, the middle-class

home of the third quarter of the nineteenth century was usually overdecorated. Drapes hung over doors and windows, pictures and prints covered the walls, and overstuffed furniture filled the rooms. All were intended to convey gentility and comfort.

Woman's Place. Industrialization had separated the workplace from the home. Protective legislation before midcentury attempted to ease women out of the work force. Middle-class women were expected to assume primary responsibility for the domestic goals of escape and status. Just as the workplace was man's world, the private world of the home was woman's domain. After 1850, magazines, handbooks, and guidebooks that instructed women on how to fulfill their domestic duties proliferated. The most famous of the instruction manuals in Britain was *Mrs. Beeton's Book of Household Management* (1861). The title is instructive. The business concept of management could now be applied to the home. Mrs. Beeton told

■ The cover of the 1890 edition of *Mrs. Beeton's Everyday Cookery and Housekeeping Book*. Preparing an elaborate table like that shown in the cover illustration was one of women's principal domestic duties, according to Mrs. Beeton.

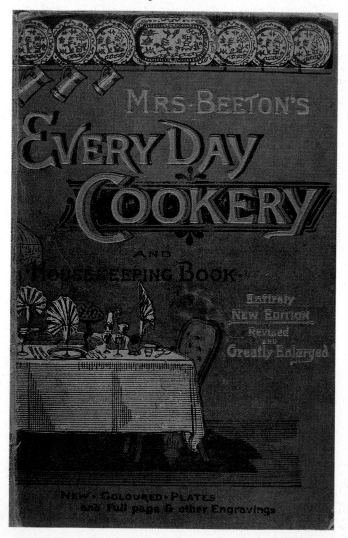

MISTRESS OF THE HOUSE

Mrs. Beeton's Book of Household Management was first published in 1861 and in less than a year sold 60,000 copies. Isabella Beeton was 23 years old when the book first appeared and she died at the age of 28 before she saw its vast success as one of the most published and reissued guidebooks of all time. The book is filled with practical advice on a wide variety of subjects ranging from wet-nursing, care of a sick child, etiquette, fashion, and cooking. Mrs. Beeton also provided a strong rationale for the importance of the domestic sphere in the modern world. The sections below are from Chapter 1: The Mistress.

Focus Questions

What is Mrs. Beeton's purpose in using military and business comparisons to describe the housewife's role? What is Mrs. Beeton's view of servants and of the mistress' responsibility as their manager? Why is an orderly household so important to the author?

As with the commander of an army, or the leader of any enterprise, so it is with the mistress of a house. Her spirit will be seen through the whole establishment; and just in proportion as she performs her duties intelligently and thoroughly, so will her domestics follow her path. Of all those acquirements, which more particularly belong to the feminine character, there are none which take a higher rank, in our estimation, than such as enter into a knowledge of household duties; for on these are perpetually dependent the happiness, comfort, and well-being of a family . . . .

Early rising is one of the most essential qualities which enter into good Household Management, as it is not only the parent of health, but of innumerable other advantages. Indeed, when a mistress is an early riser, it is almost certain that her house will be orderly and well-managed. On the contrary, if she remain in bed till a late hour, then the domestics, who, as we have before observed, invariably partake somewhat of their mistress's character, will surely become sluggards. To self-indulgence all are more or less disposed, and it is not to be expected that servants are freer from fault than the heads of houses. The great Lord Chatham thus gave his advice in reference to this subject:—"I would have inscribed on the curtains of your bed, and the walls of your chamber, 'If you do not rise early, you can make progress in nothing.'"

From Mrs. Isabella Beeton, *The Book of Household Management* (1861).

---

her readers, "The functions of the mistress of the house resemble those of the general of an army or the manager of a great business concern." "Home economics" was invented during this period. As the marketplace had its own rules and regulations that could be studied in the "dismal science" of economics, so too, women were told, the domestic sphere could benefit from the application of rational principles of organization.

Women were targeted by popular literature about how to get a man and keep him. Manuals cautioned women not to be too clever, since women with opinions were not popular with men. Mrs. Beeton's advice centered on food as the way to a man's heart. A wife's duty, she explained, was above all to provide her husband with a hot meal, prepared well and served punctually. Meals became elaborate occasions of several courses requiring hours of work. Women's magazines bombarded a growing readership with menus and recipes for the careful housewife. Status was communicated not by expensive foods, but by extravagant preparation. Meal planning was an art, women learned, one whose practice required and assumed the assistance of household servants. Before that time, women had produced in the home products they could now buy in the marketplace. Purchases of bread, beer, soap, and candles saved housewives hours of labor every week. But with rising expectations about

the quality of life in the home, women had more rather than less to do each day. Handbooks prescribed rules on etiquette and proper manners. The rituals of domestic life, from letter writing to afternoon visits and serving tea, were minutely detailed for middle-class audiences. The woman of the house was instructed in the care and education of her children; in health, cleanliness, and nutrition; and in the management of resources. Thrift, industry, and orderliness, the virtues of the business world, had their own particular meaning in the domestic sphere.

To the Victorian mind, gentility and morality were inextricably interwoven. A woman who failed in her duty to maintain a clean and comfortable home threatened the safety of her family. An 1867 English tract warned:

> The man who goes home on a Saturday only to find his house in disorder, with every article of furniture out of its place, the floor unwashed or sloppy from uncompleted washing, his wife slovenly, his children untidy, his dinner not yet ready, or spoilt in the cooking, is much more likely "to go on a spree" than the man who finds his house in order, the furniture glistening from the recent polishing, the burnished steel fire-irons looking doubly resplendent from the bright glow of the cheerful fire, his well-cooked dinner laid on a snowy cloth, and his wife and children tidy and cheerful.

Working-Class Wives and Mothers. The "ideal" was very far from the experiences of most families throughout Europe after the middle of the century. The "science" of homemaking presupposed a cushion of affluence out of reach to the men, women, and children who made up the vast majority of the population. Working-class wives and mothers often had to earn wages if their families were to survive. One Englishwoman, Lucy Luck (1848–1922), began her working career in a silk mill at the age of eight. By law allowed to work only half a day, the child Lucy returned to her foster home at the end of her shift to labor late into the night plaiting straw for baskets. In her reminiscences, she looked back over her life: "I have been at work for forty-seven years, and have never missed one season, although I have a large family of seven surviving children." Lucy, who married at the age of 18, learned that on her own she could not survive without a man's income or without resorting to the "bad life" of crime and prostitution. In the marriage, the couple could not survive without Lucy's wages.

Like Lucy Luck, many women held jobs outside the home or did piecework to supplement meager family incomes. In 1866, women constituted a significant percentage of the French labor force, including 45 percent of all textile workers. At the height of the rhetoric about the virtues of domesticity, as many as two married English women in five worked in the mills in industrial areas such as Lancashire. Working women often chose the "sweated labor" that they could perform in their home because it allowed them to care for their children while being paid by the piece. Home workers labored in the needle trades, shoemaking, and furniture making in their cramped living quarters under miserable conditions; and they worked for a third or less of what men earned.

Troubles at Home. The "haven" of the home was not insulated from the perils of the outside world. Nor was every home a happy one. Venereal diseases rose dramatically in Western nations, belying the image of the devoted couple. By the end of the nineteenth century, 14 to 17 percent of all deaths in France were attributable to sexually transmitted diseases. The diseases were blind to class distinctions. Illegitimacy rates rose in the first half of the nineteenth century and remained high after 1850 among the working classes, defying middle-class standards of propriety. Illegitimate births were highest in urban areas, where household life assumed its own distinctive pattern among working-class families, with couples often choosing free union instead of legal marriage.

Because virtue was defined in terms of woman's roles as wife and mother, working women were regarded as immoral. Social evils were, according to that reasoning, easily attributed to the "unnatural" phenomenon of women leaving the home to work in a man's world. Women continued to work and, in some cases, to organize to demand their rights. Women like Lucy Luck did not and could not accept the prescription that good mothers should not work, since their wages fed their children. The politics of homemaking defined women as mothers and hence legitimated the poor treatment and poor pay of women as workers. Yet the labor of women outside as well as inside the home remained the norm.

Nor did all middle-class women accept approved social roles. Increasing numbers of middle-class women in western Europe protested their circumscribed sphere. Critics argued that designating the home as woman's proper domain stifled individual development. Earlier in the century, Jane Austen, one of Britain's greatest novelists, had to keep a piece of muslin work on her writing table in the family drawing room to cover her papers lest visitors detect evidence of literary activity. In the next generation, Florence Nightingale refused to accept the embroidery and knitting to which she was relegated at home. That period in Western society witnessed both the creation of the cult of domesticity and the stirrings of feminism among middle-class women, whose demand for equal treatment for women was to become more important after 1870. Patterns of behavior changed within the family, and they were not fixed immutably in social practice. Woman's place and woman's role proved to be much-disputed questions in the new politics of homemaking.

Realism in the Arts

Realism in the arts and literature was a rejection of romantic idealism and subjectivity. The realist response to the disillusionment with the political failures of the post-1848 era characterized a wide array of artistic and literary endeavors. Realists depicted the challenges of urban and industrial growth by confronting the alienation of modern life.

The Social World of the Artist. The term **realism** was first used in 1850 to describe the paintings of Gustave Courbet (1819–1877). In *The Artist's Studio* (1855), Courbet portrayed himself surrounded by the intellectuals and political figures of his day. He may have been painting a landscape, but contemporary political life crowded in; a starving Irish peasant and her child crouch beneath his easel. Of his unrelenting canvases, none more fittingly portrays the harsh realism of bourgeois life than the funeral ceremony depicted in *Burial at Ornans* (1849–1850) (see p. 727) or better depicts the brutality of workers' lives than *Stone Breakers* (1849).

Other artists shared Courbet's desire to reject the conventions prevailing in the art world in favor of portraying reality in its natural and social dimensions. Jean-Francois Millet's paintings of peasants and workers (see p. 673) sought for a truth deeper than a surface beauty. Images of ordinary people, the working classes, and the poor populated realist art. Realist artists often strove to make a social commentary such as that of Honoré Daumier's *Washerwoman*, which shows a woman of the lower classes, clearly weary, climbing up a flight of stairs with a small child in tow. Daumier's *Third-Class Carriage* (see p. 652) likewise captures a scene from the daily life of the poor that would not have been considered a fit subject for art a generation before.

■ Gustave Courbet (1819–1877), *Burial at Ornans*. Courbet realistically portrays a bourgeois funeral ceremony without flattering his subjects.

Realist Novels. After midcentury, idealization in romantic literature yielded to novels depicting the objective and unforgiving social world. Through serialization in journals and newspapers, fiction reached out to mass audiences, who obtained their "facts" about modern life through stories that often cynically portrayed the monotony and boredom of daily existence. In *Hard Times* (1854), set in the imaginary city of Coketown, Charles Dickens (1812–1870) created an allegory that exposed the sterility and soullessness of industrial society through "fact, fact, fact everywhere in the material aspect of the town; fact, fact, fact everywhere in the immaterial."

Gustave Flaubert (1821–1880), the great French realist novelist, critiqued the Western intellectual tradition in his unfinished *Dictionary of Accepted Ideas* (1881). In the novel *Bouvard et Pécuchet* (1881), Flaubert satirized modern man's applications of Enlightenment ideas about the environment and progress by showing that they were foolish and often at odds with common sense. The main characters of the novel know everything there is to know about theories and applied sciences, but they know nothing about life. His best-known work, *Madame Bovary* (1856), recounts the story of a young country doctor's wife whose desire to escape from the boredom of her provincial existence leads her into adultery and eventually results in her destruction. Flaubert was put on trial for obscenity and violating public morality with his tale of the unrepentant Emma Bovary. The beautifully crafted novel is marked by an ironic detachment from the hypocrisy of bourgeois life. Mary Ann Evans (1819–1880), writing under the pseudonym George Eliot, was also concerned with moral choices and responsibilities in her novels, including *Middlemarch* (1871–1872), a tale of idealism disappointed by the petty realities of provincial English life.

The problem of morality in the realist novel is nowhere more apparent than in the works of the Russian writer Fyodor Dostoyevsky (1821–1881). Dostoyevsky's protagonists wrestle with a universe where God no longer exists and where they must shape their own morality. The impoverished student Raskolnikov in *Crime and Punishment* (1866) justifies his brutal murder of an old woman that occurs in the opening pages of the novel. Realist art and literature addressed an educated elite public but did not flinch before the unrelenting poverty and harshness of contemporary life. The morality of the realist vision lay not in condemning the evils of modern life and seeking their political solutions, as an earlier generation of romantics did, but in depicting social evils for what they were, failures of a smug and progressive middle class.

The New World of Photography. It is perhaps difficult for us to imagine a world before the existence of accurate visual images that modern photography and the media revolution of the twentieth century made possible as an integral part of our daily lives. Yet it was not until 1839 that Western men and women saw the first modern photographs.

Nineteenth-century photography was the result of wedding art and science. Although various techniques that made it possible to capture images and landscapes on paper existed in the early decades of the nineteenth century, Louis Daguerre (1789–1851) can be credited as a pioneer in the photographic process with the invention of the daguerreotype in 1839. Daguerre was both a French scene painter and a physicist, and

■ Calotype of the Adamson family, ca. 1844, by pioneer photographers Robert Adamson (shown at far right) and David Octavius Hill of Scotland. The new technology of photography enabled middle-class families to have their portraits taken, a luxury once only available to those wealthy enough to commission artists.

he brought both his sensibilities and scientific training to the process of capturing images on silver-coated copper plates treated with iodine vapor. The images were often clouded and not able to be reproduced, as from a negative. Successive discoveries of new techniques allowed for the creation and reproduction of lasting images in still photography.

The fascination with photography in the nineteenth century can be observed in its use for portraits by growing numbers of ordinary people, just as in an earlier time the wealthy and powerful sat for oil portraits. With the achievement of greater portability and precision, the camera, still a cumbersome object, was used for country landscapes, urban landmarks, and recording the horrors and glory of battle. Within a generation, cameras altered the way people understood the world around them and how they recorded human life. An increasing emphasis on the real world, reflected in literature, art, and discoveries in science was fueled by the altered worldview and the new consciousness that photography made possible.

Charles Darwin and the New Science

Science had a special appeal for a generation of Europeans disillusioned with the political failures of idealism in the revolutions of 1848. It was not an age of great scientific discovery, but rather one of synthesis of previous findings and their technological applications. Science was, above all, to be useful in promoting material progress.

Charles Darwin (1809–1882), the preeminent scientist of the age, was a great synthesizer. Darwin began his scientific career as a naturalist with a background in geology. As a young man, he sailed around the world on the *Beagle* (1831–1836). He collected specimens and fossils as the ship's naturalist, with his greatest finds in South America, especially the Galápagos Islands. He

DOCUMENT
On Darwin

spent the next 20 years of his life taking notes of his observations of the natural world. In chronically poor health, Darwin produced 500 pages of what he called "one long argument." *On the Origin of Species by Means of Natural Selection* (1859) was a book that changed the world.

Darwin's argument was a simple one: life forms originated in and perpetuated themselves through struggle. The outcome of the struggle was determined by **natural selection,** or what came to be known as "survival of the fittest." Better-adapted individuals survived, while others died out. Competition between species and within species produced a dynamic model of organic evolution. Darwin did not use the word evolution in the original edition, but a positivist belief in an evolutionary process permeated the 1859 text.

Evolutionary theory was not new, nor was materialism a new concept in organic biology. In the 1850s, others were coming forward with similar ideas about natural selection, including most notably A. R. Wallace (1823–1913), who stressed geographic factors in biological evolution. Darwin's work was a product of discoveries in a variety of fields—philosophy, history, and science. He derived his idea of struggle from Malthus's *Essay on Population* and borrowed across disciplines to construct a theory of "the preservation of favored races in the struggle for life" (part of the book's subtitle). The publication of *On the Origin of Species* made Darwin immediately famous. Scientific theory was the stuff of front-page headlines. Like Samuel Smiles, a businessman who published the best-seller *Self-Help* in 1860, Darwin spoke of struggle and discipline, though in nature, not in the marketplace. In the world of biology, Darwin's ideas embodied a new realist belief in progress based on struggle. Force explained the past and would guarantee the future as the fittest survived. Those were ideas that a general public applied to a whole range of human endeavors and to theories of social organization.

Karl Marx and The Science of Society

"Just as Darwin discovered the law of development of organic nature, Marx discovered the law of development of human history." So spoke Friedrich Engels (1820–1895), longtime friend of and collaborator with Karl Marx (1818–1883), over

■ This illustration by Gustave Doré appeared in *The Condition of the Working Class in England in 1844* by Friedrich Engels. Small and cramped industrial working-class houses with their tiny walled backyards are framed by railway lines.

Marx's grave. Marx would have been pleased with Engels's eulogy; he called himself the Darwin of sociology. Marx footnoted as corroborating evidence Darwin's "epoch-making work on the origin of species" in his own masterwork, *Das Kapital,* the first volume of which appeared in 1867. As the theorist of the socialism that he called "scientific," Marx viewed himself as an evolutionist who demonstrated that history is the dialectical struggle of classes.

The son of a Prussian lawyer who had converted from Judaism to Christianity, Marx had rejected the study of the law and belief in a deity. In exile because of his political writings, Marx was the most brilliant of the German young Hegelians, intellectuals heavily influenced by the ideas of Georg Friedrich Hegel (1770–1831), which held sway over the German intellectual world of the 1830s and 1840s. By the mid-1840s, Marx was in rebellion against Hegel's idealism and was developing his own materially grounded view of society.

The philosophy that evolved in the years of collaboration with Engels was built on a materialist view of society. Human beings were defined not by their souls but by their labor. Labor was a struggle to transform nature by producing commodities useful for survival. Their ability to transform nature by work differentiated men and women from animals. Building on that fundamental concept of labor, Marx and Engels saw society as divided into two camps: those who own

property and those who do not. Nineteenth-century capitalist society was divided into two classes: the bourgeoisie, those who owned the means of production as its private property, and the proletariat, the propertyless working class.

The Class Struggle.   This materialist perspective on society was the engine driving Marx's theory of history. For Marx, every social system based on a division into classes carries within it the seeds of its own destruction. Marx and Engels used a biological metaphor to explain the destruction: the growth of a plant from a seed is a dialectical process in which the germ is destroyed by its opposite, the plant. The mature plant produces seed while continuing its form. For Marx and Engels, the different stages of history are determined by different forms of the ownership of production. In a feudal-agrarian society, the aristocracy controlled and exploited the unfree labor of serfs. In a world of commerce and manufacturing, the capitalist bourgeoisie are the new aristocracy exploiting free labor for wages.

Marx was more than an observer: he was a critic of capitalism. His labor theory of value was the wedge he drove into the self-congratulatory rhetoric of the capitalist age. Labor is the source of all value, he argued, and yet the bourgeois employer denies workers the profit of their work by refusing to pay them a decent wage. Instead, the employer pockets the profits. Workers are separated, or alienated, from the product of their

ON THE ORIGIN OF SPECIES, 1859

For the 20 years prior to the publication of On the Origin of Species, *Charles Darwin gathered data in support of his theory of evolution. He was not alone in advancing a theory of natural selection, but he was unique in basing his conclusions on carefully compiled data.* On the Origin of Species *was based on his scientific observations resulting from a five-year cruise aboard the* Beagle, *which took him to the Galápagos Islands off the coast of Ecuador.*

Focus Questions

How did Charles Darwin construct his case and deploy his thesis for the evolution of the human species without using the word "evolution"? What words did he use? What did he mean by the term "species," and how did he see species as interrelated?

I have now recapitulated the chief facts and considerations which have thoroughly convinced me that species have changed, and are still slowly changing by the preservation and accumulation of successive slight favorable variations. Why, it may be asked, have all the most eminent living naturalists and geologists rejected this view of the mutability of species? It cannot be asserted that organic beings in a state of nature are subject to no variation; it cannot be proved that the amount of variation in the course of long ages is a limited quantity; no clear distinction has been, or can be, drawn between species and well-marked varieties. It cannot be maintained that species when intercrossed are invariably sterile, and varieties invariably fertile; and that sterility is a special endowment and sign of creation. The belief that species were immutable productions was almost unavoidable as long as the history of the world was thought to be of short duration; and now that we have acquired some idea of the lapse of time, we are too apt to assume, without proof, that the geological record is so perfect that it would have afforded us plain evidence of the mutation of species, if they had undergone mutation.

But the chief cause of our natural unwillingness to admit that one species have given birth to other and distinct species, is that we are always slow in admitting any great change of which we do not see the intermediate steps. The difficulty is the same as that felt by so many geologists, when Lyell [Sir Charles Lyell (1797–1875), English geologist] first insisted that long lines of inland cliffs had been formed, and great valleys excavated, by the slow action of the coast-waves. The mind cannot possibly grasp the full meaning of the term of a hundred million years; it cannot add up and perceive the full effects of many slight variations, accumulated during an almost infinite number of generations.

Although I am fully convinced of the truth of the views given in this volume under the form of an abstract, I by no means expect to convince experienced naturalists whose

labor. But more profoundly, Marx believed that in a capitalist system all workers are alienated from the creation that makes them human; they are alienated from their labor.

Marx predicted that capitalism would produce more and more goods but would continue to pay workers the lowest wages possible. By driving out smaller producers, the bourgeoisie would increase the size of the proletariat. Yet Marx was optimistic. As workers were slowly pauperized, they would become conscious of their exploitation and would revolt.

Marx's Legacy.   The force of Karl Marx's ideas mobilized thousands of contemporaries aware of the injustices of capitalism. Few thinkers in the history of the West have left a more lasting legacy than Marx. The legacy has survived the fact that much of Marx's analysis rested on incorrect predictions about the increasing misery of workers and the inflexibility of the capitalist system. Marx was a synthesizer who combined economics, philosophy, politics, and history in a wide-ranging critique of industrial society.

Marxism spread across Europe as workers responded to its message. Marx did not cause the increase in the organization of workers that took place in the 1860s, but his theories did give shape and focus to a growing critique of labor relations in the second half of the nineteenth century. Political parties throughout Europe coalesced around Marxist beliefs and programs. Marxists were beginning to be heard in associations of workers, and in 1864 they helped found the International Working Men's Association in London, an organization of French, German, and Italian workers dedicated to "the end of all class rule." The promise of a common association of workers transcending national boundaries became a compelling idea to those who envisioned the end of capitalism. The importance of the international exchange of ideas and information cannot be underestimated as a means of promoting labor organization in western Europe. In 1871, Marx and his followers turned to Paris for proof that the revolution was at hand.

A New Revolution?

Soundly defeated on 2 September 1870, Napoleon III and his fighting force of 100,000 men became Prussia's prisoners of war. With the emperor's defeat, the Second Empire collapsed.

minds are stocked with a multitude of facts all viewed, during a long course of years, from a point of view directly opposite to mine. It is so easy to hide our ignorance under such expressions as the "plan of creation," "unity of design," etc., and to think that we give an explanation when we only restate a fact. Any one whose disposition leads him to attach more weight to unexplained difficulties than to the explanation of a certain number of facts will certainly reject my theory.

A few naturalists, endowed with much flexibility of mind, and who have already begun to doubt on the immutability of species, may be influenced by this volume; but I look with confidence to the future, to young and rising naturalists, who will be able to view both sides of the question with impartiality. Whoever is led to believe that species are mutable will do good service by conscientiously expressing his conviction; for only thus can the load of prejudice by which this subject is overwhelmed be removed....

It may be asked how far I extend the doctrine of the modification of species. The question is difficult to answer, because the more distinct the forms are which we may consider, by so much the arguments fall away in force. But some arguments of the greatest weight extend very far. All the members of whole classes can be connected together by chains of affinities, and all can be classified on the same principle, in groups subordinate to groups. Fossil remains sometimes tend to fill up very wide intervals between existing orders. Organs in a rudimentary condition plainly show that an early progenitor had the organ in a fully developed state; and this in some instances necessarily implies an enormous amount of modification in the descendants. Throughout whole classes various structures are formed on the same pattern, and at an embryonic age the species closely resemble each other. Therefore I cannot doubt that the theory of descent with modification embraces all the members of the same class. I believe that animals have descended from at most only four or five progenitors, and plants from an equal or lesser number.

Analogy would lead me one step further, namely, to the belief that all animals and plants have descended from some one prototype. But analogy may be a deceitful guide. Nevertheless all living things have much in common, in the chemical composition, their germinal vesicles, their cellular structure, and their laws of growth and reproduction. We see this even in so trifling a circumstance as that the same poison often similarly affects plants and animals; or that the poison secreted by the gall-fly produces monstrous growths on the wild rose or oak-tree. Therefore I should infer from analogy that probably all the organic beings which have ever lived on this earth have descended from some one primordial form, into which life was first breathed.

From Charles Darwin, *On the Origin of Species* (London, 1859), pp. 480–490.

But even with the capture of Napoleon III, the French capital city of Paris refused to capitulate. The dedication of Parisians to the ongoing war with the Prussians was evident from the first. The regime's liberal critics in Paris seized the initiative to proclaim France a republic. If a corrupt and decadent empire could not save the nation, then France's Third Republic could.

The Siege of Paris. In mid-September 1870, two German armies surrounded Paris and began a siege that lasted for more than four months. Only carrier pigeons and balloon-transported passengers linked Paris with the rest of France. In the beginning, Parisian heroism, unchallenged by battle, seemed festive and unreal. Bismarck's troops were intent on bringing the city to its knees not by fighting but by cutting off its vital supply lines. By November, food and fuel were dwindling and Parisians were facing starvation. Undaunted, they began to eat dogs, cats, and rats. By December, famine threatened to become a reality. Most people had no vegetables and no meat. Rationing was ineffective, and a black market prevailed in which the wealthy could buy whatever was available. Horses disappeared from the streets and the zoo was emptied as antelope, camel, donkey, mule, and elephant became desirable table fare. The Bois de Boulogne, the city's largest park, was leveled for timber to build barricades and for fuel. But the wood was too green and would not burn. The bitter cold of one of the century's most severe winters heightened the horror. Yet the population was committed to fighting on. Men and women became part of the city's citizen militia, the National Guard, and trained for combat against the Germans. "Siege fever" swept the city. In spite of dire conditions, there were moments of euphoria. Collective delusions, perhaps intensified by empty stomachs, convinced Parisians that they were invincible against the enemy. Citizens joined clubs to discuss politics and preparedness, and probably to keep warm. Patents on inventions to defeat the Germans proliferated. Most of them were useless and silly, like the musical machine gun that was intended to lure its victims within firing range. The enemy at their gates absorbed the total attention of the urban population. There was no life other than the war.

Apparently with the goal of terrorizing the population, the Germans began a steady bombardment of the city at the beginning of January 1871. The shells fell for three weeks, but

■ The Paris Commune. French troops, under the direction of the French government sitting in Versailles, penetrated the fortifications ringing the city of Paris, and within one "Bloody Week," crushed the Parisian Communards.

women, and children poured into the streets to protect their cannons and to defend their right to bear arms. In the fighting that followed, the Versailles troops were driven from the city. Paris was in a state of siege once again.

The spontaneity of the March uprising was soon succeeded by organization. Citizens rallied to the idea of the city's self-government and established the **Paris Commune,** as other French cities followed the capital's lead. Karl Marx hailed the event as the beginning of the revolution that would overthrow the capitalist system and saw in it the beginning of the dictatorship of the proletariat. But what occurred between March and May 1871 was not a proletarian revolution. Rather, it was a continuation of the state of siege that had held Paris through the fall and early winter months. Parisians were still

Parisian resistance prevailed. However, the rest of France wanted an end to the war. The Germans agreed to an armistice at the end of January 1871 in order that French national elections could be held to elect representatives to the new government. In the elections, French citizens outside Paris repudiated the war and returned an overwhelmingly conservative majority to seek peace.

Thus the siege came to an end. Yet it left deep wounds that still festered. Parisians believed they had been betrayed by the rest of France. Through four months as a besieged city, they had sacrificed, suffered, and died. Parisians believed that they were defenders of the true republic, the true patriots. Among Parisians, disparities of wealth were more obvious than ever before. Some wealthy citizens had abandoned the city during the siege. The wealthy who did stay ate and kept warm. Poor women who stood in food lines from before dawn every day to provision their families knew that there was food—but not for them.

The Paris Commune. The war was over, but Paris was not at peace. The new national government, safely installed outside Paris at Versailles, attempted to reestablish normal life. The volatility of the city motivated the government's attempt in March 1871 to disarm the Parisian citizenry by using army troops. In the hilly neighborhood of northern Paris, men,

CHRONOLOGY	
STATE BUILDING AND SOCIAL CHANGE	
1853–1856	Crimean War
1859	Austria declares war on Kingdom of Sardinia; France joins forces with Italians
1860	Piedmont-Sardinia annexes duchies in central Italy; France gains Nice and Savoy
3 March 1861	Emancipation of Russian serfs
14 March 1861	Kingdom of Italy proclaimed with Victor Emmanuel II as king
1861–1865	American Civil War
1863	Maximilian crowned emperor of Mexico
1863	Prussians and Austrians at war with Denmark
1866	Seven Weeks' War between Austria and Prussia; Italy acquires Venetia
1867	Emperor Maximilian executed
July 1870	Franco-Prussian War begins
2 September 1870	French Second Empire capitulates with Prussian victory at Sedan
20 September 1870	Italy annexes Rome
18 January 1871	German Empire proclaimed
March–May 1871	Paris Commune

at war. It was not war against a foreign enemy, nor was it a class war. It was a civil war against the rest of France.

The social experiment of self-defense in the Commune lasted for 72 days. Armed women formed their own fighting units, the city council regulated labor relations, and neighborhoods ruled themselves. In May 1871, government troops reentered the city and brutally crushed the Paris Commune. In one "Bloody Week," 25,000 Parisians were massacred and 40,000 others were arrested and tried. Of the 10,000 rebels convicted, 5000 were sent to a penal colony in the southwestern Pacific Ocean. Such reprisals inflamed radicals and workers all over Europe. The myth of the Commune became a rallying cry for revolutionary movements throughout the world and inspired the future leaders of the Russian revolutionary state.

The Commune was important at the time, but not as a revolution. It offered two lessons to men and women at the end of the third quarter of the nineteenth century. First, it demonstrated the power of patriotism. Competing images of the nation were at stake, one Parisian and the other French, but no one could deny the power of national identity to inspire a whole city to suffer and to sacrifice. Second, the Commune made clear the power of the state. No revolutionary movement could succeed without controlling the massive forces of repression at the state's command. The Commune had tried to recapture a local, federal view of the world but failed to take sufficient account of the power of the state that it opposed. In writing of the episode two decades later, Friedrich Engels wondered if revolution would ever again be possible in the West.

CONCLUSION

Western societies had crossed the threshold into the modern age in the third quarter of the nineteenth century. Strong states from Great Britain to Russia were committed to creating and preserving the conditions of industrial expansion. The machine age, railroads, and metallurgy were spreading industrial development much more widely through western and central Europe than had been possible before 1850. Italians and Prussians, in attempting to join the ranks of nation-states, realized that the road to a strong nation could only be achieved with industrial development and social reforms.

State building in Western societies went hand in hand with growth in the social responsibilities of government. The national powers that would dominate world politics and economy in the twentieth century all underwent modernizing transitions in the 1860s. The powers included the United States, France, Great Britain, and Germany. The Austrian Empire, too, undertook programs to modernize its government and economy, and the Russian Empire established social reforms of unparalleled dimensions. New nations came into existence in this period through the limited use of armed force. With the establishment of the German Empire, Otto von Bismarck, the most realistic of politicians, was intent on preserving the peace in Europe by balancing the power of the great European states. Europeans prided themselves on being both modern and realistic in the third quarter of the nineteenth century. Peace was possible if it was armed and vigilant. Reform, not revolution, many were sure, was the key to the future progress of European societies.

QUESTIONS FOR REVIEW

1. How did the process of creating nation-states in Germany and Italy differ?
2. What social and political circumstances explain the different reforms undertaken in France, Britain, and Russia?
3. How did industrialization change women's lives, and how did such changes depend on a woman's social class?
4. What were the connections between Darwin's ideas about nature and Marx's ideas about society?
5. What forces inspired the creation of the Paris Commune, and what did its fate suggest about the possibility of revolution in the late nineteenth century?

KEY TERMS

Eastern question, *p. 706*

natural selection, *p. 728*

Paris Commune, *p. 732*

Proclamation of the German Empire, *p. 704*

realism, *p. 726*

Realpolitik, *p. 712*

Reichstag, *p. 714*

Risorgimento, *p. 707*

zemstvos, p. 721

DISCOVERING WESTERN CIVILIZATION ONLINE

You can obtain more information about state building and social change in Europe between 1850 and 1871 at the Websites listed below. See also the Companion Website that accompanies this text, www.ablongman.com/kishlansky, which contains an online study guide and additional resources.

Building Nations: The Politics of Unification

The Crimean War (1853–1856)
www.hillsdale.edu/oldacademics/history/war/19Crim.htm
Electronic texts of officers' and soldiers' accounts of the battles of the Crimean War.

Internet Modern History Sourcebook: 19th Century Italy
www.fordham.edu/halsall/mod/modsbook23.html
This site focuses on documents relating to the unification of Italy and the Risorgimento.

Modern History Sourcebook: Documents of German Unification, 1848–1871
www.fordham.edu/halsall/mod/germanunification.html
This site provides translations of major primary documents concerning the unification of Germany.

Reforming European Society

The Victorian Web
www.victorianweb.org
A comprehensive collection of links to Victorian England.

Age of Liberalism: 1848–1914
campus.northpark.edu/history/WebChron/WestEurope/LiberalAge.html
A collection of links to chronologies for the "Age of Liberalism," 1848–1914.

Internet Modern History Sourcebook: Russian Revolution
www.fordham.edu/halsall/mod/modsbook39.html
This site, a repository for links to the Russian Revolution, provides links to documents on nineteenth-century tsarist Russia.

Changing Values and the Force of New Ideas

Florence Nightingale
www.kings.edu/womens_history/florence.html
Annotated bibliography of literature on Florence Nightingale.

The Eighteenth Brumaire of Louis Napoleon
csf.colorado.edu/psn/marx/Archive/1852-18brum/
The electronic text of Karl Marx's *Eighteenth Brumaire of Napoleon*.

1851 Project: The Great Exhibition
www.nal.vam.ac.uk/projects/1851.html
This site draws upon the collection of the National Library of Art in London to chronicle the Great Exhibition of 1851.

The Darwin Page
web.clas.ufl.edu/users/rhatch/pages/02-Teaching Resources/readingwriting/darwin/05-DARWIN-PAGE.html
Web page of Professor Robert Hatch of the University of Florida, which provides links to bibliographies, texts, and other resources on Charles Darwin.

Paris Commune Archive
dwardmac.pitzer.edu/Anarchist_Archives/pariscommune/Pariscommunearchive.html
A Pitzer College political studies site providing summaries of the major players and events of the Paris Commune as well as an extensive bibliography.

Internet Women's History Sourcebook
www.fordham.edu/halsall/women/womensbook.html
This section of the Modern History Sourcebook focuses on women's history from antiquity to the present. The subchapter on modern European women's history provides links to texts on the structure of working women's lives as well as texts on feminism and the suffrage movement.

SUGGESTIONS FOR FURTHER READING

Building Nations: The Politics of Unification

Derek Beales, *The Risorgimento and the Unification of Italy* (London: Allen & Unwin, 1982). Drawing a distinction between unification and national revival, Beales situates the period of unification within the larger process of cultural and political revival.

David Blackbourn, *The Long Nineteenth Century: A History of Germany, 1780–1918* (New York: Oxford University Press, 1998). This book examines the emergence of Germany from the late eighteenth century through the First World War in terms of politics, economics, and culture.

John A. Davis, ed., *Italy in the Nineteenth Century, 1796–1900* (New York: Oxford University Press, 2000). The essays of nine specialists provide an historical analysis of Italian society, politics, and culture.

Dieter Langewiesche, *Liberalism in Germany* (Princeton, NJ: Princeton University Press, 2000). This study traces the roots of German liberalism to the late eighteenth century and emphasizes the role of individual German states, with a special chapter on the local influences on the formation of the nation-state between 1815 and 1860.

Lucy Riall, *The Italian Risorgimento: State, Society, and National Unification* (New York: Routledge, 1999). Riall examines the historiography of Italian unification and presents the turbulent period of "resurgence" as a turning point in Italian history.

Denis Mack Smith, *Cavour* (London: Weidenfeld and Nicolson, 1985). Smith contrasts Cavour and his policies with those of Garibaldi and Mazzini and considers the challenge of regionalism to the unification process.

Reforming European Society

Jane Burbank and David Ransel, eds., *Imperial Russia: New Histories for the Empire* (Bloomington: Indiana University Press, 1998). A collection of essays using new methodologies for understanding Russian history in the eighteenth and nineteenth centuries.

Judith Flanders, *Inside the Victorian Home: A Portrait of Domestic Life in Victorian England* (New York: W.W. Norton & Co., 2004). This examination of the daily lives of ordinary people reconstructs the drudgery of Victorian domesticity and "the different mental world" of that era.

Catherine Hall, Keith McClelland, and Jane Rendall, *Defining the Victorian Nation: Class, Race, Gender and the British Reform Act of 1867* (Cambridge: Cambridge University Press, 2000). This co-authored study presents a cultural, social, and gender history of the extension of the vote in 1867, accompanied by strong bibliographic aids.

Sudhir Hazareesingh, *From Subject to Citizen: The Second Empire and the Emergence of Modern French Democracy* (Princeton, NJ: Princeton University Press, 1998). In showing the relationship between the local and the national, the author provides a reevaluation of the emergence of republican citizenship in the Second Empire.

Margaret Homans, *Royal Representations: Queen Victoria and British Culture, 1837–1876* (Chicago: University of Chicago Press, 1998). Victoria is examined as a monarch, a symbol, and a wife and mother as a key to British culture.

Alain Plessis, *The Rise and Fall of the Second Empire, 1852–1871*, tr. Jonathan Mandelbaum (Cambridge: Cambridge University Press, 1985). Discusses the Second Empire as an important transitional period in French history, when the conflict was between traditional and modern values in political, economic, and social transformations.

Changing Values and the Force of New Ideas

Jenni Calder, *The Victorian Home* (London: B. T. Batsford, 1977). A cultural and social history of Victorian domestic life in which the author describes both bourgeois and working-class domestic environments.

Bonnie G. Smith, *Ladies of the Leisure Class: The Bourgeoises of Northern France in the Nineteenth Century* (Princeton, NJ: Princeton University Press, 1981). Explores the impact of industrialization on the lives of bourgeois women in northern France and demonstrates how the cult of domesticity emerged in a particular community.

Robert Tombs, *The Paris Commune, 1871* (London: Longman, 1999). A synthetic overview of the events of the Commune and their impact on the course of French and European history.

Martha Vicinus, *Independent Women: Work and Community for Single Women, 1850–1920* (Chicago: University of Chicago Press, 1985). Chronicles the choices that Victorian women made to live outside the norms of marriage and domesticity in various women's communities, including sisterhoods, nursing communities, colleges, boarding schools, and settlement houses.

For a list of additional titles related to this chapter's topics, please see http://www.ablongman.com/kishlansky.

Chapter 24

THE CRISIS OF EUROPEAN CULTURE, 1871–1914

Chapter Outline

Europeans in the late nineteenth and early twentieth centuries witnessed enormous cultural changes. Advancements in technology came at a dizzying pace, and discoveries in the sciences challenged many deeply held beliefs. Some people saw chaos and crisis in the new age, but many artists embraced the changes and saw breaks with tradition as liberation. In The Visual Record, see how Italian painter Umberto Boccioni celebrated the energy and the technology of the future. ➤

SPEEDING TO THE FUTURE

Mass Society and the Rejection of Tradition

"We want to demolish museums and libraries." These are not the words of an anarchist or a terrorist but of a poet. The Italian writer Emilio Marinetti (1876–1944) endeavored—symbolically, at least, through the power of his pen—to destroy the citadels of Western culture at the beginning of the twentieth century. Marinetti was not alone in wanting to pull down all that preserved art and learning in the West. Joined by other artists and writers who called themselves **futurists,** Marinetti represented a desire to break free of the past. By shocking complacent bourgeois society with their art, futurists hoped to fashion a new and dynamic civilization. Although they were a small group with limited influence, their concerns were shared by a growing number of intellectuals who judged European culture to be in the throes of a serious moral and cultural crisis. Futurist ideas also reflected the growing preoccupation with the future common among European men and women who spurned the value of tradition.

The futurist painter Umberto Boccioni (1882–1916) captured an aspect of the dynamic intensity of the changing world in his *Riot in the Galleria* (1910) shown here. The setting is a galleria, the equivalent of a modern shopping mall, in front of a respectable *caffé* (an Italian coffee shop), frequented by well-dressed men and women, clearly members of the middle class. It shows a modern urban scene, a public space in every way characteristic of the new age of enjoyment and consumption.

The painting tells a story. In a flurry of light and shadow, a rush of figures moves toward the middle ground of the canvas. At the center of the movement are two women engaged in a brawl that seems to pull the figures of shoppers and strollers toward it. The fact that the brawlers are female is intended to underscore the irrationality of the incident. Yet the brawl itself is not compelling our attention. Rather it is the movement of the crowd, like moths to a flame, that Boccioni intended viewers to see. It is a painting about movement. The objects in motion are little more than vibrations in space, faceless and indistinguishable as individuals. The crowd does not walk or run; it appears instead to be in flight. In his studies for the canvas, Boccioni reduced movement to a series of lines both swirling and directed.

The riot Boccioni depicts is an irrational event. It is no ordinary rabble: it is a well-dressed mob, as the blurred but sumptuously flowered hats and the occasional yellow straw boaters make clear. Movement is taking place without forethought, fueled by the attraction of violence and the possibility of participating in it. There are those on the periphery who have not joined the frenzy, but it appears likely that they will be swept up in the action as the energy of the brawl sucks everything to its center, like the vortex of a tornado. European society seemed to many contemporaries to be moving into an abyss, a world of tumultuous change but without values.

In the violence of the riot we are shown beauty of movement that surpasses that of an orderly waltz. Boccioni uses the warm glow of the electric lights, symbol of the modern age, to illuminate a "new reality." Golden tones, warm oranges and rosy hues, shadowed in delicate purples, create a mosaic whose beauty in the play of color is strangely at odds with the theme of the two brawling figures who activate the crowd. There is no meaning beyond the movement.

Riot in the Galleria reflects the preoccupation with change in the early twentieth century. Life was moving so fast that by 1900 European society seemed to have outrun its own heritage. Technology was transforming Europe with a breakneck speed unmatched in human history. Science undermined the way people thought about themselves by challenging moral and religious values as hollow and meaningless. The natural sciences threw into doubt the existence of a creator. New forms of communication and transportation—the telephone, the wireless telegraph, the bicycle, the automobile, the airplane—were obliterating traditional understandings of time and space. The cinema and the X ray altered visual perception and redefined the ways people saw the world around them. It was a period of intense excitement and vitality in the history of the West, one that traditional values did not always explain.

Like the political revolutionaries of an earlier age, futurist artists sought the liberation of the human spirit from a world that could no longer be understood or controlled. Liberation could only be achieved through immersion in mass society and rapid change. Boccioni's goal was a revolutionary one: "Let's turn everything upside down. . . . Let's split open our figures and place the environment inside them."

Boccioni has been recognized as one of the great artists of the twentieth century. In his sculpture and painting, he aimed to capture the vitality and excitement of the new age. The individual was no longer at the center of the new culture. Change, technology, and, above all, violence were exalted. As the First Futurist Manifesto urged, "Let us leave Wisdom behind. . . . Let us throw ourselves to be devoured by the Unknown." With the figures in his canvas swept up into an irrational mass, Boccioni emphasizes the rush and unpredictability of daily life. Boccioni met his own death in 1916 as a soldier in the war that he welcomed as a purifying event.

■ Umberto Boccioni, *Riot in the Galleria* (1910).

Looking Ahead

As Europe passed from the nineteenth to the twentieth century, the new, grand scale of industrial production and political life was matched by the emergence of mass society. This chapter will discuss how the need for regulation and control in mass democracy challenged the liberal, nineteenth-century emphasis on individual rights and parliamentary rule in Great Britain, Germany, France, and Austria. Mass democracy drew new social groups, workers and peasants, into the political arena, but it also continued to exclude others, including women, ethnic minorities, and Jews, whose pursuit of inclusion further challenged parliamentary forms.

The sciences and the new scientific study of society known as the social sciences contributed to attempts to understand how the physical world functioned, its predictability, and its improvement through technological and applied advances in knowledge. And a new artistic vision influenced by breakthroughs in science, technology, new knowledge about other cultures, and the study of the unconscious greatly enriched the way Europeans and the broader global community viewed the world. A new consciousness shaped ideas about family life, gender roles, and patterns of consumption as Europeans entered the twentieth century. ➤

EUROPEAN ECONOMY AND THE POLITICS OF MASS SOCIETY

Between 1871 and 1914, the scale of European life was radically altered. Industrial society had promoted largeness as the norm, and growing numbers of people worked under the same roof. Large-scale heavy industries fueled by new energy sources dominated the economic landscape. Great Britain, the leader of the first phase of the Industrial Revolution of the eighteenth century, slipped in prominence as an industrial power at the end of the nineteenth century, as Germany and the United States devised successful competitive strategies of investment, protection, and control.

Regulating Boom and Bust

The organization of factory production throughout Europe and the proximity of productive centers to distribution networks meant ever greater concentration of populations in urban areas. Like factories, cities were getting bigger at a rapid

■ This bustling Berlin street scene in 1909 in a fashionable quarter of the city is typical of European urban life at the beginning of the twentieth century.

rate and were proliferating in numbers. Berlin, capital of the new German nation, mushroomed in size in the last quarter of the nineteenth century. In the less industrialized parts of eastern Europe, cities also underwent record growth. Warsaw, St. Petersburg, and Moscow all expanded by at least 400,000 inhabitants each. Budapest, the city created by uniting the towns of Buda and Pest in 1872, tripled in size between 1867 and 1914 and was typical of the booming growth of provincial cities throughout Europe. With every passing year proportionately fewer people remained on the land. Those who did stay in the agricultural sector were linked to cities and tied into national cultures by new transportation and communications networks.

The Need for Regulation.   Between 1873 and 1895, an epidemic of slumps battered the economies of European nations. The slumps, characterized by falling prices, downturns in productivity, and declining profits, have been called the "Great Depression" of the nineteenth century. In reality, the economic downturn of the period was not a great depression like the one that followed the crash of 1929, but instead was a period of economic uncertainty and fluctuation. It did not strike European nations simultaneously, nor did it affect all countries with the same degree of severity. But the so-called Great Depression of the late nineteenth century and the boom period of intense economic expansion from 1895 to 1914 did teach industrialists, financiers, and politicians one important lesson: alternative booms and busts in the business cycle were dangerous and had to be regulated.

Too much of a good thing brought on the steady deflation of the last quarter of the nineteenth century. In the world economy, there was an overproduction of agricultural products—a sharp contrast to the famines that had ravaged Europe only 50 years earlier. Overproduction resulted from two new factors in the world economy: technological advances in crop cultivation and the low cost of shipping and transport, which had opened up European markets to cheap agricultural goods from the United States, Canada, and Argentina. The absolute numbers of those employed in agriculture remained more or less constant, but world output soared. Cheap foreign grains, especially wheat, flooded European markets and drastically drove down agricultural prices. The drop in prices affected purchasing power in other sectors and resulted in long-term deflation and unemployment.

Financiers, politicians, and businessmen dedicated themselves to eliminating the boom-and-bust phenomenon, which they considered dangerous. Why were cyclic downturns considered so dangerous at the end of the nineteenth century when they had not been before? Earlier in the century, manufacturers of textiles could endure "bust" periods of depressed prices and declining profits without great hardship. Small family firms requiring little capital could move in and out of production to meet demand. But by the last quarter of the nineteenth century that situation had changed dramatically. The application of science and technology to industrial production required huge amounts of capital. The two new sources of power after 1880, petroleum and electricity, could only be developed with heavy capital investment. Large mechanized steel plants were costly and out of reach for small family firms of the scale that had industrialized textiles so successfully earlier in the century. Heavy machinery, smelting furnaces, buildings, and transport were all beyond the abilities of the small entrepreneur. In order to raise the capital necessary for the new heavy industry at the end of the nineteenth century, firms had to look outside themselves to the stock market, banks, or the state to find adequate capital resources.

But investors, especially banks, refused to invest without guarantees on their capital. Bankers all over Europe were intent on minimizing risks, and they certainly wanted to avoid the uncertainties of the business cycle. Because investment in heavy industry meant tying up capital for extended periods of time, banks insisted on safeguards against falling prices. The solution they demanded was the elimination of uncertainty through the regulation of markets.

Cartels.   Regulation was achieved through the establishment of **cartels,** combinations of firms in a given industry united to fix prices and to establish production quotas. Not as extreme as the monopolies that appeared in the United States in the same period and for the same purpose, cartels were agreements among big firms intent on controlling markets and guaranteeing profits. Trusts were another form of collaboration that resulted in the elimination of unprofitable businesses. Firms joined together horizontally within the same industry—for example, all steel producers agreed to fix prices and set quotas. Or they combined vertically by controlling all levels of the production process, from raw materials to the finished product, and all other ancillary products necessary to or

resulting from the production process. That type of cartel was exemplified by a single firm that controlled the entire production process and the marketing of a single product, from raw materials and fuel through sales and distribution.

Firms in Great Britain, falling behind in heavy industry, failed to form cartels and for the most part remained in private hands. But heavy industry in Germany, France, and Austria, to varying degrees, sought regulation of markets through cartels. International cartels appeared that regulated markets and prices across national borders within Europe. Firms producing steel, chemicals, coke, and pig iron all minimized the effects of competition through the regulation of prices and output.

Banks, which had been the initial impetus behind the transformation to a regulated economy, in turn formed consortia to meet the need for greater amounts of capital. A consortium—paralleling a cartel—was a partnership among banks, often international in character, in which interest rates and the movement of capital were regulated by mutual agreement. The state, too, played an important role in directing the economy. In capital-poor Russia, the state used indirect taxes on the peasantry to finance industrialization and railway construction at the end of the nineteenth century. Russia industrialized with the sweat of its peasants. Russia also needed to import capital, primarily from France after 1887. The state had to guarantee foreign loans and regulate the economy to pay interest on foreign capital investment. Foreign investors were not willing to leave the export of capital to chance or the vagaries of the business cycle. The state must intervene.

Throughout Europe, nation-states protected domestic industries by erecting tariff barriers that made foreign goods noncompetitive in domestic markets. Only Great Britain

■ A cartoon from a pamphlet published in Britain by the Tariff Reform League in 1903. The tree represents Britain's free trade policy. The other nations of the world are harvesting the benefits of the British policy.

among the major powers stood by a policy of free trade. Europe was split into two tiers, the haves and the have-nots—those countries with a solid industrial core and those that had remained unindustrialized. The division had a geographic character, with the north and west of Europe more heavily developed and capitalized and the southern and eastern parts of Europe remaining heavily agricultural. For both the haves and the have-nots, tariff policies were an attractive form of regulation by the state to protect established industries and to nurture those industries struggling for existence.

Economic regulation was not a twentieth-century creation, as critics of the welfare state contend. Intervention and control began in the late nineteenth century, very much under the impetus of bankers, financiers, and industrialists. Capitalists looked on state intervention not as an intrusion but as a welcome corrective to the ups and downs of the business cycle. Regulation did not emerge from any philosophical or ideological assumption about government but came about as a result of the very real need for capital to enable heavy industry to expand and the equally compelling need to protect profits in order to encourage financiers to invest.

Challenging Liberal England

Great Britain experienced the transformation in political organization and social structure before other European nations. But after 1870, changes in politics influenced by the scale of the new industrial society spread to every European country. Mass democracy was on the rise and was pushing aside the liberal emphasis on individual rights valued by parliamentary governments everywhere.

Great Britain had avoided revolution and social upheaval. It prided itself on the progress achieved by a strong parliamentary tradition. One writer caught the self-congratulatory spirit of the age in an 1885 book on popular government: "We Englishmen pass on the Continent as masters of the art of government." Parliamentary government was based on a homogeneous ruling elite. Aristocrats and businessmen and financial leaders shared a common educational background in England's elitist educational system of the "public schools," which were really exclusive, private ones, and the universities of Oxford or Cambridge. Schooling produced a common outlook and common attitudes toward parliamentary rule, whether in Conservative or Liberal circles, and guaranteed a certain stability in policies and legislation.

Trade Unions. In the 1880s, issues of unemployment, housing, public health, and education challenged the attitudes of Britain's ruling elite and fostered the advent of an independent working-class politics. Between 1867 and 1885, extension of the suffrage increased the electorate fourfold. Protected by the markets of its empire, the British economy did not experience the roller-coaster effect of recurrent booms and busts after 1873. Nor did Britain experience severe economic crisis between 1890 and 1914, a period of growing labor unrest. But after 1900, wages stagnated while prices continued to rise.

Traditional parliamentary politics had little to offer those workers whose standard of living suffered a real decline. The quality of urban housing deteriorated, as exemplified by the severe overcrowding of London's East End.

Workers responded to their distress by supporting militant trade unions. Trade unions, drawing on a long tradition of working-class associations, were all that stood between workers and the economic dislocation caused by unemployment, sickness, or old age. In addition, new unions of unskilled and semiskilled workers flourished, beginning in the 1880s and 1890s. A Scottish miner, James Keir Hardie (1856–1915), attracted national attention as the spokesman for a new political movement, the Labour party, whose goal was to represent workers in Parliament. In 1892, Hardie was the first independent working man to sit in the House of Commons. Hardie and his party convinced trade unions that it was in their best interests to support Labour candidates instead of Liberals in parliamentary elections after 1900. Unions, as extraparliamentary groups, worked successfully toward achieving a parliamentary voice. By 1906, the new Labour party had 29 seats in Parliament.

Fabian Socialism and Parliamentary Reforms. Yet Parliament seemed to be failing the poor. So argued a group of intellectuals concerned with social welfare who called themselves **Fabians.** They named themselves after the Roman dictator Fabius, who was noted for his delaying tactics, which enabled him to avoid decisive battle with Hannibal in the Punic Wars. Fabius believed in cutting off the supplies of his enemies and engaging in skirmishes. Following his lead, the Fabians were socialists, not in a Marxist sense of ultimate revolutionary confrontation, but in a gradualist sense of a reformist commitment to social justice. Led by Beatrice Webb (1858–1943) and Sidney Webb (1859–1947), and including in their number playwright and critic George Bernard Shaw (1856–1950), theosophist Annie Besant (1847–1943), and novelist H. G. Wells (1866–1946), the Fabians proved to be successful propagandists who were able to keep issues of social reform in the public eye. They advocated collective ownership of factories and workshops and state direction of production through gradual reform. At the turn of the century, the Fabian Society threw its support and the power of its tracts on social issues behind Labour party candidates. Intellectuals now joined with trade unionists in demanding public housing, better public sanitation, municipal reforms, and improved pay and benefits for working people.

The existence of the new Labour party pressured Conservatives and Liberals to develop more enlightened social policies and programs. After 1906, under threat of losing votes to the Labour party, the Liberal party heeded the pressures for reform. The "new" Liberals supported legislation to strengthen the right of unions to picket peacefully. Led by David Lloyd George (1863–1945), who was chancellor of the exchequer, Liberals sponsored the National Insurance Act of 1911. Modeled after Bismarck's social welfare policies (see p. 744), the act provided compulsory payments to workers for sickness and unemployment benefits. In order to gain approval to pay for the new legislation, Lloyd George recognized that Parliament itself had to be renovated. The Parliament Bill of 1911 reduced the House of Lords, dominated by Conservatives resistant to proposed welfare reforms, from its status as equal partner with the House of Commons. Commons could and now did raise taxes without the consent of the House of Lords to pay for new programs that benefited workers and the poor.

Extraparliamentary Protest. Social legislation did not silence unions and worker organizations. To the contrary, protest increased in the period up to the beginning of World War I in 1914. There was little doubt about the ability of militant trade unions to mobilize workers. In 1910, three of every ten manual workers belonged to a union, and that figure doubled to 60 percent of the work force between 1910 and 1914. In those years, waves of strikes broke over England. Unions threatened to paralyze the economy. Coal miners, seamen, railroad workers, and dockers protested against stagnant wages and rising prices.

The high incidence of strikes was a consequence of growing distrust of Parliament and distrust, too, of a regulatory state bureaucracy responsible for the social welfare reforms. Workers felt manipulated by a system unresponsive to their needs. Labour's voice grew more strident. The Trade Unions Act of 1913 granted unions legal rights to settle their grievances with management directly. In the summer of 1914, a railway worker boasted, "We are big and powerful enough to fight our own battle without the aid of Parliament or any other agency. There could be no affection between the robber and the robbed." Only the outbreak of war in 1914 ended the possibility of a general strike by miners, railwaymen, and transport workers.

The question of Irish Home Rule also plagued Parliament. In Ulster in northern Ireland, army officers of Protestant Irish background threatened to mutiny. In addition, women agitating for the vote shattered parliamentary complacence. The most advanced industrial nation in the world, with its tradition of peaceful parliamentary rule, had entered the age of mass politics.

Political Struggles in Germany

During his reign as chancellor of the German Empire (1871–1890), Otto von Bismarck formed shrewd alliances that hampered the development of effective parliamentary government. He repeatedly and successfully blocked the emergence of fully democratic participation. In Germany, all males had the right to vote, but the German parliament, the Reichstag, enjoyed only restricted powers in comparison to the British Parliament. Bismarck's objective remained always the successful unification of Germany, and he promoted cooperation with democratic institutions and parties only so long as that goal was enhanced.

Bismarck and the German Parliament. Throughout the 1870s, the German chancellor collaborated with the German liberal parties in constructing the legal codes, the monetary

■ Known as the "Iron Chancellor," Otto von Bismarck hampered the development of effective parliamentary government in Germany.

and banking system, the judicial apparatus, and the railroad network that pulled the new Germany together. Bismarck backed German liberals in their antipapal campaign, in which the Catholic Church was declared the enemy of the German state. He suspected the identification of Catholics with Rome, which the liberals depicted as an authority in competition with the nation-state. The anti-Church campaign, launched in 1872, was dubbed the *Kulturkampf*, the "struggle for civilization," because its supporters contended that it was a battle waged in the interests of humanity.

The legislation of the *Kulturkampf* expelled Jesuits from Germany, removed priests from state service, attacked religious education, and instituted civil marriage. Bishops and priests who followed the instructions of Pope Pius IX (1846–1878) not to obey the new laws were arrested and expelled from Germany. Many Germans grew concerned over the social costs of such widespread religious repression, and the Catholic Center party increased its parliamentary representation by rallying Catholics as a voting bloc in the face of state repression. With the succession of a new pontiff, Leo XIII (1878–1903), Bismarck took advantage of the opportunity to negotiate a settlement with the

Catholic Church, cutting his losses and bringing the *Kulturkampf* to a halt. Bismarck had grown wary of the demands of the National Liberal party for an increasing share of political power.

The Social Democratic Party. Bismarck's repressive policies also targeted the Social Democratic party. The Social Democrats were committed to a Marxist critique of capitalism and to international cooperation with other socialist parties. Seeing them as a threat to stability in Germany and in Europe as a whole, he set out to smash them. In 1878, using the opportunity for repression presented by two attempts on the emperor's life, Bismarck outlawed the fledgling Socialist Party. The Anti-Socialist Law forbade meetings among Socialists, fundraising, and distribution of printed matter. The law relied on expanded police powers and was a fundamental attack on civil liberties and freedom of choice within a democratic electoral system. Nevertheless, individual Social Democratic candidates stood for election in the period and quickly learned how to work with middle-class parties in order to achieve electoral successes. By 1890, Social Democrats had captured 20 percent of the electorate and controlled 35 Reichstag seats, in spite of Bismarck's anti-Socialist legislation.

Throughout the 1880s, as his ability to manage Reichstag majorities declined and as Socialist strength steadily mounted, Bismarck grew disenchanted with universal manhood suffrage. Beginning in 1888, the chancellor found himself at odds with the new emperor, Wilhelm II (1888–1918), over his foreign and domestic policies. The young emperor dismissed Bismarck in March 1890 and abandoned the chancellor's anti-Socialist legislation. The Social Democratic party became the largest Marxist party in the world and, by 1914, the largest single party in Germany.

The socialism of the German Social Democrats was modified in the 1890s. Although it had never been violent or insurrectionary, social democracy moved away from a belief in a future revolution and toward a democratic **revisionism** that favored gradual reform through parliamentary participation. Those who continued to maintain a more orthodox Marxist position, such as August Bebel (1840–1913) and Karl Kautsky (1854–1938), believed capitalism would destroy itself, as Karl Marx had predicted, without any violent action by German Social Democrats. Bebel confided to Friedrich Engels in 1885 that he went to bed every night with the confidence that "the last hour of bourgeois society strikes soon."

Revisionism was both practical and democratic. Its leading advocate, Eduard Bernstein (1850–1932), introduced aspects of Fabian state socialism into the German movement. The grassroots transformation favored evolutionary rather than revolutionary political action. Workers were the primary force behind the shift away from the catastrophe theory of Bebel and Kautsky. Their standard of living had been improving in Germany, and the prospect of the imminent collapse of capitalism seemed slight to workers intent on achieving further gains. Union membership grew dramatically among unskilled workers after 1895. Working-class organizations, tolerated earlier by Social Democrats for their future potential, now became centers of power and pressed for practical benefits for their members.

During the period when the Social Democratic movement had been outlawed, Bismarck had employed carrot-and-stick methods to woo the working class away from the Marxists. The stick with which Bismarck beat back the political opposition had been the Anti-Socialist Law. The carrot that he and then Wilhelm II used to win mass support was social welfare legislation, including accident insurance, sick benefits, and old age and disability benefits introduced by the state. But such legislation did not undermine the popularity of socialism, nor did it attract workers away from Marxist political programs, as the mounting electoral returns demonstrated. Social democracy built its rank-and-file union membership by employing sophisticated organizational techniques in order to expand its mass base of support.

The success and popularity of the Social Democratic party cemented a stronger alliance on the Right among Conservatives. Realizing that they could not beat the Left, right-wing groups decided to copy it. Unable to defeat social democracy by force or by state-sponsored welfare policies, Bismarck's successors set out to organize mass support. Agrarian and industrial interests united strongly behind state policies. An aggressive foreign policy was judged as the surest way to win over the masses. Leagues were formed to exploit nationalism and patriotism among the electorate over issues of naval and military expansion and colonial development.

In the end, the Reichstag failed to defy the absolute authority of Emperor Wilhelm II, who was served after 1890 by a string of ineffectual chancellors. Despite its constitutional forms, Germany was ruled by a state authoritarianism in which the bureaucracy, the military, and various interest groups exercised influence over the emperor. A high-risk foreign policy that had mass appeal was one way to circumvent a parliamentary system incapable of decision making. Constitutional solutions had been short-circuited in favor of authoritarian rule.

Political Scandals and Mass Politics in France

The Third Republic in France had an aura of accidental origins and precarious existence. Founded in 1870 with the defeat of Napoleon III's empire by the Germans, the Third Republic claimed legitimacy by placing itself squarely within the revolutionary democratic tradition. Yet its early days were marked by bloody social conflict, and its existence was plagued by ongoing struggles among contenders on the Right and Left who sought to control it.

Creating Citizens. In spite of surface indications of political conflict, the Third Republic successfully worked toward the creation of a national community based on a common identity for its citizens. Compulsory schooling, one of the great institutional transformations of French government in 1885, socialized French children by implanting in them common values, patriotism, and identification with the nation-state. Old ways, local dialects, superstitious practices, and peasant insularity dropped away or were modified under the persistent pressure of a centralized curriculum of reading, writing, arithmetic, and civics. Compulsory service in the army for the generation of young men of draft age served the same end of communicating national values to a predominantly peasant population.

Technology also accelerated the process of shaping a national citizenry as railroad lines tied people together and the infrastructure of roads made distances shrink. People could now travel back and forth between village and city, town and countryside, with ease and frequency. Common expectations for a better life and upward mobility moved through rural populations that for most of the nineteenth century had not looked beyond the horizon of the village. Young working women were particularly influential in transferring values from urban to rural areas as they moved from villages to towns in search of domestic and industrial jobs and then returned to their villages with new outlooks and new goals for their families.

Information was controlled at the center—Paris—and distributed on a national scale. Villagers in southern France read Parisian newspapers over their morning bowls of coffee and learned—with a previously unimaginable immediacy—about French foreign exploits and parliamentary wrangles. A truly national mass culture emerged in the period between 1880 and 1914. Common symbols such as the bust of Marianne appeared in every city hall in France, and a common vocabulary of patriotism spread across the land. French people were not necessarily more political, but they were political in a new way that enabled them to identify their own local interests with national issues.

The Boulanger Affair.   A political crisis, known as the Boulanger Affair, temporarily threatened the stability of the Republic and served as a good indication of the extent of the transformation in French political life at the end of the nineteenth century. General Georges Boulanger (1837–1891) was a popular and romantic figure who captured the imagination of the French press. As minister of war, Boulanger became a hero to French soldiers when he undertook needed reforms of army life. He won over businessmen by leading troops against strikers. Above all, he cultivated the image of a patriot ready to defend France's honor at any cost. Known as "the Man on Horseback" because of his ability to look dashing in public appearances astride his black horse, Boulanger was a shallow man whose success and national popularity were created by a carefully orchestrated publicity campaign that made him the most popular man in France by 1886.

Boulanger's potential in the political arena attracted the attention of right-wing backers, including monarchists who hoped eventually to restore kingship to France. Supported by big-money interests who favored a strengthened executive and a weaker parliamentary system, Boulanger undertook a nationwide political campaign, hoping to appeal to those unhappy with the Third Republic and promising vague constitutional reforms. General Boulanger's 1889 campaign managers successfully manipulated images that were recognizable to a rural electorate. Religious lithographs carried likenesses of the modern "messiah," the blond-bearded general, in place of Jesus.

Campaign workers were recruited at the local level. Boulangists hoped that through universal suffrage an authoritarian government could be established. By 1889, Boulanger was able to amass enough national support to frighten the defenders of parliamentary institutions. The charismatic general ultimately failed in his bid for power and fled the country because of allegations of treason. But he left in his wake an embryonic mass movement on the Right that operated outside the channels of parliamentary institutions. Boulanger's success was due to a new nationalism that flexed its muscles after 1880. Cultural symbols such as the flag and the nation-in-arms moved from the revolutionary tradition of the Left to become part of the appeal of the new right-wing groups that were growing in importance.

The Dreyfus Affair.   A very different type of crisis began to take shape in 1894 with the controversy surrounding the trial of Captain Alfred Dreyfus (1859–1935) that came to be known

■ This caricature portrays Captain Alfred Dreyfus as a dragon for the alleged leaking of military secrets.

"J' Accuse"

The central role of the press during the Dreyfus Affair is nowhere more apparent than in the impact of the novelist Émile Zola's front-page letter to the president of the Third Republic published in Georges Clemenceau's newspaper L'Aurore, on 13 January 1898. "J'Accuse" was an impassioned appeal to the French nation for justice in which Zola pointed to those truly guilty of betraying France in a cascade of ringing accusations. This letter, which was ultimately instrumental in freeing Captain Dreyfus, resulted in Zola's own prosecution for libel.

Focus Questions

What institutions of the French Third Republic was Zola attacking in "J'Accuse"? Why were Zola's words considered so libelous?

I accuse Lieutenant-Colonel du Paty de Clam of having been the diabolical artisan of the judicial error, without knowing it, I am willing to believe, and then of having defended his nefarious work for three years throughout the most grotesque and culpable machinations.

I accuse General Mercier of having become an accomplice, out of mental weakness at the least, in one of the greatest iniquities of the century. . . .

I accuse the three handwriting experts, Mssrs. Belhomme, Varinard, and Couard, of having composed deceitful and fraudulent reports, unless a medical examination declares them to be stricken with an impairment of vision or judgment.

I accuse the offices of War of having conducted in the press, particularly in *L'Éclair* and in *L'Echo de Paris*, an abominable campaign designed to mislead public opinion and to conceal their wrongdoing.

Finally, I accuse the first Court Martial of having violated the law in convicting a defendant on the basis of a document kept secret, and I accuse the second Court Martial of having covered up that illegality on command by committing in turn the juridical crime of knowingly acquitting a guilty man.

In bringing these accusations, I am not without realizing that I expose myself in the process to Articles 30 and 31 of the press law of July 29, 1881, which punishes offenses of slander. And it is quite willingly that I so expose myself.

As for those whom I accuse, I do not know them, I have never seen them, I have neither rancor nor hatred for them. They are for me no more than entities, spirits of social malfeasance. And the act that I hereby accomplish is but a revolutionary means of hastening the explosion of truth and justice.

I have but one passion, one for seeing the light, in the name of humanity which has so suffered and which is entitled to happiness. My fiery protest is but the cry of my soul. Let me be brought then before a criminal court and let the investigation be conducted in the light of day!

I am waiting.

---

simply as "the Affair." Dreyfus was an Alsatian Jewish army officer accused of selling military secrets to the Germans. His trial for treason served as a lightning rod for xenophobia—the hatred of foreigners, especially Germans—and **anti-Semitism,** the hatred of Jews. Dreyfus was stripped of his commission and honors and sentenced to solitary confinement for life on Devil's Island, a convict colony off French Guiana in South America.

Illegal activities and outright falsifications by Dreyfus's superiors in order to secure a conviction came to light in the mass press. The nation was soon divided. Those who supported Dreyfus's innocence, the pro-Dreyfusards, were for the most part on the left of the political spectrum and spoke of the Republic's duty to uphold justice and freedom. The anti-Dreyfusards were associated with the traditional institutions of the Catholic Church and the army and considered themselves to be defending the honor of France. Among those who upheld the conviction were right-wing groups, monarchists, and virulent anti-Semites.

Dreyfus was eventually exonerated and granted a full pardon in 1905. On the personal level, the Affair represented the ability of an individual to seek redress against injustice. On the national level, the Affair represented an important transformation in the nature of French political life. Existing parliamentary institutions had been found wanting and unable to cope with the mass politics stirred up by Dreyfus's conviction. New groups entered public life after 1894, coalescing around the question of the guilt or innocence of an individual man. The newspaper press vied with parliament and the courts as a forum for investigation and decision making. Intellectuals, too, organized. Leagues on the left and on the right took shape; unions, cooperatives, and professional societies all raised their voices. The organizations manipulated propaganda around issues of national defense and republican justice.

The crises provoked by Boulanger's attempt at power and the Dreyfus Affair demonstrated the major role of the press and the importance of public opinion in exerting pressure on the system of government. The press emerged as a mythmaker in shaping and channeling public opinion. Émile Zola (1840–1902), the great French novelist, spearheaded the pro-Dreyfusard movement with his damning article "I Accuse!" in which he pointed to the military and the judiciary as the "spirits of social evil" for persecuting an innocent man. The article appeared in a leading French newspaper and was influential in securing Dreyfus's eventual exoneration and the discovery of the real culprit, one of Dreyfus's colleagues in the General Staff. The Third Republic had never been in danger of collapsing, but it was transformed. The locus of power in parliament was challenged by pressure groups outside it.

Defeating Liberalism in Austria

In the 1870s, the liberal values of the bourgeoisie dominated the Austro-Hungarian Empire. The Habsburg monarchy had adjusted to constitutional government, which was introduced throughout Austria in 1860. Faith in parliamentary government based on a restricted suffrage had established a tenuous foothold. After the setbacks of 1848 and the troublesome decade of the 1860s, when Prussia had trounced Austria and Bismarck had routed the hope of an Austrian-dominated German Empire, the Austrian bourgeoisie counted on a peaceful future with a centralized multinational state dedicated to order and progress.

Vienna and the Bourgeoisie.   There is no better symbol of middle-class political and cultural aspirations in the period than the monumental rebuilding of the city of Vienna that took place after 1860. The belt of public and private buildings on the Ringstrasse, or "Ring Street," girding the old central city and separating it from its suburbs was dramatic testimony to bourgeois self-confidence. Grandiose buildings, likened to "cakes on platters," glorified constitutional government, economic vitality, the fine arts, and educational values. Monumental architecture was intended to legitimize bourgeois claims to power and to link Austrian institutions with the great cultural heritage of the West. The buildings were blatant copies of past architectural styles—massive Gothic for the city hall, Renaissance for the university, and early baroque for the theater. Yet the rebuilding was more than a self-confident statement of Austria's inheritance of a rich cultural tradition. Vienna's ruling class was fortifying itself behind the edifices of Western politics and culture against the onslaught of the new age.

In reality, the Austrian bourgeoisie was weaker than its French or British counterparts. The Austrian ruling class was heavily dependent on the Habsburg emperor and identified itself with the values of the aristocracy. Rapid economic growth had strengthened bourgeois status between 1840 and 1870, but it had also unleashed new social forces that existing institutions were unable to control. Liberal values of constitutional monarchy, centralization, restricted suffrage, and multinational government came up against new and threatening forces of anti-Semitism, socialism, nationalism, and mass politics.

The New Right.   By 1900, liberal politicians were being eliminated as a directing force in national politics. The new politicians who replaced them rejected the liberal-rational values of progress and order and moved into a realm colored by charisma, fantasy, and demagoguery. A new Right wielded mass political strategies that embraced the irrational and the violent.

The new groups laying claim to political power and displacing a weak Austrian bourgeoisie were peasants, workers, urban artisans and shopkeepers, and the colonized Slavic peoples of the empire. Bourgeois politics and laissez-faire economics had offered little or nothing to those varied groups, who were claiming the right of participation. Mass parties were formed based on radical pan-Germanic feeling; anticapitalism, which appealed to peasants and artisans; hatred of the Jews, shared by students and artisans; and nationalist aspirations that attracted the lower middle classes.

In 1895, Karl Lueger (1844–1910) used anti-Semitism in his successful campaign for the office of mayor of Vienna. Lueger's election was the first serious sign of the collapse of Austrian liberalism. Jews were identified with capitalists, and the irrational hatred directed at them unified different groups and helped to sweep Lueger into office.

Austrian poet and playwright Hugo von Hofmannsthal (1874–1929) understood the rejection of bourgeois politics in the age of expanded suffrage: "Politics is magic. He who knows how to summon the forces from the deep, him will they follow." The creation of a scapegoat by means of anti-Semitism and racism became the means of uniting the masses against a common foe and in favor of a common nationalist program. In Austria, antiliberal politics grew stronger in the years before 1914. The great buildings on the Ringstrasse that had attempted to connect Austrian political life with the glories of the European past were mocked as relics of a dead age. Centrifugal forces of pan-Germanism and nationalism were pulling the parliamentary system apart. An urban and capitalist middle class that ruled Austria by virtue of a limited suffrage based on property had lost ground to new groups that were essentially anticapitalist and antiliberal in their outlook and for whom parliamentary deliberations held no promise. The rejection of liberalism was a "revolt against the fathers." A new style of leader had emerged in Vienna at the end of the century, charismatic in style and violent in appeal. The "politics of fantasy" based on a new electorate was fast becoming the nightmare of parliamentary disintegration.

The political experiences of Great Britain, Germany, France, and Austria between 1871 and 1914 make clear the common challenges confronting Western parliamentary systems in a changing era of democratic politics. In spite of variations, each nation experienced its own challenge to liberal parliamentary institutions, and each shaped its own variety of responses to a new international phenomenon—the rise of the masses as a political force.

OUTSIDERS IN MASS POLITICS

By the end of the nineteenth century, the masses were replacing the individual in political culture. A faceless, nameless electorate became the basis of new political strategies and a new political rhetoric. The growing urbanization of western Europe and central and eastern Europe between 1870 and 1914 contributed to this emphasis on mass society. A concept of class identification of workers was devalued in favor of interest-group politics in which lobbies formed around single issues to pressure European governments. But the apparently all-inclusive concept of mass society continued to exclude some groups. Women, ethnic minorities, and Jews were pushed to the margins. Outsiders in mass politics had little in common with one another except for the common experience of repression by the state. But they did not remain quietly on the periphery. Women and ethnic minorities learned to incorporate strategies and techniques of politics and organization that permitted them to challenge the existing political system. Others, including anarchists, rejected both the organizational techniques of mass society and the values of the nation-state. Outsiders, then, were both those intent on being integrated into mass politics and those who sought its destruction.

Feminists and Politics

Women's emancipation had been a recurrent motif of European political culture throughout the nineteenth century. In the areas of civil liberties, legal equality with men, and economic autonomy, only the most limited reforms had been enacted. The cult of domesticity, important throughout the nineteenth century, assigned women to a separate sphere, that of the home. Glorifying domesticity was a recognition of women's unique contribution to society in the home, but it may itself have been a means of controlling women who protested the separation between public and private space.

Women's Rights. European women were paid at most one-third to one-half of what men earned for the same work. In Great Britain, women did not enjoy equal divorce rights until the twentieth century. In France, married women had no control over their own incomes: all their earnings were considered their husbands' private property. From the Atlantic to the Urals, women were excluded from economic and educational opportunities. Serfs had been liberated. Working-class men had gained the right to vote. But the new electoral politics that emerged in the last quarter of the nineteenth century explicitly excluded women.

Growing numbers of women, primarily from the middle classes, began calling themselves "feminist," a term coined in France in the 1830s. The new feminists throughout western Europe differed from earlier generations in their willingness to organize mass movements and to appropriate the techniques of interest-group politics. The first international congress of women's rights, held in Paris in 1878, initiated an era of international cooperation and exchange among women's organizations. Women's groups now positioned themselves for sustained political action.

Feminism as a historic term is worth pondering. Like liberalism, which had pulled down kings and destroyed privilege, feminism aimed at eliminating social inequalities. Like socialism, feminism was a set of principles for action whose purpose was to build a better world. At its base, feminism recognized the equality of the sexes, without denying difference. As John Stuart Mill in Great Britain and Ernest Legouvé (1807–1903), a French dramatist and leading proponent of women's rights, had demonstrated, one need not be female to be a feminist. It was the belief that men and women were equal and should enjoy equal rights that identified the feminist. Most feminists, however, were women, and the leadership of the movement for equal rights was in women's hands. The converse—that most women were feminists—was not true. Contemporary critics often dismissed feminism on the grounds that it represented no more than a tiny minority of women. The same minority status characterized the trade union movement—which in France, for example, had a smaller membership at the end of the nineteenth century than did feminist organizations.

European feminist organizations did not share a common agenda but instead grouped themselves around a series of related concerns for legal, educational, economic, and political emancipation. Rather than speaking of a single feminism, it is more appropriate to speak of different feminisms. The General German Women's Association agitated for educational opportunities and democratic participation for women. In France, women working for the vote were a minority of the women's organizations. Many French feminists defended a "maternal politics," by which they sought protection for women's responsibilities in the home. Other feminists were involved in abortion reform, birth control issues, and repeal of state control of prostitution. The French League for the Rights of Women stood steadfastly against the vote as an end in itself and worked instead for legal and economic reforms. On the whole, however, feminist organizations were divided into two camps. In the first were those who agitated for the vote; the second included those who thought that the vote was beside the point and that the central issues were economic, social, and legal reforms of women's status. Constituting the left wing of the second group were socialist women who were dedicated to needs of women of the working class.

Movements for the Vote. The lessons of the new electoral politics were not lost on feminists seeking women's emancipation through the vote. The feminist leaders Hubertine Auclert (1848–1914) in France and Emmeline Pankhurst (1858–1928) in Great Britain recognized the need for a mass base of support. If women's organizations were to survive as competing interest groups, they needed to form political alliances, control their own newspapers and magazines, and keep their cause before the public eye. Just as cartels, trade unions, and political parties had learned the game of influence and leverage so important for survival in the modern political milieu, so too

■ Suffragist Emmeline Pankhurst is arrested at a demonstration outside London's Buckingham Palace on May 1, 1914.

did feminists rely on organization to achieve their ends. There was a growing willingness by a variety of women's organizations to hold mass demonstrations and rallies and to use violent tactics.

No movement operated more effectively in that regard than the British suffrage movement. In 1903, the Women's Social and Political Union (WSPU) was formed by a group of eminently respectable middle-class and aristocratic British women. At the center of the movement was Emmeline Pankhurst, an attractive middle-aged woman with a frail appearance but a will of iron and a gift for oratory. Emmeline Pankhurst and her two daughters—Christabel (1880–1958), a lawyer by training, and Sylvia (1882–1960), an artist—succeeded in keeping women's suffrage before the British public and brought the plight of British women to international attention. During the following seven years, the WSPU made considerable progress, attracting a growing number of followers and successfully aligning itself with parliamentary supporters.

Women's demands for political power were the basis of an unheralded revolution in Western culture. In Great Britain, the decade before the Great War of 1914 was a period of profound political education for women seeking the vote. An unprecedented 250,000 women gathered in Hyde Park in 1908 to hear more about female suffrage. Laughed at by men, ridiculed in the press, taunted in public demonstrations, women activists refused to be quiet and to "know their place." If respectable women would never demonstrate for their rights, then the suffragists were willing to cease being respectable. Because they spoke out for voting rights, feminists were demeaned, humiliated, and accused of not being *real* women by their detractors.

One of the best examples of the rebellion of women against the limitations of their social roles took place on 18 November 1910, a day that came to be known among feminists as Black Friday. On that day, suffragists marched on Parliament, which had failed to support the vote for women. In a confrontation that lasted six hours, unarmed women battled with police to hold their ground. Rather than returning home as they were ordered, the women relentlessly pushed forward, meeting the blows and the wrath of London's bobbies. Many women were injured and many arrested.

The year 1910 marked the beginning of an era of increased militancy among women, who were derisively called **suffragettes** in the press in order to distinguish them from the nonmilitant suffragists. A basic element in the new militancy was the willingness to use violence to achieve political emancipation. As Emmeline Pankhurst explained it, "The argument of the broken window pane is the most valuable argument in modern politics." Militant women set mailboxes on fire or poured glue and jam over their contents, threw bombs into country houses, and slashed paintings in the National Gallery. All over London the tinkling of thousands of shattered windowpanes ushered in a new age of women's political action.

Mrs. Pankhurst was not naive about what her followers were doing: "There is something which governments care for more than human life and that is the security of property, and so it is through property that we shall strike the enemy." Suffragettes set fires in public buildings, churches, and hotels. As frustration grew, some assaulted members of the cabinet. One suffragette, Emily Wilding Davison (1872–1913), probably intent on suicide as an act of protest, was trampled to

TREATMENT OF POLITICAL PRISONERS UNDER A LIBERAL GOVERNMENT.

■ This British suffragette poster, published by the Women's Social and Political Union, graphically depicts the extreme methods used to force-feed women prisoners. A prison guard pulls back the prisoner's head, others hold down her arms and legs, and another ties her foot to the chair. A doctor holds a hose through which he forces gruel into the woman's nose.

death when she threw herself under the king's horse on Derby Day at Epsom Downs in 1913. Mrs. Pankhurst and others advocated violence against personal property to highlight the violence done to women by denying them their rights. The tactics seemed to accomplish little before the war, although they certainly kept the issue of female suffrage in the public eye until the outbreak of war in 1914. It was not until 1918 that British women were granted limited suffrage, and not until 1928 that women gained voting rights equal to those of men.

Women suffered for their militancy, for civil disobedience evoked harsh repressive measures from the British government. Previous benevolence toward middle-class female prisoners arrested for attacks on property gave way to a new harshness that included the force-feeding of convicted suffragettes. Using tubes, hoses, and metal jaw clamps, prison guards and doctors poured gruel down the throats of imprisoned women who, as a form of protest, refused to eat. Such repressive measures only increased the solidarity within the women's movement and won the suffragettes international sympathy and support. Stymied, the government passed the Cat and Mouse Act in 1913. Imprisoned women who refused to eat were released, then reincarcerated once they had resumed eating and regained their strength. The "cat-and-mouse" pattern of release and reimprisonment could double or extend indefinitely a three-year sentence served in three-day segments. Many of the more dramatic tactics of the suffragettes, including getting arrested, were not available to working-class activists, who could not put aside their family responsibilities to serve jail sentences.

European women did not easily gain the right to vote. In France and Germany, moderate and left-wing politicians opposed extension of the vote to women because they feared that women would strengthen conservative candidates. Many

politicians felt that women were not "ready" for the vote and that they should receive it only as a reward—an unusual concept in democratic societies. Queen Victoria condemned women's agitation for the vote as a "mad, wicked folly." Only after war and revolution was the vote extended to women in the West—in Germany in 1918, in the United States in 1920, and in France at the end of World War II.

Women and Social Reform. Not all activist women saw the right to vote as the solution to women's oppression. Those who agitated for social reforms for poor and working-class women parted ways with the militant suffragettes. Sylvia Pankhurst, for example, left her mother and sister to their political battles in order to work for social reform in London's poverty-stricken East End. Differing from those who focused on woman's right to vote as a primary goal, women socialists were concerned with working-class women's "double oppression" in the home and in the workplace. The largest women's socialist movement existed in Germany, with 175,000 members by 1914. With its own newspaper, it operated independently of the men's socialist movement. German socialist women were opposed to suffrage on the grounds that giving middle-class women the vote did not address social issues.

Socialist women's lot was not an easy one, since union members often denied women's right to work and saw women's employment as a threat to men in the workplace. In Germany, socialist men opposed women industrial workers. Unions supported the concept of separate spheres for men and women and based their demands for a family wage on the need to maintain a separate private domain of the home. Socialist men argued that women's work often resulted in the neglect of children and could lead to the physical degeneration of

DOCUMENT

Working Conditions of Women in Factories

CONSTANCE LYTTON

Civil disobedience by British women demanding the right to vote often led to their arrest. In protest, incarcerated suffragettes went on hunger strikes to publicize their cause. The British government responded with a brutal policy of force-feeding of prisoners. Constance Lytton, a British aristocrat and suffragette, recounts here the agony of being forcibly fed in prison. Her own health was seriously weakened by the experience.

Focus Questions

How did Constance Lytton express civil disobedience? Why was the government intent on force-feeding women incarcerated in this way, a practice not common with other prisoners?

[The prison's senior medical officer] urged me to take food voluntarily. I told him that was absolutely out of the question, that when our legislators ceased to resist enfranchising women then I should cease to resist taking food in prison... . I offered no resistance to being placed in position, but lay down voluntarily on the plank bed. Two of the wardresses took hold of my arms, one held my head and one my feet. One wardress helped to pour the food. The doctor leant on my knees as he stooped over my chest to get at my mouth. I shut my mouth and clenched my teeth. . . . The doctor offered me the choice of a wooden or steel gag; he explained elaborately, as he did on most subsequent occasions, that the steel gag would hurt and the wooden one not, and he urged me not to force him to use the steel gag. But I did not speak nor open my mouth, so that after playing about for a moment or two with the wooden one he finally had recourse to the steel. He seemed annoyed at my resistance and he broke into a temper as he plied my teeth with the steel implement. . . . The pain of it was intense and at last I must have given way for he got the gag between my teeth, when he proceeded to turn it much more than necessary until my jaws were fastened wide apart, far more than they could go naturally. Then he put down my throat a tube which seemed to me much too wide and was something like four feet in length. The irritation of the tube was excessive. I choked the moment it touched my throat until it had got down. Then the food was poured in quickly; it made me sick a few seconds after it was down and the action of the sickness made my body and legs double up, but the wardresses instantly pressed back my head and the doctor leant on my knees. The horror of it was more than I can describe. I was sick over the doctor and wardresses, and it seemed a long time before they took the tube out. As the doctor left he gave me a slap on the cheek, not violently, but, as it were, to express his contemptuous disapproval, and he seemed to take for granted that my distress was assumed. . . . I had been sick over my hair, which, though short, hung on either side of my face, all over the wall near my bed, and my clothes seemed saturated with it, but the wardresses told me they could not get me a change that night as it was too late, the office was shut. I lay quite motionless, it seemed paradise to be without the suffocating tube, without the liquid food going in and out of my body and without the gag between my teeth. Before long I heard the sounds of the forced feeding in the next cell to mine. It was almost more than I could bear, it was Elsie Howey, I was sure. When the ghastly process was over and all quiet, I tapped on the wall and called out at the top of my voice, which wasn't much just then, "No surrender," and there came the answer past any doubt in Elsie's voice. "No surrender."

From Constance Lytton, *Prisons and Prisoners* (1914).

the family. Working women, socialist men argued, undermined existing wage scales and aided the exploitation of workers by their willingness to work for lower wages. Class oppression, countered German socialist leader and theorist Clara Zetkin (1857–1933), was the basis of women's oppression. For militants like Zetkin, socialism offered the only means to eliminate sexual inequalities.

The women's movements of the period from 1871 to 1914 differed socially and culturally from nation to nation. Yet in one sense the women's movements constituted an international phenomenon. The rise in the level of women's political consciousness occurred in the most advanced Western countries almost simultaneously and had a predominantly middle-class character. Working-class women, most notably in Germany, united feminism with socialism in search of a better life. In spite of concerted efforts, women remained on the outside of societies that excluded them from political participation, access to education, and social and economic equality.

The Jewish Question and Zionism

Two million eastern European Jews migrated westward between 1868 and 1914 in search of peace and refuge. Seventy thousand settled in Germany. Others continued westward, stopping in the United States. Another kind of Jewish migration took place in the nineteenth century—the movement of

MAP DISCOVERY

Legend:
- The Pale: area where Russian Jews allowed to live
- Other areas of large Jewish population
- • Cities with large Jewish population
- General routes of Jewish exodus

Jewish Migration

Persecution and expulsions drove two million Jews out of Russia and eastern Europe between 1868 and 1914. Some settled in central Europe, others traveled to Palestine and the Americas. According to this map, what features do the areas of large Jewish population have in common? What are the major general routes of Jewish exodus? Based on the chapter discussion, why did Jews migrate into and out of The Pale in western Russia? What were the major stopover points in the Jewish migrations to the south and west?

Differing in language, culture, and dress, they were viewed as alien in every way.

Anti-Semitism. The term anti-Semitism, meaning hostility to Jews, was first used in 1879 to give a pseudoscientific legitimacy to bigotry and hatred. Persecution was a harsh reality for Jews in eastern Europe at the end of the nineteenth century. In Russia, Jews could not own property and were restricted to living in certain territories. Organized massacres, or **pogroms,** in Kiev, Odessa, and Warsaw followed the assassination of Tsar Alexander II in 1881 and recurred after the failed Russian revolution of 1905. Russian authorities blamed the Jews, seen as perennial outsiders, for the assassination and revolution and the social instability that followed them. Pogroms resulted in the death and displacement of tens of thousands of Russian and eastern European Jews.

In western Europe, Jews considered themselves "assimilated" into their national cultures, identifying with their nationality as much as with their religion. Austrian and German Jews were granted full civil rights in 1867 on the principle that citizens of all religions enjoyed full equality. In France, Jews had been legally emancipated since the end of the eighteenth century. But western and central European politics of the 1890s had a strong dose of anti-Semitism. Demagogues such as Georg von Schönerer (1842–1921) of Austria were capable of whipping up a frenzy of riots and violence against Jews. They did not distinguish between assimilated and immigrant Jewish populations in their irrational denunciations.

Western and central European anti-Semitism assumed a new level of virulence at the end of the nineteenth century. Fear of an economic depression united aristocrat and worker

Jews from rural to urban areas within nations. In eastern Europe, Jewish migrations coincided with downturns in the economic cycle, and Jews became scapegoats for the high rates of unemployment and high prices that seemed to follow in their wake. Most migrants were peddlers, artisans, or small shopkeepers who were seen as threatening to small businesses.

■ Maurycy Minkowski, *After the Pogrom* (ca. 1910). Minkowski's works depict Jewish life in Poland before the Russian Revolution. In this painting he has expertly captured the weariness, hopelessness, and fear of the refugees who have interrupted their flight to rest. The sense of isolation and dislocation evoked in the painting may derive from the deaf and mute artist's personal perception of profound separation and detachment.

alike in blaming a Jewish conspiracy. German anti-Semitism proliferated in the 1880s. "It is like a horrible epidemic," the scholar Theodor Mommsen (1817–1903) observed. "It can neither be explained nor cured."

Fear of the Jews was connected with hatred of capitalism. In France and Germany, Jews controlled powerful banking and commercial firms that became the targets of blame in hard times. Upwardly mobile sons of Jewish immigrants entered the professions of banking, trading, and journalism. They were also growing in numbers as teachers and academics. In the 1880s, more than half of Vienna's physicians (61 percent in 1881) and lawyers (58 percent of barristers in 1888) were Jewish. Their professional success only heightened tensions and condemnations of Jews as an "alien race." Anti-Semitism served as a violent means of mobilizing mass support, especially among those groups who felt threatened by capitalist concentration and large-scale industrialization. For anti-Semitic Europeans, Jews embodied the democratic, liberal, and cosmopolitan tendencies of the culture that they were consciously rejecting in their new political affiliations.

Zionism.   A Jewish leadership emerged in central and western Europe that treated anti-Semitism as a problem that could be solved by political means. For their generation at the end of the nineteenth century, the assimilation of their fathers and mothers was not the answer. Jews needed their own nation, it was argued, since they were a people without a nation. **Zionism** was the solution to what Jewish intellectuals called "the Jewish problem." Zion, the ancient homeland of Biblical times, would provide a national territory, and a choice, to persecuted Jews. Zionism became a Jewish nationalist movement

dedicated to the establishment of a Jewish state. Although Zionism did not develop mass support in western Europe among assimilated Jews, its program for national identity and social reforms appealed to a large following of eastern European Jews in Galicia (Poland), Russia, and the eastern lands of the Habsburg Empire—those directly subjected to the extremes of persecution.

Theodor Herzl (1860–1904), an Austrian Jew born in Budapest, was the founder of Zionism in its political form. As a student in Vienna he had encountered discrimination, but his commitment to Zionism developed as a result of his years as a journalist in Paris. Observing the anti-Semitic attacks in republican France provoked by the scandals surrounding the misappropriation of funds by leading French politicians and businessmen during the construction of the Panama Canal and the divisive conflict over the Dreyfus Affair in the 1890s, Herzl came to appreciate how deeply imbedded anti-Semitism was in European society. He despaired of the ability of corrupt parliamentary governments to solve the problem of anti-Semitism. In *The Jewish State* (1896), Herzl concluded that Jews must have a state of their own. Under his direction, Zionism developed a worldwide organization and its own newspaper with the aim of establishing a Jewish homeland in Palestine.

Jews began emigrating to Palestine. With the financial backing of Jewish donors, including the French banker Baron de Rothschild, nearly 90,000 Jews had established settlements there by 1914. Calculated to tap a common Jewish identification with an ancient heritage, the choice of Palestine as a homeland was controversial from the beginning. The problems arising from the choice have persisted into the twenty-first century.

The promised land of the Old Testament, Zion is a holy place in Judaism. The Austrian psychoanalyst Sigmund Freud (1856–1939), who described himself as "a Jew from Moravia," was sympathetic to the Zionist cause but critical of the idea of Palestine as a Jewish state. He considered the idea unworkable and one bound to arouse Christian and Islamic opposition. Freud feared that Palestine would arouse the suspicions of the Arab world and challenge "the feelings of the local natives." He would have preferred a "new, historically unencumbered soil."

Some Jewish critics of Zionism believed that a separate Jewish state would prove that Jews were not good citizens of their respective nation-states and would exacerbate hostilities toward Jews as outsiders. Yet Zionism had much in common with the European liberal tradition because it sought in the creation of a nation-state for Jews the solution to social injustice. Zion, the Jewish nation in the Middle East, was a liberal utopia for the Jewish people. Zionism learned from other mass movements of the period the importance of a broad base of support. By the time of the First Zionist Congress, held in Basel, Switzerland, in 1897, it had become a truly international movement. Herzl was also well aware of the necessity for a charismatic leader and cast himself in the role of messiah for his people.

Zionism did not achieve its goals before World War I, and the Jewish state of Israel was not recognized by the world community until 1948. Before World War I, anti-Semitism and antifeminism were strongly linked in nationalist political programs, which insisted that the place for Jews was on the periphery and the place for women was in the home. Through the Zionist movement, Jews victimized by nationalism planned for their own nation-state as a solution.

Workers and Minorities on the Margins

Changes in the scale of political life paralleled the rise of heavy industry and the increasing urbanization of European populations. New industrial and financial leaders assumed positions of power among Europe's ruling elite. A new style of politics brought new political actors into the public arena at the beginning of the twentieth century. Extraparliamentary groups grew in influence and power and came to exert pressure on the political process. The politics of mass society made clear the contradictions inherent in democracy. Propaganda, the ability to control information, became the avenue to success.

Anarchism.   There was no single anarchist doctrine, but the varieties of **anarchism** all shared a hope in a future free from constraints. Mikhail Bakunin (1814–1876), a member of the Russian nobility, absorbed the works and the message of the French social critic Pierre-Joseph Proudhon. Bakunin became Europe's leading anarchist spokesman. Unlike Proudhon, Bakunin was a man of revolutionary action who espoused the use of violence to achieve individual liberation. He believed that all existing institutions had to be swept away before ownership of production could be collectivized. Bakunin broke with Marx, whom he considered a "scientific bourgeois socialist" out of touch with the mass of workers.

In 1892, the Parisian trial of a bomb-throwing anarchist named Ravachol attracted great public attention. He and other French anarchists had captured the popular imagination with their threats to destroy bourgeois society by bombing private residences, public buildings, and restaurants. Ravachol's terrorist deeds represented the extreme rejection of participation in electoral politics. The public was frightened—but also fascinated. Ravachol opposed the state and the capitalist economy as the dual enemy that could only be destroyed through individual acts of random physical violence. For his crimes he was condemned to death and publicly executed.

The best-known anarchists of the late nineteenth century were those, like Ravachol, who engaged in terrorist assassinations and bombings. Although not all anarchists were terrorists intent on destruction, all shared a desire for a revolutionary restructuring of society. Most anarchists were loners. They dreamed of the collapse of the capitalist system with its exploitation and inequality and of the emergence of a society based on personal freedom, autonomy, and justice. Anarchists spurned the Marxist willingness to organize and participate in parliamentary politics. They disdained the tyranny of new organizations and bureaucracies that worked for gradual reforms at the expense of principles of justice.

Bakunin's successor in international anarchist doctrine was also a Russian of aristocratic lineage—Prince Petr Kropotkin (1842–1921). Kropotkin joined together communism and anarchism, arguing that goods should be communally distributed, "from each according to his ability, to each according to his needs." On the basis of his own empirical observations, Kropotkin argued that competition and dominance were not laws of nature and instead stressed human interdependence.

It is difficult to measure the extent of Bakunin's or Kropotkin's influence, since whatever followers they might have inspired were not overtly or formally organized. Anarchism's greatest appeal was in the less industrialized countries of southern Europe: Spain, Italy, and southern France. In those countries, grassroots anarchism germinated in working-class communities. In the second half of the nineteenth century, Russia too had developed a strong populist tradition similar to anarchism in its opposition to state tyranny. But anarchism was primarily a western European phenomenon.

Anarchism had special appeal to workers in trades staggering under the blows of industrial capitalism. Calling themselves anarcho-syndicalists, artisans—especially in France—were able to combine local trade union organization with anarchist principles. Alienation from the political process was strong among the French working class, who had recent bitter memories of repression during the Paris Commune in 1871 and who rejected the sterility and corruption of the party politics of the Third Republic. Most of the workers were in skilled trades that suffered from high rates of unemployment and chronically depressed wages.

Unlike union movements in the industrialized countries of Great Britain and Germany, French trade unions remained small, weak, and local, without the resources to undertake sustained action. French unions had gained legal recognition in 1884, eight years after Great Britain but six years before Germany. Workers who combined trade unionism with anarchism shared an apocalyptic vision of social transformation. The contrast between the Labour party in Great Britain and the German Social Democrats on the one hand and the French anarcho-syndicalists on the other highlighted the split between advanced industrial countries and less-developed areas of Europe, where an artisan class was attempting to preserve autonomy and control.

The General Strike. The journalist and social thinker Georges Sorel (1847–1922) captured the philosophy of anarcho-syndicalism in his book *Reflections on Violence* (1908). Sorel described the "myth," or shared belief, in the "general strike," a kind of final judgment day when justice would prevail. Unlike the trade unions of other western European states, anarcho-syndicalist unions were militantly opposed to issues of improved wages and better working conditions. They believed that in order to be ready for the collapse of bourgeois society, anarcho-syndicalists must not collaborate with the existing system by accepting benefits and improvements from it. Instead, workers were to hold themselves ready by employing a technique of "direct action" to maintain worker solidarity. "Direct action" was a symbolic gesture that did not advance the revolution but did help workers remain aware of their exploitation. A typical example of "direct action" was the agreement among the militantly revolutionary barbers' union to nick their customers periodically with the razor while shaving them. Acts such as this were meaningless in themselves—except perhaps to those who experienced them—but were intended to raise the level of commitment to a common cause.

The problems of disaffected groups in general intensified before 1914. Anarchists and anarcho-syndicalist workers deplored the centralization and organization of mass society. Yet anarchism posed no serious threat to social stability because of the effectiveness of policing in most European states. As Friedrich Engels observed at the turn of the century, random violence directed against politics and the economy was no match for the repressive forces at the command of the nation-state. The politics of mass society excluded diverse groups—including women, Jews, and ethnic minorities—from participation. Yet the techniques, values, and organization of the world of politics remained available to all those groups. It was the outbreak of war in 1914 that silenced, temporarily at least, the challenge of the outsiders.

SHAPING THE NEW CONSCIOUSNESS

Both science and art contributed to the new world view that emerged in western society in the late nineteenth century. Not only was the European imagination opened up to new influences from the culture and aesthetics of other lands, but Europeans developed a critique of traditional values and rationalist thought from within through new developments in philosophy and science.

The Authority of Science

The discoveries of science had ramifications that extended beyond the laboratory, the hospital, and the classroom. What may seem commonplace at the beginning of the twenty-first century was nothing less than spectacular at the end of the nineteenth. Imagine a world that discovered how to eliminate the difference between night and day. Imagine further a civilization that could obliterate distance or shrink it. Imagine a people who could see for the first time into solid mass, into their own bodies, and send images through space. Those are the imaginings of fable and fantasy that can be traced back to prehistory. But what had always been the stuff of magic became reality between 1880 and 1914. The people of the West used science and technology to reshape the world and their understanding of it.

Discoveries in the Physical Sciences.   Scientific discoveries in the last quarter of the century pushed out the frontiers of knowledge. In physics, James Clerk Maxwell (1831–1879) discovered the relationship between electricity and magnetism. Maxwell showed mathematically that an oscillating electric charge produces an electromagnetic field and that such a field radiates outward from its source at a constant speed—the speed of light. His theories led to the discovery of the electromagnetic spectrum, comprising radiation of different wavelengths, including X rays, visible light, and radio waves. The discovery had important practical applications for the development of the electrical industry and led to the invention of radio and television. Within a generation, the names of Edison, Westinghouse, Marconi, Siemens, and Bell entered the public realm.

Discoveries in the physical sciences succeeded one another with great rapidity. The periodic table of chemical elements was formulated in 1869. Radioactivity was discovered in 1896. Two years later, Marie Curie (1867–1934) and her husband Pierre (1859–1906) discovered the elements radium and polonium. At the end of the century, Ernest Rutherford (1871–1937) identified alpha and beta rays in radioactive atoms. Building on the new discoveries, Max Planck (1858–1947), Albert Einstein (1879–1955), and Niels Bohr (1885–1962) dismantled the classical physics of absolute and determined principles and left in its place modern physics based on relativity and uncertainty. In 1900, Planck propounded a theory that renounced the emphasis in classical physics on energy as a wave phenomenon in favor of a new "quantum theory" of energy as emitted and absorbed in minute, discrete amounts.

The name Einstein became synonymous with genius in the twentieth century. In 1905, Albert Einstein formulated his special theory of relativity, in which he established the relationship of mass and energy in the famous equation $E = mc^2$.

■ Marie Curie was born Manya Sklodowska in Warsaw, Poland. She shared the Nobel Prize in physics in 1903 and was awarded the Nobel Prize in chemistry in 1911. She is one of two women interred in the French Pantheon, commemorated as a hero of France.

In 1916, he published his general theory of relativity, a mathematical formulation that created a new conception of space and time. Einstein disproved the Newtonian view of gravitation as a force and instead saw it as a curved field in the time-space continuum created by the presence of mass. No one at the time foresaw that the application of Einstein's theory—that a particle of matter could be converted into a great quantity of energy—would unleash the greatest destructive power in history. Einstein, a pacifist, lived to see atomic bombs developed in his lifetime.

Achievements in Biology.   Although there were no more dramatic discoveries than those in the physical sciences, the biological sciences also witnessed great breakthroughs. Research biologists dedicated themselves to the study of disease-causing microbes and to the chemical bases of physiology. French chemist Louis Pasteur (1822–1895) studied microorganisms to find methods of preventing the spread of diseases in humans, animals, and plants. He developed methods of

inoculation to provide protection against anthrax in sheep, cholera in chickens, and rabies in animals and humans.

The pace of breakthroughs in biological knowledge and medical treatment was staggering. The malaria parasite was isolated in 1880. The control of diseases such as yellow fever contributed to improvement in the quality of life. Knowledge burst the bounds of disciplines, and new fields developed to accommodate new concerns. Research in human genetics, a field that was only beginning to be understood, was begun in the first decade of the twentieth century. The studies of Austrian botanist Gregor Mendel (1822–1884) in the crossbreeding of peas in the 1860s led to the Mendelian laws of inheritance. Scientists at the time ignored Mendel, but after the turn of the century Mendel's discoveries were used to pursue the problem of how hereditary characteristics were transmitted.

Applied Knowledge.   Biological discoveries resulted in new state policies. Public health benefited from new methods of prevention and detection of diseases caused by germs. A professor at the University of Berlin, Rudolf Virchow (1821–1902) discovered the relationship between microbes, sewage, and disease that led to the development of modern sewer systems and pure water for urban populations. Biochemistry, bacteriology, and physiology promoted a belief in social progress through state programs. After 1900, health programs to educate the general public spread throughout Europe.

Discoveries that changed the face of the twentieth century proliferated in a variety of fields. It was a time of many firsts. Airplane flights and deep-sea expeditions based on technological applications of new discoveries pushed out boundaries of exploration above the land and below the sea. In 1909, the same year that work began in human genetics, American explorer Robert E. Peary (1856–1920) reached the North Pole. In that year, too, plastic was first manufactured, under the trade name Bakelite. In the period, Irish-born British astronomer Agnes Mary Clerke (1842–1907) did pioneering work in the new field of astrophysics. Ernest Rutherford proposed a new spatial reality in his theory of the nuclear structure of the atom, which stated that the atom could be divided and that it consisted of a nucleus surrounded by electrons revolving in orbits.

The values of an age are often revealed in the accomplishments it chooses to honor. In 1896, Swedish industrialist Alfred Nobel (1833–1896), who had invented dynamite and amassed a fortune through the manufacture of explosives, established the Nobel Prizes. To be drawn from a bequest of $9.2 million, the prizes were to recognize achievement internationally in five areas: physics, physiology or medicine, chemistry, literature, and peace. Literary figures, peacemakers, poets, and philosophers had long been recognized as shapers of Western culture. At the end of the nineteenth century, scientists assumed pride of place in their company.

Establishing the Social Sciences

Innovations in the social sciences paralleled the drama of discovery in the biological and physical sciences. The "scientific" study of society purported to apply the same methods of observation and experimentation to human interactions. After 1870, the fields of sociology, economics, history, psychology, anthropology, and archaeology took shape at the core of new social scientific endeavors. They, like the "hard" sciences, had benefits to offer Western women and men that improved the quality of life. But just as scientific advances could be applied to destructive ends, so too did the social sciences promote inequities and prejudices in the Western world.

Archaeology.

Archaeology uncovered lost civilizations. Heinrich Schliemann (1822–1890) discovered Troy. Schliemann, a German businessman, captured the imagination of Europeans when he used his own fortune to open up what he believed to be the ruins of the sites mentioned in Homeric verse. Sir Arthur Evans (1851–1941) began excavations in Crete in 1900 and over the next eight years unearthed the remains of Minoan culture. Both men used scientific procedures to reconstruct ancient cultures. Historians, too, applied new techniques to the study of the past. German historian Leopold von Ranke (1795–1886) eschewed a literary form of historical writing that

■ Hoard of metal and artifacts from Heinrich Schliemann's excavation of Troy in 1871, one of several major archaeological discoveries in the late nineteenth and early twentieth centuries.

Trésor de Priam découvert à 8½ mètres de profondeur

relied on legend and tradition in favor of objective, "scientific" history based on documentation and other forms of material evidence. Ranke produced influential multivolume histories of Prussia, England, France, and the world.

Economics.

The social scientific study of economics came to the aid of businessmen. Influenced by the quantum theory of physics, economists posited a new view of the economy that revised the classical models of Adam Smith and David Ricardo. The neoclassical economic theory of Alfred Marshall (1842–1924) and others recognized the centrality of individual choice in the marketplace, while dealing with the problem of overproduction: how could businesses know they have produced enough to maximize profits? Economists concerned with how individuals responded to prices devised a theory of marginal utility, by which producers could calculate costs and project profits in a reliable fashion based on a pattern of consumer response to price changes.

Psychology and Studying Human Behavior.

"Scientific" psychology developed in a variety of directions. Wilhelm Wundt (1832–1920) established the first laboratory devoted to psychological research in Leipzig in 1879. From his experiments he concluded that thought is grounded in physical reality. The Russian physiologist Ivan Pavlov (1849–1936) had already received the Nobel Prize for physiology and medicine for his study of the dog's digestive system when he began his famous series of experiments demonstrating the conditioned reflex in dogs. Other psychological models competed for theoretical primacy. With his theory of personality development and the creation of psychoanalysis, the science of the unconscious, Sigmund Freud (1859–1939) greatly influenced the direction of psychology. (See "A Closer Look: Sigmund Freud, Explorer of Dreams," pp. 758–759.) Freudian probing of the unconscious was a model greatly at odds with the behavioral perspective of conditioned responses based on Pavlov's work.

The new social science of criminology claimed scientific veracity after 1880. In 1885, Sir Francis Galton (1822–1911), a cousin of Charles Darwin, proved the individuality of fingerprints through scientific study and thereby initiated an important method of identifying criminals. Criminologists joined psychiatrists as expert witnesses in criminal trials for the first time at the end of the nineteenth century. Galton also propagated pseudoscientific ideas about **eugenics,** the improvement of the human race through selective breeding. Anthropological studies of primitive cultures influenced eugenic assumptions about inferiority and superiority based on racial differences.

The new specialties of forensic medicine and criminal anthropology came into being at the end of the century. *The Criminal Man* (1876), written by Italian criminologist Cesare Lombroso (1836–1909), claimed to be a scientific study of the physical attributes of convicted criminals. Through observation and statistical compilation, Lombroso discovered "born criminals," individuals whose physical characteristics proved their deviance. Criminals, he claimed, could be identified by

A Closer Look

Sigmund Freud, Explorer of Dreams

Sigmund Freud was a disciplined man, precise and punctual in his habits. In many ways, his life was typical of the life of a Viennese bourgeois professional at the end of the nineteenth century. His day was like a railway timetable, scheduled to the minute—whether seeing patients, dining with his family, or taking his daily constitutional. He even calculated his pleasures, counting as his only indulgence the 20 cigars he smoked every day.

The order in Freud's life seemed curiously at odds with his dedication to the study of disorder. He was a man of science, a medical doctor specializing in organic diseases of the nervous system. Early in his career, he began to question physiological explanations for certain nervous disorders and to search for another reason for the disorders of the mind. His exploration took him to Paris in 1885 to study with the leading French neurologist, Jean Martin Charcot (1825–1893), whose work on hysteria had won him an international reputation.

Surrounded by hysterics in Charcot's clinic, Freud wondered whether organic physical illnesses could be traced to psychological problems. Freud explored the value of hypnosis as a technique for uncovering the secret workings of the mind. He learned that emotions alone could produce physical symptoms such as blindness and paralysis. By hypnotizing patients, Freud caught glimpses of the world of the unconscious as a vast and hidden terrain. He approached the new territory as an explorer.

Freud created a new science of the unconscious, psychoanalysis, when he rejected physiological causes for nervous disorders in favor of psychological ones. He intended psychoanalysis as a theory of personality and a method of treatment or therapy. That was a dramatic break with existing theories of madness and mental disorder. On his seventieth birthday, Freud looked back over his own career and described his achievement: "The poets and philosophers before me discovered the unconscious; what I discovered was the scientific method by which the unconscious can be studied."

The hostile reaction to Freud's break with existing ideas about mental disorders was further aggravated by the importance he attributed to sexuality. Colleagues in Vienna were shocked by the direction that his work was taking. Freud began by hypothesizing that disturbed patients developed neurotic symptoms because of the repression of memories of actual sexual abuse as children. He moved away from the theory of sexual abuse to one in which the subject had *fantasized* about sex as a child and then had repressed the desire. In searching for the root of psychological disorders, Freud argued that sexual conflicts originating in early childhood were the cause of adult neuroses. Repressed sexual desire therefore became the key to understanding human behavior.

Freud's self-described scientific method, which allowed him to probe the unconscious, was free association. Patients were encouraged to talk, or "associate," in a relaxed atmosphere. The couch in the doctor's office became the enduring symbol of the psychoanalytic method. Patients were particularly encouraged to talk about their dreams. The unconscious, Freud argued, manifests itself in dreams. The role of the psychoanalyst was to examine the content of the dream and interpret it, facilitating recognition and hence a cure in the patient.

Freud's first major work, and probably the most important study of his career, *The Interpretation of Dreams* (1900), heralded the new century. Working with his own dreams and those of his patients, Freud posited that a dream was the fulfillment of a wish. He believed dreams were not literal in their meaning; that their symbols and context always had to be interpreted and that the experiences of people's conscious lives were rearranged in dreams. For Freud, nothing was accidental. Jokes, obsessions, and even slips of the tongue ("Freudian slips"), as well as dreams, were indicators of unconscious desires. In his dream theory, every object and detail had meaning in the context of the patient's associations.

Freud used his own dreams and his relationship with his parents to describe the neurotic personality and the Oedipus complex, so important to his later work on childhood sexuality.

There the child's unresolved desire for the parent of the opposite sex formed the basis for all ego development. In famous case studies such as "Dora," "The Wolf Man," and "The Rat Man," Freud described the symptoms and histories of patients to whom he assigned fictitious names. In subsequent works, Freud went on to detail the uncharted land of the unconscious he discovered in his work on dreams, using designations for the components of personality—the "ego," the "superego," and the "id."

Sigmund Freud gave Western culture a new vocabulary. His lexicon has survived into the twenty-first century and has entered common parlance as a way of explaining our daily lives in psychological terms. Freud's work sounded the death knell for the nineteenth century's faith in reason. For Freud, human beings were driven by subterranean instincts and desires. The horrors of war and destruction in the twentieth century confirmed for Freud his belief in the irrationality of Western civilization.

Freud died in exile in London in 1939, having fled from the Nazi occupation of his beloved Vienna. During his lifetime and ever since, his theories have been refuted, with critics saying that they explain nothing more than the psychic world in which Freud lived—the world of European middle-class men

■ Sigmund Freud and his wife Martha Bernays, 1886.

at the beginning of the twentieth century. But there can be no denying that Freud's exploration of the land of dreams in the world of the unconscious was a revolutionary event in the history of Western thought.

their looks. With statistics, Lombroso demonstrated, for example, that left-handed, redheaded people with low foreheads were naturally disposed to a life of crime. Even during his lifetime, Lombroso's ideas were widely disputed, and subsequently they were discredited, but their temporary legitimacy was a good indication of how scientific claims justified prejudicial assumptions. Opposing Lombroso's ideas, the French school of criminology stressed the social determinants of crime, seeing poverty and malnutrition as explanations for the different physical appearance of criminals.

The psychology of crowd behavior originated in the work of the French physician Gustave Le Bon (1841–1931). In *Psychology of Crowds* (1895), Le Bon argued that the masses were instinctively irrational. Through his "science" he arrived at the political judgment that democracy was a despicable and dangerous form of government. Émile Durkheim (1858–1917) is regarded as the founder of modern sociology. In his famous study of suicide as a social phenomenon, Durkheim pitted sociological theory against psychology and argued that deviance was the result not of psychic disturbances but of environmental factors and hereditary forces.

Heredity became a general explanation for behavior of all sorts. The novels of Émile Zola presented a popular view of biological determinism. Zola's protagonists were doomed by self-destructive characteristics they inherited from their parents. Everything from poverty, drunkenness, and crime to a declining birthrate could be attributed to biologically determined causes. For some theorists, the reasoning teetered on the edge of racism and ideas about "better blood." Intelligence was now measured "scientifically" for the first time with intelligence quotient (IQ) tests developed at the Sorbonne by the psychologist Alfred Binet (1857–1911) in the 1890s. The tests did not acknowledge the importance of cultural factors in the development of intelligence, and they scientifically legitimated a belief in natural elites. Not least of all, science was also invoked in support of a particular system of gender relations, one that itself was undergoing assault and upheaval between 1871 and 1914.

Science changed the way people thought and the way they lived. It improved the quality of life by defeating diseases, improving nutrition, and lengthening life span. But scientific knowledge was not without its costs. Scientific discoveries led to new forces of destruction. Scientific ideas challenged moral and religious beliefs. Science was invoked to justify racial and sexual discrimination. Traditional values and religious beliefs also did combat with the new god of science, with philosophers proclaiming that God was dead. Not least of all, science and the progress it promised came under attack by those like Friedrich Nietzsche (1844–1900), the German philosopher who questioned rational values as well as the emphasis on religion in Western thought.

The "New Woman" and the New Consciousness

As women continued to be excluded from national political participation, the right to vote was gradually being extended to all men in western Europe, regardless of property or social rank. New scientific ideas colluded with political prejudices to justify denying women equal rights. The natural sciences had a formative impact on prevailing views of gender relations and female sexuality and were employed to prove the inferiority of women in the species.

Biology and Woman's Destiny. In *The Descent of Man* (1871), Charles Darwin, the giant of evolutionary theory, concluded that the mental power of man was higher than that of woman. The female's need for male protection, the father of evolution reasoned, had increased her dependence over time while at the same time increasing the competition of natural selection among men. The result, Darwin argued, was inequality between the sexes. Darwin went on to reject women's emancipation as out of step with biological realities. What Darwin presented was a vicious circle in which women's dependence had made them inferior and their inferiority kept them dependent. The attitudes toward gender and race marked the advent of biological "proofs" to justify social policies. Those of Darwin's disciples who applied biological principles to society came to be known as **social Darwinists,** specialists who claimed that "survival of the fittest" was a concept that could be applied to all social interactions between races and the sexes.

Darwin was not the only man of science who had ideas about a woman's proper place. Others made a dubious case for brain size as an index of superiority. The French physiologist Paul Broca (1824–1880), a contemporary of Darwin, countered in 1873 that the skull capacity of the two sexes was very similar and that a case for inferiority could not be based on measurement. But Broca was atypical. Most scientific opinion argued in favor of female frailty and outright inferiority. Social Darwinists adapted evolutionary biology to the debate over inequality between the sexes. They complemented their race theories with evolutionary theories of sexual division: "What was decided among the prehistoric Protozoa cannot be annulled by an Act of Parliament." Sexless prehistoric protozoa held the message for social Darwinists that women should not enjoy the right to vote. In general, the natural sciences worked to reinforce the idea of women as reproducers whose proper role was nurturing and whose proper domain was the home. The social sciences, in particular sociology, echoed the findings by asserting that the male-dominated household was a proof of social progress.

The "scientific" arguments justified the exclusion of women from educational opportunities and from professions such as medicine and law. Biology became destiny as women's attempts at equal education came up against closed doors. Stalwarts broke the prohibitions, but women who gained higher education in those decades were the exception that proved the rule. The women who were able to get an education were blocked from using it. There was a generalized fear in Western societies that women who attempted to exceed their "natural" abilities would damage their reproductive functions and neglect their nurturing roles. The specter of sickly children and women with

"ANGEL" OR WOMAN?

Victorian domestic ideals viewed woman as an "Angel in the House" (the title of a poem by Coventry Patmore) who created a paradise of love and nurturance for her husband and children. By the end of the nineteenth century, many women recognized that the description, however rosy, kept women in the home and out of public life. Here Maria Desraismes, a French feminist and republican, rebuts republican and historian Jules Michelet for his popular books that romanticized women and marriage. Desraismes advocated legal rights for women.

Focus Questions

How did the formulation of woman as angel limit the rights of women at the end of the nineteenth century? What is the concept of freedom grounded on in this passage?

Of all woman's enemies, I tell you that the worst are those who insist that woman is an angel. To say that woman is an angel is to impose on her, in a sentimental and admiring fashion, all duties, and to reserve for oneself all rights; it is to imply that her specialty is self-effacement, resignation, and sacrifice; it is to suggest to her that woman's greatest glory, her greatest happiness, is to immolate herself for those she loves; it is to let her understand that she will be

generously furnished with every opportunity for exercising her aptitudes. It is to say that she will respond to absolutism by submission, to brutality by meekness, to indifference by tenderness, to inconstancy by fidelity, to egotism by devotion.

In the face of this long enumeration, I decline the honor of being an angel. No one has the right to force me to be both dupe and victim. Self-sacrifice is not a habit, a custom; it is an *extra!* It is not on the program of one's duties. No power has the right to impose it on me. Of all acts, sacrifice is the freest, and it is precisely because it is free that it is so admirable.

From Maria Desraismes, "La Femme et le droit" public address published in *Eve dans l'humanité* (1891).

nervous disorders was invoked as grounds for opposing demands for coeducation. Women's education was assigned to churches and was intended to meet the needs of the family. The creation of the first separate women's colleges in the late 1860s marked the beginning of the pioneering era of higher education for women.

The New Woman. In the age of scientific justification of female inferiority, the "new woman" emerged. All over Europe the feminist movement had demanded social, economic, and political progress for women. But the "new woman" phenomenon exceeded the bounds of the feminist movement and can be described as a general cultural phenomenon. The search for independence was overwhelmingly a middle-class phenomenon that had a psychological as well as a political significance in the years between 1880 and 1914. Victorian stereotypes of the angel at the hearth were crumbling. The "new woman" was a woman characterized by intelligence, strength, and sexual desire—in every way man's equal. The Norwegian playwright Henrik Ibsen (1828–1906) created a fictional embodiment of the phenomenon in Nora, the hero of *A Doll's House* (1879), who was typical of the restive spirit for independence among wives and mothers confined to suffocating households and relegated to the status of children. Contemporary opinion condemned Nora as immoral for abandoning her home, her husband, and her children.

The "new woman's" pursuit of independence included control over her own body. The term *birth control* was first used by an American, Margaret Sanger (1879–1966), although the reality itself was not new. Women had always known of and employed contraceptive and abortive techniques to limit family size. What was different in the period before 1914 was the militant public discussion of ways to prevent conception and an awareness of the death and debilitation that resulted from primitive methods. The development of a process of vulcanizing rubber in the mid-nineteenth century had made condoms available to a mass market, but they were little employed. A growing number of women, among whom were medical doctors, decided to take information to the public. A common result was state repression of their activities. Annie Besant, advocating birth control in Great Britain, was charged with corrupting youth by distributing books that dealt with contraception. Aletta Jacobs (1849–1929), the first woman to practice medicine in Holland, opened a contraceptive clinic in 1882. Leagues for distributing contraceptive information were formed elsewhere in Europe. Birth-control advocates aimed to preserve women's health and to give them some control over their reproductive lives.

Discussions of contraception brought into the public arena the premise that women, like men, were sexual beings. That was reinforced by the frank discussions of sexuality in the works of Sigmund Freud. The first English translation of Freud's *The Interpretation of Dreams* appeared in 1913 with a der roles at the beginning of the twentieth century makes clear, science was a way of thinking as well as a body of doctrine. Traditional ideas might be scientifically justified, but they would not go unchallenged.

Art and the New Age

In the last quarter of the nineteenth century, the world of art in western Europe and the United States was characterized by new discoveries, new subjects, and new modes of expression. At least a half dozen major and distinct art movements caught the imagination of artists and the general public. Beginning in the 1860s, impressionist painters led the way in rebelling against the conventions of the formal painting of the academic salons. Choosing unlikely subjects such as railway stations and haystacks in the works of Claude Monet (1840–1926), impressionists made a revolution in capturing on canvas the nature of light and atmosphere. Post-impressionists in the 1880s and 1890s built on the insights of their impressionist colleagues but went in new and less predictable directions, as exemplified in the work of Paul Cezanne (1839–1906), Vincent Van Gogh (1853–1890), and Henri Rousseau (1844–1910). Pointillism, well exemplified in the work of Georges Seurat (1859–1891), also followed the discoveries of the impressionists by using tiny dots to convey light and a spectrum of color.

Symbolism in painting brought a new concern with the unconscious and dream imagery to the canvas and influenced important movements in the twentieth century. The Norwegian painter Edvard Munch (1863–1944), for example, brought an eerie sense of disquiet to works such as *The Scream*. In France, Odilon Redon (1840–1916) used color and light to convey mysticism through recurrent symbols. Color took on dramatic power as well for the fauvists, who used it to convey primitive emotions, such as in the works of Paul Gauguin (1848–1903), also labeled post-impressionist, and in the bold compositions of Henri Matisse (1869–1954). In Italy, the particular movement of futurism flourished in this same period. As discussed in "The Visual Record" (pp. 738–739), futurist Umberto Boccioni embraced the new age in his art and broke free of the more sedate art that had characterized the Western tradition. Other movements that were contemporaneous with impressionism and post-impressionism included the British pre-Raphaelites and the arts and crafts movement.

All the widely varied art of this period also had certain features in common. The artists reflected the values and mores of a changing society in their work, both in their choice of subject matter and their choice of perspective. They were also influenced by breakthroughs in science and technology that allowed the understanding of how light worked through the new realism of the photographic medium and new discoveries in physics and the science of the material world. New knowledge about non-Western cultures and Europeans' widening view of the world also influenced artistic subjects and styles (see "The West and the Wider World: African Art

■ In October 1916, Margaret Sanger opened the first birth-control clinic in the United States in Brooklyn, New York. Police soon raided the clinic, and Sanger was charged with "maintaining a public nuisance." She was convicted and sentenced to 30 days in jail. The New York Court of Appeals upheld the sentence but also ruled that physicians should have broader discretion in prescribing birth control. Later in 1916 Sanger formed the New York Birth Control League to push for even broader discretion. Sanger is shown here leaving the Court of Special Sessions after her arraignment in October 1916.

warning note from the publisher that its sale should be limited to doctors, lawyers, and clerics. Richard von Krafft-Ebing (1840–1902) and Havelock Ellis (1859–1939) also contributed to the public discussion of sex in their works on sexuality and sexual deviance. By 1900, sexuality and reproduction were openly connected to discussions of women's rights.

Scientific discoveries had worked to change the world. At the same time, those intent on preserving traditional values invoked scientific authority. But as the uncertainty over gen-

■ Claude Monet, *Arrival of the Normandy Train, Gare Saint-Lazare,* 1877. French impressionist painter Claude Monet frequently painted a subject repeatedly under varying light conditions or during different seasons to emphasize light and atmosphere, hallmarks of impressionism. This painting of a bustling Paris train station is one of seven paintings of the station by Monet.

and European Artists," pp. 764–765). The new art movements of the late nineteenth century also indicated a dramatic shift in the class base of art out of the salons of the elite and the aristocracy and into the venues of middle class life—the home, the public spheres of the café, the theater, and the railway station.

The New Consumption

The great Russian novelist Lev Tolstoy (1828–1910) was an astute observer of the world in which he lived. In 1877, he condemned the materialism that characterized European society: "Money is a new form of slavery, and distinguishable from the old simply by the fact that it is impersonal—that there is no human relation between master and slave." Although he was speaking as a moral philosopher, Tolstoy had put his finger on something that economists were just beginning to understand—the extension of a money economy. Tolstoy was aware of how peasants freed from the land became entangled in a web of financial obligations that constituted a new form of serfdom.

Disposable Income.   At the end of the nineteenth century, the role of money changed in ways affecting all of Western society. Workers were beginning to share in the benefits of industrial prosperity. The prosperity differed dramatically by geographic region and occupation. But the expansion in the ranks of a salaried working class augured a shift in patterns of behavior. Lagging behind the industrial revolutions but no

less important was a revolution in consumption patterns among European populations. The new consumer age is best illustrated by the creation of the big department stores of the last quarter of the nineteenth century. The Bon Marché Department Store in Paris occupied more than 52,000 square feet and contained a vast selection of goods. Everything from initialed toilet paper to household furniture was now located under a single roof. The department store was intended to satisfy every need. Advertising and the art of display became industries in themselves, the goal of which was to encourage people to buy things they did not need. The promise of the good life, epitomized in the department store and preached by advertising, now seemed accessible to everyone.

Leisure as Consumption.   Leisure time also became a consumer item in the late nineteenth century. In 1899, the American economist Thorstein Veblen (1857–1929) published a pathbreaking work that was little appreciated at the time. *The Theory of the Leisure Class* argued that leisure was a form of "conspicuous consumption," a term Veblen coined. More than a theory, his work constituted a critique of the values of Western culture. Women and the family were, for Veblen, the primary vehicles for conspicuous consumption. Elegant dress, for example, conveyed status and served as a sign of leisure just as it had done in aristocratic society. Expensive clothing was designed to show that the wearer had no need to earn wages. For this purpose, women were actually "mutilated," in Veblen's term, by the corset that constricted their vitality and rendered them unfit for work. Women

The West and the Wider World
AFRICAN ART AND EUROPEAN ARTISTS

The limited definition of civilization held by the Western world for more than a millennium began to broaden in the late nineteenth century. Anthropologists studying non-Western cultures argued that the social structure, habits, beliefs, and products of communities elsewhere in the world formerly dismissed as primitive or exotic were, in their own way, as complex and evolved as those based on European tradition. In the late nineteenth century, the world view of Europeans was expanded by two characteristic European institutions: world fairs and public museums. European countries and the United States hosted international exhibitions such as the London Great Exhibition of 1851 and the Chicago Columbian Exposition of 1893 that introduced art and cultural artifacts from all over the world to a mass public audience. Curiosity led to awareness, and gave way to growing appreciation and understanding of the cultures of different continents. For example, European exposure to the art forms and costumes of the Far East changed European style and painting in the second half of the nineteenth century. The discovery of Japanese painting, wood-block prints, and calligraphy provided an important influence on the new direction of European impressionists and postimpressionists. Japanese design was incorporated into the work of such leading Western artists as Edgar Degas and James Whistler.

No less important was the artistic influence of Africa, portrayed as the "dark continent" and the "white man's burden" by colonizing forces (see Chapter 25), on leading lights of the European art world. Pablo Picasso encountered African carvings for the first time as a young man in the ethnographic collections of the Trocadéro Museum in Paris. The Spanish artist was so fascinated by the directness and strength of the

African aesthetic that he was inspired to abandon all traces of traditional form in his work and seek a new means of expression. In one of his best known works from the early twentieth century, *Les Desmoiselles d'Avignon* (1907, France, Figure 1), Picasso used the formula of African masks to cover the faces of the two women on the right of the canvas. Mask-like features were incorporated into the faces of the three women to the left. The denial of natural appearance in these women is coupled with the denial of a similar Western art convention, the illusion of three-dimensional space. Picasso fragments the

planes of the background and the planes of some of the bodies, breaking them into the jagged slabs that would become the hallmark of Cubism. Picasso knew little about the cultural significance of the African masks he so admired and collected; he saw them as emblems of primitivism, appropriate for the spirit of danger and mystery he wanted to convey in a portrait of Avignon prostitutes. He saw in African art the point of departure and the source of inspiration for a new and radical art in the West.

The dynamic of cultural exchange in the arts flowed in both directions. While

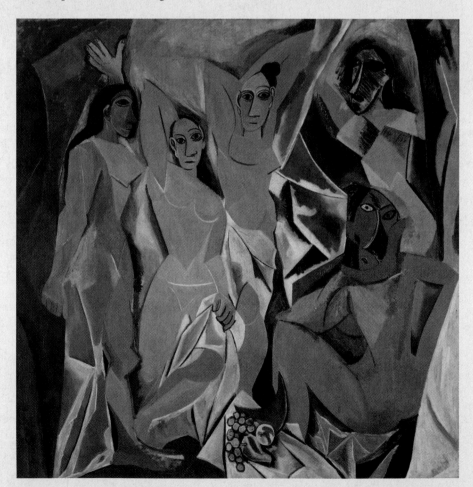

■ Figure 1. Pablo Picasso, *Les Demoiselles d'Avignon* (1907). Museum of Modern Art, New York/Art Resource, NY/© The Estate of Pablo Picasso/Artists Rights Society (ARS), New York

leading European artists such as Picasso were forging new art forms by appropriating an African art aesthetic identified as primitive, African artists were borrowing and incorporating Western-inspired forms into their art. See this staff finial from the Kongo (ca. 16th–19th century, Figure 2) of an ivory figure representing a Kongo man, indicated by his broken teeth and beardless chin, with blue eyes and dressed in Western clothing. Wooden staffs topped with ivory carvings symbolized power and status to Kongo peoples. This particular figure, reddened by pigment and use, embodies the further status conferred by Western hat, high-collared jacket, and earring typical of the earliest Westerners to trade in Africa. The man's garb positions him in a new wider world, associating Westernization with power and progress.

The Mami Wata cult of west Africa demonstrates another kind of cultural intersection. Images of this foreign water spirit seen here in a mask of the Guro peoples from the Ivory Coast in the mid-twentieth century (Figure 3) record the layering of ideas and aesthetics from abroad. Her posture and her attribute of the coiling snake have been traced back to a German color lithograph of an East Indian snake charmer, circulated throughout the Ivory Coast in the late nineteenth century. Here the Mami Wata figure is superimposed on the top of a beautiful and colorful tribal mask, demonstrating the graceful coexistence of cultures and influences. The combination of the Mami Wata icon with the traditional African mask, similar to those collected by Picasso, is intended to connote a particular spiritual force of imported ideas and influences. The cult of Mami Wata has endured through the twentieth century, and her image is associated with more than a dozen cultures from Senegal to Tanzania. Dressed according to modern Western standards, Mami Wata's form has continued to change with the times. Her iconography is a dynamic one that continues to develop.

Beyond form and content, one of the major differences that should be noted in considering the dynamic between the West and the wider world of African art is the presence of the individual artist in the Western aesthetic. We know *Les Desmoiselles d'Avignon* as the work of the great artist Pablo Picasso, but in the African examples considered here, no artist's name was recorded. We know the art by the region and the community in which it was produced. The African emphasis on the role of the community in the production of art is quite different from the Western glorification of the individual artist and his or her creative act.

■ Figure 3. Mask with carving of Mami Wata, foreign water spirit (mid–20th century, Ivory Coast).

QUESTIONS FOR DISCUSSION

What African art form influenced Picasso, and how did his use of it lead to changes in Western art? What symbols did African artists in the same period import from the West and from other cultures? What qualities did Picasso attempt to convey by using African art forms? And what qualities did African artists recognize in appropriating Western symbols?

■ Figure 2. Staff finial of the Kongo peoples (ca. 16th–19th century).

■ Ad for toys for the Bon Marché Department Store in Paris, 1911. Such advertisements lured consumers (and their children) to the big department stores with vast selections of goods on display.

well. Sports also promoted national and regional identification. Beginning in the 1860s, men began playing the games they had learned as boys in English public schools. Rugby, football (soccer), and cricket soon developed national followings. Golf originated in Scotland in the period and spread throughout Europe and to the United States. Spectator sports grew in importance, with audiences of more than 100,000 people at British soccer matches at the beginning of the twentieth century. Victorians saw the necessity of recreation and endorsed the renewing, relaxing, and entertaining aspects of organized play.

Scouting also originated at the end of the nineteenth century as another form of organized leisure. Uniformed boys were taught "manly" virtues of self-reliance and teamwork. Team spirit was tied to patriotism. Scouting organizations for girls emphasized domestic virtues and household tasks. Amateur athletics and track-and-field events grew in popularity, especially after the establishment of an international Olympics competition, modeled on the ancient Greek games. The first modern Olympiad was held in Athens in 1896, and—except for upheavals caused by war—the Olympic Games continue to be held at four-year intervals.

Cycling became a popular competitive sport on the Continent with the establishment of the Tour de France at the

■ A poster for the World Exhibition held in Paris in 1889 features the star attraction of the show—the Eiffel Tower. Most of the other exhibition buildings were subsequently demolished.

immobilized by their clothes and shoes became the ultimate symbols of social status.

The middle and upper classes controlled sufficient disposable income to allow them to spend time in such leisure pursuits as flocking to seaside resorts in Great Britain and on the Continent. However, resort vacations remained out of the financial reach of most working-class people. Instead, in pursuit of leisure-time activities, working-class men congregated in cafes and pubs. Starting in the 1880s, vaudeville and music halls rose in popularity, their low admission price attracting ever larger crowds. There were at least 30 striptease shows in Paris in the 1890s. Such activities fostered fear among the middle classes that working-class leisure was degenerate. The newly invented cinema also exercised a growing appeal for European men and women of all ages and classes.

Not least important in the new leisure was the rise of organized sports. The strict organization of work life in mature industrial societies may have made sports an attractive way of organizing leisure. Men—there were few organized sports for women—worked by the clock and now played by the clock as beginning of the twentieth century. Some saw in the new pastime of bicycling a threat to the social order. Women, attracted by the exercise and mobility afforded by the new means of transportation, altered their costumes in favor of freedom of movement. For eminently practical reasons, they discarded their corsets and bustles and shortened their skirts. As women gained greater mobility, some observers saw in the "new woman" on the bicycle seat the decline of true womanhood and Western values.

sensations when they appeared. London's Inner Circle underground railway was completed in 1884, and other lines soon followed, forming a vast urban subterranean network. In 1898, the miracle of underground transportation became a reality in Paris with the opening of the Métro, or subway. Yet some observers saw in the new age upheaval and disruption of traditional liberal values, the collapse of the family, and the disruptions of women and workers who did not know their place.

The Eiffel Tower was criticized more than it was praised. It was a building, yet it was not. Its inside and its outside were confused. The admirers of classic architecture lamented the ugliness of the girdered monument whose main function was to demonstrate structural innovation for its own sake. Critics lamented that science disrupted people's understanding of the world and their place in it in the same way. The Eiffel Tower—like the values of the new age (speed, progress, technological innovation, and mass consumption), critics warned—was hollow and would not endure.

CONCLUSION

The engineering marvel of the Eiffel Tower, built in 1889 for the World Exposition held in Paris, became a symbol not only of the French capital but of the values of the new age. New artifacts of European culture proliferated. Photography, motorcars, bicycles, motion picture cameras, and X rays all created

QUESTIONS FOR REVIEW

1. Why did European economies run through cycles of boom and bust in the late nineteenth century, and how did European governments attempt to regulate the economy?
2. What challenges did liberal ideals and institutions confront in England, Germany, France, and Austria?

3. What social forces brought women and others into the new mass politics of the late nineteenth century?
4. What new ideas were being generated in psychology and the social sciences at the turn of the century, and what impact did they have on the way Europeans thought about gender relations?

KEY TERMS

anarchism, *p. 754*

anti-Semitism, *p. 746*

cartels, *p. 741*

eugenics, *p. 757*

Fabians, *p. 742*

futurists, *p. 738*

Kulturkampf, p. 743

pogroms, *p. 752*

revisionism, *p. 744*

social Darwinists, *p. 760*

suffragettes, *p. 749*

Zionism, *p. 753*

DISCOVERING WESTERN CIVILIZATION ONLINE

You can obtain more information about the crisis of European culture between 1871 and 1914 at the Websites listed below. See also the Companion Website that accompanies this text, www.ablongman.com/kishlansky, which contains an online study guide and additional resources.

European Economy and the Politics of Mass Society

Encyclopaedia of British History: Socialism
www.spartacus.schoolnet.co.uk/socialism.htm
This is a fairly comprehensive site on the English labor movement, including texts, biographies of major figures, and other links.

Project Social Insurance in Germany
www.erziehung.uni-giessen.de/studis/Robert/inhver_e.html
A brief overview of the development of social welfare legislation in Germany in the latter half of the nineteenth century.

Habsburg Source Texts Archive
www2.h-net.msu.edu/~habsweb/sourcetexts
Sponsored by the H-Net Discussion list HABSBURG, this site provides electronic texts relating to the creation of the Dual Monarchy.

Outsiders in Mass Politics

The Emancipation of Women: 1750–1920
www.spartacus.schoolnet.co.uk/women.htm
This site contains links to biographies of major figures, essays on the major organizations and societies, and electronic texts of the women's movement in Britain.

The Genesis Project
www.genesis.ac.uk
This mapping project on women's history research sources is provided by the Women's Library of London and the Research Support Libraries Programme.

Shaping the New Consciousness

Sigmund Freud: Conflict & Culture
www.loc.gov/exhibits/freud
A Library of Congress virtual exhibit on the life and times of Sigmund Freud.

Sigmund Freud and the Freud Archives
users.rcn.com/brill/freudarc.html
An exhaustive collection of links to archives, electronic texts, bibliographies, and other resources on Freud and the history of psychoanalysis.

Internet History of Science Sourcebook
www.fordham.edu/halsall/science/sciencesbook.html
A comprehensive collection of links to primary source materials, Websites, and bibliographies on major scientists, discoveries, and theories in the nineteenth century.

Art History Resources: 19th-Century Art & 20th-Century Art
witcombe.sbc.edu/ARTHLinks5.html
witcombe.sbc.edu/ARTH20thcentury.html
The first web page contains numerous links on the artists, styles, and schools of art in the nineteenth century, including impressionism, post-impressionism, and symbolism. The second page includes links to resources on art and artists of the twentieth century.

SUGGESTIONS FOR FURTHER READING

European Economy and the Politics of Mass Society

Edward Arnold, ed., *The Development of the Radical Right in France: From Boulanger to Le Pen* (New York: St. Martin's Press, 2000). Part I examines Boulangism, Socialism, anti-Semitism, right-wing working-class politics, and roots of right-wing radicalism.

Sudhir Hazareesingh, *Political Traditions in Modern France* (New York: Oxford University Press, 1994). In examining the particularities of French political life, the author focuses on the relationship between political movements and ideologies since 1789.

Martin P. Johnson, *The Dreyfus Affair* (New York: St. Martin's Press, 1999). A concise and comprehensive overview of the Affair as a defining event in French history.

Kevin Repp, *Reformers, Critics, and the Paths of German Modernity, 1890–1914* (Cambridge, MA: Harvard University Press, 2000). The author looks at the reformers, intellectuals, and activists who shaped the modernist movement in Germany.

Carl E. Schorske, *Fin-de-Siècle Vienna: Politics and Culture* (New York: Alfred A. Knopf, 1980). A series of essays describing the break with nineteenth-century liberal culture in one of Europe's great cities as artists, intellectuals, and politicians responded to the disintegration of the Habsburg Empire.

Outsiders in Mass Politics

Richard J. Evans, *The Feminist Movement in Germany, 1894–1933* (London: Sage Publications, 1976). Considers two conflicting approaches to bourgeois feminism—one radical and the other conservative and authoritarian—and discusses the role of social Darwinism in the women's movement and the place of feminism in political life.

June Purvis and Sandra Stanley Holton, eds., *Votes for Women* (New York: Routledge, 2000). The editors have brought together a collection of essays that reappraise the history of British suffragism by examining the activities of various women's groups and individuals from the nineteenth century to the interwar period.

Richard Stites, *The Women's Liberation Movement in Russia: Feminism, Nihilism, and Bolshevism, 1860–1930* (Princeton, NJ: Princeton University Press, 1978). Situates the Russian women's movement within the contexts of both nineteenth-century European feminism and twentieth-century communist ideology and traces its development from the early feminists through the rise of the Bolsheviks to power. Includes a discussion of the Russian Revolution's impact on the status of women.

Sophia A. van Wingerden, *The Women's Suffrage Movement in Britain, 1866–1928* (New York: St. Martin's Press, 1999). A chronological overview of the history of the British suffrage movement.

Shaping the New Consciousness

Geoffrey Crossick and Serge Jaumain, eds., *Cathedrals of Consumption: The European Department Store, 1850–1939* (Aldershot, England: Ashgate Publishing, 1999). A collection of articles about the creation of department stores in different European countries from the perspectives of culture, consumption, gender, and urban life.

Stephen Kern, *The Culture of Time and Space, 1880–1918* (Cambridge, MA: Harvard University Press, 1983). Describes how late-nineteenth-century technological advances created new modes of thinking about and experiencing time and space.

Robert A. Nye, *Crime, Madness, and Politics in Modern France: The Medical Concept of National Decline* (Princeton, NJ: Princeton University Press, 1984). Nye shows how the medical concept of deviance was linked to a general cultural crisis in fin-de-siécle France.

Theodore M. Porter, *The Rise of Statistical Thinking, 1820–1900* (Princeton, NJ: Princeton University Press, 1986). This work traces the origins of modern statistical innovation of the early 1900s and shows the interdependence of the natural and social sciences.

William M. Reddy, *Money and Liberty in Modern Europe: A Critique of Historical Understanding* (Cambridge: Cambridge University Press, 1987). This essay on the role of money in modern Europe contends that its widespread use in exchange influenced social structure. Arguing that monetary exchange intensified existing social inequities, Reddy examines the expansion of commerce in France, Germany, and England.

Vanessa Schwartz, *Spectacular Realities: Early Mass Culture in Fin-de-Siécle Paris* (Berkeley: University of California Press, 1998). This work examines the formation and emergence of mass urban culture in late nineteenth-century Paris.

John Tosh, *A Man's Place: Masculinity and the Middle-Class Home in Victorian England* (New Haven, CT: Yale University Press, 1999). This work examines the roles of men in the private world of the domestic sphere and argues that Victorian masculinity was constructed not only in terms of work and male associations but also in terms of the home.

For a list of additional titles related to this chapter's topics, please see http://www.ablongman.com/kishlansky.

Chapter 25

EUROPE AND THE WORLD, 1870–1914

Chapter Outline

THE VISUAL RECORD

The Politics of Mapmaking

THE EUROPEAN BALANCE OF POWER, 1870–1914

Upsetting the European Balance of Power
The Instability of the Alliance System

THE NEW IMPERIALISM

The Technology of Empire
Motives for Empire

THE SEARCH FOR TERRITORY AND MARKETS

The Scramble for Africa: Diplomacy and Conflict
Gold, Empire Building, and the Boer War
Imperialism in Asia
The Imperialism of the United States

RESULTS OF A EUROPEAN-DOMINATED WORLD

A World Economy
Race and Culture
Women and Imperialism
Ecology and Imperialism
Critiquing Capitalism

In the imperial period of the late nineteenth and early twentieth centuries, new maps reflected the new territorial arrangements. How might mapmaking be political? Examine The Visual Record to see one map of empire and power. ➤

THE POLITICS OF MAPMAKING

The First Standardized Map of the World

People drew maps before they knew how to write. Yet in 1885 only one-ninth of the land surface of the earth had been surveyed. In the ten-year period before 1900, European and American surveyors and cartographers fanned out around the globe to every continent including Antarctica. The result was that for the first time comprehensive and accurate world maps could be drawn.

The great leap forward in knowledge of the earth's terrain did not produce a standardized map of the world. Representatives of different countries argued over the units for measurement, and even the symbols and colors that should be used on official maps. Mapmakers from Europe and the United States began to gather regularly at their own international conventions with the goal of devising a uniform map of the world that would satisfy everyone. They failed repeatedly.

The French, for example, argued that the meter should be the standard measurement for the world map. The British countered with yards and miles, unscientifically developed units of measurement to which they had been committed for centuries. Those scientists who acknowledged the logic of using the meter could not agree on which prototype meter should be taken as standard. Should the meter be measured according to the common method of the movement of a pendulum? If so, gravitation varying from one place to another on the earth's surface would result in different meter lengths. Most agreed that the meter should be measured in reference to the arc of the meridian. But where should the prime meridian, the place on the map that indicates zero longitude, be located since it was not a fixed phenomenon?

The debate over the prime meridian is a perfect example of the politics of mapmaking. Unlike the equator, which is midway between the North and South Poles, zero longitude can be drawn anywhere. Paris, Philadelphia, and Beijing were just three of the competing sites designated as zero longitude in the nineteenth century.

Uniformity, the cartographers insisted, would have advantages for everyone. Not least of all, a standardized map would make standardized timekeeping easier. Standard times could be calculated according to zones of longitude. Germany had five different time zones in 1891. In France, every city had its own time taken from solar readings. The United States had more than 200 time zones from one coast to the other. In modern industrial societies with railroad timetables and legal contracts, time had to be controlled and it had to be exact. In other words, time had to be standardized. Specialists suggested that the Royal Observatory in Greenwich, England, was the best place to locate the prime meridian in order to calculate a standard time system. The French balked, insisting on Paris as the only candidate for the designation. In the end, there was a compromise. The metric system, created during the French Revolution, prevailed as the standard of measurement, and the prime meridian passed through the Royal Greenwich Observatory, where standard time was calculated for most of the globe. Standard time zones and uniform maps were possible for the first time only at the end of the nineteenth century, and the key to standardization, its touchstone, was determined by geopolitical dominance. Great Britain, the most powerful imperial power, became the starting point for measuring time and space.

The accompanying map provides a dramatic example of the conquest of territories by the British Empire in 1886. The importance of territorial expansion is underlined by the presence of the inset in the upper right, which shows the extent of British territories a century earlier. The map is Great Britain's report card of success between 1785 and 1886. Britannia, sitting astride the "world" in the bottom center, is held up by Human Labor and attended by women of color with fans.

■ Map of the world highlighting the reaches of the British Empire in 1886.

Prospectors, explorers, men of the military, and a British schoolboy all witness Britannia's triumph. In the right panel, native women are erotically presented amid garlands and tropical flora, mirroring the people from colder climes on the opposing panel. British presence provides the only color on the world's continents, which are, it appears, ready to be suffused by the rosy glow of British rule.

In 1891, a young Viennese geographer named Albrecht Penck proposed an international map of the world. His idea was to produce a map using standard symbols and colors and omitting political boundaries. Penck's proposal came up against the harsh realities of mapmaking. In the age of imperialism, being able to indicate the extent of territorial control of nations on maps became a supreme value. The imperialist nation-states of Europe at the end of the nineteenth century sought to tout their territorial successes, not always with the greatest attention to accuracy. As technology made more accurate mapmaking possible, national pride resisted standardization. Penck's global vision remained subordinate to the limits of national boundaries and to the politics of mapmaking.

Looking Ahead

This chapter begins by considering the territorial arrangements and conflicts within Europe between 1870 and 1914 that created a new kind of foreign policy based on mutual interests and national vulnerabilities. The chapter then turns to European rivalries in the global arena and the territorial and market expansion into Africa and Asia that characterized the new imperialism. Finally, the chapter considers how imperial encounters changed both the colonized and the colonizer and produced interdependent markets and a new world economy. ➤

THE EUROPEAN BALANCE OF POWER, 1870–1914

Geopolitics, or the politics of geography, is based on the recognition that certain areas of the world are valuable for political reasons. The term, first used at the end of the nineteenth century, described a process well under way in international relations. Between 1870 and 1914, European states were locked in a competition within Europe for territorial dominance and control. Geopolitics combined with rising nationalist movements in southern Europe and the Ottoman Empire to create a mood of increasing confrontation among Europe's great powers. The European balance of power so carefully crafted by Germany's Otto von Bismarck began to disintegrate with his departure from office in 1890. By 1914, a Europe divided into two camps was no longer the sure guarantee of peace that it had been a generation earlier.

Upsetting the European Balance of Power

The map of Europe had been redrawn in the two decades after 1850. By 1871, Europe consisted of five great powers, known as the Big Five—Britain, France, Germany, Austria-Hungary, and Russia—and a handful of lesser states. The declaration of a German Empire in 1871 and the emergence of Italy with Rome as its capital in 1870 unified numerous disparate states. Although not always corresponding to linguistic and cultural differences among Europe's peoples, national boundaries appeared fixed, with no country aspiring to territorial expansion at the expense of its neighbors. But the creation of the two new national units of Germany and Italy had legitimized nationalist aspirations and the militarism necessary to enforce them.

The Three Emperors' League. Under the chancellorship of Otto von Bismarck, Germany led the way in forging a new alliance system based on the realistic assessment of power politics within Europe. In 1873, Bismarck joined together the three most conservative powers of the Big Five—Germany, Austria-Hungary, and Russia—into the Three Emperors' League. Consultation over mutual interests and friendly neutrality were the cornerstones of the alliance. Identifying enemies and choosing friends in the new configuration of power came in large part to depend on geographic weaknesses. The Three Emperors' League was one example of the geographic imperatives driving diplomacy. Bismarck was determined to banish the specter of a two-front war by isolating France on the Continent.

Each of the Great Powers had a vulnerability, a geographic Achilles' heel. Germany's vulnerability lay in its North Sea ports. German shipping along its only coast could easily be bottlenecked by a powerful naval force. Such an event, the Germans knew, could destroy their rapidly growing international trade. What was worse, powerful land forces could "encircle" Germany. As Britain's century-old factories slowly became obsolete under peeling coats of paint, Germany enjoyed the advantages of a latecomer to industrialization—forced to start from scratch by investing in the most advanced machinery and technology. The German Reich was willing to support industrial expansion, scientific and technological training, and social programs for its workers. Yet as Germany surged forward to seize its share of world markets, it was acutely aware that it was hemmed in on the Continent. Germany could not extend its frontiers the way Russia had to the east. German gains in the Franco-Prussian War in Alsace and Lorraine could not be repeated without risking greater enmity. German leaders saw the threat of encirclement as a second geographic weakness. Bismarck's awareness of those geographic facts of life prompted his engineering of the Three Emperors' League in 1873, two years after the founding of the German Empire.

Austria-Hungary was Europe's second largest nation in land and the third largest in population. The same factors that had made it a great European power—its size and its diversity—now threatened to destroy it. The ramshackle empire of Europe, it had no geographical unity. Its vulnerability came from within, from the centrifugal forces of linguistic and cultural diversity. Weakened by nationalities clamoring for independence and self-rule and by an unresponsive political system, Austria-Hungary remained backward agriculturally and unable to respond to the Western industrial challenge. It seemed most likely to collapse from social and political pressures.

Russia's vulnerability was reflected in its preoccupation with maintaining free access to the Mediterranean Sea. Russia, clearly Europe's greatest landed power, was vulnerable because it could be landlocked by frozen or blockaded ports. The ice that crippled its naval and commercial vessels in the Baltic Sea drove Russia east through Asia to secure another ice-blocked port on the Sea of Japan at Vladivostok in 1860 and to seek ice-free Chinese ports. Russia was equally obsessed with protecting its warm-water ports on the Black Sea. Whoever controlled the strait of the Bosporus controlled Russia's grain export trade, on which its economic prosperity depended.

The Ottoman Empire. To the southeast of Europe lay the Ottoman Empire, a great decaying conglomeration that bridged Europe and Asia. Politically feeble and on the verge of bankruptcy, the Ottoman Empire, with Turkey at its core, was composed of a vast array of ethnically, linguistically, and culturally diverse peoples. In the hundred years before 1914, increasing social unrest and nationalist bids for independence had plagued the Ottoman Empire. As was the case with the Habsburgs in Austria-Hungary, the Ottomans maintained power with increasing difficulty over the myriad ethnic groups struggling to be free. The Ottoman Empire, called "the sick man of Europe" by contemporaries, found two kinds of relations sitting at its bedside: those who would do anything to ensure its survival, no matter how weak, and those who longed for and sought to hasten its demise. Fortunately for the Ottoman Empire, its enemies were willing to preserve it in its weakened state rather than see one of the other rival European powers benefit from its collapse.

■ A *Punch* cartoon shows European leaders trying to keep the lid on the simmering kettle of Balkan crises.

The Ottomans had already seen parts of their holdings lopped off in the nineteenth century. Britain, ever conscious of its interests in India, had acquired Cyprus, Egypt, Aden, and Sudan from the Ottomans. Germany insinuated itself into Turkish internal affairs and financed the Baghdad Railway in the attempt to link the Mediterranean to the Persian Gulf. Russia acquired territories on the banks of the Caspian Sea and had plans to take Constantinople. But it was the volatile Balkan Peninsula that threatened to upset the European power balance. The Balkans appeared to be a territory that begged for dismemberment. Internally, the Slavs sought independence from their Habsburg and Turkish oppressors. External pressures were equally great, with each of the major powers following its own political agenda.

The Instability of the Alliance System

The system of alliances formed between and among European states was guided by two political realities: the tension between France and Germany, and Russia's fear of becoming landlocked.

Franco-German Tensions.   A major destabilizing factor in the European balance of power was the tension between France and Germany. France had lost its dominance on the Continent in 1870–1871, when it was easily defeated by Prussia at the head of a nascent German Empire. With its back to the Atlantic, France faced the smaller states of Belgium, Luxembourg, Switzerland, and Italy and the industrially and militarily powerful Germany. It had suffered the humiliation of losing territory to Germany—Alsace and Lorraine in 1871—and was well aware of its continued vulnerability. France felt trapped and isolated geographically and in need of powerful friends as a counterweight to German power.

Russian Aspirations and the Congress of Berlin.
Ostensibly, Russia had the most to gain from the extension of its frontiers and the creation of pro-Russian satellites. It saw that by championing Pan-Slavic nationalist groups in southeastern Europe, it could greatly strengthen its own position at the expense of the two great declining empires, Ottoman Turkey and Austria-Hungary. Russia hoped to draw the Slavs into its orbit by fostering the creation of independent states in the Balkans. A Serbian revolt began in two Ottoman provinces, Bosnia and Herzegovina, in 1874. International opinion pressured Turkey to initiate reforms. Serbia declared war on Turkey on 30 June 1876; Montenegro did the same the next day. Britain, supporting the Ottoman Empire because of its trading interests in the Mediterranean, found itself in a delicate position of perhaps condemning an ally when it received news of Turkish atrocities against Christians in Bulgaria. Prime Minister Disraeli insisted that Britain was bound to defend Constantinople because of British interests in the Suez Canal and India. While Britain stood on the sidelines, Russia, with Romania as an ally, declared war against the Ottoman Empire. The war was quickly over, with Russia capturing all of Armenia, forcing the Ottoman sultan, Abdul Hamid II (1842–1918), to sue for peace on 31 January 1878.

Great Britain did not share Germany's and Russia's fears of strangulation by blockade. And although the question of Irish home rule was a nationalities problem for Britain, it paled in comparison with Austria-Hungary's internal challenge. As an island kingdom, however, Great Britain relied on imports for its survival. The first of the European nations to become an urban and industrial power, Britain was forced to do so at the expense of its agricultural sector. It could not feed its own people without importing foodstuffs. Britain's geographic vulnerability was its dependence on access to its empire and the maintenance of open sea-lanes. Britain saw its greatest menace coming from the rise of other sea powers—notably Germany.

Bismarck, a seemingly disinterested party acting as an "honest broker," hosted the peace conference that met at Berlin. The British succeeded in blocking Russia's intentions for a Bulgarian satellite and keeping the Russians from taking Constantinople. Russia abandoned its support of Serbian nationalism, and Austria-Hungary occupied Bosnia and Herzegovina. The peace concluded at the 1878 Congress of Berlin disregarded Serbian claims, thereby promising continuing conflict over the nationalities question.

The Berlin Congress also marked the emergence of a new estrangement among the Great Powers. Russia believed itself betrayed by Bismarck and abandoned in its alliance with Germany. Bismarck in turn cemented a Dual Alliance between Austria-Hungary and Germany in 1879 that survived until the collapse of the two imperial regimes in 1918. The Three Emperors' League was renewed in 1881, now with stipulations regarding the division of the spoils in case of a war against Turkey.

The Alliance System Revamped.   In 1882, Italy was asked to join the Dual Alliance with Germany and Austria-Hungary, thus converting it into the **Triple Alliance,** which prevailed until the Great War of 1914. Germany, under Bismarck's tutelage, signed treaties with Italy, Russia, and Austria-Hungary and established friendly terms with Great Britain. A new Balkan crisis in 1885, however, shattered the illusion of stable relations.

Hostilities erupted between Bulgaria and Serbia. Russia threatened to occupy Bulgaria, but Austria stepped in to prevent Russian domination of the Balkans, thus threatening the alliance of the Three Emperors' League. Russia was further angered by German unwillingness to support its interests against Austrian actions in the Balkans. Germany maintained relations with Russia in a new Reinsurance Treaty drawn up in 1887, which stipulated that each power would maintain neutrality should the other find itself at war. Bismarck now walked a fine line, balancing alliances and selectively disclosing the terms of secret treaties to nonsignatory countries with the goal of preserving the peace. He was described by his successor as the only man who could keep five glass balls in the air at the same time.

After Bismarck's resignation in 1890, Germany found itself unable to juggle all the glass balls. Germany allowed the arrangement with Russia to lapse. Russia, in turn, allied itself in 1894 with France. Also allied with Great Britain, France had broken out of the isolation that Bismarck had intended for it two decades earlier. The **Triple Entente** came into existence following the Anglo-Russian understanding of 1907. Now it was the Triple Entente of Great Britain, France, and Russia against the Triple Alliance of Germany, Austria-Hungary, and Italy.

There was still every confidence that the two camps could balance each other and preserve the peace. But in 1908–1909, the unresolved Balkan problem threatened to topple Europe's precarious peace. Against Russia's objections, Austria-Hungary annexed Bosnia and Herzegovina, the provinces it had occupied since 1878. Russia supported Serbia's discontent over Austrian acquisition of the predominantly Slavic territories that Serbia believed should be united with its own lands. Unwilling to risk a European war at this point, Russia was ultimately forced to back down under German pressure. Germany had to contend with its own fear of geographic vulnerability with hostile neighbors, France and Russia, on its western and eastern frontiers.

A third Balkan crisis erupted in 1912 when Italy and Turkey fought over the possession of Tripoli in North Africa.

CHRONOLOGY EUROPEAN CRISES AND THE BALANCE OF POWER	
1871	German Empire created
1873	Three Emperors' League: Germany, Austria-Hungary, and Russia
1874	First Balkan crisis: Serbian revolt in Bosnia and Herzegovina
1875	Russo-Turkish War
1876	Serbia declares war on Turkey; Montenegro declares war on Turkey
1878	Congress of Berlin
1879	Dual Alliance: Germany and Austria-Hungary
1881	Three Emperors' League renewed
1882	Triple Alliance: Germany, Austria-Hungary, and Italy
1885	Second Balkan crisis: Bulgaria versus Serbia
1887	Reinsurance Treaty between Germany and Russia
1894	Russia concludes alliance with France
1907	Triple Entente: Great Britain, France, and Russia
1908	Austria-Hungary annexes Bosnia and Herzegovina
1912	Third Balkan crisis: Italy versus Turkey
1913	War erupts between Serbia and Bulgaria

The Balkan states took advantage of the opportunity to increase their holdings at Turkey's expense. The action quickly involved Great Power interests once again. A second war broke out in 1913 over Serbian interests in Bulgaria. Russia backed Serbia against Austro-Hungarian support of Bulgaria. The Russians and Austrians prepared for war while the British and Germans urged peaceful resolution. Although hostilities ceased, Serbian resentment toward Austria-Hungary over its frustrated nationalism was greater than ever. Britain, in its backing of Russia, and Germany, in its support of Austria-Hungary, were enmeshed in alliances that could involve them in a military confrontation.

THE NEW IMPERIALISM

Europeans in the last third of the nineteenth century did not invent the idea of empire: ancient civilizations had valued territorial conquest. Even before 1870 in Europe, the influence of Great Britain stretched far beyond the limits of its island holdings to India and South Africa. Russia held Siberia and central Asia, and France ruled Algeria and Indochina. Older empires—Spain, for example—had survived from the sixteenth century but as hollow shells. What, then, was new about the **new imperialism** practiced by England, France, and Germany after 1870?

In part, the new imperialism was the acquisition of territories on an intense and unprecedented scale. Industrialization created the tools of transportation, communication, and domination that permitted the rapid pace of global empire building. Above all, what distinguished the new imperialism was the domination by the industrial powers over the nonindustrial world. The United States also participated in the new imperialism, less by territorial acquisition and more by developing an "invisible" empire of trade and influence in the Pacific. The forms of imperialism may have varied from nation to nation, but the basically unequal relationship between an industrial power and an undeveloped territory did not.

Only nation-states commanded the technology and resources necessary for the new scale of imperialist expansion. Rivalry among a few European nation-states—notably Great Britain, France, and Germany—was a common denominator that set the standards by which the nations and other European nation-states gained control of the globe by 1900. Why did the Europeans create vast empires? Were empires built for economic gain, military protection, or national glory? Questions about motives may obscure common features of the new imperialism. Industrial powers sought to take over nonindustrial regions, not in isolated areas but all over the globe. In the attempt they necessarily competed with one another, successfully adapting the resources of industrialism to the needs of conquest.

The Technology of Empire

For Europeans at the end of the nineteenth century, the world had definitely become a smaller place. Steam, iron, and electricity—the great forces of Western industrialization—were responsible for seemingly shrinking the globe. Technology not only allowed Europeans to accomplish tasks and to mass-produce goods efficiently, but it also altered the previous conception of time and space.

Steam, which powered factories, proved equally efficient as an energy source in transportation. Great iron steamships fueled by coal replaced the smaller, slower, wind-powered wooden sailing vessels that had ruled the seas for centuries. Steam-powered vessels transported large cargoes of people and goods more quickly and more reliably than the sailing ships. Iron ships were superior to wood in their durability, lightness, water-tightness, cargo space, speed, and fuel economy. For most

of the nineteenth century, British trading ships and the British navy dominated the seas, but after 1880 other nations, especially Germany, challenged England by building versatile and efficient iron steamers. In a society in which time was money, steamships were important because, for the first time, ocean-going vessels could meet schedules as precisely and as predictably as railroads could. Just as the imperial Romans had used their network of roads to link far-flung territories to the capital, Europeans used sea-lanes to join their colonies to the home country.

Until 1850, Europeans had ventured no farther on the African continent than its coastal areas. The installation of coal-burning boilers on smaller boats permitted navigation of previously uncharted and unnavigable rivers. Steam power made exploration and migration possible and greatly contributed to knowledge of terrain, natural wealth, and resources. Smaller steam-powered vessels also increased European inland trade with China, Burma, and India.

Engineering Empire. While technology improved European mobility on water, it also literally moved the land. Harbors were deepened to accommodate the new iron- and then steel-hulled ships. One of the greatest engineering feats of the century was the construction of a hundred-mile-long canal across the Isthmus of Suez in Egypt. The Suez Canal, completed in 1869, joined the Mediterranean and Red Seas and created a new, safer trade route to the East. No longer did trading vessels have to make the long voyage around Africa's Cape of Good Hope. The Suez Canal was built by the French under the supervision of Ferdinand de Lesseps (1805–1894), a diplomat with no technical or financial background who was able to promote construction because of concessions he received from Said Pasha, the viceroy of Egypt. The canal could accommodate ships of all sizes. Great Britain purchased a controlling interest in the Suez Canal in 1875 to benefit its trade with India.

De Lesseps later oversaw the initial construction of the Panama Canal in the Western Hemisphere. The combination of French mismanagement, bankruptcy, and the high incidence of disease among work crews enabled the United States to acquire rights to the Panama project and complete the canal by 1914. Fifty-one miles long, the Panama Canal connected the world's two largest bodies of water, the Atlantic and Pacific Oceans, across the Isthmus of Panama by a waterway containing a series of locks. The passage from the Atlantic Ocean to the Pacific Ocean took less than eight hours—much less time than it took using the various overland routes or voyaging around the tip of South America. Both the Suez and Panama canals were built in pursuit of speed. Shorter distances meant quicker travel, which in turn meant higher profits.

Europeans carried the technologies of destruction as well as survival with them into less-developed areas of the world. New types of firearms produced in the second half of the nineteenth century included breech-loading rifles, repeating rifles, and machine guns. The new weapons gave the advantages of both accurate aim and rapid fire. The spears of

■ Photograph of the construction of the Suez Canal. An elaborate ceremony marked the opening of the canal to navigation on 17 November 1869.

African warriors and the primitive weaponry of Chinese rebels were no match for sophisticated European arms, which permitted their bearers to lie down while firing and to remain undetected at distances of up to a half mile.

Technology also altered time by increasing the speed with which Westerners communicated with other parts of the world. In 1830, for example, it took about two years for a person sending a letter from Great Britain to India to receive a reply. In 1850, steam-powered mail boats shortened the time required for the same round-trip correspondence to about two or three months. But the real revolution in communication came through electricity. Thousands of miles of copper telegraph wire laced countries together; insulated underwater cables linked continents to each other. By the late nineteenth century, a vast telegraph network connected Europe to every area of the world. In 1870, a telegram from London to Bombay arrived in a matter of hours, instead of months, and a response could be received back in London on the same day. Faster communications extended power and control throughout empires. Europeans could communicate immediately with their distant colonies, dispatching troops, orders, and supplies. The communication network eliminated the problem of overextension that had plagued Roman imperial organization in the third century. For the first time, continents discovered by Europeans five centuries earlier were brought into daily contact with the West.

Medical Advances.   Advances in medicine helped foster European imperialism in the nineteenth century by permitting European men and women to penetrate disease-ridden swamps and jungles. After 1850, European explorers, traders,

missionaries, and adventurers carried **quinine** pills. Quinine, the bitter-tasting derivative of cinchona tree bark, was discovered to be an effective treatment for malaria. The treatment had its first important test during the French invasion of Algeria in 1830, and it allowed the French to stay healthy enough to conquer that North African country between 1830 and 1847. David Livingstone (1813–1873) and Henry M. Stanley (1841–1904) were just two of the many explorers who crossed vast terrains and explored the waterways of Africa, after malaria—the number one killer of European travelers— had been controlled.

The new technology did not cause the new imperialism. The Western powers used technological advances as a tool for establishing their control of the world. Viewed as a tool, however, the new technology does explain how vast areas of land and millions of people were conquered so rapidly.

Motives for Empire

If technology was not the cause but only a tool, what explains the new imperialism of the late nineteenth century? Were wealthy financiers, searching for high-yielding opportunities for investments, the driving force? Was profit the main motive? Were politicians and heads of state in the game for the prestige and glory that territorial expansion could bring them at home?

There are no easy or simple explanations for the new imperialism. Individuals made their fortunes overseas, and heavy industries such as the Krupp firm in Germany prospered with the expansion of state-protected colonies. Yet many colonies were economically worthless. Tunisia and

■ The transatlantic telegraph cable was the first intercontinental communications link of the electric age. This illustration shows the *Great Eastern,* the largest ship afloat, which finally succeeded in laying the cable in 1866.

Morocco, acquired for their strategic and political importance, constituted an economic loss for the French, who poured more funds into their administration than they were able to extract. Each imperial power held one or more colonies whose costs outweighed the return. Yet that does not mean that some Europeans were simply irrational in their pursuit of empire and glory.

Economics.   The test for economic motivation cannot simply be reduced to a balance sheet of debits and credits because, in the end, an account of state revenues and state expenditures provides only a static picture of the business of empire. Even losses cannot be counted as proof against the profit motive in expansion. In modern capitalism, profits, especially great profits, are often predicated on risks. Portugal and Italy, as smaller nations with limited resources, failed as players in the game in which the great industrial powers called the shots. Prestige through the acquisition of empire was one way of keeping alive in the game.

Imperialism was influenced by business interests, market considerations, and the pursuit of individual and national fortunes. Not by accident did the great industrial powers control the scramble and dictate the terms of expansion. Nor was it merely fortuitous that Great Britain, the nation that provided the model for European expansion, dedicated itself to the establishment of a profitable worldwide network of trade and investment. Above all, the search for investment opportunities—whether railroads in China or diamond mines in South Africa—lured Europeans into a world system that challenged capitalist ingenuity and imagination. Acquiring territory was only one means of protecting investments. But there

were other benefits associated with the acquisition of territory that cannot be reduced to economic terms, and those too must be considered.

Geopolitics.   Statesmen influenced by geopolitical concerns recognized the strategic value of land. Some territory was considered important because of its proximity to acquired colonies or to territory targeted for takeover. France, for example, occupied thousands of square miles of the Sahara Desert to protect its interests in Algeria.

Other territory was important because of its proximity to sea routes. Egypt had significance for Great Britain not because of its inherent economic potential but because it permitted the British to protect access to lucrative markets in India through the Suez Canal. Beginning in 1875, the British purchased shares in the canal. By 1879, Egypt was under the informal dual rule of France and Great Britain. The British used the deterioration of internal Egyptian politics to justify their occupation of the country in 1882. Protected access to India also accounted for Great Britain's maintenance of Mediterranean outposts, its acquisition of territory on the east coast of Africa, and its occupation of territory in southern Asia.

A third geopolitical motive for annexation was the necessity of fueling bases throughout the world. Faster and more reliable than wind-powered vessels, coal-powered ships were nonetheless dependent on guaranteed fueling bases in friendly ports of call. Islands in the South Pacific and the Indian Ocean were acquired primarily to serve as coaling stations for the great steamers carrying manufactured goods to colonial ports and returning with foodstuffs and raw materials. Ports along the southern rim of Asia served the same purpose. The need for protection

LEOPOLD II OF BELGIUM, SPEECH TO AN INTERNATIONAL CONFERENCE OF GEOGRAPHERS, 12 SEPTEMBER 1876

Leopold II reigned as king of the Belgians from 1865 until his death in 1909. Although the ruler of a small European country, he had vast territorial aspirations in Africa. As the personal ruler of the Congo Free State, Leopold amassed an immense fortune until abuses of African workers forced him to hand over his authority over what is now Congo to the Belgian government. In addressing geographers, Leopold evinced some of the self-serving goals that made him the architect of the scramble for territory.

Focus Questions

How does King Leopold's speech rely on the concept of the "White Man's burden" to justify occupation of territory? What are Leopold's motives for occupying Africa?

The matter which brings us together today is one most deserving the attention of the friends of humanity. For bringing civilization to the only part of the earth which it has not yet reached and lightening the darkness in which whole peoples are plunged, is, I venture to say, a crusade worthy of this century of progress, and I am glad to find how favourable public opinion is to the accomplishment of this task. We are swimming with the tide. Many of those who have closely studied Africa have come to realize that it would be in the interest of the object they are all seeking to achieve for them to meet and consult together with a view to regulating the course to be taken, combining their efforts and drawing on all available resources in a way which would avoid duplication of effort. . . . Among the matters which remain to be discussed, the following may be mentioned:

1. Deciding exactly where to acquire bases for the task in hand . . . on the Zanzibar coast and near the mouth of the Congo, either by means of conventions with chiefs or by purchasing or renting sites from individuals.
2. Deciding on the routes to be successively opened up into the interior, and on the medical, scientific and peace-keeping stations which are to be set up with a view to abolishing slavery, and bringing about good relations between the chiefs by providing them with fair-minded, impartial persons to settle their disputes, and so forth.
3. Setting up—once the task to be done has been clearly defined—a central, international committee with national committees, each to carry out this task in the aspects of it which concern them, to explain the object to the public of all countries, and to appeal to the feeling of charity to which no worthy cause has ever appealed in vain.

These are some of the points which seem worthy of your attention. . . . My wish is to serve the great cause for which you have already done so much, in whatever manner you may suggest to me. It is with this object that I put myself at your disposal, and I extend a cordial welcome to you.

---

of colonies, fueling ports, and sea-lanes led to the creation of naval bases such as those on the Red Sea at Djibouti by the French, along the South China Sea at Singapore by the British, and in the Pacific Ocean at Honolulu by the Americans.

In turn, the acquisition of territories justified the increase in naval budgets and the size of fleets. Britain still had the world's largest navy, but by the beginning of the twentieth century, the United States and Germany had entered the competition for dominance of sea-lanes. Japan joined the contest by expanding its navy as a vehicle for its own claims to empire in the Pacific.

The politics of geography was land- as well as sea-based. As navies grew to protect sea-lanes, armies expanded to police new lands. Between 1890 and 1914, military expenditures of Western governments grew phenomenally, with war machines doubling in size. In both its impact on domestic budgets and its protection of markets and trading routes, geopolitics had a strong economic component. Governments became consumers

of heavy industry; their predictable participation in markets for armaments and military supplies helped control fluctuations in the business cycle and reduce unemployment at home. A side effect of the growing importance of geopolitics was the increased influence of military and naval leaders in foreign and domestic policy making.

Nationalism. Many European statesmen in the last quarter of the nineteenth century gave stirring speeches about the importance of empire as a means of enhancing national prestige. In his Crystal Palace speech of 1872, Benjamin Disraeli, British prime minister in 1868 and 1874–1880, put the challenge boldly to the British:

I appeal to the sublime instinct of an ancient people. . . . The issue is not a mean one. It is whether you will be content to be a comfortable England, modelled and moulded upon Continental principles and meeting in due course an inevitable fate, or whether you will be a great country, an imperial country, a country where your sons, when they rise, rise to paramount positions and obtain not merely the esteem of their countrymen but command the respect of the world.

National prestige was not an absolute value but one weighed relatively. Possessing an empire may have meant "keeping up with the Joneses," as it did for smaller countries such as Italy. Imperial status was important to a country such as Portugal, which was willing to go bankrupt to maintain its territories. But prestige without economic power was the form of imperialism without its substance. Nation-states could, through the acquisition of overseas territories, gain bargaining chips to be played at the international conference table. In that way, smaller nations hoped to be taken seriously in the system of alliances that preserved "the balance of power" in Europe.

Western newspapers deliberately fostered the desire for the advancement of national interests. Newspapers competed for readers, and their circulation often depended on the passions they aroused. Filled with tales calculated to titillate and entertain, and with advertisements promising miracle cures, newspapers wrested foreign policy from the realm of the specialist and transformed politics into another form of entertainment. The drama and vocabulary of sporting events, whose mass appeal as a leisure activity also dates from the era, were now applied to imperialist politics. Whether it was a rugby match or a territorial conquest, readers backed the "home" team, disdained the opposition, and competed for the thrill of victory. It marked quite a change for urban dwellers whose grandparents worked the land and did not look beyond the horizon of their home villages. Newspapers forged a national consciousness whereby individuals learned to identify with collective causes they often did not fully comprehend. Some observed what was happening with a critical eye, identifying a deep-seated need in modern men and women for excitement in their lives.

Information conveyed in newspapers shaped opinion, and opinion, in turn, could influence policy. Leaders had to reckon with the new creation of "public opinion." In a typical instance, French newspaper editors promoted feverish public outcry for conquest of the Congo by pointing out the need to revenge British advances in Egypt. "Colonial fever" in France was so high in the summer of 1882 that French policy makers were pressured to pursue claims in the Congo Basin without adequate assessment or reflection. As a result, the French government evicted Belgians and Portuguese from the northern Congo territory and enforced questionable treaty claims rather than risk public censure for appearing weak and irresolute.

Public opinion was certainly influential, but it also could be manipulated. In Germany, the government often promoted colonial hysteria through the press in order to advance its own political ends. Chancellor Otto von Bismarck used his power over the press to support imperialism and to influence electoral outcomes in 1884. His successors were deft at promoting the "bread and circuses" atmosphere that surrounded colonial expansion in order to direct attention away from social problems at home and to maintain domestic stability.

The printed word was also manipulated in Britain, critics asserted, by business interests during the Boer War (1899–1902) to keep public enthusiasm for the war effort high. J. A. Hobson (1858–1940), a journalist and theorist of imperialism, denounced the "abuse of the press" in his hard-

■ Great Britain originally opposed construction of the Suez Canal but soon recognized its crucial role in the route to India. In this cartoon, *The Lion's Share*, British Prime Minister Disraeli purchases a controlling interest in the Suez Canal Company from the khedive of Egypt. The British lion in the foreground guards the key to India, the symbol of the canal.

THE LION'S SHARE.

hitting *Psychology of Jingoism* (1901), which appeared while the war was still being waged. Hobson recognized **jingoism** as the appropriate term for the "inverted patriotism whereby the love of one's own nation is transformed into hatred of another nation, and into the fierce craving to destroy the individual members of that other nation."

Jingoism was not a new phenomenon in 1900, nor was it confined to Britain. Throughout Europe a mass public appeared increasingly willing to support conflict to defend national honor. Xenophobia (hatred of foreigners) melded with nationalism, both nurtured by the mass press, to put new pressures on the determination of foreign policy. Government elites, who formerly had operated behind closed doors far removed from public scrutiny, were now accountable in new ways to faceless masses. Even in autocratic states such as Austria-Hungary, the opinion of the masses was a powerful political force that could destroy individual careers and dissolve governments.

Every nation in Europe had its jingoes, those willing to risk war for national glory. Significantly, the term *jingo* was coined in 1878 during a British showdown with the Russians over Turkey. The sentiment that "the Russians shall not have Constantinople" was so strong that the acceptability of war was set to music:

> We don't want to fight,
> But, by Jingo, if we do,
> We've got the men,
> We've got the ships,
> We've got the money too.

This was the most popular music-hall song in Britain that year, and long after the crisis had faded the tune and its lyrics lingered.

To varying degrees, all of the factors—economics, geopolitics, and nationalism—motivated the actions of the three great imperialist powers—Britain, France, and Germany—and their less-powerful European neighbors. The same reasons account for the global aspirations of non-European nations such as the United States and Japan. Each of the powers was aware of what the others were doing and tailored its actions accordingly. Imperialism followed a variety of patterns but always had a built-in component of emulation and acceleration. It was both a cause and a proof of a world system of states in which the actions of one nation affected the others.

THE SEARCH FOR TERRITORY AND MARKETS

Most western Europeans who read about the distant regions that their armies and statesmen were bringing under their national flags tended to regard the new territories as no more than entries on a great tally sheet or as colors on a map. The daily press recorded the numbers of square miles gained and the captive populations taken, and for readers that was often the end of the story. Few Europeans looked on imperialism as a relationship of power between two parties and, like all relationships, one influenced by both partners. Fewer still understood or appreciated the distinctive qualities of the conquered peoples.

The areas European imperialism affected varied widely in their political organization. Throughout Africa, states were generally small or even nonexistent, and Europeans considered their governmental institutions too ineffectual to produce the economic changes and growth of trade Europe wanted. Military takeover and direct rule by European officials seemed the only feasible way to establish empire there. In Asia, on the other hand, societies such as China and India were territorially large and possessed efficient institutions of government dominated by established political hierarchies. Although they were more difficult to conquer, their leaders were also more likely to cooperate with the imperial powers because their own interests were often similar to those of the Westerners. For those reasons, European empire builders pursued a variety of models: formal military empires (as in Africa), informal empires (as in China), or formal but indirect rule over hierarchical societies (as in India). The United States provided yet another model, one that relied on hegemonic influence as well as outright control.

The Scramble for Africa: Diplomacy and Conflict

In the mid-1860s, a committee of the British Parliament recommended that Britain withdraw from the scattering of small colonies it possessed in West Africa, arguing that they were costly anachronisms in an era of free trade. In 1898, the president of France, when commenting on French policies of the previous 20 years, remarked, "We have behaved like madmen in Africa, having been led astray by irresponsible people called the 'colonialists.'" The "mad" event that had altered the political landscape in Africa was the so-called **scramble for Africa** that is usually considered as extending from around 1875 to around 1912. By its end, virtually all of Africa was under European control.

Africa is a large and complex continent, and the reasons of Europeans for pursuing specific pieces of African territory were similarly complex. The explanations for the acquisition of a particular colony, therefore, depend largely on the historical context of that particular case. In certain areas, such as the West African desert zones of the Sudan and the Sahara, ambitious French military men sought to advance their careers by carving out grand colonies.

The existence of valuable minerals motivated the scramble for the area now called Zimbabwe, the Zambian-Zairian copper belt, and other areas. Along the West African coast, chronic disputes between traders working in a souring economy seemed to demand European annexation. Some colonies, such as those in what are now Uganda and Malawi, were created to please missionaries already working there. Britain took Egypt and France took Djibouti for strategic reasons. And in Mozambique, Tanzania, Namibia, and Botswana, some Europeans seized areas to keep other Europeans from doing

JOSEPH CHAMBERLAIN'S SPEECH TO THE BIRMINGHAM RELIEF ASSOCIATION

Joseph Chamberlain (1836–1914) was an English businessman and statesman and, from 1873 to 1876, the mayor of one of Great Britain's leading industrial cities, Birmingham. He was a national advocate for an expansionist colonial policy as the means of keeping his country strong. On 22 January 1894, with no regard for African people, he spoke before a community group to convince them that British imperialism helped the working class.

Focus Questions

What are the motives evoked by Chamberlain to justify colonial expansion? How does he appeal to the patriotism of the English working classes?

Believe me, if in any one of the places [in Africa] to which I have referred any change took place which deprived us of that control and influence of which I have been speaking, the first to suffer would be the working-men of this country. Then, indeed, we should see a distress which would not be temporary, but which would be chronic, and we should find that England was entirely unable to support the enormous population which is now maintained by the aid of her foreign trade. If the working-men of this country understand, as I believe they do—I am one of those who have had good reason through my life to rely upon their intelligence and shrewdness—if they understand their own interests, they will never lend any countenance to the doctrines of those politicians who never lose an opportunity of pouring contempt and abuse upon the brave Englishmen, who, even at this moment, in all parts of the world are carving out new dominions for Britain, and are opening up fresh markets for British commerce, and laying out fresh fields for British labour. [Applause.] If the Little Englanders[i] had their way, not only would they refrain from taking the legitimate opportunities which offer for extending the empire and for securing for us new markets, but I doubt whether they would even take the pains which are necessary to preserve the great heritage which has come down to us from our ancestors. [Applause.]

When you are told that the British pioneers of civilisation in Africa are filibusters,[ii] and when you are asked to call them back, and to leave this great continent to the barbarism and superstition in which it has been steeped for centuries, or to hand over to foreign countries the duty which you are unwilling to undertake, I ask you to consider what would have happened if 100 or 150 years ago your ancestors had taken similar views of their responsibility? Where would be the empire on which now your livelihood depends? We should have been the United Kingdom of Great Britain and Ireland; but those vast dependencies, those hundreds of millions with whom we keep up a mutually beneficial relationship and commerce would have been the subjects of other nations, who would not have been slow to profit by our neglect of our opportunities and obligations. [Applause.]

From Joseph Chamberlain, M.P., *Foreign and Colonial Speeches* (1897).

[i] Britain's anti-imperialists.

[ii] A person engaged in a private military action against a foreign government.

---

the same. In seeking territorial control, Europeans were willing to use force. Only Ethiopia escaped the European grasp.

The Drive for Markets and Profits. An important factor influencing imperialist expansion was the economic downturn in Europe that lasted from 1873 until 1896. The downturn, coupled with Germany's rapid rise to economic power during the second phase of the Industrial Revolution in the 1870s and 1880s, was deeply unsettling to many Europeans. Protectionist policies springing from new economic anxieties eroded the earlier European faith in free trade. Many Europeans favored acquiring African territory just in case it should turn out to be economically useful. Even Britain, long the major champion of free trade, became ever more protectionist and imperialistic as the century neared its end.

Colonization in Africa

Historians generally agree that the person who provided the catalyst for the scramble was Leopold II, king of Belgium (1835–1909). Sheer greed motivated Leopold. In early 1876, he had read a report about the Congo Basin that claimed it was "mostly a magnificent and healthy country of unspeakable richness" that promised "to repay any enterprising capitalist." Leopold, an ambitious and frustrated king ruling over a small country, went to work at once to acquire the Congo Basin, an area one-third the size of the United States. Cloaking himself in the mantle of philanthropy and asserting that all he desired was to stamp out the remnants of the East African slave trade, in late 1876 Leopold organized the International African Association. Leopold II's association soon established trading stations on the region's rivers and coerced much valuable ivory from the people. Belgian settlers, missionaries, and traders set out to create a common

IN THE RUBBER COILS.

■ A contemporary cartoon characterized King Leopold of the Belgians as a monstrous snake crushing the life out of the black population of the Congo Free State. The territory was under the personal rule of the Belgian king from 1885 to 1908.

language among disparate tribes, and imposed Swahili on Congolese natives.

Leopold skillfully lobbied in Europe for formal recognition of his association's right to rule the Congo Basin. The action provoked objections from France and Portugal, and, after much diplomatic wrangling, an international conference was finally held in Berlin in late 1884 to decide who should rule the Congo. The Berlin Conference was important, not only because it yielded the Congo Basin to Leopold as the Congo Free State, but also because it laid down the ground rules for all other colonial acquisitions in Africa. For international recognition of a claim, "effective occupation" would be required. That meant that no longer would planting a flag in an area be considered adequate for establishing sovereignty; instead, a real presence calculated to produce "economic development" would be needed. If Leopold's actions began the scramble by panicking the European states, the Berlin

Conference organized it. However, it is clear in retrospect that the scramble would have occurred even without Leopold II's greedy intervention.

European Agreements and African Massacres. In their disputes over apportioning Africa, the Europeans were remarkably pacific with each other. Although Britain threatened Portugal with war in 1890 in a conflict over the area around Lake Malawi, and although it appeared for a while that Britain and France were headed toward armed conflict in 1898 at Fashoda in a dispute over the Nile headwaters, peaceful diplomatic settlements that satisfied the imperial powers were always worked out. Deals where states traded territory were common, and peace was maintained. Africa was not worth a war to Europeans. Yet in every instance of expansion in Africa, Europeans were ready to shoot Africans. With Hiram Maxim's invention in 1884 of a machine gun that could fire 11 bullets per second, and with the sale of modern weapons to Africans banned by the Brussels Convention of 1890, the military advantage passed overwhelmingly to the imperialists. As the British poet Hillaire Belloc tellingly observed,

> Whatever happens, we have got
> The Maxim gun, and they have not.

The conquest of "them" became more like hunting than warfare. In 1893, for example, in Zimbabwe, 50 Europeans, using only six machine guns, killed 3000 Ndebele people in less than two hours. In 1897, in northern Nigeria, a force of 32 Europeans and 500 African mercenaries defeated the 31,000-man army of the emir of Sokoto. The nature of such warfare is well summed up in a report by Winston Churchill about the battle at Omdurman, in the Sudan, in 1898:

> The [British] infantry fired steadily and stolidly, without hurry or excitement, for the enemy were far away and the officers careful. Besides the soldiers were interested in the work and took great pains. . . . And all the time out on the plain on the other side bullets were shearing through flesh, smashing and splintering bone: blood spouted from terrible wounds; valiant men were struggling on through a hell of whistling metal, exploding shells, and spurting dust—suffering, despairing, and dying.

After five hours of fighting, the number killed were 20 Britons, 20 Egyptian allies, and more than 11,000 Sudanese. Technology had made bravery and courage obsolete for the majority of Africans.

Ethiopia as an Exception. One exception to the general rule of easy conquest was Ethiopia. The history of the country illustrates the overriding importance of guns in understanding the essential dynamic of the scramble. In the middle of the nineteenth century, the emperor of Ethiopia possessed little more than a grand title. The empire had broken down into its ethnic and regional components, each of which was fueled by its own "big men," local rulers with little regard for the emperor. Yet the dream of a united empire was alive and pursued by the emperors of the time, Amharic-speaking "big men" with their political base on the fertile plateau that constituted the heartland of the country. In their campaigns to rebuild the empire, they relied increasingly on modern weapons imported from Europe. Their work went forward with some success.

By the early 1870s, however, the emperor realized that his accomplishments in recreating the Ethiopian Empire were endangered by the resistance of the people whom he was then trying to force into his empire and, more ominously, by interference from the outside world, especially Egypt to the north and the Sudan to the west. An expansionary Egypt actually invaded Ethiopian territory, and it was only the Egyptian government's bankruptcy in 1876 that gave the emperor breathing room. The opening of the Suez Canal in 1869 had made the Red Sea and its surroundings attractive not only to Egypt but also to European countries eager to ensure their trade routes to Asia. By the end of the 1870s, when the scramble for Africa was getting seriously under way, Britain, France, and Italy were all contemplating acquiring land in the region. Soon thereafter, Britain occupied Egypt (1882), France took Djibouti (1884), and Italy seized Eritrea (1885).

The Ethiopian emperor, Menelik II (1889–1913), realized that he could exploit rival European interests in the area by playing off one European power against the others to obtain the weapons he needed for expanding his empire's boundaries. Thus he gave certain concessions to France in return for French weapons. Italy, upset by the growing French influence in Ethiopia, offered weapons as well, and Menelik accepted them. Russia and Britain joined in. More and more modern weapons flowed into Ethiopia during the 1870s and 1880s and into the early 1890s, and Menelik steadily strengthened his military position, both to stop internal unrest and to block encroachment from without. Because each European power feared its rivals' influence in Ethiopia, each sold arms to Menelik, and Ethiopia remained largely unaffected by the scramble going on around it.

In the early 1890s, Menelik's stratagems began to unravel. In 1889 he had signed the Treaty of Wichale with Italy, granting it certain concessions in return for more arms shipments. Italy then claimed that Ethiopia had become an Italian protectorate and moved against Menelik when he objected. By 1896, Italy was ready for a major assault on the Ethiopian army. The Italians were heady with confident racism, believing that their forces could defeat the "primitive" Ethiopians with ease. However, General Oreste Baratieri (1841–1901), the commander of the 18,000-man Italian army in Eritrea, was wisely cautious. He understood that modern weapons functioned the same, whether they were fired by Africans or by Italians. Baratieri knew that Menelik's army of some 100,000 troops had very long supply lines, and his strategy was to wait until Menelik could no longer supply his troops with food. Then, he assumed, the soldiers would simply disappear and the Italians would walk in. But the prime minister of Italy, Francesco Crispi (1819–1901), wanted a quick, glorious victory to enhance his political reputation. Crispi ordered Baratieri to send his army of 18,000 men into battle at once. Hopelessly outnumbered, the Italians lost more than 8000 at the decisive battle of Adowa on 1 March 1896. With its army destroyed and its artillery lost to the Ethiopians, Italy had no choice but to sue for peace.

Italy's acceptance of Ethiopia as a sovereign state with greatly expanded imperial boundaries was soon ratified by France and Britain. As a consequence of its victory at Adowa—and attesting to the crucial importance of modern weaponry for survival in late-nineteenth-century Africa—Ethiopia was the only African country aside from the United States' quasi-colony of Liberia not to be occupied in the scramble for Africa. After 1896, Menelik, with his access to modern weapons assured by his country's international recognition, continued his campaign to extend his control forcefully over the Ethiopian Empire's subordinate peoples.

Gold, Empire Building, and the Boer War

Europeans fought white African settlers as well as black Africans during the scramble, as they seized their lands and resources. In South Africa, for example, the British engaged in a long war over access to the world's largest supply of gold with a group of "Afrikaners"—white settlers who had emi-

■ This cartoon shows Cecil Rhodes astride the continent of Africa like a colossus, fulfilling his dream of a British Africa from the Cape to Cairo.

THE RHODES COLOSSUS
STRIDING FROM CAPE TOWN TO CAIRO.

MAP DISCOVERY

Belgian

British

French

German

Italian

Portuguese

Spanish

Independent

Africa, 1914

By 1914, the map of Africa emerged as a colorful patchwork indicating competing European interests. Do you perceive any patterns in the way the seven European nations laid claim to territory? What were the geopolitical imperatives that motivated the British to seek a swathe of territory from north to south? What are the only two states in 1914 not under the control or oversight of European powers? Based on the chapter discussion, how do you explain why they were exceptions?

grated, mostly from the Netherlands, and settled in South Africa during the eighteenth and early nineteenth centuries.

Afrikaner Rule. After the Great Trek (1837–1844), in which a large number of Afrikaners had withdrawn from the British-controlled Colony of the Cape of Good Hope (or Cape Colony), the British had grudgingly recognized the independence of the Orange Free State and the Transvaal—the

Afrikaner republics in the interior—in a series of formal agreements. The British complacently believed that the Afrikaners, economically weak and geographically isolated, could never challenge British preeminence in the region. Two events of the mid-1880s shattered British complacency. First, in 1884, Germany—Britain's greatest rival—inserted itself into the region by annexing Namibia as a colony as part of its imperial adventures. The British, aware that the Germans and the Afrikaners were as sympathetic to one another as both were hostile to them, worried about the German threat to their regional hegemony and economic prospects.

Britain's War in South Africa.

British fear of the Germans redoubled in 1886 when, in the Witwatersrand area of the Transvaal Republic, huge deposits of gold were discovered. A group of rich British diamond-mine owners moved in quickly to develop the gold mines in the Witwatersrand area, for the gold lay deep in the ground and could be mined only with a large capital investment, which the Afrikaners lacked. The best known of the British investors was Cecil Rhodes (1853–1902), a politician and financier intent upon expanding his wealth through an expansion of British power. Rhodes and his colleagues quickly recognized that Afrikaner governmental policies on agriculture, tariffs, and labor control were major impediments to profitable gold production. Therefore, in 1895, with the connivance of members of the British government, they organized an attempt to overthrow the Afrikaner government. The attempt was led by Dr. L. S. Jameson (1853–1917), Rhodes's lieutenant. It involved the invasion of Transvaal by British South African police and came to be known as the Jameson Raid. It was faultily executed, however, and to Rhodes's utter humiliation, it failed.

The failure of the Jameson raiders prompted the British government to send a new agent, Alfred Milner (1854–1925), to the area. He was an ardent advocate of expanding the British Empire and of keeping German influence in the region to a minimum. Well aware of the importance of gold to Britain's financial position in the world, Milner was determined to push the Afrikaners into uniting with the British in South Africa, either through diplomacy or war. By 1899 war had become inevitable, and in October it broke out. The British confidently expected to win the war by Christmas, but the Afrikaners did not cooperate. Inept British commanders opposed by skillful Afrikaner guerrilla-warfare leaders guaranteed that the so-called Boer War would drag on and on.

The British eventually sent 350,000 troops to South Africa, but the forces could not decisively defeat the 65,000 Afrikaner fighting men. Casualties were high, not merely from the fighting, but because typhus epidemics broke out in the concentration camps in which the British interred Afrikaner women and children as they pursued their scorched-earth policies. By the war's end in April 1902, 25,000 Afrikaners, 22,000 British imperial troops, and 12,000 Africans had died. Britain had also been widely criticized for having treated white Afrikaners as if they were black Africans.

In April 1902, the British accepted the conditional surrender of the Afrikaners. The British annexed the Afrikaners to the empire and had the opportunity of making the gold industry efficient. However, they had to promise the Afrikaners that no decisions regarding the political role of the black African majority in a future South Africa would be made before returning political power to the Afrikaners. That crucial concession ensured that segregation would remain the model for race relations in South Africa throughout the twentieth century.

By the time World War I broke out in 1914, the scramble for Africa was over and the map of the continent was colored in imperial inks. France had secured the largest chunk of the continent—some four million square miles—but it was mostly desert and tropical forest. Britain had the second-largest empire, but it was richer in minerals and agricultural potential than France's. Germany was the proud possessor of two West African colonies, Togo and Cameroon, as well as Namibia and Tanganyika. Belgium had inherited Leopold II's Congo in 1908. Portugal had finally consolidated its feeble hold on Angola, Mozambique, and Portuguese Guinea. Italy and Spain held unimportant bits of coastal territory. Only Ethiopia and Liberia were politically independent. With the conquest of Africa, the colonial powers had to face the issue of how their new colonies could be made to pay off; Africans had to face the issue of how they might regain their political independence.

Imperialism in Asia

During the first half of the nineteenth century, strong Asian powers had grown stronger. China increased its control over Inner Asian territories; Vietnam and Siam, predecessor to modern Thailand, enhanced their powers in southeast Asia. By the end of the nineteenth century, Asian political dynasties had suffered reversals. China had been permanently weakened in Inner Asia; Vietnam had fallen under French colonial rule; Siam had lost half its territories. India had long constituted an important part of the British Empire. By contrast, Japan became an aggressive power, itself an imperialist presence.

India.

The British Parliament proclaimed that on New Year's Day, 1877, Queen Victoria (1837–1901) would add the title of Empress of India to her many honors. India, the great jewel in the imperial crown, was a land Victoria had never seen. The queen's new title, not universally popular in Britain and unnoticed by most famine-stricken Indian peasants, in fact changed nothing about the way the British ruled India. Yet it was more than merely a symbolic assertion of dominance over a country long controlled by the British.

DOCUMENT

Arrival of British in Punjab

India was the starting point of all British expansion, and it stood at the center of British foreign policy. To protect its sea routes to India and to secure its Indian markets, Britain acquired territories and carved out concessions all over the world. Devised by Prime Minister Benjamin Disraeli to flatter an aging monarch, the new title of empress was really a calculated warning to Russia—present on India's northern frontier in Afghanistan—and to France, busily pursuing its own interests in Egypt.

Formal British rule in India began in 1861 with the appointment of a viceroy, assisted by legislative and executive councils. Both of the bodies included some Indian representatives. British rule encountered the four main divisions of the highly stratified Hindu society. At the top were Brahmans—the learned and priestly class—followed by warriors and rulers, then by farmers and merchants, and finally by peasants and laborers. On the outside of Hindu society were the "untouchables"—a fifth division relegated to performing society's most menial tasks. Rather than disrupt the divisive caste system, the British found it to their advantage to maintain the status quo.

Britain's relationship with India originated in the seventeenth century, when the British East India Company—a joint-stock venture free of government control—began limited trading in Indian markets. The need for regulation and protection firmly established British rule by the end of the eighteenth century. Conquest of the Punjab in 1849 brought the last independent areas of India under British control. Throughout this period, Britain invested considerable overseas capital in India, and in turn India absorbed one-fifth of the total of British exports. The market for Indian cotton, for centuries exported to markets in Asia and Europe, collapsed under British tariffs, and India became a ready market for cheap Lancashire cotton. The British also exploited India's agricultural products, salt, and opium.

China.   At the end of the eighteenth century, the British were trading English wool and Indian cotton for Chinese tea and textiles. But Britain's thirst for Chinese tea grew, while Chinese demand for English and Indian textiles slackened. Britain discovered that Indian opium could be used to balance the trade deficit created by tea. British merchants and local Chinese officials, especially in the entry port of Canton, began to expand their profitable involvement in a contraband trade in opium. The British East India Company held a monopoly over opium cultivation in Bengal. Opium exports to China mounted phenomenally: from 200 chests in 1729 to 40,000 chests in 1838. By the 1830s, opium was probably Britain's most important crop in world markets. The British prospered as opium was pumped into China at rates faster than tea was flowing out. Chinese buyers began paying for the drug with silver.

Concerned about the sharp rise in opium addiction, the accompanying social problems, and the massive exporting of silver, the Chinese government reacted. As Chinese officials saw it, they were exchanging their precious metal for British poison. Addicts were threatened with the death penalty. In 1839, the Chinese government destroyed British opium in the port of Canton, touching off the so-called Opium War (1839–1842). British expeditionary forces blockaded Chinese ports, besieged Canton, and occupied Shanghai. In protecting the rights of British merchants engaged in illegal trading, Great Britain became the first Western nation to use force to impose its economic interests on China. The Treaty of Nanking (1842) initiated a series of unequal treaties between Europeans and the Chinese and set the pattern for exacting large indemnities.

Treaty Ports
and Boxer
Rebellion

Between 1842 and 1895, China fought five wars with foreigners and lost all of them. Defeat was expensive, as China had to pay costs to the winners. Before the end of the century, Britain, France, Germany, and Japan had managed to establish major territorial advantages in their "**spheres of influence**,"

sometimes through negotiation and sometimes through force. By 1912, more than 50 major Chinese ports had been handed over to foreign control as "treaty ports." British spheres included Shanghai, the lower Yangzi, and Hong Kong. France maintained special interests in South China. Germany controlled the Shandong peninsula. Japan laid claim to the northeast.

Spheres of influence grew in importance at the beginning of the twentieth century, when foreign investors poured capital into railway lines, which needed treaty protection from competing companies. Railways necessarily furthered foreign encroachment and opened up new territories to the claims of foreigners. As one Chinese official explained it, the railroads were like scissors that threatened to cut China into many pieces. As a result, China lost control of its trade and was totally unable to protect its infant industries. Foreigners established no formal empires in China, but the treaty ports certainly were evidence of both informal rule and indisputable foreign dominance.

Treaty ports were centers of foreign residence and trade, where rules of **extraterritoriality** applied. That meant that foreigners were exempt from Chinese law enforcement and that, though present on Chinese territory, they could be judged only by officials of their own countries. Extraterritoriality, a privilege not just for diplomats but one shared by every foreign national, implied both a distrust of Chinese legal procedures and a cultural arrogance about the superiority of Western institutions. The arrangements stirred Chinese resentment and contributed considerably to growing antiforeign sentiment.

To preserve extraterritoriality and maintain informal empires, the European powers appointed civilian representatives known as consuls. Often merchants themselves—in the beginning unpaid in their posts—and consuls acted as the chieftains of resident merchant communities, judges in all civil and criminal cases, and spokesmen for the commercial interests of the home country. They clearly embodied the commercial intentions of Western governments. Initially they stood outside the diplomatic corps; later they were consigned to its lower ranks. Consuls acted as brokers for commerce and interpreted the international commercial law being forged. Consulates spread beyond China as Western nations used consuls to protect their own interests elsewhere. In Africa, consuls represented the trading concerns of European governments and were instrumental in the transition to formal rule.

The rise of Western influence in China coincided with and benefited from Chinese domestic problems, including dynastic decline, famine, and successive rebellions. The European powers were willing to prop up the crumbling structure for their own ends, but the Boxer Rebellion of 1900 made clear to the Western powers their limited ability to control social unrest in China. The Boxers—peasants so named by Westerners because of the martial rites practiced by their secret society, the Harmonious Fists—rose up against the foreign and Christian exploitation in north China. At the beginning of the summer of

■ The claims of the Boxer troops to invulnerability were believed by millions of Chinese. In this Chinese print, the Boxer forces use cannons, bayonets, dynamite, and sabers to drive the Western "barbarians" from the Middle Kingdom.

1900, the Boxers—with the concealed encouragement of the Chinese government—killed Europeans and seized the foreign legations in Beijing. An international expeditionary force of 16,000 well-armed Japanese, Russian, British, American, German, French, Austrian, and Italian troops entered Beijing in August to defend the treaty interests of their respective countries. Led by a German general, the international force followed Kaiser Wilhelm II's urging to remember the Huns: "Show no mercy! Take no prisoners!" Systematic plunder and slaughter followed. Beijing was sacked.

Abandoning earlier discussions of partitioning China, the international powers accepted the need for a central Chinese government—even one that had betrayed their interests—that would police a populace plagued by demographic pressures, famine, discrimination against minorities, excessive taxation, exorbitant land rents, and social and economic dislocations created by foreign trade. During the previous year (1899), the United States had asserted its claims in China in the Open Door policy. The policy, formulated by U.S. Secretary of State John Hay, was as much concerned with preserving Chinese sovereignty as it was with establishing equal economic opportunity for foreign competition in Chinese markets. Europeans and Americans wanted to send bankers to China, not gunboats. A stable central government facilitated their aims. By operating within delineated spheres of influence and using established elites to further their own programs, Westerners protected their financial interests without incurring the costs and responsibilities of direct rule.

Southeast Asia and Japan.

European nations pursued imperialist endeavors elsewhere in Asia, acquiring territories on China's frontiers and taking over states that had formerly paid tribute to the Chinese Empire. The British acquired Hong Kong in 1842, Burma in 1886, and Kowloon in 1898. The Russians took over the Maritime Provinces in 1858.

European Powers in Southeast Asia

With the Dutch already well established in Java, France, Great Britain, and the United States each established a center of power in southeast Asia and sought a balance of strength there to complement their global efforts to keep any one of them from getting ahead of the others. The French creation of Indochina was administratively the most complex. Composed of five territories administered separately, only Cochinchina (south Vietnam) was a formal colony; the other four regions were protectorates—Annam (central Vietnam), Tonkin (northern Vietnam), Cambodia, and Laos. French power remained strongest in south Vietnam and weakest in the center where, as in the north, local government was under a combined French and Vietnamese rule. The French approach to colonial rule combined hierarchical administration, economic exploitation, and cultural elitism. They introduced plantation agriculture for coffee and tea; together with

CHRONOLOGY
THE NEW IMPERIALISM IN AFRICA AND ASIA

1837–1844	Great Trek
1839–1842	Opium War
1869	Suez Canal completed
1884	Berlin Conference held to regulate imperialism in Africa
1886	Gold discovered in the Transvaal Republic
1894–1895	Sino-Japanese War
1896	Battle of Adowa
1899–1902	Boer War
1900	Boxer Rebellion
1904–1905	Russo-Japanese War

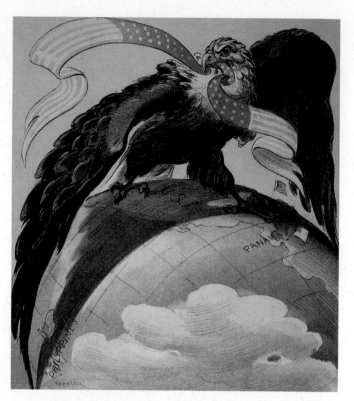

■ This 1904 cartoon of the United States' imperial expansion shows an American eagle stretching its wings from Panama to the Philippines.

rubber, the plantations were concentrated in the southern region of Indochina. Some light industry developed in the north at Hanoi. Because of its economic growth, Hanoi became the capital of the Indo-Chinese Union in 1902.

The French established their dominion in Laos at the expense of Siam (Thailand). The French provoked a crisis over Laos with the Thai, who hoped for British backing in the dispute. The British, however, saw French control over Laos as a reasonable part of the regional balance of European power. Laos, Cambodia, and central Vietnam all stagnated under French colonial rule. While the Mekong Delta in the south continued to export raw materials and crops, political power became more concentrated in the north in Hanoi.

Thailand was the only country in southeast Asia to escape direct control by the Western powers. Yet it was forced to yield half the territory it once controlled, and to accept the treaty port system with its tariffs and extraterritoriality. Through government reforms, the Thai attempted to meet the demands of facing foreign powers without forsaking their traditional institutions of Buddhist monarchy and monkhood.

In the Philippines, Spanish suppression of nationalist sentiments led to increasingly bitter feelings in the 1870s and 1880s. Separate groups of educated and poor people who opposed Spanish rule were unified by the Spanish execution of elite leader José Rizal (1861–1896). His martyrdom inspired broadly based resistance. The United States took control of the Philippines from the Spanish during the Spanish-American War over Cuba. Facing continued Filipino resistance, the United States opposed Filipino nationalism with its new colonial rule. American colonialism collaborated with a conservative landowning Filipino oligarchy that controlled huge sugar plantations. The plantations impeded the development of a more balanced agriculture that could feed the country's population. American colonial rule, like colonial regimes elsewhere in the region, fostered an acute Philippine economic dependency on the colonial power.

The Sino-Japanese War of 1894–1895 revealed Japan's intentions to compete as an imperialist power in Asia. The modernized and westernized Japanese army easily defeated the ill-equipped and poorly led Chinese forces. As a result, Japan gained the island of Taiwan. Pressing its ambitions on the continent, Japan locked horns with Russia over claims to the Liaotung peninsula, Korea, and South Manchuria. Following its victory in the Russo-Japanese War of 1904–1905, Japan expanded into all of those areas, annexing Korea outright in 1910. The war sent a strong message to the West about the ease with which the small Asian nation had defeated the Russian giant and contributed to the heightening of anti-imperialist sentiments in China.

The Imperialism of the United States

The United States provided another variation on imperial expansion. Its westward drive across the North American continent, beginning at the end of the eighteenth century, established the United States as an imperial power in the Western Hemisphere. By 1848, the relatively young American nation stretched over 3000 miles from one ocean to the other. It had met the opposition and resistance of the Native Americans with armed force, decimated them, and "concentrated" the survivors in assigned territories, and later on reservations.

At the end of the nineteenth century, the United States, possessing both the people and the resources for rapid industrial development, turned to the Caribbean and the Pacific islands in pursuit of markets and investment opportunities. By acquiring stepping stones of islands across the Pacific Ocean in the Hawaiian Islands and Samoa, it secured fueling bases and access to lucrative east Asian ports. And by intervening repeatedly in Central America and building the Panama Canal, the United States had established its hegemony in the Caribbean by 1914. Growing in economic power and hegemonic influence, both Japan and the United States had joined the club of imperial powers and were making serious claims against European expansion.

RESULTS OF A EUROPEAN-DOMINATED WORLD

Europeans fashioned the world in their own image, but in doing so, Western values and Western institutions underwent profound and unintended transformations. Family values were articulated in an imperialist context, and race emerged as a key cultural factor. The discovery of new lands, new cultures, and new peoples altered the ways in which European

MAP DISCOVERY

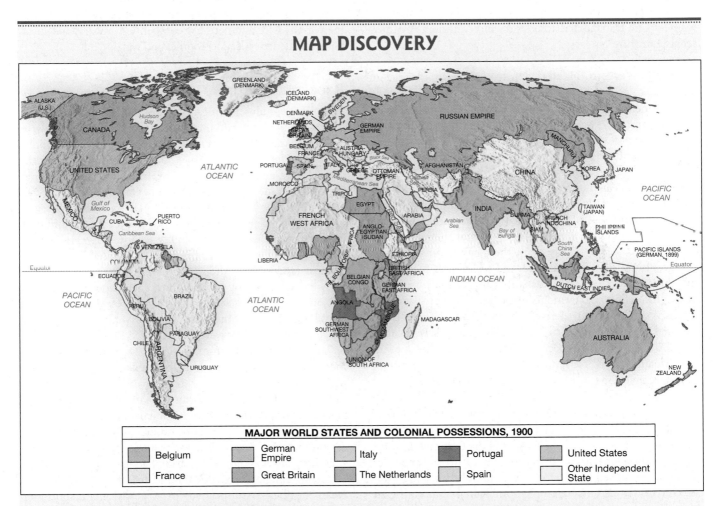

MAJOR WORLD STATES AND COLONIAL POSSESSIONS, 1900

Belgium	German Empire	Italy	Portugal	United States
France	Great Britain	The Netherlands	Spain	Other Independent State

World Colonial Holdings

The European powers, great and small, competed with each other for world empires and world influence between 1870 and 1914. In terms of territory occupied, which nation held the largest global empire? What is the meaning of the expression "the sun never sets on the British Empire"? Based on what you have read in the chapter, how do you explain the fact that the Netherlands held colonies in southeast Asia and Latin America, but had no holdings in Africa? How did the United States become an imperial power in this period? How do you explain the locations of U.S. colonial acquisitions?

women and men regarded themselves and viewed their place in the world. With the rise of new contenders for power—the United States and Japan—and growing criticism about the morality of capitalism, the Western world was not as predictable in 1914 as it had appeared to be in 1870.

A World Economy

Imperialism produced an interdependent world economy, with Europe at its center. Industrial and commercial capitalism linked together the world's continents in a communications and transportation network unimaginable in earlier ages. As a result, foreign trade increased from 3 percent of world output in 1800 to 33 percent by 1913. The greatest growth in trade occurred in the period from 1870 to 1914 as raw materials, manufactured products, capital, and men and women were transported across seas and continents by those seeking profits.

Meeting Western Needs.   Most trading in the age of imperialism still took place among European nations and North America. But entrepreneurs in search of new markets and new resources saw in Africa and Asia opportunities for protected exploitation. Opportunities were not seized but created in nonindustrialized areas of the world as new markets were shaped to meet the needs of Western producers and consumers. European landlords and managers trained Kenyan farmers to put aside their traditional agricultural methods and grow more "useful" crops such as coffee, tea, and sugar. The availability of cheaper British textiles of inferior quality drove Indian weavers away from their handlooms. Chinese silk producers changed centuries-old techniques to produce silk thread and cloth that was suited to the machinery and mass-production requirements of the French. Non-European producers undoubtedly derived benefits from the new international trading partnership, but those benefits were often scarce. Trade permitted specialization, but at the choice of the colonizer, not the colonized. World production and consumption were being shaped to suit the needs of the West.

Investment Abroad.   Capital in search of profits flowed out of the wealthier areas of Europe into the nonindustrialized regions of Russia, the Balkans, and the Ottoman Empire, where capital-intensive expenditures (on railways, for instance) promised high returns. Capital investment in overseas territories also increased phenomenally as railroads were built to gain access to primary products. Great Britain maintained its overwhelming dominance in overseas investment, with loans abroad greater than those of its five major competitors—France, Germany, Holland, the United States, and Belgium—combined.

The City of London had become the world's banker, serving as the clearinghouse for foreign investment on a global scale. The adoption of gold as the standard for exchange for most European currencies by 1874 further facilitated the operation of a single interdependent trading and investment system.

Britain remained the world's biggest trading nation, with half of its exports going to Asia, Africa, and South America and the other half to Europe and the United States. But Germany was Britain's fastest-growing competitor, with twice as many exports to Europe and expanding overseas trade by 1914. The United States had recently joined the league of the world's great trading nations and was running a strong third in shares of total trade.

Foreign investments often took the form of loans to governments or to enterprises guaranteed by governments. Investors might be willing to take risks, but they also expected protection, no less so than merchants and industrialists trading in overseas territories. Together, trade and investment interests exerted considerable pressure on European states for control through acquisition and concessions. The vast amounts of money involved help explain the expectations of state involvement and the reasons why international competition, rivalry, and instability threatened to lead to conflict and war.

Race and Culture

After 1870 pseudoscientific racist ideas spread that Europeans were a superior race and that Africans were inferior. The writings of Charles Darwin were critical in gaining broad popular acceptance for the concept of a racial hierarchy governed by natural laws and operating within an evolutionist dynamic. That was not merely because Darwin's *On the Origin of Species* (1859) and *The Descent of Man* (1871) "scientifically" legitimated the concept of evolution, but also because he himself explicitly suggested its applicability to humanity. His suggestion was quickly taken up by intellectuals such as Herbert Spencer (1820–1903) and subsequently popularized as social Darwinism. According to the notion, the various racial groups not only occupied distinct positions in a staged sequence of "development" over time, with whites the most advanced and blacks the least so, but were also engaged in a natural conflict or struggle with one another. Social Darwinism's strongest message was that the fittest were destined to prevail, an idea especially welcome to racists of the later nineteenth century because it could be used to justify as "natural" the imperial expansion upon which they were then embarked.

The West's ability to kill and conquer as well as to cure was, as one Victorian social observer argued, proof of its cultural superiority. Every colonizing nation had its spokesmen for the "civilizing mission" to educate and to convert African and Asian "heathens." Cultural superiority was only a short step from arguments for racial superiority. Prompted by the U.S. involvement in the Philippines, the British poet Rudyard Kipling (1865–1936) characterized the responsibilities of the advanced West as "the White Man's burden." The smug and arrogant attitude of his poem about the white man's mission revealed a deep-seated and unacknowledged racism toward peoples considered "half-devil and half-child."

Race and culture were collapsed into each other. If Westerners were culturally superior, as they claimed, they must be racially superior as well. The "survival of the fittest"

■ A British family in India poses with their domestic staff in front of their bungalow. An 1878 hand-book on upper-class life in India recommended 27 servants per family. Note the dimensions of the "bungalow."

came to justify conquest and subjugation as "laws" of human interaction and, by extension, of relations among nations.

Women and Imperialism

Ideas about racial and cultural superiority were not confined to books by pseudoscientists and to discussions among policy makers. Public discussions about marriage, reproduction, motherhood, and child-rearing reflected new concerns about furthering "the imperial race"—the racial identity of white Westerners. Women throughout Western societies were encouraged by reformers, politicians, and doctors to have more children and instructed to take better care of them. "Children are the most valuable of imperial assets," one British doctor instructed his readers. Healthy young men were needed in the colonies, they were told, to defend Western values. State officials paid new attention to infant mortality at the end of the nineteenth century, set up health programs for children, and provided young women with training in home management, nutrition, and child care. The programs were no coincidence in an age of imperialism. Their rhetoric was explicitly imperialist and often racist in urging women to preserve the quality of the white race.

In the poem "White Man's Burden," Kipling advised, "Send forth the best ye breed." All over Europe, newly formed associations and clubs stressed the need for careful mate selection. In Britain, Francis Galton (1822–1911) founded eugenics, the study of genetics for the purpose of improving inherited characteristics of the race. Imperialism, the propagandists proclaimed, depended on mothers—women who would nurture healthy workers, strong soldiers and sailors, and intelligent and capable leaders. High infant mortality and poor health in children were attributed directly to maternal failings and not to environmental factors or poverty. Kaiser Wilhelm II stressed that German women's attention to the "three Ks"—*Kinder, Küche, Kirche* (children, kitchen, church)—would guarantee a race of Germans who would rule the world. British generals and French statesmen publicly applied similar sentiments to their own countries and stressed that the future depended on the devotion of women to their family obligations.

Some European women participated directly in the colonizing experience. As missionaries and nurses, they supported the civilizing mission. As wives of officials and managers, they were expected to embody the gentility and values of Western culture. Most men who traded and served overseas did so unaccompanied by women. But when women were present in any numbers, as they were in India before 1914, they were expected to preserve the exclusivity of Western communities and to maintain class and status differentiations as a proof of cultural superiority.

Ecology and Imperialism

Ecology—the relationship and adjustment of human groups to their environment—was affected by imperial expansion, which

KARL PEARSON AND THE DEFENSE OF EUGENICS

The following is an excerpt from a lecture titled "National Life from the Standpoint of Science," given by a British professor of mathematics, Karl Pearson (1857–1936), in 1900. Pearson held the first chair in eugenics at the University of London, where he applied statistical methods to the study of heredity and evolution. The term eugenics *was introduced by Francis Galton, of whom Pearson was a follower. Pearson was heavily influenced by the pseudoscientific assumptions of social Darwinism and combined prejudices about race and nationalism to justify British imperialism as a proof of "survival of the fittest."*

Focus Questions

What does Pearson mean by "the scientific view of the nation"? And how "scientific" are the views he employs to arrive at that view?

The . . . great function of science in national life . . . is to show us what national life means, and how the nation is a vast organism subject as much to the great forces of evolution as any other gregarious type of life. There is a struggle of race against race and of nation against nation. In the early days of that struggle it was a blind, unconscious struggle of barbaric tribes. At the present day, in the case of the civilized white man, it has become more and more the conscious, carefully directed attempt of the nation to fit itself to a continuously changing environment. The nation has to foresee how and where the struggle will be carried on; the maintenance of national position is becoming more and more a conscious preparation for changing conditions, an insight into the needs of coming environments. . . .

If a nation is to maintain its position in this struggle, it must be fully provided with trained brains in every department of national activity, from the government to the factory, and have, if possible, *a reserve of brain and physique* to fall back upon in times of national crisis. . . .

You will see that my view—and I think it may be called the scientific view of a nation—is that of an organized whole, kept up to a high pitch of internal efficiency by insuring that its numbers are substantially recruited from the better stocks, and kept up to a high pitch of external efficiency by contest, chiefly by way of war with inferior races, and with equal races by the struggle for trade-routes and for the sources of raw material and of food supply. This is

the natural history view of mankind, and I do not think you can in its main features subvert it. . . .

Is it not a fact that the daily bread of our millions of workers depends on their having somebody to work for? That if we give up the contest for trade-routes and for free markets and for waste lands, we indirectly give up our food supply? Is it not a fact that our strength depends on these and upon our colonies, and that our colonies have been won by the ejection of inferior races, and are maintained against equal races only by respect for the present power of our empire? . . .

We find that the law of the survival of the fitter is true of mankind, but that the struggle is that of the gregarious animal. A community not knit together by strong social instincts, by sympathy between man and man, and class and class, cannot face the external contest, the competition with other nations, by peace or by war, for the raw material of production and for its food supply. This struggle of tribe with tribe, and nation with nation, may have its mournful side; but we see as a result of it the gradual progress of mankind to higher intellectual and physical efficiency. It is idle to condemn it; we can only see that it exists and recognize what we have gained by it—civilization and social sympathy. But while the statesman has to watch this external struggle, . . . he must be very cautious that the nation is not silently rotting at its core. He must insure that the fertility of the inferior stocks is checked, and that of the superior stocks encouraged; he must regard with suspicion anything that tempts the physically and mentally fitter men and women to remain childless.

From Karl Pearson, *National Life from the Standpoint of Science* (1905).

dislocated the societies that it touched. Early explorers had disrupted little as they arrived, observed, and then moved on. The missionaries, merchants, soldiers, and businessmen who came later required that those with whom they came into contact must change their thought and behavior. In some cases, dislocation resulted in material improvements, better medical care,

and the introduction of modern technology. For the most part, however, the initial ecological impact of the imperialist was negative. Western men and women carried diseases to people who did not share the Westerners' immunity. Traditional village life was destroyed in rural India, and African tribal societies disintegrated under the European onslaught. Resistance existed everywhere, but only the Ethiopians, with their defeat of the Italians at Adowa in 1896, managed to have any success in keeping out foreigners.

Education of native populations had as its primary goal the improvement of administration and productivity in the colonies. When foreigners ruled indirectly through existing indigenous hierarchies, they often created corrupt and tyrannical bureaucracies that exploited natives. The indirect rule of the British in India was based on a pragmatic desire to keep British costs low.

When Asian and African laborers started producing for the Western market, they became dependent on its fluctuations. Victimized for centuries by the vagaries of weather, they now had to contend with the instability and cutthroat competition of cash crops in world markets. Individuals migrated from place to place in the countryside and from the countryside to newly formed cities. The fabric of tribal life unraveled. Such migrations necessarily affected family life, with individuals marrying later because they lacked the resources to set up households. The situation paralleled similar disruptions in English society at the beginning of the Industrial Revolution. Women as well as men migrated to find jobs. Many women, cut free of their tribes (as was the case in Nairobi), turned to prostitution—literally for pennies—as a means of survival.

In an extreme example of the colonizers' disdain for the colonized, some European countries used their overseas territories as dumping grounds for hardened and incorrigible convicted criminals. Imitating the earlier example of the British in Australia, the French developed Guiana and New Caledonia as prison colonies in the hope that they could solve their social problems at home by exporting them.

Critiquing Capitalism

Not least significant of the consequences of imperialism was the critique of capitalism it produced. Those who condemned capitalism as exploitative and racist saw imperialism as an expression of problems inherent in it.

In 1902, J. A. Hobson (1858–1940) published *Imperialism, A Study*, a work that has remained in print ever since. In his book, Hobson argued that underconsumption and surplus capital at home drove Western industrial countries overseas in search of a cure for those economic ills. Rather than solving the problems by raising workers' wages, and thereby increasing their consumption power and creating new opportunities for investment in home markets, manufacturers, entrepreneurs, and industrialists sought higher profits abroad. Hobson considered those business interests "economic parasites," making large fortunes at the expense of national interests.

In the midst of world war, the future leader of the Russian Revolution, Vladimir Ilyich Ulyanov (1870–1924)—or to use his revolutionary name, Lenin—added his own critique of capitalism. He did not share Hobson's belief that capitalism was merely malfunctioning in its imperialist endeavors. Instead, Lenin argued in *Imperialism, the Highest Stage of Capitalism* (1916) that capitalism is inherently and inevitably imperialistic. Because he was sure that Western capitalism was in the process of destroying itself, Lenin called World War I the final "imperialist war."

Critics, historians, and economists have since pointed out that the works by Hobson and Lenin are marred by errors and omissions. Yet the works usher in almost a century of debate over the morality and economic feasibility of imperialism. Hobson as a liberal and Lenin as a Marxist highlighted the connections between social problems at home—whether in late Victorian England or in prerevolutionary Russia—and economic exploitation abroad.

Yet if electoral results and the popular press are any indication, Europeans not only accepted but warmly embraced the responsibilities of empire. Criticism of the backwardness of captive peoples prevailed. Victorian social scientist Walter Bagehot (1826–1877) told the story of an aged savage who, upon returning to his tribe, informed them that he had "tried civilization for 40 years and it was not worth the trouble." No matter how intelligent the judgment of this African might seem with hindsight, the possibility of returning to areas of the world not influenced by the civilization of the West was rapidly disappearing in the years before World War I.

CONCLUSION

From the very beginning of the competition for territories and concessions, no European state could act in Africa or Asia without affecting the interests and actions of its rivals in Europe. The scramble for Africa made clear how interlocking the system of European states had become after 1870. The development of spheres of influence in China underlined the value of world markets and international trade for the survival and expansion of Western nations.

A "balance of power" among states guaranteed national security and independence until the end of the nineteenth century. But between 1870 and 1914, industrialization, technology, and accompanying capital formation created vast economic disparities. Conflict and disequilibrium challenged European stability and balance. Ultimately, it was the politics of geography on the European continent, not confrontations in distant colonies, that polarized the European states into two camps. Despite the unresolved conflicts behind all of the crises, European statesmen prided themselves on their ability to settle disputes through reason and negotiation. Yet it was the problems at home in Europe and not abroad in the colonies that were to exacerbate geopolitical vulnerabilities and detonate a conflict far worse than the world had ever seen.

QUESTIONS FOR REVIEW

1. What geopolitical factors made the European balance of power so unstable around the turn of the century?
2. What social, political, and economic forces encouraged the nations of Europe to create overseas empires in the late nineteenth century?
3. How and why did European imperialism differ in Africa and Asia?
4. How did imperial expansion around the globe transform the lives of Europeans at home?

KEY TERMS

extraterritoriality, *p. 788*

geopolitics, *p. 774*

jingoism, *p. 782*

new imperialism, *p. 777*

quinine, *p. 778*

scramble for Africa, *p. 782*

spheres of influence, *p. 788*

Triple Alliance, *p. 776*

Triple Entente, *p. 776*

DISCOVERING WESTERN CIVILIZATION ONLINE

You can obtain more information about Europe and the world between 1870 and 1914 at the Websites listed below. See also the Companion Website that accompanies this text, www.ablongman.com/kishlansky, which contains an online study guide and additional resources.

The European Balance of Power, 1870–1914

Internet Modern History Sourcebook: World War I
www.fordham.edu/halsall/mod/modsbook38.html
This site is part of a larger site on World War I primary and secondary sources, but it contains a section on the developments among the great powers from the 1870s to 1914.

The New Imperialism

Internet Modern History Sourcebook: Imperialism
www.fordham.edu/halsall/mod/modsbook34.html
A comprehensive site of links arranged by continent to primary source materials and bibliographies on imperialism.

Colonialism and Postcolonialism: Selected Biographies
landow.stg.brown.edu/post/misc/bibl.html
Another site of links to bibliographies on colonialism and post-colonialism.

European Imperialism
www.winsor.edu/library/euroimpe.htm
This site is sponsored by the Winsor School and contains an extensive list of links by region on European imperialism.

The European Search for Territory and Markets

Francophone Africa: Bibliographies
www.hum.port.ac.uk/slas/francophone/bibliographies.htm
A collection of bibliographies on the partition of Africa and the impact of colonization in Africa.

South African War Virtual Library
www.bowlerhat.com.au/sawvl/
A virtual library of essays, photos, and further links on the Boer War.

China: A Traveling Exhibit, 1903–1904
www.chinaexhibit.org
A virtual museum exhibit of photographs taken in 1903 of the Chinese countryside after the Boxer Rebellion.

SUGGESTIONS FOR FURTHER READING

The European Balance of Power, 1870–1914

Norman Rich, *Great Power Diplomacy, 1814–1914* (New York: McGraw-Hill Higher Education, 1992). This work surveys diplomatic activities from the end of the Napoleonic Wars to the eve of World War I.

Alan Sked, *The Decline and Fall of the Habsburg Empire, 1815–1918* (London: Longman, 1989). An overview of the Habsburg Empire's history from Metternich to World War I. The author interprets the various historiographical debates over the collapse of Habsburg rule. Rather than treating the late empire as a case of inevitable decline, the book examines the monarchy as a viable institution within a multinational state.

The New Imperialism

Antoinette Burton, ed., *After the Imperial Turn: Thinking With and Through the Nation* (Durham, NC: Duke University Press, 2003). This collection provides a critical cultural analysis of nationalism and imperialism by showing the inadequacies of the nation as an analytic category.

David Cannadine, *Ornamentalism: How the British Saw Their Empire* (New York: Oxford University Press, 2001). The author approaches the history of the British Empire as interconnected with the history of the British nation and considers this "entire interactive system" in terms of a social construction and social perceptions.

Michael W. Doyle, *Empires* (Ithaca, NY: Cornell University Press, 1986). Nineteenth-century imperialism is placed in a broad historical context that emphasizes a comparative perspective of the European imperial experience.

Richard Drayton, *Nature's Government: Science, Imperial Britain, and the 'Improvement' of the World* (New Haven, CT: Yale University Press, 2000). A fascinating examination of the role scientists, and especially botanists, played as partners with bureaucratic government in British imperial expansion.

Daniel R. Headrick, *The Tentacles of Progress: Technology Transfer in the Age of Imperialism, 1850–1940* (New York: Oxford University Press, 1988). Argues that the transfer of technology to Africa and Asia by the Western imperial powers produced colonial underdevelopment.

Robert H. MacDonald, *The Language of Empire: Myths and Metaphors of Popular Imperialism, 1880–1918* (Manchester, England: Manchester University Press, 1994). In studying the new metaphors of imperialism, the author examines the role of mythmakers, such as Rudyard Kipling, and popular fiction in shaping imperial perceptions and experiences. The author argues that the very shaping of language about non-European lands and peoples helped determine the form empire took in Great Britain.

The Search for Territory and Markets

Winfried Baumgart, *Imperialism: The Idea and Reality of British and French Colonial Expansion, 1880–1914* (New York: Oxford University Press, 1982). Principally concerned with the motives that led to imperial expansion, the author argues that the motives were many and that each action must be studied in its specific social, political, and economic context.

Raymond F. Betts, *The False Dawn: European Imperialism in the Nineteenth Century* (Oxford: Oxford University Press, 1976). Explores the ideology of empire and the process of cultural transmission through colonial institutions.

Eric Hobsbawm, *The Age of Empire, 1875–1914* (New York: Pantheon, 1987). A wide-ranging interpretive history of the late nineteenth century that spans economic, social, political, and cultural developments.

Thomas Pakenham, *The Scramble for Africa* (New York: Random House, 1991). A narrative history of how Europeans subdivided Africa among themselves.

Results of a European-Dominated World

Tony Ballantyne, *Orientalism and Race: Aryanism in the British Empire* (New York: Palgrave, 2002). Ballantyne traces how the idea of an Aryan race became an important feature of British imperial culture in the nineteenth century.

Johannes Fabian, *Language and Colonial Power: The Appropriation of Swahili in the Former Belgian Congo* (Cambridge: Cambridge University Press, 1986). Demonstrates how colonial power was exercised in the Belgian Congo through the study of the growth of Swahili as a lingua franca. The author pays particular attention to the uses of Swahili in industrial and other work situations.

Leila Tarazi Fawaz and C. A. Bayly, eds., *Modernity and Culture: From the Mediterranean to the Indian Ocean* (New York: Columbia University Press, 2002). This collection of essays demonstrates how cities in this vast region were increasingly cosmopolitan loci for a new kind of modernity that responded to political, economic, social, and cultural change.

Anne McClintock, *Imperial Leather: Race, Gender, and Sexuality in the Colonial Contest* (New York: Routledge, 1995). By using novels, diaries, advertisements, and other sources, the author demonstrates the relationship between images of domestic life and an ideology of imperial domination and focuses on the role of women in the colonial experience.

Paul B. Rich, *Race and Empire in British Politics* (Cambridge: Cambridge University Press, 1986). An intellectual history of ideas about race in the imperial tradition. Focusing on the years between 1890 and 1970, the author examines the political dimensions of race and race ideology in British society.

For a list of additional titles related to this chapter's topics, please see http://www.ablongman.com/kishlansky.

Chapter 26

WAR AND REVOLUTION, 1914–1920

Chapter Outline

The sustained, devastating global war of 1914 to 1918, which came to be known as the Great War, was not what Europe was expecting when the conflict began. But total war is what it got. How did governments sell the idea of war to their citizens and maintain crucial public support as the war dragged on? Find out in The Visual Record. ➤

SELLING THE GREAT WAR

Advertising is a powerful influence in modern life. Some believe that it makes people buy goods they do not need. Others insist that advertising is an efficient way of conveying information, on the basis of which people make choices. The leaders of Western nations discovered the power of advertising during the years of World War I, from 1914 to 1918. Advertising did not create the conflict that came to be known as the Great War. Nor did it produce the enthusiasm that excited millions of Europeans when war was declared in 1914. But when death

■ "Take Up the Sword of Justice" by Sir Bernard Partridge, England, 1915.

counts mounted, prices skyrocketed, food supplies dwindled, and the frenzy and fervor for the war flagged, governments came to rely more heavily on the art of persuasion. Survival and victory required the support and coordination of the whole society. For the first time in history, war had to advertise.

By the early decades of the twentieth century, businessmen had learned that it was not enough to develop efficient technologies and to mass-produce everything from hair oil to corsets—they had to sell their goods to the public. People would not buy goods they did not know about and whose merits they did not understand. Modern advertising pioneered sales techniques that convinced people to buy. Now political leaders came to realize that the advertising techniques of the marketplace could be useful. Governments took up the "science" of selling—not products but the idea of war. It was not enough to have a well-trained and well-equipped army to ensure victory. Citizens had to be persuaded to join, to fight, to work, to save, and to believe in the national war effort. Warring nations learned how to organize enthusiasm and how to mobilize the masses in support of what proved to be a long and bloody conflict.

The poster on the facing page shows a dramatic appeal to German women to support war work. A stern soldier whose visage and bearing communicate strength and singleness of purpose is backed up by an equally determined young woman. She is in the act of handing him a grenade as she stands with him, her arm on his shoulder, facing the unseen enemy. Grenades hang from his belt and from his left hand, giving the sense that he is able to enter battle properly armed, thanks to the dedicated woman's efforts. The poster is a good representation of the centrality of women's work to the waging of a new kind of war in the twentieth century. The battlefront had to be backed up by a *home front*—the term used for the first time in the Great War—of working men, women, and even children. The poster communicates the dignity and worth that lay in the concerted partnership of soldiers and civilians to defeat the enemy.

Early war posters stressed justice and national glory. Later, as weariness with the war spread, the need for personal sacrifice became the dominant theme. The poster at left shows a sad female figure rising from a sea of suffering and death. The woman, both goddesslike and vulnerable, symbolizes Great Britain. She is making a strong visual plea for action, seeking soldiers for her cause. The appeal for volunteers for the armed forces was unique to Great Britain, where conscription was not established until 1916. Yet the image is typical of every nation's reliance on a noble female symbol to emphasize the justice of its cause. The dark suffering and death in the waters lapping at her robes are reflected in her eyes. She evinces a fierce determination as she exhorts, "Take up the sword of justice." In February 1915, Germany declared the waters around the British Isles to be a war zone. All British shipping was subject to attack, as were neutral merchant vessels, which were attacked without warning. In May 1915, the *Lusitania* was sunk, taking with it more than 1000 lives, including those of 128 Americans. The poster frames an illuminated horizon where a ship that is probably the *Lusitania* is sinking. The poster is a clear call to arms against the perfidy of an enemy who has killed innocent civilians. The female figure's determined jaw, clenched fist, and outstretched arms communicate the nobility of the cause and the certainty of success.

Civilians had to be mobilized for two reasons. First, it became evident early in the fighting that the costs of the war in terms of human lives were high. Soldiers at the front had to be constantly replaced by civilian reserves. Second, the costs of the war in terms of food, equipment, and productive materials were so high that civilian populations had to be willing to endure great hardships and to sacrifice their own well-being to produce supplies for soldiers at the front.

Deutsche Frauen arbeitet im Heimatheer!

Kriegsamtstelle Magdeburg

■ World War I poster by George Kirchbach, Germany, 1914–1918.

Advertising was used by nations at war to coordinate civilian and military contributions to a common cause. Selling the Great War required selectively communicating information and inspiring belief and a commitment to total victory, no matter how high the cost.

Looking Ahead

The European governments proudly "selling" war to their citizens in 1914 expected quick victories and a war of short duration. Instead, as this chapter will show, what they experienced was a prolonged global war, costly in human life and material destruction, stretching out over four devastating years. In adjusting to the unexpected, military technology and timetables called the tune in a defensive war fought from the trenches with sophisticated weapons capable of maiming and killing in new ways. In the case of Russia, the war signaled political and social collapse and a revolution of unprecedented scale. The intervention of the United States and German defeat preceded a peace that reshaped Europe as a whole in fundamental ways. ➤

THE WAR EUROPE EXPECTED

In 1914, Europe stood confidently at the center of the world. Covering only 7 percent of the earth's surface, it dominated the world's trade and was actively exporting both European goods and European culture all over the globe. Proud of the progress and prosperity of urban industrial society, Europeans had harnessed nature to transform their environment. They extended their influence beyond their continent, sure that their achievements marked the pinnacle of civilization.

The values of nineteenth-century liberalism permeated the self-confident worldview of European men and women in 1914. Liberalism assured the middle classes that the world was at peace, governed by rules that could be known. Europeans assumed that they could discover the rules and fashion a better world. Science and industry were their tools for controlling nature and shaping institutions. If life was not yet perfect, it could become so.

Westerners took stability and harmony for granted as preconditions for progress. Yet they also recognized the utility of war. In recent times, local confrontations between European states in Africa had been successfully contained in bids for increased territory. While warfare was accepted as an instrument of policy, no one expected or wanted a general war. Liberal values served the goals of limited war, just as they had justified imperial conquest. Statesmen decided there were rules to the game of war that could be employed in the interests of statecraft.

Science and technology also served the goals of limited war. Modern weapons, statesmen and generals were sure, would prevent a long war. Superiority in armed force became a priority for European states seeking to protect the peace.

The beginning of the modern arms race resulted in "armed peace" as a defense against war. Leaders nevertheless expected and planned for a war, short and limited, in which the fittest and most advanced nation would win. Planners believed that their rivals could not triumph. War was acceptable because it would be quick and decisive. Previous confrontations among European states had been limited in duration and destruction, as in the case of Prussia and France in 1870, or confined to peripheries, as squabbles among the Great Powers in Africa indicated. The alliance system was expected to defend the peace by defining the conditions of war.

As international tensions mounted, the hot summer days of 1914 were a time of hope and glory. The hope was that war, when it came, would be "over by Christmas." The glory was the promise of ultimate victory in the "crusade for civilization" that each nation's leaders held out to their people. Declarations of war were greeted with songs, flowers, wild enthusiasm, and dancing in the streets. Crowds welcomed the battles to come with the delirium of cheering a favorite team in a sports match. Some embraced war as a test of greatness, a purification of a society that had become lazy and complacent. When war did come in 1914, it was a choice, not an accident. Yet it was a choice that Europeans did not understand, one whose limits

■ European Alliances on the Eve of World War I. Alliance systems divided Europe into two great blocs with few countries remaining neutral.

they could not control. Their unquestioned pride in reason and progress, which ironically had led them to the war, did not survive the four years of barbaric slaughter that followed.

Separating Friends from Foes

At the end of the nineteenth century, the world appeared to be coming together in a vast international network linked by commerce and finance. A system of alliances based on shared interests also connected states to one another. After 1905, the intricate defensive alliances between and among the European states maintained the balance of power between two blocs of nations and helped prevent one bloc from dominating the other. Yet by creating blocs, alliances identified foes as well as friends. On the eve of the war, France, Great Britain, and Russia stood together in the Triple Entente. Since 1882, Germany, Austria-Hungary, and Italy had joined forces in the Triple Alliance. Other states allied with one or the other of the blocs in pacts of mutual interest and protection. Throughout the world, whether in North Africa, the Balkans, or Asia, the power of some states was intended to balance the power of others. Yet the balance of power did not exist simply to preserve the peace. It existed to preserve a system of independent national societies—nation-states—in a precarious equilibrium. Gains in one area by one bloc had to be offset by compromises in an-

■ Linguistic Groups in Austria-Hungary. The significant linguistic and cultural diversity of Habsburg lands made Austria-Hungary difficult to govern. Although Germany counted on Austria-Hungary as a key ally in promoting a balance of power, its internal challenges made it a weak partner.

other to maintain the balance. Nations recognized limited conflict as a legitimate means of preserving equilibrium.

The alliance system of blocs reflected the growing impact of public opinion on international relations. Statesmen had the ability to manipulate the newspaper images of allies as good and rivals as evil. But controlling public opinion served to lock policy makers into permanent partnerships and "blank checks" of support for their allies. Western leaders understood that swings in public opinion in periods of crisis could hobble their efforts in the national interest. Permanent military alliances with clearly identified "friends," therefore, took the place of more fluid arrangements.

Although alliances that guaranteed military support did not cause war, they did permit weak nations to act irresponsibly, with the certainty that they would be defended by their more powerful partners. France and Germany were publicly committed to their weaker allies Russia and Austria-Hungary, respectively, in supporting imperialist ambitions in the Balkans from which they themselves derived little direct benefit. Because of treaty commitments, no country expected to face war alone. The interlocking system of defensive alliances was structured to match strength against strength—France against Germany, for example—thereby making a prolonged war more likely than would be the case if a weak nation confronted a strong enemy.

Military Timetables

As Europe soon discovered, military timetables restricted the choices of leaders at times of conflict. The crisis of the summer of 1914 revealed the extent to which politicians and statesmen had come to rely on military expertise and strategic considerations in making decisions. Military general staffs assumed increasing importance in state policy making. War planners became powerful as war was accepted as an alternative to the negotiation of differences. Germany's military preparations are a good example of how war strategy exacerbated crises and prevented peaceful solutions.

The Schlieffen Plan. Alfred von Schlieffen (1833–1913), the Prussian general and chief of the German General Staff (1891–1905) who developed the war plan, understood little about politics but spent his life studying the strategic challenges of warfare. His war plan was designed to make Germany the greatest power on the Continent. The **Schlieffen Plan,** which he set before his fellow officers in 1905, was a bold and daring one: in the likely event of war with Russia, Germany would launch a devastating offensive against France. Schlieffen reasoned that France was a strong military presence that would come to the aid of its ally, Russia. Russia, lacking a modern transportation system, would not be able to mobilize as rapidly as France.

Russia also had the inestimable advantage of the ability to retreat into its vast interior. If Germany were pulled into a war with Russia, its western frontier would be vulnerable to France, Russia's powerful ally. The Schlieffen Plan recognized

MAP DISCOVERY

The Schlieffen Plan and France's Plan XVII

The Schlieffen Plan was a German plan of attack devised in the event of a war against Russia. Why was the plan based on the principle that the road to St. Petersburg (to the east) ran through Paris (to the west)? What countries on this map were neutral countries? Why was Germany willing to violate their neutrality in order to move troops across their territory? The French meanwhile were devising their own war plan, called Plan XVII. Where did they plan to concentrate their offensive? Why was it not successful?

likelihood that Germany would come to the aid of Austria-Hungary. Russia knew, too, that because of its primitive railway network it would be unable to mobilize troops rapidly. In order to compensate for that weakness, Russian leaders planned to mobilize *before* war was declared. German military leaders had no choice in the event of full Russian mobilization but to mobilize their own troops immediately and to urge the declaration of war. There was no chance of containing the conflict once a general mobilization on both sides was underway. Mobilization would mean war.

Like the Schlieffen Plan, the French Plan XVII called for the concentration of troops in a single area, with the intention of decisively defeating the enemy. The French command, not well informed about German strengths and strategies, designated Alsace and Lorraine for the immediate offensive against Germany in the event of war. Plan XVII left Paris exposed to the German drive through Belgium called for in the Schlieffen Plan.

Military leaders throughout Europe argued that if their plans were to succeed, speed was essential. Delays to consider peaceful solutions would cripple military responses. Diplomacy bowed to military strategy. When orders to mobilize went out, armies would be set on the march. Like a row of dominoes falling with the initial push, the two alliance systems would be at war.

that France must first be defeated in the west before Germany could turn its forces to the task of defeating Russia. The Schlieffen Plan thus committed Germany to a war with France, regardless of particular circumstances. Furthermore, the plan, with its strategy of invading the neutral countries of Belgium, Holland, and Luxembourg in order to defeat France in six weeks, ignored the rights of the neutral countries.

Russia's Mobilization Plan and the French Plan XVII.

Germany was not alone in being driven by military timetables when conflicts arose. Russian military strategists planned full mobilization if war broke out with Austria-Hungary, which was menacing the interests of Russia's ally Serbia. Russia foresaw the

Assassination at Sarajevo

A teenager with a handgun started the First World War. On 28 June 1914, in Sarajevo, the sleepy capital of the Austro-Hungarian province of Bosnia, Gavrilo Princip (1895–1918), a 19-year-old Bosnian Serb, repeatedly pulled the trigger of his Browning revolver, killing the designated heir of the Habsburg throne, Archduke Franz Ferdinand, and his wife, Sophie. Princip belonged to the Young Bosnian Society, a

■ Austrian Archduke Franz
Ferdinand and his wife, Sophie,
leave the Senate House in Sarajevo
on 28 June 1914. Five minutes
later, Serbian terrorist Gavrilo
Princip assassinated the couple.

group of students, workers, some peasants, Croats, Muslims, and intellectuals who wanted to free Slavic populations from Habsburg control. Princip was part of a growing movement of South Slavs struggling for national liberation who believed they were being held in colonial servitude by Austria-Hungary.

Struggle over control of the Balkans had been a long-standing issue that had involved all the major European powers for decades. As Austria-Hungary's ally since 1879, Germany was willing to support Vienna's showdown in the Balkans as a way of stopping Russian advances in the area. The alliance with Germany gave Austria-Hungary a sense of security and confidence to pursue its Balkan aims. Germany had its own plans for domination of the Continent and feared that a weakened Austria-Hungary would undermine its own position in central Europe. Independent Balkan states to the south and east were also a threat to Germany's plans. German leaders hoped that an Austro-Serbian war would remain localized and would strengthen their ally, Austria-Hungary. While Austria-Hungary had Germany's support, Serbia was backed by a sympathetic Russia that favored nationalist movements in the Balkans. Russia, in turn, had been encouraged by France, its ally by military pact since 1894, to take a firm stand in its struggle with Austria-Hungary for dominance among Balkan nationalities.

The interim of five weeks between the assassination of Archduke Ferdinand and the outbreak of the war was a period of intense diplomatic activity. The assassination gave Austria-Hungary the excuse it needed to bring a troublesome Serbia into line. Austria-Hungary held Serbia responsible for the shootings. Leaders in Vienna had no evidence at the time to justify their allegations of a Serbian conspiracy, but they saw in the event the perfect pretext for military action. On 23 July

1914, Austria-Hungary issued an ultimatum to the small Balkan nation and secretly decided to declare war regardless of Serbia's response. The demands were so severe that, if met, they would have stripped Serbia of its independence. Austria's aim was to destroy Serbia. In spite of a conciliatory, though not capitulatory, reply from Serbia to the ultimatum, Austria-Hungary declared war on the Balkan nation on 28 July 1914. Russia mobilized two days after the Austro-Hungarian declaration of war against Serbia. Germany mobilized in response to the Russian action and declared war on Russia on 1 August, and on France on 3 August. France had begun mobilizing on 30 July, when its ally, Russia, entered the war.

Great Britain stood briefly outside the fray in the futile attempt to mediate a settlement in the Austro-Serbian conflict. Britain's dependence on its alliance with France as a means of protecting British sea routes in the Mediterranean meant that Great Britain could not remain neutral once France declared war. On 4 August, after Germany had violated Belgian neutrality in its march to France, Great Britain honored its treaty obligations and declared war on Germany. Great Britain entered the war because it judged that a powerful Germany could use ports on the English Channel to invade the British Isles. Italy alone of the major powers remained for the moment outside the conflict. Although allied with Germany and Austria-Hungary, its own aspirations in the Balkans kept it from fighting for the Austrian cause in 1914.

Self-interest, fear, and ambition motivated the Great Powers in different ways in the pursuit of war. The international diplomatic system that had worked so well to prevent war in the preceding decades now enmeshed European states in interlocking alliances and created a chain reaction. The Austro-Serbian war of July 1914 became a Europewide war within a month.

A NEW KIND OF WARFARE

The expectation of a speedy war of decisive victories and domestic glory drove European leaders and their populations to embrace armed conflict as an acceptable means of mediating grievances in 1914. The peace that had been preserved from the end of the nineteenth century to 1914 was a precarious one indeed, predicated as it was on military timetables that planned for war and alliance systems that guaranteed that local disagreements would become international conflicts. The international mechanisms for keeping the peace led directly to war and guaranteed that once war broke out, it would not remain limited and local.

Early in the war, the best-laid plans of political and military leaders collapsed. In the first place, Europe experienced a war that was not quickly and decisively won, but spread throughout Europe and became global. Switzerland, Spain, the Netherlands, and all of Scandinavia remained neutral, but every other European nation was pulled into the war. In August 1914, Japan cast its lot with the **Allies,** as the Entente came to be known, and in November the Ottoman Empire joined the **Central Powers** of Germany and Austria-Hungary. In the following year, Italy joined the war—not on the side of its long-term treaty partners, Germany and Austria-Hungary, but on the side of the Allies, with the expectation of benefiting in the Balkans from Austrian defeat. Bulgaria joined Germany and Austria-Hungary in 1915, seeking territory at Serbia's expense. By the time the United States entered the war in 1917, the war had become a world war.

The second surprise for the European powers was that they did not get a war of movement, nor did they get one of short duration. Within weeks, that pattern had given way to what promised to be a long and costly war of attrition. The war started as German strategists had planned, with German victory in battle after battle. The end seemed near. But in the space of less than a month, the war changed in ways that no one had predicted. Technology was the key to understanding the change and explaining the surprises.

Technology and the Trenches

In the history of nineteenth-century European warfare, armies had relied on mobile cavalry and infantry units, whose greatest asset was speed. Rapid advance had been decisive in the Prussian victory over the French in 1870, which had resulted in the formation of the German Empire.

Digging In. Soldiers of the twentieth century were also trained for a war of movement, high maneuverability, and maximum territorial conquest. But after the first six weeks of battle, soldiers were ordered to do something unimaginable to strategists of European warfare: they were ordered to dig ditches and fight from fixed positions. Soldiers on both sides shoveled out trenches four feet deep, piled up sandbags, mounted their machine guns, and began to fight an unplanned defensive war.

DOCUMENT

Wilfred Owen (1921)

The front lines of Europe's armies in the west wallowed in the 400 miles of trenches that ran from the English Channel

■ A typical World War I trench. Millions of soldiers lived amid mud, disease, and vermin, awaiting death from enemy shells. After the French army mutiny in 1916, the troops wrung the concession from their commanders that they would not have to charge German machine guns while armed only with rifles.

ALL QUIET ON THE WESTERN FRONT

Eyewitness accounts described the horrors of the new trench warfare. But no one captured the war better than the German novelist Erich Maria Remarque (1898–1970), who drew on his own wartime experiences in All Quiet on the Western Front. *Published in 1928 and subsequently translated into 25 languages, this powerful portrayal of the transformation of a schoolboy into a soldier indicts the inhumanity of war and pleads for peace. Stressing the camaraderie of fighting men and sympathy for the plight of the enemy soldier, Remarque also underscored the alienation of a whole generation—the lost generation of young men who could not go home again after the war.*

Focus Questions

In the final paragraph, the narrator tells us his age. Would you have guessed his age from the opening three paragraphs? How does the narrator's description of his generation transcend enemy lines?

Attack, counter-attack, charge, repulse—these are words, but what things they signify! We have lost a good many men, mostly recruits. Reinforcements have again been sent up to our sector. They are one of the new regiments, composed almost entirely of young fellows just called up. They have had hardly any training, and are sent into the field with only a theoretical knowledge. They do know what a hand-grenade is, it is true, but they have very little idea of cover, and what is most important of all, have no eye for it. A fold in the ground has to be quite eighteen inches high before they can see it.

Although we need reinforcement, the recruits give us almost more trouble than they are worth. They are helpless in this grim fighting area, they fall like flies. Modern trench-warfare demands knowledge and experience; a man must have a feeling for the contours of the ground, an ear for the sound and character of the shells, must be able to decide beforehand where they will drop, how they will burst, and how to shelter from them.

The young recruits of course know none of these things. They get killed simply because they hardly can tell shrapnel from high-explosive, they are mown down because they are listening anxiously to the roar of the big coal-boxes falling in the rear, and miss the light, piping whistle of the low spreading daisy-cutters. They flock together like sheep instead of scattering, and even the wounded are shot down like hares by the airmen.

Their pale turnip faces, their pitiful clenched hands, the fine courage of these poor devils, the desperate charges and attacks made by the poor brave wretches, who are so terrified that they dare not cry out loudly, but with battered chests, with torn bellies, arms and legs only whimper softly for their mothers and cease as soon as one looks at them.

Their sharp, downy, dead faces have the awful expressionlessness of dead children. . . .

I am young, I am twenty years old; yet I know nothing of life but despair, death, fear, and fatuous superficiality cast over an abyss of sorrow. I see how peoples are set against one another, and in silence, unknowingly, foolishly, obediently, innocently slay one another. I see that the keenest brains of the world invent weapons and words to make it yet more refined and enduring. And all men of my age, here and over there, throughout the whole world see these things; all my generation is experiencing these things with me. What would our fathers do if we suddenly stood up and came before them and proffered our account? What do they expect of us if a time ever comes when the war is over? Through the years our business has been killing;—it was our first calling in life. Our knowledge of life is limited to death. What will happen afterwards? And what shall come out of us?

From Erich Maria Remarque, *All Quiet on the Western Front.*

---

to the Swiss frontier. The British and French on one side and the Germans on the other fought each other with machine guns and mortars, backed up by heavy artillery to the rear. Strategists on both sides believed they could break through enemy lines. As a result, the monotony of trench warfare was punctuated periodically by infantry offensives in which immense concentrations of artillery caused great bloodshed. Ten million men were killed in the bizarre and deadly combination of old and new warfare. The glamour of battle that had attracted many young men disappeared quickly in the daily reality of living in mud with rats and constantly facing death. The British poet Wilfred Owen (1893–1918), shortly before his own death in battle, wrote about how the soldier next to him had been shot in the head, soaking Owen in blood: "I shall feel again as soon as I dare, but now I must not."

New Weapons.   The invention of new weaponry and heavy equipment had transformed war into an enterprise of increasing complexity. Military and naval staffs expanded to meet the new needs of warfare, but old ways persisted. Outmoded cavalry units survived despite more efficient mechanization. In

DOCUMENT
Wilfred Owen
(1921)

■ The British invented the tank, which made its combat debut in 1916. The new weapon terrified the German troops when first used on the western front. The British had developed it in heavy secrecy under the pretext of constructing water tanks; hence the name.

their bright blue coats and red trousers, French and Belgian infantrymen made easy targets. The railroad made the mobilization, organization, and deployment of mass armies possible. Specialists were needed to control the new war machines that heavy industry had created.

The shovel and the machine gun had transformed war. The machine gun was not new in 1914, but its strategic value had not been fully appreciated before then. The Maxim machine gun had been used by the British in Africa. Strategists regarded the carnage that resulted as a stunning achievement but failed to ask how a weapon of such phenomenal destructive power would work against an enemy armed with machine guns instead of spears. Military strategists drew all the wrong conclusions. They continued to plan an offensive strategy when the weaponry developed for massive destruction had pushed them into fighting a defensive war from the trenches. Both sides resorted to concentration of artillery, increased use of poison gas, and unrestricted submarine warfare in desperate attempts to break the deadlock caused by meeting armed force with force.

The necessity of total victory drove the Central Powers and the Allies to grisly new inventions. Late in the war, the need to break the deadlock of trench warfare ushered in the airplane and the tank. Neither was decisive in altering the course of the war, although the airplane was useful for reconnaissance and for limited bombing and the tank promised the means of breaking through defensive lines. Chlorine gas was first used in warfare by the Germans in 1915. Mustard gas, which was named for its distinctive smell and which caused severe blistering, was introduced two years later. The Germans were the first to use flame throwers, especially effective against mechanized vehicles with vulnerable fuel tanks. Barbed wire, invented in the American Midwest to contain farm animals, became an essential aspect of trench warfare, as it marked off the no-man's-land between combatants and prevented surprise attacks.

The technology that had been viewed as proof of progress was now channeled toward engineering new instruments of death. Yet technology itself produced a stalemate. New weapons sometimes produced their antidotes. For example, the invention of deadly gas was followed soon after by gas masks. Each side was capable of matching the other's ability to devise new armaments. Deadlocks caused by technological parity forced both sides to resort to desperate concentrations of men and weaponry that resulted not in decisive battles but in ever-escalating casualty rates. By improving their efficiency at killing, the European powers were not finding a way to end the war.

The German Offensive

German forces seized the offensive in the west and invaded neutral Belgium at the beginning of August 1914. The Belgians resisted stubbornly but unsuccessfully. Belgian forts were systematically captured, and the capital of Brussels fell under the German advance on 20 August. After the fall of Belgium, German military might swept into northern France with the intention of defeating the French in six weeks.

Germany on Two Fronts.   In the years preceding the war, the German General Staff, unwilling to concentrate all of its troops in the west, had modified the Schlieffen Plan by committing divisions to its eastern frontier. The absence of the full German fighting force in the west did not appreciably slow the German advance through Belgium. Yet the Germans had underestimated both the cost of holding back the French in Alsace-Lorraine and the difficulty of maneuvering German forces and transporting supplies in an offensive war. Eventually, unexpected Russian advances in the east also siphoned off troops from the west. German forces in the west were so weakened by the offensive that they were unable

"DULCE ET DECORUM EST"

Some of the best and most moving poetry of modern times was produced in the trenches of World War I. Wilfred Owen (1893–1918), a company commander for the British Army, died in battle one week before the war ended. His poems stand as a strong testimonial to the horrors of battle and the camaraderie of the trenches.

Focus Questions

In this poem, Owen uses his schoolboy Latin to quote the patriotic sentiment that "It is sweet and fitting to die for one's country." What leads him to conclude that this noble thought is "the Old Lie"? Notice how he contrasts images of "old beggars under sacks" who are "coughing like hags" to youthful images, a reference to boys, "innocent tongues," and "children ardent for some desperate glory." What effect does his use of words like "ecstasy" and "dreams" have in conveying the horrors of war? This is a poem full of sounds; consider how those sounds are orchestrated to emphasize the poem's theme.

Bent double, like old beggars under sacks,
Knock-kneed, coughing like hags, we cursed through sludge,
Till on the haunting flares we turned our backs
And towards our distant rest began to trudge.
Men marched asleep. Many had lost their boots
But limped on, blood-shod. All went lame; all blind;
Drunk with fatigue; deaf even to the hoots
Of tired, outstripped Five Nines that dropped behind.

Gas! Gas! Quick, boys!—An ecstasy of fumbling,
Fitting the clumsy helmets just in time;
But someone still was yelling out and stumbling
And flound'ring like a man in fire or lime. . .
Dim, through the misty panes and thick green light,
As under a green sea, I saw him drowning.
In all my dreams, before my helpless sight,
He plunges at me, guttering, choking, drowning.

If in some smothering dreams you too could pace
Behind the wagon that we flung him in,
And watch the white eyes writhing in his face,
His hanging face, like a devil's sick of sin;
If you could hear, at every jolt, the blood
Come gargling from the froth-corrupted lungs,
Obscene as cancer, bitter as the cud
Of vile, incurable sores on innocent tongues,—
My friend, you would not tell with such high zest
To children ardent for some desperate glory,
The old Lie: Dulce et decorum est
Pro patria mori.

From Wilfred Owen, *Poems*, 1920.

---

to swing west of Paris, as planned, and instead chose to enter the French capital from the northeast by crossing the Marne River. The shift exposed the German First Army on its western flank and opened up a gap on its eastern flank.

First Battle of the Marne. Despite an initial pattern of retreat and a lack of coordination of forces, Allied French and British troops were ready to take advantage of the vulnerabilities in the German advance. In a series of battles between 6 and 10 September 1914 that came to be known as the First Battle of the Marne, the Allies counterattacked and advanced into the gap. The German army was forced to drop back. In the following months, each army tried to outflank the other in what has been called "the race to the sea." By late fall, it was clear that the battles from the Marne north to the border town of Ypres in northwest Belgium near the English Channel had ended an open war of movement on the western front. Soldiers now dug in along a line of battle that changed little in the long three and a half years until March 1918.

The Allies gained a strategic victory in the First Battle of the Marne by resisting the German advance in the fighting that quickly became known as the "miracle of the Marne." The legend was further enhanced by true stories of French troops being rushed from Paris to the front in taxicabs. Yet the real significance of the Marne lay in the severe miscalculations of military leaders and statesmen on both sides who had expected a different kind of war. They did not understand the new technology that made a short war unlikely. Nor did they understand the demands that the new kind of warfare would make on civilian populations. Those Parisian taxi drivers foreshadowed how European civilians would be called upon again and again to support the war in the next four years. The Schlieffen Plan was dead. But it was no more a failure than any of the other military timetables of the Great Powers.

"I don't know what is to be done—this isn't war." So spoke Lord Horatio Kitchener (1850–1916), one of the most decorated British generals of his time. He was not alone in his bafflement over the stalemate of trench warfare at the end of 1914. By that time, Germany's greatest fear, a simultaneous war on two fronts, had become a grim reality. The Central Powers were under a state of siege, cut off from the world by the great battlefront in the west and by the Allied blockade at sea. The rules of the game had changed, and the European powers settled in for a long war.

War on the Eastern Front

War on Germany's eastern front was a mobile war, fought over vast distances. The Russian army was the largest in the world. Yet it was crippled from the outbreak of the war by inadequate supplies and poor leadership. At the end of August 1914, the smaller German army, supported by divisions drawn from the west, delivered a devastating defeat to the Russians in the one great battle on the eastern front. At Tannenberg, the entire Russian Second Army was destroyed, and about 100,000 Russian soldiers were taken prisoner.

MAP DISCOVERY

World War I

The Central Powers were in the unenviable position of fighting wars on two major fronts. The inset shows the stabilized western front of trench warfare in northern France and Belgium. Why did warfare focus in the west on this area, and why did it bog down for such a long period along this front? How did warfare along the eastern front differ, and why did the eastern front cover a much greater expanse? You will note the major battles in western and eastern Europe and the Ottoman Empire. Why were none of these battles decisive in ending the war? Were the British naval blockade and the German submarine war zone effective? Finally, note the reduced Russian territory as a result of the Treaty of Brest-Litovsk. Why was Russia willing to agree to such a loss of land to Germany before the war ended?

Faced with that humiliation, General Aleksandr Vasilievich Samsonov (1859–1914), head of the Russian forces, committed suicide on the field of battle.

The German general Paul von Hindenburg (1847–1934), a veteran of the Franco-Prussian war of 1870, had been recalled from retirement to direct the campaign against the Russians because of his intimate knowledge of the area. Assisted by Quartermaster General Erich Ludendorff (1865–1937), Hindenburg followed the stunning victory of Tannenberg two weeks later with another devastating blow to Russian forces at the Masurian Lakes.

The Russians were holding up their end of the bargain in the Allied war effort, but at great cost. They kept the Germans busy and forced them to divert troops to the eastern front, weakening the German effort to knock France out of the war. In the south, the tsar's troops defeated the Austro-Hungarian army at Lemberg in Galicia in September. The Russian victory gave Serbia a temporary reprieve. But by mid-1915, Germany had thrown the Russians back and was keeping Austria-Hungary propped up in the war. By fall, Russia had lost most of Galicia, the Polish lands of the Russian Empire, Lithuania, and parts of Latvia and Byelorussia to the advancing enemy. The losses amounted to 15 percent of its territory and 20 percent of its population. The Russian army staggered, with more than one million soldiers taken as prisoners of war and at least as many killed or wounded.

The Russian army, as one of its own officers described it, was being bled to death. Russian soldiers were poorly led into battle, or not led at all because of the shortage of officers. Munitions shortages meant that soldiers often went into battle without rifles, armed only with the hope of scavenging arms from their fallen comrades. Despite the difficulties, the Russians, under the direction of General Aleksei Brusilov (1853–1926), commander of the Russian armies in the southern part of the eastern front, remarkably managed to throw back the Austro-Hungarian forces in 1916 and almost eliminated Austria as a military power. Russia's near-destruction of the Austrian army tremendously benefited Russia's allies. In order to protect its partner, Germany was forced to withdraw 8 divisions from Italy—alleviating the Allied situation in the Tyrol—and 12 divisions from the western front, providing relief for the French at Verdun and the British at the Somme. In addition, Russia sent troops to the aid of a new member of the Allied camp, Romania, an act that probably further weakened Brusilov's efforts. In response to Brusilov's challenge, the Germans established control over the Austrian army, assigning military command of the coalition to General Ludendorff. But that was the last great campaign on the eastern front and Russia's last show of strength in the Great War.

War on the Western Front

Along hundreds of miles of trenches, the French and British tried repeatedly to expel the Germans from Belgium. Long periods of inactivity were punctuated by orgies of heavy bloodletting. The German phrase "All quiet on the western front," used in military communiqués to describe those periods of silence between massive shellings and infantry attacks, reported only the uneasy calm before the next violent storm.

Verdun. Military leaders on both sides cherished the dream of a decisive offensive, the breakthrough that would win the war. In 1916, the Allies planned a joint strike at the Somme, a river in northern France flowing west into the English Channel, but the Germans struck first at Verdun, a small fortress city in northeast France. By concentrating great numbers of troops, the Germans outnumbered the French five to two. As General Erich von Falkenhayn (1861–1922), chief of the General Staff of the German army from 1914 to 1916, explained it, the German purpose in attacking Verdun was "to bleed the French white by virtue of our superiority in guns."

On the first day of battle, one million shells were fired. The battlefield was a living hell as soldiers stumbled across corpse after corpse. Against the German onslaught, French troops were instructed to hold out, though they lacked adequate artillery and reinforcements. General Joseph Joffre (1852–1931), commander in chief of the French army, was unwilling to divert reinforcements to Verdun.

The German troops advanced easily through the first lines of defense. But the French held their position for ten long, horrifying months of continuous mass slaughter from February to December 1916. General Henri Philippe Pétain (1856–1951), a local commander who had been planning an early retirement before the war, bolstered morale by constantly rotating his troops to the point that most of the French army—259 of 330 infantry battalions—saw action at Verdun. Nearly starving and poorly armed, the French stood alone in the bloodiest offensive of the war. Attack strategy backfired on the Germans as their own death tolls mounted.

Pétain and his flamboyant general Robert Georges Nivelle (1856–1924) were both hailed as heroes for fulfilling the instruction to their troops: "They shall not pass." Falkenhayn fared less well and was dismissed from his post. Yet no real winners emerged from the scorched earth of Verdun, where observers could see the nearest thing to a desert created in Europe. Verdun was a disaster. The French suffered more than half a million total casualties. German casualties were almost as high. A few square miles of territory had changed hands back and forth. In the end, no military advantage was gained, and almost 700,000 lives had been lost. Legends of the brilliant leadership of Pétain and Nivelle, who both went on to greater positions of authority, and the failed command of Falkenhayn, who retired in disgrace, obscured the real lesson of the battle: an offensive war under those conditions was impossible.

The Somme. Still, new offensives were devised. The British went ahead with their planned offensive on the Somme in July

■ Paul Nash, *We Are Making a New World* (1918), depicts the destructiveness of war. Nash was one of many artists who used their work to communicate their moral outrage against the war.

1916. For an advance of seven miles, 400,000 British and 200,000 French soldiers were killed or wounded. The American writer F. Scott Fitzgerald (1896–1940), who had served as an army officer in World War I, wrote of the battle of the Somme in his novel *Tender Is the Night* (1934). One of his characters describes a visit to the Somme Valley after the war: "See that little stream. We could walk to it in two minutes. It took the British a whole month to walk to it—a whole empire walking very slowly, dying in front and pushing forward behind. And another empire walked very slowly backward a few inches a day, leaving the dead like a million bloody rugs." German losses brought the total casualties of the offensive to one million men.

Despite his experience at Verdun, the French general Robert Nivelle planned his own offensive in the Champagne region in spring 1917, sure that he could succeed where others had failed in "breaking the crust." The Nivelle offensive resulted in 40,000 deaths, and Nivelle was dismissed. The French army was falling apart, with mutiny and insubordination everywhere.

The British believed they could succeed where the French had failed. Under General Douglas Haig (1861–1928), the commander in chief of British expeditionary forces on the Continent, the British launched an attack in Flanders throughout the summer and fall of 1917. Known as the *Passchendaele offensive* for the village and ridge in whose "porridge of mud" much of the fighting took place, the campaign resulted in the slaughter of almost 400,000 British soldiers for insignificant territorial gain. The Allies and the Germans finally recognized that "going over the top" in offensives was not working and could not work. The war must be won by other means.

■ British machine gunners wearing gas masks at the battle of the Somme in 1916.

War on the Periphery

Recognizing the stalemate in the west, the Allies attempted to open up other fronts where the Central Powers might be vulnerable. In the spring of 1915, the Allies were successful in convincing Italy to enter the war on their side by promising that it would receive, at the time of the peace, the South Tyrol, the southern part of Dalmatia, and key Dalmatian islands, which would ensure Italy's dominance over the Adriatic Sea. By thus capitalizing on Italian antagonism toward Austria-Hungary over control of that territory, the Allies gained 875,000 Italian soldiers for their cause. Although the Italian troops were in no way decisive in the fighting that followed, Great Britain, France, and Russia saw the need to build up Allied support in southern Europe in order to reinforce Serbian attempts to keep Austrian troops beyond its borders. The Allies also hoped that by pulling Germans into the southern front, some relief might be provided for British and French soldiers on the western front.

Germany, in turn, was well aware of the need to expand its alliances beyond Austria-Hungary if it was to compete successfully against superior Allied forces. Trapped as they were to the east and west, the Central Powers established control over a broad corridor stretching from the North Sea through central Europe and down through the Ottoman Empire to the Suez Canal that was so vital to British interests.

In the Balkans, where the war had begun, the Serbs were consistently bested by the Austrians. By late 1915, the Serbs had been knocked out of the war in spite of Allied attempts to assist them. Serbia paid a heavy price in the Great War: it lost one-sixth of its population through war, famine, and disease. The promise of booty persuaded Bulgaria to join Germany and Austria-Hungary. Over the next year and a half, the Allies responded by convincing Romania and then Greece to join them.

War in the Ottoman Empire.   The theater of war continued to expand. Although the Ottoman Empire had joined the war in late 1914 on the side of the Central Powers, its own internal difficulties attenuated its fighting ability. As a multinational empire consisting of Turks, Arabs, Armenians, Greeks, Kurds, and other ethnic minorities, it was plagued by Turkish misrule and Arab nationalism. Hence the Ottoman Empire was the weakest link in the chain of German alliances. Yet it held a crucial position. The Turks could block shipping of vital supplies to Russia through the Mediterranean and Black Seas. Coming to the aid of their Russian ally, a combined British and French fleet attacked Turkish forces at the straits of the Dardanelles in April 1915. In the face of political and military opposition, First Lord of the Admiralty Winston Churchill (1874–1965) supported the idea of opening a new front by sea.

DOCUMENT

Turkish Officer Describes Armenian Massacres

Poorly planned and mismanaged, the expedition was a disaster. When the naval effort in the German-mined strait failed, the British foolishly decided to land troops on the Gallipoli Peninsula, which extended from the southern coast of European Turkey. There British soldiers were trapped on the rocky terrain, unable to advance against the Turks and unable to fall back. Gallipoli was the first large-scale attempt at amphibious warfare. The Australian and New Zealand forces (ANZACs) showed great bravery in some of the most brutal fighting of the war. Critics in Britain argued that the only success of the nine-month campaign was the Allied evacuation.

Britain sought to protect its interests in the Suez Canal. Turkish troops menaced the canal effectively enough to terrify the British into maintaining an elaborate system of defense in the area and concentrating large troop reinforcements in Egypt. War with the Ottoman Empire also extended battle into the oil fields of Mesopotamia and Persia. The attempt at a new front was initially a fiasco for the British and Russian forces that threatened Baghdad. The Allies proceeded not only without plans, but also without maps. They literally did not know where they were going. Eventually, British forces recovered and took Baghdad in 1917, while Australian and New Zealand troops captured Jerusalem. The tentacles of war spread out, following the path of Western economic and imperial interests throughout the world.

War at Sea. Most surprising of all was the indecisive nature of the war at sea. The great battleships of the British and German navies avoided confrontation on the high seas. The only major naval battle of the Great War, the Battle of Jutland in the North Sea, took place in early 1916. Each side inflicted damage on the other but, through careful maneuvering, avoided a decisive outcome to the battle. Probably the enormous cost of replacing battleships deterred both the British and the Germans from risking their fleets in engagements on the high seas. With the demands for munitions and equipment on the two great land fronts of the war, neither side could afford to lose a traditional war at sea. Instead, the British used their seapower as a policing force to blockade German trade and strangle the German economy.

The German navy, much weaker than the British, relied on a new weapon, the submarine, which threatened to become decisive in the war at sea. Submarines were initially used in the first months of the war for reconnaissance. Their potential for inflicting heavy losses on commercial shipping became apparent in 1915. Undergoing technological improvements throughout the war, U-boats (*Unterseebooten*), as German submarines were called, torpedoed six million tons of Allied shipping in 1917. With cruising ranges as far as 3600 miles, German submarines attacked Allied and neutral shipping as far away as off the shore of the United States and the Arctic supply line to Russia. German insistence on unrestricted use outraged neutral powers, which considered the Germans in violation of international law. The Germans rejected the requirements of warning an enemy ship and boarding it for investigation as too dangerous for submarines, which were no match for battleships above water. The Allies invented depth charges and mines capable of blowing German submarines out of the water. Those weapons, combined with the use of the convoy system in the Atlantic Ocean and the Mediterranean Sea, produced a successful blockade and an antisubmarine campaign that put an end to the German advantage.

ADJUSTING TO THE UNEXPECTED: TOTAL WAR

The war that Europe experienced differed from all previous experiences and expectations of armed conflict. Technological advances, equally matched on both sides, introduced a war of attrition, defensive and prolonged. Nineteenth-century wars that lasted six to eight weeks, were confined to one locale, and

■ Crew on the deck of a German World War I submarine at sea.

were determined by a handful of battles marked by low casualties had nothing in common with the long, dirty, lice-infested reality of trench warfare. Warring European nations faced enemies to the west, to the east, and on the periphery, with no end to the slaughter in sight.

The period from 1914 to 1918 marked the first time in history that the productive activities of entire populations were directed toward a single goal: military victory. The Great War became a war of peoples, not just of armies. Wars throughout history have involved noncombatants caught in the crossfire or standing in the wrong place at the wrong time. But the unexpected war of attrition required civilian populations to adjust to a situation in which what went on at the battlefront transformed life on the home front. For this reason, the Great War became known as history's first **total war.**

Adjusting to the unexpected war of 1914, governments intervened to centralize and control every aspect of economic life. Technology and industrial capacity made possible a war of unimaginable destruction. The scale of production and distribution of war-related materials required for victory was unprecedented. To persuade civilians to suffer at home for the sake of the war, leaders pictured the enemy as evil villains who had to be defeated at any cost. The sacrifice required for a total war made total victory necessary. And total victory required an economy totally geared to fighting the war.

Mobilizing the Home Front

While soldiers were fighting on the eastern and western fronts, businessmen and politicians at home were creating bureaucracies to control wages and prices, distribute supplies, establish production quotas, and mobilize human and material resources. Just as governments had conscripted the active male population for military service, the Allies and the Central Powers now mobilized civilians of all ages and both sexes to work for the war.

WAR AT HOME

The total character of World War I meant that it changed life for noncombatants as much as it did for those at the front. Women had to fend for themselves, organizing relief societies, working the fields, and manufacturing weapons and war goods. They often took jobs men had held before. In London, taxi driving had been a male monopoly before the war. Articles from 16 March 1917 in the Manchester Guardian *show what could happen when both women and men shared jobs. Conflicts could break out when men felt threatened by women's new positions.*

Focus Questions

Why does this newspaper coverage consider that a strike by taxi-men "could be no more than a vain and selfish protest" against competition from women drivers? Is the question here women's competence or something else?

Women Taxi-Cab Drivers

The taxi-cab drivers of London threaten to try to bring about a strike, which will include motor-'bus drivers and conductors, if the London County Council does not abandon its intention to license women to drive taxi-cabs. To be successful a strike must in the ultimate event be in defense of a principle that commands a measure of public assent. The only principle for which the men stand in this strike is that even where women are fitted to do men's work they should be debarred from it. It is a principle never tenable in justice, and utterly discredited in the popular mind by the war. If the employment of women as motor-drivers meant a decrease in the general level of skill in the trade, a worsening of conditions, or a lowering of wages a real principle would be involved. Stress of war might make the setting aside of it temporarily necessary, but the point would be at least arguable. In this matter such considerations do not arise. Hundreds of women have taken the place of men as motor-drivers for the army and the Red Cross at home and abroad, thousands more are employed in driving commercial motors. They have proved, if proof were needed, that this work is well within their compass. The woman who can take a man's place fully in the harder sort of tasks involved in work on the railways or in agriculture is an exception, and the employment of women for such work is a war-time necessity that may not to any great extent survive when peace comes. But the woman motor-driver has come to stay, and a strike of taxi-men could be no more than a vain and selfish protest against her arrival.

"Down Cabs" Again

The London taxi-drivers are again threatening trouble—this time because the Home Office refuses to give way on the question of licensing women drivers. Sir George Cave told a deputation of the Licensed Vehicle Workers the other day that there is no intention at present of licensing women as tram and 'bus drivers, but that competent women will certainly be licensed for taxi-driving. The men are holding indignation meetings on Sunday, and threaten to bring all the cab, 'bus, and tram drivers of London out on strike—about 20,000 workers, inclusive of garage men.

Women's Roles. Women played an essential role in the mobilization of the home front. They had never been isolated from the experiences and hardships of war, but they now found new ways to support the war effort. In cities, women went to work in munitions factories and war-related industries that had previously employed only men. Women filled service jobs, from fire fighting to trolley-car conducting—jobs that were essential to the smooth running of industrial society and that had been left vacant by men. On farms, women literally took up the plow after both men and horses had been requisitioned for the war effort.

By 1918, 650,000 French women were working in war-related industries and in clerical positions in the army, and they had counterparts throughout Europe. In Germany, two out of every five munitions workers were women. Women became more prominent in the work force as a whole, as the case of Great Britain makes clear: there the number of women workers jumped from 250,000 at the beginning of the war to five million by the war's end. Women also served in the auxiliary units of the armed services, in the clerical and medical corps, in order to free men for fighting at the front. In eastern European nations, women entered combat as soldiers. Although most women were displaced from their wartime jobs with the return of men after the armistice, they were as important to the war effort as the men fighting at the front.

Government Controls. In the first months of the war, the private sector had been left to its own devices, with nearly disastrous results. Shortages, especially of shells, and bottlenecks in production threatened military efforts. Governments were forced to establish controls and to set up state monopolies in order to guarantee the supplies necessary to wage war. In Germany, industrialists Walther Rathenau (1867–1922) and Alfred Hugenberg (1865–1951) worked with the government. By the spring of 1915, they had eliminated the German problem of munitions scarcity. France was in trouble six weeks after the outbreak of the war: it had used up half of its accumulated munitions supplies in the First Battle of the Marne. German occupation of France's northern industrial basin further crippled munitions production. Through government intervention, France improvised and relocated its war industries. The British government became involved in production, too, by establishing in 1915 the first Ministry of Munitions under the direction of David Lloyd George (1863–1945). Distinct from the Ministry of War, the Ministry of Munitions was to coordinate military needs with the armaments industry.

In a war that leaders soon realized would be a long one, food supplies assumed paramount importance. Germany, dependent on food imports to feed its people and isolated from the world market by the Allied blockade, introduced rationing five months after the outbreak of the war. Other continental nations followed suit. Government agents set quotas for agricultural producers. Armies were fed and supplied at the expense of domestic populations. Great Britain, which enjoyed a more reliable food supply by virtue of its sea power, did not impose food rationing until 1917.

■ Women played a key role in the munitions industry during the war. In this ca. 1914 photograph of a British munitions factory, workers handle artillery shells.

Three factors put food supplies at risk. First, the need for large numbers of soldiers at the front pulled farmers and peasants off the land. The resultant drop in the agricultural work force meant that land was taken out of production and what remained was less efficiently cultivated, so that productivity declined. A second factor was fear of requisitioning and the general uncertainties of war that caused agricultural producers to hoard supplies. What little was available was traded on black markets. Finally, because all European countries depended to some extent on imports of food and fertilizers, enemies successfully targeted trade routes for attack.

Silencing Dissent

The strains of total war were becoming apparent. Two years of sacrificing, scrimping, and, in some areas, starving began to take their toll among soldiers and civilians on both sides.

With the lack of decisive victories, war weariness was spreading. Work stoppages and strikes, which had virtually ceased with the outbreak of war in 1914, began to climb rapidly in 1916. Between 1915 and 1916 in France, the number of strikes by dissatisfied workers increased by 400 percent. Underpaid and tired workers went on strike, staged demonstrations, and protested exploitation. Labor militancy also intensified in the British Isles and Germany. Women, breadwinners for their families, were often in the forefront of the protests throughout Europe. Social peace between unions and governments was no longer held together by patriotic enthusiasm for war.

Politicians, too, began to rethink their suspension of opposition to government policies as the war dragged on.

Dissidents among European socialist parties regained their prewar commitment to peace. Most socialists had enthusiastically supported the declarations of war in 1914. By 1916, the united front that political opponents had presented against the enemy was crumbling under growing demands for peace.

In a total war, unrest at home guaranteed defeat. Governments knew that all opposition to war policies had to be eliminated. In a dramatic extension of the police powers of the state, whether among the Allies or the Central Powers, criticism of the government became treason. Censorship was enforced and propaganda became more virulent. Those who spoke for peace were no better than the enemy. The governments of every warring nation resorted to harsh measures. Parliamentary bodies were stripped of power, civil liberties were suspended, democratic procedures were ignored. The civilian governments of Premier Georges Clemenceau (1841–1929) in France and Prime Minister Lloyd George in Great Britain resorted to rule by emergency police power to repress criticism. Under Generals von Hindenburg and Ludendorff in Germany, military rule became the order of the day. Nowhere was "government as usual" possible in total war.

Every warring nation sought to promote dissension from within the societies of its enemies. Germany provided some aid for the Easter Rebellion in Ireland in 1916 in the hope that the Irish demand for independence that predated the war would deflect British attention and undermine fighting strength and morale. Germany also supported separatist movements among minority nationalities in the Russian Empire and was responsible for returning the avowed revolutionary V. I. Lenin under escort to Russia in April 1917. The British engaged in similar tactics. The British foreign secretary Arthur Balfour (1848–1930) worked with Zionist leaders in 1917 in drawing up the **Balfour Declaration,** which promised to "look with favor" on the creation of a Jewish homeland in Palestine. The British thereby encouraged Zionist hopes among central European Jews, with the intent of creating difficulties for German and Austrian rulers. Similarly, the British encouraged Arabs to rebel against Turks with the same promise of Palestine. Undermining the loyalties of colonized peoples and minorities would be at minimum a nuisance to the enemy. Beyond that, it could erode war efforts from within.

THE RUSSIAN REVOLUTION AND ALLIED VICTORY

For the Allies, 1917 began with a series of crises. Under the hammering of one costly offensive after another, French morale had collapsed and military discipline was deteriorating. A combined German-Austrian force had eliminated the Allied states of Serbia and Romania. The Italians experienced a military debacle at Caporetto and were effectively out of the war. The peril at sea had increased with the opening of unrestricted U-boat warfare against Allied and neutral ships.

Two events proved decisive in 1917 in determining the course of the war: the collapse of the Russian army and the entry of the United States. Russia, in the throes of domestic revolution, ceased to be an effective opponent, and Germany was able to concentrate more of its resources in the west, fight a one-front war, and utilize the foodstuffs and raw materials of its newly acquired Russian territories to buoy its home front.

The war had gone from a stalemate to a state of crisis for both sides. Every belligerent state was experiencing war weariness that undermined civilian and military morale. Both Austria-Hungary and the Ottoman Empire teetered on the verge of collapse, with internal difficulties increasing as the war dragged on. Germany suffered from labor and supply shortages and economic hardship resulting from the blockade and an economy totally dedicated to waging war. It was at this point of crisis and defeatism that the entry of the United States into the war on the side of the Allies proved decisive.

Revolution in Russia

In order to understand Russia's withdrawal from the war, it is important to understand that Russia's ruler, Tsar Nicholas II (1894–1917), presided over an empire in the process of modernization with widening social divisions in 1914. Nicholas believed that a short, successful war would strengthen his monarchy against the domestic forces of change. Little did Nicholas know, when he committed Russia to the path of war instead of revolution, that he had guaranteed a future of war *and* revolution. He was delivering his nation up to humiliating defeat in global war and a devastating civil war. His own days were numbered, with his fate to be determined at the hands of a Marxist dictatorship.

The Last Tsar. In 1914, Russia was considered backward by the standards of Western industrial society. Russia still recalled a recent feudal past. The serfs had been freed in the 1860s, but the nature of the emancipation exacerbated tensions in the countryside and peasant hunger for land. Russia's limited, rapid industrialization in the 1880s and 1890s was an attempt to catch up with Great Britain, France, and Germany as a world industrial power. But the speed of such change brought with it severe dislocation, especially in the industrial city of Moscow and the capital, St. Petersburg.

Twelve years earlier, in 1905, the workers of St. Petersburg had protested hardships due to cyclical downturns in the economy. On a Sunday in January 1905, the tsar's troops fired on a peaceful mass demonstration in front of the Winter Palace, killing and wounding scores of workers, women, and children, who were appealing to the tsar for relief. The event, which came to be known as Bloody Sunday, set off a revolution that spread to Moscow and the countryside. In October 1905, the regime responded to the disruptions with a series of reforms that legalized political parties and established the Duma, or national parliament. Peasants, oppressed with their own burdens of taxation and endemic poverty, launched mass attacks on big landowners throughout 1905 and 1906. The government met workers' and peasants' demands with a return to repression in

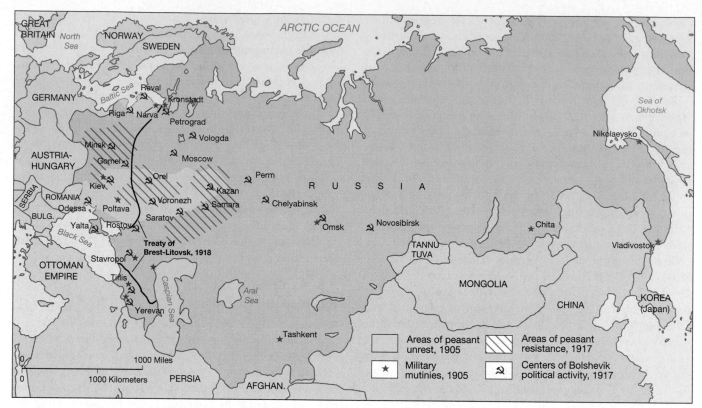

■ Revolution and Civil War in Russia, 1914–1920. Revolutionary and civil unrest was greatest in those areas of Russia with the greatest concentrations of peasants. Kulaks, the more prosperous peasants, were severely repressed for resisting the requisitioning of food after 1918.

1907. In the half-decade before the Great War, the Russian state stood as an autocracy of parliamentary concessions blended with severe police controls.

What workers had learned in 1905 was the power and the means of independent organization. Factory committees, trade unions, and **soviets,** or workers' councils, proliferated. Despite winning a grant of legal status after 1906, unions gained little in terms of ability to act on behalf of their members. Unrest among factory workers revived on the eve of the Great War, a period of rapid economic growth and renewed trade union activity. Between January and July 1914, Russia experienced 3500 strikes. Although economic strikes were considered legal, strikes deemed political were not. With the outbreak of war, all collective action was banned. Protest stopped, but only momentarily. The tsar certainly weighed the workers' actions in his decision to view war as a possible diversion from domestic problems.

Russia was less prepared for war than any of the other belligerents. Undoubtedly it had more soldiers than other countries, but it lacked arms and equipment. Problems of provisioning such a huge fighting force placed great strains on the domestic economy and on the work force. Under government coercion to meet the needs of war, industrial output doubled between 1914 and 1917, while agricultural production plummeted. The tsar, who unwisely insisted on commanding his own troops, left the government in the hands of his wife, the Tsarina Alexandra, a German princess by birth, and her eccentric peasant adviser, Rasputin. Scandal, sexual innuendo, and charges of treason surrounded the royal court. The incompetence of a series of unpopular ministers further eroded confidence in the regime. (See "A Closer Look: The Women Who Started the Russian Revolution," pp. 820–821.)

In the end, the war sharpened long-standing divisions within Russian society. Led by exhausted and starving working women, poorly paid and underfed workers toppled the regime in the bitter winter of March 1917. The event was the beginning of a violent process of revolution and civil war. The tsar abdicated, and all public symbols of the tsardom were destroyed. The banner bearing the Romanov two-headed eagle was torn down, and in its place the red flag of revolution flew over the Winter Palace.

Dual Power. With the tsar's abdication, two centers of authority replaced autocracy. One was the Provisional Government, appointed by the Duma and made up of progressive liberals led by Prince Georgi Lvov (1861–1925), prime minister of the new government, who also served as minister of the interior. Aleksandr Kerenski (1881–1970), the only socialist in the Provisional Government, served as minister of justice. The members of the new government hoped to establish constitutional and democratic rule. The other center of authority was the soviets—committees or councils elected by workers and soldiers and supported by radical lawyers, journalists, and intellectuals in favor of socialist self-rule. The Petrograd Soviet was the most prominent among the councils. The duality of power was matched by duality in policies and objectives, which guaranteed a short-lived and unstable regime.

The problems facing the new regime soon became apparent as revolution spread to the provinces and the battlefront. Peasants, who made up 80 percent of the Russian population, accepted the revolution and demanded land and peace. Without waiting for government directives, peasants began seizing the land. Peasants tried to alleviate some of their suffering by hoarding what little they had. The food crisis of winter persisted throughout the spring and summer as breadlines lengthened and prices rose. Workers in cities gained better working conditions and higher wages. But wage increases were invariably followed by higher prices that robbed workers of their gains. Real wages declined.

In addition to the problems of land and bread, the war itself presented the new government with other insurmountable difficulties. Hundreds of thousands of Russian soldiers at the front deserted the war, having heard news from home of peasant land grabs and rumors of a new offensive planned for July. The Provisional Government, concerned with Russia's territorial integrity and its position in the international system, continued to honor the tsar's commitments to the Allies by participating in the war. By spring 1917, six to eight million Russian soldiers had been killed, wounded, or captured. The Russian army was incapable of fighting.

The Provisional Government tried everything to convince its people to carry on with the war. In the summer of 1917, the Women's Battalion of Death, composed exclusively of female recruits, was enlisted into the army. Its real purpose, officials admitted, was to "shame the men" into fighting. The all-female unit, like its male counterparts, experienced high losses: 80 percent of the force suffered casualties. The Provisional Government was caught in an impossible situation: it could not withdraw from the war, but neither could it

fight. Continued involvement in the lost cause of the war blocked any consideration of social reforms.

While the Provisional Government was trying to deal with the calamities, many members of the intelligentsia—Russia's educated class, who had been exiled by the tsar for their political beliefs—now rushed back from western Europe to take part in the great revolutionary experiment. Theorists of all stripes put their cases before the people. Those who were in favor of gradual reform debated the relative merits of various government policies with those who favored violent revolution. The months between February 1917 and July 1917 were a period of great intellectual ferment. It was the Marxists, or Social Democrats, who had the greatest impact on the direction of the revolution.

The Social Democrats believed that there were objective laws of historical development that could be discovered. Russia's future could be understood only in terms of the present situation in western Europe. Like Marxists in the West, the Russian Social Democrats split over how best to achieve a socialist state. The more moderate Mensheviks (the term means "minority") wanted to work through parliamentary institutions and were willing to cooperate with the Provisional Government. A smaller faction—despite its name—calling themselves **Bolsheviks** (meaning "majority") dedicated themselves to preparation for revolutionary upheaval. After April 1917, the Bolsheviks refused to work with the Provisional Government and organized themselves to take control of the Petrograd Soviet.

Lenin and the Opposition to War. The leader of the Bolsheviks was Vladimir Ilyich Ulyanov (1870–1924), best known by his revolutionary name, Lenin. Forty-seven years old at the time of the revolution, Lenin had spent most of his life in exile or in prison. More a pragmatist than a theoretician, he argued for a disciplined party of professional revolutionaries, a vanguard that would lead the peasants and workers in a socialist revolution against capitalism. In contrast to the Mensheviks, he argued that the time was ripe for a successful revolution and that it could be achieved through the soviets.

■ As late as August 1917, the Provisional Government of Aleksandr Kerenski was determined to carry on the war, but the war-weary troops began to quit. In this scene from Galicia, demoralized Russian soldiers throw down their arms and flee after hearing that German cavalry has broken through the lines.

A Closer Look
The Women Who Started the Russian Revolution

Women in Russia, like their counterparts throughout Europe in 1914, took over new jobs in the workplace as men marched off to war. Four of every ten Russian workers were women, up from three of ten on the eve of the war. The situation was more dramatic in Petrograd, Russia's capital and principal industrial center, where by 1917 women constituted 55 percent of the labor force. Russian working women faced greater hardships than their sisters in the West. Most women workers in Petrograd held unskilled, poorly paid jobs in the textile industries and worked grueling 12- and 13-hour days. They left work only to stand for hours in long bread lines and then returned home to care for their elderly relatives and often sick children. Infant mortality was alarmingly high, with as many as half of all children dying before the age of three. Factory owners reported that nothing could be done. "The worker mother drudges and knows only need, only worry and grief," one commentator observed. "Her life passes in gloom, without light."

Russia was suffering badly in the war, with more than two million soldiers killed by the beginning of 1917. News of disasters at the front reached mothers, wives, and sisters at home in spite of the government's efforts to hide the defeats. In the less than three years since the war had begun, prices had increased 400 percent and transport lines for food and coal had broken down. Bread was the main staple of meager diets. Supplies of flour and grain were not reaching towns and cities. People were starving and freezing to death. Young children were now working 11 $\frac{1}{2}$ hour days in the factories. The situation was dire, and working women knew that something must be done if their families were to survive.

The working women of Petrograd correctly understood that the intolerable state of affairs had come about because the government was unable to control distribution and to ration limited supplies. Carrying a double burden of supporting those at home unable to work and of producing in the factory the armaments essential for the war effort, women workers began demanding that labor organizations take action to alleviate the situation. In the winter of 1916–1917, labor leaders advised exhausted and starving workers to be cautious and patient: workers must wait to strike until the time was ripe. Women workers did not agree. On 8 March 1917 (23 February by the Russian calendar), more than 7000 women went on strike in acknowledgment of International Women's Day, an event initiated in the United States in 1909 to recognize the rights of working women. The striking women were angry, frustrated, hungry, and tired of watching their families starve while their husbands, brothers, and sons were away at the battlefront. The week before, the city had been placed on severe rationing because Petrograd was down to its last few days' supply of flour. Although the principal concern of the striking women was bread, their protest was more than just a food riot. Women left their posts in the textile mills to demand an end to the war and an end to the reign of Tsar Nicholas II. They were responding not to revolutionary propaganda but to the politics of hunger. Singing songs of protest, they marched through the streets to take their cause to the better-paid and more radical male metalworkers. Women appealed to working men to join the strike. By the end of the day, 100,000 workers had left their jobs to join demonstrations against the government.

The women did not stop there. They took justice into their own hands and looted bakeries and grocery shops in search of food. In the street demonstrations of the next several days, women and men marched by the thousands, attracting growing support from workers throughout the city and the suburbs. Forty demonstrators were killed when government troops fired into a crowd. Still the women were not deterred. Bolshevik leader Leon Trotsky recalled women's bravery in going up to detachments of soldiers: "More boldly than men, they take hold of the rifles and beseech, almost command: 'Put down your bayonets—join us!'" Stories

■ Women workers on strike march through Petrograd, Russia, in 1917.

abound of how poor working women persuaded officers and soldiers of the Cossacks—the tsar's privileged fighting force—to lay down their arms. It was rumored that soldiers abandoned the tsar because they would not fire on the crowds of women. A participant in one confrontation reported that women workers stood without flinching as a detachment of Cossacks bore down upon them. Someone in the crowd shouted out that the women were the wives and sisters of soldiers at the front. The Cossacks lowered their rifles and turned their horses around. Troops like those, tired of the war, mutinied all over Petrograd. Within four days of the first action taken by women textile operatives, the government had lost the support of Petrograd workers, women and men, and its soldiers, who had joined the demonstrators. The tsar was forced to abdicate. From that point on, the Romanov monarchy and the Russian war effort were doomed.

In those first days of protest, the women of Petrograd took action into their own hands, pouring into the streets to call for bread, peace, and the end of tsardom. They rejected autocracy and war in defense of their communities and their families. The Russian Revolution had begun.

821

WAR COMMUNISM

The Bolsheviks faced many problems in trying to stabilize their new regime. Not least of these was their attempt to feed the population in the face of grain speculation and hoarding. The following is a decree on grain from 9 May 1918.

Focus Questions

How many social classes are identified in this decree, and how are they defined in opposition to each other? How does the government conceive of its role in the economic struggle?

The disastrous process of disorganization affecting the country's food supplies, the grave heritage of four years of war, continues to become increasingly widespread and increasingly acute. . . . The grain is in the hands of the village kulaks [rich peasants] and profiteers, in the hands of the rural bourgeoisie. Well fed and well provided for, having put aside huge sums of money obtained during the war years, the rural bourgeoisie remains stubbornly deaf and indifferent to the wailings of starving workers and the peasant poor. They do not bring their grain to the collecting points, reckoning on compelling the State to raise grain prices again and again while they themselves sell grain in the localities at fabulous prices to speculators. . . . The answer to the violence of the grain owners toward the starving poor must be violence toward the bourgeoisie. . . .

This policy must be implemented immediately, especially since the German occupation of the Ukraine compels us to get along with grain resources which are barely sufficient for sowing and reduced rations.

Having considered the situation created, and having taken into account that only through the strictest stock-taking and even distribution of grain reserves will Russia get out of the food crisis, the All-Russian Central Executive Committee of Soviets has resolved:

1. To reassert the firmness of the grain monopoly and fixed prices, and also the necessity of a ruthless struggle against grain speculators and bagmen; to compel each grain owner to declare the surplus above the quantity needed for sowing the fields and personal use, according to the established norms, until the new harvest, and to surrender the same within a week of the publication of this decree. . . .

2. To call upon all workers and poor peasants to unite at once for a merciless struggle against the kulaks.

3. To declare all those having surplus grain and not bringing it to the collection points, and also those squandering grain reserves on illegal distilleries, enemies of the people; to turn them over to the Revolutionary Court with a view to sending the culprits to prison for a term of not less than 10 years; to expel them from the farm community forever, all their property being subject to confiscation; to sentence illegal distillers, moreover, to socially useful hard labor.

4. That in the event of discovering that someone has not declared his surplus grain for surrender in compliance with point 1, the grain shall be taken away from him without payment; after the actual receipt of the undeclared surpluses at the collection point, half their value, calculated at fixed prices, is to be paid to the person who pointed out the concealed surpluses, and the other half to the village commune. Declarations concerning concealed surpluses are to be made to local food organizations.

Immediately upon his arrival in Petrograd from Switzerland, Lenin threw down the gauntlet to the Provisional Government. In his **April Theses,** he promised the Russian people peace, land, and bread. The war must be ended immediately, he argued, because it represented an imperialist struggle that was benefiting capitalists. Russia's duty was to withdraw and wait for a world revolution. That was more than rhetoric on Lenin's part. His years in exile in the West and news of mutinies and worker protests convinced him that revolution was imminent. His revolutionary policies on land were little more than endorsements of the seizures already taking place all over Russia. Even his promises of bread had little substance. But on the whole, the April Theses constituted a clear critique of the policies of the Provisional Government.

Dissatisfaction with the Provisional Government increased as the war dragged hopelessly on and bread lines lengthened. In the midst of the calamities, a massive popular demonstration erupted in July 1917 against the Provisional Government and in favor of the soviets, which excluded the upper classes from voting. The Provisional Government responded with repressive force reminiscent of the tsardom. The July Days were proof of the growing influence of the Bolsheviks among the Russian people. Although the Bolshevik leadership had withdrawn support for the demonstrations at the last moment, Bolshevik rank-and-file party members strongly endorsed the protest. Indisputably, Bolshevik influence was growing in the soviets despite repression and the persecution of its leaders. Lenin himself was forced to flee to Finland.

As a result of the July Days, Kerenski, who had been heading the Ministry of Justice, was named prime minister and continued the Provisional Government's moderate policies. In order to protect the government from a coup on the right, Kerenski permitted the arming of the Red Guards, the workers' militia units of the Petrograd Soviet. The traditional chasm between the upper and lower classes was widening as the policies of the Provisional Government conflicted with the demands of the soviets.

The October Revolution.

The second revolution came in November (October according to the Russian calendar). It was not a spontaneous street demonstration by thousands of working women that triggered the second revolution, but rather the seizure of the Russian capital by the Red Guards of the Petrograd Soviet. The revolution was carefully planned and orchestrated by Lenin and his vanguard of Bolsheviks, who now possessed majorities in the soviets in Moscow and Petrograd and in other industrial centers. Returning surreptitiously from Finland, Lenin moved through the streets of Petrograd disguised in a curly wig and head bandages, watching the Red Guards seize centers of communication and public buildings. The military action was directed by Lev Bronstein, better known by his revolutionary name, Leon Trotsky (1879–1940). The Bolshevik chairman of the Petrograd Soviet, Trotsky used the Red Guards to seize political control and arrest the members of the Provisional Government. Kerenski escaped and fled the city.

The takeover was achieved with almost no bloodshed and was immediately endorsed by the All-Russian Congress of Soviets, which consisted of representatives of local soviets from throughout the nation who were in session amid the takeover of the capital. A Bolshevik regime under Lenin now ruled Russia. Tsar Nicholas II and the royal family were executed by the Bolshevik revolutionaries in July 1918.

The Treaty of Brest-Litovsk.

Lenin immediately set to work to end the Great War for Russia. After months of negotiation, Russia signed a separate peace with the Germans in March 1918 in the **Treaty of Brest-Litovsk.** By every measure, the treaty was a bitter humiliation for the new Soviet regime. The territorial losses sustained were phenomenal. In a vast amputation, Russia was reduced to the size of its Muscovite period: it recognized the independence of the Ukraine, Georgia, and Finland; it relinquished its Polish territories, the Baltic States, and part of Byelorussia to Germany and Austria-Hungary; it handed over other territories on the Black Sea to Turkey. Lenin believed that he had no choice: he needed to buy time in order to consolidate the revolution at home, and he hoped for a socialist revolution in Germany that would soften the results of the treaty.

The Treaty of Brest-Litovsk was judged a betrayal, not only outside Russia among the Allied powers, but also inside Russia among some army officers who had sacrificed much for the tsar's war. To those military men, the Bolsheviks were no more than German agents who held the country in their sway.

CHRONOLOGY
THE RUSSIAN REVOLUTION

January–July 1914	Protests and strikes
30 July 1914	Russia enters World War I
March 1917	First Russian Revolution: Abdication of Tsar Nicholas II
March 1917	Creation of Provisional Government
April 1917	Bolsheviks take control of Petrograd
July 1917	Massive demonstration against Provisional Government; Lenin is forced to flee Russia
November 1917	Bolsheviks and Red Guards seize political control in what comes to be known as the October Revolution
March 1918	Russia withdraws from World War I and signs Treaty of Brest-Litovsk
July 1918	Tsar Nicholas II and family are executed

To deal with the anarchy caused by the fratricidal struggle, Lenin had to strengthen the government's dictatorial elements at the expense of its democratic ones. The new Soviet state used state police to suppress all opposition. The dictatorship of the proletariat yielded to the dictatorship of the repressive forces.

In the course of the civil war, Lenin was no more successful than Kerenski and the Provisional Government had been in solving the problems of food supplies. Human costs of the civil war were high, with more than 800,000 soldiers dead on both sides and two million civilian deaths from dysentery and diseases caused by poor nutrition. Industrial production ceased, and people fled towns to return to the countryside.

The United States Enters the Great War

The Allies longed for the entry of the United States into the war. Although the United States was a neutral country, from the beginning of the war it had been an important supplier to the Allies. U.S. trade with the Allies had jumped from $825 million in 1914 to $3.2 billion in 1916. American bankers also made loans and extended credit to the Allies to the amount of $2.2 billion. The United States had made a sizable investment in the Allied war effort, and its economy was prospering.

Beginning with the sinking of the *Lusitania* in 1915, German policy on the high seas had incensed the American public. Increased U-boat activity in 1916 led U.S. President Woodrow Wilson (1856–1924) to issue a severe warning to the Germans to cease submarine warfare. The Germans, however, were driven to desperate measures. The great advantage of submarines was in sneak attacks—a procedure against international rules, which required warning. Germany initiated a new phase of unrestricted submarine warfare on 1 February 1917, when the German ambassador informed the U.S. government that U-boats would sink on sight all ships, including passenger ships—even those neutral and unarmed.

The United States Declares War.

German machinations in Mexico were also revealed on 25 February 1917, with the interception of a telegram from Arthur Zimmermann (1864–1940), the German foreign minister. The telegram communicated Germany's willingness to support Mexico's recovery of "lost territory" in New Mexico, Arizona, and Texas in return for Mexican support of Germany in the event of U.S. entry into the war. U.S. citizens were outraged. On 2 April 1917, Wilson, who had won the presidential election of 1916 on the promise of peace, asked the U.S. Congress for a declaration of war against Germany.

The entry of the United States was the turning point in the war, tipping the scales dramatically in favor of the Allies. The United States contributed its naval power to the large Allied convoys formed to protect shipping against German attacks. In a total war, control and shipment of resources had become crucial issues, and it was in those areas that the U.S. entry gave the Allies indisputable superiority. The United States was also able to send "over there" tens of thousands of conscripts fighting with the American Expeditionary Forces under the leadership of General John "Black Jack" Pershing (1860–1948). They reinforced British and French troops and gave a vital boost to morale.

However, for such a rich nation, the help that the United States was able to give at first was very little. The U.S. government was new to the business of coordinating a war effort, but it displayed great ingenuity in creating a wartime bureaucracy that increased a small military establishment of 210,000 soldiers to 9.5 million young men registered before the beginning of summer 1917. By July 1918, the Americans were sending a phenomenal 300,000 soldiers a month to Europe. By the end of the war, 2 million Americans had traveled to Europe to fight in the war.

The U.S. entry is significant not just because it provided reinforcements, fresh troops, and fresh supplies to the beleaguered Allies. From a broader perspective, it marked a shift in the nature of international politics: Europe was no longer able to handle its own affairs and settle its own differences without outside help.

U.S. troops, though numerous, were not well trained, and they relied on France and Great Britain for their arms and equipment. But the Germans correctly understood that they could not hold out indefinitely against the superior Allied force. Austria-Hungary was effectively out of the war.

Germany had no replacements for its fallen soldiers, but it was able to transfer troops from Russia, Romania, and Macedonia to the west. It realized that its only chance of victory lay in swift action. The German high command decided on a bold measure: one great, final offensive that would knock the combined forces of Great Britain, France, and the United States out of the war once and for all by striking at a weak point and smashing through enemy lines. The great surprise was that it almost worked.

German Defeat.

Known as the *Ludendorff offensive,* after the general who devised it, the final German push began in March 1918, almost a year after U.S. entry into the war. Secretly amassing tired troops from the eastern front pulled back after the Russian withdrawal, the Germans counted on the element of surprise to enable them to break through a weak sector in the west. On the first day of spring, Ludendorff struck. The larger German force gained initial success against weakened British and French forces. Yet in spite of breaches in its defense, the Allied line held. Allied Supreme Commander General Ferdinand Foch (1851–1929)

CHRONOLOGY	
FIGHTING THE GREAT WAR	
1905	Development of the Schlieffen Plan
28 June 1914	Assassination of Archduke Franz Ferdinand and his wife, Sophie
28 July 1914	Austria-Hungary declares war on Serbia
30 July–4 August 1914	Russia, France, Britain, and Germany declare war in accordance with system of alliances
August 1914	Germany invades Belgium
6–10 September 1914	First Battle of the Marne
1915	Germany introduces chlorine gas
April 1915–January 1916	Gallipoli Campaign
May 1915	Sinking of the *Lusitania*
February–December 1916	Battle at Verdun
1917	First use of mustard gas
2 April 1917	United States enters war
March 1918	Russia withdraws
11 November 1918	Armistice

■ British soldiers, blinded by gas in Germany's final offensive in the spring of 1918, lead each other toward a medical aid station.

coordinated the war effort that withstood German offensives throughout the spring and early summer of 1918.

The final drive began in mid-July. More than one million German soldiers had already been killed, wounded, or captured in the months between March and July. German prisoners of war gave the French details of Ludendorff's plan. The Germans, now exposed and vulnerable, were placed on the defensive. The German army was rapidly disintegrating. On the other side, tanks, plentiful munitions, and U.S. reinforcements fueled an Allied offensive that advanced steadily throughout the summer of 1918. The German army retreated, destroying property and equipment as it went. With weak political leadership and indecision in Berlin, the Germans held on until early November, when their efforts collapsed. On 11 November 1918, an armistice signed by representatives of the German and Allied forces took effect.

Thus came to an end a war of slightly more than four years in duration that had consumed the soldiers, material, and productive resources of the European nations on both sides. Europeans had prided themselves on representing the pinnacle of civilization against the barbarism of other continents. Yet nothing matched the destructiveness of the Great War. Of the 70 million who were mobilized, about one in eight were killed. Battlefields of scorched earth and mud-filled ditches, silent at last, scarred once-fertile countrysides as grim memorials to history's first total war. Home fronts, too, served as battlefields, with those who demanded peace silenced as traitors. In the end, only the entry of the United States into the war on the side of the Allies brought an end to the human misery and staggering bloodletting. The war to end all wars was over; the task of settling the peace now loomed.

SETTLING THE PEACE

In the aftermath of war, the task of the victors was to define the terms of a settlement that would guarantee peace and stabilize Europe. Russia was the ghost at the conference table, excluded from the negotiations because of its withdrawal from the Allied camp in 1917 and its separate peace with Germany in March 1918. The Bolsheviks were dealing with problems of their own following the revolution, including a great civil war which lasted through 1920. Much of what happened in the peace settlements reflected the unspoken concern with the challenge of revolution that the new Soviet Russia represented. A variety of goals marked the peace talks: the idealistic desire to create a better world, the patriotic pursuit of self-defense, a commitment to the self-determination of nations, and the desire to fix blame for the outbreak of the war. In the end, the peace treaties satisfied none of those goals. Meanwhile, Russia's new leaders carefully watched events in the west, looking for opportunities that might permit them to extend their revolution to central Europe.

From January to June 1919, an assembly of nations convened in Paris to draw up the new European peace. Although the primary task of settling the peace fell to the Council of Four—Premier Georges Clemenceau of France, Prime Minister David Lloyd George of Great Britain, Prime Minister Vittorio Emanuele Orlando of Italy, and President Woodrow Wilson of the United States—small states, newly formed states, and non-European states, Japan in particular, joined in the task of forging the peace. The states of Germany, Austria-Hungary, and Soviet Russia were excluded from the negotiating tables where the future of Europe was to be determined.

Wilson's Fourteen Points

President Wilson, who captured international attention with his liberal views on the peace, was the central figure of the conference. He was firmly committed to the task of shaping a better world: before the end of the war he had proclaimed the **Fourteen Points** as a guideline to the future peace and as an appeal to the people of Europe to support his policies. Believing that secret diplomacy and the alliance system were responsible for the events leading up to the declaration of war in 1914, he put forward as a basic principle "open covenants of peace, openly arrived at." Other points included the reduction of armaments, freedom of commerce and trade, self-determination

of peoples, and a general association of nations to guarantee the peace that became the League of Nations. The Fourteen Points were, above all, an idealistic statement of the principles for a good and lasting peace. Point 14, which stipulated "mutual guarantees of independence and territorial integrity" through the establishment of the League of Nations, was endorsed by the peace conference. The League, which the United States refused to join in spite of Wilson's advocacy, was intended to arbitrate all future disputes among states and to keep the peace.

Georges Clemenceau of France represented a different approach to the challenge of the peace, one motivated primarily by a concern for his nation's security. France had suffered the greatest losses of the war in both human lives and property destroyed. In order to prevent a resurgent Germany, Clemenceau supported a variety of measures to cripple it as a military force on the Continent. Germany was disarmed. The territory west of the Rhine River was demilitarized, with occupation by Allied troops to last for a period of 15 years. With Russia unavailable as a partner to contain Germany, France supported the creation of a series of states in eastern Europe carved out of former Russian, Austrian, and German territory. Wilson supported the new states out of a concern for the self-determination of peoples. Clemenceau's main concern was self-defense.

Much time and energy were devoted to redrawing the map of Europe. New states were created out of the lands of three failed empires. To allow self-determination, Finland, Latvia, Estonia, Lithuania, Poland, Czechoslovakia, Austria, Hungary, and Yugoslavia were all granted status as nation-states. However, the rights of ethnic and cultural minorities were violated in some cases because of the impossibility of redrawing the map of Europe strictly according to the principle of self-determination. In spite of good intentions, every new nation had its own national minority, a situation that held the promise of future trouble.

■ The representatives of the victorious Allies at Versailles: (left to right) David Lloyd George of Great Britain, Vittorio Orlando of Italy, Georges Clemenceau of France, and Woodrow Wilson of the United States.

Treaties and Territories

The peace conference produced separate treaties with each of the defeated nations: Austria, Hungary, Turkey, Bulgaria, and Germany. The Austria settlement acknowledged the fundamental disintegration of the Austrian Empire, recognizing an independent Czechoslovakian republic and preparing the way for a fusing of Croatia, Dalmatia, Bosnia and Herzegovina with the Kingdom of Serbia, into the nation of Yugoslavia. Hungary and Poland also emerged as independent nations thanks to territorial losses by Germany and Austria Hungary. Bulgaria lost territory on the Aegean Sea to Greece, and Yugoslavia assumed control of Bulgarian holdings in Macedonia. Romania gained Hungarian and Bulgarian territory.

In the Middle East, a separate treaty acknowledged Great Britain's mandate in Palestine, Mesopotamia, and Transjordan; and France's mandate in Syria. Hejaz emerged as an independent state. Many aspects of the post-war settlement affecting Turkey and the Middle East were renegotiated in the early 1920s, but British and French gains were preserved, and Hejaz remained as an independent state.

In November 1917 the British affirmed its support of the creation in Palestine of a national home for the Jewish people. This affirmation, known as the Balfour Declaration, was made by Lord Balfour on behalf of "His Majesty's Government" and was considered as a violation of promises made to the Arabs during the war that they would be given control of Palestine in return for supporting the Allied war effort. Although Arab rulers were given control of British mandates, and Prince Faisal assumed the title of king of Iraq, Arab resentment festered as increased numbers of European Jews moved into Palestine and Arab hopes for the creation of an Arab kingdom were dashed.

Amidst these other treaty negotiations, the treaty signed with Germany on 28 June 1919, known as the **Treaty of Versailles,** dealt exclusively with defeated Germany. In that treaty, signed in the great Versailles palace outside of Paris, the Allies imposed blame for the war on Germany and its expansionist aims in the famous War Guilt Clause. According to that Clause, the war was Germany's fault, and Germany must be made to pay. According to the treaty, "compensation will be made by Germany for all damage done to the civilian population of the Allies and their property by the aggression of Germany by land, by sea and from the air." Reparations, once the price of defeat, were now exacted as compensation for damages inflicted by a guilty aggressor.

The principle of punitive reparations was included in the German settlement. Germany learned it had to make a down

■ Europe After World War I. The need for security on the continent led France to support a buffer zone of new nations between Russia and Germany, carved out of the former Austrian Empire. German territory along the French border was demilitarized out of the same concern for protection.

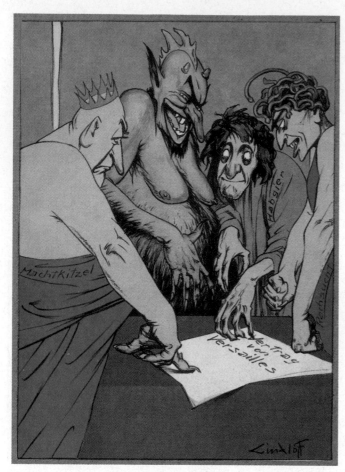

■ A German cartoon by Lindloff depicts German reaction to the terms of the Treaty of Versailles and to the Allies' brand of justice. Greed, revenge, and other devils gloat over the settlement.

than any other aspect of the peace settlement, came to haunt the Allies in the succeeding decades.

In the end, no nation obtained what it wanted from the peace settlement. The defeated nations believed that they had been badly abused. The victorious nations were aware of the compromises they had reluctantly accepted. Cooperation among nations was essential if the treaty was to work successfully. It had taken the combined resources, not only of France and the British Empire but also of Russia with its vast population and the United States with its great industrial and financial might, to defeat the power of Germany and the militarily ineffective Austro-Hungarian Empire. A new and stable balance of power depended on the participation of Russia, the United States, and the British Empire. But Russia was excluded from and hostile to the peace settlement, the United States was uncommitted to it, and the British Empire declined to guarantee it. All three Great Powers backed off from their European responsibilities at the end of the war. By 1920, all aspects of the treaty, but especially the reparations clause, had been questioned and criticized by the very governments that had written and accepted them. The search for a lasting peace had just begun.

Conclusion

By every measure, the Great War was disastrously expensive. Some European nations suffered more than others, but all endured significant losses of life, property, and productive capacity. The cost in human lives was enormous. In western Europe, 8.5 million were dead; total casualties amounted to 37.5 million. France lost 20 percent of its men between the ages of 20 and 44, Germany lost 15 percent, and Great Britain 10 percent. The war also resulted in huge losses in productive capacity. National economies buckled under the weight of foreign debts, and governments resorted to a variety of methods to bail themselves out, including taxes, loans, and currency inflation. The people of Europe continued to pay for the war long after the fighting had ended.

The big winner in the war was the United States, now a creditor nation owed billions of dollars in loans from the Allies and operating in new markets established during the war. The shift was not a temporary move but a structural change. The United States now took its place as a great power in the international system. The world that had existed before 1914 was gone, and what was to replace it was still very much in flux. To the east, Russia was engaged in the vast experiment of building a new society. In the west, the absence of war was not peace.

payment of $5 billion against a future bill of $32 billion; had to hand over a significant proportion of their merchant ships, including all vessels of more than 1600 tons; had to lose all German colonies; and had to deliver coal to neighboring countries. In addition, Germany lost the territory gained from Russia in 1918; returned Alsace and Lorraine to France; ceded territory to Belgium and eventually to Lithuania; and gave up parts of Prussia with large Polish populations. Furthermore, Germany lost control of the Saar, a coal-producing region, to France for fifteen years; and the German Baltic port of Danzig was declared an international "free city." By stripping Germany of key resources, territory and population, its ability to pay reparations was also weakened. These harsh clauses dictated by the determination of German war guilt, more

QUESTIONS FOR REVIEW

1. Why did so many in Europe look forward to war by the summer of 1914, and what had they done to bring it about?

2. How and why did the Great War differ so much from the expectations of both the generals and the majority of Europeans?

3. What is total war, and what made World War I the first such war in history?

4. How was peace achieved, and what were the terms of that peace?

5. In what ways did the Great War contribute to revolution in Russia?

KEY TERMS

Allies, *p. 806*

April Theses, *p. 822*

Balfour Declaration, *p. 817*

Bolsheviks, *p. 819*

Central Powers, *p. 806*

Fourteen Points, *p. 826*

Schlieffen Plan, *p. 803*

soviets, *p. 818*

total war, *p. 815*

Treaty of Brest-Litovsk, *p. 823*

Treat of Versailles, *p. 827*

DISCOVERING WESTERN CIVILIZATION ONLINE

You can obtain more information about war and revolution between 1914 and 1920 at the Websites listed below. See also the Companion Website that accompanies this text, www.ablongman.com/kishlansky, which contains an online study guide and additional resources.

The War Europe Expected

Photos and Posters of the Great War

www.geocities.com/SoHo/Gallery/8054

These are sites of posters, photos, and art of World War I.

A New Kind of Warfare

Military History: World War I (1914–1918)

wps.cfc.dnd.ca/links/milhist/wwi.html

Sponsored by Canadian Forces College, this site provides an extensive set of links about World War I with emphasis on military history.

Adjusting to the Unexpected: Total War

World War I: Trenches on the Web

www.worldwar1.com/

This site on World War I is sponsored by the History Channel.

The Great War (1914–1918)

www.pitt.edu/~pugachev/greatwar/ww1.html

A comprehensive site containing primary text, summaries, and photos of the major events in World War I.

The War Poems & Manuscripts of Wilfred Owen

www.hcu.ox.ac.uk/jtap/warpoems.htm

This site contains 57 of Wilfred Owens' war poems.

The Russian Revolution and Allied Victory

Russian Revolution Resources

www.historyguide.org/europe/rusrev_links.html

This site provides electronic texts in English of Lenin and Trotsky and several other links to sites on the Russian Revolution.

Settling the Peace

The Versailles Treaty

history.acusd.edu/gen/text/versaillestreaty/vercontents.html

This site is devoted to the Versailles Treaty, including the text of all articles of the treaty.

SUGGESTIONS FOR FURTHER READING

The War Europe Expected

Keith Robbins, *The First World War* (Oxford: Oxford University Press, 1984). The author explores the major cultural, political, military, and social developments between 1914 and 1918, including the course of the land war and modes of warfare.

Jeffrey Verhey, *The Spirit of 1914: Militarism, Myth, and Mobilization in Germany* (Cambridge: Cambridge University Press, 2000). The author captures the fervor and patriotism that surrounded the August experiences and the declaration of war and chronicles the survival of the memory of the "spirit of 1914" in the postwar period.

A New Kind of Warfare

Roger Chickering, *Imperial Germany and the Great War, 1914–1918* (Cambridge: Cambridge University Press, 1998). The author offers a synthetic treatment of the history of the war and its impact on German society.

Frans Coetzee and Marilyn Shevin-Coetzee, eds., *Authority, Identity and the Social History of the Great War* (Providence: Berghahn Books, 1995). Recognizing that 1914 marks the beginning of the twentieth century, contributors examine the variety of national responses involved in waging total war and stress the interrelatedness of the home fronts and the battlefronts in affecting individual lives and identities.

Mark Cornwall, *The Undermining of Austria-Hungary: The Battle for Hearts and Minds* (New York: St. Martin's Press, 2000). This study presents extensive research on how propaganda was used by and against Austria-Hungary as a weapon of war.

Paul Fussell, *The Great War and Modern Memory* (New York: Oxford University Press, 2000). This twenty-fifth anniversary edition is a cultural history of World War I that treats the patterns and tendencies in war literature within the framework of a literary tradition.

John Keegan, *The First World War* (New York: Alfred A. Knopf, Inc., 1998). Keegan offers the definitive military history of the war based on diaries, letters, and reports, and in so doing illuminates the origins and progress of the war and the experience of the combatants.

Hew Strachan, ed., *The Oxford Illustrated History of the First World War* (Oxford: Oxford University Press, 1998). This extensively illustrated volume contains 23 chapters on key themes in the history of the Great War covering military issues, the home front, and the role of propaganda.

Adjusting to the Unexpected: Total War

Roger Chickering and Stig Förster, eds., *Great War, Total War: Combat and Mobilization on the Western Front, 1914–1918* (Cambridge: Cambridge University Press, 2000). In a collection of specialist essays, the authors consider the nineteenth-century origins of total industrialized warfare in search of a consensus on what constitutes total war.

Claire A. Culleton, *Working-Class Culture, Women, and Britain, 1914–1921* (New York: St. Martin's Press, 1999). A cultural and social history of British working-class women's experiences.

Belinda J. Davis, *Home Fires Burning: Food, Politics, and Everyday Life in World War I Berlin* (Chapel Hill: University of North Carolina Press, 2000). This thorough study examines the actions of women, especially poorer women, in Berlin during the war and the impact they had on politics and policy.

Patrick Fridenson, ed., *The French Home Front, 1914–1918* (Providence: Berg Publishers, 1992). The collection of articles demonstrates that unity on the home front concealed deep divisions, which led to open resistance and a redefined political universe at the end of the war.

Susan R. Grayzel, *Women's Identities at War: Gender, Motherhood, and Politics in Britain and France During the First World War* (Chapel Hill: University of North Carolina Press, 1999). A carefully documented cultural history of women's roles in World War I on the French and British home fronts.

Aviel Roshwald and Richard Stites, eds., *European Culture in the Great War: The Arts, Entertainment, and Propaganda, 1914–1918* (Cambridge: Cambridge University Press, 1999). This volume encompasses Europe to include western and eastern Europe and the South Slavic lands and examines the relationship between culture and politics during the war.

Jay Winter, Geoffrey Parker, and Mary Habeck, eds., *The Great War and the Twentieth Century* (New Haven, CT: Yale University Press, 2000). This volume of essays by leading scholars contributes to a comparative history of total war in the twentieth century.

The Russian Revolution and Allied Victory

Jane Burbank, *Intelligentsia and Revolution: Russian Views of Bolshevism, 1917–1922* (New York: Oxford University Press, 1982). The author examines the thinking of Russian intellectuals from the beginnings of revolution to the consolidation of Bolshevik power.

Sheila Fitzpatrick, *The Russian Revolution, 1917–1932* (Oxford: Oxford University Press, 1982). An analysis of the October Revolution of 1917 from the perspective of Stalinist society. The February and October revolutions of 1917, the civil war, and the economic policies of the 1920s are treated as various aspects of a single revolutionary movement.

Jane McDermid and Anna Hillyar, *Midwives of the Revolution: Female Bolsheviks and Women Workers in 1917* (Athens, OH: Ohio University Press, 1999). This work provides a good overview of the importance of women's actions in the Russian Revolution.

Settling the Peace

Manfred E. Boemeke, Gerald D. Feldman, Elisabeth Glaser, eds., *The Treaty of Versailles: A Reassessment After 75 Years* (Cambridge: Cambridge University Press, 1998). The volume is a synthetic reappraisal of the peace treaty, divergent peace aims, and postwar context in which it was developed.

David Stevenson, *The First World War and International Politics* (Oxford: Oxford University Press, 1988). A study of the global ramifications of World War I, this work traces the development of war aims on both sides, the reasons peace negotiations failed, and why compromise proved elusive.

For a list of additional titles related to this chapter's topics, please see http://www.ablongman.com/kishlansky.

Chapter 27

THE EUROPEAN SEARCH FOR STABILITY, 1920–1939

Chapter Outline

In the aftermath of the Great War, unstable economies and runaway inflation extended the suffering and devastation in countries such as Germany. In The Visual Record, see how one German artist depicted the forces behind such misery and how one German citizen coped with the painful reality. ➤

THE HARD LESSONS OF INFLATION

For many who survived the horrors of the Great War, worse disruptions were in store. Inflation, like combat, wreaked havoc with people's lives. During the war, prices had doubled in Great Britain, the United States, Germany, Canada, and Japan. Prices had tripled in France and Sweden; in Italy, they had quadrupled. But all of that was nothing compared to what happened after the war in Germany, Austria, Hungary, Poland, and Russia. Inflation was so great, with prices increasing astronomically— by tens of thousands of times as much—that a new term had to be created for the runaway inflation: *hyperinflation*. As prices reached staggering heights, currencies collapsed. In Germany in 1918, one prewar gold mark was worth two paper marks; by 1923, it took one billion paper marks to match a single gold mark in value. The currency was worthless. German people's hopes and futures disappeared into the abyss of the nine zeroes it took to write a numerical billion.

In war it is important to identify the enemy. So too in hyperinflation did people seek out the adversary. The German expressionist artist George Grosz (1893–1959) was renowned for portraying the decadence and corruption of bourgeois society in the 1920s. In the painting shown here entitled *The Pillars of Society,* Grosz caricatured postwar Germany as composed of corrupt judges, greedy businessmen, mercenary militarists, and hypocritical pacifists.

Many believed that the postwar republican government of Germany was to blame because it had accepted a harsh peace treaty and made reparations payments. Socialists and Communists were singled out for special disdain. Jewish politicians, bankers, and financiers became scapegoats for Germany's economic problems. Confidence in the state evaporated. The German people learned that the economy was neither stable nor self-correcting. They learned in the harshest way possible that the economy responded to political choices and international events. Social groups accused one another. Small businessmen blamed big capitalists. Civil servants saw unionized workers as the problem. Retailers blamed wholesalers.

Men and women who spend money on food, clothing, and shelter do not have to be schooled in basic facts about money;

■ George Grosz, *The Pillars of Society*. bpk, Berlin/Art Resource, NY/© Estate of George Grosz/Licensed by VAGA, New York, NY

they learn on a daily basis how the prices of coffee, orange juice, or gasoline fluctuate in relation to factors far beyond their control. But no amount of sophistication in the marketplace could have prepared people for the harsh realities of the German economy in the 1920s.

832

Inflation began in Germany during the war. It was caused by the government's decision to print money rather than levying taxes to pay off war debts. After the war, inflation continued because big business in need of new capital and organized labor in search of jobs benefited from it. The inflation was further aggravated by depreciation of the currencies in central and eastern European countries. Depreciation was prompted by the hollow hope that by making currencies worth less, exports would be more attractive and would earn the foreign exchange so necessary for prosperity. The Allied demands for reparations payments further undermined confidence in the mark. The result was that double-digit inflation turned into hyperinflation in the spring of 1922. When the French army occupied the Ruhr and the German government printed money to subsidize the miners and trainmen who were conducting passive resistance, inflation became astronomical.

More and more paper money came into circulation without any corresponding increase in the amount of goods and services. Almost 2000 printing presses ran around the clock. As the value of money plummeted, prices soared. A handful of apples cost cartloads of paper currency—hundreds of billions of marks at the height of the inflation in the summer of 1923. People were paid twice a day so that they could rush to stores during their breaks and spend their earnings before their money became worth even less.

Working people were malnourished, the unemployed starved. Only one in three German workers was fully employed by the end of 1923. Death rates rose as sicknesses related to poor diets spread. Few people could afford hospital care or doctors' fees. The middle classes suffered most from hyperinflation. Their savings were wiped out, their investments destroyed, their property stripped from them. Widows and the aged living on pensions were reduced to poverty, and civil servants and teachers became paupers overnight, as previously comfortable salaries dwindled. Hyperinflation gave new meaning to the old saying that the money wasn't worth the paper it was printed on, a saying that is seen in action here in the photograph of a German housewife lighting her stove with millions of marks because it was cheaper to use the currency for kindling than to buy wood with it. With soaring prices, people lost security and stability just as surely as if they had been in a military upheaval.

■ A German housewife uses worthless currency to light her stove.

Looking Ahead

In this chapter, we shall begin with a geographical tour of Europe that allows us to consider how economic and security issues fueled national and territorial tensions. The Germans blamed the French for their reparations demands, and their invading troops for the plight of Germany. Hyperinflation had extremely negative repercussions for democracy, as extremists on both the left and right blamed their liberal political leaders. When the Great Depression that began in 1929 hit European economies, the fear of new inflation prevented governments from using deficit spending to bring back prosperity. The Soviet Union, isolated from international politics and international markets, pursued its own separate path of forced economic development at great human and social costs. In Italy and Germany, fascist dictatorships promised solutions to all economic problems. People, having grown cynical and defiant through suffering, sought security in extraordinary and extrademocratic solutions. ➤

GEOGRAPHICAL TOUR
Europe After 1918

The armistice that ended World War I in 1918 did not stop the process of social upheaval and transformations challenging attempts to restore order throughout Europe (see **Map A**). In 1918, parts of war-torn Europe faced the possibility of revolution. Russia, where revolution had destroyed tsardom, expectantly watched revolutionary developments in countries from the British Isles to eastern Europe. The Bolshevik leaders of Russia's revolution counted on the capitalist system to destroy itself. That did not happen. By 1921, revolutions had been brutally crushed in Berlin, Munich, and Budapest. The Soviets, meanwhile, had won the civil war against the Whites and survived the intervention of the British, French, Japanese,

and Americans. But the new Russian regime was diplomatically isolated and in a state of almost total economic collapse.

In 1917–1918, the United States had played a significant and central role in the waging of war and in the pursuit of peace. Under U.S. President Woodrow Wilson, who urged his country to guarantee European security and guide Europe's future, the United States seemed promising as an active and positive force in international politics. By 1921, however, the United States had retreated to a position, not of isolation, but of selective involvement. With one giant, Russia, devastated and isolated, and the other, the United States, reluctant, Europeans faced an uncertain future.

New Nation-States, New Problems

Before World War I, east-central Europe was a region divided among four great empires—the Ottoman, the Habsburg, the Russian, and the German. Under the pressure of defeat, those

■ **Map A. Europe After World War I.** The peace settlement dismantled the four great empires in Europe—the Ottoman, Habsburg, Russian, and German—and created new sovereign states.

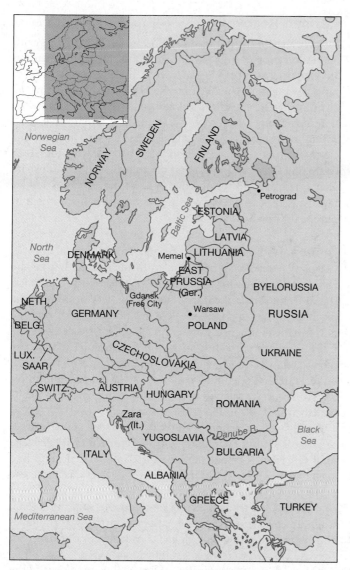

■ **Map B. East-Central Europe.** A dozen sovereign states were created in east-central Europe in the hope that they would serve as an independent buffer between Russia and Germany and guarantee peace.

states. Yugoslavia was pieced together from a patchwork of territories. Romania swelled, fed on a diet of settlement concessions. The new nations assured the victorious powers, especially France, that the new political geography of east-central Europe would guarantee the peace.

The Instability of Self-Determination. World War I victor nations hoped that the new states would stabilize European affairs; they could not have been more wrong. They erred in three important ways in their calculations. Many of the new states were internally unstable precisely because of the principle of national self-determination, the idea that nationalities had the right to rule themselves. Honoring the rights of nationalities was simple in the abstract, but application of the principle proved complicated and at times impossible. Religious, linguistic, and ethnic diversity abounded in the newly formed nations, and recognizing nationality often meant ignoring the rights of minorities. In Czechoslovakia, for example, the Czechs dominated the Slovaks and the Germans even though the Czechs were fewer in number. Ethnic unrest plagued all of eastern Europe. Minority tensions weakened and destabilized the fragile governments.

The struggle for economic prosperity further destabilized the new governments. East-central Europe was primarily agricultural, and the existence of the great empires had created guaranteed markets. The war disrupted the economy and generated social unrest. The peace settlements only compounded the economic problems of the region. When the Habsburg Empire disintegrated, the Danube River basin ceased to be a cohesive economic unit. New governments were saddled with borders that made little economic sense.

Creating cohesive economic units proved an insurmountable task for newly formed governments and administrations that lacked both resources and experience. Low productivity, unemployment, and overpopulation characterized most of east-central Europe. Attempts to industrialize and to develop new markets confronted many obstacles. Much of the land was farmed on a subsistence basis. What agricultural surplus was created was difficult to sell abroad. East-central Europeans—including Poles, Czechs, Yugoslavs, and Romanians, all tied to France through military and political commitments—were excluded from western European markets and were isolated economically from their treaty allies. Economic ties with Germany endured in ways that perpetuated economic dependence and threatened future survival.

Border Disputes. Common borders produced tensions over territories. The peace settlements made no one happy. Poland quarreled with Lithuania; Czechoslovakia vied with Poland over territorial claims. War broke out between Poland and Russia for six months in 1920 over the creation of an independent Ukrainian state. The Bolsheviks counterattacked and tried to turn the conflict into a revolutionary war in order to spread communism to central Europe. The Poles turned the Russians back. The Treaty of Riga, signed in March 1921, gave Poland much but not all of the territory it claimed.

empires collapsed into their component national parts, and when the dust of the peace treaties had settled, the region had been molded into a dozen sovereign states (see **Map B**). The victorious Allies hoped that independent states newly created from fragments of empire would buffer Europe from the spread of communism westward and the expansion of German power eastward.

New independent states emerged at the center of Europe because of national movements and local leadership. Finland achieved independence from Russia in 1917. Estonia, Latvia, and Lithuania, also formerly under Russian rule, comprised the now independent Baltic states (see **Map B**). After more than a century of dismemberment among three empires, Poland successfully laid claim to being a single nation once again. Czechoslovakia was carved out of former Habsburg lands. Austria and Hungary shriveled to small, independent

■ **Map C. Germany.** France hoped to hem Germany in, according to the terms of the peace settlement. France regained from Germany the territories of Alsace and Lorraine that France had lost in the Franco-Prussian War in 1870. In the 1920s, the French began building massive fortifications, known as the Maginot Line, along the frontier with Germany.

Hungary, having lost the most territory in World War I, held the distinction of having the greatest number of territorial grievances against its neighbors—Czechoslovakia, Romania, and Yugoslavia. Yugoslavia made claims against Austria. Bulgaria sought territories controlled by Greece and Romania. Ethnicity, strategic considerations, and economic needs motivated claims for territory. Disputes festered, fed by the intense nationalism that prevented the cooperation necessary for survival.

Germany, the Soviet Union, and Italy further complicated the situation with their own territorial claims against their east-central European neighbors. The new German government refused to accept the loss of the "corridor" controlled by Poland that severed East Prussia from the rest of Germany. Nor was Germany resigned to the loss of part of Silesia to Poland (see **Map C**). Russia refused to forget its losses to Romania, Poland, Finland, and the Baltic states. Italy, too weak to act on its own, nevertheless dreamed of expansion into Yugoslavia, Austria, and Albania. The redefined borders of eastern and central Europe produced animosity and the seeds of ongoing conflict. The new states of eastern Europe stood as a picket fence between Germany and Russia, a fence that held little promise of guaranteeing the peace or of making good neighbors.

German Recovery

Germany, the most populous nation in western Europe with 60 million people, emerged apparently strong from defeat. In 1919, the German people endorsed a new liberal and democratic government, the **Weimar Republic,** so named for the city in which its constitution had been written. The constitution of the new government was unusually progressive, with voting rights for women and extensive civil liberties for German citizens. Because World War I had not been fought in Germany, German transportation networks and industrial plants had escaped serious damage. Its industry was fed by raw materials and energy resources unsurpassed anywhere in Europe outside Russia.

Territorial Advantages and Goals. In east-central Europe, Germany had actually benefited from the dismantling of the Habsburg Empire and the removal of Poland and the Baltic states from Russian control. Replacing its formerly large neighbor to the east were weak states potentially susceptible to Germany's influence. Because the governments of east-central Europe feared communism, they were not likely to ally themselves with the Soviet state. The existence of the small buffer states left open the possibility of German collaboration with Russia, since the two large nations might be able to negotiate their interests in the area.

On its western frontier, Germany's prospects were not so bright. Alsace and Lorraine had been returned to France (see **Map C**). From German territory, a demilitarized zone had been created in the Rhineland. The Saar district was under the protection of League of Nations commissioners, and the Saar coal mines were transferred to French ownership until 1935, when a plebiscite returned the region to Germany. Humiliated and betrayed by the geographic consequences of its defeat, Germany looked to recover its status.

Germany's primary foreign policy goal was revision of the treaty settlements of World War I. German politicians and military leaders perceived disarmament, loss of territory, and payment of reparations as serious obstacles in restoring Germany's position as a great power. German statesmen sought liberation of the Rhineland from foreign military occupation, return of the Saar basin, and recovery of the Corridor and Upper Silesia from Poland.

German leaders set economic recovery as the basis of their new foreign policy. In 1922, Germany signed the Treaty of Rapallo with Russia, a peacetime partnership that shocked the Western powers. Economics motivated the new Russo-German alliance: German industry needed markets, and the Russians needed loans to reconstruct their economy. Both states wanted to break out of the isolation imposed on them by the victors of World War I. However, Germany quickly learned that markets in Russia were limited and that hopes for recovery depended on financial cooperation with western Europe and the United States. At the end of 1923, Gustav Stresemann (1878–1929) assumed direction of the German Foreign Ministry and began to implement a conciliatory policy toward France and Britain. By displaying peaceful intentions, he hoped to secure American capital for German industry and win the support of the West for the revision of the peace settlement.

The Locarno Treaties. Stresemann joined his French and British counterparts, Aristide Briand (1862–1932) and Austen Chamberlain (1863–1937), in fashioning a series of treaties at Locarno, Switzerland, in 1925. In a spirit of cooperation, Germany, France, and Belgium promised never again to go to war against each other and to respect the demilitarized zone that separated them. Britain and Italy "guaranteed" the borders of all three countries and ensured the integrity of the demilitarized zone. The treaties initiated an atmosphere of goodwill, a "spirit of Locarno," that heralded a new age of security and nonaggression.

However, Germany did not renounce its ambitions in eastern Europe. Stresemann expected Germany to recover the territory lost to Poland. He also knew that Germany must rearm and expand to the east. From the early 1920s until 1933, Germany secretly rearmed. Undercover, Germany rebuilt its army and trained its soldiers and airmen on Russian territory. In violation of Versailles treaty agreements, Germany planned to be once again a great power with the same rights as other European countries.

France's Search for Security

Having learned the harsh lessons of 1870–1871 and 1914–1918, France understood well the threat posed by a united, industrialized, and well-armed Germany. During the years immediately following World War I, France deeply distrusted Germany. France had a smaller population of 40 million people and lower industrial production than Germany. France had been devastated by the war, and Germany had not. But France did have certain advantages in 1921. It had the best-equipped army in the world. Germany was disarmed. The Rhineland was demilitarized and occupied. But France knew that without the support of Great Britain and the United States, it could not enforce the Treaty of Versailles and keep Germany militarily weak.

The Americans and the British refused to conclude a long-term peacetime alliance with the French. In search of allies on the Continent, therefore, France committed itself to an alliance in the east with Poland and the Little Entente nations of Czechoslovakia, Romania, and Yugoslavia. Treaties with the four states of east-central Europe gave France some security in the event of an attack. But the treaties were also liabilities because France would have to fight to defend east-central Europe.

To keep Germany militarily and economically weak, the French attempted to enforce the Treaty of Versailles fully in 1921–1923. They were willing to do so alone if necessary. In 1923, the French army invaded the Ruhr district of Germany and occupied it with the intention of collecting reparations payments. But the Ruhr invasion served only to isolate France further from its wartime allies. France depended on loans from American banks to balance its budget, and the Americans disapproved of the French use of military might to enforce the treaty.

In 1924–1925, France decided to cooperate with the United States and Great Britain rather than continue a policy of enforcing the treaty alone and attempting to keep Germany weak. France withdrew its army from the Ruhr and some troops from the Rhineland. It agreed to lower German reparations payments. In addition, by signing the Locarno treaties, France cooperated with the Anglo-American policy that rejected the use of military force against Germany and promoted German economic recovery.

French anxiety about security continued, however. Nothing indicated the nature of that anxiety more clearly than the construction, beginning in the late 1920s, of the Maginot Line, a system of defensive fortifications between Germany and France (see **Map C**).

Throughout the 1920s, French political leaders tried to engage Great Britain in guaranteeing the security of France and Europe. The British agreed to defend France and Belgium against possible German aggression. They stopped short, however, of promising to defend Poland and Czechoslovakia. After settling the matter at Locarno, Britain largely reverted to its prewar pattern of withdrawing from continental Europe and concentrating its attention on the demands of its global empire.

The United States in Europe

The Treaty of Versailles marked the demise of European autonomy. American intervention had boosted French and British morale during the crucial months of 1917. In providing financial help, ships, troops, and supplies, the United States had rescued the Allied powers. After the war, a balance of power in Europe could not be maintained without outside help. Germany had been defeated, but if it recovered, France and Britain alone probably would not be able to contain it. Security and peace now depended on the presence of the United States to guarantee a stable balance of power in Europe and to defend Western hegemony in the world.

The United States was unwilling to assume a new role as political leader of Europe and mediator of European conflict. It refused to sign a joint peace, arranging instead a separate peace with Germany. It also refused to join the League of Nations. Following the war, the League had been devised as an international body of nations committed, according to article 10 of its covenant, to "respect and preserve as against external aggression the territorial integrity and existing political independence" of others. Germany was excluded from membership until 1926, and the Union of Soviet Socialist Republics (USSR) was denied entry until 1934. Otherwise, the League of Nations claimed a global membership. But the absence of U.S. support and the lack of any machinery to enforce its decisions undermined the possibility of the League's long-term effectiveness. Hopes that the international body could serve as a peacekeeper collapsed in 1931 with the League's failure to deal with the crisis of Japanese aggression against Manchuria.

The United States persisted in avoiding political and military obligations in Europe, with the idea of protecting its own freedom and autonomy. Instead, it sought to promote German economic recovery and reasoned that a peaceful and stable Europe would be reestablished without a real balance of power in Europe and without a commitment from the United States.

Many feared that territorial settlements of the peace held the promise of another war. Even efforts at comprehensive international cooperation such as the League of Nations did not overcome the problem of competitive nations, nor did the Kellogg-Briand Pact, signed by 23 nations in 1928. Named for U.S. Secretary of State Frank B. Kellogg (1856–1937) and French foreign minister Aristide Briand, who devised the plan, the pact renounced war. In the atmosphere of the 1920s, a time of hope and caution, the agreement carried all the weight of an empty gesture.

CRISIS AND COLLAPSE IN A WORLD ECONOMY

In 1918, the belligerent nations—winners and losers alike—had big bills on their hands. Although nations at war had borrowed from their own populations through the sale of war bonds, private citizens could not provide all the money needed to finance four years of war.

International Loans and Trade Barriers

France borrowed from Great Britain. Both Great Britain and France took loans from the United States. When all else failed, belligerent nations could and did print money not backed by productive wealth. Because more money had claims on the same amount of national wealth, the money in circulation was worth less. When the people who had purchased war bonds were then paid off with depreciated currency, they lost real wealth. Inflation had the same effect as taxation. The people had less wealth and the government had less debt.

The United States, for the first time in history the leading creditor nation in the world, had no intention of wiping the slate clean by forgiving war debts. Nor did it intend to accept repayment in less valuable postwar currencies: loans were tied to gold. Britain, France, and Belgium counted on reparations from Germany to pay their war debts and to rebuild their economies. Reparations were calculated on the basis of the damages Germany had inflicted on the Allies. The postwar Reparations Commission determined that Germany owed the

MARRIED AGAIN

IRELAND, *THE COLUMBUS DISPATCH*

■ "Married Again." This 1928 cartoon shows the wicked world once again pledging eternal fidelity to peace with the signing of the Kellogg-Briand Pact. The cynical attitude of the artist was vindicated by the events of the later twentieth century.

PASSING THE BUCK.

■ A British cartoonist's view of the reparations problem following World War I.

victors 132 billion gold marks ($33 billion), to be paid in annual installments of 2 billion gold marks ($500 million), plus 26 percent of the value of German exports.

For the German people and for German leaders, reparations were an unacceptable punitive levy that mortgaged the prosperity of future generations. Germany, too, wanted to recover from the years of privation of the war. Substantial reparations payments would have transferred real wealth from Germany to the Allies. Transferring wealth would have cut into any increase in the German standard of living in the 1920s, and it would have diminished the investment needed to make the German economy grow. Instead, the German government printed huge amounts of currency. The mark collapsed and world currencies were endangered.

With financial disaster looming, the British and Americans decided to intervene. A plan had to be devised that would permit Germany to prosper while funneling payments to France, which was so dependent on reparations for its own recovery and for its war debt payments to the United States. In 1924, the American banker Charles G. Dawes (1865–1951), along with a group of international financial experts appointed by the Allied governments, devised a solution to the reparations problem. The Dawes Plan aimed to end inflation and restore economic prosperity in Germany by giving Germany a more modest and realistic schedule of payments and by extending a loan from American banks to get payments started.

As important as reparations and war debts are in understanding the Western world in the 1920s, they cannot be considered in isolation. Debtor nations, whether Allies paying back loans to the United States or defeated nations paying reparations to the victors, needed to be able to sell their goods

in world markets. They saw trade as the principal way to accumulate enough national income to pay back what they owed and to prosper domestically without burying their citizens under a mountain of new taxes.

If trade was to be the stepladder out of the financial hole of indebtedness, open markets and stable currencies were its rungs. The United States recognized that a stable Europe would give it a market for its own agricultural and industrial products and provide a guarantee for recovery of its loans and investments. Yet the proverbial monkey wrench in a smoothly functioning international economy was the trade policy of the United States. Republican political leaders in the United States insisted on high tariffs to protect domestic goods against imports. But high tariffs prevented Europeans from selling in the United States and earning the dollars they needed to repay war debts.

While blocking imports, the United States planned to expand its own exports to world markets, especially to Europe. The problem for American exporters, however, was the instability of European currencies in the first half of the 1920s. All over Europe, governments allowed inflation to rise with the expectation that depreciating currencies would make their goods cheaper in world markets and hence more salable.

Depreciating European currencies on the one hand meant an appreciating dollar on the other. For the "grand design" of U.S. trade expansion, a strong dollar was no virtue. More and more German marks, British pounds, and French francs had to be spent to purchase American goods. The result was that fewer American exports were sold in European markets. Because two-thirds of Germany's long-term credits came from the United States, Germany's fate was directly linked to the fortunes of American financial centers. Conversely, the soundness of American banks depended on a solvent Germany, which now absorbed 18 percent of U.S. capital exports.

Despite the scaled-down schedule of the Dawes Plan, reparations remained a bitter pill for German leaders and the German public to swallow. In 1929, American bankers devised another plan under the leadership of the American businessman Owen D. Young (1874–1962), chairman of the board of General Electric. Although the Young Plan initially transferred $100 million to Germany, Germans saw the twentieth century stretching before them as year after year of nothing but humiliating reparations payments. To make matters worse, after 1928 American private loans shriveled in Germany as American investors sought the higher yields of a booming stock market at home.

Europe as a whole made rapid progress in manufacturing production during the second half of the decade, and by 1929 it had surpassed its prewar (1913) per capita income. Yet structural weaknesses were present, although they went almost unnoticed. The false security of a new gold standard masked the instability and interdependence of currencies. Low prices prevailed in the agricultural sector, keeping the incomes of a significant segment of the population depressed. But the low rate of long-term capital investment was obscured in the flurry of short-term loans, whose disappearance in 1928 spelled the beginning of the end for European recovery. The protectionist trade policy of the United States conflicted with its insistence on repayment of war debts. Germany's resentment over reparations was in no way alleviated by the Dawes and Young repayment plans. The irresponsibility of American speculation in the stock market pricked the bubble of prosperity. None of those factors operated in isolation to cause the collapse that began in 1929. Taken together, however, they caused a depression of previously unimagined severity in the international economic system.

The Great Depression

In the history of the Western world, the year 1929 has assumed mythic proportions. During one week in October of that year, the stock market in the United States collapsed. That crash set off the **Great Depression** in an international economic system already plagued with structural problems. It also marked the beginning of a long period of worldwide economic stagnation and depression.

Dependence on the American Economy. A confluence of factors made Europe and the rest of the world vulnerable to reversals in the American economy. Heavy borrowing and reliance on American investment throughout the 1920s contributed to the inherent instability of European economies. Even Great Britain, itself a creditor, relied on short-term loans; "borrowing short and lending long" proved to be disastrous when loans were recalled. Excessive lending and leniency were fatal mistakes of creditor nations, especially the United States. When, in the summer of 1929, American investors turned off the tap of the flow of capital to search for higher profits at home, a precarious situation began to get worse.

A depression is a severe economic downturn marked by sharp declines in income and production as buying and selling slow down to a crawl. Depressions were not new in the business cycles of modern economies, but what happened in October 1929 was more serious in its extent and duration than any depression before or since. The bottom was not reached until three years after the Great Depression began. In 1932, one in four American workers was without a job. One in three banks had closed its doors. People lost their homes, unable to pay their mortgages; farmers lost their land, unable to earn enough to survive. The great prosperity of the 1920s had vanished overnight.

DOCUMENT
Oral Account of the Great Depression

The plight of the United States rippled through world markets. Americans stopped buying foreign goods. The Smoot-Hawley Tariff Act, passed by the U.S. Congress in 1930, created an impenetrable tariff fortress against agricultural and manufactured imports and hampered foreign producers. The major trading nations of the world, including Great Britain, enacted similar protectionist measures. American investment abroad dried up as the lifelines of American capital to Europe were cut.

European nations tried to staunch the outward flow of capital and gold by restricting the transfer of capital abroad. Large amounts of foreign-owned gold ($6.6 billion from 1931 to 1938) nevertheless were deposited in American banks. In 1931, President Herbert Hoover (1874–1964) supported a moratorium on the payment of reparations and war debts. The moratorium, combined with the pooling of gold in the United States, led to a run on the British pound sterling in 1931 and the collapse of Great Britain as one of the world's great financial centers.

Political Repercussions. The gold standard disappeared from the international economy, never to return. So, too, did reparations payments and war debts when the major nations of Europe met without the United States at a special conference held in Lausanne, Switzerland, in 1932. Something else

■ This poster for the October 1931 British General Election reflects the National Government's concern over mass unemployment and industrial stagnation. The coalition National Government swamped the opposition Labour Party, taking 556 Parliament seats to Labour's 51.

THE DEPRESSION FOR WOMEN

Winifred Holtby (1898–1935) was a British novelist, journalist, and social reformer who covered European political events throughout the interwar period. In this selection from her writings she chronicles the differential impact that war and economic depression had on women's lives. Expectations about woman's proper role, whether of housewife and mother or serving her country in the workplace, were profoundly political and hotly contested.

Focus Questions

What are the resentments Holtby describes caused by the gender division of labor? Why does Holtby place the word "natural" in quotes when speaking of "house-keeping and child-bearing"?

The effect of the slump upon women's economic position is most obvious, not only in the problems of unemployment among both industrial and professional women, but still more in the bitterness surrounding the question of married women's paid employment, "pin money" office girls, unorganized casual female factory labour, and claims to alimony, maintenance, and separation allowances. These are the dilemmas of scarcity. It is here that the shoe pinches when national purchasing power has failed to distribute adequately the products of industry.

During the War, women entered almost every branch of industry and most of the professions. . . . In transport, engineering, chemicals, textiles, tailoring and woodwork, women took the places which, ever since the sorting-out process which followed the first disorganized scramble of the Industrial Revolution, had been reserved to men. They took and they enjoyed them.

Then the men returned, and on demobilization demanded again the jobs which they had left. The position was not simple.

Some of the men had received promises that their work should be kept for them; but of these, some did not return. Some women surrendered their shovels, lathes, and hoes without a grievance. Their work had been "for the duration of the war" and they had no desire to retain it.

But others thought differently. Women, they told themselves, had been excluded from the more highly-skilled and better-paid industrial posts for two or more generations. They had been told that certain processes were beyond their power. It was a lie. During the war they had proved it

to be so, by their own skill and efficiency. Why surrender without a word opportunities closed to them by fraud and falsehood? They had as much right to wheel, loom, or cash-register as any man. Why then pretend that they were intruders in a world which was as much their own as their brothers'? . . .

After 1928, jobs became not duties which war-time propaganda taught girls that it was patriotic to perform, but privileges to be reserved for potential bread-winners and fathers of families. Women were commanded to go back to the home.

The bitterness began which has lasted ever since—the women keeping jobs and the men resenting it—the men regaining the jobs and the women resenting it. . . .

In Italy, Germany, and Ireland a new dream of natural instinctive racial unity was arising, which designed for women a return to their "natural" functions of house-keeping and child-bearing; while in the English-speaking countries a new anti-rational philosophy combined with economic fatalism, militated against the ebullient hopes which an earlier generation had pinned to education, effort, and individual enterprise.

All generalizations are false. In every civilized country are little groups of older women with memories of suffrage struggles, and young women who grew up into the post-war optimism, and whose ideas remain unchanged by the fashions of the hour. It is they who still organize protests against reaction; who in national and international societies defend the political, civil, and economic equality of men and women; who invade new territories of achievement; who look towards a time when there shall be no wrangling over rights and wrongs, man's place and woman's place, but an equal and cooperative partnership, the individual going unfettered to the work for which he is best suited, responsibilities and obligations shared alike.

From Winifred Holtby, *Women in a Changing Civilization* (1934).

died at the end of the 1920s: confidence in a self-adjusting economy, an "invisible hand" by which the business cycle would be righted. During 1932–1933, the Great Depression, showing no signs of disappearing, reached its nadir and became a global phenomenon. Economic hardship transformed political realities. The Labour cabinet in Great

Britain was forced to resign, and a new national government composed of Conservative, Liberal, and Labour leaders was formed to deal with the world economic emergency. Republican government was torn by bitter divisions in France. In the United States, the Republican party, which had been in power since 1920, was defeated in 1932. Franklin D.

CHRONOLOGY
INTERNATIONAL POLITICS

1919	Creation of the League of Nations
1920	War between Poland and Russia
1921	Treaty of Riga
1922	Germany and Russia sign Treaty of Rapallo
1923	French and Belgian troops invade the Ruhr district
1924	Dawes Plan
1925	Locarno Treaties
1928	Kellogg-Briand Pact
1929	Young Plan
October 1929	Collapse of the U.S. stock market; beginning of the Great Depression
1935	Saar region returned to German control
1936	Germany stations troops in the Rhineland in violation of the Versailles Treaty

In the decade following the Great War, peace settlements did not promote a stable international community. Instead, self-determination of peoples created new grounds for national rivalries in eastern Europe, and the lack of any effective means of guaranteeing the peace only exacerbated prewar animosities. The economic interdependence of nation-states through an international system of reparations payments and loans increased the vulnerability of governments to external pressures. With the collapse of the international finance system in 1929, political stability and international cooperation seemed more elusive than ever.

THE SOVIET UNION'S SEPARATE PATH

In the 1920s, the Soviet state was also faced with solving its economic problems. Lenin's successor, Joseph Stalin (1879–1953), obliged the Soviet people to achieve in a single generation and in isolation what it had taken the West a century and a half to accomplish.

The Soviet Regime at the End of the Civil War

Echoing Karl Marx, the Bolshevik leader Lenin declared that the revolution and the civil war had been won in the name of "the dictatorship of the proletariat." The hammer and sickle on the Soviet flag represented the united rule of workers and peasants and were symbolic reminders of the commitment to rule from below. But at the end of the civil war in 1921, the Bolsheviks, not the people, were in charge.

DOCUMENT

Lenin Calls for Electrification of All Russia

Roosevelt (1882–1945), a Democrat, was elected president in a landslide victory with a mandate to transform the American economy. German democratic institutions were pulled down in favor of fascist dictatorship.

■ As members of the Politburo, Leon Trotsky (left), Nikolai Bukharin (center), and Joseph Stalin (right) each tried to direct Soviet economic policy. Only the politically shrewd Stalin would emerge victorious.

The industrial sector, small as it was, was in total disarray by 1921. Famine and epidemics in 1921–1922 killed and weakened more people than the Great War and the civil war combined. The countryside had been plundered to feed the Red and White armies. The combination of empty promises and a declining standard of living left workers and peasants frustrated and discontented. Urban strikes and rural uprisings defied short-term solutions. The proletarian revolutionary heroes of 1917 were rejecting the new Soviet regime. The Bolshevik party now faced the task of restoring a country exhausted by war and revolution, its resources depleted, its economy destroyed.

At the head of the Soviet state was Lenin, the first among equals in the seven-man Politburo. The Central Committee of the Communist party decided "fundamental questions of policy, international and domestic," but in reality the Politburo, the inner circle of the Central Committee, held the reins of power.

Among seven members of the Politburo, three in particular attempted to leave their mark on the direction of Soviet policy: Leon Trotsky, Nikolai Bukharin (1888–1938), and Joseph Stalin. The great drama of Soviet leadership in the 1920s revolved around how the most brilliant (Trotsky) and the most popular (Bukharin) failed at the hands of the most shrewdly political (Stalin).

The two extremes in the debate over the direction of economic development were, on the one hand, a planned economy totally directed from above and, on the other hand, an economy controlled from below. In 1920–1921, Leon Trotsky, at that time the people's commissar of war, favored a planned economy based on the militarization of labor. Trade unions opposed such a proposal and argued for a share of control over production. Lenin, however, favored a proletarian democracy and supported unions organized independently of state control.

The controversy was resolved in the short run at the Tenth Party Congress in 1921, when Lenin chose to steer a middle course between trade union autonomy and militarization by preserving the unions and at the same time insisting on the state's responsibility for economic development. His primary goal was to stabilize Bolshevik rule in its progress toward socialism. He recognized that nothing could be achieved without the peasants. As a result, Lenin found himself embracing a new economic policy that he termed a "temporary retreat" from Communist goals.

The New Economic Policy, 1921–1928

In 1921, Lenin ended the forced requisitioning of peasant produce that had been in effect during the civil war. In its place, peasants were to pay a tax in kind, that is, a fixed portion of their yield, to the state. Peasants, in turn, were permitted to reinstate private trade on their own terms. Party leaders accepted the dramatic shift in economic policy because it held the promise of prosperity so necessary for political stability. The actions of Lenin to return the benefits of productivity to the economy, combined with those of the peasants to

reestablish markets, created the **New Economic Policy (NEP)** that emerged in the spring and summer of 1921.

Bukharin's Role.   It remained for Nikolai Bukharin to give shape and substance to the economic policy that permitted Russian producers to engage in some capitalist practices. As one of the founding fathers of the Soviet state and the youngest of the top Bolshevik leaders, Bukharin took his place on the Central Committee of the Communist party and on the Politburo as well.

Bukharin set about solving Russia's single greatest problem: how could Russia, crippled by poverty, find enough capital to industrialize? Insisting on the need for long-term economic planning, Bukharin counted on a prosperous and contented peasantry as the mainstay of his policy. Bukharin was also strongly interested in attracting foreign investment to Soviet endeavors as a way of ensuring future productivity.

Bukharin appreciated the importance of landholding to Russian peasants and defended a system of individual farms and private accumulation. Agriculture would operate through a market system, and the peasants would have the right to control their own surpluses. Rural prosperity would generate profits that could be used for gradual industrial development. Bukharin's policy stood in stark contrast to Stalin's later plan to feed industry by starving the agricultural sector.

Collective and large-scale farming had to be deferred indefinitely in order to reconcile the peasantry to the state—a policy profoundly at odds with the programs of the Communist state to pull down the capitalist system and establish socialism. In 1924, the tax in kind was replaced with a tax in cash. With that shift, the state now procured grain through commercial agencies and cooperative organizations instead of directly from the peasants. The move toward Western capitalist models seemed more pronounced than ever to critics of the NEP.

Beginning in 1922, Lenin suffered a series of strokes, which virtually removed him from power by March 1923. When he died on 21 January 1924, the Communist leadership split over the ambiguities of the NEP. The backward nature of agriculture did not permit the kind of productivity that the NEP policy makers had anticipated. Cities demanded more food as their populations swelled with the influx of unskilled workers from rural areas. In 1927, peasants held back their grain. The Soviet Union was then experiencing a series of foreign policy setbacks in the West and in China, and Bolshevik leaders spoke of an active anti-Soviet conspiracy by the capitalist powers, led by Great Britain. The Soviet state lowered the price of grain, thereby squeezing the peasantry. The war scare, combined with the drop in food prices, soon led to an economic crisis.

Stalin Takes Charge.   By 1928, the NEP was in trouble. Stalin, general secretary of the Communist party of the Soviet Union, saw his chance. Under his supervision, the state intervened to prevent peasants from disposing of their own grain surpluses. The peasants responded to requisitioning by hoarding their produce and violently rioting. Bukharin and the NEP were in danger. Stalin exploited the internal crisis and external dangers to eliminate his political rivals. Trotsky had been expelled from the Communist party in November 1927 on charges that he had engaged in antiparty activities. Banished from Russia in 1929, he eventually found refuge in Mexico, where he was assassinated in 1940 at Stalin's command.

Bukharin's popularity in the party also threatened Stalin's aspirations. Bukharin was dropped from the Politburo in 1929. Tolerated throughout the early 1930s, he was arrested in 1937, and tried and executed for alleged treasonous activities the following year. The fate that befell Trotsky and Bukharin was typical of what happened to those who stood in the way of Stalin's pursuit of dictatorial control. Stalin was, in a colleague's words, "a gray blur." Beneath his apparently colorless personality, however, was a dangerous man of great political acumen, a ruthless behind-the-scenes politician who controlled the machinery of the party for his own

ends and was not averse to employing violence in order to achieve them.

Stalin's Rise to Power

Joseph Stalin was born Iosif Vissarionovich Dzhugashvili in 1879. His self-chosen revolutionary name, Stalin, means "steel" in Russian and is as good an indication as any of his opinion of his own personality and will. Stalin, the man who ruled the Soviet Union as a dictator from 1928 until his death in 1953, was not a Russian. He was from Georgia, an area between the Black and Caspian seas, and spoke Russian with an accent. Georgia, with its land occupied and its people subjugated by invading armies for centuries, was annexed to the expanding Russian Empire in 1801.

As the youngest of four and the only surviving child of Vissarion and Ekaterina Dzhugashvili, Stalin endured a

THE RESULTS OF THE FIRST FIVE-YEAR PLAN

Under Joseph Stalin the Soviet Union embarked on rapid industrialization that transformed the peasant-based economy into a leading iron and steel producer. The Five-Year Plan achieved in four years what the Western industrialized nations took 150 years to accomplish. The Soviet leader did not tally the cost in human lives or the impact on the quality of life that such brutal economic transformation entailed.

Focus Questions

How is capitalism depicted as the enemy in this document? How are the impacts of the First Five-Year Plan similar for industry and agriculture? What elements of style and tone in the document indicate the propagandistic intent of Stalin, the author?

The fundamental task of the five-year plan was to transfer our country, with its backward, and in part medieval, technique, to the lines of new, modern technique.

The fundamental task of the Five-Year Plan was to convert the USSR from an agrarian and weak country, dependent upon the caprices of the capitalist countries, into an industrial and powerful country, fully self-reliant and independent of the caprices of world capitalism.

The fundamental task of the Five-Year Plan was, in converting the USSR into an industrial country, fully to eliminate the capitalist elements, to widen the front of socialist forms of economy, and to create the economic base for the abolition of classes in the USSR, for the construction of socialist society....

The fundamental task of the Five-Year Plan was to transfer small and scattered agriculture to the lines of large-scale collective farming, so as to ensure the economic base for socialism in the rural districts and thus to eliminate the possibility of the restoration of capitalism in the USSR.

Finally, the task of the Five-Year Plan was to create in the country all the necessary technical and economic prerequisites for increasing to the utmost the defensive capacity of the country, to enable it to organize determined resistance to any and every attempt at military intervention from outside, to any and every attempt at military attack from without....

What are the results of the Five-Year Plan in four years in the sphere of *industry*?

Have we achieved victory in this sphere?

Yes, we have....

We did not have an iron and steel industry, the foundation for the industrialization of the country. Now we have this industry.

We did not have a tractor industry. Now we have one.

We did not have an automobile industry. Now we have one.

We did not have a machine-tool industry. Now we have one.

We did not have a big and up-to-date chemical industry. Now we have one.

We did not have a real and big industry for the production of modern agricultural machinery. Now we have one.

childhood of brutal misery. Stalin's father was a poor and often unemployed shoemaker who intended that his son be apprenticed in the same trade. Under his mother's protection, young Iosif received an education and entered a seminary against his father's wishes. Iosif's schooling, extraordinary for someone of his poverty-stricken background, gave him the opportunity to learn about revolutionary socialist politics. At the turn of the century, Georgia had a strong Marxist revolutionary movement that opposed Russian exploitation. Iosif dropped out of the seminary in 1899 to engage in underground Marxist activities, and he soon became a follower of Lenin.

Stalin's association with Lenin kept him close to the center of power after the October Revolution of 1917. First as people's commissar for nationalities (1920–1923) and then as general secretary of the Central Committee of the Communist party (1922–1953), Stalin showed natural talent as a political strategist. His familiarity with non-Russian nationalities was a great asset in his dealings with the ethnic diversity and unrest in the vast Soviet state. Unlike party leaders who had lived in exile in western Europe before the revolution, Stalin had little knowledge of the West.

After Lenin's death in 1924, Stalin shrewdly bolstered his own reputation by orchestrating cult worship of Lenin. In 1929, Stalin used the occasion of his fiftieth birthday to fashion for himself a reputation as the living hero of the Soviet state. Icons, statues, busts, and images of all sorts of both Lenin and Stalin appeared everywhere in public buildings, schoolrooms, and homes. He systematically began eliminating his rivals so that he alone stood unchallenged as Lenin's true successor.

The First Five-Year Plan

The cult of Stalin coincided with the First Five-Year Plan (1929–1932), which launched Stalin's program of rapid

---

We did not have an aircraft industry. Now we have one.

In output of electric power we were last on the list. Now we rank among the first.

In output of oil products and coal we were last on the list. Now we rank among the first.

We had only one coal and metallurgical base—in the Ukraine—which we barely managed to keep going. We have not only succeeded in improving this base, but have created a new coal and metallurgical base—in the East—which is the pride of our country.

We had only one center of the textile industry—in the North of our country. As a result of our efforts we will have in the very near future two new centers of the textile industry—in Central Asia and Western Siberia.

And we have not only created these new great industries, but have created them on a scale and in dimensions that eclipse the scale and dimensions of European industry.

And as a result of all this the capitalist elements have been completely and irrevocably eliminated from industry, and socialist industry has become the sole form of industry in the USSR.

And as a result of all this our country has been converted from an agrarian into an industrial country; for the proportion of industrial output, as compared with agricultural output, has risen from 48 percent of the total in the beginning of the Five-Year Plan period (1928) to 70 percent at the end of the fourth year of the Five-Year Plan period (1932). . . .

The object of the Five-Year Plan in the sphere of agriculture was to unite the scattered and small individual peasant farms, which lacked the opportunity of utilizing tractors and modern agricultural machinery, into large collective farms, equipped with all the modern implements of highly developed agriculture, and to cover unoccupied land with model state farms. . . .

The party has succeeded, in a matter of three years, in organizing more than 200,000 collective farms and about 5000 state farms specializing mainly in grain growing and livestock raising, and at the same time it has succeeded, in the course of four years, in enlarging the crop area by 21,000,000 hectares.

The party has succeeded in getting more than 60 percent of the peasant farms, which account for more than 70 percent of the land cultivated by peasants, to unite into collective farms, which means that we have *fulfilled* the Five-Year Plan *threefold*.

The party has succeeded in creating the possibility of obtaining, not 500,000,000 to 600,000,000 poods[1] of marketable grain, which was the amount purchased in the period when individual peasant farming predominated, but 1,200,000,000 to 1,400,000,000 poods of grain annually.

The party has succeeded in routing the kulaks as a class, although they have not yet been dealt the final blow; the laboring peasants have been emancipated from kulak bondage and exploitation, and a firm economic basis for the Soviet government, the basis of collective farming, has been established in the countryside.

The party has succeeded in converting the USSR from a land of small peasant farming into a land where agriculture is run on the largest scale in the world.

Such, in general terms, are the results of the Five-Year Plan in four years in the sphere of agriculture.

From Joseph Stalin, *Selected Writings* (1942).

[1]Pood—a unit of weight equivalent to 36.1 pounds.

■ This 1931 Soviet political poster exhorts workers "Join our kolkhoz [collective farm]." A year later, the process of collectivization of Soviet agriculture was nearly complete.

soared between 1929 and 1932. The Russian people were constantly reminded that no sacrifice could be too great in producing steel and iron.

When he first began to deal with the grain crisis of 1928, Stalin did not intend collective agriculture to be a solution. But by the end of 1929, the increasingly repressive measures instituted by the state against the peasants had led both to **collectivization** and to the deportation of *kulaks,* the derisive term for wealthy peasants that literally means "the tight-fisted ones." Stalin achieved forced collectivization by confiscating land and establishing collective farms run by the state. Within a few months, half of all peasant farms were collectivized. By 1938, private land had been virtually eliminated. The state set prices, controlled distribution, and selected crops with the intention of ensuring a steady food supply and freeing a rural labor force for heavy industry. More as a publicity ploy than a statement of fact, the First Five-Year Plan was declared a success after only three years. It was a success in one important sense: it did lay the foundations of the Soviet planned economy, in which the state bureaucracy made all decisions about production, distribution, and prices.

Collectivization meant misery for the 25 million peasant families who suffered under it. At least 5 million peasants died between 1929 and 1932. Collectivization ripped apart the fabric of village life, destroyed families, and sent homeless peasants into exile. Peasants who resisted collectivization retaliated by destroying their own crops and livestock. Rapid industrial development shattered the lives of millions of people. In attempting to develop an industrial sector overnight, Stalin, like tsars before him, saw that Russia could be carried into the future only on the backs of its peasants.

The Comintern, Economic Development, and the Purges

In addition to promoting its internal economic development, the Soviet Union had to worry about survival in a world political system composed entirely of capitalist countries.

After the Bolshevik revolution in 1917, Lenin had fully expected that other socialist revolutions would follow throughout the world, especially in central and western Europe. Those revolutions would destroy capitalism and secure Russia's place in a new world order. But as the prospects for world proletarian revolution evaporated, Soviet leaders sought to protect their revolutionary country from what they saw as a hostile capitalist world. They used diplomacy to that end. The end of the Allied intervention in Russia allowed the Bolshevik state to initiate diplomatic relations with the West, beginning with the Treaty of Rapallo signed with Germany in 1921. By 1924, all the major countries of the world—with the exception of the United States—had established diplomatic relations with the Soviet Union. In 1928, the USSR cooperated in the preparation of a world disarmament conference to be held in Geneva and joined western European powers in a commitment to peace.

industrialization. Between 1929 and 1937, the period covered by the first two five-year plans (truncated because of their proclaimed success), Stalin laid the foundation for an urban industrial society in the Soviet Union. By brutally squeezing profits out of the agricultural sector, Stalin managed to increase heavy industrial production between 300 and 600 percent.

Stalin committed the Soviet Union to rapid industrialization as the only way to preserve socialism. The failure of revolutionary movements in western Europe meant that the Soviet Union must preserve "socialism in one country," the slogan of the political philosophy that justified Stalin's economic plans. Stalin made steel the idol of the new age. The Soviet state needed heavy machinery to build the future. An industrial labor force was created virtually overnight as peasant men and women were placed at workbenches and before the vast furnaces of modern metallurgical plants. The number of women in the industrial work force tripled in the decade after 1929. The reliability of official indices varied, but there is little doubt that heavy industrial production

DOCUMENT

Stalin Demands Rapid Industrialization

The United States and the Soviet Union exchanged ambassadors for the first time in 1933.

The Comintern.

In addition to diplomatic relations, the Soviet state in 1919 encouraged various national Communist parties to form an association for the purpose of promoting and coordinating the coming world revolution. The Communist International, or Comintern, was based in Moscow and by 1920 included representatives from 37 countries. As it became clear that a world revolution was not imminent, the Comintern concerned itself with the ideological purity of its member parties. Under Lenin's direction, the Soviet Communist party determined policy for all the member parties.

Bukharin and Stalin shared a view of the Comintern that prevailed from 1924 to 1929: since the collapse of capitalism was not imminent, the Comintern should work to promote the unity of working classes everywhere and should cooperate with existing worker organizations. In 1929, however, Stalin argued that advanced capitalist societies were teetering on the brink of new wars and revolutions. As a result, the Comintern must seek to sever the ties between foreign Communist parties and social democratic parties in order to prepare for the revolutionary struggle. Stalin purged the Comintern of dissenters, and he decreed a policy of noncooperation in Europe from 1929 to 1933. As a result, socialism in Europe was badly split between Communists and democratic socialists.

The Second Five-Year Plan, announced in 1933, succeeded in reducing the Soviet Union's dependence on foreign imports, especially in the areas of heavy industry, machinery, and metal works. The basic physical plant for armaments production was in place by 1937, and resources continued to be shifted away from consumer goods to heavy industrial development. The industrial development and the collectivization of agriculture brought growing urbanization. By 1939, one in three Soviet people lived in cities, compared to one in six in 1926. In his commitment to increased production, Stalin introduced into the workplace incentives and differential wage scales at odds with the principles and programs of the original Bolshevik revolution. Stricter discipline was enforced; absenteeism was punished with severe fines or loss of employment. Workers who exceeded their quotas were rewarded and honored.

The Great Purge.

Amid the rapid industrialization, Stalin inaugurated the **Great Purge,** which actually was a series of purges lasting from 1934 to 1938. Those whom Stalin believed to be his opponents—real and imagined, past, present, and future—were labeled *class enemies.* The most prominent of them, including leaders of the Bolshevik revolution who had worked with Stalin during the 1920s, appeared in widely publicized *show trials.* They were intimidated and tortured into making false confessions of crimes against the regime, humiliated by brutal prosecutors, and condemned to death or imprisonment. Stalin wiped out the Bolshevik old guard, Communist party members whose first loyalty was to the international Communist movement rather than to Stalin himself, and all potential opposition within the Communist party. Probably 300,000 people were put to death, among them engineers, managers, technical specialists, and officers of the army and navy. In addition, seven million people were placed in labor camps. Stalin now had unquestioned control of the Communist party and the country.

The purges dealt a severe blow to the command of the army and resulted in a shortage of qualified industrial personnel, slowing industrial growth. The Great Purge coerced the Soviet people into making great sacrifices in the drive for industrialization. It prevented any possible dissension or opposition within the USSR at a time when the "foreign threat" posed by Nazi Germany was becoming increasingly serious.

■ Soviet women were mobilized into the labor force. Here four women are shown in a factory in the 1930s.

The human suffering associated with the dislocation and heavy workloads of rapid, coerced industrialization cannot be measured. Planned growth brought with it a top-heavy and often inefficient bureaucracy, and that bureaucracy ensured that the Soviet Union was the most highly centralized of the European states. The growing threat of foreign war meant an even greater diversion of resources from consumer goods to war industries beginning with the Third Five-Year Plan in 1938.

Women and the Family in the New Soviet State

The building of the new Soviet state exacted particularly high costs from women. Soviet women had been active in the revolution from the beginning. Lenin and the Bolshevik leaders were committed to the liberation of women, who, like workers, were considered to be oppressed under capitalism. Lenin denounced housework as "barbarously unproductive, petty, nerve-wracking, stultifying, and crushing drudgery." In its early days, the Soviet state pledged to protect the rights of mothers without narrowing women's opportunities or restricting women's role to the family.

After the October Revolution of 1917, the Bolsheviks passed a new law establishing equality for women within marriage. In 1920, abortion was legalized. New legislation established the right to divorce and removed the stigma from illegitimacy. Communes, calling themselves "laboratories of revolution," experimented with sexual equality. Russian women were enfranchised in 1917, gaining the right to vote before women in the industrialized countries of western Europe. The Russian revolution went further than any revolution in history toward the legal liberation of women within such a short span of time.

Those advances, as utopian as they appeared to admirers in western European countries, did not deal with the problems faced by the majority of Russian women. Bolshevik legislation did little to address the special economic hardships of peasant and factory women. Although paid maternity leaves and nursing breaks were required by law, those guarantees became a source of discrimination against women workers, who were the last hired and first fired by

THE LAW ON THE ABOLITION OF LEGAL ABORTION, 1936

In his drive to industrialize the Soviet Union as rapidly as possible, Stalin recognized the economic importance of women's roles both as workers and as mothers. At the height of the Second Five-Year Plan, many women's rights were revoked, including the right to an abortion. The "New Woman" of the revolutionary period gave way to the post-1936 woman, depicted by the state as the perfect mother who matched her husband's productivity in the workplace, ran the household, and raised a large family.

Focus Questions

In this excerpt, can you identify why Stalin considers abortion a threat to the Soviet state? Why does a working woman fulfill her duties as a citizen through motherhood?

When we speak of strengthening the Soviet family, we are speaking precisely of the struggle against the survivals of a bourgeois attitude towards marriage, women and children. So-called "free love" and all disorderly sex life are bourgeois through and through, and have nothing to do with either socialist principles or the ethics and standards of conduct of the Soviet citizen. Socialist doctrine shows this, and it is proved by life itself.

The elite of our country, the best of the Soviet youth, are as a rule also excellent family men who dearly love their children. And vice versa: the man who does not take marriage seriously, and abandons his children to the whims of fate, is usually also a bad worker and a poor member of society.

Fatherhood and motherhood have long been virtues in this country. This can be seen at the first glance, without searching enquiry. Go through the parks and streets of Moscow or of any other town in the Soviet Union on a holiday, and you will see not a few young men walking with pink-cheeked, well-fed babies in their arms. . . .

The toilers of our land have paid with their blood for the right to a life of joy, and a life of joy implies the right to have one's own family and healthy, happy children. Millions of workers beyond the frontiers of our land are still deprived of this joy, for there unemployment, hunger and helpless poverty are rampant. Old maids and elderly bachelors, a rare thing in our country, are frequent in the West, and that is no accident.

We alone have all the conditions under which a working woman can fulfill her duties as a citizen and as a mother responsible for the birth and early upbringing of her children.

A woman without children merits our pity, for she does not know the full joy of life. Our Soviet women, full-blooded citizens of the freest country in the world, have been given the bliss of motherhood. We must safeguard our family and raise and rear healthy Soviet heroes!

CHRONOLOGY
The Soviet Union's Separate Path

November 1917	Bolsheviks and Red Guard seize power
1919	Creation of the Communist International (Comintern)
1920	Legalization of abortion and divorce
1921	End of the civil war
1921	Introduction of the New Economic Policy
3 April 1922	Stalin becomes secretary general of the Communist party
21 January 1924	Lenin dies
1924–1929	Comintern policy of "Unity of the Working Classes"
1927	Dissatisfied peasants hoard grain
November 1927	Trotsky expelled from Communist party
1928	Stalin introduces grain requisitioning
November 1929	Bukharin expelled from Politburo
1929	Introduction of First Five-Year Plan and the collectivization of agriculture
1929–1933	Comintern policy of noncooperation with Social Democratic parties
1933–1937	Second Five-Year Plan
1934–1938	Great Purge
1936	Abortion declared illegal
1938	Third Five-Year Plan

employers trying to limit expenses. Divorce legislation was hardly a blessing for women with children, since men incurred no financial responsibility toward their offspring in terminating a marriage. Even as legislation was being passed in the early days of the new Soviet state, women were losing ground in the struggle for equal rights and independent economic survival.

By the early 1930s, reforms affecting women were in trouble due in large part to a plummeting birthrate. The decline created special worries for Soviet planners, who forecast doom if the trend was not reversed. In 1936, a woman's right to choose to end a first pregnancy was revoked. In the following decade, all abortions were made illegal. Homosexuality was declared a criminal offense. The family was glorified as the mainstay of the socialist order, and the independence of women was challenged as a threat to Soviet productivity. While motherhood was idealized, the Stalinist drive to industrialize could not dispense with full-time women workers.

Women's double burden in the home and workplace became heavier during Stalin's reign. Most Russian women held full-time jobs in the factories or on the farms. They also worked what they called a "second shift" in running a household and taking care of children. In the industrialized nations of western Europe, the growth of a consumer economy lightened to some extent women's labor in the home. In the Soviet Union, procuring the simplest necessities was woman's work that required waiting in long lines for hours. Lack of indoor plumbing meant that women spent time hauling water for their families at the end of a working day. In such ways, rapid industrialization exacted its special price from Soviet women.

In the 1920s and 1930s, the Soviet search for stability and prosperity took the Soviet Union down a path very different from that of the states of western Europe. Rejecting an accommodation with a market economy, Stalin committed the Soviet people to planned rapid industrialization that was accomplished through mass repression and great human suffering. Insulated from world markets and the devastation of the Great Depression, the Soviet Union relied on a massive state bureaucratic system to achieve socialism in one country and to make the Soviet state into an industrial giant.

THE RISE OF FASCIST DICTATORSHIP IN ITALY

Throughout western Europe, parliamentary institutions, representative government, and electoral politics offered no ready solutions to the problems of economic collapse and the political upheaval on the left and the right. **Fascism** promised what liberal democratic societies failed to deliver—a way out of the economic and political morass. Fascism, which emerged first in Italy out of the political and social upheaval following World War I, is a totalitarian political system that glorifies the state and totally subordinates the individual to the state's needs. Italy was the first fascist state, followed in the 1930s by Germany and Spain. In all three cases, fascist rule meant dictatorship by a strong, charismatic leader. It promised to those subjected to its rule an escape from parliamentary chaos, party wranglings, and the threat of communism. Fascism promised more: by identifying ready enemies—scapegoats for failed economic and national ambitions—fascism promised that it held the answer for those who sought protection and security.

Fascism sounded very like socialism. In the Soviet Union, Bolshevik leaders reassured their people that socialism was the only way of dealing with the weaknesses and inequities of the world capitalist system laid bare in the world war. In their initial condemnations of the capitalist economy and liberal political institutions and values, fascists employed revolutionary language similar to that of the Left while manipulating in radically new ways the political symbols of the Right—the nation, the flag, and the army. However, fascism rejected the socialist tenet of the collective or government ownership of production and property. It was violently opposed to socialist egalitarianism. Instead, fascism promised to steer a course between the uncertainties and exploitation of a liberal capitalist system and the revolutionary upheaval and expropriation of a socialist system. Fascism was ultranationalist, and the use of force was central to its appeal.

The word *fascism* is derived from the Latin *fasces,* the name for the bundle of rods with ax head carried by the magistrates of the Roman Empire. Fascism was rooted in the mass political movements of the late nineteenth century, which glorified the nation, emphasized antiliberal values, and pursued a politics of violence. The electoral successes of the German variant—National Socialism, or **Nazism**—were just beginning in the late 1920s. In the same period, fascist movements were making their appearance in England, Hungary, Spain, and France. But none was more successful and none demanded more attention than the fascist experiment in Italy, which inspired observers throughout Europe to emulate it.

Mussolini's Italy

Italy was a poor nation. Although Italy was one of the victorious Allies in World War I, Italians believed that their country had been betrayed by the peace settlement of 1919 by being denied the territory and status it deserved. A recently created electoral system based on universal manhood suffrage had produced parliamentary chaos and ministerial instability. The lack of coherent political programs only heightened the general disapproval with government that accompanied the peace negotiations. People were beginning to doubt the parliamentary regime's hold on the future. It was under those circumstances that the Fascist party, led by Benito Mussolini (1883–1945), entered politics in 1920 by attacking the large Socialist and Popular (Catholic) parties.

The Rise of Mussolini.   Mussolini had begun his prewar political career as a Socialist. The young Mussolini was arrested numerous times for Socialist political activities and placed under state surveillance. An ardent nationalist, he volunteered for combat in World War I and was promoted to the rank of corporal. Injured in early 1917 by an exploding shell detonated during firing practice, he returned to Milan to continue his work as editor of *Il Populo d'Italia* ("The People of Italy"), the newspaper he founded in 1914 to promote Italian participation in the war.

Mussolini yearned to be the leader of a revolution in Italy comparable to that directed by Lenin in Russia. Although his doctrinal allegiance to socialism was beginning to flag, Mussolini, like Lenin, recognized the power of the printed word to stir political passions. Emphasizing nationalist goals and vague measures of socioeconomic transformation, Mussolini identified a new enemy for Italy—bolshevism. He organized his followers into the Fascist party, a political movement that, by utilizing strict party discipline, quickly developed its own national network.

Many Fascists were former Socialists and war veterans like Mussolini who were disillusioned with postwar government. They dreamed of Italy as a great world power, as it had been in the days of ancient Rome. Their enemies were not only Communists with their international outlook but also the big businesses, which they believed drained Italy's resources and kept its people poor and powerless. Panicky members of the lower middle classes sought security against the economic uncertainties of inflation and were willing to endorse violence to achieve it. Unions were to be feared because they used strikes to further their demands for higher salaries and better working conditions for their members while other social groups languished. Near civil war erupted as Italian Communists and Fascists clashed violently in street battles in the early 1920s. The Fascists entered the national political arena and succeeded on the local level in overthrowing city governments. In

■ Gerardo Dottori, *Portrait of the Duce* (1933). Dottori was one of a group of Italian Futurist artists whose works reflected their fascination with aircraft, flight, and extraterrestrial fantasy. In 1929, they published a manifesto in which they launched the idea of an art linked to the most exciting aspect of contemporary life. During the 1930s the artists sought to align themselves with Mussolini's Fascist regime.

spite of its visibility on the national political scene, however, the Fascist party was still very much a minority party when Mussolini refused to serve as a junior minister in the new government in 1922.

The March on Rome.

His refusal to serve as representative of a minority party reflected Mussolini's belief that the Fascists had to be in charge. On 28 October 1922, the Fascists undertook their famous March on Rome, which followed similar Fascist takeovers in Milan and Bologna. Mussolini's followers occupied the capital. The event marked the beginning of the end of parliamentary government and the emergence of Fascist dictatorship and institutionalized violence. Rising unemployment and severe inflation contributed to the politically deteriorating situation that helped bring Mussolini to power.

Destruction and violence, not the ballot box, became fascism's most successful tools for securing political power. *Squadristi*—armed bands of Fascist thugs—attacked their political enemies (both Catholic and Socialist), destroyed private property, dismantled the printing presses of adversary groups, and generally terrorized both rural and urban populations. By the end of 1922, Fascists could claim a following of 300,000 members endorsing the new politics of intimidation.

The Fascists achieved their first parliamentary majority by using violent tactics of intimidation to secure votes. One outspoken Socialist critic of Fascist violence, Giacomo Matteotti (1885–1924), was murdered by Mussolini's subordinates. The deed threatened the survival of Mussolini's government as 150 Socialist, Liberal, and Popular party deputies resigned in protest. Mussolini chose that moment to consolidate his position by arresting and silencing his enemies to preserve order. Within two years, Fascists were firmly in control, monopolizing politics, suppressing a free press, creating a secret police force, and transforming social and economic policies. Mussolini destroyed political parties and made Italy into a one-party dictatorship.

Dealing with Big Business and the Church.

In 1925, the Fascist party entered into an agreement with Italian industrialists that gave industry a position of privilege protected by the state in return for its support. Mussolini presented the partnership as the end to class conflict, but in fact it ensured the dominance of capital and the control of labor and professional groups.

A corrupt bureaucracy filled with Mussolini's cronies and run on bribes orchestrated the new relationship between big business and the state. In spite of official claims, Fascist Italy had not done well in riding out the Great Depression. A large rural sector masked the problems of high unemployment by absorbing an urban work force without jobs. Corporatism, a system of economic self-rule by interest groups promoted on paper by Benito Mussolini, was a sham that had little to do with the dominance of the Italian economy by big business. By lending money to Italian businesses on the verge of bankruptcy, the government acquired a controlling interest in key industries, including steel, shipping, heavy machinery, and electricity.

Mussolini, himself an atheist, recognized the importance of the Catholic Church in securing his regime. In 1870, when Italy had been unified, the pope had been deprived of his territories in Rome. That event, which became known as the "Roman Question," proved to be the source of ongoing problems for Italian governments. In February 1929, Mussolini settled matters with Pope Pius XI in the Lateran Treaty and the accompanying Concordat, which granted to the pope sovereignty over the territory around St. Peter's Basilica and the Vatican. The treaty also protected the role of the Catholic Church in education and guaranteed that Italian marriage laws would conform to Catholic dogma.

By 1929, *Il Duce* (the leader), as Mussolini preferred to be called, was at the height of his popularity and power. Apparent political harmony had been achieved by ruthlessly crushing fascism's opponents. The agreement with the pope, which restored harmony with the Church, was matched by a new sense of order and accomplishment in Italian society and the economy.

Mussolini's Plans for Empire

As fascism failed to initiate effective social programs, Mussolini's popularity plummeted. In the hope of boosting his sagging image, *Il Duce* committed Italy to a foreign policy of imperial conquest.

Italy had conquered Ottoman-controlled Libya in North Africa in 1911. Now, in the 1930s, Mussolini targeted Ethiopia for his expansionist aims and ordered Italian troops to invade the east African kingdom in October 1935. Using poison gas and aerial bombing, the Italian army defeated the native troops of Ethiopian Emperor Haile Selassie (1892–1975). European democracies, under the pressure of public opinion, cried out against the wanton and unwarranted attack, but Mussolini succeeded in proclaiming Ethiopia an Italian territory.

The invasion of Ethiopia exposed the ineffectiveness of the League of Nations to stop such flagrant violations of its covenant. Great Britain and France took no action other than to express their disapproval of Italy's conquest. Yet a rift opened between the two western European nations and Italy. Mussolini had distanced himself from the Nazi state in the first years of the German regime's existence, and he was critical of Hitler's plans for rearmament. Now, in light of disapproval from Britain and France, Mussolini turned to Germany for support. In October 1936, Italy aligned itself with Germany in what Mussolini called the Rome-Berlin Axis. The alliance was little more than a pledge of friendship. However, less than three years later, in May 1939, Germany and Italy agreed to offer support in any offensive or defensive war. The agreement, known as the Pact of Steel, in fact bound Italy militarily to Germany.

Mussolini pursued other imperialist goals within Europe. The small Balkan nation of Albania entered into a series of agreements with Mussolini beginning in the mid-1920s that

■ Ethiopian chieftain and armed forces wait to encounter Mussolini's invading troops, 1935.

made it dependent financially and militarily on Italian aid. By 1933, Albanian independence had been undermined by its "friendship" with its stronger neighbor. In order not to be outdone by Hitler, who was at the time dismantling Czechoslovakia, Mussolini invaded and annexed Albania in April 1939, ending the fiction that Albania was an Italian protectorate.

HITLER AND THE THIRD REICH

Repeated economic, political, and diplomatic crises of the 1920s buffeted Germany's internal stability. Most Germans considered reparations to be an unfair burden, so onerous that payment should be evaded and resisted in every way possible. The German government did not promote inflation in order to avoid paying reparations, but rather to avoid a postwar recession, revive industrial production, and maintain high employment. But the moderate inflation that stimulated the economy spun out of control into destructive hyperinflation.

The fiscal problems of the Weimar Republic obscure the fact that, in the period after World War I, Germany experienced real economic growth. German industry advanced, productivity was high, and German workers flexed their union muscles to secure better wages. Weimar committed itself to large expenditures for social welfare programs, including unemployment insurance. By 1930, social welfare was responsible for 40 percent of all public expenditures, compared to 19 percent before the war. All those changes, apparently fostering the well-being of the German people,

aggravated the fears of German big businessmen, who resented the trade unions and the perceived trend toward socialism. The lower middle classes also felt cheated and economically threatened by inflation. They were a politically volatile group, susceptible to the antidemocratic appeals of some of Weimar's critics.

Growing numbers of Germans expressed disgust with parliamentary democracy. The Great Depression dealt a staggering blow to the Weimar Republic in 1929 as American loans were withdrawn and German unemployment skyrocketed. By 1930, the antagonisms among the parties were so great that the parliament was no longer effective in ruling Germany. As chancellor from 1930 to 1932, Centrist leader Heinrich Brüning (1885–1970) attempted to break the impasse by overriding the Weimar constitution. The move opened the door to enemies of the republic, and Brüning was forced to resign.

Hitler's Rise to Power

One man in particular knew how to exploit the Weimar Republic's weaknesses for his own political ends. Adolf Hitler was that man. He denounced the betrayal of reparations. He made a special appeal to Germans who saw their savings disappearing, first in inflation and then in the Great Depression. He promised a way out of economic hardship and the reassertion of Germany's claim to status as a world power.

Just as Stalin was born a Georgian and not an ethnic Russian, Adolf Hitler (1889–1945) was born an Austrian outside the German fatherland he came to rule. Hitler, the son of a customs agent who worked on the Austrian side of the border with Germany, came from a middle-class family with social pretensions. Aimlessness and failure marked Hitler's early life. Denied admission to architecture school, he took odd jobs to survive. Hitler welcomed the outbreak of war in 1914, which put an end to his self-described sleepwalking. He volunteered immediately for service in the German army. Wounded and gassed at the front, he was twice awarded the Iron Cross for bravery in action.

Hitler later described what he had learned from war in terms of the solidarity of struggle against a common enemy and the purity of heroism. The army provided him with a sense of security and direction. What he learned from the peace that followed was an equally powerful lesson that determined his commitment to a career in politics. Hitler profoundly believed in the stab-in-the-back legend: Germany had not lost the war, he insisted, it had been defeated from within—or stabbed in the back by Communists, Socialists, liberals, and Jews. The Weimar Republic signed the humiliating Treaty of Versailles and continued to betray the German people by taxing wages to pay reparations. Hitler's highly distorted and false view of the origins of the republic and its policies was the basis for his demand that the "Weimar System" must be abolished and replaced by a Nazi regime.

The Beer Hall Putsch of 1923. For his failed attempt to seize control of the Munich municipal government in 1923, in an event that became known as the Beer Hall Putsch because of the locale in which Hitler attempted to initiate the "national revolution," he served nine months of a five-year sentence in prison. There he began writing the first volume of his autobiography, *Mein Kampf* ("My Struggle"). In that turgid work, he condemned the decadence of Western society and singled out for special contempt Jews, Bolsheviks, and middle-class liberals. From his failed attempt to seize power, Hitler learned the important lesson that he could succeed against the German republic only from within, by coming to power legally. By 1928, he had a small party of about 100,000 Nazis. Modifying his anticapitalist message, Hitler appealed to the discontented small farmers and tailored his nationalist sentiments to a frightened middle class.

Hitler as Chancellor. Adolf Hitler became chancellor of Germany in January 1933 by legal, constitutional, and democratic means. The Nazi party was supported by farmers, small businessmen, civil servants, and young people. In the elections of 1930 and 1932, the voters made the Nazi party the largest party in the country—although not the majority one. President Paul von Hindenburg (1925–1934) invited Hitler to form a government. Hitler claimed that Germany was on the verge of a Communist revolution and persuaded Hindenburg and the Reichstag to consent to a series of emergency laws, which the Nazis used to establish themselves firmly in power. Legislation outlawed freedom of the press and public meetings and approved of the use of violence against Hitler's political enemies, particularly the Socialists and the Communists. Within two months after Hitler came to office, Germany was a police state and Hitler was a "legal" dictator who could issue his own laws without having to gain the consent of either the Reichstag or the president. After carrying out the "legal revolution" that incapacitated representative institutions and ended civil liberties, the Nazis worked to consolidate their position and their power. They abolished all other political parties, established single-party rule, dissolved trade unions, and put their own people into state governments and the bureaucracy.

Many observers at the time considered the new Nazi state to be a monolithic structure, ruled and coordinated from the center. That was not, however, an accurate observation. Hitler actually issued few directives. Policy was set by an often chaotic jockeying for power among rival Nazi factions. Hitler's political alliance with traditional conservative and nationalist politicians, industrialists, and military men helped give the state created by Adolf Hitler a claim to legitimacy based on continuity with the past. Hitler called that state the **Third Reich.** (The first Reich was the medieval German Empire; the second Reich was the German Empire created by Bismarck in 1871.)

The first of the paramilitary groups so important in orchestrating violence to eliminate Hitler's enemies was the SA (Sturmabteilung), or the storm troopers, under Ernst Röhm (1887–1934). Röhm helped Hitler achieve electoral victories by beating up political opponents on the streets and using other thuglike tactics. SA followers, also known as Brownshirts, adopted a military appearance for their terrorist operations. By the beginning of 1934, there were 2.5 million members of the SA, vastly outnumbering the regular army of 100,000 soldiers.

Heinrich Himmler (1900–1945) headed an elite force of the Nazi party within the SA called the SS (Schutzstaffel, or protection squad), a group whose members wore black uniforms and menacing skull-and-crossbones insignia on their caps. Himmler seized control of political policing and emerged as Röhm's chief rival. In 1934, with the assistance of the army, Hitler and the SS purged the SA and executed Röhm, thereby making the SS Hitler's exclusive elite corps, entrusted with carrying out his extreme programs and responsible later for the greatest atrocities of the Second World War.

Nazi Goals

Hitler identified three organizing goals for the Nazi state: *Lebensraum* (living space), rearmament, and economic recovery. The goals were the basis of the new foreign policy Hitler forged for Germany, and they served to fuse that foreign policy with the domestic politics of the Third Reich. These goals served the ultimate purpose of securing totalitarian power for the German state. All three were based on Hitler's version of social Darwinism—that the German race was the fittest and would survive and prosper at the expense of others.

■ Adolf Hitler salutes a huge crowd of Hitler Youth at a rally. The mass meetings were used by the Nazi mythmakers to enhance Hitler's image as the savior of Germany.

Living Space.   Key to Hitler's worldview was the concept of *Lebensraum,* living space, in which he considered the right and the duty of the German master race to be the world's greatest empire, one that would endure for a thousand years. Hitler first stated his ideals about living space in *Mein Kampf,* where he argued that superior nations had the right to expand into the territories of inferior states. Living space meant for him German domination of central and eastern Europe at the expense of Slavic peoples. The Aryan master race would dominate inferior peoples. Colonies were unacceptable because they weakened rather than strengthened national security; Germany must annex territories within continental Europe.

Hitler's primary target was what he called "Russia and her vassal border states."

Rearmament.   Hitler continued the secret rearmament of Germany begun by his Weimar predecessors in violation of the restrictions of the Treaty of Versailles. He withdrew Germany from the League of Nations and from the World Disarmament Conference, signaling a new direction for German foreign policy. In 1935, he publicly renounced the Treaty of Versailles and announced that Germany was rearming. The following year he openly defied the French and moved German troops into the Rhineland, the demilitarized

NATIONAL INCOME OF THE POWERS IN 1937 AND PERCENTAGE SPENT ON DEFENSE

	National Income (billions of dollars)	Percentage Spent on Defense
United States	68	1.5
British Empire	22	5.7
France	10	9.1
Germany	17	23.5
Italy	6	14.5
USSR	19	26.4
Japan	4	28.2

security zone that separated the armed forces of the two countries. Hitler also reversed the cooperative relationship his nation had established with the Soviet Union in the 1920s. In 1933, the German state was illicitly spending 1 billion Reichsmarks on arms. By 1939, annual expenditures to prepare Germany for war had climbed to 30 billion.

Hitler knew that preparation for war meant more than amassing weapons; it also required full economic recovery. One of Germany's great weaknesses in World War I had been its dependence on imports of raw materials and foodstuffs. To avoid a repetition of that problem, Hitler instituted a program of autarky, or economic self-sufficiency, by which Germany aimed to produce everything that it consumed. He encouraged the efforts of German industry to develop synthetics for petroleum, rubber, metals, and fats.

Economic Recovery.   The state pumped money into the private economy, creating new jobs and achieving full employment after 1936, an accomplishment unmatched by any other European nation. Recovery was built on armaments as well as consumer products. The Nazi state's concentration of economic power in the hands of a few strengthened big businesses. The victims of corporate consolidation were the small firms that could no longer compete with government-sponsored corporations such as the chemical giant I. G. Farben.

In 1936, Hitler introduced his Four-Year Plan, dedicated to the goals of full-scale rearmament and economic self-sufficiency. Before the third year of the Four-Year Plan, however, Hitler was aware of the failure to develop synthetic products sufficient to meet Germany's needs. But if Germany could not create substitutes, it could control territories that provided fuel, metals, and foodstuffs. Germany had been importing raw materials from southeastern Europe and wielding increasing economic influence over the Balkan countries. Hitler now realized that economic self-sufficiency could be directly linked to the main goal of the Nazi state: *Lebensraum.*

Thus Hitler was committed to territorial expansion from the time he came to power. He rearmed Germany for that purpose. When economists and generals cautioned him, he refused to listen. Instead, he informed them of his commitment to *Lebensraum* and of his intention to use aggressive war to acquire it. He removed his critics from their positions of power and replaced them with Nazis loyal to him.

Propaganda, Racism, and Culture

To reinforce his personal power and to sell his program for the "total state," Hitler created a Ministry of Propaganda under Joseph Goebbels (1897–1945), a former journalist and Nazi party district leader in Berlin. Goebbels was a master of manipulating emotions in mass demonstrations held to whip up enthusiasm for Nazi policies. Flying the flag and wearing the swastika signified identification with the Nazi state. With his magnetic appeal, Hitler inspired and manipulated the devotion of hundreds of thousands of those who heard him speak. Leni Riefenstahl, a young filmmaker working for

Hitler, made a documentary of a National Socialist party rally at Nuremberg. In scenes of swooning women and cheering men, her film, called *Triumph of the Will,* recorded the dramatic force of Hitler's rhetoric and his ability to move the German people. Hitler's public charisma masked a profoundly troubled and incomplete individual capable of irrational rage and sick hatred of his fellow human beings. His warped views of the world were responsible for the greatest outrages ever committed in the name of legitimate power. Yet millions, including admirers in western Europe and the United States, succumbed to his appeal.

Targeting the Young and Women.   Family life, too, was carefully regulated through the propaganda machinery. Loyalty only to the state meant less loyalty to the family. In 1939, 82 percent of all German boys and girls between the ages of 10 and 18 were members of Nazi-controlled organizations. Special youth organizations, including the Hitler Youth, indoctrinated boys with nationalistic and military values. Organizations for girls were intended to mold them into worthy wives and mothers.

■ The *Frauen Warte* was the Nazi Party's official magazine for women. In this cover from an August 1938 issue, a happy family is presented as the best foundation of the German people.

ADOLF HITLER ON "RACIAL PURITY"

The purity of German blood was a recurrent theme in Hitler's speeches and writings from the beginning of his political career. In attacking both liberalism and socialism, Hitler offered racial superiority as the essence of the National Socialist "revolution." This speech, delivered in Berlin on 30 January 1937, lays out his attack on the concept of individual rights and humanity in favor of the folk community.

Focus Questions

In this diatribe, how does race function to promote the "folk" and to undermine the individual's rights? Is Hitler's goal here to create "a better understanding" among nations?

The most important plank in the National Socialist program is to abolish the liberal idea of the individual and the Marxist idea of humanity and to substitute for them the folk community rooted in the soil and held together by the bond of common blood. This sounds simple, but it involves a principle which has great consequences.

For the first time and in the first country our people are being taught to understand that, of all the tasks we have to face, the most noble and the most sacred for all mankind is the concept that each racial species must preserve the purity of blood which God has given to it.

The greatest revolution won by National Socialism is that it has pierced the veil which hid from us the knowledge that all human errors may be attributed to the conditions of the time and hence can be remedied, but there is one error that cannot be set right once it has been made by men—that is, the failure to understand the importance of keeping the blood and the race free from intermingling, and in this way

to alter God's gift. It is not for human beings to discuss why Providence created different races. Rather it is important to understand the fact that it will punish those who pay no attention to its work of creation. . . .

I hereby prophesy that, just as knowledge that the earth moves around the sun led to a revolutionary change in the world picture, so will the blood-and-race doctrine of the National Socialist movement bring about a revolutionary change in our knowledge. . . . It will also change the course of history in the future.

This will not lead to difficulties between nations. On the contrary, it will lead to a better understanding between them. But at the same time it will prevent the Jews, under the mask of world citizenship, from thrusting themselves among all nations as an element of domestic chaos. . . .

The National Socialist movement limits its domestic activities to those individuals who belong to one people. It refuses to permit those of a foreign race to have any influence whatever on our political, intellectual, or cultural life. We refuse to give any members of a foreign race a dominant position in our national economic system.

In our folk community, which is based on ties of blood, in the results which National Socialism has obtained by training the public in the idea of this folk-community, lies the deepest reason for the great success of our Revolution.

Woman's natural function, Hitler argued, was to serve in the home. Education for women beyond the care of home and family was a waste. Adult women had their own organizations to serve the Nazi state. The German Women's Bureau under Gertrud Scholtz-Klink instructed women in their "proper" female duties. In an effort to promote large families, the state paid allowances to couples for getting married, subsidized families according to their size, and gave tax breaks to large families. Abortion and birth control were outlawed, and women who sought such measures risked severe penalties and imprisonment.

By 1937, the need for women workers conflicted with the goals of Nazi propaganda. With the outbreak of war in 1939, women were urged to work, especially in jobs such as munitions manufacture formerly held by men. For working women with families, the double burden was a heavy one, as women were required to work long shifts—60-hour workweeks were not unusual—for low wages. Many women resisted entering the work

force if they had other income or could live on the cash payments they received as the wives of soldiers. At the beginning of 1943, the German people were ordered to make sacrifices for a new era of "total war." Female labor became compulsory, and women were drafted into working for the war.

Enemies of the State. Propaganda condemned everything foreign, including Mickey Mouse, who was declared an enemy of the state in the 1930s. Purging foreign influences meant purging political opponents, especially members of the Communist party, who were rounded up and sent to concentration camps in Germany. Communism was identified as an international Jewish conspiracy to destroy the German *Volk*, or people. Nazi literature also identified "asocials," those who were considered deviant in any way, including homosexuals, who were likewise to be expelled. Euthanasia was used against the mentally ill and the mentally disabled in the 1930s. Concentration camps were expanded to contain enemies of the state. Later, when concentration camps became sites of extermination and forced labor, gypsies, homosexuals, criminals, and religious offenders had to wear insignia of different colors to indicate the reason for their persecution. The people who received the greatest attention for exclusion from Nazi Germany, and then from Europe, were the Jews.

Scapegoating Jews. The first measures against German Jews—their exclusion from public employment and higher education—began almost immediately in 1933. In 1935, the Nuremberg Laws were enacted to identify Jews, to deprive them of their citizenship, and to forbid marriage and extramarital sexual relations between Jews and non-Jews. On the night of 9 November 1938, synagogues were set afire and books and valuables owned by Jews were confiscated throughout Germany. Jews were beaten, about 91 were killed, and 20,000 to 30,000 were imprisoned in concentration camps. The night came to be

■ An anti-Semitic campaign poster from Germany in 1933 for the Nazis reads: "Free from misery! Free from the Jews! Vote list no. 1, National-Socialists."

called *Kristallnacht,* meaning "night of broken glass," which referred to the Jewish shop windows smashed under orders from Goebbels. The government claimed that *Kristallnacht* was an outpouring of the German people's will. An atmosphere of state-sanctioned hate prevailed.

Racism was nothing new in European culture, nor was its particular variant, anti-Semitism—hatred of Jews—the creation of the Third Reich. The link the Nazis cultivated between racism and politics was built on cultural precedents. In the 1890s, in France and Austria and elsewhere in Europe, anti-Semitism was espoused by political and professional groups that formed themselves around issues of militant nationalism, authoritarianism, and mass politics. Hitler was a racist and an anti-Semite, and he placed theories of race at the core of his fascist ideology. "Experts" decided that sterilization was the surest way to protect "German blood." In 1933, one of the early laws of Hitler's new Reich decreed compulsory sterilization of "undesirables" in order to "eliminate inferior genes." The Nazi state decided who the undesirables were and forced the sterilization of 400,000 men and women.

The Third Reich was a government that delivered on its promises to end unemployment, to improve productivity, to break through the logjam of parliamentary obstacles, and to return Germany to the international arena as a contender for power. Hitler's Nazi state ruled by violence, coercion, and intimidation. With a propaganda machine that glorified the leader and vilified groups singled out as scapegoats for Germany's problems, Hitler undermined democratic institutions and civil liberties in his pursuit of German power.

DEMOCRACIES IN CRISIS

Democracies in the 1930s turned in on themselves in order to survive. In contrast to the Fascist mobilization of society and the Soviet restructuring of the economy, European democracies took small, tentative steps to respond to the challenges of the Great Depression. Democratic leaders lacked creative vision or even clear policy. Both democratic France and Great Britain were less successful than Nazi Germany in responding to the challenges of the Great Depression. France paid a high price for parliamentary stalemate and was still severely depressed on the eve of war in 1938–1939. Great Britain maintained a stagnant economy and stable politics under Conservative leadership. Internal dissension ripped Spain apart. Its civil war assumed broader dimensions as the Soviet Union, Italy, and Germany struggled over Spain's future while Europe's democratic nations stood by and accepted defeat.

The Failure of the Left in France

France's Third Republic, like most European parliamentary democracies in the 1930s, was characterized by a multiparty system. Genuine political differences often separated one party from another. The tendency toward parliamentary stalemate

MAP DISCOVERY

Dictatorships by 1938

Democracies dismantled by dictatorships, 1938 – 1940

Remaining democracies in 1940

Europe: Types of Government

Note the prevalence of dictatorships throughout Europe in 1940. How many democracies were dismantled by dictatorships between 1938 and 1940? What were the similarities and differences among these dictatorships? By 1940, most European nations were ruled by dictatorships. What five countries were the exceptions? What generalizations, if any, might you make about those five democracies? Were European dictatorships allied or ideologically similar?

problem. Distrusting both the New Deal model of the United States and the Nazi response to depression politics, the Third Republic followed a haphazard, wait-and-see policy of insulating the economy, discouraging competition, and protecting favored interests in both industry and agriculture. Stimulating the economy by deficit spending was considered anathema. Devaluation of the franc, which might have helped French exports, was regarded by policy makers as an unpatriotic act. France stood fast as a bastion of liberal belief in the self-adjusting mechanism of the market, and it suffered greatly for it. Party politics worked to reinforce the defensive rather than offensive response to the challenges of depression and a sluggish economy.

In 1936, an electoral mandate for change swept the Left into power. The new premier, Léon Blum (1872–1950), was a Socialist. Lacking the votes to rule with an exclusively Socialist government, Blum formed a coalition of Left and Center parties intent on economic reforms known as the **Popular Front.** Before Blum's government could take power, a wave of strikes swept France. Although reluctant to intervene in the economy, the Popular Front nevertheless was pushed into some action. It promised wage increases, paid vacations, and collective bargaining to French workers. The reduced workweek of 40 hours caused a drop in productivity, as did the short-lived one-month vacation policy. The government did nothing to prevent the outflow of investment capital from France. Higher wages failed to generate increased consumer demand because employers raised prices to cover their higher operating costs.

German rearmament, now publicly known, forced France into rearmament, which it could ill afford. Blum's government failed in 1937, with France still bogged down in a sluggish and depressed economy. The last peacetime government of the

was aggravated by the Great Depression and by the increasingly extremist politics on both the left and the right in response to developments in the Soviet Union and Germany.

The belief of the French people in a private enterprise economy was shaken by the Great Depression, but no new unifying belief replaced it. Some believed that state planning was the answer; others were sure that state intervention had caused the

1930s represented a conservative swing back to laissez-faire policies that put the needs of business above those of workers and brought a measure of revival to the French economy.

The radical Right drew strength from the Left's failures. Right-wing leagues and organizations multiplied, appealing to a frightened middle class. The failure of the Socialists, in turn, drove many sympathizers further to the left to join the Communist party. A divided France could not stand up to the foreign policy challenges of the 1930s posed by Hitler's provocations.

Muddling Through in Great Britain

Great Britain was hard hit by the Great Depression of the 1930s; only Germany and the United States experienced comparable economic devastation. The socialist Labour government of the years 1929–1931 under Prime Minister Ramsay MacDonald (1866–1937) was unprepared to deal with the 1929 collapse and lacked the vision and the planning to devise a way out of the morass. It took a coalition of moderate groups from the three parties—Liberal, Conservative, and Labour—to address the issues of high unemployment, a growing government deficit, a banking crisis, and the flight of capital. The National Government (1931–1935) was a centrist, nonpartisan coalition whose members included Ramsay MacDonald, retained as prime minister, and Stanley Baldwin (1867–1947), a Conservative with a background in iron and steel manufacturing.

Slow Recovery. In response to the endemic crisis, the National Government took Britain off the international gold standard and devalued the pound. In order to protect domestic production, tariffs were established. The British economy showed signs of slow recovery, probably due less to the government measures than to a gradual improvement in the business cycle. The government had survived the crisis without resorting to the kinds of creative alternatives devised in the Scandinavian countries, where, for example, consumer and producer cooperatives provided widespread economic relief. Moderates and classical liberals in Great Britain persisted in defending the nonintervention of the government in the economy, despite new economic theories such as that of John Maynard Keynes (1883–1946), who urged government spending to stimulate consumer demand as the best way to shorten the duration of the Great Depression.

The British Union of Fascists.   In 1932, Sir Oswald Mosley (1896–1980) founded the British Union of Fascists (BUF), consisting of goon squads and bodyguards. The BUF was opposed to free trade liberalism and communism alike. Mosley developed a corporate model for economic and political life in which interest groups rather than an electorate would be represented in a new kind of parliament. He favored, above all, national solutions by relying on imperial development; he rejected the world of international finance as corrupt.

The BUF shared similarities with European Fascist organizations. BUF squads beat up their political opponents and began attacking Jews, especially the eastern European émigrés living in London. The British fascists struck a responsive chord among the poorest working-class people of London's East End; at its peak the group claimed a membership of 20,000. Public alarm over increasingly inflammatory and

■ A British Union of Fascists unit salutes founder Sir Oswald Mosley in London, October 1936.

A Closer Look
The Screams from Guernica

Rarely does a piece of art scream out. The mural *Guernica* is different. *Listen* to the painting shown here. It is a painting whose images convey sounds: the shrieks of terror, fear, suffering, and death. There is a chaos of noise here that seems at odds with the drab grays, black, and white, the monochromatic colorlessness of the artist's palette. But no, the lack of color only heightens the noise and allows us to focus on the sound, the screams that come from the open mouths of human and beast on the canvas. Death and brutality reverberate throughout the painting. The open mouths of the dead baby's mother, the bull standing behind her, the small bird to the right of the bull, and the wounded horse at the center of the canvas emit fear like projectiles— beak and tongues thrusting forth in pointed daggers.

The artist Pablo Picasso (1881–1973) painted the great mural in May and June 1937 for the Spanish Pavilion of the International Exhibition to be held in Paris. He called it *Guernica* in commemoration of the bombing of the small Basque town in Spain by German planes at the end of April 1937. The destruction of Guernica was an event that shocked the world and devastated the Spanish artist, then living in France.

Working in collaboration with the insurgent forces of Francisco Franco (1892–1975), German planes dropped bomb after bomb on the ancient city, destroying it in three and a half hours. Their purpose was to cut off the retreat of loyalist government troops and to terrorize civilians through saturation bombing. Picasso demonstrates here vividly that noncombatants, represented by the women and child, were no longer just hapless bystanders but were, in fact, the very targets of indiscriminate killing.

Guernica is a huge canvas, measuring more than 11 feet high and 25 feet wide. It dwarfs spectators who stand before it, enveloping them in a modern-day apocalypse of contorted bodies. We do not look at war directly in the mural but at the terror it creates in this vision of needless slaughter. Picasso deliberately used the traditional religious symbols of the Madonna and Child and the Pietà as models for his terrifying image of maternity. The lips of the baby, who hangs like a rag doll in the arms of its despairing mother on the far left of the canvas, are sealed in the silence of death. The mother finds her counterpoint in the figure of the limping woman in the right foreground, who

drags behind her a wounded arm and a swollen knee. Above her a woman, gaping in disbelief and clutching her breasts in anguish, raises a lamp over the scene. On the far right, a fourth woman, trapped in the flames of a burning building, appears to be exploding upward in terrified petition. On the ground under the horse lies a dead man with his head and arm severed from his body, clutching a broken sword and flower whose petals wait to be picked in his right hand. The presentation of his head as a piece of statuary fallen from its pedestal reinforces the bloodless horror of his death. His left palm is crisscrossed with the lines of fate, or perhaps marked with the toil of heavy labor. Suspended over the scene like a huge eye is a naked light bulb, a modern image illuminating the timelessness of the theme of the horror of war.

In one of his rare moments of self-interpretation, Picasso explained to a public eager to grasp the mural's symbolism that the horse whose side is opened by a terrible gash is "the people," victimized by incomprehensible cruelty. The bull is an enigmatic figure symbolizing, Picasso said, darkness and brutality. The horned beast appears as a powerful and vulnerable

■ Pablo Picasso, *Guernica*, 1937. Museo del Prado, Madrid. © 2000 Estate of Pablo Picasso/Artists Rights Society (ARS), New York

witness to the scene of needless destruction.

Guernica has been hailed as the most significant painting of the twentieth century. His greatness as an artist, Picasso claimed, derived from his ability to understand his time. In the stripped-down, almost cartoonlike figures of *Guernica*, Picasso presents a picture of European society that is brutal and horrible. It is a condemnation of the modern technological war that targets civilian populations; there on the horrifying canvas are portrayed the consequences of totalitarianism and the failure of democracy that characterized the European search for stability between 1920 and 1939. Subsequent events made Germany's actions in the Spanish Civil War seem like a dress rehearsal for atrocities against the population centers of Warsaw, Rotterdam, and London and made this canvas seem a prophecy of horrors to come. Some years later, during the Second World War, a Nazi official challenged Picasso with a photograph of the great mural: "So it was you who did this." The artist answered, "No, you did."

anti-Semitic rhetoric converged with parliamentary denunciation. Popular support for the group was already beginning to erode when the BUF was outlawed in 1936. By that time, anti-Hitler feeling was spreading in Great Britain.

Mosley's response to harsh economic times had proven to be no match for the steady and reassuring strength of Stanley Baldwin's National Government, which seemed to be in control of an improving economic situation. The traditional party system prevailed not because of its brilliant solutions to difficult economic problems but because of the willingness of moderate parliamentarians to cooperate and adapt, however slowly, to the new need for economic transformation.

The Spanish Republic as Battleground

In 1931, Spain became a democratic republic after centuries of Bourbon monarchy and almost a decade of military dictatorship. In 1936, the voters of Spain elected a Popular Front government. The Popular Front in Spain was more radical than its French counterpart. The property of aristocratic landlords was seized; revolutionary workers went on strike; the Catholic Church and its clergy were attacked.

The social revolution initiated three years of civil war. On one side were the Republicans, the Popular Front defenders of the Spanish Republic and of social revolution in Spain. On the other side were the Nationalists, those who sought to

■ The Spanish Civil War. The Civil War in Spain lasted from 1936 to 1939, with the Nationalists controlling only the south and west until they defeated the Republicans in their strongholds in the north and east.

Spanish capital (Republican stronghold)

★ Nationalist provisional capital

✸ Major battles or bombings

CHRONOLOGY	
THE RISE OF FASCISM AND DEMOCRACIES IN CRISIS	
28 October 1922	Italian Fascists march on Rome
November 1923	Beer Hall Putsch in Munich
1924	Fascists achieve parliamentary majority in Italy
1929	Lateran Treaty between Mussolini and Pope Pius XI
1932	Nazi party is single largest party in German parliament
January 1933	Hitler becomes chancellor of Germany
30 June 1934	Purge of the SA leaves Hitler and the SS in unassailable position
March 1935	Hitler publicly rejects Treaty of Versailles and announces German rearmament
15 September 1935	Enactment of Nuremberg Laws against Jews and other minorities
3 October 1935	Italy invades Ethiopia
1936	Popular Front government elected in Spain
July 1936	Beginning of Spanish Civil War
October 1936	Rome-Berlin Axis Pact, an Italo–German accord
1936–1937	Popular Front government in France
27 April 1937	Bombing of the Spanish town of Guernica
9 November 1938	*Kristallnacht* initiates massive violence against Jews
March 1939	Fascists defeat the Spanish Republic
April 1939	Italy annexes Albania
May 1939	Pact of Steel between Germany and Italy

overthrow the Republic—aristocratic landowners, supporters of the monarchy and the Catholic Church, and much of the Spanish army.

The Spanish Civil War began in July 1936 with a revolt against the Republic from within the Spanish army. It was led by General Francisco Franco (1892–1975), a tough, shrewd, and stubborn man, a conservative nationalist allied with the

■ A Spanish Civil War propaganda poster of the *Izquierda Republicana* (the Republican Left Party) supporting the Popular Front against the international threat of fascism.

Falange, the Fascist party in Spain. The conflict soon became a bloody military stalemate, with the Nationalists led by Franco controlling the more rural and conservative south and west of Spain and the Republicans holding out in the cities of the north and east—Madrid, Valencia, and Barcelona.

Almost from the beginning, the Spanish Civil War was an international event. Mussolini sent ground troops, "volunteers," to fight alongside Franco's forces. Hitler dispatched technical specialists, tanks, and the Condor Legion, an aviation unit, to support the Nationalists. The Germans regarded Spain as a testing ground for new equipment and new methods of warfare, including aerial bombardment. (See "A Closer Look: The Screams from Guernica," pp. 860–861.) The Soviet Union intervened on the side of the Republic, sending armaments, supplies, and technical and political advisers. Because the people of Britain and France were deeply divided in their attitudes toward the war in Spain, the British government stayed neutral, and the government of France was unable to aid its fellow Popular Front government in Spain. Although Americans volunteered to fight with the Republicans, the American government did not prevent the Texas Oil Company from selling 1.9 million tons of oil to Franco's insurgents, nor did it block the Ford Motor Company, General Motors, and Studebaker from supplying them with trucks.

The Spanish government pleaded, "Men and women of all lands! Come to our aid!" In response, 2800 American volunteers—among them college students, professors, intellectuals, and trade unionists—joined the loyalist army and European volunteers in defense of the Spanish Republic. Britons and antifascist émigrés from Italy and Germany also joined the International Brigades, which were vital in helping the city of Madrid hold out against the Nationalist generals. The Russians withdrew from the war in 1938, disillusioned by the failure of the French, British, and Americans to come to the aid of the Republicans. Madrid fell to the Nationalists in March 1939. The government established by Franco sent one million of its enemies to prison or concentration camps.

CONCLUSION

The fragile postwar stability of the 1920s crumbled under the pressures of economic depression, ongoing national antagonisms, and insecurity in the international arena. Europe after 1932 was plagued by the consequences of economic collapse, Fascist success, and the growing threat of armed conflict. Parliamentary institutions were fighting and losing a tug-of-war with authoritarian movements. A Fascist regime was in place in Italy. Political and electoral defeats eroded democratic and liberal principles in Germany's Weimar Republic. Dictatorships triumphed in Spain and in much of eastern and central Europe. Liberal parliamentary governments were failing to solve the economic and social problems of the postwar years. In the democratic nations of France, Great Britain, and, during the brief period from 1931 to 1936, Spain, parliamentary institutions appeared to be persevering. But even there, polarization and increasing intransigence on both the left and the right threatened the future of democratic politics.

The exclusion of the Soviet Union from Western internationalism in the 1920s both reflected and exacerbated the crisis. The Bolshevik revolution had served as a political catalyst among workers in the West, attracting them to the possibility of radical solutions. That potential radicalization aggravated class antagonisms in the 1930s, when mass politics prevailed and drove political leaders to seek conservative solutions as a means of stabilizing class politics.

QUESTIONS FOR REVIEW

1. What problems for European stability were created or left unresolved by the armistice ending World War I?
2. What did Stalin's victory over Trotsky mean for economic development in the Soviet Union?
3. What is fascism, and why was it so alluring to Italians, Germans, and other Europeans?
4. How were rearmament, anti-Semitism, and autarky all part of Hitler's vision of *Lebensraum*?
5. Why did Europe's remaining democracies prove to be so frail during the 1930s?

KEY TERMS

collectivization, *p. 846*

fascism, *p. 849*

Great Depression, *p. 840*

Great Purge, *p. 847*

Kristallnacht, *p. 857*

Lebensraum, *p. 853*

Nazism, *p. 850*

New Economic Policy (NEP), *p. 843*

Popular Front, *p. 858*

Third Reich, *p. 853*

Weimar Republic, *p. 836*

DISCOVERING WESTERN CIVILIZATION ONLINE

You can obtain more information about the European search for stability between 1920 and 1939 at the Websites listed below. See also the Companion Website that accompanies this text, www.ablongman.com/kishlansky, which contains an online study guide and additional resources.

Geographical Tour: Europe After 1918

League of Nations Statistical and Disarmament Documents

www.library.nwu.edu/govpub/collections/league/index.html
This is the home page of a project to digitize documents published by the League of Nations.

Internet Modern History Sourcebook: Age of Anxiety

www.fordham.edu/halsall/mod/modsbook40.html
A collection of links to electronic texts and materials on the interwar period, focusing on the cultural crisis in European and American societies as a result of World War I.

Internet Modern History Sourcebook: The Depression

www.fordham.edu/halsall/mod/modsbook41.html
Comprehensive collection of primary sources and links to materials on the Great Depression in Europe and the United States.

The Soviet Union's Separate Path

NEP: A Bibliography of Soviet and Western Literature

www.lib.duke.edu/ias/slavic/nep.htm
This site contains an exhaustive bibliography on Soviet history during the period of the New Economic Policy.

Revelations from the Russian Archives

www.loc.gov/exhibits/archives
A virtual exhibit by the Library of Congress on material from the secret archives of the Central Committee of the Communist Party of the USSR.

The Rise of Fascist Dictatorship in Italy

Internet Modern History Sourcebook: Fascism in Europe

www.fordham.edu/halsall/mod/modsbook42.html
This site refers to fascism in general, but it focuses on a speech of Mussolini and Spanish Civil War materials.

Hitler and the Third Reich

The National Socialist Era, 1933–1945

www2.h-net.msu.edu/~german/gtext/nazi/index.html
Sponsored by the H-German list, this is a small collection of electronic texts relating to the rise of the Nazis, the creation of the Third Reich, and World War II.

Internet Modern History Sourcebook: Nazism

www.fordham.edu/halsall/mod/modsbook43.html
A collection of primary documents and links on the Weimar Republic and the rise of Nazism.

Third Reich Stamps

www.geocities.com/WallStreet/Exchange/5456/third.html
A Web site of stamps issued during the Third Reich with brief descriptions depicting the cultural values propagated by the Nazis.

Democracies in Crisis

Spanish Civil War Archive

dwardmac.pitzer.edu/anarchist_archives/spancivwar/Spanishcivilwar.html
This site was created by a political studies professor at Pitzer College (see link for Paris Commune in Chapter 23) and contains essays, bibliography, and photographs.

SUGGESTIONS FOR FURTHER READING

Geographical Tour: Europe After 1918

Manfred E. Boemeke, Gerald Feldman, and Elisabeth Glaser, eds., *The Treaty of Versailles: A Reassessment After 75 Years* (Cambridge: Cambridge University Press, 1998). This collection of essays constitutes a reappraisal of the divergent peace aims of the United States, France, Germany, and Great Britain and a new understanding of the period of temporary stability created by the treaty after the war.

Igor Lukes, *Czechoslovakia Between Stalin and Hitler: The Diplomacy of Edvard Beneš in the 1930s* (New York: Oxford University Press, 1996). By examining the Czech statesman Edvard Beneš role this book provides an important perspective on the Munich crisis of 1938 and of Czechoslovakia's fate in the battle between East and West.

Crisis and Collapse in a World Economy

Gerald Feldman, *The Great Disorder: Politics, Economy, and Society in the German Inflation, 1914–1924* (New York: Oxford University Press, 1993). Feldman's monumental study of the German inflation provides a detailed historical account of the economic conditions and monetary policy in Germany during and after the war.

The Soviet Union's Separate Path

Stephen F. Cohen, *Bukharin and the Bolshevik Revolution: A Political Biography, 1888–1938* (Oxford: Oxford University Press, 1980). This millestone work is a general history of the period, as well as a political and intellectual biography of Bukharin, "the last Bolshevik," who supported an evolutionary road to modernization and socialism and whose policies were an alternative to Stalinism.

Sheila Fitzpatrick, *Everyday Stalinism—Ordinary Life in Extraordinary Times: Soviet Russia in the 1930s* (New York: Oxford University Press, 1999). The author explores the rituals, family life, and institutions of the Stalinist era, what the author calls the "distinctive Stalinist habitat" of Russian urban life in the 1930s.

Arch Getty and Roberta Manning, *Stalinist Terror: New Perspectives* (Cambridge: Cambridge University Press, 1994). Leading revisionist scholars of the Stalinist period provide a reassessment of the regime.

Robert C. Tucker, *Stalin in Power: The Revolution from Above, 1928–1941* (New York: W.W. Norton & Company, 1992). The author portrays how Stalin deliberately chose terror, mass murder, forced resettlement, and prison camps as a means of enforcing "revolution from above."

Chris Ward, ed., *The Stalinist Dictatorship* (New York: Oxford University Press, 1998). A collection of leading Soviet scholars examine Stalin's character, his role within the Soviet Union, and how Stalinism was a lived experience.

The Rise of Fascist Dictatorship in Italy

MacGregor Knox, *Dictatorship, Foreign Policy, and War in Fascist Italy and Nazi Germany* (London: Cambridge University Press, 2000). Expanding on his earlier work on Mussolini's foreign policy, the author offers a comparative perspective of Italy's and Germany's moves from unification to militant dictatorships, the similar forces that shaped their creation, and the differences in expansionist zeal, military traditions, and fighting power.

Zeev Sternhell with Mario Sznajder and Maia Asheri, *The Birth of Fascist Ideology: From Cultural Rebellion to Political Revolution* (Princeton, NJ: Princeton University Press, 1994). Approaches fascism as an ideology rather than a social movement and argues that it was already fully formed before World War I.

Hitler and the Third Reich

Ian Kershaw, *Hitler, 1889–1936: Hubris* (New York: W.W. Norton & Company, 1998); and *Hitler, 1936–1945: Nemesis* (New York: W.W. Norton & Company, 2000). The definitive two-volume biography provides a history of Germany society through Hitler's extraordinary political domination.

Dieter Langewiesche, *Liberalism in Germany.* Translated by Christiane Banerji. (Princeton, NJ: Princeton University Press, 2000). This translated work traces the history of German liberalism from the early nineteenth century to post-1945 politics in West Germany as it was embodied in political movements, organizations, and values.

Bernd Widdig, *Culture and Inflation in Weimar Germany* (Berkeley: University of California Press, 2001). Through literary and filmic sources, the author provides a cultural analysis of a defining economic event in Germany history.

Democracies in Crisis

Ivan T. Berend, *Decades of Crisis: Central and Eastern Europe Before World War II* (Berkeley: University of California Press, 1998). The author offers a comprehensive overview of central and eastern Europe in the first half of the twentieth century and argues that the region "embarked on a historical 'detour'" in rejecting the parliamentary system and turning to nationalist authoritarian regimes.

John Hiden and Patrick Salmon, *The Baltic Nations and Europe: Estonia, Latvia, and Lithuania in the Twentieth Century* (London and New York: Longman, 1991). Surveys the development of the Baltic states in the twentieth century, discussing Baltic independence, the period between the wars, and the states' incorporation into the Soviet Union, as well as renewed efforts toward independence in the Gorbachev era.

Julian Jackson, *The Popular Front in France: Defending Democracy, 1934–1938* (Cambridge: Cambridge University Press, 1988). An in-depth study of Léon Blum's government, with a special emphasis on cultural transformation and the legacy of the Popular Front.

Michael Jackson, *Fallen Sparrows: The International Brigades in the Spanish Civil War* (Philadelphia: American Philosophical Society, 1994). A careful description of the members and activities of the International Brigades, which were organized under the direction of the Comintern to save the Spanish Republic.

Stanley G. Payne, *Fascism in Spain, 1923–1977* (Madison: The University of Wisconsin Press, 1999). The author presents a comprehensive history of Spanish fascism from its origins to the death of Franco.

Michael Richards, *A Time of Silence: Civil War and the Culture of Repression in Franco's Spain, 1936–1945* (Cambridge: Cambridge University Press, 1998). This work examines Spanish society during and after the Spanish Civil War in relation to Franco's policy of "moral and economic reconstruction" based on self-sufficiency.

For a list of additional titles related to this chapter's topics, please see http://www.ablongman.com/kishlansky.

Chapter 28

GLOBAL CONFLAGRATION: WORLD WAR II, 1939–1945

Chapter Outline

In 1938, Europe watched as Adolf Hitler made one bold move after another. One year later, the world was once again at war. Turn the page to see how The Visual Record captures the spectacle of Hitler's 1938 entry into Austria. ➤

PRECURSOR OF WAR
The Annexation of Austria

Adolf Hitler's entry into Vienna, capital city of his native country of Austria, was planned as a media event. The accompanying photograph displays a triumphant Hitler leading what appears to be a parade on 14 March 1938. Standing in his open Mercedes in order to be visible to thousands of cheering Austrians and protected by thirteen police cars, Hitler was no less the conqueror. The motorcade of limousines moved slowly along the Ringstrasse, Vienna's most important street of monumental public buildings, greeted by wildly cheering crowds. The Nazi swastika fluttered on flagpoles and draped facades. The viewer is left to wonder how the flags and banners could have been manufactured and positioned over the course of a weekend to greet the Fuhrer's unannounced and "friendly visit." The independent nation of Austria had, overnight and with virtually no bloodshed, become part of the German Reich.

On the first page of *Mein Kampf,* Hitler had promised, "Germany-Austria must return to the great German mothercountry, and not because of any economic considerations. . . . One blood demands one Reich." By 1938 Hitler had consolidated power at home by removing the non-Nazi conservatives from positions of power in Germany. Now he alone determined foreign policy. As a cornerstone of that policy, Hitler aimed to unite all German people in one nation by extending German control over territories including those not ethnically German, but which could provide "living space" and economic self-sufficiency for the German race. (See "Nazi Goals" in Chapter 27.) Becoming increasingly impatient, Hitler feared that Germany could fail to achieve its destiny as a world power by waiting too long to act. He became more aggressive and willing to use military force as he set out to remove, one by one, the obstacles to German domination of central Europe—Austria, Czechoslovakia, and Poland.

The annexation of Austria was the first step in Hitler's plans for conquest. Using the threat of invasion, Hitler intimidated the Austrian government into legalizing the Nazi party, which thereby brought pro-Nazis into the Austrian cabinet and German troops into the country. Many Austrians wanted to be joined to Germany; others had no desire to be led by Nazis. A rigged plebiscite in April 1938, organized by Goebbels's Propaganda Ministry, delivered a 99.75 percent vote of approval in Austria for annexation by Germany. With the union of Austria and Germany, the Third Reich claimed a population of 80 million people as it prepared itself for a war to the east. What appeared to be a parade of pomp and circumstance in March 1938 was really the precursor of a terrible conflagration that would last for six years and claim 50 million lives around the globe.

Looking Ahead

This chapter considers the events leading to the outbreak of the war in 1939 and how collaboration and resistance developed across Europe as the German army advanced. Virulent racism played a central role in directing the war against Jews, Slavs, and others identified as inferior by Nazi racial policies. The power of Soviet patriotism and bravery and the entry of the United States into the war ensured Allied victory. Allied cooperation gave way, however, even as the peace was being forged under the direction of the two superpowers. The dropping of the atom bomb on Japan hastened the war's end, but would taint the ensuing peace. ➤

■ A triumphant Hitler enters Austria in 1938.

AGGRESSION AND CONQUEST

The years between 1933 and 1939 marked a bleak period in international affairs when the British, the French, and the Americans were unwilling or unable to recognize the dire threat to world peace posed by Hitler and his Nazi state. The leaders of those countries did not comprehend Hitler's single-minded goal to extend German living space eastward as far as western Russia. They failed to understand the seriousness of the Nazi process of consolidation at home. They took no action against Hitler's initial acts of aggression. The war that began in Europe in 1939 eventually became a global conflict that pitted Germany, Italy, and Japan—the **Axis Powers**—against the British Empire, the Soviet Union, and the United States—the Grand Alliance.

Even before war broke out in Europe, there was armed conflict in Asia. The rapidly expanding Japanese economy depended on Manchuria for raw materials and on China for markets. Chinese boycotts against Japanese goods and threats to Japanese economic interests in Manchuria led to a Japanese military occupation of Manchuria and the establishment of a Japanese puppet state there in 1931–1932. When the powers of the League of Nations, led by Great Britain, refused to recognize that state, Japan withdrew from the League. Fearing that the Chinese government was becoming strong enough to exclude Japanese trade from China, Japanese troops and naval units began an undeclared war in China in 1937. Many important Chinese cities—Peking, Shanghai, Nanking, Canton, and Hankow—fell to Japanese forces. Relentless aerial bombardment of Chinese cities and atrocities committed by Japanese troops against Chinese civilians outraged Europeans and Americans. The governments of the Soviet Union, Great Britain, and the United States, seeking to protect their own ideological, economic, and security interests in China, gave economic, diplomatic, and moral support to the Chinese government of Chiang Kai-shek. Thus the stage was set for major military conflicts in Asia and in Europe.

Hitler's Foreign Policy and Appeasement

For Hitler a war against the Soviet Union for living space was inevitable. It would come, he told some of his close associates, in the years 1943–1945. However, he wanted to avoid fighting anew the war that had led to Germany's defeat in 1914–1918. World War I was a war fought on two fronts—in the east and in the west. It was a war in which Germany had to face many enemies at the same time, and a war that lasted until German soldiers, civilians, and resources were exhausted. In the next war, Hitler wanted above all to avoid fighting Great Britain while battling Russia for living space. He convinced himself that the British would remain neutral if Germany agreed not to attack the British Empire. Would they not appreciate his willingness to abolish forever the menace of communism? Were they not Aryans too?

The Campaign Against Czechoslovakia.   Encouraged by his success in the annexation of Austria in March 1938, Hitler provoked a crisis in Czechoslovakia in the summer of the same year. He demanded "freedom" for the German-speaking people of the Sudetenland area of Czechoslovakia. His main objective, however, was not to protect the Germans of Czechoslovakia but to smash the Czech state, the major obstacle in central Europe to the launching of an attack on living space farther east.

Western statesmen did not understand Hitler's commitment to destroying Czechoslovakia or his willingness to fight a limited war against the Czechs to do so. Hitler did everything possible to isolate Czechoslovakia from its neighbors and its treaty partners. France, an ally of Czechoslovakia, appeared distinctly unwilling to defend it against Germany's menace. Britain, seeking to avoid a war that the government did not think was necessary and for which the British were not prepared, sent Prime Minister Neville Chamberlain (1869–1940) to reason with Hitler. Believing that transferring the Sudetenland, the German-speaking area of Czechoslovakia, to Germany was the only solution—and one that would redress some of the wrongs done to Germany after World War I—Chamberlain convinced France and Czechoslovakia to yield to Hitler's demands.

Appeasement at Munich.   Chamberlain's actions were the result of British self-interest. British leaders agreed that their country could not afford another war like the Great War of 1914–1918. Defense expenditures had been dramatically reduced to devote national resources to improving domestic social services, protecting world trade, and fortifying Britain's global interests. Britain understood well its weakened position in its dominions. In the British hierarchy of priorities, defense of the British Empire ranked first, above defense of Europe; Britain's commitment to western Europe ranked above the defense of eastern and central Europe.

Hitler's response to being granted everything he requested was to renege and issue new demands. One final meeting was held at Munich to avert war. On 29 September 1938, one day before German troops were scheduled to invade Czechoslovakia, Mussolini and the French prime minister, Édouard Daladier (1884–1970), joined Hitler and Chamberlain at Munich to discuss a peaceful resolution to the crisis.

At Munich, Chamberlain and Daladier again yielded to Hitler's demands. The Sudetenland was ceded to Germany, and German troops quickly moved to occupy the area. The policy of the British and French was dubbed **appeasement** to indicate the willingness to concede to demands in order to preserve peace. Appeasement became a dirty word in twentieth-century European history, taken to mean weakness and cowardice. Yet Chamberlain was neither weak nor cowardly. His great mistake in negotiating with Hitler was in assuming that Hitler was a reasonable man, who like all reasonable persons wanted to avoid another war.

Chamberlain thought his mediation at Munich had won for Europe a lasting peace—"peace for our time," he reported. The people of Europe received Chamberlain's assessment with a sense of relief and shame—relief over what had been avoided, shame at having deserted Czechoslovakia. In fact, the policy of appeasement further destabilized Europe and accelerated Hitler's plans for European domination. Within months, Hitler cast aside the Munich agreement by annihilating Czechoslovakia. German troops occupied the western, Czech part of the state, including the capital of Prague. The Slovak eastern part became independent and a German satellite. At the same time, Lithuania was pressured into surrendering Memel to Germany, and Hitler demanded that Germany control Gdansk and the Polish Corridor. No longer could Hitler be ignored or appeased. No longer could his goals be misunderstood.

Hitler's War, 1939–1941

In the tense months that followed the Munich meeting and the occupation of Prague, Hitler readied himself for war in western Europe. To strengthen his position, in May 1939 he formed a military alliance, the Pact of Steel, with Mussolini's Italy. Then Hitler and Stalin, previously self-declared enemies, shocked the West by joining their two nations in a pact of mutual neutrality, the Non-Aggression Pact of 1939. Opportunism lay behind Hitler's willingness to ally with the Communist state that he had denounced throughout the 1930s. A German alliance with the Soviet Union would, Hitler believed, force the British and the French to back down and to remain neutral while Germany conquered Poland—the last obstacle to a drive for expansion eastward—in a short, limited war. Stalin recognized the failure of the western European powers to stand up to Hitler. There was little possibility, he thought, of an alliance against Germany with the virulently anti-Communist Neville Chamberlain. The best Stalin could hope for was that the Germans and the Western powers would fight it out while the Soviet Union waited to enter the war at the most opportune moment. As an added bonus, Germany promised not to interfere if the Soviet Union annexed eastern Poland, Bessarabia, and the Baltic republics of Latvia and Estonia.

Finally recognizing Hitler's intent, the British and the French also signed a pact in the spring of 1939 promising assistance to Poland in the event of aggression. Tensions mounted throughout the summer as Europeans awaited the inevitable German aggression. On 1 September 1939, Germany attacked Poland, which was ill-prepared to defend itself. By the end of the month, in spite of valiant resistance, the vastly outnumbered Poles surrendered. Although the German army needed no assistance, the Russians invaded Poland ten days before its collapse, and Germany and Russia divided the spoils. Not trusting his alliance with Hitler, Stalin almost immediately took measures to defend Russia against a possible German attack. The Soviet Union assumed military control in the Baltic states and demanded of Finland territory and military bases from which the city of Leningrad could be

■ A German motorized detachment rides through a bomb-shattered town during the Nazi invasion of Poland in 1939. The invasion saw the first use of the *blitzkrieg*—lightning war—in which air power and rapid tank movement combined for swift victory.

defended. When Finland refused, Russia invaded. In the snows of the "Winter War" of 1939–1940, the Finns initially fought the Russian army to a standstill, much to the encouragement of the democratic West. The Finns, however, were eventually defeated in March 1940.

War in Europe. Hitler's war, the war for German domination of Europe, had begun. But it had not begun the way he intended. Great Britain and France, true to their alliance with Poland and contrary to Hitler's expectations, declared war on Germany on 3 September 1939, even though they were unable to give any help to Poland. In the six months after the fall of Poland, no military action took place between Germany and the Allies as Hitler postponed offensives in northern and western Europe because

MAP DISCOVERY

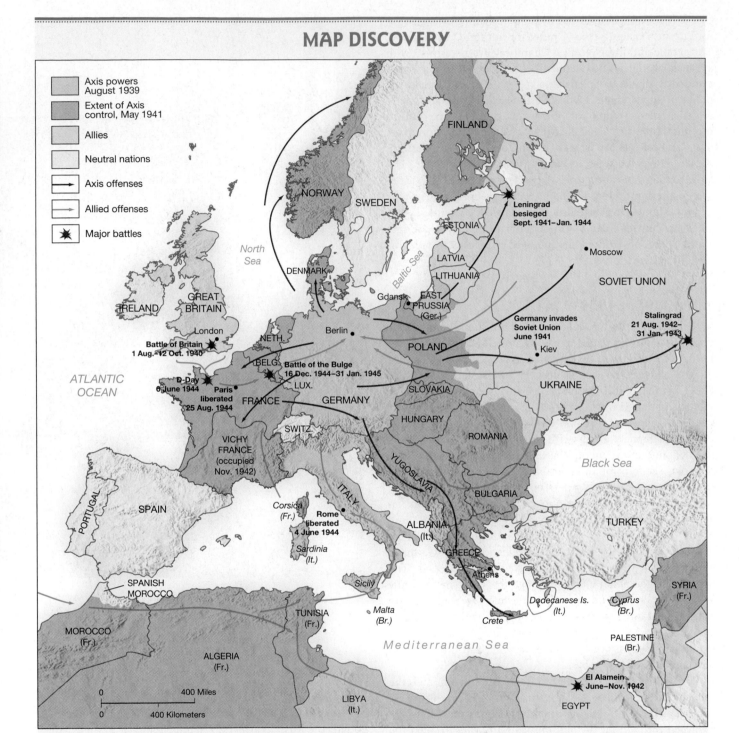

Legend:
- Axis powers August 1939
- Extent of Axis control, May 1941
- Allies
- Neutral nations
- Axis offenses
- Allied offenses
- Major battles

World War II in Europe

Note the movement of Axis armies in four different directions: north, south, east, and west. How were the Axis forces able to sustain a multi-front war? The Axis Powers controlled most of Europe and north Africa by 1941. How do you explain the success of major Allied offensives?

of poor weather conditions. That strange interlude, which became known as "the phony war," was a period of suspended reality in which France and Great Britain waited for Hitler to make his next move. Civilian morale in France deteriorated among a population that still remembered the death and destruction that France had endured in the Great War. An attitude of defeatism germinated and grew before the first French soldier fell in battle.

With the arrival of spring, Germany attacked Denmark and Norway in April 1940. Then, on 10 May 1940, Hitler's armies invaded the Netherlands, Belgium, and Luxembourg. By the third week of May, German mechanized forces were racing through northern France toward the English Channel, cutting off the British and Belgian troops and 120,000 French forces from the rest of the French army. With the rapid defeat of Belgium, the forces were crowded against the Channel and had to be evacuated from the beaches of Dunkirk. France, with a large and well-equipped army, nevertheless relied on Allied support and was in a desperate situation without it.

In France, the German army fought a new kind of war called a *blitzkrieg,* or "lightning war," so named because of its speed. The British and the French had expected the German army to behave much as it had in World War I, concentrating its striking forces in a swing through coastal Belgium and Holland in order to capture Paris. French strategists believed that France was safe because of hilly and forested terrain they thought was impassable. They also counted on the protection of the fortress wall known as the Maginot Line that France had built in the period between the wars. The Maginot Line stretched for hundreds of miles but was useless against mobile tank divisions, which outflanked it. With stunning speed, Germany drove its tanks—panzers—through the French defenses at Sedan in eastern France.

The Fall of France.

The French could have pinched off the advance of the overextended panzers, but the French army, suffering from severe morale problems, collapsed and was in retreat. On 17 June 1940, only weeks after German soldiers had stepped on French soil, Marshal Henri-Philippe Pétain, the great hero of the Battle of Verdun in World War I, petitioned the Germans for an armistice. Three-fifths of France, including the entire Atlantic seaboard, was occupied by the German army and placed under direct German rule. In the territory that remained unoccupied, Pétain created a collaborationist government that resided at Vichy—a spa city in central France—and worked in partnership with the Germans for the rest of the war. Charles de Gaulle (1890–1970), a brigadier general opposed to the armistice, fled to London, where he set up a Free French government in exile.

The Battle of Britain.

French capitulation in June 1940 followed Italian entry into the war on the side of Germany in the same month. The British were now alone in a war against the two Axis Powers as Germany made plans for an invasion of the British Isles from across the English Channel. To prepare the way, the German air force, under Reich marshal Hermann Göring (1893–1946), launched a series of air attacks against England—the Battle of Britain. The German air force first attacked British aircraft, airfields, and munitions centers and then shifted targets to major population centers such as London and industrial cities such as Coventry. Between 7 September and 2 November 1940, the German air force bombed the city of London every night, inflicting serious damage on the city and killing 15,000 people.

■ The Division of France, 1940–1944. The collaborationist Vichy regime governed the southern portion of France, while the Germans occupied the north and west and reannexed the provinces of Alsace and Lorraine.

The British resisted the attacks under the leadership of Winston Churchill, who had succeeded Chamberlain as prime minister in 1940. Churchill was a master public speaker who, in a series of radio broadcasts, inspired the people of Britain with the historic greatness of the task confronting them—holding out against Nazism until the forces of the overseas British Empire and the United States could be marshaled to liberate Europe. The British Royal Air Force inflicted serious losses on German aircraft, while British industry was able to maintain steady production of planes, bombs, and armaments. Civilians endured the nightly destruction and air raids in what Churchill termed Britain's "finest hour." Recognizing his lack of success in establishing air superiority over the Channel or in breaking the will of the British people, Hitler abandoned the Battle of Britain and canceled the invasion.

The Balkans at War.

It was not in Great Britain but in the Balkans that Hitler was able to engage the British enemy and inflict serious losses. The British had a presence in the Greek Peloponnese, where their air units were deployed to support the valiant resistance of the Greeks against Italian aggression. In his original plans for a limited war, Hitler hoped to establish control over the Balkans by peaceful diplomatic means. But Mussolini's disastrous attempt to achieve military glory by conquering Greece impelled Hitler to make his own plans

■ The London Underground was pressed into service as a bomb shelter during the persistent Nazi attacks on London in the Battle of Britain.

to attack Greece in Operation Marita. Using Bulgaria as the base of operations, Germany invaded Yugoslavia, whose government had been weakened by a recent military coup. The capital of Belgrade fell in April 1941. Internal ethnic enmity between the Croats and the Serbs led to the mutiny of Croatian soldiers and to the formation of an autonomous Croatian government favorably disposed to the Germans in Zagreb.

German troops then crossed the Yugoslav border into Greece. Moving quickly down the Greek mainland, German soldiers captured the capital of Athens on 27 April 1941. German forces then turned their attention to the Greek island of Crete, where fleeing British soldiers sought refuge. In the first mass paratroops attack in history, Crete was rapidly subdued, forcing the British to evacuate to Egypt. The British were routed and experienced humiliating defeat by the German blitzkrieg.

The Balkans were important to Hitler for a number of reasons. Half of Germany's wheat and livestock came from the countries of southeastern Europe. Romanian and Hungarian oil fields supplied Germany's only non-Russian oil. Greece and Yugoslavia were important suppliers of metal ores, including aluminum, tin, lead, and copper, so necessary for industry and the war effort.

The necessity of protecting resources, especially the oil fields in Romania, also gave the area geopolitical importance for Germany. In launching an attack against the Soviet Union, Hitler was well aware of the strategic significance of controlling the straits linking the Mediterranean and Black seas. The British lifeline to its empire could also be cut by control of the eastern Mediterranean.

Collaboration and Resistance

No one nation has ever controlled the Balkans, and Hitler understood that he must rule not by occupation but by collaboration. Some Balkan collaborators joined puppet governments out of an ideological commitment to fascism. They were hostile to communism and believed that Hitler's Nazism was far preferable to Stalin's communism. They saw in the German victory the chance to put their beliefs into practice.

Motives for Collaboration.   Some governments collaborated with the Germans out of national self-interest. Just as the government of Hungary allied with Germany in the hope of winning back territory lost at the end of World War I, Romania allied with Russia. The government of Slovakia was loyal to the Third Reich because Hitler had given it independence from the Czechs. A German puppet state was set up in the Yugoslav province of Croatia. Other collaborators were pragmatists who believed that by taking political office they could negotiate with the German conquerors and soften the effects of the Nazi conquest on their people. Hitler had little affection for local ideological fascists and sometimes smashed their movements. He preferred to work with local generals and administrators. Pragmatic collaborators often could not or would not negotiate with the German authorities. The help they gave in rounding up opponents of Nazi Germany—resistance fighters and Jews—resulted in their punishment after the war.

Forms of Resistance.   Resistance against German occupation and collaborationist regimes took many forms. Resisters wrote subversive tracts, distributed them, gathered intelligence information for the Allies, sheltered Jews or other enemies of the Nazis, committed acts of sabotage or assassination or other violent acts, and carried on guerrilla warfare against the German army. Resisters ran the risk of endangering themselves and their families, who, if discovered, would be tortured and killed. Resistance movements developed after the German attack on the Soviet Union in 1941, when the Communist parties of occupied Europe formed the core of the violent resistance against the Nazi regime. Resistance grew when the

Germans began to draft young European men for work on German farms and in German factories. Many preferred to go underground rather than to Germany.

One of the great resistance fighters of the Second World War was Josip Broz (1892–1980), alias Tito. He was a Croatian Communist and a Yugoslav nationalist. Instead of waiting to be liberated by the Allies, his partisans fought against Italian and German troops. Ten or more German divisions that might otherwise have fought elsewhere were tied up combating Tito's forces. He gained the admiration and the support of Churchill, Roosevelt, and Stalin. After liberation, Tito's organization won 90 percent of the vote in the Yugoslav elections, and he became the leader of the country in the postwar era. Resistance entailed enormous risks and required secrecy, moral courage, and great bravery. On the whole, however, the actions of resistance fighters seldom affected military timetables and did little to change the course of the war and Hitler's domination of Europe.

By the middle of 1941, Hitler controlled a vast continental empire that stretched from the Baltic to the Black Sea and from the Atlantic Ocean to the Russian border. Either the German army occupied territories and controlled satellites, or Hitler relied on collaborationist governments for support. Having destroyed the democracies of western Europe, with the exception of Great Britain, Hitler's armies absorbed territory and marched across nations at rapid speed with technical and strategic superiority. Military conquest was not the only horror that the seemingly invincible Hitler inflicted on European peoples.

RACISM AND DESTRUCTION

War, as the saying goes, is hell. But the horrors perpetrated in World War II exceeded anything ever experienced in Western civilization. Claims of racial superiority were invoked to justify inhuman atrocities. The Germans and Japanese used spurious arguments of racial superiority to fuel their war efforts in both the European and Asian theaters of battle. But the Germans and the Japanese were not alone in using racist propaganda. The United States employed racial stereotypes to depict the inferiority of the enemy, and the government interned Japanese-Americans living on the West Coast in camps and seized their property.

Nowhere, however, was the use of racism by the state more virulent than in Germany. German racist ideology distorted pseudoscientific theories for the purpose of separating those they deemed racially superior from those considered racially inferior. The phrase "the master race" was used to identify those human beings worthy of living; those not worthy were designated "subhuman." Hatred of certain groups fueled both politics and war. Hitler promised the German people a purified Reich of Aryans free of the Jews and the racially and mentally inferior. Slavic peoples—Poles and Russians—were designated as subhumans who could be displaced in the search for "living space" for German citizens and German destiny.

With the war in eastern Europe, anti-Semitism changed from a policy of persecution and expropriation in the 1930s into a program of systematic extermination beginning in 1941.

Enforcing Nazi Racial Policies

Social policies erected on horrifying biomedical theories discriminated against a variety of social groups in the Third Reich. Beginning in 1933, police harassment of those identified as gypsies began in earnest. In 1936, the Nazi bureaucracy expanded to include the Reich Central Office Against the Gypsy Nuisance, where files on gypsies were assiduously maintained. They were subject to all racialist legislation and could be sterilized because of their "inferiority" without any formal hearing process. In September 1939, even as the war was beginning, high-ranking Nazis planned the removal of 30,000 gypsies to Poland. More than 200,000 German, Russian, Polish, and Balkan gypsies were killed in the course of the war by internment in camps and by systematic extermination.

Mixed-race children were also singled out for special opprobrium under Nazi racial policies. A generational cohort of children born of white German mothers and black fathers was a consequence of the presence in the Rhineland of French colonial troops from Senegal, Morocco, and Malaga as part of the French occupation forces during the 1920s and 1930s. The press during both the Weimar Republic and the Nazi regime attacked the children of those unions, probably numbering no more than 500 to 800 individuals, as "Rhineland bastards." In 1937, the Nazis decided to sterilize them without any legal proceedings.

Those suffering from hereditary illnesses were labeled as a biological threat to the racial purity of the German people. Illegitimate medical tests were devised by state doctors to establish who was feeble-minded and genetically defective. Since the society of the Third Reich was treated as one huge laboratory for the production of the racially fit and the "destruction of worthless life," categories were constructed according to subjective criteria that claimed scientific validation. Medical officials examined children, and those judged to be deformed were separated from their families and transferred to special pediatric clinics where they were either starved to death or injected with lethal drugs. In the summer of 1939, euthanasia programs for adults were organized, and 65,000 to 70,000 Germans were identified for death. Asylums were asked to rank patients according to their race, state of health, and ability to work. The rankings were used to determine candidates for death. In Poland, mental patients were simply shot; in other places they were starved to death. The uncooperative, the sick, and the disabled were purged as racially undesirable.

The umbrella covering hereditary illnesses was broad but not broader than the category covering the "asocial." In that designation, asocial behavior itself came to be interpreted as a hereditary trait. Criminals, beggars, vagrants, and the homeless could be compulsorily sterilized. Alcoholics, prostitutes, and

Schreibers rassenkundliche Anschauungstafel: Deutsche Rassenköpfe
Bearbeitet von Dr Alfred Eydt

Nordisch   Westisch

Fälisch   Dinarisch

Ostbaltisch   Ostisch

■ The Nazis attempted to cloak their self-serving racial theories in scientific respectability. A Nazi "race-identification table" displays what were asserted to be the typical heads of different German "races"—a classification that has no basis in anthropology.

people with sexually transmitted diseases could be labeled asocial and treated accordingly. Those forms of behavior were considered to be hereditary and determined by blood.

Homosexuals were likewise treated as "community aliens" by Nazi social policies. The persecution of homosexual men intensified after 1934, when any form of "same-sex immorality" became subject to legal persecution. "Gazing and lustful intention" were left to the definition of the police and the courts. Criminal sentences could involve a term in a concentration camp. But because homosexuality was judged to be a sickness rather than an immutable biological trait, gays did not become the primary object of Nazi extermination policies that began to be enforced against the "biologically inferior." Instead, Nazi treatment of homosexuality might involve castration or indefinite incarceration in a concentration camp.

Gay men in Nazi concentration camps during the war were singled out with the badge of a pink triangle. Although it is not clear how many gay men were actually killed by the Nazis, estimates run as high as 200,000. Gay men rather than lesbian women were singled out by officials of the Third Reich because their behavior was considered a greater threat to the perpetuation of the German race.

The Destruction of Europe's Jews

Although anti-Semitism was an integral part of Hitler's view of the world, he did not think the peoples of Germany and

Europe were ready for harsh measures against the Jews. When they came to power in 1933, the Nazis did not have a blueprint for the destruction of Europe's Jews; the anti-Semitic policies of the Third Reich evolved incrementally in the 1930s and 1940s.

After 1938, German civil servants expropriated Jewish property as rightfully belonging to the state. When the war began, Jews were rounded up and herded into urban ghettos in Germany and in the large cities of Poland. For a time, the German foreign ministry considered the possibility of deporting the more than three million Jews under German control to Madagascar, an island off the southeast coast of Africa. Until 1941, Nazi policies against the Jews were often uncoordinated and unfocused.

The "Final Solution."   Confinement in urban ghettos was the beginning of a policy of concentration that ended in annihilation. After having identified Jews, seized their property, and then confined them to ghettos, German authorities began to implement a step-by-step plan for extermination. There appears to have been no single order from Hitler that decreed what became known to German officials as the "**Final Solution**"—the total extermination of European Jews. But Hitler's recorded remarks make it clear that he knew and approved of what was being done to the Jews. A spirit of shared purpose permeated the entire administrative system, from the civil service through the judiciary. Administrative

■ The Holocaust. The greatest loss of Jewish life in the Holocaust took place in Poland and the Soviet Union.

Jewish Population (in thousands)

1939 Population
      annihilated
      by 1945

Map shows
1938 boundaries

agencies competed to interpret the Führer's will. SS guards in the camps and police in the streets embraced Hitler's "mission" of destruction. Those involved in carrying out the plan for extermination understood what was meant by the Final Solution and what their responsibilities were for enforcing it. To ensure that the whole process operated smoothly, a planning conference for the Final Solution was conducted by Reinhard Heydrich (1904–1942), leader of the Sicherheitsdienst (SD), or Security Service of the SS, for the benefit of state and party officials at Wannsee, a Berlin suburb, in January 1942.

Mass racial extermination began with the German conquest of Poland, where both Jews and non-Jews were systematically killed. It continued when Hitler's army invaded the Soviet Union in 1941. That campaign, known as Operation Barbarossa, set off the mass execution of eastern Europeans declared to be enemies of the Reich. The tactics of the campaign pointed the way to the Final Solution. To the Nazi leadership, Slavs were subhuman. Russian Jews were, by extension, the lowest of the low, even more despised than German Jews. Nazi propaganda had equated Jews with Communists, and

Hitler had used the expression *Judeocommunist* to describe what he considered to be the most dangerous criminal and enemy of the Third Reich, the enemy who must be annihilated at any cost.

The executions were the work of the SS, the elite military arm of the Nazi party. Special mobile murder squads of the SD under Heydrich were organized behind the German lines in Poland and Russia. Members of the army were aware of what the SS squads were doing and participated in some of the extermination measures. In the spring of 1941, Hitler ordered a massive propaganda campaign to be conducted among the armed forces. The army was indoctrinated to believe that the invasion of the Soviet Union was more than a military campaign: it was a "holy war," a crusade that Germany was waging for civilization. SS chief Heinrich Himmler set about to enforce the Führer's threats with concrete extermination policies. Fearful that the SS would be outstripped by the regular army in the Führer's favor, Himmler exhorted his men to commit the worst atrocities.

Firing squads shot Russian victims en masse, then piled their bodies on top of each other in open graves. Reviewing

■ Seizing Jews in Warsaw. Nazi soldiers rounded up men, women, and children for "resettlement" in the east.

the procedures for mass killings, Himmler—ever competitive with other Nazi agencies—suggested a more efficient means of extermination that would require less manpower and would enhance the prestige of the SS. As a result, extermination by gas was introduced, using vans whose exhaust fumes were piped into the enclosed cargo areas that served as portable gas chambers. In Poland, Himmler replaced the vans with permanent buildings housing gas chambers using Zyklon B, a gas developed by the chemical firm I. G. Farben for the purpose. The chambers could annihilate thousands at a time.

The Third Reich began erecting its vast network of death in 1941. The first extermination camp was created in Chelmno, Poland, where 150,000 people were killed between 1941 and 1944. The camps practiced systematic extermination for the savage destruction of those groups deemed racially inferior, sexually deviant, or politically dangerous. The term **holocaust** has been used to describe the mass slaughter of European Jews, most of which took place in the five major killing centers in what is now Polish territory— Chelmno, Belzec, Sobibor, Treblinka, and Auschwitz. *Holocaust,* drawn from the Greek term for "burnt sacrifice," came to be used more generally after World War II to describe genocide and nuclear annihilation.

Many victims died before ever reaching the camps, transported for days in sealed railroad cars without food, water, or sanitation facilities. Others died within months as forced laborers for the Reich. People of all ages were starved, beaten, and systematically humiliated. Guards taunted their victims verbally, degraded them physically, and tortured them with

false hope. Promised clean clothes and nourishment, camp internees were herded into "showers" that dispensed gas rather than water. Descriptions of life in the camps reveal a systematized brutality and inhumanity on the part of the German, Ukrainian, and Polish guards toward their victims. In all, 11 million people died by the extermination process—6 million Jews and almost as many non-Jews, including children, the aged, homosexuals, Slavic slave laborers, Soviet prisoners of war, Communists, members of the Polish and Soviet leadership, various resistance elements, gypsies, and Jehovah's Witnesses.

The words ARBEIT MACHT FREI ("Work Makes You Free") were emblazoned over the main gate at Auschwitz, the largest of the concentration camps. It was at Auschwitz that the greatest number of persons died in a single place, including more than one million Jews. The healthy and the young were kept barely alive to work. Hard labor, starvation, and disease—especially typhus, tuberculosis, and other diseases that spread rapidly because of the lack of sanitation—claimed many victims.

On entering the camps, the sick and the aged were automatically designated for extermination because of their uselessness as a labor force. Many children were put to work, but some were designated for extermination. Many mothers chose to accompany their children to their deaths to comfort them in their final moments. Pregnant women were considered useless in the forced labor camps and were sent immediately to the "showers." The number of German Jewish women who died in the camps was 50 percent higher than the number of

DOCUMENT

Memoirs from Commandant of Auschwitz

German Jewish men. Starvation diets meant that women stopped menstruating. Because the Nazis worried that women of childbearing age would continue to reproduce, women who showed signs of menstruation were killed immediately. Women who were discovered to have given birth undetected in the camp were killed, as were their infants. Family relations were completely destroyed, as inmates were segregated by sex. It soon became clear that even those allowed to live were only intended to serve the short-term needs of the Nazis.

Resisting Destruction.   The impossibility of any effective resistance was based on two essential characteristics of the process of extermination. First, the entire German state and its bureaucratic apparatus were involved in the policies, laws, and decrees of the 1930s that singled out victims, while most Germans stood silently by. There was no possibility of appeal and no place to hide. Those who understood early what was happening and who had enough money to buy their way out emigrated to safer places, including Palestine and the United States. But most countries blocked the entry of German and eastern European refugees with immigration quotas. Neither Britain nor the United States was willing to deal with the mass influx of European Jews. Jews in the occupied countries and the Axis nations had virtually no chance to escape. They were trapped in a society where all forces of law and administration worked against them.

A second reason for the impossibility of effective resistance was the step-by-step nature of the process of extermination, which meant that few understood the final outcome until it was too late. Initially, in the 1930s, many German Jews believed that things could get no worse and obeyed the German state as good citizens. Even the policy of removing groups from the ghetto militated against resistance because the hope was that sending 1000 Jews to "resettlement" would allow 10,000 Jews remaining behind to be saved. The German authorities deliberately controlled information to cultivate misunderstanding of what was happening.

Isolated instances of resistance in the camps—rioting at Treblinka, for example—only highlight how impossible rebellion was for physically debilitated people in the heavily guarded centers. In the Warsaw ghetto, a resistance movement was organized with a few firearms and some grenades and homemade Molotov cocktails in April 1943. Starvation, overcrowding, and epidemics made Warsaw, the largest of the ghettos, into an extermination camp. As news reached the ghetto that "resettlement" was the death warrant of tens of thousands of Polish Jews, armed rebellion erupted. It did not succeed in blocking the completion of the Final Solution against the Warsaw ghetto the following year, when the SS commandant proclaimed, "The Jewish Quarter of Warsaw is no more!" Polish and Russian Jews accounted for 70 percent of the total Jewish deaths.

Who Knew?   It is impossible that killing on such a scale could have been kept secret. Along with those who ordered extermination operations, the guards and camp personnel involved in car-

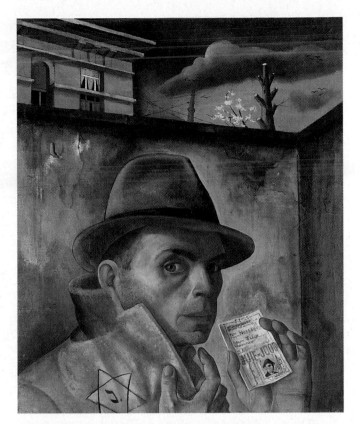

■ Felix Nussbaum, *Self-Portrait with a Jewish Identity Card* (1943). Nussbaum left Germany when the Nazis came to power in 1933. During the Holocaust he went underground, moving from place to place in constant fear of discovery. He painted this work, which captures his deep anxiety, while he was in hiding. Nussbaum and his wife were arrested in 1944, and both perished at Auschwitz. Kulturgeschichtliches Museum, Osnäbruck, © Auguste Moses-Nussbaum and Shulmait Jaari/© 2004 Artists Rights Society (ARS), New York/VG Bild-Kunst, Bonn

rying out the directives were aware of what was happening. Those who brought internees to the camps, returning always with empty railroad cars, knew it too. People believed for a time that their disappearing neighbors were being resettled in the east. But as news got back to central and western Europe, it was more difficult to sustain belief in the ruse. People who lived near the camps could not ignore the screams and fumes of gas and burning bodies that permeated the environs.

Although it never publicly announced its extermination program, the German government convinced its citizens that the policies of the Nazi state could not be judged by ordinary moral standards. The benefits to the German state were justification enough for the annihilation of 11 million people. Official propaganda successfully convinced millions that the Reich was the supreme good. Admitting the existence of the extermination program carried with it a responsibility on which few acted, perhaps out of fear of reprisals. There were some heroes such as Raoul Wallenberg of Sweden, who interceded for Hungarian Jews and provided Jews in the Budapest ghetto with food and protection. The king of Denmark, when informed that the Nazis had ordered Danish Jews to wear the yellow star,

MANIFESTO OF THE JEWISH RESISTANCE IN VILNA, SEPTEMBER 1943

In May 1943, in spite of the valiant resistance of Jewish fighting groups, the Warsaw ghetto was destroyed by the German SS. In August of the same year, inmates revolted in the concentration camp at Treblinka in the face of insurmountable odds. News of the Warsaw ghetto revolt had spread to the camp, where it inspired Jews to rise up and fight against their captors. Few survived the revolt, although considerable damage was done to the gas chambers, the railway station, and the barracks by the armed inmates. The Jews of the ghetto of Vilna (Vilnius) organized active resistance to the Nazis.

Focus Questions

What is the meaning of the rallying cry, "Jews, we have nothing to lose"? What kind of armed resistance was possible?

Offer armed resistance! Jews, defend yourselves with arms!

The German and Lithuanian executioners are at the gates of the ghetto. They have come to murder us! Soon they will lead you forth in groups through the ghetto door.

Tens of thousands of us were dispatched. But we shall not go! We will not offer our heads to the butcher like sheep.

Jews, defend yourselves with arms!

Do not believe the false promises of the assassins or believe the words of the traitors.

Anyone who passes through the ghetto gate will go to Ponar [death camp]!

And Ponar means death!

Jews, we have nothing to lose. Death will overtake us in any event. And who can still believe in survival when the murderer exterminates us with so much determination? The hand of the executioner will reach each man and woman. Flight and acts of cowardice will not save our lives.

Active resistance alone can save our lives and our honor.

Brothers! It is better to die in battle in the ghetto than to be carried away to Ponar like sheep. And know this: within the walls of the ghetto there are organized Jewish forces who will resist with weapons.

Support the revolt!

Do not take refuge or hide in the bunkers, for then you will fall into the hands of the murderers like rats.

Jewish people, go out into the squares. Anyone who has no weapons should take an ax, and he who has no ax should take a crowbar or a bludgeon!

For our ancestors!

For our murdered children!

Avenge Ponar!

Attack the murderers!

In every street, in every courtyard, in every house within and without the ghetto, attack these dogs!

Jews, we have nothing to lose! We shall save our lives only if we exterminate our assassins.

Long live liberty! Long live armed resistance! Death to the assassins!

Vilna, the Ghetto, 1 September 1943.

---

stated that he and his family would also wear the yellow star as a "badge of honor." Heroic acts, however, were isolated and rare.

Collaborationist governments and occupied nations often cooperated with Nazi extermination policies. The French government at Vichy introduced and implemented a variety of anti-Jewish measures without German orders and without German pressure. By voluntarily identifying and deporting Jews, the Vichy government sent 75,000 men, women, and children to their deaths.

As the war dragged on for years, internees of the camps hoped and prayed for rescue by the Allies. But such help did not come. The U.S. State Department and the British Foreign Office had early and reliable information on the nature and extent of the atrocities. But they did not act. American Jews were unable to convince President Franklin D. Roosevelt to intercede to prevent the slaughter. Appeals to bomb the gas chambers at Auschwitz and the railroad lines leading to them

were rejected by the United States on strategic grounds. Those trying to survive in the camps and the ghettos despaired at their abandonment.

The handful of survivors found by Allied soldiers who entered the camps after Germany's defeat presented a haunting picture of humanity. A British colonel who entered the camp at Bergen-Belsen in April 1945 gave a restrained account of what he found:

> As we walked down the main road of the camp, we were cheered by the internees, and for the first time we saw their condition. A great number were little more than living skeletons. There were men and women lying in heaps on both sides of the track. Others were walking slowly and aimlessly about, vacant expressions on their starved faces.

The sight of corpses piled on top of one another lining the roads and the piles of shoes, clothing, underwear, and gold

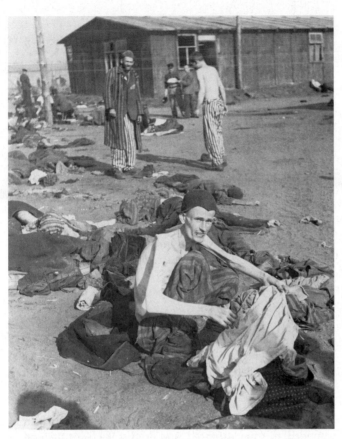

■ Internees at Bergen-Belsen upon liberation of the camp by British troops in April 1945.

teeth extracted from the dead shocked those who came to liberate the camps. One of the two survivors of Chelmno summed it all up: "No one can understand what happened here."

The Final Solution was a perversion of every value of civilization. The achievements of twentieth-century industry, technology, state, and bureaucracy in the West were turned against millions to create, as one German official called it, murder by assembly line. Mass killing was not prompted by military or security concerns. Nor was the elimination of vital labor power consistent with the needs of the Nazi state. The international tribunal for war crimes that met in 1945 in the German city of Nuremberg attempted to mete out justice to the criminals against humanity responsible for the destruction of 11 million Europeans labeled as demons and racial inferiors. History must record, even if it cannot explain, such inhumanity.

ALLIED VICTORY

The situation at the end of 1941 appeared grim for the British and their dominions and for the Americans who were assisting them with munitions, money, and food. Hitler had achieved control of a vast land empire covering all of continental Europe in the west, north, south, and center. The empire, which Hitler

called his "New Order," included territories occupied and directly administered by the German army, satellites, and collaborationist regimes. It was fortified by alliances with Italy, the Soviet Union, and Japan. Hitler commanded the greatest fighting force in the world, one that had knocked France out of the war in a matter of weeks, brought destruction to British cities, and conquered Yugoslavia in 12 days. Much of the world was coming to fear German invincibility.

Then, in June 1941, Hitler's troops invaded the Soviet Union, providing the British with an ally. In December, the naval and air forces of Japan attacked American bases in the Pacific, providing the British and the Russians with still another ally. What was a European war became a world war. It was the war Hitler did not want and that Germany could not win—a long, total war to the finish against three powers with inexhaustible resources: the British Empire, the Soviet Union, and the United States.

The Soviet Union's Great Patriotic War

Hitler had always considered the Soviet Union Germany's primary enemy. His hatred of communism was all-encompassing: Bolshevism was an evil invention of the Jewish people and a dangerous ideological threat to the Third Reich. The 1939 Non-Aggression Pact with Stalin was no more than an expedient for him. Hitler rebuked a Swiss diplomat in 1939 for failing to grasp the central fact of his foreign policy:

> Everything I undertake is directed against Russia. If those in the West are too stupid and too blind to understand this, then I should be forced to come to an understanding with the Russians to beat the West, and then, after its defeat, turn with all my concentrated force against the Soviet Union.

Soviet Unpreparedness. On 22 June 1941, German armies marched into Russia. They found the Soviet army larger but totally unprepared for war. In contrast to German soldiers, who had fought in Spain, Poland, and France, Soviet troops had no firsthand battle experience. Nor were they well led. Stalin's purges in the late 1930s had removed 35,000 officers from their posts by dismissal, imprisonment, or execution. Many of the men who replaced them were unseasoned in the responsibilities of leadership.

Russian military leaders were sure they would be ready for a European war against the capitalist nations by 1942, and Stalin refused to believe that Hitler would attack the Soviet Union before then. British agents and Stalin's own spies tried to warn him of German plans for an invasion in the spring of 1941. When the Germans did invade Russian territory, Stalin was so overwhelmed that he fell into a depression and was unable to act for days.

In his first radio address after the attack on 3 July 1941, Stalin identified his nation with the Allied cause: "Our struggle for the freedom of our country will merge with the struggle of the peoples of Europe and America for their independence, for democratic liberties." He accepted offers of support from the United States and Great Britain, the two nations that had worked consistently to exclude the Soviet Union from European power politics since the Bolshevik revolution in 1917. With France defeated and Great Britain crippled, the future of the war depended on the Soviet fighting power and American supplies.

German Offensive and Reversals. Hitler's invasion of Russia involved three million soldiers from Germany and Germany's satellites, the largest invasion force in history. It stretched along an immense battlefront from the Baltic to the Black Sea. Instead of exclusively targeting Moscow, the capital, the German army concentrated first on destroying Soviet armed forces and capturing Leningrad in the north and the oil-rich Caucasus in the south. In the beginning, the German forces advanced rapidly in a blitzkrieg across western Russia, where they were greeted as liberators in the Ukraine. The Germans took 290,000 prisoners of war and massacred tens of thousands of others in their path through the Jewish settlements of western Russia.

Within four months, the German army had advanced to the gates of Moscow, but they concentrated their forces too late. The Red Army rallied to defend Moscow as thousands of civilian women set to work digging trenches and antitank ditches around the city. The Soviet people answered Stalin's call for a scorched-earth policy by burning everything that might be useful to the advancing German troops. German troops had also burned much in their path, depriving themselves of essential supplies for the winter months ahead. The German advance was stopped, and the best ally of the Red Army—the Russian winter—settled in. The first snow fell at the beginning of October. By early November, German troops were beginning to suffer the harsh effects of an early and exceptionally bitter Russian winter.

Hitler promised the German people that "final victory" was at hand. So confident was Hitler of a speedy and decisive victory that he sent his soldiers into Russia wearing only light summer uniforms. Hitler's generals knew better and tried repeatedly to explain military realities to the Führer. General Heinz Guderian (1888–1954), commander of the tank units, reported that his men were suffering frostbite, that tanks could not be started, and that automatic weapons were jamming in the subzero temperatures. Back in Germany, the civilian population received little accurate news of the campaign. They began to suspect the worst when the government sent out a plea for woolen blankets and clothing for the troops.

By early December, the German military situation was desperate. The Soviets, benefiting from intelligence information about German plans and an awareness that Japan was about to declare war on the United States, recalled fresh troops from the Siberian frontier and the border with China and Manchuria and launched a powerful counterattack against the poorly outfitted German army outside Moscow. Under the command of General Gyorgi Zhukov (1896–1974), Russian troops, dressed and trained for winter warfare, pushed the Germans back in retreat across the snow-covered expanses. By February, 200,000 German troops had been killed, 46,000 were missing in action, and 835,000 were wounded in battle and by the weather. Thus the campaign cost the German army more than one million casualties. It probably cost the Soviets twice that number of wounded, missing, captured, and dead soldiers. At the end of the Soviet counterattack in March, the German army and its satellite forces were in a shambles reminiscent of Napoleon's troops, who 130 years earlier had been decimated in the campaign to capture Moscow. An enraged Hitler dismissed his generals for retreating without his permission, and he himself assumed the position of commander in chief of the armed forces.

■ Russian villagers search for loved ones among civilians slain by German troops. Noncombatants were frequent victims of the Nazi policy of enslavement or annihilation.

Hitler was not daunted by the devastating costs of his invasion of Russia. In the summer of 1942, he initiated a second major offensive, this time to take the city of Stalingrad. Constant bombardment gutted the city, and the Soviet army was forced into hand-to-hand combat with the German soldiers. But the German troops, once again inadequately supplied and unprepared for the Russian winter, failed to capture the city. The Battle of Stalingrad was over in the first days of February 1943. Of the original 300,000 members of the German Sixth Army, fewer than 100,000 survived to be taken prisoner by the Soviets. Of those, only 9,000 returned to Germany in 1955, when German prisoners of war were repatriated.

Soviet Patriotism.   The Soviets succeeded by exploiting two great advantages in their war against Germany: the large Soviet population and their knowledge of Russian weather and terrain. There was a third advantage that Hitler ignored: the Soviet people's determination to sacrifice everything for the war effort. In his successive Five-Year Plans, Stalin had mobilized Soviet society with an appeal to fulfill and surpass production quotas. In the summer of 1941, as Hitler's troops threatened Moscow, he used the same rhetoric to appeal to his Soviet "brothers and sisters" to join him in waging "the Great Patriotic War." The Russian people shared a sense of common purpose, sacrifice, and moral commitment in their loyalty to the nation.

The advancing Germans themselves intensified Soviet patriotism by torturing and killing tens of thousands of peasants who might have willingly cooperated against the Stalinist regime. Millions of Soviet peasants joined the Red Army. Young men of high school age were drafted into the armed forces. Three million women became wage earners for the first time as they replaced men in war industries. Women who remained on the land worked to feed the townspeople and the soldiers. Because the Red Army had requisitioned horses and tractors for combat, grain had to be sown and harvested by hand—and that often meant women's hands. Tens of thousands of Russians left their homes in western Russia to work for relocated Soviet industries in the Urals, the Volga region, Siberia, and Central Asia.

More than 20 million Soviet people, soldiers and civilians, men, women, and children, died in the course of World War II. In addition to those killed in battle, millions starved as a direct result of the hardships of war. In 1943, food was so scarce that seed for the next year's crops was eaten. One in every three men born in 1906 died in the war. But Soviet resistance did not flag. The Great Patriotic War had a profound impact on Soviet views of the world and the Soviet Union's place in it. The war left the Soviet people with an enduring fear of invasion. The official falsification of all published maps of the Soviet Union in order to mislead spies and foreign armies was just one indication of the Russian expectation of treachery. (That practice was as recent as 1988.) Today, a visitor to Stalingrad, renamed Volgograd, can still find old tanks in city parks and on streets as reminders of the front

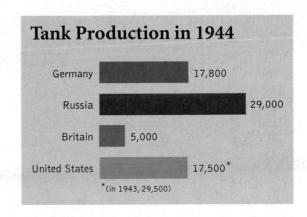

Tank Production in 1944

Germany	17,800
Russia	29,000
Britain	5,000
United States	17,500*

*(in 1943, 29,500)

line of the Red Army in the Great Patriotic War. Ruins of buildings have been left standing as grim monuments to the need for continued preparedness. The few remaining trees that endured through the war's devastation bear plaques that make their survival a memorial.

The Soviet Union sacrificed 10 percent of its population to the war effort, incurring more than 50 percent of all the deaths and casualties of the war. Few families escaped the death of members in the defense of the nation. Soviet citizens correctly considered that they had given more than any other country to defeat Hitler. For the Soviet people, their suffering in battle made World War II the Soviet Union's war and their sacrifice made possible the Allied victory.

The United States Enters the War

Victory still eluded the Allies in western Europe, where now another nation, the United States, had entered the fray. Although a neutral power, the United States began extending aid to the Allies after the fall of France in 1940. Since neither Britain nor the Soviet Union could afford to pay all the costs of defending Europe against Hitler, the U.S. Congress passed the Lend-Lease Act in 1941. The act authorized President Roosevelt to provide armaments to Great Britain and the Soviet Union without payment. America became the "arsenal of democracy." The United States and Britain sent 4100 airplanes and 138,000 motor vehicles, as well as steel and machinery, to the Soviet Union for the campaign of 1943. In all, America pumped $11 billion worth of equipment into the Soviet war effort between 1941 and 1945. Stalin later told Roosevelt that the USSR would have lost the war with Germany without the help of the Americans and the British.

Japan Attacks.   President Roosevelt and his advisers considered Germany, not Japan, to be America's primary target for a future war. Japan nevertheless had been threatening American trade interests in Asia and had embroiled the United States in disputes over Japanese imperialist expansion in the late 1930s. The United States understood Japan to be an aggressive country determined to expand its control over China and southeast Asia, which it opposed initially through economic embargoes. The presence of the Soviet Union pressing eastward across Asia,

PRESIDENT FRANKLIN ROOSEVELT'S REQUEST FOR A DECLARATION OF WAR ON JAPAN, 8 DECEMBER 1941

On 7 December 1941, the Japanese naval and air forces attacked the American naval base at Pearl Harbor in Hawaii, killing and wounding 3457 military personnel and civilians. Most of the U.S. Pacific fleet was moored in Pearl Harbor, and it sustained severe destruction of its naval vessels, battleships, and aircraft. U.S. military and political leaders were taken completely by surprise by the Japanese attack.

Focus Questions

Why is December 7, 1941, called a "day which will live in infamy"? How does Roosevelt's declaration of war reflect outrage over the "infamy"?

To the Congress of the United States:

Yesterday, December 7, 1941—a date which will live in infamy—the United States of America was suddenly and deliberately attacked by naval and air forces of the Empire of Japan.

The United States was at peace with that Nation and, at the solicitation of Japan, was still in conversation with its Government and its Emperor looking toward the maintenance of peace in the Pacific. Indeed, one hour after Japanese air squadrons had commenced bombing in Oahu, the Japanese Ambassador to the United States and his colleague delivered to the Secretary of State a formal reply to a recent American message. While this reply stated that it seemed useless to continue the existing diplomatic negotiations, it contained no threat or hint of war or armed attack.

It will be recorded that the distance of Hawaii from Japan makes it obvious that the attack was deliberately planned many days or even weeks ago. During the intervening time the Japanese Government has deliberately sought to deceive the United States by false statements and expressions of hope for continued peace.

The attack yesterday on the Hawaiian Islands has caused severe damage to American naval and military forces. Very many American lives have been lost. In addition, American ships have been reported torpedoed on the high seas between San Francisco and Honolulu.

Yesterday the Japanese Government also launched an attack against Malaya.

Last night Japanese forces attacked Hong Kong.

Last night Japanese forces attacked Guam.

Last night Japanese forces attacked the Philippine Islands.

Last night the Japanese attacked Wake Island.

This morning the Japanese attacked Midway Island.

Japan has, therefore, undertaken a surprise offensive extending throughout the Pacific area. The facts of yesterday speak for themselves. The people of the United States have already formed their opinions and well understand the implications to the very life and safety of our Nation.

As Commander-in-Chief of the Army and Navy I have directed that all measures be taken for our defense.

Always will we remember the character of the onslaught against us.

No matter how long it may take us to overcome this premeditated invasion, the American people in their righteous might will win through to absolute victory. . . .

With confidence in our armed forces—with the unbounded determination of our people—we will gain the inevitable triumph—so help us God.

I ask that the Congress declare that since the unprovoked and dastardly attack by Japan on Sunday, December seventh, a state of war has existed between the United States and the Japanese Empire.

Franklin D. Roosevelt

---

coupled with the colonial presences in Asia of Great Britain, France, and the United States, severely constrained Japan's capacity to expand its frontiers and ensure its security. The war in western Europe and the German invasion of the Soviet Union in June 1941 meant that the Japanese could concentrate their attention farther south in China, Indochina, and Thailand. Japan's limited reserves of foreign currency and raw materials made it increasingly vulnerable to economic disruptions. Japanese leaders accepted the necessity of grasping oil and raw materials in southeast Asia.

In September 1940, Japan joined forces with the Axis Powers of Germany and Italy in the Tripartite Pact, in which the signatories, promising mutual support against aggression, acknowledged the legitimacy of each other's expansionist efforts in Europe and Asia. Japanese–American relations deteriorated following the Japanese invasion of southern Indochina in July 1941. The United States insisted that Japan vacate China and Indochina and reestablish the open door for trade in Asia. The United States knew, however, that it was only a matter of time until Japan attacked U.S. interests but was uncertain about where that attack would take place.

On Sunday morning, 7 December 1941, Japan struck at the heart of the American Pacific Fleet stationed at Pearl Harbor, Hawaii. The fleet was literally caught asleep at the switch:

JAPAN'S DECLARATION OF WAR ON THE UNITED STATES AND GREAT BRITAIN, 8 DECEMBER 1941

Japan's sense of its mission in East Asia is embodied in Emperor Hirohito's declaration of war against the United States and Great Britain on 8 December 1941, the day after Japanese forces attacked the American fleet in Hawaii. Interestingly, the Japanese declaration speaks of "world peace" and "friendship among nations." In spite of marked cultural differences in the form of the two declarations, both the Japanese and the American leaders make clear their country's dependence on the total support of their people to win the war.

Focus Questions

Why in a declaration of war against the United States and the British Empire does the Emperor talk about China? What are "the true intentions of Our Empire" to which Emperor Hirohito is referring?

We, by grace of heaven, Emperor of Japan, seated on the Throne of the line unbroken for ages eternal, enjoin upon ye. Our loyal and brave subjects.

We hereby declare war on the United States of America and the British Empire. The men and officers of Our Army and Navy shall do their utmost in prosecuting the war, Our public servants of various departments shall perform faithfully and diligently their appointed tasks, and all other subjects of Ours shall pursue their respective duties; the entire nation with a united will shall mobilize their total strength so that nothing will miscarry in the attainment of our war aims.

To insure the stability of East Asia and to contribute to world peace is the far-sighted policy which was formulated by Our Great Illustrious Imperial Grandsire and Our Great Imperial Sire succeeding Him, and which We have constantly to heart. To cultivate friendship among nations and to employ prosperity in common with all nations has always been the guiding principle of Our Empire's foreign policy. It has been truly unavoidable and far from Our wishes that Our Empire has now been brought to cross swords with America and Britain. More than four years

have passed since the government of the Chinese Republic, failing to comprehend the true intentions of Our Empire, and recklessly courting trouble, disturbed the peace of east Asia and compelled Our Empire to take up arms. . . .

Patiently have We waited and long have We endured, in the hope that Our Government might retrieve the situation in peace. But our adversaries, showing not the least spirit of conciliation, have unduly delayed a settlement; and in the meantime, they have intensified the economic and military pressure to compel thereby Our Empire to submission. This trend of affairs would, if left unchecked, not only nullify Our Empire's efforts of many years for the sake of the stabilization of east Asia, but also endanger the very existence of Our nation. The situation being such as it is, Our Empire for its existence and self-defense has no other recourse but to appeal to arms and to crush every obstacle in its path.

The hallowed spirits of Our Imperial Ancestors guarding Us from above, We rely upon the loyalty and courage of Our subjects in Our confident expectation that the task bequeathed by Our Forefathers will be carried forward, and that the sources of evil will be speedily eradicated and an enduring peace immutably established in East Asia, preserving thereby the glory of Our Empire.

The 8th day of the 12th month of the 16th year of Showa.
Hirohito

2300 people were killed, and eight battleships and numerous cruisers and destroyers were sunk or severely damaged. The attack crippled American naval power in the Pacific as the American navy suffered its worst loss in history in a single engagement. The attack on Pearl Harbor led to the United States' immediate declaration of war against Japan. In President Roosevelt's words, 7 December 1941 was "a date which will live in infamy."

In the next three months, Japan captured Hong Kong, Malaya, and the important naval base at Singapore from the British, taking 60,000 prisoners. Like its earlier march into China, the Japanese invasion of southeast Asia moved swiftly

to establish control, outstripping the Japanese military's own timetables for advance. In December 1941, the Japanese landed in Thailand and secured immediate agreement for Japanese occupation of strategic spots in the country. They then turned to the Malayan peninsula, decisively defeating the British fleet off Malaya and pushing on the ground toward Singapore, which they conquered in February 1942. They conquered British Borneo in January, drove the Dutch from all of Indonesia but New Guinea, pushed American forces in the Philippines into the Bataan Peninsula, occupied Burma, and inflicted severe defeats on British, Dutch, and American naval power in East Asia. U.S. General Douglas MacArthur

■ The battleship USS *West Virginia* in flames at Pearl Harbor. The attack was carried out entirely by carrier-based aircraft—a sign of things to come in naval warfare.

(1880–1964) surrendered the Philippines to the Japanese on 2 January 1942 with the promise to return. With the armies of Germany deep in Russian territory, Australia had little hope of Allied help against a Japanese invasion.

Germany Declares War on the United States. Hitler praised the Japanese government for its action against the British Empire and against the United States and its "millionaire and Jewish backers." Germany, with its armies retreating from Moscow, nevertheless declared war against the United States on 11 December 1941. Hitler, in fact, considered that the United States was already at war with Germany because of its policy of supplying the Allies. Within days, the United States, a nation with an army smaller than Belgium's, had gone from neutrality to a war in two theaters. Although militarily weak, the United States was an economic giant, commanding a vast industrial capacity and access to resources. America grew even stronger under the stimulus of war, increasing its production by 400 percent in two years. It devoted itself to the demands of a total war and the unconditional surrender of Germany and then Japan.

Winning the War in Europe

The Allies did not always share the same strategies or concerns. President Roosevelt and Prime Minister Churchill had already discussed common goals in the summer of 1941 before the U.S. entry into the war. The United States embraced the priority of the European war and the postponement of war in the Pacific. Stalin pleaded for the Anglo-Americans to open up a second front against Germany in western Europe to give his troops some relief and save Soviet lives. Anglo-American resources were committed to the Pacific to stop the Japanese advance, and the Americans and the British disagreed as to where a second front in Europe might be opened.

Because of British interests in the Mediterranean, Churchill insisted on a move from North Africa into Sicily and Italy. That strategy was put into effect in 1942. The Italian government withdrew from the war in September, but German troops carried on the fight in Italy. The Anglo-American invasion of Italy did little to alleviate Russian losses, and the Soviet Union absorbed almost the entire force of German military power until 1944. Stalin's distrust of his allies increased. Churchill, Roosevelt, and Stalin met for the first time in late November 1943 at Teheran, Iran. Roosevelt and Churchill made a commitment to Stalin to open a second front in France within six months. Stalin, in turn, promised to attack Japan to aid the United States in the Pacific. The great showdown of the global war was at hand.

On 6 June 1944, Allied troops under the command of American General Dwight D. Eisenhower (1890–1969)

■ A United States Army unit joins Allied forces at the beachheads of Normandy during Operation Overlord in 1944. The invasion began the opening of the second front that Stalin had been urging on the Allies since the German armies thrust into Russia in 1941.

■ Soldiers raise the hammer-and-sickle flag over the ruins of the Reichstag as Soviet troops occupy Berlin in May 1945. At war's end, the Soviets occupied most of eastern Europe, which gave Stalin an advantage at the Yalta Conference.

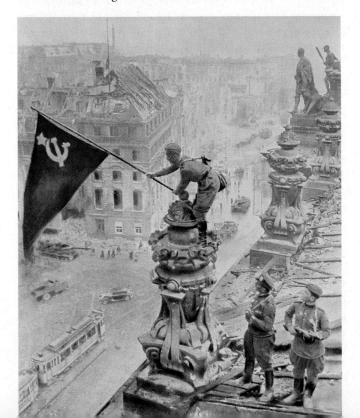

came ashore on the beaches of Normandy in the largest amphibious landing in history. In a daring operation identified by the code name Operation Overlord, 2.2 million American, British, and Free French forces, 450,000 vehicles, and 4 million tons of supplies poured into northern France. Allied forces broke through German lines to liberate Paris in late August. The Germans launched a last-ditch counterattack in late December 1944 in Luxembourg and Belgium. The Battle of the Bulge only slowed the Allied advance; in March 1945, American forces crossed the Rhine into Germany. Hitler, meanwhile, refused to surrender and insisted on a fight to the death of the last German soldier. Members of his own High Command had attempted unsuccessfully to assassinate Hitler in July 1944. The final German defeat came in April 1945, when the Russians stormed the German capital of Berlin. Hitler, living in an underground bunker near the Chancellery building, committed suicide on 30 April 1945.

Japanese War Aims and Assumptions

Japan and the United States entered the Pacific War with very different understandings of what was at stake. The Japanese appealed to southeast Asian leaders, presenting themselves as the liberators of Asian peoples from Western colonialism and imperialism.

Japanese Hegemony in Asia. The approach struck a responsive chord as the Japanese established what they called the Greater East Asia Co-Prosperity Sphere. Ba Maw, Burma's leader, said at the Assembly of the Greater East Asiatic Nations held in Tokyo in November 1943, "My Asiatic blood has always called to other Asiatics. . . . This is not the time to think with our minds; this is the time to think with our blood, and it is thinking with the blood that has brought me all the way from Burma to Japan." But the passionate and positive welcome Ba Maw extended to the Japanese liberators did not last long. As he bluntly explained in his memoirs, "The brutality, arrogance, and racial pretensions of the Japanese militarists in Burma remain among the deepest Burmese memories of the war years; for a great many people in southeast Asia these are all they remember of the war."

The Greater East Asia Co-Prosperity Sphere began in 1940 and lasted until the summer of 1945. The reorganization of east and southeast Asia under Japanese hegemony constituted a redefinition of world geography, with Japan at the center. The Japanese fashioned a romanticized vision of the family living in harmony, each member knowing his place and enjoying the complementary division of responsibilities and reciprocities that made family life work smoothly. Behind the pleasant image lurked the reality of a brutal power structure forcing subject peoples to accept massively inferior positions in a world fashioned exclusively for Japanese desires and needs. The Japanese viewed southeast Asia principally as a market for Japanese manufactured goods, a source of raw materials, and a source of profits for Japanese capital invested in mining, rubber, and raw cotton. Plans were made for hydroelectric power and aluminum refining facilities.

Wartime Japanese nakedly displayed their disdain for the people they conquered in southeast Asia. All subject peoples were to bow on meeting a Japanese. At public assemblies a ritual bow in the direction of the Japanese emperor was required, to the dismay of southeast Asians such as Indies Muslims or Philippine Catholics, who regarded Japanese emperor worship as pagan and presumptuous. Japanese holidays, such as the emperor's birthday, were enforced as Co-Prosperity Sphere holidays, and the calendar was reset to the mythical founding of the Japanese state in 660 B.C.E.

The Japanese were less brazen toward the Chinese in their rhetoric, in part because so much of east Asian civilization had its roots in China. But even if more temperate in their pronouncements, the realities of Japanese aggression in China included one of the worst periods of destruction in modern warfare. When they took over the Nationalist capital of Nanjing in December 1937, 20,000 women were raped, 30,000 soldiers killed, and another 12,000 civilians died in the more than six weeks of wanton terror inflicted by Japanese soldiers.

Japan's View of the West. With regard to Westerners, Japanese propaganda avoided labeling them as inferior. In part this reflected Japan's economic and political emulation of the West since the late nineteenth century. Rather than denigrating Western people, the Japanese chose to elevate themselves as a people descended from divine origins. Stressing their unique mythical history gave the Japanese a strong sense of superiority neither intellectual nor physical, but moral. They believed that virtue was on their side in their mission to stop Western expansion in Asia and to take their "proper place" as the leading people in Asia by tyrannizing the Co-Prosperity Sphere.

To achieve their moral superiority, the Japanese government urged their people to "purify" themselves. Although purification rituals occur in the world's great religions, rarely do governments urge people to cleanse their souls. For the average wartime Japanese citizen, purification meant accepting extreme material poverty and scarcity, rejecting foreign influences, and if called upon, dying for the emperor. The Japanese elevation of patriotism to the level of human sacrifice lay outside Western sensibilities of the time; to expect the spirit to become more purified made little sense to large numbers of Westerners. A bit more comprehensible, perhaps, were Japanese wartime views of Americans as beasts because of the atrocities that American soldiers committed. The grotesque quality of the American soldier's desire for war trophies was captured by a *Life* magazine photograph of a blond young American woman holding a Japanese skull sent to her by her GI sweetheart. What *Life* magazine considered "human interest" the Japanese found racist. However reasonable that assessment may have been, Japanese impressions of Westerners definitely proved fatally false in another matter. The Japanese assumed that individual selfishness and egoism would make Americans and Europeans incapable of mobilizing for a long fight.

Winning the War in the Pacific

The tide in the Pacific War began to turn when the planned Japanese invasion of Australia was thwarted. Fighting in the jungles of New Guinea, Australian and American troops under the command of General Douglas MacArthur turned back the Japanese army. U.S. Marines did likewise with a bold landing at Guadalcanal and months of bloody fighting in the Solomon Islands. In June 1942, within six months of the attack at Pearl Harbor, American naval forces commanded by Admiral Chester Nimitz (1885–1966) inflicted a defeat on the Japanese navy from which it could not recover. In the battle of Midway (June 3–6, 1942), Japan lost 4 aircraft carriers, a heavy cruiser, more than 300 airplanes, and 5,000 men. Midway was the Pacific equivalent of the Battle of Stalingrad.

In the summer of 1943, as the Soviet Union launched the offensive that was to defeat Germany, America began to move across the Pacific toward Japan. Nimitz and MacArthur conceived a brilliant plan in which American land, sea, and air forces fought in a coordinated effort. With a series of amphibious landings, they hopped from island to island. Some Japanese island fortresses, such as Tarawa, were taken; others, such as Truk, were bypassed and cut off from Japanese home bases. With the conquest of Saipan in November 1944 and Iwo Jima in March 1945, the U.S. Air Force acquired bases from which B-29 bombers could strike at the Japanese home

MAP DISCOVERY

World War II in the Pacific, 1941–1945

Japan extended control throughout east and southeast Asia until the Japanese Empire reached its pinnacle in August 1942. Note the direction of major Allied offensives and the necessity of coordinated land, sea, and air offensives. Why were Hiroshima and Nagasaki chosen as atomic bomb targets?

"GLITTERING FRAGMENTS"

Hara Tamiki (1905–1951) was a Japanese poet who was living in Hiroshima when the atomic bomb exploded there on 6 August 1945. His poem "Glittering Fragments" tells about what he saw. A victim of the bomb's radioactivity, he committed suicide in 1951.

Focus Questions

How does the economy of words in this poem convey the horror of the atomic bomb for its victims? Why does the title seem to convey a pleasing image?

Glittering fragments
Ashen embers
Like a rippling panorama,
Burning red then dulled.
Strange rhythm of human corpses.
All existence, all that could exist
Laid bare in a flash. The rest of the world
The swelling of a horse's corpse
At the side of an upturned train,
The smell of smoldering electric wires.

---

islands. In the summer of 1945, in the greatest air offensive in history, American planes destroyed what remained of the Japanese navy, crippled Japanese industry, and mercilessly firebombed major population centers. The attack ended with the dropping of atomic bombs on the cities of Hiroshima and Nagasaki. (See "A Closer Look: The Atomic Wasteland," pp. 892–893.) The Japanese government accepted American terms for peace and surrendered unconditionally on 2 September 1945 on the battleship *Missouri* in Tokyo Bay. Four months after the defeat of Germany, the war in Asia was over.

DOCUMENT

An Eyewitness
to Hiroshima

The Fate of Allied Cooperation: 1945

The costs of World War II in terms of death and destruction were the highest in history. Fifty million lives were lost. Most of the dead were Europeans, and most of the Europeans were Russians and Poles. The high incidence of civilian deaths distinguished the Second World War from previous wars—more than 50 percent of the dead were noncombatants. Deliberate military targeting of cities explains that phenomenon only in part. The majority of civilian deaths were the result of starvation, enslavement, massacre, and deliberate extermination.

Civilian Populations.   The psychological devastation of continual violence, deprivation, injury, and rape of survivors cannot be measured. Terrorizing citizens became an established means of warfare in the modern age. Another phenomenon not matched in the First World War emerged in 1945: mass rape. The Russians, brutally treated by Hitler's army, returned the savagery in their advance through eastern and central Europe. The Soviet officer corps encouraged the advancing Russian army to use sexual violence against German women and girls.

■ Photographer Yosuke Yamahata was one of three men sent by the Japanese Army to document the effects of the atomic bomb dropped on Nagasaki on 9 August 1945. The three arrived in Nagasaki just before dawn on August 10, and as the sun rose Yamahata immediately began to take pictures. One of his first was this photo of a young boy and his mother holding riceballs, the only emergency rations available to survivors of the atomic blast.

CHRONOLOGY
WORLD WAR II

1937	Japan begins undeclared war on China
March 1938	Germany annexes Austria to the German Reich
29 September 1938	Chamberlain, Daladier, Mussolini, and Hitler meet at Munich conference
May 1939	Pact of Steel: military alliance between Italy and Germany
1939	Non-Aggression Pact between Germany and the Soviet Union
1 September 1939	Germany attacks Poland
3 September 1939	Great Britain and France declare war on Germany
April 1940	Germany attacks Denmark and Norway
May 1940	Germany invades the Netherlands, Belgium, Luxembourg, and then France
June 1940	Italy enters the war on the side of Germany
17 June 1940	French Marshal Pétain petitions Germany for an armistice and creates a collaborationist government at Vichy
September 1940	Japan, Germany, and Italy sign Tripartite Pact
September–November 1940	The Battle of Britain
22 June 1941	Germany invades the Soviet Union
1941	First extermination camp created in Chelmno, Poland
7 December 1941	Japan attacks Pearl Harbor; the following day, the United States declares war on Japan
11 December 1941	Germany declares war on the United States
January 1942	Wannsee Conference, where the Final Solution is planned
June 1942	Battle of Midway
September 1942	Italian government withdraws from the war
April 1943	Unsuccessful uprising in the Warsaw ghetto
November 1943	Churchill, Roosevelt, and Stalin meet at Teheran conference
6 June 1944	Allied forces land in northern France—D-Day
February 1945	Churchill, Roosevelt, and Stalin meet at Yalta
March 1945	American forces march into Germany
30 April 1945	Hitler commits suicide
July and August 1945	Churchill, Truman, and Stalin meet at Potsdam
6 August 1945	United States drops atomic bomb on Hiroshima
2 September 1945	Japan surrenders

Collective rape became a means of direct retaliation. Victorious Japanese soldiers raped Chinese women as part of the spoils of war. Regardless of which country was involved, victorious armies practiced rape against civilian populations as one of the unspoken aspects of conquest.

Material destruction was great. Axis and Allied cities, centers of civilization and culture, were turned into wastelands by aerial bombing. The Germans bombed Rotterdam and Coventry. The British engineered the firebombing of Dresden. Warsaw and Stalingrad were destroyed by the

A Closer Look
The Atomic Wasteland

The sixth of August 1945 was a typical summer day in southwestern Japan. In the city of Hiroshima at 8:15 A.M., people were walking to work, sitting down at office desks, riding buses, weeding gardens, and clearing away breakfast dishes. Suddenly a noiseless flash lit the sky over the city and its environs for miles. A mammoth column of smoke in the shape of a mushroom cloud ballooned up. The United States had dropped history's first atomic bomb.

The explosion had the intensity of a huge blast furnace. In some areas, the brilliant light created by the explosion bleached everything it touched. Near the epicenter of the blast, human bodies were charred to cinders or turned into frightening statues. Flesh melted and bones fused. Buildings were reduced to ashes. Stones bled. Hiroshima, a city renowned in prewar Japan for its relaxed and agreeable atmosphere, was leveled in an instant by the terrifying force of a single atomic bomb.

There were 78,000 dead in Hiroshima on 6 August. By December, the number had reached 140,000 as the sickness caused by radioactive poisoning continued to take its toll. Rescue workers inhaled the dense dust and became contaminated by radioactivity. Surviving victims often lost their hair and eyebrows and experienced nausea, vomiting, diarrhea, and bleeding. Others suffered from internal hemorrhaging, blindness, chronic weakness, and fatigue. Many developed cancers such as leukemia, sometimes years later. The bomb scarred and disfigured.

Atomic radiation released by the bomb caused unseen damage by attacking the lungs, heart, bone marrow, and internal organs. It poisoned the lymph glands. It worked unobserved to alter genetic structure, deforming unborn babies and those not yet conceived.

Harry Truman, who became president of the United States on 12 April 1945 following the death of Franklin D. Roosevelt, later spoke of his decision to drop the atomic bomb to bring the war to a speedy end. In July 1945, Truman issued an ultimatum to Japan to surrender immediately or face dire consequences. The Japanese ignored the warning. Hiroshima was targeted, according to Truman, to make a point to the Japanese, to demonstrate the unimaginable force of the new American weapon. The city was a military center, a major storage and assembly point that supplied the armed forces. Nagasaki, bombed three days after Hiroshima with an experimental plutonium bomb, was targeted as an industrial center and the place where the torpedoes that had destroyed American ships were manufactured.

It is undoubtedly true that the bombings were responsible for the Japanese surrender a few days later. The atomic bomb did bring the Asian war to an immediate end. But critics of the bombings pointed out that Japan was already close to defeat. Secret U.S. intelligence studies that came to light in the 1980s indicate that American leaders knew in 1945 that Japan had been weakened by intense American incendiary bombing of its cities. Twenty-six square miles of the working-class and industrial section of Tokyo had been burned at the cost of more than 100,000 lives. Many refugees from other Japanese cities had fled to Hiroshima to live with relatives. The Sea of Japan had been heavily mined, cutting off Japan from its armies on the Asian mainland. Some radical young officers of the Japanese army, however, were preparing to kidnap Emperor Hirohito to keep him from capitulating, and the planned American landing on Japan was expected to be costly. U.S. forces had already suffered more than 100,000 casualties in the conquest of the Japanese island of Okinawa in April. Truman and his advisers were now prepared to use any means possible to prevent further American casualties. Defenders of the decision have argued that any responsible American leader would have made the same decision to use the atomic bomb. Modern total wars acquire a life of their own, and desperate nations use the science, technology, and weapons available to them.

In the summer of 1945, General Dwight D. Eisenhower, then the victorious Supreme Allied Commander in the European theater of war, was informed by U.S. Secretary of War Henry L. Stimson of what was about to take place in Hiroshima. Eisenhower voiced "grave misgivings" based on his "belief that Japan was already defeated and that the dropping of the bomb was completely unnecessary" to end the war. He was not alone among military men in questioning the use of nuclear force on strategic and moral grounds. Strong opposition to nuclear weapons began to surface among scientists working on the bomb. In opposition to many of their colleagues, they warned that the atomic bomb was an undiscriminating weapon that could not pinpoint supply depots and military targets but would destroy entire civilian populations. The peace movement based on banning nuclear weapons actually began among horrified scientists who were aware, before the rest of the world could know, of the terrible force that they had helped to create.

■ Painting by Yasuko Yamagata.

At the Potsdam Conference in July 1945, Stalin had informed President Truman and Prime Minister Winston Churchill that the Soviet Union was about to invade Manchuria, honoring the promise Stalin had made at Teheran in 1943 to join the war against Japan after Germany was defeated. The Soviet Union would now play a role in determining the future of Asia. Truman told Stalin of the powerful new weapon America had developed. Stalin seemed unimpressed. Secretary of War Stimson was aware that the atomic bomb would be an important weapon to have in the American arsenal when the time came to negotiate a postwar world settlement with the Russians. Truman and his advisers, however, never deviated from their insistence that saving the lives of thousands of American and Japanese soldiers was their only consideration in dropping the bomb.

An American observer called the bombing of Hiroshima "the immersion in death." Survivors repeatedly described Hiroshima after the "flash" as what hell must be like. Photographs of the city record the total destruction of buildings and vegetation. Japanese photographers avoided taking pictures of the devastation the bomb had done to human bodies, believing that what they saw was too horrible to record. Yet the brutality of nuclear war could not be ignored and nuclear weapons continue to be a central issue of international politics in the twenty-first century. The decision to drop the atomic bomb has had enduring moral and political consequences. On that August morning in 1945, the world had its first terrifying glimpse of the power of total annihilation. In an instant—0.3 second—Hiroshima became an atomic wasteland. The world now lived with the knowledge that it could happen again.

German army. Hiroshima and Nagasaki were leveled by the United States. The nations of Europe were weakened after World War I; after World War II, they were crippled. Europe was completely displaced from the position of world dominance it had held for centuries. The United States alone was undamaged and stronger after the war than before, its industrial capacity and production greatly improved by the war.

The Big Three.   What would be the future of Europe? The leaders of the United States, Great Britain, and the Soviet Union—the **Big Three,** as they were called—met three times between 1943 and 1945: first at Teheran; then in February 1945 at Yalta, a Russian Black Sea resort; and finally in July and August 1945 at Potsdam, a suburb of Berlin. They coordinated their attacks on Germany and Japan and discussed their plans for postwar Europe. After Allied victory, the governments of both Germany and Japan would be totally abolished and completely reconstructed. No deals would be made with Hitler or his successors; no peace would be negotiated with the enemy; surrender would be unconditional. Germany would be disarmed and denazified, and its leaders would be tried as war criminals. The armies of the Big Three occupied Germany, each with a separate zone, but the country would be governed as a single economic unit. The Soviet Union, it was agreed, could collect reparations from Germany. With Germany and Japan defeated, a United Nations organization would provide the structure for a lasting peace in the world.

Stalin expected that the Soviet Union would decide the future of the territories of eastern Europe that the Soviet army had liberated from Germany. This area was vital to the security of the war-devastated Soviet Union; Stalin saw it as a protective barrier against another attack from the west. Romania, Bulgaria, Hungary, Czechoslovakia, and Poland, the Big Three decided, would have pro-Soviet governments. Since Soviet troops occupied these countries in 1945, there was little that the Anglo-Americans could do to prevent Russian control unless they wanted to go to war against the USSR. Churchill realistically accepted this. But for Americans who took seriously the proclamations of President Roosevelt that their country had fought to restore freedom and self-determination to peoples oppressed by tyranny, Soviet power in eastern Europe proved to be a bitter disappointment.

CONCLUSION

The war that broke out in 1939 was caused by German aggression, which the appeasement policies of the British failed to contain. Within two years Hitler ruled continental western Europe by either occupation or collaboration. Although pockets of resistance existed, the activities of the resisters had little impact on the course of the war. Hitler undertook the destruction of Europe's Jewish population and attempts to eliminate other minorities deemed inferior by Nazi racial policies.

The year 1941 was a critical turning point in the war because of the German attack on its former ally, which brought Russia to the Allied cause. And in December of that same year, the Japanese attack on an American naval base in Hawaii brought the United States into the war. The war became a truly global conflagration. The Allies were able to coordinate the war effort on several fronts. American technology and resources proved critical in the Allied success. The dropping of two atom bombs also set the tone for determining the peace. And the ideological divide between East and West would sow the seeds of future dissension. Meanwhile the Allies celebrated their victory in a war in which 50 million people died. With the defeat of Germany and Japan, the United States and the Soviet Union stood as the undisputed giants in world politics.

■ Churchill, Roosevelt, and Stalin— the Big Three—at the Yalta Conference. Stalin invoked the Yalta agreements to justify the Soviet Union's control over eastern Europe after the war.

QUESTIONS FOR REVIEW

1. What factors made possible Hitler's diplomatic and military successes between 1933 and 1941?
2. Why did the Nazi regime believe that it needed to destroy the Jews, gypsies, and other outsiders, and how did it attempt to justify that policy?
3. How did Hitler's invasion of the Soviet Union and the entry of the United States into the war transform the military situation?
4. How did the Allies coordinate their efforts, and what factors strained relations between them?
5. How did the three Allied victors envision the future of Europe, and what steps did they take to ensure the peace?

KEY TERMS

appeasement, *p. 870*

Axis Powers, *p. 870*

Big Three, *p. 894*

blitzkrieg, p. 873

Final Solution, *p. 876*

holocaust, *p. 878*

DISCOVERING WESTERN CIVILIZATION ONLINE

You can obtain more information about World War II at the Websites listed below. See also the Companion Website that accompanies this text, www.ablongman.com/kishlansky, which contains an online study guide and additional resources.

Aggression and Conquest

The Avalon Project: Munich Pact 9/29/38

www.yale.edu/lawweb/avalon/imt/munich1.htm
Electronic text of the Munich agreements.

The Avalon Project: World War II Documents

http://www.yale.edu/lawweb/avalon/wwii/wwii.htm
An important collection of documents from the pre-war years, the war years, and the subsequent peace settlements.

Racism and Destruction

United States Holocaust Memorial Museum

www.ushmm.org
Home page of the United States Holocaust Museum. The site contains a searchable online catalog of both documentary and photographic sources.

Simon Wiesenthal Center

www.wiesenthal.com
Home page of the Simon Wiesenthal Center and the Museum of Tolerance. It has an extensive collection of materials related to the Holocaust and anti-Semitism.

The Vidal Sassoon International Center for the Study of Antisemitism (SICSA)

sicsa.huji.ac.il/
The site of the Vidal Sassoon International Center for Anti-Semitism that contains an extensive bibliography on the Holocaust.

Allied Victory

Internet Modern History Sourcebook: World War II

www.fordham.edu/halsall/mod/modsbook45.html
A collection of primary source documents and links to materials on World War II.

World War II

www.archives.gov/digital_classroom/teaching_with_documents.html#great_depression
War documents from the U.S. National Archives and Research Administration.

Russian Photography Collection—War Photography

www.schicklerart.com/auto_exh/RPCWar
Images of World War II from the Soviet perspective.

Women Come to the Front

www.loc.gov/exhibits/wcf/wcf0001.html
A virtual exhibit by the Library of Congress on women journalists, photographers, and broadcasters during World War II.

SUGGESTIONS FOR FURTHER READING

Aggression and Conquest

Paul Kennedy, *The Realities Behind Diplomacy: Background Influences on British External Policy, 1865–1980* (London: Allen & Unwin, 1981). Essays dealing with the continuity of appeasement in British foreign policy across two centuries.

Ian Kershaw, *The Nazi Dictatorship* (London: Edward Arnold, 1985). A fine synthesis of key problems of interpretation regarding the Third Reich. Special attention is paid to the interdependence of domestic and foreign policy and the inevitability of war in Hitler's ideology.

Donald Cameron Watt, *How War Came: The Immediate Origins of the Second World War* (London: Heinemann, 1989). An international historian chronicles the events leading to the outbreak of the war.

Racism and Destruction

Renate Bridenthal, Atina Grossmann, and Marion Kaplan, eds., *When Biology Became Destiny: Women in Weimar and Nazi Germany* (New York: Monthly Review Press, 1984). A volume of essays pursuing common themes on the relation between sexism and racism in interwar and wartime Germany.

Raul Hilberg, *The Destruction of the European Jews,* 3 vols. (New York: Holmes and Meier, 1985). An exhaustive study of the annihilation of European Jews beginning with cultural precedents and antecedents. Examines step-by-step developments that led to extermination policies and contains valuable appendixes on statistics and a discussion of sources.

Charles S. Maier, *The Unmasterable Past: History, Holocaust, and German National Identity* (Cambridge, MA: Harvard University Press, 1988). A thoughtful discussion of the historical debate over the Holocaust and the comparative dimensions of the event. Especially valuable in placing the Holocaust within German history.

Michael R. Marrus, *The Holocaust in History* (New York: New American Library, 1987). A comprehensive survey of all aspects of the Holocaust, including the policies of the Third Reich, the living conditions in the camps, and the prospects for resistance and opposition.

Allied Victory

John Campbell, ed., *The Experience of World War II* (New York: Oxford University Press, 1989). This richly illustrated work provides an overview of the Second World War in both the Asian and European theaters in terms of origins, events, and consequences.

Akira Iriye, *The Origins of the Second World War in Asia and the Pacific* (London: Longman, 1987). Examines the events of the 1930s leading up to hostilities in the Pacific theater, with a special focus on Japanese isolation and aggression.

John Keegan, *The Second World War* (New York: Viking, 1990). Provides a panoramic sweep of "the largest single event in human history," with special attention to warfare in all its forms and the importance of leadership.

Gerhard L. Weinberg, *A World at Arms: A Global History of World War II* (New York: Cambridge University Press, 1994). An overview of the interactions among Germany, the Soviet Union, and Japan, which provides an integrated history of World War II with a helpful bibliographic essay.

For a list of additional titles related to this chapter's topics, please see http://www.ablongman.com/kishlansky.

Chapter 29

THE COLD WAR AND POSTWAR ECONOMIC RECOVERY: 1945–1970

Chapter Outline

After World War II, Europe faced enormous challenges as it began the process of rebuilding and recovery. Material damage during the war had been great, and some cities were almost completely destroyed. In The Visual Record, see one stark example of a city in ruins in 1946 and find out how it was saved. ➤

EUROPE IN RUINS

Warsaw, 1946

When the dust from the last bombs settled over Europe's cities, the balance sheets of destruction were tallied. Great cities including London, Cologne, Berlin, Stalingrad, and Warsaw incurred serious damage and human loss. Millions of refugees on the Continent found themselves homeless, having lost their loved ones, often all of their personal belongings, and the roofs over their heads. Millions more returned home from battlefronts and concentration camps to rubble, with wounds beyond healing. There were no jobs; there was nothing to eat. Peacetime rationing dipped below wartime levels. What was not measured in the statistics on physical and human destruction, at least not immediately, was the psychological devastation that succeeded such loss. There could be no returning to life as normal. For many, the war was far gentler than the peace. For the combatants of peacetime, often women and children, digging out and surviving were the greatest battles of all.

Warsaw in 1946 stands as a stark example of extreme destruction and of startling renewal. At the close of the war, Warsaw was an almost completely destroyed city, consisting of little more than dust, ashes, and the charred hulks of destroyed buildings, with no inhabitants and no water, electricity, or sanitation. The scene here, captured by a photographer in early 1946, is not an isolated perspective but rather a landscape typical of Poland's capital after the war. By contrast with this image, Warsaw was recognized in the interwar period of the 1920s and 1930s as a metropolitan center of charm and culture, known for its artists and intellectuals and vibrant urban life.

Warsaw's devastation was not achieved in the same way that Hiroshima and Nagasaki were each destroyed by a single atomic bomb. Instead, Warsaw was annihilated in stages over a five-year period by conventional weapons like flamethrowers, tanks, and dynamite. Unrelenting aerial attacks by German planes against the city and its population began first on September 1, 1939. The Nazi occupiers systematically destroyed people and buildings in order to bring the civilian population to its knees. The Jewish ghetto was completely eliminated in 1943. The destruction, building by building, was premeditated and methodical. By the end of 1944, Warsaw was no more than a heap of rubble with almost 90 percent of its buildings destroyed. A large portion of its population was wiped out, and those who survived were in detention camps or in flight. Warsaw became known as "the vanished city."

But that is where the postwar story of recovery begins. With the liberation by the Red Army of what was left of the city, the Polish people almost immediately planned for the rebuilding of their capital, helped raise the necessary funds, and volunteered their labor to the great task. Women and children joined the men in clearing the rubble and sweeping the path for recovery. Aid in the form of food, clothing, and shelter from organizations such as the United Nations Relief and Rehabilitation Administration supported the healing and rebuilding of Warsaw. Civilians returned to the city. By 1951 the population reached 815,000, although still below its 1.3 million inhabitants in 1939.

In rebuilding Warsaw, the Polish people did not ignore the city's historic past by building a modern, postwar metropolis, as the people of Frankfurt, for example, did. Instead they sought to reconstruct Warsaw as it had been in 1939 by recreating monuments and historic buildings in their original form. Often that required architects to consult unconventional sources, including paintings and postcards, in the absence of blueprints and plans. Palaces and castles were reborn, baroque

■ Street scene in Warsaw, 1946.

buildings rose up, ornamental gardens were replanted, and ancient vistas and panoramas were brought back to life. The achievement of historical preservation was astounding. By 1951 a large part of the city had been rebuilt, perhaps one of the best examples of how Europeans met the postwar challenge of urban reconstruction and economic revival.

Looking Ahead

In this chapter, we shall see how, under the tutelage of the two superpowers, the United States and the Soviet Union, Europe diverged on two separate paths of reconstruction and economic integration after 1945. Europe dismantled its global empires. Cold war replaced the hot war of global conflagration. In the West and in the Eastern Bloc, different welfare state models emerged for the regulation and social distribution of economic expansion. Slowed prosperity in the late 1960s, combined with the growth of an independent youth culture, helped fuel protests in the East and the West. Dissent, prosperity, and rising and unmet consumer expectations characterized Western societies within twenty-five years—the span of a generation—after the end of World War II. ➤

THE ORIGINS OF THE COLD WAR

For victors and vanquished alike, the situation in Europe at the end of the Second World War was dire. Economies geared totally toward war efforts were incapable of the kind of reorientation needed to reconstruct markets and eliminate economic distress. Governments faced political crises as they attempted to restore or establish democratic principles. Moreover, Europe did not have the capital necessary to begin the process of rebuilding. Political disorganization reigned in Berlin, which was divided into sectors, in Germany, which was divided into zones, and in the former European empires, which were in the process of being dismantled. Even the winners were losers as survivors faced a level of human and material destruction unknown in the history of warfare. As one American military observer reported to his superiors in 1947, "Millions of people in the cities are slowly starving." Could Europe rise from these ashes and, if so, in what form?

Cold War conflict initially developed because of differing Russian and American notions regarding the economic reconstruction of Europe. The Soviet Union realized that American aid to Europe was not primarily a humanitarian program; it was part of an economic offensive in Europe that would contribute to the dominance of American capital in world markets. The United States recognized that the Soviet Union hoped to achieve its own recovery through outright control of eastern Europe.

The World in Two Blocs

With the cessation of the "hot" war that had ripped Europe apart from 1939 to 1945, the armies of the United States and the Soviet Union met on the banks of the Elbe River in 1945. Greeting each other as victors and allies, the occupying armies waited for direction on how to conduct the peace. Europe and Japan had been destroyed, leaving the United States and the

MAP DISCOVERY

American zone
British zone
French zone
Soviet zone
Berlin airlift 1948–1949

The Division of Germany

Examine the division of Germany after World War II. Why did the four victor nations divide Germany into zones at the end of the war? How did Berlin come to be divided into two zones? What was the Soviet goal in blockading West Berlin, and why did the blockade fail?

■ The Berlin airlift of 1948–1949 broke through the Soviet blockade of the city. Called "Operation Vittles," the airlift provided food and fuel for the beleaguered West Berliners. Here children wait for the candy American pilots dropped in tiny parachute handkerchiefs. The Soviets ended the blockade in the spring of 1949.

THE IRON CURTAIN

Winston Churchill (1874–1965), prime minister of England during World War II, captured the drama of the post-war international order in a speech he delivered in Missouri in 1946. Churchill had long been suspicious of the political motives of the Soviet Union, though he welcomed Stalin as an ally in defeating Hitler. The term that he coined, iron curtain, described graphically the fate of Europe that many feared: a Europe rigidly divided between East and West, no more than a pawn in the struggle of the superpowers.

Focus Questions

What are "the Communist fifth columns" in countries such as France and Italy to which Churchill refers? What does Churchill mean by the "grand pacification of Europe," and how does he hope it will be achieved?

From Stettin in the Baltic to Trieste in the Adriatic, an iron curtain has descended across the Continent. Behind that line lie all the capitals of the ancient states of Central and Eastern Europe. Warsaw, Berlin, Prague, Vienna, Budapest, Belgrade, Bucharest and Sofia, all these famous cities and the populations around them lie in what I must call the Soviet sphere, and all are subject in one form or another, not only to Soviet influence but to a very high and, in many cases, increasing measure of control from Moscow. Athens alone—Greece with its immortal glories—is free to decide its future at an election under British, American, and French observation. The Russian-dominated Polish Government has been encouraged to make enormous and wrongful inroads upon Germany, and mass expulsions of millions of Germans on a scale grievous and undreamed-of are now taking place. The Communist parties, which were very small in all these Eastern States of Europe, have been raised to preeminence and power far beyond their numbers and are seeking everywhere to obtain totalitarian control. Police governments are prevailing in nearly every case, and so far, except in Czechoslovakia, there is no true democracy.

The safety of the world requires a new unity in Europe, from which no nation should be permanently outcast. It is from the quarrels of the strong parent races in Europe that the world wars we have witnessed, or which occurred in former times, have sprung. Twice in our own lifetime we have seen the United States, against their wishes and their traditions, against arguments, the force of which it is impossible not to comprehend, drawn by irresistible forces, into these wars in time to secure the victory of the good cause, but only after frightful slaughter and devastation had occurred. Twice the United States has had to send several millions of its young men across the Atlantic to find the war; but now war can find any nation, wherever it may dwell between dusk and dawn. Surely we should work with conscious purpose for a grand pacification of Europe, within the structure of the United Nations and in accordance with its Charter. That I feel is an open cause of policy of very great importance.

In front of the iron curtain which lies across Europe are other causes for anxiety. In Italy the Communist Party is seriously hampered by having to support the Communist-trained Marshal Tito's claims to former Italian territory at the head of the Adriatic. Nevertheless the future of Italy hangs in the balance. Again one cannot imagine a regenerated Europe without a strong France. All my public life I have worked for a strong France and I never lost faith in her destiny, even in the darkest hours. I will not lose faith now. However, in a great number of countries, far from the Russian frontiers and throughout the world, Communist fifth columns are established and work in complete unity and absolute obedience to the directions they receive from the Communist centre. Except in the British Commonwealth and in the United States where Communism is in its infancy, the Communist parties or fifth columns constitute a growing challenge and peril to Christian civilization. These are somber facts for anyone to have to recite on the morrow of a victory gained by so much splendid comradeship in arms and in the cause of freedom and democracy; but we should be most unwise not to face them squarely while time remains.

Soviet Union as indisputably the two richest and strongest nations in the world.

The Soviets understood that they ran a sorry second to American military superiority—the United States was alone in possessing the atomic bomb—and to American wealth, which, measured in Gross National Product (GNP), was 400 percent greater than that of the Soviet Union. Stalin, nevertheless, committed the Soviet Union to an arms race in which he refused to accept American dominance. War had made the two superpowers wary allies; peace promised to make them once again active foes. In the three years that followed the war, a new kind of conflict emerged between the two superpower victors, a war deemed "cold" because of its lack of military violence, but a bitter war nonetheless.

The Cold War was rooted in the ideological opposition between communism and capitalist democracies, dominated by the two superpowers, the Soviet Union and the United States. It affected the entire world. Drawing on three decades

MAP DISCOVERY

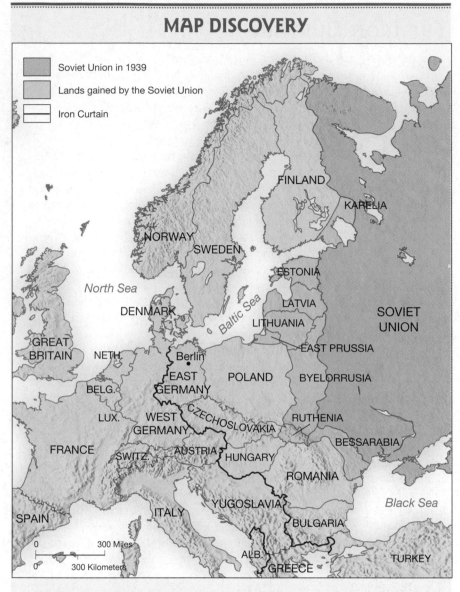

Soviet Union in 1939

Lands gained by the Soviet Union

Iron Curtain

The Soviet Union and the Soviet Bloc

Notice the boundary of the Soviet Union before 1939 and the territory it gained after World War II. Which countries in eastern Europe did the Soviet Union annex after the war and why? In other countries of eastern Europe the Soviet Union established economic and political control without annexation. Which countries constituted the Soviet bloc?

The Division of Germany. In central Europe, Cold War tensions first surfaced over the question of how to treat Germany. The United States and the Soviet Union had very different ideas about the future of their former enemy. In fostering economic reconstruction in Europe, the United States counted on a German economy transfused with American funds that would be self-supporting and stable. To the contrary, the Soviet Union, blaming Germany for its extreme destruction, was explicit in its demands: German resources must be siphoned off for Soviet reconstruction. Stricken as the Soviets were with 20 million dead, millions of homeless refugees in dire poverty, and 1700 cities in ruins, commandeering German labor and stripping Germany of its industrial plant seemed to them only fair.

With Germany's defeat, its territory had been divided into four zones, occupied by American, Soviet, British, and French troops. An Allied Control Commission consisting of representatives of the four powers was to govern Germany as a whole in keeping with the decisions made at Yalta before the end of the war. As Soviet and American antagonisms over Germany's future deepened, however, Allied rule polarized between the East and the West, with the internal politics of each area determined by the ideological conflicts between communism and capitalist free enterprise.

Allied attempts to administer Germany as a whole faltered and failed in 1948 over a question of economic policy. The zones of the Western occupying forces (the United States, Great Britain, and France), now administered as a single unit, issued a uniform and stable currency that the Russians accurately saw as a threat to their own economic policies in Germany. The Soviets blockaded the city of Berlin, which, though behind the frontier of the Russian sector, was being administered in sectors by the four powers and whose western sector promised to become a successful enclave of Western capitalism. With the support of the people of West Berlin, the Allies responded by airlifting food and supplies into West Berlin for almost a year, defending it as an outpost that had to be preserved from the advance of communism. The Russians were forced to withdraw the blockade in the spring of 1949. The Berlin blockade hardened the commitment on both sides to two Germanys.

of distrust between the East and the West, the Cold War was related to the economic and foreign policy goals of both superpowers.

Winston Churchill captured the drama of the new international order in a speech he delivered in Missouri in 1946: "From Stettin in the Baltic to Trieste in the Adriatic an iron curtain has descended across the continent." The term **iron curtain** described graphically for many the new fate of Europe rigidly divided between East and West, a pawn in the struggle of the superpowers.

NATO countries, 1955

Warsaw Pact countries, 1955

ALASKA (U.S.)

ARCTIC OCEAN

North Pole

NORTH AMERICA

CANADA

UNITED STATES

GREENLAND (DENMARK)

ATLANTIC OCEAN

ICELAND

NORWAY

DEN.

GREAT BRITAIN

NETH.

BELG.

LUX.

FRANCE

W. GER.

E. GER.

CZECH.

POLAND

HUNG.

ITALY

PORTUGAL

AFRICA

ASIA

SOVIET UNION

E U R O P E

ROMANIA

BULG.

Black Sea

TURKEY

GREECE

ALBANIA

Mediterranean Sea

1200 Miles

1200 Kilometers

■ The Cold War: U.S. and Soviet Alliances. The U.S. and Soviet blocs (NATO countries and Warsaw Pact countries, respectively) constituted a balance of power in global politics.

The two new states came into existence in 1949, their founding separated by less than a month. The Federal Republic of Germany (West Germany), within the American orbit, was established as a democratic parliamentary regime. Free elections brought the Christian Democrat Konrad Adenauer to power as chancellor. The German Democratic Republic (East Germany) was ruled as a single-party state under Walter Ulbricht, who took his direction from the Soviet Union. The division of Germany became a microcosm of the division of the world into two armed camps.

Eastern Europe and the Soviet Bloc. With the support of local Communist parties, Soviet-dominated governments were established in Poland, Hungary, Bulgaria, and Romania in 1947. The following year, Czechoslovakia was pulled into the Soviet orbit. Czechoslovakia served as a significant marker in the development of Cold War confrontation. The tactics of the Communists in Czechoslovakia taught the West that coalition governments were unacceptable and undoubtedly hardened the resolve of U.S. policy makers in support of two Germanys. Needing the stability of peace, the Soviets saw in eastern Europe, hostile as the area may have been to forced integration, a necessary buffer against Western competition. The Soviet Union feared U.S. intentions to establish liberal governments and capitalist markets in the states bordering its own frontiers and viewed such attempts as a threat to Soviet interests. For those reasons, Stalin refused to allow free elections in Poland and, by force of occupying armies, annexed neighboring territories that

included eastern Finland, the Baltic states, East Prussia, eastern Poland, Ruthenia, and Bessarabia. With the exception of East Prussia, the annexations were limited to territories that had once been part of tsarist Russia.

NATO and Other Treaty Alliances. With the aim of containing the USSR, a policy known as **containment,** the United States entered into a series of military alliances around the world. In order to provide mutual assistance should any member be attacked, the United States joined with Belgium, Britain, Canada, Denmark, France, Iceland, Italy, the Netherlands, Norway, and Portugal in 1949 to form the **North Atlantic Treaty Organization (NATO).** Greece and Turkey became members in 1952, West Germany in 1955, and Spain in 1982. The potential military threat of the Soviet Union in Western Europe prompted the peacetime military alliance.

A challenge to Cold War power politics came from within the NATO alliance. General Charles de Gaulle, as president of the French Fifth Republic, rejected the straitjacket of American dominance in Western Europe and asserted his country's independent status by exploding the first French atomic bomb in 1960. Refusing to place the French military under an American general who served as Supreme Allied Commander for NATO, de Gaulle completely withdrew France from participation in NATO in 1966. He forged an independent French foreign policy, taking advantage of the loosening of bloc politics in the mid-1960s.

The Southeast Asia Treaty Organization (SEATO) in 1954 and the Baghdad Pact of 1955 (known as the Central Treaty Organization after 1959) followed. The United States strengthened its military presence throughout the period by acquiring 1400 military bases in foreign countries for its own forces.

In 1955, Albania, Bulgaria, Romania, Czechoslovakia, Hungary, Poland, and East Germany joined with the Soviet Union to form a defensive alliance organization known as the **Warsaw Pact.** The USSR intended its Eastern European allies to serve as a strategic buffer zone against the NATO forces.

The Nuclear Club

The nuclear arms race began in earnest during World War II, well before the first atomic bomb was dropped in August 1945. The Germans, the Russians, and the British all had teams exploring the destructive possibilities of nuclear fission during the war, but the Americans had the edge in the development of the bomb. Stalin understood the political significance of the weapon and committed the Soviet Union to a breakneck program of development following the war.

The USSR ended the American monopoly and tested its first atomic bomb in 1949. Both countries developed the hydrogen bomb almost simultaneously in 1953. Space exploration by satellite was also deemed important in terms of the detection and deployment of bombs, and the Soviets pulled ahead in this area with the launching of the first satellite, *Sputnik I,* in 1957. Intercontinental ballistic missiles (ICBMs) followed, further accelerating the pace of nuclear armament.

The atomic bomb and thermonuclear weapons contributed greatly to the shape of Cold War politics. The incineration of Hiroshima and Nagasaki sent a clear message to the world about the power of total annihilation available to those who controlled the bombs. The threat of such total destruction made full and direct confrontation with an equally armed enemy impossible. Both the United States and the Soviet Union, the first two members of the "**nuclear club,**" knew that they had the capability of obliterating their enemy, but not before the enemy could retaliate. They also knew that the technology necessary for nuclear arms was available to any industrial power. By 1974, the nuclear club included Great Britain, France, the People's Republic of China, and India. Those countries joined the United States and the Soviet Union in spending the billions of dollars necessary every year to expand nuclear arsenals and to develop more sophisticated weaponry and delivery systems.

A new vocabulary transformed popular attitudes and values. *Missile gaps, deterrence, first strike, second strike, radioactive fallout,* and *containment* were all terms that heightened popular fears. Citizens in the Soviet Union learned of American weapons stockpiling and American deployment of military forces throughout the world. Americans learned that the Soviets had the ability to deliver bombs that could wipe out major U.S. cities. Paranoia on both sides was encouraged by heads of state in their public addresses throughout the 1950s. Traitors were publicly tried while espionage was being sponsored by the state.

DOCUMENT

Krushchev Challenges the West to Disarm

The Nuclear Test Ban Treaty of 1963, the first of its kind, banned tests in the atmosphere and inaugurated a period of lessening tensions between the Eastern and Western blocs. Arms limitation and nonproliferation were the subjects of a series of conferences between the United States and the Soviet Union in the late 1960s and pointed the way to limitations eventually agreed on in the next decade. The United Nations (UN), an organization created by the Allies immediately following World War II to take the place of the defunct League of Nations, established

■ The first hydrogen bomb test, on November 1, 1952, destroyed an entire island in the Pacific.

■ Interior view of *Sputnik I* before its launch. The news of the Soviet breakthrough galvanized the Western nations. The United States redoubled its efforts to enter the space age and reorganized school curricula to stress math and science.

international agencies for the purpose of harnessing nuclear power for peaceful uses. By the early 1970s, both the United States and the Soviet Union recognized the importance of closer relations between the superpowers. The USSR and the United States had achieved nuclear parity. On the whole, however, the arms race persisted as a continuing threat in Cold War politics. The race required the dedication of huge national resources to maintain a competitive stance. Conventional forces, too, were expanded to protect Eastern and Western bloc interests.

Decolonization and the Cold War

No part of the globe escaped the tensions generated by the Cold War. By the end of the Second World War, European colonial empires had been weakened or destroyed by the ravages of battle, occupation, and neglect. Nationalist movements had been growing in power in the 1930s, and many nationalist leaders saw the war as a catalyst for independence. Former colonies were no longer directly controlled but as newly independent countries, they had to contend with Cold War pressures to belong in one or the other superpower camp. Hence, **decolonization** often meant continued dependence.

Soviet leader Joseph Stalin limited the Soviet Union's foreign involvement following the Second World War to Communist regimes that shared borders with the USSR in Eastern Europe and Asia. But after Stalin's death in 1953, the Soviet Union turned to the **third world.** Former colonies played an important new role in the Cold War strategies with the accession to power of Nikita Khrushchev (1894–1971) in the mid-1950s. The Soviet Union abandoned its previous caution and assumed a global role in offering "friendship treaties," military advice, trade credits, and general support for attempts at national liberation in Asia, Africa, and Latin America. Both East and West took advantage of tribalism and regionalism, which worked against the establishment of strong central governments. Military rule and fragmentation often resulted. Instability and acute poverty continued to characterize former colonies after

emancipation, regardless of whether the new leaders joined the communist or democratic camps.

Asia. Great Britain knew that it no longer commanded the resources to control India, historically its richest colony, which under the leadership of Mohandas Gandhi (1869–1948) had been agitating for independence since 1920. Given the title of "Mahatma," or "great-souled," by his people, Gandhi advocated passive resistance to achieve independence. He sought to bring pressure on the colonizers by means of civil disobedience, boycotts, and public fasts instead of violence. The British granted self-government to India in 1946 with the proviso that if the bitter conflict between Hindus and Muslims was not settled by mutual agreement, Great Britain would decide on the division of power. As a result, Muslim and Hindu representatives agreed to the division of British India into the independent states of India and Pakistan in 1947. Ceylon (now Sri Lanka) and Burma (now Myanmar) achieved full independence in 1948.

Gandhi on Civil Disobedience

In its march through Asia during the war, Japan had smashed colonial empires. Japan's defeat created a power vacuum that nationalist leaders were eager to fill. Civil wars erupted in China, Burma, Korea, and Indochina. In 1950, the United States and the United Nations intervened when North Korea attacked South Korea. Korea, formerly controlled by Japan, had been divided following the war as a result of the presence of Russian and American troops. Communist-dominated North Korea refused to accept the artificial boundary between it and Western-dominated South Korea. China, a Communist state following the victory of Mao Zedong (1893–1976) in 1949, intervened in the Korean conflict when American troops advanced on Chinese frontiers in October 1950. After three years of military stalemate, Korea was partitioned on the 38th parallel in 1953. The Soviet Union was not party to the conflict in Korea, but the United States considered China to be in the Soviet camp rather than an independent contender for power.

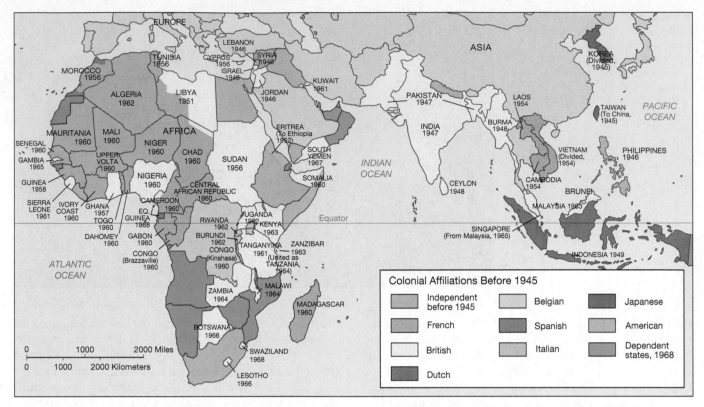

■ Decolonization. Few nations in Africa and south and southeast Asia were independent before 1945. Few remained dependent after 1968.

The United States was heavily committed as a military presence in Southeast Asia after the French withdrawal from Indochina following the French defeat at Dien Bien Phu in 1954. The North Vietnamese state was established under the French-educated leader Ho Chi Minh. South Vietnam was declared a republic, and the United States sponsored a regime that was considered favorable to Western interests. Arguing the domino theory—that one Southeast Asian country after another would fall like a row of dominoes to Communist takeover—the United States also intervened in Laos and Cambodia. Between 1961 and 1973, the United States committed American troops to a full-scale war—though officially termed only a military action—against Communist guerrilla forces throughout the region. After almost two decades of escalating involvement, in 1973 American troops were finally withdrawn from a war in Vietnam that they could not win.

Africa.   The first wave of decolonization after 1945 had been in Asia, but it wasn't until the late 1950s and early 1960s that a second wave crested and crashed in Africa. Wartime experiences and rapid economic development fed existing nationalist aspirations and encouraged the emergence of mass political demands for liberation. A new generation of leaders, many of them educated in European institutions, moved from cooperation with home rule to demands for independence by the early 1960s. British Prime Minister Harold MacMillan (1894–1986) spoke of "the winds of change" in 1960, the year that proved to be a turning point in African politics. Britain and Belgium yielded their colonies. In 1960, Patrice Lumumba (1925–1961)

became the first prime minister of the Republic of the Congo (present-day Democratic Republic of the Congo). White European rule continued in Rhodesia (now Zimbabwe) and South Africa, despite continued world pressure. African leader Kwame Nkrumah (1909–1972) of Ghana denounced the situation of African dependence as "neocolonialism" and called for a united Africa as the only means of resistance. He led Ghana in a policy of nonalignment in the Cold War. With Jomo Kenyatta (1894–1978) of Kenya, Nkrumah founded the Pan-African Federation, which promoted African nationalism.

DOCUMENT

Kwame
Nkrumah on
African Unity

The French, having faced what its officer corps considered a humiliating defeat in Indochina, held on against the winds of change in North Africa. France's problems in Algeria began in earnest in 1954 when Muslims seeking independence and self-rule revolted. Although the Algerian rebels successfully employed terrorist and guerrilla tactics, European settlers and the French army in Algeria refused to accept defeat. Facing political collapse at home, the French, under the leadership of General Charles de Gaulle, ended the war and agreed to Algeria's independence, which was achieved in 1962.

The Middle East.   The United States and the Soviet Union used aid to win support of "client" states in the Middle East. The withdrawal, sometimes under duress, of British and French rule in the Middle East and North Africa and the creation of the state of Israel in 1948 destabilized the area and created opportunities for new alliances. Egypt and Syria, for example, sought

Soviet support against the new Israeli state, which had been formed out of the part of Palestine under British mandate since 1920 and which was dependent on U.S. aid.

Oil, an essential resource for rapid industrialization, was the object of Soviet politicking in Iran after World War II. Western oil companies, long active in the area, had won oil concessions in Iran in 1946, but such rights eluded the Soviets. In 1951, a nationalist Iranian government sought to evict Westerners by nationalizing the oil fields. The British blockaded Iranian trade in the Persian Gulf, and the newly formed American espionage organization, the Central Intelligence Agency (CIA), subverted the nationalist government and placed in power the shah of Iran, a leader favorable to American interests.

In 1956, a crisis came in Egypt. Egyptian President Gamal Abdel Nasser (1918–1970), a nationalist in power by virtue of a military coup d'état in 1952, oversaw the nationalization of the Suez Canal. British and French military forces attacked and were forced to withdraw by pressure from both the Soviet Union and the United States, which cooperated in seeking to avert a disaster. The Middle East, however, remained a Cold War powder keg, with Israeli and Arab nationalist interests and Soviet and American aid running on a collision course. The expansion of the Israeli state at the expense of its Arab neighbors further exacerbated tensions.

Latin America.   The United States was also experiencing Cold War problems closer to home. In 1954, the CIA plotted the overthrow of Guatemala's leftist regime to keep Soviet influence out of the Western Hemisphere. In 1958, President Dwight D. Eisenhower sent his vice president, Richard M. Nixon, on a tour of Latin American countries. Crowds everywhere jeered the American vice president and hurled stones and eggs at his motorcade in response to U.S. policies. In 1959, a revolution in Cuba, an island nation only 90 miles off the American coast, resulted in the ejection of U.S. interests and the establishment of a Communist regime under the leadership of a young lawyer, Fidel Castro. In 1962, a direct and frightening confrontation occurred between the United States and the USSR over Soviet missile installations in Cuba. Following the Russian withdrawal from the island, both U.S. President John F. Kennedy and Soviet leader Nikita Khrushchev pursued a policy of *peaceful coexistence,* intent on averting nuclear confrontation. Both sides recognized how close they had come to mutual annihilation in the showdown over Cuba.

DOCUMENT
John F. Kennedy and Cuba

POSTWAR ECONOMIC RECOVERY IN EUROPE, JAPAN, AND THE SOVIET UNION

In contrast to the Soviet Union, the United States had incurred relatively light casualties in World War II. Because the fighting had not taken place on the North American continent, U.S. cities, farmlands, and factories were intact. As the chief producer and supplier for the Allied war effort, even before its entry into the conflict, the United States had benefited from the conflict in Europe and actually expanded its economic productivity during the war. In 1945, the United States was producing a full 50 percent of the world's GNP—a staggering fact to a displaced Great Britain, whose former trade networks were permanently destroyed. Furthermore, the United States held two-thirds of the world's gold. A United States bursting with energy and prosperity was a real threat to the Soviet Union viewing the rubble of its destroyed cities and counting the bodies of its dead. However, the United States knew that it lacked one important guarantee to secure its growth and its future prosperity: adequate international markets for its goods. After World War I, American officials and businessmen understood that America's productive capacity was outpacing its ability to export goods. In the 1920s, the United States had exported capital to Europe in the form of private loans with the hope that trade would flourish as a result. The decade following the Great Depression of 1929 witnessed the search for a policy to expand U.S. markets. Both Europe and Japan were recognized as potential buyers for American goods, but both areas parried with protectionism to foster their own post-depression recovery.

The Economic Challenge

Economists judged that Europe would need at least 25 years to regain its prewar economic capacity. The worst was also feared: that Europe would never recover as a world economic power. Large-scale population movements made matters worse. Displaced persons by the millions moved across Europe. Just as the war had caused dislocation, so too did the peace create millions of refugees seeking asylum and a better life. The release of prisoners of war and slave workers imprisoned during the Third Reich strained already weak economies. Germans were expelled from territories that Germany had controlled before the war. Soviet expansionist policies forced others to flee Estonia, Latvia, and Lithuania. Jews who survived the concentration camps resettled outside Europe, primarily in Palestine and the United States.

European industrial production in 1945 was one-third of its level in 1938. Housing shortages existed everywhere. France had lost one-fifth of its housing during the war years; Germany's 50 largest cities had seen two-fifths of their buildings reduced to rubble. Frankfurt, Düsseldorf, Dresden, Warsaw (see "The Visual Record," pp. 898–899), and Berlin were virtually destroyed. The transportation infrastructure was severely damaged: railways, roads, and bridges were in shambles all over Europe. Communications networks were in disarray. In some cases, industrial plants had not been as adversely affected as urban centers. Yet machinery everywhere had been worn out in wartime production, and replacement parts were nonexistent. German equipment was dismantled and seized by Soviet soldiers to be used in Russia in place of what the Germans had destroyed.

Agriculture, too, suffered severe reversals in wartime economies and was unable to resume prewar production in 1945. In general, European agriculture was producing at 50

■ A brother and sister on the way home from school walk down a deserted street in a bombed-out section of Berlin. They carry tin cans for the hot meals they receive in school.

percent of its prewar capacity. Livestock had been decimated during the war years—in France, for example, 50 percent of all farm animals had been killed—and it was estimated that restoring herds would take decades. Italy suffered greatly, with one-third of its overall assets destroyed. The scarcity of goods converged with ballooning inflation. Black markets with astronomical prices for necessities flourished, while currency rates plummeted. Everywhere the outlook was bleak. Yet in less than a decade, the situation was reversed. The solution came from outside of Europe.

The Economic Solution: The Marshall Plan

World War II facilitated the success of an international economic policy consistent with international economic goals identified by U.S. policy makers as early as 1920. In both Europe and Japan, the United States intervened to aid reconstruction and recovery of war-torn nations. Those economies, hungry for capital, no longer opposed U.S. intervention or erected trade barriers against American goods. The prospect of a Europe in chaos economically, socially, and politically and on the verge of collapse justified immediate action by the United States.

By the spring of 1947 it was clear to American policy makers that initial postwar attempts to stabilize European economies and promote world recovery were simply not working. The United States had, earlier in the same year, engineered emergency aid to Turkey and Greece, both objects of Soviet aspirations for control. President Truman articulated a doctrine bearing his name: "I believe that it must be the policy of the United States to support free people who are resisting attempted subjugation by armed minorities or by outside pressures." The aid emerged in an atmosphere of opposition between the United States and the Soviet Union over issues of territorial control in eastern and southern Europe. The Cold War coincided with and reinforced the U.S. need to reconstruct western Europe.

DOCUMENT

Truman Doctrine

On 5 June 1947, Secretary of State George C. Marshall (1880–1959) delivered the commencement address at Harvard University. In his speech, Marshall introduced the European Recovery Act, popularly known as the **Marshall Plan,** through which billions of dollars in aid would be made available to European states, both in the east and in the west, provided that two conditions were met: (1) the recipient states had to cooperate with one another in aligning national economic policies and improving the international monetary system, and (2) they had to work toward breaking down trade barriers.

Participating countries included Austria, Belgium, Denmark, France, West Germany, Great Britain, Greece, Iceland, Italy, Luxembourg, the Netherlands, Norway, Sweden, Switzerland, and Turkey. The Soviet Union and eastern European countries were also eligible for aid under the original formulation. But the Soviets opposed the plan from the first, wary of U.S. intentions to extend the influence of Western capitalism. Soviet opposition encouraged members of the U.S. Congress, afraid of a Communist takeover in Europe, to support the plan.

The amount of U.S. aid to Europe was massive. More than $23 billion was pumped into western Europe between 1947 and 1952. By every measure, the Marshall Plan was judged a success in the West. American foreign aid restored western European trade and production while at the same time controlling inflation. Dean Acheson (1893–1971), Marshall's successor as secretary of state, described the plan in terms of "our duty as human beings" but nevertheless considered it "chiefly as a matter of national self-interest." Soviet critics and Western observers differed dramatically in describing self-interest and domination as the primary motives for the plan.

Western European Economic Integration

As significant as the gift of funds to European states undoubtedly was, no less important was the whole administrative apparatus that American aid brought in its wake. In order to expend available monies most effectively and comply with stipulations for cooperation and regulation, the states of western Europe resorted to intensified planning and limited nationalization.

THE MARSHALL PLAN

In the rituals that are part of graduation ceremonies, guest speakers often address the challenges of the future awaiting graduates. Not many commencement addresses change the world. The speech given by U.S. Secretary of State George C. Marshall at Harvard University in June 1947 was different. By pledging gifts in aid, the United States helped rebuild war-torn Europe and transform the world's economy.

Focus Questions

What does Marshall mean when he states that this policy is "directed not against any country or doctrine"? How does Marshall explain that the plan for economic recovery is not intended as charity?

The truth of the matter is that Europe's requirements for the next three or four years of foreign food and other essential products—principally from America—are so much greater than her present ability to pay that she must have substantial additional help or face economic, social, and political deterioration of a very grave character.

The remedy lies in breaking the vicious circle and restoring the confidence of the European people in the economic future of their own countries and of Europe as a whole. The manufacturer and the farmer throughout wide areas must be able and willing to exchange their products for currencies the continuing value of which is not open to question.

Aside from the demoralizing effect on the world at large and the possibilities of disturbances arising as a result of the desperation of the people concerned, the consequences to the economy of the United States should be apparent to all. It is logical that the United States should do whatever it is able to do to assist in the return of normal economic health in the world, without which there can be no political stability and no assured peace. Our policy is directed not against any country or doctrine but against hunger, poverty, desperation, and chaos. Its purpose should be the revival of a working economy in the world so as to permit the emergence of political and social conditions in which free institutions can exist. Such assistance, I am convinced, must not be on a piecemeal basis as various crises develop. Any assistance that this Government may render in the future should provide a cure rather than a mere palliative. Any government that is willing to assist in the task of recovery will find full cooperation, I am sure, on the part of the United States Government. Any government which maneuvers to block the recovery of other countries cannot expect help from us. Furthermore, governments, political parties, or groups which seek to perpetuate human misery in order to profit therefrom politically or otherwise will encounter the opposition of the United States.

From Department of State Bulletin, 15 June 1947.

Planning for Recovery.

The ideas of intensified planning and limited nationalization were not new in the experience of European states: Vichy France, for example, had emphasized the importance of planning and specialization in its corporatist approach to economic development and social welfare policies. Regulation and state intervention dominated the formulation of economic policy. Special attention was given to workers' welfare through unemployment insurance, retirement benefits, public health, and housing policies. European states recognized the need to provide a safety net for their citizens in order to avoid reexperiencing the disastrous depression and stagnation of the 1930s while attempting to rebuild their shattered economies. Those were lessons that had been learned as much from the attempts at recovery before 1939 as from the experiences of running wartime economies.

It was the economic theory of John Maynard Keynes that influenced the planning process. His economic concepts had been applied successfully by neutral Sweden to its economic policies during the war, came into vogue throughout Europe in 1945, and triumphed in the postwar era. Keynes favored macroeconomic policies to increase productivity and argued for an active role for government in "priming the pump" of economic growth. The government should be responsible, according to Keynes, for the control and regulation of the economy, with the goal of ensuring full employment for its people. Governments could and should check inflation and eliminate boom-and-bust cycles, incurring deficits by spending beyond revenues if necessary.

European Economic Cooperation.

U.S. foreign aid contributed mightily to the extension of central planning and the growth of the welfare state throughout western Europe. But money alone could not have accomplished the recovery that took place. The chief mechanism for administering Marshall Plan aid was the Office of European Economic Cooperation (OEEC). That master coordinating agency made the requirements for recovery clear. European states had to stabilize their own economies. Cooperation between the public and private sectors was intended to free market forces, modernize production, and raise productivity. Planning mechanisms,

■ A train carrying iron ore crosses the France-Luxembourg border, celebrating the joint community in coal and steel that became effective in 1953. The European Coal and Steel Community was the first step in the economic integration of Europe.

including transnational organizations and networks, resulted in the modernization of production and the assimilation of new techniques, new styles of management, and innovative business practices from the United States. The modernization of economies through centrally coordinated planning made Europe once again a major contender in the international economic arena.

The major exception to the establishment of central planning agencies and the nationalization of key industries was West Germany. Deciding against the British and French models of planned growth, the West Germans endorsed a free market policy that encouraged private enterprise while providing state insurance for all workers. What has been described as "a free enterprise economy with a social conscience" produced the richest economy in western Europe by the mid-1950s. Some West German industries had been dismantled, but much of West Germany's productive capacity remained intact in the late 1940s. The wealth of great industrialists who were serving prison sentences as war criminals had

not been expropriated, and their commercial empires stood ready to direct the economic revival. The Krupp munitions and I. G. Farben chemical empires were successfully broken up into smaller units. Industries forced to start afresh benefited from the latest technology.

European integration, discussed before and during the war, received added impetus in the postwar period. The Marshall Plan reconciled western Europe with West Germany through economic cooperation, although that was by no means its original purpose.

Realizing that Europe as a region needed the cooperation of its member states if it was to contend in world markets, associations dedicated to integration began to emerge alongside economic planning mechanisms. The Council of Europe dealt with the "discussion of questions of common concern and by agreements and common action in economic, social, cultural, scientific, legal, and administrative matters and in the maintenance and further realization of human rights and fundamental freedoms." Although not itself a supranational institution with its own authority, the Council of Europe urged a federation among European states. Britain alone rejected all attempts to develop structures of loose intergovernmental cooperation.

Belgium, the Netherlands, and Luxembourg were the first European states to establish themselves as an economic unit—Benelux. Internal customs duties among the three states were removed, and a common external tariff barrier was erected. The Schuman Plan joined France and West Germany in economic cooperation by pooling all coal and steel resources, beginning in 1950. The creators of the plan, Jean Monnet (1888–1979) and Robert Schuman (1886–1963) of France, saw it as the first step toward the removal of all economic barriers among European states and as a move toward eventual political integration. In 1951, the Netherlands, Belgium, Luxembourg, France, Italy, and West Germany formed the European Coal and Steel Community (ECSC). While constantly confronting domestic opposition on nationalist grounds, the ECSC succeeded in establishing a "common market" in coal and steel among its member states. In 1957, the same six members created the **European Economic Community (EEC)** and committed themselves to broadening the integration of markets. It was the beginning of what became known as the Common Market.

DOCUMENT

A Common Market and European Integration

The Common Market aimed to establish among its member states a free movement of labor and capital, the elimination of restrictions on trade, common investment practices, and coordinated social welfare programs. National agricultural interests were to be protected. Great Britain was initially a vocal opponent of the Common Market and continued to defend its own trading relationship with its Commonwealth countries, eventually founding its own free trade association in 1959. In 1973, Great Britain became a member of the Common Market and joined with other European nations in defining common economic policies. The EEC meanwhile achieved the support of the United States in its transitional period, in which it had 15 years to accomplish its aims.

European union was a phenomenon of exclusion as much as inclusion. It sharpened antagonisms between the West and the East by its very success. While promoting prosperity, European economic unification favored concentration and the emergence of large corporations. Vast individual fortunes flourished under state sponsorship and the rule of the experts. National parliaments were sometimes eclipsed by new economic decision-making organizations that aimed to make western Europe into a single free trade area.

Japan's Recovery

Japanese economic challenges in the postwar era were similar to those of western Europe. As a defeated and occupied nation in 1945, Japan faced a grim future. U.S. aims for Asia were similar to those for Europe: American policy makers sought to create a multilateral system of world trade and preserve America's sphere of influence against Communist encroachment. The American general Douglas MacArthur was appointed the Supreme Commander for the Allied Powers and the head of occupation forces in Japan. His mission in Japan was to impose rapid economic change from above. The occupation government set out to erect institutions to promote political democratization and to eliminate militaristic institutions, official patronage, and censorship. Planning, both formal and informal, reshaped the economy as U.S. aid flowed into Japan during the late forties and early fifties. The changes in Japan, as in western Europe, took place alongside growing American fears of communism in the region.

Japan turned its wartime devastation into an advantage by replacing destroyed factories with the latest technology, obtained by license from foreign firms. Through a combination of bureaucracy and patronage devoted to planned growth, Japan's GNP reached prewar levels by 1956. By 1968, Japan had turned defeat into triumph and stood as the third largest industrial nation in the world. Japanese growth paralleled the "economic miracle" of West Germany, with the Japanese economy growing at a rate three times faster than that of the United States between 1954 and 1967.

The abolition of the army and navy was a boon for the Japanese economy, since 16 percent of prewar GNP had been devoted to support of the military. Postwar demilitarization freed Japan of the financial exigencies of the arms race. Funds formerly used for arms now flowed into investment and new technology. (See "The West and the Wider World: Made in Japan," pp. 912–913.) Slowed population growth after 1948 and an increased volume of foreign trade contributed to Japanese prosperity. In the 1960s, Japan emerged as an affluent society undergoing a revolution in consumer durables, including televisions, washing machines, refrigerators, and automobiles.

Recipients of American aid surpassed U.S. goals. A multilateral system of world trade emerged out of the ashes of war. The effects of the Great Depression, which the world had been unable to shake throughout the 1930s, had been laid to rest by global war and its consequences.

The Soviet Path to Economic Recovery

The Soviet Union countered economic integration in the West with its own alliances and organizations. In 1949, the USSR established the Council for Mutual Economic Assistance, or **Comecon,** with bilateral agreements between the Soviet Union and eastern European states. Comecon was Stalin's response to the U.S. Marshall Plan in western Europe. Rather than providing aid, however, Comecon benefited the Soviet Union at the expense of its partners, seeking to integrate and control the economies of eastern Europe for Soviet gain. The Soviet Union implemented an expansion of its territorial boundaries as a way of reversing some of its drastic losses in the war. Above all, it wanted a protective ring of satellite states as security from attack from the West. Stalin also was eager to see the Soviet Union surrounded by "friendly" governments in eastern Europe to replace the hostile regimes with which the Soviets had had to contend in the period between the wars. Picking up territory from Finland, Poland, and parts of East Prussia and eastern Czechoslovakia; forcibly reincorporating the Baltic states of Estonia, Latvia, and Lithuania; and recovering Bessarabia, the Soviet Union succeeded in acquiring sizable territories. The Soviet state then began to dedicate itself to economic reconstruction behind a protective buffer of satellite states—Poland, East Germany, Czechoslovakia, Hungary, Romania, and Bulgaria—over which Soviet leaders exercised strong control. Yugoslavia and Albania chose to follow a more independent Communist path. Lacking the capital necessary to finance recovery, the Soviets sought compensation from eastern and central European territories.

Under Stalin's direction, the Soviet Union concentrated all its efforts on reconstructing its devastated economy and, to that end, sought integration with eastern European states, whose technology and resources were needed for the rebuilding of the Soviet state. U.S. dominance threatened the vital connection with eastern Europe that the Soviet Union was determinedly solidifying in the postwar years. In the years before his death in 1953, Joseph Stalin succeeded in making the Soviet Union a vital industrial giant second only to the United States. The Soviet economy experienced dramatic recovery after 1945, in spite of the severe damage inflicted on it during the war. The production of steel, coal, and crude oil skyrocketed under state planning. Heavy industry was the top priority of Soviet recovery, in keeping with prewar commitments to rapid modernization. In addition, the postwar Soviet economy assumed the new burdens of the development of a nuclear arsenal and an expensive program for the exploration of space. Stalin maintained the Soviet Union on the footing of a war economy, restricting occupational mobility and continuing to rely on forced-labor camps.

In the years following World War II a revolution was taking shape in manufacturing and marketing that would change the world. The revolution began in an unlikely place—war-crippled Japan—and it was all the more startling because, with the rise of Japanese industry, American and European producers were left behind in key electronics markets that came to symbolize the new consumption.

Japan's economic competitiveness commanded notice beginning in the late nineteenth century because it combined the new industrialization techniques of the West with traditional values of family and nation. The Japanese were influenced certainly by modes of production in the West and rapidly advanced their own productivity through the 1930s and the wartime economy.

With atomic destruction and military defeat many Japanese faced starvation and severe hardship. The Supreme Command of Allied Forces under General Douglas MacArthur brought in an occupying army whose emphasis was education and revitalization of the economy. Yet what happened in Japan after the war cannot be explained by the one-way transmission of ideas and institutions of a Western occupying force. When the occupation ended in 1952, Japan was already on its way to sustained high economic productivity through innovation, adaptability, and the application of its own cultural values to new management practices.

The rise of the Sony Corporation provides a good case study of the Japanese transformation. Sony's founders, according to the company's own history, were committed from the very beginning to capturing a mass consumer market and appropriating whatever tools available to do so. Working in less than optimum surroundings in an abandoned department store, Sony's founders stressed the importance of the team in production. After failed beginnings in rice cookers and heating pads but greater success with tape recorders, Sony struck on the radio and its potential in a mass market. Sony was the first to develop transistor radios for the home by applying a technology developed in the West and available to but not utilized by American and European producers. The Japanese company developed technical superiority and soon became a leader in the world market. The great success of Japanese industry resided in its ability to mass produce quality products at cheap prices.

How were the Japanese able to achieve such resounding success in the fifteen years following World War II? One way, of course, was by the appropriation of lessons learned in the West. Japanese industrial leaders visited the United States regularly, met with American business leaders, visited assembly lines, and studied management as a science. One American in particular, W. Edwards Deming, became a Japanese hero because of his seminars taught in Japan during the occupation on "statistical quality control." In 1960 the Japanese government created a prize in Deming's honor which is awarded annually to industries for their use of consumer research in improving the design of

■ Sony TR-55 from ca. 1955, Japan's first all transistor radio.

■ Toyota automobile construction at the Motomachi factory, Japan, ca. 1960s.

products and production. Sony, Matsushita, and Toyota are just a few of the industries that employed Deming's methods and those of other Western consultants who favored "total quality management." Such a total approach to the production process was not utilized by Western competitors until it was rediscovered in the West in the 1980s, thanks to Japan's success story.

In its unique culture of the workplace, the Japanese method put emphasis on the values of the individual worker and the importance of working in small teams. Management fully participated in production and respected employees' opinions and insights. The founders of Sony launched their enterprise immediately after the war by treating their employees like family, providing daily rice to them for their lunch breaks, and organizing joint recreation and vacations. Such

emphasis on family and the values of caring and responsibility for employees resonated strongly with Japanese culture and traditions. The emphasis in this new workplace culture was on the participation of the employees and the needs of the customers. Explicitly rejected was the Ford assembly-line model of mass-production as dehumanizing and destructive of quality in the goods produced. The Japanese innovators appropriated selectively from Western industrial theory and models and applied this knowledge to their own strategies.

So successful were the management innovations of the Japanese producers that Western industries began sending observers to study Japanese methods. Japanese auto producers in the United States at the present time use their own production methods based on Japanese cultural values with their

American employees. And industrialists from the European Union continue to send their business leaders to learn "the Japanese way." Perhaps no industry better demonstrates the two-way cultural exchange of ideas, institutions, and practices than consumer electronics in the global economy. Japan succeeded in dominating world markets because it understood that production and success must be rooted in the culture and values of its own people.

....

▨ QUESTIONS FOR DISCUSSION

How did Japan develop new goods and new markets in the 1950s? Why was the mass-marketing of small electronics so well-suited to postwar Japan? In what ways did the United States and western Europe learn lessons from innovations in Japanese production?

....

REPORT TO THE TWENTIETH PARTY CONGRESS

Like Stalin before him, the Soviet leader Nikita Khrushchev perceived that the Soviet Union was locked in a worldwide struggle with the United States and Western capitalist nations. The experiences of the Korean War and the escalation of the nuclear arms race prompted him to proceed with wariness in foreign policy. In his now-famous speech before the Twentieth Party Congress in February 1956, Khrushchev, as first secretary of the Communist party, accused the United States, England, and France of imperialism and pleaded for the peaceful coexistence of communism and capitalism, confident that, in the end, communism would win the day.

Focus Questions

How does Khrushchev portray the Soviet Union as a victim? How does he describe the origins and the purposes of the Cold War?

Soon after the Second World War ended, the influence of reactionary and militarist groups began to be increasingly evident in the policy of the United States of America, Britain, and France. Their desire to enforce their will on other countries by economic and political pressure, threats, and military provocation prevailed. This became known as the "positions of strength" policy. It reflects the aspiration of the most aggressive sections of present-day imperialism to win world supremacy, to suppress the working class and democratic and nation-liberation movements; it reflects their plans for military adventures against the socialist camp.

The international atmosphere was poisoned by war hysteria. The arms race began to assume more and more monstrous dimensions. Many big U.S. military bases designed for use against the USSR and the People's Democracies [East European countries under Soviet control] were built in countries thousands of miles from the borders of the United States. "Cold war" was begun against the socialist camp. International distrust was artificially kindled, and nations set against one another. A bloody war was launched in Korea; the war in Indochina dragged on for years.

. . . The Leninist principle of peaceful coexistence of states with different social systems has always been and remains the general line of our country's foreign policy. . . . To this day the enemies of peace allege that the Soviet Union is out to overthrow capitalism in other countries by "exporting" revolution. It goes without saying that among us Communists there are no supporters of capitalism. But this does not mean that we have interfered or plan to interfere in the internal affairs of countries where capitalism still exists.

When we say that the socialist system will win in the competition between the two systems—the capitalist and the socialist—this by no means signifies that its victory will be achieved through armed interference by the socialist countries in the internal affairs of the capitalist countries. Our certainty of the victory of communism is based on the fact that the socialist mode of production possesses decisive advantages over the capitalist mode of production. Precisely because of this, the ideas of Marxism-Leninism are more and more capturing the minds of the broad masses of the working people in the capitalist countries, just as they have captured the minds of millions of men and women in our country and the People's Democracies. [*Prolonged applause.*] We believe that all working men in the world, once they have become convinced of the advantages communism brings, will sooner or later take the road of struggle for the construction of socialist society.

De-Stalinization. In 1953, Stalin, who had ruled the Soviet Union for almost three decades, died. The vacuum that he left provoked a struggle for power among the Communist party leadership. It also initiated almost immediately a process of **de-Stalinization** and the beginnings of a thaw in censorship and repression. A growing urban and professional class expected improvements in the quality of life and greater freedoms after years of war and hardship. In 1956, at the Twentieth Party Congress, Nikita Khrushchev (1894–1971), as head of the Communist party, denounced Stalin as incompetent and cruel. After five years of jockeying for power among Stalin's former lieutenants, Khrushchev emerged victorious and assumed the office of premier in 1958.

De-Stalinization also took place in eastern Europe. Discontent over collectivization, low wages, and the lack of consumer goods fueled a latent nationalism among eastern European populations resentful of Soviet control and influence. Violence erupted in 1953 in East Berlin as workers revolted over conditions in the workplace, but it was quickly and effectively suppressed. Demands for reforms and liberalization in Poland also produced riots and changes in Communist party leadership. Wladislaw Gomulka (1905–1982), a Communist with a nationalist point of view who had survived Stalin's purges, aimed to take advantage of the power vacuum created by the departure of Stalinist leaders. Gomulka refused to back down in the face of severe Soviet pressure and the threat of a Soviet invasion to keep him from power. Elected as the first secretary of the Communist party in Poland, Gomulka sought to steer his nation on a more liberal course.

Hungarians followed suit with their demands for the withdrawal of Hungary from the Warsaw Pact. On 23 October 1956, inspired by the events in Poland, Hungarians rose up in anger against their old-guard Stalinist rulers. Imre Nagy (1896–1958), a liberal Communist, took control of the government, attempted to introduce democratic reforms, and relaxed economic controls. The Soviets, however, were unwilling to lose control of their sphere of influence in Eastern Bloc nations and to jeopardize their system of defense in the Warsaw Pact. Moscow responded to liberal experimentation in Hungary by sending tanks and troops into Budapest. Brutal repression and purges followed. The Hungarian experience in 1956 made clear that too much change too quickly would not be tolerated by the Soviet rulers. The thaw following Stalin's death had promoted expectations among eastern Europeans that a new era was dawning. The violent crushing of the Hungarian revolution was a reminder of the realities of Soviet control and the Soviet Union's defense priorities in eastern Europe.

The Soviet Standard of Living.

The Soviet Union's standard of living remained relatively low in the years when western Europe was undergoing a consumer revolution. Soviet consumption was necessarily stagnant, since profits were plowed back as investments in future heavy industrial expansion. In the Soviet Union and throughout the Eastern Bloc countries, women's full participation in the labor force was essential for recovery. In spite of their presence in large numbers in highly skilled sectors such as medicine, Soviet and Eastern Bloc women remained poorly paid, as did women in the West. Soviet men received higher salaries for the same work on the grounds that they had to support families.

The Soviet population was growing rapidly, from 170 million in 1939 to 234 million in 1967. Nikita Khrushchev promised the people lower prices and a shorter workweek, but in 1964, when he fell from power, Soviets were paying higher prices for their food than before. With a declining rate of development, the Soviet economy lacked the necessary capital to advance the plans for growth in all sectors. Defense spending nearly doubled in the short period between 1960 and 1968.

Eastern Bloc Economies and Dissent.

The nature of planned Soviet growth exacted heavy costs in the Eastern Bloc countries. Adhering to the Soviet pattern of heavy industrial expansion at the expense of agriculture and consumer goods, East Germany nearly doubled its industrial output by 1955, despite having been stripped of its industrial plants by the Soviet Union before 1948. Czechoslovakia, Bulgaria, Romania, and Yugoslavia all reported significant industrial growth in this period. Yet dislocations caused by collectivization and heavy defense expenditures stirred up social unrest in East Germany, Czechoslovakia, Poland, and Hungary. The Soviet Union responded with some economic concessions but on the whole stressed common industrial and defense pursuits, employing ideological persuasion and military pressure to keep its reluctant partners in line.

East Berlin in the late 1950s and early 1960s posed a particular problem for Communist rule. Unable to compete successfully in wages and standard of living with the capitalist western sector of the city, East Berlin saw increasing numbers of its population, especially the educated and professional classes, crossing the line to a more prosperous life. In 1961, the Soviet Union responded to the problem by building a wall that cordoned off the part of the city that it controlled. The Berlin Wall eventually stretched for 103 miles, with heavily policed crossing points, turrets, and troops and tanks facing each other across the divide that came to symbolize the Cold War.

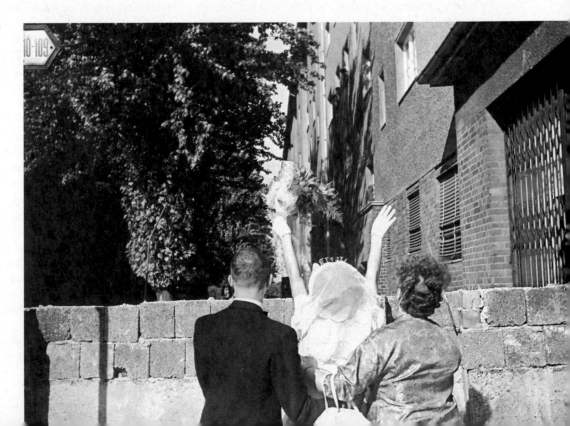

■ A West Berlin bride waves her wedding bouquet over the Berlin Wall to friends and family isolated on the other side.

■ Soviet tanks rumbled through Prague as troops from the Warsaw Pact countries invaded the Czechoslovakian capital in 1968, bringing an end to Alexander Dubcek's reform movement. Dubcek was rehabilitated in the liberalization of 1989 and elected chairman of the parliament.

The process of liberalization that had begun after Stalin's death and continued under Khrushchev certainly experienced its setbacks and reversals in the case of Budapest and Berlin. But in 1968 the policy of de-Stalinization reached a critical juncture in Czechoslovakia. Early in 1968, Alexander Dubcek, Czech party secretary and a member of the educated younger generation of technocrats, had supported liberal reforms in Czechoslovakia that included decentralization of planning and economic decision making, market pricing, and market incentives for higher productivity and innovation. He acted on popular desire for nationalism, the end of censorship, and better working conditions. Above all, he called for democratic reforms in the political process that would restore rule to the people. Dubcek spoke of "socialism with a human face," although, unlike the Hungarians in 1956, he made no move to withdraw his country from the Warsaw Pact or to defy Soviet leadership. Moscow nevertheless feared the erosion of obedience within the Eastern Bloc and the collapse of one-party rule in the Czech state and sent in thousands of tanks and hundreds of thousands of Warsaw Pact troops to Prague and other Czech cities to reestablish control. The Czechs responded with passive resistance in what became known as the **Prague Spring** uprising. The Soviet invasion made clear that popular nationalism was intolerable in an Eastern Bloc nation.

Alone among eastern European leaders, Marshal Tito of Yugoslavia resisted Soviet encroachment. As a partisan leader of the Communist resistance during World War II, Tito had earned the reputation as a war hero for his opposition to the Germans. Ruling Yugoslavia as a dictator after 1945, he refused to accede to Soviet directives to collectivize agriculture and to participate in joint economic ventures. For its defiance of Soviet supremacy, in 1948 Yugoslavia was expelled from the Cominform, the Soviet-controlled information agency that replaced the Comintern after 1943.

The slowed growth of the 1960s, the delay in development of consumer durables, and the inadequacy of basic foodstuffs, housing, and clothing were the costs that Eastern Bloc citizens paid for their inefficient and rigid planned economies dedicated to the development of heavy industry. In eastern Europe and the Soviet Union, poverty was virtually eliminated, however, as the state subsidized housing, health care, and higher education, which were available to all.

THE WELFARE STATE AND SOCIAL TRANSFORMATION

The **welfare state,** a creation of the post–World War II era throughout Europe, grew out of the social welfare policies of the interwar period and out of the war itself. Welfare programs aimed to protect citizens through the establishment of a decent standard of living available for everyone. The experiences of the Great Depression had done much to foster concern for economic security. In France, the primary concern of the welfare state was the protection of children and the issue of family allowances. In Great Britain, as in Germany, emphasis was placed on unemployment insurance and health care benefits. Everywhere, however, the welfare state developed a related set of social programs and policies whereby the state intervened in the cycles of individual lives to provide economic support for the challenges of birth, sickness, old age, and unemployment.

Protection of the citizenry took varied forms according to Cold War politics. In the Warsaw Pact countries, the need to industrialize rapidly and to dedicate productive wealth to armament and military protection resulted in a nonexistent consumer economy in which the issues of quality of life and protection took a very different direction. Based on a concept of equal access to a minimum standard of living, welfare states did not treat all their members equally. Women were often disadvantaged in social welfare programs as family needs, men's rights, and the protection of children led to different national configurations.

Prosperity and Consumption in the West

Despite the different paths toward reconstruction following World War II, every western European nation experienced dramatic increases in total wealth. Per capita income was clearly on the rise through the mid-1960s, and there was more disposable wealth than ever before. Prosperity encouraged new patterns of spending based on confidence in the economy. That new consumerism, in turn, was essential to economic growth and future productivity.

The New Consumption.   The social programs of the welfare state played an important role in promoting postwar consumption. People began to relax about their economic futures, more secure because of the provisions of unemployment insurance, old-age pensions, and health and accident insurance. The state alleviated the necessity of saving for a rainy day by providing protection that had formerly been covered by the savings of workers. In the mid-1950s, all over western Europe, people began to spend their earnings, knowing that accidents, disasters, and sicknesses would be taken care of by the state.

The main items in the new consumption were consumer durables, above all televisions and automobiles. Refrigerators and washing machines also developed mass markets, as did the increased consumption of liquor and cigarettes. Increased leisure resulted in a boom in vacation travel. In addition to spending their salaries, western Europeans began to buy on credit, spending money they had not yet earned. That, too, was an innovation in postwar markets. People sought immediate gratification through consumption by means of delayed payment against future earnings.

Welfare programs could be sustained only in an era of prosperity and economic growth, since they depended on taxation of income for their funds. Such taxation did not, however, result in a redistribution of wealth. Wealth remained in the hands of a few and became even more concentrated as a result of phenomenal postwar economic growth. In West Germany, for example, 1.7 percent of the population owned 35 percent of the society's total wealth.

Women's Wages.   Just as the welfare state did not redistribute wealth, it did not provide equal pay for equal work. In France, women who performed the same jobs as men received less pay. In typesetting, for example, women, who on average set 15,000 keystrokes per hour at the keyboards compared to 10,000 by men, earned 50 percent of men's salaries and held different titles for their jobs. Separate wage scales for women drawn up during the Nazi period remained in effect in West Germany until 1956. The skills associated with occupations performed by women were downgraded, as were their salaries. Women earned two-thirds or less of what men earned throughout western Europe. Welfare state revenues were a direct result

■ A traffic jam on the Place de la Concorde in Paris in 1962. Western Europeans learned that prosperity had its price as nineteenth-century cities were thrust into the automobile age.

of pay-scale inequities. Lower salaries for women meant higher profits and helped make economic recovery possible.

Family Strategies

The pressures on European women and their families in 1945 were often greater than in wartime. Severe scarcity of food, clothes, and housing required careful management. Women who during the war held jobs in industry and munitions plants earned their own money and established their own independence. After the war, in victorious and defeated nations alike, women were moved out of the work force to make room for returning men. Changing social policies affected women's lives in the home and in the workplace and contributed to the politicization of women within the context of the welfare state.

Demography and Birth Control.   Prewar concerns with a declining birthrate intensified after World War II. In some European countries, the birthrate climbed in the years immediately following the war, an encouraging sign to observers who saw in the trend an optimistic commitment to the future after the cessation of the horrors of war. The situation was more complicated in France and the United States, where the birthrates began to climb even before the war was over. Nearly everywhere throughout Europe, however, the rise in the birthrate was momentary, with the United States standing alone in experiencing a genuine and sustained "baby boom" until about 1960. In Germany and in eastern Europe (Poland and Yugoslavia, for example), the costs of the war exacted heavy tolls on families long after the hostilities ended. On average, women everywhere were having fewer children by choice.

Technology had expanded the range of choices in family planning. In the early 1960s, the birth control pill became available on the European and American markets, primarily to middle-class women. Europeans were choosing to have smaller families. The drop in the birthrate had clearly preceded the new technological interventions that included intrauterine devices (IUDs), improved diaphragms, sponges, and more effective spermicidal creams and jellies. The condom, invented a century earlier, was now sold to a mass market. Information about their reproductive lives became more accessible to young women. Illegal abortions continued to be an alternative for women. Abortion was probably the primary form of birth control in the Soviet Union in the years following the war. Controversies, however, surrounded unhealthy side effects of the pill and the dangerous Dalkon shield, an IUD that had not been adequately tested before marketing and that resulted in the death or sterilization of thousands of women. Religious leaders also spoke out on the moral issues surrounding sexuality without reproduction. And in France and Italy, birth control information was often withheld from the public.

The Family and Welfare.   Concurrent with a low birthrate was a new valuing of family life and domestic virtues in the years after the war. Those who had lived through the previous 20 years were haunted by the memories of the Great Depression, severe economic hardships, destructive war, and the loss of loved ones. Women and men throughout western Europe and the United States embraced the centrality of the family to society, even if they did not opt for large families. Expectations for improved family life placed new demands on welfare state programs. They also placed increased demands on mothers, whose presence in the home was now seen as all-important for the proper development of the child. Handbooks for mothers proliferated, instructing them in the "science" of child rearing. The best-seller *Baby and Child Care* by Dr. Benjamin Spock was typical of such guides.

European states implemented official programs to encourage women to have more children and to be better mothers. **Pronatalism,** as the policy was known, resulted from an official concern over low birthrates and a decline in family size. It is unlikely that pronatalism was caused by a fear of a decline in the labor force, since the influx of foreign workers, refugees from eastern Europe, and migrant laborers from poorer southern European nations provided an expanding labor pool. Other considerations about racial dominance and women's proper role seem to have affected the development of policies. In 1945, Lord Beveridge (1879–1960), the architect of the British welfare state, emphasized the importance of women's role "in ensuring the adequate continuance of the British race" and argued that women's place was in the home: "During marriage most women will not be gainfully employed. The small minority of women who undertake paid employment or other gainful employment or other gainful occupations after marriage require special treatment differing from that of single women."

Welfare state programs differed from country to country as the result of a series of different expectations of women as workers and women as mothers. Konrad Adenauer, chancellor of West Germany, spoke of "a will to children" as essential for his country's continued economic growth and prosperity. In Great Britain, the welfare system was built on the ideal of the mother at home with her children. With the emphasis on the need for larger families—four children was considered desirable in England—English society focused on the importance of the role of the mother. Family allowances determined by the number of children were tied to men's participation in the work force; women were defined according to their husbands' status. The state welfare system strengthened the financial dependence of English wives on their husbands.

In Great Britain, anxiety over the low birthrate was also tied to the debate over equal pay for women. Opponents of the measure argued that equal pay would cause women to forgo marriage and motherhood and should therefore be avoided. There was a consensus about keeping women out of the work force and paying them less in order to achieve that end.

The French system of *sécurité sociale* defined all women, whether married or single, as equal to men; unlike English women, all French women had the same rights of access to welfare programs as men. That may well have reflected the different work history of women in France and the recognition of the importance of women's labor for reconstruction of

■ Many basic needs are provided for under Britain's cradle-to-grave social welfare system. Here mothers and children line up to receive orange juice. Vitamins and milk are also provided for growing children.

the economy. As a result, family allowances, pre- and post-natal care, maternity benefits, and child care were provided on the assumption that working mothers were a fact of life. French payments were intended to encourage large families and focused primarily on the needs of children. More and more women entered the paid labor force after 1945, and they were less financially dependent on their husbands than were their British counterparts.

Both forms of welfare state—the British that emphasized women's role as mothers and the French that accepted women's role as workers—were based on different attitudes about the nature of gender difference and equality. Women's political consciousness developed in both societies. The women's liberation movements of the late sixties and early seventies found their roots in the contradictions of differing welfare policies.

The Beginnings of Women's Protest. The 1960s were a period of protest in Western countries as people demonstrated

for civil rights and free expression. In Europe and America, protests against U.S. involvement in Vietnam began, emulating patterns of activism established in the movement for black civil rights. Pacifist and antinuclear groups united to "ban the bomb." Women participated in all of the movements, and by the end of the 1960s had begun to question their own place in organizations that did not acknowledge their claims to equal rights, equal pay, and liberation from the oppression of male society. A new critique began to form within the welfare state that indicated there were cracks in the facade.

One book in particular, written after World War II, captured the attention of many women who were aware of the contradictions and limitations placed on them by state and society. *The Second Sex* (1949), written by Simone de Beauvoir (1908–1986), a leading French intellectual, analyzed women's place in the context of Western culture. By examining the assumptions of political theories, including Marxism, in the light of philosophy, biology, history, and psychoanalysis, de Beauvoir uncovered the myths governing the creation of the female self. By showing how the male is the center of culture and the female is "other," de Beauvoir urged women to be independent and to

■ French novelist and feminist Simone de Beauvoir participated in demonstrations for women's issues such as family planning.

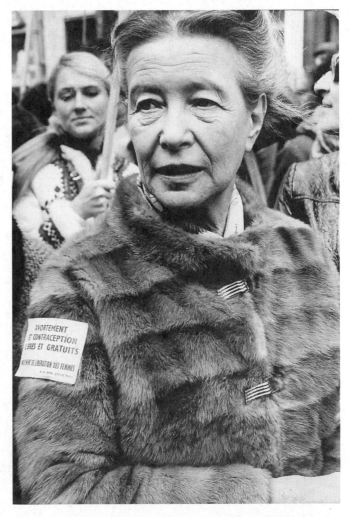

THE SECOND SEX

Simone de Beauvoir, one of France's leading intellectuals, wrote philosophical treatises, essays, and novels that drew on a wide variety of cultural traditions and synthesized philosophy, history, literary criticism, and Freudian psychoanalysis in her studies of the human condition. The Second Sex, which first appeared in French in 1949, has subsequently been translated into many languages and has appeared in numerous editions throughout the world. It has served as a call to arms for the feminist movement, provoking debate, controversy, and a questioning of the fundamental gender arrangements of modern society.

Focus Questions

What does de Beauvoir mean when she says that men and women occupy separate economic castes? From her analysis, can you tell if de Beauvoir is "very well pleased with [woman's] role as the Other*"?*

A man never begins by presenting himself as an individual of a certain sex; it goes without saying that he is a man. The terms *masculine* and *feminine* are used symmetrically only as a matter of form, as on legal papers. In actuality the relation of the two sexes is not quite like that of two electrical poles, for man represents both the positive and the neutral, as is indicated by the common use of man to designate human beings in general; whereas woman represents only the negative, defining by limiting criteria, without reciprocity. In the midst of an abstract discussion it is vexing to hear a man say: "You think thus and so because you are a woman"; but I know that my only defense is to reply: "I think thus and so because it is true," thereby removing my subjective self from the argument. It would be out of the question to reply: "And you think the contrary because you are a man," for it is understood that the fact of being a man is no peculiarity. A man is in the right in being a man; it is the woman who is in the wrong. It amounts to this: just as for the ancients there was an absolute vertical with reference to which the oblique was defined, so there is an absolute human type, the masculine. Woman has ovaries, a uterus; these peculiarities imprison her in her subjectivity, circumscribe her within the limits of her own nature. It is often said that she thinks with her glands. Man superbly ignores the fact that his anatomy also includes glands, such as the testicles, and that they secrete hormones. He thinks of his body as a direct and normal connection with the world, which he believes he apprehends objectively, whereas he regards the body of woman as a hindrance, a prison, weighed down by everything peculiar to it. "The female is a female by virtue of certain lack of qualities," said Aristotle; "we should regard the female nature as afflicted with a natural defectiveness." And Saint Thomas for his part pronounced woman to be an "imperfect man," an "incidental" being. This is symbolized in Genesis where Eve is depicted as made from what Bossuet called "a supernumerary bone" of Adam.

Now, woman has always been man's dependent, if not his slave; the two sexes have never shared the world in equality. And even today woman is heavily handicapped, though her situation is beginning to change. Almost nowhere is her legal status the same as man's, and frequently it is much to her disadvantage. Even when her rights are legally recognized in the abstract, long-standing custom prevents their full expression in the mores. In the economic sphere men and women can almost be said to make up two castes; other things being equal, the former hold the better jobs, get higher wages, and have more opportunity for success than their new competitors. In industry and politics men have a great many more positions and they monopolize the most important posts. In addition to all this, they enjoy a traditional prestige that the education of children tends in every way to support, for the present enshrines the past—and in the past all history has been made by men. At the present time, when women are beginning to take part in the affairs of the world, it is still a world that belongs to men—they have no doubt of it at all and women have scarcely any. To decline to be the Other, to refuse to be a party to the deal—this would be for women to renounce all the advantages conferred upon them by their alliance with the superior caste. Man-the-sovereign will provide women-the-liege with material protection and will undertake the moral justification of her existence; thus she can evade at once both economic risk and the metaphysical risk of a liberty in which ends and aims must be contrived without assistance. Indeed, along with the ethical urge of each individual to affirm his subjective existence, there is also the temptation to forgo liberty and become a thing. This is an inauspicious road, for he who takes it—passive, lost, ruined—becomes henceforth the creature of another's will, frustrated in his transcendence and deprived of every value. But it is an easy road; on it one avoids the strain involved in undertaking an authentic existence. When man makes of woman the *Other,* he may, then, expect her to manifest deep-seated tendencies toward complicity. Thus, woman may fail to lay claim to the status of subject because she lacks definite resources, because she feels the necessary bond that ties her to man regardless of reciprocity, and because she is often very well pleased with her role as the *Other.*

From Simone de Beauvoir, *The Second Sex* (1949).

resist male definitions. *The Second Sex* became the handbook of the women's movement in the 1960s.

A very different work, *The Feminine Mystique,* appeared in 1963. In that book, author Betty Friedan voiced the grievances of a previously politically quiescent group of women. Friedan was an American suburban homemaker and the mother of three children when she wrote about what she saw as the schizophrenic split in her own middle-class world between the reality of women's lives and the idealized image of the perfect homemaker. After World War II, women were expected to find personal fulfillment in the domestic sphere. Instead, Friedan found women suffering from the "sickness with no name" and the "nameless desperation" of a profound crisis in identity.

A new politics centering on women's needs and women's rights slowly took root. The feminist critique did not emerge as a mass movement until the 1970s. Youth culture and dissent among the young further influenced growing feminist discontent. But the agenda of protest in the sixties, reinforced by social policies, accepted gender differences as normal and natural.

Youth Culture and Dissent

Youth culture was created by outside forces as much as it was self-created. Socialized together in an expanding educational system from primary school through high school, the young came to see themselves as a social force. They were also socialized by marketing efforts that appealed to their particular needs as a group.

The prosperity that characterized the period from the mid-fifties to the mid-sixties throughout the West provided a secure base from which radical dissenters could launch their protests. The young people of the 1960s were the first generation to come of age after World War II. Although they had no memory themselves of the destruction of that war, they were reminded daily of the imminence of nuclear destruction in their own lives. The combination of the security of affluence and the insecurity of Cold War politics created a widening gap between the world of decision-making adults and the idealistic universe of the young. To the criticisms of parents, politicians, and teachers, the new generation responded that no one over 30 could be trusted.

New styles of dress and grooming were a rejection of middle-class culture in Europe and the United States. Anthropologists and sociologists in the 1960s began studying youth as if they were a foreign tribe. The "**generation gap**" appeared as the subject of hundreds of specialized studies. Adolescent behavior was examined across cultures. Sexual freedom and the use of drugs were subjected to special scrutiny. But, above all, it was the politics of the young that baffled and enraged many observers. When the stable base of economic prosperity began to erode as a result of slowed growth and inflation in the second half of the sixties—first in western Europe and then in the United States—frustrated expectations and shrinking opportunities for the young served as a further impetus for political action.

The Sexual Revolution.   Increased emphasis on fulfillment through sexual pleasure was one consequence of the technological revolution in birth control devices, and it led to what has been called a revolution in sexual values in Western societies in the 1960s. The sexual revolution drew attention to sexual fulfillment as an end in itself. Women's bodies were displayed more explicitly than ever before in mass advertising in order to sell products from automobiles to soap. Sex magazines, sex shops, and movies were part of an explosion in the marketing of male sexual fantasies in the 1960s.

Sweden experienced the most far-reaching reforms of sexual mores in the 1960s. Sex education became part of every school's curriculum, contraceptive information was widely available, and homosexuality was decriminalized. Technology allowed women and men to separate pleasure

■ Isle of Wight Festival, England, 1969. Open-air music festivals were a popular feature of the sixties—the era of pacifism, when young people experimented with sexual liberation, the drug culture, and Eastern mysticism.

from reproduction but did not alter men's and women's domestic roles. Pleasure was also separated from familial responsibilities, yet the domestic ideal of the woman in the home remained. Some women were beginning to question their exploitation in the sexual revolution. In the early 1970s, that issue became part of mass feminist protest.

The New Drug Culture.

Just as sexuality was invested with new meaning within the context of protest, so was the use of drugs. Drug use was not new in history: through the ages drugs have been taken as painkillers or pleasure enhancers and used in religious and cultural rituals. Soldiers in nineteenth-century wars in Europe and America returned home addicted to opium and morphine, which they were given when treated for their wounds. In the 1960s, American soldiers in Vietnam turned to drugs as an escape from the horrors of war.

Drugs began to pervade Western cultures in apparently harmless ways. At the end of the nineteenth century in the United States, the newly created Coca-Cola was originally made with cocaine, a drug derived from the coca shrub. Another ingredient in the soft drink formula was the kola nut, which contains the stimulant caffeine. In the 1950s and 1960s, chemical technology made possible the manufacture of synthetic drugs. Pharmaceutical industries in Europe and the United States expanded by leaps and bounds with the mass marketing of amphetamines, barbiturates, and tranquilizers. Doctors prescribed the new drugs for a variety of problems from obesity to depression to sleeplessness. People discovered that the drugs had additional mood-altering effects.

Marijuana grew in popularity as a safe "recreational" drug, especially among college and university students in the 1960s. In fact, young people were the primary users of drugs of all sorts, including synthetic drugs such as the hallucinogen LSD (lysergic acid diethylamide). Hallucinogens were considered by their proponents to be mind-expanding drugs that permitted the achievement of new levels of consciousness. Drugs used by young people affluent enough to afford them served to widen the gap between the generations still further.

The Anti-War Movement and Social Protest.

Student protest, which began at the University of California at Berkeley in 1964 as the Free Speech movement, by the spring of 1968 had become an international phenomenon that had spread to other American campuses and throughout Europe and Japan. A common denominator of protest, whether in New York, London, or Tokyo, was opposition to the war in Vietnam. Growing numbers of intellectuals and students throughout the world condemned the U.S. presence in Vietnam as an immoral violation of the rights of the Vietnamese people and violent proof of U.S. imperialism.

Student protesters shared other concerns in addition to opposition to the war in southeast Asia. The growing activism on American campuses was aimed at social reform, student self-governance, and a recognition of the responsibilities of the university in the wider community. In West Germany, highly politicized radical activists, a conspicuous minority among the students at the Free University of Berlin, directed protest out into the wider society. Student demonstrations met with brutal police repression and violence, and rioting was common.

European students, more than their American counterparts, were also experiencing frustration in the classroom. European universities were unprepared to absorb the huge influx of students in the 1960s. The student–teacher ratio at the University of Rome, for example, was 200 to 1. In Italian universities in general, the majority of more than half a million students had no contact with their professors. The University of Paris was similarly overcrowded.

For the most part, student protest was primarily a middle-class phenomenon. In France, for example, only four percent of university students came from below the middle class. Higher education had been developed after World War II to serve the increased needs of a technocratic society. Instead of altering the social structure, which politically committed student protesters thought it should do, mass education served as a certifying mechanism for bureaucratic and technical institutions. Many of the occupations that students could look forward to were in dead-end service jobs or in bureaucratic posts.

■ Czech students distribute underground literature in Wenceslas Square, Prague, in protest against the Soviet occupation of their country.

"SUBTERRANEAN HOMESICK BLUES"

The gap between the generations yawned into a gulf as rock music became political in the mid-1960s. Bob Dylan, an American rock performer, introduced folk music to the genre with songs of social protest such as "Blowin' in the Wind" and "Only a Pawn in Their Game." Rock music was denounced as a communist plot as performers urged their audiences to "make love, not war." Dylan's "Subterranean Homesick Blues" targeted the hypocrisy of his society.

Focus Questions

Can you find examples of social protest against the government and a questioning of law and order in this song? How does Dylan target hypocrisy in these verses?

Subterranean Homesick Blues
Bob Dylan

Johnny's in the basement
Mixing up the medicine
I'm on the pavement
Thinking about the government
The man in the trench coat
Badge out, laid off
Says he's got a bad cough
Wants to get it paid off
Look out kid
It's somethin' you did
God knows when
But you're doin' it again
You better duck down the alley way
Lookin' for a new friend
The man in the coon-skin cap
In the big pen
Wants eleven dollar bills
You only got ten

Maggie comes fleet foot
Face full of black soot
Talkin' that the heat put
Plants in the bed but
Look out kid
You're gonna get hit
But users, cheaters
Six-time losers
Hang around the theaters
Girl by the whirlpool
Lookin' for a new fool
Don't follow leaders
Watch the parkin' meters

Ah get born, keep warm
Short pants, romance, learn to dance
Get dressed, get blessed
Try to be a success
The phone's tapped anyway
Maggie says that many say
They must bust in early May
Orders from the D.A.
Look out kid
Don't matter what you did
Walk on your tip toes
Don't try "No Doz"
Better stay away from those
That carry around a fire hose
Keep a clean nose
Watch the plain clothes
You don't need a weather man
To know which way the wind blows

Get sick, get well
Hang around a ink well
Ring bell, hard to tell
If anything is goin' to sell
Try hard, get barred
Get back, write braille
Get jailed, jump bail
Join the army, if you fail
Please her, please him, buy gifts
Don't steal, don't lift
Twenty years of schoolin'
And they put you on the day shift
Look out kid
They keep it all hid
Better jump down a manhole
Light yourself a candle
Don't wear sandals
Try to avoid the scandals
Don't wanna be a bum
You better chew gum
The pump don't work
'Cause the vandals took the handles

Protest and the Economy. Student dissent reflected the changing economy of the late 1960s. Inflation, which earlier in the decade had spurred prosperity, was spiraling out of control in the late sixties. In the advanced industrial countries of western Europe and later in the United States, the growth of the postwar period was slowing down. Economic opportunity was evaporating and jobs were being eliminated. One survey estimated that only one in three Italian university graduates in

1967 was able to find a job. The dawning awareness of shrinking opportunities in the workplace for students who had attained their degrees and been properly certified further aggravated student frustration and dissent. Anger about the uncertainties of their future mixed with the realization of the boredom of the careers that awaited them upon graduation.

By the late sixties, universities and colleges provided the students a forum for expressing their discontent with advanced industrial societies. In their protests, student activists rejected the values of consumer society. The programs and politics of the student protesters aimed to transform the world in which they lived. Student protesters in France chanted *"Métro, boulot, dodo,"* a slang condemnation of the treadmill-like existence of those who spent their lives in a repetitive cycle of subway riding (*Métro*), mindless work (*boulot*), and sleep (*dodo*). The spirit of protest was expressed in the graffiti and posters that seemed to appear overnight on the walls of Paris:

"Action must not be a reaction—but a creation"

"Power to the Imagination"

"The revolution will be won when the last bureaucrat is strangled in the entrails of the last cop"

"The state is each one of us"

In May 1968, French protest spread beyond the university when workers and managers joined students in paralyzing the French economy and threatening to topple the Fifth Republic. Between 7 and 10 million people went on strike in support of worker and student demands. White-collar employees and technicians joined blue-collar factory workers in the strike. Student demands, based on a thoroughgoing critique of the whole society, proved to be incompatible with the wage and consumption issues of workers. But the unusual, if short-lived, alliance of students and workers shocked those in power and induced reforms.

CONCLUSION

The division of the world into two camps framed the recovery of combatant nations dealing with the losses of World War II. The Cold War instilled fear in the populations who lived on both sides of the divide. Yet the Cold War also created the terms for stability following the upheaval of war. It promoted prosperity that preserved the long-term policies of both the United States and the Soviet Union in the twentieth century. The Soviet Union had buffered itself from the West by creating a ring of friendly nations on its borders and had continued its race to industrialize. The belief that the USSR had won the war for the Allies and the sense of betrayal that followed the war determined the outlook of grim distrust shared by postwar Soviet leaders who had survived the years from 1939 to 1945.

The United States, on the other hand, found itself playing the role of rich uncle in bankrolling the European recovery. Its

CHRONOLOGY	
COLD WAR AND ECONOMIC RECOVERY	
1947	Marshall Plan starts U.S. aid to European countries; pro-Soviet governments established in Poland, Hungary, Bulgaria, and Romania
1948	Pro-Soviet government established in Czechoslovakia
1949	European states and United States form North Atlantic Treaty Organization (NATO); Federal Republic of Germany and German Democratic Republic established; Soviet Union creates Council for Mutual Economic Assistance (Comecon); Soviet Union tests its first atomic bomb
1950–1953	Korean War, ending with the partition of Korea
1953	United States and Soviet Union develop hydrogen bombs
1955	Formation of Warsaw Pact
1956	Hungarian uprising and subsequent repression by Soviet military forces
1957	The Netherlands, Belgium, Luxembourg, France, Italy, and West Germany form the European Economic Community (EEC), also called the Common Market; Soviet Union launches first satellite, *Sputnik I*
1961	Berlin Wall built
1961–1973	U.S. troops engaged in Vietnam
1962	Cuban missile crisis
1963	Soviet Union and United States sign Nuclear Test Ban Treaty
1968	Prague Spring uprising in Czechoslovakia, quelled by Soviet Union

long-term commitment to promoting its own economic interests by helping future trading partners led it also into playing the role of police officer throughout the world. The escalating war in Vietnam made America vulnerable to growing world criticism and to growing domestic discontent.

The gains of economic recovery began to unravel in the mid-1960s. The protests of 1968 were a response to changing economic conditions. In the West, rising expectations of consumer societies came up against the harsh realities of slowed growth. In the East, frustrated nationalism, the lack of consumer goods, and repressive conditions resulted in low morale, demonstrations, and outright conflict. After Stalin's death, resources were diverted to consumer goods, but there was little measurable improvement in the quality of life. By 1970, changing economies in both East and West affected the goals of the Cold War, still very much an organizing reality in the international arena. Created out of the aftermath of war, the Cold War now faced the challenges of prosperity both at home and abroad.

QUESTIONS FOR REVIEW

1. What did it mean for postwar European politics that the Continent was divided by an "iron curtain"?
2. What factors encouraged decolonization in the decades after World War II?
3. Why did western Europe's economy recover so rapidly, and how did that contribute to a gradual process of European economic integration?
4. How did the Soviet Union's strategy for recovery differ from that of western Europe?
5. What is the welfare state, and how did it transform the lives of ordinary Europeans?
6. What were some of the concerns that provoked protests from women, students, and others in the 1960s?

KEY TERMS

Berlin Wall, *p. 915*

Cold War, *p. 900*

Comecon, *p. 911*

containment, *p. 903*

decolonization, *p. 905*

de-Stalinization, *p. 914*

European Economic Community (EEC), *p. 910*

generation gap, *p. 921*

iron curtain, *p. 902*

Marshall Plan, *p. 908*

North Atlantic Treaty Organization (NATO), *p. 903*

nuclear club, *p. 904*

Prague Spring, *p. 916*

pronatalism, *p. 918*

third world, *p. 905*

Warsaw Pact, *p. 904*

welfare state, *p. 916*

DISCOVERING WESTERN CIVILIZATION ONLINE

You can obtain more information about the Cold War and postwar economic recovery at the Websites listed below. See also the Companion Website that accompanies this text, www.ablongman.com/kishlansky, which contains an online study guide and additional resources.

The Origins of the Cold War

The Berlin Airlift: Documents, Images, History

www.trumanlibrary.org/whistlestop/study_collection/berlin_airlift/large/berlin_airlift.htm
A virtual exhibit with electronic texts on the Berlin Airlift as presented by the Harry S Truman Library and Museum.

Internet Modern History Sourcebook: A Bipolar World

www.fordham.edu/halsall/mod/modsbook46.html
A collection of primary source documents and links to the creation of the United Nations and the outbreak of the Cold War.

Cold War International History Project

wwics.si.edu/index.cfm?topic_id=1409&fuseaction=topics.home
This site, sponsored by the Woodrow Wilson International Center for Scholars, provides a comprehensive list of primary documents and images, secondary sources, bibliographies, and working paper series on all aspects of the Cold War.

Soviet Archives Exhibit

www.ibiblio.org/expo/soviet.exhibit/entrance.html
A Soviet archive exhibit on the Cold War with images and electronic texts by the Library of Congress.

Postwar Economic Recovery in Europe, Japan, and the Soviet Union

Internet Modern History Sourcebook: Eastern Europe Since 1945

www.fordham.edu/halsall/mod/modsbook50.html
Two collections of links to primary sources and other sites on postwar western and eastern Europe.

The European Recovery: The Fiftieth Anniversary of the Marshall Plan

www.loc.gov/exhibits/marshall

A virtual museum exhibit with images and electronic primary and secondary texts on the Marshall Plan.

The Welfare State and Social Transformation

Internet Modern History Sourcebook: Modern Social Movements

www.fordham.edu/halsall/mod/modsbook56.html

A collection of primary source documents and links to sites on modern social movements including feminism, black power, and gay and lesbian rights.

The Sixties Project Home Page

lists.village.virginia.edu/sixties/

Web site of The Sixties Project, which brings together discussion lists, primary documents, bibliographies, museum exhibits, and personal testimonies about the 1960s and the Vietnam War from an exclusively American perspective.

Paris 1968 Posters

burn.ucsd.edu/paris.htm

A collection of posters of the 1968 protest movement in Paris.

SUGGESTIONS FOR FURTHER READING

The Origins of the Cold War

Franz Ansprenger, *The Dissolution of the Colonial Empires* (London: Routledge, 1989). An analysis of Europe's withdrawal from Asia and Africa following the Second World War, beginning with an examination of post–World War I imperialism.

Edward H. Judge and John W. Langdon, eds., *The Cold War: A History Through Documents* (New York: Prentice-Hall, 1998). Includes about 130 edited documents covering the period from 1945 to 1991.

Charles S. Maier, *In Search of Stability: Explorations in Historical Political Economy* (Cambridge: Cambridge University Press, 1987). Covers a wide variety of issues affecting twentieth-century Europe, including the foundation of American international economic policy after World War II and the conditions for stability in western Europe after 1945.

Bruce D. Porter, *The USSR in Third World Conflicts: Soviet Arms and Diplomacy in Local Wars, 1945–1980* (Cambridge: Cambridge University Press, 1984). A case study approach to the Soviet Union's changing postwar policies toward the third world that centers on local wars in Africa and the Middle East.

Postwar Economic Recovery in Europe, Japan, and the Soviet Union

Eric Hobsbawm, *The Age of Extremes: A History of the World, 1914–1991* (New York: Vintage Books, 1996). This volume covers what the author calls "the short twentieth century" from the outbreak of World War I to the fall of the Soviet Union. Of particular interest is the section on the 30 years following World War II, which the author sees as a "golden age" of extraordinary economic growth and social transformation.

Michael J. Hogan, *The Marshall Plan: America, Britain, and the Reconstruction of Western Europe* (Cambridge: Cambridge University Press, 1987). A thoroughly researched argument on the continuity of U.S. economic policy in the twentieth century. Hogan counters the belief that the Marshall Plan was merely a response to the Cold War.

Derek W. Urwin, *Western Europe Since 1945: A Political History,* 4th ed. (London: Longman, 1989). An updated general survey of postwar politics, with a special focus on the problems of reconstruction and the role of the resistance after 1945.

The Welfare State and Social Transformation

Simone de Beauvoir, *The Second Sex* (New York: Knopf, 1963). The author, one of France's leading intellectuals in the twentieth century, describes the situation of women's lives in the postwar West by placing them within the context of the history and myths governing Western culture.

Jane Jenson, "Both Friend and Foe: Women and State Welfare," *Becoming Visible: Women in European History,* ed. Renate Bridenthal, Claudia Koonz, and Susan Stuard (Boston: Houghton Mifflin, 1987). This essay illuminates the mixed blessing of the welfare state for women after 1945 by focusing on the experiences of women in Great Britain and France.

Walter Laqueur, *Europe Since Hitler: The Rebirth of Europe* (New York: Penguin Books, 1982). Surveys politics, economy, society, and culture in order to explain Europe's postwar resurgence.

Susan Pederson, *Family, Dependence, and the Origins of the Welfare State: Britain and France, 1914–1945* (Cambridge: Cambridge University Press: 1994). Although this work covers the earlier period, the comparative approach to differing attitudes and policies provides an essential background to understanding family policy in postwar Europe.

Denise Riley, *War in the Nursery: Theories of the Child and Mother* (London: Virago Press, 1983). Treats social policies of postwar pronatalism within the context of the popularization of developmental and child psychologies in Europe, with special attention to Britain and the United States and an emphasis on the postwar period as a turning point in attitudes toward women and the family.

Mary Ruggie, *The State and Working Women: A Comparative Study of Britain and Sweden* (Princeton, NJ: Princeton University Press, 1984). A sociological study comparing the economic status of women in two European welfare states.

David Caute, *The Year of the Barricades: A Journey Through 1968* (New York: Harper & Row, 1988). More than its title suggests, this work is an overview of postwar youth culture on three continents. The politics of 1968 is featured, although other topics regarding the counterculture, lifestyles, and cultural ramifications are considered.

John R. Gillis, *Youth and History: Tradition and Change in European Age Relations, 1770–Present* (New York: Academic Press, 1981). Connects the history of European youth to broad trends in economic and demographic modernization over the last 200 years.

Margaret Mead, *Culture and Commitment: The New Relationships Between the Generations in the 1970s* (New York: Columbia University Press, 1978). This series of essays, written by one of America's premier anthropologists, explores the origins and consequences of the generation gap, with special attention to Cold War politics, historical conditions, and technological transformations.

For a list of additional titles related to this chapter's topics, please see http://www.ablongman.com/kishlansky.

Chapter 30

THE END OF THE COLD WAR AND NEW GLOBAL CHALLENGES, 1970 TO THE PRESENT

Chapter Outline

For three decades the Berlin Wall stood as a symbol of the division between East and West in the Cold War. In November 1989 the Wall came down. The Visual Record examines the end of the ideological divide and the beginning of a new era. ➤

THE BERLIN WALL COMES DOWN

The American poet Robert Frost captured a basic aspect of human nature when he wrote, "Good fences make good neighbors." The uneasy coexistence of Communist East Germany and liberal and capitalist West Germany reached a confrontation point 16 years after the end of World War II, with the building of a "fence"—the Berlin Wall. In August 1961 the Wall, erected by the East German government under Soviet direction, bifurcated the former German capital and served its intended purpose of keeping East Germans confined behind it.

Why the Wall? East Germany's chief problem in the 1950s was the exodus of over two million East Germans in search of a better life in the West. The flow of emigration throughout the 1950s turned into a torrent in the first eight months of 1961. The Berlin Wall was, more than anything else, erected to keep skilled and professional workers in East Germany. German leaders in the West continued to voice their long-term commitment to reunification, while East German leaders insisted on the independence and autonomy of their state.

Throughout its 28-year life, the Berlin Wall served as a chilling reminder of the great ideological divide between East and West in the Cold War. Cutting through neighborhoods, streets, and railway lines, the Wall also divided families in two. Yet the Wall was porous, if even only slightly so. Passes could be authorized for holidays and special family events, funerals, weddings, and births so that East Berliners could visit their relatives. But long lines through checkpoints with passport and currency controls prevented circulation. Individuals attempting escape from East Berlin to the West were gunned down from watch towers along the Wall. Consisting of over 90 miles of concrete slabs and barbed wire, the Wall stood as a scar through the center of Berlin and around West Berlin. In 1963 President John F. Kennedy visited West Berlin and proclaimed in solidarity with citizens on both sides of the Wall, "Ich bin ein Berliner" (I am a Berliner). In that same speech, Kennedy stated, "There are some who say that communism is the wave of the future. Let them come to Berlin." President Ronald Reagan used the occasion of his visit to West Berlin in 1987 to highlight the apparently increasing openness of the Soviet bloc.

Applications for authorized immigration to West Germany increased in the 1980s, and in 1984 East Germany allowed 30,000 citizens to emigrate to the West. Throughout the late 1980s, the emigration rate remained high, with an average exodus of 20,000 a year. With Hungary's refusal to continue to block the passage of East Germans into West Germany, the floodgates were opened: 57,000 East Germans migrated via Hungary within a matter of weeks. In the face of angry demonstrations, Erich Honecker, head of the East German state, was forced to resign.

The new government opened the Berlin Wall on November 9, 1989, ending all restrictions on travel between East and West. The toppling of communism, already underway, was captured in that moment. Robert Frost wrote of good fences, but he concluded, "Something there is that doesn't love a wall." With the rise of democratic institutions, open markets, and civil liberties, the Cold War had come to an end.

Looking Ahead

By 1970 the postwar restrictions of a bipolar world were giving way to signs of republicanism, democracy, and self-rule. Some transformations were achieved with violence. Most notably, the history of ethnic differences led to war in the Balkans and the former Soviet republics. The United States was embroiled in conflicts throughout the Middle East. The place of the West in the global community continued to depend on social and gender inequalities. And a new kind of war based on the terrorism of civilian populations emerged as the weapon of choice of dispossessed groups around the globe. ➤

■ In a scene that symbolizes the end of the Cold War, people dance atop the Berlin Wall in November 1989.

THE END OF THE COLD WAR AND THE EMERGENCE OF A NEW EUROPE

The Cold War, while it lasted from the post-1945 period to the late 1980s, provided a way of ordering the world. It served to divide friend from foe, to create spheres of economic interest, and to promote market relations among blocs of nations. Also, in a seemingly contradictory sense, it was a conflict that promoted stability and peace between the superpowers, no matter how uneasy. Yet chinks in the façade of Communist unity were already present by the mid-1960s, as we have seen in the previous chapter. As the Soviets faced growing discontent within the Soviet bloc, and as the nuclear threat made cooperation necessary, the bipolar security of the Cold War began to crumble.

The Brezhnev Doctrine and Détente

The use of military intervention to resolve the Czech crisis (Chapter 29) opened a new era governed by what came to be known as the **Brezhnev Doctrine.** Leonid Brezhnev (1906–1982), general secretary of the Communist party and head of the Soviet Union from 1966 to 1982, established a policy whereby the Soviet Union claimed the right to interfere in the internal affairs of its allies in order to prevent counterrevolution. Brezhnev was responsible for the decision to intervene in Czechoslovakia, arguing that a socialist state was obliged to take action in another socialist state if the survival of socialism was at stake. The Brezhnev Doctrine influenced developments in eastern Europe throughout the next decade. After 1968, rigidity and stagnation characterized the Soviet, East German, and Czechoslovakian governments, as well as Communist party rule in other eastern European states.

In the international arena, the Soviet Union had achieved nuclear parity. Now, from positions of equality, both sides expressed a willingness to negotiate. The 1970s became the decade of **détente,** a period of cooperation between the two superpowers. The Strategic Arms Limitation Treaty, known as SALT I, signed in Moscow in 1972, limited defensive anti-ballistic missile systems.

The refusal of the United States in 1979 to sign SALT II to limit strategic nuclear weapons ushered in the "dangerous decade" of the 1980s, when the possibility of peaceful coexistence seemed crushed. U.S. President Ronald Reagan, during his first term in office, revived traditional Cold War rhetoric and posturing. Nuclear strategists on both sides were once again talking about nuclear war as possible and winnable. Popular concern over the nuclear arms race intensified in the United States, in the Soviet Union, and throughout Europe as the United States pursued the Strategic Defense Initiative (SDI), popularly called "Stars Wars" because of its futuristic, science-fiction quality of promised superiority through technology to a single power. At the least, the new system threatened an escalation in nuclear defense spending on both sides

in an attempt to end the stabilizing parity between the United States and the Soviet Union.

In spite of grandstanding gestures such as the Star Wars initiative, East–West relations after 1983 were characterized by less confrontation and more attempts at cooperation between the Soviet Union and the United States. The world political system itself appeared to have stabilized, with a diminution of conflict in the three main arenas of superpower competition—the third world, China, and western Europe. By the end of 1989, leaders in the East and West declared that the ideological differences that separated them were more apparent than real. They declared an end to the Cold War and sought a new and permanent détente.

The New Direction in Soviet Politics

By the mid-1980s, Soviet leaders were weighing the costs of increasing conflict within the Soviet bloc, which the Brezhnev Doctrine failed to control, and the promise of benefits from improved relations with the West. Growing dissent from intellectuals within the Soviet Union joined the voices of those from abroad who criticized Soviet repression. In response to the same forces of change, a different kind of leader was being forged in the ranks of the Communist party among a generation that favored more open political values and dynamic economic growth.

Soviet Dissent. With the repression sanctioned by the Brezhnev Doctrine came growing protest within the Soviet Union. In response to state repression in the period from the late 1960s to the early 1980s, dissidence took on a variety of forms. Some dissenters sought an international forum for their cause. At first weak but increasing in volume, dissent from within communist countries commanded international attention in the mid-1970s.

Growing numbers of Soviet Jews, for example, petitioned to emigrate to Israel in order to escape anti-Semitism within the Soviet Union and to embrace their own cultural heritage. Some of the 178,000 who were allowed to emigrate found their way to western Europe and the United States, and stories of persecution were published in the world press. In May 1976, a number of Soviet dissidents, including Jewish protesters, commanded international attention by openly declaring themselves united for the purpose of securing human rights in the Soviet Union. The state retaliated by charging organizers with anti-Soviet propaganda and handing out harsh prison sentences or relegating protesters to mental asylums, drawing the criticism of democratic states.

One vehicle of protest was the self-published, privately circulated manuscripts in either typed or mimeographed form, known as *samizdat,* which became the chief means of dissident communication. For the most part, dissidents were members of a university-trained professional elite. The leading Soviet dissident of the period was Andrei Sakharov

(1921–1989), internationally renowned as the father of the Soviet hydrogen bomb and a scientist of great eminence. In 1968 he wrote *Thoughts on Progress, Peaceful Coexistence, and Intellectual Freedom,* a work that opposed Communist party rule in favor of a liberal democratic system. For his dissident activities and criticism of the invasion of Afghanistan, Sakharov was sentenced to a life in exile in Gorky in 1980.

Sakharov was not the only figure of stature to engage in protest. The novelist Alexander Solzhenitsyn denounced the abuses of Soviet bureaucracy in *Cancer Ward, The Gulag Archipelago,* and *One Day in the Life of Ivan Denisovich,* works that were highly respected in the West. The historian Roy Medvedev also criticized Stalinism and continued to speak out in favor of peace and democratic principles in the Gorbachev years.

For almost three decades, dissidents waged a lonely battle within the Soviet Union for civil liberties, democratic rights, and the end of the nuclear arms race. In the 1980s it became clear to Soviet watchers in the West that demands for recognition of nationalities were an important part of the dissident movement in the Soviet Union that echoed similar demands throughout eastern Europe. Cultural, religious, ethnic, and ecological concerns and demands for national autonomy joined forces with protests for civil liberties and economic freedom. The reinstatement of Sakharov, one of the Soviet Union's most visible dissidents, as a national hero just before his death and after years of persecution was one of the best barometers of the social revolution that was transforming Soviet politics in the 1980s.

Gorbachev's Economic Reforms.   Typical of the new generation of political leaders was Mikhail Gorbachev, who was,

■ Mikhail Gorbachev's rule ushered in a new age of openness in the Soviet Union. Here, Gorbachev and his wife, Raisa, are shown making a public appearance before a crowd in September 1988.

above all, a technocrat, someone who could apply specialized technical knowledge to the problems of a stagnant Soviet economy. In 1985, the accession to power of Mikhail Gorbachev as general secretary ushered in a new age of openness.

As the youngest Soviet leader since Stalin, Gorbachev set in motion in 1985 bold plans for increased openness, which he called **glasnost,** and a program of political and economic restructuring, which he dubbed **perestroika.** The economic challenges that Gorbachev faced were enormous. Soviet citizens were better fed, better educated, and in better health than their parents and grandparents had been. Yet while economic growth continued throughout the postwar years, the rate of growth was slowing down in the 1970s. Some planners feared that the Soviet Union could never catch up to the United States, Japan, and West Germany. Soviet citizens were increasingly aware of the sacrifices and suffering that economic development had cost them in the twentieth century and of the disparities in the standards of living between the capitalist and communist worlds. Due to outmoded technology, declining older industries, pollution, labor imbalances, critical shortages of foodstuffs and certain raw materials, and a significant amount of hidden unemployment in unproductive industries, discontent became more widespread.

DOCUMENT

Gorbachev on the Need for Economic Reform

Consumer products were either of poor quality or not available. Because of limited provisions, people queued on the average of two hours every day to purchase food and basic supplies. Housing, when it was available, was inadequate, and there were long waiting lists for vacancies. The black market flourished, with high prices on everything from Western blue jeans to Soviet automobiles. People saw corruption in their ruling elite, who drove Western cars, wore Western clothes, had access to material goods not available to the general population, and lived in luxury.

The problem was not salaries. Workers were well paid, with more disposable income than ever before. But purchasing power far outstripped supplies. The state system of production, which emphasized quantity over quality, resulted in overproduction of some goods and underproduction of others. The state kept prices low in order to control the cost of living, but low prices were a problem because they did not provide sufficient incentive for the production of better-quality goods.

Gorbachev's programs between 1985 and 1988 promised more than they delivered. The promises were part of the problem since they created unmet expectations. Modest increases in output were achieved, but people's demands for food and consumer goods were rising faster than they could be met. The Soviet Union did not increase imports of consumer durables or food to meet the demand, nor did the quality of Soviet goods improve appreciably. Rising wages only gave workers more money that they could not or would not spend on Soviet products. The black market was a symbol both of the economic failures of the state and of the growing consumerism of Soviet citizens. Rather than purchase poor-quality goods, Soviets chose to purchase foreign products at vastly inflated prices.

Although his economic reforms broke sharply with the centralized economy established by Stalin in the 1930s, Gorbachev candidly warned that he would not implement a consumption revolution in the near future. Many critics, including fellow communist Boris Yeltsin, believed that Gorbachev did not go far or fast enough with his economic reforms. In place of a controlled economy, Gorbachev offered a limited open market free of state controls for manufacturing enterprises organized on a cooperative basis and for light industry. He loosened restrictions on foreign trade, encouraged the development of the private sector, and decentralized economic decision making for agriculture and the service sector.

Reforming the Soviet State.

In contrast to the ingrained conservatism of his predecessors, Gorbachev represented experimentation, innovation, vitality, and a willingness to question old ways. Gorbachev appointed men who shared his vision to key posts, especially in the foreign ministry. And he extended the olive branch of peace to the West, meeting with President Ronald Reagan in a superpower summit in Geneva.

Furthermore, he argued that economic and political reforms had to be accomplished in concert; the economy, in other words, could only be restructured by "a democratization of our society at all levels." Therefore, Gorbachev's foreign policy also served his economic goals. Military participation in decision making declined as state expenditures on defense were cut. Moscow had always borne larger military costs than Washington. Gorbachev recognized that Cold War defense spending must decline if the Soviet Union was to prosper: consumer durables had to take the place of weapons on the production lines. But there the transformation was bound to be slow.

Gorbachev and Reagan agreed to systematic arms reduction and greater cooperation. In 1988, Soviet troops began the withdrawal from Afghanistan and completed the process by the following year. Also in 1989, in a stunning reversal of the Brezhnev Doctrine, the Soviet state refused to intervene in the upheavals that were sweeping eastern Europe. By 1989, many observers inside and outside the Soviet Union believed that a new age was at hand as the Soviet leader loosened censorship, denounced Stalin, and held the first free elections in the Soviet Union since 1917.

Reform in Eastern Europe

The Soviet example of restructuring and Gorbachev's calls for reforms and openness gave the lead to eastern Europe. In 1988, Gorbachev, speaking before the United Nations, assured the West that he would not prevent eastern European satellites from going their own way: "Freedom of choice is a universal principle," the Soviet head of state declared.

Poland and Grassroots Protest.

Poland's first free elections in 40 years were part of a vast mosaic of protest from which a pattern began to emerge in the spring of 1989. Poland, the most populous nation in eastern Europe, had played an important role in the Soviet bloc because of its strategic location as a corridor for supplies to the Soviet Union's 380,000 troops in East Germany. Yet its economy was never robust, and it had a 20-year history of worker protest and resistance. Throughout the 1970s, the Polish government, based on one-party rule, drew loans from abroad for investment in technology and industrial expansion. The government increased its foreign indebtedness rather than raise prices at home. In 1976, however, price increases were again decreed. A new wave of spontaneous strikes erupted, forcing the government to rescind the increases.

■ Strike leader Lech Walesa addresses shipyard workers in Gdansk, Poland, on 30 August 1980.

1. **Poland.** Solidarity party sweeps elections, June 1989.

2. **Czechoslovakia.** Communist leadership ousted, Nov. 1989; Vaclav Havel named president, Dec. 1989.

3. **Germany.** Berlin Wall breached, Nov 1989. Reunification of East and West Germany, Oct. 1990.

4. **Yugoslavia.** Government decides to hold free elections, Dec. 1989.

5. **Romania.** Communist dictator Ceauşescu overthrown and executed, Dec. 1989; Salvation Front led by dissident former Communists wins elections, May 1990.

6. **Albania.** Communist party still retains Leninist orientation, Jan. 1990. Parliament backs liberal reforms, May 1990.

7. **Bulgaria.** Government disavows "dominant role" for Communist party; pledges free elections and new constitution in 1990.

8. **Lithuania** declares independence, March 1990; Moscow calls move illegal.

9. **Hungary.** Free election sweeps non-Communists into power, April 1990.

10. **Latvia and Estonia** begin process of separation from Soviet Union, April 1990.

■ Events in Eastern Europe, 1989–1990. The events of 1989 and 1990 seemed to indicate that peaceful democratic change through free elections and liberal reforms would fill the void left by the collapse of communist rule.

Poland's indebtedness to the West rose from $2.5 billion in 1973 to $17 billion in 1980. Poland was sinking into the mire of ever higher interest payments that absorbed the country's export earnings. At the beginning of July 1980, the government was forced yet again to raise food prices. Shipyard workers in Gdansk were ready, solidly organized in a new noncommunist labor union called **Solidarity** under the leadership of a politically astute electrician named Lech Walesa. The union staged a sit-down strike that paralyzed the shipyards. Union committees coordinated their activities from one factory to the next and succeeded in shutting down the entire economy. The government agreed to a series of union-backed reforms known as the Gdansk Accords, which, among other measures, increased civil liberties and acknowledged Solidarity's right to exist.

Within a year, Solidarity had an astounding 8 million members out of a population of 35 million. The Catholic Church lent important support to those who opposed Communist rule. Dissident intellectuals also cast their lot with the organized workers in demanding reforms. General Wojciech Jaruzelski became prime minister in February 1981, but the situation of shortages did not change appreciably. Jaruzelski attempted to curb the union's demands for democratic government and participation in management by harsh measures: he declared martial law on 13 December 1981.

Jaruzelski was trying to save the Polish Communist party by using the Polish military to crack down on the dissidents. The Soviet response was to do nothing. Soviet leaders knew that the size of the Polish protest would require a massive retaliation, which they were unwilling to undertake—especially since to do so would fly in the face of Western opinion that supported the Solidarity movement. In addition, the Soviet Union had other problems in this period: in 1979, it began a war in Afghanistan to secure Communist rule. Moscow feared that the Islamic fundamentalism at its border threatened to stir up the rapidly growing Muslim populations in six Soviet republics—Azerbaijan, Kazakhstan, Uzbekistan, Tadzhikistan, Turkmenistan, and Kirgizia. Poland, as a result, was left to Polish rule.

Martial law in Poland produced military repression. Solidarity was outlawed and Walesa was jailed. The West did not lose sight of him: in 1983, the union leader was awarded the Nobel Peace Prize for his efforts. After years of negotiations and intermittent strikes, Solidarity was legalized once again in 1989. The economy was in dire straits, and Jaruzelski knew that he needed Solidarity's cooperation: he agreed to open elections. At the polls, Solidarity candidates soundly defeated the Communist party. Poland was the first country anywhere to turn a Communist regime out of office peacefully. Yet Poland did not pull out of the Warsaw Pact. As Lech Walesa explained in 1989 on West German television, "Poland cannot forget where it is situated. You know we are in the Warsaw Pact. That cannot be changed."

The great challenge before the Solidarity government, as for the Communist regime that preceded it, was economic recovery. Inflation drove food prices up at the rate of 50 percent a month. The Polish government committed itself to freeing the zloty from state control and making it a convertible currency, one that could be bought and sold for other currencies on the international currency market, so that Polish goods could compete in world markets. Poland faced the task of earning enough foreign trade credits to alleviate its indebtedness and to justify foreign investment. In the mid-1990s, Poland continued its pursuit of a free market economy by attracting Western companies and corporations to open subsidiaries and to do business within its borders, as inflation slowed to a still high 20 to 30 percent, and a prosperous management class began emerging.

Hungary, Czechoslovakia, and Romania. In the same period as the Polish free elections, Hungary dismantled the barbed-wire fences on its Austrian border; all of its borders to the West were opened in September 1989. People wanted freedom of movement and freedom of expression. Everywhere Eastern Europeans demanded democratic institutions modeled on those of Western nations. "People power" swept away Communist leaders and ousted the Communist party, many believed for good. The leader of the New Socialist Party in Hungary, Imre Pozsgay, declared: "Communism does not work. We must start again at zero." Unlike other eastern European countries, Hungary had begun experimenting cautiously with free markets and private control as early as the 1970s. As a result, Hungary was best positioned to engage in serious trade with western Europe and made the most prosperous adjustment to democratic autonomy.

Czechoslovakia's revolution began with angry university students. Singing Czech versions of protest songs such as "We Shall Overcome," student protesters were reminiscent of the student activists of 1968. They tried to give flowers to police, who responded by bludgeoning the protesters. That spark touched off a mass movement that within days drove out the Czech Communist party. Idealism and growing public sympathy were on the side of the protesters. The dissident playwright Václav Havel, released from jail just before the demonstrations began, emerged as the leader of the democratic opposition and was elected president of the new government. He became a powerful spokesperson for democratic institutions and oversaw a relatively peaceful separation of the Czech Republic from Slovakia. All of the countries underwent what were considered "velvet revolutions," characterized by a lack of violence and an apparently smooth passage to a new order and the achievement of independence.

The year 1989 did not end, however, without bloody upheaval. Romania under communist dictator Nicolae Ceaucescu appeared to be pursuing a peaceful path. It had evaded its military responsibilities in the Warsaw Pact; it alone of the member states had refused to participate in the Czechoslovakian intervention of 1968. Yet Romania was a state that could not tolerate internal protest. In December 1989, Ceaucescu ordered his troops to fire on demonstrators. Thousands of men, women, and children were killed and buried unceremoniously in mass graves. The slaughter set off a revolution in which Ceaucescu and his wife and co-ruler, Elena, were captured, tried, and executed by a firing squad. They were charged with genocide—the slaughter of 64,000 people—and the mismanagement of the economy. In the days that followed, Romanians spoke in the international media of

■ "Nothing Lasts Forever" reads the sign hanging from the battered bust of Communist dictator Joseph Stalin being carried through the streets of Prague by Czech demonstrators celebrating the end of the Communist regime in their country.

their newly won freedom, as videotaped images of the slain leaders were broadcast to the world. (See "A Closer Look: Televisions, Computers, and the Media Revolution," pp. 938–939.) The events of 1989 made it clear that Ceaucescu was far from an enlightened leader; instead he ruled in the most totalitarian fashion, with repressive policies and a cadre of thugs who enforced them.

The Unification of Germany

The crumbling façade of Communist unity within the Soviet bloc was nowhere more evident than in East Germany. The German Democratic Republic (East Germany) and the German Federal Republic (West Germany), divided by the victorious Allies following World War II, continued to develop after 1968 as two separate countries with different social, economic, and political institutions. On the surface, the differences seemed insurmountable. The erection of the Berlin Wall in 1961 (see The Visual Record, pp. 930–931) cutting the city in two stood as a continual reminder of the ideological divide between East and West.

The two Germanys had been linked economically, if not politically, throughout most of the postwar period. When West Germany entered the European Community in 1957, it insisted that in matters related to trade the two Germanys were to be treated as one country. As a result, East Germany benefited from its free trade relationship with West Germany. That advantage provided an important part of East Germany's prosperity since the 1960s. West Germany, in turn, achieved much of its prosperity through export-led growth, and it found markets in East Germany.

In the 1980s, West Germany stood as an economic giant, second in foreign trade only to the United States and far ahead of Japan. East Germany also established itself as an important trading nation—fifteenth in the world in 1975. Nevertheless, citizens in East Germany were lured by the

■ Reunified Germany, October 1990. Divided into zones as a consequence of its defeat in World War II, East and West Germany were reunited by peaceful means after 45 years of separate rule.

greater prosperity of the West. The lure proved too great in the 1980s and East Germany increasing allowed its citizens to emigrate. The dismantling of the Berlin Wall in 1989 was symbolic of a greater opening of borders as greater numbers of East Germans chose the West.

BALANCE SHEET: EAST AND WEST GERMANY ON THE EVE OF UNIFICATION

East Germany built the strongest economy in the Soviet bloc, but its standard of living lagged far behind that of West Germany, creating challenges for the unified German state after 1990.

	Federal Republic of Germany (West)	German Democratic Republic (East)
Population	61 million	17 million
Life Expectancy	Men, 71.2 years; women, 78.1 years	Men, 69.5 years; women, 75.4 years
Gross National Product	$1.12 trillion	$207.2 billion
Public Spending on Education	9.4% of all government expenditures	5.5% of all government expenditures
New Books Published	50,903 volumes	5636 volumes

Sources: *Statistical Yearbook*, UNESCO, 1988; *Demographic Yearbook*, United Nations; *CIA World Factbook*, 1988.

A Closer Look
Televisions, Computers, and the Media Revolution

A media revolution that transformed communications in the second half of the twentieth century, television became the principal means of communicating current events to mass populations. It was one of the chief consumer durables purchased by the newly prosperous populations of Europe and the United States beginning in the 1950s. Many intellectuals in the West feared that television, because of its uninspired programming, would dull the sensibilities of the masses and serve as a kind of opiate to cloud political judgment. In the same way, a new generation of critics feared that the computer revolution of the 1990s would cause reading and analytical skills to wither away.

Television has been a force for political reform and social change. East Germans in large numbers began buying televisions in the 1960s and 1970s, in order to watch West German television programs, in violation of East German law. East German leaders feared that the "corrupt" and "decadent" images of West Germany might attract their citizens. They were right. The East German head of state, Walter Ulbricht, warned ominously in 1961 that "the enemy of the people stands on the roof." He was talking about television antennas. The East German ban was impossible to enforce. Millions of East German viewers tuned in daily to West German programs and were able to compare the different standards of living in the two German nations and to learn of their own deprivation. The irony of awareness was that as East Germans achieved a higher standard of living and were able to buy more televisions, they became more and more discontented over their relatively low standard of living. Television contributed to rising expectations and the exodus of East Germans to the West.

Television also played a central role in the Romanian revolution of 1989, spreading information and encouraging coordinated action throughout the country. One of the first acts of the Bucharest revolutionaries was to seize the headquarters of the state television station in order to transmit their own view of the conflict. When Nicolae and Elena Ceausescu were executed, the event was videotaped for broadcast to the Romanian nation and the world. In a still heavily rural society undergoing modernization, television provided the essential link between city and countryside. Television promoted concerted action. Romanians in Timosoara, a small city near the Hungarian border, and Bucharest, the nation's capital, simultaneously espoused the same revolutionary program and adopted the same symbols, as similarly doctored national flags made clear. The new regime governed by means of the television screen.

Politicians on both the left and the right used television for political ends. The political utility of television was exploited in France, where 60 percent of the population owned TV sets in 1968. Charles de Gaulle, president of the Fifth Republic, used the medium to appeal directly to the French people against the student-worker revolt that began in Paris in May 1968. Television was decisive in maintaining de Gaulle in power and mobilizing conservatives against the activists. Two decades later, Soviet President Mikhail Gorbachev was so successful in creating his own televised publicity that he became a popular figure within the Western capitalist world as well as within Soviet bloc countries.

Above all, television contributed to the revolution in expectations in Communist countries in the last quarter of the twentieth century. The contrast between the quality of life in the East and the West became inescapable for many educated eastern European and Soviet men and women who had access to travel and to television.

While ownership of televisions was widespread around the globe in the last quarter of the twentieth century, access to computers and the Internet was still restricted to the educated elite and those with discretionary wealth at the beginning of the twenty-first century. The Internet held out the promise of an even greater revolution in beliefs and habits than that achieved by the television. In addition

■ At a Pristina café, ethnic Albanians watch television for the latest news and information after fighting broke out near the northern Kosovo village of Lapastica. Television and computers bring word of war and revolution to the general public in ways never before imagined.

to transmitting information and images, the Internet provided users with the ability to communicate with each other and to create virtual communities of interest, which could transcend national boundaries and geographic limits. Access to the World Wide Web made the world a smaller, if not less complicated place by connecting the local with the global in an immediate way. In one widely publicized example, a Bosnian teenaged girl established a pen-pal correspondence over the Internet with a teenager in Berkeley, California. Her plight captured the attention and sympathy of

the world during the 1999 war in Kosovo.

Communities dispersed through emigration and exile sought reunion on the Internet. Some believed that the Internet could facilitate plots and terrorism. A growing paranoia about the Internet grew with fears that Year 2000 (Y2K) computer glitches might immobilize Western societies that increasingly depended on advanced technologies. As Westerners entered the twentieth-first century, the uses to which the great tool of information technology could be dedicated continued to be discovered.

Modern television technology did not cause revolutions, but it did convey information and provide political platforms. Television publicized revolutions and, in some cases, sold dreams. Computers and the World Wide Web likewise are powerful forces in spreading information, although that information lacked any demonstrated claim to accuracy at the beginning of the twenty-first century. For those who argued that increased communication could lessen hatred and violence, the latest media revolution of the late twentieth century held the promise of prosperity and understanding throughout the world.

An East Germany with open borders could no longer survive as its citizens poured into the promised land of the West in record numbers. The West German government intervened to assist East Germany in shoring up its badly faltering economy; the West German deutsche mark was substituted for the East German currency. Monetary union prefigured political unification. In October 1990, Germany became a single, united nation once again.

Germans represent the largest nationality in Europe west of Russia. Other Europeans feared the prospect of a united Germany, although publicly European leaders endorsed the principle of the self-determination of peoples. In addition, western Europeans were troubled by the impact a united Germany might have on plans for European unification in the European Union. Not least of all, Germans themselves feared reunification. Former East Germans were wary about marginalization and second-class citizenship, while West Germans worried that their poor cousins from the east would act as a brake on West Germany's sustained economic expansion. Nevertheless, Germany committed itself to a course of action to make of the German nation a unified people whose economy would continue to dominate European and world markets.

Russia and the New Republics

As eastern and central European nations were choosing self-rule and greater independence from the Soviet Union, the Soviet Union's own Communist party faced a dilemma. How could party rule and centralization be coordinated with the demands for freedom and autonomy that Gorbachev's own reforms fostered?

To gain credibility and backing, Gorbachev supported the formation of new parliamentary bodies, including a 2250-member Congress of People's Deputies in 1988. Yet the new Congress soon became the forum for attacks on the Communist party and the KGB. In March 1989, in the first

CAREER ADVANCEMENT, COMMUNIST-STYLE

Interviewed in 1990, Klara Paramova, a Soviet lecturer who taught the English language in Moscow, told of her decision to join the Communist party as a means of upward mobility. Although fluent in English and "the best pupil in the class," she realized that membership in the Party was the only way of getting the job she wanted in higher education. Her disillusionment with the tenets of communism was typical of many Soviet citizens of her generation and younger.

Focus Questions

Why does the speaker find dignity of the individual lacking in communism? Why does she continue to be a member of the Party in spite of her criticisms?

I'm thirty-nine and I joined the party at twenty-four so that means fifteen years as a member in, what is the phrase, good standing—paying my dues, sometimes going to a meeting to elect a delegate to this conference or a representative for that occasion, but not much else. I'm not an active member, I don't take my share of responsibilities. Why? Well, because I am not a good Party member, as I told you. And I'm not a good Party member because I don't believe in Communism, it is as simple as that. Nor do a lot of Party members, does that surprise you? It should not. . . . Joining the Party was for me entirely a calculated way of furthering my career. It had nothing at all to do with ideals. . . .

But . . . I am still a member of the Party and I shall remain one. At its simplest it is because if I was to do something that would draw attention to me, like not continuing my membership and stepping down from it—well, then I think, almost certainly, I would lose my present job as senior lecturer. I got it because of those who were in contention for the vacancy, I was the only one who was in the Party—and from this it is correct to deduce, yes, the members of the appointments committee were nearly all themselves members of the Party. . . .

I am not a Communist, and don't believe in Communism, for the simple reason that I think it takes too rosy a view of human beings and it doesn't work. You could say I am not a Christian either, for almost the same reasons. I know there are good Communists and bad Communists, and not all the bad things done in the name of Communism are the fault of the system of itself. But I think it lacks things, and some of the things it lacks are serious. First I would put self-respect or a feeling of the value of people as individuals. I have never been to the West, but of course at the place where I work I have met a lot of people from the West—and there is something about their manner, their self-assurance, which is unlike that of Russian people. I think this can only be the fault of Communism: it may have done, it has done, many good things, but it has never somehow built up dignity in people. There are many catch-phrases, "the dignity of labour" and such sayings; but there isn't one for the dignity of a person as a person, it's an idea which doesn't even exist.

I think I will not change in my views very much now, not at the age of forty: I think I will remain as I am, a Party member but not a good one because I don't share its beliefs.

free elections held in the Soviet Union since 1917, Communist party officials suffered further reversals. Early in 1990, Gorbachev ended the Party's constitutional monopoly of power; the Party now no longer played a leading role in Soviet political life. New political parties proliferated, some defending the old order but many demanding a total break with the past and with Communist ideology and programs.

Among Gorbachev's harshest critics was his former ally and supporter, the former Moscow Party leader Boris N. Yeltsin, who began in 1987 to criticize Gorbachev's caution in implementing reforms. Later, as the popularly elected president of the Russian Republic in 1990, Yeltsin called for a true democracy and decisive economic action.

Aware of his precarious political position, Gorbachev appeared to retrench by increasing control over the media and by attempting to consolidate his base of power. As a result of the attempts, many believed that the regime was becoming authoritarian. Gorbachev was clearly walking a fine line in attempting to maintain stability, yet he was making no one happy—neither Communist party hard-liners nor Western-oriented supporters of capitalism.

Boris Yeltsin in Power.

The shocking end to the Gorbachev experiment came in August 1991. A quasi-military council of Communist hard-liners seized power in order to restore Communist rule and reverse democratic reforms. Gorbachev was taken prisoner in his vacation home in the Crimea. Soviet citizens from the Baltic republics to Siberia protested the takeover, and tens of thousands of Muscovites poured into the streets to defy the tanks and troops of the rebel government. Three people were killed outside Russia's parliament building, which had become a rallying point for the protesters. The timing of the coup was probably determined by the fact that Gorbachev was scheduled to sign a new union treaty with nine of the republics the day following his house arrest, which would have effectively broken up the Soviet empire.

Boris Yeltsin became a hero overnight, publicly defying the plotters, rallying popular support behind him, and helping convince Soviet army troops to disobey orders to attack the White House, as the parliament building in Moscow is called. After only two days, the coup d'état failed; Gorbachev returned to Moscow and banned the Communist party. Although Gorbachev retained his title of Soviet president, his prestige had been seriously damaged by the coup and by the challenge of Yeltsin's new dominance as a popular hero. In the national elections for the Congress of People's Deputies that followed, Boris Yeltsin, who had been dismissed as the head of the Moscow party in 1987, garnered 89 percent of the popular vote. As Yeltsin's star was on the rise, the Soviet Union was now in full collapse.

Economic Challenges.

Embarking on a drive toward westernization and playing catch-up with capitalist nations, liberal reformers in Russia pressed after August 1991 for privatization of industry and the lifting of price controls. There was hope inside and outside Russia that the new state would easily enter the capitalist marketplace. The long lines in front of stores disappeared. But inflation ominously galloped to new heights, wiping out savings and pensions overnight. The black market, always in the shadows even in the most repressed of times,

DOCUMENT

Scientists on Russia's Economy and Environment

emerged boldly as a corrupt "mafia," and its people became the new business leaders of Russia. New markets relied on dollars, and neither banks nor police had the power to stem illegal activities. Visitors to St. Petersburg (the former Leningrad) could ride in taxis whose meters registered the fare in dollars and could eat in restaurants in sections reserved for dollar-paying customers where the service and the food were

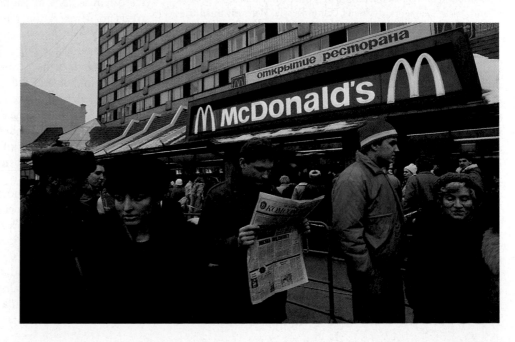

■ The Big Mac comes to Moscow. McDonald's opened its first Soviet fast-food outlet in 1990, just a few blocks from the Kremlin. Muscovites stood in long lines for milkshakes, fries, and the "Bolshoi Mak."

■ Economic problems, including high prices and shortages of food and goods, plague post–Soviet Union Russia. Here a woman tries to exchange a used sweater for fish at a flea market in Moscow.

better—all violations of government policy and law, because dealing in dollars was outlawed. The combined crises of inflation and rule by a gangster elite weakened the barely emergent market economy and undermined the Russian ruble, whose value crashed in October 1994. While a new wealthy class was emerging, as many as 30 percent of the population had become indigent and lived below the poverty line. In 1996, the average monthly salary amounted to about $140 in its U.S. currency equivalent.

The Nationalities Problem. A crucial element in understanding the end of the Soviet Union was the **nationalities problem** within its borders—the claim to self-determination made by Soviet minorities. The Soviet Union listed 102 separate nationalities in its 1979 census. Twenty-two of those nationalities had populations of one million or more people. That very diversity contributed to the disintegration of the

Soviet Union from within. As Gorbachev supported the demands for self-determination in eastern Europe, he faced similar claims to autonomy in a growing number of Soviet republics. The nationalities problem proved to be even more challenging to Gorbachev's regime than the free market economy. In fact, the demands for more freedom in the marketplace went hand in hand with demands for greater cultural self-expression and political autonomy among minority nationalities.

The three major areas of nationalist conflict—Central Asia, Armenia, and the Baltic states—had been voicing grievances against the Soviet state since the 1920s. The protests of the 1980s differed from earlier outcries because a new and educated urban elite, formed after World War II, were now the protesters. Moscow relied on those groups of university-educated and upwardly mobile professionals to further its economic reforms. The groups also became the driving force behind demands for nationalist reforms. Gorbachev's challenge was to harness their protests for autonomy without undermining the Communist party's authority, and to make the Party the vehicle for the new social groups and their local needs. Because of the Party's inability to accommodate these new political ends, Gorbachev ultimately failed.

Ethnic minorities, especially in the Soviet Baltic republics of Latvia, Lithuania, and Estonia, threatened the dominance of Party rule in favor of immediate self-determination. Endorsing diversity of opinion, individual rights, and freedom as the bases of good government, Gorbachev now had to deal with vocal nationalities who took him at his word. Large-scale riots erupted in Lithuania over demands for nationalist rights. In 1988, Estonians demanded the right of veto over any law passed in Moscow. The Russian minority in Estonia protested attacks and prejudicial treatment in the Estonian republic. In the same year, outright violence erupted in Azerbaijan as tens of thousands of Armenians took to the streets to demand the return of the Armenian enclave of Nagorno-Karabakh, incorporated into Azerbaijan in 1921. In the Azerbaijan capital of Baku, the center of Russia's oil-producing region, demonstrators demanded greater autonomy for their republic and the accountability of their deputies in Moscow. Violence between Azerbaijanis and Armenians resulted in 32 deaths and the displacement of tens of thousands. The state upheaval climaxed in December 1988, when an earthquake in Armenia killed 25,000 people. Soviet troops were placed in the area, ostensibly to deal with the aftermath of the natural disaster.

In 1986, university students in the Central Asian republic of Kazakhstan incited two days of demonstrations and rioting over the removal of a corrupt local leader who was replaced with a Russian Party official. The Soviet government's attempts to clean up politics in the area betrayed a clumsy disregard for ethnic issues and seemed at odds with Gorbachev's commitment to decentralization. Crimean Tatars, who had been exiled in Islamic fundamentalist Kazakhstan since World War II, agitated for a return home.

The Breakaway Republics Lead the Way.   One by one, all 15 of the Soviet republics proclaimed their independence, following the lead of the breakaway Baltic republics of Estonia, Lithuania, and Latvia. Having failed to agree on a new plan for union, Gorbachev and the leaders of ten republics transferred authority to an emergency State Council in September 1991 until a plan could be devised. By the end of the year, the Soviet Union was faced with serious food shortages and was bankrupt, unable to pay its employees and dependent on the financial backing provided by Yeltsin as head of the Russian state. Rejecting all Soviet authority, Russia, Belarus, and Ukraine joined together in December 1991 to form the Commonwealth of Independent States (CIS). Eight other republics followed their lead. The Soviet Union thereby came to its end on 21 December 1991 with the resignation of Mikhail Gorbachev, who had become a man without a state to rule. Russian President Yeltsin moved into Gorbachev's Soviet presidential offices at the Kremlin.

Many issues remained unresolved. The new political organization did not address the endemic problems of economic hardship and left unanswered the questions of who would control the former Soviet Union's vast military machine, including its nuclear arsenal, and how trade networks and a stable monetary policy would be determined. Just as there were millions of Russians living beyond the borders of the Russian state with the rise of independent republics, there continued to be ethnic minorities within Russia who sought independence. Russia, on a smaller scale than its Soviet predecessor, was a federation of different ethnic minorities and a Russian majority population with no clear policy for autonomy or self-rule.

In the elections of December 1993, a post-Soviet constitution was approved. Ominously, ultranationalists became a troubling presence in Russian politics as they combined forces with communists and other groups to receive almost 50 percent of the votes cast. Yeltsin's grasp of the reigns of power slipped as he faced challenges both from inside and outside

MAP DISCOVERY

Republics of the Soviet Union

The Soviet Union broke up into 15 independent nations, which embraced a variety of ethnic groups. Note the correspondence between ethnicity/language and independent nation status. What new republics have only one language? In the nation of Uzbekistan how many ethnicities and languages are there? How many different ethnic groups remained in the new Russian state?

CHRONOLOGY
THE VELVET REVOLUTIONS

1989	Free elections in Poland lead to the ouster of the Communist regime
September 1989	Hungary opens its borders to the West
November 1989	German Democratic Republic lifts travel restrictions between East and West Germany; the Berlin Wall comes down
December 1989	Václav Havel elected president of Czechoslovakia
July 1990	Havel reelected as president of the Czech and Slovak Federated Republic
1990	Boris Yeltsin elected president of the Russian Republic
1990	Gorbachev ends the Communist party's monopoly of power
1990	Lech Walesa elected president of Poland
October 1990	Federal Republic of Germany and German Democratic Republic reunited
December 1991	Eleven former Soviet republics form Commonwealth of Independent States (CIS); Mikhail Gorbachev resigns, and the Soviet Union is dissolved

the government. In the vacuum of power that resulted from the collapse of Soviet rule, regions operated autonomously and local rule was often supreme. After easily winning the national election in the summer of 1996, Yeltsin began his second term in failing health, hidden from public view, and under a heavy cloud of doubt about his ability to lead.

The year 1989 marked a watershed in the history of European politics. The beginnings of transformation were first signaled by the Soviet Union, followed by dramatic events in central and eastern Europe. The democratic tide appeared irreversible as symbols of freedom and cooperation proliferated throughout the former Warsaw Pact countries. One million people joined hands in a widely publicized event to form a 370-mile-long human chain that stretched across the Soviet Baltic republics of Estonia, Latvia, and Lithuania in protest against Soviet annexation in 1940. Other bodies defied borders, as in September 1989, when East Germans began a mass

exodus into West Germany, voting with their feet for economic prosperity and democracy. Poland and Hungary opted for democratic regimes, and Bulgarians ended the 35-year reign of the dictator Todor Zhivkov and endorsed parliamentary government. Tens of thousands of Czech demonstrators in the capital city of Prague typified the peaceful "velvet revolution" of the democratic movement that swept through eastern and central Europe as they poured into the streets to sing songs about freedom and cheer their new heroes, dissidents persecuted and jailed under the former communist regime.

ETHNIC CONFLICT AND NATIONALISM

Yet freedom was not the only force unleashed with the collapse of communism. Ugly battles based on long-standing grievances erupted. Groups intent on autonomy and independence vied with each other over territories and borders. Chechnya struggled to be free of Russian rule. The Balkans, where borders had been imposed at the end of World War I, erupted into genocidal strife that shocked the world.

In Bosnia, where a bloody war dragged on for years in the former Yugoslavia, the term **ethnic cleansing** laid bare the barbarity and genocide that were still very much a part of the Europe of the late twentieth century. The international arena seemed bereft of solutions to the troubling problem of borders at the beginning of the twenty-first century as terrorism and state repression defined the Chechen-Russian struggle.

The Chechen Challenge

In the midst of its own crisis of rule, in December 1994, Russia committed itself and 30,000 Russian troops to a war with one of its ethnic minorities, the secessionist Chechens, who had declared themselves independent of Russia in 1991. Chechnya, a territory of plains and peaks in the Caucasus, had also posed a problem for the former Russian Empire. In the nineteenth century, Muslims of the area waged a series of what they called "holy wars" to fend off the Russian invaders, but to no avail.

Russian Invasion, 1994–1996. Following in the footsteps of their forebears and in a long tradition of resistance, secessionist Chechens challenged Russian rule that appeared insensitive to local needs. In December 1994, Russia launched a full-scale invasion, seizing control of the Chechen capital of Grozny. After almost two years of battle, Russian officials estimated that the death toll stood at 80,000, with some 240,000 wounded. The war was denounced in the international arena because of Russian attacks against the civilian population. Reportedly, 60 percent of schools, kindergartens, and nurseries were partly or fully destroyed. An estimated 80 percent of the war dead were civilian. Russian warplanes bombed rebel-occupied villages, and thousands of refugees fled their homes in search of shelter. By the summer of 1996, Russia appeared to have lost the war, despite the fact that it possessed the largest army in Europe deployed against an enemy estimated to be about 4000. Russian estimates were undoubtedly low, but the disparity in forces was nonetheless real.

The Truce.

Yeltsin promised to end the war, which proved so unpopular among Russians, in his 1996 reelection campaign. Yet critics of the truce negotiations that took place in August 1996 believed that he had attracted votes in bad faith. Yeltsin appeared to be reverting to his hawkish ways, with renewed bombing. Chechen forces responded by regaining control of Grozny in August 1996. A Chechen rebel leader also claimed responsibility for two terrorist bombings in Moscow during that period. Russian troops began a systematic withdrawal from Chechen cities following the retaking of Grozny. Both sides agreed to a truce, similar to a half dozen such efforts in the preceding two years. The development of a peace plan that would acknowledge Chechen autonomy within the Russian state was acceptable to the rebels, who saw the advantage of regrouping their forces and the need for a break in the hostilities. The agreement proposed in the summer of 1996 called for a referendum in Chechnya in the year 2001 for the purpose of determining the future of the republic.

But attempts at implementation of a peace plan demonstrated the fissures in Russian leadership. Yeltsin continued to remain out of public view, increasing speculation about his ability to rule. Kremlin officials expressed dismay that the move toward Chechen autonomy threatened "Russian territorial integrity."

Renewed War and Terrorism.

In the summer of 1999 conflict again escalated into open warfare because of terrorist bombings of apartment buildings and barracks in and around Moscow that killed hundreds. The terrorist deeds were attributed to Chechen rebels. Affected by arguments of self-defense against terrorists, Russian popular opinion now turned in favor of repressing the Chechen bid for independence. Russia had important economic motives for subduing the runaway republic. Chechnya's location was central to the oil pipeline routes near the Caspian Sea. Several former Soviet states had begun building a new pipeline in the 1990s in order to circumvent the Russian supply and to sell directly to Western buyers.

What had begun as a period of openness, restructuring, and commitment to democratic values had turned by the late 1990s into conflict, instability, and political uncertainty. Just as the ethnic question had ultimately pulled down the Soviet Union, it posed the single greatest threat to the stability of Russia, at least as powerful as economic hardship in threatening the future of the new Russian state. And economic hardship was great. Tied for most of the twentieth century to the control of a state-run economy, Russia appeared to lack the resources—infrastructural, financial, and human—to join the top ranks of productive nations.

In 2001, Russian president Vladimir Putin declared the war in Chechnya over. Yet violence continued as Chechens protested the presence of Russian troops. Following terrorist attacks in the United States on 11 September 2001, the Russians escalated their war against terrorism in Chechnya. The Chechens responded with terrorist tactics within the Russian state. Atrocities against Russian civilians escalated in 2004. Plane bombings on two flights leaving Moscow and the killing of 339 hostages held in a schoolhouse, half of whom were children, provoked global denunciation. Russian president Putin responded to these atrocities by limiting democracy and civil liberties for the Russian population, a move that unleashed popular discontent within Russia and international criticism.

■ Chechen women and Russian soldiers' mothers united in a peace march to try to bring an end to the war in Chechnya. Russian troops halted the women, who were on their way to the village of Samashki in western Chechnya, the site of an alleged massacre by Russian soldiers.

A Woman Reporter Behind the Lines of the War in Chechnya

Anne Nivat was the Moscow correspondent for the French daily newspaper Libération *in October 2000 when she interviewed the rebel president of Chechnya. Fluent in Russian and holding a doctorate in political science, Nivat began traveling as a young journalist through Chechnya at the end of the first Russian-Chechen war in 1996. After a year's break as a Fulbright Fellow at Harvard's Russian Research Center, she returned to southern Russia and, disguised as a Chechen woman, traveled alone covering the war from the Chechen side. Nivat concludes her recent book recounting her experiences, "In my coverage of this war, I have tried to avoid assigning guilt to one side or the other. Instead, I have tried to show that the Russian-Chechen conflict will not cease until first the Russians and then the rest of the international community work toward that end. . . . We must not forget the countless humiliations and acts of violence that these Chechens suffer in their daily lives." Her newspaper reports led to antiwar protests against Russia in Paris.*

Focus Questions

What indications does the Chechen rebel leader give that he sees guerrilla warfare within Chechnya as the best means of defeating Russia? What are his motives for opposition to the presence of Russian troops in Chechnya?

I finally find Maskhadov. He is wearing a military uniform with a pistol in his belt and appears to be in perfect health. Seated on a comfortable sofa in a "safe house," he seems relaxed and eager to share his thoughts on the situation in Chechnya. Outside, Russian armored vehicles pass through the autumn mist. Since he left Grozny the previous winter, the rebel president hasn't spent more than two consecutive days in any one spot. He usually communicates with his men and with the outside world by means of audiotapes. Few journalists take the trouble to hunt him down and interview him. In any case, he's very suspicious of the press. We talk for several hours over a meal of soup.

"The Russian intervention in Chechnya is about one year old. Where are we now?" I ask Maskhadov.

The fugitive leader answers simply: "As far as we're concerned, it all began on September 5, 1999, when the Russians bombed our country for the first time, and not on October 1. This time we're not so naïve to throw ourselves into all-out combat with the Russians, as we did in the first war. We know that's not the way to make any headway against their army. All we can do is mount a series [of] diversionary actions," he explains. "Our goal is not to halt their army but to conserve our own forces. While they occupy our territory—that is, while they remain inactive—their forces grow weaker, while ours get stronger. Our men are everywhere. The Russians know it, and yet they never mount an offensive. Their army is demoralized."

I ask Maskhadov why the rebels didn't counterattack during the summer when it would have been easier. "We intended to. We had set plans for retaking Grozny and Gudermes and Argun," he answers. "But at a meeting of the GKO,[1] we opted for guerilla action instead. Our strength lies in our invisibility, when we're everywhere and nowhere at the same time. We also want to keep our losses to a minimum." . . .

Maskhadov is silent for a moment. He lets out a deep sigh. The Chechens, he admits, are tired of this war. "I recognize that the situation is difficult for the civilian population, which has become the target of the Russian army. I also regret that thousands of my countrymen have had to leave for Ingushetia or elsewhere. But each time I send out my representatives, they come back with the same message: 'Continue the fight. We're with you.' We can't afford to lose face, and the population knows it as well as I do. One way or another, the Russians will be forced to come to the negotiating table. I am constantly reminding Putin that he will be better off negotiating with me, as long as I am alive. It will be worse without me. And the Russians will leave in the end. Last time they led us to believe that they would never leave and then they disappeared. The worse thing would be if they stayed and we had to defend their troops here in Chechnya!" . . .

Maskhadov repudiates the idea of a religious component to the conflict. "This is a war of national liberation. We are fighting to deprive Russia of the right to destroy us as a nation. I am forty-nine years old. I have lived through the Chechen deportation and two wars. I know what I'm talking about. We're followers of Islam, but 'Wahhabism'[2] isn't part of our tradition. Chechens are not going to let themselves be turned into Arabs."

Maskhadov is enjoying our discussion. It is rare that he has the full attention of a member of the foreign press. He has a hard time tearing himself away, but he finally gets up to leave, followed by his Minister of Defense and two bodyguards. His old car starts up crankily. It carries him away to the edge of the forest. From there he will go on horseback to his camp.

From Anne Nivat, *Chienne de Guerre: A Woman Reporter Behind the Lines of the War in Chechnya,* translated by Susan Darnton (New York: Public Affairs Press, 2001), pp. 251–255.

[1]The State Defense Committee, comprising some forty key leaders of secessionist Chechnya.

[2]Wahhabis are Muslim religious fundamentalists, an extremist group that rejects secular forms of government.

War in the Balkans

Hopes for social transformation and liberal economic reforms were highest for Yugoslavia in 1989 with the waning of Soviet power and the end of the Cold War. Yugoslavia, after all, was the success story of the Soviet bloc with open borders and its escape from the Stalinist grasp in 1948. Many Europeans believed it was moving toward a market economy with its liberal economic policies and trade agreements.

Yugoslavia was a federation of six people's republics, with Serbia, Croatia, and Bosnia and Herzegovina the three largest in descending order. In 1991 festering differences erupted in civil war between Serbs and Croats, as Serbian nationalists overran multiethnic Bosnia and Herzegovina in a bid for territorial aggrandizement of Serbia. Serbia and Croatia were more than long-standing rival enemies with a history of hostility that had been masked by their federated status in the Yugoslav state.

The History of Ethnic Differences. The question of national independence in the Balkans had caused war before in the twentieth century. A Serbian nationalist intent on independence for Serbia from Austria-Hungary assassinated an Austrian archduke in 1914, sparking the outbreak of World War I. The nation of Yugoslavia had been created in 1918 by consolidating different ethnic groups as part of the peace that settled the war. The divide between the Serbs and Croats was partly identified with religious differences—the Croats were historically Catholic, the Serbs Orthodox—but for the most part, their enmity was based on the competing claims over the South Slavic lands, Bosnia and Herzegovina, that were part of the former Ottoman and Austro-Hungarian empires.

Various historic milestones have been commemorated on both sides as part of their litany of grievances against each other. In 1928, for example, a Croation nationalist was assassinated in the Serbian city of Belgrade, capital of Yugoslavia. In World War II, Croatians sympathized with the Nazi occupiers and committed atrocities against the Serbs. The legacy of those and similar events was the creation of an unauthorized history of ethnic identity distinct from that of the official Yugoslav history that stressed the independence of the Yugoslav state within the Soviet bloc.

Conflicting territorial claims of the Serbs and Croatians were considerably exacerbated by two facts. First, a large number of Serbs lived in Croatia, and, of course, Croatians were present in the Serbian-claimed lands of Bosnia. Under Tito's rule, ethnic differences were held in check. After 1991, land claims were considerably complicated by the mixed population of Bosnia and Herzegovina. Second, another group, neither Catholic nor Orthodox but Muslim, amounting to 9 percent of the population of the former Yugoslavia and a majority of the Bosnian population, got caught in the crossfire of the war between Serbs and Croats and became a target for massacre and atrocities by the Serbs.

In 1992, the Serbian army evicted 750,000 Muslim civilians from their homes in Bosnia. Serb forces also continued to bomb civilians in the Bosnian capital of Sarajevo. It later came to light that in 1992 Serb leaders had authorized a policy of ethnic cleansing—including concentration camps, rape, and starvation—against Muslims. In 1995, the Serb military was also responsible for the mass killings of Muslims from Srebrenica. Such barbarity contributed heavily to forging a strong sense of national identity among Bosnian Muslims, who controlled the Bosnian army and the presidency.

■ Bosnian soldiers in 1996 show the solidarity of their cause with the Muslim "holy war" by wearing headbands with Muslim phrases and chanting their readiness to die in Allah's name in pursuit of Bosnian independence.

■ Balkans. New republics, federations, and sectors were carved out of the former Yugoslavia in the 1990s, with conflicts still unresolved at the turn of the new century.

Beginning in 1992, Muslims from other parts of the world, including Afghanistan, Iran, Turkey, Pakistan, and Arab countries such as Egypt, volunteered to fight alongside the soldiers of the Bosnian army as Muslim holy warriors or *moujahedeen* against the Serb nationalists. Used as shock troops by Bosnia commanders, they quickly earned a reputation as fierce fighters who inspired religious fervor among the Bosnian army.

In the course of the war, with more than a quarter of a million lives lost and two million people displaced, the Bosnia conflict was recognized as the bloodiest ground war in Europe in 50 years, and Bosnian Serb leaders were indicted as war criminals. The United Nations placed forces in Bosnia on a peace-keeping mission, which allowed it to take neither side in the war. NATO intervened against the Serbian attempt to overrun Bosnia after the outbreak of hostilities, and in September 1995 NATO stepped up the bombing of Bosnian Serb military installations and Serbian-held positions in Bosnia with the policy of avoiding civilian targets.

The Dayton Peace Accords brokered by the United States brought Muslim, Croat, and Serb leaders together in Ohio in November and December 1995. As part of the commitment to the accord, the Clinton Administration sent 20,000 U.S. troops to join the 60,000 NATO troops already present to help enforce the peace. The aim of the Accords was to create a unified country in Bosnia while recognizing ethnic interests. The settlement called for a shared three-person presidency chosen by free elections. In the judgment of some Western diplomats, such an arrangement offered little hope of a stable and enduring peace. Despite the Accord, Bosnia remained a partitioned country, with Croats, Serbs, and Muslims still struggling for separate rule.

Kosovo and the Ongoing Conflict in Eastern Europe.
Yet another arena of bloodshed opened up in 1998. Kosovo, one of the six former Yugoslav republics, had been known as the "autonomous province" of Serbia. With the breakup of Yugoslavia, there had been movement toward an independent Kosovo, and even talk of a "Greater Albania," which would reunify Albanians in Kosovo, western Macedonia, and Albania. Checking attempts at Kosovo independence, Serbia proceeded to strip it of its autonomous status after 1990. In addition, there was overwhelming evidence that the Serb state intended to drive more than one million Kosovo Albanians from the province. The Kosovo Liberation Army responded with guerrilla actions against the Serbs.

Civil rights abuses and atrocities against Kosovo Albanians by Kosovo Serbs shocked the world into action in 1998. On the night of 24 March 1999, NATO forces began attacking Serbian targets in Kosovo in a massive military campaign of air strikes that lasted for almost 11 weeks. The war, a first in NATO's history, marked a failure in its policy of deterrence. As the lead partner, the United States justified an unpopular war at home by promising not to commit ground troops in battle. The air war succeeded, and United Nations peace-keeping forces, including U.S. troops, entered Kosovo in June 1999. The Serbs were probably responsible for the deaths of at least 10,000 and the expulsion of 800,000 Kosovo Albanians. With the defeat of Serb forces, Kosovo Albanians took the place of their Serb oppressors and committed new atrocities, now under the nose of peace-keeping forces, with the aim of driving non-Albanians out of the province. Intolerance and the desire for revenge boded ill for the future of peace in the region.

The new Serbia remained a tightly controlled state economy. Privatization was unconstitutional in Serbia. Former communist officials continued to run things, as before, as feudal fiefdoms for the profit of a few. Bosnia had no economy at all, and foreign investors, so necessary for economic recovery and trade, avoided putting funds in a country lacking financial institutions and a market orientation. In 2002, Serbia and Montenegro, both part of the former Yugoslavia, began discussions that resulted in the formation of a federation of the two republics, the new state of Serbia and Montenegro, in 2003.

But Albania, a tiny nation of 3.5 million people, was in the worst economic shape of all at the end of the twentieth century. As the poorest nation, with the highest infant mortality rate and the lowest life expectancy rate in Europe, Albania faced the challenges of the post-communist era with its industrial infrastructure in ruins, its government in shambles, and its environment polluted. Without the authoritarian control of communist rule, Albania disintegrated into a primitive society ruled by bandits, blood feuds, and vendettas.

Other eastern European states also were riddled with ethnic troubles—including Czechs and Slovaks, the Hungarians and Romanians over the border region of Transylvania, and the Bulgarians and Turks in Bulgaria—but none of those disputes involved the degree of violence that had occurred in the Balkans.

THE WEST IN THE GLOBAL COMMUNITY

The phenomenal growth and prosperity of western Europe came up against a new set of harsh realities in the 1970s with skyrocketing oil prices, inflation, and recession. Western European nations saw greater cooperation as the best response in world markets dominated by the American superpower. A key component in achieving growth was not only the U.S. capital that helped fuel recovery, but also the availability to western European economies of a floating labor pool of workers from southern Europe and from former colonies in Asia and Africa. The permanent presence of foreign workers, many of them unemployed or erratically employed during the economic downturns of the 1970s and 1980s, came to be seen as a problem by welfare-state leaders and politicians of the New Right. Europe's new working class became the brunt of racist antagonism.

With the goal of reviving the economy in the 1980s the 12 member states of the European Economic Community devoted themselves to making western Europe competitive as a bloc in world markets. They hoped that by uniting they could serve as a counterweight to American economic hegemony in the West. At the same time that Russian satellites in eastern Europe were breaking free of Soviet control and attempting to strike out on their own, the nations of western Europe were negotiating a new unity based on a single market and centralized policy making.

Europe, both east and west, seemed on the verge of a renaissance, united economically, committed to democratic institutions, and looking forward to the twenty-first century as a global power in its own right. Yet social and economic problems persisted, the costs of the welfare state rose, terrorism tyrannized democratic societies, and a new nationalism vied with cooperation across borders. The rosy vision of the West in a global community that many foresaw in 1990 seemed to have a cloudy future as the West faced the new century.

European Union and the American Superpower

In 1957, the founders of the European Economic Community, Robert Schuman and Jean Monnet, envisioned the idea of a United States of Europe. Both men perceived that Europe's only hope of competing in a new world system was through unity. The European Community (EC) had been created in 1967 by merging the three transnational European bodies—the European Coal and Steel Community, the European Economic Community, and the European Atomic Energy Community. It operated with its own commission, parliament, and council of ministers, though it had little real power over the operations of member states. In 1974, a European Council was created within the European Community, made up of heads of government who met three times a year. Almost since its inception, the European Community has been committed to European integration.

The Politics of Oil.   The oil crisis of the 1970s encouraged isolationism among the members of the EC and eroded foreign markets, causing growing dependence on national suppliers and thereby undercutting the goals of the Common Market. In 1973, the international politics of oil prices provoked an economic crisis followed by a recession. The Organization of Petroleum Exporting Countries (OPEC) raised prices and cut back production. Western European countries depended heavily on imported oil, which they used to fuel their prosperity through the early 1970s. As the crisis abated, competition and efficiency reemerged as priorities within the EC. Europeans were well aware that the United States and Japan had surged ahead after the 1973 crisis. The Common Market had been successful in promoting European growth and integration since 1958. Western European leaders realized that integration was the only defense against the permanent loss of markets and dwindling profits. In unity there was strength, as the aggregate economic indicators for 1987 later made clear.

Toward a Single Europe. In 1985, the EC negotiated the Single European Act, which by 1987 had been ratified by the parliamentary bodies of all the member nations. Final steps were initiated to establish a fully integrated market by 31 December 1992. The 12 members of the EC intended to eliminate internal barriers and to create a huge open market among the member states with common external tariff policies. In addition, the elimination of internal frontier controls with a single-format passport was intended to make travel easier and to avoid shipping delays at frontiers, thereby lowering costs. An international labor market based on standardized requirements for certification and interchangeable job qualifications would result. The easier movement of capital to areas where profitability was greatest was encouraged. All aspects of trade and communication, down to electrical plugs and sockets, had to be standardized. The goal behind the planning was to make the EC think and act as a single country. Supporters compared it to the 50 individual American states participating in one nation.

In 1989, there were 320 million European citizens of the 12 countries of the EC: the original Common Market six of France, West Germany, Belgium, the Netherlands, Luxembourg, and Italy were joined by Britain, Denmark, and Ireland in 1973, Greece in 1981, and Portugal and Spain in 1986.

Plans for European economic integration moved dramatically forward in October 1991 when the 12-nation European Community and the 7 nations of the European Free Trade Association (EFTA) joined forces to form a new common market to be known as the European Economic Area. The EFTA countries that joined forces with the EC included Austria, Finland, Iceland, Liechtenstein, Norway, Sweden, and Switzerland. Several of the EFTA nations announced plans to join the EC as well. The European Economic Area constituted the world's largest trading bloc, stretching from the Arctic Circle to the Mediterranean and consisting of about 380 million consumers. The nations of the EFTA agreed to abide by the EC's plans for economic integration and adopted the vast array of laws and regulations that governed the EC.

The European Union. Meeting in Maastricht, the Netherlands, in December 1991, the heads of the 12 EC countries ratified a treaty momentous for the European Union. They agreed that a common currency, the **euro,** would replace the national currencies of eligible nations, and that a single central banking system, known as the European Monetary Institute, would guide member nations in reducing inflation rates and budget deficits. Economic union would be reinforced by political union, with member states sharing a common European defense system and common social policies regulating immigration and labor practices. In that sense, the new **European Union (EU)** was intended as something more than the European Community (EC), which had been primarily an economic entity to promote free trade. In the words of French President François Mitterrand the goals of the European Union were: "One currency, one culture, one social area, one environment."

On 1 January 2002, Europeans in 12 of 15 member nations began using the new common currency, the euro. Since 1999

■ A young boy in Nicosia, Cyprus, waves a European Union flag to celebrate entrance of Cyprus into the EU on 1 May 2004.

the euro had been a virtual currency, existing as a bookkeeping device. In 2002, the new hard currency replaced national monetary units including the French franc, the German mark, the Spanish peseta, the Greek drachma, and the Dutch guilder. Hailed as the European Union's boldest achievement, the new currency was intended to solidify the basis of integrated European markets and be competitive in international markets against the dollar. Within two months of the introduction of the euro, at the end of February 2002, the member nations of the European Union held a convention for the purpose of considering the creation of a Europe-wide constitution.

European Money Before the Euro

Many worried, however, that the long histories, traditions, and national identifications of the individual member states would stand in the way of a fully integrated and politically united Europe. Britain was the most reluctant of the member states at the prospect of European integration. British negotiators strongly resisted plans for monetary union because they feared losing national sovereignty rights. Nonetheless, Prime Minister Margaret Thatcher and her successor, John Major, solidly committed Great Britain to the EU. As Thatcher explained it: "Our destiny is in Europe." In addition to resisting

Original EU member
in 1992

Became member in 1995

Became member in 2004

0   500 Miles

0   500 Kilometers

NORWAY

FINLAND

SWEDEN

ESTONIA

RUSSIA

LATVIA

North
Sea

Baltic Sea

LITHUANIA

RUSSIA

IRELAND

DENMARK

BELARUS

GREAT
BRITAIN

NETHERLANDS

POLAND

BELGIUM

GERMANY

ATLANTIC
OCEAN

LUX.

CZECH
REPUBLIC

UKRAINE

SLOVAKIA

SWITZ.

AUSTRIA

HUNGARY

MOLDOVA

FRANCE

SLOVENIA

ROMANIA

CROATIA

BOSNIA &
HERZEGOVINA

SERBIA &
MONTENEGRO

Black Sea

Corsica

ITALY

BULGARIA

PORTUGAL

SPAIN

MACEDONIA

ALBANIA

Balearic
Islands

Sardinia

TURKEY

Mediterranean Sea

GREECE

Sicily

MOROCCO

ALGERIA

TUNISIA

MALTA

Crete

CYPRUS

■ European Union. The most stable and prosperous European nations formed the 12 original
member states of the European Union in 1992, soon joined by three additional members. These
members agreed to share a common currency, economic and social policies, and planning. In
2004, 10 new nations joined the EU.

monetary union, British public opinion polls reflected cynicism over the 1991 Maastricht negotiations and a social policy
affecting working hours, minimum wages, and conditions of
employment throughout Europe. Prime Minister Tony Blair
continued to be committed to the European Union, although
the British pursued a separate path to full membership.

The biggest expansion in the European Union came on 1
May 2004 when 10 new states, all from eastern Europe, be-
came members of the EU. The inclusion of Cyprus, the Czech
Republic, Estonia, Hungary, Latvia, Lithuania, Malta, Poland,
Slovakia, and Slovenia now brought EU membership to 25.

Some planners were wary about the prospect of including
eastern European nations whose troubled economies, they
feared, would dilute the economic strength of the EU. More
optimistic predictions recognized the potential of an available
labor pool and the possibility of new markets in the former
Soviet bloc. In its English-language homepage, the European
Union explained its enlargement in this way: "In taking this
decision, the European Union was not simply increasing its
surface area and its population. It was putting an end to the
split in our continent—the rift that, from 1945 onwards, separated the free world from the Communist world."

With four other candidate countries in the wings, two of which—Bulgaria and Romania—were slated for membership in 2007, the European Union worked toward achieving true European integration. The plan for European unity affected more than just economics. Education, too, faced standardization of curricula and requirements for degrees. There were proposals for a common European history textbook that, in place of national perspectives, would emphasize the values of a single political entity in its discussion of battles, wars, social change, and culture. The EU also had its own flag—a circle of twelve gold stars on a field of blue—and its own anthem, Beethoven's "Ode to Joy."

Export-producing nations, including Japan and the United States, expressed concerns over "Fortress Europe," that is, Europe as a global trading bloc with a common external tariff policy that would exclude them. A united Europe, with the world's largest volume of trade and the highest productivity, would constitute a formidable presence in the world arena.

Originally intended to offset American dominance in European markets, in the 1990s the EU offered the opportunity of a closer economic relationship with the United States. The EU became the largest customer for American products. In addition, Ford, IBM, Digital, Boeing, Unisys, Otis, General Electric, Pratt & Whitney, McDonnell Douglas, and Pacific Telesis were just a few of the American companies that entered into partnerships and joint ventures with EU firms. The possibility of the emergence of a truly global marketplace seemed, paradoxically, more likely with the creation of the EU and other regional associations throughout the world. By fostering market economies, economic competition, political stability of democratic institutions, as well as common political, economic, and social policies, the EU offered a counterbalance to the void filled by the end of the Cold War and the promise of peace based on productivity and trade.

A New Working Class: Foreign Workers

Foreign workers played an important role in the industrial expansion of western Europe beginning in the 1950s.

Western European nations needed cheap, unskilled laborers. Great Britain, France, and West Germany were the chief labor-importing countries; their economic growth in the fifties and sixties had been made possible by readily available pools of cheap foreign labor. The chief labor-exporting countries included Portugal, Turkey, Algeria, Italy, and Spain, whose sluggish economic performance spurred workers to seek employment opportunities beyond national borders. Great Britain also imported workers from the West Indies, Ireland, India, Pakistan, Africa, and southern Europe.

Migrant employment was by definition poorly paid, unskilled or semiskilled manual work. Italian workers in West Germany, for example, commonly worked factory night shifts that German workers refused. France employed a large number of foreign laborers in agriculture, public works, commerce, and engineering. Foreign male workers found employment on construction sites all over western Europe. Foreign women worked in domestic service, personal care, and factories.

Commonly, married men migrated without their families, with the goal of earning cash to send home to those left behind. Switzerland actually discouraged family migration with restrictions on income and housing. Nevertheless, prosperous and underpopulated Switzerland had Europe's highest percentage of foreign workers—16 percent of the total Swiss population in 1975. The prohibition against permanent settlement, however, hampered assimilation among this sizable percentage of foreign workers.

Most immigrants who came looking for jobs carried with them the "myth of return," the belief that they would someday go back home. For the most part, however, foreign workers stayed in the host country. Irish workers were alone in returning to their home country.

Working Conditions and Rights. The lot of foreign workers was difficult and sometimes dangerous. Onerous and demanding labor was common. Foreign workers were often herded together in crowded living quarters, socially marginalized, and identified with the degrading work they performed. Street cleaning and refuse collection in France were

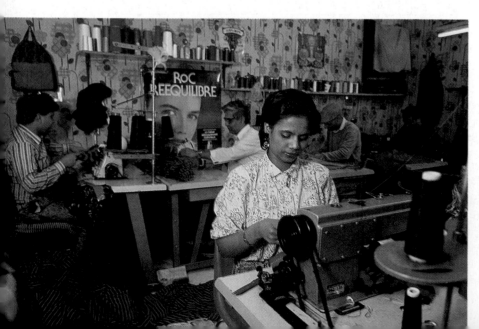

■ Indian immigrants in France sewing in a sweatshop. Immigrant workers in European countries took low-paying, menial jobs. They faced resentment from xenophobic native Europeans.

jobs typically performed by black Africans. Foreign workers were frequently denied the rights of citizenship and subjected to the vagaries of legislation. In economic downturns they were the first to be laid off. Yet the obligations of foreign workers to send money back home to aged parents, spouses, children, and siblings persisted. Children who resided in the host country with their foreign-worker parents suffered from severe identity problems, experiencing discrimination in schools in the countries in which they were born and with which they identified. A rising incidence of violence among second-generation Algerian adolescents in France, for example, indicated tensions and a new kind of rebellion among migrant populations in the 1970s and 1980s. Third and fourth generations of foreign workers born on West German soil were refused the rights of citizenship and denied the possibility of naturalization.

Women endured special problems within the foreign work force. Between 1964 and 1974, the majority of Portuguese immigrants to France came with families, but there were few social services to support them on their arrival. Dependable child care was either too expensive or unavailable to female workers with children. Increasing numbers of single women began migrating to western Europe independently of their households. Like men, they worked in order to send money back home. Often housed in dormitories provided by their employers, Spanish and Portuguese women factory workers in Germany and France were isolated from the communities of their compatriots.

Opposition and Restrictions. Opposition to the presence of foreign workers was often expressed in ultranationalist rhetoric and usually flared up in periods of economic reversals. Right-wing politicians sometimes complained that foreign workers deprived native workers of jobs. That argument seemed baseless, since many of the jobs filled by migrants were spurned by native workers as too menial, too poorly paid, or too physically demanding. Opposition to foreign workers

nonetheless became virulent. In 1986 in France, the xenophobic National Front campaigned on a platform of "France for the French" and captured 10 percent of the vote in national elections. Racism was out in the open in Western countries that had depended on a foreign labor force for their prosperity. Arab and black African workers in France resorted to work stoppages to protest police discrimination and identity controls that they likened to the yellow Stars of David that Jews had been required to wear in Nazi Germany. In 1996, the French government chartered planes to return undocumented Africans to Africa. Riots in Great Britain in 1980 and 1981, particularly in the London ghetto of Brixton, were motivated by racial discrimination against blacks, severe cuts in social welfare spending, and deteriorating working conditions.

Before 1973, most countries in western Europe, including Great Britain, had actively encouraged foreign labor. After that date, restrictions became the order of the day. It is no coincidence that restrictions on foreign labor followed the 1973 oil crisis. Western governments enforced new conservative policies throughout the 1970s and 1980s aimed at keeping out third world refugees. Exceptions were made for political refugees from eastern Europe. Racial considerations lay beneath the surface of discussions about political asylum. In 1989, the British government sent back to Vietnam the "boat people" who had escaped to Hong Kong in search of a better life. Britain earned the condemnation of other Western governments and humanitarian groups for its refusal to provide a haven for Asian refugees, many of whom were children.

The European Union attempted to impose uniform standards and quotas on immigration but these were often resisted by member nations. One reason they resisted was the lack of skilled workers to do certain jobs. For instance, at the beginning of the new century, Spain's economy was one of the fastest growing in western Europe. Yet Spain suffered labor shortages in the construction and agricultural sectors. Spanish employers relied heavily on illegal immigrants in spite of the fact that

■ A weeping African woman and her child leave St. Bernard Church in Paris after riot police stormed the church to disperse the 300 African immigrants who had gathered there to protest French treatment of immigrants.

THE RETURN OF FASCISM?

In the following two excerpts from the New York Times *(2 December 1992), neo-Nazi attacks in Germany by gangs of skinheads gave rise to renewed fears about the resurgence of racism in Europe. Attacks on foreigners—gypsies, Cambodians, Turks, and other ethnic groups—were not unique to Germany in the last decade of the twentieth century. With renewed emphasis on nationalism, extremist groups have designated enemies based on racist terms throughout central, eastern, and western Europe.*

Focus Questions

What kinds of symbols do the skinheads in these articles employ to identify with a Nazi past? Who are the targets of their racism?

Music of Hate Raises the Volume in Germany

Were it not for the lyrics, it might be just another teen-age rock show. But this is a concert in Zwickau, in eastern Germany, by Störkraft, a Düsseldorf-based skinhead band whose name means "destructive force." They are performing hits like their 1990 song "Kraft für Deutschland," or "Strength for Germany," and the lead singer, Jörg Petrisch, howls the words:

> We fight shaved, our fists are hard as steel,
> Our heart beats true for our Fatherland.
> Whatever may happen, we will never leave you,
> We will stand true for our Germany,
> Because we are the strength for Germany,
> That makes Germany clean.
> Germany awake!

"Germany awake!" is a slogan the Nazis used during their rise to power in the early 1930s. When the concert ends, the audience of about 1,000 young people begins chanting "Sieg Heil." Some give the stiff-armed Fascist salute. Several young men unfurl a black-white-and-red Third Reich battle flag emblazoned with the swastika.

Two Germans Admit Arson Attack That Killed Three Turkish Nationals

BERLIN, Dec. 1 (AP)—German officials said today that two men arrested in connection with the firebombing that killed a Turkish grandmother and two girls had confessed to their part in the attack, the country's worst case of neo-Nazi violence.

The two right-wing radicals have been charged with murder, attempted murder and arson after confessing to the attack on November 23 in the northern town of Mölln, Alexander von Stahl, the chief federal prosecutor, said.

Moving to counter a wave of violence by right-wing groups, officials have banned a neo-Nazi political party and expanded federal antiterrorist operations over the last week.

Justice Minister Sabine Leutheusser-Schnarrenberger said in Bonn today that dozens of neo-Nazi and skinhead hate-music bands would be investigated under the new ban. Critics say that the bands' racist lyrics, set to a derivative of punk and metal music, may have inspired some attacks.

Rightists have made nearly 1,800 attacks that have killed 16 people in Germany this year.

Officials are worried that the violence is hurting Germany's image abroad and could harm the export-dependent economy, leading to boycotts of German products or declining foreign investment.

In a statement issued in Cologne today, the Federation of German Industries said the world must know that "Germany is not an anti-foreigner country."

In the Mölln firebombing case, Lars Christiansen, 19 years old, and Michael Peters, 25, confessed to carrying out two bombings on houses where Turks lived, Mr. von Stahl said.

After each attack, the prosecutor said, Mr. Peters called the police from a telephone booth to claim responsibility, closing each call by shouting "Heil Hitler!"

Spain had the highest unemployment rate in the European Union in the year 2000. Germany likewise suffered from high unemployment, yet sought increased numbers of professional workers from abroad because of the limited skills in the available pool of workers. A declining birth rate in western European countries also contributed to labor shortages and reliance on imported labor. On the whole, restrictions failed to achieve what they set out to do—remove foreign workers from Western countries by repatriation in spite of numerous policies to restrict and police illegal immigration.

The presence of foreign workers in European Union countries heightened racism and overt antagonism from a resurgent extreme Right. In the late 1980s, when movements for democratic freedom and human rights were being endorsed in eastern Europe, the problem of permanent resident "aliens" was without a solution in western Europe. Yet the need for cheap labor made the preservation of such a labor pool likely.

The issue of immigration became a prominent one in electoral campaigns throughout Europe in the 1990s. Opposition to the presence of foreign workers and concerns about protecting small business interests fueled ballot-box victories for the far right in Austria, the Netherlands, and France. In the first presidential election of the twenty-first century in France, the National Front candidate Jean-Marie Le Pen ran on the party's "France for the French" platform and garnered an unprecedented 18 percent of the electorate, giving pause to the democratic leadership of many European countries. In 2004, debate raged in the industrialized countries about how to deal with the apparently contradictory demands of high rates of endemic unemployment and labor shortages.

French Laws on Secularity.   The presence of populations from north Africa and southern and eastern Europe in western Europe resulted in a clash of cultures, values, and religious beliefs. In France these issues came together around a particular item of clothing prohibited for school children at the primary and secondary levels. Muslim girls began wearing veils and head scarves in school in growing numbers beginning in the late 1980s. A long national debate in France ensued following the expulsion of two young girls for wearing head scarves. Citing French laws on the separation of church and state, authorities ultimately banned all accessories and clothing that indicated religious affiliation, including crosses and yarmulkes. An amendment to the law in 2004 raised enforcement to the national level. The public debate about assimilation and citizenship reinforced the idea that citizenship required adherence to a common code and common cultural values. This situation highlights the challenges that cultural diversity presented to all European nations with growing minority populations. Although in the first week of school in September 2004 only 240 girls out of nearly 12 million students came to school wearing head scarves, the issue captured the attention of the world by exposing the tensions within Western societies caused by the influx of new, often foreign-born Muslim minorities.

Women's Changing Lives

During the last quarter of the twentieth century, the lives of Western women reflected dramatic social changes. Women were more educated than ever before. Access to institutions of higher learning and professional schools allowed women to participate in the work force in education, law, medicine, and business throughout the world, whether in France, the United States, or the Soviet Union. Women had been active in calling for the liberation of oppressed groups in the 1960s. Those activities served to heighten women's collective awareness of the disparities between their own situations and those of men in Western societies: women worked at home without pay; in the workplace, women received less pay than men for the same work.

In that period of increased educational and work opportunities, an international women's movement emerged. International conferences about issues related to women were media events in the 1970s. In 1975, the United Nations Conference on the Decade for Women was convened in Mexico City. Women activists believed that something more was needed than the conference, which was accused of seeking only to integrate women into existing social structures dominated by men. On 8 March 1976—International Women's Day—the International Tribunal of Crimes Against Women was convened in Brussels.

Modeling the conference on tribunals such as the Nuremberg Commission, which dealt with Nazi atrocities in World War II, the feminists who convened in Brussels concentrated on crimes against women for the purpose of promoting greater political awareness and action. Fertility and sexuality were at the center of the new politics of the women's movement, justified in the slogan "The personal is political." Rape and abortion were problems of international concern. "Sisterhood is powerful!" gave way to a new organizing slogan, "International sisterhood is *more* powerful!"

■ French Muslim schoolgirls wearing head scarves outside of Lille High School, France. French laws on separation of church and state resulted in a ban in public schools of all accessories and clothing that indicate religious affiliation, including head scarves, crosses, and yarmulkes.

Reforms and Political Action.   In Italy, political action by women yielded a new law in 1970 that allowed divorce under very restricted circumstances. Italian feminists used the legal system as a public forum. In France, the sale of contraceptives was legalized in 1968. French feminists, like their Italian counterparts, worked through the courts to make abortion legal: they achieved their goal in 1975. Important in the victory were two manifestos: one signed in 1971 by 343 French women, many of them prominent, who acknowledged having had an abortion; the other signed in 1975 by 345 French doctors who acknowledged having performed abortions. Widespread opposition from religious and conservative groups did not reverse the legal gains. With the increasing integration of Europe in the 1990s, differing national practices in child care, health care, and gender parity were reviewed by the deliberative bodies of the European Union. Yet national differences of women's social and family roles still prevailed among European countries, including differences in education, healthcare, and reproductive rights.

The feminist movement created a new feminist scholarship that sought to incorporate women's experiences and perspectives into the disciplines of the humanities and the social sciences. Women's studies courses, which emphasized the history of women and their contributions to civilization, became part of university and college curricula throughout Europe and the United States. Reformers also attempted to transform language, which, they argued, had served as a tool of oppression.

In addition to promoting political action throughout Europe, issues of domestic violence, incest, and sexual orientation entered the political arena. In 1970, Western feminism was discovering that "socialism was not enough," and that women had to address problems of discrimination in terms of gender as much as class. As two French feminists explained in 1974: "If we maintain that our sex unites us across all class differences because we are oppressed as women, regardless of class, race, and age, then even those men who serve the revolution start to react violently and brutally against us. Since we conceive of ourselves as an oppressed sex, we naturally resist those who oppress us." That was a declaration of war between the sexes. In its most radical form, lesbian separatism meant a total rejection of men as enemies, and separatists provoked a rift in the women's movement.

Western feminists continued to be politically active in the 1970s and 1980s in the peace movement, in antinuclear protests, and in the 1990s in ecological groups concerned with protecting the environment. As Petra Kelly, the West German leader of the Green party, an ecological and pacifist coalition, described it: "Women all over the world are rising up, infusing the antinuclear, peace, and alternative movements with a vitality and creativity never seen before." At the turn of the new century feminists, student activists, environmentalists, and internationalists found common ground in the concerns of exploitation of a global work force, sweatshops, ecological devastation, and the pollution and exploitation of the environment. The biggest of these demonstrations occurred in Seattle, Washington, in November and December 1999, when thousands of protesters, women and men from around the world, converged for a week to protest the actions of the World Trade Organization and international corporations, perceived as prime culprits in global exploitation and pollution.

■ French women demonstrate for the right to choose. The sign says, "A baby, no baby, ten babies if I wish."

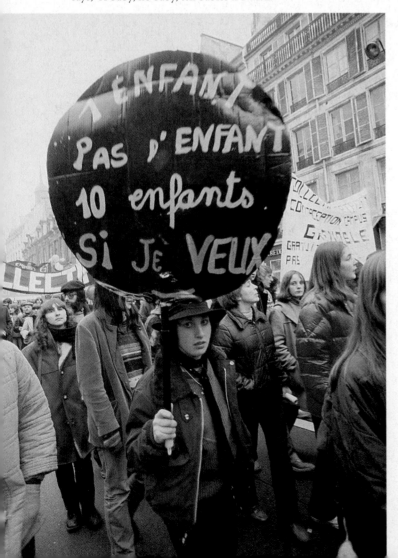

Soviet Women's Experiences.   In the last quarter of the twentieth century, women in socialist countries were also engaged in the process of redefining women's social roles and political participation. The Soviet Union provides an interesting case study of comparison and contrast. Increasingly, well-educated Soviet women demanded reforms, and the beginnings of a women's protest literature in the 1970s indicated an awakening concern for women's issues. Soviet women enjoyed more representation in parliamentary bodies than women in the West. More than half of the 2.3 million deputies to the local Soviets in the 1980s were women. One-third of the 1500 members of the Supreme Soviet were women. Gorbachev appointed a woman as one of the 12 Central Committee secretaries—the most politically influential people in the country. In spite of greater participation, however, women enjoyed little real authority in the higher echelons of political life, and most Soviet women rejected feminism as a political movement.

The same pattern held true for women in the work force. More than 85 percent of Soviet women worked, compared to about 60 percent of women in the West. Although 70 percent of doctors and 73 percent of teachers were women, women held few positions of authority. Both their pay and their status were lower than men's, as the example of primary school teaching reveals: 80 percent of primary school teachers were women, but two out of three head teachers were men, a phenomenon similar to that in other Western countries.

Unlike western European women, many Soviet women—two out of three on average, according to censuses in the 1970s—performed heavy manual labor. Older women, for example, still chopped ice from Soviet streets. The practice had begun 40 years earlier because of the heavy losses of men in World War II—15 million had died in the war. In her doctoral dissertation on the sociology of the rural village of Stavropol, Raisa Gorbachev, wife of the Soviet leader, argued that while men were trained to run machines and tractors, women were expected more and more to perform the heavy physical labor associated with farm work.

Birthrates fell in the Soviet Union as in Western countries; women were bearing fewer children. Technology had made controlled fertility possible in safer, more dependable ways, but most birth control devices remained unavailable to Soviet women, and what was available was often unreliable. Abortion continued to be a common form of birth control in the Soviet Union, with two abortions for every live birth. Women were also choosing to have their children later, often because of work and financial considerations, with a growing percentage delaying childbearing until their thirties. Women complained of lack of quality in maternity hospital care. As one young mother explained, "The only experience worse than an abortion is having a baby in a Soviet hospital."

In the late 1980s, Soviet President Mikhail Gorbachev made direct appeals for women's support by promising preschool nurseries and kindergartens for every child. Gorbachev also committed himself to supporting increased sick leave for mothers of sick children, paid maternity leave for a period of 18 months, increased child-care allowances, and shorter workdays for women who worked at home. In support of women's voice in the workplace, women's councils were to be revived.

Women's work experience in the East and the West varied in degree, but a startlingly similar pattern of home and work life prevailed at the beginning of the twenty-first century. Neither state institutions nor the law met the needs of women.

Terrorism: The "New Kind of War"

A new kind of warfare emerged globally as disfranchised groups rejected the avenues of cooperation and reform and instead chose violence as the sole means of achieving their political ends. The history of contemporary terrorism began after World War II. The creation of the state of Israel in part of the land of Palestine in 1948 led to conflict between the Israelis and the Palestinian Arabs, who refused to accept the new Jewish state. Israel's Arab neighbors went to war to support the Palestinians but were defeated by Israel in late 1948. Hundreds of thousands of Palestinians became refugees in neighboring Arab states, and Palestinian guerrillas decided that the best way to attack Israel and its protectors was with a global strategy of terrorist violence. The first Palestinian hijacking took place in the summer of 1968. Ejected from Jordan, Palestinian guerrillas set up their headquarters in Syria and Lebanon in order to continue their terrorist activities.

Another influence figured prominently in terrorism of the late twentieth century: Islamic fundamentalism. Muslim militants intent on waging a "holy war" for the oppressed could be found throughout the world in areas as different as Algeria, Bosnia and Herzegovina, France, and the Philippines. Muslim radicals in those and other countries shared a truly global commitment and were often heavily influenced by their formative volunteer experiences in the Afghan war of the 1980s. Conceiving of their mission as a holy one, they were able to form a series of loose connections with Muslims from other countries for the purposes of recruitment, training, and deployment of dedicated fighters. A taxi driver from Egypt, for example, who fought in the Afghan war was convicted for the 1993 bombing of New York's World Trade Center. Conspirators led by the convicted Egyptian cleric Omar Abdel Rahman plotted to bomb the United Nations building, FBI headquarters in lower Manhattan, and the Lincoln and Holland tunnels linking Manhattan with New Jersey. The French blamed Afghan trained Algerian Muslims for the 1994 Christmas Eve hijacking of an Air France airbus in which three passengers were killed in the initial shoot-out in Algiers.

Terrorists came from many nations and religious backgrounds. Peace-loving Muslims were maligned in Europe and the United States because of fundamentalists' actions. Following the 1995 bombing of the federal building in Oklahoma City, Arabs and Muslims across the United States were singled out for reprisals and intimidation until it was discovered that the Oklahoma City bombing was the act of domestic terrorists protesting U.S. government policies. The Oklahoma City attack, which terrorized the nation, fit the essential definition of the new terrorism as a violent act against innocent civilians for the purpose of undermining the power of the government.

Terrorism in the Last Quarter of the Twentieth Century.

By the late 1970s, a strategy of terrorist violence appealed to European revolutionaries intent on advancing a variety of political causes. Political killings became a tactic of choice for terrorists throughout the world. Victims were targeted by terrorists not because they merited any punishment themselves but as a means of attracting international attention to the terrorists' cause. Although motivated by different political agenda, terrorist groups often formed cooperative networks on an international basis, sharing training, weapons, and information. A small group of West German left-wing radicals known as the Red Army Faction executed key industrial, financial, and judicial leaders. The Red Army Faction was also responsible for a number of bombings, including that of the West German embassy in Stockholm. In Italy, a small group known as the Red Brigades was responsible for violent incidents, including the "kneecapping"—permanent crippling of people by shooting them in the knees—of leading Italian businessmen and the kidnapping and murder of the former Italian prime minister Aldo Moro. In 1981, the Red Brigades targeted the United States for their terrorist reprisals when they abducted an American general, James Dozier.

Western Europe served as an important arena for terrorist acts by non-European groups. To succeed—that is, to terrify mass populations—terrorists needed publicity. Terrorists relied on media exposure and claimed responsibility for acts only after they had been successfully completed. In September 1972, members of the Palestinian Black September movement kidnapped 11 Israeli athletes at the Olympic Games in Munich. An estimated 500 million people watched their televisions in horror as all 11 were slaughtered during an American sports broadcast. In a dramatic shoot-out, also televised, five of the terrorists died as well. Incidents such as the taking hostage of the OPEC oil ministers later in the decade in Vienna made urban populations aware of their vulnerability to gratuitous acts of violence. In 1979, 52 Americans were kidnapped from the American Embassy in Teheran and were held hostage for 444 days by a group of young Iranian revolutionaries who claimed to be battling against the "great Satan."

A recurrent pattern of terrorism prevailed throughout the 1980s with Israel and the United States often the targets of attacks. Incidents highlighted by international media coverage

■ A hooded Arab terrorist stands on a balcony during the attack on the Israeli Olympic team headquarters at the Munich Olympics in 1972.

included: the attempted assassination of the pope in 1981 by a Turkish fascist; the blowing up of the U.S. Marine garrison in Beirut in 1983 by a Lebanese Shi'ite, whose act took the lives of 241 American soldiers as well as his own; the 1985 hijacking of a cruise ship, the *Achille Lauro,* by Palestinian ultranationalists, who killed one aged Jewish American passenger; and the bombing of TWA and El Al registration counters at two of Europe's busiest airports, in Rome and Vienna, in 1985. In December 1988, hundreds of people died when a Pan American plane on which a bomb had been planted exploded in flight over Lockerbie, Scotland. The bombing was probably in retaliation for the downing of an Iranian passenger airliner by the U.S. Navy in the Persian Gulf.

Terrorist activities against the United States escalated following the U.S. military action against Iraq in 1991 known as the Persian Gulf War. In February 1993, the explosion of a bomb planted in a small truck parked in the basement garage of the World Trade Center in New York killed six people, wounded a thousand, and did limited damage to the structure. Two terrorist attacks in Saudi Arabia in 1995 and 1996 killed 24 Americans. In August 1998, two major assaults against American embassies, one in Tanzania and the other in Kenya, killed 224 people and injured hundreds of others. In October 2000, a suicide attack against the USS *Cole* in the port of Aden took the lives of 17 sailors.

All of these attacks were attributed to the network of a single man, Osama bin Laden, a Saudi Arabian millionaire, who had been trained by the U.S. Central Intelligence Agency and who, between 1980 and 1989, had fought against the Russians in Afghanistan. In June 2001, bin Laden called on the Muslims of the world to mobilize themselves into a general **jihad,** or holy war, against their enemies. Three months after this call-to-arms, terrorists dealt their most extreme blow against the United States.

September 11, 2001: A Turning Point.   On 11 September 2001, four U.S. passenger planes were hijacked and used as flying bombs in a coordinated action that targeted the World Trade Center in New York City and the Pentagon just outside of Washington, DC. Two of the four hijacked planes slammed into the twin towers of the World Trade Center, and a third plane hit its mark by diving into the Pentagon. The fourth plane crashed in a field in Pennsylvania, its suicide attack foiled by passengers who opposed their captors. More than 3,000 people were killed, thousands more were wounded, and the loss of property was unprecedented in the worst terrorist attack in history. The events horrified people around the world who understood that two symbols of American global financial and military dominance had been singled out in a carefully planned and executed mission of destruction. Once again, Osama bin Laden was identified as the mastermind of terrorist devastation. President George W. Bush declared, in the wake of the terrorist attacks, that the United States was entering "a new kind of war," one not waged between nations but one whose stateless enemy would be sought out and hunted down. Terrorism had long plagued Europe and the Middle

■ This photograph captures the massive explosion caused when a second hijacked plane crashed into the World Trade Center in New York on 11 September 2001. The landmark twin towers were destroyed in the attack, and thousands of people were killed.

East, but the September 11 attacks marked the first time in history that an act of terrorist warfare by an external enemy took place on American soil. The event marked a turning point in the struggle against terrorism and a new focus in state security measures of Western governments. It also marked the beginning of a new war.

In October 2001, less than a month after the attacks, the United States and Great Britain undertook war in Afghanistan in pursuit of bin Laden, who was believed to have been harbored there by the Taliban, the fundamentalist Muslim ruling group. Though bin Laden was not captured, the Taliban was removed from power. In the fall of 2004, free elections were conducted throughout Afghanistan under the eyes of military observers for the nation's first elected president.

After 9/11, the Americans and their allies in Europe and throughout the world joined forces in pledging to eradicate terrorism. Stringent security measures in airports and public places were instituted worldwide as nations faced harsh new political realities, including incidents of bioterrorism—germ warfare against civilians—in the months following the September terrorist attacks. When the European Union and the United States passed new laws and directives to combat terrorism, critics feared the curtailment of civil liberties. Such a curtailment in fact took place in Russia following terrorist incidents in the summer of 2004. Racist incidents against Muslims and Arabs mounted, even as European and American leaders stressed that bin Laden and his network was a non-representative and fanatical fringe within the Muslim world.

Throughout the post-9/11 era, Iraq and its leader Saddam Hussein continued to be singled out by the U.S. government as sympathetic to the terrorist cause and committed to developing "weapons of mass destruction." As a consequence of a United Nations' resolution, UN inspection teams entered Iraq in mid-November 2002 in a search for such weapons. None were found. In further pursuit of such weapons and with the intention of removing Hussein from power, President Bush ordered U.S. troops in coalition with British forces to lead an attack against Iraq in March 2003. Saddam Hussein was captured, but some insurgent forces resisted the military occupation. Terrorist actions continued to take American and Iraqi lives as the American government attempted to rebuild the Iraqi economy during the peace. American involvement in this war was greatly unpopular and resulted in undermining Western alliances and increasing criticism of American foreign policy throughout the world.

Terrorism and Counterterrorism. Terrorism in the last quarter of the twentieth century was not a single movement but a wide variety of groups and organizations on both the left and right. Some organizations were Marxist; some were nationalist; some were Islamic fundamentalists. All defined the enemy as an imperialist and a colonizer. Industrial nations, especially the United States and Israel, were common targets of terrorist attacks. Terrorists all shared a vision of the world based on the commonly held belief that destruction of the existing order was the only way to bring about a more equitable system. Palestinian terrorists were willing to sacrifice their lives to ensure the establishment of an independent Palestinian state. In the case of bin Laden's fundamentalist Muslim terrorists, holy war was perceived as the only way to create an Islamic state free of Western influence and the corruption of a U.S.-dominated global economy.

Terrorists justified their violent actions in terms of the legitimacy of their cause. The Provisional Wing of the Irish Republican Army, for example, explained that it bombed crowds of Christmas shoppers in London as a means of uniting Northern Ireland with the Independent Irish Republic. Terrorists argued that just as resistance fighters in World War II had used bombs and assassinations as their means of fighting a more powerful enemy, they themselves were engaged in wars of liberation, revolution, and resistance and were using the only weapons at their disposal to fight great imperialist powers. Plastic explosives in suitcases, nearly impossible to detect by available technology, became the weapon of choice. If all was fair in war—and in World War II, both sides bombed innocent civilian victims in pursuit of victory—then, terrorists countered, they were fighting their war with the only weapons and in the only arena they had.

By the mid-1990s it was clear that terrorism was an effective challenge to the tranquility of industrial nations. Modern terrorists were often able to evade policing and detection. Surveillance had not prevented terrorists from striking at airplanes and cruise ships. Yet terrorists accomplished little in the way of bringing about political change or solutions to problems.

West European governments often refused on principle to bargain with terrorists. Yet at times, European nations and the United States have been willing to negotiate for the release of kidnapped citizens. They have also been willing to use violence themselves against terrorists. Israel led the way in creating antiterror squads. In 1976, Israeli commandos succeeded in freeing captives held by pro-Palestinian hijackers of an Air France plane in Entebbe, Uganda. The following year, specially trained West German troops freed Lufthansa passengers and crew held hostage at Mogadishu, Somalia, on the east coast of Africa. The Arab kidnappers had hoped to bargain for the release of the imprisoned leaders of the Red Army Faction; the West German government refused. In 1986, the United States bombed Libya, long recognized as a training ground for international terrorist recruits, in retaliation for the bombing of a discotheque frequented by U.S. service personnel in West Germany. Israel bombed refugee camps to retaliate against Palestinian nationalists. The greatest mobilization in counterterrorist efforts came with U.S. leadership following the events of 11 September 2001. The goal of the "counterterrorism" was to undermine support for terrorists among their own people; its tactics and ends opened counterterrorism to the criticism that it was very similar to the terrorism it was opposing. In fact, torture of prisoners and interrogations in violation of the Geneva conventions at the hands of American soldiers and civilian personnel came to light in an Iraqi prison in the summer of 2004.

In spite of tactics of meeting violence with violence, the advanced industrial states of western Europe and the United States remained vulnerable to an invisible terrorist enemy. That elusive enemy could terrorize populations and incapacitate the smooth functioning of the modern industrial state. With the dawn of a new century, terrorism continued to threaten peace and paralyze security, at the very moment when people all over the globe celebrated the hope for a better world. After the large-scale terrorist attacks of 2001, the promise of a new and better world seemed, for many, to move further out of reach.

CONCLUSION

In 1970 Western nations had managed to put the destruction, hardship, and sacrifice of the Second World War behind them in the space of a single generation. Yet economic downturn and rising expectations of a better life continued to fuel protest and discontent. The escalating costs of nuclear parity were in conflict with the growing demands of consumer societies, and this conflict helped to end the Cold War. With the collapse of the Soviet Union, a period of new hope and international cooperation dawned.

The world of 1989 was now a world dominated by one superpower, the United States. It was also a world characterized by the rise of new political entities and the search for integration and stability in Europe. The Western world was undoubtedly a different place in the last quarter of the twentieth century from all that had gone before. But was the world really so transformed that one could speak of its being ordered in a different way? The iceberg of communism had melted. As democrats replaced dictators, some observers wondered if counterrevolution was waiting in the wings, should the new capitalist experiments fail. In other countries, the dictators did not leave; they only changed their political allegiances. Proto-fascist and anti-Semitic groups became more vocal in the early 1990s amid the economic chaos.

One potentially unifying force was the marketplace. Democratic institutions seemed most stable in those countries with developed market economies. In the former Yugoslavia, for example, little had changed for the better since the fall of the communist regime. Russia itself suffered from a similar problem of economic readjustment and restructuring. Even where political reforms had been accomplished, economic reforms lagged behind or were nonexistent.

Western Europe and the United States realized the devastation that industrialization had wrought in their own countries after a century and a half of development, and were taking steps to control pollution and to clean up the air and the environment. Yet in eastern Europe, ecological concerns were considered a luxury as industries struggled uncontrolled to establish footholds in competitive markets. In spite of the emergence of a new world order of democratic states, many Europeans, both in the East and in the West, saw an uncertain future of misery and repression fueled as long as virulent nationalism remained unchecked.

Problems that plagued Western states in the modern era persisted. The triumph of the nation-state in the nineteenth century had carried the seeds of violence and destruction, as two world wars and countless local conflicts had proven.

Democracy, likewise viewed as the best hope for a better world, struggled in new settings that lacked the institutions, the culture, and the experience of democratic values. Elected elites from Russia to Romania used positions of power for aggrandizement, both political and economic.

As the benefits of the welfare state in the West dwindled with slowed economic growth, the gap between the rich and the poor widened. The widening gulf characterized the new capitalist economies of the former Soviet bloc as well as those of the West. In the United States, the richest 1 percent of households controlled about 40 percent of the nation's wealth. In Germany, high-wage-earning families earned about two and a half times as much as low-wage workers. And the gap between rich and poor on a global scale yawned even wider into a gulf.

What lay ahead for Western societies? Would the third millennium be so different? Arthur Miller, the renowned American playwright, commented in the aftermath of the terrorist attacks of 11 September 2001, "It is so simple to destroy a city." Citizens of Western industrial societies had a new and shocking sense of their own vulnerability as they stood at the beginning of a new age of anxiety and fear. Symbols of civilization and economic achievement—skyscrapers and office buildings—could appear to melt in an instant, taking the lives of all those trapped inside. What was best in civilization at the beginning of the third millennium—selflessness, self-sacrifice, and willingness to help others in spite of personal cost—came face to face with mindless destruction and attacks on civilian populations but gave hope that the best values of civilization would prevail.

QUESTIONS FOR REVIEW

1. What caused the end of the Cold War?
2. What was the nature of dissent in the Soviet Union?
3. How did the ideas of *glasnost* and *perestroika* help bring about the end of the Soviet Union?
4. How did the collapse of communist regimes in Russia and eastern Europe promote national and ethnic conflict?
5. What social, economic, and political forces contributed to German reunification?
6. How did the treaty signed by the nations of the European Community at Maastricht in 1991 create both hopes and fears of European unity?

7. In what ways have women's lives in eastern and western Europe been similar and in what ways have their experiences differed since the 1960s?
8. What is the difference between the European Community and the European Union?
9. How have democracy and nationalism come into conflict since 1989?
10. What nations and populations experienced terrorism in the late twentieth and early twenty-first centuries? What were the causes of terrorism and from what did terrorism derive its power?

KEY TERMS

Brezhnev Doctrine, *p. 932*

détente, *p. 932*

ethnic cleansing, *p. 944*

euro, *p. 950*

European Union (EU), *p. 950*

glasnost, *p. 933*

jihad, *p. 958*

nationalities problem, *p. 942*

perestroika, p. 933

samizdat, p. 932

Solidarity, *p. 935*

DISCOVERING WESTERN CIVILIZATION ONLINE

You can obtain more information about the end of the Cold War and new global challenges at the Websites listed below. See also the Companion Website that accompanies this text, www.ablongman.com/kishlansky, which contains an online study guide and additional resources.

The End of the Cold War and the Emergence of a New Europe

Mikhail Sergeyevich Gorbachev

www.almaz.com/nobel/peace/1990a.html
A biography of Mikhail Gorbachev with electronic texts compiled by the Nobel Prize Internet Archive.

A Research Guide to Soviet History

www.unc.edu/depts/slavlib/html/guides/history_0.htm
A research guide to Soviet history sponsored by the University of North Carolina libraries.

Chronology of Russian History: Post-Soviet Period

www.departments.bucknell.edu/russian/chrono4.html
A chronology of Russian history since 1991 with links to additional resources.

Boris Yeltsin

www.cs.indiana.edu/hyplan/dmiguse/Russian/bybio.html

A chronology of Yeltsin's presidency with links to further materials on key events and personalities.

The Fall of the Berlin Wall 1989

www.remote.org/frederik/culture/berlin

A photo tour of the fall of the Berlin Wall supplemented by text from several German newspapers (in English).

A Concrete Curtain: The Life and Death of the Berlin Wall

www.wall-berlin.org/gb/berlin.htm

A virtual exhibit to commemorate the tenth anniversary of the fall of the Berlin Wall with links to further readings.

Post-Soviet Russia: Library and Internet Resources

www.libraries.wright.edu/libnet/subj/pol/pls460.html

A research guide to post–Soviet Russian library and Internet resources sponsored by the Wright State University libraries.

Ethnic Conflict and Nationalism

International Helsinki Federation for Human Rights

www.ihf-hr.org/

Official Website of the International Helsinki Federation for Human Rights, a nonprofit organization. This site is useful as a resource for the latest developments in the Balkans and in Chechnya from a human rights activist perspective.

Physicians for Human Rights: Chechnya Resources

www.phrusa.org/research/chechnya/chech_resources.html

Part of the Physicians for Human Rights official Web page with links devoted to the conflict on Chechnya, including current newspaper and journal articles.

Bosnia HomePage at Caltech

www.its.caltech.edu/~bosnia/

This site provides links to essays and documents on the history of the disintegration of Yugoslavia and subsequent developments in the region.

Bosnia and Herzegovina Web Links

www.usip.org/library/regions/bosnia.html

The United States Institute of Peace provides links to Web resources on the Balkan conflict and its resolution.

The West in the Global Community

History of European Integration Site

www.let.leidenuniv.nl/history/rtg/res1

This site provides primary source materials and bibliographies of the history of European integration. It also includes links to statistical data relating to the European Union and its organizations. It provides annotated links to the broader theme of Cold War history.

The New Europe@nationalgeographic.com

magma.nationalgeographic.com/ngm/0201/feature3/

This National Geographic feature on the New Europe includes articles, multimedia resources, and a downloadable map, as well as links to related sites.

The Terrorism Research Center

www.terrorism.com/index.shtml

The home page of the Terrorism Research Center. The site provides essays, documents, and links to additional materials on terrorism and political violence.

SUGGESTIONS FOR FURTHER READING

The End of the Cold War and the Emergence of a New Europe

Timothy Garton Ash, *In Europe's Name: Germany and the Divided Continent* (London: Jonathan Cape, 1993). An original and complex thesis that looks at German reunification from its origins in the 1970s.

Archie Brown, *The Gorbachev Factor* (New York: Oxford University Press, 1996). Traces Gorbachev's career and examines in detail his attempts to convert the Soviet Union into a social democratic variant of socialism.

Geoffrey Hosking, *The Awakening of the Soviet Union* (Cambridge, MA: Harvard University Press, 1990). Published in the midst of the dramatic changes taking place in the Soviet Union, this study emphasizes the social bases of reform and the challenges to Soviet leadership.

Michael Ignatieff, *Blood and Belonging: Journeys into the New Nationalism* (Toronto: Viking Press, 1993). A companion to a BBC television series, the volume provides a sophisticated exploration of expressions of nationalism throughout Europe.

Walter Laqueur, *The Dream That Failed: Reflections on the Soviet Union* (New York: Oxford University Press, 1994). This work recognizes the tenuous hold of capitalism in Russia and the possibility of a Communist party return.

Martin Malia, *The Soviet Tragedy: A History of Socialism in Russia, 1917–1991* (New York: Maxwell Macmillan International, 1994). A reevaluation of the failure of communism by a leading Russian historian.

Adam Michnik, *Letters from Freedom: Post–Cold War Realities and Perspectives* (Berkeley: University of California Press, 1998). Michnik, a journalist, politician, and writer imprisoned for his political views in the 1980s, is widely regarded as a hero in Poland today. This volume includes his articles, speeches, and interviews with leading European political figures and addresses the political realities of Europe after the end of the Cold War.

Joseph Rothschild, *Return to Diversity: A Political History of East Central Europe* (New York: Oxford University Press, 1989). A historical and analytical survey of Poland, Czechoslovakia, Hungary, Yugoslavia, Romania, Bulgaria, and Albania that appeared just before the great changes that swept through eastern Europe in 1989. Rothschild highlights the tensions between nationalist aspirations and Communist rule.

Henry Ashby Turner, Jr., *The Two Germanies Since 1945* (New Haven, CT: Yale University Press, 1987). A political history of the postwar division of Germany until 1987 that bridges a period the author contends was one of increasing involvement and underlying mutual interests between the two nations.

Ethnic Conflict and Nationalism

Richard Holbrooke, *To End a War* (New York: The Modern Library, 1998). The author offers a firsthand account of the intense diplomatic negotiations surrounding the Dayton Accords and a clear understanding of the problems plaguing Bosnia.

Tim Judah, *Kosovo: War and Revenge* (New Haven, CT: Yale University Press, 2000). Based on careful research, the author analyzes "the last great European war of the twentieth century."

Noël Malcolm, *Kosovo: A Short History* (New York: Harper Collins, 1999). The author is a historian who traces Kosovo's history to medieval times and challenges myths and debates about national origins.

Julie A. Mertus, *Kosovo: How Myths and Truths Started a War* (Berkeley: University of California Press, 1999). Having spent two years in Kosovo interviewing people affected by the conflict, the author is able to offer an understanding from the perspective of the victims of what is happening there.

Michael A. Sells, *The Bridge Betrayed* (Berkeley: The University of California Press, 1996). The author stresses the role of religious nationalists, Serbian Orthodox and Croatian Roman Catholic, in waging a holy war resulting in genocide and destruction.

Susan L. Woodward, *Balkan Tragedy: Chaos and Dissolution After the Cold War* (Washington, DC: The Brookings Institution, 1995). This important study explains, in terms of the breakdown of political and civil order, why Yugoslavia disintegrated into ethnic hatreds so rapidly after 1989.

The West in the Global Community

Michael Emerson et al., *The Economics of 1992: The E.C. Commission's Assessment of the Economic Effects of Completing the Internal Market* (Oxford: Oxford University Press, 1988). A work replete with empirical data that give a comprehensive assessment of the potential impact of establishing a single internal market in the European Economic Community.

Mark Juergensmeyer, *The New Cold War? Religious Nationalism Confronts the Secular State* (Berkeley: The University of California Press, 1994). The author examines the growing significance of religious nationalism from a global perspective.

Geir Lundestad, *"Empire" by Integration* (New York: Oxford University Press, 1998). Provides a comprehensive overview of U.S. policy toward European integration.

Wolfgang Mommsen and Gerhard Hirschfeld, eds., *Social Protest, Violence and Terror in Nineteenth- and Twentieth-Century Europe* (London: Macmillan, 1982). Places terrorism within a historical context in Europe over the last century and a half in a series of articles that takes a national case-history approach.

Richard E. Rubinstein, *Alchemists of Revolution: Terrorism in the Modern World* (New York: Basic Books, 1987). Examines the local root causes of terrorism in historical perspective and argues that terrorism is the social and moral crisis of a disaffected intelligentsia.

For a list of additional titles related to this chapter's topics, please see http://www.ablongman.com/kishlansky.

GLOSSARY

CREDITS

INDEX

MAP OF EUROPE

GLOSSARY

absolutism Government in which power was consolidated in the hands of a divinely ordained monarch; typified by reverence for the monarch, weakening of representative institutions, and expansion of military.

agricultural revolution Changes in the traditional agricultural system during the eighteenth century that included enclosure, introduction of fodder crops, intensified animal husbandry, and commercial market orientation.

alchemy Study of metals in an effort to find their essence through purification. Medieval alchemists attempted to find precious metals such as silver and gold as the essence of base metals such as lead and iron.

Allies In World War I, the United States, Great Britain, France, and Russia—the alliance that opposed and defeated the Central Powers of Germany and Austria-Hungary and their allies.

Anabaptists Part of the radical Reformation, Protestant groups that varied in belief but agreed on the principle of adult baptism.

anarchism A political movement based on rejection of extant political systems; most prominent in less industrialized Western nations.

anti-Semitism Hostility toward and discrimination against Jews.

appeasement British policy of making concessions to Germany in the 1930s in order to avoid war. It allowed Hitler to militarize the Sudetenland and eventually take all of Czechoslovakia.

April Theses Lenin's promise to the Russian people and challenge to the Provisional Government to provide peace, land, and bread. These three issues became the rallying cries for the second Russian revolution and for the withdrawal of Soviet Russia from World War I.

Arians During the early Christological controversies, followers of the Alexandrine theologian, Arius, who believed that Jesus was not equal to God the Father.

Axis Powers In World War II, the alliance of Germany, Italy, and later Japan.

balance of power Distribution of power among nations in alliances so that any one nation is prevented from dominating the others.

Balfour Declaration The commitment by the British government issued in 1917 to support a Jewish homeland in Palestine.

Berlin Wall Barrier built by East Germany in 1961 to halt an exodus of skilled professionals to the West; opened in 1989 as a prelude to the reunification of East and West Germany.

Big Three The British, Soviet, and U.S. leaders who coordinated defeat of Germany and Japan in World War II and negotiated postwar settlements. Referred to Churchill, Stalin, and Roosevelt until 1945; Attlee, Stalin, and Truman by summer 1945.

Black Death The virulent combination of bubonic, septicemic, and pneumonic plagues that destroyed between one third and one half of the population of Europe between 1347 and 1352.

blitzkrieg "Lightning war"; the rapid advance accompanied by armored vehicles that typified the German military during World War II.

Bolsheviks Radical faction of Marxist Social Democrats following a political theory based on necessity of violent revolution. The Bolsheviks came to power with Lenin in November 1917.

bourgeoisie A French term referring to the commercial classes of Europe after the seventeenth century; primarily an urban class.

Brezhnev Doctrine Policy of Soviet leader Leonid Brezhnev that approved the use of military intervention in the internal affairs of Soviet allies to prevent counterrevolution.

broad-spectrum gathering A technique of subsistence common in the Neolithic era that preceded permanent settlement in one place and relied on the exploitation of many seasonal sources of food over a limited area.

cahiers de doléances Lists of grievances sent with representatives to the French Estates-General in 1789; demonstrated the existence of a widespread public political culture in France.

caliph The successors of Muhammad who served as political and religious leaders of the Islamic world (see Umma).

capitularies The written instructions for the implementation of royal directives at the local level produced by the clerics of the Carolingian court.

caravels Small Portuguese ships developed in the fifteenth century that were ideal for ocean travel.

Carnival One of the traditional sixteenth-century festivals, the feasts and carousing of which preceded the onset of Lent.

Carolingian Renaissance The cultural revival of classical learning sponsored by the emperor Charlemagne. New schools and the copying of manuscripts were among its important achievements.

cartels Combinations of firms in a given industry to fix prices and establish production quotas.

Cartesianism Philosophy of René Descartes that rested on the dual existence of mind and matter, a principle that enabled the use of skepticism to create certainty.

Central Powers Germany and Austria-Hungary during World War I.

chartism An English working-class reform movement that flourished in the 1830s and 1840s and that demanded universal male suffrage (right to vote), payment for parliamentary service, equal electoral districts, and secret ballots.

chivalry The ideals of knighthood, most notably fighting, that spread from northern France across Europe in the High Middle Ages.

Christian humanism The application of the principles of humanistic education, particularly philology, to the documents of Christianity. It resulted in a program of reform through better education.

Christological controversies The debate about the Christian Trinity (Father, Son, and Holy Spirit) and the relationship between humanity and divinity within it. It caused great division and conflict in the Church and society from the third to the fifth centuries.

city-states Self-governing political units centered upon an urban area. During the fifteenth and sixteenth centuries, city-states took on various forms of government, including republics such as Venice and oligarchies such as Milan.

civic humanism The use of humanistic training and education in the service of the state. Many humanists became advisors to princes or republican governments, holding high office and helping to establish policy.

Cold War The diplomatic and ideological confrontation between the Soviet Union and the United States that began in the aftermath of World War II, dividing the world into two armed camps.

collectivization Soviet plan under Stalin to create large communal state farms to replace private farms owned by peasants.

coloni Tenant farmers who worked on the estates of wealthy landowners in the Roman Empire.

colonization Process by which colonies, or new settlements with links to a parent state, are established.

Columbian Exchange The transfer of microbes, animals, and plants in the encounters between Europeans and Native Americans during the age of exploration.

Comecon The Council for Mutual Economic Assistance established in 1949 with bilateral agreements between the Soviet Union and eastern European states. Comecon was Stalin's response to the U.S. Marshall Plan in western Europe, but rather than providing aid it sought to integrate and control the economies of eastern Europe for Soviet gain.

Communist Manifesto, The A call to arms written in 1848 by Karl Marx and Frederich Engels in which they defined in general terms the class struggle in industrializing Europe.

conciliarism The movement proposed by church lawyers in which only a general council of bishops could end the Great Schism.

condottiere A mercenary military leader who sold his services and that of his private army to the highest bidder; used in the wars between the Italian city-states.

Congress of Vienna A meeting of European powers after the Napoleonic wars in 1815; established a balance of power to preserve the status quo in post-revolutionary Europe.

conquistadores "Conquerors." Spanish adventurers who led the conquests in the Americas in the sixteenth century.

conscription Compulsory service of citizens in the army. France was the first modern state to enforce conscription. The ability to draft all able-bodied men was a key component in the Revolutionary and Napoleonic wars.

conservatism Nineteenth-century ideology that favored tradition and stability and only gradual, or "organic," growth and change.

containment Cold War policy of resisting the spread of Soviet communism.

Continental System The economic boycott of England by Napoleon during the wars beginning in 1803.

Counter-Reformation Catholic response to repel Protestantism.

Crusades Religious wars of conquest directed against non-Christians and heretics in the eleventh through the thirteenth centuries.

Crystal Palace Exhibition This international exhibition, held in London in 1851 in a specially built see-through exhibition hall, featured the greatest technological advances of the day and served as a spur for further industrialization.

culture Those shared beliefs, values, customs, and practices that humans transmit from generation to generation through learning.

cuneiform A form of writing from Mesopotamia characterized by wedge-shaped symbols pressed into wet clay tablets to record words.

Cycladic culture The artistically and economically sophisticated culture which flourished on islands in the Aegean Sea during the early and middle Greek Bronze Age (3000–1500 BCE).

Cynics Followers of a Hellenistic Greek philosophy that rejected the world as the source of evil and unhappiness and advocated the reduction of possessions, connections, and pleasures to the absolute minimum.

Declaratory Act A statute enacted in England in 1766 that stated that Parliament held sovereign jurisdiction over the North American colonies.

decolonization Withdrawal of Western nations from colonies in Africa and Asia after World War II.

decurions Members of the city councils in the Roman Empire. Initially, they were the backbone of the provincial elite but by the third and fourth centuries were crippled by their personal responsibility for provincial taxes.

deists Those who believed that God created the universe but then did not intervene in its operation.

Delian League League of Greek cities formed to drive out the Persian invaders. Its leader, Athens, turned it into its own empire.

demesne Land kept by a medieval lord for his direct profit and worked a specified number of days each week by his peasants.

democracy Form of government in which the citizens choose their leaders; began in Athens, Greece, in the fifth century B.C.E.

de-Stalinization Process initiated by Nikita Khrushchev beginning in 1956 that reversed many of Stalin's repressive policies in the Soviet Union.

détente From the French word meaning a relaxation in tension, cooperation between the two superpowers, the Soviet Union and the United States. This policy was characterized by improved U.S.-Soviet diplomatic relationships in the 1970s to lessen the possibility of nuclear war.

dictator In the Roman Republic, an official who was granted unlimited power to rule the state for a period up to six months in a time of emergency. Sulla and Caesar both used the dictatorship for political ends.

diplomas The records of royal grants and decisions produced by clerics in medieval courts.

divine rights of kings Political theory that held that the institution of monarchy had divine origin and that the monarch functioned as God's representative on earth.

doge Chief magistrate of the Venetian Republic who served for life.

Eastern Question The "question" posed by the Great Powers about the future of the Ottoman territories.

Edict of Nantes The proclamation by Henry IV of France granting limited toleration to Huguenots.

ekklesia The assembly of all free male Athenian citizens.

emirs Local military commanders who took control of provincial administration in the Islamic world at the expense of the caliphs by the tenth century.

empiricism The philosophy propounded by Aristotle which rejected Plato's idea of abstract Forms in favor of practical observation and explanation, building general theories from particular data.

enclosure In the eighteenth century, the closing off of common and public land within the open field system to foster private landholding.

Enlightenment Philosophical and intellectual movement that began in Europe during the eighteenth century. The movement was characterized by a wave of new learning, especially in the sciences and mathematics, and the application of reason to solve society's problems.

entrepôt A place where goods were brought for storage before being exchanged; a commercial concept originated by the Dutch.

Epicureans Those who adhered to a Hellenistic Greek philosophy that the world was a random collection of atoms (atheistic and materialistic), and that one must pursue pleasure, but only in moderation as excess causes pain.

equestrians In the early Roman Republic, the equestrians were one of the richest classes in the Roman army, those who could afford to maintain a horse. By the late republic, their role expanded into banking and commerce.

Estates-General An official body assembled periodically by the medieval French state, consisting of representatives from three separate groups or "estates": those who prayed (the Church), those who fought (the aristocracy), and those who worked (commoners). Long in disuse by the monarch, it was convened by Louis XVI in 1789.

ethnic cleansing Term introduced in the Balkan war of the 1990s to describe the systematic killing and forcible removal of one ethnic group by another.

ethnos Large rural territorial units in the Dark Age and Archaic Greece focused around a central religious sanctuary and dominated by a local oligarchy, such as in Aetolia.

Etruscans Peoples native to Italy who influenced the formation of the Roman state.

eugenics An ersatz scientific theory that promoted the improvement of the human race through selective breeding.

eunomia The good order and obedience to the law which was the ideal of Sparta's militaristic society.

euro Common currency of the European Union; accepted as common currency by all members of the European Union except the United Kingdom.

European Economic Community (EEC) Formed in 1957 by Belgium, the Netherlands, Luxembourg, Italy, France, and West Germany to provide a single, integrated European market. Also known as the Common Market.

European Union (EU) Formed in 1992 to succeed the European Community in terms of economic integration; members share defensive, social, and economic policies as well.

extraterritoriality Exempted all foreigners in China from Chinese legal jurisdiction; practiced within foreign "spheres of influence" in China.

Fabians Members of a late nineteenth-century socialist movement in Britain who advocated gradual reform rather than revolution and supported the Labour party.

Factory Act (1833) British Parliamentary legislation that prohibited factory work by children under age nine, provided two hours of daily education for factory children, and limited labor for adults to twelve hours each day.

fascism Rooted in mass politics of the late-nineteenth century, a totalitarian political system that glorifies the state and subordinates the individual to the state's needs. First emerging in Italy after World War I, fascism appeared in virtually all European countries, but particularly Germany.

feudalism Anachronistic term used by early modern lawyers to describe medieval relations of vassalage.

fief A parcel of productive land along with the serfs and privileges attached to it granted by a lord to a knightly follower (vassal) in return for loyalty and military service.

Final Solution The term used by the Third Reich to refer to the extermination of all people deemed unfit; resulted in the execution of 11 million men, women, and children, 6 million of them Jews.

first triumvirate Political alliance between Pompey, Crassus, and Caesar to share power in the Roman Republic.

fodder crops Crops that were grown not for human consumption but to improve the nutrients in the soil. Some, such as turnips, were also used as animal feed.

Forms In Plato's philosophy, the perfect ideal that underlies all worldly objects. In recollecting them from one's previous existence one communes with all that is good, true, and beautiful.

Fourteen Points U.S. President Woodrow Wilson's idealistic set of guidelines drawn up as part of the peace process whose goal was to create a lasting peace after World War I.

French wars of religion Violent clashes between French Catholics and Calvinists (Huguenots) from 1562–1598.

Fronde An aristocratic revolution in France beginning in 1648 during the minority of Louis XIV, which was initiated by the tax policies of the minority government under Cardinal Mazarin.

futurists Artists and intellectuals of the late nineteenth and early twentieth century who wished to create a new culture free from traditional Western civilization. Futurists lionized technology, the masses, violence, and upheaval.

generation gap The baby boom following World War II resulted in a generation that came of age in the 1960s. The gap refers to the divergence in values between a large cohort of adolescents and young adults and their parents that resulted in more liberal values and socio-cultural mores.

geopolitics Politics of geography; based on recognition that certain areas of the world are valuable for political reasons.

Girondins French revolutionary faction that was more moderate than the Jacobins.

glasnost A Russian term meaning openness; one of the programs of reform initiated by Mikhail Gorbachev in the 1980s.

Glorious Revolution Change of government in England in 1688–1689 when the Catholic monarch James II was replaced by the Dutch ruler William of Orange. Called "glorious" because it supposedly was accomplished without bloodshed.

Gnostics An early Christian group that interpreted scripture as gnosis, or secret wisdom, and believed that Jesus had no human element. They were opposed by many bishops.

Golden Bull The edict of emperor Charles IV in 1356 recognizing that German princes and kings were autonomous rulers.

Great Chain of Being A hierarchic model of social organization common in the fifteenth and sixteenth centuries in which all parts of creation held a specific place in a divinely ordered universe.

Great Depression Devastation of the global economy that began in 1929 with the U.S. stock market crash and lasted through the 1930s.

Great Purge A series of executions between 1934 and 1938 in the Soviet Union that removed all of Joseph Stalin's political enemies.

Great Reform Bill of 1832 An extension of the right to vote in England to men of the middle class that resulted in a 50 percent increase in those eligible to vote.

Great Schism The conflict (1378–1415) between two sets of rival popes based in Rome and Avignon that divided the loyalties of states and individuals across Europe.

guilds Professional associations of merchants or artisans that offer protection of members and regulation of a particular trade or craft.

hadith The written form of the Sunnah, practices established by the prophet Muhammad that guide the interpretation of the Qur'an.

Hanseatic League A commercial and political alliance of northern German towns established in the late fourteenth century to monopolize the grain and fish trade of the Baltic Sea.

Hijra In early Islam, the journey undertaken by Muhammad from Mecca to Medina in 622 in order to govern Medina and calm its internal political dissension.

holocaust During World War II, mass extermination of Jews by the Nazis under Adolph Hitler.

Holy Alliance Prussia, Austria, and Russia, under the leadership of tsar Alexander I, agreed to protect the peace and the Christian religion following the Congress of Vienna.

honestiores The privileged classes of the later Roman Empire: senators, municipal gentry, and the military.

hoplites In Archaic Greece, armed infantry soldiers.

Huguenots French Calvinists led by Henry of Navarre. Huguenots were victims of the St. Bartholomew's Day Massacre, a slaughter of numerous Protestants in Paris in 1572 during the French wars of religion.

humanists Scholars who studied and taught the humanities, the skills of disciplines like philology—the art of language—and rhetoric—the art of expression; concentrated on ancient texts.

humiliores The lower classes of the later Roman Empire whose status declined from the period of the *Pax Romana* and who suffered disproportionately from the tax increases of the period.

Hundred Years' War A series of military engagements between England and France (1337–1452) over territorial and dynastic rivalries.

Hussites Followers of Jan Hus who attacked the sale of indulgences and German political dominance in the kingdom of Bohemia. After his execution, they led a partially successful revolt.

iconoclasts Breakers of icons; opponents of the mediating use of icons (religious images) in worship. Most emperors supported this faction in eighth- and early ninth-century Byzantium.

iconodules Venerators of icons; the ecclesiastical faction that resisted the iconoclasts. Most of the people and lesser clergy were iconodules.

icons Sacred images.

imperium The powers conferred on magistrates by the Roman people: the supreme power to command, to execute the law, and to impose the death penalty.

indulgences Remission of temporal punishment in Purgatory due to one's sins. Originally granted for performing pious acts, but later acquired through a grant to the church treasury. In the sixteenth century, indulgences were sold to raise money for the papacy; a critical issue in the Lutheran reform.

industrialization Process by which production becomes mechanized.

Industrial Revolution Sustained period of economic growth and change brought on by technological innovations in the process of manufacturing; began in Britain in the mid-eighteenth century.

intendants Officials appointed by the central government in France to oversee the local administration of the regional aristocracy; a critical component of the centralization of the French state.

iron curtain The term coined by former British Prime Minister Winston Churchill to describe the ideological divide between western and eastern Europe after World War II.

Jacobins One of the political factions of the French National Convention that seized the initiative provided by the sans-culottes to take control of the radical revolution in the late eighteenth century; led by Maximilien Robespierre.

Jacquerie The revolt of French peasants against the aristocracy and crown in 1358. It was part of the struggle for rights caused by the labor shortage after the Black Death.

jihads Holy wars waged by Muslims against their religious enemies.

jingoism Use of public opinion to stir support for one's own nation and hatred for another nation; used extensively by political leaders to justify imperial expansion.

joint-stock companies Business enterprises that raise capital by selling shares to individuals who receive dividends on their investments.

kouros Nude statues of young men that were a common subject in Archaic art. The stiff posture demonstrates the influence of Egyptian sculpture.

Kristallnacht "Crystal night" in German; refers to the night of 9 November 1938 when mobs directed by the Nazis destroyed the homes, businesses, and synagogues of German Jews.

Kulturkampf "Struggle for civilization"; legislation of the German Empire against the Catholic Church in the 1870s.

laissez-faire An economic theory that required government to cease interference with private economic activity; Adam Smith and the Physiocrats were its leading proponents.

latifundia The vast rural estates of the Roman patricians which were worked by slaves or free but dependent tenant farmers.

lay investiture The practice by which kings and emperors appointed bishops and invested them with the symbols of their office. It led to conflict between the Papacy and the emperors in the eleventh century.

Lebensraum "Living room"; one of Hitler's foreign policy objectives to extend the borders of Germany in eastern and central Europe.

lectio divina In monastic life, the process of reading and studying the Old and New Testaments that formed an important part of each day's activities.

liberalism A political philosophy based on freedom of the individual and the corruptibility of authority; associated with constitutional reform in the first half of the nineteenth century.

Linear B A syllabic form of writing from the late Greek Bronze Age which preserves the earliest known form of Greek. It was used by Mycenaean elites almost entirely for record-keeping.

linear perspective A technique developed in painting to give a flat surface the appearance of depth and dimension.

Long Parliament An English Parliament that officially met from 1640 to 1653. It forced reforms under Charles I, defeated the royal armies during the English Civil War, and tried and executed the king.

maat In Egyptian thought, the ideal state of the universe and of society which the pharaoh was supposed to uphold.

Magna Carta The "great charter" limiting royal power that King John was forced to sign in 1215.

manses Farms worked by slaves, serfs, and freemen in the Middle Ages.

Marchfield The assembly of all free warriors in the early Germanic kingdoms in which the king's authority was all-powerful.

Marshall Plan The U.S. economic aid program for European countries after World War II; intended to establish U.S. economic influence in European markets.

mercantilism A popular state economy of the seventeenth century; involved bullionism, protective tariffs, and monopolies.

metics The non-Athenian residents of Athens who comprised about half of the free population of the city. They were active in commerce and banking.

Minoan civilization The culture of Crete in the Middle Bronze Age (2000–1550 B.C.E.) in which elites based at great palaces, such as Knossos, dominated the island politically, economically, and religiously.

minuscule New style of handwriting developed in the Carolingian Renaissance to preserve texts; later adopted as standard script.

Mishnah In Jewish law, the oral interpretation of the Torah (scripture) which was developed by the Pharisees and later developed into an extensive written body of legal interpretation.

missi dominici Teams of counts and bishops that examined the state of each county in the Carolingian Empire on behalf of the king.

monasticism The life of monks devoted to God, from the fourth century onwards, either as part of communal organization or in solitary life. Monasticism began in Egypt as a rejection of the worldliness of civilization.

monopoly Exclusive control of a market or industry; a form of economic regulation in which special privileges are granted in return for financial considerations and an agreement to abide by the rules set out by the state.

Museum The shrine to the Muses in Hellenistic Alexandria to which was added the Library containing all the great works of Greek literature and learning.

Mycenaean Late Greek Bronze Age civilization that arose ca. 1600 B.C.E. at Mycenae and that encompassed the Greek mainland and parts of Asia Minor. Myceneans developed the Linear B script.

mystery cults Religions that promised immediate, personal contact with a deity that would bring immortality.

Napoleonic Code The recodification of French law carried out during Napoleon's reign.

nationalities problem The existence of numerous ethnic minorities within the borders of the Soviet Union leading to demands for self-determination and political independence.

natural selection A theory advanced by Charles Darwin that accounted for evolution of species; a realist scientific approach.

Navigation Acts English economic legislation providing that colonial goods could only be shipped in English ships.

Nazism National Socialism; German variant of fascism.

Neolithic era The New Stone Age (8000–6500 B.C.E.) in which modern man developed agriculture and the first villages.

Neoplatonism Use of the writings of Plato to advance modern ideas about science, particularly mathematics and the health sciences.

New Economic Policy (NEP) A state-planned economic policy in the Soviet Union between 1921 and 1928; based on agricultural productivity, it required set payments from peasants; surpluses could be sold on the free market.

new imperialism Imperialism practiced by European countries after 1870 that was, in essence, the domination by industrial powers over the non-industrial world. Distinguished from the earlier acquisition of territory, new imperialism took a variety of forms including territorial occupations, colonization, exploitation of labor and raw materials, and development of economic spheres of influence.

New Monarchies The more centralized European governments of western Europe created in the fifteenth and sixteenth centuries.

New Piety An aspect of the Roman Catholic reform movement; originated among the Brethren of the Common Life with an emphasis on simplicity and more personalized religious practice.

nominalism The doctrine of William of Ockham that argued that human reason could not aspire to certain truth.

North Atlantic Treaty Organization (NATO) An organization founded in 1949 the members of which signed a defense pact to protect those countries bordering the North Atlantic.

nuclear club The group of nations in possession of atomic weapons, originally consisting of the United States and the Soviet Union. By 1974, the nuclear club included Great Britain, France, the People's Republic of China, and India.

Old Regime The old order; political and social system of France in the eighteenth century before the French Revolution.

oligarchy Government by an elite few.

optimates The traditionalist Roman political faction that succeeded the Gracchi and sought to preserve the senatorial oligarchy against the populares.

Orthodox Christianity The official "right-teaching" faith of Constantinople as opposed to the heterodox peoples on the margins of the Byzantine Empire.

ostracism A practice in Athenian democracy by which anyone deemed to threaten the constitution could, by popular vote, be exiled for ten years without the loss of property.

Paleolithic era The Old Stone Age (600,000–10,000 B.C.E.) in which advanced primates developed into Neanderthals and also modern man. They hunted food or collected it by gathering.

Paris Commune Created in 1871 in the aftermath of the Franco-Prussian War; crushed by the national army after a brief struggle; symbol of revolution for radical politicians, including Marxists.

parlements Provincial courts in France; the Parlement of Paris, the main law court of the state, was the most powerful of these.

parties A form of political organization in which members of the British parliament divided into groups with identifiable interests. Whigs and Tories were the first political parties.

Patent of Toleration An edict of Joseph II of Austria in 1781 that granted freedom of worship to Protestants and members of the Greek Orthodox Church, in addition to Roman Catholics.

paterfamilias The male head of household in the Roman family. His power was absolute, including the power of life and death.

patricians Leaders of the gentes, or clans, in early Roman society.

Pax Romana The two centuries of peace and stability in the early Roman Empire inaugurated by the emperor Augustus.

perestroika A Russian term meaning restructuring; part of Mikhail Gorbachev's attempts to reform the Soviet government and economy in the 1980s.

Peterloo Massacre In August 1819, the English army troops policing a political crowd gathered near Manchester, England, lost control resulting in the deaths of 11 and the injury of hundreds of others.

phalanx A tightly ordered and well-disciplined body of elite Greek warriors in heavy armor that attacked in close formation with long spears.

philology The art of language; one of the most important aspects of humanist studies, based on models of ancient texts.

philosophes A French term for the intellectuals of the eighteenth-century Enlightenment. Voltaire, Diderot, and Condorcet were leading philosophes.

Physiocrats A group of French thinkers who subscribed to the view that land was wealth and thus argued that improvements in agricultural activity should take first priority in state reforms.

pictograms The earliest form of writing in Mesopotamia, ca. 3500 B.C.E., in which pictures represented particular objects, such as animals.

Pietà A painting or sculpture of Mary mourning the dead Jesus. The most famous was carved by Michelangelo and is in St. Peter's Basilica.

plebs Families not organized into gentes, or clans, in early Roman society. The lower classes.

pogroms State-organized massacres of Jews.

polis The city-state of Archaic and Classical Greece, particularly found on the shores of the Aegean. A city formed the center of government (tyranny, oligarchy, or democracy) and of religious life with temples on its citadel (Acropolis).

politiques During the sixteenth-century French wars of religion, a group of Catholics who joined with Huguenots to demand a practical settlement of the wars.

populares The Roman political faction that succeeded the Gracchi whose leaders appealed to the masses as a source of power.

Popular Front Socialist governments established in both France and Spain in the 1930s; the French version failed to solve the Depression and was voted out of office; the creation of a socialist republic in Spain initiated a civil war.

Pragmatic Sanction The document that attempted to secure the recognition of Maria Theresa as heiress to the Habsburg possessions of Charles VI.

Prague Spring Popular uprising and reform movement in 1968 Czechoslovakia, ended by Soviet invasion in August 1968.

predestination A fundamental principle of Calvin's theology: the belief that all Christians are predestined to either heaven or hell from the act of creation.

presbyters The priests of the early Christian tradition who were subordinated to bishops as hierarchy developed in the Church.

Price Revolution The dramatic price inflation of the fifteenth and sixteenth centuries; caused by monetary debasement and the influx of bullion from the New World.

princeps "First citizen"; the title assumed by the emperor Augustus to reassure public opinion by preserving the traditional constitutional forms.

Proclamation of the German Empire The creation in 1871 of the nation-state of Germany by uniting the 38 German states into a single national entity.

proletariat The industrial working class.

pronatalism State programs implemented after the Second World War to encourage women to have larger families.

Puritans English Protestants who sought to purify the Church of England of all traces of Catholicism.

putting-out system Mobilization of the rural labor force for commercial production of large quantities of manufactured goods; raw materials put out to homes of workers where manufacture took place.

quadrivium Part of a medieval liberal arts education that included arithmetic, geometry, astronomy, and music.

Quadruple Alliance Pact signed in 1815 by the four powers who defeated Napoleon—Great Britain, Austria, Russia, and Prussia—for the purpose of protecting Europe against future French aggression.

quinine An important nineteenth-century medical advance derived from cinchona that was an effective treatment for malaria; it permitted large numbers of Europeans to travel without risking death and disease.

raison d'état Reason of state; placing the needs of the nation above the privileges of its most important groups.

realism An artistic and literary style that criticized industrialized society and rejected bourgeois concepts of morality.

Realpolitik Pragmatic political theory advanced by Otto von Bismarck; ruthless pursuit by any means, including illegal and violent ones, in the interests of the state.

reconquista The Christian reconquest of the Iberian peninsula from the Spanish Muslims or Moors; completed in 1492 under Ferdinand and Isabella.

Reformation A movement to reform and purify the Catholic Church that resulted in the creation of new religious denominations in Europe collectively known as Protestants.

Reichstag The national legislative body of the German Empire; elected by universal male suffrage.

Reign of Terror The period from 1793 to 1794 when Maximilien Robespierre assumed leadership of the Committee of Public Safety and oversaw the revolutionary tribunals that sentenced about 40,000 people to execution.

Renaissance A "rebirth" of classical learning and emphasis on humanity that characterized the period between 1350 and 1550.

revisionism A German socialist school that favored gradual reform through the parliamentary system; led by Edouard Bernstein.

rhetoric The art of expression and persuasion.

Risorgimento The nineteenth-century movement to reunite Italy.

robot Labor service that peasants owed to their lord; more typical in eastern Europe after the fifteenth century.

romanticism An artistic and literary tradition based on emotions rather than the intellect; rejection of classical traditions in favor of "nature"; often associated with nationalism.

salons Informal social gatherings during the Enlightenment, frequently organized by women, in which topics of intellectual interest were discussed.

samizdat Self-published, privately circulated manuscripts; chief vehicle for circulating information among dissidents in the Soviet Union.

sans-culottes Literally "those without knee-breeches"; working-class revolutionaries who initiated the radical stage of the French revolution in 1792.

Schlieffen Plan The strategy of the German high command at the outset of World War I, predicated on knocking France out of the war.

Scholastic method The combination of legal analysis from the new university at Bologna with Aristotelian logic; established by Peter Abelard in the twelfth century.

scientific revolution In the sixteenth and seventeenth centuries, a period of new scientific inquiry, experimentation, and discovery that resulted in a new understanding of the universe based on mathematical principles and led to the creation of the modern sciences, particularly astronomy and physics.

scramble for Africa The colonization of Africa as part of the new imperialism. This domination of Africa by Germany, Britain, and France ended with the crisis at Fashoda.

second triumvirate Alliance of Octavian, Mark Anthony, and Lepidus following the assassination of Julius Caesar to defeat the assassins and control the Roman Empire.

seigneur Manor lord responsible for maintaining order, administering justice, and arbitrating disputes among tenants.

serfs Peasants of degraded status and very limited legal rights who were dependent on the lords in the High Middle Ages. They formed the great bulk of the population.

Shi'ites Muslims who follow the tradition that legitimate leadership of Islam can only come through the descendants of 'Ali, whom they regard as the last orthodox caliph.

social Darwinists Those who applied the theory of evolutionary biology, particularly the concept of "survival of the fittest," to human society.

sola fide A fundamental principle of Luther's theology: justification of Christians by faith alone.

sola scriptura By the word alone; emphasis on scriptural authority in preference to the canons of the Church, a fundamental element of Luther's theology.

Solidarity A non-communist Polish labor organization founded by Lech Walesa in the Gdansk shipbuilding yards; legalized in 1989 as a political movement, it won a victory in the first Polish democratic elections.

Sophists Professional teachers in fifth-century Greece who traveled from city to city instructing students, for a fee, in rhetoric, the art of persuasion.

soviets Councils of workers in Russia formed after 1905 that became one center of power after the overthrow of the tsar; source of power for Lenin and Bolsheviks.

Spanish Armada The Spanish fleet sent in 1588 to transport troops from the Low Countries for an invasion of England; defeated by the English fleets of Elizabeth I.

Spanish Inquisition An ecclesiastical tribunal utilized to combat heresy and non-Christians; used by Ferdinand and Isabella against the conversos, or converted Jews of Spain.

spheres of influence Diplomatic term used to connote territorial influence or control of weaker nations not necessarily occupied by the more powerful ones. The term was first used to explain one kind of control of western European powers in the 1800s during African imperialism, and was later used to describe European and Japanese territorial control and influence over markets in China at the end of the nineteenth century.

Stoics Followers of the Hellenistic Greek philosophy propounded by Zeno, which teaches that orderliness is proper to the universe and that happiness derives from embracing one's divinely ordained role and unhappiness from rejecting it.

strategoi Generals, the military commanders of themes in the Byzantine Empire. They were responsible for civil and military administration.

suffragettes Militant members of the English feminist movement led by Emmeline Pankhurst who engaged in acts of violence against private property in order to secure the vote.

sunnah In Islamic theology, the practices established by the prophet Muhammad. They were initially preserved by oral tradition.

Sunnis The majority tradition of Islam that accepts that political succession should be based on consensus, the existing political order, and a leader's merits.

synod A meeting of bishops called to debate Church policy, such as that at Whitby in 664, which established the customs of the Roman Church among Angles and Saxons.

Table of Ranks Official state hierarchy in Russia under Peter the Great that established the social position or rank of individuals according to categories of military service, civil service, and ownership of landed estates.

tetrarchy Rule by four; Diocletian's attempt to regulate the suggestion of the Roman Empire by dividing the empire into eastern and western parts, with both an augustus and a junior emperor, or caesar, ruling each part.

Thermidorian Reaction Revolt beginning in July 1794 (the month of Thermidor) against the radicalism of the French Revolution, leading to the downfall and execution of Robespierre and the end of the Reign of Terror.

Third Estate Branch of the French Estates-General consisting of the bourgeoisie and the working classes; separated from the other estates to form the National Assembly in 1789.

Third Reich "The Third Empire"; Hitler's government, established after 1933.

third world The former colonies of European and Asian imperialism; sought to separate themselves from European economic control after independence; operated in the United Nations as a non-aligned bloc.

Thirty Years' War War lasting from 1618–1648.

three-field system An efficient agricultural system in which one-third of the land was planted in autumn with wheat or rye, one-third remained fallow, and one-third was planted in spring with a crop that added nutrients to the soil.

Time of Troubles The period of disruption within Russia following the death of Ivan the Terrible; only ended with the Polish invasion of Russia.

Torah The body of law in Hebrew scripture.

Tories Members of a political party in England that in the seventeenth century defended the principle of hereditary succession to the crown; in opposition to the Whigs. The Tories sought to preserve the traditional political structure and supported the authority of the Anglican church.

total war War that requires mobilization of the civilian population in addition to the military; typified by centralized governments with limits on economy and civil rights.

Treaty of Brest-Litovsk The Treaty between Russia and Germany signed in March 1918 whereby Soviet Russia withdrew from World War I.

Treaty of Tordesillas A 1494 agreement that recognized Portugal's claims to Brazil, but gave all of the remainder of the New World to Spain.

Treaty of Versailles Peace settlement with Germany at the end of World War I; included the War Guilt Clause fixing blame on Germany for the war and requiring massive reparations.

triangular trade A three-way trade system during the seventeenth century involving the shipment of calicoes to Africa for slaves who were transported to the East Indies in exchange for sugar, which was shipped to Europe.

Triple Alliance An alliance founded in 1882 between Germany, Austria-Hungary, and Italy at Germany's instigation for the purpose of securing mutual support on the European continent.

Triple Entente Alliance founded in 1907 between France, Britain, and Russia. With the defection of Russia from the Three Emperors' League, it hemmed in Germany on both eastern and western borders.

trivium The basic education in cathedral schools of the Middle Ages: grammar, rhetoric, and logic.

tyrants Rulers who had seized power illegally. Tyrannies replaced oligarchies in many *poleis* in Archaic Greece, such as at Corinth and Athens. The term did not have the negative connotations it does today, as many tyrants were popular leaders welcomed by their subjects.

Umma The community of all believers in the Islamic faith. Initially, it was both a political and religious supertribe of Arabs.

universitas The guilds of students that formed the first true universities from the twelfth century onwards.

utilitarianism Jeremy Bentham's philosophical plan to ensure social harmony through measurement of pleasure and pain or the greatest happiness of the greatest number; a liberal philosophy.

vassals Knights sworn to fealty or loyalty to a lord; in return the lord granted the vassal a means of support, or fief.

Victorian Compromise The balance between freedom and protectionism achieved by liberal parliamentary reform during the reign of Queen Victoria.

Villanovans Peoples of the first Iron Age culture in Italy (1000–800 B.C.E.), which was based in the north. They made iron tools and weapons and placed the ashes of their dead in large urns.

Warsaw Pact Defensive alliance organization formed in 1955 by Albania, Bulgaria, Romania, Czechoslovakia, Hungary, Poland, East Germany, and the Soviet Union. The alliance served as a strategic buffer zone against NATO forces.

Weimar Republic German government founded at the end of the First World War; used by German general staff as scapegoat for German defeat and harsh peace terms; overthrown in 1933.

welfare state The tendency of post–World War II states to establish safety nets for citizens in areas of birth, sickness, old age, and unemployment.

wergeld In Germanic society, the payment in reparation for crimes in place of blood vengeance. Tribal leaders used it to reduce internal hostilities.

Whigs Members of a political party in England that in the seventeenth century supported the Protestant succession and a broad-based Protestantism and advocated a constitutional monarchy that limited royal power; in opposition to the Tories. The Whigs were later identified with social and parliamentary reform.

zemstvos Local elected assemblies in Russia during the reign of Alexander II; representatives elected by landowners, townspeople, and peasants.

ziggurat Babylonian tiered towers (or step-pyramids) from ca. 2000 B.C.E. that were dedicated to gods and stood near temples. They were among the most important buildings of Babylonian cities.

Zionism A program initiated by Theodor Herzl to establish an independent Jewish state in Palestine.

Zollverein A unified trading zone created by Prussia in which member states adopted the liberal Prussian customs regulations; an attempt to overcome the fragmented nature of the German economy.

Zoroastrianism A monotheistic religion founded by Zoroaster in sixth-century B.C.E. Persia that emphasized the personal choice between good (light) and evil (darkness).

CREDITS

DOCUMENT CREDITS

Introduction

"Hector and Andromache": From *The Iliad of Homer*, translated by Richmond Lattimore. Copyright © 1951 by the University of Chicago. Reprinted by permission of the University of Chicago Press.

"The Two Faces of Athenian Democracy": Excerpts from Thucydides, *History of the Peloponnesian War*, translated by Rex Warner.

"The Twelve Tables": From *Roman Civilization*, Volume I, by Naphtali Lewis and Meyer Reinhold. Copyright © 1951 Columbia University Press. Reprinted by permission of the publisher.

"Peter Announces the Good News": Excerpts from Acts 3:17–26. Scripture quotations are from the Revised Standard Version of the Bible. Copyright 1946, 1952, 1971 by the Division of Christian Education of the National Council of Churches of Christ in the United States of America. Used by permission. All rights reserved.

"Love in the Two Cities": From Saint Augustine, *The City of God*. (Garden City, NY: Image Books, 1958), pp. 321–322. By permission.

"The Qur'an": From the *Qur'an*, sura 2.

"Saint Francis of Assisi on Humility and Poverty": From *The Rule of St. Francis of Assisi*, in E. F. Henderson, ed., Select Historical Documents.

Chapter 10

"The Black Death in Florence": From Boccaccio's *Decameron*.

"A Woman Before the Inquisition": From "Jacques Fournier, Inquisition Records." Original Source: Jean Duvernoy, *Le Registre d'Inquisition de Jacques Fournier* (Paris: Editions de l'Ecole des Hautes Etudes en Sciences Sociales, 1978). Reprinted by permission.

Convivencia: Excerpt from *Las Siete Partidas*, translated by Samuel Parson Scott (Chicago: Published for the Comparative Law Bureau of the American Bar Association by Commerce Clearing House, Inc., 1931).

Chapter 11

"On the Family": From Leon Battista Alberti, "On the Family" in *The Family in Renaissance Florence* by Renee Watkins. Reprinted by permission of Renee Watkins.

"The Renaissance Man": From Giorgio Vasari, "Life of Leonardo da Vinci," in *Lives of the Most Eminent Painters, Sculptors, and Architects*, translated by Gaston du C. de Vere (London: Warner, 1912–14).

"The Lion and the Fox": From *The Prince* (1513) by Niccolo Machiavelli, translated and edited by Robert M. Adams (New York: Norton, 1977).

"The Siege of Constantinople": From Kritovoulos, *The History of Mehmed the Conqueror*, pp. 324–325.

Chapter 12

"A Momentous Discovery": From Christopher Columbus, "Letter from the First Voyage" (1493), in *Letters of Christopher Columbus*, translated by R. H. Major (London: Hakluyt Society, 1947).

"The Halls of Montezuma": From Bernal Diaz, "The True History of the Conquest of New Spain," in *The Bernal Diaz Chronicles*, translated and edited by Albert Idell, pp. 169–171.

"Last Words": From Anne Boleyn, "Scaffold Speech," 1536.

"The Kingdom of France": From Claude de Seyssel, *The Monarchy of France*, translated by J. H. Hexter and edited by Donald R. Kelley. Copyright © 1981 by Yale University Press. All rights reserved. Reprinted by permission.

Chapter 13

"A Dutch Wit": From Desiderius Erasmus, *In Praise of Folly* (London: Reeves & Turner, 1876).

"Luther on Marriage": From Martin Luther, *On Good Works*, translated and edited by William Hazlitt (London: George Bell and Sons, 1895).

"The Eternal Decree": From John Calvin, "Institutes of the Christian Religion," in John Calvin, *Selections from His Writings*, edited and with an introduction by John Dillenberger.

"Heavenly Vision": From *The Life of St. Teresa of Avila* (1611), translated by David Lewis.

Chapter 14

"Catholics and Huguenots": From "The Edict of Nantes," translated by James Harvey Robinson, in *Readings in European History, Volume II: From the Opening of the Protestant Revolt to the Present Day* (Boston: Ginn & Company, 1906).

"Cannibals": Excerpts from Donald M. Frame, translator, *The Complete Essays of Montaigne*. Copyright © 1958 by the Board of Trustees of the Leland Stanford Junior University. All rights reserved. Used with the permission of Stanford University Press, www.sup.org.

"War Is Hell": From Hans Jacob Cristoph Von Grimmelshausen, *The Adventurous Simplicissimus*, translated by A. T. S. Goodrick (1912).

"Fire and Sword": From *The Destruction of Magdeburg*.

Chapter 15

"Living by One's Wits": From *The Life of Lazarillo Des Tormes*, translated and edited by Louis How, with an introduction by Charles Philip Wagner (New York: Mitchell Kennerly, 1917).

"The Peasants' Revolt": From "The Twelve Articles of the Peasants of Swabia" in *Readings in European History, Volume II: From the Opening of the Protestant Revolt to the Present Day*, edited by James Harvey Robinson (Boston: Ginn & Company, 1906).

"A Feminine Perspective": From Arcangela Tarabotti, "Innocence Undone," translated by Brendan Dooley. Reprinted by permission of Brendan Dooley.

"The Devil's Due": From "Medieval Witchcraft" in *Translations and Reprints from the Original Sources of European History*, Volume III. Reprinted by permission of The University of Pennsylvania Press.

Chapter 16

"A Glimpse of a King": From *Memoirs of the Duke of Saint-Simon*, translated by Bayle St. John (London: Swan Sonnonschein & Co., 1900).

"A Short, Sharp Shock": From an eyewitness account of the execution of Charles I, 1649, excerpted from *The Execution of Charles I*.

"The Nature of Man": From Thomas Hobbes, *Leviathan* (London: 1651).

"A Close Shave": From "DeMissy's Life of Peter" in *Readings in European History, Volume II: From the Opening of the Protestant Revolt to the Present Day*, edited by James Harvey Robinson (Boston: Ginn & Company, 1906).

Chapter 17

"Stargazing": From Copernicus, "On the Revolutions of Heavenly Spheres" (1543), in *Movement of the Earth* by Thomas S. Kuhn.

"The Telescope": From *Discoveries and Opinions of Galileo* by Galileo Galilei, translated by Stillman Drake, copyright © 1957 by Stillman Drake. Used by permission of Doubleday, a Division of Random House, Inc.

"Descartes Experiments": From *Discourse on Method and Related Writings* by Rene Descartes, translated by Desmond Clarke (Penguin Classics, 1999). Copyright © Desmond Clarke, 1999. Reproduced by permission of Penguin Books Ltd.

"Defining Commerce": From Adam Smith, *The Wealth of Nations*, edited by James E. Thorold Rogers, Volume I, 2nd ed. (Oxford: Clarendon Press, 1880).

Chapter 18

"Captain Cook Encounters the Tahitians": From *The Journals of Captain Cook*, edited by Philip Edwards, 1999, pp. 39–41. Reprinted by permission of Hakluyt Society.

"A King's-Eye View": From Frederick the Great, *An Essay on Forms of Government*, translated by T. Holcroft.

"Military Discipline": Excerpt from Marshal de Saxe, "Memoirs on the Art of War" (1757) in *War, Diplomacy, and Imperialism, 1618–1763*, edited by Geoffrey Symcox. Copyright © 1974 by Geoffrey Symcox. Reprinted by permission of the author.

"Unalienable Rights": From *The Declaration of Independence*, 1776.

Chapter 19

"The All Knowing": From Denis Diderot, *Encyclopedia* (1751–1752).

"The Human Condition": From Voltaire's *Philosophical Dictionary*, Volume One, by Peter Gay, 1962. Reprinted by permission of the author, Peter Gay.

"The Good of All": From Jean-Jacques Rousseau, *The Social Contract*, translated by Rose M. Harrington, 1906.

"Love and Marriage": From *The Old Maid*, Number 1, by Frances Brooke, November 15, 1755.

Chapter 20

"What Is the Third Estate?": From *A Documentary Survey of the French Revolution* by John Hall Stewart. Copyright © 1951. Reprinted by permission of Prentice-Hall, Inc., Upper Saddle River, NJ.

"Declaration of the Rights of Man and Citizen": From *Readings in European History, Volume II: From the Opening of the Protestant Revolt to the Present Day*, edited by James Harvey Robinson (Boston: Ginn & Company, 1906).

"Declaration of the Rights of Woman and Citizen": From Olympe de Gouges, "Declaration of the Rights of Woman and Female Citizen," in *Women in Revolutionary Paris, 1789–1795*, translated by Darline Gay Levy, Harriet Branson Applewhite, and Mary Durham Johnson (Urbana: University of Illinois Press, 1979).

"The Civil Code of the Code Napoléon": From Henry Cachard, *The French Civil Code* (London: Stevens and Sons, 1895).

Chapter 21

"The Wealth of Britain": From Edward Baines, *The History of the Cotton Manufactures in Great Britain* (1835).

"The Sin of Wages": From Robert Owen, *Observations on the Effect of the Manufacturing System* (1815).

"Exploiting the Young": From "Child Labor in the Coal Mines," Testimony to the Parliamentary Investigative Committee (1842).

"The Slavery of Labor": From Friedrich Engels, *The Condition of the Working Class in England in 1844*, translated by Florence Kelley Wischnewetsky (London: Allen and Unwin, 1892).

Chapter 22

"Young Italy": From *Young Italy* by Giuseppe Mazinni in *Metternich's Europe*, edited and translated by Mack Walker, 1968.

The Communist Manifesto: From Karl Marx and Friedrich Engels, *Manifesto of the Communist Party* (1848).

"Flora Tristan and the Rights of Working Women": From "Flora Tristan" in *L'Union Ouvriere*, 3rd ed. (Paris and Lyons, 1843) as translated by Giselle Pincetl in Harvest Quarterly, 7 (Fall 1977). Reprinted by permission of Giselle Pincetl.

Chapter 23

"The Russian Emancipation Proclamation, 1861": From *Diary of a Russian Censor: Aleksandr Nikitenko*, abr., ed., tr. by Helen Saltz Jacobson (Amherst: The University of Massachusetts Press, 1975). Copyright © 1975 by The University of Massachusetts Press. Reprinted by permission.

"Mistress of the House": From *Mrs. Beeton's Book of Household Management*, 1861.

On the Origin of Species: From Charles Darwin, *On the Origin of Species* (London, 1859).

Chapter 24

"J'Accuse": From *The Affair: The Case of Alfred Dreyfus* by Jean-Denis Bredin. Copyright © 1986 by George Braziller, Inc. Reprinted by permission of George Braziller, Inc.

"Constance Lytton": From Constance Lytton, *Prisons and Prisoners*, 1914.

"Angel or Woman?": From Maria Desraismes, "La Femme et le droit," in *Eve Dans L'Humanite* (Paris, 1891).

Chapter 25

"Leopold II of Belgium": From *French Colonialism, 1871–1914: Myths and Realities* by Henri Brunschwig. Reprinted by permission of Armand Colin, Editeur.

"Joseph Chamberlain's Speech to Birmingham Relief Association": From Joseph Chamberlain, M.P., *Foreign and Colonial Speeches* (1897).

"Karl Pearson and the Defense of Eugenics": From Karl Pearson, *National Life from the Standpoint of Science* (1905).

Chapter 26

All Quiet on the Western Front: From Erich Maria Remarque, *All Quiet on the Western Front* (1928).

"Dulce Et Decorum Est": From *Poems* by Wilfred Owen, with an introduction by Sigfried Sassoon, 1920.

"War at Home": From "Women Taxi-Cab Drivers" and "Down Cabs' Again," *Manchester Guardian*, Friday, March 6, 1917, in *Newspapers of the First World War*, Ian Williams, ed.

"War Communism": From "Decree on Grain, May 9, 1918," copyright © S. Pollard and C. Holmes from *Documents of European Economic History*, Volume III, by S. Pollard and C. Holmes. Reprinted with permission of Palgrave.

"Proclamation of the 'Whites'": From "Proclamation of the 'Whites'" in *Intervention, Civil War and Communism in Russia, April–December 1918* by James Bunyon. Published by Octagon Books, a Division of Hippocrene Books, Inc. Reprinted by permission.

Chapter 27

"The Depression for Women": From Winifred Holtby, *Women and a Changing Civilization*. Copyright © 1934 by The Bodley Head Ltd. Selections reprinted by permission of Paul Berry and Marion Shaw, literary executors for Winifred Holtby.

"The Results of the First Five-Year Plan": From "The Results of the First Five-Year Plan" in Joseph Stalin, *Selected Writings* (New York: International Publishers, 1942). Reprinted by permission of International Publishers Company.

"The Law on the Abolition of Legal Abortion": Excerpt from Rudolph Schlesinger, *The Family in the USSR: Documents and Readings* (London: Routledge & Kegan Paul, 1949), pp. 251–254. Reprinted by permission of the publisher.

"Adolf Hitler on Racial Purity": From "Racial Purity: Hitler Reverts to the Dominant Theme of the National Socialist Program, January 30, 1937" in Hitler's *Third Reich*, edited by Louis L. Snyder. Copyright © 1981 by Louis L. Snyder. Reprinted by permission of Nelson-Hall, Inc.

Chapter 28

"Manifesto of the Jewish Resistance": From *An Anthology of Holocaust Literature*, edited by J. Glatstein, I. Knox, and S. Margoshes. Reprinted by permission of the Jewish Publication Society.

"President Franklin Roosevelt's Request for a Declaration of War on Japan, 8 December 1941": From *World War II: Policy and Strategy* by Hans Adolf Jacobsen and Arthur J. Smith, Jr. Reprinted by permission.

"Japan's Declaration of War on the United States and Great Britain, 8 December 1941": From *World War II: Policy and Strategy* by Hans Adolf Jacobsen and Arthur J. Smith, Jr. Reprinted by permission.

"Glittering Fragments": "Glittering Fragments" by Hara Tamiki from p. 221 in *The Penguin Book of Japanese Verse*, translated by Geoffrey Bownas and Anthony Thwaite (Penguin Books, 1964). Translation copyright © Geoffrey Bownas and Anthony Thwaite, 1964. Reproduced by permission of Penguin Books Ltd.

Chapter 29

"The Iron Curtain": From Winston Churchill, "The Sinews of Peace" in Vol. VII: 1943–1949 of *Winston S. Churchill: His Complete Speeches 1897–1963*, edited by Robert Rhodes James. © 1974. Reprinted by permission of Chelsea House Publishers, LLC.

"The Marshall Plan": From Department of State Bulletin, 15 June 1947.

"Report to the Twentieth Party Congress": From "Report to the Twentieth Party Congress" by Nikita S. Khrushchev, reprinted from *Current Soviet Policies II: The Documentary Record of the Twentieth Party Congress and Its Aftermath*, translation copyright by The Current Digest of the Soviet Press, Columbus, Ohio. Used by permission.

"The Second Sex": From *The Second Sex* by Simone De Beauvoir, trans., H. M. Parshley. Copyright 1952 and renewed 1980 by Alfred A. Knopf, a Division of Random House, Inc. Used by permission of Alfred A. Knopf, a Division of Random House, Inc.

"Subterranean Homesick Blues": "Subterranean Homesick Blues" by Bob Dylan. Copyright © 1965 by Warner Bros. Music. Copyright renewed 1993 by Special Rider Music. All rights reserved. International copyright secured. Reprinted by permission.

Chapter 30

"Career Advancement, Communist-Style": From *Russian Voices* by Tony Parker. Copyright © 1991. Reproduced by permission of the author c/o Rogers, Coleridge and White Ltd., 20 Powis Mews, London W11 1JN.

"A Woman Reporter Behind the Lines of the War in Chechnya": From *Chienne de Guerre* by Anne Nivat. Copyright © Librairie Artheme Fayard, 2000. Reprinted by permission of PublicAffairs, a member of Perseus Books, L.L.C.

"The Return of Fascism?": From "Music of Hate Raises the Volume in Germany" by Ferdinand Protzman, *The New York Times*, December 2, 1992. Copyright © 1992 by The New York Times Co. Reprinted with permission.

"The Return of Fascism?": From "Two Germans Admit Arson Attack That Killed Three Turkish Nationals" as appeared in *The New York Times*, December 2, 1992. Reprinted by permission of the Associated Press.

PHOTO CREDITS

Unless otherwise acknowledged, all photographs are the property of Pearson Education, Inc. Page abbreviations are as follows: (T) top, (B) bottom, (L) left, (R) right, and (C) center.

Introduction
xxxiv, xxxv Augustin Ochsenreiter/South Tyrol Museum of Archaeology **xxxvii (L)** © The Trustees of the British Museum, **(R)** Hirmer Fotoarchiv, Munich **xxxviii** AKG-Images **xl** Bridgeman Art Library **xli** Lee Boltin Picture Library **xliii** Réunion des Museés Nationaux/Art Resource, NY **xlv** Staatliche Museen zu Berlin-Antikensammlung/bpk Berlin/Art Resource, NY **xlvi** Hirmer Fotoarchiv, Munich **l** American Museum of Classical Studies at Athens: Agora Excavation **li** Ping Amranad/© SuperStock, Inc. **liii** Archaeological Museuj Salonica/Dagli Orti/The Art Archive **lviii** Bibliothèque Nationale de France, Paris **lxii** Romische-Germanisches Zentralmuseum Mainz **lxiii** Scala/Art Resource, NY **lxv** Erich Lessing/Art Resource, NY **lxix** Erich Lessing/Art Resource, NY **lxx** Erich Lessing/Art Resource, NY **lxxv** Courtesy of The Freer Gallery of Art, Smithsonian Institution, Washington, D.C.: Purchase, F1930.60a **lxxvi** National Museum of China, Beijing **lxxvii** Photo: Ann Münchow © Domkapitel Aachen **lxxviii** Bibliothèque Nationale de France, Paris (MS ARABE 5847, fol. 94v) **lxxxi** Dagli Orti/The Art Archive **lxxxii** Fototeca Unione, American Academy, Rome/Bridgeman Art Library **lxxxiii** British Museum/Eileen Tweedy/The Art Archive **lxxxvii** University Library, Heidelberg/Dagli Orti/The Art Archive **xc** Bodleian Library, University of Oxford (MS. Bodl. 264 fol. 218r)

Chapter 10
291, 292, 293, 296 Erich Lessing/Art Resource, NY **299** Lambeth Palace Library (MS.6,f.43) **300** Giraudon/Art Resource, NY **301** By Permission of the British Library (MS ADD 27695, fol. 8r) **302** Psalter and Prayer

Book of Bonne of Luxembourg, Duchess of Normandy: folio 322 recto: The Three Dead. Grisaille, color, gilt and brown ink on vellum. H. 4 15/16 in. W. 3 9/16 in. (12.5 x 9.1 cm.) The Metropolitan Museum of Art, Cloisters Collection, 1969 (69.86) Photograph © 1991 The Metropolitan Museum of Art **305** By Permission of the British Library (MS ROY 20 CVII, fol 41v) **307** Stadtarchiv Soest (Bestand A Nr. 2771) **312** Rosgarten Museum, Städtische Museen Konstanz (Hs1,fol.58a) **315** Biblioteca Apostolica Vaticana (Vatican) (URB LAT 365, Inferno, Canto VIII, fol. 20r) **317** By Permission of the British Library (MS Harl. 4431, fol. 3r)

Chapter 11
321, 323, 326 Scala/Art Resource, NY **329(L), (R)** Galleria degli Uffizi Florence/Dagli Orti/The Art Archive **331** Erich Lessing/Art Resource, NY **332, 333, 334, 335, 336** Scala/Art Resource, NY **338** Bridgeman Art Library **339, 344, 345** Scala/Art Resource, NY **346** Erich Lessing/Art Resource, NY **349** Bibliothèque Nationale de France, Paris (MS Fr. 9087, fol. 207v)

Chapter 12
353, 355 Walker Art Gallery, National Museums Liverpool **358** Giraudon/Art Resource, NY **361** Institut Amatller d'Art Hispanic **362(T)** The Granger Collection, New York, **(B)** Laurie Platt Winfrey, Inc. **366** Reproduced by courtesy of the Trustees, © The National Gallery, London (NG1287) **372** Czartoyski Collection, Krakow **373** National Portrait Gallery, London (NPG668) **375** Giraudon/Art Resource, NY **380** Scala/Art Resource, NY **381** Musée du Louvre, Paris/Bridgeman Art Library, London/© SuperStock, Inc. **382** Erich Lessing/Art Resource, NY **383** Topkapi Palace Museum

Chapter 13
387, 388, 389 Library of Congress **390** Private Collection/Bridgeman Art Library **396** Erich Lessing/Art Resource, NY **397** Kunstsammlungen Der Veste Coburg **398** Courtesy of the Fogg Art Museum, Harvard University, Cambridge, MA; Gift of Meta and Paul J. Sachs (1955.164) **401** Giraudon/Art Resource, NY **403** University Library of Geneva/Dagli Orti/The Art Archive **404** Bibliothèque Publique et Universitaire, Geneva, Switzerland/Bridgeman Art Library **406** François Martin, Geneva/Document BPU **408** M. Schneiders/Artephot **410, 412** Scala/Art Resource, NY **413** Erich Lessing/Art Resource, NY **414** Giraudon/Art Resource, NY

Chapter 14
419, 421 Giraudon/Art Resource, NY **423** Art Resource, NY **425** National Portrait Gallery, London (NPG429) **426** Musée Cantonal des Beaus Arts, Lausanne **428** Réunion des Musées Nationaux/Art Resource, NY **429** Erich Lessing/Art Resource, NY **432** Palazzo Pitti FLorence/Dagli Orti/The Art Archive **435** © Rijksmuseum, Amsterdam **437** Erich Lessing/Art Resource, NY **442** Musée des Beaux-Arts de Strasbourg (2.86.12970) **445** Kunsthistorisches Museum (Inv.Nr.GG1071)

Chapter 15
449, 450, 451 Roudnice Lobkowicz Collection/Bridgeman Art Library **453** Scala/Art Resource, NY **455** Museum of Art, Tula, Russia/Bridgeman Art Library **456** Erich Lessing/Art Resource, NY **459** Giraudon/Art Resource, NY **461** Bridgeman Art Library **463** La Tour, Georges de (1593–1652) *The Fortune Teller*. Oil on canvas. J. 40 /8 in. W. 48 5/8 in. (101.9 3 123.5 cm.) Signed (upper right): G. de La Tour Fecit Luneuilla Lothar: Metropolitan Museum of Art, Rogers Fund, 1960 (60.30) Photograph © 1982 The Metropolitan Museum of Art **464** Reproduced by courtesy of the Trustees, © The National Gallery, London (NG944) **465, 469** © Rijksmuseum, Amsterdam **471** Victoria & Albert Museum, London/Art Resource, NY **473** Reproduced by courtesy of the Trustees, © The National Gallery, London (NG186) **474** Erich Lessing/Art Resource, NY **478** bpk Berlin/Art Resource, NY

Chapter 16
483, 485 Réunion des Musées Nationaux/Art Resource, NY **486** National Portrait Gallery, London (NPG2561) **488** Reproduced by courtesy of the Trustees, © The National Gallery, London (NG1449) **489(L)** Courtesy of the Hispanic Society of America, New York, **(R)** National Portrait Gallery, London (NPG3840) **492** The Granger Collection, New York **494** The Art Archive **496** Chateau de Versailles, France/Bridgeman Art Library **499** By permission of the Earl of Rosebury, on loan to the Scottish National Portrait Gallery **507, 508, 509** Scala/Art Resource, NY

Chapter 17
513, 515 Photograph © Maritshuis, The Hague **517** By Permission of The British Library (Maps C6C3. between 22–23) **519** Newberry Library **521(L)** Erich Lessing/Art Resource, NY, **(R)** National Library of Medecine **522** Scala/Art Resource, NY **523** Bridgeman Art Library **525** Städelsches Kunstistitut, Frankfurt/Gnamm-Arthotek **528 (L)** Hanging (Kalamakari): Indian notable, wife and child, surrounded by household scenes, with European figures introduced. Detail #1: Bottom center, three women. Cotton, resist dyed. Whole: H. 99 1/2 in. W. 77 in. (2.53 x 1.96 m) The Metropolitan Museum of Art, Gift of Mrs. Albert Blum, 1920 (20.79) Photograph © 1980 The Metropolitan Museum of Art, **(R)** Tate Gallery, London/Art Resource, NY **529** Library Company of Philadelphia (Rare Il Pome 95.Q) **531** Museum Boijmans Van Beuningen, Rotterdam **533** © Amsterdams Historisch Museum **535, 536** © Rijksmuseum, Amsterdam **538** From the private collection of Peter V. Lape **539** Biblioteca Nacional, Lisbon, Portugal **541** Reproduced by courtesy of the Trustees, © The National Gallery, London (NG896)

Chapter 18
547, 549 Reproduced by courtesy of the Trustees, © The National Gallery, London (NG681) **556** Russian Historical Museum Moscow/Dagli Orti/The Art Archive **557** Michael Holford **559** Scala/Art Resource, NY **562** bpk Berlin/Art Resource, NY **565** Kunsthistorisches Museum, Vienna **566** Giraudon/Art Resource, NY **570** The British Library/The Art Archive **571** India Office Library/The Art Archive **573** Library of Congress

Chapter 19
577, 579 Sameul H. Kress Collection, © Board of Trustees, National Gallery of Art, Washington, D.C. (1946.7.7[772]/PA) **580** Mozarteum Salzburg/Dagli Orti/The Art Archive **581** Giraudon/Art Resource, NY **583** Mary Evans Picture Library **584** Scottish National Portrait Gallery (PG1057) **585** bpk Berlin/Art Resource, NY **589** The Landsdowne Dining Room. Room from Landsdowne House, Berkeley Square, London. Originally begun by John Stuart (1713–1792), third Earl of Bute, and completed for William Petty Fitzmaurice (1737–1805), second earl of Shelbourne, later first Marquess of Landsdowne. Furnished with Neoclassical Adam-style furniture and silver not original to the room. View #1: Fireplace wall and serving area with two columns. L. 47 ft. (14.31 m.) W. 24 ft. 6 in. (7.47 m.) H. 7 ft. 11 in. (5.46 m.) The Metropolitan Museum of Art, Rogers Fund, 1932 (32.12) Photograph © 1995 The Metropolitan Museum of Art **590** Reproduced by courtesy of the Trustees, © The National Gallery, London (NG114) **592** Michael Holford **593** Scala/Art Resource, NY **595** Victoria & Albert Museum, London/Art Resource, NY **601** Musée du Louvre Paris/Dagli Orti/The Art Archive **603** © The Trustees of the British Museum

Chapter 20
607, 609 Spencer Collection, The NewYork Public Library, Astor, Lenox and Tilden Foundations **611** Giraudon/Art Resource, NY **612** "Abus à Surprimé" ("Abuses to Suppress"), Musée de la Révolution Française (mfr 88–133) **614** Réunion des Musées Nationaux/Art Resource, NY **616** Giraudon/Art Resource, NY **617** Library of Congress **622** Giraudon/Art Resource, NY **623** University of Maryland Libraries (DC187.7 C655 [1794]) **627** Goya, Francisco. Spanish, 1746–1828, *Y No Hai Remedio (And there is no remedy)*, from *Los Desastres de la Guerra*. Etching, fourth

state. The Metropolitan Museum of Art, Schiff Fund, 1992 (22.60.25[15]). Photo © 2002 The Metropolitan Museum of Art **630** Musée de Beaux-Arts, Rouen **631** Olin Library, Rare Books, Cornell University (Cornell nap. 31)

Chapter 21

635, 637 The Tate Gallery, London/Art Resource, NY **641** Mary Evans Picture Library **642** Bedfordshire & Luton Archives & Records Service **646** The Board of Trustees of the National Museums and Galleries of Merseyside (Walker Art Gallery, Liverpool [WAG 659]) **647** AKG-Images **648** The Granger Collection, New York **652** Daumier, Honore (1808–1879) *The Third Class Carriage.* Oil on canvas. H. 25 3/4 in. W. 35 1/2 in. (65.4 3 90.2 cm.) The Metropolitan Museum of Art, H. O. Havemeyer Collection, Bequest of Mrs. H. O. Havemeyer, 1929. (29.100.129) Photograph by Malcolm Varon. Photograph © 1984 The Metropolitan Museum of Art **653** Victoria & Albert Museum, London/Art Resource, NY **657** John R. Freeman/Fotomas, London **658** The Royal Collection © 2004, Her Majesty Queen Elizabeth II **660** Mansell Collection/Time Life Pictures/Getty Images **663** Giraudon/Art Resource, NY **666** Courtesy of the Print and Picture Department, Free Library of Philadelphia

Chapter 22

671, 673 *Potato Planters,* about 1861; Jean-Fraonçois Millet, French (1814–1875), oil on canvas; 82.5 3 101.3 cm (32 1/2 x 39 7/8 in.) Gift of Quincy Adams Shaw through Quincy A. Shaw, Jr. and Mrs. Marian Shaw Haughton (17.1505). Courtesy, Museum of Fine Arts, Boston. Reproduced with permission. © 2002 The Museum of Fine Arts, Boston. All Rights Reserved. **677** Bibliothèque Nationale de France, Paris **680** Image by courtesy of the Wedgwood Museum Trust Limited, Barlaston, Staffordshire (England). **683** AKG-Images **684** Giraudon/Art Resource, NY **689** Mary Evans Picture Library **690** Eileen Tweedy/The Art Archive **697** bpk Berlin/Art Resource, NY

Chapter 23

703, 705 bpk Berlin/Art Resource, NY **709** Hulton Archive/Getty Images **710** © Hulton-Deutsch Collection/Corbis **712** bpk Berlin/Art Resource, NY **716** Bibliothèque Nationale de France, Paris **717** Erich Lesing/Art Resource, NY **718** Bridgeman Art Library **719** Mary Evans Picture Library **722** By courtesy of the Board of Trustees of the Victoria & Albert Museum **724** Mary Evans Picture Library **727** Giraudon/Art Resource, NY **729** Hulton Archive/Getty Images

Chapter 24

737, 739 Bridgeman Art Library **740** Stadtmuseum Berlin (PC9890) **743** Hulton Archive/Getty Images **745** AKG-Images **749** Hulton Archive/Getty Images **750** Mary Evans Picture Library **753** Jewish Museum/Art Resource, NY **756** AP/Wide World Photos **757** Hulton-Deutsch Collection/Corbis **759** Corbis **762** Sophia Smith Collection, Smith College (SRSM5) **763** Claude Monet, French, 1840–1926, *Arrival of the Normany Train, Gare Saint-Lazare,* oil on canvas, 1877, 59.6 x 80.2 cm, Mr. and Mrs. Martin A. Ryerson Collection, 1933. 1158, photograph © 1994 The Art Institute of Chicago. All Rights Reserved. **764** Museum of Modern Art, New York/Art Resource, NY/© 2004 The Estate of Pablo Picasso/Artists Rights Society (ARS), New York, **765(L)** Staff finial, (mvuala), Kongo peoples, Democratic Republic of the Congo, Congo, Angola, 16th–19th century, Ivory, ceramic, camwood, resin. 6.5 x 5.1 x 6 cm (6 1/2 x 2 x 2 3/8 in.), Museum purchase. National Museum of African Art, Smithsonian Institution, Washington, D.C. (85-15-4), **(R)** Face mask, Guro peoples, Côte d'Ivoire, Mid 20th century, wood, paint, 54 x 28.6 x 17 cm (21 1/4 x 11 1/4 x 6 11/16 in.). Bequest of Eliot Elisofon. National Museum of African Art, Smithsonian Insitution, Washington, D.C. (73-7-167). **766(T)** Mary Evans Picture Library, **(B)** L. Degraces/© Photothèques des Musées de la Ville de Paris (AFF.2479)

Chapter 25

771, 773 Corbis **778** Rue des Archives/The Granger Collection, New York **789** Eileen Tweedy/The Art Archive **790** The Granger Collection, New York **793** By Permission of The British Library (154 f. 31d, neg. B6140)

Chapter 26

800 "Take Up the Sword of Justice" by Sir Bernard J. Partridge, England, 1915. From copy in Bowman Gray Collection, Rare Book Collection, University of North Carolina Library, Chapel Hill **799, 801** "Deutsche Frauen Arbeitet im Heimate-Heer! Kriegsamtstelle Magdeburg" ("German Woman Work in the Home-Army! Amgdeburg War Office") by George Kirchbach, Germany, 1914–18. From copy in Bowman Gray Collection, Rare Book Collection, University of North Carolina Library, Chapel Hill **805** Corbis **806** Imperial War Museum, London (Q3990) **808** National Archives **812** *We Are Making a New World,* 1918 (oil on canvas) by Paul Nash (1889–1946) Imperial War Museum, London, UK/Bridgeman Art Library **813** Imperial War Museum, London (Q3995) **814** Imperial War Museum, London (Q20220) **816** Mansell Collection/Time Life Pictures/Getty Images **819** *Illustrated London News,* August 9, 1917 **821** Sovfoto **825** Imperial War Museum, London (Q11586) **826** Brown Brothers **828** Mary Evans Picture Library

Chapter 27

832 © bpk, Berlin/Art Resource, NY/© Estate of George Grosz/Licensed by VAGA, New York, NY **831, 833** Bettmann/Corbis **838** Reprinted, with permission, from The Columbus (Ohio) Dispatch **839** Stock Montage, Inc. **840** Michael Holford **842(L)** © Collection Roger-Viollet/Getty Images, **(C), (R)** Liaison International/Getty Images **846** Novosti/Sovfoto **847** Sovfoto **850** Erich Lessing/Art Resource, NY **852** Bettmann/Corbis **854** Corbis **855** German Propaganda Archive **857** Corbis **859** AP/Wide World Photos **861** Museo del Prado, Madrid. © 2004 Estate of Pablo Picasso/Artists Rights Society (ARS), New York **863** © Archivo Iconografico, S.A./Corbis

Chapter 28

867, 869 Österreichische Nationalbibliothek, Vienna (435573/BRF) **871** Corbis **874** Imperial War Museum, London (D1568) **876** © Wiener Library, London **878** © Collection Roger-Viollet/Getty Images **879** Kulturgeschichtliches Museum, Osnäbruck. © Auguste Moses-Nussbaum and Shulmait Jaari/© 2004 Artists Rights Society (ARS), New York/VG Bild-Kunst, Bonn **881** AKG-Images **882** Sovfoto **887(T)** US Army Military History Institute, **(B)** bpk Berlin/Art Resource, NY **890** Yosuke Yamahata/Shogo Yamahta **893** Nippon Hoso Shuppan Kyokai, Japan **894** Courtesy Franklin D. Roosevelt Library

Chapter 29

897, 899 Bettmann/Corbis **900** Courtesy Consulate General of Germany **904** Los Alamos National Laboratory **905** Hulton Archive/Getty Images **908** Corbis **910** Council of the European Union **912** Sony Coporation **913** Rene Burri/Magnum Photos, Inc. **915** Courtesy German Information Center **916** Popperfoto/Robertstock **917** AP/Wide World Photos **919(L)** AP/Wide World Photos, **(R)** Gilles Peress/Magnum Photos, Inc. **921** David Hurn/Magnum Photos, Inc. **922** Liaison International/Getty Images

Chapter 30

929, 931 AP/Wide World Photos **933** Sovfoto **934** Bettmann/Corbis **936, 939** AP/Wide World Photos **941** Vlastimir Shone/Liaison International/Getty Images **942** Corbis **945, 947** AP/Wide World Photos **950** Getty Images **952** Steve McCurry/Magnum Photos, Inc. **953, 955** Corbis **956** Nogues/Corbis Sygma **958** AP/Wide World Photos **959** AFP/Corbis

INDEX

A boldface entry indicates a key term and the page number where its definition can be found. Terms and definitions also appear in the Glossary on pages G-1–G-7.